Y0-BYP-589

STRATEGIC MANAGEMENT
Analysis and Action

Kenneth J. Hatten
Boston University

Mary Louise Hatten
Graduate School of Management
Simmons College

Mayank V. Vadodaria
Nashua, NH.
Sept. 1 '88

Prentice-Hall, Inc., Englewood Cliffs, New Jersey 07632

Library of Congress Cataloging-in-Publication Data

Hatten, Kenneth J.
Strategic management.

Includes index.
1. Strategic planning. 2. Strategic planning—Case studies. I. Hatten, Mary Louise. II. Title.
HD30.28.H384 1987 658.4'012 86-30453
ISBN 0-13-850694-9

To *Meredith, Sydney,* and *Toby*

Editorial/production supervision and
interior design: *Pamela Wilder*
Cover design: *Bruce Kenselaar*
Cover photo: *Ralph King*
Manufacturing buyer: *Ed O'Dougherty*

Printed in the United States of America
10 9 8 7 6 5 4 3 2 1

ISBN 0-13-850694-9 01

Prentice-Hall International (UK) Limited, *London*
Prentice-Hall of Australia Pty. Limited, *Sydney*
Prentice-Hall Canada Inc., *Toronto*
Prentice-Hall Hispanoamericana, S.A., *Mexico*
Prentice-Hall of India Private Limited, *New Delhi*
Prentice-Hall of Japan, Inc., *Tokyo*
Prentice-Hall of Southeast Asia Pte. Ltd., *Singapore*
Editora Prentice-Hall do Brasil, Ltda., *Rio de Janeiro*

Contents

PART FOUR
STRATEGIC ADMINISTRATION

CASES

PART FIVE
DIVERSIFIED AND INTEGRATED COMPANIES

PART SIX
STRATEGY AND LEADERSHIP

Preface

A Preface normally tells readers how to use the book and what they will learn from reading it. We will depart from this tradition and begin by telling you what we have learned while writing the book.

Of course, we've learned that writing a strategy text is a formidable undertaking—the valuable research of this field has rarely been cataloged and then mostly on a piecemeal basis. We've learned that linking the traditions of the field with its modern literature is complex and difficult, because the modern research tradition is science-based whereas the field itself is anchored strongly in general management practice. We've learned that there are substantial gaps in the current research thrusts of the field: Certain topics are amenable to statistical research, while others are by their nature more qualitative. It is the former that are receiving attention in the literature, while the others may indeed be more valuable to management practice.

We have attempted to communicate what the field knows about strategy formulation and implementation. Of necessity, the book separates the two activities, although we know that managers have to engage in both virtually simultaneously.

One objective of this book is to present an integrated perspective of the field, drawing upon our personal experiences of policy research, the different research traditions at Purdue and Harvard as well as the social-issue thrusts of research at Boston University and Boston College and the administrative perspective of Simmons College. Unifying these different perspectives is a common administrative point of view that is critical to effective management. It is the administrative point of view that makes the combination of text and cases so powerful in the classroom.

Strategic management is a pragmatic field, influenced by practice and the administrative point of view as well as science. Ultimately founded in judgment, it is enriched by many academic contributions and conceptual frameworks.

Strategic management has more to do with structuring problems as opportunities to create value than with problem-solving *per se*. It is about what is feasible more than it is about what is right, because it is a field where results matter more than initial decisions—where making things work is more important than knowing you are right.

Strategic management is about analysis and action, and in practice the two are inseparable. Of course, you cannot learn analysis and action by reading about it—you must practice. To help you, we have selected cases that illustrate a broad range of strategic management issues in a wide variety of settings, such as small businesses, large corporations, manufacturing and service firms, and not-for-profit organizations. In all these situations, strategic management can be used to improve organizational performance.

As you will see, strategic management encompasses many concepts. Each case is an opportunity to develop your experience in the use of these concepts. Learning which ones are most productive for you in a particular situation requires familiarity with a wide range of approaches. Each person may find different concepts more helpful. Each concept is like the side of a many-faceted prism—a tool that lets each of us see something new about a particular situation. But remember, ours is only one view of reality; we must learn to use the analytical tools to sharpen our initial view of a situation and learn to use discussion to benefit from the views of others.

We hope that this book will enrich readers whose experience is at various stages of development. For those new to strategic thinking, it offers structures, including functional analysis, industry analysis, and competitive analysis to facilitate strategy identification,  evaluation, and improvement. For academics and executives familiar with strategic management, it offers our interpretation of the strategic management literature. Rather than being encyclopedic, we have been selective and stressed contributions to the field that are fundamental and most relevant in the classroom and current management practice. We believe that the analytical structures provide a powerful framework for corporate and industry analysis and, therefore, a foundation for successful strategy formulation and implementation in the organization. We believe that strategic management literacy is an important aid to successful professional education and self-development.

Ultimately, our most important objective for this book is to help you help yourself develop the skills to select from the various concepts and experiences of this book, your education, and life, those that will work best for you in particular situations. As you accumulate experience in using these resources, you will probably, increasingly and selectively, abbreviate analytical processes in the interests of efficiency. Moreover, we will be surprised if you don't quickly synthesize a strategy on some occasions as you size up a situation and then selectively use analysis to test your strategy before advocating its merits. However, on some occasions, relatively exhaustive fundamental analysis may be needed before you begin to see what to do.

We recommend viewing the book as a "resource in the whole." You may consider skimming the whole text so that you know what is in it and where particular ideas are discussed. Focus on particular ideas that interest you and appear useful in a specific context—perhaps a particular case—while being careful to remember the administrative point of view. In doing so, you will be acting more like senior executives and administrators who generally have to deal with all aspects of their organizations and their environments concurrently, rather than approaching issues in a piecemeal fashion.

The book is built upon our professional and personal backgrounds, and we want to acknowledge the many colleagues who have played critical roles in our professional development. Dan Schendel and Arnold Cooper of the Krannert Graduate School of Management at Purdue University introduced us to strategic management. At Harvard, the former Dean, Lawrence Fouraker, and the current Dean, John McArthur, as well as Frank Aguilar, Norman Berg, Joe Bower, Neil Churchill, John Matthews, Bill Poorvu, Malcolm Salter, Howard Stevenson, Tom Raymond, Hugo Uyterhoeven, and also Mark Teagan and the late Jack Glover have influenced our lives in important and subtle ways. Dan Thomas, Ken Hatten's colleague at Harvard, who later taught at Stanford before founding his own consulting firm, was particularly helpful in the development of initial teaching plans for some of our cases, both at Harvard and Stanford. The late Bill Glueck of the University of Georgia was influential in attracting our attention to the pedagogical value of some of the cases we've included here.

At Boston University, Deans Henry Morgan and John Russell as well as Ken Hatten's department chairmen, Fred Foulkes and later Ted Murray, provided him with welcome professional assignments that gave us the opportunity to develop the text and the teaching plans that accompany the book. Boston University colleagues Bob Dickie, Liam Fahey, John Mahon, Jim Post, and Jules Schwartz have each contributed insights to the refinement of the text and teaching material. Special thanks are due to Tim Edlund for his careful and constructive comments on the text as well as to the people who reviewed the manuscript for Prentice-Hall. At Boston College, Dean John Neuhauser was remarkably supportive of Mary Louise Hatten's concurrent efforts as department chairwoman and author, and Walter Klein reacted to the social issues discussed in the text. Deans Margaret Hennig and Anne Jardim at Simmons College provided Mary Louise with an hospitable and encouraging environment in which to complete the manuscript. By influencing our thinking and writing, all these people, as well as our students in graduate, undergraduate, and executive classes at Boston University, Simmons, and Boston College, as well as Vanderbilt, Harvard, and Purdue have played a critical role in the development of this material.

Special thanks are due to Audrey Barrett of Harvard's Division of Research for her gracious help in clearing the cases for publication. The word processing staff at Boston College, particularly Joanne Brennan and Tricia Thomas, provided cheerful help with the manuscript.

To conclude, our families deserve our personal thanks for the values they instilled and for the ''don't quit'' attitude: Books can't be finished if you stop too soon. To our children Meredith, Sydney, and Toby, thanks for being so terrific through the stresses and tribulations that make textbook writing such a memorable experience for all of us. To Pam Wilder, thanks for sounding as if you believed us when we began every conversation with, ''We've got to get this thing out of here.'' It's out!

Kenneth J. Hatten
Mary Louise Piccoli Hatten

chapter 1

What Is Strategy?

DEFINITIONS AND AN EXAMPLE

Strategic management is the process by which an organization formulates objectives and is managed to achieve them. Strategy is the means to an organization's ends; it is the way to achieve organizational objectives.

A strategy is a route to a destination; an objective is the destination. Picking a destination is the choice of an objective. Selecting a route represents a decision. Driving along it is the implementation of that decision. Of course, both decision and implementation are necessary if you are to reach your strategic objective.

Strategic management is an artful blending of insightful analysis and learning used by managers to create value from the skills and resources which they control. Let us use a brief example to see how management, with an appreciation of the resources it controls, attempts to find an opportunity to create value and sustain the growth of a company. In 1969, senior management at Philip Morris, a major US cigarette manufacturer, explained to its shareholders:

> Inevitably our [Philip Morris's] domestic cigarette business will level off as our market share increases and growth in consumption stabilizes around one to two percent per year. Our cash flow will increase dramatically at that time and we need growth businesses in which to invest this cash flow. . . . [However] it's hard to find another business that is as good as this one. . . . Beer probably comes closest to matching our skills with a market opportunity. (Philip Morris, Annual Report, 1970, p. 25)

In May, 1969, Philip Morris purchased 53 percent of Miller Brewing. Twelve months later Philip Morris increased its shareholding to 100 percent of Miller and shortly thereafter management said:

> We believe the long-range potential of Miller will be best served by increasing its share of the growing premium beer market rather than by emphasizing short-term profit goals. (Philip Morris, Annual Report, 1970, p. 25)

Strategies and objectives evolve as problems and opportunities are identified, resolved, and exploited. Philip Morris's strategy was to enter the brewing industry by acquisition. This decided, it first tried one route, Canadian Breweries. When a better opportunity, Miller, presented itself, the first was allowed to die and the second seized. Recognizing the inconsistency of its objectives with the interests of Miller's minority shareholder, the DeRance Foundation (which wanted dividends for the Miller family and the foundations which the family funded), Philip Morris took time to gain complete control and then defined its objectives for Miller: growth before short-term profit.

Miller's management developed a strategy which encompassed a program of massive advertising, product development, and capacity expansion. Miller's image was changed from the "Champagne of Bottled Beers" to "Miller Time" as the reward at the end of a day of hard work. The former champagne of beers was sold in a wider range of packages, bottles, and cans than ever before. Miller Lite, a low-calorie beer similar to those which the Rheingold and Meister Brau companies had introduced unsuccessfully as diet beers for women, was reformulated to taste like Coors and promoted to appeal to the heavier-drinking males. As sales rose, new, larger breweries were built to meet the growing demand.

Strategies and objectives exist and have relevance at all levels of management. At Miller, specific strategies and objectives at the product level were made to fit with higher-level strategies at the brewing business level. Miller's management, in turn, had to develop strategies and objectives which were consistent with Philip Morris's corporate strategies, objectives, and resources. While the overall thrust of Philip Morris's entry into the brewing business was determined at the top, much of the impetus for change at the product level came about because of the actions and insight of specific people, often middle managers.

Other companies' histories can also illustrate the link between objectives and strategy. When Coca Cola bought Taylor Wine, its objective was to own a nationally known vintner. Under Coke's aegis, Taylor's strategy shifted from producing New York State wines with heavy East Coast distribution to include producing nationally distributed California wines with a new brand name, Taylor California Cellars. Polaroid wanted to revolutionize instant photography and establish new patents to protect its business from competitors. To do so, it developed the new SX-70 camera and film and manufactured them itself rather than contract production to Timex and Kodak as it had done previously.

Interlocking objectives and strategies characterize the effective management of organizations; they bind, coordinate, and integrate the parts into a whole. Effective organizations are tied by means-ends chains into a purposeful whole (in our terminology, *means* refers to strategy, and *ends* are objectives). Indeed, a high-level manager's strategy to achieve corporate goals can itself provide objectives for lower-level managers. For example, Miller's top management could have seen the introduction of Lite beer as a strategy to boost Miller's market share growth, but it was the task of Lite's product managers to develop the product and the promotional strategy necessary for the success of Lite beer.

KEY STRATEGIC CONCEPTS

To design successful strategies, there are two key rules:

1 Do what you do well.
2 Pick competitors you can beat.

Distinctive competence is the term that describes the first rule: Work out what you are best at, what your special or unique capabilities are, and do those things (Selznick, 1957). Philip Morris saw its distinctive competence as marketing ability in the package goods industry; it has been a successful marketer of leading cigarette brands, including Marlboro and Merit. Polaroid's distinctive competence during the 1948–1976 reign of its founder, Edwin Land, was product research and development.

Competitive advantage comes from the selection of markets where you can excel and where your competence gives you an edge: Choose markets where you can beat your competitors or avoid them. Indeed, if there is no competitive advantage, there is no ability to earn a true economic profit (returns higher than the average returns in the industry). Philip Morris entered the brewing industry at a time when smaller regional brewers could not afford the investments in capacity and advertising required to match the operating and marketing efficiency of the nationals like Anheuser-Busch. Bic moved into the US ball-point pen market in the late 1950s against very small, no-name competitors when Scripto, which had been the major branded popularly-priced competitor, was showing signs of internal decay and when its corporate interests were moving beyond pens, Scripto's mainstay. In this situation, Scripto opened a strategic window for Bic's entry to the market (Abell, 1978).

Strategists and researchers have confirmed the importance of focusing on what you do well and choosing your competition so that you can succeed. Sun Tzu, a Chinese military strategist, wrote circa 500 BC:

> He who knows when he can fight and when he cannot will be victorious. . . . [Know] the enemy and know yourself and in one hundred battles you will never be in peril. (Sun Tzu, 1963, pp. 82,84)

Chester Barnard (1966), who distinguished managerial effectiveness from efficiency, stressed the need for focus and self-knowledge when he defined the strategic factors as the limiting factors which are crucial to success in a changing environment. More recently, Peter Drucker (1973) described effective management as doing the right things as opposed to doing things right, again stressing the need to focus on what matters and the factors that can make a difference. Selznick (1957) also believed that one of the critical roles of the chief executive officer was to understand what was different about his or her organization and to protect and develop the firm's distinctive competence. Andrews (1980) extended this idea, stating that the corporation must be organized and administered to implement a unique strategy which must be based on its distinctive competence.

GOOD MANAGERS CREATE VALUE

The job of the manager is ultimately to create value: to allow the firm to capture (more of) the returns from its productive activities. Strategy is the means used to create value, since management allocates resources to opportunities which contribute to the implementation of strategy and manages opportunities to achieve results which increase the value of the firm.

Opportunities where the competence of the firm can be leveraged with its other resources to give the firm a competitive advantage must be recognized. To identify these opportunities and to make them profitable, a manager must answer the following important questions:

1 What business are we in?
2 What business should we be in?
3 How can we get the resources and commitments we need to succeed?

On the surface, these questions are simple. But in fact they are very difficult to answer. Their simplicity gives them power, yet at the same time makes them hard to handle.

Managers, however, can only do their jobs and create value if they can answer these questions and use their answers as the foundation of a strategy which demands the purposeful commitment of resources—people and capital and all else that is needed to make an idea a valuable opportunity. For example, Dr. Edwin Land's ideas for instant photography themselves had a certain value, but he increased their value substantially by building the Polaroid Corporation to manufacture and sell the products developed from those ideas.

Commitment to a strategy and the conversion of that strategy into an operating plan has an inherent value for managers seeking to improve performance. ''It [a plan] suppresses or reduces hesitancy, false steps, unwarranted changes, of course, and helps to improve personnel. It is a precious managerial instrument,'' wrote Henri Fayol (1972), a very successful early twentieth-century French manager.

ANALYSIS AND ACTION ARE INTEGRAL TO STRATEGIC MANAGEMENT

Strategy is a means to the organization's objectives. But selection of the route is not enough; implementation is required to actually achieve objectives. Strategies must be formulated then implemented if they are to have results, and it is on results that organizations and managers are measured. *Analysis and action are essential.* Robert Adler, the President of the Bic Pen Corporation, said:

> What's important once a decision is made is to make sure that it comes out right. The decision is not so important; it's the outcome. A president must say to himself: "I will now make my decision successful."[1]

In successful organizations, a review of results achieved leads to more successful strategies. Analysis and action are linked over time and strategic management is, in a sense, learned. Argyris (1977) has termed this type of process ''double-loop learning,'' distinguishing it from ''single-loop learning'' which is restricted to attempts to correct specific errors. Double-loop learning, in contrast, requires thinking which questions fundamental premises and assumptions to determine how a company's resources can be put to better use.

Some authors have focused on the learned nature of strategic action, pointing out that the learning is slow and occurs one step at a time. Quinn (1980) used the term ''incrementalism,'' since future strategy is generally based on past experience and modifi-

[1]Bic Pen Corporation (A) and (B) HBS Case Services No's 374-305, 374-306, 1974.

cations of past strategy. Ohmae (1982) sensibly pointed out, however, that although strategy may be learned and developed through an iterative process, creative insights founded in experience are the hallmarks of the outstanding strategist and of successful value creation.

The competition between General Motors and Ford in the 1920s illustrates the interplay of analysis and action, learning and insightful creativity. At a time when the favorite quotation of Henry Ford's observers was his dictum, "You can have it in any color as long as it's black," General Motors chose to provide "a car for every pocketbook." GM's strategy addressed the individual needs of its customers in a way Ford could not. Instead of competing head-on with Ford on a cost basis, Ford's strength, GM broadened its product line to offer more value to its customers through their choice of GM's Chevrolet, Pontiac, Buick, Oldsmobile and Cadillac automobiles. Ford saw its earnings decline substantially as the market changed. Only after GM had successfully taken the leadership position in the industry did Ford respond by broadening its product line to imitate GM.

Analysis and action, learning and creativity, are also evident in the early story of Timex. Joachim Lehmkuhl, Timex's founder, competed with the established Swiss watchmakers by offering a mass produced pin lever watch which everyone could afford, in a market where people were used to buying a watch as "the gift of a lifetime." Lehmkuhl wanted to sell Timex watches at low prices and low margins, but jewelers rebuffed him. Turning to drugstores as an alternative channel, Lehmkuhl added a one-year guarantee to affirm his watch's reliability. Timex's strategy eventually captured 50 percent of the US watch market. As Timex watches grew more popular, the company promoted watches as fashion goods in its efforts to continue to increase sales. Greater volume allowed Timex to lower its costs still further and enhance its already superior assembly skills.

In the recent past, Bic has fought Gillette with various degrees of success in a number of markets, including the ballpoint pen and the disposable lighter markets. In its most recent attack on Gillette, Bic has used all its experience and resources to develop and execute its strategy in the razor market. It attacked Gillette's enormous strength in razorblades with the single-unit disposable razor—certainly a creative and insightful attempt to unseat the Goliath of the world razor business.

STRATEGIES AND OBJECTIVES AT ALL MANAGEMENT LEVELS

Although the stories of strategic change in organization sometimes make strategy formulation and implementation sound like the prerogative of the chief executive officer (CEO) and board of directors, strategic analysis and action is spread throughout every organization. Strategy is, therefore, relevant to every manager, senior or junior, top-level and middle. Strategies are implemented by people at all levels in the organization, not just people at the top. The analytical inputs and creative insights required to define or formulate a strategy, as well as the actions needed to implement it, occur at every level in an organization. Strategic analysis encompasses the likely reactions of affected people to the proposed strategic actions as well as likely market responses. Managers at every level have different roles to play in the formulation and implementation of strategy.

Consequently, strategies and objectives must be designed to link the levels of the organization together so that efforts are focused and coordinated and the desired results are achieved. The hierarchy of strategies and objectives is, therefore, one of the underlying rationales for the administrative and organizational structure of the firm. For example, when there are corporate, divisional, product, and functional strategies and objectives, there should be a parallel organizational structure. All these organizational levels are linked by the ends-means chain, the hierarchy of objectives and strategies, and each level provides results and environmental data needed for management of the firm. The strategies at one managerial level define the objectives of the next lower level of management, with the firm's top-level objectives reflecting the goals of its major stakeholders.

WHY LEARN ABOUT STRATEGIC MANAGEMENT?

As a future manager, ability to understand your firm's strategy is an important skill for it will enable you to be a more effective manager of the resources for which you are responsible. As you use this book, you will develop experience in case discussions. On the job, the sooner you think and act like a manager, the faster you will be one—and an effective one.

Strategic management training helps you develop a sense of what an organization's critical problems and priorities are. If you recognize what your organization wants of you, you can make yourself more valuable in the organization. By producing results that matter, you can enhance your power to get things done. You need power to get results, and results beyond expectations enhance power. Salancik and Pfeffer (1977) wrote, "Power adheres to those who can cope with the critical problems of the organization."

The worth of strategic management, then, extends to personal career management. The skills you will develop in sizing up environments and organizations can help you make better personal career decisions. They will help you recognize the opportunities which really match your skills, interests, and needs.

PREVIEW

This text is structured to help you understand and use the concept of strategy. The strategic management process is outlined in Chapter 2 and the steps needed to formulate and design strategies for single-business firms are discussed in detail in Chapters 3 through 10. Implementation is discussed in Chapters 11 to 14. We examine the complexities of the multibusiness firm, the use of strategic management concepts in diversified corporations, and the global corporation in Chapters 15 through 19, and conclude with a discussion of leadership in Chapter 20.

The cases in this book have been selected to allow you to practice strategic analysis and to explore the merits of alternative actions in real managerial situations. You will meet strategists who are brilliant and those who are not, managers who are effective implementers and some who are not. You will see for yourself how the systematic approach of strategic management can improve the effectiveness and efficiency of many kinds of organizations.

Your reading and discussion of the case material will uncover personal factors, beliefs, and values which affect the workings of an organization and the choices it makes. The personal feelings of the firm's stakeholders have meaning and implications for the efficient functioning of an organization and affect the contributions they are willing to make (Barnard, 1966). Individuals are a major influence on organizational performance.

To sum up, strategic management requires analysis and action. An effective strategic manager adds value, marshalling resources and people to work effectively and efficiently in the environment of the firm and within its organization to achieve its objectives. To be a successful manager, you must develop strategic management skills. Take this opportunity to learn to think and act strategically.

chapter 2

The Strategic Management Process

INTRODUCTION TO THE MODEL

In this chapter, we introduce and outline the strategic management process. The framework will guide you through the book as you develop your own capacity to think and act strategically. Your understanding of this process will develop as you focus in turn on each of its stages in the following chapters.

The model presented here is shown in *Figure 2-1*. It is founded in the reality of good management practice, since it moves from the *present* strategy of the firm, supported by the resources and strengths generated in the *past,* to the design and implementation of a strategy which will carry the firm successfully into the *future*. It is an iterative process, that is, a process repeated over time, since the strategy in use must be evaluated from time to time to determine whether it is likely to succeed in the future.

The strategic management process is consistent with the best traditions of management. For example, Henri Fayol in 1916 described the administrative system he used at the French steel company, Comambault, as

> . . . concerned with each and every part of the undertaking. It shows the situation in the present, in the past, and in the probable future. The historical part . . . deals with the considerations that led to the formation of the enterprise, the changes that have taken place, and the results that have been achieved. The present situation is shown in full detail as to the resources and needs of the undertaking, looked at from every point of view. The probable future is arrived at by taking into account the past, present, and the prevailing circumstances, economic, political, and social. (Fayol, 1972, p. xi)

You will see it is related to our model. This was essentially the model upon which James McKinsey developed the analytical practices of McKinsey and Company, one of the most successful international management consulting firms (Wolf, 1978).[1]

[1]Gilmore (1970, 1971) used a model of the strategic management process which began like ours with the reality of current strategy and its subsequent evaluation. So did Henderson (1979).

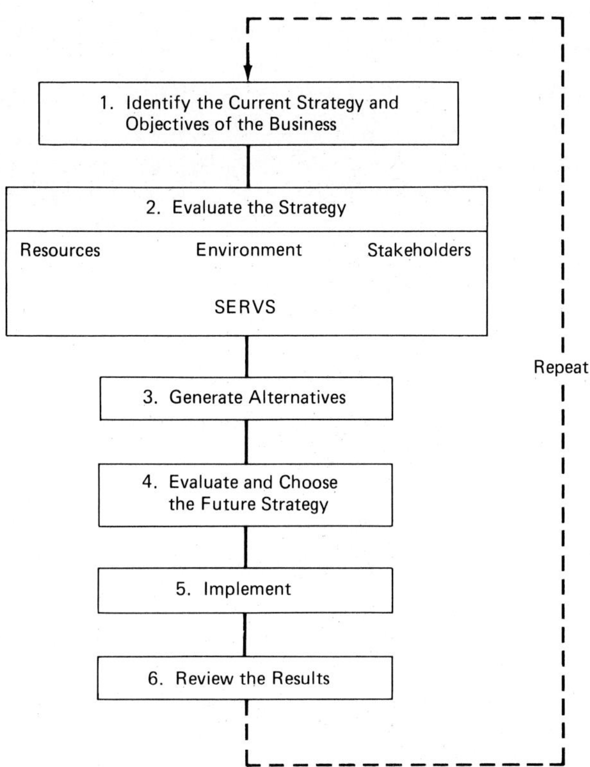

FIGURE 2-1 The Strategic Management Process

With this outline of the entire strategic management process, you will be able to move quickly into an active, participative role in case discussions. Of course, your performance in the various stages of the strategic management process will improve as you learn more and put your knowledge to work. The overview of the complete model is, therefore, a roadmap which you can use to develop your understanding of the cases you study. You can also use it to monitor your mastery of the strategic management process as you become more experienced with each step. Let us now outline each step of the process.

STEP 1: IDENTIFY THE CURRENT STRATEGY AND OBJECTIVES

To reach any destination, you need to know where you are, your starting point. Identification of the organization's current strategy and objectives gives you a starting point: the management approach currently being followed.[2]

Current strategy need not be explicit, but it always exists. Current strategy is what the company is doing presently. Its objectives are what it is trying to do. Managers have to make decisions and get results in some way. Even if they cannot articulate their strategy

[2]Even the product champions who have succeeded in bringing major innovations to market have controlled the risks they have faced by first demonstrating results and winning the allegiance of more powerful sponsors who can absorb early losses (Schoen, 1969).

precisely, it can be discovered in the pattern of actions, decisions, and commitments they have made in each of the functional areas and operations which comprise the business, or in each of the businesses which comprise the activities of the multibusiness corporation. Their objectives are similarly revealed by their results.

Since strategy in the context of a single business coordinates the functional areas, the functions represent the starting point for strategic analysis anchored in current reality. Awareness of the functional activities—for example, marketing, finance, production, human resources management—is the key to identifying the business strategy. At Miller Brewing (to use a single-business example), the marketing strategy was to reposition the Miller brand for broader appeal, extend the product line, and advertise extensively. The production strategy was to increase capacity and technical efficiency by building new, large-scale breweries. The financial strategy used resources from the parent, Philip Morris, to increase the fixed assets and working capital available to expand and operate Miller. The human resource strategy brought Philip Morris's cigarette managers with package goods marketing skills into the brewing company. All these strategies were linked together by their objective, the commitment to growth in the marketplace. Indeed, Miller's overall strategy could be characterized as sales growth to gain a dominant competitive position in the industry. Since objectives and strategies form an ends-means chain linking all levels of the corporation, it is logical that functional objectives carry information on the higher-level business strategy, and business strategy defines the objectives of the lower-level managers.

STEP 2: EVALUATE THE STRATEGY: RESOURCES, ENVIRONMENT, AND VALUES

Once identified, a strategy must be evaluated to determine whether it should be changed. Since strategies are designed to achieve objectives, they are evaluated by focusing on the results they have achieved or promise.

Strategies are evaluated by examining their present or expected results in the light of the firm's resources, its probable environment, and the interests of its stakeholders. Evaluation first requires a consideration of results against the resources available to support them. Are the resources applied against consistent objectives? Are the goals consistent, coordinated, and mutually supportive? Do the results to date represent a satisfactory return on the resources invested? Can the resources available yield the desired results in the future? Secondly, evaluation requires an analysis of the probable results of the strategy in the likely future environment of the firm. Will the strategy work in the future? Finally, it is important to determine whether the strategy's likely results will satisfy the interests of the organization's stakeholders, since their opposition may prevent the successful implementation of the strategy.

Evaluating strategies with respect to the *resources* available will reveal the firm's competences, strengths, and weaknesses. But there are no strengths or weaknesses in an absolute sense; they exist only in relation to the competition in the probable future environment (Stevenson, 1976). For example, Polaroid's strategy and resources appeared weaker after Kodak entered the instant photography market in 1976.

Probably one of the most serious errors which can be made in strategy evaluation is to ignore the *environment* in which the strategy will be implemented, behaving as if the strategy had a life of its own independent of the industry, the macroeconomy, and the social-political environment. Environmental assessment is a necessary component of strategy evaluation. The future environment must be forecast to estimate what the likely future results of a strategy will be.

The environment important to the firm's success is multifaceted. Obviously, the environment exists at the level of the industry—the competitive arena. But it also includes the macroeconomic environment which affects demand, prices, capital costs and returns within an industry. It further encompasses the social-political environment which can rapidly alter stakeholder power and objectives and thereby affect the viability of a particular strategy or objective.

The *values and objectives of the firm's stakeholders* must be understood to assess the strengths of commitment or resolve behind any strategy. Managers must become conscious of the interests, power, and objectives of their internal (e.g., employee) and external (e.g., outside stockholders, suppliers) stakeholders, because stakeholder groups can either support or block implementation of a particular strategy. We need to remember what Cyert and March (1963) wrote: "Organizations do not have objectives; only people do." Action, and particularly unified action, is only possible when sufficient numbers of critical people can be induced to support the strategy—at reasonable cost.

People typically have to get something or expect future rewards before they give their support to a cause. Unless people support a strategy, its results are likely to be unsatisfactory (Bourgeois, 1980). Hence, in evaluating the strategy, it is important to determine who is getting what, and why. This is also a preliminary step to developing more effective and efficient action; strategic action will succeed only if the firm's stakeholders are managed. If people do not like the results they get, they are unlikely to act as they must for the strategy to achieve the objectives it was designed to realize. Dr. Edwin Land of Polaroid, for example, wanted to develop instant photography. He believed that instant photography was superior to conventional photography and he would not commit resources in the older field. Even though 35 mm. photography has become popular as a large segment of the photography market, Dr. Land's values and beliefs prevented Polaroid from taking timely advantage of this market, ignoring it until more than thirty-five years after the corporation was formed.

To summarize, an organization's resources, its environment, and its stakeholder objectives must all be considered in evaluating a strategy. The essence of good strategy is internal consistency and a good fit with the current and future environments. A good strategy will be one where the firm has the resources it needs to succeed; where the functional strategies and resources are internally consistent and support the business strategy; where environmental trends will increase its likelihood of success; and where the objectives of sufficient numbers of the firm's stakeholders are achieved in order to garner support and commitment.

A simple acronym may be helpful to you in developing a strategic perspective in your early case analyses: SERVS, which stands for current strategy – environment – resources – values – future strategy. To formulate a new strategy, a firm's current strategy, environment, resource base, and stakeholders' values must all be balanced and integrated. A strategy for the future which integrates all of these factors and takes their interdependencies into account will "serve" the organization well. The "S" on the ends of SERVS should remind you that strategic management is an ongoing process, reassessing and modifying the organization's commitments and objectives when improved performance is possible and worth the effort.

STEP 3: GENERATE ALTERNATIVES

Of course, if there is nothing wrong with a firm's strategy, don't fix it. The status quo is always an option which deserves consideration, often because it has the lowest monetary and organizational costs since it is already in place. The status quo option can be used to highlight risks and rewards of other options if they are compared to the current course.

But what if the fit between the current strategy and the environment, resources, and values in the firm is not good, if the firm's resources, environment, and some of its stakeholders' objectives do not match its current strategy? Then there is a strategic problem. In many companies, the strategy evaluation process reveals problems which must be resolved and new opportunities whose potential should be assessed. A manager seeking to improve the organization's performance first must determine what problems and opportunities exist and then decide which are worth the effort and will contribute to the organization's future success. In this context, it is important to realize that every problem or threat is an opportunity to implement an improved strategy which may result ultimately in far greater success than the original strategy could promise.

Generation of alternatives is the step which requires shifts between analysis and synthesis, because it demands both types of thinking. One useful way to generate alternatives is to work out what is needed, through analysis of resources, environment, and stakeholder objectives, and then determine what actions will achieve the desired position.

Typically, your sense of problems within a business will come from a failure to meet objectives, from organizational strife, from inconsistencies you have identified, from a sense that your competence has been declining or that you are losing financial vigor. While these are all signs and symptoms of problems, it is important to address causes when you develop solutions. Your sense of opportunity will come from your successes, from the enthusiasm your organization has for a particular project, from your sense of an unserved market ignored by your competitors, and a realization that you have money to invest—that is, underused resources.

Concentrate your efforts on the critical issues and the most promising opportunities. Typically, 80 percent of the problems are in 20 percent of your operations and 20 percent of your initiatives will contribute 80 percent of your successes. Your planning and information system should be designed to separate the good from the bad.

When evaluation shows the firm would benefit from rethinking its strategy, what kinds of alternatives are sensible and attractive? Strategists rarely move directly to new and untested concepts; strategic change is rarely radical. It is generally evolutionary, exploiting the firm's resource base and momentum with trials and experiments, with "incremental" changes to the original (Quinn, 1980). Few managers will "bet a company" or a career on a completely unknown and untried course; the risk of failure and its costs are too high.

Another way to develop alternatives exploits "brainstorming," focused on ideal solutions instead of problems. This approach works best when there is a strong foundation of fact and experience on which to begin, and when traditional problem solving is unproductive (Emshoff, Mitroff, and Kilmann, 1978). It moves from the ideal to the possible, seeking ideas which contain the germ of a strategy that will work. Creativity without immediate evaluation and discarding of ideas is important if you use this approach, however, since nay-sayers at this stage only constrain the organization to traditional and limited views of itself and its options. Levitt's message in "Marketing Myopia" (1960), Ansoff's concept, "common thread" (1965), and Ohmae's *The Mind of the Strategist* (1982) all stress the value of creative or insightful thinking as a base for strategic change. Unbridled creativity is the essence of brainstorming, although criticism is useful later when the raw ideas are honed for use in the organization. Note, too, that the leap from idea to practical insight, invention and innovation is, to quote Thomas Edison, "95 percent perspiration and 5 percent inspiration."

STEP 4: EVALUATE ALTERNATIVES AND CHOOSE THE FUTURE STRATEGY

To evaluate alternative strategies, their results must be anticipated and again considered with respect to their fit with resource availability, the environment, stakeholder objectives, and current direction of the firm. New strategies require implementation, so the plan to make the proposed strategy work in the organization must be developed and evaluated in light of the organization's ability to marshall the necessary resources and garner internal organizational support. Thus, the proposed strategy's fit with the organization must be examined both analytically in the context of the competitive market, and for its ability to induce commitment and actions in the organization and thereby succeed.

STEP 5: IMPLEMENT

A decision alone does not solve a strategic problem. Action must follow analysis. It is at least as important to think about how something will be done, who will do it, and when, as it is to think about what is to be done, the strategy itself.

Implementation must fit the current and likely future organizational realities. It must be practical within the organization's culture and acceptable to the organization's stakeholders, particularly its internal stakeholders, since their support is critical to its implementation.

Thinking through the implementation process first is likely to alert a good strategic manager to contingencies which could weaken the strategy's effectiveness. Predetermined milestones, or bench marks, facilitate a "try and check" approach, allowing review of the strategy while it can still be modified. Limited commitments represent a practical approach to the problem of strategic innovation and the management of corporate and personal, or career, risk exposure.

STEP 6: REVIEW RESULTS

Effective managers limit commitment and use time to develop results which they use to justify greater resource commitments. Argyris (1977), Quinn (1980), and Braybrooke and Lindbloom (1970) all stress the use of milestones to facilitate learning about what works and what does not and thereby improve strategic performance on an ongoing basis. The availability of milestones and your ability to modify particular alternative strategies must be considered when you evaluate strategies.

Good managers make decisions while there is still time to choose among alternatives. They thus limit the risk associated with the new strategy and gain the freedom to experiment. This freedom and flexibility can be preserved over time if the results of the selected strategy can be monitored and the strategy modified when the results are not satisfactory.

SUMMARY

Strategy is the means used to achieve an organization's ends. Good strategic management requires marshalling the resources, accumulated by the organization during past and current operating cycles, to perform effectively in the likely future. It requires creative generation and rational evaluation of alternative strategies using information on the past and forecasts of the future, followed by reviews of results to ensure that the organization is performing as desired and maintaining a viable relationship with its environment and its stakeholders.

Strategic management is a learning process. Organizations and strategists can learn from their past and current results what works in the market and in their organization, and what does not. The objective of this learning is effectiveness. Indeed, strategic management is an ongoing organizational activity; it is always seeking a better match between an organization's strategy and its components, its resources, its environments, and its stakeholders' objectives.

Strategy must serve the organization while the organization serves the strategy. The concept is simple, yet its simplicity is both a source of frustration and a source of power. Effective strategies work, ineffective strategies do not. This is a very simple principle, much like the stockbrokers' rule, "Buy low, sell high"—easy to understand but difficult to implement. Similarly, there are only eight notes in a musical scale, yet they can be arranged in an infinite number of ways. The rules are simple, but only practice leads to mastery. So it is in the field of strategic management: you must practice to master it.

chapter 3

Identifying the Strategy and Objectives of a Business

INTRODUCTION: THE SHORT CUT TO STRATEGY

Management must assess the current reality of its business before trying to move an organization in a new direction toward some future position. The first step of the strategic management process, then, requires identification of an organization's current strategy and objectives as a prelude to deciding whether changes are necessary. There is another important reason to learn how to identify strategy and objectives: understanding your competitors means understanding their strategy. This chapter shows you how to identify the strategy of a business using a technique we call Functional Analysis.

Identifying a strategy means discovering or isolating the critical and essential elements of what the firm does in the competitive marketplace. Suppose we met an organization's chief executive officer at a party and asked, "What does your company do?" The answer we would receive would probably be a summary of the firm's strategy. The response requires clarity, directness, and brevity, and it would highlight the special elements of that organization which distinguish it in the marketplace. For example, an entrepreneur in the shoe industry might say, "We make and distribute fashionable children's shoes using the latest available technology." Dr. Land of Polaroid might have answered, "We develop the technology of instant photography." Both answers express the focus of the firm and the CEO's perceptions of his or her own activities.

Indeed, "What does your company do?" can generate quite a conversation. The verbs used to respond to the question describe the key actions of the firm, its strategy. Subsequent discussion in response to an implicit question, "Why?"—as, for example, "We want to be the biggest in the industry," or, "Because man has always wanted an instant record of his activities"—reveal the objectives of the firm.

OBJECTIVES AND STRATEGY

Objectives are very important. They point towards desired future achievements rather than describe current activities, and so must be differentiated from strategies. Objectives are the ends of business strategies; strategies are the means used to achieve them.

Strategy identification encourages managers to reduce the activities of a business to its essentials, and so requires a view of the linkages between the business's various activities. Levitt (1960) advises managers to define their business in a few words and so get at the essential kernel of their activities. However, although abstractions like "railroads are in the transportation business," and "oil companies are in energy," may be provocative and useful in certain circumstances, they tend to be too generalized and brief for managers who need tangible products and plans to guide them. To satisfy this need, we can follow Andrews (1980) and advise managers to focus on their own organization's distinctive competence and to develop their future strategies from that base.

An ability to see things freshly by selectively exploiting abstractions or tangible product-based or resource-based approaches is important when you are developing and evaluating strategic alternatives. Applying established skills and using the resources you control is easier and less risky than tackling opportunities which require totally new skills and new resources. Levitt (1960) pointed out that "marketing myopia" (too narrow a view of the firm's activities) can blind managers to the opportunities on which they might build future markets. Nevertheless, research suggests that wandering too far afield is rarely profitable (Rumelt, 1974, 1982; Salter and Weinhold, 1978; Salter, 1979).

The job of adding value is simpler when you put your current skills and resources to work, using your distinctive competence to gain a competitive advantage. This means you must know your current strategy and understand both the opportunities it presents and the constraints it imposes on your future actions.

IDENTIFYING BUSINESS STRATEGY: FUNCTIONAL ANALYSIS

If organizations always clearly and explicitly stated their own strategies, identifying strategy would be easy for most people. But this happens infrequently and, besides, organizations drift; what they intend is not always realized (Mintzberg, 1978). Normally, we must discover the strategy in the practices of the organization, that is, by looking at what people do at the functional level. We call this Functional Analysis.

The first step in Functional Analysis is to develop a description of what the company is doing in each of its functions. We simply record what is done in each function—marketing, finance, operations, human resource management, for example. Next, we identify the objectives of each function and extend the analysis by tracing the relationships between subfunctional elements within functions and across functions. Awareness of the important elements within each functional area helps us gain significant insights into the firm's current strategy, its distinctive competence, and the sources of its competitive advantage.

Figure 3-1 is illustrative of the functions and subfunctional strategies which a manufacturer might consider. Service organizations use similar, if not exactly the same, activities to deliver their services. Let us briefly examine each function before discussing how functional actions reveal business strategy.

FIGURE 3-1 Functional Analysis

Marketing	*Production/Operations*	*Finance*	*Administrative Strategy*

Market:
Geographic scope and target segments
Unserved potential
 	
Product:
Physical or tangible product
Supplementary service/benefits
Technology level
Extent of product line
Focus of development
 	
Price:
Relative price level and range
Use of price changes
 	
Promotion:
Use and role of sales force
Choice and use of media, discounts
Push or pull emphasis
 	
Place (Distribution):
Number of channels
Channel role(s) services rendered
Margins allowed
 	
Product Development
	Scope of Operations:
	Extent of vertical integration
	  Owned
	  Contracted
	
	Functions Performed:
	Sourcing
	Number, size, location of plants
	Logistical spread
	Value added
	Product line
	
	Type of Operations:
	Process type
	Flexibility/specialized
	Breakeven volume
	Operations leverage/contribution margin
	Focus of plants
	Capital/labor intensity
	
	Development:
	Process/product
	Technology risk level
	Engineering content
	
	Operations Control:
	Plant focus
	Stability of line
	Size and role of inventory
	Control
	  Operations/scheduling
	  Quality
	  Cost reduction practices
	Labor
	  Skill level
	  Supervision needed
	  Union status
	
	Cost Position
	
	Experience Level
		Source of Funds:
		Use of debt
		
		Deployment of Funds:
		Dividend payout percentage
		Additions to fixed assets and working capital
		
		Liquidity Position
		
		Capital Structure
		
		Earnings per Share Pattern:
		Smoothed or varying
		
		Growth:
		Internal
		Acquisition—
		  Stock
		  Cash
			Structure:
			Type
			Role of hierarchy
			Span of control
			Formal/informal structure
			
			Systems:
			Clarity of objectives
			Performance measures
			Performance appraisal
			Resource allocation
			Planning and control information
			
			Human Resources:
			Recruiting
			Development
			Compensation
			Bonuses
			Promotion
			Job security
			
			Culture:
			Principles
			Attitude to risk/reward
			Fit

Marketing Strategy

Marketing manages the relationships between a firm and its markets, the demand relationships for its products. To describe a firm's marketing strategy, we must begin by identifying the firm's market as well as take note of the firm's views of the served and potential markets for its products or services.

We recommend that you use the "4 P's" of marketing to describe the significant elements of marketing activities: *Product, Price, Promotion,* and *Place* (distribution) (McCarthy, 1960). By examining in turn what the organization is doing on each of the 4 P dimensions, its current marketing strategy will become clear.

Sometimes it is useful to categorize marketing strategy as "Push" or "Pull." *Push* means that the firm attempts to force its product through the distribution system with dealer discounts or promotions slanted toward the distributor, raising the distributor's margins, and so inducing the distributor to sell more of the product. Procter and Gamble, for example, may reduce its price to distributors by 20 percent for a two-week period and so push its Duncan Hines cake mixes through the system.

Pull strategies, in contrast, appeal to the product's final consumers with brand advertising, promotion, or "cents off" coupons, for example. Wisk laundry detergent's "ring around the collar" ads provide an example of Lever Brothers' use of a pull marketing strategy, with the corporate message focused on the final consumer. New products may greatly benefit from a pull strategy when distributors are reluctant to add to their line. A pull strategy might make consumers sufficiently aware of the new product to ask store managers for it; store managers may, in turn, demand it from their distributors.

Operations Strategy

Operations strategy refers to the elements of production, or supply, which are materials, labor and plant. Knowing how the product or service is sourced, produced, and delivered is essential, because control of a major source of raw material or a unique process may provide a cost, quality, or reliability advantage for the business. To identify the operations strategy, examine the operations tradeoffs management has made. For example, how specialized is the production process, and how close to capacity does the company operate its production facilities? Concerning capacity expansion, it is important to note what risks the firm takes. Does it "frontload" by building capacity ahead of sales, or "backload" by building sales and market share before committing to capacity additions? In the brewing industry in the 1970s, Schlitz followed a financially risky and expensive front-loading production strategy, betting that management could quickly develop new markets, while Miller backloaded and risked having some unsatisfied customers rather than inexorable fixed costs and lower returns.

Financial Strategy

Financial management must fund the organization's strategy while satisfying the needs of its financial stakeholders. The company's sources of funds and its use of those funds reveal its financial strategy. Operations, debt, and equity are the principle sources of funding for most organizations. Their proportions reveal who has what stake in the organization and where the potential sources of additional funds are.

Financial strategy gives insights into the firm's ability to change direction, its flexibility. Liquidity can be used to balance business and financial risk and give the firm staying power in bad times or an ability to take advantage of opportunity. A liquid position is often maintained by firms who differentiate their products with additional services, such as inventory or credit availability to customers and cooperative advertising with distributors.

A firm's deployment of its assets points to what management thinks about its future. Heavy commitment to fixed assets signals confidence in the stability of future demand, for example. Likewise, a firm's choice of growth strategy—internal development of markets or products, or acquisition, as well as its choice of acquisition terms (stock or cash)—tells of its expectations about its future, reveals the importance of personal control to management, and shows where the company sees future opportunity.

Administrative Strategy

Administrative strategy is concerned with the ways managers work through others to get things done. Managers do not do everything themselves. They design structures and systems, and choose people to manage the firm's resources and produce the results demanded by its strategy and objectives.

The administrative strategy defines how human needs are met, how roles are defined, and how the formal and informal interrelationships within the company are used to achieve business results. *Structure* is necessary to put experienced people in the right places—positions where their experience will add value and reduce risk. *Systems* are needed to measure results and provide information to key people so they can control the firm's operations and improve the allocation of the firm's resources. Results are the basis for reward. Plans and budgets specify results wanted. *People* must be recruited, trained, compensated, and selected for promotion. Management must allocate resources, give appropriate people authority over resources and hold them accountable for results.

Since people are a major resource (ironically, they never appear on the balance sheet, although a few figure in the annual report), human resource strategy is a major aspect of administrative strategy. Indeed, labor may be the only resource which has the potential to generate virtually limitless returns, since it is the only creative resource. Thus, a firm's strategy for handling its people—executives *and* workers both—plays an important role in its business strategy. Specifications of who works in what roles, and how they are chosen, retained, developed, and managed provides important information about the organization.

Managerial time spent on human resource problems is particularly revealing of the strategy followed by the firm. Senior management's time should be spent on people who count, those who can contribute most. In small organizations particularly, management time has a very high opportunity cost since it can be used profitably on many other tasks, and its use in one task precludes its use on another.

For example, the owner of a Midwestern food processing company has limited the time he spends on human resource management, illustrating a simple, understandable, but not necessarily effective human resource strategy. In his firm, over sixty members of the owner's extended family have managerial positions, so their retention depends on their continued good personal relationship with the owner rather than on performance. Retention in this firm is high while accountability is low. The owner spends the bulk of his time on the firm's critical customer relationships and has centralized all strategic decision making. With this strategy, he has done nothing to develop the management capabilities of his firm and has denied his family the opportunity to develop their own strategic management capabilities. He has thereby put his enterprise in long-term jeopardy, since it is unlikely that there will be effective leadership for a lengthy period when he ultimately leaves the company.

This discussion of the components of Functional Analysis points you towards the types of data you will need to collect and categorize to fully describe the functional strategies of the single business firm or business unit. Next, we turn to the important interrelationships between the functions which are critical to business success. Let us now comment briefly on the importance of the interconnections and interdependencies among the components of the strategy.

INTERRELATIONSHIPS AMONG FUNCTIONS: KEYS TO IDENTIFYING BUSINESS STRATEGY

We have noted that to understand strategy at any level in an organization, it is necessary to look down one level at the parts of the organization and catalog what is done and how the parts are interconnected. Indeed, business strategy coordinates the actions of the firm in the market and uses the functions to relate the firm to its environment. Interconnections and interrelationships among functions reveal the important elements of business strategy. In extending your functional analysis, therefore, look for the interrelationships which link the functions.

Among the most important connections are functional objectives. Each functional objective gives insights to the strategy of the business, because it is the higher-level business strategy which specifies the ends, or objectives, of lower-level functional management.

Identification of the functional interrelationships should also help you identify the firm's distinctive competence—the asset or skill upon which its competitive strength has been developed. The interrelationships will also let you develop your view of how that competence is leveraged with the firm's other resources to develop a competitive advantage. Recognizing the distinctive competence and competitive advantages of a business provides more insight into what the business does—its strategy. An illustration which demonstrates the use of Functional Analysis will help you understand these ideas.

STRATEGY AND ITS COMPONENTS: AN ILLUSTRATION

We will use Functional Analysis to identify the business strategy of the Dr. Pepper Company, a soft drink firm, during the 1970s. Since we are interested in a business, we examine its functions and collect data which describe what the company has been doing.

This information has been tabulated for Dr. Pepper, function by function, in *Figure 3-2*. If you study this figure for a few minutes and reflect on what you may already know about Dr. Pepper, you will almost instinctively begin to make connections between the parts.

Functional Analysis uses these connections or interrelationships first to identify functional objectives, and then key elements of business strategy. What were the principal components of Dr. Pepper's strategy and the keys to its success? Try to specify the interconnections, so you can see what is central to its success and what is peripheral.

First, focus on identifying the objectives of the functions. Why does the company do what it does? What results would constitute success for the manager of each function?

At the bottom of *Figure 3-2,* we present our view of Dr. Pepper's functional objectives. Note that they are not single-word objectives in this case; they are what we believe Dr. Pepper's managers wanted, function by function:

1 Marketing: Stable controlled growth. Pull via trial; push via service and relationships with distributors.
2 Production/Operations: Volume sales with limited asset commitment.
3 Finance: Small-company atmosphere. Large dividend payout, liquidity, and tight control.
4 Administrative Strategy: Tight control and stable relationships with distributors cemented by service.

Also, note that Dr. Pepper's objectives, function by function, "add up." They support one another. In fact, they reveal the company's strategy, because the firm is the level above the functions, and it is the firm's strategy which defines the objectives of the functions in the ends-means chain.

What was Dr. Pepper's strategy? Dr. Pepper was a tightly held family-dominated company whose marketing was characterized by consumer pull and distributor push. Its operations were piggybacked onto the operations of the strong franchises of its much larger soft drink rivals, Coke and Pepsi. Dr. Pepper marketed soft drinks by having the soft drink industry's distribution giants carry it to the market. And it was successful because Dr. Pepper is an incremental income opportunity which imposes low costs on its distributors' operations. Its growth was limited by opportunity in the marketplace, or demand, and controlled by its takeout—or, inversely, its willingness to invest.

Note at this point that we have an operational definition or description of Dr. Pepper's strategy which summarizes a very large amount of data. Note, too, that we have not troubled ourselves about what Dr. Pepper's managers said their objectives were. We have inferred the functional objectives for ourselves by looking at results.

Recognize that objectives can be inferred, like strategies, from the pattern of decisions and actions which a company makes and the results it produces. Later in our analysis, we will contrast stated and unstated objectives and seek the managerial and strategic significance of any differences we observe.

Now, we will extend the functional analysis to determine why the company made money during the 1970s and achieved the results it had—over forty years of dividends and market share growth. Consider the functions, one by one. What substrategies are most important? How are the substrategies interconnected? The more linkages there are, the better focused the functional strategy will be. What function is most important and how are the functions themselves linked? The more linkages there are between the functions

FIGURE 3-2 Functional Analysis: The Dr. Pepper Company

Marketing

Market:
Principally the southwest US; covers rest but penetration still comparatively low. Customers "hooked."

Targets:
Regular: 8-18.
Diet: women 18-49.

Product:
Concentrate, fountain syrup, and carbonated soft drink. Regular and sugar-free. Unique, fruit-flavored. 6-8 repeats after trial creates loyal customer.

Price:
Above competition to bottlers. Competitive at retail level. Rare price promotions.

Promotion:
Heavy (20% sales). Intense personal selling/service to bottler. Focused spending on strong markets. Uses coop programs on 2:1 basis to supplement bottler effort. Packaging/point-of-sale important. Advertising emphasis is local (60%). Fountain business pushed to build trial and volume.

Place:
Bottlers 59%; fountain 20%; canners 21%. Franchised bottlers are strong businesses, usually Coke or Pepsi franchises with territory under contract to Dr. Pepper.

Production/Operations

Plants:
2 concentrate plants, Dallas and Birmingham, AL. Texas operation integrated forward as producer of own canned and bottled drinks. Serves largest markets as canner and bottler.

Product:
A secret formula or recipe mixing 23 fruit flavors. Sold as concentrate. Fountain syrup and carbonated drink, not a cola.

Quality:
"Must taste right." 4 checks on bottler annually.

Sourcing:
Sugar is major ingredient; fructose substitution possible in part.

Wholesale Operations:
Principally through strong bottlers of Coke and Pepsi. Usually the #1 distributor in territory. Since Pepper is not a cola, law and other agreements allow this arrangement. Company provides market planning, subsidizes fountain business development. Provides extra minor flavors for those who need them. Travel award incentive program. Maintains personal business relationship. Franchise department tries to limit taxes for franchisees.

Finance

Source Funds:
Operations. Uses no debt financing. Stock tightly held.

Use Funds:
Limited fixed investment. Maintains high cash or liquidity position. Limited need for working capital. High dividend payout (60% earnings). Concentrate and fountain sales contribute most income to company. Company operates integrated plant in Texas, its most deeply penetrated and largest market.

Note: In 1975, company was $138 million sales, $58 million assets; equity $150 million; income $12 million.

Administrative Strategy

Structure:
Simple functional structure, divided geographically in marketing area. 7 layers between CEO and bottler. 2 areas, 7 zones, 34 divisions.

People:
Experienced top management. Emphasis on marketing. Depth developing. Internal promotion favored. "Messianic belief in product."

Culture:
"Golden Rule: "Do unto others as you would have them do unto you."

Principles of Marketing:
- *perfect product*
- *availability via strong distribution*
- *sampling/trial*
- *point of sale advertising*
- *media advertising.*

"Pepper Family." Performance rewarded.

Functional Objectives

Marketing	Production/Operations	Finance	Administrative Strategy
Stable controlled growth. Pull via trial; push via service and relationships.	Volume sales with limited asset commitment.	Small-company atmosphere; large takeout, liquidity, and control.	Tight control and relationship with distributors through service.

(and between the parts of each function), the better focused the firm's total competitive effort will be. The more all of the parts support common objectives and each other, the more effective that focus is likely to be in creating a competitive advantage for the firm.

At Dr. Pepper, there were some powerful linkages. Dr. Pepper's uniqueness appears to be, as the company's advertising tells us, its "original flavor." Dr. Pepper asked for and got a high price from its distributors because the flavor and promotion appeal to a "want to be different" market segment, "the Peppers" who really like and are loyal consumers of Dr. Pepper. The high price allowed high promotional expenditures which facilitated Dr. Pepper's distribution relationships with dominant cola bottlers.[1] Note that marketing and production functions were synergistic; both, in our view, sought volume by reinforcing the company's relationships with its distributors.

In addition, Dr. Pepper's production strategy—piggybacking on Coke or Pepsi distributors and, like Coke, principally supplying only concentrate—both minimized Pepper's fixed asset commitments and limited its rate of growth. These two outcomes lifted dividend potential and increased management's control, since the company had the ability to plow large amounts of money back into the business through promotion and franchisee services. Pepper's high returns were due to uniqueness, focus, and reinvestment in controlled growth, along with a genuine commitment to follow the Golden Rule in its business dealings: sharing the rewards of a coordinated business effort with its distributors. Note that those distributors who were more committed to Dr. Pepper got more resources spent in their markets and so reaped bigger rewards—as did Dr. Pepper.

To conclude this analysis, let us consider what the distinctive competence of Dr. Pepper was, and see if we can determine how that competence was applied in the market to earn the company a competitive advantage which yielded high returns. Dr. Pepper's unique asset is its "most original flavor," but, in our judgment, its distinctive competence was its marketing skills. These are the skills with which "Foots" Clements, Dr. Pepper's Chairman and CEO was most concerned. It was in marketing, too, that Clements enumerated his five principles, which are listed in *Figure 3-2* under Culture. Clements once commented:

> . . . there is one absolute and rigid criterion for every market. Every program for every market must be built around and with the complete utilization of the basic fundamentals—not just one—but all five. J.C. Penney once said they don't rewrite the Bible every Sunday; the same applies to these basic fundamentals.[2]

Dr. Pepper's management was most concerned with marketing, not operations. Essentially, they have delegated the operations function to the experts, the Coke and Pepsi bottlers.

Dr. Pepper's choice of operational strategy allowed them to avoid competition and turn their rivals' strengths to their own company's advantage. Pepper's competitive advantage stemmed from its ability to produce a large incremental profit for its distributors. By applying its own financial and marketing resources forcefully in those markets where it had market share and a strong active distributor, Dr. Pepper cemented its relationship with

[1]Because the courts have ruled that Dr. Pepper is not a cola drink, cola distributors are permitted to sell Dr. Pepper without violating their exclusive flavor bottling agreements with Coke or Pepsi.

[2]Dr. Pepper Co. HBS, 377–146 p. 7.

these same distributors and created a competitive advantage, a low cost position, for itself and them. Again, Dr. Pepper followed ''Foots'' Clements's personal philosophy—to practice the Golden Rule:

> I don't hesitate to profess my beliefs in God and in my business. He gave you whatever talents you have. You can't just take; you have to put something back.[3]

Indeed, one explanation of Dr. Pepper's poor performance in the early 1980s and subsequent leverage buyout by Forstman Little in 1984 was that it moved away from the Golden Rule. It sought a growth level by going national with Dr. Pepper and by purchasing Canada Dry, a strategy which diverted management attention and corporate resources from bottlers in the best Dr. Pepper sales areas.

STRATEGIC EVALUATION: THE NEED FOR CONSISTENCY

Of course, strategies once identified must be evaluated to determine whether they are serving the organization well. But there is one initial criterion that seems to characterize successful businesses: Their functions are balanced, coordinated, and ultimately focused on the same business objectives. Functional strategies must be internally consistent and seek the same ends. Indeed, if a particular function is allowed to dominate the organization, the organization may not be strong enough in its other areas to sustain itself if the conditions which presently suit the business strategy change. On the other hand, if the functions work at cross-purposes, resources will be wasted. Abraham Lincoln understood this when he said, ''A house divided against itself cannot stand.''

Robert Adler, the CEO of Bic, once gave a vivid example of the importance of balance when he likened his business to a car in which all four wheels (the functions) must be on the ground and pointing in the same direction before the car can move. Dominance by one function—the strategic equivalent of a car with a spinning wheel—can generate a source of power which may be inappropriate for the firm's current or future resources and environment. If the wheels are unbalanced and misaligned, tires and gas will both be wasted. So, in business, inconsistencies and misalignments waste resources.

PREVIEW

In this chapter, we have begun the strategic management process by sizing up the reality of the organization. Of course, being able to identify your own strategy means that you have developed the ability to be able to identify and, later, evaluate the strategies of others. It is the critical step in competitive analysis. Knowing your competitors and yourself is important.

[3]*Ibid.* p. 29.

In Chapter 4, we move to strategy evaluation. We go beyond internal consistency to test current strategy for its fit with current and future resources and with the environment, and for its ability to deliver performance deemed important by stakeholders—individuals whose views influence the organization's choices and whose support is important to effectively implement the organization's strategy.

chapter 4

The Strategy Evaluation Process

This chapter introduces strategy evaluation and provides an overview of the following, more detailed chapters on evaluation. The next three chapters deal with the data that managers need to collect and analyze to evaluate their strategy thoroughly. The fifth chapter of the set, Chapter 8, is concerned with the synthesis of the analysis and the summarization of the evaluative effort.

The purpose of this chapter is to alert you to the key concepts used by strategists as they evaluate their own and their competitors' strategies and to explain why evaluation warrants so much attention. If you keep the key concepts of strategy evaluation in mind as you read the following chapters, you will read them more purposefully and find them more valuable than if you use a less deliberate approach.

EVALUATION: AN OVERVIEW

A thorough identification of an organization's current strategy and objectives, its distinctive competence, and its perceived competitive advantage reveals important parts of the reality confronting management. But they are only parts. Moreover, since the thrust of strategic management is to move the organization successfully into the future, then the future environment, the resources available to get the firm there, and the people whose support is needed, must all be considered before the firm commits its resources.

Evaluating a strategy means evaluating its results—past, present and probable. Resources are the accumulated results of past actions. The results of the current operating cycle are the best indicators of what aspects of our current strategy are working in the present environment. Together, past and current results point out the current direction of the organization and reveal likely near-term futures.

Every organization reaches its future by moving from the past through the present to that future. Strategy is a bridge between past and future. Current strategy has a momentum which both constrains an organization's freedom to change and facilitates change if it is exploited. The future results of the current strategy must be anticipated, therefore, before management can prudently recommit to or change its strategy.

When we evaluate a strategy, we focus on results. Resources, future environment, and stakeholder interests are the factors that we have to consider when we look at the firm's current strategy and resources and try to determine what to do next.

Essentially, evaluation helps us to make sense of experience, to determine the meaning of our current results—what led to them, and what they are likely to be in the future. At this point, we can note that managers never *know* what will work. They can only judge what is likely to work best and act on their judgment. They can tell if they're right only after the event (Vickers, 1965).

Usually, managers cannot wait for perfect or complete information but must act in a state of uncertainty. They must be aware that mistakes, errors of judgment, and errors of commission will occur; inappropriate and mistaken actions will be taken. They are not expected to be prophets, merely forecasters. Accountability means that they are responsible for results—what actually happens. They are not expected to be always right—merely to make things work out properly.

With these factors in mind, what managers need first of all is a process that is comprehensive, so that they have an opportunity to review *all* the information that is available to enlighten their judgment. Second, they need a process which is structured to focus their judgment on what counts while protecting them from hastily drawn false conclusions. Finally, it should be possible to abbreviate or collapse the process so that managers facing a developing situation can quickly and effectively bring their experience to bear on the data available and act in their own and their company's best interests.

In the next chapters, we will evaluate a strategy sequentially by reviewing its results in the light of its resources, its environment, and its stakeholder interests. In each chapter, as we collect new data and review the strategy's results, we will reach the following conclusions which indicate key concepts in strategy evaluation:

1 In looking at our results in light of resources, we will identify the *strengths and weaknesses* of the firm and get a sense of what we can do.
2 In examining the environment and anticipating our future performance, we will identify *opportunities and threats* lying ahead and get a sense of what might be done.
3 In determining what our stakeholders' interests, power and objectives are and how they are changing, we will develop a sense of what is *wanted, or possible, or unthinkable,* what actions will serve our interests and others'.

Thus, evaluation means assessing the results produced by our past actions and gauging the likely future success of our current strategy to set the stage for the development of more appropriate and vital objectives and future strategies. Following the sequence—past,

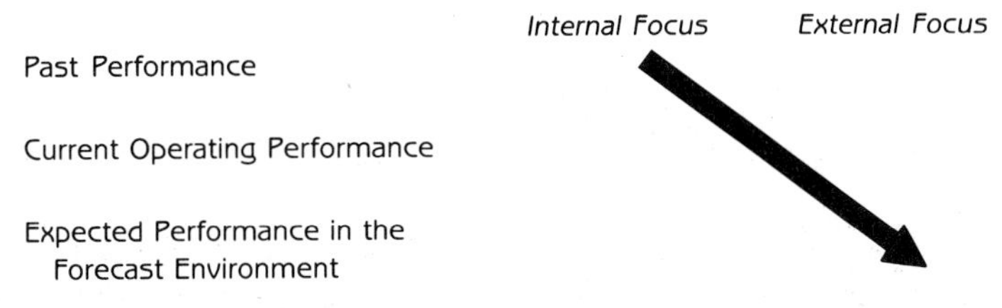

FIGURE 4-1 The Shifting Focus of Strategy Evaluation

present, and future—the strategist shifts the focus of his or her analysis from internal to external factors, as the line in *Figure 4-1* suggests.

Now, before we develop each chapter in detail, let us outline the rationale underlying Chapter 5's emphasis on resources, Chapter 6's focus on the environment, and Chapter 7's concentration on stakeholders. Once this is done, we will develop our synthesis and summarize strategy evaluation.

RESOURCES

Resources are the results of the firm's past strategies. They are the sources of strengths and weaknesses which will affect current and future performance. Resources which have a positive effect on performance are strengths; those which have a negative effect on performance we call weaknesses. For example, a strong brand name would be a positive resource for new product introduction, while poor relations with distributors would be a negative resource and would handicap a new product entry.

Resources can generally be identified with functions—marketing resources in the above example—or with businesses in a diversified enterprise. Since resources are the results of strategies, it is helpful to turn again to functional analysis. In this instance, however, we differentiate between strategies, which are the action verbs, and results, the nouns that are the output of strategies over sequential operating cycles. Of course, a successful past strategy will have produced the results desired and achieved the objectives set earlier. Large disparities, however, will exist between the objectives of unsuccessful strategies and the results they achieved.

Resources come from the past, but the focus of the strategy evaluation process is on the future. Resources link the past and the future; that is, they sit between the past and the future, because they are what the firm has available for its future competitive efforts. Resources are our basis for competing in the future.

Distinguishing those resources which are critical for future competitive success puts us in a position to improve the current strategy. The strategic factors, or keys to success, are the functional strategies which either exploit or result in critical resources. Indeed, one mark of a good manager is that he or she develops and protects the firm's most important resources since, as Chester Barnard (1966) wrote, "Critical resources limit or sustain a company's power and are 'strategic.'" Strategies which focus on critical resources will be successful. Losing strategies neglect what matters most and waste resources, thereby constraining future options and, ultimately, performance.

ENVIRONMENT

While it is important to determine whether the current strategy is working now, it is also important to determine how it will work in the likely future environment. How will today's strategy work in the likely future?

In assessing the environment, we have to be demanding but also realistic. The environment is the outside world; it encompasses everything outside the firm itself. Hence it is unlikely that we can be right about the future all the time and in every detail. Forecasts are needed to guide our actions and a logic is needed to guide our forecasting efforts.

The principle that we advocate is relevance. Focus just on what is most relevant to what you do and avoid aimless "blue-sky" speculations. This principle means that we emphasize what is most critical to the future success of the enterprise and the changes that appear likely, and then broaden our perspective selectively. Thus we first examine the industry of the firm, our suppliers, customers, and competitors, their power and their impact on our strategy. Next we focus on the macroeconomy and its likely impacts on our industry and our firm's strategy. We finally move to our stakeholders, those who constitute the most relevant social and political environment of the firm and who can seriously affect our ability to implement certain strategies.

Environmental assessment is *not* simply environmental extrapolation. We may expect a future like the past, but acting on this opinion requires judgment about the future. Casual extrapolation is an easy way to avoid thinking carefully about the future, that is, about the elements of the past likely to carry over into the future and those likely to be very different. Extrapolation is a common mistake in firms where success has come easily and critical strategic elements have never been carefully assessed. Thinking about the unthinkable and seeking new insights signify assessment rather than extrapolation.

By assessing the likely future—within the industry and competition, at the level of the macroeconomy, and in the larger social-political environment of the firm—we hope to be effective as well as efficiently exhaustive. Thinking through likely competitive reactions to your current strategy prevents many surprises. Understanding the impact of the business cycle and macroeconomic policies on your strategies prepares you to cope with macroeconomic change on a strategic level. Because the firm does not operate solely on an industrial or financial basis, it is better to assess the future social-political environment of the firm early. Early, there is time to prepare to meet it. Later, your actions or reactions are more tightly constrained and so may not be as effective.

Environmental assessment focuses attention on the results you are likely to achieve in the expected future. By first identifying the factors in the environment critical to your success, you can put research and time-consuming forecasting efforts where they are most warranted. You can determine where the strategy must be closely monitored to be sure the future is unfolding in a way consistent with the assumptions you have made about it, and the resources available, thus insuring the success of the strategy.

STAKEHOLDER OBJECTIVES

Organizations are people, not things. And people have a stake in organizational performance. Both internal and external stakeholders in an organization have values which influence their personal objectives, their views of the organization's results, and, ultimately, the objectives of the organization. To manage your stakeholders, it is important to distinguish your stakeholders' "wish lists" from those objectives they will actively support.

Stakeholder objectives which have been internalized by the organization may be discovered by asking, "What is the organization trying to accomplish?" The firm's objectives may be explicitly stated, or they may be unstated and implicit in the firm's priorities and past behavior. But whether explicit or implicit, recognition of stakeholder objectives is important in determining how a strategy will be implemented.

While maximizing profit is the economist's view of a firm's objective, actual objectives are not always or necessarily profit-dominated. For example, John K. Hanson, the founder and major shareholder of Winnebago, the Iowa-based recreational vehicle (RV) manufacturer, probably limited his firm's success by refusing to open plants throughout the country which might have cut transportation costs of the finished RV's and increased the firm's ability to hire professional managers. As a major stakeholder, however, one of his objectives may have been to maintain employment in his home town of Forest City, Iowa. In any event, Winnebagos were manufactured only in Forest City for many years. His actions as a manager certainly were consistent with his personal values. Understanding this key stakeholder is important in evaluating Winnebago.

In evaluating a strategy, it is important to note that a strategy which conflicts with major stakeholder objectives is likely to be very difficult to implement because it has no clear mandate to support it. On the other hand, strategies which appear to be supported by powerful stakeholders are unlikely to be blocked by less powerful individuals inside or outside the organization.

EVALUATION WITHIN THE STRATEGIC MANAGEMENT PROCESS

Evaluation involves analysis, then synthesis, and is a necessary prelude to strategic action. Considering resources in relation to the environment, improved strategies build on strengths and selectively repair weaknesses which are likely to impair future success. Good strategists take advantage of selective opportunities and work to avoid threats in the environment. Strategies can be implemented successfully only if they fulfill major stakeholder objectives and thereby win stakeholders' support and commitment. Of course, because stakeholder objectives will fit to varying degrees with the good of the firm, an element of strategic implementation is developing support for appropriate objectives and choosing which stakeholders to satisfy and which to disappoint.

To summarize, strategy must be made to serve the organization, moving it from the past, through the present, to the future. The important elements which management must synthesize and balance to develop a new strategy are (current) strategy, environment, resources, and values. In the following chapters, we discuss resources, the future environment, and stakeholders in greater depth. Only by increasing our understanding of these factors can we develop our ability to evaluate the current strategy of complex organizations (and competitors) and set the stage for strategic change and improved performance.

chapter 5

Resource Assessment

OVERVIEW

When we outlined the strategic management process, we said that strategy evaluation requires a consideration of both current and likely future results against the resources committed to the strategy. Do the results to date represent a satisfactory achievement given the resources committed? Can the resources available yield the future results required?

Answering these two questions is never easy. The first question, concerning "satisfactory achievement," points to opportunities to improve the performance of current operations. The second, involving "future results," tests the more venturesome entrepreneurial activities of the firm for feasibility—that is, consistency with the firm's capabilities. Answering the questions requires an integrative judgment encompassing results, resources, the future, and competition, as well as objectives and strategy.

Both strategy identification and resource assessment require an understanding of the firm's current situation. Using the current reality as an anchor for thinking about the future, the strategic management process moves from an organizational consensus about facts toward areas of uncertainty where different judgments can be reached by reasonable people. Thus, while strategy identification forces us to confront the reality of what we are doing, resource assessment forces us to review how well we are doing and the reality of what we have. Resources are what we have available for tomorrow's competition. You must know yourself to know what to look for in others; our objective in assessing resources is to identify our competitive strengths and weaknesses.

WHAT ARE STRATEGIC RESOURCES?

Strategic resources are the results of our past strategy. While strategies are verbs, resources are nouns. Strategies are actions, and resources are outcomes.

Resources range well beyond finance and the bottom line. Successful strategic action builds market relationships, arranges supply contracts, and constructs world-scale plants. It develops relationships with distribution channels, confidence in the capital markets, and human and technological capabilities within the firm, as well as earning a profit. Even though most strategic results are nonfinancial, they enhance the firm's market value because they contribute to future earnings growth. Although the board may allow some resources to flow out of the firm as dividends to shareholders, most of the results of successful action accrue to the company and are available for recommitment in subsequent operating cycles.

Resources are enhanced by success, debilitated and wasted by neglect and failure. Of course, when a current strategy is totally successful in achieving its objectives, plans are realized and the current resource inventory will be what was expected. Flaws in a strategy or in its execution will be exposed if the firm does not have resources where management expects or needs them, or if important resources are underutilized.

Having resources allows freedom of action. Having to pursue resources when you are under pressure is a trap which turns energies away from the pursuit of future opportunities. To use resources well, you must know what resources you have. Prudent strategists work within the constraints of their current resource base. In assessing the competitive value of an organization's resources, remember that different resources can have a positive or negative impact on the success of a particular strategy. Positive or negative implies that resources can be strategic assets or liabilities. Assets will generally be the result of past success, while liabilities stem from underachievement, dissipation, or failure.

Note that resources are not absolute quantities but are relative and have a time dimension. Assessing resources involves comparisons with the competition over time. It is the competitive value of resources at a particular time that determines whether they afford a firm advantage or disadvantage, whether the firm is strong or weak. In the real estate industry, for example, prudent people never commit to a project without an understanding of the revenue and cost streams of comparable projects. It should be the same in every business, since it is relative competitive strength in the future which will determine the success of our strategic actions.

In this chapter, we will discuss the various types of resources available to an organization by focusing on each function in turn. Resources exist in marketing, finance, production, and administrative functions, and it is substantially easier to inventory and examine them within those categories than in any other way. Since we identified a firm's business strategy by examining functional strategies, our functional approach to resource assessment exploits a parallel structure and facilitates integrative thinking.

MARKETING RESOURCES

Market power is a firm's ultimate marketing resource. Customers', distributors', and competitors' views of your firm in the marketplace underpin your organization's marketing resources. Their perceptions of your ability to use the 4 P's of marketing (product, price, promotion, and place) to manage your relationships with them affect the firm's market power.

In assessing current market reality, it is reasonable to begin with your customers—your chosen market. How many customers do you have? Who buys what? These may seem like simple questions, but many firms have been surprised by the answers. A

frequently cited but astoundingly accurate rule of thumb is that, for most firms, 20 percent of the customers buy 80 percent of the goods. The strength of these relationships with the top 20 percent of the customers and the nature of the relationship—for example, the relative power and security of customers and supplier—provide information on the basic strength of the business situation.

Different definitions of markets can provide useful information on well-served and underserved (therefore potential) market segments. Majaro (1977) writes of a British pharmaceutical manufacturer which found that an allergy drug had different market shares:

> Stanton, a British ethical drug manufacturer, held 20% of a £5 million retail market for anti-asthma drugs. Trying to sharpen its strategic marketing practices, Stanton researched its markets and discovered that the drug had a 30% share of total prescriptions issued for anti-asthma drugs, although only 18% of doctors actually prescribed Stanton's drug. When asthma sufferers were contacted, 40% were found using Stanton's drug.

This example points to the information content and diagnostic potential of alternate market share definitions. Such information provides important market data to use as a resource in reformulating strategies to hit more effectively the segments that are most profitable to the firm.

In addition to knowing who your customers are, it is also important to know who actually makes purchase decisions. Supermarkets, for example, are finding that men are doing the family shopping more often than some advertisers assumed. The length, quality, and closeness of customer relationships and the quality and quantity of customer contact also give insights into the worth of a customer base as a marketing resource, as well as the costs of servicing certain customers. A positive market resource may be a loyal customer base needing little encouragement, while a fickle, very price-sensitive, or disappointed customer base is obviously a negative marketing resource.

The firm's *products* are a resource, as is the breadth or specialized depth of the product line. Breadth or depth is a positive resource if it contributes to profitability, negative if it contributes excessively to costs or if it has weak elements or gaps which limit sales. Keep in mind the 80 : 20 rule here, too—80 percent of the profits are likely to come from 20 percent of the products. Value to the firm and its customers is the telling product characteristic. It is important to examine each product line's reputation or perceived quality level to understand the roles of function, associated service levels, and socio-psychological benefits, both before and after the sale.

Indeed, the most important aspect of a product as a marketing resource is its perceived value, or the relationship between price and quality. The product's technology also may be important to the market's perception of quality. For example, for the producer of a high-technology product which has a sketchy in-service record, reputation may be a negative resource. This judgment may be softened, however, if the older technology is becoming prohibitively expensive or if the market is made up of early adopters tolerant of in-service difficulties.

Time makes a difference to the value of a product as a strategic resource. What is acceptable early in the product life cycle may be unacceptable later. At what stage of their life cycles are your products? Is demand building, stable, or declining? The product life cycle, shown in *Figure 5-1,* has been criticized because few products experience the

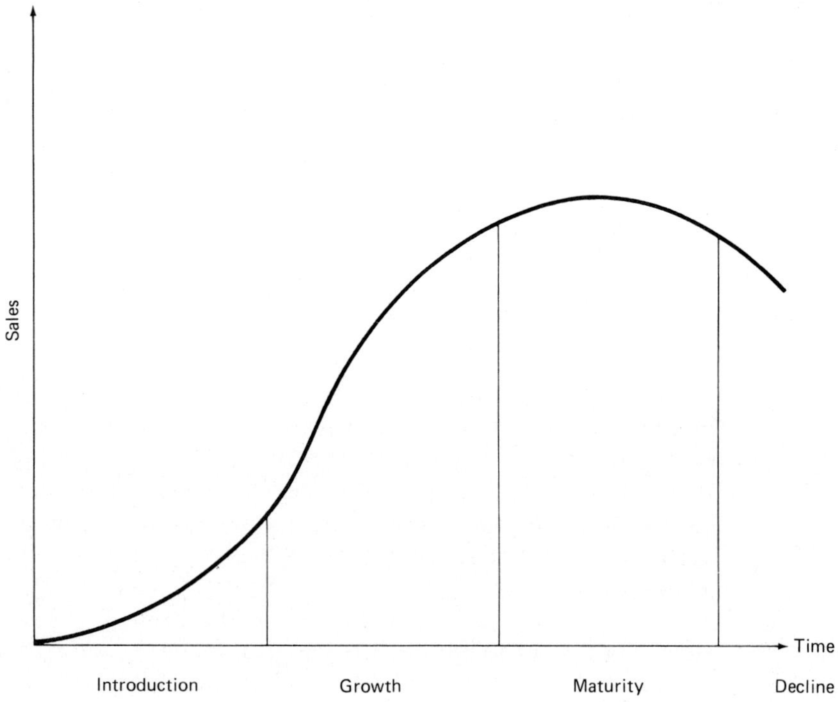

FIGURE 5-1 The Product Life Cycle

classic S-shaped growth pattern, beginning slowly with early adopters, speeding up as the product's reputation spreads, and leveling off as the market is saturated and the product matures. Nevertheless, the life cycle is a useful forward-looking tool for strategic managers and alerts managers to the forces which are likely to affect future sales and profits (Webster, 1979). We will refer to the product life cycle later in this chapter as we inventory the firm's resources in relation to the product's growth stage, and elsewhere in this book when we evaluate strategy and discuss strategic alternatives.

Price position and pricing power in the marketplace refer to another strategic area. Price elasticity of demand, (ϵ) (the absolute value of the percentage change in quantity divided by the percentage change in price), tells much about the firm's ability to charge high prices and gain revenue in the process. A product with an inelastic demand ($\epsilon < 1$) is one where volume responds very little to price increases, allowing the firm to raise total revenue by raising prices.

Firms often are reluctant to raise prices, but when they test their price elasticity, they are sometimes surprised to find the customer willing to pay a much higher price than they had expected. Indeed, this points to a situation where the firm has given away much of the value of its product over time. Successfully raising the product's price proves that it was more valuable to consumers than was originally thought, and the firm has not captured that value for itself by charging a higher price earlier. Relative elasticity, a firm's elasticity compared with others in its industry, summarizes a firm's ability to raise price, or its price leadership. The firm with the lowest elasticity in its industry is the one with the most price power in the marketplace.

Value added is another important characteristic of a product and is related to price. Value added refers to the value added in production, that is, the product's selling price minus its materials costs. A high value added and a high margin demonstrate that the firm's product is highly regarded by the market and that some price cutting may be a feasible strategic option. A high value added and a low margin point to a high capital- or labor-intense business with little market power, dependent on high turnover to earn a satisfactory return.

Price robustness, another marketing resource, is the firm's ability to hold its price in apparently unfavorable situations, such as drops in industry demand (for example, recession), or price cutting by competitors. A robust-priced product can withstand these crises because the customer believes it is still worth paying for. Price robustness is a sign of perceived value and possibly price leadership.

Pricing may also vary over the product life cycle, and management should evaluate its pricing pattern to see if it has enhanced profitability over the life cycle. Polaroid, for example, has used a "cream-skimming" pricing strategy for its instant cameras, setting high prices in the product introduction phase followed by lower prices as the product line gains volume. Kodak, however, typically enters the market with moderate price. It did this with its instant camera product line, possibly believing that a moderate entry price would be more consistent with its mass market strategy. Each company's pricing strategy fit its corporate strategy—Polaroid was a camera company, while Kodak made its money on film and film processing.

Price splits value between the producer and the consumer, resulting in a particular profit-level for the producer and an overall product satisfaction for the consumer. High prices allow the producer to retain more value, while lower prices raise the product's value to the consumer. A wise manager will generally price to retain value of the product, realizing that drastic price reductions will always sell more units but may annihilate producer margins. And past producer margins can be a valuable resource to aid the manager in pursuing an expensive but pre-emptive long-term strategy against competitors.

Figure 5-2 illustrates this price/value concept by showing the producers' and consumers' surpluses for a particular product. Producers' surplus, BCP, refers to the gain over costs which efficient producers experience at the P price level. Consumers' surplus, ABP, refers to the satisfaction gained by consumers who would have been willing to pay more than P to get the product. A price P_1 below P would raise the consumers' surplus and lower the producers' surplus.

In discussing price resources, elasticity, robustness, and value, a useful summary question is: "Are you pricing to value or giving it away?" While lowering prices is often the only way that managers refer to price as a competitive variable, the ability to raise prices unscathed certainly demonstrates competitive power and can achieve a firm's profit objectives without more difficult cost controls. Indeed, having the image of a price cutter can sometimes sully the reputation of a quality product. Raising prices successfully, however, is the mark of a price leader with obvious market power.

Promotion, the third of marketing's 4 P's, is also a repository for marketing resources. What is the organization's media position? Does it do well with the most effective media? How has promotion enhanced the product's quality perception or name

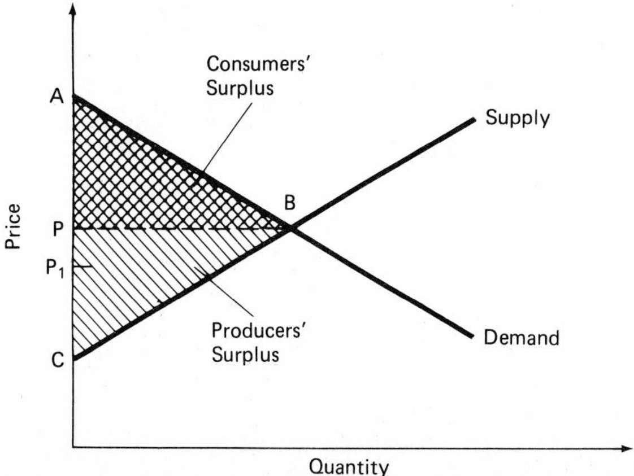

FIGURE 5-2 Producers' and Consumers' Surpluses

recognition? Can its brand, such as Bic or Timex or Kodak, successfully carry new and different products to the marketplace? Are its promotional efforts expected and ineffective, or do they generate interest and excitement? Is its sales force exceptional? Do its customer services cement relationships?

How well do the firm's promotional resources match the product's life cycle stage? Firms introducing products to the mass market early in the life cycle may need only limited promotional resources. A late entrant may need very substantial sums of money to promote its products and achieve a successful entrance. Bic, a \$60-million company in 1973, spent amounts equivalent to 30 percent of its \$10 million operating cash flow to introduce its disposable cigarette lighter into the US market against Gillette. Bic still had cash and securities of \$10 million on hand to prime the promotional pump for subsequent new product introductions, since its strategy has been late entry in emerging markets and such a risky strategy demands high promotional expenditures and reserves should an entry attempt fail.

Firms with more mature products, with substantial brand recognition, may be able to spend differently and spend less on promotion than their competition. Anheuser-Busch, for example, time-pulses its advertising (that is, heavy advertising in a market, followed by no advertising, followed by intense advertising again) across the media to maximize promotional efficiency and limit expenditures (Ackoff and Emshoff, 1975). Coca-Cola is in a similar enviable position in the soft drink market.

Under the promotional heading, too, remember the sales force. Lincoln Electric's salesmen are all trained welders and so are expert sales engineers who can help their customers solve problems at the cutting edge of welding technology. Tasty Baking, manufacturers of the famous Philadelphia Tastykake, has a waiting list of qualified, experienced salesmen stretching out two years ahead of its needs, each one waiting for a call to start work—a remarkable resource, indeed.

To evaluate *place* as a marketing resource, we examine both position in the distribution chain and geographic market. Channel power, power in the distribution chain, is achieved by a firm when the rewards are heavy for little risk, and when the services rendered by the chosen channels are high—for example, the distributors hold title, carry inventory, or provide after-sales service.

In discussing a product's geographic market, we also consider the geographic barriers around our markets, or the barriers around others' markets—a firm could hold a geographic niche. If place is a positive market resource, geographic barriers around us will be high, and those around others very low. The Japanese computer manufacturers, for example, operate in a system where the barriers around them are high due to import restrictions; the barriers around US competitors are low, due to virtually free trade in electronics equipment in the US.

An assessment of market power is a convenient summary of a business's marketing resources. Market power encompasses power in the channel, the ability to raise price, and the ability to set a quality standard. It is important to identify the firm's source of power—the dimension on which it offers great value—and to consider whether it can be sustained.

PRODUCTION RESOURCES

In order to assess production resources, we must understand the production process. What is the technology and process used in production? Is it proprietary or otherwise unique to the firm? Is the product hand-produced or automated, job shop or continuous process? How does the firm relate to suppliers, by contract or integration? What kind of control or planning exists to avoid *ad hoc* coping responses to production snags? Do inventory policies smooth production, yet limit the risks of loss of business and obsolescence appropriately?

How well does the production process fit with the company's marketing strategy and the marketplace? Hayes and Wheelwright (1979) link what they call process life cycles with the product life cycle. They argue that different processes fit better with specific product structures and use *Figure 5-3* to illustrate their case. Note that there are some absolute mismatches, since the further the firm departs from the diagonal, the more complex it is to maintain a useful effective and efficient match between marketing and production. Generally, stable product lines will fit below the diagonal—with heavier investments in plant—while more diverse and changing product lines will fit above the diagonal.

Another indicator of the fit between marketing and production is focus (Skinner, 1974). Are manufacturing and marketing well-coordinated and mutually supportive? Are the plants focused on a limited number of objectives or many? Plants which have a limited number of objectives tend to have higher effectiveness and efficiency, that is, they can more readily and more cheaply achieve their objectives. Focus is a resource.

Costs of production are an indication of managerial flexibility and skill. How are fixed and variable costs balanced, relative to market, and what is the operating leverage? How is the bulk/value tradeoff managed, and do the logistics of transporting supplies and products make economic sense?

Costs of production also shift over time. Here, too, cost escalation or lack of control becomes obvious. How has the cost position changed? Are costs under control? Have cost cutting measures been used? How is quality controlled?

Learning and experience in production should enable unit costs to drop. A firm which has taken advantage of its production experience and opportunities to modify its operating technology should have a production resource or strength contributing to its overall profitability. Firms which have ignored the potential of experience will have high cost positions. We discuss experience in detail in Chapter 6.

Process technology plays an important role in many industries. Specialized, rather than flexible, technology may increase efficiency or quality, but the commitment carries with it strategic risk for the firm because it locks the firm into particular products or processes. The organization's current production technology may be a positive or negative

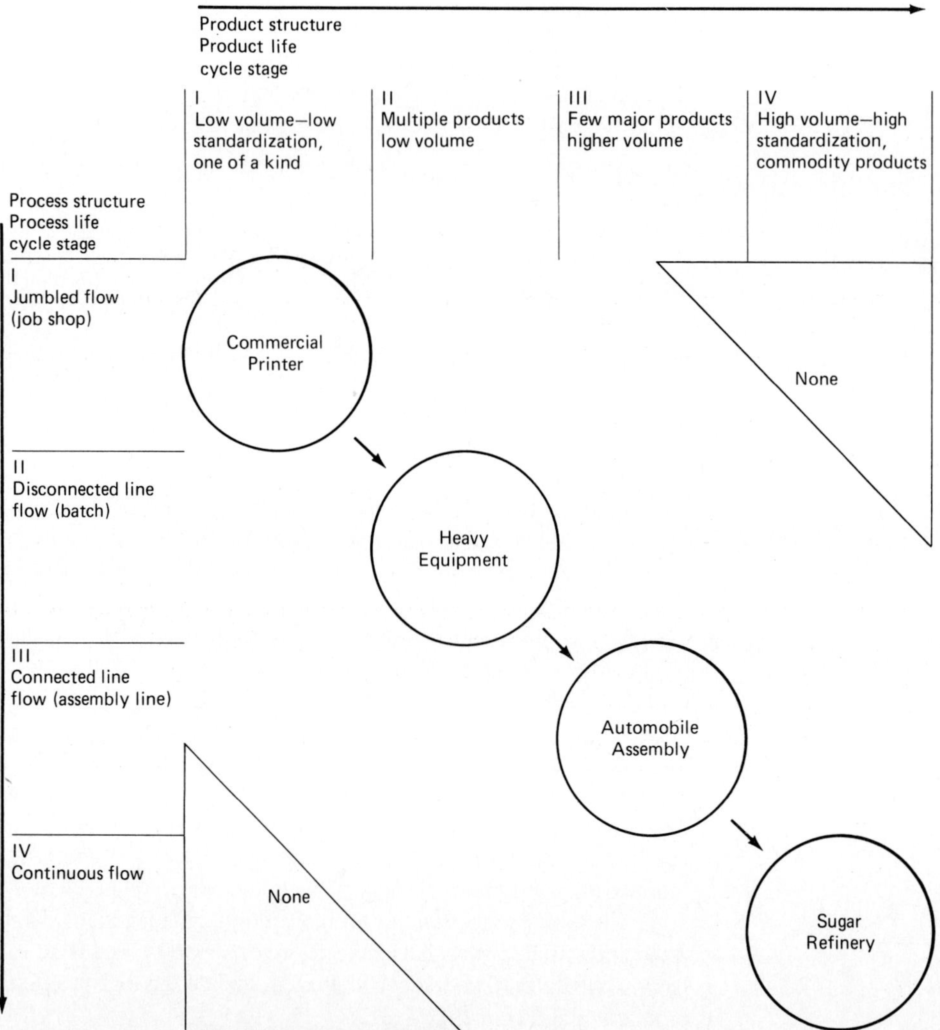

FIGURE 5-3 Matching Major Stages of Product and Process Life Cycles

Source: Robert Hayes and Steven Wheelwright, "Dynamics of Process-Product Life-Cycles," March 1979. Reprinted by permission of the *Harvard Business Review*. Copyright © 1979 by the President and Fellows of Harvard College; all rights reserved.

resource; the same is true of its ability to learn a new technology. Most technologies require significant skill, labor and capital tradeoffs, and have certain efficient operating ranges with different breakeven volumes which may contribute to or hinder the success of particular strategies.

Research and development (R&D) skills are also a production resource. Product or process R&D, and expertise for basic or applied research may be among the resources of a firm. R&D capability can enhance a firm's competitive ability, or it can be a poorly managed and costly activity.

Utterback and Abernathy (1975) provide a useful model of process and product innovation which is relevant in our assessment of R&D skills. As *Figure 5-4* shows, the Utterback and Abernathy model hypothesizes a declining rate of production innovation concurrent with a rising and then falling track of process innovation, with innovation being stimulated by different corporate and market needs as the product matures. The key question for management is: Are the R&D resources appropriately deployed for the competition ahead? However, to answer this, we need to know just what resources are available now and how they are employed.

Finally, let us discuss capacity. While underutilized capacity is a problem, when conditions change slack capacity becomes a resource. What is critical is the match between sales and capacity, that is, between demand and supply. As a market grows, capacity in place may deter others from entering a market. In some businesses, the competition becomes so intense that overcapacity conditions prevail and marginal operators leave the industry. Nevertheless, slack capacity can be an expensive and fleeting asset, since competitors can build capacity themselves and reduce any market response advantage held by the firm with slack. Also, capacity and location are intimately linked: *where* it is may have a larger impact than *what* it is.

FINANCIAL RESOURCES

Financial resources reflect the numerical reality of a company, the numbers measuring its performance under the current strategy. Indeed, an increase in financial resources will generally confirm or suggest the existence of positive resources or strengths in other areas, while a decline in financial resources indicates problems.

An initial question to assess financial resources is obvious: Is the firm wealthy? A wealthy organization is one which has assets appropriate for its business needs as well as a cushion for likely contingencies. Such a cushion requires liquidity to cope with the unexpected. This liquidity can be in the form of idle working capital—for example, marketable securities, expected cash flow—or funding in reserve, such as unused credit lines or the owners' willingness to provide further backing. Heavy fixed assets also have a bearing on a firm's liquidity, since they often necessitate heavy fixed costs and leave the firm constrained in its other spending.

Assessing who owns the firm, who controls its financial destiny, is also important when you evaluate the firm's financial staying power, or, if you like, the quality of the firm's money. Trade creditors can be an important source of funding; their ability to give the firm flexible financing arrangements represents a resource area. Lenders to the firm are also important as *de facto* owners who represent resources of credit or constraint. Legal owners have the right to the residual value of the firm and are its final call for more

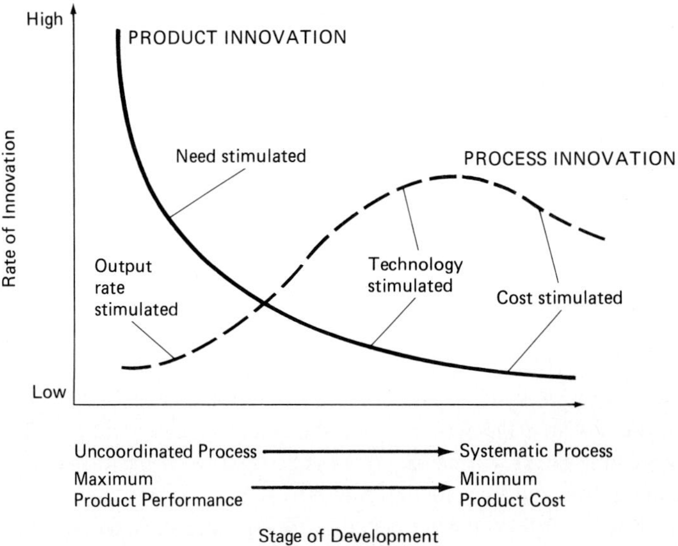

FIGURE 5-4 Innovation and Stage of Development

Source: Reprinted with permission from *OMEGA, the International Journal of Management Science,* vol. 3, Utterback and Abernathy, "A Dynamic Model of Process and Product Innovation," © 1975, Pergamon Press, Ltd.

capital; their present willingness and ability to commit more capital to the firm is a major resource.

Although this discussion of financial resources has thus far centered on balance-sheet issues, current income is a resource because profits enhance and losses deplete the firm's long-term financial base. A firm with a record of strong current income is likely to understand and increase its revenue sources and manage costs, including the impact of high or rising fixed costs. Current income flows represent an important financial resource; changes here are an alert to new strengths or flaws in a firm's current strategy. The DuPont formula links return on equity with sales margins, with asset turnover (a product of both current activity and balance-sheet resources), and with leverage, from the balance sheet, allowing us to analyze profitability.

How has the firm generated its profits? We will use the DuPont formula to analyze profitability:

$$\frac{\text{Profit}}{\text{Equity}} = \frac{\text{Profit}}{\text{Sales}} \times \frac{\text{Sales}}{\text{Assets}} \times \frac{\text{Assets}}{\text{Equity}}$$

Profitability analysis will point to changing competitive strengths as the margin shifts, to new efficiency as turnover rises, and to heightened leverage as debt use increases. A sense of past financial resource development will give important insights into how the firm currently makes its money and into the skills on which its profitability is founded.

A critical resource is cash flow. Whether from operations or financial transactions, the firm's cash flow links balance-sheet and income statements. If current operations can produce surplus funds, the firm's financial strength will be enhanced. If external sources are tapped, usually the firm suffers some loss of flexibility, although additional leverage may enhance profitability. What probably matters most is how the firm deploys its assets and, in particular, its cash flow. Are they invested in businesses and projects which enhance the firm's value, or are they wasted in low-return ventures, relics of the past, or spread so thinly that they have no competitive weight?

A firm whose product is at an early growth stage will be pumping cash from operations back into the company (and even taking on debt) to add to capacity and working capital, and to buy promotion necessary to stimulate future growth. A mature product, however, may allow asset redeployment. A mature volume product may be able to win financial concessions from suppliers and buyers who now depend on its high volumes as the mainstay of their own businesses. For example, they may be able to operate with large payables and small receivables, since they have power in their relationships with suppliers and customers.

Over the life cycles of its products, the firm's cash flow should shift from investment to return. Even in the smallest businesses, the successes of the past supply the seed corn of the future. Shareholders who eat too much in the form of dividends are a problem and will destroy the value of the firm if not restrained.

The value of the firm is the ultimate corporate resource. Stock market values reflect current earnings and financial strength and the market's perception of the future success which management is likely to enjoy. While stock market value does not always quickly result from good management, the job of the manager is to create value. Stock market value is a resource in acquisition or a defense against takeover; it should be enhanced by effective strategic management.

ADMINISTRATIVE AND HUMAN RESOURCES

Administrative and human resources consist of the people in an organization, their skills (by level and by function), and the way they are organized. These resources may be the most important of all because a firm's distinctive competence is frequently based on the skills of its people. Indeed, Stevenson (1976) found that higher-level managers, those who are most responsible for the long-term success of the organization, are more concerned with human resources than with any other functional resource.

The organization's strategic management capability and experience, too, rest in its human resources at both the managerial and administrative levels, and so strategic management ability must be assessed within a human resource audit. Employee and management stability and loyalty are important to firms which consciously attempt to develop their people-based distinctiveness. Appropriate compensation for performance also affects the quality of the firm's human resources.

The memory of critical experiences in a firm can seriously affect current operations, sustain its *esprit de corps,* and define a code for employee behavior. Such an *esprit de corps* may provide the basis for a future strategy and is a valuable resource. Timex's critical experiences include the collapse of its bomb fuse business after World War II and its rebuff by jewelry stores which refused to distribute its low-priced watches in the early

1950s. Timex turned to the drugstores and the emerging discount chains. Indeed, volume was exactly what Timex needed to enhance its manufacturing skills and enable it to lower its costs. These were the only channels available, but channels which better matched Timex's product and market, since the discounters and drugstores needed volume sales and only low-priced watches could sell in volume. Timex has moved very deliberately since that time. The company seems unfazed by the rapid rise of the electronic watch and has never been tempted too far from its manufacturing and assembly competence.

Critical experience, however, may hinder a firm from taking appropriate action. It can become a negative resource, a source of weakness. Some firms which have survived recessions with judicious, controlled penny pinching find their managers become too conservative to reap the full benefits of the succeeding prosperity. The retailer Montgomery Ward is a notable example. Thirty years after the Great Depression, Ward maintained its liquidity as a reserve for the next depression, sacrificing its competitive position to its past experience. As Sears moved aggressively into the suburbs and malls of America, Montgomery Ward watched and waited with its cash for a "future" which never developed (in the way Ward expected). The result was prosperity and growth for Sears and years of decline and ultimately a takeover for Ward, ironically with its own cash (reserves) being used to pay for the purchase.

Personal values are an important element of human resources: What do the people in the organization want? Examples of employees with differing values include the professional interested in the job, the man or woman interested in "the company" and its role in the community, and the individual interested in the paycheck. An organization's value structure is a resource which can support or limit a firm's strategic success. For example, when times are tight, employees who believe in the organization may continue to work even for reduced or deferred pay; personal values may be a strong strategic resource.

Power is an important organizational resource. Because power can be used to grant authority over other resources, a person or group with power can shift the organization's priorities and strategies. Thus, it is important to note who has power and why, how power is used and shared. Who has autonomy? How does structure reflect power, and how does the administrative system enhance the organization's ability to focus resources where they are needed for strategic success? The question, "Who's in and who's out?" reveals where power resides in the organization. Remember the old adage, "If you're not in, you're out" (Jennings, 1980).

To summarize the human resource assessment, identify the firm's distinctive competence and the critical people by whom it has been built and maintained. For the modern strategic thinker, people are the ultimate source of value. People are the only resource which can determine the effective, creative use of human and nonhuman resources. Ohmae (1982) calls this creative factor insight; the right person will always defeat a machine because only a man can create beyond experience.

RESOURCES: AN ILLUSTRATION

We will discuss resource assessment for Dr. Pepper, the firm whose strategy we identified in Chapter 4. *Figure 5-5* shows the resources of Dr. Pepper, arranged in a functional structure parallel to that used for strategy identification. Resources are the result of past functional strategies.

FIGURE 5-5 Resource Assessment—Dr. Pepper: Mid-1970s

Marketing	*Production*	*Finance*	*Human Resources*
Market: Primarily in the Southwest, but sold throughout US with some international sales, including Japan. In 1982, dropped from 3rd to 4th in national market share, behind Coke, Pepsi, and 7-Up. *Product:* Unique taste of 23 flavors, identified by some as similar to rootbeer, almonds and/or cherries. Also, sugar-free Dr. Pepper. Often available in fewer sizes than competitors. Mature product in Southwest, small market share in Northeast. *Price:* Often higher-priced than competitors. Inelastic and robust to loyal drinkers, less inelastic and robust in new markets. *Promotion:* Point-of-sale ads, in conjuction with ads and samplings through local bottlers. Some national promotion. *Place:* Primarily manufacturer of concentrate, some co-owned manufacturing and bottling plants. Strongest in Southwest, which has a growing population, although nationally distributed via strong local cola bottlers. Strong in traditional markets, recently growing but now slipping nationally.	Concentrate production requires few employees and simple equipment; low capital investment needed to increase capacity. High fixed cost stage of production and expensive transportation of soft drinks provided by strong, local cola bottlers. Canning and bottling require more employees, working capital and capital investment. Presold bulk palletized delivery (on pallets moveable by forklift) to large grocery chains saves money and provides better service than traditional route delivery. Large user of sugar, paying current commodity prices. High quality. *R&D:* Use of new containers, development of powdered Dr. Pepper for hot drinks. Powerful as low cost concentrate producer. Powerful in distribution chain, due to quality and taste.	History of growing profits; profits fell in 1982. Formerly heavy cash, but now increasing debt to acquire Canada Dry. Falling sales margin. Stock price: depressed from previous high. Uses financial strength of bottlers with its own. Quarterly dividends. Resources spent in acquisition and national distribution. Power as a concentrate producer.	Employees as believers in Dr. Pepper's uniqueness, quality, and position in industry and community, illustrating Golden Rule in business. Led by W. W. ("Foots") Clements as chairman. Recently hired president from Procter and Gamble replaced after less than 3 years, in Nov. 82, by R. Q. Armstrong, president of Canada Dry when Dr. Pepper acquired it (1982). Cadre of loyal employees, spreading "word" of Dr. Pepper to raise market penetration.

You will note after analyzing *Figure 5-5* that the resources for Dr. Pepper are generally strong in its Southwest markets, signifying that the past strategy in its traditional operating area has been successful. For a firm whose past strategies have earned mixed results, the resource assessment will show weaknesses as well as strengths. Weaknesses are areas of past strategic failure which may require additional effort if they leave the firm vulnerable to a competitor's strengths. Dr. Pepper's falling national market position, following an expensive bid for national market share, was a sign of growing weakness.

Dr. Pepper was a substantially weaker company earlier when bottlers were not willing to risk their franchise agreements with the major colas (which specified that they could bottle only one cola) in order to add another brown soft drink with a unique, possibly cola-like taste. This situation limited its bottlers to those who were weaker number three's in the local markets and who could not afford the advertising and sampling expenses required to win Dr. Pepper drinkers. Thus, until the court ruling that Dr. Pepper was not a cola,[1] Dr. Pepper was vulnerable against the richer, stronger cola manufacturers even when it sought to expand slowly outside its original Southwest markets.

Resource assessment gives you information about what Dr. Pepper is, to add to the strategy identification data on what it is doing. Current position as well as strategic thrust are important in assessing where Dr. Pepper is likely to go in the future. Current position also provides a base, questions, and priorities on which to begin an analysis of the likely relevant future environment in which Dr. Pepper will operate. And, although we have not yet discussed alternative strategies in detail, this strategy and resource analysis of Dr. Pepper provide a strong foundation for W. W. Clements's 1983 statement:

> We lose the effectiveness of our marketing money when we try to paint with too broad a brush. This doesn't mean we'll abandon the Northeast, but we'll certainly try to strengthen our position where we're already strong. (Clements, 1983)

RESOURCES AND THE FUTURE

A resource inventory is a foundation for assessing the competitive strengths and weaknesses of your organization. The full synthesis required to determine your relative competitive power will be made later when you understand your competitors' objectives, strategy, and resource bases, and have developed your own sense of the future.

In moving towards that identification of strategic strengths and weaknesses, some relevant empirical research can guide us. Be careful: relative competitive strength is what matters, yet that is not where managers often focus. Stevenson (1976) found that managers typically use different criteria to define strengths and weaknesses. Historical criteria, such as experience, intra-company comparison, and budget are used to judge strength; weaknesses are judged against normative criteria such as consultants' opinions, management's understanding of the business literature, rules of thumb, and opinion. He also found managerial position affecting interpretation of the importance of certain resources, with functional managers giving more weight to marketing and production issues and top

[1]In 1962, Pepsi-Cola sued Dr. Pepper for trademark infringement over the use of the word ''pep'' by Dr. Pepper. Pepsi won, but Dr. Pepper countersued and won a ruling, later supported by the Food and Drug Administration, that Dr. Pepper was a unique and separate flavor rather than a cola.

managers giving more weight to financial and human resources. But it is important to take an integrative and competitive view, no matter what your position.

Because the job of management is to create value, the ultimate test of management is that the cumulative impact of the resources in the current and future marketplace exceeds the sum of its parts. If management cannot create such a synergy, it cannot justify the costs of administering the parts of the organization to develop a united front in the marketplace. Since synergy or value creation can occur in a number of ways in the future, resources must be evaluated qualitatively, integratively, and competitively, focusing extra selective attention on those resources whose presence or absence is crucial for strategic success (Barnard, 1966).

PREVIEW

Resource assessment is, initially, a static analysis, to identify and inventory the current base, the foundation for future strategy. But resource evaluation takes place in the light of current and future needs. One of the reasons we introduced the product life cycle and mentioned the experience concept in this chapter is to give some attention to the likely future, even as we inventory our resources. Both models thrust us toward the future, have a competitive content and help us forecast what our future resource needs are likely to be. We discuss experience as a concept summarizing resource strength in Chapter 6. We move from a current resource base to the future as we explore the industry, competitive and social-political environment in Chapters 7, 8 and 9.

Resource identification links current strategy with past results, while resource evaluation requires a look at the likely future to fully assess resource strengths and weaknesses in light of future needs. Some guidelines will enhance the productivity of your analysis of the strengths and weaknesses of your firm in relation to the competition.

1 Be selective. Not all weaknesses are correctable or worth correcting, and there are some you must live with. Of course, all weaknesses inhibit our ability to fulfill purpose (Stevenson, 1976). Knowledge of what they are means that you can avoid putting strain on areas that cannot withstand it (Hussey, 1968).
2 Be sensitive to what is opinion and what is fact. Stevenson (1976) has found that managers are more willing to judge strengths against historical comparisons than against competitive factors. And managers rely on outsiders' opinions to highlight weaknesses rather than their own assessment of the competition.
3 Do not be absolute. Use your resource inventory to alert you to areas for competitive comparison rather than to what are absolute strengths or weaknesses.

Ultimately, one of the principles of competition is to focus strength against your rivals' weakness. This means you must exploit others' errors and weaknesses and guard your own. Sun Tzu wrote, circa 500 B.C., "Know the enemy and know yourself; in a hundred battles you will not be in peril" (Sun Tzu, 1963, p. 84). Experience, as we address it in Chapter 6, summarizes our knowledge of our own resources.

In Chapters 7 to 9, we move to an analysis of the future environment. Environmental assessment must be married to resource assessment to gain a full view of the world in which our strategy must work.

chapter 6

Experience, Price and Value: Summarizing Resources

INTRODUCTION

Experience, price and value collectively tell us a great deal about our most significant competitive resource, our relative strength in the market. Experience is the strategist's shorthand for the track of unit costs over time. Price is a measure of market power. With cost, it determines margin, revealing how much of the value created by a particular product or service offering is being captured as profit. Indeed, it is profit dollars that ultimately fund growth.

In this chapter, we will describe in detail the experience curve, its slow application in the strategic management area and its strategic implications. We will show how price and value are affected by strategies based on the experience curve.

LEARNING AND EXPERIENCE: A BRIEF HISTORY AND DEFINITION

In 1925, aeronautical engineers observed that the manufacturing labor content of airplanes fell as the total output accumulated. They attributed the decline to learning. People doing repetitive tasks, like building an airplane, learn to do it better and so save time on later units.

In the early 1960s, the Boston Consulting Group (BCG) staff observed similar price and cost patterns across a number of industries and across all costs. They called the phenomenon "the experience curve" and promoted its use in the strategic management arena through their 1968 publication, *Perspectives on Experience* and their professional work. Typically, total real unit costs decline at some "characteristic rate" each time accumulated production is doubled—from almost nothing to a rate as high as 60 percent each time accumulated production doubles (Ghemawat, 1985). In the electronics industry, for example, real costs typically decline by 30 percent as production is doubled.

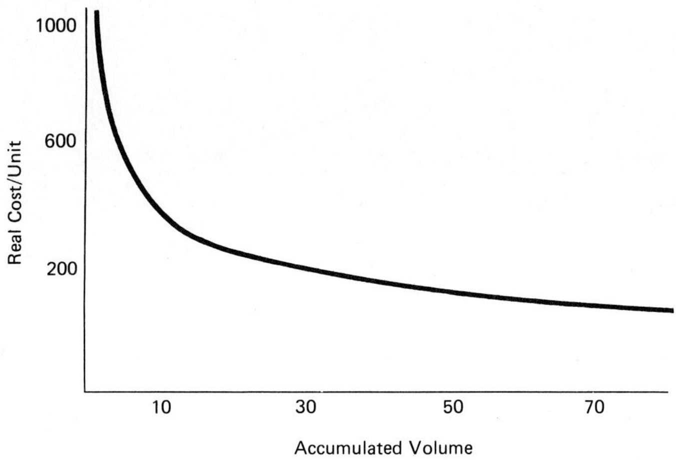

FIGURE 6-1 An 80 Percent Experience Curve: Linear Scale

The experience curve, then, is simply a trace of real unit costs as volume accumulates. The usual formulation, shown in *Figure 6-1*, is:

$$C_x = a\, x^{-b}$$

where c_x = cost of x-th unit

a = cost of the first unit

b = a constant that depends on the learning rate.

Figure 6-2 illustrates this as a function linear in the log:

$$\log c_x = \log a - b \log x$$

while *Table 6-1* lists the values of the exponent b for various experience curves.

We can note here first that accounting practices within firms and across industries often complicate "cost" estimates and make comparability difficult. Secondly, we note that the cost of any multicomponent product is probably complicated by different cost curves for those components (Hax and Majluf, 1984). Moreover, the cost of the first unit and accumulated experience at a particular time point is rarely known. BCG advised:

> Estimates of the cumulative unit volume obtained by the first year in the series were made by the Boston Consulting Group. The rule used was: previous experience about equals the amount added in doubling the annual unit rate. Thus, if 5 years are required to double the annual rate, the sum of production in the 5 years approximates the cumulative experience at the beginning of the 5 years. This rule is accurate in all cases in which a constant growth rate applies. It should be noted that the estimate on initial cumulative volume is significant on logarithmic scales only when long prior experience and slow sales growth apply. (1968, p. 69)

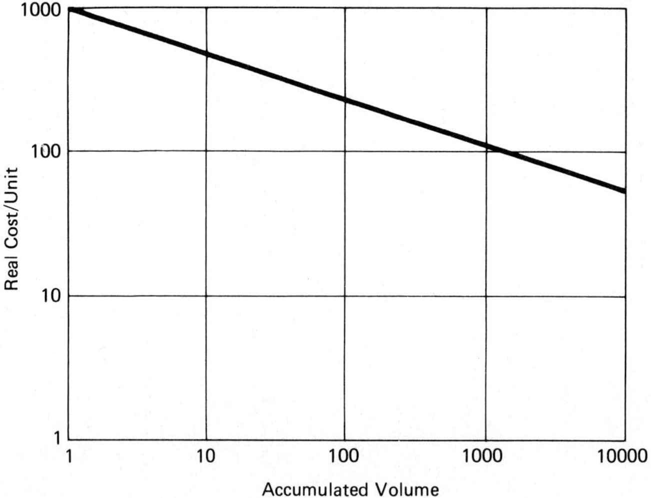

FIGURE 6-2 An 80 Percent Experience Curve: Logarithmic Scale

By 1981, however, *Fortune* reported that the strategic importance of the experience curve had passed (Kiechel, 1981). It seemed business had begun to use the tool in an uninformed manner. Inexperienced managers had begun to misuse it, for example, applying it slavishly in inappropriate contexts. Nevertheless, it seems inappropriate to discard a powerful tool simply because it has been poorly understood and applied improperly.

Let us examine the experience curve in more depth so that it can be properly applied as an aid to strategic analysis. We can learn more about its strengths and limitations if we follow its history.

THE EVOLUTION OF THE EXPERIENCE CONCEPT

People have long recognized the value of experience, learning to do things well and more efficiently. For example, experienced tradesmen, like experienced managers, are more valued and more highly paid than others because they have met the test of experience. It is

TABLE 6-1 Value of Exponent for Various Experience Curves

Experience Curve	*b*
100%	0.000
90	.152
80	.322
70	.515
60	.738

not only mastery of repetitive tasks that characterizes such people but their ability to use what they know in new and difficult situations to define problems so they can be solved. In this way, experienced people extend their experience. Let us see how the notions of learning and experience entered the lexicon of the strategic manager.

Noting the advantages of automation in the Industrial Revolution, Chauncey Jerome, a pioneer clock manufacturer, wrote in 1860:

> The business of manufacture of them has become so systematized of late that it has brought the prices exceedingly low and it has long been the astonishment of the whole world that they could be made so cheap yet be good. (Abell and Hammond, 1979, p. 106)

Yet, despite the obvious need to explain this industrial productivity, little systematic study took place.

Indeed, it was not until 1925 that the commander of the Wright-Patterson air base observed "learning" and reported that the number of direct labor hours required to assemble a plane decreased as the number of aircraft assembled increased. Moreover, his observations were not made public until 1936 when T. P. Wright, then CEO of Curtis-Wright, Buffalo, New York, published "Factors Affecting the Cost of Airplanes" in the *Journal of Aeronautical Sciences* and suggested an exponential model of the learning phenomenon of the same form as the model cited above.

World War II provided many opportunities to observe learning, not only on planes but on Liberty Ships and other major and minor military equipment and munitions. Rapping (1965) reported that the cost index of Liberty Ships fell from 100 in December, 1941, to 45 by December, 1944—a 40 percent productivity gain made possible in part because of the new scale of shipbuilding needed to satisfy the war effort. New designs, the use of mass production techniques, initially inexperienced labor like "Rosie the Riveter," and managers who were ignorant of shipbuilding, were all crucial elements of a naive start-up scenario followed by long and large production runs which "exaggerated" the learning effect over the cost declines normally observable in industry.

Nevertheless, the use of the "aircraft learning curve" was restricted to the defense and allied industries and their government customers. Upper management as well as business educators appeared not to see the relevance of the learning concept.

Only in 1954 was business generally given its first public view of learning by Frank J. Andress in the *Harvard Business Review*. Andress, who argued that the concept could be applied outside the aircraft industry, began with a description of the following incident:

> During World War II an executive of a home appliance manufacturing company chanced to cross paths with an executive of a large West Coast aircraft firm. The appliance executive mentioned that it had taken his company two years to determine the exact cost of the electric refrigerator which it manufactured.
>
> The aircraft executive pointed out that in many cases his company had been forced to determine costs on similar items in a matter of a few minutes, and said, "I'll bet you a steak dinner that I can predict the cost of your 200,000th refrigerator within 120% accuracy by using a learning curve based on aircraft production."
>
> The manufacturing executive accepted the bet. The only information he furnished was the weight of the refrigerator and the cost of the first unit produced.

During the next few minutes he watched while the aircraft executive worked with pencil, ruler, and log-log graph paper.

When he had completed plotting the curve, the aircraft executive stated: "Your 200,000th unit should cost you $162.50."

"Just drop the 50 cents," the appliance executive said. "It was actually $162.00."

Andress advised business that learning by repetition led to efficiency, that the scope and pace of cost improvement was regular and predictable, and he argued that the concept could be widely applied across industry. Indeed, in 1954, Andress anticipated the application of the learning curve to the nonmanufacturing operations of a business, and he argued that growing competition would make such a search for efficiency a necessity.

We must emphasize that Andress published this in 1954, twenty-nine years after the learning phenomenon was first measured. Note, too, that it was fourteen years later that the Boston Consulting Group published its treatise on experience, applying learning in just the way Andress had forecast. It had taken forty years for business to begin applying the lessons of experience, and according to *Fortune* only twelve years or so to misapply it and then begin to discard it (probably out of ignorance). The experience curve is a classic example of the difficulty of innovating in business.

Andress made other contributions which demonstrate the value to managers of thoroughly using research. Moreover, his contributions suggest that little progress has been made in developing greater universal knowledge of the experience phenomenon in the past thirty years, perhaps because users of the experience concept have ignored Andress's and others' cautions about the tool. Andress wrote, "From the management viewpoint, there is a real problem in the constant need to be on guard against errors creeping into the data for the learning curve and distorting it," and he warned against errors which contemporary authors have also cited.

- He distinguished between productivity and learning because learning is repeated whenever a new model is introduced while productivity gains per se are sustainable.
- He pointed out that the slope of the curve could be expected to differ depending upon the labor content of the work—a higher labor content afforded greater opportunities for learning.
- He also advised that the slope of the curve (the rate of labor cost reduction) could be expected to change as output accumulated noting that "subsequent factors entered the picture, and the curve became quite unpredictable."
- He warned that the cost of proceeding down the learning curve had to be weighed against the benefits of a lower cost position and he attracted attention to the significance of the anticipated length of the production run in making that decision.
- He warned that it is the cost portion of value which is subject to learning and that changes in operating methods and labor costs (and even purchasing practices where sales prices are constrained by competition) all affect the short-term rate of cost decline.
- Finally, he cautioned that rate of production and capacity utilization affect labor costs.

In 1959, Conway and Schultz presented a paper on the "Manufacturing Progress Function" and noted that increased efficiency and cost reductions stemmed from other sources besides learning. They added considerably to our knowledge of the variability and difficulty of using learning curves and also introduced rate or production and total accumulated volume (as well as duration of production) as factors to be considered in managing costs. Tooling methods, design changes, quality incentives—all were held to contribute to cost declines.

Significantly, they noted a problem associated with the aggregated cost of many products, for example, airplanes. Airplanes are assembled from many products and components, some unique to one plane or model, others used in many. Thus the cost of an airplane is an aggregated cost, and they pointed out that the sum of a series of exponential functions is not another exponential function unless the bases are identical. They stated their conviction that, for various types of operations, the powers or characteristics of learning curves differed—"hence the attainment of a convex shape rather than a linear shape would follow their addition" (p. 44).

It is worth noting the full range of their conclusions and advice on the use of learning curves:

- First cost is difficult to estimate *de novo*. Most engineering estimates are better made for a "stable" level of production, say the one-hundredth or two-hundredth, or one-thousandth or two-thousandth unit, depending on the expected production run, and the earlier curve estimated based on expected slopes. Typically, early points are overemphasized when plotting log-log lines.
- Model fit is not stable; for example, if redesign occurs or if rework is eliminated, a new model may be necessary.
- Wide ranges of slopes occur.
- Once a control or quantitative objective is imposed on an organization, there are strong forces created to make the performance fit the objective; thus use of an experience curve as a control mechanism will affect the data.
- Effort is needed to get cost down, and central to marshalling that effort is expectation. Progress does not occur unless it is expected *and* rewarded.

Conway and Schultz concluded:

> There are significant differences in patterns of progress for different industries, firms, and products and type of work. There is no such thing as a fundamental law of progress such as the 80% learning curve used in the aircraft industry. *No particular slope is universal, and probably there is not even a common model.* (p. 53, emphasis added)

WHAT MAKES COSTS GO DOWN?

Alchian (1959) and Hirschleifer (1962) were among the first economists to attempt to reconcile the classic U-shaped cost curve of static economic analysis (where unit costs fall and then rise) with the dynamics of the experience curve and its seemingly endless unit cost decline. Hirschleifer noted the paradox: Although economic theory teaches that at equilibrium in a competitive market marginal cost must be rising (since it becomes increasingly costly to raise output to meet successive increments of demand with stable technology and input prices—the law of diminishing returns), managers feel that additional units are *not* increasingly costly to produce, except under extreme and exceptional conditions.

Alchian moved towards a resolution of this inconsistency between theory and practice by proposing that cost is a function of *rate* of output and scheduled *volume* of output. Economics heretofore had largely focused on total volume per period and ignored accumulated volume. Nevertheless, expected volume additions and total historical volume are both cues to management's assessment of the strength of demand over time. Thus, Alchian and Hirschleifer brought Conway's and Schultz's notions of accumulated volume into the economists' purview—rate of growth, duration, and cumulative expected production all became relevant. Engineers and managers, of course, have dealt with these distinctions in many different circumstances over the years. Power station design, for example, requires a long-term commitment to both peak and base loads, and utility regulation necessitates an assumption about the life of a project and the total demand for the services it can provide.

Accumulated volume and volume growth are crucial issues in management decision making. An assessment of total demand and the rate of demand growth over the life of a production facility is necessary before committing to an initial cost position, and these same factors determine whether there will be opportunities for cost reduction. The duration of high demand affords opportunities for both learning and technological progress in both product and process design. Total expected production will influence the primary choice of process and scale—in accounting terms, the commitment of fixed capital and a commitment to a particular mix of variable costs.

Faddish goods, such as hula hoops, require subcontracted production rather than commitments to high fixed costs. By comparison, Coleco's phenomenal and relatively long-lasting success with its Cabbage Patch dolls warranted plant commitments, while its inability to supply the huge market it found was a result of its initial decision to subcontract production.

PRICE AND EXPERIENCE

In 1968, the Boston Consulting Group published its *Perspectives on Experience* and hypothesized:

> Prices follow the same patterns as cost, if the relationships between competitors is stable. If they don't, the relationship between competitors becomes increasingly unstable.
>
> If cost is a function of accumulated experience, then profit is a function of sustained market share, which therefore has an intrinsic and calculable value. (1968, p. 19)

The importance of these two hypotheses in practice is considerable. They suggest that management should consider attempts to reduce its costs so that it can cut prices and capture market share. Cutting costs thus gives the firm an opportunity to develop a defensible and increasing competitive advantage.

These general propositions and their obvious implications were intended as a platform for company-specific research by BCG on particular consulting engagements. Nevertheless, they led many companies to foolhardy cost and price reduction programs without benefit of counsel and with no consideration of the long-run implications of their growing capital investments and price cutting decisions in their particular industry circumstances. Paradoxically, these companies were ignoring the accumulated experience of many industries and, indeed, the experience we have just reported—the experience which had accumulated over time in the application of learning curves in industry. The Boston Consulting Group warned its readers of just these dangers—but apparently its cautions went unnoticed as many companies jumped on the "cost cutting" bandwagon and began what ultimately became destructive and profitless fights for market share (Fruhan, 1972; Chevalier, 1974).

LEARNING VERSUS EXPERIENCE

The major difference between the aircraft industry's 80 percent learning curve and the Boston Consulting Group's experience curve was BCG's emphasis on price and total costs, rather than manufacturing costs, and its emphasis on the competitive value of high market share. BCG's empirical support for its propositions was restricted to price-based experience curves, which presented a remarkably consistent set of patterns ranging across a wide variety of industries, including electronics, petrochemicals, and primary metals. The evidence supported their case that prices declined by constant percentages with each doubling of total units produced. But the critical part of their argument was that, if prices declined (according to a predictable pattern), sellers' costs had to decline quickly enough to stay below prices and preserve margins. And, they argued, if costs declined more quickly than price, the margins would grow, signalling competitors of an opportunity worth investigating. More competition, and more capacity, would put new pressure on prices to bring them back in line with the consistent cost decline pattern, as *Figure 6-3* shows.

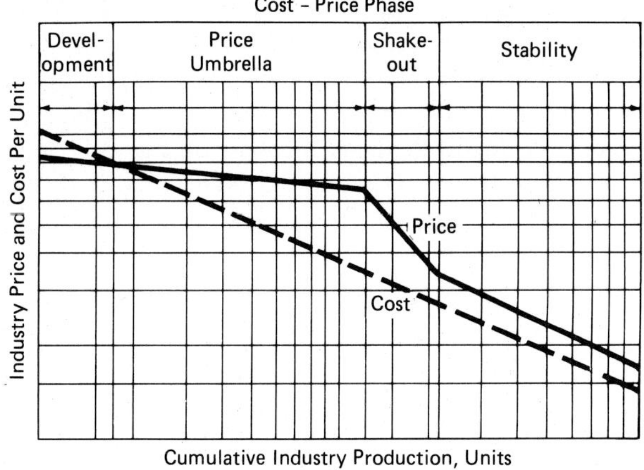

FIGURE 6-3 Typical Price-Cost Relationship

Source: Adapted from *Perspectives on Experience* (Boston: The Boston Consulting Group, 1972), p. 21

EXPERIENCE AND COMPETITIVE STABILITY

BCG's most important conclusion was that competitive relationships cannot be stable when one company has a large market share and manages it so that its incremental accumulated experience allows it to lower costs relative to the competition (BCG, 1968). Lower costs, of course, in simple terms, lead to market power and potentially to further market share gains.

BCG proposed that stable competitive relationships can only occur where price and cost closely follow the same pattern—that is, when prices and costs decline at the same rate and where all competitors are able to maintain the same relative cost positions, as indicated by stable market shares.

The implications of such an "iron law" of market share and market power are powerful, *if it holds*. It would mean that ultimately any market will be dominated by one competitor, so long as that competitor follows the BCG cost control prescriptions.

MARKET SHARE, MARKET POWER, AND SECURITY

A firm's performance from the pursuit of market share does not depend on *whether* the law of market share power holds, but rather the strategy will work *while* the law holds. Businesses survive so long as they are able to stay in touch with the market. Thus, it is not share that counts, but creating value in the eyes of the customer and being responsive to the customer's needs. Changes in taste or demographic shifts in the market, revised prices for substitutes or complementary goods, all influence demand for the product and the ultimate size of the market.

Remember, the strength that comes from having a low cost position can become a weakness if the market changes—for example, if consumers or buyers find their needs have changed or if some creative and innovative competitor, or new entrant, has found a way to satisfy these same needs in a way which offers the consumer more value. In such circumstances, the fixed asset commitments required to reach a low cost position in many markets can become a mill-stone around the corporate neck. Timex's efficient assembly operations had been the source of its competitive strength in the low-priced watch industry worldwide for over twenty years, but they became largely irrelevant when Texas Instruments (TI) entered the market with digital watches. On entry, TI probably enjoyed a lower cost position than Timex and the TI watch was an electronic product on which TI could anticipate a fast "start-up" cost decline—one that Timex's old technology could not duplicate.

The real point of BCG's theory, in simple terms, was that ultimately profit margin is a function of sustained market share. Essentially, however, that is a tautology, since it was share that yielded low cost and price power and further market share gains. It's akin to the "buy low, sell high" rule for stock market success—true, but difficult to practice, as BCG warned.

Market share is only an indicator of strength, not a security guarantee. A danger with strategies heavily dependent on the experience curve is that the people of the organization may become inward-looking, operations-dominated and myopic. An experience curve strategy is often erroneously believed to be a production strategy. Some managers forget that sensitivity to the market and customers' needs is necessary if they are to sell the product. Sustained willingness to buy is the only guarantee of an opportunity to double sales volume over any time period.

The cost declines promised by the experience curve are most germane during the start-up and early growth stages of the life cycle. Here accumulated volume grows quickly, almost certainly before substitutes are developed by competitors. And here costs can be expected to decline rapidly, if managerial emphasis is put on this objective. The puzzle for management is to take advantage of the opportunity to reach a dominant position without being trapped in a destructive competition by an overcommitment based on false expectations of continuing growth for an unchanged product.

A LESSON FROM WELFARE ECONOMICS

The reason competition based on aggressive price cutting is so destructive is that it is naive. It does not manage value effectively. Let us reflect for a moment on one of the concepts used by welfare economists, *surplus,* particularly the consumers' surplus, and use it to help us see how value can be mismanaged by short-sighted price cutting.

As time passes, an aggressive firm attempting to build market share and market power is likely to advertise and improve its product to increase demand. At the same time, it is likely to invest in new designs and new high-capacity equipment to lower its average cost position. However, these decisions give it higher fixed costs while cutting variable costs. Success, and the urge to build share, may lead the company to cut prices, too. Hence, the supply and demand charts at times 1, 2, and 3 in *Figure 6-4* reflect a successful marketer improving production capabilities and cutting prices to build additional volume and share.

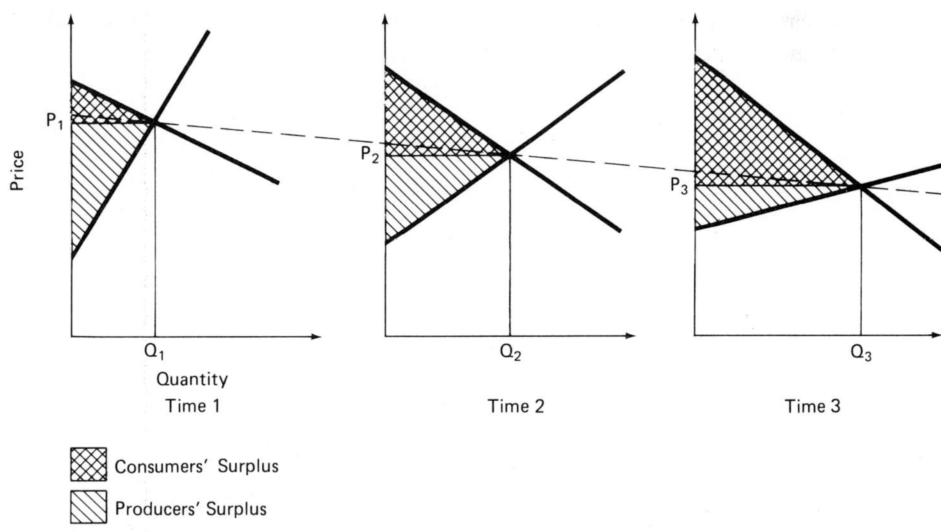

FIGURE 6-4 The Reallocation of Value with "Experience"-Based Pricing

Imagine that price cuts, new distribution channels, quality improvements and advertising combine to move the demand curve to the right and make it more inelastic, as *Figure 6-4* shows between times 1 and 2. Such success encourages the firm to expand its capacity and improve its operating efficiency again. Improved production capabilities and new capacity flatten the supply curve and move it to the right. Its aggressive competitive practices and its success are likely to prompt the firm to cut its prices again, ultimately reaching the situation portrayed as time 3 in *Figure 6-4*.

Obviously, prudent managers would invest in advertising and plant only if they believed there will be a return. This is likely, however, only if the demand curve stays up—that is, stays well to the right. Moreover, they should cut price only if they believe building market share is likely to be profitable and defensible once captured.

Yet price splits the value created by the product offering into two components: One, the consumers' surplus,[1] shown by the closely hatched area(s) above the market price between and to the left of the supply and demand curves; and two, the producers' surplus,[2] below the market price, between and to the left of the supply and demand curves. Note the reduction in the proportion of the value created by the producer but kept by the consumer, the consumers' surplus, versus that kept or captured by the producer, the producers' surplus, when the producer cuts prices.

Figure 6-4, therefore, illustrates one of the costs of building share with aggressive price cutting: the producers' retention of less and less of the value created within any time period as prices are cut. This means it will take longer and longer to recover the investments, and recovery is possible only if demand can be maintained. If for any reason this is not so, the cash invested may be lost and unrecoverable. Indeed, there are many "possible causes" of such a situation, including new product offerings by existing or new competitors. The dwindling producers' surplus also signals that profits are falling, leaving less money to wage marketing or production wars in the future.

Thus, whenever the value of market share is threatened or the certainty of having time to get capital out of a business is low, the experience curve is likely to be inapplicable. Abell and Hammond (1979) suggest that care is needed in using experience-based strategies in these situations:

- if value added is low;
- if competitors have low cost positions because of some non-experience-based resource or relationship;
- if technology is rapidly transferred among firms by equipment manufacturers or licensing, for example;
- when the effects of scale are low.

They warn that patents, as well as seasonal, and cyclical factors, can also complicate the use of the experience concept.

[1]The consumers' surplus is a measure of the value captured by those buyers who, although willing to purchase a good at a price above market, are able to buy at market. The market price is a "deal" in their eyes and the indifference between the price they were willing to pay and market is a surplus or benefit they enjoy—the consumers' surplus.

[2]The producers' surplus measures the difference between market price and a lower price at which some (efficient) producers are willing to supply.

THE ABUSE OF THE EXPERIENCE CONCEPT

Nevertheless, these warnings—like those of Alchian and Hirschleifer, Conway and Schultz, and later BCG—concerning the importance of the total market and the prospect of market saturation, have sometimes been ignored by management intent on achieving a low cost position. Some managers, in the interests of capturing the value of "experience," have committed to expensive plants completed as the market was nearing saturation.

Management can be a victim of "mob psychology," as McKinsey noted in 1932. Spurred by naive overconfidence, managers may pursue a growing market with plant additions without considering the implications of competitive plant expansions (and consequent potential loss of manufacturer power) in the market. The US color TV industry in the late 1960s and the US chain saw industry in the mid 1970s suffered this fate.

Similarly, managers may pursue cost reductions with such gusto that they lose sight of the danger in the (cost) advantage: reduced flexibility in the face of market or technological change. Henry Ford discovered this danger to his great chagrin in 1927 when General Motors' multidivisional strategy forced the discontinuation of the Model T and a twelve-month shut-down for retooling for the Model A (Abernathy and Wayne, 1974). Indeed, there are "limits to the learning curve," as Abernathy and Wayne wrote.

SOME IMPORTANT CONSIDERATIONS IN MANAGING EXPERIENCE

Earlier we noted that costs go down because of the rate of output and scheduled volume and that these factors combine to create opportunities for commitments to scale (economies), technological progress, and learning. These appear to be the levers for cost management. Sultan (1975) estimated that the prices of steam turbine generators fell between 1904 and 1970 on an 87 percent experience curve—that is, the ratio of price decline per unit with each doubling of experience was 87 percent. As he explained it, if the total output of steam turbine generators on a cumulative throughput basis climbed from 6 million to 12 million kilowatts, the cost per kilowatt would decline from an index of 100 to an index of 87. However, he found that there were two principal components for this cost decline: a 93 percent curve for cumulative production experience, or learning, and a 93 percent curve for product technology. The effects are multiplicative, hence the 87 percent product experience curve ($.93 \times .93 - 87$).

Figure 6-5 illustrates one of the critical issues in using the experience curve: it is important to define the area of investigation carefully. On the figure, the 87 percent slope applies to generating units of a particular size. Considering the total costs of generating capacity, a 70 percent curve holds, according to Sultan. Experience developed as the industry itself acquired the capability to produce increasingly large-scale units and took advantage of learning and technological progress.

In a study of the petrochemicals market, Stobaugh and Townsend (1975) reported on the effects of competition, product standardization, experience and scale as causes of lower prices. They summarized as follows:

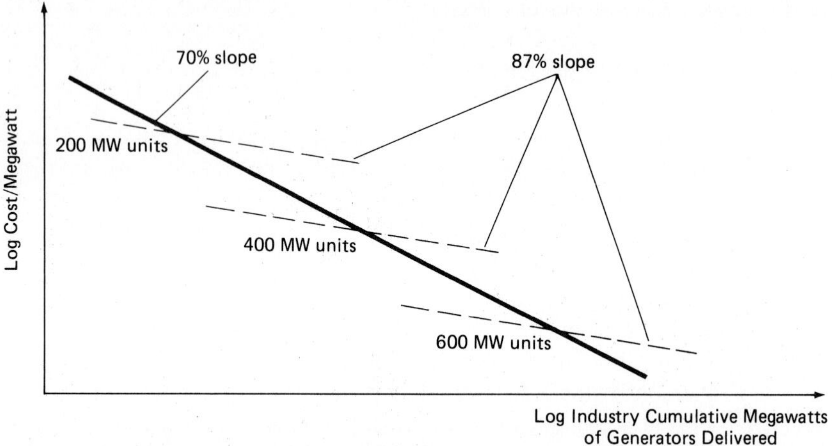

FIGURE 6-5 **Cost Experience for Steam Turbine Generators**
Source: Day and Montgomery, "Diagnosing the Experience Curve," *Journal of Marketing*, 47, Spring 1983, 47.

> Competition, product standardization, experience, and static scale are all significant factors in petrochemical price declines and act in the expected directions. They become important over the 3 to 7 year interval relevant for investment decisions. By the time a petrochemical has three or more producers, experience and the combined effect of the unidentified time-related variables generally have a larger effect than the number of producers, product standardization, or static scale. (p. 26)

They presented their findings on the price declines of eight petrochemicals over a five-year period as shown in *Table 6-2*.

Note that Sultan's and Stobaugh and Townsend's research was founded on price-based experience curves. Experience curves can be estimated for price or cost for products, for industries, or for companies, and they can be estimated across time or across companies or both. Each form of analysis presents its own insights and presents its own

TABLE 6-2 **Sources of Price Decline for Eight Petrochemicals**

Average 5-Year Change (Allowed) in Factor(s)	*Percent Relative Reduction of Real Price over 5-Year Interval*
40% more competitors	5%
Standardized quality	5
150% more accumulated experience	12
60% more output per producer	5
Other time-related factors over 5 years	12
All factors*	34%

*Again, individual factors are multiplicative, not additive. Thus, individual reductions multiply to give total reduction: (1-.05) (1-.05) (1-.12) (1-.05) (1-.12) = (1-.34)
Source: Stobaugh and Townsend, "Price Forecasting and Strategic Planning: The Case of Petrochemicals," *Journal of Marketing Research*, 12, February 1975, 19–29.

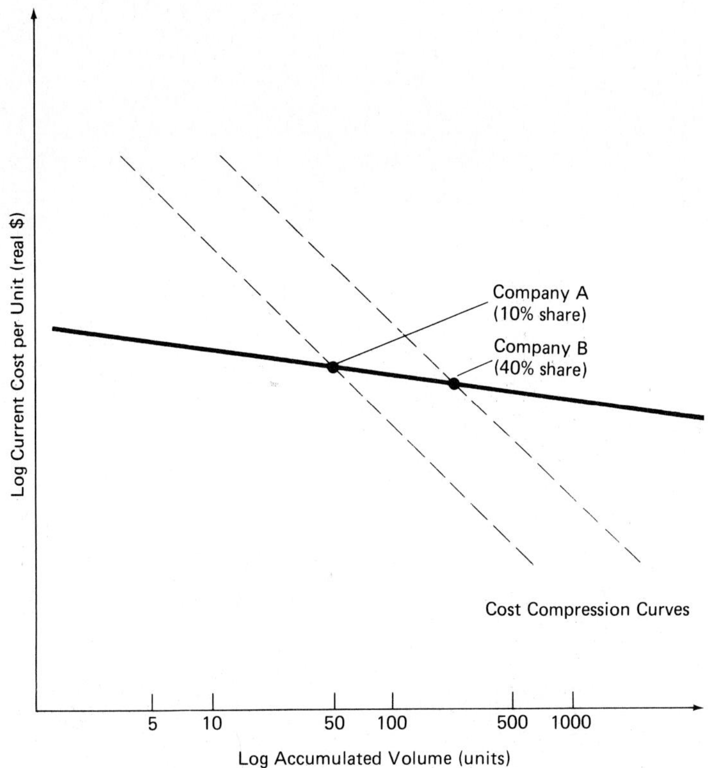

FIGURE 6-6 Competitive Cost Comparison Curves

Source: Day and Montgomery, "Diagnosing the Experience Curve," *Journal of Marketing,* 47, Spring 1983, 49.

problems. Day and Montgomery (1983) point out that the cross-sectional experience curves encompassing the output of many separate producers are likely to be shallower than curves calculated on the experience of a single decision maker. Biggadike (1977) reported that the real price per unit of a split-system central air conditioner has been declining on an 80 percent curve with each doubling of industry experience, yet a cross-sectional curve describing several major competitors' costs had a slope of 92 percent.

Figure 6-6 illustrates the difference between industry and firm experience curves. Day and Montgomery offer the following explanations for the steeper curves achieved by a corporation (when compared with an industry):

1 Followers may enjoy lower initial costs than the pioneer—if they can learn from the pioneer's successes and mistakes by hiring key personnel, or reverse-engineering its products, or by duplicating its manufacturing and distribution or service systems.

2 Followers may be able to leapfrog the early entrant by using new manufacturing technology or by building a plant to a larger scale, and by sourcing components from producers whose own experience is larger than the innovators'—that is, take advantage of shared experience.

TABLE 6-3
Experience and the Relative Contribution of Various Cost Components

	Cost Component									
	A (75% Curve; 1 Item Per Unit)			*B (80% Curve; 1 Item Per Unit)*			*C (80% Curve; 2 Items Per Unit)*			
Experience with the Product	*Component Experience*	*Cost Per Unit*	*% of Total Unit Cost*	*Component Experience*	*Cost Per Unit*	*% of Total Unit Cost*	*Component Experience*	*Cost Per Unit*	*% of Total Unit Cost*	*Total Unit Cost*
100 units	100	$70.00	70.0%	10,100	$20.00	20.0%	1,000,200	$10.00	10.0%	$100.00
1,000 units	1,000	26.92	47.8	11,000	19.46	34.5	1,002,000	9.99	17.7	56.37
10,000 units	10,000	10.35	28.4	20,000	16.05	44.2	1,020,000	9.94	27.4	36.34
100,000 units	100,000	3.98	17.5	110,000	9.27	40.9	1,200,000	9.43	41.6	22.68
1,000,000 units	1,000,000	1.53	11.7	1,010,000	4.53	34.6	3,000,000	7.02	53.7	13.08

Source: Abell and Hammond, *Strategic Market Planning: Problems and Analytical Approaches*, Englewood Cliffs, NJ: Prentice-Hall, 1979, p. 126.

SHARED EXPERIENCE

Shared experience is an important confounding factor in the interpretations of relative cost positions in nearly every industry. For example, a diversified wire producer making steel, copper, and aluminum wire might well have a considerable advantage over a specialist because of its ability to spread its development, marketing, and overhead costs over a larger sales volume.

While shared experience often frustrates measurement and has to be estimated, it is clear that a company which has produced 900,000 units has an advantage over two major competitors who have produced 700,000 and 400,000 units, respectively. But if this leading competitor's product incorporates components which are used in another related product with a 600,000 accumulated volume, it shares components with a total effective accumulated experience of 1.5 million, making it an even more formidable competitor.

The difficult question, as in many strategic studies, is the issue of what is a relevant market. Shared experience is relevant where the production process has built on earlier products' components and where costs are shared. For example, a smart manager of a "first-in" competitor can confound potential entrants by his or her ability to produce innovative products at low cost, by re-using tried components in innovative ways to create value in the marketplace. The relevant experience curves to the cost position of such a producer concern components rather than the new product per se.

For companies which exploit shared experience within a product line which assembles components or modules or systems in different configurations, it is important to note that the strategic cost factor changes over time and as experience accumulates. The impact of cutting the cost of a particular component of the final product varies over time, as *Table 6-3* shows. Components have different relative cost impacts over time because the company's length of experience with each component varies. It is sensible that management's attention should turn towards the component where the current impact of a cost cut on overall production cost is the highest. And, when cost reduction is achieved on such a component, the manager's interest must shift to the next component where cost reduction can significantly affect the product's costs. In *Table 6-3*, the "critical" component is A at first, then B and finally C.

EXPERIENCE, PRICE, AND VALUE

Business decisions necessitate tradeoffs between objectives, such as profit and growth, short-term advantage and long-term security, and value creation and profit-taking. In evaluating the resource base of the firm, experience is a summarization of the firm's success at combining the critical functions of marketing, production and finance in a cost-efficient way. Effectiveness, however, is best represented by the value created in the market by the firm's product or service offerings, and a firm's ability to hold its sales volume *and* its prices and maintain its share of the market, especially when that market is growing.

Managing experience, too, means making tradeoffs. To illustrate, there is potential inflexibility in a capital-intensive production strategy. For example, a company which has integrated backwards to gain control of raw materials sources, in order to provide a greater percentage of the total value added in the industry chain, is less flexible than one which buys its inputs on the open market. Yet there is tremendous strategic flexibility in having a relative cost advantage. This strategic flexibility may be the ultimate advantage of experience-based cost reductions. The low-cost producer may or may not make a decision to lower price, but the option, at a profit, is always available to such a producer. Faced with the prospect of new entrants, for example, a price cut may deter entry. And with no new entrants, and the other competitors operating at higher costs, a strategy of price maintenance can pay handsome profits to the low-cost producer.

Experience, prices, and value are, as we have shown above, inextricably interconnected. Simple, generic strategies based on low cost or low price can be useful reference points during the strategy formulation process. However, business success rarely comes from the simple application of generic strategies. In this chapter, for example, we have seen the long-term inflexibility that may be the result of some cost cutting and value adding strategies.

Value added and profit, the share of the value added captured by the firm, are ultimately the firm's critical competitive resources. Value added stems from a concentration on the customers' needs. Profitability and, ultimately, profit stem from the firm's ability to meet these needs in a creative as well as cost-effective manner.

Experience, properly applied, creates value by meeting consumer needs, while continuing efforts to control costs promote efficiency. So long as the firm understands the necessity to be sensitive to changing consumer needs, a low-cost position can give it competitive (pricing) flexibility against new entrants or price cutting competitors who did not pay attention to *both* demand and supply.

CUTTING COSTS IS MANAGEMENT'S RESPONSIBILITY

George Santayana wrote, "Those who don't understand the past are doomed to repeat it." For all its truth, this maxim is largely honored in the breech by US managers who, as a group, sometimes seem to hurry toward the future (or the latest management fad) with little sense of the tremendous resource of their past experience and its relevance to their mission of cost control. Indeed, the recent vogue of factory "quality circles," where workers gather to suggest ways to improve quality, is an attempt to capitalize on the experience of those most closely associated with the production process and use that information to raise productivity and lower costs. It is difficult to move beyond the past and create beyond experience if you don't know how you came to the present.

While the quest for lower costs must be tempered with a realistic understanding of the future longevity of the market and the prospects of profit, ultimately costs will not decline unless management acts as if it believes a cost decline is possible. Simply put, this is because cost management is ultimately a social activity. Cost improvements are always possible if people are encouraged to seek them and rewarded when they do:

> The industrial learning curve thus embraces more than the increasing skill of an individual by repetition of a simple operation. Instead, it describes a more complex organism—the collective efforts of many people, some in line and others in staff

> positions, but all aiming to accomplish a common task progressively more efficiently. (Hirschman, 1964, p. 128)

Experience thus summarizes management's coordination of its own organization and, as well, requires an understanding of the forces at work in the industrial and competitive environment of the organization. We explore the firm's economic environment, the industry and competition, in Chapters 7 and 8.

chapter 7

The Industry Environment

INTRODUCTION

For managers, the purpose of environmental analysis is to understand the forces changing their industry. They have to understand the reasons for turbulence and the reasons for periods of relative stability and calm. Ultimately, they have to be alert to the forces of change. Some of these will undoubtedly come from within their own organizations, from dissatisfaction with present results or a realization that some corporate resource can be turned to greater advantage in the marketplace. Others will stem from the actions of one competitor or even many competitors in their industry.

Yet senior managers seldom study their industry. It is a time-consuming task, typically delegated to staff whose conclusions are tested against the experience of senior management.

Industry analysis should, therefore, result in conclusions which help managers evaluate and formulate strategies on the basis of reliable information. Reliable information is vital when critical tradeoffs have to be made between long-term and short-term profit—in other words, between short-term profit and current corporate growth. Analysis must help managers understand the forces driving change, anticipate the actions of competition and the consequences of those actions, and help them anticipate consequences of any commitments the firm might make to change.

Managers don't like surprises, and they don't like to be caught unaware. Consequently, they have to develop an understanding of their environment, the source of most surprises, and an ability to use that understanding. Fayol (1972) went so far as to say, ''managing means looking ahead . . . to foresee . . . to assess the future and make provision for it'' (p. 43).

We have split environmental analysis into three sections. In this chapter, we examine the industry, where the primary choice is what role to take. In Chapter 8, we examine how to compete, once you have chosen your industry role or have recommitted to it. And Chapter 9 discusses the greater environment which affects all industries, that is, society itself.

In this chapter, then, we deal with the industry environment. We have chosen an approach which is exhaustive, so that you'll have a reference point for any complete study you may wish to make. Indeed, a complete industry analysis will give less experienced people significant insights into the workings of both their industry and their firm. We caution you, however, that the scope of a complete industry analysis is well outside normal managerial experience. Typically, managers will select from this framework those pieces which they believe are likely to reveal the sources of change and the opportunities and problems which industry change presents for them. Experienced people tend to be more accurate in their assessment than those with less experience.

A complete assessment is most relevant in times of turbulence, where the strategic decision is to change or recommit to an historical industry position. If the industry is changing drastically, however, "all previous bets are off," and the strategist must take a long, hard look at the firm's industry and competitive position in it. At such times, the strategist seeks a target for reinvestment so that the firm can move with the times, preserving the value that has been created in the past and adding to it by investing in the center of future profit opportunity—for example, by taking a new role in the firm's traditional industry chain.

A comprehensive framework is invaluable, because it tells you where to begin and what to do, and it gives you confidence about completing the task. And, as your experience accumulates, the industry analysis framework will help you quickly pinpoint sources of vulnerability and opportunities evolving in the marketplace.

FUNDAMENTALS OF ENVIRONMENTAL ANALYSIS

When managers allocate human and capital resources to a project, they commit or recommit their oganization to a strategy they believe will succeed and will enhance the value of the firm. No matter what results have been achieved already, the firm's commitment is based on an expectation of future results. But results depend not only on what is done; they are also conditional on the future.

Because of this, prudent managers try to become aware of trends and recognize events which will make their jobs easier—*opportunities*—and those trends or events which will make achieving their objectives more difficult—*threats*. Opportunities exist when we are able to work with or use the environment; in sailing, being able to run with the wind is an opportunity. Threats exist in both management and sailing when the winds change against us. Yet even when the environment is threatening, so long as we know where we are and where we want to be, we may be able to move towards our objective, albeit slowly. In other cases, we may find the environment so alien to our cause that we have to alter some of our objectives and seek new ones, even if only temporarily.

The purpose of environmental analysis is to identify the significant trends—that is, those likely to affect our results—early enough for management to provide for them. Such an analysis relies on two principles: one, that the future will evolve out of the present from the past; and two, although the future evolves from the past, that the future world will be different.

Insight is required. Environmental assessment and the forecasting inherent to it are more than simply projecting or extrapolating current trends and results. What management must do is to interpret current events and discover their meaning for the firm.

A realistic view of management's capability for effective environmental assessment is also necessary. Only if change can be interpreted in the light of earlier experience will it be noted, have meaning, and be intelligible to management (Johnson, 1967). Sharing this view of management's limitations in environmental assessment, while still stressing the importance of environmental data, McKinsey wrote during the Great Depression:

> The human mind . . . cannot make perfect decisions with reference to the variable factors which affect our business actions. Although this is true, we should not be discouraged of doing as well as we can. . . . [We] should guard against mistakes by securing all the information we can as a protection from our inherent tendency to be guided by mob psychology. (1932, p. 8)

Good managers make a healthy skepticism work for them in environmental analysis. They use all the information available. They avoid being slaves to tradition and are not closed-minded. They think for themselves, realizing that they cannot know when specific events will occur nor how important they will be. By knowing their organization and their environment, however, they prepare their firms for the future. When the unexpected occurs, they are able to understand quickly its real impact on their firms' interests and act appropriately.

A STAKEHOLDER APPROACH TO EFFECTIVE ENVIRONMENTAL ANALYSIS

What are the significant trends? Traditionally, strategic managers have considered competitive, technological, economic, political, and social (including demographic) trends. The dilemma is where to begin. All these trends are important, because each affects the level of demand or the conditions of supply which the firm meets in its markets.

Supply and demand describe the conditions of exchange between the firm's products and its environment, and we can note that very few organizations can exist for long without some form of exchange of input for output (Williamson, 1975; Pfeffer and Salancik, 1978). Indeed, the impacts of the environment on the terms of exchange—that is, the market price and quantity produced—demonstrate the interdependence of the firm and its environment. The firm's performance is the result of its exchanges with its environment.

We have therefore come to use an approach to environmental analysis which focuses on the stakeholders of this firm-environment exchange. *Figure 7-1* illustrates the range of stakeholders in the environment of a typical larger US firm. A stakeholder is any individual or organization whose behavior can directly affect the firm's future but is not under the firm's control (Freeman, 1981). Such groups have a stake in the firm, relationships with it, and interests in its results, as well as direct and indirect influence on those results. In short, there is an exchange of goods or services for money, or of approval for results, between the firm and such groups. The exact number of stakeholders to be considered will depend on the organization, and the weight given them is likely to vary depending upon the issues at hand and the circumstances surrounding the issues (Freeman, 1981; Emshoff and Freeman, 1979).

It is obvious that this stakeholder environment is wide and the interconnections among all the participants are likely to be complex. To manage this complexity, and to allocate our efforts where the environmental effect on the firm is greatest, we will work selectively and sequentially through our stakeholder set. Focusing on one group of

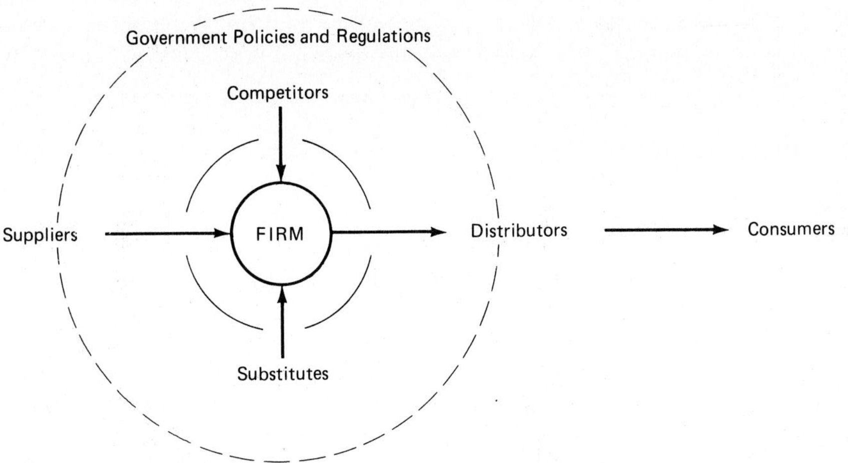

FIGURE 7-1 Stakeholders of the Firm

stakeholders at a time limits errors. The sequence helps make the relevant environmental issues clear and keeps the task manageable for those who have operating responsibilities in the organization.

Keep in mind that, in environmental analysis, our approach is to assess whether our strategy is consistent with the environment and to anticipate the future path of current events and their impact on our performance. Our objectives are to be realistic and to accurately distinguish minor change from structural changes, which are likely to have greater consequences for the viability of our strategy. The most important changes are those which:

1 affect the role of stakeholders and their power in our affairs;
2 alter the relative power of the players in our competitive arena; and
3 point to improved methods of operations.

These changes are likely sources of opportunities and threats. And whatever trends we identify, we must identify them in a timely manner because we want time to consider whether and how we should position our organization to take advantage of them, or, at worst, accommodate them.

Now, let us describe the order in which we analyze stakeholders to fully assess the firm's environment. First, we explore the production-distribution relationships in the industry, because these supplier and customer stakeholders have the most exchanges with the firm and therefore the most impact on it. Next, we move to competitors—indeed, competitors are stakeholders since their financial performance depends on the activities of the firm. Finally, we discuss the firm's social and political stakeholders, some of whom may have the power to forbid the firm to operate.

In this chapter, however, we will concentrate on the economic relationships between the firm and its stakeholders. Of course, some industrial stakeholders have social-political relationships with the firm, too. We will not deal with these here. This aspect of the industrial stakeholders as well as the firm's relationships with other, primarily non-economic, stakeholders will be discussed in Chapter 9.

THE INDUSTRIAL ENVIRONMENT

Although the firm is affected by many environmental factors, our analysis begins in the environment usually most relevant to the firm's operating and strategic decisions: its industry. We want a framework which organizes industry data to help us understand the basic economics of our industry and the behavior of our competitors. Amazingly, few firms have more than vague notions about their industry's structure and the future significance of their competitors' behavior.

The data we need are usually easy to collect, and, although there may be gaps, very rarely are these critical. Lack of information should not hamper industry analysis. Trade magazines and shows, customers, suppliers, and salespeople are all rich sources of information on industry and competitor performance. So, too, are annual reports, industry associations, and government statistics. Indeed, it is amazing how much information on a firm's industrial environment is available at minimal cost from government agencies, public libraries, or conversations with industry participants. Even small pieces of strategic intelligence can lead to important inferences about the industry and our competition.

STAKEHOLDERS IN THE INDUSTRY CHAIN

Every firm holds a position or *role* in the chain of activities necessary to convert natural and human resources into more valued goods or services and market them. The firm's role describes what it does—for example, it may be a miner, grower, manufacturer, distributor, or retailer.

Industrial power allows a firm to pursue its own objectives in its own ways. Firms without power are very dependent on those ahead and behind them in the industry's natural sequence of activities. To evaluate a firm's power in the industry, then, it is important to assess the interdependencies which exist between the firm and others in its chain.

The industry chain, also known as the commercialization chain, the production-distribution chain, and the value adding chain, is a subset of the firm's stakeholders, as shown within the dotted lines in *Figure 7-1*. The industry chain is illustrated separately in *Figure 7-2* and focuses attention on the exchanges between buyers and sellers—input/output relationships (McLean and Haigh, 1954). We will use the chain as the foundation of a framework for industry analysis.[1]

[1]While the graphics of the industry chain show suppliers and customers in a visually horizontal relationship to the firm, it is important to note that any merger between these parts is referred to as vertical integration, since the economist views the relationships from suppliers, through manufacturers, to customers as vertical. Similarly, economists refer to mergers between those competitors at the same stage in the chain—i.e., competitive manufacturers or competitive distributors—as horizontal. Following the tradition of strategic management, however, competitors are shown in a vertical relationship with the firm in *Figure 7-2*.

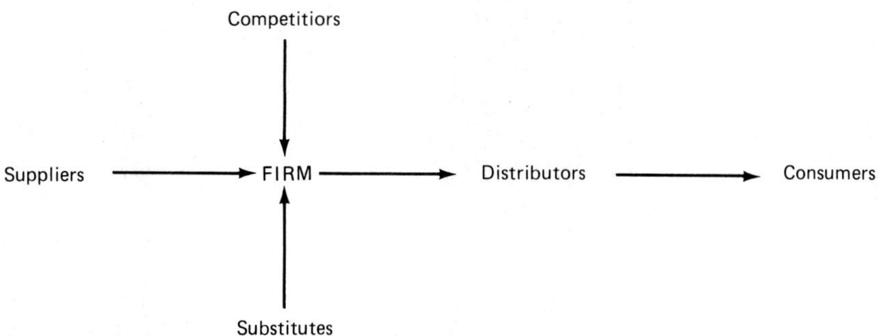

FIGURE 7-2 The Industrial Environment of the Firm

FRAMEWORK FOR INDUSTRY ANALYSIS

The Framework for Industry Analysis (*Figure 7-3*) organizes industry data so we can view the industry as a whole. The framework requires that we identify the major players in the industry and then collect data to describe its essential economics, competitive practices and trends, risk/reward structure, and the macroeconomy's impact on industry members. We will use this information to determine which roles have or promise greater relative power and to identify trends, and thereby the opportunities and threats, within the industry. A study of the industry and its structure is in fact akin to industry demographics: we are interested in corporate births and deaths, movement within the industry chain, geographical movements, and income and wealth statistics.

We begin by identifying the groups holding various roles in the industry and then describe the rest of the data needed for a very thorough industrial analysis. We simply work through the framework addressing each issue in turn. First, we need to know how many stages are in the industry chain and the identity of the key players and their relative importance. Then we need to know how they compete—what are the key economic characteristics and competitive variables, the results, the risks taken and rewards received at each stage as value is added.

The Players

Identifying the players requires us to consider who is in the industry, stage by stage. It is useful to record how many competitors there are at each stage and even how they are distributed by size or class. In most instances, it is useful to note the major competitors by name, and whether they serve a distinct or special market segment. Large corporations often play multiple roles with sister divisions acting as both suppliers and customers.

Suppliers, of course, include sources of raw material as well as manufacturers of intermediate goods. Ford, for example, buys tires but makes glass. Hence, it is a customer of Firestone and Goodyear as well as a buyer of silica sands. Prior to Polaroid's introduction of its SX-70 system, Kodak supplied instant film negatives to Polaroid.

Buyers include other manufacturers as well as wholesale and retail distributors and, ultimately, consumers. It is important to identify who the buyer is, and what type of demand influences sales. Sometimes the ultimate buyer may be strongly influenced by others. For example, although elevators are purchased by developers, architects usually

FIGURE 7-3 **Framework for Industry Analysis**

	Raw Material Supplier	*Intermediate Goods Manufacturer*	*Final Manufacturer*	*Wholesaler*	*Retailer*	*Customer*
The Players						
Names						
Number and size distribution						
Segments addressed						
Government's roles						
Entry/Exit trends						
Historical Elements of Competition						
Type of demand						
Product differentiation						
Price/Cost						
Quality/Service						
Value						
Capacity						
Timing of intense activity						
Likely changes						
Economic Characteristics (of operations)						
Growth						
Product life cycle stage						
Technology/Process						
Capital/Labor intensity						
Value added						
Fixed/Variable cost levels						
Breakeven volume						
Operating leverage						
Labor skills required						
Length of operating cycle						
Inventory position						
Receivables/Payables position						
Experience						
Macroeconomic Response						
Impact of business cycle						
Impact of fiscal policy						
Impact of monetary policy						
Inflation						
Robustness of demand						
Risk/Reward						
Profitability analysis						
Margin						
Turnover						
Leverage						
Profit share/Market share						
Sustainable growth rate						
Conclusions						
Risks taken						
Power, and rewards of power						
Problems						
Outlook						
Likely future competitive entrants						

make the specification decision. Because elevators have a derived demand function, sales occur only if developers expect a healthy primary demand for residential and commercial space. A peek inside a children's shoe store will show that, while parents purchase the shoes, even very young children have strong preferences which heavily impact the purchase decision.

Beyond identifying the players, an assessment of the profit impact of size may provide insights into the current and future importance of particular firms in the industry. Market share, or relative market share (your market share divided by that of your biggest competitor) is a useful measure of size and points to the market power of firms at different stages in the industry chain. Research by the Strategic Planning Institute and its associates on the Profit Impact of Market Strategy (PIMS) data base has pointed to a positive relationship between market share and profitability (Schoeffler, et al., 1974; Buzzell, et al., 1975), although others (Gale, 1972; Rumelt and Wensley, 1981; Hatten and Hatten, 1985; Woo, 1983) have challenged the general application of the finding.

Profits, profitability, and profit share all carry important information on the viability of a business. The crucial factor for management is not whether profitability and market share are correlated generally, but how they are related *in their own business*. The answer may help us evaluate alternative strategies, the adequacy of our present strategy, and the vulnerability of our present position in our industry. In fact, a firm's management should be alert to growing competitors who are earning profits greater than its own and holding a profit share greater than its own market share. Such companies are building not only market share but probably also cash reserves for additional expansion, productivity improvements and, thereby, increased market power (Hatten and Hatten, 1985).

In addition to identifying the major players and the size distributions of the industry's members, it is worth noting the multiple roles of government in the industry. In the auto industry, for example, government's role has changed over the years. As well as providing the legal structure for corporate activity via limited liability, the government has mandated safety and pollution standards and the 55 mph speed limit. It guaranteed the Chrysler bail-out loans and is a customer, tax collector, and source of information for the industry. Furthermore, government's fiscal and monetary policies can stimulate or reduce private demand for cars.

A knowledge of entry and exit trends can enrich our analysis and understanding of an industry's competitive environment (Porter, 1980). Entry to the ranks of a firm's suppliers may mean opportunity for lower-priced inputs. Exit may mean more power to the survivors, since competition is reduced. Additionally, entering and exiting capacity can signal efficient scale in the industry. Entrants can be presumed to be making their best commitments with plant design, and so point to currently efficient scale. Plant closures should point to size which is marginally profitable (Scherer, 1970).

Historically Exploited Competitive Weapons

Having identified who is in the industry, it is useful to consider how they compete. Many weapons exist: price, quality and service, value, capacity and availability, and product differentiation, to name a few. Porter (1980) says there are three generic strategies which are successful: cost leadership, differentiation, and focus. While we will defer our discussion of the firm's competitors until later, historic patterns of competition throughout the industry point to strategies that have worked at a particular industry stage in the past and to those that may be used again. Intense competition upstream at supplier stages may lead to lower manufacturers' costs. Intense competition downstream by distributors may lead to higher manufacturers' margins.

In considering competition in each stage, try to determine what events lead to outbursts of intense competitive behavior and whether these conform to any sequence or pattern. Knowledge of when competitive battles erupt or how they are timed may help you anticipate future competitive events in your stage elsewhere in the industry. For example, price wars afflict the soft drink industry early in the summer when Pepsi or Coke lowers prices. Awareness of this strategy and its timing is important to retailers who are dealing with other soft drink producers and planning their inventories to synchronize with price reductions and advertising in the industry.

Economic Characteristics

Economic logic suggests that certain industries work in certain ways. Understanding the economic rationale for industry behavior should help you develop your personal view of what the characteristics of a successful company in each industry role should be. For example, because iron ore is heavy and has a relatively low bulk value, the steel industry tends to concentrate or partially refine the ore before it is transported to the steel mills. The paper industry usually locates its mills near forest reserves, although the paper recyclers, like the scrap metal industry, locate near or in old urban centers where supply is plentiful and reliable.

Determining the basic economic characteristics at each stage of the industry chain is important, because that knowledge can help you develop an economic rationale for your own strategy. The characteristics of the industry tend to generate rules. For example, in the auto industry, some dealers use the following rule to control their used car inventories: "Don't let the sun set on a forty-five-day used car." Meat packers have an even more vivid inventory rule: "Sell it or smell it." Unconsciously violating industry rules often leads to failure. And innovations which consciously break with the conventional wisdom of the industry must be thoroughly analyzed and tested before commitment. McDonald's, for example, broke the traditional rule of the hamburger industry, "fresh to order," but Ray Kroc had the experience and success of the McDonald brothers' operation in California to bolster his confidence in the method and its product when he successfully automated (Kroc, 1977).

Certain basic data are needed to describe an industry and its economics. What type of demand drives the market? Farm equipment and fire engines may be favored by some buyers because the products are red or green or yellow, but they are certainly not consumer goods and are difficult to sell when farm income or local tax revenues are down.

Where are property, plant, and equipment located? Why? What is an industry's geographic scope? Bulk value of raw materials and transport costs, limited sources of supply, or the need for large energy or water resources may restrict some industry stages to particular locations. Food distribution, for example, tends to be a regional business. Brewing has developed a national scope as the US population migrated from the Northeast and Midwest to the West and South, as efficient scale rose, and as national advertising became feasible.

Capital and labor intensity, efficient scale, breakeven volume, and operating leverage available are all characteristics of the operating processes used by firms at every stage. They highlight the importance of volume and market scope, and their relative importance tends to change over time. Sometimes industries are surprising. Can manufacturing, for example, is seen as capital-intensive by many people. However, although can lines are costly, they are durable. An analysis of the costs of a can shows that, due to the high cost of setting up the line, the costs of line maintenance, and the skills required to do these jobs well, labor is the largest part of the value added in can manufacturing. Labor cost control is therefore more important in the can industry than most people believe, explaining why the industry has been known to accept a strike rather than a wage increase it believes is too high and explaining why modern canning plants often have idle lines set up for specific product runs. The lesser importance of capital also explains why the potential for entry is high. Many sources of competition exist, keeping prices low. The large brewers, for example, have their own canning operations, supplementing external capacity.

The operating cycle (days of inventory plus days of receivables) is another important characteristic because it determines how much working capital is needed to operate the business, that is, to synchronize its operations with those ahead and behind it in the industry chain. As cash is converted to inventory and inventory to receivables and receivables to cash, the business links itself to suppliers and customers and moves through an operating cycle. In some businesses, such as agriculture and leisure goods, the cycles are seasonal and therefore very long. In others, there are many cycles per year; for example, supermarkets have very short operating cycles.

Where the working capital is invested points to the security of the credit risk and the importance of the service role that the business plays in its industry. For example, brewers carry large receivables from their distributors. Iowa Beef faces the following credit cycles in the meat packing industry:

Farms to Iowa Beef	0 to 1 day
Iowa Beef to wholesaler	9 days
Wholesaler to distributor	26 days
Distributor to restaurant	45 to 60 days
Restaurant to patron	0 days (cash or credit card)

Note that for a distributor, working capital is needed to pay its suppliers (inventory) and finance its sales (receivables).

Typically, those with power command better terms and may receive credit and even on-time inventory delivery. For example, the Japanese auto industry uses the Kanban system where auto manufacturers receive inventory "just in time" for production, without the expense or risk of storing materials. Sears Roebuck and the large English retailer Marks and Spencer use their heavy buying power to gain much credit and service in their dealings with suppliers.

The Product Life Cycle

Growth is another important characteristic of an industry. Fast growth situations attract entrants, while slow growth promotes exit. One of the most powerful analytical tools in the strategist's armory, the Product Life Cycle, addresses growth directly and helps us speculate on the evolution of a product, market, or industry.

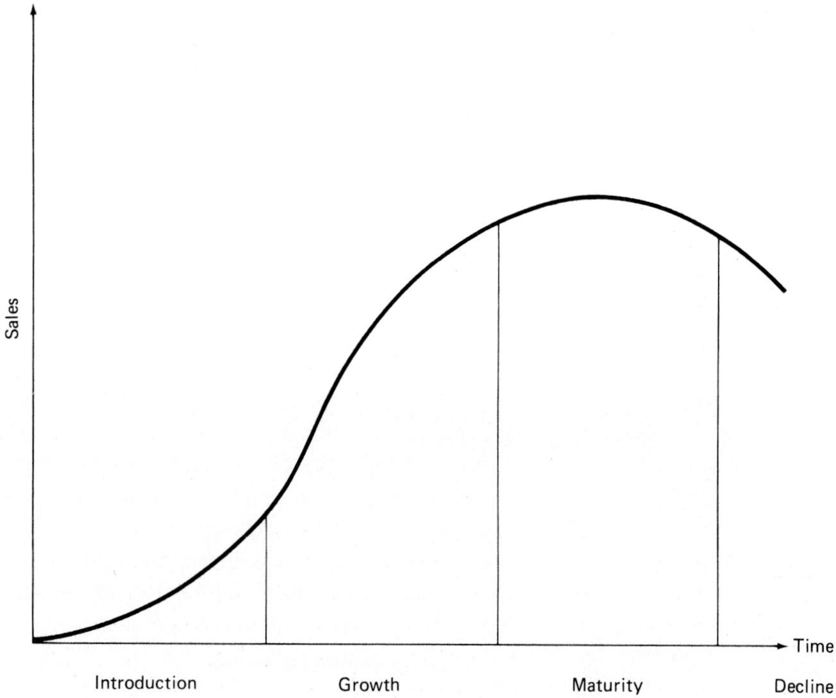

FIGURE 7-4 The Product Life Cycle

The life cycle model suggests that most product-markets develop along an S-shaped path (*Figure 7-4*) with slower early sales growth, faster midterm development, and tapering sales growth as the product saturates its market and competition appears. Common sense and experience suggest that management practices should change to earn the best possible results at each stage as the product moves along the life cycle.

But the value of the concept lies in the way it helps us anticipate industry evolution and the future track of most competitive variables. *Figure 7-5* illustrates this point by showing likely evolutionary paths for capital investment, profit, cash flow, competition, and innovation over the life cycle. Since businesses are economic systems, each element of the system is interdependent and must move consistently with the others. This systematic consistency gives the product life cycle its analytical power and explains its popularity.

In a discussion of the product life cycle, it is necessary to note that the classic S-shaped life cycle holds exactly for very few products (Gaston, 1961; Gold 1964). Gold tracked thirty-five single-product industries over a seventy-year-period, 1885 to 1955, and found that twenty-nine of them fitted four basic patterns: eight showed constant growth, nine showed slow growth, eight had growth followed by stability, and four had growth followed by decline. Although these basic patterns appeared to hold, he observed wide short-term deviations from the long-term growth path and argued that it is dangerous to use projections of recent experience in lieu of forecasts of future demand. He explained that managers try to overcome sales declines and to continue success, thereby altering the

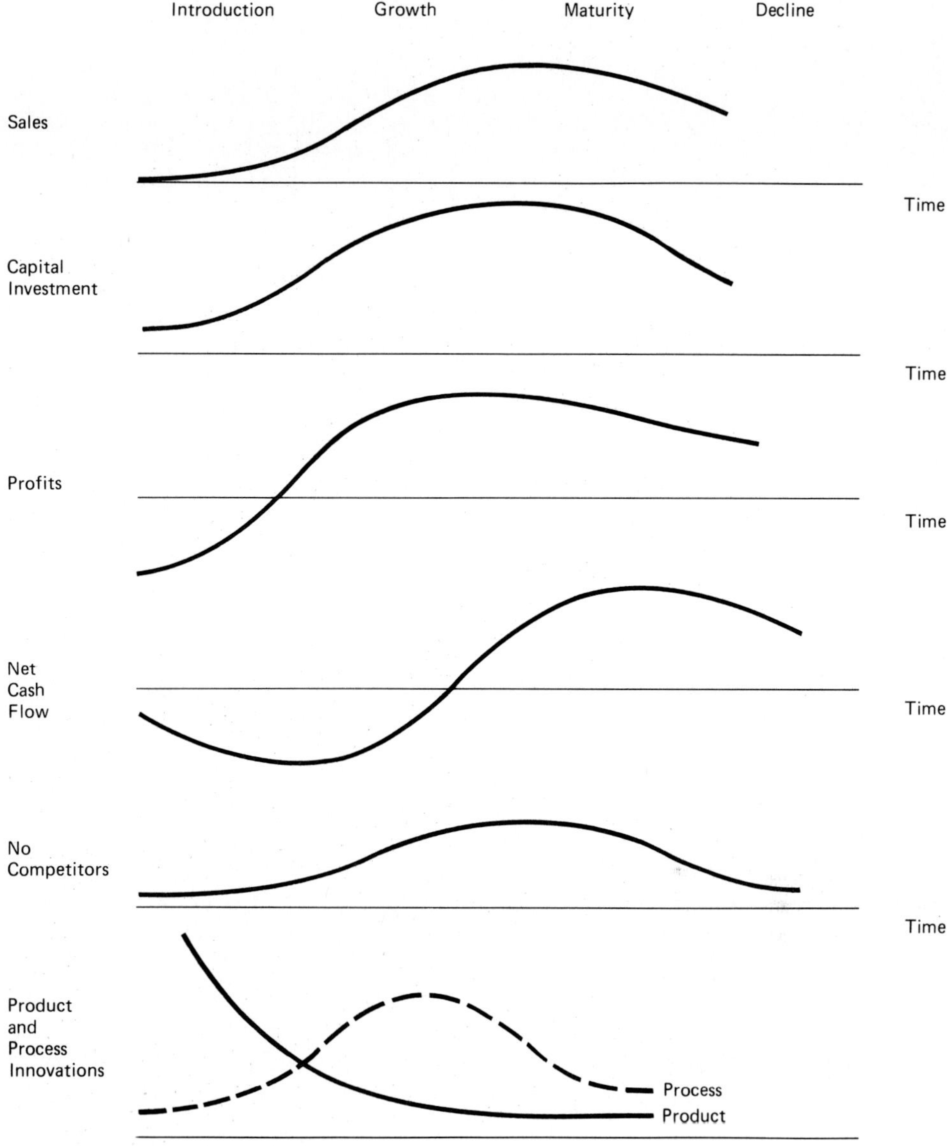

FIGURE 7-5 Impact of the Product Life Cycle

growth path. Managers elongate the 'S' pattern rather than allowing the product to decline as the model suggests.

Evidence of this type of behavior is presented by Yale (1964) and by Levitt (1965) in their discussions of the nylon industry. As *Figure 7-6* shows, nylon's sales were repeatedly revitalized as new uses and new users were found for the product. Each extension postponed the time of maturity. Cox (1967) in his study of the ethical drug

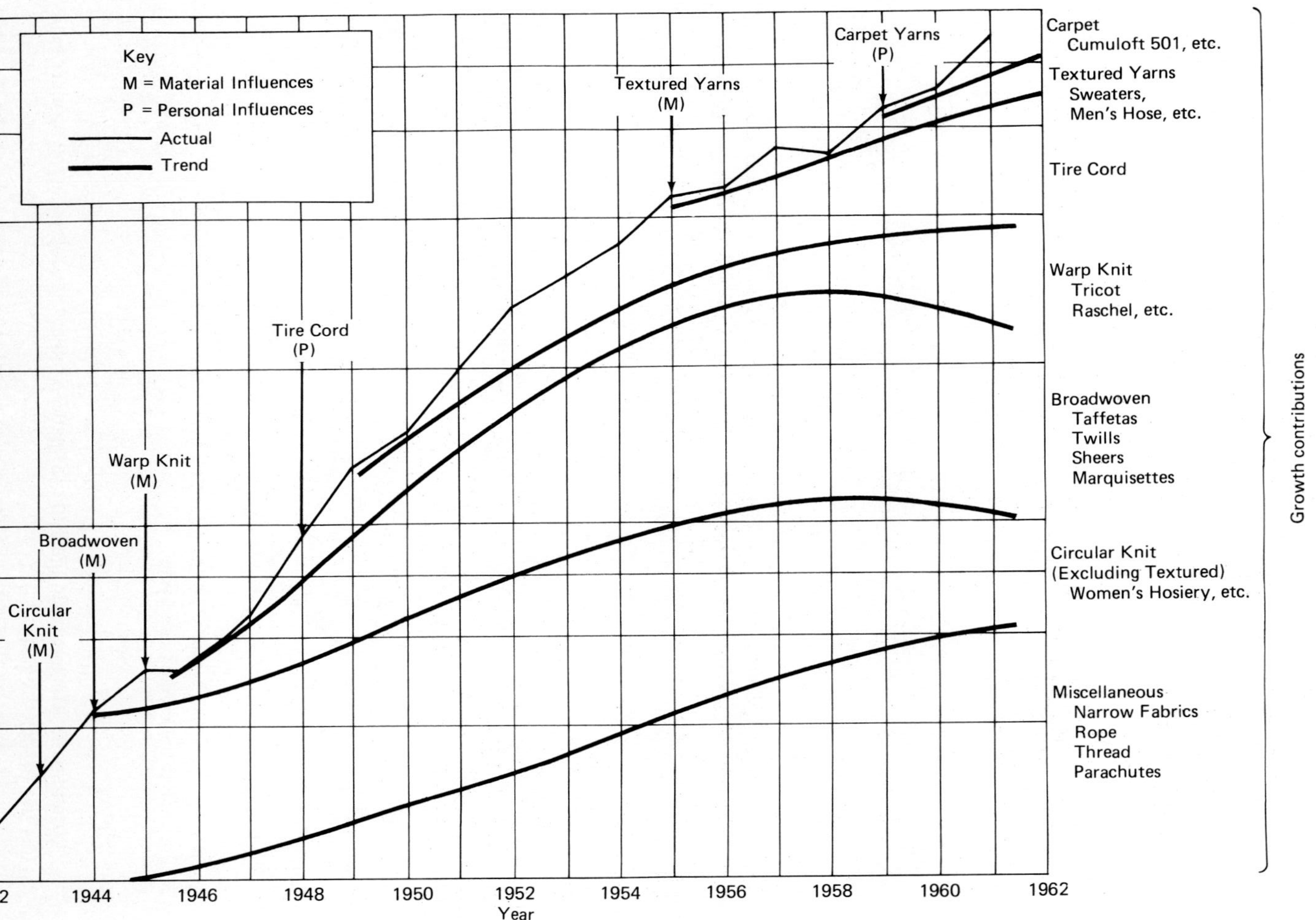

FIGURE 7-6 Innovation of New Products in the Nylon Industry

Source: Reprinted by permission of the *Harvard Business Review.* Theodore Levitt, "Exploit the Product Life Cycle," Nov.-Dec. 1965.

	1955 to 1963 (258 products)		%
I.		$y = a + bx + cx^2$	28.3
II.		$y = a + bx$	5.4
III.		$y = a - bx$	12.8
IV.		$y = a$	5.1
V.		$y = a + bx + cx^2 + dx^3$	9.3
VI.		$y = a + bx + cx^2 + dx^3 + ex^4$	39.0
			100.0

FIGURE 7-7 Growth Patterns in the Ethical Drug Industry

Source: Adapted from Cox, "Product Life Cycles as Marketing Models," *Journal of Business,* 40, 4, Oct. 1967. Reprinted by permission of the University of Chicago Press.

industry found six life cycle patterns (*Figure 7-7*). Note that most drug sale curves ultimately experienced decay, probably as more effective drugs were substituted for old.

Substitution of one product form for another is quite common, as is the substitution of one technology for another. Examples include water- and oil-based paint, electric furnaces replacing open hearth steel furnaces, and jet planes replacing those driven by propellers (Fisher and Pry, 1971; Lenz and Lanford, 1972).

Polli and Cook (1969) investigated 140 nondurables and made the following observations, consistent with Gaston's, Levitt's, and Cox's work:

1 Stability does not mean saturation unless no new product forms are possible with current technology or no new uses exist.
2 Several periods of decline may apply to a product form but are unlikely to apply to a product class.
3 A mature market may mask turbulence among product forms or brands.
4 The life cycle model fits more narrowly defined products better than it fits broad product classes and industries.

Bass (1969) and Nevers (1970) used an epidemiological model of first purchase behavior based on the first few years' sales experience of the air conditioning and color TV industries to estimate cumulative market size, peak sales, and sales rates. At the time, Bass predicted a decline in color TV sales, while the industry projected continued growth and committed to substantial new plant additions. Bass was right and the industry wrong; new plants were idle, draining the competitive strength of the industry and perhaps indirectly leading to the later successful Japanese entry to the US market. In beer, the life cycle is thousands of years long. In electronics, it is probably months long.

For us, the life cycle model should focus attention on change and the need for adaptation, as well as the likely character of the future market and competition. For the strategist, the issue is less likely to be short-run sales forecasts and product planning than it is plant size, capital commitments, and commitments to businesses themselves. Fast growth is increasingly difficult to sustain in any business, and it is in this context that the life cycle model raises useful questions and prompts us to be alert to signs of change.

Indeed, many industries run into trouble and overcapacity when their members assume current sales growth rates will be sustained forever. *Figure 7-8* shows a graph of projected growth of the personal computer industry done in 1983 (Stipp and Hill, 1983). This is a simple "northeasterly," where sales have been forecast as running up the northeast corner of the chart at a constant rate. Serious overcapacity and price cutting could occur if the personal computer industry did not grow as expected and, indeed, by mid-1985 this was the case. The industry was in decline and Steven Jobs, Apple's founder and chairman, was dethroned.

Growth also affects technology. As markets grow and competitors enter, the strategic problem shifts from product specification to process efficiency and perhaps to service capability. Utterback and Abernathy (1975) have described the parallel evolution of process and product innovation which highlights the reasons for change. As *Figure 7-9* shows, they hypothesize different innovation priorities as time passes and the product life cycle evolves.

Hayes and Wheelwright (1979) applied these ideas to process and product life cycles, advocating coordination. Note that there are some very fundamental economic pressures driving competitors in fast-growing markets toward standardized products and

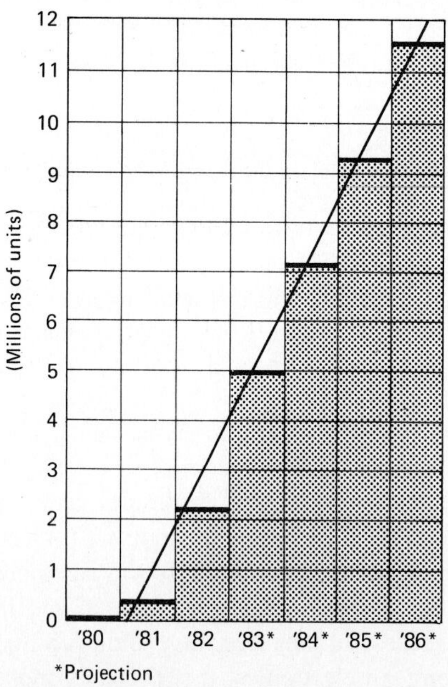

FIGURE 7-8 Sales of Home Computers Costing Less Than $1000

Source: David Stipp and G. Christian Hill, "Texas Instruments' Problems Show Pitfalls of Home-Computer Market," *The Wall Street Journal*, Dow Jones & Co., 1983. All rights reserved.

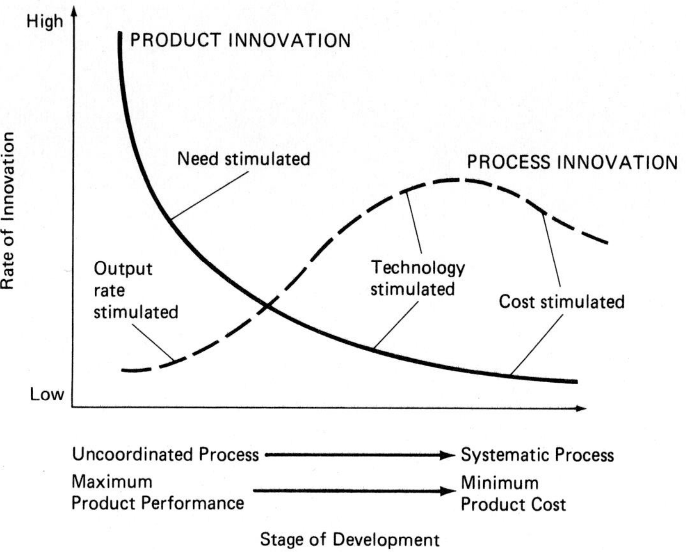

FIGURE 7-9 Innovation and Stage of Development
Source: Adapted from Utterback and Abernathy, 1975, p. 645

mass or continuous processes, as implied by the arrows down the diagonal of *Figure 7-10*. These pressures include:

1 Competitors' need to lower costs, particularly variable costs. With demand rising, investments in fixed assets appear supportable, and so fixed costs rise.
2 The immediate benefits of scale. As the Lang effect shows, the costs of a production facility do not grow as fast as outward capacity:

$$\text{Cost of new plant} = \text{Cost of old plant} \times \left(\frac{\text{Capacity of new}}{\text{Capacity of old}} \right)^{L}$$

where L, the Lang factor, is about 0.7. Costs rise with the surface area of materials used to build the plant and capacity with volume, hence the .7, roughly 2/3, power factor.[2]
3 The effects of experience and learning. Costs of production fall as managers and workers learn to improve production techniques.

Remember, though, that asset commitments imply risk, even in a period of growth. High productivity may be at a cost of reduced flexibility and innovative capacity. Competition from other industries and process changes by customers may severely affect the business (Abernathy and Utterback, 1978). On the other hand, of course, the rise of

[2]Compare the surface area of a cube, roughly proportional to its cost, with its volume. A cube of sides 1 has a surface area of 6 enclosing a volume of 1; a cube with sides 2 has surface area of 6×2^2 with a volume of 2^3 or 8. Hence costs increase slower than capacity, roughly measured by volume.

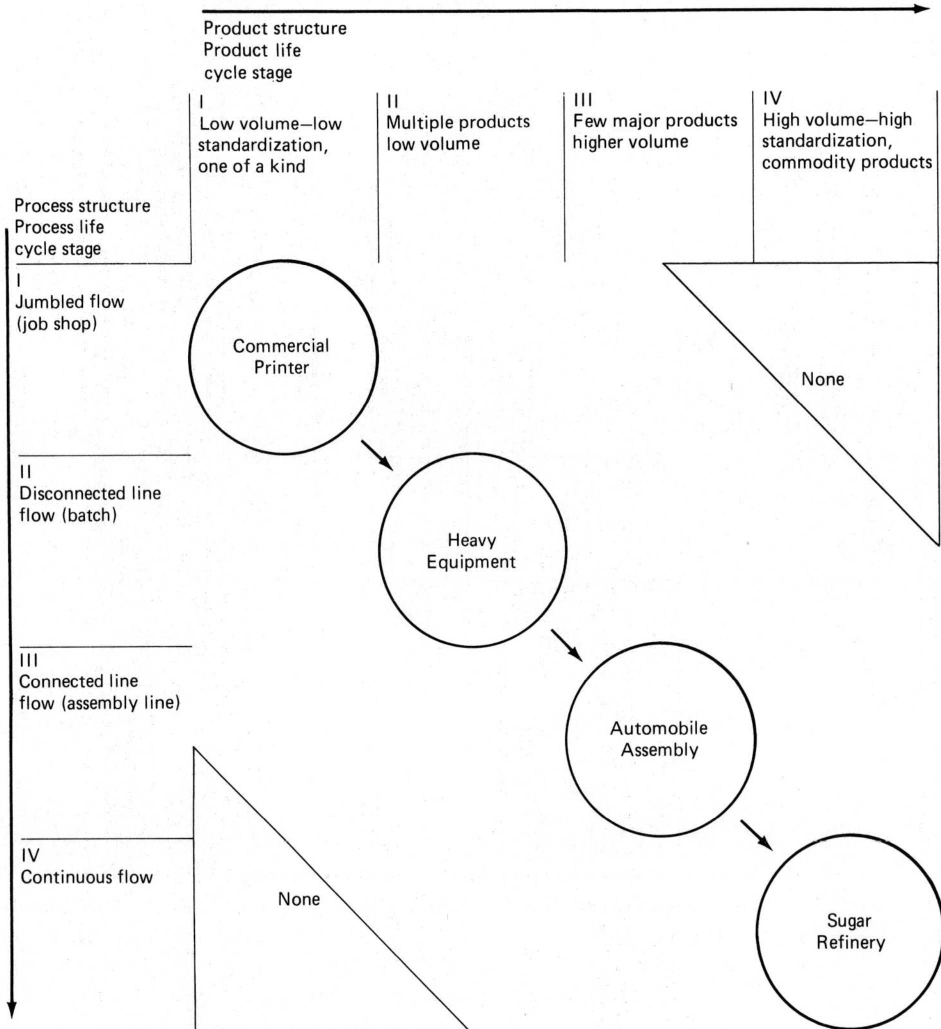

FIGURE 7-10 Matching Major Stages of Product and Process Life Cycles
Source: Hayes & Wheelwright, 1979, p. 128

world-scale plants, especially if demand is controlled by contract or vertical integration, may prevent competition from entering a market for many years, since competition at such a scale is enormously expensive. And if demand is contracted, a window of opportunity does not exist. Demand and market scope must be balanced with plant size; massive marketing efforts and research accompany the building of world-scale plants, to ensure that an efficient market exists and is tapped prior to such a plant commitment.

Value Added Analysis

Value added is another economic characteristic which we should investigate. Value added shows which parts of the industry chain make major contributions of value to the final customer and thus gain major rewards for their effort. Value added is the difference between the selling price and the costs of materials inputs for that stage (that is, it includes labor, plant and profit). For example, in the lobster fishing industry, the prices per pound at various stages of production might be (Uyterhoeven et al., 1977, p. 208):

Ex vessel	$1.08 per pound
To wholesale	$1.48
To retail	$1.88
To consumer	$2.49

and the percent value added for each stage is:

By fisherman	$1.08/$2.49 = 43% (includes fishing costs)
By dealer	$ .40/$2.49 = 16%
By wholesaler	$ .40/$2.49 = 16%
By retailer	$ .61/$2.49 = 25%

Value added is particularly revealing when compared with risk and gives insight to the power held by the major players. If both value added and risk are assessed at each stage, the favorable positions (high reward for low risk) and unfavorable positions (low reward for high risk) in the industry chain can be seen. In the lobstering example above, the fishermen have high risk while adding little value (when costs are considered), but wholesalers add much value at relatively little risk for themselves. The risk in the industry comes in finding supply, and this is obviously high for the fishermen while the wholesaler only sells what he can get. The economics of the lobster industry, then, supports the concept of independent fishermen operating at small scales with relatively low capital investment, because low financial risk is more appropriate in this low value added situation. Large companies operating capital-intensively at this stage with technology substituting for labor would actually raise the risk (with high fixed costs) and so be uneconomical in this industry. Effort on a larger scale might make sense if lobster farming (in tanks) were perfected to be a reliable source of supply; the risk of supply would be substantially reduced and could thus justify higher capitalization. Similarly, large-scale effort may be worthwhile in lobster wholesaling because the rewards are high and the lower risk factor can justify higher fixed costs.

Macroeconomic Sensitivity

The macroeconomic sensitivity of the industry refers to the effect of the business cycle (*Figure 7-11*) and macroeconomic policy on firm performance at different stages in the industry. Macroeconomic phenomena include unemployment, inflation, and interest rate

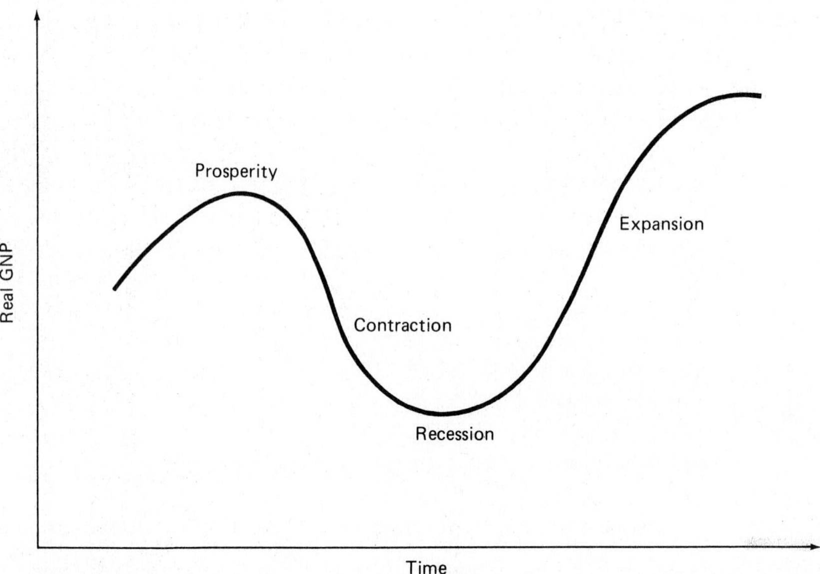

FIGURE 7-11 The Business Cycle

fluctuations which accompany the business cycle, and the monetary and fiscal policies which influence the cycle. The 1974 and 1981–82 recessions demonstrated that monetary and fiscal policies which had been seen as keys to extended post-World War II prosperity in the US were not a macroeconomic insurance scheme; the business cycle continues to have a severe impact on certain industries, an impact amplified by the industries' own purchasing and inventory policies as well as government monetary policy affecting interest rates.

The macroeconomy can affect different businesses' sales in a variety of ways, depending upon whether buyers see the good as discretionary or essential, a prestige or a make-do item. Cyclical goods are those for which demand moves with the business cycle; demand is strong during periods of prosperity and weak during recessions. Firms selling cyclical goods are more vulnerable in recession, although their performance is very strong in periods of economic prosperity. Automobiles are cyclical, as are large home appliances, carpeting, and Coke and Pepsi.

Countercyclical goods are those for which demand runs against the business cycle: demand slows in prosperity and increases in recession. Starches, such as rice and pasta, as well as movie tickets, moderately priced alcohol, and generic colas are countercyclical. Similarly, dry-cleaning and shoe-repair services are countercyclical, as people make do with the old rather than buy new clothes or shoes in recessions.

We shall term "robust" those businesses which can withstand the swings of the macroeconomy and enjoy stable demand throughout the business cycle. These goods include high-priced, prestige items, such as Mercedes-Benz automobiles, fur coats, and expensive alcohol, since the rich are generally less severely affected by recessions than blue-collar workers. Essentials, such as toothpaste, respond very little to small changes in GNP. Interestingly, Dr Pepper has had a history of demand apparently unaffected by recession, perhaps because its drinkers must have the ''most original soft drink'' no matter what the state of the economy.

Goods with a derived demand are those for which demand depends on the demand for other goods. If the primary good is cyclical, countercyclical, or robust, goods which have demand derived from it will be similarly influenced. Elevator demand, for example, is a derived demand from the primary demand for commercial or residential space; hence elevator demand is cyclical, as is construction.

If some firms are particularly vulnerable to certain macroeconomic situations, the likely effects of attempted macroeconomic stabilization policies of government and the central bank will be important for them. Taxation and monetary policies can seriously affect particular products' customers, and these must be monitored carefully by the managers of affected companies. For example, Chrysler's recovery was slowed and the fate of International Harvester made bleaker by the Federal Reserve Bank's high interest rates and the federal government's tight fiscal policies in the early 1980s, effectively restricting demand in Chrysler's and International Harvester's markets. Restauranteurs fear Congressional tirades against the ''three-martini lunch'' and expense-account meals when tax reform is debated. Construction is sensitive to both interest rates and the interest payment and depreciation expense deductions allowed by the federal tax system.

The macroeconomic environment affects industries on the demand side through the impact of the business cycle and economic policies on customers. Its impact is also felt on the supply side, as competitors enter or leave the industry due to prosperity or failures as the business cycle shifts. It is felt as capital becomes more expensive and less available when government borrows heavily in the capital markets and forces interest rates up. Also, unions become more powerful in prosperity and more aggressive in periods of inflation.

The manager must be aware both of how the macroeconomy affects his or her business directly, and also how it can or might shift power in the industry chain. For example, in a recession, a high fixed cost producer of a cyclical good has less power in relation to customers, since volume is essential for its survival. The power of cyclical goods producers rises in periods of prosperity, since supply may not match the exploding demand levels felt by their distributors.

Lincoln Electric, a manufacturer of welding equipment and consumables, provides an interesting example of a firm structured so that every phase of the business cycle can be used to enhance its business strength. Lincoln takes a proactive position in the macroeconomy and moves with the times.

Lincoln has a ''no layoff'' policy. It controls or limits its growth in expansionary times and so avoids overhiring. Its costs are constantly cut by serious management effort and with employee cooperation. With general prosperity, its sales of highly cyclical arc welding equipment soar. Lincoln turns down orders or accumulates a backlog, but it never raises prices to restrict demand. Nor does it hire extra employees to cope with short-term production problems. Indeed, it tries to lower its prices constantly as its costs drop. In recession, its low prices and competent technical services make it the preferred supplier and give it a robust position in its industry. Rather than laying off experienced people,

Lincoln sees recessions as periods of slack capacity and uses them to prepare for the next upswing. James F. Lincoln, a founder of Lincoln Electric, explained:

> Continuous employment is the first step to efficiency. But how? First, during slack periods, manufacture to build up inventory; costs will usually be less because of lower material costs. Second, develop new machines and methods of manufacturing; plans should be waiting on the shelf. Third, reduce prices by getting lower costs. When slack times come, workers are eager to help cut costs. Fourth, explore markets passed over when times are good. Fifth, hours of work can be reduced if the worker is agreeable. Sixth, develop new products. In sum, management should plan for slumps. They are useful. (*Civil Engineering*, American Society of Civil Engineers, January, 1973, p. 78)

Lincoln has actively limited its exposure to macroeconomic change. Most firms, however, are passive reactors to macroeconomic change, but that is their choice. An understanding of the macroeconomy's impact on firms at different industrial stages should help managers understand how and why their firm is affected and thereby help them take the first steps to limiting those effects by developing a strategy which uses the macroeconomic cycle to enhance their firm's competitive strengths.

Returns and Profitability Analysis

One of the great clichés of business is that business is about results, about returns at the "bottom line." And, of course, returns are the primary signal for entry and exit, for investment and divestment. Returns summarize the success of firms at each industry stage and reflect their robustness in the face of macroeconomic change.

Returns point the way of industry change. Stages with high returns may be attractive targets for future corporate migration; others, the low-return stages, may be reduced in importance. For decades, the oil companies have moved away from low-return stages and placed more resources in high-return stages (McLean and Haigh, 1954). Xerox, as another example, enjoyed very high returns in its copier business, a factor which ultimately made its markets attractive targets for Japanese competitors such as Savin and Ricoh and for re-entry by former competitors like Kodak.

Because returns point to the future, they must be thoroughly understood. Possibly the best tool for this purpose is Profitability Analysis founded upon the DuPont formula:

$$\text{Return on Equity} = \text{Margin} \times \text{Asset Turnover} \times \text{Leverage}$$

$$\frac{\text{Profit}}{\text{Equity}} = \frac{\text{Profit}}{\text{Sales}} \times \frac{\text{Sales}}{\text{Assets}} \times \frac{\text{Assets}}{\text{Equity}}$$

By applying this formula to the major players or class of competitors stage by stage, and by tracking the evolution of margin, asset turnover and leverage over time, we can learn not only how strong the stage is, but where its members may be vulnerable to competition and entry, and how they are changing their business.

As an example of the application of profitability analysis, notice that a strike would hurt firms where volume or asset turnover—that is, a large sales/asset ratio—is an important contributor to profitability. A price war could be started by a firm whose profits are founded in its asset turnover, hurting both competitors dependent on sales margin and their suppliers. Rising interest rates could severely affect a competitor or customer whose equity is highly leveraged with funds borrowed at variable rates.

Similarly, if return on equity (ROE) is stable while return on assets (ROA), and either margin or turnover or both, fall, the company must be leveraging up. This, of course, raises questions: why and how long can this strategy be sustained? A falling ROA, that is:

$$\frac{\text{Profit}}{\text{Sales}} \times \frac{\text{Sales}}{\text{Assets}}$$

may be a natural transitional cost of far-sighted expansion. On the other hand, it may be due to foreign competition. In the second case, prudence may suggest divestment and a reduction of equity investment. Hence, the company's increased leverage could be the owner's deliberate strategy to survive in a different competitive world.

It is important, therefore, to recognize how firms earn their profits in each stage of the industry chain. The components of profitability should relate to the economic character of the industry stage. Where sales are growing and returns are high, entry is likely. Where margins are high, turnover is likely to be low. Where turnover is high, margin is likely to be low. If ROA is high, debt may be used to accelerate growth. If ROA is low, the risk of leverage rises. Bankers try to lend only to those who will pay their loans off, to businesses they believe have low risk and high return.

For every business, this conservatism of financing institutions raises a question: How fast can we grow? John Chudley of Letraset, a British company, answers it this way:

> The long-term rate of growth that a company can afford under normal conditions is about two-fifths of the rate of return it earns on its capital employed. (1974, p. 81)

Chudley's personal experience-based response was founded on a British corporate tax rate of 40 percent and a 33 percent dividend payout, but there is a universally applicable formula for the sustainable growth rate which we can use in any corporation. The sustainable growth rate, g_S, is the rate of growth a firm can finance independently:

$$g_S = \frac{\text{Profit after Tax} - \text{Dividends}}{\text{Equity}} - \text{Inflation}$$

This calculation is based upon two implicit assumptions: First, that the firm's asset turnover is fixed (i.e., sales/assets is constant), and second that its leverage is unchanged (i.e., assets/equity is constant).

Quite simply, the sustainable growth rate is the ratio of new capital to capital employed, adjusted for inflation. Here, of course, the new capital is raised the old-fashioned way: It is earned *and* retained in the business, hence the name sustainable growth. Inflation slows real growth because it reduces the purchasing power of the dollars retained.

The sustainable growth formula gives us a simple way to monitor market power in our industry analysis. It also can help us identify opportunities and points of likely industry change. When a company has a sustainable growth rate which exceeds the growth of its industry or industry stage, $g_S > g_{industry}$, a company is financially capable of expanding its market share, integrating, or diversifying. The competitors who are threats may be in a high growth position or, conversely, desperately trying to escape from a low growth position. A low growth capability nearly always is due to low margins and limited market power. In family companies, it may be due to years of generous dividends.

Risk/Reward

The balance of risk and reward at each stage in the industry provides important data on the power and flexibility of the players in each industry role. Identifying where firms put their assets at risk and where they reap their rewards gives insights to their vulnerability or strength. Recognizing the ways in which a firm successfully controls the risks inherent to its position—by choosing to operate in a strong local market rather than risk costly national competition, for example—may indicate the future strategies which management believes are useful and those which are unthinkable.

The financial statements help us pinpoint where the firm is at risk. The balance sheet, for example, shows where fixed assets are heavy, how suppliers support the firm through its operating cycle, and how the firm serves its customers by providing financial support. A strong, low-risk firm will be integrated financially with its suppliers through large payables, for example, possibly cutting its own fixed asset exposure. A powerful firm will have small receivables, since its distributors will carry large inventories on their own books; its distributors view themselves as dependent on the firm.

As an example of a low-risk, high-power firm, consider AT&T, the old "Ma Bell." From 1956 until its 1982 settlement of a Justice Department suit, AT&T was the largest, if not sole, customer for certain telephonic products in the United States. Its suppliers extended substantial trade credit to AT&T, to the extent that AT&T's working capital was often negative. Indeed, AT&T's working capital need was reduced because of its access to its suppliers' working capital. A less powerful firm would not be treated so favorably by its suppliers.

Conversely, the terms which a less powerful firm received on raw materials would be shorter and more expensive; it would have to fund its own working capital. This is the situation in which Chrysler Corporation found itself soon after its brush with insolvency in 1980. To continue to operate, Chrysler had to generate its own working capital by selling fixed assets and entire non-automobile businesses; suppliers and bankers were understandably wary of Chrysler's ability to pay in its weakened condition.

A firm's choice of customers in the industry chain also influences risk. A small manufacturer selling exclusively to Sears Roebuck in the US is very dependent on Sears, and so is at risk should Sears redirect its purchasing. The small manufacturer may be asked to extend liberal credit, may cut its prices, or may even invest in plant rather than risk the loss of a large customer like Sears or General Motors. On the other hand, a speciality shoe manufacturer with one hundred equal-sized accounts can negotiate tough prices and payment terms with each of them, since the loss of any one customer's business represents only a small risk. The shoe manufacturer can limit its receivables and use the capital elsewhere in its business rather than bankroll a large customer.

Risk and reward are therefore important in determining what the viable opportunities and real threats in the industry are. Obviously, no firm will consciously choose a position in the industry with low returns and high risk, but if that is the reality of the present situation, then it must be recognized before management can correct it. Knowledge of the behavior of other players in the industry and the rewards and risks they take should help an organization improve its operating performance, either by imitating others in limiting risk or by gaining larger rewards in new markets where the returns are high.

An understanding of where returns are rising and where they are falling can be used to develop alternative strategies which move the firm toward more powerful roles or which reduce the risks or costs incurred with low-return activities. In the long run, risk/reward data should help strategists add value, by entering high-return businesses which have low risk, while cutting their high-risk/low-return operations.

SYNTHESIS: POWER, OPPORTUNITY, AND THREAT WITHIN THE INDUSTRY CHAIN

The data we have described as being used in the Framework for Industry Analysis are detailed and exhaustive; collectively, they give us an industry map which we can use to guide us in evaluating our current strategy and later to formulate new strategies. In practice, experienced managers will emphasize some parts of the framework at the expense of others in particular situations. Similarly, complete data are available in some case studies, while in others they are not. What we need to know is simple enough: What does the map mean for us? It will probably suggest focusing on some industry roles and some industry characteristics more than others.

The signs of industry power are revealed in the linkages, exchanges, and results of the industry chain. *Figure 7-12* focuses first on vertical integration, then on results and the industry's reaction to those results. It lists the signs of shifting industrial power. By focusing on the role(s) we play and comparing the data on our role with those on the others, we can judge who has power and who earns the largest rewards—they should be the same companies. Then we try to discern what present changes portend for the future success of our current strategy and for the likely development of competition in our stage (or stages) of the industry.

The locations of power in an industry can make or break a strategy; identifying them is therefore critical to strategic management. Are we making the best use of the power we have in the chain? Could that power be enhanced? Will the power of others block our strategy? Certain strategies will be aided by the power we have in the chain, while other strategies may depend heavily on other players in the chain and could be stymied by our own lack of power against them. Research suggests the obvious: market power, if managed properly, should enhance returns now, by raising revenue or controlling costs, or both; it should also reduce risk in the future, thereby enhancing value.

Likely future problems will emerge from a detailed study of an industry. Is entry by potentially strong competitors likely in certain stages? Have large players inappropriately evaluated the risks they have taken, making exits from some positions in the industry likely? Are certain companies ignoring the economics of their industry roles, and are their returns starting to slide?

After analyzing the industry, a strategic manager should have a better sense of likely

FIGURE 7-12 Linkages Within the Industry Chain

Vertical Integration
- Who does business with whom
- Ownership
- Contractual relationships
- Business linkages (e.g., inventory/credit support)

Pattern of Result
- Value added
- Risks taken
- Profits
- Growth

Reactions
- Asset deployments (signals ROA expectations)
- Entry/Exit/Migration
- New investments
- Capacity additions (signals demand expectations)
- Technology push
- Price shifts

Summation
- Who has power
- What is the outlook—problems/opportunities
- Likely future completion
- Key to future success

future developments in the industry. Insight into future developments reveals areas where opportunities or threats to our current strategy may lie. Perhaps, recently, one firm has successfully taken on a preceding or subsequent role in the chain; others may follow, leading to the integration and consolidation of a number of production stages. If an extended period of prosperity seems to lie ahead, some firms in the more cyclical portions of the industry will grow substantially stronger and become more powerful forces in the industry.

Your assessment of which stages of the industry chain are powerful and where there are opportunities to increase power can be corroborated by checking asset deployment of the major players at those stages. Resource deployments by industry members, if consistent with changing patterns of risk and reward, point to opportunities where additional rewards can be gained at low risk. Resource redeployment from certain areas may indicate threats where low rewards are accompanying high risk. You would expect assets to be invested where power is greatest, supporting strength and taking advantage of opportunities, and likewise that assets should be moved out of areas of weakness. If actual asset deployments are consistent with your power assessment, your assessment is shared by the industry and you are probably correct. If, however, asset deployments are different than you expected, there are two possible explanations: either the firms in the industry are misreading the environment, or they have additional information which leads them to a different assessment of emerging power, opportunities, and threats. Either explanation points to a need for further analysis before you complete your work assessing the industry.

Managers adopt strategies which conflict with the conventional wisdom of their industry only if they have good reasons to do so.

PREVIEW

Now, having taken the industry chain out of the full stakeholder set, limiting our focus to those stakeholders most closely related to the firm's operations, and having a sense of how the industry is evolving, we focus on competition per se. Hence, we put the firm's chosen industry role under a microscope, narrowing the breadth of the analysis and intensifying its depth. We focus on those who share that role, the competitors, and those who may share it in the future, potential entrants. First, we try to determine what their strategies and objectives are now and are likely to be in the future. Second, we explore what we might do to improve our performance. Finally, we examine how the results of our present or new strategy will be affected by our competitors' actions and reactions.

chapter 8

Competitive Analysis and Competing

OVERVIEW

This chapter focuses on competition, that is, on the activities of players in a particular industry role. It examines forces affecting the competition between organizations playing the same roles within an industry chain.

The selection of an industry role presupposes an analysis of where the firm can add most value with manageable risk and capture an appropriate profit. This done, the task is how to compete in your chosen role with others who have made similar role selection decisions. It is here, as we examine how other firms compete and anticipate how they will respond to competitive pressure, that competitive analysis can add value for the manager.

Competitive analysis and competing go hand in hand. It is virtually impossible to be an effective competitor unless you have a good understanding of your competitors' objectives, strategies, perceptions and resources. Without an informed sense of who your competitors are and what they are trying to do, you are managing blindly; sooner or later (probably sooner) you will be vulnerable to them.

The essence of competition is to focus strength against weakness. Competition places strategy against strategy. We must be able to move a little faster and a little harder than the competition. There are two principles to keep in mind:

1 *Focus strength against weakness*. Note, however, that smart competitors will focus their strengths against our weaknesses. Consequently, this principle is quite difficult to put into practice unless you thoroughly understand yourself and your competitors.
2 Before you seize an advantage or avoid a danger, *consider the danger in the advantage and the advantage in the danger*. In competing, the danger very often stems from vulnerabilities exposed by errors in attempting to do too much too soon with insufficient resources.

The objective of business competition is not so much to damage the competitor as to win the market. And we must remember the advice of Alfred Sloan, an early Chairman of General Motors: Companies compete with all their resources, not just specific products.

Indeed, all the fundamental tools of competitive analysis have been developed earlier in this book. You have to be able to look at your competitors as thoroughly as you look at yourself. You must understand their strategies, objectives, motives, perceptions and responses to pressure. You must identify their strengths and resources and understand the competitive arena where you meet.

To understand the competitive market, you have to understand your own role in the industry chain and the pressures that affect your competitive position. You have to work to develop your power in the marketplace and in this you will have to contend with the power of your suppliers and customers, those preceding and following you in the industry chain, as well as the power of your rivals, and the competitive strengths of substitutes and new entrants.

In this chapter, we will emphasize the nature of competition: its structure and the forces that enhance or destroy competitive advantage. These, indeed, are the forces of structural change and we shall discuss various ways to assess them. In doing this, we shall discuss strategic groups and competitive information and the ways in which alternative models can be used to formulate better strategies on the one hand, and to anticipate the consequences of competitive action on the other.

Competing is a mind game. We believe that, although industry structure may influence decision makers, essentially competition is about people, not structure. For this reason, identifying and understanding competing managements is a critical element in developing your sense of the competition and your ability to anticipate the likely course of future events.

DEFINITIONS OF THE INDUSTRY: THE COMPETITIVE ARENA

One of the principal difficulties of competitive analysis (and business) is determining exactly what the competitive arena is. There is always a risk in a competitive situation of defining the arena too narrowly. One way to avoid this error is to be alert to changes in the pressures stemming from those around you in the industry chain. It is particularly important to think about your product or service as satisfying certain consumer needs; then, look to consumer behavior to tell you what alternative ways they see to satisfy those needs.

Substitutes

Defining the competitive arena is the equivalent of defining the relevant market, and it is a matter where considerable debate is both possible and useful. Economists, however, have dealt with this problem for many years, particularly in the antitrust courts. They have developed an approach to determine substitutes: By calculating cross-elasticities, they judge which goods indeed substitute for others in the market. Cross-elasticity, ϵ_x, is calculated as:

$$\epsilon_x = \frac{(\%\text{ change in quantity sold of Good A})}{(\%\text{ change in price of Good B})}$$

that is, the responsiveness of the quantity sold of another good when your price changes. Obviously, if you increase your prices and consumers buy more of a good you had not considered a substitute for yours, the market has indeed spoken. Buyers apparently believe the other good satisfies about the same function as yours, and you must reconsider your definition of the competitive marketplace.

Competitive substitutes are those goods which fulfill the same consumer need. Recognition of the range of consumer substitutes can also give a manager insights to likely potential market entrants. We emphasize that what is a substitute is market-determined rather than based on the producer's perception alone. Indeed, a producer might emphasize product quality while failing to notice that quality is not a major factor for the consumer who considers goods of lower quality attractive substitutes. For example, a consumer might see a cheaper set of soft-sided luggage as a substitute for a longer-wearing, better-made line if he or she focused on the fashion aspects of the product rather than viewing it as "luggage for life," the term used by the producer.

Entry

Another purpose in defining relevant competitive scope broadly is to assess sources of likely entry, the sources of future competition. While not every firm is a potential competitor, it is helpful to think about where entry could come from. A firm making a separate product but sold in the same market as yours, or a firm with a good relationship with your industry's suppliers, has eliminated some of the costs of entering the market with a product like yours. A profit in its current business may provide capital for expansion, diversification, and entry to your business. A handbag manufacturer, for example, could readily introduce a line of casual soft-sided luggage, because it has access to the same suppliers and distribution channels as those already in the casual luggage industry. Other firms may integrate forward or backward to become new competitors in a particular industry role.

Let us consider an example showing an old industry subject to extreme competitive pressures from both traditional competitors and new entrants. For top management, this threatened a total change of the basis of competition and required fresh thinking about the definition of their industry. This was the situation facing Polaroid and Kodak when Kodak entered the instant photography market in 1976. Was the market "instant photography," or photography generally? Was it amateur photography, or all photography? We might have expected Polaroid to adopt a narrower definition because of its past successes in instant photography, while Kodak, because of its diverse activity as a chemically-based photography company, might have adopted a broader definition.

However, at the time Kodak was entering the instant photography market, Japanese manufacturers of 35 mm. cameras, such as Olympus and Canon, were beginning to drop the prices of their products. Basically, consumers had three choices: the traditional Kodak-type product using 110 film, the instant products exemplified by Polaroid, and the newly price-reduced 35 mm. systems. Further complicating the world of Polaroid and Kodak was the competition among Kodak's Super 8 movie systems, Polaroid's instant movie system (Polavision), and amateur video technology with Sony's Beta system.

Indeed, the growth segment in photography during the late 1970s and early 1980s was the 35 mm. market. Instant photography has been relatively stable since the end of the 1970s. Polavision was a commercial failure, although, in the company's eyes, a considerable technical success. Sony, the innovator with its Betamax system, did not become the industry standard; amateur video in 1985 was dominated by the VHS systems. Furthermore, the intrusion of Sony and video into photography heralded a change in photography from being a chemical-based industry to being electronic-based. The traditional dominance of Kodak, based on chemicals, is perhaps at risk because of the entrance of new competitors from outside the boundaries of the traditional industry, competitors whose technical skills are primarily electronic.

However, as these examples demonstrate, for top management the definition of relevant market is more than a strategic sleight of hand. For the strategist, the definition of market means a target of opportunity and a target of effort. Helicopters, for example, is a broad market, while heavy military helicopters is a more narrowly defined market with different requirements for success. Corporations which identify viable niches, those groups of customers who need special services or who cannot be served economically by larger corporations, have opportunities to survive profitably in markets seemingly dominated by larger competitors. If such a company has a strategy to pull business to it with superior differentiated service or product design, and coordinates this marketing effort with an efficient cost position based upon judicious sourcing and subcontracting, it can turn profit opportunity to reality.

THE FORCES OF COMPETITION: THE ELEMENTS OF MARKET STRUCTURE

Recall the Stakeholder Diagram, *Figure 7-1,* and the industry chain which we drew from it in *Figure 7-2. Figure 8-1* is nothing more than part of this chain, the part relevant for a firm focusing on one industry role. The forces of competition, described by Porter (1979), are the power of suppliers and customers and the threats of new entrants and substitutes, together with the rivalry between competitors within the industry.

Porter (1979) lists elements of supplier and buyer power which can be summarized by noticing that industry roles with few players have relatively more power than industry

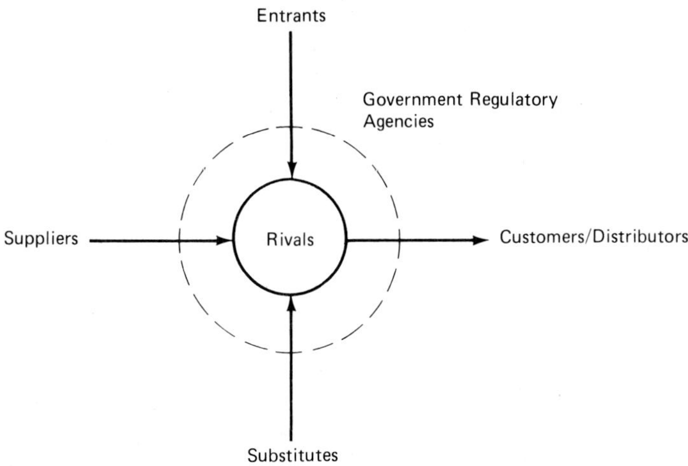

FIGURE 8-1 The Industry Chain

roles with many players. A few players are powerful. For example, a manufacturer with few customers must please them, perhaps setting prices to please them, or lose significant market share. Likewise, a firm with few suppliers has few alternative sources and so must often bear with price rises or quality downgrades or be unable to produce its product.

Let us recall some examples of market power. The old AT&T (''Ma Bell''), the regulated ''monopolist,'' nearly always operated with negative working capital as its suppliers were forced to give it favorable terms. The English retailer Marks and Spencer as well as the American Sears Roebuck have sufficient power in the marketplace that their suppliers realize that losing such a large customer would indeed be disastrous; such suppliers live with severe pressure on their own margins as a result of these retailers' power.

Porter, and Richard Caves (1964), echoed Joe Bain's work in 1956 and listed the important structural elements for competitive analysis as:

- seller concentration
- product differentiation
- barriers to the entry of new firms
- buyer concentration
- height of fixed costs and barriers to exit
- growth of market demand

As in all economic analysis, the players with the scarce goods have power. This notion characterizes Caves's first four elements, which refer to current market power. Information on the last two is useful in forecasting the sustainability of those who are currently powerful and the future location of market power in the industry chain.

Exit barriers are seldom discussed, but they can be relevant in some industries. For example, in the brewing industry, thc substantial fixcd costs of an efficient-scale plant limit entry and also force medium-sized brewers already in the market but operating with minimal profits to stay in longer than ROA alone might justify—the old plants have low market value.

As another example of exit barriers, the glass industry was substantially overcapacitied at the end of the 1970s, yet the large firms which owned much of the capacity were unwilling to write down their fixed assets and take a loss because of the expected negative impact on their share prices. Moreover, the potential buyers of some of these overcapacitied plants were foreign glass manufacturers who wanted the additional US capacity and customer relationships to compete in the glass companies' basic, still profitable markets. Both these factors meant that exit from unprofitable operations was nearly impossible, both financially and strategically.

THE STRUCTURE OF US INDUSTRY

Henderson (1979) argued that a stable competitive market rarely has more than three significant competitors, the largest of which has no more than four times the market share of the smallest. He argued that the ratio of 2 : 1 between the market shares of any two competitors seems to be large enough to keep the smaller one small. This is so, he believed, because substantial growth by the smaller players requires such high spending that it is impractical and so market structure is relatively stable. Henderson also said that any competitor with a relative market share position of less than 1/4 of the largest can hardly be effective.

This finding is based on the power of experience, discussed in Chapter 6. Recall that the basic theory of the value of experience goes something like this: A sustained high market share gives a company a larger accumulated experience than its competitors and, hence, if it is managed forcefully, a low cost position and, because of this, a potentially high profitability.

Subject again to the complexities of defining a market in any exact way, the Boston Consulting Group's position has been that where the number of competitors is large and where scale economies and opportunities for technological progress exist, a shakeout is nearly inevitable and, *by definition,* only those firms which grow faster than the market can survive. In the Boston Consulting Group's terms, this means, to all practical purposes, that the ultimate market structure will consist of only two large-share competitors who will be profitable while a few other firms will survive so long as they are prepared to live in a position of marginal profitability.

The research of Cooke (1974) and Cox (1977) as well as Bass (1977) and Miller (1977) is relevant here because it suggests industry-specific bench marks of relative competitive strength. Cooke, working with Cox, identified a structural relationship of firm market shares within industries, approximated by a semi-logarithmic function, so that the market share of the j-th firm is a constant percentage, c, of the next highest ranked firm:

$$s_j = c\, s_{j-1}$$

For the leading firm, this means the proportionality constant is the reciprocal of the relative market position it enjoys, and relative market share of the leading firm is 1/c.[1]

Perhaps more important is the significance of the relationship between c and the number of *important* firms in the industry. Bass (1977) reports that the leader's market share in what we will call a stable competitive equilibrium is approximated by the relationship:

$$s_1 = 1/\sqrt{n}$$

where n is the number of important firms. Also notice that, by definition, the total market must be 100 percent (or at least approximately so), so that:

$$1 = \sum_{j=1}^{n} s_n$$

[1] $\log s_j = k_0 - k_{1j}$
$c = \text{antilog } k1$
where s_j = the market share of the j-th firm in the market
j = the market share rank of the firms in the market, k_0 and k_1, are regression coefficients.
c is a proportionality constant, the transformed slope of a semilogarithmic function which describes the structural relationship of the market shares held by firms within an industry.

that is,

$$1 = s_1\ (1+c+c^2+\ .\ .\ .\ +c^{n-1})$$

and

$$s_1 = 1/(1+c+c^2+\ .\ .\ .\ +c^{n-1})$$

which is the same as:

$$s_1 = (1-c)/(1-c^n)$$

so that we can say:

$$s_1 = (1-c)/(1-c^n) = 1/\sqrt{n}$$

Hence, knowing any two of the s_1 or n or c, we can estimate the other and then contrast the estimated structure of the industry with the actual.

When c is small and therefore the leading company enjoys substantial relative competitive strength, and when estimated structure is close to actual, we might consider the market in a state of "equilibrium." Where estimated and actual structures diverge, it seems likely that the competitive situation is unsettled. Under such conditions, efforts to build market share are likely to be more successful than attempts to take cash out of the business. Moreover, the leaders' market positions, in particular, may be in jeopardy. *Table 8-1* is a sample of s, c, and n statistics for a series of US industries in 1974.

When linked with the product portfolio in Chapter 16, this relationship between leader market share and industry structure gives you both a bench mark and a shorthand way of exploring the structure of the market, estimating relative market sharcs and the number of significant competitors. All these factors have a bearing on the attractiveness of

TABLE 8-1 Industry Structure and Relative Size

Industry	*c*	*Number of Important Firms*	*Cox**	*Leading Share 1/n**	*Actual '74*
Automobiles	.420	4	59.9%	50.0%	49.6%
Sulphur	.539	6	54.8	40.8	
Diesel engines	.566	6	44.9	40.8	
Ready-to-eat cereals	.599	7	40.8	37.8	41.0
Cigarettes	.735	6**	31.5	40.8	
Air transport	.785	11	23.1	30.2	
Steel	.812	16	19.5	25.0	
Trucks	.850	6**	22.1	40.8	36.1
Beer	.893	25	11.4	20.0	
Gasoline	.898	40	10.3	15.8	

*Estimates

**Cox notes these as exceptions to the direct relationship between c and n

Source: Adapted from Cox, "Product Portfolio Strategy, Market Structure and Performance," and Miller, "Comments on the Essay by William E. Cox, Jr.," in *Strategy + Structure = Performance,* Hans B. Thorelli, ed., 1977. Bloomington, IN: Indiana University Press.

the market for entry and, depending on your actual size, the desirability of attempting to sustain your position in the market.

CONTESTABILITY, GROWTH, AND MARKET NICHES

The importance of entry has received renewed attention in economic theory with the notion of contestability advanced by Baumol (1982) and others. Contestability, a revisionist theory of industrial economics, is somewhat controversial because of its view of entry. Baumol hypothesized a perfectly contestible market where potential free entry and exit is possible and used this assumption as a foundation to explore competition. He argued that the pressure of entry can replace the less realistic free competition assumptions and requires competitors to maintain a low cost position to survive. In this regard, Baumol's theories and the experience-based theories of Bruce Henderson and BCG appear to be on convergent courses. Each view stresses the importance of long-run cost control and the possibility of very long-run cost declines if demand continues to grow or is sustained at high levels for a long time.

Using the concept of contestability and the BCG emphasis on profitability through controlled costs, managers in those firms where the competitive environment appears rosy should be alert to the importance of monitoring potential competitors and the strength of their own competitive advantage in the marketplace. Xerox once believed that it had a virtual monopoly in the copier business, but Japanese competitors, Savin in particular, made successful inroads to the Xerox market share by producing low-cost, high-quality, easy-to-service machines. Xerox's profits fell drastically as it tried to cope with cost-conscious consumers who had a choice for the first time. Xerox's complex high-performance and high service-requirement copiers positioned Xerox at the high-cost, high-quality end of the copier business, but in an inflexible position when confronted with competition from low-cost producers of reliable simple copiers. Xerox apparently had limited control of its costs, making it difficult to compete with low-cost producers. If Xerox, however, had controlled its manufacturing and service costs and limited its prices earlier, entry by these competitors would either not have happened or would have been unsuccessful.

Contestability theory and Henderson's work suggest to something very important in theory of market structure: Most markets encompass tenable and untenable niches and it is a tricky factor to decide when a niche is defensible and therefore tenable. Indeed, this issue can be summarized in terms of growth and barriers to entry.

In particular, Baumol's theoretical development makes references to efficient scale and draws implications about the number of competitors of efficient scale who can operate in a market, allowing for the type of capacity growth referred to by Hirschmann (1964) in his discussion of the petrochemical industry and also observed in the work of the Boston Consulting Group.

Baumol suggests that, over time, an efficient-scale plant can work effectively and at approximately minimal cost over a reasonable range of production. For example, if an efficient-scale plant of design capacity 1000 is capable of working over a range of, say, up to 1250 units—that is, 1.25 times capacity—the number of efficient plants in the market will be 1 when the market demand is between 1000 and 1250. If the market is 2000 units,

2 plants may compete—however, one of them may be producing 1.25 of capacity and the other 750 units. In effect, if the first plant gets up to full scale quickly and achieves a large market share, there is less room for a second plant and the second producer may have to operate at less than efficient scale or with multiple products. If the market demand grows up to 3000 units, there is room for 2 plants operating between efficient design capacity and realizable capacity, plus one smaller plant. The smaller plant is the classical low relative market share producer of Henderson's theory. Ideally, this producer will become a niche producer but this requires innovation or customizing or some other barrier to entry so the larger producers cannot affect it. At 4000 units in the market, there is room for 3, not 4, production facilities of efficient scale. At 5000 units, there is certainly room for 4 but probably not room for 5. And think about what happens if efficient scale rises—the weak, smaller-scale competitors will be squeezed out by the lower-cost, large-scale producers with excess capacity.

As *Figure 8-2* suggests, however, potentially untenable niches exist between "efficient operating conditions." Where the market demand is bigger than 1 to 1.25 times the size of the "best" capacity plant, but smaller than 2 efficient plants, small competitors may find niches. But if the market growth is fast enough, the larger competitors will themselves increase their capacity and the small niches between truly efficient suppliers will become untenable. Thus, if the larger competitors are growing faster than market demand and are profitable, and particularly if the scale of efficient plants is rising, niches are likely to collapse. The situation deteriorates still further for the niche player when market growth slows and the larger players fight to sustain their corporate growth rates.

Demand or market growth is indeed an important factor in competitive analysis.

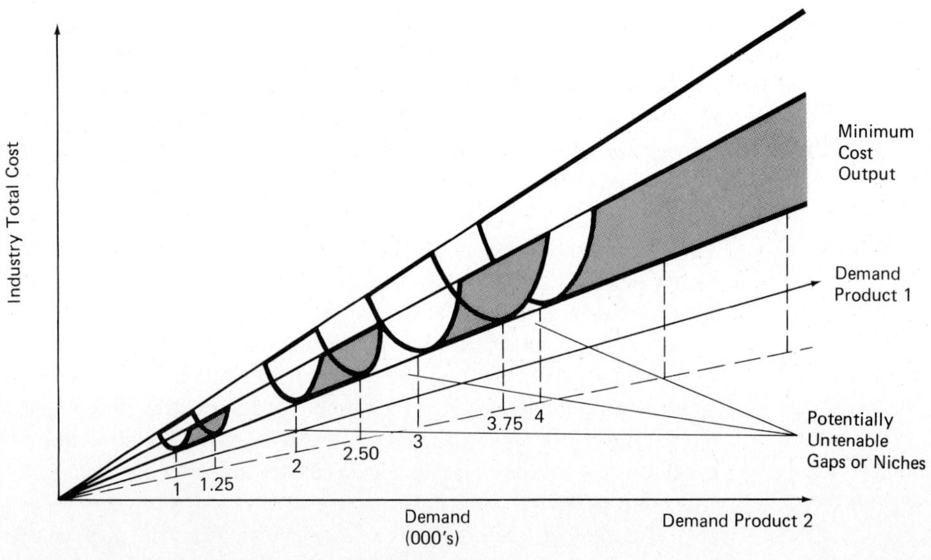

FIGURE 8-2 Satisfying Demand with Efficient-Scaled Plants

Source: Adapted from Baumol, "Contestable Markets: An Uprising in the Theory of Industry Structure," *American Economic Review*, 72, 1, March 1982.

Growth makes for easy entry and it promotes changes in market structure, sometimes changes unobserved by many players, although such changes have long-term consequences. The effects on industry structure are particularly acute, however, when the growth rate slows, because then accumulated experiences and cost positions are a potentially sustainable competitive advantage and promote relative stability in market structure. Such relative stability may, however, include unfortunate consequences for some who are trapped in untenable positions. These trapped competitors are either forced to innovate their way into a defensible niche, or get out of the business. They may only be able to exist if someone for other reasons, including fear of antitrust action, allows them to continue in the marketplace. Another reason for the survival of such businesses is that their sponsors see some of these businesses' attributes, such as completeness of product line, as having strategic value, and so are willing to support a relatively inefficient producer of certain items.

COMPETITIVE MAPS

There are two essential issues that motivate competitive analysis: Efforts to determine profit improvements or to formulate new strategies, and investigations to evaluate their likely consequences before committing resources to a particular competitive stance. In this regard, there are several tools which are closely related: Competitive maps, strategic groups, and structural analysis. Strategic groups are groups of companies with similar resources who compete in similar, although not identical, ways.

Depending on your purposes and knowledge of the market, competitive maps are probably an ideal way to develop a sense of competition. To use a competitive map, it is not necessary to develop a sense of strategic groups; however, most strategic groups are ultimately presented to the executive audience in a map form. Begin simply by identifying what you believe are key dimensions of competition—for example, in hosiery it may be distribution channel and price. Then, map each major competitor on these dimensions.

Let us use the US hosiery market to illustrate the power of a simple competitive map, structural analysis, and the strategic group concept. Some years ago, as *Figure 8-3* shows, the market was defined primarily on the basis of price (and quality) and distribution. Boutiques which sold the highest-priced hosiery were differentiated from department stores selling mid-priced hosiery while supermarkets sold unbranded cheaper products. At the end of the 1960s, the mini-skirt was introduced and women moved from stockings to pantyhose. To make matters difficult for hosiery manufacturers, taste then turned from the brief mini-skirt to the pants suit and women began to wear less hosiery. The largest-scale producers, Hanes, Burlington, Kayser-Roth, with their high-capacity plants, faced a decision. Was the downward shift of demand for hosiery a temporary or permanent phenomenon?

The large-scale hosiery manufacturers appeared to have judged that the market shift was at least long-lived, so Hanes' L'Eggs was born. L'Eggs was followed by No Nonsense and Activ. These brands, designed for supermarket distribution, pitted the largest manufacturers against the weakest. Their entrance to the lowest-priced end of the market was accompanied by lower prices, higher promotion, more creative and innovative pack-

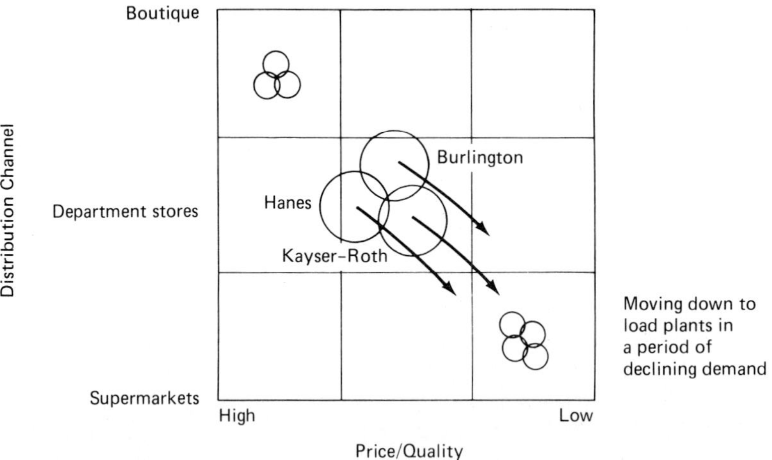

FIGURE 8-3 US Hosiery Market, 1970

aging, and intense national-scale sales efforts all designed to gain distribution and market share at the expense of weaker competitors. The number of plants and companies in the US hosiery business fell precipitiously during the early 1970s.

The consequent restructuring of the market can be illustrated on another map of the hosiery market, again framed by distribution and price (*Figure 8-4*). It shows boutiques with a specialized high-fashion product, supermarkets with the L'Eggs, No Nonsense, and Activ brands as well as the survivors at the ''no-name'' end, and leaves the department stores without committed sources of supply. As the map shows, the largest firms, as a strategic group, moved out of the middle market to the lower right-hand side, leaving behind them a gap, a market vacuum into which a few companies moved. And one of them was the French-owned DIM company which, after some attempts to enter the US

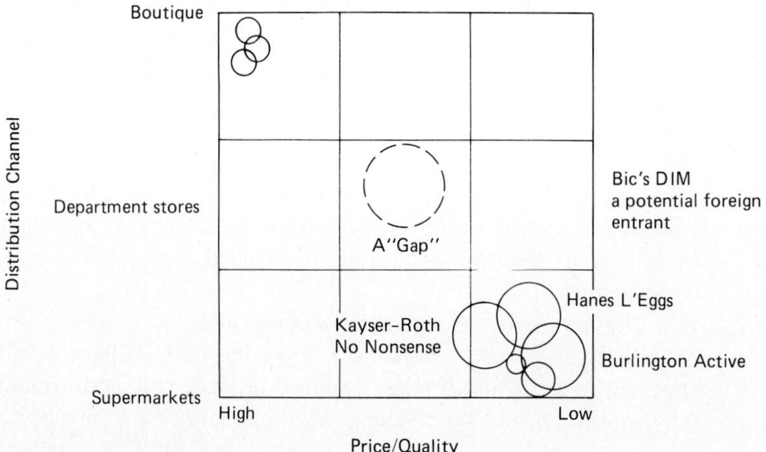

FIGURE 8-4 US Hosiery Market, 1974

market through supermarkets and drugstores (perhaps because its parent company, Bic, had experience in these channels), ultimately began to sell "French" hose retailing for a price roughly three times that of L'Eggs, through the department store and even boutique channels.

Note that a series of competitive maps like *Figures 8-3* and *8-4* would have made this development very obvious to all the competitors. It might have led some American hosiery manufacturers to renew their attentions in the department store market sooner, moving to a new strategic group, rather than allowing an additional entrant to take advantage of the gap in the distribution net. However, we can note that DIM was a world-scale producer in France and probably interested in incremental business, *not* a major market position in the US. Its interests and those of the US majors were asymmetric.

This kind of a map is very simple and can serve the creative and realistic manager well. And, indeed, competitive maps are sometimes very powerful in picking up the direction of change in a competitive environment. Most successful small companies use strategies that are variations on the simple theme of identifying and servicing an industry void, doing things large companies do not or will not do.

You will probably find mapping and a traditional policy focus on companies helpful in recording what people are doing and indeed what they may do next. Recall that strategic models are tools to help you organize business data. Also remember that certain models will capture different information in a more strategically meaningful form (for different people). Often you will identify the most useful information only when you have taken a number of different approaches to organizing industry facts.

USING STRUCTURAL ANALYSIS

The dilemma facing an executive who has developed a competitive map is to determine what the consequences of any pattern shifts are. For example, if there is an apparent gap, a sensible question is: "Is it real or illusory?" In the competitive environment, there is an ambient set of economic conditions that can be catalogued quickly. For example, use the Industry Framework of Chapter 7 to see what results deter competitive entry into the gap, as well as barriers to exit or entry. It is here that the structural models favored by industrial organization theorists can be of greatest value to the strategist, for they help us assess the consequences of collective corporate actions.

Take, for example, a simple mapping which suggests that a large number of competitors are beginning to turn from their traditional markets to a common, growing market, as the American chain saw manufacturers did in the early 1970s. Under these conditions, prompted by both external opportunity and, it seems, by the internal pressures of the large corporations which owned them, the US chain saw manufacturers began to chase the rapidly growing high-volume consumer market for chain saws. This market, which may have developed in response to the oil price shocks of 1973, had many signs of a market "bubble"—for example, its rate of growth was over 50 percent per year. After four years, the market penetration had reached a level of about 20 percent of US homes; similar products, like lawn mowers, had penetrations of about 30 percent. Moreover, an executive considering the consequences of all this movement might have observed that the number of competitors serving the mass consumer market was beginning to increase and that these same competitors were adding capacity, apparently on the assumption of increased demand and increased market share.

A structural analysis would have pointed to:

1 Increased competition and therefore lower margins.
2 The prospects of declining growth rates promising intense competition and additional pressure on margins.
3 Lower margins which were very likely to be associated with higher fixed asset investments and, therefore, lower turnover.
4 A transfer of power from the manufacturers to the large mass market retailers such as Sears and Penney's.

The combined pressures of competition and higher fixed costs in a bubble market can be lethal when the bubble bursts and growth slows. Price discipline is likely to be nonexistent as some competitors begin to cut prices to preserve volume and obtain some contribution to their fixed costs.

The perceptive manager might have seen this migration away from traditional chain saw outlets toward the consumer markets as an opportunity, however. As in hosiery, a gap was opening in the market. Producers could serve those buyers who, being heavier users, needed service, parts, and more heavy-duty equipment than the consumer market. No US manufacturer deliberately made this choice. Due to a consent decree in an earlier antitrust case, McCulloch was prevented from moving further toward the mass market, precluding Black and Decker, its owner at the time, from using the company as it had planned. McCulloch, therefore, appeared to be a handicapped player yet to some extent was forced to behave in its own long-range best interests.

The real beneficiaries in the market, however, were the European manufacturers who for a number of reasons (primarily because of their commitments to growth in Europe and their highly integrated manufacturing strategies) stuck with their old, high-quality, service-supported dealer network in the US and in addition began to pick up the better capitalized and market-linked dealers of the American manufacturers. The result was that while the unit market share in the industry shifted substantially toward the American manufacturers, the profit share went toward the Europeans. Interestingly enough, the lifetime expenditure by a buyer in the higher-quality, heavy-use segment of the market—for both the initial equipment and consumables such as chains, bars, and other parts—was estimated at between five and ten times as large a dollar amount as the lifetime expenditures of the high unit growth consumer market. The US manufacturers appeared to have focused on share, not profit.

As we stated earlier, the industrial organization model popularized by Porter in the strategic management literature is most useful in anticipating just what the consequences of a collected competitive action will be. Corporate actions such as those we have described in the chain saw industry have consequences: industry structures change. And, with the structural changes come changes in competitive power. New entrants in the form of conglomerates pressuring growth in similar ways within one market segment dominated by a few retail chains, such as Sears, were the set of conditions that heralded a major transfer of power from manufacturer to distributor in the chain saw industry. The dealers serving the heavy-use market were ignored by their old suppliers while the consumer market became overpopulated with suppliers.

A COMPANY PERSPECTIVE ON STRUCTURAL ANALYSIS

In looking at a competitive environment, the strategist focuses on the competitors to determine what is likely to happen and on the structural model to determine what the consequences of their expected actions will be. It is, then, a matter of judgment: Are the competitors as well-informed and as diligent in analyzing the situation? What pressures will they respond to? Often managers suffering from short-run pressure for immediate results within their corporation will gain those results at the expense of their long-run competitive position and ultimately the long-run welfare of their company.

Indeed, a focus on earnings, perhaps prompted by the pension fund ownership structure of the US stock market, can have major long-run disadvantages. Ironically, senior management of the type which says, ''Get me the results today,'' and rewards short-term performance, itself magnifies the pressure for results with its strategically inappropriate measurement and reward systems. Smart people do what you pay them to do. These matters are discussed further in Chapter 15, but suffice it to say that a firm populated by smart people rewarded with inappropriate incentives can find itself in a great deal of (strategic) trouble.

STRATEGIC GROUPS AND STRATEGIC INFORMATION

A strategic group is an analytical tool used for purposes of investigation to group companies which pursue similar strategies with similar resources. The term was first used by Hunt (1973) and then by others studying a variety of industries.

Strategic groups have been used in two distinctly useful ways in the literature. First, primarily Harvard-based doctoral research (Hunt, 1973; Porter, 1974; Newman, 1978) has used the strategic group concept where the focus has been to simplify the industry structure, reducing the number of competitive variables considered to two and then mapping firms on those dimensions. Those firms with similar map positions are referred to as strategic groups. The alternative use of the term strategic groups is in the work of Hatten and others who used groups of firms to explore the strategies of individual firms. The Harvard research primarily addressed the question: What is the structure of the industry? By contrast, Hatten, Schendel and Cooper (1978) and later Schendel and Patten (1978) at Purdue focused on the strategies of companies and attempted to define those strategies in multivariate terms.

Although the simple bivariate map and group technique we described for hosiery and chain saws is quite powerful in the classroom, there are circumstances where it is insufficient and indeed could be misleading for a practicing manager. Getting data into high relief can be effective for analysis, but throwing away data by summarizing it too severely can be very costly for a strategist.

Indeed, the costs of data compression are highest when you are looking at ways *to creatively formulate a new strategy* to difference yourself from the competition. Formulation—asking, ''What next?''—requires much more information and it is here that multivariate methods, although expensive in terms of data and time required, have value.

Strategy formulation requires creativity which requires information—and often the critical information for the strategist is not similarities but rather differences. The group formulations using bivariate rather than multivariate data simply focus on similarities and do not provide sufficient information to allow you to pin down and evaluate new and different directions or options.

We can note here that the use of the bivariately defined strategic group stems from a number of factors—the first being the question asked in the original Harvard research, which was primarily concerned with structure itself and focuses on modestly capital-intensive industries where distribution played a very big role (white goods, bicycles, chain saws). Thus, their research correlated or mapped quality against distribution.

In contrast, the Purdue research pursued a different question: could strategy be modeled econometrically? This research began with a different premise, that strategy involves many variables and certainly at the business level encompasses more than one function. And there was a particular problem: the data available to model the firm in any strategically meaningful way are scarce and complicated—and strategic models are data-intense. One way to handle this problem was to pool the data to preserve information and study groups of firms which were alike but not exactly like each other, to establish a range across every variable. In this way, the researchers could look at the impact of manipulations of that variable on profitability or other performance goals over a reasonable range—for example, over a range of plant capacities or advertising expenditures per unit. This allowed them to highlight relationships so they could later *compare the results of the econometric investigation and the data* on all these companies, first, to test the validity of the model and, second, to determine whether manipulations of a particular variable indeed affected performance in ways that were both desirable and feasible for a particular company. Firms were grouped not because they were the same but because they were alike or comparable yet different.

Then, separate groups were formed to facilitate the analysis of the strategies of firms which were unalike because of size or strategy. Under these circumstances the researchers could then look not only at how different companies might compete, but how they might use the results and experiences of their competitors to enhance their own performance (see also McGee, 1982).

For example, only one strategic group in the beer industry studies, the regional brewers, shows multiple brands positively correlated with profitability. Yet an examination of the data on the separate firms being analyzed as a group showed that only one, Heileman, exploited multiple brands extensively and profitably. Note that in this use of the strategic group, it was the preservation of information and subsequent investigations or checking of empirical conclusions against data that led to:

1 Increased understanding of a competitor on a number of relevant competitive dimensions.
2 Asking whether other companies should try to do what a successful and different competitor did.

Another difference between the Harvard and Purdue research is that Harvard researchers tended to view a group as a competing unit rather than an analytical unit. This may have stemmed from the types of industries they studied, where, for example, the scope of the industry was national rather than regional with geographical restrictions. The key difference is that the Harvard formulation involves only companies that are competing with each other and this is not a general case, but a special one. It is, of course, a very powerful technique where the fit is perfect, but it is not so valuable for strategy formulation and the development of alternative strategies. Again, the critical distinction is really alternative uses of information.

The Purdue research used data on the beer market, a geographically dispersed market. In such a situation, it became obvious that groups did not have to be made up of companies which competed with each other or in any meaningful way as a cohort against a common larger rival. Indeed, groups were composed of members who were active in the market and competing against other market members—that is, small companies competing in different markets against the national-scale brewers. Information on companies competing like you, but not with you, may suggest alternative strategies for you—strategies such as those that companies similar to you have employed successfully against larger rivals.

COMPETITORS AND COMPARABLES AS SOURCES OF INFORMATION

Strategies are best evaluated in light of their results, both ours and our competitors'. An old adage illustrates this focus on results in competitive analysis: ''He who has the power has the gold.'' Indeed, conclusions on strategic history and forecasts of the likely locus of future strategic power can be drawn from competitors' financial results, that is, by analysis of the financial ratios of competing and comparable companies across the competitive spectrum of the industry. A powerful competitor will be one who is prospering, while less powerful players are likely to have a weaker cash flow.

Competitors leave a financial trail of success or failure in the marketplace which can point to potential improvements or problems in our own operations. Similarly, companies preparing to enter a market leave tracks which will be clear to astute managers who search for them. Using comparable profitability (DuPont) analyses, product life cycles, experience curves, and technology analyses, we can examine the results of competitors' functional activities in finance, marketing, and production, and later discuss how different values among competitors can affect future strategic choices and results. This requires considerably less effort than the econometric approach referred to above, although the skill needed to gain real insight is one that is slowly honed by experience.

Applying the DuPont formula to current and potential competitors can demonstrate how they are making money, where they are at risk, as well as how their sources of profitability have shifted over time. For example, brewing industry data shown in *Table 8-2* illustrate how Heileman's success depends on its extraordinary turnover relative to the national brewers, Anheuser-Busch, Miller and Schlitz. The explanation is that Heileman bought older, smaller breweries depreciated by their former owners; Heileman purchased these facilities after these companies failed or left the industry. Note, too, with high fixed costs and declining market share, Schlitz was also becoming heavily dependent on leverage as turnover slowed in the 1970s. Yet Schlitz's ROA was only 2.65 percent in a world of 12 to 20 percent prime rates, so that such high interest rates would make financial strategy still more expensive as time passed. As another example, Dr. Pepper had a much higher asset turnover than Coke or Pepsi in the past, but its desire to bottle more of its own packaged products severely affected its asset turnover and profitability.

Use of the *product life cycle* and estimation of *experience curves* and the impact of

TABLE 8-2 Profitability Analysis Applying the DuPont Formula, US Brewing, 1977

	ROE	=	Margin	×	Turn	×	Leverage
	Profit / Equity	=	Profit / Sales	×	Sales / Assets	×	Assets / Equity
Anheuser-Busch	13.5%		4.6%		1.43		2.06
Heileman	22.8%		4.5%		2.70		1.86
Miller	16.7%		4.3%*		1.62		2.40*
Schlitz	5.6%		1.7		1.56		2.04

*Assumes Miller's interest expenses and leverage are the same percentage of Philip Morris' corporate interest and equity as brewing assets are of the company's total assets, 41.8%

new technology (both process and product) for current or possible competitors can also indicate the likely strength of future competition and those firms' ability to control their costs. Timex controlled costs very well on its mature product, the pin lever watch, but Texas Instruments' ability to base a watch on semi-conductor technology lowered costs by a scale factor which Timex's more traditional methods could not match. Timex remained a watch manufacturer, but used its distinctive competence as an assembler, working for growing firms which had little manufacturing capacity, such as Polaroid in the 1960s and early 1970s, and more recently Sinclair Computer with their under $100 personal computer. Timex chose not to invest heavily in the watch business in the early days of semiconductors, when it was at a comparative disadvantage without electronic technology.

Competitors' experience can be used to enhance a firm's own experience, both in marketing and in production. Indeed, if the experience curve is considered for components as well as products, then identifying the competitions' sources of shared experience and their respective cost positions could provide a new entrant with clues to the technology and market expertise needed to be more efficient than the innovator. Zenith is a very good example of a smart "number two" which essentially has used the development efforts of RCA, the innovator in the television industry, as real-life market research. Repeatedly, Zenith has introduced its version of RCA's radio and television products after RCA, avoiding RCA's errors and capitalizing on its successes but without assuming the costly risks of the innovator. In the cigarette industry, too, Phillip Morris is not considered an innovator but rather a firm which follows the successful innovations of others. Phillip Morris brings to market products which are even more successful than those of the innovator, including Virginia Slims cigarettes for the women's market, Vantage cigarettes for the health-conscious smoker, and Miller Lite low-carbohydrate beer. Indeed, contrary to popular belief, Miller did not invent the low-carbohydrate concept in beer. Instead, Miller took market research which had been done on an early low-carbohydrate entrant and determined what features made it appealing to heavy drinkers in order to formulate its product and advertising strategy for Miller Lite.

COMPETING: THE MIND

Competition is not an analytical exercise—it's a matter of personal commitments. Analysis may shape those commitments, but analysis of organizations as objects rather than structures populated and manipulated by people is sterile.

A manager who sees an opportunity and says, "The limits are within myself," is likely to look for ways to change an industry and may even succeed. The manager who looks at an evolving competitive situation and sees all his competitors moving in the same direction, risking their power, and joins them because he can think of nothing better to do, merely subscribes to short-sighted competitive greed.

The game is one of minds. Bruce Henderson recognized that in 1967 in his article, "Brinksmanship in Business," which dealt with the advantages of being perceived as an irrational player. We can examine a modern example where the obvious may not be true. Coca-Cola and Pepsi surrounded themselves with subsidiary brands like Tab, Sprite, and Diet Pepsi and in the early 1980s introduced caffeine-free and non-saccharine sweetened diet drinks—a difficult competition. Then in 1985 Coca-Cola changed its Coke formulation to one, it said, which would be more appealing to Pepsi drinkers. Two months later, responding to what it said were consumer and bottler demands, Coke reintroduced "Coke Classic," splitting the brand and apologizing to its customers for its error. At last, Coke had taken an action that Pepsi could not publicly emulate in the short run; who would want to emulate an error? But it is the result that counts, not the decision. Coke's actions sparked interest in an old brand and perhaps gained shelf-space for two colas, their sugar-free and caffeine-free products, as well as Cherry Coke. In this example, Coke may, indeed, "be it."

COMPETITIVE SIGNALLING

Competitive signalling is the term strategists use to describe this kind of game. Competing on paper with signals about capacity and new products is used by the petrochemical and computer industries where the cost of adding capacity is enormous. In the chemical photography industry, Kodak has to inform its film competitors about its new products eighteen months in advance of their introductions, as part of an earlier antitrust decree. And it could be argued that when Polaroid produced its own film for its SX-70 system rather than continue to buy it from Kodak, Polaroid signalled Kodak to either leave the instant market or compete.

Ultimately, we have to keep in mind that competitors are people, too. They respond to pressure—pressures from inside their organization, pressures to perform and excel and to win quickly, the pressures of the marketplace, particularly the capital market. And they will respond to the pressure of competition.

Remember, a major purpose of competitive analysis, whether the comparable or structural approach, is to be able to anticipate your competitors' likely reaction to your strategy changes. Indeed, strategic action and reaction in the industry set off competitive signals, and the competitive signals sent by a firm can be managed in order to help create a favorable competitive environment for itself. A firm which has an elastic demand, for example, could drop prices and, while raising its own revenue, wreak havoc with firms who have built inelastic demands for themselves. Similarly, a firm with a strong inelastic demand could raise prices and make itself powerful financially, perhaps even increasing the prestige value of its product, while its competitors with more elastic demand suffered through lower prices with limited profits and minimal prospects for improvement. This last strategy was followed in the German automobile market by BMW and Mercedes-Benz, leaving Volkswagen's base products in a poor competitive position and probably putting pressure on it to strengthen its more luxurious Audi line.

An interesting case of competitive signalling was the Pepsi Challenge taste test. The Coke-Pepsi cola market demand is elastic, since the substitutes are closely matched to most palates. The taste test represented Pepsi's signal for competition on quality rather than cut-throat competition on prices, in an industry where price competition is self-destructive for the major competitors, particularly the smaller Pepsi. Similarly, Dr Pepper's claim to being "deliciously different" and "the most original soft drink" represents a competitive signal to other soft drink producers. It removes Dr Pepper from being considered a cola substitute and thus allows it to charge higher prices as a soft drink whose unique flavor is the base of an inelastic demand.

Analysis of competitors (and substitutes) should also include an assessment of their own managers, whose experience and values may either preclude or emphasize certain kinds of reactions or strategies. Indeed, competitors are people, too. For example, the inventive Dr. Edwin Land at Polaroid was unlikely to compete with processed photographic developments at Kodak, even when 35 mm photography grew in popularity—he stood for instant photography. Baron Bich, who had made his fortune with the Bic ballpoint pen, was slow to develop felt-tipped writing instruments because he believed felt-tipped pens would not be used by consumers in a world of carbon-copy technology. Bic thus opened a "strategic window" (Abell, 1978) for the entry of Gillette into the mass pen market with the Flair felt-tipped pen. Swiss watch industry leaders, as precision jewelry manufacturers, probably found it ludicrous that Timex could sell $6.95 watches in American drugstores in the 1950s, and, again, that twenty years later Timex itself could be underpriced by a new electronic entrant to the watch industry, Texas Instruments. The bulk of the Swiss watch manufacturers chose not to compete with either "industry upstart," and thus opened a strategic window for Timex and, later, the electronics industry, to successfully enter watch manufacturing.

THE ROLE OF ERROR

The biggest cause of competitive failure is error—not what the competition does, but what you do as you respond to the wrong information, the wrong set of competitive signals, or the wrong pressures from your own organization.

In this context, the market share-profit relationship, often generalized as positive by structural analysts of industries, bears verifying in the industry's particular competitive environment. Looking at the historical market share-profit relationship and how it has changed over time, many managers, and too many strategists, assume that high market share will ensure profitability. Nevertheless, it is worth looking at competitive experience to validate this belief for a particular firm in a particular industry. While the PIMS data seem to indicate that a positive market share-profitability relationship holds for large, diversified firms (Schoeffler et al., 1974; Buzzell et al., 1975), this is not necessarily true for firms of different sizes or in particular industries. Hatten and Hatten (1985) found that the market share-profitability relationship varied substantially for different sized brewing firms, and the differences called for the small firms to gain profitability from very different competitive behaviors than those which brought profits to the larger firms.

A misunderstanding of their potential market share-profit relationships can be particularly dangerous for firms with a monopoly position in their industries, such as those

FIGURE 8-5 Evaluating Competitors

To evaluate a firm's competitors, ask:

1. Who are our current competitors? What is their strategy and objectives?
2. What kind of power do we have, relative to them?
3. What kinds of products are substitutes for ours? Would the consumer agree?
4. How much power do we have against substitutes?
5. Who are potential competitors?
6. What would make it attractive for the potential competitors to enter? What would be their entry strategy?
7. Are we powerful enough to keep potential competitors out, or be unaffected by their entry?
8. How can we enhance our power and use it to increase our returns?
9. What are our vulnerabilities?

with patented technologies. Such firms may feel that their high market share and profit levels are impenetrable by potential competitors. That feeling can blind them to substitute technologies or to international competitors who gain market share by paying more attention to cost control, service, and quality than the richer monopolist.

To sum up, the power of competitors must be realistically assessed for the firm to gauge the likely success of its strategic behavior. A powerful competitor may mean that certain strategies are not worth pursuing, and its presence may encourage a firm to seek strategies avoiding direct competition. Knowing your competitors is essential if you are to forecast the future environment of the firm responsibly.

Figure 8-5 lists important issues to be addressed in evaluating competitors, substitutes, and potential entrants. Indeed, the best way to avoid surprises from unexpected sources is to be aware of the motivations behind such unexpected, and possibly unwelcome, events. The firm's power in relation to its current and potential competitors must be assessed, since competitive power will facilitate certain strategies while weakness may make the success of some strategies impossible.

EVALUATION OF THE FIRM IN ITS COMPETITIVE ENVIRONMENT

Just as resource assessment required a listing of various kinds of resources before the critical ones could be assessed, environmental assessment encompasses various industrial, competitive, macroeconomic, and stakeholder observations as a prelude to evaluation. Here, the environmental evaluation criterion is overall fit with the probable world to come. The important question is, "Will the firm's current strategy work in its likely future environment?" In order for a firm's strategy to continue to perform well, the distinctive competence of the firm must remain relevant and advantageous in the likely future environment.

Both the distinctiveness and the advantage—that is, the firm's ability to perform on this critical dimension and its ability to leverage it—must be retained in the emerging environment. Advantage comes from differences. An environment in which many competitors have the same ability, or where it is no longer possible to do business in the manner in which the firm excelled, is hostile to the firm. The firm's strategy no longer fits in the firm's emerging environment.

Future strategic success requires that the firm's competences continue to provide distinction and advantage in the marketplace. Thus, full assessment of the competitive environment requires that the firm have answers to the following questions:

1 How will industrial power shift?
2 Will the distinctive competence still yield a competitive advantage?
3 Will the firm's competitive advantage still exist in its old markets?
4 Should new markets be sought where the competitive advantage can be claimed, or will the environment and competition change so that a new distinctive competence must be developed?

Economic relationships are interdependent by their nature. Cross-impacts of likely futures will exaggerate some vulnerable areas as well as strengths, competencies, and weaknesses. Complete environmental assessment should generate sets of opportunities and threats which strategists must consider if the firm is to successfully achieve its objectives.

SUMMARY: THE SILVER LINING OF THE BLEAKEST ENVIRONMENTS

A strategist may make an unpleasant discovery about the likely future, one which will hinder his firm; the firm may appear doomed in a crisis. In these circumstances, remember the Chinese character for "crisis," a combination of the characters for "danger" and "opportunity." Indeed, every environment is a source of both opportunities and threats. Management must design strategies which make and take advantage of opportunities while neutralizing threats in the environment.

Insight is often the key to responding to a seemingly hostile environment. Groups of knowledgeable participants may be able to engage in loosely structured (Delphi-type) discussions to brainstorm about issues which seem unworkable and unthinkable, to identify what or who could change an industry's structure to make it more conducive to the firm's strategic success. Vulnerability and cross-impact analysis can also allow more realistic assessments of the options and actions available and their effect in the likely future environment.

The environment itself is neither totally negative or positive. Keep in mind the advice of Ecclesiastes 9:11:

> Again, I saw that under the sun the race is not to the swift, nor the battle to the strong, nor bread to the wise, nor riches to the intelligent nor favor to men of skill, but time and chance happen to them all.

For success, analysis must be followed by action which capitalizes on opportunities and minimizes the risk of threatening situations.

PREVIEW: SOCIAL-POLITICAL AND INTERNATIONAL ENVIRONMENTS

Major changes in a firm's social-political environment, such as society's attitude toward the firm's products, or in the international environment, such as reduced tariffs or new import restrictions, will affect the firm. In contrast to changes in the industrial environment—which generally allow the firm to continue to operate—social, political, and international changes can have very abrupt effects, and may actually require a firm to cease operations immediately and totally. Examples of such immediate changes are the nationalization of the firm's subsidiary in a developing country or regulations which declare a firm's product outside safety or trade limits. Monsanto's plastic bottle (one of its major intended uses was as soft drink packaging) was for a time declared an unsafe receptacle for food by a government agency.

Social-political organizations and international political changes can affect costs, prices, and power in the industrial chain as taxes and regulation raise costs or as tariffs significantly raise prices to consumers and open or shut markets to producers. By forbidding or interfering with the sale of certain goods, constituencies of the firm can even break links in the chain and so represent a significant loss of market and competitive power.

Thus, social, political and international power, although it is apparently non-economic, can have severe economic consequences for the firm in its industry. Regulations, political power, and ethical considerations can shift their emphasis, so that the manager must constantly be aware of their changing economic implications. Stakeholder values and objectives—major aspects of the social-political and international environments, and sometimes basic causes of changing industrial structure—will be discussed in Chapter 9.

chapter 9

Stakeholder Analysis and the Organization's Objectives

INTRODUCTION: A DIFFERENT APPROACH TO OBJECTIVES VIA STAKEHOLDER ANALYSIS

Strategists have been known to develop plans which they consider logical, pre-emptive, and efficient in their use of resources and almost certain to succeed in the firm's future environment. But the plans have not worked, and the planners have scratched their heads and wondered why.

Sometimes plans do not work because the objectives or strategies could not win support. Indeed, strategists cannot simply concentrate on the rational elements of the organization—they must take its heart into account, too. And the organization's heart is revealed by its objectives and values, what it wants and the actions which its members will accept. Dill wrote:

> All efforts to move in new directions entail risks that important side costs and consequences will be overlooked, and that failure to consult and inform will breed resistance from those whose help is needed. (1976, p. 125)

Of course, social values and objectives will shift over time. Indeed, when an organization's objectives are being reviewed or developed, the issue is to synthesize and accommodate internal and external stakeholder interests appropriately. The firm's relationships with its stakeholders have to be managed in an interactive way. Cyert and March (1963) noted, ''Organizations do not have objectives; people do,'' and the stakeholders of the organization are represented by people. Hence, stakeholder management necessitates developing relationships with people, some of whom act independently while some act as agents of others, for example, unions. Stakeholders may have stakeholders themselves! To be effective, management must earn stakeholder support, commitment, or acceptance for the organization's strategy (Bourgeois, 1980).

Internal stakeholders are those involved in the operations of the business—the employees, both blue- and white-collar, as well as outside members of the board of directors. They are the organization's personnel resource and the source of its human energy (Selznick, 1957). Their values, preferences and needs, and the firm's ability to satisfy them, are major factors in determining what is organizationally possible. Barnard wrote, "The life of an organization depends upon its ability to secure and maintain the personal contributions of energy necessary to effect its purposes" (1966, p. 92).

While the boundary between internal and external stakeholders is sometimes fuzzy, external stakeholders generally come from the wider environment first discussed in Chapter 7. Stakeholders evident from the industry chain include suppliers, customers, and bankers. Others are shareholders and competitors. External stakeholders also come from the social-political, macroeconomic, and internal environments and encompass the neighbors of a plant, local politicians and journalists, state and federal regulators, and even industrial policymakers in other countries.

The sensitive strategic manager must recognize the full range of actual and potential stakeholder pressures and identify their sources in the objectives and strategies of particular stakeholders. As in resource and economic environmental assessment, the full identification of the firm's current stakeholders, their objectives, and the firm's ability to satisfy them improves both the quality of analysis and the prospects of successful action. We can note, however, that not all who claim to be stakeholders are legitimate; some, in fact, may be opportunists attempting to use the organization to serve their own ends (Dill, 1976).

The first step to improved constituent or stakeholder management is fully identifying stakeholder interests and power. The second is to recognize their ongoing and changing contextual power. The third is to distinguish superficial differences among stakeholders from those that are fundamental (Andrews, 1980). This approach highlights the tradeoffs required to develop support for a particular strategy or set of objectives. Knowing the range of your stakeholders' interests and how they are changing allows a rational consideration of the noneconomic issues which can dominate or constrain strategy for very valid reasons (Murray, 1978). Understanding that the stakeholders of different firms are likely to be different implies that varying accommodations will be made by each firm, to some extent explaining the differences in chosen strategies within industries and across regional and national cultures. For example, it is likely that employees in the computer industry, who have prospered because of growth and innovation, are much more favorably disposed toward technological change than shoe industry employees whose experiences when automation displaced labor have made them more wary of innovation. As a result, innovative strategies are easier to pursue in the computer industry and more difficult to implement in the shoe industry.

STAKEHOLDER ANALYSIS

Analysis before action is the watchword of the strategist, as Sun Tzu wrote 2500 years ago: "With many calculations, one can win; with few, one cannot. How much less chance of victory has one who makes none at all!" (1963, p. 71). This is true in the societal arena, just as it holds in the industrial and competitive environments.

To manage our stakeholders effectively, we need to know ourselves and them. We need to learn how our strategy affects their success, and how theirs affects ours.

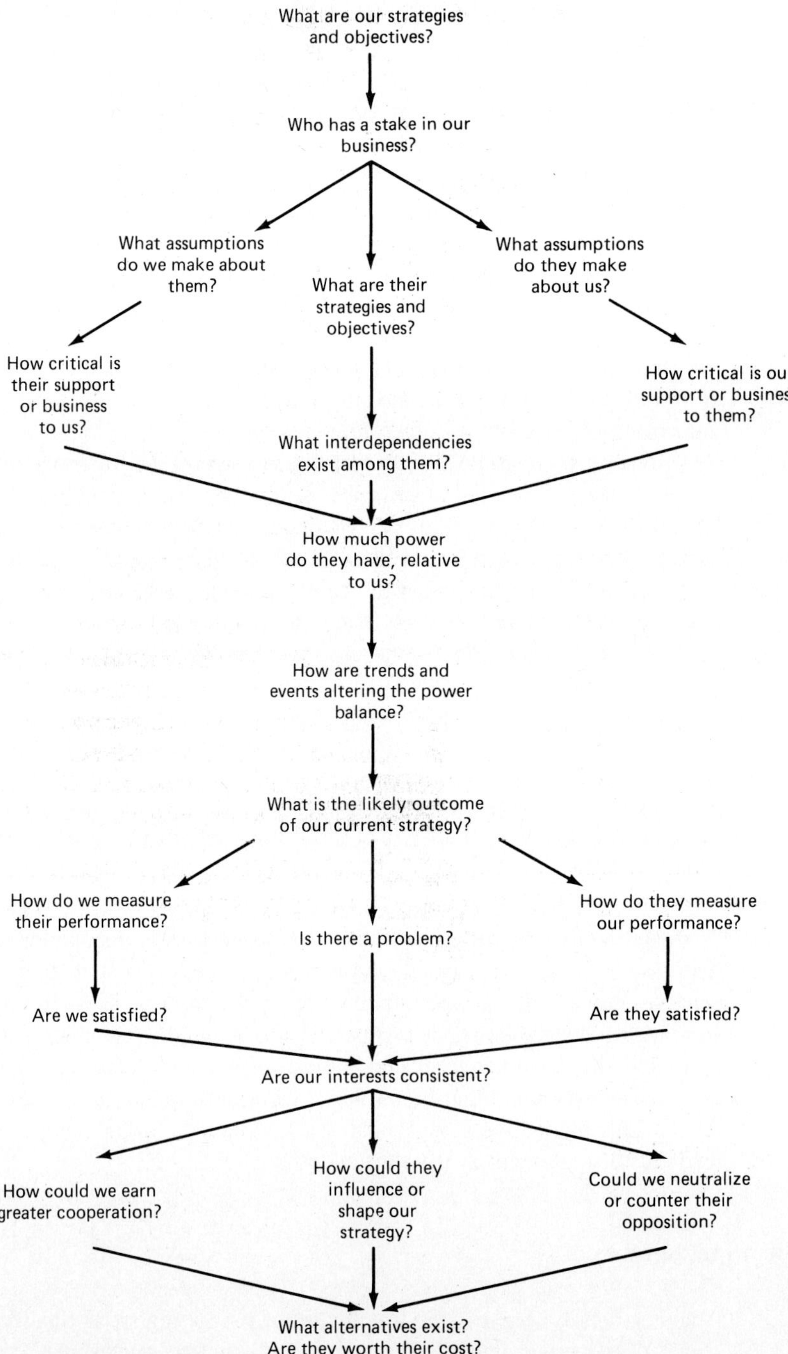

FIGURE 9-1 Stakeholder Analysis

Stakeholder analysis, like competitive analysis, requires us to be ''other-centered'' (Rogers, 1977) and to see the complementary nature of stakeholder relationships.

In a simple sense, our task is to collect data so that we can understand our stakeholders' objectives and behavior, recognize their power and use that knowledge and our creative ability to anticipate the stakeholder implications of our current strategy. Later, this analysis will help us determine what our alternative strategies are and which is likely to contribute most to our future success. *Figure 9-1* illustrates the flow of this process of analysis within the stakeholder environment.

THE STAKEHOLDER AUDIT

To organize our analysis, we need a framework which will lead us to an understanding of our stakeholders and their satisfaction with our performance as well as their power with respect to our organization. Following Emshoff and Freeman (1979), we want to recognize all our stakeholders, not just the highly visible ones. In addition, we want to develop a sense of the overall cooperative potential of our stakeholders and of our capability to deal simultaneously with several of them. Once we have evaluated our current strategy, our responsibility is to the future. Thus, evaluating stakeholders will lead to considerations of managerial action appropriate within the stakeholder environment.

Figure 9-2, The Stakeholder Audit, is an important framework to organize, investigate and analyze stakeholder interests. It focuses attention first on the nature of our stakeholders' interests in our current strategy and objectives. Then, it organizes what we know and believe about our stakeholders and our relationships with them, emphasizing the complementary nature of the relationships. The sequences and titles—Actions, Beliefs, Cooperative Potential, and Stakes—are designed to help us recall and use what must be considered—the ABC's of stakeholder management. We have to understand the ABC's in order to be effective stakeholder managers. Stakeholder analysis begins with identification of who the stakeholders are and which are currently most important. The stakeholder mix can be expected to change over time and from issue to issue so that stakeholder analysis is ongoing and dynamic. We can refer to *current* and *potential* stakeholders in every corporate action and for every corporate issue, and we can judge whether they are supporters or opponents.

Actions

For all significant stakeholders, it is important to examine their actions to determine what they are doing, what they want, and what they will tolerate. What they do may be more important for a manager than what they say. Some stakeholders want much and tolerate little divergence from their ideal, while others are more relaxed about their personal stake in the firm and will tolerate greater divergence, except perhaps on one or two sensitive issues which move them to activism.

We need to learn what stimulates stakeholder activism. Stakeholders are particularly important when they demand an active role in corporate decisions. Simon (1976) and Barnard (1966) believed that individuals and organizations who could affect the corporation had thresholds beyond which they became active participants rather than passive

FIGURE 9-2 The Stakeholder Audit

	Supporters (Active)	Uncommitted (Nonactive)	Opposition (Active)
Who are the stakeholders?			
Currently active?			
Not active?			
Potentially active?			
For or against?			
Actions:			
What are they doing, e.g., what pressures and procedures are they using, and what actions have they taken to get what they want?			
What are the thresholds between their indifference and activism? What has or could trigger their response? What are their sensitive areas?			
What are they asking for, or what will they ask for, and what do they want?—i.e., what are their objectives?			
Beliefs:			
What do their executives believe in? Is their knowledge of us accurate or inaccurate?			
What assumptions do they make about us? What assumptions about them are *implicit* to our strategy?			
How do they think we affect their success, and they ours?			
What is their power relative to us? What is our power over them?			
How do they measure our performance, and we measure theirs?			
What do we really want? Are these objectives legitimate? Are they satisfied? Are we satisfied? What do they really want?			
How will time and current trends affect their satisfaction, relative power, and activism?			
Cooperative potential:			
With which of our stakeholder sets are they related or dependent?			
What differences are there between them and us, or our other stakeholders? Are these differences fundamental or superficial?			
How could they be influenced, and by whom, at what cost?			
Stakes:			
What is their stake in us, and what is our stake in them? How important are these stakes?			
What is their real power in our affairs? Is theirs an *equity* interest, or is it economic? Do they seek influence for some other reason?			
What power do we have in their affairs?			

observers of corporate affairs. Because stakeholder activism can sometimes lead to major constraints on normal operations and because circumstances alter thresholds, we must identify the relevant thresholds between stakeholder indifference and action. While linked with the issue of what they will tolerate this also requires the strategist to think critically about the unthinkable: "What will they do if provoked? How could it happen?" A very simple example of the costs of threshold violation can be seen in the vastly different responses people receive if they ask, ''May I step to the front of the line?'' or if they barge in. The first approach respects the stakeholders involved, the second does not.

Stakeholders may have unstated as well as stated objectives, and the unstated objectives can have surprising and undesirable impacts on the success of future strategies. Here, an historical perspective on the stakeholders' patterns of behavior is important: What situation precipitated actions which were unexpected and inconsistent with their public statements and espoused values? What unstated values and objectives are implied?

For example, the flat administrative structure of a small firm may hinder an entrepreneur's much publicized attempts to expand, but his refusal to hire a general manager and share power is a very strong behavioral signal that one of his important values may be the maintenance of close personal control of the organization. Like the biblical tree, the entrepreneur must be judged by the fruit of his actions, as well as by his talk! Unstated and implicit objectives often have greater weight in management than highly publicized slogans. Actions alert us to stakeholder strategies and let us infer what their objectives are, with respect to us.

Beliefs

Beliefs—theirs about us and ours about them—play a large role in stakeholder relations. Beliefs may be founded in fact or in misinformation. Clues to the real state of affairs are usually found in the statements and memoranda of stakeholders and their representatives, and in their actions. Although we will have internal data for ourselves only, our experience and their public posture should enable us to say what we think their key people believe in and what they will find unacceptable. We can speculate on the assumptions they make about us, and we should be careful to look at the complementary assumptions we make about them.

The assumptions implicit in our strategy must be made explicit if we are to manage our relationships with our stakeholders; management is essentially a conscious activity. Typically, the assumptions which managers fail to specify relate to the real sources and scope of stakeholder power (or powerlessness), and to the respective objectives of managers and stakeholders. These assumptions apply to the criteria our stakeholders use to monitor our performance and what we use to gauge theirs. Politicians, for example, have a limited personal responsibility for performance in the marketplace; their currency is measured in votes at the polling booth. If we wish to understand our stakeholders, we need to learn how they measure their own performance and how they believe we affect it. We have to judge whether they are satisfied with us and determine whether we are satisfied with them. We must look at them through their eyes and not through our eyes only.

Cooperative Potential

In assessing the cooperative potential of stakeholders, note that most stakeholders should be expected to act in their own self-interest, ensuring that their contributions to the firm provide an appropriate benefit to themselves. It is management's job to ensure that cooperating with management and supporting its work is within the stakeholders' interests. This is particularly important when opposition could undermine the firm's vitality and reduce its options. Likewise, management has a responsibility to ensure that the firm's contributions to its stakeholders benefit the firm.

Every stakeholder can support, ignore, or oppose management's initiatives and programs, and vice versa. Because resources are scarce, management must determine how to allocate them among its stakeholders and their developing interests over time and in changing circumstances. Common sense and experience suggest that powerful contributors will demand a share in the organization's success and that some people and organizations will attempt to frustrate management at almost every turn in their efforts to achieve some tangentially related purpose of their own.

Between the extremes of active proponents and active opponents, there are likely to be many stakeholders who are indifferent and uncommitted unless mobilized. Mobilization may not be necessary for success on most corporate initiatives. But for those where opposition can be seen or anticipated, management should begin to seek its friends and identify its foes.

The factor which we should consider is whether interests are shared or are superficially or fundamentally different among stakeholders. For particular stakeholders, much will depend on the relationships between us and them, their real interests and ours. If they and we are highly interdependent and are threatened by the same forces, the cooperative potential will be high. If they are loosely connected to us and highly dependent on others, they will be less likely to support us in tough situations. Moreover, as time passes and events unfold, some potential coalitions are likely to break, while others may strengthen.

Grefe (1982) makes a practical and even finer distinction when he describes ''family'' and ''friends'' in the stakeholder context. ''Family'' matter most, share your interests, and will suffer or benefit with you; they are a loyal and usually constant stakeholder group. ''Friends,'' according to Grefe, are merely allies and are likely to be less constant, shifting their allegiance to suit their permanent interests, issue by issue.

Stakes

Ultimately, the effort we put forth and the strength of our support or opposition will depend on the importance of the stake each group sees in us, and likewise the stake we see in them. Freeman (1981) uses the terms ''equity, economy, and influence'' to describe the nature of most constituents' stakes in a business enterprise.

Stakeholder analysis has a simple purpose. It is to help us construct a reasoned explanation of stakeholders' behavior and an understanding of their power in our affairs. It should help us distinguish between the legitimate stakeholders' demands and those of the opportunists who seek to use the organization. Government in some instances chooses the easy way and makes business responsible for the implementation of government objectives rather than using tax revenues to finance programs designed to achieve the same ends. Housing policy, highway safety, and pollution control are just a few areas where government has used business to achieve its social objectives, by mandating the availability of bank financing for certain construction projects and by requiring safer and less polluting automobiles.

We use stakeholder analysis to alert us to which stakeholders are satisfied with our performance and which are not. We have to look at the data, judge who is with us and who can be persuaded, and judge whether our present and potential support will outweigh that of any opposition by a sufficient degree to ensure organizational commitment and the ultimate success of our current stragegy. This evaluation done, we may have to develop a new strategy to manage our stakeholders. The key factors in our deliberations then will be: First, are our stakeholders content and satisfied with our performance, and we with theirs? Secondly, what is their real power in our affairs, and our power in theirs?

STAKEHOLDER MANAGEMENT

In a well-managed organization, objectives exploit the flexibility which current success gives in the interests of future vitality. Success is an opportunity to run the company as it should be hereafter (Bower, 1966). We will only have the opportunity to manage as long as our stakeholders are satisfied. This is why the audit of stakeholder satisfaction is important, and why stakeholder management is critical.

Stakeholder management is founded in performance. If our results and actions satisfy our stakeholders, we will have earned the right to manage our organization autonomously, we will have leeway, and we will be able to manage our relationships with our stakeholders to ensure the survival and vitality of our organization and the maintenance of an economic system that values such business-society relationships. Where we can anticipate problems with particular stakeholders, we can work to reduce them, resolve them, or maybe redefine them. We can use time and power to influence the process whereby they will be addressed, and the forum in which this will take place.

Knowledge of who has power and who may use it, plus an explicit consideration of how our current strategy is likely to affect our stakeholders, will lead us to seek strategies which eliminate difficulties. For any remaining, we may make tradeoffs consistent with both our own interests and our stakeholders' interests, or attempt to develop coalitions to help us get what we believe is best. Stakeholder analysis is essential to the rational, skillful use of power. Some examples illustrate the need to implement strategies with stakeholder interests in mind.

In the mid-1950s, Martin Halen, the founder of Green Stamps, successfully mobilized all the businesses which supplied the trading stamp companies with premiums as a powerful political constituency to head off legislative efforts to abolish trading stamps (Grefe, 1982). New England Telephone attempted to use a similar stakeholder strategy in its efforts to charge users rather than all subscribers for directory assistance calls (Emshoff and Freeman, 1979). New England Telephone identified stakeholders it believed could influence the Massachusetts Department of Public Utilities and then disseminated information to them, interacted with them, and accommodated to their concerns. The company also polled the public on the issue, finding support. In opposition, however, was the company's union which, through skilled political coalition-building in the Massachusetts House of Representatives, was able to block the change. Directory assistance is a labor-intense service and, despite the company's guarantee of job security, the union would not negotiate about it.

SOCIAL RESPONSIBILITY

Social responsibility issues typically arise when there has been a failure in stakeholder management. For example, a firm may have ignored or misread one or more external stakeholders and allowed the second-order effects of its operations or products to pass the threshold of community or political activism—perhaps allowing an offensive effluent to pass into an adjacent stream, or selling a car of questionable safety. Once aroused, stakeholder activism can threaten the normal operations of the firm. Such situations demand skilled stakeholder management.

We believe, like Ackerman (1975) and Post (1978), that the firm can operate more smoothly and effectively if its relations with its societal stakeholders are managed like any other function, such as production or marketing, before thresholds for stakeholder activism have been passed. Indeed, since responsibility issues arise at the shared boundaries of the organization and its social and political stakeholders, it is operations managers who are on the front line. Unless there is a responsive corporate culture supported by senior management to guide these people, the firm is likely to live from crisis to crisis in its relations with its publics (Simon, 1976). In fact, social responsibility issues are often simply signs of a failure of corporations to adapt to present-day realities of reasonable and legitimate stakeholder demands.

Milton Friedman writes that the only "social" responsibility of the firm is its fiduciary responsibility to maximize returns to shareholders (Friedman, 1962). The reality of today's business environment, however, indicates that poor management of the firm's important relationships with its constituents can affect operations and profits. A loss of flexibility, exorbitant legal fees, and the diversion of senior management time are all inefficient results of poor stakeholder management.

We believe stakeholder management is good business. Social responsibility is a responsibility of the strategic manager; Freeman goes so far as to say that "strategic management is building bridges to the firm's stakeholders" (1981, p. 20). It is not a matter of taste, nor is it just enlightened self-interest, to manage stakeholder relationships well.

Proactive Versus Reactive Management

Management can be proactive rather than reactive. Managers have choices about which stakeholders' interests to serve, whom to satisfy and whom to disappoint, and to what degree, and they can anticipate stakeholder interests. They must choose how to balance their organization's short- and long-term financial performance needs with critical social demands which, if ignored, may sorely affect its ability to do business (Barnard, 1966; Selznick, 1964; Andrews, 1980). Just as he or she prepares for an expected change in the industrial environment by altering variables such as prices, production methods, or debt source, so, too, in the societal arena, the manager can consider which stakeholders have priority, how interests can be balanced, and how the firm's actions on social issues or for specific stakeholders can be timed to do the most good.

Reactive managers, by comparison, tend to use strategies in the societal arena designed upon the base of their competitive experience. Managers who are exclusively reactive risk heavy costs in situations where the firm is allowed to drift into conflict with powerful stakeholders. Such issues could be quickly resolved or negotiated if they were identified and understood earlier. A crisis situation in a social issue has the same impact as an unexpected economic crisis: the manager loses flexibility.

One pharmaceutical company avoided the high research and development costs which characterize the industry by acquiring smaller companies with proven new products and then using its marketing and financial resources to stimulate growth and improve operating performance. They waited, watched, and reacted in the competitive arena, and did the same when one of their products became the target of drug abuse. By waiting to see what would happen next, they lost their ability to control their future. Their concern became news, and then a political issue. They found their product placed by the US Drug Enforcement Agency on the restricted manufacturing and sales list, forbidding its production or sale. What worked competitively failed in the world of societal and regulatory stakeholders (Schwartz, 1978).

The second-order effects of social responsibility situations can go substantially beyond the original issue as the situation evolves. Depending on the values and power of the affected stakeholders, social responsibility issues can create events and investigations which attract media, political, and government attention to a number of a firm's activities, sometimes virtually unrelated to the original issue. Enough managers have been caught flat-footed and open-mouthed by TV cameras to realize that Post's view of social responsiveness as a necessary, ongoing activity of corporate managers is reasonable. Insincerity robs management of credibility and influence.

If social responsiveness is treated as a managerial responsibility, a strategic view can enhance performance in dealing with sometimes seemingly intractable social issues and stakeholder demands. Cohen (1982) writes that information, time, power, and involvement are critical variables in every negotiation. It is useful, therefore, to evaluate our use of information, time, and power in our relations with our stakeholders—that is, to evaluate our stakeholder strategies.

Empathetic Management: Thinking It Through

Responsible management means knowing what effects our operations have on the well-being of employees and neighbors. It means anticipating or resolving issues before they are politicized and before new actors or stakeholders enter with additional expectations which have to be satisfied (Post, 1979). A firm should develop a system or process of self-governance to ensure that it knows what it is doing and that it is not knowingly violating the rights of others (Sclznick, 1964; Dalton and Cosier, 1982).

It is important to consider the strategy, objectives, resources and environments of the stakeholders involved in a social responsibility issue, to recognize their power and anticipate their reactions to a firm's various planned (and implicit) stakeholder strategies. For example, immediacy, frequent coverage and relevance to a broad spectrum of the population are important objectives of the broadcast media. They have a particularly difficult time finding newsworthy items on weekends or over holidays. Ralph Nader certainly understood this when he called a press conference to describe the Corvair's failures late on a Friday afternoon, in the summer of 1963. His pronouncements were the most important event for the news reports of the weekend, and General Motors' executives did not offer a response until business hours on Monday. Understanding the strategic significance of Nader's timing would have made GM management more effective and responsive spokesmen in their company's behalf.

Similarly, government regulators have objectives which are important to them. And government officials have methods, such as the use of delays for permits or meetings, by which to achieve their objectives. Thinking through a regulatory agency's likely response to various strategies and the procedural actions available to it would improve the likelihood of choosing a strategy which could allow the firm to function effectively and with low legal costs.

Interactive Management

Interactive stakeholder management, where management realizes likely stakeholder reactions and responds to stakeholder interests and actions, is better than either reactive or proactive stakeholder approaches. Post (1976) writes that the best stakeholder management is generally interactive, since reactive management is rarely in control of the situation and a proactive stance may address the wrong problem. Interaction allows the firm to influence both the process by which an issue is resolved and the outcome of that process. While sometimes the firm has no choice but to be reactive, being reactive indeed limits the firm's choices.

Choices are enhanced and increased when stakeholder objectives can be thought through ahead, when time is available to handle issues interactively and to negotiate, and when you know how stakeholders measure your performance and you understand how you value theirs. Indeed, time and knowledge are both the most important results of anticipatory, interactive stakeholder management and so are the most valuable resources to carry out that management function effectively. Knowledge is a major source of power in social responsibility situations. Time provides the opportunity to use it.

TOWARD EVALUATION

In the last two sections, we have addressed not analysis per se, but analysis in a context of relationship management, linking analysis and action. This shift of emphasis is deliberate, for although we believe analysis is a necessary prelude to effective action, analysis and action are not totally separable. Analysis is most useful when the analyst appreciates the context of prospective action. Context for the strategist is the net of stakeholder relationships which exists and changes with success and failure, including failures of responsibility.

Before we act, we have to judge what the facts are and then what they mean for the organization. This last phase necessitates making value judgments—judgments about the significance of the facts for ourselves or our organization. Knowing what the facts are, we attach weight or significance to them and thereafter regulate our behavior (Vickers, 1965). Hence, our movement from facts for analysis to relationship management and responsibility is designed to focus attention on the need for judgment and the influence of values in strategic management.

Values matter in strategic management. Personal values give strategies vitality.

Indeed, how long do people support unprincipled leaders, or those without a cause? Sun Tzu wrote that the first factor in (military) success was the moral factor, explaining:

> By moral influence, I mean that which causes the people to be in harmony with their leaders, so they will accompany them in life and unto death without fear of moral peril. (1963, p. 64)

Arjay Miller vividly reminds managers of the importance of personal values and "doing good," when he advises that in thinking about the ethical, moral, and legal aspects of their decisions, managers should apply what he called the TV test and ask themselves, "How would I explain my actions on TV?" His advice is simple: Don't do anything you wouldn't be willing to explain on TV (Miller, 1980). The question demonstrates that while managers can choose both strategies and implementation methods, their responsibility and position place them in the public eye. They must be willing to live publicly with the results of their decisions. Results are generally easier to live with when they have been anticipated and judged appropriate *before* commitment, while there is time to choose courses of action.

THE MORAL FACTOR: JUDGMENT

What is moral judgment? Barnard (1966) defines morals as

> . . . personal forces . . . which tend to inhibit, control, or modify inconsistent immediate specific desires, impulses, or interests and to intensify those which are consistent with such propensities. (p. 261)

Judgment is a subtle quality. It is labeled by others as good or bad, responsible or irresponsible, insightful or pedestrian. Yet, the calculus of judgment is largely unknown, as Vickers notes:

> There is no means by which any of their judgments can be proved right or wrong—even, I shall suggest, after the event. Judgment, it seems, is an ultimate category, which can only be approved or condemned by a further exercise of the same ability. (1965, p. 13)

Despite this difficulty, managers and others agree that good judgment is restrained. While seeking, indeed creating, opportunity, it is not opportunistic. It is essentially moral, in that it seeks something greater than merely an immediate advantage.

Moral restraint is needed to promote and protect the best interests and well-being of the organization. Selznick calls the source of this well-being the integrity of the organization. Indeed, opportunism threatens integrity, and Selznick writes:

> To take advantages of opportunities is to show that one is alive, but institutions no less than persons must look to the long-run effects of present advantage. In speaking of the "long run" we have in mind not time, as such, but how change affects personal or institutional identity. (1957, p. 143)

Barnard (1966) eloquently presents the case for moral management. Responsibility gives dependability and determination to human conduct, and foresight and idealism to purpose (p. 260). Management's resources root it in the past, while the future is endless (p. 284). Foresight, high ideals, and long purposes are the basis for persistent cooperation in this context. Thus, the chief executive responsibility is to develop a capacity "to bind the wills of men to accomplishment of purpose beyond their immediate ends, beyond their times" (p. 283).

A critical responsibility for a leader is, therefore, to inculcate his or her organization with a moral code to guide its decisions. In Simon's terms, a good manager creates a moral culture (Simon, 1976). Indeed, this is not needed simply to avoid failure in some relationship or exchange; it is needed to create and protect the organization, its "self." "Do unto others as you would have them do unto you" is the essence of organizational morality which restrains and protects the institution.

OBJECTIVES

Ultimately, organizations exist because they serve a purpose: they have objectives which are worth winning. The essence of leadership is choice and the assumption of responsibility for a commitment to a particular path. Sometimes the leader must transcend disagreement and subordinates must follow (Andrews, 1980, p. 85).

Failure by leadership default very often comes from trying to avoid internal conflict or appeasing the illicit claims of some opportunist stakeholder. When businesses fail, it is often by default rather than error. As managers, we can, do, and will make errors. But we do not have to live with repeated errors. If we demand performance of ourselves, that is, if we have objectives, we can demand performance of others.

Selznick (1957) noted that without specific or legitimate objectives, organizations drift, "exposed to vagrant pressures, readily influenced by short run opportunistic trends" (p. 25). He attributes this type of drift to a failure of nerve and a fundamental inability to see what corrupts an organization and makes it vulnerable. As Andrews (1980) puts it, management can allow everyday pressures to rob it of a capacity for self-criticism.

EVALUATING STRATEGY AND OBJECTIVES

Since strategies are what we do to achieve our objectives, when we evaluate our strategy and its results, there is a legitimate question: What were our objectives? Remember, as managers, we may choose to modify our objectives, but it is necessary to evaluate them first. Were they ambitious, inspirational and far-sighted, or mundane? Were they feasible, or impossible?

These are vital issues and it is stakeholder behavior which is the best indicator of our success. Stakeholder behavior, commitment, and enthusiasm all point to stakeholder satisfaction. If there is no enthusiasm or if there is waning commitment, it could mean inadequate or unrealistic objectives or dissatisfaction with our strategy.

We need a capacity for self-criticism to answer the question, "What do the symptoms mean?" One way to find out is to seek meaningful patterns in the Stakeholder Audit

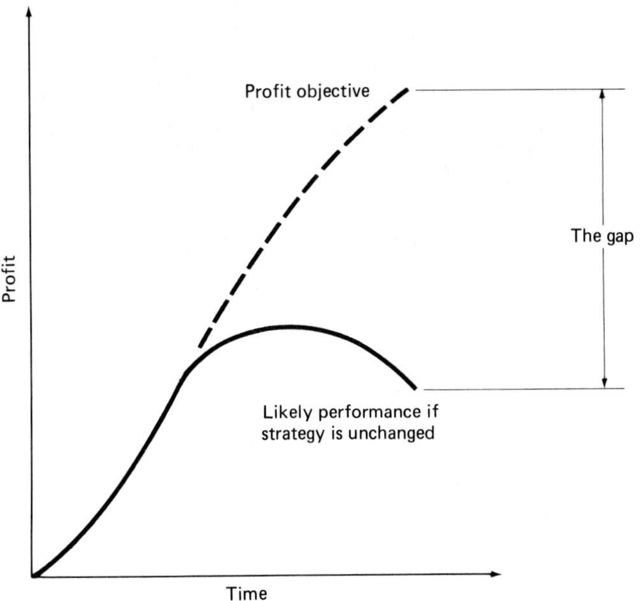

FIGURE 9-3 Gap Analysis

data. For example, we can identify any gap between our performance and our stakeholders' objectives. Secondly, we can compare our performance gaps with our stakeholders' power. Is there a pattern of satisfaction or dissatisfaction? Do the powerful or powerless receive satisfaction in return for their support?

Gap Analysis focuses management attention on the difference between what was wanted and what was achieved. Following Ansoff (1965) and Kami (1969), the identification of the gap is a stimulus for a strategy to close it. *Figure 9-3* describes a profit gap, and similar gap analysis can be done for other objectives. We will discuss gap analysis in more detail in Chapter 11 where we use it as an aid to develop alternatives.

Although normally restricted to financial and market performance, gap analysis can be applied to any performance measure, including the secondary and more remote effects of operations on the environment or stakeholder satisfaction. To do this, the more you know about your stakeholders and how they measure your performance, the better. Likewise, the more you are able to specify and measure your own performance, the better. Explicitness in gap analysis facilitates self-criticism.

SOME CONCLUDING COMMENTS

Just as the summary of the resources and environment of the firm moves the strategist closer to analyzing how they fit together and fit with the strategy, so, too, our concluding comments on objectives will focus on fit. Do the objectives of the firm which the strategist has identified fit with and synthesize stakeholder interests? Do they inspire the firm or constrain it? Do they represent tradeoffs and accommodations of extreme interests so that the firm can operate normally? If a firm's objectives run counter to a major stakeholder's interests, the "fit" is bad, and many strategies which may satisfy simple economic objectives may be unworkable. In practice, if the lack of fit is great enough, key stakeholders may act to constrain operations and remove management.

Indeed, objectives and constraints come from people's values. The heart operates differently than the head, and the heart is indeed an important component of the firm and of great interest to the strategic manager. In the context of stakeholder management, objectives may be considered positive imperatives, what the firm will do. Constraints, in contrast, are negative imperatives, corresponding to "will not do" (Simon, 1964). Both objectives and constraints are important, as the strategist seeks to satisfy the former and avoid violating the latter.

In evaluating our strategy, we consider the quality of the results it has produced and promises; we must blend analysis and synthesis. We have a view of the strategy itself and we have a perspective of the economic environment, the firm's resources, and its stakeholders and their values and objectives. Essentially, each view by itself is only part of the whole picture. In the next chapter, we put them together and gain the benefits from the many perspectives we have developed to evaluate our strategy as we move towards the future.

chapter 10

Strategy Evaluation

INTRODUCTION

Strategy evaluation is one of the most important steps in the strategic management process. Evaluation marks a watershed stage in our efforts to formulate strategy. Before evaluation, we collect and analyze facts. After evaluation, we synthesize new alternatives. Evaluation requires both analysis and synthesis, because it is the step in the process where we have to pull information together.

To evaluate, we look back and we look ahead. In evaluating a strategy, we set the stage for improvement and change. Evaluation requires judgment because evaluation precedes our determination of what to do next.

Evaluation permeates good management systems. Not only do managers evaluate their current strategy's performance, they later must evaluate alternative strategies. As part of their work, they must evaluate their competitors' strategies and the strategies of their organization's stakeholders. Moreover, each manager has to learn to evaluate his or her own performance and the work of others before supporting a new venture, promoting or rewarding subordinates, or considering a new position. Much depends on knowing how to evaluate strategy and people and being right—your career, the survival of your organization, and the jobs of the people who work for you and with you.

In the context of evaluation, what does "being right" mean? Simply put, it means ensuring that the actions you take, based on the evaluation, work out. It does not mean making the right decision. Managers do not just make decisions. Indeed, that is really a very small part of the job (Mintzberg, 1973), and, quite often, a number of alternative courses of action could give satisfactory results (Simon, 1976). Being right as a manager means getting the right result.

Evaluation forces us to look at multiple dimensions of strategy in the organization. *Figure 10-1* illustrates the complexity of the situation facing managers. Getting results is not simply a matter of evaluating the current strategy and selecting a strategy likely to be effective in the *future* environment. The strategy has to be implemented through the organization with its structures, systems, and people. Behavior—action—produces results. When results are unsatisfactory, therefore, the problem may not be the strategic decision. Problems may be due to structural or administrative errors, the personal actions of key people in the organization, or environmental changes.

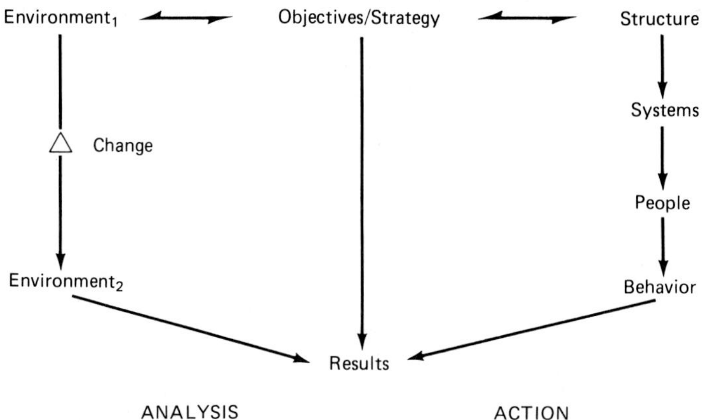

FIGURE 10-1 The Strategic Management System

THE NEED FOR JUDGMENT

Judgment is needed in evaluation because we are under pressure to be right. When we are under pressure, we are likely to pay too much attention to the present or to our prior experience and too little to the future. Moreover, it is never really clear what the facts available mean—for example, what are symptoms and what are causes of problems? Furthermore, as our planning horizon extends, our confidence in the details of any forecast declines. For example, managers of an electric utility face construction periods of five to ten years and an operating life of perhaps as much as fifty years when they commit to new generation and distribution facilities. They have to commit knowing that unexpected change is inevitable. Judgment is essential in these circumstances.

Judgment is required because evaluation leads to a determination of what to do next and where to intervene in the system. Should objectives or strategy be changed, or is it the organization's structure or administrative systems which need modification? Is it a person who must be replaced?

When we evaluate a strategy and take the first steps to determine what to do next, we address a situation marked by complexity and interdependence—and by uncertainty, because the future is uncertain. The effectiveness of the strategy is interdependent with each element in the system that is needed to gain the desired result. Evaluation—sorting out what is needed—requires judgment.

EVALUATION FROM MANY POINTS OF VIEW

To cope with multiple sources of complexity and uncertainty in the evaluation process, we need information and we must break with conventional ways of thinking which limit our ability to be insightful and put unnecessary bounds on our thinking (Simon, 1976; Williamson, 1975). We have to learn to evaluate the strategy from many points of view and we have to learn how to weigh our findings.

Each evaluation perspective we will use tests the strategy. Each test points to potential strengths or weaknesses, to opportunities and threats, to problems, to the benefits and costs of either a continued commitment to the current strategy or of a change. Note that few strategies will receive a perfect score on each dimension. It is the pattern as a whole which we have to use to guide us towards a judgment. The multiplex view, however, helps organize and integrate the information available to us, adds value to our evaluation effort, and, later, will help us generate alternative strategies and develop more efficient operations. The many perspectives and tests pull all the data together and thereby reduce the possibility of our evaluation being dominated by a single error of judgment. Ultimately, the multiple perspectives free us from conventional views alone and so help us intervene in the strategy-structure system more effectively and more efficiently.

EVALUATION AND TIME

Strategy is essentially a bridge between past and future. We stand in the present, straddling the past and the future. Thus, time is a critical factor in the evaluation process:

1 We use the track of performance from the past through the present to the future to judge the merits of a strategy.
2 Our judgment also may be affected by *when* we look.

To make sure the evaluation does not give undue weight to our own present, the evaluation process is more effective when it examines the results of a strategy in the past, present, and future. In this way, it gives weight to current trends, particularly to those originating outside the organization.

Moreover, strategy evaluation is not simply a matter of how results change over time. How the company or organization uses time and times its actions is a strategic choice and this, too, must be considered in evaluating strategies. The following excerpt from *A Book of Five Rings,* written in Japan in 1645, captures some of the subtle relationships between strategic success and time:

> In strategy there are various timing considerations. From the onset you must know the applicable timing and the inapplicable timing, and from the large and small things and the fast and slow timings find the relevant timing, first seeing the distant timing and the background timing. This is the main thing in strategy. It is especially important to know the background timing, otherwise your strategy will become uncertain. (Musashi, 1974)

Looking at past, present, and future results helps us develop insight to the quality of strategy design and its execution, and insight as to whether the strategic management process is becoming more effective. It helps us isolate the proven, real strengths and weaknesses in the business—the resources we have for future competition. Finally, it helps us judge whether the firm's management has been awake to opportunity, timely and far-sighted in its actions and thus building the organization's competitive strength—or short-sighted, wasting resources to create short-term but temporary success—or reckless, needlessly placing the organization's future in jeopardy for short-term, opportunistic gain.

It is worth noting here that the emphasis we give to past, present, and future in strategy evaluation is traditional in business. The accounting system provides us with data along that same time track. The balance sheet is an accumulation of the results of our past strategies. The income statement tells us how we are doing currently, while the sources-and-uses-of-funds statements essentially tell us where the firm believes its future lies, since the use of funds reveals the firm's investment in the future.

The DAAG Example

In this chapter, we will refer repeatedly to the DAAG example to highlight the critical elements of strategy evaluation; here we introduce it and illustrate the importance of the time element in evaluation. During the early 1960s, DAAG, the disguised name for the European division of a US multinational elevator company, adopted an aggressive growth strategy in the market for Class B elevators (those designed for three- to five-floor buildings). By standardizing its product line, initially in Germany and later throughout Europe, and by rationalizing its production operations, the company cut its costs. At the same time, however, it cut its prices even faster to build volume and market share. By 1969, DAAG had reached the point where elevator prices were below manufacturing costs, and questions were raised about the value of the strategy. Critics noted that it is usually possible to build volume if you give goods away. *Figure 10-2* illustrates the situation facing DAAG.

It is important to understand that, for DAAG, 1969 was about half-way through the thirteen-year period which the managing director had believed necessary to complete the changes required to make his strategy successful inside DAAG and in the market. He had planned for losses on current sales and maintained his division's profitability by expanding and emphasizing his elevator service business. In fact, he may have used his losses on

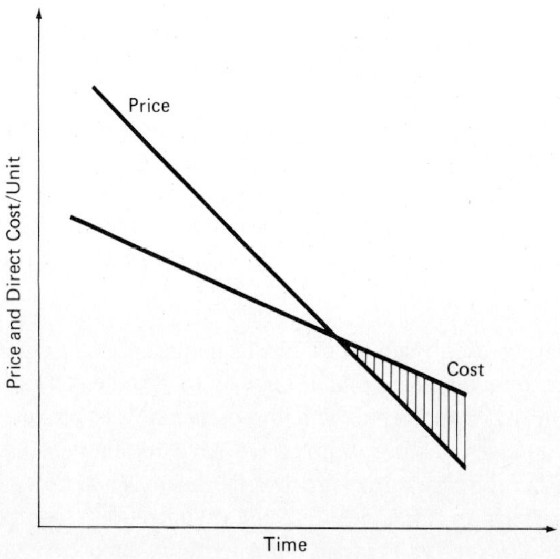

FIGURE 10-2 Price and Direct Cost of a Standard Elevator, c. 1963–69

new elevator sales to force manufacturing efficiency on his company and change in his industry. Because elevators are critical to convenient access to larger buildings, yet are a small part of total building cost, they add considerable value and enjoy relatively inelastic demand, although the level of demand varies with the fortunes of the construction industry. While the company's price cuts forced internal reorganization to reduce costs, the strategy stimulated industry restructuring as some competitors yielded share and sought less competitive niches, while others operated at reduced margins until they either left the industry or imitated DAAG's operating methods, albeit slowly.

Note how time can affect the evaluation of DAAG's strategy. In 1969, an evaluation which heavily weighed losses on new sales might have led to the abandonment of the strategy. A more thorough evaluation would have seen that the strategy was taking advantage of reductions of trade barriers due to the existence of the European Economic Community (the EEC or Common Market) and of the then-current building boom in Europe to develop an unusually robust competitor from a once very ordinary company. Four years later, in 1973, the company's profits demonstrated the success of the strategy and the good judgment of the parent board which had allowed the division to follow its strategy.

In 1969, however, this success was not assured, although the track over time indicated that DAAG's competitive strength was growing. By 1969, the company had been successful in moving its cost structure to a steeper experience curve than it had enjoyed earlier, a steeper curve than any of its competitors. As DAAG garnered volume in its standardized lines, it achieved a new scale of production, exploited processes which allowed learning, and focused and rationalized its factories and selling operations.

Figure 10-3 illustrates DAAG's experience curve for its most successful model. Note the cost break around 1966 or 1967. A competitor tracking DAAG might have fitted

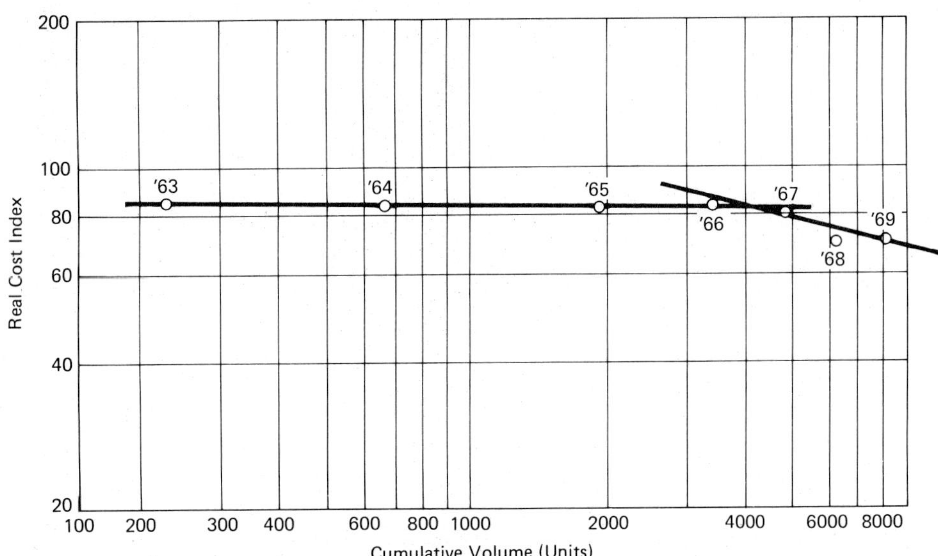

FIGURE 10-3 **DAAG: Experience Curve MOD-S Elevator (Log/Log)**

a single curve to the company's cost data through 1969, reasoning that, like the other elevator manufacturers in Europe, DAAG had done nothing to improve its operations. This would have been a potentially very costly underestimation of a competitor whose scale of operations had changed dramatically.

Even in this abbreviated example, it is easy to imagine reaching a different conclusion on DAAG's strategy if we had evaluated the results in 1965 or 1966 when the experience effect had not been captured by DAAG, or if we took a different point of view—for example, that DAAG was out of control. But if we could foresee the longer-term benefits of the operating strategy then underway, would we have given support to the strategy? Indeed, evaluation requires the use of the tracks of many results over time.

SOME PRINCIPLES OF SUCCESSFUL STRATEGIES

While the past, present, and future track of results over time gives us one framework with which to evaluate strategy, we need others to widen our perspective and to enlarge our analytical armory. Let us use experience and consider what makes a strategy effective or ineffective.

First, *the strategy must be consistent with the environment.* It is tough sailing into the wind. It is easier to move with the environment than against it. DAAG, for example, standardized its product line and rationalized its production operations across national boundaries during a period when barriers to international trade were falling in Europe. Similarly, it expanded its Class B operations at a time when construction of three- to five-floor buildings was booming, making its entry to the market easier.

Second, *the strategies of the parts must be consistent with each other and the whole.* For example, marketing must be consistent with manufacturing. For many years, US farm equipment manufacturers such as J.I. Case and International Harvester sought volume in the market to help them cut costs, but marketing continuously broadened the product line, denying manufacturing any opportunity to reach efficient scale. The two functions, production and marketing, were seeking volume but at cross-purposes for the firm's profitability.

Third, *effective strategies focus resources rather than spread or scatter them.* Few weak companies have prospered by diversifying, for example. Some have made money by cutting back and focusing their energy on one market segment, however. Joan Fabrics, once a diversified fabric producer, eliminated almost its entire product line and specialized in upholstery fabrics for the auto industry in the late 1970s. The company has prospered as velour seat-covers have supplanted vinyl in US-made cars.

Fourth, *effective strategies usually focus strength against weakness, seize an advantage, and exploit their competitors' errors to limit costs.* DAAG, a large, well-capitalized multinational company, attacked not multinationals but small family-owned regional elevator companies. It used strategy to pressure these companies into error. If they held their prices, after DAAG cut its prices 9 percent from its former 10 percent premium to match the smaller companies, DAAG gained share. Its new low price, buttressed by its image as a quality international producer, gave DAAG the advantage. If its small competitors cut prices, DAAG saw them cut margins and underinvest in the future. Only a few could identify small, specialized niches out of the thrust of DAAG's strategy.

Fifth, *resources are critical.* Strategy is the art of the possible. Do what is feasible. Resource shortages lead to constraints and vulnerabilities. DAAG moved deliberately, constrained by the profitability of its service business.

Sixth, *risks should not be taken casually.* They should be limited, managed, and reduced—usually by using time rather than fighting it, and by finding others who will absorb the risk for a fee, a reward you can afford to pay if things work out. Resources and relationships can be used to absorb the costs of failure.

Seventh, *a good strategy is controlled.* Its success or difficulties can be anticipated and milestones defined to monitor performance. It should be ''self-correcting'': managers should learn from their successes and failures. Surprises are failures of control.

Eighth, *strategy should build on its successes.* Internally, success should be traded for autonomy. Externally, success should be used to manage effectively and build more success. Many companies pursuing growth and low-cost strategies see volume leading to cost efficiency and so to opportunities to lower prices again and stimulate sales, gaining more volume, and thereby allowing the cycle of success to continue. Once the strategy is in place, it strengthens itself until the environment changes, as it did for Timex when low-priced electronic watches were introduced to the market.

Ninth, *a sign of strategic success is support by the organization's stakeholders, particularly by top and middle management.* Support is not only a commitment, but a confirmation by others that the course is right.

CONSISTENCY CHECKS

Consistency is the most important characteristic of a successful strategy (Tilles, 1963; Andrews, 1980). In fact, consistency is the shared characteristic of all the principles listed above—consistency with the times and the external environment, and consistency within the firm, including consistent, focused functional strategies. Attacking weakness with strength and exploiting others' errors to limit costs is consistent with maintaining your resource base. Attempting what is impossible is inconsistent with resource maintenance, as it implies taking risks you cannot absorb.

External Consistency

Probably one of the most useful ways of evaluating a strategy is to focus on external and internal consistency. External consistency asks, is it timely? Does the strategy use the environment and ride the wave of change or fight it?

Another form of external consistency is robustness. Robustness refers to a strategy's competitive strength under different environmental contingencies. Strategies which build competitive strength under conditions of prosperity, stability, and recession, for example, are robust and may even be pre-eminent, since these strategies ensure competitive strength and therefore prosperity for the firm under all scenarios.

DAAG, the elevator company we described earlier in this chapter, built a Europe-wide organization using its existing plants for the most part, thereby limiting its capital commitments and so its risk exposure. It made standardized rather than custom elevators and sold them at low prices. Standardization led to volume production, scale economies,

FIGURE 10-4 DAAG's Strategy, 1969, a Robustness Test

Building Industry Conditions	*Major Customer Needs*	*Standardized Producer's Competitive Strength v. Unstandardized*
Boom	Delivery	High
Stability	Reduced construction time, service	Growing
Recession	Price	High

and new manufacturing processes which enhanced the company's existing capacity and lowered costs, as well as allowing faster service and installation time.

Figure 10-4 illustrates the robustness test for DAAG under different industry conditions. DAAG's customers have different needs in different industry conditions. The standardized producer's competitive strength is affected by those conditions. The company's competitive strength grew as it reorganized, reduced costs, and trained its field staff to work with and install the standardized elevators. Because it had not substantially altered its fixed costs, its relative competitive strength was robust in bad times as well as good. Moreover, in good times DAAG could deliver its standard product faster than any of its nonstandardized competitors. Again, it had a competitive advantage. The strategy was robust.

Internal Consistency

Internal consistency is a test focusing attention on functional operations, the business's internal components. If they are coordinated and if each serves the firm's strategy by striving for objectives which are consistent, the strategy of the business will be internally consistent. Adler of Bic used the analogy of business as a car to emphasize the need for coordination and balance within an organization; the analogy stresses the importance of internal consistency.

An organization in which the marketing staff's success depends on maintaining its size and stable relationships with its customers will probably fit with an operations group organized to deliver quality goods. Relationships with customers and internal relationships will probably be smoother in this case if price stability is more important than cost reduction. In contrast, an organization like Bic's emphasizes growth, volume, and volume-based cost reductions. Bic's strategy, too, is internally consistent and, operating cycle after cycle, it built the company's resources and competitive strengths.

Resource Adequacy

Another form of internal consistency relates directly to resources. Are the resources available when they are needed? Abundance allows flexibility and reduces the costs of error. Scarcity constrains freedom and intensifies uncertainty and internal conflict (Pfeffer and Salancik, 1978). A small brewery which aspires to growth is a typical example of a business which cannot afford success. If it promotes its product and fills capacity, the costs of additional capacity are high. If incremental expansion is impractical, the investment required for a new discrete plant is usually too big. New York's Schaeffer Brewing perished as an independent company because it did not have the financial resources needed to implement its strategy of converting its production operations to efficient scale. Although debt was available to the company, rising interest costs through the 1970s and intense competition combined to create losses, and the company failed. The resources were inconsistent with the needs of Schaeffer's strategy.

Consistency with Stakeholders

Consistency is also needed between the strategy and objectives of the firm and the objectives of its stakeholders. Inconsistency here is likely to lead to conflict and a lack of support for the strategy, and so to ineffective implementation. Persistent internal disharmony or conflict with major input-making or output-taking stakeholders is likely to lead to a lack of consensus at the top of the firm and to ambiguity and inconsistency in the market. Without support, top management has no clear power or mandate to do anything, and the organization typically begins to decay. Curtis Publishing Company was a company owned largely by the Curtis and Bok families. Although it published the *Saturday Evening Post,* a very successful magazine in its heyday of the 1920s, the company floundered because in the end, by the 1960s, no one involved in the organization had the power to act decisively and put the survival of the company before the survival of its products.

COMPETITIVE ADVANTAGE

Essentially, companies survive and succeed when they have a competitive advantage and fail when they do not. Even if the advantage is local (for example, a seaside hotel), or temporary (for example, a new but imitable product), the prosperity of the business depends on its ability to defend its relative advantage and on the abilities of its rivals to reduce it. And, we should remember that advantages are rarely absolute or permanent; they apply to a particular segment or niche or time.

Evolutionary theory suggests that niches are the result of a confluence of environmental conditions, have a finite capacity, and may close when the environmental conditions needed to sustain them change (Zammuto, 1982). When change occurs, companies have to learn to survive in a different world and use their resources and competencies to create a new competitive advantage. Timex's dominance of the watch industry ended with the advent of the electronic watch although it continued to use its manufacturing competence to assemble Polaroid cameras and, later, Sinclair computers. Coors's Western markets were isolated from competition by the Rocky Mountains and the Western plains as well as by taste distinctions, until the 1970s. Increased saturation of the Eastern and Midwestern markets led successful national brewers such as Anheuser-Busch to move west into competition with Coors, while Miller targeted its Miller Lite beer to compete directly with Coors. Hence, Coors lost its geographic niche and its taste advantage concurrently and has been unable to maintain its profitability and market stature, or to revive its product's distinctiveness, since that time.

Being the same is never enough. You have to be better than your competitors and different from them. It is your differences which allow you to develop an advantage (Henderson, 1979). The issue as we evaluate our strategy is: What are the differences between us and our competition? Does our strategy exploit those differences to give us an advantage?

Later, we will have to find ways either to enhance our advantage or to start new businesses, in which our competitive profile, our resources, can be used to create an advantage. It may include upsetting an existing competitive situation by entry, acting to induce competitors to avoid us, or deliberately avoiding competitors. We will discuss the generation of alternatives based on a firm's competitive advantage in more detail in Chapter 11.

RISK AND REWARD BALANCE

A principle which permeates strategic management is that *risks must be balanced by rewards*. Managers should strive to increase rewards and cut risks. In the framework of conventional finance theory, a generally upward sloping relationship is posited between risk and reward. One version shows return on assets plotted against β, relative variability of market price, a proxy measure of risk, as *Figure 10-5* shows. The dots[1] under the curve show the investment options facing a portfolio manager who can choose between a treasury bill with a steady return (if held to maturity) and other investments. An efficient investor will mix a portfolio between treasury-bills with low relative risk and the most efficient investment in terms of reward for risk taken. The only ways to increase value are to increase reward or cut risk, or both.

Theory and the realization that value is enhanced when reward is increased or risk is cut should lead us to examine the risk/reward balance of our strategy. Where are the risks? Can they be reduced by different operating procedures or different strategies? Can the rewards earned justify the investments in money and time required?

Are risks taken adequately rewarded? This should be a major concern for management. What risks are inherent in the current strategy? There are many possibilities because some risk is associated with every balance sheet and income statement account. Risk relates to what may happen in the future, and any of these accounts can change due to risk. Of course, the financial statements themselves describe situations of little risk, since financial data rely primarily on historic or market costs.

The Sources of Risk

What are the risks? Liquidity means foregoing the opportunity to invest. Accounts receivable involve credit risks; inventories may carry a fashion or obsolescence risk, as well as the possibility of disaster, theft, or deterioration. Fixed assets expose a company to the technological risk of obsolescence and even nationalization, in some cases. Short-term

[1]It is interesting to note that the feasible set of investments (the dots in *Figure 10-5*) are mostly losers who took too much risk and so destroyed value.

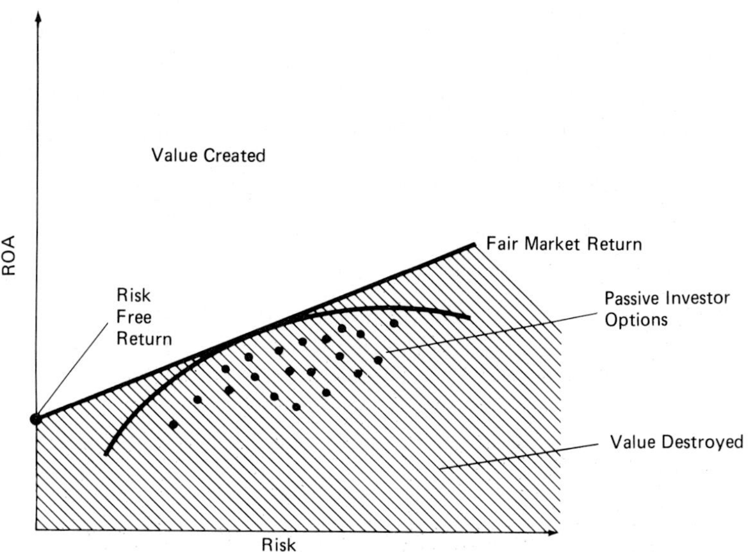

FIGURE 10-5 Risk and Reward

and long-term debt carry the risk of insolvency and negative leverage. Poor equity placements may lead to risk of control.

There are risks of short supply from scarcity, strike, or breakdowns in the plant which interrupt business. Risk is also associated with demand. Product failure or tampering, such as Tylenol experienced in 1982 and 1986, and promotional failures such as Schlitz experienced in the late 1970s with its "Drink Schlitz or else" campaign, are examples of demand-related risk.

Risks are popularly seen as environmental contingencies which carry potential loss, that is, financial risk. But risks also exist within the organization and for its people. For example, the risk that failure will lead to a loss or diffusion of power with the organization is a very real problem with some strategies, making future action more difficult.

The point here is not to be exhaustive about strategic risks, but simply to note that in business there are many sources of risk. The more you are able to specify and identify the risks you take, the more likely it is that you will find ways to manage them explicitly and the fewer risks you will overlook.

Reducing Risk

How can risks be reduced? Managers can use time instead of fighting time, and accumulate resources. Managers can also develop relationships or commitments which not only share the risk but, in doing so, reduce it. In real estate and in major petrochemical projects, for example, risks are reduced by prior commitments. In a shopping center or commercial development, a signed commitment by a leading tenant—for example, a major department store chain—substantially reduces the risk of the venture. In the petrochemical business, "take or pay" contracts from major customers have the same effect, since the customer essentially guarantees payment in all cases by signing such a contract—the customer must take it or pay for it anyway.

DAAG provides us with superb examples of risk management over time. DAAG's managing director limited his own and his organization's risk by taking one step at a time and making each step work out before taking the next. First, he had his engineering staff design a B-class elevator which he called "standard." Then he sold the elevators. Not until he had sold more than 200 did he need anything, and then he asked the parent for a dedicated plant for the now-proven product. (Remember that, until this time, European elevators were custom-designed.) Next, he found an acquisition target in the B market and bought it, saving 2 years of plant construction time and picking up a 15 percent market share, giving DAAG a 35 percent share, about 800 units per annum. The next year DAAG's elevator sales in Germany rose to almost 1500 units, where they plateaued. The next request was for more sales territory, so the parent put the managing director in charge of European operations, but there was little risk. By this point, the strategy was proven and it remained only to replicate and exploit the competitive strength already established, country by country.

By being patient and by using time to accumulate results, the managing director was able to limit risks. Because each move was predicated by business success, each move was reversible at only minor incremental cost, and the incremental costs were low. Moreover, each additional commitment increased the company's competitive strength, making it more robust. The timing used to implement the strategy reduced the risks attached to the strategy.

Willingness to take risk varies with individuals and with situations (Luce and Raiffa, 1957; Swalm, 1966). A full assesment of the risk/reward profile of a strategy thus requires that the "who" and "under what conditions" inherent in the risk component be clarified. "Who" may reinforce the notion that certain stakeholders in the business may be sources of support who could reduce the perceived risk of the strategy. And "under what conditions" may also reveal resources, strengths, weaknesses, or critical experiences which may alter an initially simple risk/reward assessment. Indeed, since risks are viewed more subjectively than most rewards, the values, resources, and risk tolerance of key stakeholders are most relevant when we evaluate a strategy, our own or another's.

CONTROL

One factor which tends to reduce stakeholders' perceptions of risk is control. People will support a strategy which requires substantial investment and operating losses if management comes to the pump for money once, can live within an initial budget, and can sustain itself. Smart managers learn this early since they know that when you ask you have to give, and what you give up for the privilege of using other people's money is autonomy or independence; control and constraints come along with the money.

Another aspect of control is "controlled" results. DAAG's strategy was to sell at prices set in anticipation of later cost efficiencies—a practice followed in many industries. For example, in airplane manufacturing, and in the electronics and auto industries, prices are set based on costs estimated on forecast unit sales. DAAG's strategy was questioned in 1969 when prices fell below manufacturing cost, yet the company had lost money on elevator sales every year from 1966 to 1969. What reassured the critics was the fact that the average loss per elevator had stayed close to 100 Deutsch Mark (DM), falling as low as 90 DM and rising as high as 108 DM. Because the company retained over 80 percent of its elevator customers as service customers and earned a 10 to 12 percent margin on service, and because elevators need regular service, the small loss of 100 DM, or about 1 percent of sales, gave little cause for alarm. It could be recouped within a reasonable time by the service business which was generated by sales growth. DAAG's total strategy was under control.

ACHIEVEMENT AND GAP ANALYSIS

As we have noted already, managers, strategies, and organizations are judged by the results they produce. But there are more kinds of results than the commonly measured profit, growth, and market share, for example. Results are generated in all the exchanges that occur between the organization—that is, its stakeholders—and its environment.

For example, the ability of an organization (and its management) to achieve its objectives and satisfy its stakeholders is a key test of a strategy and the organization. DAAG's management had a solid record of accomplishment to reassure its stakeholders:

1. management had standardized the company's product line so that 80 percent of DAAG's sales throughout Europe were accounted for by only five different models;
2. it established a European organization and engineering group;
3. it cut costs by almost 20 percent in six years;
4. it captured 25 percent of the European market in units (18 percent in dollar volume);
5. it rationalized manufacturing across Europe;
6. its installed base grew significantly, spreading the fixed costs of their service over higher volume;
7. it earned profit each year.

Top management won the support of its parent company, its peers and its subordinates for what had been viewed by many as a controversial and risky strategy.

Although past achievement is important and gives us confidence in the worth of a strategy, the future is more important. Will the company be able to achieve its objectives, develop or maintain a competitive advantage, and satisfy its stakeholders? Declining advantage and growing stakeholder dissatisfaction should be alerts that the longevity of current profitability, market share, and growth rates is suspect. Even if current results are good in numeric terms, their quality is poor if advantage is declining. The cost of maintaining current earnings is sometimes to sacrifice the organization's future.

An analytical tool which can help us focus new attention on management's investment in the future is Gap Analysis. We introduced the gap concept in Chapter 9, in the stakeholder context. Gap analysis leads us to question not only our likely future achievements, but also our aspirations for the future (Ansoff, 1965). Are our results likely to be adequate? Are we working hard enough? Are we overreaching? Should our strategy or our objectives be changed? Gap analysis is usually applied to an organization's principal objectives and interests. But it can be extended to apply to competitive advantage and the firm's critical stakeholders.

As *Figure 10-6* indicates, gap analysis compares achievement and aspiration, specifically expected (forecast) achievement on an explicit objective against what is required. In this example, the future sales of the organization, if it pursues its current strategy unchanged (the bold line), appear likely to fall, although management is intent on very substantial growth (the dotted line). The gap is the difference between target and likely accomplishment.

If the gap is negative, as in *Figure 10-6,* we may wish to consider whether our resources, including our competencies and competitive advantages, are up to the task. A more modest ambition might be more rewarding and less risky, because it is feasible. Alternatively, we might seek projects, programs, and strategies to close the gap, as Ansoff (1965) suggests. If the gap is positive and performance exceeds aspiration, we should consider the merits of greater ambition and upwardly revised objectives.

Gap analysis forces managers to measure their performance and to audit their gap-closing capabilities (Kami, 1969). Indeed, if you apply gap analysis to nontraditional objectives, such as the satisfaction of explicit stakeholders or stakeholder groups, or to competitive advantage, the analysis forces some hard thinking about measurement. What do stakeholders want? On what dimension is our competitive advantage? Specificity is often the first step towards better management and better results, even with nonfinancial or nonmarket objectives.

The identification of a gap of any substance allows management, for example, to identify and prioritize their on-the-shelf growth projects. How many are there? Kami suggests that a successful organization is *unlikely* to be successful on more than 30 percent of its growth programs; he argues for programs with a total potential of three times the gap over five to ten years. In making that self-assessment, management is advised to monitor

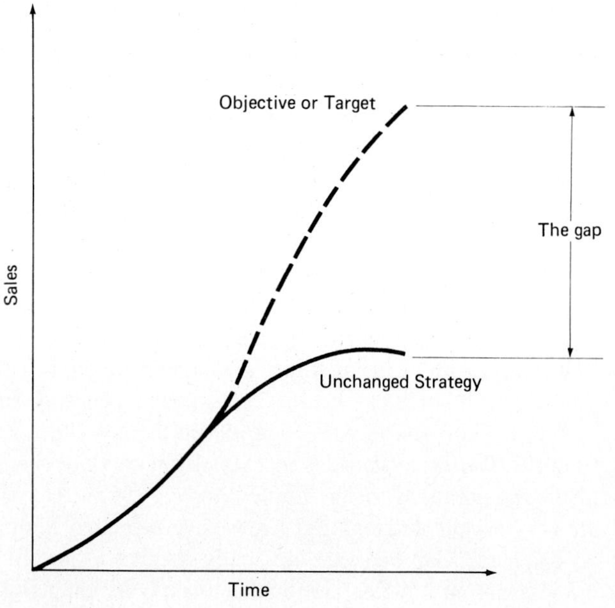

FIGURE 10-6 Gap Analysis

and review the track record of past new ventures (Crawford, 1966). How many were successful? How capable is management of tracking their success and setting practical milestones to measure performance? Kami (1968), after experience at IBM and Xerox during their periods of high growth, suggested that forecasts which were essentially extrapolations typically exceeded actual performance by 100 percent, that is, a factor of two!

Obviously, finding a gap forces a search for both gap-closing strategies and more realistic objectives. Ansoff (1965) broke these two alternatives into two principal classes, expansion and diversification, either internally or by acquisition. We shall deal with these again in Chapter 12.

AN INTEGRATIVE MULTIPLEX VIEW

Multiple assessments, done simultaneously, are necessary for a full and competent strategy evaluation—a multiplex approach—because there are so many aspects to consider. The track of time from the past, through the present, to the future, sets out trends. Trends alert us to opportunities and threats more quickly and reliably than data from a single period. We judge performance by results or achievements; these are the ultimate merits of a strategy. Risks must be reduced and rewards increased to create value. To gain competitive advantage is almost always the reason why we strategize; prosperity in business stems from creating and exploiting an advantage.

Understanding the need for a multiplex perspective, how can we put all these issues together so that busy managers can make a preliminary evaluation of a strategy with reasonable prospects of success? Tilles (1963) used six criteria: internal and environmental consistency, resource adequacy, risk acceptability, the appropriateness of the time horizon, and workability. Under "risk," Tilles emphasized the time and size of the commitments required; "workability" refers to the future. Andrews (1980) used nine different criteria: identifiability and explicitness; the extent to which the strategy uses opportunity (gaps in the market are vulnerabilities); consistency with respect to competence and resources; internal consistency; feasible corporate and personal risk; consistency with values of management; level of contribution to society; stimulus to organizational commitment; and early signs that the strategy works in the market.

These writers, as well as the experiences of good managers, make it clear that many criteria are needed to fully evaluate a strategy. There are many sources of uncertainty and vulnerability in business. Each point of view we take in evaluating strategy adds to our understanding of the situation facing management, although a particular point of view or form of analysis may have limited immediate value.

Strengths, Weaknesses, Opportunities, and Threats

What we strive for is a synthesis of all our information, a view of the whole situation which will help us bring the critical factors into high relief. By focusing on the critical factors, we create a shorthand way to send the most relevant information to management and so expedite action, where it will pay off. Two sets of ideas which have stood the test of time as summary statements of a strategy evaluation are strengths and weaknesses, opportunities and threats. Some writers use the acronym SWOT to describe the combinations. They are, of course, a matched set, since strengths can be used to take advantage of opportunities and threats and can be made more serious by weaknesses.

Strengths are the characteristics and resources that give a company power in the market and make it uniquely capable in specific ways. Weaknesses limit the organization and make it vulnerable to attack. While closely related to resource evaluation, strengths and weaknesses have a dynamic and time-specific character; they relate to the competitive environment ahead and to what the firm needs to succeed. Strengths may include high brand recognition and consumer perceptions of product quality and value in an industry where branded products have premium prices, or perhaps a cost advantage due to scale or process efficiency. A weakness could be a temporary or chronic overdependence on debt during a time of rising interest rates, intense competition, and an imminent need for capital to maintain a competitive cost position. Both strengths and weaknesses are situation-specific and occur in time. They wax and wane as competitors and the world change, sometimes converting strength to weakness and leaving management with the task of creating strength again.

Opportunities and threats seem more linked to the external environment than strengths and weaknesses, but this is not always the case. Opportunities for improvement and new ventures exist within the organization and threats can come from within, too. An overcompetitive battle for succession, for example, may leave the company with an exhausted victor, a divided board, and a decimated senior executive cadre.

What are opportunities and what are threats depend on the resources available and uncommitted. Liquid companies can weather different and more severe storms than overextended organizations. An opportunity may be the discovery that the firm's products have a different consumption pattern with a particular market segment. After Miller Brewing acquired a small brewing company primarily to recapture an important Chicago Miller distributorship, an alert manager noticed an unusually heavy consumption of low-calorie beer in the blue-collar town of Anderson, Indiana—an observation which ultimately led to the phenomenally successful Miller Lite beer. A threat may be the actions of a regulatory agency or a competitor which seem likely to interfere with our normal way of business.

Strengths and weaknesses ultimately must be matched with opportunities and threats to generate alternative strategies and select among them; hence the name SWOT analysis, because all four factors are important. However, we should keep in mind the value of comparative and competitive analysis in identifying each component. Not only do they help us appreciate our industry position and how it may shift, but the collective experience of other organizations is available to us to test our ideas, to learn from, and to confirm or refute the conventional wisdom of our industry.

AN EVALUATION FRAMEWORK

Figure 10-7 shows a matrix which collects and summarizes the major concepts used in strategy evaluation. Vertically, it shows how strategies are evaluated by their results over time. The horizontal dimension lists the many components of the firm and its environment which must be addressed. The matrix suggests the use of comparability to evaluate past

FIGURE 10-7 An Evaluation Framework

Track Record	Company Objectives	Your Stakeholders' Objectives	Company Resources	Industry	Competition	Environment	Stakeholders
Past			Comparables				
Current Near-term Future			Control and Risk Exposure				
Long-term Future			Consistency, Robustness, Gap Analysis				
Strengths							
Weaknesses							
Opportunities							
Threats							

results; risk exposure and control for current and near-term performance; and consistency, robustness, and gap analysis for the long-term future environment. In addition, *Figure 10-8* suggests a series of pragmatic evaluative questions. Note that strengths, weaknesses, opportunities, and threats appear on both of the figures to summarize the evaluation process.

By looking to the past, try to determine whether performance is improving or decreasing and why, in addition to how well resources are used. In looking at the most recent cycle, try to see what problems are being created by your actions and what opportunities lie in underutilized resources. Looking to the future, try to determine whether the concepts and assumptions that underlie your strategy are likely to be valid and consistent with the trends of the environment and robust under likely contingencies, including competitors' responses and initiatives. In addition, ask whether your assumptions are consistent with stakeholders' values for future activity and performance.

Consider what the past performance of your strategy has been, what results you have achieved, and why. Consider the consequences of your current mode of operating—for example, what are the results of undermaintaining your facilities or replacing professional staff with less experienced or less capable people in order to hold costs or salaries down? Finally, consider how well your current strategy will function in the environment you see ahead.

By contrasting your most recent results with your earlier record, you can see where your performance has slipped and where you are doing well. In contrasting your results with your objectives, you can see where improvements are needed and where you can proceed confidently. Examining the record of comparable and competitive organizations and contrasting their record with yours, and asking a simple question—"Why?"—you may identify new opportunities, potential improvements, and sources of useful information.

FIGURE 10-8 Strategy Evaluation Questions

	Your Track Record	*Your Objectives*	*Your Stakeholders' Objectives*	*Performance of Comparable Organizations*	*Forecast Environment*	*Resource Base*
Past Performance	Where have you done better or worse and why?					
Current Operating Performance	Are the trends positive or negative?	Are you meeting your objectives, and why? What are they?	Who is satisfied? Who is not? Are thresholds violated?	Who is doing better or worse, and why?	Are you creating future problems for yourself? Are you moving with or against the environment?	Are you fully utilizing your resources? Consistently?
Expected Performance in Future Environment		Is there a gap? Are your objectives achievable or can they be modified?	How will your current strategy affect your stakeholders? Their power, their relative power, and activism?	What will these and competing organizations do to counter your efforts?	What trends will hinder you and which will help you achieve your objectives?	Do you have the resources to succeed in competition?

Strengths
Weaknesses
Opportunities
Threats

Evaluate your current strategy against the environment you see ahead. Can it succeed, substrategy by substrategy? Will your strategy do the job for you in the future world you see ahead? Do you have the resources you need to make it a success?

Evaluation requires systematic thinking. Inconsistency is typically the signal of problems, the alert. Inconsistencies between results and objectives, resource needs and capabilities, between what we are doing and what will be needed, are likely to appear. Evaluation is necessary so that we can determine what to change.

To conclude the evaluation, decide what you think your problems and opportunities are. Typically, your sense of problems will come from a failure to meet objectives, from organizational strife, from inconsistencies you identify, from a sense that your competence has been declining, perhaps in marketing or service delivery, or from a sense that your organization is losing its competitive or financial vigor. These are all symptoms, however. It is important to determine why these symptoms exist, if you can, so that your future actions can be more effective. By contrast, your sense of opportunities will come from your successes, the enthusiasm which organization members have for particular programs, your identification of unserved needs which your communities or competitors have ignored, and your realization that you have discretionary funds available to invest.

THE PRACTICAL BENEFITS OF EVALUATION

Managers who do not manage well always seem to be surprised. Their best-laid plans appear to go astray, or, as one president of Scripto said, ''I lie awake all night wondering how things will work out.'' The president of another company told a consultant, ''If only we'd called you in sooner.'' Bottom-line blindness had led that company to monitor profit closely, but poor asset deployment had allowed the company to put too much money into its inventory, and the inventory was obsolete. A multiplex evaluation would have uncovered that strategic flaw. A rigorous strategic evaluation can head off surprises and insomnia, since a strategy evaluation can flag potential problems while they can be successfully handled, before they become real problems.

Strategic evaluation allows the manager to anticipate responses to expected problems. It is a necessary step before generating alternative strategies, because alternatives responding to specific problems and needs are likely to be more valuable than alternatives based on gazing into a crystal ball. And strategic evaluation is an ongoing process. The continuous evaluation of the results of an implemented (alternative) strategy creates an opportunity to constantly refine and improve the strategy.

Management has to develop sufficient confidence in its analysis and evaluation to act, but management must also expect change and understand the need for reaction. If the objectives of the organization are far-sighted, management can change its strategy in small and even large ways, but stick to the course selected.

The task is never easy. Strategic success comes from creating a situation where your organization has an advantage over its competitors and then acting to exploit that advantage to achieve your objectives. Mastering the situation requires information and hard thinking: evaluation. Remember, the only competitive situations you should enter are those you can win and defend. Otherwise, why invest resources?

PREVIEW: DEVELOPING SOLUTIONS, NEW OR IMPROVED STRATEGIES

Once you have a sense of what your organization's problems and opportunities are, it is your job to develop potential solutions. In developing these solutions or responses, you are moving to modify your current strategy, improve your performance, and turn your organization toward new opportunities. These are the subjects of Chapter 11.

chapter 11

Generating Alternatives

INTRODUCTION

Generating alternatives, the strategies and actions organizations could take to exploit their opportunities or resolve their problems, is a challenging and exciting part of every manager's work. The task holds the challenge of making organizations work better and the challenge of resolving an organization's really difficult problems. Freewheeling creative thinking and participation in the definition of an organization's future can be very exciting.

Once you have developed a deep understanding of a business's current strategy, the alternatives you need will often come to mind quickly. This is natural, because strategic analysis is a problem-finding process (Ansoff, 1971; Bower, 1967, 1982). With the organization's situation defined as strengths, weaknesses, opportunities and threats, solutions develop as natural responses to each type of problem. In most instances, the alternatives which fit this natural response category exploit traditional or standard strategies which are evolutionary rather than radical.

For most successful organizations, the outcomes of a strategic audit are minor changes to the existing strategy, fine-tuning of operations, and limited trials of a new strategy. Successful performance implies maintaining what works. In successful organizations, management is concerned with preservation of what it has and with continuity rather than change, so change is slow and adaptive. Braybrooke and Lindbloom (1970) and Quinn (1980) call such changes logical incrementalism, since they build from a successful base in ways which improve performance still further.

Yet even in a world where continuity is valued highly, sometimes radical change is required. When the problems or opportunities facing the organization are too large, complex, or intractable for incremental and evolutionary solutions, radical solutions may be needed. But we must determine the real cause of management's difficulty in certain situations so that we do not undertake the risks of radical solutions needlessly. Narrow-mindedness, tunnel vision, or a loss of flexibility in management's thinking may be blocking the creative elements of the strategic management process. Alternatively, perhaps the change ahead in the environment is truly large and does have grave consequences for the organization. In this case, developing a response is indeed a major challenge not readily amenable to normal approaches. Radical solutions and significant strategic change may be necessary.

The purpose of this chapter is to help you generate alternatives effectively and efficiently and help you understand the role you can play in defining your organization's future. Alternatives are best generated with an attitude which is opportunity-seeking rather than problem-solving. We will describe the generic strategy options that are available to every organization. We will then suggest what ''blocks'' mean in the process of generating alternatives and how to get out of them. We will also outline ways to deal with more extreme situations where major change is required. Finally, we will illustrate how all levels of management must contribute to the process of generating alternatives if the organization's strategic performance is to improve significantly.

SELECTION OF PROBLEMS TO SOLVE

As we begin this chapter, we should note that although the strategic audit process which encompasses strategy identification and evaluation often ''finds'' problems, and although many of them can be addressed quickly and at low cost, this is not always so. Nor is the problem always the best starting point for generating alternatives. Indeed, we do not have to solve problems simply because we find them.

In management and administration people must learn to stop solving problems indiscriminately and start thinking about addressing problems selectively to create value and keep it. Very little time in our society is spent determining which problems warrant effort. We honor problem solvers and our education system institutionalizes the myth that problems should be solved. Indeed, ''good'' students are often thought to be those who solve the most problems during their education.

The job of management is not to solve problems, nor is it to define problems for others to solve. At its best, managing is an opportunity-seeking activity (deBono, 1977). Problems are nothing more than opportunities to act and thereby achieve our objectives.

Indeed, because management's job is not to solve problems but to define and achieve objectives so that the value of the organization is enhanced, management must be selective. Managers must select from among the problems and opportunities revealed by strategic analysis (and day-to-day events) those few which warrant attention. Managers must select problems which, if addressed, will move the company furthest toward the accomplishment of its objectives. Selectivity is key: Management must choose which problems and opportunities to address, which to ignore, and which to monitor.

So before working hard to exploit opportunities or to reduce the number of problems facing an organization, reflect on the outcome of your work to identify and evaluate your firm's strategy. What is the firm's business and what is making the greatest contribution to its success or impeding its progress most severely? Put your effort where the payoff is likely to be greatest. Address both strategic and operating problems and opportunities. Not every problem is inherently strategic, and neglected operating problems can lead to corporate failure.

BEGINNING THE PROCESS OF GENERATING ALTERNATIVES

Strategy evaluation provides us with opportunities to understand what we do now and to do it better, as well as time to prepare and provide for the future. It tells us what is working and what is not. Evaluation alerts us to the likely future course of events and to the need to modify our objectives. Therefore, evaluation is the logical starting point as we seek to generate alternatives.

Either our business is working well and is properly positioned for the future, or change is needed. If we have a successful strategy and understand the reasons for its success, we should most probably follow this advice: "If it works, don't fix it!" If our strategy has problems, our efforts to identify a response should be guided, first, by the source of the difficulty, and then by the fact that useful strategies have common characteristics.

Each component of our analysis contributes issues to be addressed in the process of generating alternatives and points toward solutions. Strategy identification, for example, focuses attention on internal consistency, competence, and competitive advantage. If there is inconsistency, we can seek ways to reduce it. If our competence is unclear or declining, we can attend to it. In evaluation, the principles introduced in Chapter 10 define the characteristics of successful strategies: internal and external consistency, focus, strength against weakness, feasibility, control, and support. Does our strategy have these characteristics?

As we attempt to respond to issues coming from the evaluation process, we should make our moves deliberately. Remember that the least change is often the best change, and almost always it is the least costly and has the lowest risk. The results of small changes are easiest to monitor and control.

GENERIC STRATEGIES AND STANDARD ALTERNATIVES

The more extensive the problem, the more thought and insightfulness seems required to solve it. Yet, in addressing this task of designing a new strategy, remember the advice of Ecclesiastes 1:9:

> What has been is what will be and what has been done is what will be done; and there is nothing new under the sun.

Management need not innovate in every aspect of its strategy to succeed. Imitation can be very helpful (Levitt, 1966), and generic strategies suggest approaches known to improve performance.

So much of what people herald as new is simply something, once forgotten, which has been rediscovered and repackaged. In business, for example, the profits of the old product line have always been the primary source of funds for new ventures, long before the concepts of "cash cow" and "wildcat" were conceived and popularized by the Boston Consulting Group (see Chapter 18). Many sophisticated dictums are basically simplistic, although not necessarily simple to implement. For many years now, our neighbor, a successful stockbroker, has heard his mother-in-law's parting advice after every visit: "Remember, Mel, buy low and sell high." Obvious, of course, but correct—simple to say and difficult to do.

So it is in strategic management. Generic strategies such as Porter's differentiation, overall cost leadership, and focus (1980), and Utterback and Abernathy's performance maximizing, sales maximizing, and cost minimizing (1975), are little different from the buy low, sell high advice our friend receives from his mother-in-law.[1] They each point to ways to raise revenue or lower costs, both sure-fire methods to increase profits!

Typically, the generic strategy's emphasis on one or two variables maximizes its visceral impact and intuitive appeal, but complicates its use. Business-level strategies by their nature are integrative; they encompass many variables. ''Overall cost leadership'' is a dangerously flexible strategy definition. But the question, ''How could a company attain overall cost leadership?'' should provoke useful thinking. Often the value of generic strategies lies more in the questions they provoke than in any simple effort to implement them independently.

Other standardized strategic options come to mind. A company might choose between a change in its strategy and no change. Changes could include liquidating all its assets or part only, perhaps to specialize in one particular industry role by harvesting (slowly liquidating) its activities in another business. Alternatively, it might diversify. Vertical integration is another option. Growth may be by business development, emphasizing product or market expansion, and market expansion might be regional or international.

Figure 11-1 suggests the large number of options available to the strategist. To change or not to change, of course, is a very basic choice. But change may encompass contraction (liquidation), growth via specialization after consolidation, or diversification. Whether liquidation is fast, via divestment, or slow by harvesting over time, may depend on factors such as potential buyers or shared facilities. Consolidation, or narrowing scope, may occur with or without integration. Joan Fabrics, for example, began its consolidation strategy by moving out of all its former markets except the automobile upholstery fabrics market. It then integrated its auto fabrics activities by becoming involved in more stages of the production process.

We have included market scope and research emphasis as other dimensions of generic strategy development in *Figure 11-1,* but we have certainly not exhausted the sources of generic strategies. Each managerial dimension adds flexibility to management's choices, helping managers differentiate their company from its competitors. Such flexible thinking ensures that the strategy ultimately adopted has the greatest promise of serving the organization, since it has resulted from thoughtful combinations of strategy options. Henderson (1979) emphasized the importance of differences among firms when he wrote that advantage stems from differences and, unless there is an advantage, we note there can be no real economic profit.

Liquidation

Liquidation refers to decisions to leave a certain business or product sector. Divestment is a single-step liquidation and refers to the sale of a business. Harvest is the term frequently applied to a slower liquidation process in which the business continues to function but in a contracting form. In a harvest, little additional investment is made in the business, and resources are typically removed from the business and redeployed.

[1]See Galbraith and Schendel, 1983. These options could be used concurrently. Combinations of generic strategies may be helpful, e.g., a low-cost position in one segment to maximize sales, accompanying cost reductions on another product line. Marketing, production, and finance variations of the generic strategies create many potential combinations which can differentiate one company from another.

FIGURE 11-1 Generic Alternatives

GENERIC STRATEGIC ALTERNATIVES	
No Change	Options
Change:	
Liquidate	Harvest or Divest
Specialize	Consolidate or Integrate
Diversify	Product or Market

GENERIC TARGETS FOR DEVELOPMENT

Market	Operations
Niche	Product
Segment	Process
Regional	Purchasing
National	Service
Multi-National	Cost
Global	

For example, if change appears necessary, a company may choose to specialize by consolidating in a regional market, perhaps reevaluating its purchasing strategy and deciding to assemble components rather than self-manufacture.

Liquidation is popularly seen as the result of poor business performance, something which necessarily happens to losers, rather than as an active approach to improving performance. However, the liquidation strategy simply implies that some activities have been found to be more attractive than others. These attractive activities warrant more of the firm's resources, which are sensibly redeployed from low-return businesses to those with higher earnings. Ultimately, the liquidation strategy should improve overall corporate performancc. The harvest or partial liquidation strategy represents a very deliberate attempt to improve performance by limiting, rather than ending, commitment to certain low-return businesses. If, as is hoped, rates of return improve when less capital is devoted to the business, the harvest strategy will successfully demonstrate that resources were being used inefficiently in that area.

Integration

Integration into other components of the product-distribution chain can be an attractive alternative for managers who feel their objectives would be better served if they had more control of their suppliers or customers. Forward integration moves the firm's activities toward the consumer; for example, adding distribution to manufacturing capabilities is forward integration. Backward integration involves the firm in supplier activities in addition to its own. Both forward and backward integration are examples of vertical integration in the terminology of industrial organization economists. Horizontal integration, by contrast, refers to buying competitors at the product-distribution stage in which the firm is already operating. This strategy can be used to gain access to supply or distribution components which a competitor has and the firm itself wants; its purpose may really be vertical integration.

Classic vertical integration is costly and may not earn an appropriate return. Yet, integration need not be by ownership; fixed assets can be rented or coopted as well as owned. Contractual arrangements for input or output or for operating services can also accomplish the objectives of integration—that is, control and power—with much lower fixed cost commitments. Contracts, for example, can provide supply or distribution rights with less risk than the suppliers or distributors themselves carry. Sears and the Japanese auto makers are examples of powerful firms whose contracts with suppliers give them power with less risk than the suppliers themselves carry. Cartels are contractual arrangements dividing markets among a number of suppliers, and are thus an example of a contractual approach to horizontal integration. Cartels are common in business dealings outside the US; they are illegal restraints of competition in the US.

Integration can result in interdependence as well as power. Williamson (1975) rationalizes integration by describing the reduction in transaction costs between integrated components as more than compensating for less independence. The integrated oil industry is an example of a situation where the interdependencies between integrated components probably provide more effective, faster signals of market movements and so better responses than the independent components could generate individually.

McLean and Haigh (1954) take the example of integration still further as an alternative when they note that US oil companies have continuously changed positions in the chain, even jumping stages rather than simply moving one stage forward or backward. Changing position can be a valuable strategic alternative. In addition to investing in the most rewarding industry stages, an industry participant changing positions may bring valuable information, contacts, and experience which could raise the rewards and lower the risks of entry. For example, large shoe manufacturers in the US are now major retailers and importers, apparently using their traditional and tested fashion and distribution skills more profitably in merchandising imports rather than American-manufactured shoes. Such experience can be a source of synergy in the new position in the chain, enhancing performance beyond the level historically expected or available to other new entrants. And it may be a very appropriate way of transforming a company or revitalizing it—for example, in consolidating industries which no longer provide opportunities for the number of participants currently operating.

Diversification: The Product-Market Matrix

The product-market matrix shown in *Figure 11-2* provides a frequently overlooked framework for assessing served and neglected potential markets. In the matrix, customers define the market; product encompasses the current product, a simpler version of the same product, related and more technically advanced product forms, and unrelated product technologies. The results of the interactions of markets and product technologies when a

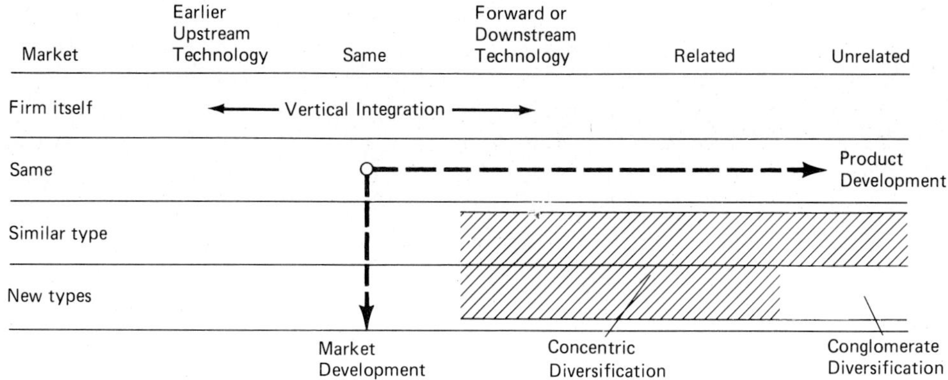

FIGURE 11-2 The Product-Market Matrix

firm is serving its own supply needs include integration and point to improvements in its own operations.

Product development occurs when the firm serves the same customers with an expanded product line. Market development uses the current technology to service additional markets. Concentric diversification is Ansoff's (1971) term for attempts to service additional markets with expanded technology offerings. Conglomerate diversification refers to business strategies offering unrelated products to new, unrelated customers.

The product-market matrix suggests directions for single-business expansion. In cases where no profitable potential markets or related technologies are apparent, it can point to diversification away from a single-business focus as a major strategic alternative—the single-business commitment may be considered too risky, while it seems that risk may be reduced by diversification.

MANAGING THE PROCESS OF GENERATING ALTERNATIVES

Creativity, Flexibility, and Timing

While we have described types of alternatives, we have thus far said little about the process of generating alternatives. Yet the process is a delicate one, and careful management of the process is likely to improve its results.

Probably the most important thing to remember about the process is that the likelihood of generating good-quality alternatives is increased if many alternatives are considered (DeBono, 1968; Janis and Mann, 1977). Few alternatives often indicate a stymied, nonproductive situation. Consider the following list of possible alternative types:

1. Status quo—"business as usual" is always an option.
2. Generic strategies to raise revenue and lower costs.
3. Actions which may alter stakeholder support and power.
4. The unthinkable—those actions that violate conventional wisdom.

Each of these strategic types holds a number of actions open to the firm. If they are never explicitly listed, they are unlikely to be adopted—and a very good approach to an opportunity or problem may be lost.

The objective of the process is to develop strategic alternatives which differentiate an organization from its competitors. Often the best alternative may integrate elements of some apparently inappropriate alternatives. Inhibiting creativity during the process—for example, by committing to an idea or evaluating it too soon—will limit the number and quality of suggestions with useful characteristics. Avoiding hasty evaluations and judgments which induce you to discard alternatives will allow you to rethink, rework, or combine them to make them more attractive. The practice of discarding suggestions too soon inhibits the creativity needed to develop alternatives. Nevertheless, creativity is needed to generate a relatively large number of alternatives, although the need for originality can be tempered if we realize that alternatives which represent strategic improvements are likely to have certain characteristics and comply with the principles described in the evaluation process (Chapter 10).

As we seek advantage and try to employ our resources as distinctively as possible, flexibility is important—call it adding degrees of strategic freedom, if you like. Flexibility to see things freshly and an ability to question current practice are important skills, yet they are difficult to maintain in practice. Familiarity, pressures for action and results, and other factors lead to an inability to think flexibly and insightfully.

Some flexibility is truly creative, although sometimes necessity is its mother. Indeed, many entrepreneurial ventures are successful only because the new owner "did not know it could not be done and had nothing to lose anyway" (Uyterhoeven et al., 1977, p. 49). Yet, expertise and market dominance can often lead to blindness, just as wealth can turn venturers into conservatives. People may fail to see the significance of current events or be unable to respond to them appropriately.

For example, many technological innovations have been made outside the bounds of the industries they have later captured. Presumably the incumbents had too large a commitment to the old way. As Cooper and Schendel (1976) found in their studies of technological threat, in mature industries, the outsider is likely to be the innovator; management and users alike are distracted by the new product's minor characteristics; managers rarely identify what it will take to succeed with the new technology; and established firms rarely make the right commitment early enough and large enough to win. Management was simply too inflexible to rethink the product, or found the situation too complex to handle well.

Timing is another variable sometimes neglected in the process of generating alternatives. Some alternatives will not work as expected without prior groundwork, and staging their implementation in steps can increase the probability of success as well as management's control. Management can react to results if those results unfold slowly rather than cataclysmically.

Thus, alternatives are best considered as actions to be taken at certain times, rather simply than as actions—with no sense or control of timing. Argyris (1977) writes of our need to monitor success, and this is facilitated if timing is a managerially controlled variable. Indeed, a limited early commitment provides results to guide further action.

Mental Blocks

Although many of the changes managers make to their strategies and operations are clearly straightforward responses to problems found in a strategy audit, these are usually minor in scope and are essentially a fine-tuning of the organization's strategy and the

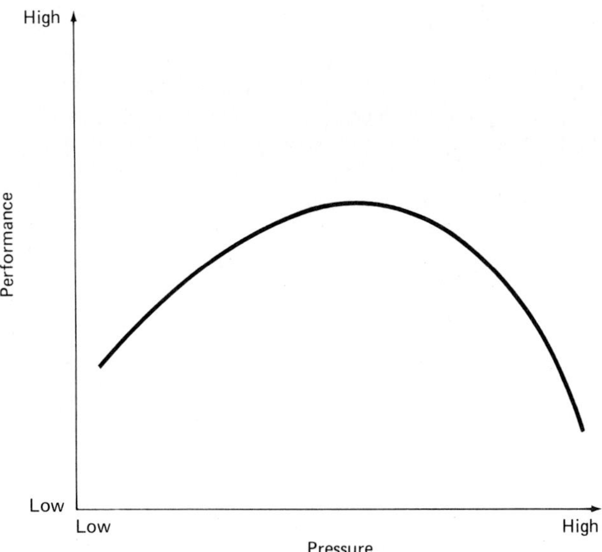

FIGURE 11-3 Pressure and Performance

operating systems which implement it. When larger changes are called for, generic and standardized "cookbook" strategies can often be adapted to serve the needs of the organization—raising revenues and lowering costs generally raises profits!

Sometimes, however, management is blocked. Being blocked is usually experienced as a feeling before it is recognized as a fact. Nonetheless, the feeling is usually a real sign that something is wrong in the process. Despite hard work and the passage of time, the company can find no way to improve its position and resolve the problems it sees.[2]

Mental blocks typically occur when the pressure is greatest. In fact, it is precisely when we need a broad perspective and some flexibility that we seem most prone to narrow our vision and find ourselves trapped in a mental block (DeBono, 1977; Ohmae, 1982). Although a little pressure prompts successful effort, too much quickly becomes dysfunctional and performance tends to falter, as the conceptual diagram of *Figure 11-3* suggests.

The block phenomenon is so pervasive that it warrants explicit attention. You are probably blocked when:

- you feel pressured and you are simultaneously unproductive;
- you recognize growing intolerance of others' points of view and an instinct to defend your point of view, a pattern repeated by your colleagues;
- priority is given to the loudest and most insistent voice, although you feel something is wrong but cannot specify what it is.

To some extent, these symptoms apply whether you are working alone or with others.

[2]The same thing often happens to students working on a case. Despite continued effort over time, progress is elusive and their frustration with the case and their colleagues grows.

FIGURE 11-4 Behavior Blocking New Thoughts

1. "Tunnel vision," when all attention is focused on the wrong response, like a wild animal frozen by the headlights of an oncoming car.
2. "The all-or-none fallacy," when management defines its options as a 0:1, go–no-go situation—for example, defining action against competitive entry as a success if the entry is completely prevented and as a total loss otherwise. It might be possible to take advantage of the entry by a competitor to have the overall market grow while preserving a powerful market position. Essentially this is a perverse form of greed.
3. "Perils of perfectionism": an unwillingness to commit to action until even subtle and often irrelevant details are attended to. An example might be to delay market entry until a totally pre-emptive strategy is developed, although you have developed a strategy which promises a relative competitive advantage.
4. "Loss of perspective": focusing on the details to the exclusion of the key factors that truly make a difference—for example, worrying about the costing details of a TV advertising campaign while your manufacturing costs substantially exceed your competitor's.
5. Failure to challenge constraints, especially self-imposed constraints. For example, consider the plight of a product manager, who controls only the marketing strategy for his product, confronting a corporate pressure for higher margins. Not controlling overhead or fixed or variable manufacturing costs, he feels trapped but does not consider price or service charges which may help sales and margins, at least in the short run.

Source: Adapted from Ohmae, *The Mind of the Strategist,* New York, NY: McGraw Hill, 1982.

Different types of blocking observed by Ohmae (1982) are listed in *Figure 11-4*. In all these circumstances, management's thinking is inflexible. Typically, under pressure, people are blind to opportunity. To break out of their own personal boxes, managers need to take a different point of view, perhaps their boss's or their customers', and change their perspective. They should use the new point of view to add new variables and flexibility to their thinking.

Recognizing the block is the first step toward a cure and possibly the way to a breakthrough. Blocked problems tend to be ''we can't do's'' seeking solutions. Ohmae says that a ''can do'' attitude is needed; DeBono says we should focus on the benefits of opportunity. One way to gain perspective is to concentrate on the key factors of success and drop the detail—that is, administratively delegate the less urgent and focus on the most important.

Essentially, blocks are not simply cognitive failures. They involve cognitive, social, and emotional factors (Emshoff, Mitroff and Kilman, 1978). They involve self-centeredness rather than other-centeredness, for example, a focus on operations rather than on the customers, or on divisional operations rather than on the corporate strategy.

Breaking Mental Blocks

Breaking blocks requires hard work and smart flexible thinking. Remember, Edison said invention is 98% perspiration and 2% inspiration. Moreover, we should not be content with a satisfactory solution. We should strive for flexibility, new perspectives, and choice.

More alternatives provide an opportunity for wiser and more confident choices. Having choices means we have degrees of strategic freedom, an ability to follow variations on strategic themes to achieve our objectives. Such freedom does not come from the presence of slack resources alone. Choices can be provided by insightful and creative management, too. Sometimes an abstract concept of the business promotes innovation, although most businesses begin with very tangibly defined products and services and never change. Levitt (1975) addressed such conservatism and the potential costs of a narrowly defined and inflexible concept of the business in ''Marketing Myopia.''

A New Concept of the Business

The Bic Pen Corporation is a good example of a flexible company whose self-concept changed. It began making ballpoint pen refills and gradually expanded its product line to include disposable ballpoint pens, retractable pens, and porous-tip pens. Later, it added cigarette lighters, pantyhose, and disposable razors. In the process, management changed its self-concept from ''pens'' to ''writing instruments,'' then to ''manufacturers and marketers of high quality, everyday disposable products distributed through writing instrument channels,'' and next to a ''marketing company.'' Management moved from tangible to abstract in its concept of its business. The test of such a concept is its productivity: Does it lead the company to new products? *Figure 11-5* illustrates Bic's conceptual evolution.

Adaptation and flexibility such as Baron Bich's at Bic is often a result of exerience. When logic does not work, try intuition to develop a new approach—intuition is your collective experience at work. The work of the Applied Research Center at the Wharton School of the University of Pennsylvania, for example, emphasizes stakeholders and stakeholder interests as opposed to the strategic and environmental analysis we emphasized. A focus on customer, competition, and company is a three-phased check list which Ohmae (1982) uses to generate ideas. The test, of course, is always productivity.

Exploiting Analogy

While it sometimes pays to be very detail-oriented, identifying key factors and restructuring them in the light of simple widely shared analogies is offen productive. This particularly is true of one-on-one competitive situations.

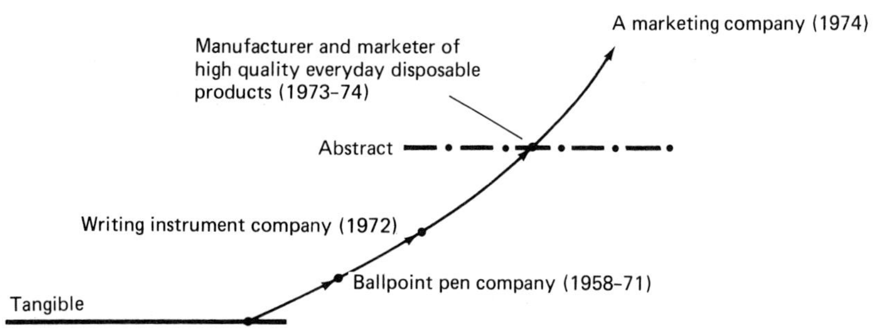

FIGURE 11-5 Conceptual Evolution of a Business: Bic

When Kodak entered the instant camera business in 1976, observers rated Polaroid and Kodak as shown in *Figure 11-6* on each of seven factors (the plus signs indicate advantage). Kodak was judged to have a more experienced and accomplished marketing force, with more numerous and more loyal outlets than Polaroid. Yet many felt that Polaroid, as the innovator in instant photography, had product technology as well as brand recognition on its side. In 1976, Polaroid had its SX70 operations running profitably at about 40 percent capacity, producing 2 million units per year, while Kodak was not yet producing instant cameras or film in commercial quantities. Kodak had broken with its traditional practice of simultaneous national and worldwide new product introduction—the company planned a phased North American rollout beginning in Canada in May and later in Florida. Also, many felt Polaroid had a short-run advantage in its manufacturing operations that Kodak would ultimately erode. Kodak was about five times larger than Polaroid and so had the financial advantage. Polaroid had Edwin Land, a brilliant inventor but an apparently inflexible man, as CEO. Kodak had professional, institutionalized management and had managed succession well.

Focusing on the details and attempting to develop options quickly is an overwhelming task. However, focusing on the skeletal outline of relative advantage can be quite productive. Putting ourselves in the shoes of Polaroid's managers, we could apply the principle of strength against weakness, which would suggest a Polaroid assault head-on against Kodak's new product, avoiding Kodak's marketing and financial strengths.

Using an analogy from the martial arts and self-defense, we might begin to think of ways to actually use Kodak's money and marketing muscle to Polaroid's advantage. A military analogy would tell us to attack when Kodak enters the instant-camera market and before its presence is well-established. A lesson of the fairy tale of "The Three Little Pigs" is that wolves shouldn't climb down chimneys but work in the open range where their strengths give them an advantage. What is Polaroid's range? Is it technology? Could Polaroid manufacture and supply the market in advance of Kodak's entry and cut price either to stimulate its own sales and Kodak's response, and thereby delay Kodak's achievement of breakeven, or else to gain sales in a growing market stimulated by Kodak's introductory advertising? The point here is not to be exhaustive or detailed, nor do we intend to explicitly consider Kodak's and Polaroid's responses and reactions.

FIGURE 11-6 Relative Advantage: Polaroid vs. Kodak

	Polaroid	*Kodak*
Marketing		+
Product technology	+	
Brand	+	
Operations		
Short-term	+	
Long-term		+
Finance		+
Management		+
Edwin Land	+/−	

Rather, we have briefly demonstrated how analogy and focus on a few key factors can quickly stimulate the development of useful strategy alternatives in a tough situation.

A New Perspective: An Industry Focus

While our focus in the Polaroid/Kodak situation was on companies, sometimes our concentration should shift to the industry. The paper industry is capital-intense and employs very large-scale plants. The biggest producers, like International Paper, are vertically integrated back to the forests and have their own fuel supplies. How could a small company operate in this industry? How could it position its plant close to its source of materials and overcome the large companies' scale advantage? One company, Clevepak, entered the industry as a manufacturer by using scrap paper as its raw material. Clevepak created a supply advantage by locating not in the woods but near its supply in the city. It countered International's cost economies due to scale by choosing value-conscious small markets characterized by relative price inelasticity. It then buttressed its position with unusually generous service. It developed a niche by servicing not the large paper-users but small specialty-goods manufacturers who needed small numbers of special packaging boxes and cardboard containers which could not be supplied economically by the largest paper manufacturers. Clevepak, a small company, recognized every characteristic of the major players in its industry and found a way to neutralize or duplicate each characteristic's competitive impact.

Intractable Problems

Clevepak's strategy, systematically creating competitive capability in an industry by overcoming the rules of the game, is an example of the experience-founded thinking required when a strategic problem is truly difficult, but sometimes problems arise which are outside our available experience. For example, large environmental changes which threaten the continued viability of the organization may develop or are foreseen. What to do then?

When normal methods do not work, we must take a different tack and turn from logic, or vertical thinking, to what DeBono (1968) called lateral thinking. He describes it:

> Instead of proceeding step by step . . . you take up a new and quite arbitrary position. You then work backwards and try to construct a logical path between this new position and the starting point. (p. 15)

Emshoff, Mitroff, and Kilman (1978) offer advice in the form of a question we might use to get us started with lateral thinking in a business context: ''How would you redesign your organization and its environment so that it is perfect or ideal?'' They term this approach ''idealized planning.''

Idealized Planning: Strategic Assumptions Analysis

Such an approach to intractable problems discards the constraints which block thinking, drops details that confuse things, and focuses attention on the whole organization. The purpose is to identify new solutions or opportunities and then find strategies to realize their potential. By specifying an ideal and then the implicit assumptions needed to support that ideal, we may be able to develop a framework which is consistent with those assumptions and reality, and so form the basis for a feasible new strategy. This approach has been formalized by Mitroff and Emshoff (1979) in the strategic planning context as Strategic Assumptions Analysis and will be discussed in detail in Chapter 16.

Various techniques can be used to develop a vision of a perfect world. We can simplify complexity and reduce the number of factors we have to deal with simultaneously. We can brainstorm—accept spontaneous thoughts and even absurd ideas from members of a group, and work off them in every way we can. We can use analogy, approximation, or the distortion of a dominant constraint, we can bridge polarized ideas to help everyone see things differently, or even take exactly opposite points of view to help us see things freshly.

It is not a matter of working hard and long on intractable problems in order to achieve results. Rather, it is important to create a climate of trust so that people can explore their environment and their strategy and envision a better future. Once that future is seen, a path can be built back to current reality, and then direction can be reversed to achieve the desired future.

Organizations need the inspiration of radical change when the apparent alternatives fail the test of evaluation and when the portents are bleak. If management sees this need early it can prepare, test alternatives, and develop the organization by conditioning it for change.

No Apparent Problem

If there is no problem, DeBono (1968) wrote, there is no chance of progress, either. One function of management is to shape problems, even to create them. When the absence of widely recognized problems looms large, the ingenuity and energy of general management is needed most.

Andrews (1980) refers to the role of general managers as "architects of strategy." By serving as architects of the possible future and as proponents of a vision which they can use to shape problems and opportunities, garner support and guide action, general managers make one of their major contributions to their firms. Vision, plus the energy, patience, and sense of timing to implement it, add up to success.

EVERY MANAGER CAN CONTRIBUTE

The excitement and the responsibility of generating alternatives is not the exclusive province of top management. Top, middle, and functional managers all have roles to play and contributions to make.

Generating alternatives is followed by evaluation, commitment, and implementation. The first three of these steps encompass the resource allocation process (Bower, 1970), a process which requires the interaction of many managerial levels. To advance through the resource allocation process, a proposal or an alternative has to be given definition and then impetus. *Definition* refers to fleshing out an alternative, giving it substantive content and the technical details which differentiate it from others. *Impetus* is the outcome of committed support within the organization, the phase when the alternative's merits are argued and advocated to move it towards approval.

During the resource allocation process, the *context* of the organization will be felt. Context determines what is acceptable and influences both definition and impetus. Context results from the culture and practices of the organization. It is affected by the way strategy is articulated, by the way work is organized and controlled and rewarded, and by the example set by top management. DeBono describes how two contributors to context, rewards and example, can thwart innovation in many large companies:

> You almost have the paradox [in large companies] that anyone intelligent enough to innovate is intelligent enough not to, because the chances of success are pretty small and if you make a mistake it can hang around your neck for the rest of your career. (1977, p. 57)

Addressing the roles of managers in developing alternatives, Bower (1970) notes that in most mature organizations lower-level managers define the problem while middle managers give it impetus and top management sets context. At the lowest level, specialists and functional managers confront specific problems and use their expert knowledge to solve them. At the second level, the middle managers who are the generalists integrate the work of the specialists they supervise and so give impetus to alternatives by:

1 deciding which proposals will go forward for approval;
2 providing liaison between senior management and specialists, clarifying corporate purpose for the specialists, and abstracting and translating technical detail for senior managers (Uyterhoeven, 1972);
3 accepting personal risk by staking their own reputation on proposals, that is, underwriting them.

These roles illustrate practice, but are not necessarily normative guides.

In reality, managers at every level must play a part in definition, impetus, and context development, depending upon their expertise, their interest and the strength of the management resources of the firm. For example, in small firms, one person may take every role. In rapidly growing firms, there may be few experienced managers to give a proposal impetus. Other mechanisms, including involvement of board members and consultants, will have to be used to test ideas and underwrite them.

Participation in developing alternatives is part of every manager's job, for it is only through the alternatives it generates that the organization implements its strategy and moves from analysis to action. Here, we have introduced the ideas leading to implementation to make the point that there are many roles that must be played in developing an alternative strategy for an organization or one of its parts. We will extend the administrative aspect of our discussion later in Chapter 14.

PREVIEW

The Strategic Management System, *Figure 11-7*, reminds us that strategic management is more than strategy formulation alone. Although our work thus far has focused on the left-hand side of the model, emphasizing the results of strategic action in a changing environ-

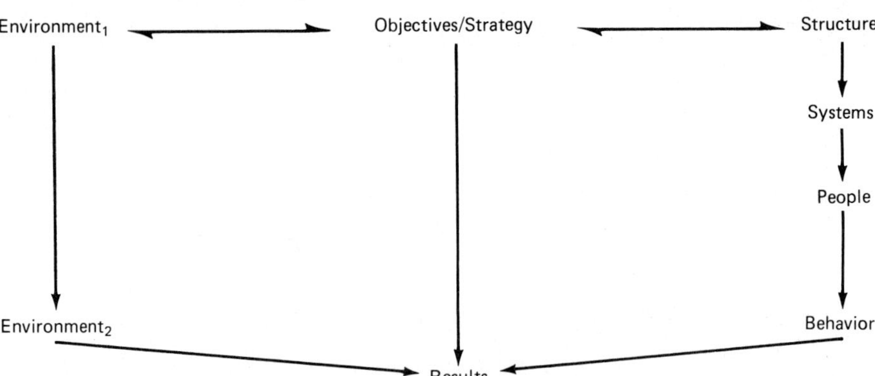

FIGURE 11-7 The Strategic Management System

ment, the results earned are not only conditional on the future but also on the behavior of the people in our organization. When evaluation points to problems, there are many possibilities for adjustment within the organization, short of a strategy change. These include the structure, systems, and people of the organization. In all these change sites, of course, less change is normally less costly and quicker. Indeed, the problems worth solving in the firm may be primarily administrative rather than strategic. We will discuss administrative aspects of the firm in detail in Chapter 14.

chapter 12

Evaluating Alternatives

INTRODUCTION

Evaluating alternatives is similar to evaluating a firm's current strategy, since we must consider how each alternative fits with the firm's resources, environment, and stakeholder objectives and values. But, unlike a strategy in use, new alternatives do not have a history, a track of results, to give us confidence in their future success. For this reason, the evaluation of new alternative strategies is more uncertain than attempts to evaluate a firm's current strategy, and so there is a greater risk of error.

Because a wrong course puts the firm's resources, its gain from earlier ventures, at risk, a commitment to the wrong strategy can be costly. Management may miss opportunity by conservatively sticking with an old strategy too long. The opposite type of error is adopting a new strategy which a more thorough analysis could have proven unfeasible. Whether we are too conservative or too casual in our evaluation, the sources of error lie in our own capabilities and in the uncertain future environment.

As we evaluate our alternatives, we must deal with the consequences of perceived uncertainty and limited information and with the fear that a competitor knows something we do not. We may feel internal discord stemming from personal limits and desires for personal advantage, gaps in our information base, uncertainty about the future, and the possibility that we are wrong. We may have misunderstandings and conflict over resources with powerful adversaries, and the possibility exists that we have oversimplified our world in the search for alternatives.

Strategists have recognized these problems for many years and have learned to live with and even enjoy uncertainty. Robert Price, former President and Chief Operating Officer of Control Data Corporation, wrote:

> Contrary to conventional wisdom, however, uncertainty is a positive force. Consider a world with no uncertainty—that is, perfect knowledge of everything. What would business look like? Every market would be dominated almost completely by one major supplier. That supplier would have no effective competitors because it would be making every decision with perfect knowledge. . . . Uncertainty gives rise to opportunities. (1982, p. 3)

Uncertainty, information gaps, and opportunity go together. Uncertainty leads to errors, and errors to opportunity. People see the future and interpret the present differently, so they act differently and get different results. DeBono (1968) points out that problems and opportunities ''jolt us out of the smooth rut of adequacy.'' In this sense, problems are the gateway to progress, and alternatives are the keys to opportunity. In this chapter, we discuss ways to evaluate alternatives which limit the risk and reduce the attendant uncertainty while creating viable opportunities for the firm.

COPING WITH UNCERTAINTY

The Importance of Choice

Probably the most important characteristic of the effective decision making process is choice: a larger list of alternatives will normally include more good quality alternatives than a brief set. Indeed, Janis and Mann (1977) make a ''wide range of alternatives'' the first of their seven ideal procedural criteria for quality decision making. When you have more choices, the evaluation process will give you more confidence that you have selected the best, because the ultimate choice won out over so many.

Such confidence is particularly important for organizations facing a need for radical strategic changes, changes for which there is no relevant history or experience. Radical changes are inherently riskier to implement because of the organization's lack of relevant experience, so selecting an alternative which has prevailed over many others increases our ability to ''sell'' it to the organization. Confidence stemming from a broadly based comparison process can actually induce greater commitment from those who would otherwise have been indifferent or hostile to major, untried change. DeBono wrote:

> Confidence in a decision does not depend on the lack of any alternative, for that might only indicate a lack of imagination, but on the ability to see many alternatives, all of which can be rejected. (1968, p. 149)

If management has compared a new strategy with many alternatives, we may safely say that although the prospective change may be untried, it certainly cannot be criticized as untested.

Thoroughness

Thoroughness in evaluation is especially important when considering future alternatives, because fit with a firm's resources, environment, and stakeholder objectives and values constitutes the sole source of evaluatory information. Without historical experience, we must be confident about fit. It is tempting to skip steps in strategic management, but skipping steps in the evaluation of alternatives can have dire consequences because already minimal information is further reduced.

Thorough evaluation must encompass the resources needed to support the alternative. While uncertainty about the future and risk are ever-present in untried alternatives, it is foolish to put the firm at risk because its strategy cannot be supported by the firm's resource base. Indeed, defining resource requirements is one part of evaluating alternatives which can be done with virtual certainty. Evaluating resource adequacy thus is an important, although frequently overlooked, test which can increase confidence in a chosen alternative. With adequate resources, the risks of a new strategy are somewhat reduced. Resources ensure that the firm can operate in the future. Strategies supported by inadequate resources endanger the firm, because they may destroy the firm's financial independence.

Unfounded Optimism

Thorough evaluation can remedy one of the most common errors of alternative evaluation: unfounded optimism. It has been vividly described by Hirschman in his study of international economic development projects:

> People typically take on and plunge into new tasks because of the erroneously presumed absence of a challenge, because the task looks easier and more manageable than it will turn out to be. (1967, p. 13)

Hirschman found that when planning their activities, people have a tendency to overlook threats to the viability of a strategy and a complementary tendency to overlook remedial actions which could be taken if a threat materializes. He called this ability to implement remedial actions the work of the ''Hiding Hand,'' which actually protects the outcome of the strategy. He warned that the champions of innovation (see Schoen's article, 1969) and new ideas tend to exaggerate the benefits of the strategy and discount its difficulties. Hirschman alerts us to typical errors:

- Pseudo-transferability: imitation of well-known successes elsewhere. If it is said to be like other successful ventures, we believe we understand it and that it has low risk.
- Pseudo-comprehensiveness: solving all the sponsor organization's problems in one fell swoop.

Hirschman concludes that individuals really do not believe in creativity and so see it as a surprise when it occurs. He says we essentially underestimate ourselves and tend to limit ourselves to problems we think we can solve, thereby falling into error—and occasionally opportunity.

Hirschman suggests a simple remedy for these errors: thorough identification of vulnerabilities and interdependencies, and the specification of the steps and results along the way. Thorough evaluation allows the interdependencies inherent in any strategy to be tested early and the outcomes of change to be monitored while adaptation is still possible.

Henderson (1979) cited three advantages of a rigorous and objective examination of a problem, that is, of a situation where something has gone awry: the discovery of invalid assumptions underlying the strategy; the discovery of neglected interactions resulting in suboptimization; and, finally, the discovery of a new, more powerful conceptual framework to explain the source of the problem and the likely impact of change. This third point suggests the opportune nature of strategic problems and links us again to Hirschman's ''Hiding Hand,'' bringing successful strategic results.

Contingency Plans

Contingency planning is another way to cope with uncertainty. It is based on an explicit recognition that the situation may not proceed as desired. Contingency planning prepares managers for uncertain situations and gives them practice in adapting to an unfolding reality.

Contingency plans specify actions needed to achieve our objectives if the original plan does not work out. Contingency planning is appropriate when alternatives are under evaluation. Alternatives which achieve desired objectives even with contingencies are superior, since they are robust across a wider variety of situations.

Using Intuition in Evaluation

Along with being as thorough as possible, do not devalue the contribution of intuition in the evaluation process. Intuition is experience at work. In an apparently irrational way, but in fact almost super-rationally, an experienced manager's intuition will give him or her insights to the overall effect of an alternative strategy by testing it against all his or her previous experience.

Intuition is usually active at the beginning and end of the strategic management process. Intuition is initially used to select problems worth pursuing, and intuition is finally used to synthesize all the evaluation information generated into a judgment and a decision which can be implemented by the organization. Henderson (1979) writes that consensus plays an important role in tapping the intuitive skills of management, because consensus is founded on "the wisest intuitive judgment of diversely experienced people."

Consensus and Support

Consensus building garners intuitive experience from many and so is a form of political thoroughness. As well, it has the side benefit of facilitating action. To cite Henderson:

> Implementation . . . is difficult if discussion and consensus have not been continued long enough to make the relationship between the overall objectives and the specific action seem clear to all who must interpret and implement required policies. Otherwise, the intuition of those who do the implementation will be used to redefine the policies which emerged from analysis. (1979, p. 45)

One CEO described his way of enforcing consensus development during his twenty-two-year term as president:

> If you're responsible for an area of the business and you report to me, you have all my authority to make decisions. The only requirement is that after the fact you have to convince me that you have thought through the rationale of your action, and that you had discussed it with everybody in the company who would be affected or who, on the basis of past experience, could contribute to your decision. You talk to me only if you aren't sure about your rationale for a decision, or you aren't sure who you ought to talk to.[1]

[1]Fletcher Byron of the Koppers Co., quoted by Myerson and Carey (1982).

Consensus about both means and ends, strategies and objectives, deserves consideration. Bourgeois concluded his study of the strategic decision making in twelve non-diversified public corporations of the Pacific Northwest as follows:

> Consensus on means always yields higher performance than disagreement on means, while allowing disagreement on less tangible goals tends to be associated with better performance. Also, the worst performance results come from goals agreement combined with means disagreement—i.e., when a firm agrees on where it wants to go but can't agree on how to get there! (1980, p. 243)

Because successful performance requires implementation, consensus on means is critical.

OPPORTUNITIES TO REDUCE UNCERTAINTY

Although managers must always cope with uncertainty when dealing with the future, some types of evaluation thinking and planning can reduce the level of uncertainty and so increase confidence that the alternative chosen will perform as expected. Methods to reduce uncertainty include careful analysis of assumptions and evaluation of stakeholder interests. Thinking about how to time implementation and how to monitor results over time also reduces the unknowns in the implementation process and allows adaptation to achieve the desired results, as Hirschman pointed out.

While the historical track of an alternative strategy cannot normally be evaluated, the assumptions underlying its expected future can be analyzed. Such analysis serves to reduce uncertainty because the outcome is more likely to be as expected if the assumptions seem plausible. Strategy which depends for its success on unsupportable assumptions is very dangerous and cannot be recommended.

Careful evaluation of stakeholder interests can also reduce the uncertainty stemming from unknown stakeholder reactions. Any strategy needs stakeholder support, particularly that of stakeholders within the organization. Thus, the strategy most likely to succeed should accommodate and build on stakeholder interests. Alternatives which violate important stakeholder values are in for tough sledding, and alternatives which require the formation of different stakeholder values carry more risk and require more managerial effort than those which build on current values. An understanding of stakeholders' interests gives us insight to their likely reactions under pressure; thus the uncertainty due to unknown reactions is limited.

Strategies to be implemented over time can be evaluated over time. This allows the firm's commitment to be limited and the period of uncertainty shortened, making the situation easier to understand and handle. If we evaluate an alternative strategy's likely implementation sequence, we can interpret results that vary from the expected and develop contingency plans to get back on track.

To emphasize the value of experiments, trials, and market tests, note that time and results achieved over time help build organizational support for a new strategy. Certain values, such as pride in a distinctive competence, can be nurtured and developed over time to ensure success. But when we evaluate an alternative, we must weigh the managerial costs in time and effort of building consensus support against the likely rewards of success.

EVALUATING ALTERNATIVES: A SUMMARY

Good managers don't just make strategic decisions; they make chosen strategies work. *Figure 12-1* provides a set of questions to test alternatives. These questions are organized within the resources–environment–stakeholder framework to address internal uncertain-

FIGURE 12-1 Tests to Evaluate a Future Strategy

Internally Focused:
Resources and Internal Stakeholders

RESOURCES

Resource Adequacy/Feasibility

Does the company have the resources to succeed?

Can it afford the risks of the strategy?

Flexibility

Will the commitment necessary preserve the company's flexibility?

Are the risks taken warranted by the rewards expected?

Can the decision be reversed, and at what cost?

Controllability

Can the company afford to succeed?

Does management know how to gauge whether the strategy is working?

What problems will be resolved? What will be created?

INTERNAL STAKEHOLDERS

Stakeholder Adequacy

Will it satisfy internal stakeholder objectives?

Value Compatibility

Will the organization's critical stakeholders go along with it?

Impact on Management Harmony

Who opposes the strategy commitment?

What is the organizational and personal cost of commitment?

Externally Focused:
Environment and External Stakeholders

ENVIRONMENT

Competitive Advantage

Does the strategy enhance the company's competitive strengths?

Is the company competitively early, late, or "on time"?

Is it far-sighted or merely expedient?

Does the strategy create and exploit a situation of imbalance—i.e., does it focus maximum resources against minimum opposition?

Does it preserve the firm's distinctive competence?

Is it robust?

Conventional Wisdom

Does the strategy violate conventional wisdom?

How do you know it will work?

Contingency Tests

What assumptions are implicit in the strategy? Are they viable—e.g., does the success of the strategy depend on an economic upswing?

EXTERNAL STAKEHOLDERS

Reactions

Does the strategy assume that the company's competitors are smart?

Does it allow for intelligent reactions by the competitors? Does it allow for irrational or emotional reactions by the competitors?

Vulnerabilities

What are the strategy's vulnerabilities?

Could it be caught in cross-impact?

The Ultimate Test

Does the strategy provide value to the ultimate customer?

Is the strategy consistent with the reality of the industry chain?

Does it acknowledge the real power of competitors, suppliers, distributors, customers, and regulators?

ties within the organization and external uncertainties originating in the environment. They test the strength of the strategy in relating the firm and its environment. The ultimate test, of course, is whether the strategy will create value.

With the information of *Figure 12-1,* the manager can anticipate problems or spot signs of trouble, monitor trends which herald their occurrence, and plan for contingencies. Evaluation provides managers with information on their chosen strategy before they commit to it. For example, it should identify potentially troublesome issues likely to affect the success of the strategy.

Time is a manager's ally. By understanding and using the flexibility that time gives, the manager can adapt and change resource commitments to keep the organization in phase with its developing environment, opportunities, and resource base. It is, of course, better to ride trends than to fight them. The latter is a risky approach while the former, by using the environment, accepts reality and turns it to advantage.

An evaluation of alternatives will identify areas of bad fit between strategies and the firm's resources, environment, and stakeholders. Using this information, the manager can modify and rework any alternative he or she believes is an opportunity, using the better elements of one option to reinforce the positive characteristics of another, and using other elements to neutralize the negative characteristic of otherwise acceptable strategies. The result can be a "super option" whose results in terms of value creation will surpass the original, and with lower risk.

Unless the manager is confident that a strategy will work within the constraints of the firm's resources, environment, and stakeholder values, the strategy should not be implemented. Companies and careers should be bet on "very likely" results, not "maybe's" or "possibly's." This is why the most commonly implemented strategic alternatives are modifications of the original strategy with which the firm has experience and so less risk. Vickers (1965) wrote of the need for judgment in the strategic management process; judgment is obviously necessary when alternative future strategies are being evaluated.

chapter 13

Reading the Corporate Culture: Prelude to Executive Action

INTRODUCTION

Throughout this book we have stressed the importance of fact-founded decision making, that is, making decisions in the light of facts and what we believe those facts mean. With this chapter, we turn from analysis to strategy implementation, and our principal concern becomes the design of the administrative strategy. In the design of that strategy, again the facts of organizational life matter.

In particular, in this brief chapter we want to attract your attention to the informal organization and to behavior that is not defined in any formal way. Experience demonstrates that practice varies from design in most organizations, sometimes supportively and sometimes not. In designing an administrative strategy, organizational practices and beliefs must be honored: The realities of organizational life must be the foundations of executive action. For this reason, we now examine "culture," an umbrella concept which encompasses all the actual behavior and beliefs of the organization, and the role of culture in administration.

CULTURE

Organizational culture has many faces or manifestations in every organization and is important to every firm. Schwartz and Davis (1981) say that culture ". . . may be the most accurate reflection of why things work the way they do, and of why some firms succeed with their strategies while others fail."

What is culture? Marvin Bower's (1966) simple definition, "it's the way we do things around here," expresses the informal nature of culture. Attempts to change an organization and its strategy that are incompatible with ''the way we do things'' are likely to be met with resistance, confusion, and ultimately failure.

Another definition of culture that fits with our strategic concerns is that of anthropologist Clyde Kluckhohn. Culture is

> . . . the set of habitual and traditional ways of thinking, feeling and reacting that are characteristic of the ways a particular society meets its problems at a particular point in time. (1949)

The words ''habitual'' and ''characteristic'' point to patterns of behavior which reflect the shared attitudes and values of management and, as Schwartz and Davis (1981) point out, particularly reflect the values, beliefs, and norms that served top managers and their company well during their own rise to power. Citing another anthropologist, C.S. Ford (1967), Schwartz and Davis note that culture is ''composed of responses that have been accepted because they met with success.'' They add, ''It is these choices that continually reaffirm the corporation's culture and reinforce the expected behavior across the organization'' (1981, p. 35).

Culture, then, is a manifestation of deeply rooted behavior. Ultimately, it may become an almost instinctive behavioral characteristic of an organization (and its management). It defines what is expected of the members of the organization in every situation and is transmitted from manager to manager informally, that is, by example.

STRATEGY AND CULTURE

Learning to understand organizational culture is important to fit in, create change, and even break the norms effectively on occasion. You need to be able to read the organization quickly and accurately if you are to:

1. formulate strategies that fit the organization;
2. implement them efficiently and effectively; and
3. survive within the organization and prosper.

Our strategies and personal actions must be consistent with the organization's culture, or we signal that we or our ideas do not fit. Consequently, only if we have the power and resources to sustain a very extended commitment can we consider taking the risk of culture change. Schwartz and Davis write:

> All steps must be prefaced by strong top leadership creating the pressure for change coupled with new top management behavior that sets the example. It is also necessary to have a united front at the top for the sake of sending consistent messages to other managers. The pivotal word is commitment—the commitment to initiate the cultural change and the staying power to see it through. (1981, p. 44)

Nevertheless, however, what Deal and Kennedy (1982) call ''outlaws'' can be tolerated in an existing strong culture. Usually very competent people, outlaws deliberately violate cultural norms, and survive. Their survival stems from the contributions they make, such as contributions to continued organizational evolution, new product development, or even the relief of pressure, as the jester did in the king's court. Even so, they satisfy the main requirements of the culture—their loyalty is never in doubt.

To illustrate the concept of the outlaw in the organization, Deal and Kennedy (1982) cite a story told about Thomas Watson, Jr., the son of the founder of IBM, and himself its chairman. "The duck who is tame will never go anywhere anymore," he said. "We are convinced that business needs its wild ducks and in IBM we try not to tame them." The story continues to describe an employee who once told Watson, "Even wild ducks fly in formation." Watson added this characteristic of organizational outlaws to his analogy, noting that their contributions were in a single (corporate) direction.

Culture is founded in shared values and indeed is a manifestation of those values. Culture affects the people and people affect the culture. The culture supporting the underlying values largely controls behavior in such organizations as Hewlett Packard, Lincoln Electric, and McDonald's. Indeed, we can note that:

> The main point of reference for analyzing the structure of any social system is its value pattern. This defines the basic orientation of the system (in this case the organization) to the situation in which it operates; hence it guides the activities of participant individuals. (Parsons, 1956, p. 67)

Thus, culture is a key element of strategy implementation and is anchored in the values of the organization's internal stakeholders.

IDENTIFYING CULTURE

The pattern of values gives us a ready handle on an organization's culture, and vice versa. If we can identify these values from what the company says are the reasons for its success, from the myths and analogies used to describe it, and from the behavior it is organized to encourage, we will be able to trace the values' influence throughout the organization.

A fruitful avenue for culture indentification is to track the powerful. Can we identify those who really succeed? For example, are they generalists or specialists? What career tracks pay off? What managerial roles are powerful? How long have the top people been with the company? What was the critical organizational problem which they solved? These questions point to patterns which reveal the corridors of organizational power which top management believes serve the organization well.

By identifying powerful organizational roles and by tracking the careers of those who hold them, we can learn how power is gained and lost. If we want to do so and have the self-discipline to persist, we can use this information to guide our own success. Moreover, by understanding how power is networked and structured in the organization, we may be able to influence its locus and even change it, if change is needed and we have sufficient power to do so.

A definite parallel exists between organizations in industries and the managers in organizations. Success in both contexts depends on a capacity to mobilize power. Given its industry role, an organization's success depends on its power to accumulate and use resources to achieve its objectives. Within an organization, a manager, too, has a role and must develop power to mobilize resources and achieve objectives.

In the earlier chapter on industry analysis, we examined the firm's role and power and used that knowledge to formulate business strategy. Here we advocate the use of the concepts of managerial role and power to analyze the organization and ultimately mobilize its resources. Reading the culture and understanding roles and power in the organization are first steps toward developing effective administrative strategies and successful executive action.

READING THE CULTURE

Given the two concepts of role and power, how can we use them to read the organization? We have already suggested the identification of superordinate objectives and tracking the careers of those who are powerful. Moreover, our earlier chapters evaluating strategy emphasized results. What are the actions and results that reveal how the organization works?

Culture is revealed by shared, repeated, and habitual behavior—that is, by the patterns of action—while the organization's reactions to the results which those actions deliver reveal what is valued. Hence, to read culture, we must study how managers work; how they work through, with, and around others to get results; and how they use those results to increase their autonomy and power.

How are critical problems defined, critical relationships formed, and tasks carried out? Schwartz and Davis (1981) suggest identifying the ways critical management tasks are carried out in the context of particular key relationships and tasks, and offer a simple Culture Matrix, shown in *Figure 13-1,* to assemble the data. In *Figure 13-1,* each line

FIGURE 13-1 Corporate Culture Matrix

	Relationships			
Tasks	*Companywide*	*Boss-subordinate*	*Peer*	*Interdepartment*
Innovating				
Decision making				
Communicating				
Organizing				
Monitoring				
Appraising and rewarding				

Source: Reprinted by permission of the publisher, from Howard Schwartz and Stanley M. Davis, "'Matching Corporate Culture and Business Strategy," *Organizational Dynamics,* Summer 1981, pp. 36, 38. © 1981 AMACOM, a division of American Management Associations; all rights reserved.

describes how a critical task is managed in the context of particular relationships. While serving as a check list, the table highlights interactions and can help you give meaning to the anecdotes or corporate myths and legends which convey organizational norms. *Figure 13-2* summarizes the culture matrix for the international banking division of a large US bank and suggests the kinds of data needed to understand how things are done. The data for such an inventory could come from company interviews or documents, the business press, or simply from your observations of the company at work. Note, however, that Schwartz and Davis restrict both matrices to internal matters. In some organizations, relationships with outsiders, such as suppliers and customers, are managed culturally—that is, the relating is culturally consistent and fits the organization's sense of self.

FIGURE 13-2 Summary of Cultural Risk Assessment (international banking division)

Relationships	*Culture Summary*
Companywide	Preserve your autonomy. Allow area managers to run the business as long as they meet the profit budget.
Boss-subordinate	Avoid confrontations. Smooth over disagreements. Support the boss.
Peer	Guard information; it is power. Be a gentleman or lady.
Interdepartment	Protect your department's bottom line. Form alliances around specific issues. Guard your turf.

Tasks	*Culture Summary*
Innovating	Consider it risky. Be a quick second.
Decision making	Handle each deal on its own merits. Gain consensus. Require many sign-offs. Involve the right people. Seize the opportunity.
Communicating	Withhold information to control adversaries. Avoid confrontations. Be a gentleman or lady.
Organizing	Centralize power. Be autocratic.
Monitoring	Meet short-term profit goals.
Appraising and rewarding	Reward the faithful. Choose the best bankers as managers. Seek safe jobs.

Source: Schwartz and Davis, 1981, p. 38. Reprinted by permission.

ROLE VERSUS JOB: THE USE OF POWER WITHIN A CULTURE

Strategy is implemented through others, that is, by people with particular roles in the organization's culture. For effective implementation, we must distinguish between roles and jobs. People in certain jobs may not take the role nominally associated with the job, but role-takers—that is, those who control resources and influence perceptions in the organization—are critical to the success of strategy implementation.

Separating reality within the organization from job description in a personnel file is critical for a strategist considering effective implementation. For example, an executive education director, by the impact he or she has on the thinking of powerful people in the organization, may be a more important force in the ongoing strategic management of a firm than someone who holds the job of strategic planner. A marketing vice president may make only promotional decisions, while product and pricing decisions are really made by the manufacturing manager.

A realistic perception of power within the organization's culture is important, too. Power is not formal authority. Morris West, in *The Clowns of God,* provides interesting definitions of power and authority:

> Power implies that we can accomplish what we plan. Authority signifies only that we may order it to be accomplished. . . . By the time it gets to the people who have to do it, it loses most of the force of its meaning . (1981, p. 342)

West's insightful view highlights the strategist's problem: Power is needed to effectively implement strategy, and formal authority is rarely sufficient to the task. We organize, as Parsons (1956) put it, to mobilize resources to achieve an objective. Yet, once organized, we are frustrated by our inability to keep things working.

Some people, however, gain the power to get things done. Moreover, the best corporations have learned to identify these people. They test managers by making their responsibility greater than their authority. Only those who can garner power, who can extend their authority by negotiation and trading while managing personal risks, succeed. And, because negotiation requires understanding the needs of those around you and trading things you do not want for things you do, the ability to gain power requires a highly developed understanding of what makes resources relevant and valuable, and what makes the environment threatening.

Ironically, managers worry about the costs of exceeding their authority. In reality, to satisfy the responsibilities of their job, they must extend their formal power informally (Uyterhoeven, 1972). Only if they succeed in integrating their actions with those of others around them in the organization can they earn the formal mantle of power which comes with senior management and facilitate the implementation of a chosen strategy.

CULTURE, ROLE, AND POWER IN ACTION

Changing culture is never easy, but sometimes cultural norms thwart necessary strategic change. In such cases, roles must be changed and power realigned to change long-standing institutionalized habits. Ineffective cultural beliefs must be exposed in such a way that those who hold them have an opportunity to change with their dignity intact.

Consider a large and today very profitable US shoe manufacturer. Originally a family company, its management believed its flagship brand shoes could be made only in its own plant to maintain their quality. Some years ago, it purchased a manufacturer of cheaper shoes in a deal that gave the owner a large block of stock in the parent company along with executive and board positions. This man had learned from his own salesmen that the quality of the parent company's flagship brand's quality was slipping, placing his own financial future at risk. After some weeks of investigation, he had his own factory make a set of flagship brand shoes and presented two racks of shoes at the next board meeting, those he had made on one rack, and the parent company's on the other. He simply asked family members to identify their own company's shoes. Looking at the two racks, they unanimously pronounced one definitely inferior and the other obviously up to their quality standards—picking the shoes made at the acquired company's factory as their own! Today, all the company's brands are made in factories best suited to their production, with desired quality and large profits.

A few months before the rack demonstration, this same man had won the confidence of family members by advising them against a buy-out offer from a conglomerate which itself later merged with the failing Penn Central Railroad. Thus an outsider gained power beyond his role with timely advice. He then used that power to violate the norms of the family board meeting and ask some very difficult questions, revealing the existence of a major business problem caused by an adherence to an ineffective way of doing business, an ineffective culture. His merger advice had demonstrated to family members that his interests in the company's financial future were the same as theirs, and he used his resulting credibility with them in the two-rack demonstration to vividly portray the faltering of their base business. Today he is CEO of the large company and on his windowsill is a brick carrying the words, "Why not?"

SUMMARY

Strategy works through organizations, and culture has an important impact on how organizations work. Culture can be the boon or bane of an organization's strategic future, facilitating or impeding performance. The strategist has two choices: Select a strategy which will achieve the desired results within the organization's culture, or work within the culture to earn and develop power which can be used to make certain aspects of the culture more hospitable to the selected strategy. Either way, culture must be recognized before the strategist can gauge the likely success of strategy or the best way to implement it within the organization.

chapter 14

Administration: Using the Organization's Structure and Systems to Implement Strategy

OVERVIEW

In Chapter 13, we introduced culture to alert you to the importance of the informal rules of corporate life. Culture can serve to align the shared power of the organization so that it will be more effective in strategy implementation. But strategic changes which are essential for a firm's health sometimes need to be implemented in organizations where the structure and culture will not facilitate, and may even hinder, administration. In this chapter, we discuss how one administrative concept, structure, can be used to develop an organization in which strategy can be successfully implemented and, if necessary, changed.

Of course, structural change is an additional and difficult step in the strategy implementation process. Biologically, and apparently organizationally, there is no growth without crisis. The administrative changes required to build an organizational structure to accommodate a chosen strategy illustrate that crises can indeed facilitate growth.

ADMINISTRATION

Administration has one basic purpose: to implement strategy. ''The corporate strategy must dominate the design of organizational structure and process,'' says Andrews (1980), emphasizing his point with the statement that the principal decision criterion in organizational design should be "relevance to the achievement of corporate purpose." Thompson put it this way:

> Perpetuation of the complex organization rests on an appropriate co-alignment in time and space not simply of human individuals but of streams of institutionalized action. (1967, p. 147)

Co-alignment is an important concept. Co-alignment does not require the standardization of action across the organization; it necessitates a strategic focus. Thompson explains that administration

> . . . is not a simple combination of static components. Each of the elements involved in the co-alignment has its own dynamics. Each behaves at its own rate, governed by forces external to the organization. (p. 147)

For example, marketing is influenced by customers and competitors; operations is influenced by suppliers, customers, and technology; finance is influenced by fiscal and monetary policy.

The co-alignment of streams of action suggests an analogy which may help make the point that we administer to focus our energy. In the *Art of War*, a commentator writing on the disposition of troops on the battlefield explained:

> The nature of water is that it avoids heights and hastens to the lowlands. When a dam is broken, the water cascades with irresistible force. Now the shape of an army resembles water. Take advantage of an enemy's unpreparedness; attack him when he does not expect it; avoid his strength and strike his emptiness, and, like water, no one can oppose you. (Sun Tzu, 1963, p. 89)

Administration means channeling the energy of the firm's separate parts so that they come together to create an irresistible force in the marketplace. Each specialized part of the organization has its own life and its own role to play. However, the combined effects of the parts create competitive power.

Skilled administrators accept and exploit the forces that motivate the different specialized parts of their organizations. By manipulating the strategic variables that produce co-alignment, they ensure that what is good for the whole organization is done, rather than what is best for one part.

THE STRATEGIC VARIABLES

What are the strategic variables? Barnard wrote:

> Now, if we approach this system or set of circumstances, with a view to the accomplishment of a purpose, . . . the elements or parts become distinguished into two classes: those which if absent or changed would accomplish the desired purpose, provided the others remain unchanged; and the others. (1966, pp. 202–3)

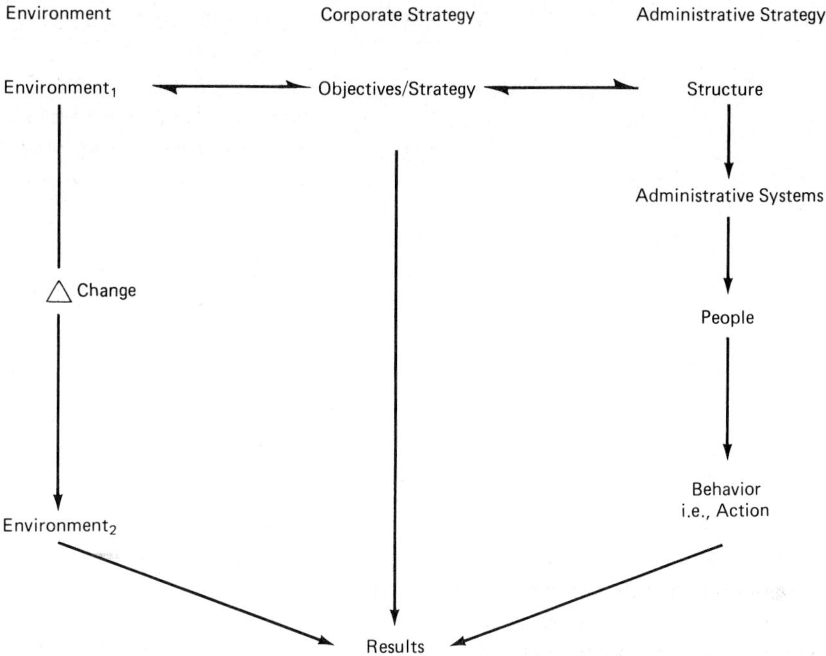

FIGURE 14-1 The Strategic Management System

The first set he called the limiting or strategic factors—"the ones whose control, in the right form, at the right place and time, will establish a new system or set of conditions which meets the purpose" (p. 203).[1]

Collectively, then, the literature alerts us to the importance of purpose in administration: we organize for a purpose and administer to achieve it. We administer both resources and action. Co-aligned actions maximize our impact, just as channels focus running water. In channeling or co-aligning our actions, we strive for economy, intervening as little as possible in the administrative system, but as powerfully as we can by manipulating the few elements that really matter, the strategic factors.

The model of the strategic management system introduced in Chapter 11 and illustrated in *Figure 14-1* puts strategy and results in the center to emphasize the importance of strategy in explaining performance. However, it gives prominence to the conditional effects of the environment, environmental change and the key elements of administrative strategy in the development of those results. Furthermore, double-headed arrows illustrate interdependencies between the environment and strategic decisions; between strategic decisions and administration; and, by implication, between the environment and the first element in the administrative strategy, structure.

[1]This concept anticipates the search for strategic factors and new strategies in Strategic Assumptions Analysis, which we referred to in Chapter 11 and which will be discussed in Chapter 16.

STRATEGY, FORMAL STRUCTURE, AND THE STAGES OF GROWTH

Structure is the configuration of the organization's human, financial, and physical resources used by management to coordinate action within the organization so that the firm's objectives are attained. Strategy and structure are interdependent.

Although we subscribe to the view that the purpose of administration is to implement strategy, we believe that strategic design flexibility should be constrained by what the firm's organizational capabilities or organizational resources are. Hence, although strategy influences structure, existing structure likewise influences our strategic decisions.

Chandler (1962) in his study of the evolution of a number of large American corporations, including DuPont, General Motors, Standard Oil (New Jersey), and Sears Roebuck and Company, advanced the thesis that structure follows strategy. In large measure, he believed that in the United States, demographic changes, prosperity, and technology led to new opportunities to employ existing resources more profitably:

> Expansion of volume led to the creation of an administrative office to handle one function in one local area. Growth through geographical dispersion brought the need for departmental structure and headquarters to administer several local field units. The decision to expand into new types of functions called for the building of a central office and a multi-departmental structure, while the developing of new lines of products or continued growth on a national or international scale brought the formation of a multi-divisional structure with a general office to administer the different divisions. (p. 14)

Essentially, Chandler observed the evolution of managerial specialization to cope efficiently with growth and complexity, just as Adam Smith's pin factory illustrated the benefits of manufacturing specialization in 1776.

In a later book, *The Visible Hand* (1977), Chandler gives great importance to the development of professional management in the evaluation of American industry. Vertically integrated and geographically diverse companies could not evolve until industry developed its administrative specialization, the managerial hierarchy. Chandler thus implied that structure influences strategy.

The problem is that structure has two faces. The face apparent outside the organization is the competitive or customer service side of organizational structure, while the face seen inside the organization emphasizes coordination and control. Researchers such as Lippitt and Schmidt (1967), Salter (1970), Scott (1971), Greiner (1972), and Clifford (1973) have all reported on the need for an appropriate match between the inside and outside faces of the organization—a consistent personality or identity. If there is a mismatch, dysfunctional behavior tends to develop.

Greiner (1972), using developmental psychology (Erikson, 1963) as well as Chandler's research, posits a ''predictable'' developmental track for the growing organization with periods of stable evolution culminating in revolutionary crises which are critical growth stages that few companies escape. In Greiner's model, organizations face critical experiences from time to time. As with people, the choices made are both effects of the previous phases and causes of the next phase's crisis. Greiner's phases of growth are

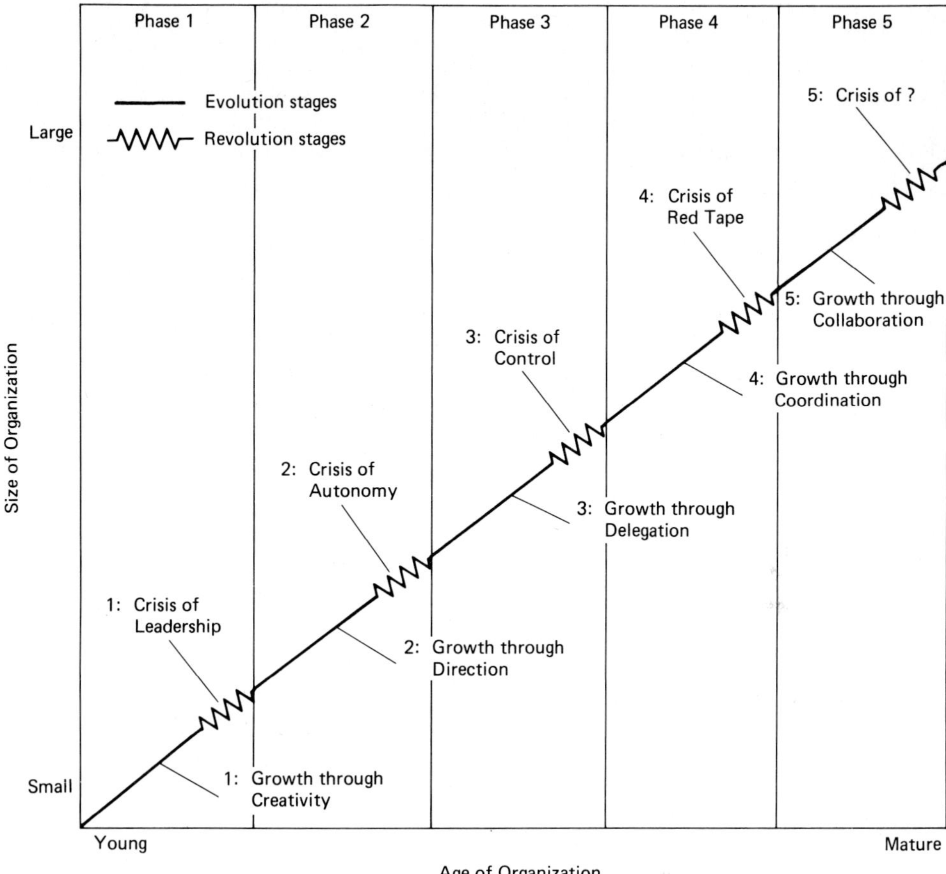

FIGURE 14-2 **The Five Phases of Growth**

Source: Reprinted by permission of the *Harvard Business Review.* Lawrence Greiner, "Evolution and Revolution as Organizations Grow," July-Aug. 1972. Copyright © 1979 by the President and Fellows of Harvard College; all rights reserved.

presented in *Figure 14-2*. The dominant component of this theory is, of course, that continued growth depends on management's ability to weather crisis.

As *Table 14-1* suggests, continued growth implies changes in strategy and structure as well as in the administrative systems used to coordinate the organization. Moreover, Greiner points out that we can anticipate and be alert for the next crisis if we recognize our present stage of growth. Typically, with size and age come new product markets and increased product market scope, formalization, specialization, and conflict between management's need for control and information and its ability to stay informed at low cost. Integration is a straightforward effort to reduce the organization's dependence on the external environment. Hierarchies and decentralized management are direct attempts to put decision making where the information is.

TABLE 14-1
Organization Practices During Evolution in the Five Phases of Growth

Category	*Phase 1*	*Phase 2*	*Phase 3*	*Phase 4*	*Phase 5*
Management Focus	Make & sell	Efficiency of operations	Expansion of market	Consolidation of organization	Problem solving & innovation
Organization Structure	Informal	Centralized & functional	Decentralized & geographical	Line-staff & product groups	Matrix of teams
Top Management Style	Individualistic & entrepreneurial	Directive	Delegative	Watchdog	Participative
Control System	Market results	Standards & cost centers	Reports & profit centers	Plans & investment centers	Mutual goal setting
Management Reward Emphasis	Ownership	Salary & merit increases	Individual bonus	Profit sharing & stock options	Team bonus

Source: Reprinted by permission of the *Harvard Business Review.* Lawrence Greiner, "Evolution and Revolution as Organizations Grow," July-Aug. 1972.

MESHING STRUCTURE INSIDE AND OUTSIDE

If the external world addressed by the organization becomes more complex, and ultimately more uncertain, because of the organization's decisions to diversify or because of externally generated change or both, the organization must develop specialized internal capabilities to relate with that world in a controlled way. The crises Greiner describes all occur when those relationships become uncontrolled, usually because simple choices were made naively in the glow of earlier success. Hirschman (1967) observed that people take on difficult tasks, thinking they are easy and then something goes wrong. He argued that from the crisis that follows comes the opportunity for growth and development—the principle of the hiding hand. Hirschman's "hiding hand" is never too far away from the successful manager. The structural choices facing management always have two sides, internal and external. On the side of internal structure, or control, is centralization or decentralization, each with its specialized management roles. On the side of external structure in the market, the external relationship and strategic choice, comes diversity and interconnectedness, interdependence and, ultimately, integration.

Figure 14-3 relates the two dimensions of structure and control and makes the point that while there is no simple prescription for the right degree of centralization for every strategy, there are some highly probable mismatches, here represented by the empty zones. In simple terms, more integrated businesses with centralized internal structures appear more controllable than diverse organizations. Diversified organizations, being highly differentiated in the marketplace, require a differentiated management structure, that is, one which is decentralized.

Of course, if the environment becomes more complex and less stable due to interconnected industry chains, small numbers of competitors, scarcity of resources, or be-

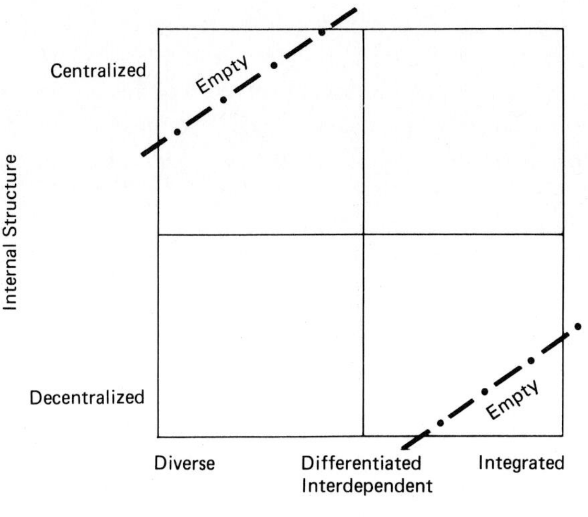

FIGURE 14-3 Matching Competitive and Administrative Structures

cause of governmental action, or technological or demand changes, our choice of external structure becomes complicated. Thompson's (1967) work suggests the following simple prescription: As our environment becomes more complex and less stable, we should move to even more independent and decentralized organizational units, adding layers of specialized management (for example, the groups or sectors at General Electric) to coordinate the parts into a responsive, purposeful whole. *Figure 14-4* points toward likely choices of structural design within various environments.

The issue for the manager is how to develop an organization capable of adaptation

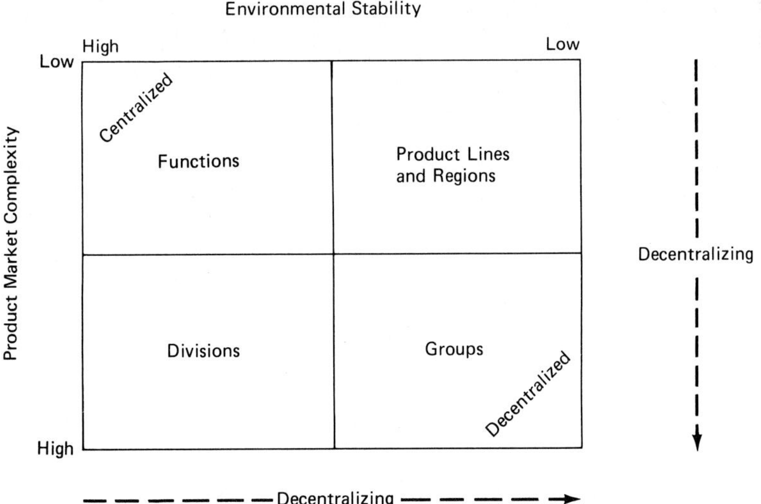

FIGURE 14-4 Organization Design Focus

to the marketplace on one hand, while maintaining operational efficiency on the other. A complex and unstable environment requires boundary-spanning activity to search for information and interpret it. Efficiency, however, requires commitment and sheltering the organization from change—hence the typical tension between marketing, as a differentiating, boundary-spanning unit, and operations, the efficiency-driven technical core. As in many other areas of management, Thompson's prescription presents a paradox and creates an administrative tension: Management must reduce uncertainty to maintain its operational efficiency and implement its strategy, yet it needs flexibility to change that strategy at every level if opportunity or crisis warrants it.

Matrix Organizations

The matrix organizational form which some organizations have adopted addresses these concerns directly. The matrix is an organization that abandons the principle, "for any action whatsoever, an employee should receive orders from one superior only" (Fayol, 1972), in favor of a multiple command system (Davis and Lawrence, 1977). Individuals in a matrix organization explicitly serve two masters. Concerning the matrix form of organization, even Davis and Lawrence advise, "If you don't really need it, leave it alone. There are easier ways to manage organizations" (p. iv).

Matrices penetrate only the top layers of the hierarchy, as *Figure 14-5* suggests, with the bulk of the structure outside and below the matrix. Essentially an integrating device for upper and middle management, matrices may suit situations where there is a

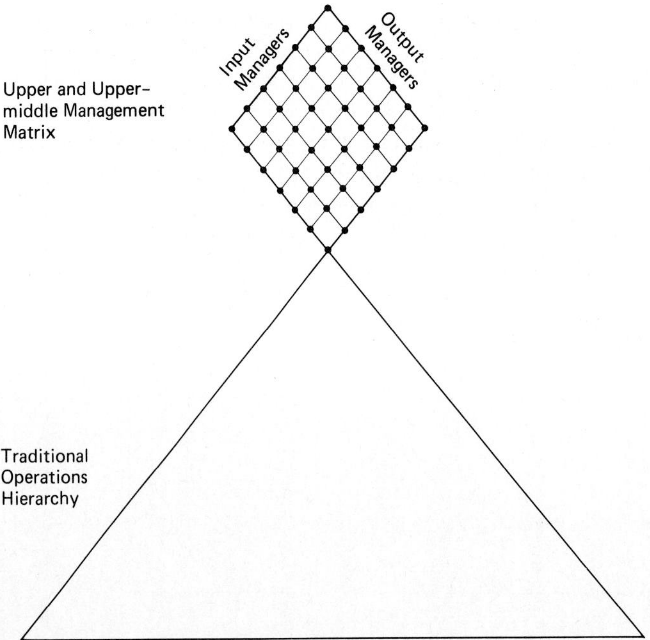

FIGURE 14-5 A Matrix Organization

Source: Adapted from Davis and Lawrence, *MATRIX*, Reading, MA: Addison-Wesley, © 1977.

very large need for information. For example, managers need information when external uncertainty exists and when their roles are highly interdependent. Likewise, information is needed where multiple and critical boundary-spanning functions exist within one organization and many resources are shared. Finally, we believe that information is highly valuable where there exists an imperative to isolate operations from the world because of the technological or security demands placed on them, for example, in the aerospace industry or international banking. Matrixing an organization requires its own supportive culture and administrative system, including simultaneous, overlapping information processing and resource allocation, outside arbitration to limit conflict, and dual personnel and reward functions.

THE INTERNAL CONTEXT: THE INFORMAL ORGANIZATION

So far in this chapter, we have offered a rationale for administration and some broad prescriptions for structuring organizations. Now we move to the inside, that part of the organization concerned with coordination and control. First, let us explore the context of the internal organization.

The decisions managers make and the actions they take occur inside the organization. Such decisions are founded on information, but not perfect or complete information. Williamson (1975) points out that in the face of uncertainty, managers often find themselves in an ''information impacted'' state, meaning that they are blocked, with only limited capacity for ''rational action.''

In these circumstances, people make the difference. They interpret information using their experience to intuit not only its meaning but its significance for the future, and for their fellow managers. Yet, their interpretations and judgments are likely to be idiosyncratic (McCaskey, 1982), especially when uncertainty is great and the pressure for action and better results is high.

Keep in mind the relationship between pressure and performance, shown in *Figure 14-6*. Managers should understand their own responses to different types of pressure and the reactions of others with whom they interact, so they can accurately evaluate the information received and respond appropriately—that is, in a way that gets the result needed.

For us, these observations set the stage for a particular view of the inner organization. Organization is not simply a structural design but a framework of formal and informal relationships among people. External complexity forces differentiation; internal interdependence necessitates communication, coordination, and hierarchies. Formal organizations reflect the outside face of the organization; they typically are rational designs that exploit specialization and hierarchy, and specify policies to control and guide action.

Informal organizations rely on interaction and behavior and example and exist wherever formal organizations exists. Barnard noted that ''An important and often indispensible part of a formal system of cooperation is informal'' (1966, p. 120). Barnard explains that the informal organization facilitates, speeds, and increases communication within the organization, promotes its culture and cohesiveness, and maintains individual feelings of autonomy and self-respect. In fact, formal and informal are not two organizations, but one (Hunt, 1972). We separate them, conceptually, for convenience, but inevitably manage one organization only.

FIGURE 14-6 Pressure and Performance

These views are consistent with research on the job of the general manager, which reveals the importance of the informal organization in administrative success. Initially, successful general managers create an agenda for their area of responsibility, drawing on their knowledge of the business and organization, their intelligence, relationships and interpersonal skills and

> . . . using an ongoing, incremental largely informal process which involved a lot of questions and produced a largely unwritten agenda of loosely connected goals and plans. . . . They used those same personal assets to develop a network of cooperative relationships, above and below them, inside their organization and out, upon whom the job and their emerging agenda made them dependent. (Kotter, 1982, p. 127)

After six months to a year, Kotter reports, these successful managers began to spend more time seeing that their networks implemented their agendas rather than establishing new agenda items or new relationships.

There is, of course, no map of the informal organization complementing the formal organization chart. Each manager has to identify the relevant people for his or her job success. Each manager must build the relationship network and a power base to get the job done.

While authority can be given formally with the position, it is confirmed informally by those around you, above you, next to you, and below you in the organizational hierarchy. Wise managers therefore build personal relationships within the organization and learn to understand how people feel and what their behavior means. Climate is an encapsulating concept which describes this collective feeling—it reflects how people's expectations are being met (recall that culture defines what is expected).

DEVELOPING POWER IN THE ORGANIZATION

The purpose of all this activity within the organization is to develop the general managers' power to do their job. Control of resources gives power, and more resources tend to be allocated to higher performers. Some resources are scarce and have more value and create more power than others.

Just as some types of performance are more highly valued by the organization, information can be valuable, too, especially if it makes others dependent on you. Relationships can give you credibility, especially if they are with more powerful people. They can give you an opportunity to create a sense of obligation or encourage others to identify with you or your ideas (Kotter, 1979).

Kotter reports on the actions one manager took in a critical turnaround situation to quickly take charge and create a climate of dependency on him. Arriving at the division on two hours' notice in a large limousine with six aides, he immediately called a meeting of the top forty managers, outlined his assessment of the situation and his strategy. He fired the top four managers in the room, telling them to be gone in two hours, and stated he would dedicate himself to destroying the career of anyone who tried to thwart his turnaround effort. He ended the sixty-minute meeting by announcing that his assistants would schedule appointments for him with each manager beginning at 7 a.m. the next day.

We can note the manager's quick action and the use of formal position, supplemented by informal action to create dependency, and imagine how those managers left must have felt. Turnarounds sometimes necessitate seemingly draconian methods. The severity of the crisis and the short time available for change sometimes force an exaggerated use of formal and informal power. Managers have to use both the formal and informal trappings of power to be effective and efficient.

Now, having made a case for the importance of the informal organization, particularly as a source of the power for the manager who seeks to implement strategy, let us take a fresh look at the organization. Structure will vary with the environment and the job to be done. It must contribute to the satisfaction of the people who work within it and it will have formal and informal aspects. All these affect the manager through his or her position in the organization.

A MODEL FOR DIAGNOSIS AND DESIGN

A practical model which captures these key factors is illustrated below; it is adapted from Hunt (1972). *Figure 14-7* shows the organization in its environment and then breaks the organization into its major components: formal structure, informal structure, task technology, and individual needs. In *Figure 14-7,* we have emphasized the letters FIT'N, which help us remember what the key factors are: formal and informal structures, technology, and needs. All of these influence the manager's role and can be manipulated by the manager to some degree. Whatever configuration is adopted, however, it must fit the situation and the strategy, and it must fit the parts together purposefully.

For example, consider a company where technology is highly interconnected across its businesses. The technology, with its machines and processes, imposes a pace on operations and demands on the manager. It may be programmed and highly dependent on

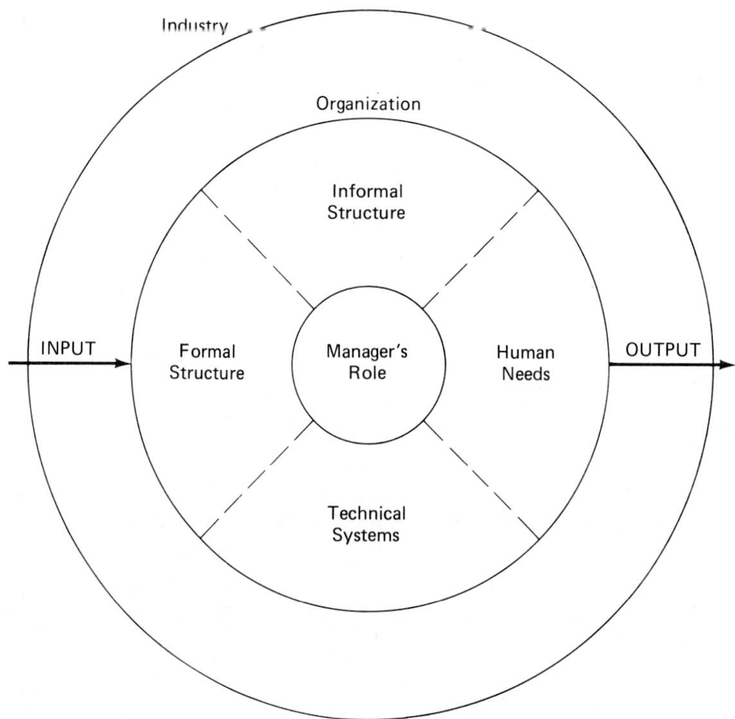

FIGURE 14-7 The Organization and Its Environment
Source: Adapted from Hunt, *The Restless Organization,* Brisbane, Australia: John Wiley & Sons, 1972.

scale for its operating efficiency. If these conditions hold, the technology itself makes the organization slow to adapt, since it is comprehensive and requires a large capital commitment. If this organization is administered through a very formal organization structure, with strict hierarchical divisions, tight controls and evaluation and compensation systems that are used to measure and punish deviation from plan, the manager is likely to have little room for initiative. Here, the organization will probably have an intense informal organization which its members use to humanize their work but not to achieve corporate objectives.

As described, the technology and formal structure stiffen the organization. If the environment becomes unstable and a change of strategy becomes necessary, the organization is likely to fail from simple inflexibility and nonadaptiveness. From the lower and middle managers' points of view, the task of the job is largely technical with very little strategic significance. For them, work is a matter of following orders and serving the "machine." Such managers are unlikely to cope successfully with external change.

THEORIES X, Y, AND Z

In the context of this discussion, it is interesting to examine McGregor's Theory X and Theory Y organizations (1960) and Ouchi's Theory Z (1981). McGregor describes the Theory X model as a "carrot and stick" organization which works so long as people are highly dependent on authority for the means to satisfy their basic needs. He believed that, with prosperity, organizations which relied on this principle would fail. The people in them would be indolent, passive, and unwilling to accept responsibility; they would resist change, follow demagogues willingly, and make unreasonable demands for economic benefits—which were all they received for their work. In our model, the Theory X organization would be highly formally structured, seek productivity through technology and the substitution of capital for labor, and deny the existence of all but the most elemental human needs. Such a business—a traditional US business, McGregor believed—would fail due to lack of adaptiveness.

McGregor described Theory Y as founded on an assumption that people are self-directing and self-controlling in the achievement of organizational objectives to the degree that they are committed to those objectives. In a Theory Y organization, authority is used less and is used less overtly. Theory Y organizations gain commitment by rewarding performance, allowing ego satisfaction and self-actualization. In our model, formal structure would be reduced in the Theory Y organization, and informal structure would take its place, moving control from the organization to its members. A less stiffly structured organization would result which would be inherently more adaptive and innovative, because whatever flexibility and adaptiveness exist in an organization stem from its people. Managers in the Y type organization have roles which extend beyond the technical towards the strategic and so have experience in adapting to change.

Ouchi (1980) in his *Theory Z* contrasts a classic American type of organization with a classic large Japanese organization, and then introduces what he calls the Type Z organization. As *Table 14-2* shows, Type Z's dominant characteristics are very similar to the Japanese model, varying mainly on the locus of responsibility and on length of employment—essentially accommodations to the "ecology of US industry and US culture." Ouchi's examples of Z-like companies included Hewlett Packard, IBM, Rockwell International, Dayton Hudson, Procter & Gamble, Eli Lilly and McDonald's. Ouchi makes the point that they are not all Z companies but share many Z characteristics.

Applying our model of *Figure 14-7* to the Z organizations which are high-technology companies, we can note that they have highly competitive and technologically unstable environments. Yet their own technologies are rigorous taskmasters. Companies

TABLE 14-2 The Theory Z Organization

	American	*Z*	*Japanese*
Term of Employment	Short	Long-term	Life
Frequency of Evaluation and Promotion	Frequent and Rapid	Infrequent	Slow
Nature of Career Path	Specialized	Nonspecialized	Nonspecialized
Explicitness of Formality of Control Mechanisms	Explicit and Formal	Implicit and Informal	Implicit
Type of Decision Making	Individual	Collective	Collective
Locus of Responsibility	Individual	Individual	Collective
Scope of Concern for the Person in the Organization	Segmented	Wholistic	Wholistic

Adapted from Ouchi and Johnson, "Types of Organizational Control and Their Relationship to Emotional Well Being," *Administrative Science Quarterly*, 23, no. 2, June 1978, 294, and from Ouchi, *Theory Z*, Reading, MA.: Addison-Wesley. © 1981.

in the computer industries have difficulty retaining the most able contributors to innovation—they can leave and do it themselves with the assistance of eager venture capitalists. The Z organizational type helps these companies retain their all-important resource, their people.

Generally, a highly formal X-type structure would be inflexible and inhospitable to innovators. Placing the control mechanisms in the informal arena maintains a more flexible and hospitable world that is likely to attract and retain the technologists these companies need. Hence, the Z organization with its consistent culture and long and stable employment satisfies corporate needs and employee needs, too.

IBM is formally structured and tightly controlled, of course, but its strategic diversity, technological leadership and dominance of its industry are legend. Yet matching its formal structures is an equally imposing, harmonizing informal culture which further strengthens IBM's control of its operations. IBM is a rigid defender of its technology in the courts. People think carefully before migration from IBM with technology learned inside. Size and diversity necessitate hierarchy, but the combined impact of formal structure and technology on the people of the organization is ameliorated, without reducing control, by IBM's career-oriented, company-loyal culture.

McDonald's, with its massive franchising operations and its part-time labor force, is a special Z organization; the organization the public sees is well outside of the corporation itself. Because McDonald's must deal with so many independents, held to it by contract and culture, informal relationships are used to keep things moving, avoid conflict, and maintain uniformity. McDonald's motto, "Quality, Service, Convenience, Value (QSCV)," is its culture. Again, a Z-like form, with stable employment at the top and a culture founded on simple, constantly communicated values like QSCV, appears to suit the needs of the situation well.

Our organization model focuses attention on the environment and the organization when the control systems are being designed or attuned to the needs of a particular strategy or strategic change. The elements of the organization have to fit together to serve the strategy. If the strategy places severe task demands on the organization, and if the environment is uncertain or unstable, management must carefully locate its control systems. Keeping the needs of the individuals who work in the organization in mind as you balance formal and informal is an important part of that organizational design activity.

STRESS AND PRESSURE WITHIN THE ORGANIZATION

The formal structure pressures managers for results, but the stress caused by this pressure is lessened if a consistent informal structure exists and allows the manager to develop the extra power necessary to get results. Inconsistent informal structure or a weak informal structure can turn pressure into dysfunctional stress.

Stress itself stems from our uncertainty about what to do and about how we will be judged. Thus, in a dysfunctional stress situation, a major real or perceived difference exists not only between responsibility and authority, but also between opportunities available to develop power informally and the power necessary to do what must be done.

Pressure is received by a manager and can be passed through to subordinates to raise their responsibility levels and so pressure them to gain power and use it. Good managers control pressure as they control resources, using it to increase output. Managers choose how much pressure to absorb and how much to pass through to their subordinates. Too much pressure retained or too much passed on, however, can be dysfunctional. Indeed, managers who let pressure become dysfunctional for themselves or their subordinates, who feel stressed or contribute to stress in those below, are not using their human resources well.

Good organizational structures place resources and pressure where they should be, while testing the people who must use them. You earn the next job (and demonstrate yourself to be ready for it) by getting the people below you ready for your job and integrating yourself into the next level, by using your resources *and* power to make your boss's job easier. Failure to delegate and failure to promote yourself are both deadly. Results must be traded for increased autonomy—that is, power must be used continuously to extend authority.

CHANGING STRUCTURE

Minimum change has the least organizational cost. The resulting strategic aphorism is: "If it works, don't fix it!" And the corollary is that if you don't understand the organization well enough to anticipate reactions and costs, you're doing the strategic equivalent of shooting bullets into a crowd when you attempt strategic implementation. "Ready, Fire, Aim!" doesn't work. A responsible manager minimizes organization costs as well as resource costs, and acts so that no cost is blindly incurred.

The costs of change are high. For example, as Barnes and Hershon (1976) have shown within the family company, strategic change usually requires a change in power, because those formerly in power had developed and supported an earlier strategy. This is also true in large organizations since people are influential in maintaining the status quo (Mintzberg, 1978). In larger firms, however, strategies are not always as closely linked with a single personality as they are in family firms. In this context, it is important to remember that a change in power is always evident on the organization chart, since it requires a change of people, of their roles *or* of their resources. We can add that for the formal and informal structures to be consistent components of a new administrative strategy, the organization chart recording the formal organization *will* change, if not by people's names and levels, then by job titles and classifications.

To consistently link the formal and informal structures, the formal structure will change to make role changes (that is, power changes) binding. Greiner (1972), for example, discussed the kinds of structures which firms will find most effective in different growth stages, noting that there are likely to be common kinds of administrative failure at thresholds between different growth stages. At these thresholds, the old power structure has become dysfunctional, since it serves the old strategy rather than the evolving strategy of the firm and so constrains performance. In family businesses, the essence of this conflict is summarized by the question: "What is family and what is business?" People may not change as the business changes; the thresholds between types of organizations illustrate how specific managers have failed to develop with the organization and so have constrained the organization's growth.

Along with formal structural changes, the reporting systems must be modified to support on administrative change. For example, suppose a marketing manager reports to a powerful production vice president. Perhaps appropriate when the firm was developing a new technology, this reporting relationship now gives the firm a dull market reputation. The breadth of its product line is limited because the production vice president controls costs by standardization although the competition offers a differentiated and fuller product line. If the marketing manager is given the title vice president and budget responsibility, while still reporting to the production executive, power has not changed. The problematic production dominance is likely to continue until both production and marketing vice presidents report independently to the CEO.

Quinn (1980) writes of strategic incrementalism, where strategic change is effected slowly. The concept is indeed a strategic adaptation of the economic concept of marginalism: small improvements improve the whole, and results at the margin indicate where further actions should be directed. Marginal actions which have negative results should be halted and those which provide positive results should be expanded. At different points in their history, GM, Timex, and Polaroid all needed to learn what customers' reactions to new, nontraditional products would be. Learning improved their ability to serve emerging market needs over time.

The concept applies inside the organization, too. Time is among the most important managerial variables. One of the best ways to control the costs of organizational change is to do it gradually, review results, and adapt while there is still strategic flexibility. Setting strategic mile-stones at definite time points is an appropriate way to avoid organizational shock and maintain control of change. Actions spread over time minimize risk and allow any losses that arise to be absorbed gradually.

SUMMARY: USING THE ORGANIZATION TO ACHIEVE RESULTS

How best to achieve results in an organization? As a manager, it is important to know your role and the roles of others. Consider how the formal and informal structures and the technical systems affect your role, and the skills needed to fulfill it, and how they satisfy your needs as well as those of others. Also, consider how parts bind the company together and facilitate its strategic success in its own environment. In this way, you will be able to define strategic roles for your managers, and put them in a logical, formal organizational context.

Knowledge of the organization requires seeing, listening, and learning. Observe the signals, spoken and unspoken. Learn by observing what risks are taken and how, particularly by the successful. Normally, successful managers take few risks, and, when they do, limit their exposure to carefully chosen dimensions along which they can absorb any possible losses. Do likewise. Only risk those losses you can absorb. And remember, a diverse set of organizational interests can help you absorb losses on one dimension while maintaining your power in other areas.

Middle management is a testing ground to develop organizational implementation skills. At the middle-management level, ambiguity is high due to the tension between the demand for results and low levels of formal authority. But those who can gain power and manipulate pressure to get results will demonstrate their ability to implement strategy at the higher levels of the organization. Middle managers who cannot do this find pressure becoming stressful.

Since power is important in implementation, managers must be aware of their positions in the informal organization. It is important to trust personal feelings, since they are the best and only documentation of your place in the informal system. A good rule for evaluating your position in the informal organization is, "If you don't know you're in, you're out" (Jennings, 1980). And being outside the important formal structure can severely limit your power and so limit the success of your efforts. In these circumstances, it may be time to find a new job and recapture the feeling of power that comes to those who are in.

chapter 15

Human Resource Strategy

INTRODUCTION

Human resource management is the humane side of enterprise in too few organizations. In many, there is neither humane administration nor effective human resource management, in spite of the nearly universal conclusion of corporate annual reports in which the "contributions of our most valued asset, our employees" are acknowledged.

People are important, and, in the best organizations, they are valued. People, however, are not corporate assets. They are willing to work for pay, given authority over the organization's assets, and given the responsibility to create value.

Some corporations recognize the importance of having the right people in the right positions and have a strategy to attract and retain them. Consider for a moment the following two statements, one from Walter Wriston, then Chairman and CEO of Citicorp, one of the largest US banks, and the other from Alan Zakon, at the time the newly elected chairman of the Boston Consulting Group, BCG. Wriston said:

> I believe the only game in town is the personnel game. . . . My theory is that if you have the right person in the job, you don't have to do anything else. If you have the wrong person in the job, there's no management system known to man than can save you. . . . The selection of the people that hold the key jobs is a principal function of the chief executive officer.[1]

Zakon wrote:

> BCG is a people business. Our creativity, our effectiveness with our clients can be no better than our staff. It is they who build our intellectual base and they who apply it. We are dedicated to recruiting the very best people. We are committed to maintaining an internal environment which encourages their rapid personal growth.[2]

People are important. And, as these two senior managers have stated, top management has to recruit and select people for particular jobs and create a structure and system that helps them do their jobs successfully and with enthusiasm.

[1]Wriston, as quoted in Foulkes, Fred K. and E. Robert Livernash, *Human Resources Management: Text and Cases,* Prentice-Hall, Inc., Englewood Cliffs, NJ, 1982.

[2]Zakon, BCG 1981 *Annual Perspective.*

Organization charts can describe positions and formal relationships between positions, but only people can make an organization come to life and use it to implement strategy, and only people can innovate. Rudyard Kipling put it this way:

They copied all they could follow
But they couldn't copy my mind
And I left 'em sweating and stealing
A year-and-a-half behind.[3]

People are valuable because of their minds. The job of managers is to get them to use their minds for the organization.

AN EARLY HUMAN RESOURCE CONSULTANT

Human resource strategy is, on the surface of things, simple: identify the tasks that need to be done and the skills required to do them; provide enough talented people to complete the work; place these people in the right jobs; and make each individual productive for the organization. In practice, this is a tall order, a difficult prescription to follow.

Jethro, Moses' father-in-law, paid him a visit during the Exodus and observed a classic failure to delegate. Jethro asked Moses:

> "What is this that you are doing for the people? Why do you sit alone, and all the people stand about you from morning till evening?" And Moses said to his father-in-law, "Because the people come to me to enquire of God; when they have a dispute. . . ." Jethro then said to Moses, "What you are doing is not good. You and the people with you will wear yourselves out, for the thing is too heavy for you; you are not able to perform it yourself alone. Listen now to my voice; I will give you counsel, and God be with you! You shall represent the people before God, and bring their cases to God; and you shall teach them the statutes and decisions, and make them know the way in which they must walk and what they must do. Moreover, choose able men from all the people such as fear God, men who are trustworthy and who hate a bribe, and place such men over the people as rulers of thousands, of hundreds, of fifties, and of tens. And let them judge the people at all times; every great matter they shall bring to you, but any small matter they shall decide themselves; so it will be easier for you, and they will bear the burden with you."

Jethro, perhaps acting as a management consultant, understood the limits of his role and his own capabilities. He recognized he was a counsellor and not the decision maker, and, notice, he wished Moses "God be with you," whatever his decision. He then laid out the principles of organization, in what is perhaps one of the most succinct and effective consulting reports ever. He defined Moses' role and the need for policies to guide everyday affairs. He specified the attributes required for the position of judge and established a hierarchy of positions. And he defined the central principle of delegation—"let them judge" according to the rules, with Moses making the decisions in exceptional cases.[4]

[3]From "Mary Gloster" by Rudyard Kipling.

[4]Our attention was drawn to the managerial significance of this biblical passage (Exodus 18:14–22) by Marvin Bower in his *Will to Manage,* p. 123.

Jethro said it all. Successful human resource management hinges on defining the roles of each level of management and creating a context so that managers know how to make a decision and which decisions to make. There has to be a supervising hierarchy and the people hired have to be able, qualified for the job, and capable of doing it responsibly.

Essentially, tasks are set by the strategy of the firm. What is it that has to be done to implement strategy? Where should responsibility for that task be placed so that the probability of a successful outcome is maximized? Is the task large enough to attract talented, high-calibre people? One question must be kept in mind whether you are accepting a new position or designing it: Is the job or the task to be done worthwhile? If it is not, then it is a poor choice for all concerned.

Remember, the mix of skills needed changes as people are advanced to higher managerial responsibilities. Initial appointments primarily require technical skills with only limited managerial and strategy skills to support them. In the middle-management positions of most enterprises, managing—that is, supervising and motivating others, translating abstract requests into explicit, tangible, coordinated, sequenced action—is more important. In top management positions, strategic management skills become most important. Indeed, some of these strategy skills are quite subtle, for example, the ability to identify the few key elements in the unwieldy flow of information that point the way of future strategy, or the ability to see how isolated minor incidents can be used to contribute to the well-being of the whole organization.

SELECTION

Strategic priority should be given to the well-being of the organization whenever a personnel appointment can contribute to the maintenance and development of the firm's distinctive competence or its superordinate goals, the values that define its culture. Moreover, such appointments warrant top management's attention. Selznick explained:

> When selection must take account of more than technical qualification, as when leading individuals are chosen for their personal commitment to precarious aims or methods, . . . where the social composition of the staff significantly affects the interplay of policy and administration, personnel selection cannot be dealt with as routine management practice. (1957, p. 57)

With the tasks defined and with a sense of what the critical appointments are, recruiting—that is, attracting qualified candidates and selecting the best—is very important. This is a difficult job. As Homer warned in the *Iliad,* c. 700 BC, skills are widely dispersed:

> You will certainly not be able to take the lead in all things yourself, for to one man a god has given deeds of war, and to another the dance, to another the lyre and song, and in another wide sounding Zeus puts a good mind.

The key to success, of course, is to identify the skills people have and the values they live by, and give them responsibilities that suit. The problem of matching people and task is as old as man and organization. Chang Yu, a commentator on Sun Tzu writing during the Sung Dynasty, explained:

> Now the method of employing men is to use the avaricious and the stupid, the wise and the brave, and to give responsibility to each in situations that suit him. Do not charge people to do what they cannot do. Select them and give them responsibilities commensurate with their abilities. (Sun Tzu, 1963, p. 94)

Chang Yu and Sun Tzu before him were writing about war. But, note, the quotation refers to the fit of both skill *and* personal values to the job and specifies the character of a successful match between person and responsibilities: "Do not charge people to do what they cannot do."

In management, board members are advised to select executives whose personalities and experience match both business conditions and the explicit objectives of the corporation. Suggesting that things have changed very little since 500 BC, Gerstein and Reisman present a senior executive's simple statement on selection:

> Some people are better at starting things up, some are better at squeezing the most out of them once they are running, and some are better at fixing them when they go wrong. Right now, the start up is complete, and it's time for a new man. (1983, p. 33)

During the early growth stages of a business, market definition may be the primary strategic problem; later it may become capacity balancing. Still later, in the mature stage of the life cycle, aggressive differentiated merchandising may be crucial to success. And, if a decision is made to get out of a business or to harvest it, cost control may be seen as the big issue. A close match of person and mission would suggest an executive with an entrepreneurial marketing orientation in the first position and a cost-conscious accountant in the latter. However, few companies have taken their senior middle management selection process to a stage where it is *formally* committed to making such a close match between corporate or business objectives, such as growth or liquidation, and the personal management orientation of particular men and women (Govindarajan and Gupta, 1981).

Rather, companies consider personal orientations *intuitively* when making senior assignments. Although senior managers will always prefer to put implementation into the hands of those most likely to succeed, there is at least one simple reason why personal orientation is dealt with intuitively and not always weighted heavily: the technology available to type managers is "primitive" (Stybel, 1982). Furthermore, although matching executive personality and mission may make sense, carried to an extreme it could deny the organization access to generally experienced people at the top should things change. Unless some of the firm's managers have weathered storms, experienced high growth, and learned how to cut costs in a crisis, it is difficult to see how they could direct a multi-business enterprise with any aplomb as top management. A firm subscribing too narrowly to type-matching would be shortchanging itself and its managers by failing to provide them with opportunities for executive development.

"Life cycle" management selection at the top of the ongoing divisions of a large diversified business places specialists in delivering certain objectives, not generalists, near the apex of the managerial hierarchy. Such selection practices suggest three probable consequences:

1 there will be few proven internal candidates for advancement to the leadership position of the corporation whose businesses are in different life cycle stages;
2 the significance of differences across the firm will be emphasized, rather than common bonds and integrative internal relationships, reducing management flexibility;
3 if taken to its extreme, such close matching of manager and managed is unlikely to hold talented people within the firm when times change. Their prospects of advancement will have declined.

Moreover, such selection practices suggest that the objectives of business units will not be changed for some time and cannot be changed without a senior management change. Top management's ability to adapt to changing circumstances and opportunities is thus reduced.

TENSIONS AFFECTING HUMAN RESOURCE STRATEGY

There are obvious tensions between the short-run needs of an explicit situation and the long-run welfare of an organization, and between each of these and the career needs of a particular person, the executive, or candidate. These tensions have to be addressed. If their existence is acknowledged, any selection process can be monitored and refined based on experience.

The tensions in the selection process are not dissimilar to the tensions between the need for executive autonomy and the need for central coordination—each is a valid principle of organization (Sloan, 1963). Yet ultimately the cause of the tensions must be addressed. A decision to act has to be made by those involved, trading off the anticipated benefits and costs on each side of the spectrum. Here, experience is likely to outweigh science, since it is confidence rather than theoretical rigor that is telling in determining how to satisfy the long run needs of the organization.

In 1983, Ralph Lauren, the designer and also the founder of a clothing and cosmetics company with 1983 sales volume of $450 million, told the story of his experience in selecting a president for the company seven years earlier when its volume was $12 million:

> I trust my gut feelings about everything. . . . I picked the president of my company, Peter Strom, against the advice of experts. He's a low-key guy, doesn't come on like dynamite. He's got the kind of personality that grows on you. He's not a one-shot personality, someone who immediately convinces you he's going to take over the world. . . . The experts asked me what I saw in this guy. I told them: "He's the kind of guy I'd like to say hello to every morning, someone you *know* will be on your side, no matter what. That's saying a lot."[5]

Lauren appears to have weighted shared values higher than technical skill or ''market orientation.'' Knowing intuitively that the personal relationship between the new presi-

[5]Quoted in the *Boston Globe*, Sept. 24, 1983, p. 10.

dent and himself would shape the future of the firm, Lauren selected a man who would help him create the kind of company he wanted. Ralph Lauren wanted as president someone with whom he could cooperate and a person who would cooperate with him rather than become his competitor. That's what we believe "on your side, no matter what" means. And, we agree, it is saying a lot.

CLIMATE: COMPETITION AND COOPERATION

Lauren hit upon one of the big issues of human resource management, the issue which ensures that you and your co-managers are productive. And that is fit. Strom fit with Lauren to make a cooperative team at the top. Lauren's intuition told him that he and his company would fare best with a cooperative internal climate in the highly competitive environment of the fashion industry.

Cooperation is necessary to co-align the actions of the firm to maximize their external impact. Other organizations might make different choices. For example, a more competitive internal climate might protect an organization from the slow draining of vitality which often afflicts monopolies, protected regulated businesses, and many governmental and charitable organizations, all of which are insulated from competition (at least in the minds of their managers and administrators).

Consider an observation which poses a dilemma for human resource management: If the climate created is too competitive, cooperation is diminished and the organization's best people will destroy each other; if the climate is too cooperative, the best are likely to be suffocated and the stimulus of their initiative snuffed out. Managers have to judge how competitive and how cooperative a climate is needed, given the organization's environment and its strategy. This relationship between competitiveness and cooperation is just one more tension which has to be manipulated with administrative skill to effectively implement strategy.

"Success in business is in almost exact ratio to the calibre of executive talent at management's command," was the conclusion reached by Marvin Bower after a long career at McKinsey and Company. But, he added, ". . . to be effectively at management's command, this executive talent must be working productively" (1966, p. 157). Management has the responsibility to make sure this is possible, that is, that managers can succeed. The culture, climate, and administrative systems of the organization have to be designed and managed so that they help managers do their jobs better, and thereby help the organization attract and retain high-calibre people.

ADMINISTRATIVE SYSTEMS: CHANNELS OF COMMUNICATION

Delegation is vital to the organization, and every executive has a critical responsibility to see that the organization's communications systems are established and maintained to aid delegation (Barnard, 1966, p. 218). Most people relish autonomy. Given a choice (in an organization that has policies delegating authority and lives by them), they prefer to be more than mere order-takers and to make decisions for themselves if they know what decisions they can make—and, we argue, if they know how they will be judged. Although management typically recognizes this priority, the number and power of the available channels of communication are often overlooked.

Administrative systems are communications channels. Recall that administration means co-aligning action. The communications sent through the administrative systems, therefore, should help the organization's managers co-align their actions—and note that "co-align" implies cooperation, not coercion.

Climate and Systems

The example of top management, the hierarchy of objectives and strategies used to focus action, the organization structure, the policies that guide day-to-day decision making, the financial information and control systems, systems for performance measurement and evaluation, and compensation and reward systems—these are the tools of administration and the threads, fibers, and lines of the communications system which management uses to influence the cooperative and competitive behavior of the people working in the organization. Their effects are interdependent. What is decided in one system influences the choices available in others and the ultimate effectiveness of the whole administrative strategy.

Management has to communicate its policies so that most people know what they can do. Example is probably one of the most powerful communicators in this regard. Another is the resource allocation process. Management delegates authority when it gives the custody of resources to specific managers. The allocation of resources makes authority tangible.

To ensure that there is a shared view of what is appropriate and correct, management designs a financial measurement system to emphasize what specific people are responsible for and what they should worry about. The explicitness of the financial system limits ambiguity but does not eliminate it. Ambiguity itself necessitates interaction and so stimulates more communication between managers. Its purpose is to promote a dialog between managers, not to make their lives uncomfortable. Now, let us see how the administrative systems work and what types of communications each system best fits.

Authority, Accountability, and Ambiguity

As we have noted already, one of the ways coordination is achieved without suffocating initiative is to design tensions into the administrative systems of the organization: authority and accountability is one of those tensions. Increased size and increased diversity both necessitate specialization of management and choices of how and where to allocate resources and how to coordinate action throughout the organization. When managers delegate, they maintain some control. They give authority—the physical custody of some corporate resources—to subordinate managers, but they hold their subordinates accountable for certain results.

Figure 15-1 demonstrates the sources and outcomes of the tension between authority and accountability, and the resulting ambiguity. The diagram puts policy first, since policy in our view is the sole foundation for delegation. On the next line, we see delegation which gives authority, subject to accountability for specific results. In structuring the organization, position by position and office-holder by office-holder, authority

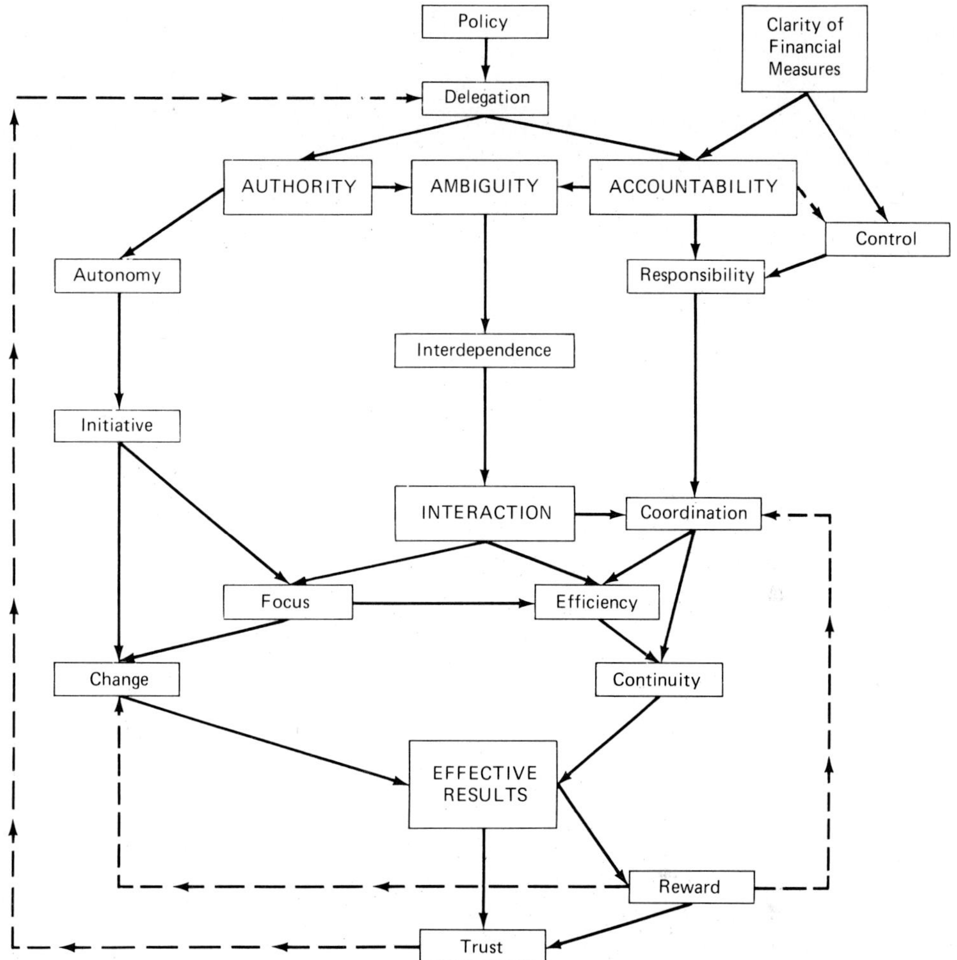

FIGURE 15-1 Authority and Accountability

over resources is given and accountability specified in reporting relationships. Authority, on the left side of *Figure 15-1,* promotes autonomy, which leads to the taking of initiative and to a search for possibilities for change. Accountability, on the right side, facilitates control and promotes both responsibility and coordination throughout the organization.

Now, consider how authority and accountability interact. For managers below the top, authority is usually less comprehensive in scope than the results required by the accountability system. Hence, the junior or middle manager's autonomy is restricted and he or she does not have custody of all the resources needed to succeed. The result is ambiguity.

Ambiguity, seen in the center of *Figure 15-1* under Delegation, stems from the fact that the activities and ultimately the results for which the manager is accountable exceed the capability of the resources in his or her custody. He or she is therefore dependent on others and, since the manager cannot simply make things happen by allocating his or her own resources, he or she has to interact with others to get the job done. Ambiguity therefore leads to interdependence and interaction. These interactions will include negotiation and attempts to influence others, for example, but in all their forms they force communication.

The Purpose of Ambiguity

Because the burden of accountability without autonomy often causes frustration, which leads to stress and career blocks for inexperienced managers, it is important to recognize the purpose of ambiguity so that you use it rather than suffer from it. Some managers incorrectly see accountability without authority as an impediment to their progress, rather than as a signal to talk. They try to work alone and fail, instead of working *through* others to succeed.

The result of delegation is not dysfunctional conflict between the accountability system and the authority system, the right- and left-hand sides of *Figure 15-1,* but rather effectiveness. The two systems are not in conflict but in tension, a tension which promotes communication and a focus on efficiency on the one hand, and a focus on the things that matter on the other, and so, ultimately, leads to effectiveness.

Authority leads to initiative-taking and accountability leads to coordination and efficient resource use. Together the two systems promote effectiveness stemming both from changes made for the sake of the future of the organization and from continuity which maintains the values of its resources. These resources are, of course, the building blocks for the organization's future.

Ultimately, it is the quality of the managers' contributions both to change and to continuity which establishes trust between managers, justifying rewards and further delegations of authority with increased autonomy to the achieving subordinate manager. The speed and certainty with which additional responsibility and authority are won will depend on the practices of the firm and its needs—for example, its growth and the degree to which advancement is competitive. The certainty with which reward follows results will influence any manager's subsequent behavior.

With this overview of the authority/accountability tension in mind, let us examine the roles of policy, delegation, and control, and the importance of trust within the administrative system. This done, we will examine measurement, appraisal, and compensation from a strategic viewpoint and conclude the chapter by summarizing how human resources shape strategy and are shaped by it.

Policies and Delegation

Policies are the foundation of delegation. If position in the managerial hierarchy is assigned on the basis of the organization's strategic needs to those with requisite knowledge, skill, perspective, and experience, and if authority is specified in light of the calibre of the human resources available, then each manager can act confidently within the scope of the authority delegated to him or her, and, importantly, with the confidence of the boss.

As *Figure 15-1* shows, policies are necessary whenever decision making is decentralized. Decentralization creates centers of initiative where specialized or informed managers can act in a timely and responsive way. Delegation specifies the authority of the managers of the decentralized unit so that they can take the initiative and succeed. Yet, if there are no policies to guide their decisions and to ensure them that they share a view of what is right with top management, delegation is a sham, initiative is reserved for those at the top, and all decisions of moment are centralized.

If managers are not allowed to decide, or if they are uncertain about what they can do or how their actions will be judged, survival dictates that they take orders and power is concentrated at the top. However, if policies exist which specify and communicate what decisions executives in certain positions can take, and if top management's practice or example is consistent with those policies, subordinate or junior managers can act confidently within the scope of whatever authority is delegated to them. They can use their minds for the organization.

Good practice is to act consistently with what you say and say what you believe. That is good example. Organizations have to let their members know what the limits of their authority are, what types of decisions are appropriate in various prescribed circumstances, and how the results they achieve will be evaluated. Inconsistent rhetoric and action are bad communicators and lead to uncertainty, shrinking confidence and a limiting of people's willingness to take the initiative. People learn quickly how their organization deals with success and failure, and change their behavior to attune themselves to the reality which is practice.

Delegation and Trust

The shared confidence underlying delegation and action is based on *trust:* delegation is a relationship which is, in essence, a contract. The terms of the contract are specified in large measure by policy, so that management as a whole is coordinated and discriminating in deciding what is the right thing to do. The contract is administered personally and develops on each side through interaction. Learning and results on both sides —that is, experience—accumulate to build either trust and confidence or mistrust (Barnes, 1981). Cooperative self-discipline on each side of the contract builds trust. Furthermore, the results achieved by the subordinate and the rewards given by the supervisor cement their trust in each other.

The paradox is that trust is only developed or extended when initiative is allowed and both executive capability and the relationships between supervisor and subordinate are tested. Policies are the framework within which this testing and executive development can occur at tolerable risk to all parties to the delegation contract, each member of the organization, and the organization as a whole. Policies in fact provide what Bower (1966) termed the backbone of the organization and the executive "will to manage," since they help all members understand what the values and plans of the organization are and adhere to them.

Control by Policy

Putting policies explicitly in place allows people to act confidently and with dispatch and to exercise initiative consistent with their capabilities and the organization's confidence in them. Allowing policy to evolve from practice, however, reduces management's control of action within the organization.

Control by policy makes good organizational sense. Control is needed to manage initiative, not to limit it. For example, the organization will be more effective if it focuses its efforts on specific targets of opportunity rather than dissipating its resources on many. It will be less exposed to risk if the scope of authority throughout the organization is matched with executive capability so that the cost of potential failure is personally and corporately absorbable.

If not consciously based on strategy, the facts of the situation, and organizational needs, policies which set out "how to do things" evolve out of practice. For example, subordinates tend to assume that their supervisors will act or make the same decisions as they do, if not advised otherwise (that is, controlled), and those below them will watch and do likewise—thereby establishing *de facto* policies. Such informal policies are likely to suit the parts of the organization better than they serve the whole and thus constitute an abdication of authority rather than delegation to serve the organization's needs. Such practices allow the dissipation of authority and weaken control.

"Loose but tight" is a term coined by Peters and Waterman (1982) in their book, *In Search of Excellence,* to describe how control by policy works. "Loose" refers to our freedom to act and use our judgment. "Tight" refers to doing what we do the "company way" in accord with policies so that our actions are focused on implementing strategy. Controls must be loose to allow action which is timely and responsive. They must be tight to ensure that decisions are made with the best available information and are co-aligned throughout the organization rather than being idiosyncratic. The concept is also found in other books on administrative practice, including those by Barnard (1966), Selznick (1957), and Bower (1966).

Policies and Administration

Policies enable delegation and control and so are a pervasive element in the administrative systems of the firm. These systems are like a light harness which helps the people of an organization pull together in the same direction. Policies promote efficiency, because they promote responsible self-coordination and allow people to act quickly in certain matters, and because they allow managers to discriminate between regular or routine circumstances and the exceptional. Policies provide a framework of criteria for managerial decision making.

Policies should be based on strategy and serve it, linking plan and practice. They should, therefore, be founded in the past and its experience but not stuck there. They should point to the future by laying out how certain things should be done in prescribed circumstances, as, for example, how employees, suppliers, or customers will be treated.

Policies should be simple and brief, focusing on the key factors rather than the minute—delegation means not doing the jobs of the people you supervise. Simplicity aids communication and promotes clarity and focus, since it reduces the need for individual interpretation and change. Simplicity also facilitates control, especially self-control, the least onerous form of control, thereby giving policy its administrative power.

THE ADMINISTRATIVE PURPOSES OF FINANCIAL MEASUREMENT SYSTEMS

Once management has established policies and decided to delegate authority, it has to communicate its intentions to the organization. There is a problem, however: how does management ensure that the message intended is received? In addressing this problem, the financial measurement system makes one of its less visible but crucial contributions to the welfare of the firm. Our discussion of financial measurement here will be administrative in spirit. We are concerned with communication between top and middle management, rather than with their respective reactions to the results of the current operating cycle.

With authority, the manager is given physical custody of some of the organization's assets. Custody makes the scope of the manager's autonomy explicit and tangible. By making the manager accountable for the use of those assets, the stage is set for a review of his or her stewardship. The financial measurement system should specify what the manager is accountable for, in a way which is:

> . . . consistent with, but more detailed than, the charter which describes his business responsibility. By deciding whether or not to assign a portion of the operating costs and asset values of shared resources to a profit center manager, corporate managers convey their intent about his or her need to be concerned with the effective utilization of those resources. . . . The design of the measurement system helps to ensure that the message gets through, reminding the profit center manager periodically whether and to what extent he should be concerned with the management of shared resources. (Vancil, 1979, pp. 129–30)

The exactness or specificity introduced by the financial measurement system is like a lens focusing management's attention on things that count. The administrative signals from the financial measurement system are important because they flesh out the fundamental contract between the manager and his or her boss. The measurement system also ensures that managers will establish a basis for a continuous dialogue about their collective use of the firm's resources, so that the benefits of any interdependency between profit centers or businesses are not lost. The ambiguity inherent in the administrative system is, therefore, nothing more or less than an alert signalling both the need for interaction and the possibility that tradeoffs between differing interests and objectives may be needed.

A secondary administrative function of the financial measurement system is to supply data documenting the outcomes of the continuous series of decisions which test the mettle of managers in every organization. This is important, because most organizations can only adapt by changing the authority and power of their managers (Barnes and Hershon, 1976). They can only do this if information on management's current performance and experience is available.

Administrative Signals from Financial Results

Current results give obviously powerful signals—probably the most difficult signals management receives if results are below expectations or if there is an unexpected loss. Note the words "expectation" and "unexpected." The delegation contract is violated by surprise, and surprise often leads to precipitous intervention by top management. "You help where you can," says top management, although such actions often reduce the autonomy of profit center management, focusing effort on the short run—since if you can't survive the short run, the long run doesn't matter.

Results are actually a mixed signal, however. They reveal something of how the market received our offerings and how we fared against our competitors, as well as something about how effectively and efficiently we operated our business. Thus, they have to be interpreted with care. In a crisis, or when they're surprised, managers are likely to overreact and the care needed in the situation is rarely given. Robert Uihlein, President and CEO of the Joseph Schlitz Brewing Company from 1961 to 1976, said when he took office, "The first thing I'm going to do is to give some fo the men around here a chance to make a mistake." What he was unable to foresee at that time was how he would react under pressure when a mistake occurred and what the net impact of encouraging rhetoric and discouraging follow-up action would be.

In the context of reacting appropriately to signals from the financial measurement system, we can note that, although some managers believe that a focus on details keeps them "on their toes," focusing on details can create a downward series of misallocations of management attention, interfering in the operations of those below and risking a failure of delegation. In general, the supervising manager should work with less rather than more detail because then the signal on subordinates' performance is clearer and there is less temptation to take on subordinates' problems, unintentionally usurping the authority delegated earlier.

Indeed, doing their subordinates' job is a common failing of anxious, newly-promoted managers who, instead of integrating themselves further up into the organization, return to whence they came—where they have mastery and feel less ambiguity. They do their old job, denying their subordinates the opportunity for development and themselves the opportunity for advancement. Rather, managers should react to the signals relevant to them, focus on the things that count, those things that contribute to the implementation of strategy, to the success of their own job, and the evaluation of their subordinates.

HUMAN RESOURCE EVALUATION: DEALING WITH SUCCESS AND FAILURE

The USCO-Euroco Example

Some years ago, while working with two separate companies each with sales substantially in excess of $10 billion, we had opportunities to learn how middle managers saw the possibilities for personal reward in the light of their companies' reactions to success and failure. The results for USCO and Euroco, as we will call them, are shown in *Figure 15-2*. The score, positive or negative, indicates the size of reward or penalty which managers believed they would receive when right or wrong.

Figure 15-2 shows that in USCO, if the manager was right in a judgment of what to support and what not to—that is, if the ultimate result favored the manager's decision—he or she was rewarded, but *only if* the company won. He or she got very little if the company was simply saved from losses. If the manager was wrong, he or she suffered and in fact was often fired. In Euroco, managers were rewarded differently. *Figure 15-2* shows there was a premium for being right at Euroco, but also a reward for championing a new venture.

In USCO, risk-taking was promoted by top management's speeches, but only winners were wanted. Full responsibility for failure was placed on individual managers. In Euroco, risk-taking was promoted at the top, but responsibility for results was shared. Because commitments to its new ventures were viewed as organizational as well as

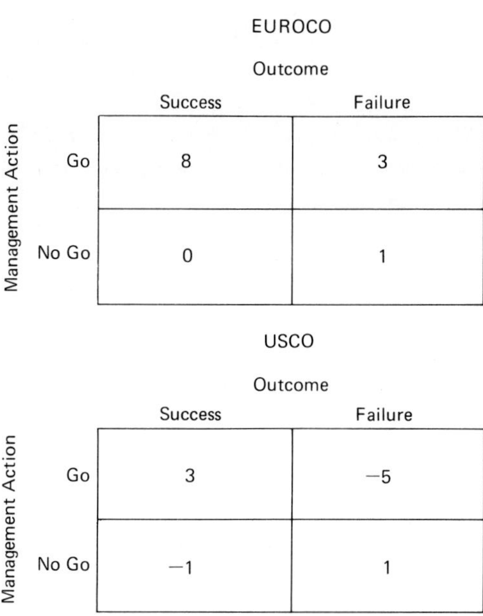

FIGURE 15-2 The Payoff for Success and Failure

individual commitments, management viewed short-term results as a signal that their internal or operating procedures needed review. They assumed, to start, that the decision to enter was right.

USCO was fast of foot, while Euroco was a little slower, since consensus was needed for action. The European company viewed businesses as commitments which, if worth initiating, were worth persevering in. Its ventures were precision rifle shots while USCO's were shotgun blasts. USCO's ventures were initially more numerous, but they were also less focused, received less early corporate support, and had a high failure rate. Ultimately, because failure was followed by firing, venturing at USCO slowed and its rate of innovation declined. Poor results severely test management's commitment to delegation.

REACTION TO POOR RESULTS

The handling of poor results affects an organization's ability to innovate and change. If venturing is punished, venturing stops. In too many organizations, the evolution of a new venture follows a deteriorating path, because of the way management deals with failure. Initial enthusiasm for the venture is followed by disappointment when the first results are reported. "Disappointment is relieved by a search for the guilty, although the innocent are punished while honor goes to the uninvolved," is an observation made by the Director of Research of a large British company. It seems to fit US experience, too.

When results are poor, how they're handled is less a matter of style than a matter of confidence and responsibility. A simplistic view suggests that either you intervene or you let the managers on the spot find their own way out of the dilemma. Another choice is to put pressure on the manager in trouble.

Management at Marks and Spencer,[6] the famous UK retailing firm, seems to disagree with such simple approaches. Management's policy for dealing with poor results is founded on two guiding principles:

1 external conditions do not justify results below plan;
2 departments where performance is smooth are closely monitored; in the face of difficult problems, pressure is relaxed.

Senior managers explain that their policy is founded on an assumption that good performance will deteriorate if not continuously pressured. Problems, however, necessitate effort and a clear head. Marks and Spencer's management believes that administrative pressure is unlikely to help the managers keep their heads when the going is tough and they are under the pressure of the problem and their own needs to succeed. At Marks and Spencer, they believe their human resource assignments are sound and that delegation means letting the manager on the spot solve the problem, drawing on (the experience of) others for aid as he or she needs it.

Of course, intervention may be necessary—for example, if a quick remedy is needed to ensure the welfare of the firm—but even in such a circumstance, managers should consider the signal they send and the way any intervention on their part will be received. Too early an intervention violates the delegation contract, too little may threaten the organization. Allowing too much pressure to reach a manager may stimulate errors rather than effectiveness. Indeed, crises reflect not only upon the manager on the scene but upon the wisdom and judgment of those who put the manager there and the quality of their supervision.

PERFORMANCE APPRAISAL

Performance appraisal or evaluation, salary determination, promotion, demotion, and termination often rely on the financial information system for much of their primary data. Managers similarly use the financial information system to help their subordinates assess where change is needed and to motivate them to change. Thus, the financial measurement system is used as a primary source of information for other administrative purposes besides communication of the intent and results of delegation.

Douglas McGregor (1960) made some observations about performance appraisal which are still valid. First, he noted a tendency for salary administrators to unconsciously discriminate to much finer levels than "outstandingly good," "satisfactory," and "unsatisfactory," and he charged that this was unrealistic. He maintained that different people used different standards, some were biased and prejudiced, and, moreover, each person's performance is ". . . to a considerable extent a function of how he is managed" (p. 83), all factors which make fine distinctions of performance impossible.

[6]Marks and Spencer, Ltd (A), ICCH 9-375-358.

McGregor found that when appraisals were used simply as a basis for consultation between superior and subordinate, they were more honest than when they were used for salary and other administrative decisions. However, he noted how difficult it is for any of us to hear and accept criticism: Too general and the subordinate finds it difficult to correct his or her behavior; too specific and the subordinate will argue that specific extenuating circumstances existed. Moreover, McGregor believed the effectiveness of the communication is often inversely related to the subordinate's need to hear—he even wondered whether people really wanted to know how they were doing—and that this tendency is exacerbated by making an event out of the appraisal interview.

Indeed, although we call it performance appraisal, the fact is that it is a personal appraisal. It is rarely an objective activity but a social-emotional one, quite subjective in most circumstances. At the top of the organization, where time horizons are longer and the job more complex, completely objective and certain evaluations are often impossible. Because appraisal leads to promotion or to termination, it is costly to individuals and organizations both. It must be made informed and equitable. Precedents exist for court intervention if this is not so.

Illustrating the frequent subjectivity of performance appraisal and one of its organizational costs, Bower wrote,

> Although I can't prove it, I believe that the insider who seems 65 percent qualified for the job is likely to outperform the typical outsider who seems 90 percent qualified, because the weaknesses of the insider are known, while those of the outsider are hard to learn accurately in advance. (1966, p. 170)

The insider, about whom more is known, faces a harder standard on the performance appraisal, while the outsider fares better. The organization, of course, is the loser as it opts for relative inexperience.

Multiple sources and multiple dimensions are needed to evaluate senior managers. Because strategies unfold over time and because results accumulate slowly, the overall pattern should normally outweigh one aberrant result. Strategic concept, control, achievements, risks taken, and support within the organization all point to the quality of executive performance. A wise boss turns the appraisal into a source of information for the manager being evaluated and motivates him or her to better performance.

MOTIVATION AND DEVELOPMENT

The shared purpose of appraisal, motivation, and development is to identify and communicate the need for change, to encourage the acquisition of knowledge and skill, and to develop the attitudes and perspectives that people need to do more comprehensive jobs. Semiannual or annual appraisal is not a particularly effective motivator to change. This is true, first, because most appraisal sessions focus on the need for improvements and what's wrong, and, second, because they occur too late. McGregor wrote,

> People do learn and change as a result of feedback. In fact, it is the only way they learn. However, the most effective feedback occurs immediately after the behav-

ior. . . . Three or four months later, the likelihood of effective learning from the experience is small. (1960, p. 87)

The One Minute Manager (Blanchard and Johnson, 1982) offers a prescription for fast feedback. The "hero," the one minute manager, tries to "catch" people doing good and praises them for it so they will learn what good management practices are. He manages by example. When reprimands are warranted, he gives them briefly and as soon as possible. He waits to let the reprimand sink in so that they can feel how he feels and then reassures the subordinate that he or she still has the boss's respect and support—touching (by shaking hands) to authenticate the full exchange and to end it.

The theme of *The One Minute Manager* is consistent with McGregor's advice that fast feedback motivates best. Fast feedback reinforces useful behavior. It deals one at a time with dysfunctional behaviors so that it is clear what behavior is being criticized and that it is the inappropriate behavior which is to be eliminated, not the person. In most corporate settings, managers eliminate people because it's easier—especially since they let a person's negative score accumulate until their frustration is so great that they take the simple way out and fire him.

Most executive development occurs on the job (Livingston, 1969). Such development occurs because a mentor or coach is on hand to reinforce discipline and to encourage. Deutsch (1983) describes what a mentor does, noting that if you turn the organization chart upside down, then your responsibility is to help those persons above you. Zaleznick (1977) says this was the concept motivating Donald Perkins, Jewel Tea's innovative president during the 1970s. Simple praise, notes, phone calls, and other acknowledgements of purposeful behavior can modify behavior if used consistently and insistently, especially early in the association when flexibility exists. The contribution of an effective mentor or coach is to bring forth what protégés have not discovered for themselves—the potential to do better—and to help them fit themselves into the organization.

Development is finally self-development. The classic transformation of the flower girl, Eliza Doolittle, to a lady in Shaw's *Pygmalion*, is an example of potential realized through coaching, although, as you may recall, the pupil ultimately had to fight for her independence. Like Eliza, executives ultimately have to be independent. Only independent minds are likely to innovate, for example.

The organization should be managed to give us the opportunity to develop ourselves. We have to integrate ourselves into the organizations we join and learn to discipline ourselves so that we are effective members. Ultimately, we are each responsible for our own development. As Kotter (1982) said, we have to set our own agenda to define our job and we have to build our own networks to facilitate our work. We have to think for ourselves since our minds and the minds of our employees are the ultimate sources of value and the sources of the satisfaction that should be associated with purposeful action and organizational membership.

From a corporate point of view, executives need to find ways to help managers develop themselves and test their mettle. Job rotation, including movement across organizational boundaries and between units, reduces barriers to communication and leads to new knowledge, skills, and perspectives. Communication and familiarity help free bottlenecks and reduce dysfunctional conflict. Temporary assignments to higher positions, during vacations, for example, allow testing and observation of performance at modest risk for all concerned. This is, however, a sadly neglected practice if potential successors and understudies are not identified for all general management positions.

Such trial and error learning experiences as those we describe can go a long way towards limiting the influence of the "Peter Principle," the observation that executives ultimately are promoted to the level of their incompetence where they become either failures or afraid to act. The incentives for promotion must be real. Compensation and the threat of termination are both used to encourage self-development and self-confidence throughout the organization.

COMPENSATION

Compensation is a difficult matter, probably handled too mechanistically in most firms. Here, our interest is in implementing strategy, and compensation is one of the most powerful communicators in the administrative armory.

Compensation cements the contract between employer and employee, between managers, no matter how humble or exalted. When you compensate or reward someone, you have a significant opportunity to reaffirm what your intent is and what your priorities are. The way you pay them tells them what is really important.

Figure 15-3 contrasts two views of salary, one of the most basic forms of compensation. One view is mechanistic, the other strategic. Possibly both are artificial, because practical salary schemes necessarily share characteristics of each. The key point we wish to make, however, relates to attitude. Salary is either market-driven—that is, it merely pays in some equitable way for services rendered—or it (and indeed all compensation) is an incentive to tune the organization to more effective strategy implementation. The mechanistic view is pedestrian and only partially relevant to the strategist, while the strategic view is challenging. Note, in *Figure 15-3,* that the needs of the firm are given

FIGURE 15-3 Alternative Views of Salary

Mechanistic	Strategic
1. Sets salaries systematically to divide a fixed pie.	Must convert salary payments to incentives.
2. Sees salary as a payment for job done.	Uses salary to reward past and present effort and to encourage future contributions and cooperation.
3. Sees salary as a monthly payment.	Uses salary to influence relationships among peers. Considerations of relative status and salary are keys to "perceived" peer group membership.
4. Tends to award salary on technical factors, for example: —contributions to profit —number of personnel supervised —nature and impact of decisions made —market availability (or replacement cost).	Must decide what kind of competitive or cooperative environment is wanted and use salary to create it. Hence will give weight to the relationship of the job to the distinctive competence of the firm in determining salary level.

greater prominence under "strategic." The strategist takes a different time perspective, emphasizing future contribution to a greater extent.

If the strategy of the firm is to have priority, management will design its full compensation scheme to communicate its purpose, to support its efforts to promote competitive and cooperative behavior throughout the organization, and to focus attention appropriately on the time horizons, long or short, of particular actions. For example, peaked salary structures promote competitiveness, while flat structures promote cooperation. The rate at which the structure narrows, whether there are a few steps or many steps or smooth transitions, signals whether internal competitiveness or cooperation is important.

Consider which of the three patterns of compensation in *Figure 15-4* is likely to be associated with the most internally competitive organization. Which do you think will be the most cooperative organization? In our view, the second (or mid) pattern is likely to be most competitive, because compensation narrows at precise points creating sets of "equals"—particularly near the top in ranks 2 to 5. Remember, money in the corporation confers status. On the other hand, the third or bottom chart is most cooperative. There are few large gaps and few gates between levels.

BONUS

Bonus is one of the classic compensation devices used in industry. It, too, allows the strategic manager an opportunity to focus management's attention on specific factors and to fine-tune the reward system. To illustrate this point, let us examine how some companies have designed and used their bonus systems.

At Analog Devices, a Massachusetts-based high technology company, management believed that no simple, one-dimensional bonus plan could satisfy its needs. As Stata and Madique (1980) tell the story (being Chairman and President, and former Vice President, the authors are primary witnesses), management settled on two dimensions, return on assets (ROA) and sales growth, to focus attention on the critical factors of profitability to fund growth and growth itself—a short-term factor and a long-term factor.

On the growth dimension, management used a twelve-quarter moving average. The period chosen matched the time it typically took Analog to realize the potential of a new product, and related to the typical tenure of an eligible executive in a single position or assignment. Shorter periods would have been too close in time to judge; longer periods would probably be too long and too distant from the perspective of an executive.

On the other hand, Analog expected its managers to adapt to changing conditions and make things work. Hence, it adopted a three-quarter average on the ROA dimension. This gave managers one quarter to pick up a result, one to change operations, and one to judge its effects.

To focus attention on the competition, Analog set its goals on each dimension to match industry peer performance—25 percent growth and 23 percent pretax ROA for the "better" semi-conductor instrument and computer companies over the prior three years. To help ensure that the company's financial strategy (funding its own growth) was feasible, management weighted the bonus in favor of ROA. As *Figure 15-5* shows, a full

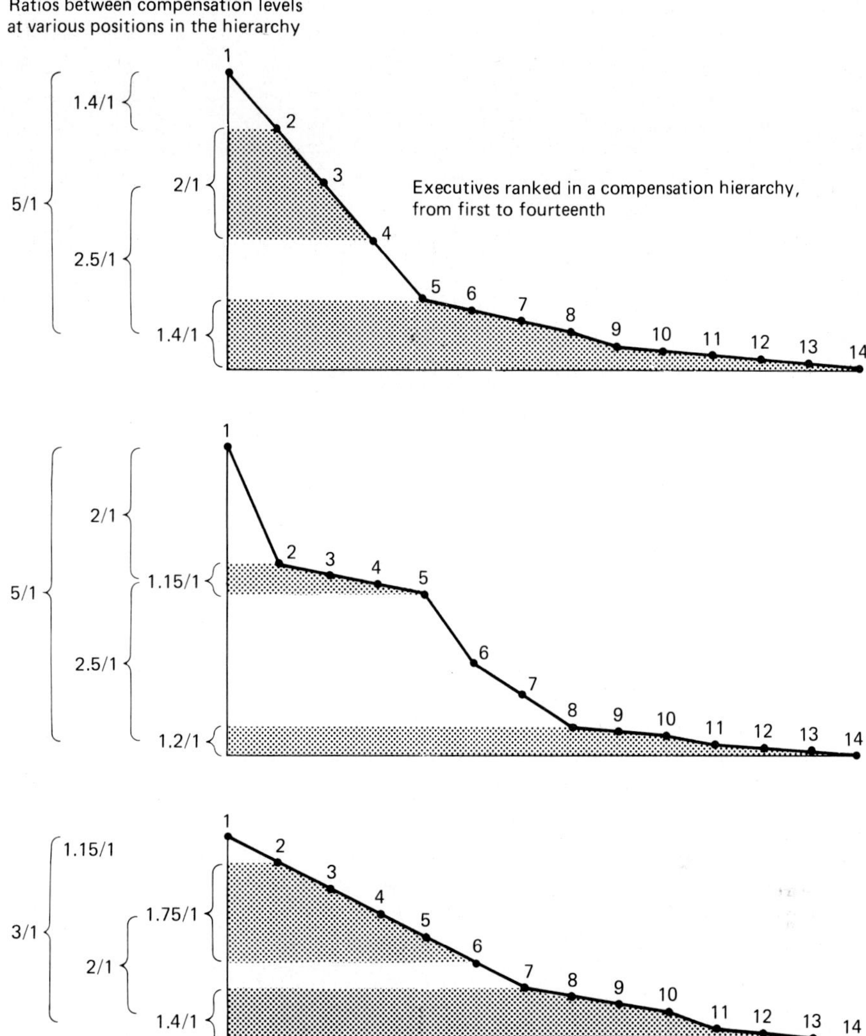

Note: These patterns are plotted on a semilogarithmic scale, such that the slopes of any one pattern may be directly compared with the others.

FIGURE 15-4 Three Patterns of Compensation in an Executive Hierarchy Having 14 Levels of Personnel

Source: Andrew Towl, "Patterns of Executive Compensation," July/August 1951. Reprinted by permission of the *Harvard Business Review.*

bonus would be paid only if goals were met. But for those who exceeded goals, bonus eligibility jumped very quickly indeed.

Analog further tuned its compensation strategy by varying the potential salary and bonus mix by rank. Those at the top could earn a bonus of up to 100 percent of salary, while those three levels below could earn only 10 percent of salary. Stata and Madique report Analog's management believed that although outstanding corporate results de-

12-quarter average sales growth rate*

3-quarter average return on assets as biased		14.9% Poor	15%	20%	25% Goal	30%	35%	40%	45% Outstanding
16.9%	Poor	0	0	0	0	0	0	0	0
17.0%		0	0.29	0.29	0.41	0.56	0.75	1.00	1.00
19.0%		0	0.29	0.41	0.56	0.75	1.00	1.30	1.30
21.0%		0	0.41	0.56	0.75	1.00	1.30	1.67	1.67
23.0%	Goal	0	0.56	0.75	1.00	1.30	1.67	2.12	2.12
25.0%		0	0.75	1.00	1.30	1.67	2.12	2.66	2.66
27.0%		0	1.00	1.30	1.67	2.12	2.66	3.29	3.29
29.0%		0	1.30	1.67	2.12	2.66	3.29	4.04	4.04
31.0%	Out-standing	0	1.30	1.67	2.12	2.66	3.29	4.04	4.04

*The bonus payout factor can be calculated from the following formula:
Bonus payout factor =

$$K = \left(\frac{\text{ROA\%} + \text{bias} + .4 \text{ sales growth\%}}{33} \right)^{4.5}$$

Note: The payout is deliberately nonlinear, generating higher incremental payoffs at higher levels of performance. Note the "cut-off" and "saturation" levels. The bias factor allows management to adjust the expected payout from year to year to compensate for unusual circumstances, for example, a year in which deliberate, heavy strategic expenditures are committed that will depress operating ROA. The bias factor is set at the beginning of the year-coincident with the annual plan-and then held constant through the planning period.

FIGURE 15-5 Bonus Payoff Function for 1979

Source: Ray Stata and Modesto Madique, "Bonus System for Balanced Strategy," Nov.-Dec. 1980. Reprinted by permission of the *Harvard Business Review*.

served an outstanding reward, junior managers should not risk such a large percentage of their compensation because higher-level decisions affect their performance, sometimes negatively. Analog paid its bonus quarterly in an effort to co-align management and stockholder interests.

At General Electric in the 1970s, management developed a three-factor bonus system to focus management attention on different factors across divisions according to their corporate missions, that is, the objectives set for them in the light of GE's corporate strategy. Invest or grow managers were more heavily rewarded for actions and programs geared to future benefits than for short-term results. Harvest or divest managers were rewarded more heavily for short-term earnings, as *Figure 15-6* shows.

Other schemes exist which incorporate more factors in bonus compensation. Stonich (1981) refers to a scheme using four factors—ROA, cash flow, strategic funds programs, and market share increase—with each factor rated differently according to the SBU (Strategic Business Unit) category of a particular operating entity. Strategic funds programming is a specific effort to emphasize long-run efforts in product development, innovation, and management development, for example, by separating normal operating expenses from ''expendable'' investments in the future well-being of the firm.

Stonich also refers to an income statement where the top part relates to operations and the bottom to strategic funds, so that operating and overall performance are

Market Growth
Market Size
Segmentation
Cyclicality
Nature of Demand
Ease of Entry and Exit
Number and Size of Competitors
Capacity in Place
Scale Economies
Break Even Positions
Length of Operating Cycle
Profitability
Roles of Price, Quality, and Cost
Product and Process Life Stage
Contingent Liabilities and Risks
Social Impact

INDUSTRY ATTRACTIVENESS

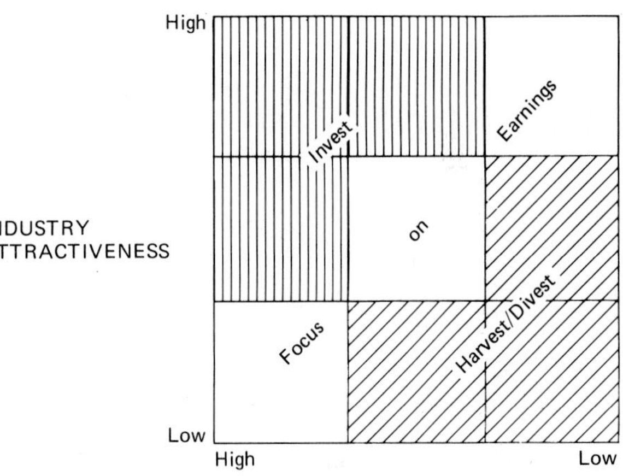

Market Share	Management
Product Technology	Labor Productivity
Process Technology	Plant Capacity
Price Premium	Cost Position
Product (Brand) Image	Flexibility and Service
Sales Force	Material Cost
Distribution Strength	Environmental Impact

Matching Bonus to Business Mission

	Bonus Weight (measure)		
Objective	*Current Financial Performance*	*Competitive Position Future Performance*	*Other Factors*
Invest	30%	60%	10%
Focus on Earnings	50%	40%	10%
Harvest/Divest	70%	20%	10%

FIGURE 15-6 Business Unit Assessment

TABLE 15-1 SBU P & L Segregation of Strategic Funds

Sales	$12,300,000
Cost of sales	−6,900,000
Gross margin	$5,400,000
Operating SG & A	−3,700,000
Operating ROA	$1,700,000 or 33%
Strategic funds	−1,000,000
Pre-tax profit (ROA)	$700,000 or 13.6%

Source: Stonich, "Using Rewards in Implementing Strategy," *Strategic Management Journal*, 2, 351. © 1981 by John Wiley & Sons.

monitored. Note the placement of strategic funds below the operating ROA in Table 15-1. Stonich comments:

> Using the strategic funds deferral method, managers can be given incentives to invest strategic funds where, under a conventional ROA measurement, the incentive is to hold them down in the same way as operating expenses. Managers can be encouraged to follow their natural inclination to manage to the "bottom line," where, in this case, current operating ROA is the measure. Thus, current operations of the company can be made as profitable as possible at the same time that critical future investments through strategic funds are encouraged. (1981, p. 350)

Hart Hanks Newspapers specified objectives on six dimensions of performance for its subsidiary, Independent Publishing of Anderson, South Carolina, in 1975,[7] specifying for each objective "must," "good," and "outstanding" levels of performance. No bonus was to be paid until "good" was reached on "managerial margin." Thereafter John Ginn, the Independent's publisher, received a personal bonus which varied according to the number of goals achieved out of the total possible. He, as all Hart Hanks managers, received a corporate bonus based on corporate performance ranging up to 15 percent of salary, while the individual bonus could amount to 20 to 35 percent of base salary.

In all these examples, the effort to use compensation to focus effort on specific objectives is deliberate. Note the use of standards so that the quality of performance is essentially rewarded contractually. These examples show the use of multiple objectives which encourage managers to make the right tradeoffs for the organization.

CONCLUSION: HUMAN RESOURCES SHAPE STRATEGY

The theme of this chapter is that administrative systems are communications systems. Signals have to be clear and clearly received to help the people of the organization work together.

Sun Tzu wrote:

> When one treats people with benevolence, justice, and righteousness, and reposes confidence in them, the army will be united in mind and will be happy to serve their leaders. (1963, p. 64)

[7]Hart Hanks Newspapers, ICCH 9-377-062.

He also stated:

> Generally, management of many is the same as management of few. It is a matter of organization. And to control many is the same as to control few. This is a matter of formations and signals. (p. 90)

These ancient prescriptions are still applicable. There is no justice in asking people to fail. Selection must be informed and careful. Confidence necessitates mutual trust founded on results. Thus, assignments should be used to give people, high and low, opportunities to build experience and trust. Benevolence is a principle of doing to others as you would like them to do to you. As Chesterton said, it isn't that it's been tried and found wanting, it simply isn't tried.

James F. Lincoln a co-founder of the Lincoln Electric Company wrote:

> Competition means there will be losers as well as winners in the game. Competition will mean the disappearance of the lazy and incompetent. . . . It is a hard taskmaster. It is necessary for anyone, be he worker, user, distributor or boss, if he is to grow. . . . There is not danger from a hard life. . . . Danger is from a life . . . made soft by lack of competition.

Yet he also stated:

> The worker (which includes management), the customer, the owner and all those involved must be satisfied that they are properly recognized or they will not cooperate, and cooperation is essential to any and all successful applications of incentives.[8]

George E. Willis, Lincoln Electric's president in 1971, explained how Lincoln could simultaneously promote competitiveness and foster cooperation:

> If our employees did not believe management was trustworthy, honest and impartial, the system could not operate. . . This ties back to a trust and understanding between individuals and all levels of the organization.[9]

In a world where competitiveness is honored on the playing field, in the classroom, and in professional life, it is easy to overlook the need for cooperation. When we join an organization, we should recognize that we will have to work with and through others and that most of our interactions are fundamentally cooperative.

Size and diversity in organizations typically necessitate a specialization of labor and choices of where and how to allocate resources. But such divisions necessitate coordination and a coordinator, and so a hierarchy of managers. Hierarchy and specialization each imply selective recruiting and development and mechanisms to influence behavior. Managers will use universal and individual incentives to influence behavior, rewarding what is functional rather than dysfunctional, making allied decisions about the use of pressure and the scope of delegation based on both the needs of the situation and their personal styles.

[8]Lincoln Electric Company, ICCH 9-376-028.
[9]*Ibid.*

Concluding, we want to stress the needs of the organization for initiative and change and for coordination and continuity. We stress the use of competitive and cooperative behavior to implement strategy, noting that managers do not work alone but together, subject to their being individually responsible (to each other) for results. The organization needs initiative and change as well as coordination and continuity.

chapter 16

Planning and Control

INTRODUCTION

Planning at its best institutionalizes strategic management. With an effective planning and control system in place, management periodically reviews its current situation and results, looks ahead, and acts to position the firm for the future. Planning may be ineffective where management has failed to act, out of timidity for example, or because management has failed to use its results to improve its plans and control its actions.

Keep in mind as you read this chapter that planning is useful only if it helps us manage. The besetting sin of planners is to give undue importance to planning, plans, and the planner. Planning is not an end in itself, but simply an institutional approach for strategic management.

Planning means not only foreseeing the future but providing for it (Fayol, 1972). Control means predicting the outcomes of our actions, collecting information on performance, comparing plan and performance. Where our decision or action proves inadequate or successful, we can use control to correct the one and reinforce the other (Ackoff, 1970).

Describing a business plan in 1916, Fayol wrote, "The plan of action is, at one and the same time, the result envisaged, the line of action to be followed, the stages to go through, and the methods to be used" (1972, p. 43). Today, we would use the words, "the objectives sought and the strategies to be used to achieve them," but Fayol's principles are relevant. Action is needed. We also note the importance Fayol gave to timing and the fact that he recognized that planning is costly, difficult, necessitates control, and must be repeated:

> Compiling the annual plan is always a delicate operation and especially lengthy and laborious when done for the first time, but each repetition brings some simplification and when the plan has become a habit the toil and difficulties are largely reduced. Conversely, the interest it offers increases. The attention demanded for executing the plan, the indispensable comparison between predicted and actual facts, the recognition [of] mistakes made and successes attained, the search for means of repeating the one and avoiding the other—all go to make the new plan a work of increasing interest and increasing usefulness. (p. 49)

Planning is important but not easy. Introducing his book, *A Concept of Corporate Planning,* Russell Ackoff eloquently describes the difficulty:

> Planning is the design of a desired future and of effective ways of bringing it about. It is an instrument that is used by the wise but not by the wise alone. When conducted by lesser men it often becomes an irrelevant ritual that produces short run peace of mind, but not the future that is longed for. (1970, p. 1)

Hunsicker (1980) quotes a typical executive complaint which suggests that Ackoff is right:

> We spend an awful lot of time planning but I find it hard to point to a clear case where our business is better off or even substantially better off for it.

Paradoxically, this same executive said the process worked ''reasonably well'' (p. 8).

DOES PLANNING PAY?

Despite management's occasional doubts, managers do plan, and researchers have generally concluded that over time the objective evidence is that planning pays. Using an extensive questionnaire to survey the acquisition practices of ninety-three US manufacturing firms over the twenty-year period 1946 to 1966, Ansoff and his colleagues (1970) concluded, ''the firms that exhibited extensive planning of their acquisition programs significantly outperformed the firms that did little formal planning'' (p. 5). Thune and House (1970) found that, when considered as a group, companies that engaged in formal long-range planning historically outperformed a comparable group of informal planners. However, Thune and House found differences in the efficacy of planning across industries and concluded:

> Successful economic results associated with long-range planning tend to take place in rapidly changing industries and among companies of medium size. . . . It is most likely that formal planning is a characteristic of a well-managed firm rather than the single cause of successful economic performance. (p. 87)

Thune's and House's work was extended by Herold (1972) who found that, collectively, formal planners' sales and profit growth outperformed informal planners' in the two industries he studied, drugs and chemicals. Reinforcing Thune and House's view that planning is associated with well-managed firms, Herold showed that the R&D expenditures of formal planners were greater than the informal planners'. Herold argued that planning and increased R&D expenditures each contributed to the increased success of the planners over comparable nonplanners and that this, too, was evidence that well-managed companies planned.

Although the research cited is not conclusive that planning per se pays, the evidence is that well-managed companies plan and outperform many others. However, in interpreting the research literature, recall that planning is only one of the administrative systems

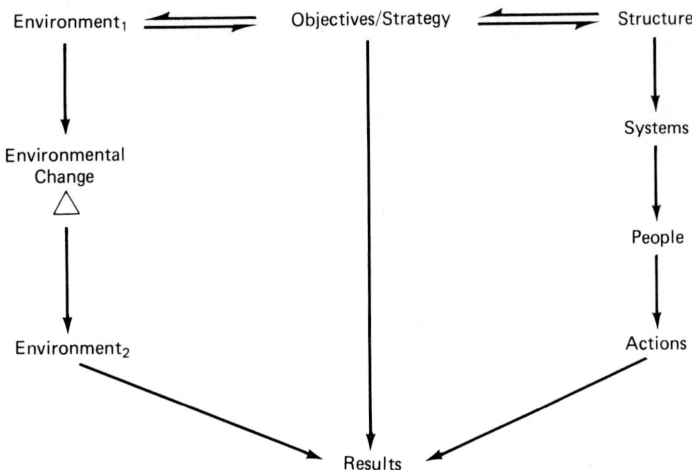

FIGURE 16-1 The Strategic Management System

management has at its disposal to enhance corporate performance. Our model of the Strategic Management System, repeated here as *Figure 16-1,* points to the separate but interdependent influences of the environment and the organization on the results earned by a particular strategy. And, although Ansoff and colleagues, Thune and House and Herold controlled for "time" and the environment, they did not have data on "good" and "poor" plans, control systems, nor the quality of the organization.

It is surprising that the research is as conclusive as it is, given the complexities of the full administrative system and the influences of the environment. Armstrong (1982) concluded in his review of the research on planning that planning is useful. He added, however, that the research to date says little about how or when to plan.

We believe planning is best when it is anchored in reality, when management "owns" its plans—that is, commits to them—and when top management uses its experience to add value to the corporation by strengthening the plans of separate business or business units in a thorough review process. Furthermore, plans are only useful when they promote commitment for coordinated action. Agreement on strategies is more critical than consensual objectives in the short run (Bourgeois, 1980), while organizations which promote and ultimately live consistently with superordinate objectives, appear to outperform all their competitors over time (Pascale and Athos, 1981; Peters and Waterman, 1982).

PLANNING PRACTICE

Formal planning for business was advocated by Fayol in 1916 and given a substantial boost in the United States by the consulting work of James McKinsey in the 1930s (McKinsey, 1932) and by his successors at McKinsey and Company and A.T. Kearney (Wolf, 1978). Since the 1960s, when "having a plan" became fashionable, management has wrestled with the wisdom of planning and the difficulty of doing it right. Wrapp questioned the wisdom of having a specific detailed plan at all:

> The top management must think out objectives in detail, but ordinarily some of the objectives must be withheld, or at least communicated to the organization in modest doses. A conditioning process which may stretch over months or years is necessary in order to prepare the organization for radical departures from what it is currently striving to attain. (1967, p. 95)

Plans are only tools. Wrapp, of course, advocated thinking about the future, although he cautioned managers about "published" plans. Used ineptly, plans can promote a set and inflexible position. Used well, they can promote coordination and focused effort. Wrapp warned management about the sacred character plans can acquire when they are seen as more than tools, and about the holy "hands-off" mantle which planners can gather about themselves in a large organization.

For example, during the 1960s and 1970s planning staffs bloomed in many large corporations, a growth aided by the availability of corporate computer power and econometric modelling techniques. While available today to planners and line managers alike, the computer languages available in those years preserved and enhanced the power of the planning staffs at the expense of line management and in some companies isolated the planners from action. In fact, although the Arab-Israeli wars in 1967 and 1971 foreshadowed dramatic structural shifts in the US economy, it was only after the 1974 oil embargo and recession that line managers began to regain influence in the planning process.

In 1976 Naylor and Schauland reported that econometric and financial models were often developed as the bases for corporate plans. Yet by 1980 some of the largest corporations, including General Electric which largely disbanded its corporate planning staff, had reduced their reliance on econometric and other planning models and put the responsibility for planning back on line managers. Although models are now used extensively to explore the implications of various strategic options, the turbulence of the late 1970s led companies to put responsibility for planning closer to the marketplace where current data and managerial experience can play a greater role in determining strategy.

In making this change to line-dominated planning, however, there is a risk. The older planning models placed great weight on analysis, but very little on synthesis. The danger is that the line-dominated approaches may place too little weight on the need for quality analysis as the foundation for the plan.

Mintzberg (1976), drawing on the research of neurologists and psychologists, noted that analysis and synthesis are two very different processes and rarely highly developed in one individual. He then proposed that there is probably a similar difference between formal planning and informal managing. Planners appear to work in a logical and orderly manner, while Mintzberg argues that many effective managers are intuitive and work with relatively little order, noting, "They tend to underemphasize analytical input that is often important as well" (p. 58).

In a speech before the Conference Board's 1981 Marketing Conference in New York City, John F. Welch, Jr., then Chairman and CEO of the General Electric Company, explained his views on why planning practice has turned, for now, back to line management and away from staff:

> At financial planning, at resource allocation . . . , the internalities, . . . strategic planning did well . . . but not too well at marketing, . . . the crucial externality. Comfortable with quantification, strategic planning mapped the external world beautifully—market size and share. It made huge contributions to resource allocation . . . but strategic planning didn't, or couldn't, *chart a market course*. . . . It didn't navigate . . . it didn't lead . . . and, unfortunately, too often it was seen to replace marketing. (1981, p. 3)

A sense of buyers' needs, ultimately seeking opportunity and creating value, is often lacking in formal planning practice. Planning promotes continuity rather than innovative change.

PLANNING PROBLEMS

As we will see, the problems that beset planning are simply a subset of those which afflict management, because planning is, as noted earlier, nothing more than one of the tools in management's administrative armory. As a result, the steps management might take to eliminate the problems of planning are likely to simultaneously facilitate and enhance the quality of planning and the effectiveness and efficiency of management as a whole.

Planning rarely works if top management does not support it. It can't work if insufficient resources are allocated to the job. Nevertheless, experience suggests that the law of diminishing returns quickly sets in if too many planners are put to work in one organization. Plans, like actions, must be founded in reality. The process used should be tailored to the needs and experience of the firm and its management rather than being abstracted from a planning text or workbook. The process will function more effectively if its results are monitored and if "good" planning is rewarded. Planning will be more fruitful if the process is modified from time to time to stimulate fresh thinking and to focus attention on different issues. Finally, planning will get results only if it is enacted—that is, if commitment follows plan and action follows commitment—and if the results of those actions are fed back into the thinking that occurs in subsequent planning cycles. Unfortunately, this rarely happens if a "planner" prepares the plan.

Consequently, an effective planning system should not rely too much on professional planners, or use too much of top and lower management's time. It should not cost too much to staff, and it should help line management day to day and thereby earn its keep. Remember, managers, not "planners," are ultimately responsible for results, including short-term results.

Top Management's Role

Probably the most critical audience for formal planning is top management. In most companies, if top management will not demonstrate support for a formal planning system, for whatever reasons, the system will be devitalized and will degenerate to empty ritual. A sure sign of a lack of top management commitment and a ritualistic planning system is middle managers who say, ''We've finished the plan. Now let's get back to work.'' Indeed, George Steiner says:

> There can be no effective comprehensive corporate planning in any organization where the chief executive does not give it firm support and makes sure that others in his organization understand his depth of commitment. (1969, p. 2)

Steiner adds, ''This principle should be obvious, but it is not.''

Since it is usually CEO's who initiate planning and whose support is critical, why do they sometimes withdraw that support? The answer is unclear, but often it comes from frustration with the time consumed and the difficulty they meet when they try to use the planning system to address their big problems. Recognizing a hole (problem), they allow the digging (planning) to continue because planning is supposed to be good for a company.

Instead, they should follow Taylor's First Rule of Holes: When you know you're in a hole, stop digging! Bruce Taylor, Executive Vice President of the Greater Boston YMCA in 1983, introduced us to this ''law.'' When applied to planning, it suggests a cure: if your present approach doesn't work, change it. Harold Henry (1977) wrote, ''If one solution doesn't work, others should be tried. There is no cookbook ingredient which can be applied in every firm, but the most important ingredient is to find or develop managers who want to do a better job of managing'' (p. 45).

The problem, as we warned earlier, is in treating planning as a sacred art rather than a tool, and planners as priests. This can be changed. Lorange and Vancil (1976) note that an effective planning system requires ''situational design'' appropriate to the organization's circumstances and resources.

Planners Are People Too (and Vice-Versa)

Of the resources affected by planning, it is the human resources that are most critical. People are responsible for planning, for its inputs and its outputs. People are accountable for the plan, the effect the process has on those involved, and ultimately for the actions taken and their results.

Remember, although planning appears to be a realistic, logical and intellectual activity, it is a social and emotional activity too. As Reichman and Levy (1975) point out, planning ''prompts illogical, irrational emotional responses that actually inhibit'' it (unless these responses are recognized and used, for example, to generate widely different alternatives as Emshoff, Mitroff and Kilman (1978) report).

Lyles and Lenz (1982) in their survey of planning practices of six regional commercial banks found that managers were aware of a large number of behavioral problems afflicting their planning efforts. We have classified the critical subset of these problems into three groups in *Figure 16-2,* reflecting our diagnosis of the types of people likely to behave in the ways Lyles and Lenz describe. The ''incapable,'' perhaps because of lack of native talent or timidity, try to plan it safe. The ''gamesmen'' try to use the planning system for their personal gain, to play it for all it's worth. The ''priests'' play planning for its own sake. For the incapable, training may be necessary. For the gamesmen, top

FIGURE 16-2 Critical Behavioral Problems* in Planning

Incapable or Afraid

- Project current trends rather than analyze the future for opportunities
- Resist changes in the status quo
- Fear making mistakes
- Avoid thinking beyond short-run, day-to-day activities
- Are uncertain about the expectations of upper-level managers
- Become bored with the planning process

Gamesmen

- Primarily bargain for resources rather than identify new resources
- "Pad" their plan to avoid close measurement
- Resist the discipline that planning requires
- View their part of the organization as more important than other parts
- Comply with rather than being committed to goals

Priests

- "Pad" their plan to avoid close measurement
- File their plan away until next year and do not look at it
- Are judged on the basis of their credibility in the organization rather than upon reaching planned objectives

*A critical problem was shared by 65 percent or more of 72 managers in 6 regional banks with assets ranging from $1.8 to $2.3 billion, who, on a 1 to 5 scale (1, no reduction in effectiveness of planning, to 5, great reduction), gave it a score greater than 3.0.

Source: Adapted from Lyles and Lenz, "Managing the Planning Process: A Field Study of the Human Side of Planning," *Strategic Management Journal,* 3, 105–18. © 1982 by John Wiley & Sons.

management review and example are likely to effect a cure, while for the priests there may be no remedy within their present employer's organization.

CAUSES OF POOR PLANNING

Planning problems are merely symptoms. What are the ultimate causes of poor planning? Bales (1977), then a principal of McKinsey and Company, cited three reasons why senior executives become dissatisfied with the results of their strategic planning efforts:

1 superficial analysis;
2 monolithic planning;
3 inadequate review.

Superficial analysis means that important environmental and internal input to the planning process is ignored or overlooked by those who define the plan. Monolithic planning implies centralization, a standardized format and a process that suffocates thought and denies managers a right to commit personally to the plan—after all it is not theirs. Inadequate review, as with the other symptoms, suggests an uninvolved or an inappropriately involved top management and a poor administrative context.

Superficial analysis occurs when form masks substance, when people omit steps in the process and create plans without a firm fact-based foundation. Its symptoms are static business definitions and casual segmentation schemes, an internal rather than a customer or competitive view, simple extrapolations of past trends, "hopeful hockey stick" forecasts of future performance improvements (that is, beginning next year, but every year being one more year forward on a longer sloping stick, promising turnaround after an ever-lengthening history of decline). A continuous record of unrealistic forecasts, time horizons frequently varied waiting for a particular result, and undifferentiated plans and planning formats in use across business units, similarly signal superficial analysis.

Most planning problems can be remedied if there is a *review process* where experienced managers or board members focus on the key competitive factors and ask how results will be earned and how competition is likely to affect those results. If reviews during the planning process are used to develop managers and educate them about their business, rather than as a lever to extract commitments, top management can participate in the process, broaden the definition of issues and add the value of its experience to the planning effort of the organization.

Monolithic plans tend to the "top-down" variety and, as Pennington (1972) said, few plans that are handed down are carried out. But the suffocating climate of the monolithic plan is usually the result of a dysfunctionally overformal process and sometimes of overabundant central direction, either from top management or staff planners. Too many forms or the "we're done planning—now we can get back to work" comment are other symptoms.

If the forms are too numerous, or the nature of the plan review is too detailed or spread over too long a time, or if responsibility for the plan is dissipated, line management will be driven out of the planning process. Perversely, the situation will then get worse as "staff" fill the gaps left by the withdrawing managers, hastening their flight with plans that are irrelevant to operating management.

Ultimately, it is top management's responsibility to change things and make the planning process work. But the task is not always easy to accomplish. We plan to manage, but to use Marvin Bower's phrase, "the will to manage" is easily sapped. A cursory review devalues the planning process while too close an involvement by top management brings its own problems. Bower described this condition well:

> Either giving too-detailed instructions in advance or making a too-detailed review after action has been taken results in poor delegation. Any subordinate already has certain automatic performance guides: policies, plans, and budgets. If, in addition, his superior tells him step by step how to take action, the subordinate feels too much like a puppet. His freedom to think for and learn by himself is limited, and his opportunity to learn through mistakes is denied. The results are virtually the same when the subordinate knows his actions will be subject to detailed review: instead of using his own judgment, he will then try to learn or guess what the superior would do. (1966, p. 176)

Bower's conclusions are supported by Lyles and Lenz's (1982) research. When operating managers' perceptions of behavioral problems were compared with top management's, one of the few problems identified only by lower management as having a large, deleterious effect on planning was "a fear of mistakes"; perhaps this fear was due not to a failure of courage but to too detailed supervision.

Ultimately, we must emphasize "managing." Planning is itself uninteresting. We plan to manage better. If managing is kept paramount, few planning problems cannot be solved. Planning problems persist when planning takes on a life of its own and becomes independent of managing and management.

DESIGNING THE PROCESS

Problems in planning are often similar to the problems which firms have in adopting a strategic management perspective. The solutions are generally the same kinds of things which would improve most firms' strategic performance: Start from reality, think through how proposed actions will be implemented, monitor results, and use a strategic management process tailored to the context of your firm rather than generalized approaches abstracted uncritically from a planning guide or text.

To formulate strategy, we must weigh and integrate the current strategy, the state of the environment, the resources available, and the values, objectives, and commitments of key stakeholders. In designing a planning system, the critical decisions concern who will be responsible for which tasks, how the separate roles will be coordinated, and when and how information will be communicated to other participants in the planning process and other members of the firm.

Structure

In a decentralized organization, most of the critical decisions that are inputs to strategy definition will be pushed down in the organization to a point where relevant information is available and understood. In a centralized organization, many more factors will be determined at the top.

Here we should note that Alfred Sloan, a member of General Motors board for forty-five years and its CEO for twenty-three years, and Ralph Cordiner, once CEO of General Electric and the architect of its initial decentralized organization structure, both recognized an inherent contradiction at the crux of managing a decentralized organization. The contradiction lies between profit center or business unit managers' needs for autonomy and the corporate need for control. Many years after drafting his principles of organization at General Motors, Sloan described the contradiction as follows:

> I am amused to see that the language is contradictory, and that its very contradiction is the crux of the matter. In point 1, I maximize decentralization of divisional operations in the words "shall in no way be limited." In point 2, I proceed to limit the responsibility of divisional chief executives in the expression, proper control. (1963, p. 58)

Sloan continues by saying that one aspect or another is given priority or asserted at different times. "Interaction is the thing," he adds, presumably between executives negotiating a proper balance in the light of the facts defining the situation of each part of the organization and the whole.

Hence, one of the crucial inputs to the design process will be corporate need. If the corporation is in crisis, perhaps precipitated by external factors, a top-down approach is likely and subordinate managers' roles are probably restricted. When the corporation is doing well, a more decentralized competitive process is likely to be used, since internal risks are more affordable.

Things to Consider

Lorange and Vancil (1976) make some simple prescriptions for system design based on the typical managerial capabilities and environmental complexity of small and large companies. *Table 16-1* focuses on the nature of the goal-setting process and the explicitness with which objectives or goals are usually communicated to the organization. In the small company, face-to-face contact reduces the need for explicitness. In large, diverse companies, top management has limited ability to judge the appropriateness of the match between corporate objectives and divisional capabilities and so is likely to make less explicit statements of objectives at first and more explicit statements as planning experience accumulates and the organization itself matures.

Scanning the environment is typically centralized in small companies where only a few managers cross the organization's boundaries. In a large, diverse organization, however, the various transactions and relationships of the organization cross many boundaries, forcing top management to rely on middle management for information which describes the different environments in which the firm operates.

Lorange and Vancil's other issues reflect on the roles played by middle managers and staff planners as company size is increased and as planning experience accumulates. As the company matures and becomes more complex, Lorange and Vancil observed that

TABLE 16-1 Approaches to Planning System Design Issues

	Situational Settings		
Issues	*"Small" Companies*	*"Large" Companies New Planning System*	*"Large" Companies Mature Planning System*
Communication of corporate goals	Not explicit	Not explicit	Explicit
Goal-setting process	Top-down	Bottom-up	"Negotiated"
Corporate-level environmental scanning	Strategic	Statistical	Statistical
Subordinate managers' focus	Financial	Financial	Strategic
Corporate planner's role	Analyst	Catalyst	Coordinator
Linkage of planning and budgeting	Tight	Loose	Tight

Source: Adapted from Lorange and Vancil, "How to Design a Strategic Planning System," Sept./Oct. 1976. Adapted by permission of the *Harvard Business Review.*

strategic decision making is increasingly delegated and the staff planners' direct influence on the process declines.

How quickly should the process reduce options, fix on objectives, and convert high-level strategy to an explicit and committed budget? If fast, there will be little time for innovation and change. What should happen first?

The decision is, we believe, contingent upon the situation facing the organization. Let us note that planning follows the simple thought process set out by Dewey (1933) and includes steps which identify:

1 objectives
2 problems
3 alternatives
4 choices
5 actions

But the order is not (necessarily) fixed, although most plans are presented in a sequence such as that shown above. In some circumstances, it may pay to differ from Dewey's sequence and start the planning process at a different point. Our view is that where control and continuity are important, objectives can be set early. Where change is needed, objectives can be set late to allow time to develop options and evaluate them, to rework the best, and develop support within the organization.

SOME ADDITIONAL PRACTICAL CONSIDERATIONS

Strategy is converted to action through a hierarchy of interlocked plans of increasing specificity. Corporate strategy and objectives influence the content of investment programs, changes in business strategy, new projects, and ultimately precise operating budgets.

Sometimes the influence of strategy is direct and the planning sequence is logically developed to implement strategy directly, but most of the time it is not. Top management uses corporate strategy, the formal structure of the organization, the administrative systems that support it, and its own example to set the rules by which decisions are and will be made. In all but the smallest firms, where no middle-management level exists, it is middle managers who put their personal energy behind projects and new strategies to win corporate approval, thereby giving them impetus in the corporation. For the most part, explicit projects are largely defined by junior managers and technology specialists (Bower, 1970).

The decision process is therefore more likely to flow from bottom to top rather than top-down. The development of new computers illustrates the typical process well. In *The Soul of a New Machine,* Tracy Kidder (1981) describes how recent graduates essentially created the architecture of a new Data General computer in 1979. Tom West, the project manager, coordinated their efforts but, more importantly, motivated them with encouragement and underwrote the project by putting his career on the line. Top management's role was to set the context. Thus the project team could predict how top management would judge the new venture and they could develop and shape it to win.

As Thompson (1967) indicated, administration means channeling the ongoing actions of the separate parts of the organization so that they serve a common purpose. Planning, budgeting, and the decision process that is part of planning help managers focus the actions of the firm. The more steps there are between strategy formulation and the budget, the more time there will be for participation and innovation, and the more the process will contribute to the development of general management skills within the firm.

Managers have other design parameters at their disposal, too. Shank and his colleagues (1973) pointed out that management can influence the output of the planning process by modifying the linkages that exist between the various plans management creates. The more links there are, the tighter the control management exercises. Shank and his colleagues argue that control trades creativity for practicality, and so they recommend care in making these linkages.

Content linkages are potentially numerous. They may be as simple as the levels of financial detail and numeric rounding used in strategic plans and the budget. Are differences allowed—a loose link—or is a tight linkage necessary, with identical numbers required? How many years' data—none, or one, or more? Again, more links will restrict the innovative range of the plan. Do the strategic plans and the budget draw on the same data sources or not? What time horizons does each employ?

Content links are joined to organizational links to modify the range of the plan. If plans and budgets are reviewed by the controller, practicality and control are likely to have priority. Are plans and budgets prepared for the same units? In some organizations, administrative organizational units budget while plans are prepared by separate planning teams in an effort to encourage innovation.

Timing, too, is important. Which plans are prepared first? If the budget precedes the strategic plan, we can predict that the plan itself will be conservative and at best evolutionary. Timing of plan and budget initiation and approval will also influence the type of plan produced. As with the other links, more links give more control and constrain the forward reach and innovative scope of the planning effort.

INTRODUCING PLANNING TO AN ORGANIZATION

Unfortunately, planning is often introduced to an organization as an extension of the budget. This usually fails; it doesn't solve the big problems. Each linkage between plan and budget makes planning like budgeting. For example, if plan and budget are subject to similar reviews (although this may suit the purposes of organizations caught in a cash crisis) it is unlikely to make planning itself a useful tool for change. This is not surprising, of course; organizations have to stretch and change to handle their big problems and they have to learn their business and how to plan before they grapple with the big issues.

Experienced executives have suggested repeatedly that planning should be introduced simply with limited initial objectives. ''Start small and make it useful'' is their advice. Demonstrate that planning can earn its keep. For example, in a primary planning effort, management might focus on a study of its market, build understanding, and mount a new segmented marketing strategy because it senses the need for both change and an opportunity for growth and cost efficiency.

In a second round of planning, the focus of data collection and analysis might turn to operations, product costs and prices. The outcome could be rationalization and a focused new product development effort. In later cycles, when the process is working smoothly and knowledge of the business and its market is more extensive, more comprehensive planning can be initiated. Comprehensiveness becomes possible simply because data and experience accumulate as we plan and act. When we plan, we learn, and when we learn, we change things.

Kami (1968), who worked in planning at IBM and Xerox between 1952 and 1967, writes, "Anybody can plan five years ahead; it takes real management to leap from crisis to crisis." Offering some useful guidelines for planning and for plan review, he emphasizes that plans are never perfect—for example, few plans are entirely credible. However, he implies that this is not a problem. Based on his experience, Kami suggests that reviewers seek proposals promising at least three times the dollar volume the organization needs to close the gap between current performance and its objectives. He has learned to expect that estimated costs and time needed will double, while the market will rarely be greater than half the initial projection. Yet he advises managers to make the necessary adjustments privately: "But don't say anything out loud—that will kill the project. Just watch carefully that it's growing in the right direction."

All this implies constancy to purpose (Bower, 1966). Senior managers have to develop a sense of purpose in their organization and direct their organization towards it, albeit indirectly. Constancy is necessary to maintain focus. The Theory of the Big Wheel explains why. An organization, Kami (1968) says, is like a set of interconnected gear wheels. The efforts of every senior executive, a big wheel, are multiplied by the efforts of those below. But if the big wheel makes half a turn, the people at the bottom, many wheels below, are likely to be revolved twenty-six times. In every organization, there is only a limited ability to adapt. The more change is needed quickly, the greater the effort required, especially from top management. The puzzle is that continuity promotes efficiency and change destroys it, although change is often necessary.

AN ALTERNATIVE PLANNING MODEL

Planning is, as Bower (1967, 1982) and Ansoff (1971) say, a problem finding process. But what if the problem cannot be solved? What if, after repeated planning meetings, research and discussion, the corporation is faced with an insolvable problem? What do you do if experience assessment methods (based on current strategy identification and evaluation) fail?

Following the advice of DeBono (1968) and Henry (1977), we change the way we plan. All planning mechanisms cycle through the steps described in this book, that is, through an assessment of the current strategy, the organization's resources, and its stakeholder objectives, coupled with a forecast of the likely future environment. But some alternative planning processes change the order of the steps, beginning with elements other than reality. In some circumstances, for example, when you are blocked by an intractable problem, planning can fruitfully begin with idealized solutions. A vision of the future may be more fruitful as a starting point in developing new strategies than an understanding of the present.

One method for solving unstructured and intractable strategic problems, which

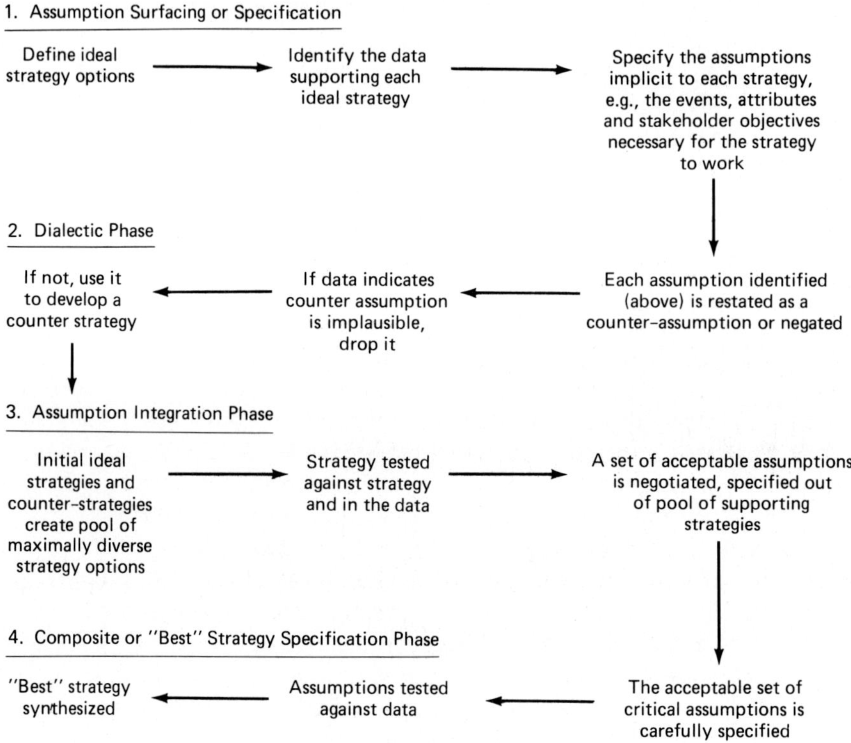

FIGURE 16-3 The Four Basic Steps of Strategic Assumptions Analysis

Source: Mitroff and Emshoff, "On Strategic Assumption-Making: A Dialectic Approach to Policy and Planning," *Academy of Management Review,* 4, no. 1, 1979, 5.

exploits this approach, is Strategic Assumptions Analysis (SAA). This has been advanced by Emshoff, Mitroff, and Kilman (1978)[1] and Mitroff and Emshoff (1979) who argue that their approach ensures that:

1 strongly different strategic options are considered;
2 thereby, the force of continuity, tradition, and organizational inertia is countered; and
3 the analysis that results is deep and so the organization is less vulnerable to non-penetrating thinking, which allows it to fall victim to unconsciously-made yet critical implicit assumptions.

The thinking behind the assumptions approach is that unless a strategy is tested against maximally challenging alternatives, it is likely to have undiscovered flaws.

As Mitroff and Emshoff (1979) describe it, the process has four phases, as illus-

[1]Strategic Assumptions Analysis and Dialectic Inquiry Systems have been described in a series of papers authored by Emshoff, Mitroff and Kilman, (1978); Emshoff and Finnel, (1979); Mitroff, Emshoff and Kilman (1979); Mitroff and Emshoff, (1979); Mason and Mitroff (1979) and Mitroff and Mason, (1980). Cosier and Aplin (1980) and Cosier (1981) offer criticism of the approach. Further comments are contained in Mitroff and Mason (1981) and Cosier (1981a).

trated in *Figure 16-3*. It begins with an assumptions specification stage which specifies ''ideal'' or uncompromising strategies. This is followed by a dialectic phase which exploits counter-assumptions to those underlying the initial strategies in order to develop an inventory of new strategies. In Phase 3, the pool of strategies and assumptions is purged of the irrelevant, the implausible and the unimportant, and finally effort it directed to identifying a practical best strategy in Phase 4.

The appeal of Mitroff and Emshoff's approach is that it breaks the block of the unsolved problem. Essentially, it is a planning methodology that takes advantage of one of DeBono's lateral thinking approaches, the use of direct opposites. Likewise, it relates to ''double-loop learning'' described by Argyris (1977), because it promotes challenges to conventional wisdom within the organization. SAA explicitly uses an Hegelian dialectic to test strategies and assumptions—strategy against strategy, assumption against assumption.

The originators of SAA, or idealized planning as it is sometimes called, warn that it is a difficult planning methodology in practice. Explicitly, they recommended its use only if experience assessment methods have been blocked. In addition, they point out that unless the initial strategies are dramatically different, the power of the approach wanes.

To obtain maximal initial divergence, they recommend the use of groups whose psychological characteristics or commitments are known. Groups of individuals are selected to represent different points of view. Each group would be composed of people of like persuasion (for example, supporters of a high or low price strategy or make or buy strategy), or of people sharing a similar psychological bent (optimists, pessimists, pragmatists, abstractionists, intuitive or logical decision makers). The point is to select groups likely to develop extreme positions.

Each group is then given the assignment to specify an ideal strategy and future environment, and to specify the assumptions underlying them. The following questions are illustrative of those used to initiate the process: What resources do you need? What environment will be most hospitable to your plan? What have you been assuming about the stakeholders or what have you had to assume about them so that if you started with these assumptions you would be able to develop your strategy?

With this done, the groups separately or together try to understand each others' points of view (not to reach consensus) and develop a set of opposite or negative assumptions. They then consider whether these negative assumptions imply a need for change in their strategies. If one of them does not, that original assumption is regarded as possibly irrelevant rather than critical.

Attention is then focused on the critical nature and certainty of the remaining assumptions and effort is directed to reduce the pool of assumptions as we noted earlier. (For example: in the circumstances shown in *Figure 16-4* research might be used to help specify the impact of Assumption C because it is both ''critical'' and ''certain.'' A and B, being neither critical nor certain, appear to need little research and might be dropped from consideration for the time being.) Then, the pool of assumptions left is used to develop a ''best strategy.'' Effort at this point is focused on integrating the robust elements of each separate analysis.

Emshoff, Mitroff, and Kilman (1978) suggest the need for an experienced facilitator to manage the dialectic and to help prepare an organization for the experience. Because groups are used one against another, trust is needed and unless this exists within the organization, no outsider is likely to develop it. For this reason, SAA is not for all.

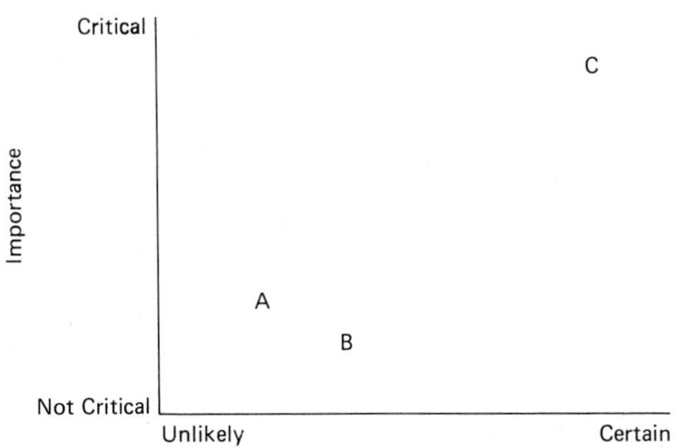

FIGURE 16-4 Importance-Certainty of Assumptions

Source: Emshoff and Finnell, "Defining Corporate Strategy: A Case Study Using Strategic Assumptions Analysis," *Sloan Management Review,* Spring 1979, p. 48. © 1979 by the Sloan Management Review Association; all rights reserved.

CONCLUSION

Top management must promote innovation and renewal as well as control the organization. Rigid formal planning systems do not innovate, since increased formality tends to generate inflexibility, while innovation requires flexibility. Planning systems therefore need some flexibility to encourage innovation and generate creative insight.

Yet, if top management must both control and innovate in the planning process, exactly how do these apparently contradictory tasks get done? The answer is leadership and an administrative system that communicates top management's leadership and example throughout the organization.

Both analysis and action are necessary for success. Action is a sign of effective planning. Performance is a sign of good management. Continued and growing performance is a sign of good planning and control. Thus, the current organization's definitions of its strategy, resources, and environmental assumptions are important. But the impetus to action must also be considered; the context and culture of the organization are an essential aid to implementation. Strategies which are properly implemented get results. And attaining desired results is the goal of successful strategic management and effective planning.

To conclude our discussion of alternative planning models, it is appropriate to mention that Jack Welsh, soon after his election as GE's Chairman, refused to publicly define GE's corporate strategy. He instead articulated a series of objectives. This, of course, does not mean that GE has no corporate strategy. Rather, GE's management has found its old centrally administered formal planning process no longer relevant for its needs. GE wants new products and new ventures and needs people ''behind'' the company's ideas. It has therefore changed its planning practices to encourage initiative, corporate flexibility and personal responsibility.

chapter 17

Corporate Strategy in Diversified and Integrated Multibusiness Firms

INTRODUCTION

Corporate strategy defines the scope of the firm's operations and how the management allocates or deploys its resources to make the whole firm a vital, competitive enterprise. The whole firm must be "vital" and "competitive"; unless the organization can function as a whole, with corporate management adding value, it is difficult to justify keeping all the parts under one corporate umbrella.

Indeed, corporate strategy is concerned more with the question of where to compete than with how to compete in a particular business—the latter is the province of business strategy. At the corporate level, the issues are what businesses to be in and how to deploy resources between them, what kind of organization to become and how to use the firm's resources to create value.

The management of the multinational health care company, Becton Dickenson, once explained:

> A large corporation is like an army: Without a clear strategy, its divisions can easily aim toward several different objectives at once. The principal challenge confronting the managers of a corporation—like the generals of an army—is to define a strategy that enables each component unit to contend effectively against its competitors, and then to array their divisions so that the entire organization marches toward the overall objective.[1]

Becton Dickenson's statement makes the point that the job of corporate management is to develop objectives and a corporate strategy that dominates, and so integrates,

[1]Becton Dickenson Annual Report 1978.

the operating business units of the corporation. Within a multibusiness firm, each business should have its own strategy and objectives so that it can contend effectively against its competition while serving the interests of the corporation. From time to time, the interests of the corporation may be best served by changes in the objectives and strategies of one or more of the businesses which it controls—the corporation must be more important than its parts.

The principle that corporate objectives and strategies must be made to dominate the parts is central to our view of a multibusiness organization. Corporate management can only do its job and add value if the parts serve the whole. Only if the parts, the business units of the firm, are managed as resources, to be used now or developed for later use by the corporation, will corporate management have an enacted strategy and the opportunity to use its accumulated experience to create value.

To distinguish corporate strategy from business strategy, the discussion in these three chapters on diversification is restricted to multibusiness firms where the corporate level is distinct from the business level. This distinction is clearer when separate or separable businesses have to be managed simultaneously. Hence, our focus is on multibusiness firms, particularly those which have diversified. We will explore diversification and the basic strategic options which diversity allows. We will examine US business practice, the rationale for diversification and its relationship to risk, and the results achieved by diversified companies.

In Chapter 18, we examine portfolio analysis and see how portfolio models can be used to track the firm's resource deployments and thereby the objectives of the firm's operating (business) units. The technique of Business Analysis is introduced in Chapter 19 as a tool for corporate strategy identification and is illustrated with the history of the Bic Corporation. The discussion of diversification will conclude, in Chapter 20, with multinational and global businesses and the administrative dilemmas faced by their corporate managements.

WHAT IS DIVERSIFICATION?

In simple terms, strategy is what you do to get what you want. Corporate strategy is what corporations do to achieve their objectives. What have they been doing? During most of the twentieth century, the largest corporations have been diversifying, and the extent of diversification has been increasing, particularly in industries based on newer and more sophisticated technologies (Rumelt, 1974).

The product-market matrix which we introduced in Chapter 11 and have extended into the international sphere in *Figure 17-1* illustrates the basic options available. As a company diversifies and moves away from a simple commitment to one product (or product line) for one market, a number of alternative directions is available. Note that *Figure 17-1* could be expanded by adding simple price and channel distinctions, or process technologies, for example.

The basic choices are simple. A movement from the "same-same" cell to the upper left of *Figure 17-1* implies vertical integration, forward or backward depending on whether the product technology is upstream or downstream in the industry chain. A

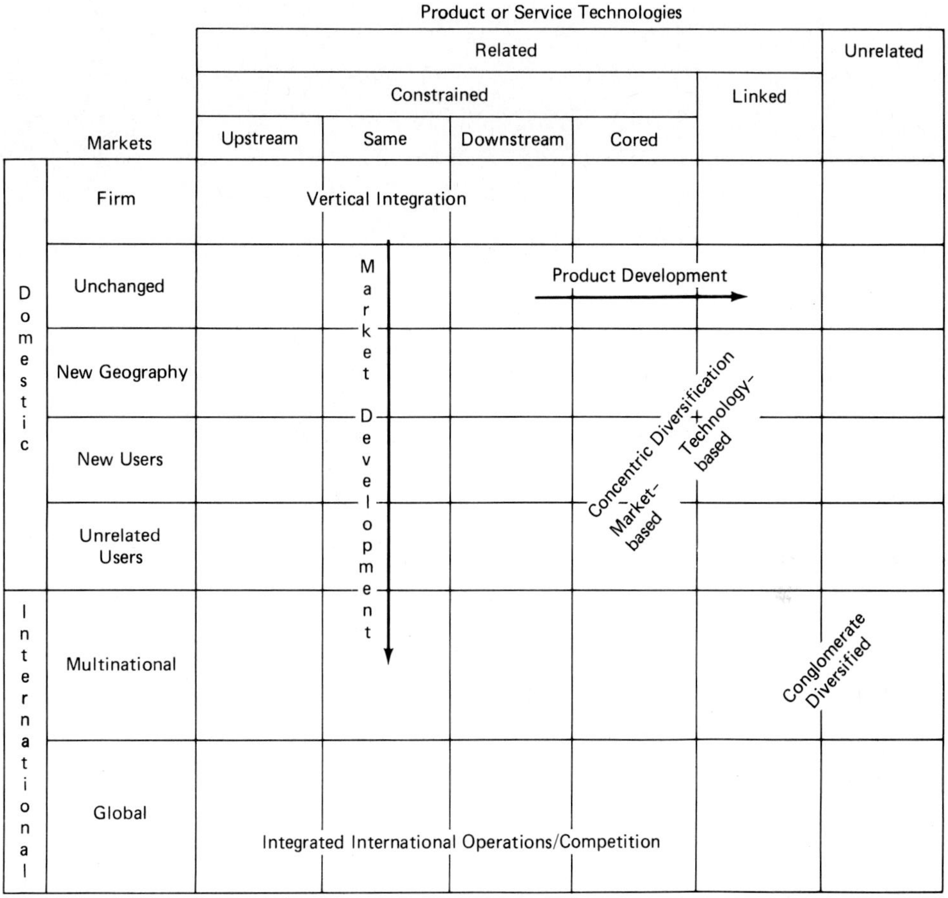

		Product or Service Technologies					
		Related					Unrelated
		Constrained				Linked	
	Markets	Upstream	Same	Downstream	Cored		
Domestic	Firm	Vertical Integration					
	Unchanged		Market Development ↓		Product Development →		
	New Geography					Concentric Diversification	
	New Users				Market-based	Technology-based	
	Unrelated Users						
International	Multinational						Conglomerate Diversified
	Global	Integrated International Operations/Competition					

FIGURE 17-1 The Product/Market Matrix

movement towards the bottom of the figure implies a market development strategy, while a movement to the right implies a product development strategy. Simultaneous addition of new markets and products and technologies amounts to diversification (Ansoff, 1965).

When diversification strategies are pursued, the character of the strategy is important. For example, is it concentric or conglomerate? If the diversification is distinguished by a *common thread* which relates past, present, and future markets and products so that insiders can guide the future development of the organization and outsiders can see where it is going, the diversification is concentric. A conglomerate is a firm where product market choices are unrelated (Ansoff, 1965).

Since Ansoff's work on diversification, researchers have focused their efforts on understanding the significance of product-market relationships within the diversified firm and have divided the related and concentric diversification category into two types: constrained and linked. A constrained diversification is characterized by a dominant core,

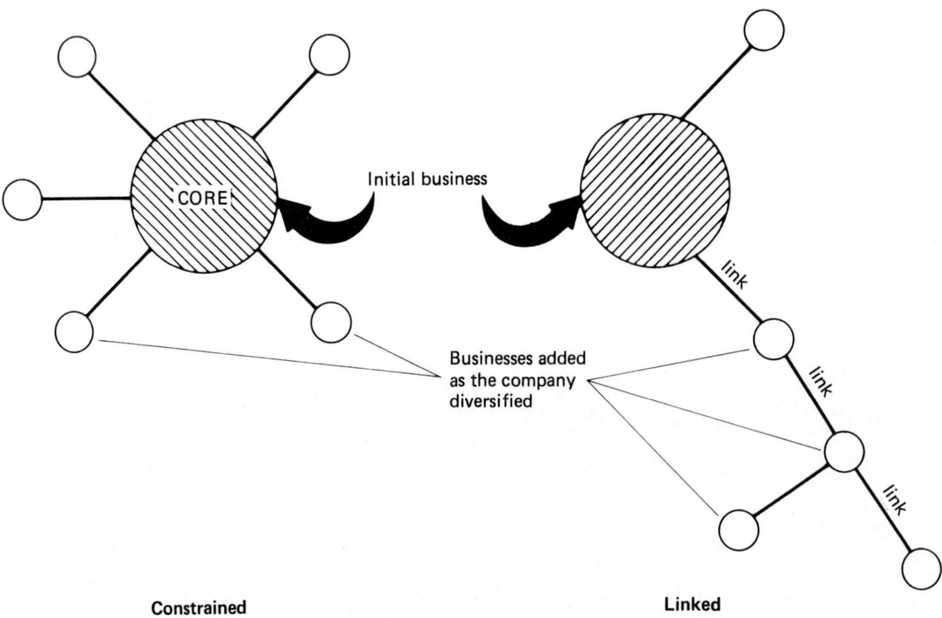

FIGURE 17-2 Types of Related Diversification

either market- or technology-based, while a linked diversification is characterized by simple links between one business and another. In simple terms, the archetypes are illustrated in *Figure 17-2*. The constrained firm has a core, the linked firm resembles a chain. Obviously, the common thread is weaker in the linked company.

Figure 17-3 fleshes out Carborundum's diversification and illustrates an additional point: US corporations have been moving from a constrained form of diversification to a linked type. Carborundum's strategic evolution has been similar to that of many US and European corporations (Rumelt, 1974).

Research by Chandler (1962), Channon (1973), Scott (1973), and Rumelt (1974) shows that big businesses worldwide have diversified and become more loosely diversified in their product market scope—in some cases adopting global strategies to operate across the world as one integrated and coordinated competitor, sometimes in many industries.[2]

Let us examine US practice. From *Table 17-1,* we can see just how extensive the trend towards product market diversity has been. *Table 17-1* catalogs the scope and type of diversification of the *Fortune* 500 over the period 1949 to 1974. Note in the top half of the table the shrinking proportion of those dominated by a single business. Similarly, note the growth of the related and unrelated categories. Within the dominant and related categories, linked diversification has become more common over time (Rumelt, 1982).

[2]Chandler (1966), Wrigley (1970), Channon (1973), Pavan (1972), Dyas (1972), Thanheiser (1972), Scott (1973).

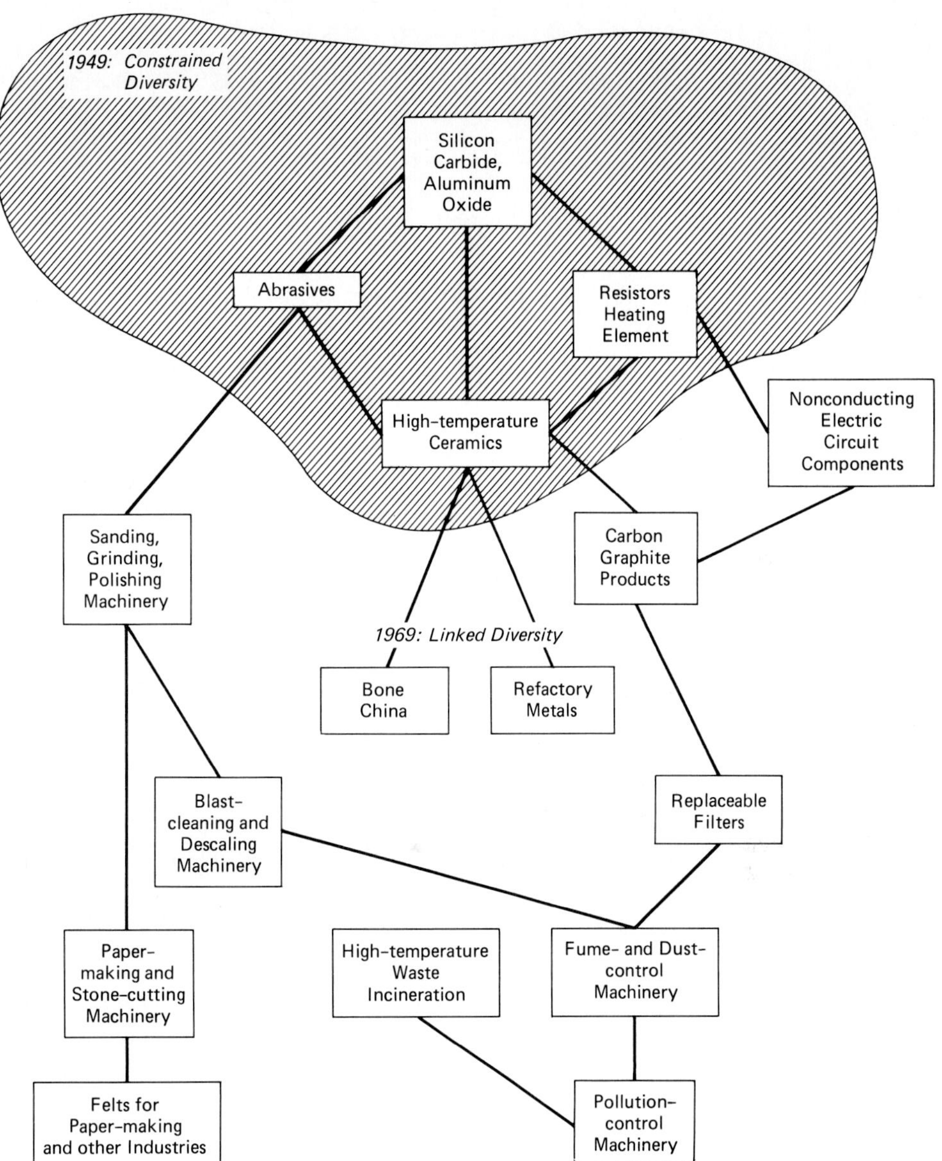

FIGURE 17-3 Carborundum, Inc., Strategic Diversification, 1949–1969, from Constrained to Linked

Source: Rumelt, *Strategy, Structural and Economic Performance,* Boston, MA: Division of Research, Harvard Business School, 1974.

TABLE 17-1
Diversification of the Fortune 500, 1949–1974

Major Category	Approx. % Revenue from Single Production-Distribution Chain*	Examples**	Estimated % of Fortune 500 Firms in Each Category					
			1949	1954	1959	1964	1969	1974
Single-Business	95	Maytag, Iowa Beef, Crown Cork & Seal, American Motors	42.1	34.1	22.8	21.5	14.8	14.4
Dominant	70–95	ARCO, Caterpillar, Hershey, Xerox, Deere, IBM	28.2	29.6	31.3	32.4	25.1	22.6
Related	45–70	GE, Merck, Dow 3M, Bristol Myers, Dupont	25.7	31.6	38.6	37.4	41.4	42.3
Unrelated	45	LTV, Rockwell Mfg., Litton, TRW	4.1	4.7	7.3	8.7	18.7	20.7
			100.0	100.0	100.0	100.0	100.0	100.0

**Strategic Management Journal* 81, Mimeo 1 (77; 2) undated mimeo
***Strategy, Structure and Economic Performance* 74
Source: Adapted from Rumelt, "Diversification Strategy and Profitability," *Strategic Management Journal*, 3, no. 4, Oct.-Dec. 1982, 359–70. © 1982 by John Wiley & Sons.

MULTIBUSINESS OBJECTIVES

Since the facts point strongly toward diversification as the strategy of choice, we can speculate about management's motives. In 1978, Wesley J. (Jack) Howe, by then President of Becton Dickinson for six years, was quoted in his company's annual report as follows: "The purpose of this diversification is both to allow steady growth in earnings and to reduce business risks by limiting the company's overall reliance on any single product." Writing about Beckton Dickenson in the same annual report, Peter Vanderwicken, consultant to the company, noted:

> The single-business company has a relatively easy task: Its strategy must be to nurture and protect its business. But a diversified company—and Beckton Dickinson is the most diversified in its industry—risks diluting its resources, neglecting its best opportunities, and doing little right.

Howe explains this risk associated with diversification:

> Our [planning] process is a continual review of the portfolio of businesses we're in, examining their characteristics and making appropriate conclusions. We are continually challenging, questioning, testing, and correcting. It's a living process. Its virtue is that we can't try to hold onto a dying business too long, or overlook some embryonic gem, because it's overshadowed by something that's bigger right now.

Note that Howe says his company has diversified to allow *steady* growth and to reduce the risk of over-reliance on one product. However, Howe acknowledges the existence of a different risk—the risk of neglecting opportunities and of being dominated by the past—which he implies is exacerbated by diversification itself.

FINANCIAL MOTIVATION FOR DIVERSIFICATION

Passive investors can eliminate nonsystematic risk of investment in their personal affairs by diversifying. Rumelt linked personal investment and corporate diversification this way:

> Until fairly recently it was commonly assumed that the smaller the commitment made to any particular security (or business) the more perfect the diversification. The application of the modern Markowitz diversification theory [theory that diversified portfolios spread risk] to the securities market has shown that the best possible diversification is achieved by portfolios consisting of a few carefully selected securities (often less than ten). The key requirement for efficient diversification is that negatively correlated returns be sought—if one goes up the other goes down. This result suggests that "too much" diversification can increase the risk faced by a corporation and that optimal diversification, in the statistical sense, is *not* necessarily obtained by investing in completely unrelated areas. For example, the ultimate diversified company, participating in all sectors of the economy would, by definition, have an average return and still bear the risk associated with major economic cycles. A firm active in military, space, and consumer electronics might earn an equal or better return and obtain superior protection against economic cycles. (1974, p. 80)

Nevertheless, although prudent investors may reap some benefits from diversification, we believe that their fate is different from that of a diversified corporation which operates businesses. Investors accept the risks attached to one stock or another, subject to the high degree of liquidity offered by the market. Managers have a more complex task: they have to manage risk, eliminating it if they can, and many of their corporate commitments are illiquid.

The major difference between business and investment portfolio diversification is that management has to *work* to create value: Management has an active role, not a passive one like an investor. Furthermore, ''Although a decrease in non-systematic risk is the rationale for portfolio diversification of marketable securities, there is no evidence that firms can create value through the simple ownership of diverse assets'' (Rumelt, 1982, p. 364).

While the risk of commitment to one business may be avoided by diversifying, a price of that risk avoidance is ''absorbing'' inexperience. *Figure 17-4* illustrates this point. If a company puts all its eggs in one basket, it can watch it more carefully. As it diversifies into areas where it has less experience, management has more and more difficulty controlling its operations. It may be possible to become too diversified.

Of course, there are many risks in business. The acquisition of a countercyclical business may reduce the impact of a downcycle on a corporation's earnings, but reduce the benefits of the upswing. Indeed, other strategies more closely tuned to the cycle of the

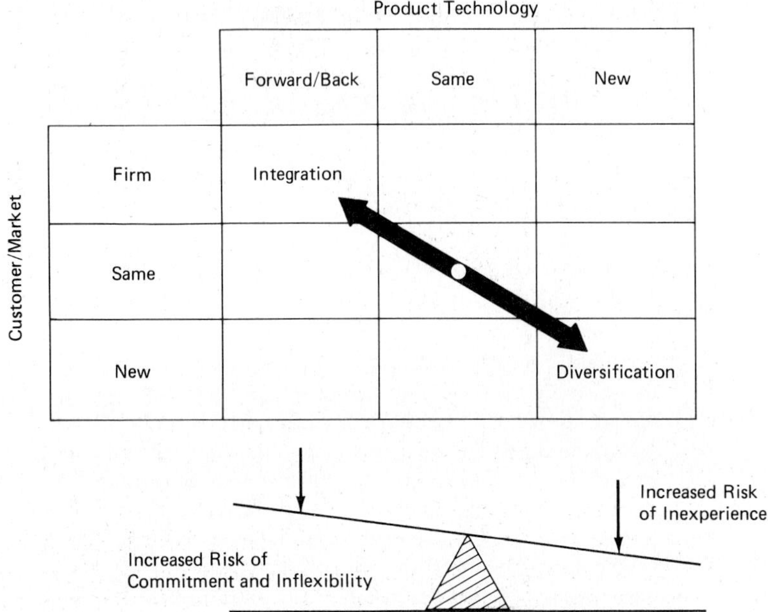

FIGURE 17-4 Risk and Diversification

corporation's dominant business—for example, using reduced financial leverage and just-in-time inventory, or lowering fixed costs and breakeven volume—may protect a corporation from the effects of a downswing in the economy without adding the risk of inexperience to the company through increased diversification.

This leaves management in a quandary. While management seeks stable growth and reduced risk, the evidence points to a need for considerable effort and self-discipline if the advantages of diversification are to be realized. Moreover, at the level of the firm, there must be some doubt that diversification per se can reduce risk—leaving us with growth as the more certain primary objective of diversification.

Such a position fits closely with the theories of the economists Baumol (1967) and Marris (1964), who argued that the fundamental motivation for growth is managerial compensation and prestige which seem to increase with growth rather than with simple profitability. Bass and his colleagues (1977), while admitting the validity of the growth objective, argued that companies diversified because their primary markets were saturated, leaving management short of opportunity close to home. He labeled many diversification programs "defensive." Others have seen diversification, particularly conglomerate diversification by acquisition, as seizing opportunity. Lewellen (1971), for example, saw many conglomerate mergers as opportunities to seize, leverage, and redeploy underutilized assets.

Although Ansoff is an early and much-quoted writer on diversification, his thinking is different from that of most others who have written on diversification. He did not mention risk reduction as an objective of diversification; moreover he seems to have omitted this deliberately because he recognized that *diversification is risky:*

> By its very definition diversification is the more drastic and risky of the two strategies [expansion is the other] since it involves a simultaneous departure from familiar products and familiar markets. (Ansoff, 1965, p. 113)[3]

Ansoff (1965) explained motivations for diversification as follows: corporations diversify if they can't meet their objectives within the scope of their current product markets; if their profitability is high and they have idle resources; if the opportunity for profit in another product-market promises to be larger than what they presently enjoy; and if management is unsure of what lies ahead. Ansoff also used the term "synergy" to describe opportunities attractive to the diversifying corporation's managers.

SYNERGY

Synergy promises a combined return on resources greater than the sum of the parts because of joint effects and shared costs; "2 + 2 = 5" is its popular form, although we know of a successfully diversified firm whose annual report refers to synergy as "2 + 2 = 7." Synergy may exist, for example, in sales via the use of common distribution channels or shared sales administration, in shared production experience, in transferred research and development, or, possibly, in management experience. Synergy should result from more intensive use of corporate resources. Hence, synergy promises added value at low cost.

Ansoff (1965) noted that synergistic potentials often exceeded actual performance in both start-ups and ongoing operations. Echoing President John F. Kennedy's "Ask not what your country can do for you but what you can do for your country," Drucker stated his primary rule of a successful acquisition:

> An acquisition will succeed only if the acquiring company thinks through what it can contribute to the business it is buying. Not what the acquired company will contribute to the acquirer, no matter how attractive the expected "synergy" may look. (1981, p. 31)

During the merger booms that sweep US industry periodically, few recall Ansoff's warnings or Drucker's rule. Indeed, "2 + 2 = 3"is negative synergy that can develop when mergers miscarry, as they often do (Kitching, 1967). In this regard, Ansoff wrote:

> In the absence of synergy, the performance of a conglomerate firm will in general be no better than it would have been if the divisions operated as independent firms . . . [with] no operating competitive advantage (e.g., lower costs). . . . There is evidence that under abnormal conditions, such as recession, conglomerate firms have less staying power than concentric ones and hence suffer sharper reversals. (1965, p. 119)

[3]Ansoff saw the strategy of expansion as the alternative to diversification, expansion being growth by market penetration or product development.

HOW CAN DIVERSIFICATION CREATE VALUE?

Whatever motivations are attributed to management, financial theorists and policy researchers alike essentially argue that the one motive that embraces all business activity is the drive to create value. This is the ultimate objective, the ultimate purpose of management and so of management action.

Classic finance and common sense point to price as the best measure of value. The price of a share of common stock represents the value of the cash flows expected by the buyer because of ownership—dividends and any receipts on sale. In the simplest of terms, value is the price paid to own the future earnings of a business, share by share if you like.

However, price is a fickle measure of value, real as it is, and price can vary substantially over time, doubtless as market expectations shift (Beaver and Morse, 1978); *Table 17-2* illustrates this. This result is relevant for diversified companies, since their purchases are generally illiquid and they are "stuck" with portfolios of businesses developed earlier. In *Table 17-3,* for example, we can see how stock price movements are explained by the performance of the economy, industry, and company. We can note that only the economy-related price changes can be regarded as systematic—indeed systemic might be a better word (Mullins, 1982). Moreover, of the rest, 49 percent of stock price changes are associated with industry, mostly with industry narrowly defined (at the four-digit Standard Industry Code (SIC) level).

These data, along with Ansoff's warnings, should give managers pause: The *big*

TABLE 17-2 Rank Correlations of Portfolios Formed by Price/Earnings Ratios in Subsequent Years

	Years Following Base Year													
Base Year	*1*	*2*	*3*	*4*	*5*	*6*	*7*	*8*	*9*	*10*	*11*	*12*	*13*	*14*
1956	0.96	0.87	0.88	0.65	0.78	0.70	0.82	0.85	0.69	0.74	0.62	0.36	0.41	0.59
1957	0.85	0.91	0.83	0.84	0.89	0.89	0.90	0.81	0.86	0.72	0.51	0.67	0.78	0.44
1958	0.95	0.73	0.64	0.52	0.43	0.55	0.49	0.30	0.60	0.22	0.24	0.49	0.41	0.18
1959	0.96	0.91	0.91	0.73	0.57	0.88	0.74	0.69	0.33	0.46	0.69	0.56	0.40	0.56
1960	0.94	0.94	0.93	0.89	0.88	0.79	0.70	0.63	0.80	0.73	0.61	0.61	0.50	0.24
1961	0.98	0.96	0.86	0.89	0.85	0.76	0.74	0.87	0.83	0.87	0.76	0.72	0.55	0.64
1962	0.92	0.89	0.93	0.94	0.87	0.69	0.86	0.73	0.78	0.76	0.87	0.78	0.77	
1963	0.99	0.98	0.95	0.89	0.71	0.77	0.75	0.61	0.79	0.93	0.77	0.76		
1964	0.95	0.96	0.94	0.72	0.88	0.89	0.72	0.88	0.90	0.81	0.82			
1965	0.99	0.93	0.83	0.83	0.77	0.86	0.93	0.91	0.80	0.71				
1966	0.96	0.89	0.95	0.96	0.84	0.95	0.89	0.80	0.79					
1967	0.98	0.98	0.94	0.89	0.85	0.58	0.57	0.69						
1968	0.98	0.95	0.88	0.84	0.63	0.53	0.35							
1969	0.89	0.92	0.95	0.74	0.80	0.82								
1970	0.95	0.79	0.63	0.72	0.73									
1971	0.96	0.80	0.70	0.67										
1972	0.96	0.96	0.96											
1973	0.99	0.97												
1974	0.97													
Median Correlation	0.96	0.92	0.91	0.83	0.80	0.78	0.74	0.76	0.79	0.73	0.69	0.64	0.50	0.44

Source: Beaver and Morse, "What Determines Price/Earnings Ratios?" *Financial Analysts Journal,* July/Aug. 1978, p. 66.

TABLE 17-3 Stock Price Effects

Economy (general market)	31%	
Industry (broad definition)	12%	49% total
Industry (narrow definition)	37%	
Company (sample of large, single-industry firms)	20%	

Source: Benjamin F. King, "The Latent Statistical Structure of Security Price Changes," unpublished Ph.D Dissertation, University of Chicago, 1964.

decision is what industry to be in. The critical action in a diversifying corporation is, therefore, the redeployment of its resources to a more attractive industry, exploiting its existing and continuing operations as resources to fund change.

AN ACID TEST FOR DIVERSIFICATION

Price is a function of current earnings, expected earnings growth, and the risks attached to that future earnings stream, that is:

$$\text{price} = f(\text{earnings, risk}).$$

We can state quite normatively that managers should diversify only if the diversification will add value to the firm by increasing income and decreasing risk and the vulnerability of the corporation to an earnings decline.

This is the acid test for diversification: Only if management can *realistically* expect to create value should it diversify. In terms of *Figure 17-5*, this will be accomplished if we lift our return above the ''fair'' rate by redeploying our resources:

1 to increase our return, our reward;
2 to reduce risk; or
3 to do both, increase rewards and cut risk.

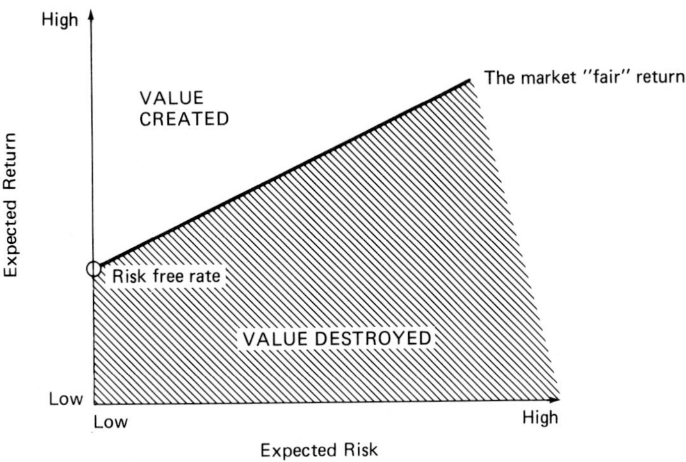

FIGURE 17-5 The Market Price of Risk

Note that any of these outcomes would lift performance into the top section of *Figure 17-5*.[4] Obviously, action should be taken only if expected rewards exceed expected costs, here measured by the market's ''fair'' return.

The test could be applied to both current or proposed new business activity. If an existing business neither adds earnings to the corporation nor cuts risk, the business adds no value and should be examined closely to determine how it might be improved or how it can be liquidated. If the test is applied to a proposed acquisition or new venture and the results are negative, there is prima facie evidence that the proposal is without merit, at least until it is reworked, repriced, or perhaps until demand or the competitive situation changes.

Furthermore, note the importance of resource allocation. Corporations operate through businesses by allocating resources to some and taking resources from others. Usually the trend of results earned by ourselves or our competitors in this or similar businesses points the way.

A straightforward rule is to take resources from the low-return businesses and allocate them to those earning a high return: Move out of businesses promising low ROA and invest in those promising a high ROA if they each allow a similar degree of financial leverage. If their leverage differs significantly, as it does for example in financial services, discriminate on a return on equity basis (ROE). Obviously, this is one of the simplest canons of finance, as simple as the ''buy low, sell high'' rule and as difficult to implement. Managers will increase value if they take money out of low return-on-asset ventures and redeploy it into higher-return businesses, *ceteris paribus*. Of course, all is rarely equal, especially in the expected future and with respect to risk. That is why managers are needed and why many companies engage specialist consultants to help them develop their corporate and business strategies.

The problem is that, although past and present earnings and returns point to the future, the future requires investment now. Thus, managers must give the likely future, about which they know little, the heaviest weight in their investment decisions. And when we analyze a set of competitors, it is their investments that we have to monitor, so that we can identify what they think the future will be.

Common sense suggests, as we have demonstrated, that there are some very simple rules to guide management investment activity. Violations of these rules carry a penalty, specifically wasted resources, lost opportunities, and the destruction of value. Let us state the rules explicitly:

1. *Invest* where returns promise to be high and reliable, that is, where you'll have a competitive advantage. Remember, no advantage, no profit.
2. *Divest* from businesses where earnings and growth are falling and risk is rising.
3. Try to *eliminate* those risks that you can; manage the rest.
4. Take as little risk as possible, but as much as necessary.
5. Diversify *only* if value will be created by increased earnings, reduced risk, or a redeployment of assets from a low ROA or ROE to a higher ROA or ROE business.

[4]*Figure 17-5* is based on the simple premise that investors demand a return for the use of their funds—even if the investment is free of ''risk''—and demand a higher return if risk increases. If net present value is positive, a diversifying action is expected to add value; if the internal rate of return equals the fair return, the net present value is zero; and, if the net present value is negative, value is destroyed. Note that this model suggests that managers can manipulate value upwards by increasing return or cutting risk (Harrington, 1983).

6 Don't diversify if current returns are high and future earnings growth is likely to be strong. In these circumstances, continued focused investment will probably pay off.

Remember that value-creating managers must develop relationships and opportunities to get the resources they need. Managers who act like conservators trying to preserve assets are likely to underachieve and earn inferior returns. If they follow the "prudent man" rule and seek a fair return, for example, they'll probably underachieve and lose value. Managers must strive for more than prudence in order to create value.

Now, given that we know that the largest corporations are diversified, and since we have a robust normative position to guide us, how has diversification served its devotees in practice?

DIVERSIFICATION RESULTS

Since so many large corporations have diversified, how have things turned out—especially for their shareholders? Has diversification led to enhanced earnings, reduced risk, and higher stock prices?

Diversifying Acquisitions

With respect to diversifying acquisitions, Salter and Weinhold (1978) presented evidence that the answer to the second question is, "No." Between 1967 and 1977, acquisitive diversifiers earned 20 percent less on assets than the average *Fortune* 500 company—a relatively diverse set of companies, as we have seen. On December 31, 1977, the diversified acquisitors in Salter and Weinhold's sample had a price earnings ratio 30 percent less than that of the average New York Stock Exchange company. (The New York listed companies, about 2200 in 1984, are on average less diverse than the *Fortune* 500.) Although the diversified acquisitors enjoyed a return on equity 20 percent greater than the *Fortune* 500 average in 1967, Salter and Weinhold reported that in 1975, the acquisitors' return on equity was 18 percent below the 500's average. Ansoff's (1965) position seems vindicated. Commenting on the effects of diversification on risk, Salter and Weinhold wrote:

> Gulf and Western's systematic risk adjusted for financial leverage differs insignificantly from that of a comparable portfolio. . . . Whatever benefits Gulf and Western provides its shareholders, reduction of investment risk apparently is not one of them. (1978, p. 168)

Comparing such corporations to mutual funds, Salter and Weinhold point out that for the investor, widely diversified companies may actually be *less* attractive investments because of the illiquidity of their asset commitments.

Salter and Weinhold continue by prescribing a set of rules to create value: Acquire and diversify only if income is increased or its variability is expected to be reduced. As we might expect, they recommend the exploitation of joint effects of synergy, more intense exploitation of *shareable* resources, leveraging underutilized financial assets, internal redeployments of funds to higher return businesses, and sticking close to home—that is, to businesses you know and to those where you can reach competitive scale.

It seems that these recommendations are little different from what can be deduced from basic finance. Yet they were not made idly. Although management is surely aware of the rules, they are difficult to live by and difficult to implement. Besides, we should not be surprised by Salter and Weinhold's negative findings. Ansoff (1965) warned that diversification was risky; Kitching (1967; 1974) pointed out that many mergers miscarry. Diversifying by acquisition adds risk to risk and we should expect the results to reflect the costs of these risks.

Acquisitions promise an easy remedy: They may appear cheaper than a start-up venture (but recall the maxim, "You get what you pay for"). But it is easy for management to be caught up in deal fever, forgetting that the price of a business may be bid up by competition to such an extent that the opportunity for value creation is lost, or at best long delayed.

Diversification in Practice

Indeed, one of the less obvious but very important social issues in business is whether the management is fulfilling its fiduciary responsibilities to the corporation's shareholders and creating value by retaining earnings for investment in diversification. Is management creating more value than the shareholders could get by investing dividends at market rates? So it is appropriate to ask, how successful is diversification per se—that is, in its many forms besides acquisition?

For a few moments, let us look at the results of diversification in the US. Rumelt (1974) reported that corporate profitability varied with diversification, pointing to a correlation between scope and type of diversity and results earned. *Figure 17-6* illustrates some of his observations.

As *Figure 17-6* shows, performance differences seem related more to type of diversification than to scope or amount of diversity—that is, related more to the way in which a firm's businesses are related to each other than to the number of products or markets offered or served. Both *Figures 17-6* (*a*) and (*b*) show the "constrained" diversifiers doing better than the rest—they are companies that drew on or added to some central strength or competence. The unrelated diversifiers and the vertically integrated companies (the very diversified and the companies intensely committed to one business) were the apparent low performers. The acquisitive conglomerates used high leverage to multiply their returns on capital to greater returns on equity. Among dominant and related businesses, those firms whose diversification was further afield did worse over the 1949 to 1969 period than those Rumelt described as having "chosen or been able to limit their product market scopes."

Yet, when Rumelt examined price/earnings ratios, he found the market statistics contrary to other measures of corporate performance. The related business category, particularly the related linked group of firms, enjoyed unusually high price/earnings ratios, even when the effects of growth, earnings stability and retention were taken into account, as *Table 17-4* shows. Rumelt commented, "The only plausible explanation for the continued existence of this difference over twenty years is that investors believe the related linked firms to be more likely to maintain their performance over the long term,"

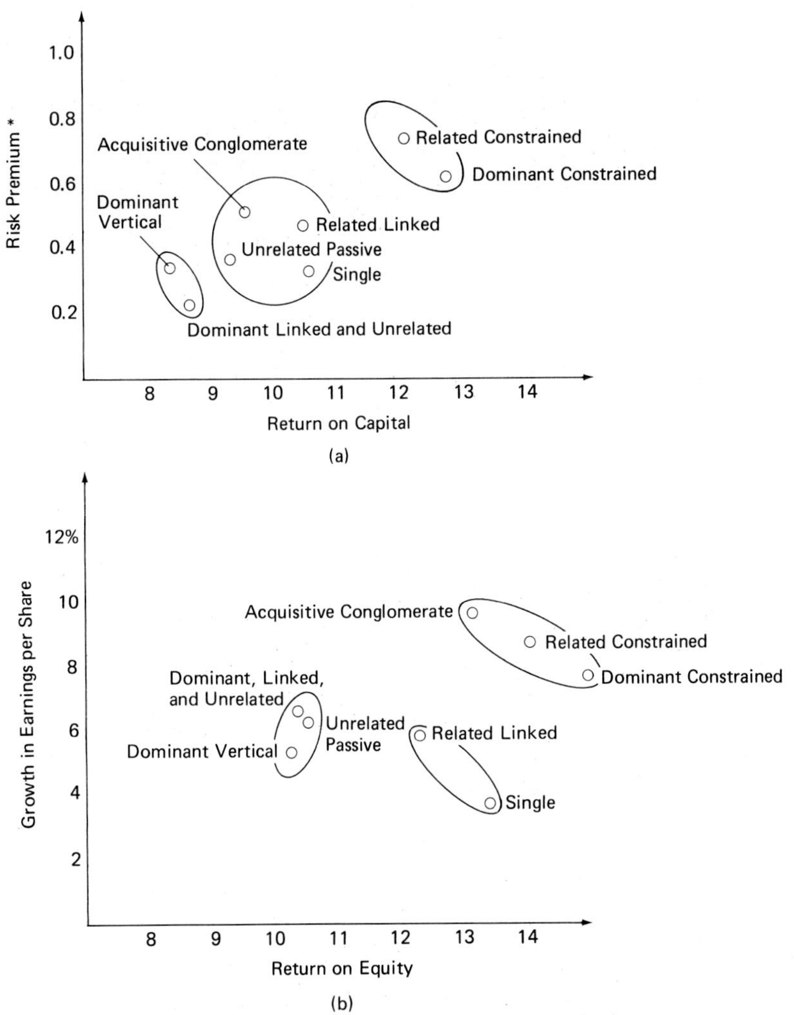

*Rumelt defined the Risk Premium as the ratio of (GEPS – 0.015)/SDEPS, i.e., as an adjusted ratio of EPS growth to the variability in the rate of EPS growth. 1.5% was his estimate of the after-tax risk-free rate.

FIGURE 17-6 Risk and Return Category Means

Source: Rumelt, *Strategy, Structural and Economic Performance*, Boston, MA: Division of Research, Harvard Business School, 1974.

perhaps because a single business is ultimately more transient than one growing from diversity.

The research results do not mean that vertically integrated companies should be transformed to related constrained or related linked companies (Rumelt, 1974, p. 101). Vertical integration implies commitment to one industry and may preclude rapid redeployment to other industries—although not precluding revolutionary redeployments of financial commitments within one industry chain (McLean & Haigh, 1954). The oil industry has had more success redeploying its assets among the different production and distribu-

TABLE 17-4
Price-Earnings Multiple Gap

	Single	*Dominant-Vertical*	*Dominant-Constrained*	*Dominant-Linked and Unrelated*	*Related-Constrained*	*Related-Linked*	*Unrelated-Passive*	*Acquisitive Conglomerate*	*All Firms*
Actual Price-Earnings Ratio	14.60	15.68	15.92	15.41	19.19	19.27	13.77	17.43	17.02
Calculated Price-Earnings Ratio*	17.02	16.64	16.84	17.19	17.50	16.94	16.55	16.89	17.02
Difference	−2.42	−.96	−.92	−1.78	+1.69	+2.33	−2.78	+.54	0.00
t-Ratio	−2.44	−1.15	−.81	−.81	+2.34	+2.11	−1.59	+.33	—
Level of Significance	.02	—	—	—	.01	.02	.06	—	—

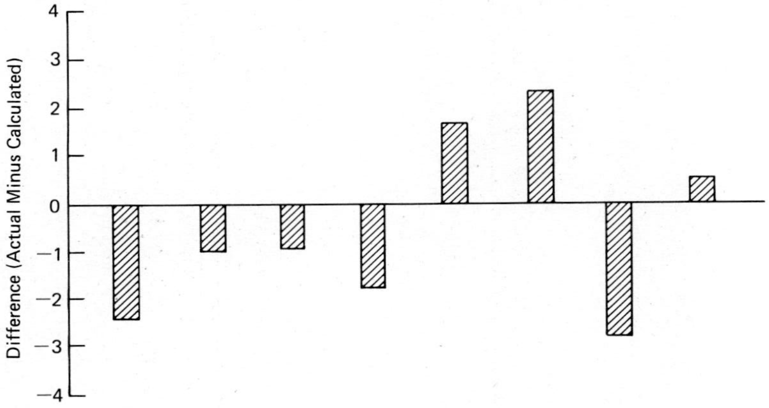

*PE = 10.97 + 4.8 Time + 0.127 GEPS −0.075 SDEPS + 3.72 RTN
R^2 = 0.48 F ratio = 24.9 (4,337).
Source: Rumelt, "Diversification Strategy and Profitability," *Strategic Management Journal,* 3, no. 4, Oct.-Dec. 1982, 367. © 1982 by John Wiley & Sons.

tion stages commercializing crude than it has in diversification—witness Mobil Oil's acquisition of Montgomery Ward and Exxon's acquisition of Reliance Electric, both apparently unsuccessful.

Advising us to interpret his research carefully, Rumelt warned that he had observed an association between performance and diversity, not causality: it may be that high performance eliminates the need for diversity rather than that diversity leads to high performance (Rumelt, 1974, p. 124). This observation is in line with Bass's hypothesis that the major motivation for diversification is defensive, as primary markets mature. Rumelt concluded:

> While it may be that these strategies tend to produce good results, it is more likely that firms already rapidly growing and profitable think it wise to restrict their scopes of activity to businesses that directly relate to their currently successful areas of competence. Nevertheless, the intensive cultivation of a single field has proven, on the average, financially more successful than bold moves into uncharted areas. (1974, p. 156)

Addressing his own questions about the fit of certain strategies to particular industries and whether the differences he observed were due more to ''industry'' than to ''diversification,'' Rumelt's investigations were frustrated by the data available. Extreme observations and small numbers of observations within industry groups precluded meaningful statistical analysis. He wrote:

> Taking a broader point of view, it seems evident that more of the strategy-related performance differences are due to industry differences, but that the two effects are simply not separable. The higher performing industries tend to consist of mostly Related Business firms, and Related Business firms tend to belong to higher performing industries. Which came first? The answer seems to be that they came together; the same conditions that produce above average performance—science-based proprietary strengths, growth in markets served along with rapid product innovation—produce diversified firms. (p. 100)

Subsequent research by Christensen and Montgomery (1981), Bettis and Hall (1981), and Rumelt (1982) has accumulated evidence indicating that industry choice is probably the most important factor in determining the success of a diversified firm. Christensen and Montgomery extended a subset of Rumelt's data to 1977, exploiting ''line of business data'' in the Securities and Exchange Commission data in Corporate Form 10-K's. Working with data for the period 1972 to 1977, these researchers found ''no statistical grounds for asserting that significant performance differences exist'' between categories of diversified firms (p. 333).

However, when data on thirty-one vertically integrated firms were added to their sample, certain performance variables became significant. Since ''the vertical integrated companies were distinctly low performers'' in their own and Rumelt's sample data, Christensen and Montgomery suggested cautious inference-making—statistics can be sensitive to extremes, as *Figure 17-7* illustrates. Lines A and B may be reasonably representative of the two groups of firms, but Line C is likely to be a poor representative of each and lead to incorrect inferences, since it is probable that the data is heterogeneous

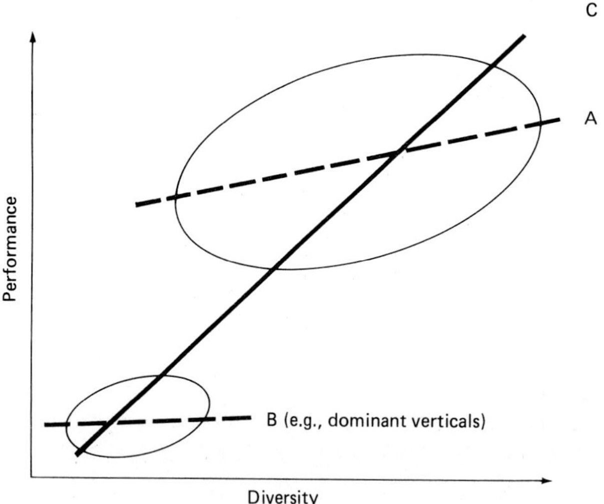

Consider the impact of including the data B in a regression with A. The true relationships A and B are masked by the aggregation, and C is the estimate.

FIGURE 17-7 Statistics and Extreme Values

rather than homogeneous (Rumelt, 1974; Hatten and Schendel, 1977; Hatten, Schendel and Cooper, 1978).

Continuing their analysis to separate out the effects of market structure—that is, industry profitability rates and company market shares—on the performance of diversified companies, Christensen and Montgomery found that the unrelated portfolio firms (Rumelt's unrelated passive and acquisitive conglomerates) had lower market shares, were positioned in less profitable and less concentrated markets, and were smaller than other firms in the sample. Related constrained firms, in contrast, were in more profitable, faster-growing, and more highly concentrated markets than other firms. They concluded:

> First, following a strategy of constrained diversification is not sufficient to assure high earnings. The constrained diversifiers appear to be more profitable in part because they operated in very profitable, highly concentrated markets, and were able to acquire large shares in those markets. These firms' above-average market shares also suggest that they possess a sufficient level of the skills and resources critical to success in these high opportunity markets—a condition which may have developed due to diversification close to the original business. Successful performance is the outcome of market opportunity combined with the capacity to take advantage of that opportunity. In diversification planning, it is unwise to fail to analyze either.
>
> Second, the rather uninspiring performance of unrelated-portfolio firms suggests the dangers of inattention to market structure in entry decisions or of knowingly entering highly fragmented, low profit markets. To the degree such markets are entered because businesses can be purchased for attractive prices, a longer-run point of view is needed. If these businesses are acquired because of unrealistic expectations of improving performance with new ownership, a hard look at market structure variables can lead to more realistic assessments of turnaround potential. (1981, pp. 339–40)

Like Christensen and Montgomery, Bettis and Hall (1981) focused on the related category, linked and constrained, again supplementing Rumelt's sample with later data but adding data on new firms as well. Observing that many of Rumelt's related constrained category were pharmaceutical companies, they asked the question whether Rumelt's findings were more representative of pharmaceutical companies (another extreme group) than related diversification. The results pointed to the influence of extremes, the pharmaceutical companies: With them included, significant differences were observed; without them, the differences were not significant. Bettis are Hall concluded that the differences Rumelt observed between the performance of the groups labelled related and unrelated diversified were due probably to the presence of the pharmaceutical firms in the related category rather than to differences in the efficacy of diversification strategies per se. They found no evidence of significant risk reduction with increased diversity.

Rumelt (1982) worked with 1970–1973 data and contrasted actual and expected return based on industry investment patterns using a straight-forward model:

$$R_j = \sum_i P_{ij} R_i$$

^{R}j, the expected return on the j-th firm, is the sum of the firm's returns in each of i industries. Those returns are simply the product of the proportion of firm capital invested in each industry, P_{ij}, and the average return on capital earned in that industry, R_i. By simply examining the return premium, the difference, P, between the actual return on capital, ROC, and the expected return based on industry participation, $\hat{R}$, that is,

$$P = ROC - \hat{R}$$

Rumelt could "test" the efficacy of alternate diversification strategies. The results are shown in *Table 17-5*.

TABLE 17-5 Return, Expected Return, and the Return Premium

Category	*Observations*	*ROC*	R	P	$P\text{-}P_{UB}$
SB	23	10.4	9.30	1.64[b]	3.53[a]
DV	33	8.48[b]	8.80[a]	−0.32	1.57[b]
DC	12	11.78	9.83	1.96[b]	3.85[a]
DLU	9	10.97	9.96	1.02	2.91[b]
RC	41	11.63[a]	10.68[a]	0.95	2.85[a]
RL	38	9.33	9.77	−0.44	1.45
UB	31	7.55[a]	9.44	−1.89[a]	—
Total/average	187	9.82	9.70	0.12	
Estimated σ		4.34	2.15	3.88	
F-statistic	[6, 180]	3.98[a]	2.60[b]	3.17[a]	

Significance tests for ROC, R, and P test hypothesis that value displayed is equal to the population mean. Significance tests for $P\text{-}P_{UB}$ test hypothesis that value displayed is zero.

[a]Level of significance = 99 per cent.

[b]Level of significance = 95 per cent.

Source: Rumelt, "Diversification Strategy and Profitability," *Strategic Management Journal,* 3, no. 4, Oct.-Dec. 1982, 367. © 1982 by John Wiley & Sons.

Rumelt commented:

> According to the F-statistic, the observed R's are not homogeneous across the categories (p = 0.05); the major contributors to this result are the low expected return, R, of the DV group and the high expected return, R, of the RC group. . . . These data show that the high ROC of the related constrained group was primarily an industry effect and that the RC firms perform as would be expected given the industries in which they participate. (1982, pp. 367–68)

He concluded, and we agree, "More remains to be understood about why firms diversify and the proper management of different patterns of diversification."

Summary on the Results of Diversification Research

The growing evidence is that for most corporations, diversification per se does little to reduce risk or increase returns. In fact, Rumelt's results under P, the return premium in *Table 17-5,* point to increased diversity's being associated with lower than expected performance once industry choice is taken into consideration.

It seems that in many corporations management has diversified, but it has not learned to make diversity pay. The high performance of the related and dominant constrained groups points to the advantage of staying close to home and building off a core technology. The dominant constrained and related constrained firms may be the beneficiaries of opportunity, or their skill may be to enter businesses where the renewal and extension of products is technologically possible. Rumelt writes that diversification succeeds "by replacing products that are stagnant or declining with close functional substitutes that are profitable and growing for reasons related to the decline of the original products" (1974, p. 157). This interpretation is substantially consistent with Bass and colleagues' (1977) position that diversification is a defensive strategy used by firms with stagnant products and markets.

Note, however, that most of the research available is based on averages which extend across large numbers of companies. Our own research within industries and the experiences cited above point to the dangers of pooling heterogeneous data. To understand more about diversity, we need to look at the exceptions, too—the high and low performers—to learn what makes them successful and unsuccessful (Hatten and Schendel, 1976; Hatten and Hatten, 1985).

One step in this direction was reported by Dundas and Richardson (1982). By contrasting high- and low-performing conglomerates, they were able to identify some of the characteristics apparently associated with successful conglomerates. These were a "narrow focus" on like industries, a limited commitment or dependence on any one business (not more than 30 percent of revenues or assets in one), and market leadership, full control, growth by friendly acquisition, and consistent administrative practices—including executive compensation to Return on Investment (ROI). They concluded, however, that the key administrative requirement was to allocate the firm's capital effectively.

NEEDED: CORPORATE STRATEGY

Corporate strategy is about being in the right businesses. Many have overlooked this message from the diversification research: Diversification has added little value per se, but it is a tool which allows corporate renewal. We should focus, therefore, on "the industries they're in" and the reasons and organizational structures and systems used to get there, as we analyze successful management techniques for diversification.

Research has shown that few companies outperform their industry choices, and that risk reduction and increased returns are elusive. Henderson commented:

> A multidivision company without an overall strategy is not even as good as the sum of its parts. It is merely a portfolio of non-liquid, non-tradable investments, with added overhead and constraints. Such closed-end investments properly sell at a discount from the sum of the parts. Intuition alone is an inadequate substitute for an integrated strategy. (Henderson, 1979, p. 28)

Henderson suggests that many corporations lack an *integrating* corporate strategy. Without integrating objectives and strategies, it is unlikely that managers can administer their corporations effectively or efficiently—they will neither be doing the right thing nor doing things right.

The question confronting management is how to judge what is right, how to create value more effectively. As noted in our discussion of single-business companies, it is difficult to modify a company's present strategy and do so responsibly until you know what you are doing and how well it is working. You have to identify your strategy before you fix it—before you know whether it needs fixing at all.

At this point, let us review what we know about diversification. First, it succeeds or fails principally because of industry choices. Second, it promises great advantages if the businesses can be related—if the skills and resources of one business can be used in concert with those of another to strengthen one or the other or both. Third, the simple rules of investment apply: increase returns and cut risk by skilled redeployment of resources from low-return businesses to those where you can earn high returns hereafter, thereby using the successes of the past to establish strength for the future. In Chapter 18, we focus our thinking on resource deployment, and on portfolio models, laying the foundation for Business Analysis, a tool for corporate strategy identification presented and demonstrated in Chapter 19.

chapter 18

Portfolio Analysis: Tracking the Deployment of Funds

INTRODUCTION

Resource deployment is the critical task of the corporate-level strategist. The principles of diversification are well-known, but the results are disappointing. Why?

In the first place is the problem and cost of entry and exit. Businesses are not liquid investments, and it is difficult to redeploy assets. Second, relatedness is difficult to realize quickly and at best takes time to develop. Third, the simple rule of investment—put your capital in higher-return businesses—is difficult to live by. All this adds up to what Henderson (1979) called a lack of an integrating corporate strategy. Few managers would disagree, yet most would point to the difficulties they have in conceiving such a strategy and living it.

Living the strategy and living by the rules that facilitate administration and that we have enumerated in Chapter 15 is difficult because it threatens the established power bases of the firm. Redeploying resources means reallocating power, and typically those who have power act to preserve it. Remember, they had to struggle to get it. We believe that any failure to appreciate the social consequences of power changes puts a strategy into jeopardy. Power and resources go hand in glove.

Diversification means change in resource deployments and priorities. It threatens power. Those who have power find it hard to let go—even if they themselves are the architects of change. We know of CEO's who have wisely initiated diversification programs committing to new product development and acquisitions, yet have not let go of their old power base in the business that made them a success. Instead of sharing power with the managers of their new venture, they have held it, losing valuable people, pouring disproportionate resources into the old businesses, and unconsciously restricting the new. It is a failure to let go of the past. Revealed by inappropriate resource deployments and a failure to delegate, it is an administrative failure which threatens the success of their diversification.

Successful change, and diversification is change, comes only when power is shifted to implement the strategy. Power has to shift ahead of the strategic change and be committed to the corporate future, not the past. Diversification programs often atrophy because this timely marriage of power and strategy is not consummated (Barnes and Hershon, 1976).

The fault lies at the top. Except when resources are committed not only to the act of diversification but to the diversified way of life, we believe diversification will be a failure. The evidence we have seen in corporation after corporation is that the successes of the past can consume the resources needed for the future. In fact, a failure to appreciate the consequences of an enacted strategy which probably unconsciously suits the old power structure but not the future vitality of the corporation is probably the reason why diversification per se has been associated with nonperformance.

PORTFOLIO ANALYSIS

Since the mid-1960s, such unconscious misallocations of capital and people have become less easy to explain, because of the simple analytical tools available to audit resource deployments—the portfolio models. Although they do little more than a straight sources-and-uses-of-funds statement could do, they provide most managers with data in a more readily digestible form.

Portfolio analysis is an analytical approach which asks managers to view corporations as portfolios of businesses to be managed for the best possible return. Linking industry characteristics, the company's competitive strengths, and resource deployment patterns, portfolio analysis gives managers an opportunity to see their companies from a different point of view and think about the future implications of their current resource commitments.

The value of the portfolio lies in its simplicity. The matrices or portfolio charts we will describe are superficially easy to understand; they confront management with particular views of their business anchored in fact. They thus facilitate discussion and thinking about the firm's competitive positions and provoke questions about the contribution of the firm's current resource allocations to its long-run vitality.

Most importantly, portfolio approaches help management relate its separable businesses to each other and so to the corporation *through* their respective objectives. Since portfolio analysis helps management see how its resources are being deployed and suggests achievable objectives for each business, it gives corporate management an opportunity to use its businesses as resources to achieve corporate objectives. We will explain portfolio analysis in this chapter, and you will see it used as one of the important elements in our approach to corporate strategy identification developed in Chapter 19.

ITS SUPPORTERS

Portfolio analysis has been held partly responsible for the improved profit performance of many companies. For example, General Electric during the 1970s substantially increased its return on equity and attributed its success to portfolio analysis, among other things. The Mead Corporation's and Armco Steel's managements also attributed their success in part to their use of portfolio concepts. William Verity, Armco's Chairman and CEO, wrote:

> We are now committed to the Product Portfolio concept of planning. If there were one single answer I could give to the question . . . Why a portfolio of businesses? . . . it would be that a balanced portfolio is necessary for the survival of the multiproduct company and essential for its profitable growth. Actually, we had always managed our business as one of many products serving many markets, but by grouping our products and markets into discrete business units, and identifying the position of each such unit vis à vis its competitors, we make better use of present investments and can make better plans for future investments. (1975, p. 50)

Armco is one of many corporations which have used portfolio concepts in their planning. Haspeslagh (1982) estimated that 36 percent of the *Fortune* 1000 and 45 percent of the *Fortune* 500 have employed the approach to some extent. Commenting, he wrote, "Most important, however, portfolio planning seems to have profoundly affected the way executives think about the management of their businesses" (p. 59).

TYPES OF PORTFOLIO ANALYSES

Portfolio analysis takes the view that a corporation is a portfolio of investments to be managed to produce the best *total* return. Most portfolio analysts recognize that each business has unique competitive problems and opportunities and is capable of making different contributions to corporate performance if it is allocated resources appropriate to its task, the objectives or mission given it by the corporation. Portfolio analysis helps management determine what those objectives should be—that is, what corporate objectives are most attainable for the portfolio of companies.

Many different portfolio analysis approaches are used across the world. *Figure 18-1* illustrates some more common examples. Growth is combined with market share in 1, the Boston Consulting Group's two-by-two product portfolio. The McKinsey matrix, 2, a three-by-three matrix, is usually associated with General Electric and Shell and combines industry attractiveness and business strength. The Strategic Planning Institute, well-known as the proprietor of the PIMS (Profit Impact of Market Strategy) study, contrasts industry average profitability with the corporation's profitability within that industry in 3.

In 4, Marakon Associates' profitability matrix allows users to compare profitability and relative growth. Arthur D. Little & Company use business strength and life cycle stage in 5. Industry market/book ratios are contrasted with the internal deployment of funds in matrix 6, which links deployment directly to the stock market and so to value creation. Matrix 7 is an adaptation of the concept to the eleemosynary sector, contrasting social need and the revenue-generating potential of a portfolio of Young Men's Christian Association (YMCA) programs. Almost every matrix is associated with one strategy consultant; a skeptic could be excused if he or she saw the differences between the matrices being due more to different consultants' needs for market differentiations than to distinct theoretical positions.

These different portfolios all share a common parentage in the rules of successful diversification: Enter businesses where future returns are likely to be high; strive for synergies and the efficiencies promised by relating one business to another; deploy your assets in a disciplined way, withdrawing assets from low-return or low-value situations; and invest where returns are high and highly valued. All the matrices help management track its deployment of funds. They relate to market value, since most encompass the major correlates of value, earnings, growth, and risk, either directly or via some other variable or set of variables which correlate with one or more of these.

Each portfolio or matrix suggests generic strategies. For example, BCG's product portfolio in *Figure 18-2* with its dogs, cows, wildcats, and stars categorizes businesses in terms of their cash use or generation and implies a prescription to withdraw from dogs, milk cows, build wildcats, and sustain or maintain the growth and market shares of stars. If a business plots in a specific quadrant, say as a cow, then we can suggest it as a primary candidate for management as a cow to be milked of the cash flow it produces each operating cycle. Each grid is populated by bubble charts proportionately representing the corporation's separable business activities by sales or assets or some other measure of commitment.

McKinsey's (GE/Shell) matrix differs from the BCG matrix because industry attractiveness is a multidimensional characteristic, either simply judged or computed based on weighted judgements about such factors as cyclicality, regulation, vulnerability to inflation and technological obsolescence, capital intensity, and pricing flexibility. Business strength embraces supply, market share, distribution strengths, service capability, production cost position, capacity, product and process engineering, quality, and, indeed whatever characteristics give a business strength (Hussey, 1978). In principle, corporations should invest in attractive businesses where they have strengths or can develop them at reasonable cost.

In contrast with the GE matrix, which is based on judged multidimensional characteristics, the Strategic Planning Institute's matrix under the PIMS (Profit Impact of Market Strategy) banner is based on cross-sectional, multidimensional regression studies of the profitability of more than 2000 businesses. It compares business average profitability, an "industry" characteristic, with performance in the business. Loomis (1980), President of the Dexter Corporation at the time, implies that the choice of industries to be in is a strategic issue and can be addressed in part on the basis of average (that is, PAR) ROI, while deviation from an industry PAR ROI is an operating outcome (he calls it tactical). Because it is regression-based, the PIMS model avoids judgmental weightings of the importance of the components of strength and attractiveness and substitutes statistical relationships estimated from past experience. Although statistically derived and scientifically inspired, the PIMS models have been criticized, primarily because the population used is heterogeneous—that is, contains many apparently dissimilar businesses—and the models largely neglect the impact of time since they are cross-sectional and do not distinguish one time period from another (Anderson and Paine, 1977; Hatten and Schendel, 1976).

Marakon, a San Francisco-based firm, has developed a different approach based on earnings above the cost of equity capital and growth relative to market. Attractive opportunities are those in the upper right-hand side and unattractive options are those in the lower left. Marakon (1981) also labels the businesses of the firm according to their cash reinvestment ratio (our internal redeployment ratio).

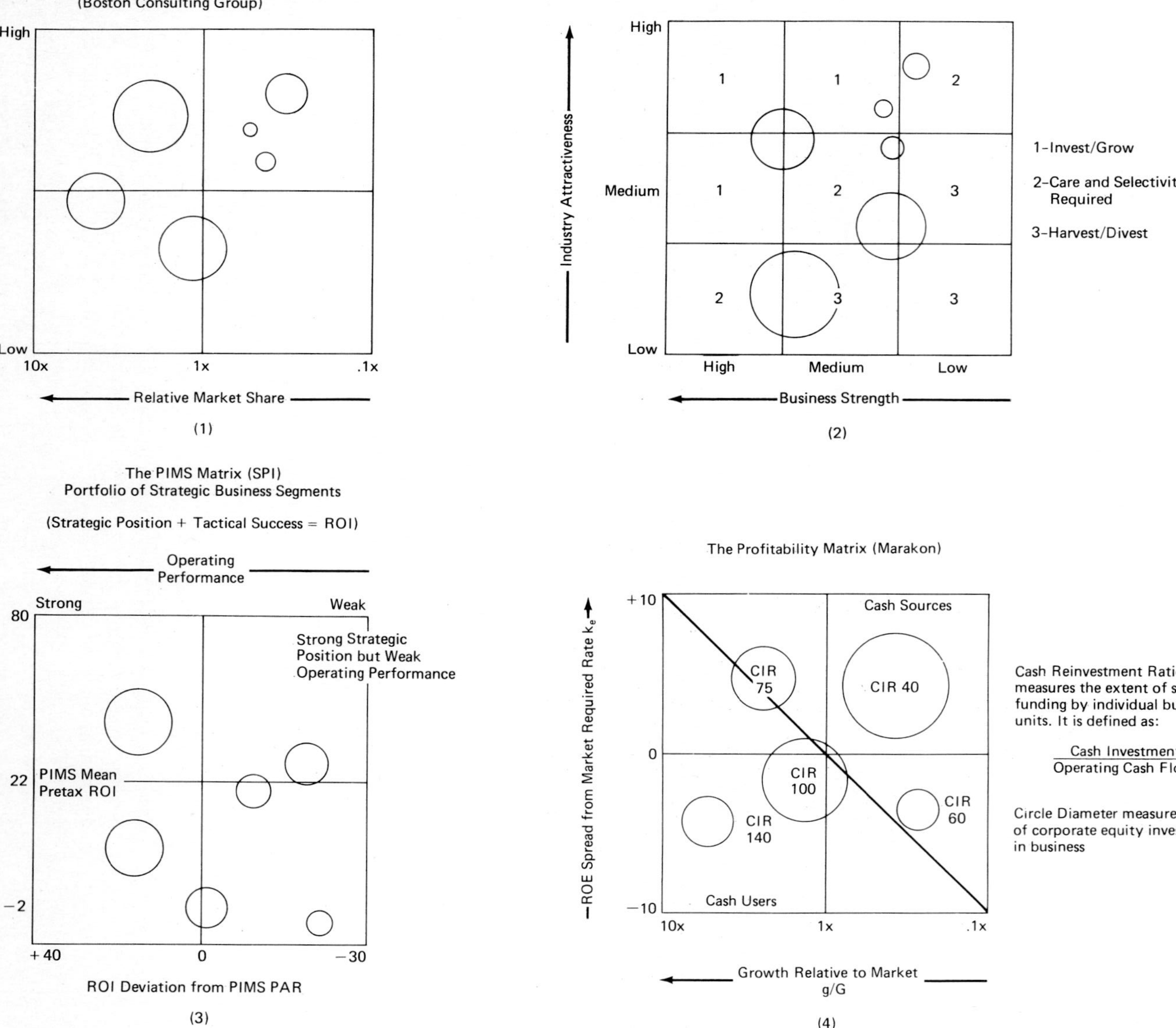
The Product Portfolio/The Market Share Growth Matrix
(Boston Consulting Group)
High
Low
Real Market Growth
10x
1x
.1x
Relative Market Share
(1)
High
Medium
Low
Industry Attractiveness
1
1
2
1
2
3
2
3
3
High
Medium
Low
Business Strength
1–Invest/Grow
2–Care and Selectivity Required
3–Harvest/Divest
(2)
The PIMS Matrix (SPI)
Portfolio of Strategic Business Segments
(Strategic Position + Tactical Success = ROI)
Operating Performance
Strong
Weak
80
22
–2
Strategic Position
Strong Strategic Position but Weak Operating Performance
PIMS Mean Pretax ROI
+40
0
–30
ROI Deviation from PIMS PAR
(3)
The Profitability Matrix (Marakon)
+10
0
–10
ROE Spread from Market Required Rate k_e
Cash Sources
CIR 75
CIR 40
CIR 100
CIR 140
CIR 60
Cash Users
10x
1x
.1x
Growth Relative to Market g/G
Cash Reinvestment Ratio (CIR) measures the extent of self-funding by individual business units. It is defined as:
$\frac{\text{Cash Investment}}{\text{Operating Cash Flow}}$
Circle Diameter measures percent of corporate equity invested in business
(4)

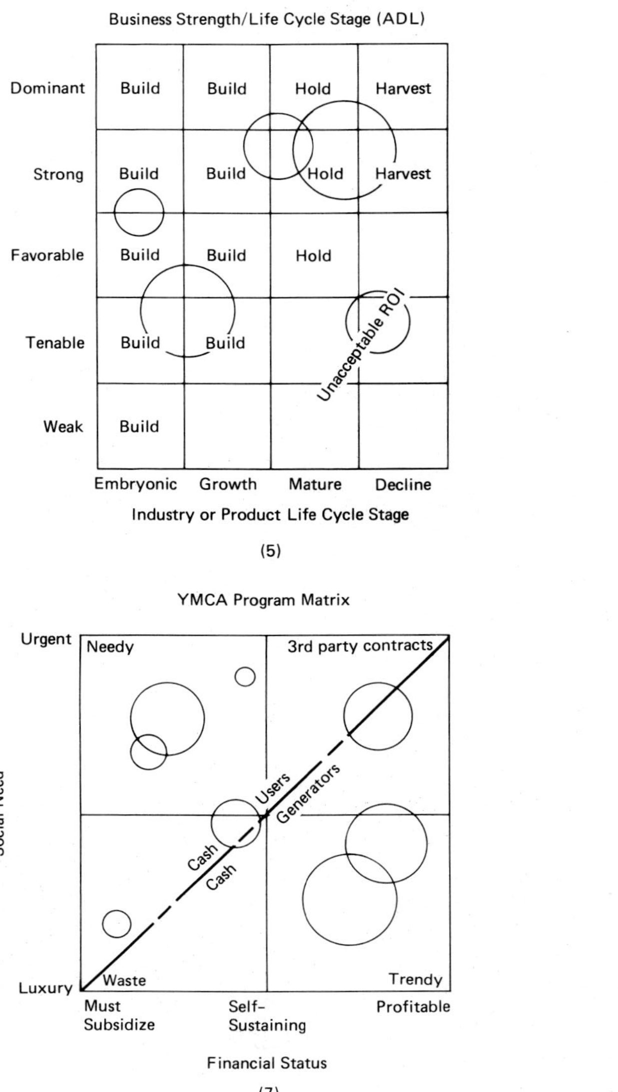

Value Management Matrix

Industry Market/Book Value: 3x, 1x, .5x

Create Value | "Starved" | Squander | Redeploy

Investing — Balance — Harvesting

Internal Deployment of Funds

(6)

Strategic Profile Analysis

Relative Product/Service Advantage \ Relative Delivered Cost	High	Average	Low
High	Average	Leader	Leader
Average	Marginal	Average	Leader
Low	Disaster	Marginal	Average

(8)

FIGURE 18-1 Portfolio Matrices

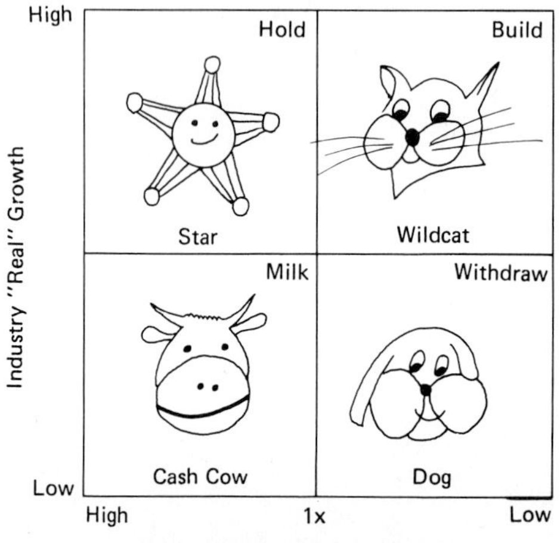

FIGURE 18-2 BCG's Product Portfolio

Source: Adopted from Bruce D. Henderson, *The Product Portfolio*. Boston: Boston Consulting Group, 1970

Arthur D. Little & Company's matrix links business strength and the product life cycle. The value management matrix contrasts market/book value with a company's internal deployment of funds. As drawn in 6, we have a company squandering value on A and B, apparently low-value businesses, while starving potentially value-creating businesses D and E. Ansoff and Leontiades (1976) offered another variation on these themes with an ROI/product life cycle portfolio.

Matrix 7, the YMCA matrix, shows a simple adaptation of the portfolio format to a not-for-profit charitable organization. By contrasting social need and financial character, the organization's management, here a YMCA executive team, could use the matrix to think about program and service mix and its ability to financially sustain the organization while serving the community. MITI, the Japanese central planning organization, is reputed to use a similar need/national resources approach in identifying those Japanese industries which deserve investment priority. Matrix 8 shows yet another variation on the theme: a simple mapping of two critical dimensions of competitive ability (Hall, 1980).

THE USEFULNESS OF PORTFOLIO ANALYSIS

Let us emphasize our view that, while differences in axis and category names appear important at first glance, a little thought shows that for the most part they are not highly differentiated, one from another. First, the dimensions on the axes of most portfolio approaches could normally be expected to be correlates of industry growth or profitability and market share, whether they encompass only one or many variables directly or through a regression model (as in the PIMS portfolio). This means we are considering *similar* types of situations, whatever portfolio we use.

Second, and more importantly, these matrices are not exact tools, despite their apparent graphic precision. They do not give answers but help us raise questions. We question the need for precision and the value of subtle distinction, since any portfolio model is really a tool to isolate crude patterns of funds deployments, misallocation of funds, and glaring gaps in the mix of businesses. Their virtue is simplicity, not precision. They point to the need for research, not to simple answers. The prescriptions of the matrices are catalysts for simple "what if" questions about the future investments of the firm.

Probably the most distinctive and usable portfolios are those which most closely relate to "estimated" market value, the matrices numbered 4 and 6 in *Figure 18-1*. Estimated market value is not stable, however, a point we made in Chapter 17 where we cited Beaver and Morse's (1978) work demonstrating the instability of price/earnings ratios over time. Businesses lose their stock market popularity—cosmetics and oil services were the darlings of the 1960s and the 1970s markets; bioengineering and computers enjoyed brief periods of market favor in the early 1980s. Note, we use estimated value because the business units of few diversified firms are publicly traded and their values, therefore, must be estimated based on "industry P/E ratios and risk levels" in the jargon of finance. This is a nontrivial task for any large corporation and one where, of necessity, apparent precision masks many assumptions, including substantial assumptions about the liquidity of business units and the stability of market value.

We can note here that portfolio models can be applied to both a corporation and its competitors, so that the cash commitments and resources of each can be quickly compared. Furthermore, they can be applied at the corporate group and business level and even at the level of the product line. In every situation, they can be used to bring facts to management's attention so that it can see its firms or businesses through different lenses. Portfolio models provide opportunities for managers to take fresh views anchored in reality. Mixing metaphors, they allow managers to "call a spade (in the matrix) a spade," as they identify in the BCG case, for example, the animals populating the matrix.

A CLOSE LOOK AT THE PRODUCT PORTFOLIO

Figure 18-3 presents BCG's product portfolio again. The two axes are real industry growth and relative market share, where relative share is simply defined as the ratio of your share to your leading competitor's share. Only the market leader has a relative share greater than one, since only the leader enjoys the second-rank company as its "leading" competitor (General Motors' lead competitor in the US auto industry is Ford; Ford, Chrysler, and AMC all have General Motors as their lead competitor).

The portfolio links an industry characteristic (growth) and an indicator of competitive strength (market share) setting the stage for a visual display of the firm's market commitments and, indirectly, of its current resource deployment (since sales-to-assets ratios are normally stable over moderate time periods across industries). The logic of this portfolio is that growing while maintaining or building market share requires investment, whereas the operations of a competitively strong business in a low-growth industry will throw off cash which corporate management can redeploy. Cash generated can be balanced with cash used, as *Figure 18-3* suggests; growth uses cash, while market strength and profitability are potential sources of cash. Notice the line drawn above the matrix in *Figure 18-3* indicating the increased expected cash-generating potential of businesses with

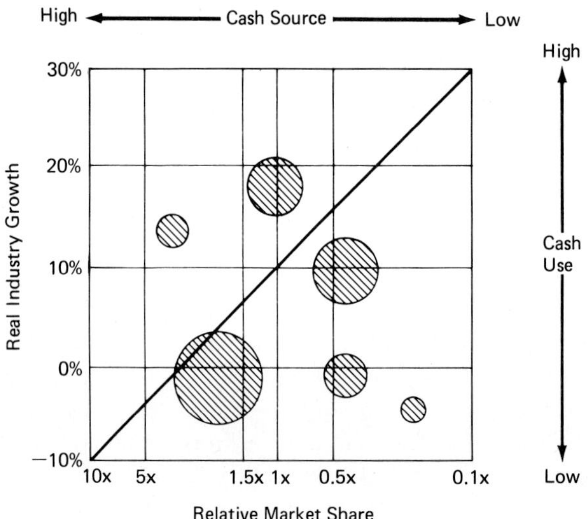

FIGURE 18-3 **The Product Portfolio**

increasing market share. To the right is the cash use characteristic of a typical cow, dog, wildcat, or star business, with cash use increasing as market growth accelerates. Here cash use and cash source are used deliberately to emphasize the explicit relationship of the product portfolio to the firm's funds statement. Note the net cash balance, category by category. More funds generated is indicated by plus (+), less by minus (−); more funds used is indicated by a minus, less funds used by plus:

BCG Category	*Source/Use*
Cow	+/+ Funds Available
Dog	−/+
Wildcat	−/− Funds Needed
Star	+/−

By positioning each of the corporation's businesses according to its industry's growth and its achieved market share, managers can see where their commitments are and judge their "quality." Relative market share (your share divided by your largest competitor's share) is the measure of relative competitive position used in the market share/growth matrix. It is plotted on a logarithmic scale. Hedley, then a BCG director, advised that this is necessary:

> . . . to be consistent with the experience curve effect which implies that profit margin or rate of cash generation differences between competitors will tend to be related to the ratio of their relative competitive positions (market shares). (1977, p. 12)

Hedley explains that 10 percent "volume" growth is a typical but arbitrary dividing line for high and low growth, adding that for high-growth and low-growth businesses, different ratios of "competitive positions" or market share divide cash users and cash generators. In high-growth industries, Hedley suggests a relative share of 1.5x, to distinguish stars from wildcats. Hedley advises us to use a relative share of 1x to separate cows and dogs in low-growth industries.

These divisions, it seems, "ensure a sufficiently dominant position that the business will have the characteristic of a star in practice" (p. 12). Hedley comments on cows that "acceptable cash-generation characteristics are occasionally, but not always, observable at relative strength as low as 1 times" (p. 13). He warns that these dividing lines are "only approximate guides," advice justified by the findings of MacMillan and his colleagues (1982), Hambrick and MacMillan (1982), and Christensen and colleagues (1982), whose collective research shows that dog businesses can outperform—or indeed underperform—their simple category expectation. Hambrick and MacMillan sensibly point out that in the simple structure of the matrix, most US businesses are dogs, yet many prosper and enjoy a positive cash flow. They conclude:

> Certain strategic factors are associated with high performance among dogs. The notable factors are low capital intensity, attention to efficiency, a narrow focus, high product quality, and low to moderate prices. (1982, p. 94)

Keep in mind that business classification is a crude tool. But it can help us uncover fundamental deployment patterns and glaring inconsistencies. And it can alert us to explore just how many opportunities for performance improvement and resource redeployment exist.

The significance of each business unit's position is its cash use or generative characteristics in practice—its growth, capital intensity, and profitability. An ability to manage a business as a cow or a star, or to avoid falling into the dog trap, depends on your ability to realistically appraise your business's relative competitive advantage. If it is sufficiently large and the competitive structure is stable, then it is probably safe to take cash out; if it is too low or erratic, then any effort to improve the situation is almost certainly unwarranted, given the firm's other opportunities.

By centering a "bubble" or "balloon" on each business's portfolio position so that the area of the bubble is proportionate to the percentage of corporate sales generated by each business, management can see not only where its businesses lie, but the likely cash balance of the firm, where cash is *probably* being generated and where it is *probably* being used. Biggadike (1978) advises those who wish to draw a product portfolio precisely that

> the radius, r, of a circle representing a product is equal to the square root of the product of the percentage, p, (expressed as a decimal) of total sales represented by that product and the square of the radius R of the large circle representing total company sales.
>
> $$r = \sqrt{pR^2}$$
>
> As a rule of thumb, the radius of the total sales circle should be about half of the distance from any axis to the interception of the index lines (the lines dividing high and low market share), along either one of the index lines. This rules ensures that a circle representing the total sales of the company will fit within one quadrant. Some trial and error may be necessary. (p. 4)[1]

[1]Within an industry where sales/asset ratios are stable and similar among companies, assets might be used as an alternate to sales.

Notice, too, that "probably" is a necessary qualifier, since portfolio position suggests a likely or expected funds balance for each business—reality could be different. When analysing diversified companies, always check the actual cash flow. For example, perhaps because of "when we look," a business whose management has determined to increase market share may be increasing its share by cutting prices but still be reaching for a stable, profitable position; it could have relatively high market value, but not a positive cash flow. Unless volume allows a firm to garner market power over its customers and so receive higher prices, or unless volume allows experience to accumulate—experience that is associated with a sustainable cost advantage—efforts to expand market share may not pay.

SOME THOUGHTFUL CRITICISM

Portfolio models are not without their critics, of course, as these last remarks suggest. Again, the BCG model can serve as a bench mark for our discussion; nevertheless, the user must beware of the implicit assumptions underlying it.

The product portfolio suggests four archetypical sets of objectives and strategies for the business units (or products) of a corporation, depending upon their positions within the matrix, as noted earlier:

- Cow—milk and redeploy cash flow
- Dog—divest and redeploy proceeds
- Star—build competitive position and grow
- Wildcat—invest heavily and selectively to improve competitive position.

Market share is assumed to be valuable because it is profitable. BCG explains the profits as the fruit of an advantageous cost position due to the rapid accumulation of experience. It is also assumed that market growth ultimately slows to allow the market leader to take cash out of the cow business.

The product portfolio is a pictorial representation of a sources and uses of funds statement. The model assumes that market share gains are associated with profitability and that growth will be followed by a decline, giving the firm an opportunity to deploy its funds.

Yet:

1. Gaining market share is costly, and some never recover the investment,
2. Many products have short and even attenuated life cycles, e.g., electronics.
3. Some products have extremely long life cycles and require continued investment.

Hence, there is no guarantee that there will be an opportunity to redeploy funds in every case.

The assumptions underlying the model are not always applicable. *Figure 18-4* suggests sources of potential error. Growing market share, the horizontal axis of the product portfolio, is not always profitable. Some believe that market share has to pass a threshold to be profitable, others that there is a U-shaped function, similar to 'ACD' in

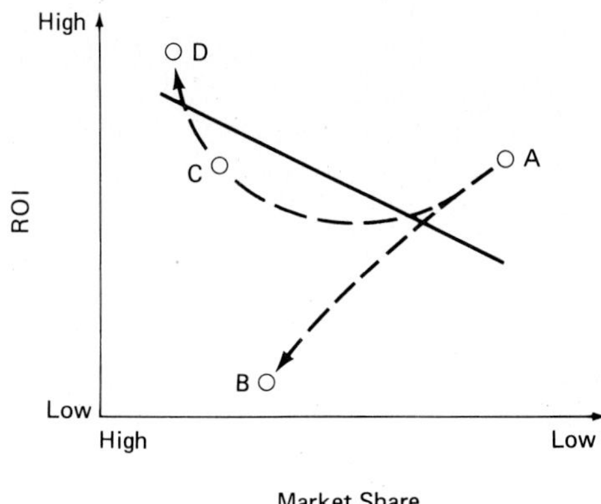

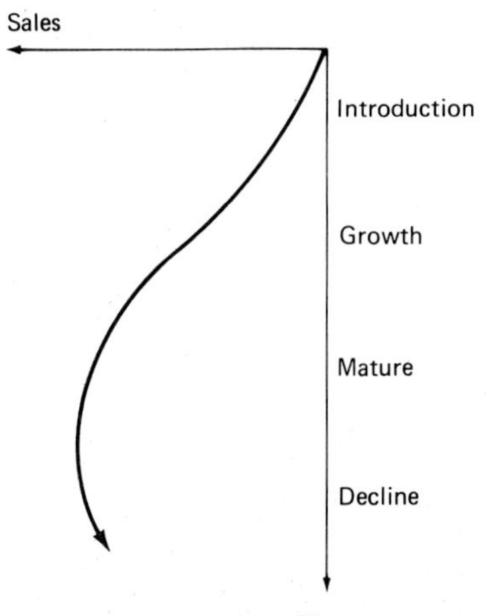

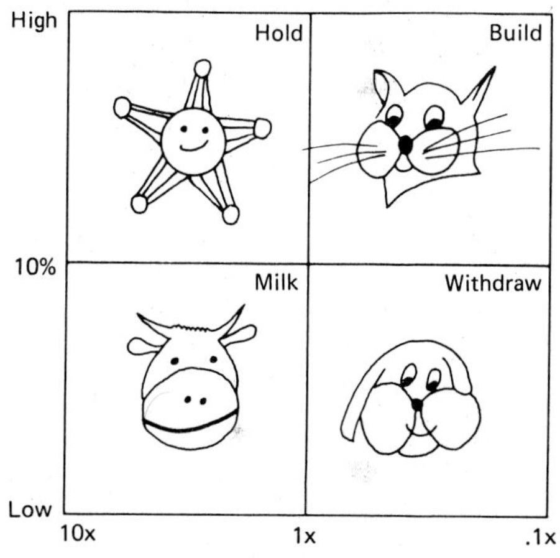

FIGURE 18-4 The Assumptions of the Product Portfolio

Figure 18-4(A), with untenable middle ground between high and low share positions (Porter, 1980). Fruhan (1974) and Chevalier (1974) documented the costs of building market share and the uncertain payoff associated with increased share, much like AB in Fig 18-4(A). Moreover, the model is a static representation of the firm. Attempting to change share is always risky. Attempts to increase share usually cut profits, at least in the short run, and so violate the implicit positive profit market share assumption of the model, the solid line in Fig 18-4(A).

With respect to the assumption as to growth and decline which underlies the vertical axis of the product portfolio, we can note again that the product life cycle (Figure 18-4B) is an unreliable descriptive model of business evolution. Some staples (bread, for example) are very long-lived while some electronic components and fashion goods are very short-lived. Bread is, of course, a very wide product category—particular bread types may come and go, although bread's ''popularity'' endures. Assumptions relating to the profit-market share relationships over time are relatively simple to expose, but the model also makes implicit assumptions about the timing a firm should use to capture its share of the value it creates by entering a particular market.

However, whenever the value of market share is threatened or the certainty of having time to get capital out of a business is low, the product portfolio is likely to be inapplicable. Abell and Hammond (1979) suggest that care is needed if value added is low; if competitors have low cost positions because of some resource or relationship that is not experienced-based; if technology is rapidly transferred among firms by equipment manufacturers or licensing, for example; or when the effects of scale are low. Patents, seasonality and cycles can also complicate the use of the portfolio concept.

Abell and Hammond (1979) and Day (1977) point out one important issue in the use of the product portfolio: market definition. Is it helicopters, heavy helicopters, or heavy military helicopters; is the geographic scope the US or the world? It's the same problem as with bread. The answer is important, of course, not simply to drawing the matrix and placing the business within it, but to helping the management of a particular firm or product line identify the relevant customers and competitors and focus effort accordingly.

Wensley (1981) makes another critical comment, applicable to most portfolio models, which relates to an implicit assumption about the firm's sources of funds. First, he points out that the portfolio approaches tend to view the corporation as an ''independent cash recycling'' entity. This is itself a useful model, but taken to an extreme, it may be unnecessarily constraining. If projects are sufficiently rewarding, debt or equity can be raised without earnings dilution.

Continuing, Wensley criticizes the implicit value of the ''high growth business'' in the BCG model. He argues that, because high growth markets generate demands for capital anyway, these businesses don't have to be highlighted. Moreover, Wensley maintains that, because the preference for high growth seems to depend upon the ease and value of gaining share, there is little evidence that share is valuable per se.

Finally, we suggest you take particular care in using product portfolio models whenever the capital intensiveness of mapped businesses differ greatly, for example, in the analysis of a multi-profit-centered company with manufacturing and service businesses such as many computer companies. Similarly be careful when the businesses you analyze enjoy the possibility of markedly different leverage: Financial service companies may have businesses leveraged 15:1 or 20:1 on an asset/equity basis, such as banks or near banks, and others whose leverage is as low as 5:1.

Remember, there is validity in the picture and in the numbers which describe the real cash flows. When dealing with diversified companies, always review the numbers on a business-by-business basis and explore any inconsistencies between numbers and pictures carefully.

To sum up, we suggest a relaxed but informed use of the models. The portfolio approaches really have stimulated managers to think about their businesses in new ways. They helped some companies purge themselves of wasteful relics of bygone ages and considerably improve their performance.

The managements of GE, Becton Dickenson, Dexter, Mead, Olin, and other companies all saw these models as valuable. In 1970, GE enjoyed a margin of 3.7 percent; by

1976 it had reached 5.9 percent and by 1984 increased to 8.2 percent. Bettis and Hall (1981) report on the performance of another portfolio user lifting its return on total capital from 6.0 to 12.9 over a period of ten years. Remember that most portfolio models were used first as marketing tools by strategy consultants. Although they contain really nothing new, they document resource deployment in a helpful way. They are the product of the creative insights of people who made fundamentals fresh and, for a time, contributed to the efficient use of internal capital. Their creators never intended that they be used alone, but as one of a set of analytical tools to help managers define better questions and talk about solutions.

SOME COMMENTS FROM USERS

William Verity, then Chairman and Chief Executive Officer of Armco Steel, described his company's application of BCG's product portfolio concept as follows:

> Obviously we want to distribute our cash . . . and assets, where they will provide the best possible return with the least possible risk exposure. The desired end result is the balanced portfolio.
>
> Portfolio management also means definition of our market position for each business as against those of our competitors . . . and delineation of cost advantage in those markets we choose to enter. Do our costs drop, as they should, as we gain experience? This is the experience curve effect, so important to portfolio management. We found that if we did not treat steel as a monolithic block but as one composed of discrete business units, which it is, we could manage it as a portfolio of business. By discrete business units we mean: "Those with clearly defined markets . . . that have their own marketing group, . . . their own manufacturing . . . and an identifiable investment in property, plant and equipment." (1975, pp. 57–58)

Loomis of Dexter commented on his use of the GE/Shell matrix:

> I was, at first, startled by the idea of forcing a distribution of one's business into the best, middle, and worst thirds and then looking upon the bottom third as a source of capital for the top two-thirds of one's portfolio. At the time that seemed like dropping the baby off the back end of the sled to prevent the wolves from running down the horses. However, as inflation takes bigger and bigger bites of capital, more firms are finding that they lack the resources to expand all of their businesses. Divestiture and liquidation are rational alternatives. (1980, p. 8)

Howe of Becton Dickinson, which employed the ADL model in the late 1970s, described the objectives as follows:

> The overall objective of the system is to maintain a strategic balance at the late growth stage. That means we must build or acquire enough new and early-growth businesses to offset the natural maturing of our existing portfolio. With its portfolio balanced at the late growth phase, the substantial cash flow from mature businesses should equal the cash needs of embryonic and early-growth ones, thus balancing the

company's overall investment requirements. In addition, profits increase most dramatically at the late growth stage. With the entire company poised at that point, it should be able to achieve its primary financial objective—a sustainable average of 15 percent annual growth in earnings per share.

With care, the product portfolio can be used to identify or design links between the operating units of a diversified corporation. Properly used in situations where its assumptions are met, it can provide good information to a manager, helping him or her add value while managing diversification. The product portfolio focuses management's attention on resource deployments and in this way is a major managerial aid in corporate strategy identification, as we will show in the next chapter.

chapter 19

Identifying Corporate Strategies

INTRODUCTION

Since corporate strategy is what corporations do to get what they want, we will focus on what they are doing and use that knowledge to identify the corporate strategy and infer its objectives, so that ultimately we can determine whether change is warranted. As we noted in our discussion of single-business companies, it is difficult to modify a company's present strategy and do so *responsibly* until you know what you are doing and how well it is working. Again, this means you have to identify your strategy before you fix it and, we suggest, in order to know whether it needs fixing. Identification is the starting point for any discussion of corporate strategy.

Let us define an approach for indentifying strategies at any level: To identify the strategy of any level, look down at its parts and seek the interrelationships between them; strategy will be revealed by these interrelationships. At the *business* level, we look down to the functions, infer their objectives, and seek interrelationships between them. At the *corporate* level, we look to the businesses of the firm, infer their objectives, and seek interrelations between them. At the *business* level, we exploit *functional analysis*. At the *corporate* level, we turn to *business analysis*. And, as we did when we identified a business's strategy from its functional actions and objectives, at the corporate level we will move from analysis to synthesis, from the separate actions of the businesses of the firm to the integrative objectives and relationships that bind them to the whole corporation.

BUSINESS ANALYSIS

As noted, the purpose of business analysis is to highlight the key relationships between the businesses of the corporation so that we can synthesize its strategy. What are these relationships?

Research on diversification suggests that industry choice is critical, that the growth strategy and relatedness are important, and that the administrative discipline which guides strategy implementation and the deployment of resources is a major determinant of success. *Figure 19-1* lists these four components and suggests some guidelines and caveats that are well-founded in research. We note that these four components encompass Ansoff's (1965) components of corporate strategy: Product-market scope, the growth factor, synergy, and competitive advantage. Ansoff suggested that these components plus the corporate objectives defined the concept of the firm's business. As noted in Chapter 17, research since 1965 has confirmed the wisdom of his choices. Competitive advantage is included here under the heading Industry Choice because we believe that it is foolish for a corporation to enter a business where it enjoys no advantage and is unlikely to attain it. Relatedness is the potential source of synergy, although experience suggests that synergy is elusive and difficult to attain. We add administrative discipline because it is the lynchpin between strategic design and implementation.

In business analysis, we examine all of the corporation's businesses—how it entered them, manages them, and deploys its assets between them. Analagous to functional analysis, business analysis structures data to highlight patterns of behavior and the relationships across businesses which reveal corporate strategy. Portfolio deployments of funds, using the idea of some business activities funding others, will guide our analysis.

Figure 19-2 provides a framework for business analysis which encompasses the components of corporate strategy, although it may require customized adaptation to suit particular needs. Note that the character of the corporation and its repeated actions suggest areas of emphasis within the business analysis framework. For an aggressively diversify-

FIGURE 19-1 Components of Corporate Strategy

Industry Choice (product-market scope)
- Keep it narrow.
- Focus.
- Enter where you have or can develop a competitive advantage.

Growth: Acquisition or Internal
- They're different.
- Acquisitions are risky.
- Diversification is risky.

Relatedness
- Synergy is elusive—and is a result of management.
- Stick close to what you know.
- Develop your distinctive competences.

Administrative Discipline
- Redeploy your assets from low-return to high-return opportunities.
- Manage risk: Limit to what you can absorb, or share it.
- Share power so that decisions can be made by those with the information to make them.

		Business	#1	#2	#3	#4	#5 ...
Entry/Growth							
Industry Characteristics							
Management	Marketing						
	Operations						
	Resource Deployment						
	Administrative Discipline						
Results							
Business Objectives							

FIGURE 19-2 Identifying the Corporate Strategy: Business Analysis

ing corporation, we might pay particular attention to the condition of the target company and the target industry at entry. For a company whose product-market mix has been stable for many years, we might emphasize operations more than entry and be careful to understand the degree and type of vertical integration the company employs. For a high-technology company, we might specify technology and research function more closely.

Note, too, that consistent patterns of resource deployments and results point to sound administrative strategies. If they are inconsistent, some closer examination of administrative practices is warranted.

In using *Figure 19-2,* we suggest that you track the diversification of the firm over time, that you seek patterns in entry strategy and the principal economic characteristics of the target industries. Under the heading Management, look for patterns which indicate marketing and operating relatedness and try to explain the firm's resource deployments in the light of the results earned and objectives sought. Many diversified firms' activities will be characterized by market relatedness or integrated operations or financial asset redeployment; only very large, mature, and successful firms, like General Electric, are likely to use the three types of managerial interrelatedness concurrently.

Figure 19-3 details the preceding framework and suggests the types of data required for a complete analysis. *Figure 19-4* lists a set of questions you might address once the basic descriptive data are collected. As in the case of the single-business firm, we should expect the objectives of the separable businesses to reveal much of the corporate strategy.

		Business	#1	#2	#3	#4	#5 ...
Entry/Growth		Entry Year Scale of Entry Acquisition/Internal Condition Terms					
Industry Characteristics		Average ROA Leader Share Sales Growth Profit Variance Key to Success Number of Competitors Key Competitor(s) Risk Sources					
Management	Marketing	Customers Product/Service Price Promotion Place-Channel					
	Operations	Sources Product Technology Process Technology Number of Plants Scale Value Added Productivity Integration					
	Resource Deployment	Percent of Assets Committed Internal Investment Personnel Quality					
	Administrative Discipline	Locus of Power Investment Criteria Performance Rewards Nature of Controls					
Results		ROA Relative Share Growth Profit Variance Technical Strength Competitive Strength					
Business Objectives		Stated Objectives					
		Unstated/Enacted Objectives					

FIGURE 19-3 Identifying Corporate Strategy: Business Analysis Detailed Information

FIGURE 19-4 Identifying the Corporate Strategy

1. What are the firm's businesses?
2. How has the firm entered those businesses? By acquisition or internal development?
3. What common characteristics are shared by the businesses? For example, along the industry chain, are there common suppliers, competitors, or customers; perhaps similar marketing or operations strategies? Are there shared resources, joint effects, or other managed synergies?
4. Are the businesses integrated in any way? By ownership, business relationships, or operations?
5. How are the firm's resources deployed? How are they being redeployed? How do the resource deployments trade off risk for reward?
6. Business by business, what are the results and how does the firm react to them?
7. Are the firm's resources being deployed in a manner consistent with the results earned and the potential earnings of each business?
8. What are the roles of headquarters and divisional management? How does power vary by business and function? How is control exercised?
9. What are the objectives of each business? How do the objectives of each business relate, one to the other?
10. What does the pattern of objectives mean? Looking down from the corporate level, what is the strategy they add up to?

THE HIERARCHY OF OBJECTIVES AND STRATEGIES

The corporation is partly, perhaps principally, coordinated by the hierarchy of strategy and objectives. In corporations, higher-level strategies define lower-level objectives in the same way that business strategy "defined" functional objectives and the synthesized "sum" of the functional objectives specified the strategy.

Remember, too, an important feature of strategic analysis: What looks like a strategy from above is likely to be seen as a set of objectives from below. Top management's strategy defines the objectives of those who report to them. Middle management's objectives are to implement the top management's strategy. Middle management's actions are means to ends, specified in turn by higher-level means and ends. Thus, the corporation's actions are coordinated by a hierarchical chain of means and ends which we call strategies and objectives.

BUSINESS ANALYSIS FOR A DIVERSIFIED CORPORATION: THE BIC CORPORATION

Let us examine one small, moderately diversified company, the Bic Corporation, to illustrate business analysis. Bic, well known for its ballpoint pens, disposable lighters, and razors, has for many years been an increasingly pressing and successful competitor of Gillette.

Put yourself in the position of the general manager of Gillette's razor division. Now for the first time you have a personal stake in the outcome of Gillette's competition with Bic. An important question for you is: What is Bic's strategy?

To answer this question, we will first outline Bic's history, describing its operations and its efforts to diversify. Then we will use the frameworks for functional and business analysis to identify Bic's corporate strategy so that we will be able to better understand its strategy in the razor business.

In 1958, Marcel Bich, a successful French businessman, acquired the Waterman Pen Company in Waterbury, Connecticut. Waterman was a troubled company whose product, fountain pens, had been declining for many years. Bich was the French manufacturer of low-priced, throwaway ballpoint pens, and he intended to produce ballpoints in the Waterbury plant.

Between 1958 and 1964, the Bic Pen Corporation (USA) lost money. But although it was losing money, Bic was building market share, a distribution channel, and a brand image. In 1961, Bic cut the price of its original crystal pen from 29¢ to 19¢ and began to promote its product more heavily. In essence, Bic had converted the Waterbury plant to ballpoint pens, developed its manufacturing capabilities as the crystal pen's sales increased, and invested some of the resulting cash flow in promotion. During this period, the French parent presumably subsidized its US offspring. By 1964, however, Bic broke even and then achieved an after-tax profit of 26.6 percent in 1975.

During the seven years between 1958 and 1965, Bic had matched its mass production capabilities with a mass marketing capability. It had developed a brand name and two distinct channels of distribution—the first through the ma and pa stores of America and the second through the then rapidly growing discount retail chains. In addition, the Bic Company had mastered the use of television mass advertising to complete its conquest of the American pen market.

Figure 19-5 is our functional analysis of Bic Corporation, circa 1972. At this point Bic was a ballpoint pen company. We have already outlined the marketing strategy of the company but it is important to note the sophisticated manufacturing strategy adopted by Bic. Its cost position was low and the company had in fact used almost every opportunity available to reduce its costs, including, you may note, the adoption of stable and secure employment conditions for its workers (in many ways, Bic has been managed like a Japanese company or perhaps as a Z-type organization). Under the heading Finance, we can note that Bic at this time was highly liquid, with about one year's operating cash flow on hand. It had no budgets, yet was tightly controlled. The explanation, of course, lies in its management practices. Bic's was an informally managed but tightly knit family of managers who enjoyed close personal supervision by their President, Robert Adler, and Marcel Bich.

Function by function, Bic's objectives can be readily inferred. Marketing strove for volume, manufacturing for a low cost position subject to meeting all product specifications. The financial objective appears to have been to ensure that funds were available for investment when needed, while the management objective was to maintain a low-cost, flexible, controlled corporation. Bic's strategy at this time was to be a ballpoint pen company operating at high volume, low cost, constantly reinvesting to improve both its volume and cost positions while managing itself as leanly as possible.

The reinvestment into promotion stimulated volume by "pulling" product into the market. Its constant reinvestment in manufacturing combined with its volume production

FIGURE 19-5 Functional Analysis: Bic Pen Corporation, 1973

Marketing	*Operations/Productions*	*Finance*	*Management*
Market: Retail Big commercial share in crystals **(not porous in '73)** *Product:* Quality ballpoint pens *Price:* Cut in 1961 Products low-priced 19¢ pen stable '61-'72 *Promotion:* Explosive introduction Emphasis on "Bic" name Heavy introduction use of TV Point of purchase advertising Jobbers and company salesforce Discounts, etc. *Distribution:* Two-channel -Direct to mass market -indirect to *old* base Ma and Pa stores (NB, 19¢ retail receipt 8.5¢ to manufacturer)	*Plant:* Single plant *Process:* Highly automated and integrated (brass bought from France) *Cost Position: Recipe for Low Cost:* -Integrated -Automated assembly -Invest to cut costs -Simple line -Standard parts -Simplified design -Relatively specialized -Intense quality control by workers (25%) -Smoothed production -Inventory buffer *Labor:* Unionized (rubber) Secure jobs: no layoffs Promotion within Retraining/Flexible use Wages high Family recruiting Experienced Workers	*Source:* Earned *Liquidity:* Very high *Dividend:* 25% payout EPS (Earnings per Share): Smooth growth No budgets No R&D	*Structure:* Informal Tightknit family Big bonuses Few rank differences Information widely shared Understaffed Personal control by Bich and Adley
Volume	+ Specified Quality at Low Cost	+ Funds Available	+ Control at Low Cost

Source: Data from Bic Annual reports

cut costs and gave the company an ability to keep its prices low and stable. This helped "push" product into the distribution channels and so to the market.

Bic had developed a consistent and tightly knit business strategy in the pen business. In 1973, however, it became apparent that the crystal pen's sales had begun to decline: Its market share had fallen from 36 percent in early 1972 to 31 percent by 1973. Bic's response was to introduce a series of new products in relatively quick succession. As *Figure 19-6* shows, the company added porous pens in late 1972, disposable lighters in 1973, pantyhose in 1974, and the disposable razor in 1976. It is significant to note that over this period of time, Bic's self-concept changed from ballpoint pens to writing instruments; then to the manufacturer and marketer of everyday, throwaway, mass pro-

FIGURE 19-6 Product & Concept Evolution—Bic Pen Corporation (USA)

Year	*Product Added*	*Corporate Concept*
1958	Crystal ballpoint pen	A ballpoint pen company
1968	Clic retractable ballpoint pen	
1972	Porous pen	A writing instrument company
1973	Disposable lighter	A company in the inexpensive, disposable, mass produced, high-quality goods business distributed through writing instrument channels.
1974	Pantyhose	A marketing company
1976	Disposable razor	

duced, high-quality, low-priced goods distributed through writing instrument channels; and finally, to a marketing company.

Let us look at Bic's performance, the results. *Figure 19-7* shows Bic's sales, profits, and profit margin between 1964 and 1973. Note the flat sales and earnings over the period 1969 to 1971. The subsequent results point to the reason for diversification: To stimulate the continuing growth of the company.

But note that in 1968, 1972, and 1973, the years when new product lines were introduced by the company, profit margins fell. The estimated pretax margins for each

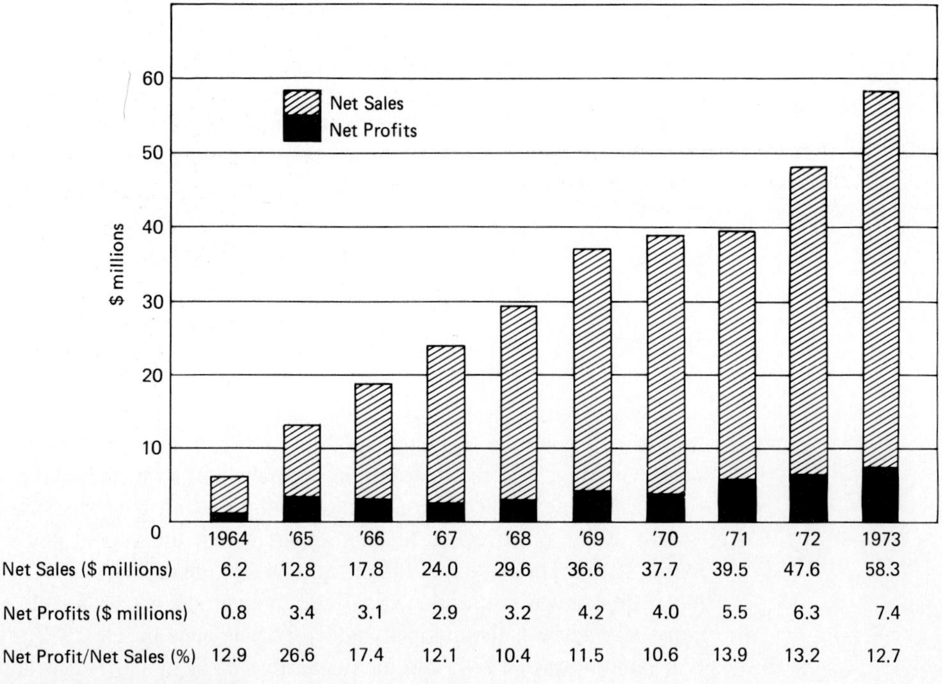

	1964	'65	'66	'67	'68	'69	'70	'71	'72	1973
Net Sales ($ millions)	6.2	12.8	17.8	24.0	29.6	36.6	37.7	39.5	47.6	58.3
Net Profits ($ millions)	0.8	3.4	3.1	2.9	3.2	4.2	4.0	5.5	6.3	7.4
Net Profit/Net Sales (%)	12.9	26.6	17.4	12.1	10.4	11.5	10.6	13.9	13.2	12.7

FIGURE 19-7 Bic Pen Corporation (USA)

Source: BIC Pen Corporation Annual Report, 1973

TABLE 19-1 Estimated Profit Margins: Bic Pen Corporation (USA) (c. 1974)

Product	*Profitability*
Crystal pen	>30%
Clic pen	≤10%
Porous pen	≃30%
Lighter	15-21%
Hose	15%

product line, circa 1974, are estimated in *Table 19-1*. These estimates suggest that each time the Bic company diversified, its profit margin declined.

One explanation of this profit decline is the presence of competition. In its later product introductions Bic confronted more established and more significant competition. Its crystal pen had been introduced into the market against no-name brands at a time when the Scripto Company withdrew from the low-priced pen market, allowing Bic a window to enter. Its porous pen, in contrast, confronted Gillette's Flair which then enjoyed a 45 percent share of the porous pen market. Its lighter again confronted Gillette. At the time of Bic's entry, Gillette's Cricket held one-third of all disposable lighter sales.

Are there other explanations for Bic's decline in profitability? *Figure 19-8* shows Bic's products on a generic life cycle curve. Referring to *Table 19-1,* we can see that Bic's early products are profitable and its late products appear to have been less successful. There appears to be some correlation between Bic's time of entry to the market and its long-run profitability, as shown at the top of *Figure 19-9*. Bic's profitability appears to be dependent upon its market share, as the lower part of *Figure 19-9* suggests. As *Table 19-2* shows, since 1972 Bic has become an increasingly alert and timely competitor, entering the market for razors virtually coincidentally with Gillette's introduction of disposable razors.

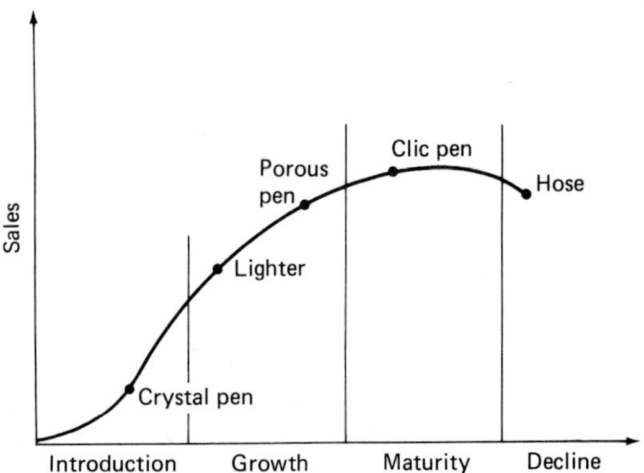

FIGURE 19-8 Life Cycle Stages, Bic Products

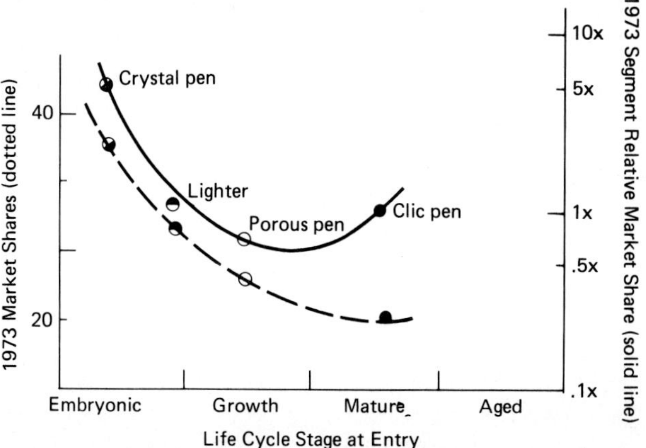

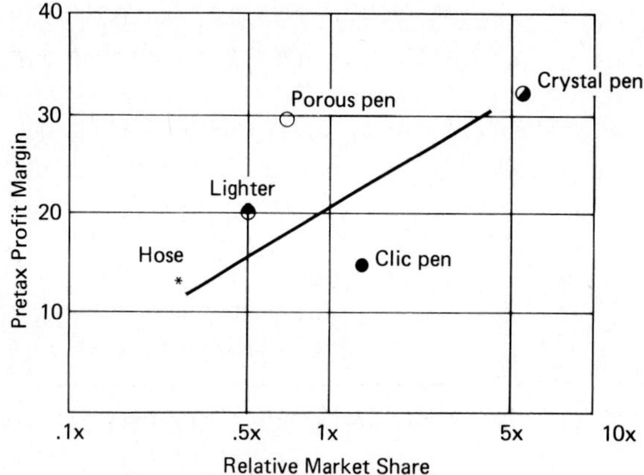

FIGURE 19-9 Bic's Performance (c. 1973)
Source: Data from Bic annual reports

TABLE 19-2 Time of Bic Entry Compared with Leader

Bic Products	*Bic Entry*	*Time after Competitor's Market Entry*
Porous pen	1972	6 years
Lighter	1973	2 years
Hose	1974	1 year
Razor	1976	6 weeks

TABLE 19-3 Financial Results: Bic (USA)

Year	*Sales*	*ROA*	*Leverage*	*ROE*	*EPS*
1972	47.6mil	18.8	1.14	21.5	1.00
1973	58.3	17.8	1.15	20.5	1.15
1974	74.5	11.6	1.30	15.1	.96
1975	93.0	11.2	1.46	16.4	1.16
1976	122.8	12.1	1.60	19.3	1.55
1977	134.8	6.9	1.72	11.9	1.06
1978	153.6	7.4	1.84	13.6	1.31
1979	179.0	6.8	1.91	13.0	1.36
1980	192.0	8.8	1.86	16.4	1.91
1981	217.7	5.4	1.83	9.9	1.27
1982	218.1	5.0	1.66	8.3	1.11

Source: Data from Bic annual reports

Table 19-3 shows some additional financial results for Bic. Note how Bic's return on assets is falling, although its return on equity was generally maintained until 1981. The company has continued to grow and, for many years, its shareholders have enjoyed higher earnings, in spite of the profit margin declines we have seen.

A Changing Strategy

Let us consider how Bic's corporate strategy changed. In *Figure 19-10* we take the Framework for Business Analysis and apply it to the Bic Pen Corporation. The first line shows how Bic entered each of its product lines in the US. The entry to the US market was by acquisition from France, the crystal and porous pens were developed from French products but inside the US market. However, the fourth, fifth, and sixth products—lighters, pantyhose, and razors—were all initially imported to the US from other Bich-owned companies.

Moving to the next line, Industry Characteristics, we can note, as we observed before, that Bic is entering the market against more established and significant competitors, and, in the case of the last three products, against competitors who view lighters, pantyhose, and razors as increasingly important parts of their respective business.

Under Marketing, we can see that Bic introduced its first three products to the market at low prices. With the second three, Bic's initial prices more closely matched those of its competitors. With the first three products, its relative advertising expenditure was high compared to the competition, while with the last three, Bic's relative advertising intensity was lower.

Under Operations, we note that Bic manufactured the first three products in the United States, while it purchased the latter three products from the French company or its subsidiaries. Under Resource Deployments, in the case of the first three products, Bic was essentially self-financing from 1964 on. In the case of lighters, pantyhose, and razors, however, the Bic Company increasingly relied on debt to fund its business development. Leverage increased from 1.15 times equity in 1973 to 1.6 times equity in 1976, the year

		Crystal pen	Clic pen	Porous pen	Lighter	Hose	Razor
Entry/ Growth	Year	1958	1968	1972	1973	1974	1975
	Scale	Large	Medium	Large	Small	Small	Small
	Method	Acquisition Turnaround	Internal	Internal	Import	Import	Import
Industry Characteristics		No-Name's Limited capitaliza-tion Scripto leaving low end	Established brands	Gillette has 50% market	3 majors, Gillette holds 30%	3 majors, largest holds 9% Shrinking industry	Gillette has 55% ROA and very dominant share (gives razors away)
Management	Marketing	Low price High relative advertising	Low price High relative advertising	Low price Equal Advertising	Equal price Small relative advertising	Equal price Small relative advertising	Equal price Small relative advertising
	Operations	Single, highly automated plant	Same plant	Same plant	Importing from French parent, later own plant	Importing from French parent	Importing from French parent, later own plant
	Resource Deployment	Initial subsidy from French parent	Self-financed	Self-financed	Marketing investments only until position established	Marketing only	Marketing only until market position established
	Administrative Discipline	Pace of diversification controlled by French parent					
Results		Sales rising, margin and ROA falling, market position well-established, a dominant or #2 competitor. Company has achieved low-cost position technically dependent on French parent.					
Business Objectives		Growth has been given priority over profitability, moving company into a negative leverage position on sub-stantial short-term loans. EPS growth sustained with leverage until 1981.					

FIGURE 19-10 Business Analysis—The BIC Corporation (USA)

Source: Data from Bic annual reports

FIGURE 19-11 **Bic's Competitive Advantages Through 1974**

	Crystal Pen	Clic Pen	Porous Pen	Lighter	Hose
Quality	+	=	−	=	?
Price	+	=/+	+/−	=	−/=
Cost	+	+	+	=/?	=/−
Promotion	+	+	+/=	+	−
Distribution	+	+	+/=	+/=	−
Number of Competitors	5	6	Gillette and others	Gillette and others	Burlington Kayser/Roth Hanes

Bic introduced its disposable razor to the US market, reaching a high point of 1.9 times equity in 1979.

In *Figure 19-11,* we show the pattern of competitive advantages which a group of executives believed held for Bic's product line in the marketplace. You may note that above the diagonal line the signs are predominantly negative (''disadvantage Bic'') while below the lines the signs are generally positive (''advantage Bic''). Although not a perfect pattern, this is evidence which we believe means that each time Bic has diversified, there has been a tendency for it to lose competitive advantages. And, we note that it was losing those advantages in a market of increasingly well-funded and increasingly aggressive competitors, such as the Hanes company in the hosiery market and Gillette in razors. The Bic company appears to have moved into an increasingly risky competitive situation while at the same time adopting an increasingly risky debt position.

Before we proceed, let us note two other factors. First, the Bic company has continued to grow and its earnings per share continued to increase until 1981. Second, we might wonder whether the company's asset commitments were as risky as they might appear to the casual observer. However, note in *Figure 19-10* that since 1973 Bic's entry to the market with new products has been as a distributor of imported products only. As one company executive said at the time, ''Bic USA has increasingly become a marketing company.''

Obviously, Bic is using its basic strategy but adapting it to a particular market. Its results are not clear. Without completing the section on Business Objectives in detail, we can note that the company gave growth priority over profits. We can suspect that the early products were being used to help fund the development of later products and that for some reason, the corporation decided that earnings per share growth warranted a risky financial profile, since returns on assets dropped from 12.1 percent in 1976 to 6.8 percent in 1979, and to 5 percent in 1982 as the company's use of debt expanded.

In 1982, the Bic Company had very little long-term debt, but carried $42.8 million of ''notes payable—bank'' on its balance sheet, an amount equivalent to approximately 28.4 percent of its total assets. By this time the company's short-term debt position had placed it in a position of negative leverage, with the company earning less on its debt-financed assets than it was paying to its banks. The company's average interest rate on its outstanding balance during 1982 was 14 percent, that is, nine percentage points greater than its ROA.

Summary

With this in mind, let us think carefully about summarizing Bic's strategy as a corporation, and, in particular, let us return to our imagined Gillette general manager and think about the advice we could offer him or her about Bic's activities in the razor business. Bic is a diversified company. As its old products decay in the market place, Bic has introduced new products to sustain the growth of the company. Its old products, in part, fund the development of the market of the new products, in the classical cow to wildcat cashflow. As *Figure 19-12* shows, the crystal pen division's success has funded in large measure the development of the porous pen, lighters, hose, and razor businesses, moving them one by one to the left side of the matrix in the late 1970s and 1980s.

However, the company has not done this alone. Underpinning the Bic Company's US activity is its relationships with its French parent. The Bic Company has entered the market as a distributor of European (Société Bic) manufactured products. Recall that when Bic USA's market position for a particular product reaches what we call efficient scale, the company has invested in US-based manufacturing plant and severed its trading

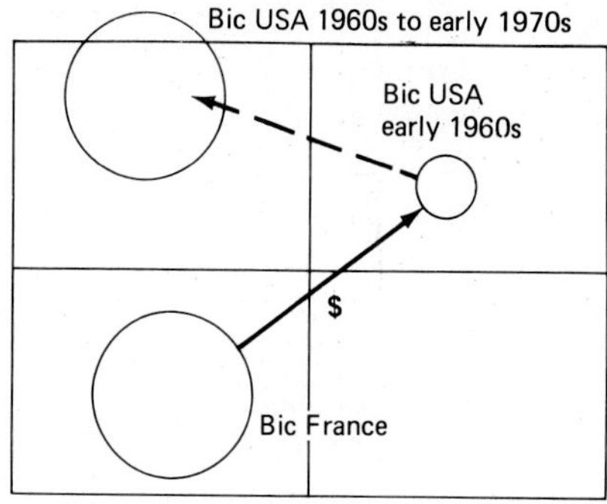

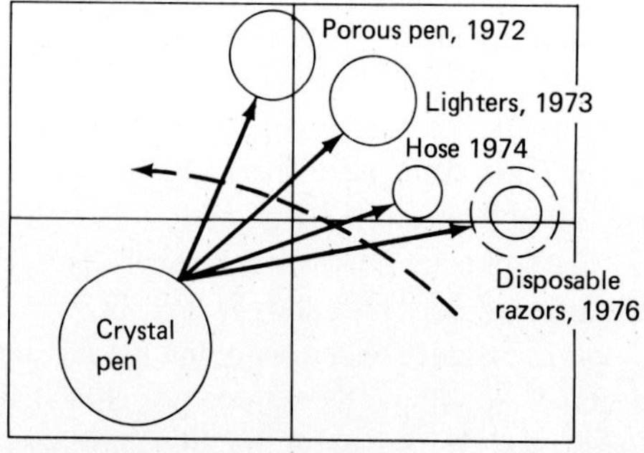

FIGURE 19-12 Portfolio Views of Bic

Source: Data from Bic annual reports

relationship with the French for that product. Essentially, Baron Bich reduces the risk of market entry by backloading capacity, that is, creating production capacity in the US *only after the market has been developed.* Bic USA is, in fact, part of a global corporation.

What do we tell the Gillette executive? He is competing with a company that is more than it seems. He is not competing with Bic USA but with the international resources of Société Bic. To properly hone his strategy, we could suggest that Gillette compete, not as a US-based company in the razor business, but as global merchandiser.

In Chapter 20, we will extend our examination to the global strategy of the Société Bic and consider its implications for Gillette's razor business.

chapter 20

International Competition and the Evolution of Global Businesses

INTRODUCTION

In Chapter 19, we completed our discussion of the diversification strategy of the Bic Corporation, the US member of Marcel Bich's international corporate empire. Indeed, the French presence is a significant part of Bic USA. The Bich family and Société Bic controlled 72 percent of the Bic Corporation as of March 1, 1983. The directors and officers of the Bic Corporation held an additional 7 percent of the corporation and the public the remainder. The Société Bic is a global business, and Bic Corporation is its US manufacturing arm and to a lesser extent one of its important distribution channels.

The Bic Corporation's existence in the United States, as *Figure 20-1* reminds us, stems from the early investments of its French parent. Recall that from 1958 to 1964 the then Bic Pen Corporation lost money, although it was growing. The French company has always controlled the R&D activity of Baron Bich's companies, presumably increasing the margin in the USA. The French company has always been a supplier to Bic USA, supplying the brass points of the crystal pen and later, as we have noted, lighters, hose, and razors—at least until the Bic Pen Corporation's US market position warranted fixed asset investments.

Global corporations play a different and broader competitive game than do purely national companies. We have already noted that Bic (USA) suffered a return on asset decline during the late 1970s and early 1980s, possibly exposing it to negative leverage, apparently as a cost of growth. However, we suggested that the risk associated with its growth was moderated by the relationships, both ownership and trading, between the French company and its US subsidiary. The ultimate challenge for our imaginary Gillette executive is to increase his understanding of Société Bic and to develop his own strategy for the Gillette razor business in light of that understanding. For a moment, then, let us

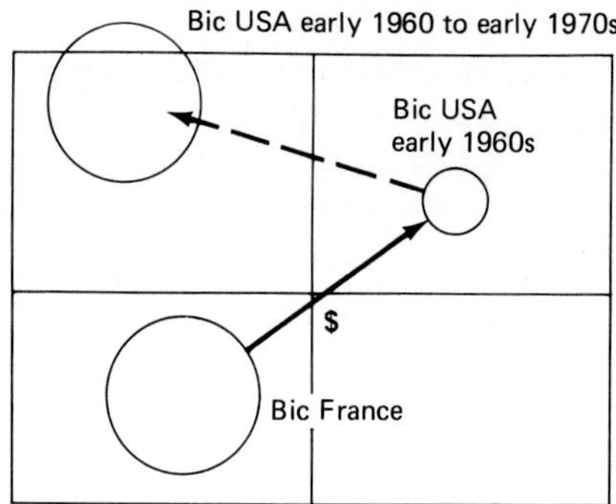

FIGURE 20-1 The Strategic Evolution of the Bic Group, Step 1
Source: Data from Bic annual reports

consider the implications of international competition and then turn to the evolution of Société Bic, S.A. as a global competitor.

THE GLOBAL CORPORATION

In his book, *My Years at General Motors,* Alfred Sloan wrote, "Again let me say that companies compete in broad policies as well as in specific products" (1964). The essence of a global competitor is that it views the world as one market, and positions itself to use all of its resources to become an effective competitor in that market. In Sloan's terms, it is competing with different policies than those of national firms. Such global strategies pose some particular problems for the managers of both the global company and its competitors, particularly those competitors who are essentially multinational, that is, companies who define competition in terms of discrete national markets.

A number of factors cause concern for managers engaged in global competition. First, global companies may be integrated by ownership, long-term sourcing contracts and trading relationships, R&D contracts, or board representation, for example (Williamson, 1975). Their perspective is necessarily broader and longer than simply national markets or single products in the short run.

Second, because of their global scope, these companies must address the concerns of wider constituent groups. Their stakeholder sets cross national boundaries and may include, to a greater extent than those of most U.S. companies, the governments of host countries. Indeed, state-owned enterprises may be suppliers, customers, and competitors simultaneously, and national competitors may be helped by product or employment regulations from their native governments, in addition to direct subsidization.

Third, the global nature of the enterprise complicates the task of business definition. In a global enterprise, the welfare of the whole must be given prominence over the welfare of the parts. Each business must be defined and managed in such a way as to make it as effective a competitor as possible, no matter who its competitors are and wherever they might be. Only in special circumstances, however, will the company's full competitive pressure be exerted simultaneously worldwide. It is more likely to be orchestrated market by market, and business by business, to maximize the value of the (parent) company as a whole. A worldwide competitive initiative at full strength is only practical when the resources available are enormous relative to the competition. In other circumstances, value is more likely to result from prudent and limited risk-taking across an interdependent set of markets, rather than across all.

Fourth, business definition and performance measurement go hand in hand. When interpreting the strategies and evaluating the competitive performance of the divisions or subsidiaries of a global enterprise, it is dangerous to place too much weight upon short-term results, for example, product level returns on assets (ROA). This caveat applies both to the firm's managers and to competitors. It is the performance of the enterprise as a whole and its long-run return on assets that counts more, and one of the best indicators of long-run performance is relative competitive strength. In a market where a globally oriented company is active and at low profit rates, the prudent competitor will pay particular attention to the development of local market strengths and international cost positions.

Fifth, global companies will for the most part work at efficient scale, that is, at efficient worldwide scale. In some markets, the scale of the enterprise will necessitate large domestic as well as export sales; in others exports will be used to lift local production to an efficient scale within a domestic or multicountry regional market. Market by market around the world, a global company will operate only world-scale efficient plants.

Let us note here that world scale applies to the current state of the art and to the technologies of production, not to worldwide demand. An alternative concept is a world standard cost advantage. Such a plant may, in fact, be capable of supplying only a region of a country, if that country is as large as the US; or it may be able to supply as much as half of Europe. World-scale production does not mean one plant but may involve many specialized and efficient-scale plants in a complex system of component production, transfer pricing, and assembly, taking advantage of technology and volume production while maintaining the political independence of the global enterprise.

Sixth, in a global enterprise, the ownership, administrative, and planning structures of a company are unlikely to be coincident across countries and businesses. This will complicate the administrative task of management at every level, particularly for those outside the strategy-formulating cadre of managers. Professional success for middle managers will likely depend on the ability to understand the reasons for the resource allocation and priorities given to their part of the whole corporation, yet it is unlikely that they will ever be privy to the true strategy of the enterprise. In essence, the middle managers of a company like Bic are in the same spot as the managers of Gillette: they have to determine for themselves what Bic's strategy is, and act accordingly.

Seventh, in a global enterprise, the company's regional and national investment strategies are likely to be conditioned by the status of the international currency markets. Exchange rates may affect the timing at which financial and competitive strength is built in certain markets. Repatriations of profits and redeployments of funds around the world are complicated by shifting exchange rates, although the need for profit repatriation can be modified by trading among corporate components and by shifting transfer prices in response to government action, tax policies, or internal interest rates. While these fiscal practices may mask the real competitive strategies of the enterprise, they demonstrate the impact of the widened stakeholder net on the pace of strategy implementation for the global corporation.

Société Bic: Global Operations

Let us now return to the Bic Corporation, broadening our analysis of a diversifying firm in Chapter 18 to that of a global competitor. In *Figure 20-1,* we showed the initial redeployment of funds from Société Bic, the French company, into the US market. In *Figure 20-2,* we show the relative status of the French company and its US subsidiary in the mid-1970s. Now let us return to the Framework for Business Analysis and consider how the Bic has evolved globally (*Figure 20-3*).

The French company was established in 1945 by Marcel Bich and his friend Edouard Bouffard in what was essentially a classical "garage type" entrepreneurial start-up, with capital of about $1000. The initial business was not ballpoint pens but ballpoint pen refills. It wasn't until Bich got the idea that a disposable pen would need no refills that the company began to look like the Bic Company of today.

In 1958, Bich acquired the Waterman Pen Company in Waterbury, Connecticut, a classic turnaround situation. The porous pen line appears to have been an internal development prompted in large measure by the management of Bic Pen US, suffering at the hands of Gillette's Flair. The decision concerning disposable lighters dates back to 1971 and Bich's purchase of Flaminaire, a French company. It is said that his objective was to market a substitute for matches, which are not freely available in Europe. The French business supplied the US for some years. In 1973, Bich took control of DIM S.A.—a $100-million company and the leading French hosiery maker—and, in 1974, began to supply the US market with pantyhose. Around 1975, Bich bought a Greek razor factory and again began to supply the US market.

In essence, we see a pattern which is production-driven. Acquisitions are followed by turnarounds founded upon volume built up both in a domestic market and interna-

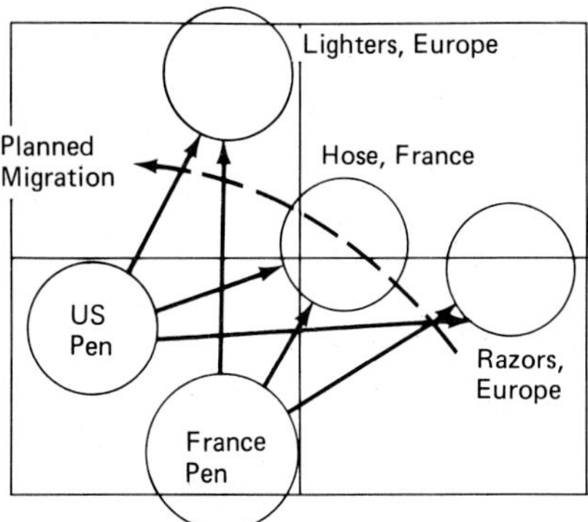

FIGURE 20-2 The Strategic Evolution of the Bic Group, Step 2
Source: Data from Bic annual reports

FIGURE 20-3 Business Analysis: Société Bic

	Pens		*Lighters*		*Hose*		*Razors*	
	France	*US*	*France*	*US*	*France*	*US*	*France*	*US*
Entry/Growth	1945	1958	1971	1973	1973	1974	1975	1976
	Garage start-up	Acquisition turnaround subsidized by French parent		Acquisition turnaround French investments strengthened by US market distribution				
Industry Characteristics	Weak competitors			Gillette	Largest in France		Gillette	
Management		Uses volume to achieve a low cost position and invests in cost improvements and promotion to strengthen market position, to build profitability. Initial profits sometimes take up to 7 years to achieve.						
Results		Worldwide sales and profit are rising. Company is achieving efficient scale production with a relative cost advantage, plant by plant.						
Business Objectives		Seizes opportunities to buy European manufacturers of low cost, disposable products. Uses US to build volume and gain manufacturing efficiencies in Europe. If US market position warrants world-scale plant, builds plant in US to exploit opportunity.						

Source: Data from Bic annual reports

tionally, particularly in the US. Where the US market has proven penetrable and of sufficient scale, Bich has later invested in manufacturing facilities to take full advantage of the business opportunity inherent to the market position created by his import distribution strategy.

Essentially, under Industry Characteristics *Figure 20-3,* we could suspect that Bich has always taken advantage of market trends. He has tended to enter markets when other companies leave them. He has been able to turn them around because he has been able to replicate his basic marketing and production strategies, business by business, country by country, around the world. In many ways, Baron Bich operates and manages his companies in a now-classical "Japanese" way: he has used his domestic market and export sales to reach efficient scale, to provide secure employment conditions, and to build brand recognition, in an integrated and consistent effort to turn competence to competitive advantage.

Bich's resource deployments, however, suggest his true business acumen. In *Figure 20-4,* we show a more complex series of portfolio charts which can help us track Bic's redeployment of its funds and, more importantly, its evolution as a global competitor.

Figure 20-4(a) shows Bic France and with it, the development of Bic (USA) through the early 1970s. Essentially, over time, the French investment converted a wildcat into a star. In *Figure 20-4(b)*, we show the Bic (USA) subsidiary alone, with its crystal pen in the apparent cash cow position for a sequence of new product introductions—porous pens, lighters, hose, and razors. The corporate objective appears to have been to convert these wildcats into stars.

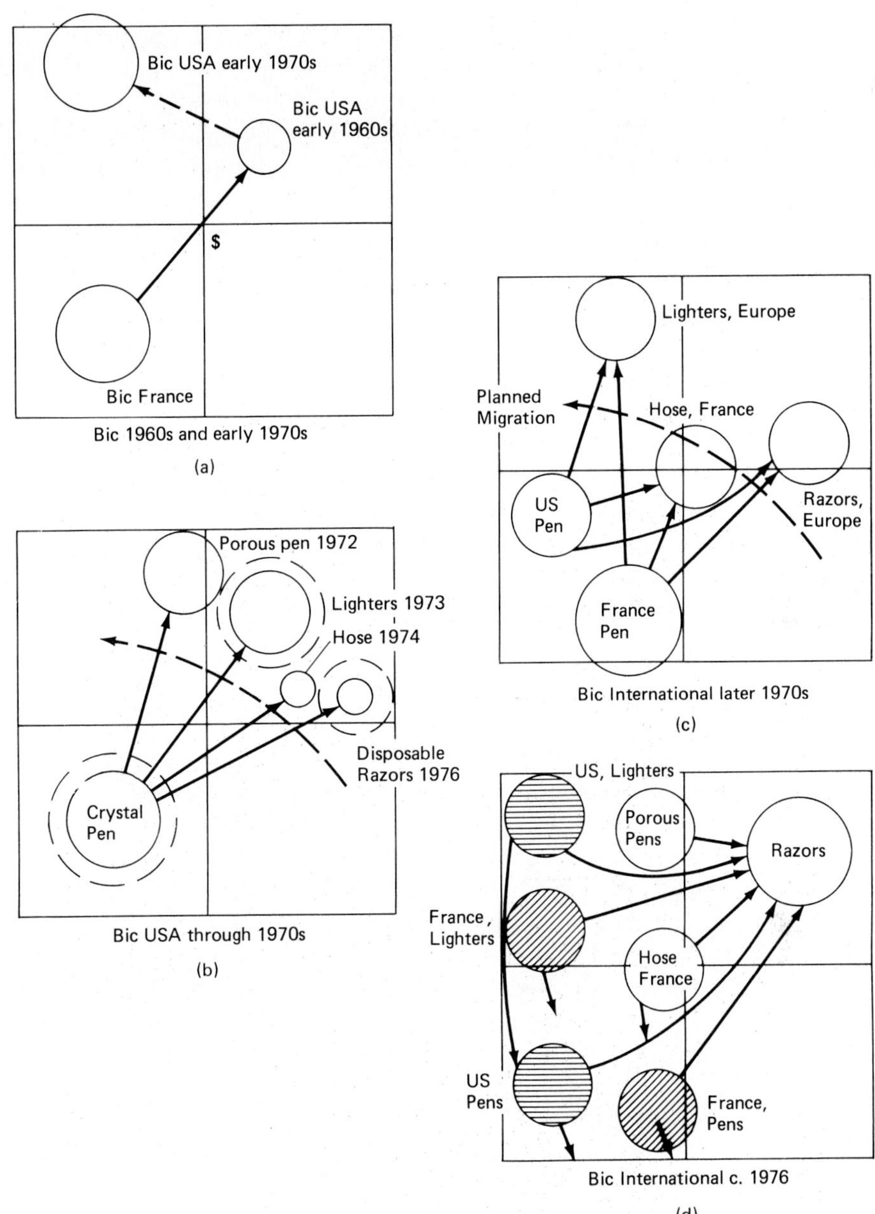

FIGURE 20-4 The Strategic Evolution of the Bic Group
Source: Data from Bic annual reports

Let us now take the perspective of the Société Bic in the mid-1970s. By this time, the US-based Bic Pen Corporation's initial products were declining in market share, in part due to new competitive entries by Gillette and other companies. From an international point of view, by the late 1970s, the Société Bic probably had two cows, the US crystal pen business and the French crystal pen business. Again from an international point of view, the major investments of the company were its newly acquired European corporations which manufactured lighters, hosiery, and razors.

We can suspect that, first, in either turning around or expanding the lighter and razor businesses, Baron Bich's objective was to convert them from wildcats to stars. Also, it is likely that the hosiery division, DIM, was essentially a dog which the Baron had to turn around before he could convert it to wildcat status.

We can note here that Baron Bich probably had the advantage of buying fixed assets in an industry that was essentially overcapacitied: hosiery in the 1970s. We would expect him, therefore, to have acquired his fixed assets at a discount so that, although a late entrant into the hosiery business, he may well have been one of the low fixed cost operators in Europe. We must also realize that the advent of low-cost supermarket hosiery distribution had taken place in the US in 1973 with Hanes's "L'Eggs" and Burlington's "No Nonsense," *only* a few months before his planned entry.

Over time, as *Figure 20-4(d)* shows, the Baron has been successful in converting not only his French and European operations into cash cows but in converting many of the US and French product lines into cash cows as well. With this herd of cows funding his entry to the disposable razor business, Baron Bich appears to have been willing to take on Gillette in its own pasture. He perceived that funding resources and his consistently successful global strategy outweighed his risk.

Bic and Gillette

For a moment, let us turn to Gillette. Gillette's razor-blade business is one of the most remarkable businesses in the world. In 1982, Gillette's profits from operations in its razor and blade divisions was $250 million on identifiable assets of $455 million—an operating return of 55 percent. This result must be viewed in the light of intense competition which the company was experiencing with Bic, and, in this context, it is worth noting 55 percent was the same rate of return which Gillette enjoyed in 1977. In 1976, however, shortly before Bic's entry to the razor market with its disposable razor, Gillette executives speculated that it was unlikely that the disposable razor would ever play any significant role in the US market. Only three years later, disposable razors made up over one-third of US razor sales, with Gillette and Bic holding roughly equivalent shares of this new market.

In a company like Gillette, with its razor and blade business earning such substantial rates of return, it would not be surprising to find the general managers of less profitable divisions under constant pressure for results. In this context, it is worth noting that the Gillette Company's commitment to the low-priced pen market waned at various times in the 1970s, with the result that Bic's share of the pen business jumped from about 60 percent to about 80 percent for a time. It is possible that by putting too high an ROA hurdle on its pen division, Gillette may have inadvertently created a larger and stronger cow in the Bic herd.

Later, as Gillette's lighter division suffered the onslaughts of competition from Bic, Gillette again seems to have wavered for a time, again inadvertently creating the window of opportunity which Bic needed. In a series of aggressive price cuts, Bic challenged Gillette for leadership of the lighter business and won. The results are shown in *Table*

TABLE 20-1 US Disposable Lighters—Bic Market Share

Year	*Bic's Percentage*	*Number of Units Sold*
1973	17	60 million
1974	25	110
1975	33	160
1976	41	225
1977	52	275
1978	50	320
1979	53	370
1980	52	400
1981	52	420
1982	52	430

Source: Bic Annual Reports, 1981 and 1982

20-1. Bic jumped to the leadership share position in the lighter business about 1977, a position it still held in 1984. More significant was the relative profit positions of Bic and Gillette in the 1980s: Bic's lighter division was profitable and probably a cash cow, while Gillette may have lost money in lighters and have had cash sink, possibly a dog. Bic reported a profit on lighters of $15.4 million in 1982. Gillette's "other" business segment, which included its Cricket disposable lighter (and other products), reported 1982 *loss* on operations of $11.5 million.

Figure 20-5 shows a different representation of the Bic empire, circa 1976, in a structural model. At this point in time, the heart of the Bic Company remained in France while its manufacturing operations were scattered about the world, in France, the US, and Greece. An example of global operations is the way in which these different manufacturing arms trade with the different distribution arms of Bic.

Consider the differences between the organizational forms and administrative practices of Bic and Gillette. To us it seems that Bic is further along in its evolution to a global enterprise than Gillette. Gillette, with its profit-centered management, product by product and region by region, is a classic American-managed multinational, a multibusiness enterprise which Hout, Porter and Rudden (1982) would call a multidomestic company. Power, for the most part, rests firmly within the United States and within the blade division.

Only in the last few years has the Gillette Company appeared to realize the benefits of competing with Bic on more fronts than one. By investing in its low-priced pen line, Write Brothers, and reintroducing it into the commercial market—ironically a market neglected by Bic because the distributors in that market demand large margins—Gillette has been able to make the pen business more competitive and less profitable for Bic. By competing in the pen business more aggressively, Gillette successfully cut the cash flow from Bic's pen business to its razor business. Bic reported a $2.1 million loss in its writing instrument business in 1982 on reduced sales of $73.9 million, down from $85.4 million in 1983.

Gillette may in fact have adopted Sloan's policy and begun to use all of its resources in the competition with Bic: Gillette suffered substantial losses in its "other" business segment (which encompasses lighters) in 1980, 1981, and 1982. However, we also noted

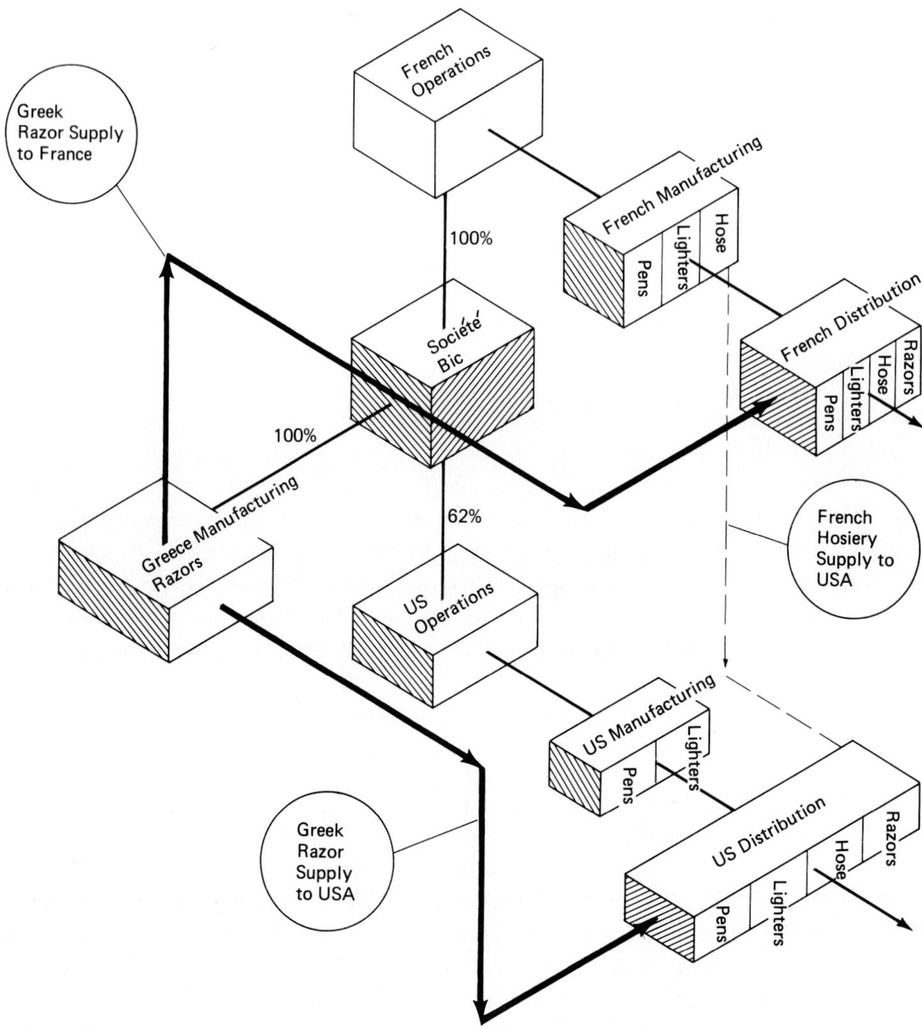

FIGURE 20-5 **Société Bic—circa 1976**
Source: Data from Bic annual reports

Gillette's stable 55 percent profit on operation in its blade and razor business across the full 1977 to 1982 period, some evidence that Gillette has protected its traditional cow successfully.

The Future for Gillette in Global Competition

Bic, we believe, is a global company. Thus, the challenge for Gillette was not to simply cut out the US-based cash cows in the Bic herd, but to compete on a global basis across all of the markets where the two companies operate. Indeed, the remainder of the world may provide the window of opportunity which Gillette needs. Bic, with its manufacturing competence, is a formidable competitor for its much larger rival, for a number of reasons.

Baron Bich's control of the Bic Companies rested in ownership, while Colman Moeckler's chairmanship of Gillette rested primarily on professional management skill and the results he earned. Moeckler's stakeholders were primarily those who believed in blue-chip investments—the institutions, widows, and orphans of America—all exerting tremendous pressure for steady and stable dividends. This demand for dividends represented a nontrivial constraint in the competition with an entrepreneur like Baron Bich.

Baron Bich's distinctive competence was manufacturing. Over time, in a number of countries, he built world-scale manufacturing capability in each of the industries in which he competed. Certainly Gillette is a world-scale competitor, but internationally it appears to operate at domestic rather than international scale. Gillette, moreover, seems accurately viewed by most people as a marketing company which is managed financially. Thus, when the competition is most intense and the margins low, it is more difficult for Gillette to invest in up-to-date manufacturing capability and capacity. By contrast, it is Baron Bich's advantage to have the most efficient production capability when margins are squeezed.

What does all this mean for the managers in Gillette's razor-blade division? In 1980, Bic lost $6.3 million in the disposable razor business. In 1981, the loss was only $2.2 million. Significantly, in 1982, Bic, by this time an integrated marketer and producer in the US, reported a profit of $2.2 million in its US operations. We would suggest that the prudent strategy for the Gillette Company is not going to be built upon simple rates of return in its US razor and blade business, but, rather, in a competition that encompasses all of its product lines and all of its resources in all of its markets, particularly those where it meets Bic.

GLOBAL CORPORATIONS AND THE FUTURE DIRECTION OF INTERNATIONAL BUSINESS

In a powerful critique of the misapplication of the marketing concept in the international business arena, Levitt (1983) suggests that it is unwise to assume that customers are kings who *know* what they want. Levitt makes the point that there is often a substantial difference between what is wanted and what would be preferred were it available. The experience of global businesses has shown that in one product market after another, low prices will shift preference structures from customized, national products to internationally standardized products.

The companies which produce customized products in the international markets are essentially those that Hout, Porter, and Rudden (1982) call *multidomestic,* that is, multinational companies functioning through independent market-based profit centers, each of which enjoys considerable autonomy to customize the product to local preferences. These companies typically compete with other companies on a market-by-market basis. Their multidomestic nature often locks them into a high cost position, with low scale economies, making them vulnerable to the price competition of a global firm which serves the world as one market.

The *global* firm is typically centrally managed and pits its worldwide resources against its competitors wherever they may be. It exploits interdependencies, sourcing, trading, and subsidizing its parts so that the competitive position of the corporation as a whole is enhanced across the world. Such corporations tend to adopt competitive measures of performance for their subsidiaries as opposed to simple financial measures such as ROA or ROI.

Bic is, as we have shown, an evolving global corporation. Gillette appears to us to be closer in kind to the multidomestic corporation. This is understandable because, for years, American companies like Gillette have enjoyed one of the world's largest standardized markets—the US. Companies that have evolved in Europe and Japan have had to export to survive and have had to find new ways to compete. The choice they have made of necessity is a movement towards globalization.

A CONFLICT WITH TRADITION

If the world is moving toward globalization, Levitt's counsel against customizing products must be heeded. Levitt has said that the twin forces of technological change and globalization will permanently change the character of the international marketplace. Technology is changing the preference structure of markets worldwide. And, technologies that provide value, that is, higher quality products and services at lower prices, have always prevailed (Burns and Stalker, 1959; Schon, 1967; Cooper and Schendel, 1976). Globalization is changing the economic realities of world competition, because global companies are seizing the opportunities presented by technological change and increasingly offering standardized goods worldwide at low competitive prices to increasingly homogenized markets.

The tradition of international business, however, is one of congenial adaptation to local conditions, accepting vestigial national differences without question, to paraphrase Levitt. Levitt describes this adaptation process as a respectful but thoughtless accommodation to what are believed to be fixed local preferences. The problem is that respectful sensitivity to local preferences, customs, and mores has led many otherwise capable firms into high-cost, many-featured product lines across the world. Each domestic market is managed idiosyncratically and economies of scale are lost in the quest to customize products.

Dealing with these markets one by one has made international business expensive and administratively complex. Worse, as noted earlier, cultural responsiveness has not made the market positions of these firms stronger. In fact, it has left them vulnerable to the aggressive price competition of global corporations.

The point is not to advocate insensitivity to local preferences, but to promote an awareness of the real value of using all the corporation's resources to their full competitive capability. Levitt points out that global corporations accept and adjust to local differences only after efforts to circumvent and reshape them. Even then, the global corporation will persist in its efforts to standardize its production across markets. For example, although Caterpillar could not fully standardize its earth-moving equipment, the components of the equipment are standardized, giving Caterpillar both production and service economies and quality.

It is perplexing that although competitive strength has come from exploiting the national market within the United States, the traditional international business approach, particularly of the American international business community, has been characterized by respectful responsiveness. Few American firms produce and serve America's regional markets with differentiated products and services, yet outside America totally differentiated products are common.

The differences between life in Boston and New York and the complexities of doing business between the two cities, as real as they may have been in 1690, are of only moderate importance to business in the twentieth century. Technology has removed the relevant differences. In like manner, the complexities of doing business between Boston and Paris in the 1980s are disappearing. Ultimately, technology will reduce the complexity of all of today's international business.

Technological advances in communication and greater ease of transportation are accelerating the trend towards worldwide markets. People everywhere want what people everywhere else have, from Coca-Cola to Hondas. Levitt writes:

> People understandably treat (money) with respect. . . . If the price is low enough, they will take highly standardized world products, even if these aren't exactly what mother said was suitable, what immemorial custom decreed was right, or what market-research fabulists asserted was preferred. (1983, p. 96)

Price sensitivity is the economic foundation of the global corporation.

Today's high-technology products are the commodities of tomorrow. Corporations which control their costs on such products are in a much better position to become global competitors, recognized for giving their customers value. As the Bic example has shown, the incremental market volume that multinational distribution can provide the units of the global corporation can quickly shift their production to world-scale efficiency. This is what Bic did in France when it used its US subsidiary as a distribution channel in the hose, lighter, and razor businesses.

GUIDELINES FOR INTERNATIONAL COMPETITION

As we noted earlier, some factors cause concern for the managements of global enterprises. Because of their integration and market scope, managing global enterprises is complicated by the complexity of business definition and the difficulty of performance measurement. Managing the global business requires, as Hout, Porter, and Rudden (1982) agree, apparently unconventional administrative practices.

The global corporation will normally choose volume over precise market matches. Its efforts will go to standardizing a product line and developing a relative cost advantage over its competitors. This means that in some markets the global corporation will offer overdesigned and underpriced products—that is, it will provide some consumers or users with exceptional value.

The appropriate point at which to measure return is at the higher level of the global corporation, not the business level. On a country-by-country basis, management is likely to approve of projects with varying degrees of profitability and quite different short-run financial performance characteristics. In making its investment decisions, the global corporation will distinguish between local projects which develop its competitive strength and the global businesses themselves. While the short-run return on investment characteristics of a narrowly defined project within a particular market may even be negative for a time, their value to the corporation is in the contributions they make to the competitive strength of the worldwide business. Global corporations do not invest without the promise of an economic profit at the higher level, over time. Their single-product, single-market decisions, however, may have apparently negative ROI's.

The Bic Corporation's history illustrates this point. In 1974, the Bic Pen Corporation (USA) was asked by its parent to introduce pantyhose into the US market. At the time, many observers wondered whether pantyhose fit well with Bic's concept of its business. They assumed that Bic's objectives in the US would be to dominate the hosiery market as it had dominated the pen business. At the time, Bic's competition was formidable indeed. Burlington, Hanes, and Kayser Roth, the three largest US competitors in an overcapacitied industry were many times larger than the Bic Company. In fact, their collective advertising budgets approximated the Bic Pen Corporation's total assets.

However, the mission that Société Bic (now) appears to have asked Bic USA to carry out was not market domination, but, rather, to gain additional volume for an underutilized French plant that Bich had recently acquired. Because the US market is over five times as large as the French market, even a small percentage of the US market would contribute a large incremental volume to the French company, and, presumably, was seen as being easier to get than a substantially larger share in France. This incremental volume helped move Bic's DIM subsidiary into a stronger competitive position in Europe and then to profitability. It is a classic example of apparent irrationality within a narrowly defined market being an opportunity for considerable market leverage and profitability when viewed from a higher and indeed broader perspective.

As this example suggests, *the management of global enterprises views national markets as interdependent entities rather than as single discrete businesses*. Moreover, in the more developed multibusiness global corporations, even businesses are managed interdependently. As we have shown in our description of the competition between Bic and Gillette, the battle for the worldwide razor business extends into the pen and lighter businesses, too, not only because Bic and Gillette compete for positions in the same distribution channels but because the cash flow earned in one business can be used to compete more aggressively in another.

Because of its own potential to compete across business and national borders, *the global corporation must consider what is a proper competitive practice in the countries in which it operates*. For the US-based global corporation, this poses something of a dilemma, for although the US Justice Department has attempted to apply the antitrust laws internationally, sovereignty is real and across the world there are different views about appropriate employment practices, the merits of industry consolidation, and predatory pricing, for example. In many countries, governments play a more active and explicit role in corporate affairs than in the US, and so are more critical stakeholders.

Country by country, a US global company is likely to confront competitors which are owned or subsidized by national governments, a situation which plagues the US-based international airlines as well as the international telecommunication industry. In fact, in telecommunications across the world, quite subtle forms of vertical integration exist between private and semi-public suppliers and the utilities which operate national telephone services. R&D subsidies, strong national preferences for locally-made products, safety, and reliability requirements characterize both explicit and implicit national industry policies.

In locating its plants behind national boundaries, the global company will have to consciously assess its own needs for power in negotiations with foreign governments, whose industry policies may favor domestic corporations. This may mean the creation of rationalized international manufacturing systems where critical components have multiple sources. Thus, the problems in any one location will not affect the business as a whole, while, at the same time, the global corporations will have bargaining chips in its inevitable dealings with sovereign governments.

By fostering interdependencies across its subsidiaries, the global corporation can increase the probabilities that the national government's interest in employment and international earnings are co-aligned with its own interests in smooth operations. Essentially, a global corporation enhances its monopoly power by operating as a single seller of products produced at coordinated multiple locations. Ultimately, the global corporation will tend toward cellular operating structures where the success of the whole is not dependent on the continuity or longevity of a particular cell, but rather on the network of communications and exchanges that produce, assemble, and distribute its products.

Over time, the global corporation's markets and productive strengths develop, enhancing its least-cost, high-volume position and usually giving it a long-lasting competitive advantage. Thus, for the global competitor confronting domestic or even multidomestic competition, time is an ally. The more time the competition allows the global company before responding to its initiatives, the stronger the global competitor will become over time.

Few competitive advantages last forever. Yet a strategy which is robust because of its delivery capabilities, service levels, and cost advantage can earn customer loyalty over time and so becomes difficult to beat whether times are good or bad. Indeed, the good times allow the firm to accumulate a "war chest" of profits which it can use to defend itself from future competitors.

In the pen industry, it would have been dangerous for companies like Gillette to assume that Bic's 1982 losses in its US writing instrument business were associated with operating difficulties across the world. The Bic Company is contending with a series of product innovations as well as direct competition. The Rolling Writer, erasible pens, ceramic-tipped pens, thin-point porous and calligraphic instruments are all recent entrants to the low-priced pen market. Bic's US losses may be associated with problems or with heavy investments of "expensible" funds into business renewal.

For a global business, success requires a top management patient enough to wait for the opportunities it needs to develop its competitive strength. It takes time to renew a business and it takes time to build a business. It takes even more time to build a global business, and taking time requires patience. Bich once said, "We just try to stick close to reality, like a surfer to his board. We don't lean forward or backward too far or too fast. We ride the wave at the right moment."[1]

THE ESSENCE OF GLOBAL COMPETITION

Some think the essence of competition is to beat the competition. The real principle of competing successfully in business, however, is simultaneously to avoid competition and strengthen oneself. Business confrontations cost a great deal of money and management

[1]"Going Bananas Over Bic," *Time,* December 18, 1972, p. 93.

time. In business as in war, winning battles is not the same as winning the war. In business, a competitive war holds no victory unless the peace is won, too. In business, this usually means the biggest piece of the market, a particularly important consideration for high-volume global firms.

Henderson (1967) pointed out that in most countries, governments will tolerate neither collaboration among competitors nor wholesale competition resulting in the annihilation of a competitor and the reduction of competition. Competing successfully on a global basis demands balance between moving too fast and too slowly vis à vis the competition and the broader environment. We believe this balance can be found if management constantly keeps in mind the need to strengthen its own corporation—rather than the havoc it can wreck on others.

The real essence of competition is to use all of your resources to achieve your objectives as efficiently as possible. Competition between companies ultimately comes down to competition between concepts of what their business is. At the top, no one defines the industry or the business. Management has to do it itself. Different concepts ensure competition without confrontation.

Creating such concepts requires vision. Garnering the resources needed to implement the concept requires patience, self-discipline, and leadership. Indeed the purpose of all management is entrepreneurial, that is, to create value. Businesses must create value by creating customers and keeping them. This is best done by giving the customers value, so they have no reason to shift their business to others.

Market niches will always exist, even in the globalized setting of tomorrow's international business community. As they are discovered by other corporations seeking volume, however, these niches are likely to be limited in growth potential and increasingly at risk. For the value-creating managers of the future, profitability, growth, and risk management are the keys to prosperity. And we believe, like Baron Bich, that prosperity is easier to gain if you ride the waves of the times.

Riding the waves of the industrial environment and determining their significance means you can commit your resources confidently to (your) future. Levitt (1983) wrote, "Data do not yield information except with the intervention of the mind. Information does not yield meaning except with the intervention of imagination" (p. 99). Change is unlikely to be well directed without considerable thought, imagination, and effort. However, for those who make the effort, the reward is the opportunity to lead their organizations into the future. We discuss leadership in Chapter 21.

chapter 21

Leadership, Values, and Objectives

INTRODUCTION: WHAT IS LEADERSHIP?

Is leadership a superior or mystical quality beyond the reach of ordinary men and women? "Leadership is the force that selects your dreams and sets your goals. It is the force that propels your endeavors to success." So wrote Robert Schuller, a Reformed Church minister, in his 1983 book, *Tough Times Never Last, But Tough People Do!* He was writing not for managers but for people everywhere. There is leadership potential in us all.

Schuller's buoyant definition and his implicit assumption that we all have some potential for being leaders are inspiring. And, it is inspired self-leadership that is needed in organizations confronting change.

Yet, at times, our potential for self-leadership is unrealized. We need a leader to set the direction, motivate us and mediate for us in the world or in the environment in which we work. Perversely, people often take leadership for granted while they enjoy its benefits. Nevertheless, they eventually become acutely aware of the absence or failure of leadership. Selznick explains:

> When institutional leadership fails, it is perhaps more often by default than by positive error or sin. Leadership is lacking when it is needed; and the institution drifts, exposed to vagrant pressures, readily influenced by short-run opportunistic trends. This default is partly a failure of nerve, partly a failure of understanding. It takes nerve to hold a course; it takes understanding to recognize and deal with the sources of institutional vulnerability. (1957, p. 25)

Leadership, in fact, like strategy, may be more noticeable when it is absent than when it is present. The drift and wandering to which Selznick refers will be revealed by a failure to maintain vital objectives, by poor results and a waning reputation, by failures to foresee impending crises, by capricious and inconsistent actions which waste resources which might otherwise be the basis for future prosperity, and by missed and wasted opportunities. In leaderless organizations, other symptoms often observed include an isolated top management, a second-tier management characterized by internecine conflict and high turnover, privileged cadres of low performers, devitalized junior positions, and a failure to plan for succession in the ongoing business.

Barnard wrote:

> Among those who cooperate the things that are seen are moved by things unseen. Out of the void comes the spirit that shapes the ends of men. (1966, p. 284)

This spirit, we say, is the spirit of leadership. It is this spirit that must be sparked. Barnard uses the word ''fulminator'' to describe the leader's role.

A ''fulminator'' provides the fire or lightning that sets things moving, that sparks creative, focused cooperation throughout the organization and infuses countless decisions with consistency even as the environment changes. Discussing this ''necessary'' leadership role, Barnard says that,

> Reflecting attitudes, ideals, hopes, derived largely from without themselves, [leaders] are compelled to bind the wills of men to the accomplishment of purpose beyond their immediate ends, beyond their times. (p. 283)

Leaders, indeed, change their times.

Leaders give organizations direction and drive; they represent the purpose of the organization inside and outside its boundaries. Direction comes from objectives which articulate what can be and make the leader's vision of the future tangible and realizable. Direction reduces uncertainty about what should be done and so promotes coordination and focus. Drive describes an organization where people want to achieve their objectives. Leaders promote drive with their vision of the future and by example.

Leaders motivate their followers by driving themselves to do more and by rewarding results, thereby reinforcing purposeful action. They symbolically represent the organization inside and outside by carefully and artfully explaining its mission, its purpose, its objectives and strategies, and by educating the organization so that its members can appreciate the significance of environmental change (Smith, 1975). After many years, their presence alone may contribute substantially to the organization's ability to stay the course.

The environment flows and change occurs; the trick for the leader is to move with the flow to accomplish purpose. To cite Sun Tzu: ''A skilled commander seeks victory from the situation and does not demand it of his subordinates'' (1963, p. 93). Chang Yu, a commentator, explained: ''One must take advantage of the situation exactly as if he were setting a ball in motion on a steep slope. The force applied is minute but the results are enormous.'' Leaders are a minute part of organizations, but they fulminate enormous releases of focused human energy so that their followers get results.

Successful leaders take such great advantage of the flow of events that often they themselves are considered lucky rather than smart; leadership may often be unrecognized. Sun Tzu writes, ''And therefore the victories won by a master of war gain him neither reputation for wisdom nor merit for valor'' (p. 87). And a commentator echoes, ''When you subdue your enemy without fighting who will pronounce you valorous?'' Indeed, both leadership and strategies are often best noticed by the chaos apparent when they are absent. They are generally identifiable backwards, through time, except by those few who can move men and women to the accomplishment of purpose and indeed strategize and lead.

Leaders inspire people to lead themselves, by articulating their personal vision of a better future and by changing the way people think about ideal performance (Zaleznick, 1977; Henderson, 1979). In the language of the strategist, leaders set new objectives and make new strategies realizable. They use objectives and strategies to give dreams substance.

THE LEADER OF THE ORGANIZATION

It is important to remember that in choosing objectives, leaders are not unfettered. Earlier, we cited Barnard: the leader is "compelled" and reflects "ideals, hopes, derived largely from without." Yet leaders must be of the organization.

"Of the organization" deserves emphasis because it encompasses one of the great contradictions of leadership: The leader leads the organization, yet is compelled by its members' desires and ideals and hopes to action.

How can this be? The answer is that leaders need followers as badly as followers need leaders; one without the other is only a potential source of energy. Something has to be done to get the two together. Followers are the resource that is critical to leadership.

Leadership can exist only in a social context and only if the leader has support. Such support will be forthcoming only if the leader is *of* the organization, not simply its highest ranking member, but its first follower. Without depreciating the importance of a "concept of the organization," the limiting factor in organizational life and in the management of change is cooperation. And, as Barnard tells us, the limiting factor in cooperation is leadership.

The leader must be of the organization and hold its values with conviction. Although he or she can order action, the leader is not independent and may in fact be impelled to certain actions by the values he and the organization share. At once, the leader is constrained by the organization and able to unleash its resources (Salanacik et al., 1975; Lieberson and O'Conner, 1972).

How does the leader come to share the followers' values? Hegel writes:

> Leadership is possible not only on the condition that fellowship has been learned, but on the more radical condition that the leader has known subjection and thralldom. The mature leader not only must have known the travail of the follower; he must here and now incorporate within himself all that the follower is. (Litzinger and Schaefer, 1982)

The paradox is that the leader must be more follower than the followers, while acknowledging that there is leadership in the followers, too. "People," folklore says, "get the leaders they deserve." Leaders promote leadership so that an organization with a leader is an organization with many leaders. Barnard writes:

> Purposeful cooperation is possible only within certain limits of a structural character, and it arises from forces derived from *all* who contributed to it. The work of cooperation is not a work of leadership, but of organization as a whole. (p. 259)

Leadership is a complex endeavor. Nerve and understanding are needed in those who would take charge of an organization, control it and change it. It takes nerve to take charge and hold the course; it takes nerve and understanding to redefine the mission and set a new course.

But these alone are insufficient to the task: organizations only exist through cooperation—that is, when others pursue the objectives set. A leader with no followers is no leader at all. And, one test of mettle as a leader is whether followers can move from the present to the future in a timely way and at a rate acceptable inside the organization and adequate without. This means managing the tension between the need for continuity and the need for change, viewing resistance as a signal that something needs investigation (Lawrence, 1969), rather than as a phenomenon to be overcome. The Zen saying, "You can only dam a river if you allow it to flow" (Pascale, 1978), applies to the management of resistance. A leader must have not only highly-tuned abilities for analysis and synthesis to allow him or her to appreciate the total situation, but highly developed human skills to manage the rate of change productively (Katz, 1955).

THE CONTRADICTIONS OF LEADERSHIP

As we have suggested, leadership is an elusive quality. It is characterized, like life, by contradiction. Already we have mentioned that:

- it is easier to recognize the absence of leadership than its presence;
- organizations need leadership to define a vision in realizable terms, yet that personal vision must reflect the organization's ideals, hopes, and values;
- leaders lead, although they may be compelled to do so;
- leaders can only exist in a social context of followership.

From the social scientist's point of view, leadership is more easily understood looking backwards, although the important aspect of leadership is its forward-thrusting vision. The Danish philosopher Kierkegaard once wrote: "Life can only be understood backwards but must be lived forward." Research looks back to project forwards, but the very intangibility of leadership frustrates the researchers' methods.

The leader is at once directing and supporting the organization. People in the organization look to the leader for direction. Usually this is described as looking to the top, and so we have the image of the powerful leader issuing directives. Yet we are all aware of the burden of leadership. Looking up, the leader sees the organization needing support, and often the burden is great. The leader is at once on the top of and supporting the organization.

While the leader is on top, contrariwise the leader is also at the bottom and the helper of all. The Catholic Church uses the title, "The Servant of the Servants of God" for the Pope. Litzinger and Schaefer write,

> Where leader and follower alike are held in obedience to defined doctrine, neither may act on his own autonomous will alone. Leadership endures so long as it assumes a posture of humility, a spirit of followership. (1982, p. 79)

Moreover, just as leadership and followership fuse to create a leading organization, objectives and strategies fuse to create purposeful action. In what seems like another contradiction, however, just as it makes little difference whether we talk of a hierarchy of leaders or a hierarchy of followers, it makes little difference whether we talk about a hierarchy of objectives or a hierarchy of strategies. The statements that strategies are objectives and leaders are followers are both true because they model reality from different viewpoints or perspectives.

The leader must be a representative of the organization's members and indeed a member, too. Yet Zaleznick (1977) focuses on another contradiction of leadership by suggesting that the leader must be apart as well:

> Leaders tend to be twice born personalities, people who feel separate from their environment, including other people. They may work in organizations but never belong to them. Their sense of who they are does not depend upon membership, work roles, or other indicators of identity. (p. 74)

Zaleznick notes that managers, by comparison, are once born and their sense of self stems from harmony with the environment. Leaders, the twice born, have had less straightforward and peaceful lives, marked by a continual struggle to attain order. Zaleznick added that

> . . . for such people, self-esteem no longer depends solely upon positive attachment and real rewards. A form of self-reliance takes hold along with expectations of performance and achievement, and perhaps even the desire to do great works. (p. 75)

THE VALUES OF A LEADER

Values set leaders apart from other people, yet make them one with others. Values are the common bond with followers. The leader represents and is a custodian of the ideals and values of the organization. To the extent he or she can, the leader must live those values and not falter. This willingness to serve the values, even at a personal cost, promotes those values, distinguishes leader and follower, and concurrently unifies leader and follower through those shared values.

What leaders do that others cannot is to synthesize the old and new. They forge new values which encompass the old out of the organization's successes and failures. This ability allows leaders to choose a path while less able people have to wait until they can proceed (tentatively) or decide with confidence because they have information to be right. Hirschman's "Hiding Hand" (1967) should alert us to the fallacy of the words "right decision" in any really important matter, since the hiding hand implies that solutions beget problems and those problems new solutions.

In being apart and one with others simultaneously, the leader must reconcile belonging on one hand and separateness on the other. First, the leaders fit with the new orthodoxy rather than the old. Second, they fit the context, internal and external, and personally fulminate change by mentoring others, insisting on performance and demonstrating their personal integrity. Third, by controlling the rate of change so that time's passage allows experience to accumulate to satisfy their followers' needs for security, they give those people the opportunity to follow. Fourth, they maintain their separateness because for them reward, status, money, and even power are not personally valued per se but recognized as tools to help them implement their strategies and achieve their objectives.

The sage comment that a leader's self-esteem no longer depends on positive attachments and real rewards (Zaleznick, 1977), explains how leaders keep themselves free from the trapping of office that are characteristics of dysfunctional bureaucracies. This freedom allows a leader to use his or her person as a resource and to use rewards as tools to accomplish purpose.

THE MAKING OF A LEADER

Where do leaders come from? Vince Lombardi, at the time the head coach of the Green Bay Packers football team, explained it in a speech on leadership before the American Management Association. He believed leadership has a personal price that each of us has to determine for ourselves:

> No one person has all the qualities that grow up to make a leader. We've more or less developed a blend of them. No one has every particular quality. You develop your own blend . . . they are not born. They are made . . . only through one way . . . through work. That's the price we all pay. . . .
>
> If we would create something, we must be something. You can't dream yourself into character. You must hammer one out for yourself. You must forge one out for yourself. . . . The difference between a group and a leader is not so much in lack of strength, not so much in lack of knowledge, but rather in lack of will. (c. 1965)

It seems that the forge that makes leaders is nothing less than life's experiences of success and failure. Zaleznick's "born" and Lombardi's "made" are words used in a kindred spirit and are consistent with Hegel's view that the leader must have known the travail of the follower, both success and failure.

People who are sheltered from life's vicissitudes cannot lead. People who have never known failure cannot appreciate success. Only those who have known success and have experienced failure—and who have mastered themselves in both conditions, forging a set of values for themselves—have confidence founded in self-trust that is the ultimate source of cooperation. People who do not trust themselves cannot trust others or earn their trust. Without trust, cooperation is impossible and without cooperation, leadership and followship alike cannot develop.

The evidence is that each of us has to train ourselves for leadership. If you want to lead or share in the leadership of business corporations and other organizations, you have to develop a "will to lead," and prepare yourself by learning who you are and what you stand for.

RULES FOR PRESERVING LEADERSHIP*

Self-knowledge is important to a leader. So is the knowledge of how to preserve leadership. However, knowledge alone is insufficient. Discipline is necessary, too. A leader must follow certain rules.

The importance of the leader's relationship with the organization is stressed by the sociologist George C. Homans in *The Human Group* (1950), where he identifies eleven rules of leadership. First, he says, *the leader will maintain his position,* establish and maintain his rank and even delay any effort for change until his position is established.

Second, *the leader will live up to the norms of the group,* because any failure to do so undermines his rank and the presumption that his orders are to be obeyed. Homans makes the point that the relevant norms are the group's, not those the leader thinks ought to be. The leader, he warns, should look after his people in the matters they think are important.

The third rule is *the leader will lead.* If the decision is his, he must decide. Fourth, *the leader will not give orders that will not be obeyed.* Such orders would confuse his followers and raise questions about his competence.

Fifth, *the leader will use established channels in giving orders,* since in maintaining his subordinates' position he maintains his own. Sixth, *he will not thrust himself upon his followers on social occasions,* also to preserve the structure that supports him and facilitates action.

Seventh, *the leader will neither blame, nor in general, praise a member of his group before members.* Again, Homans explains, this is to preserve the rank of the followers on one hand and, on the other, to allow the organization to accept change in its own time.

Eighth, *the leader will take into consideration the whole situation.* Homans points out that "nothing succeeds like success." The leader has to foresee the consequences of social action and understand how interrelationships of technology and the internal and external social system will be affected. Homans made an impassioned plea that is as valid today as it was in 1950:

> Americans are taught adequate ways of thinking about technology and organization; they are not taught adequate ways of thinking about social systems. A leader cannot examine the whole situation inside and outside his group unless he has a method for taking up each element of the situation in order and in its relations to the other elements. It is not enough to have a mystic sense of the whole; nor is it enough to have intuitive "social skills" that, all too easily, lead up a dead-end street to the "big-time operator." What is needed is explicit, conscious, intellectual understanding. Even this is not enough, but, by all that is holy in the human spirit, without this the rest is dust and ashes. (p. 435)

Ninth, *in maintaining discipline, the leader will be less concerned with inflicting punishment than with creating the conditions in which the group will discipline itself.*

*George C. Homans, abridged excerpts from "The Behavior of the Leader," *The Human Group*, copyright 1950 by Harcourt Brace Jovanovich; renewed 1978 by George C. Homans. Reprinted by permission.

Essentially, unless we understand the reasons people disobey orders and resist change, the resistance is likely to persist and our haphazard efforts to overcome it could lead to resentment (Lawrence, 1969). The leader's job is to ensure that the mistake does not happen again and to encourage self-correction. Punishment may be necessary, but only if it serves the group (which includes preserving its leadership structure).

In the tenth rule, Homans advises that *the leader will listen,* adding that he or she must be informed about the whole situation inside and outside the group (and for us, the organization). Since authority and rank cut down interaction and break down free communications, the leader must show by action that he or she is friendly and interested and encourages interaction.

Homans also warns leaders to take no moral stand ''while listening to someone else trying to say what is on his mind.'' Accept it and show you want to hear everything; any statement by the leader is carried with the weight of authority and may constrain further communication. He must ''keep his mouth shut and listen.''

Know yourself is Homans's eleventh and final rule. He writes:

> How often has the leader acted and later wished fervently he had not! He must be under great self-control in a situation where control is difficult. If, therefore, he must know his men well, he must know himself still better. He must know the passions in him that, unchecked, will destroy him as a leader, and he must know their sources in his personality. For how can we control a force, the source of whose energy we do not know? Self-knowledge is the first step in self-control. (p. 440)

Homans emphasizes the maintenance of the social order as critical in sustaining leadership, the importance of self-knowledge, and the leader's knowing and understanding organizational norms and the values underlying them. Especially when values are in conflict, the organization must come first.

VALUES AND THE PRESERVATION OF LEADERSHIP

We have put great stress on values, self-knowledge and self-control. Why? It is because the leader is, paradoxically, the greatest threat to the organization because he or she, more than any other, can put it into jeopardy.

Edward Boland Smith (1975) explained the pressure that hits the leader because of his role: ''. . . a leadership role . . . complicates and intensifies his moral position. Additional moral codes [that is, sets of values besides his personal values] must now be answered to. Conflicts of codes now arise.'' Smith, drawing heavily on Barnard, notes that executives must not only be responsible but be capable of enduring complex moral conditions:

> Otherwise he will be "overloaded," and either ability, responsibility, or morality, or all three, will be destroyed . . . (with) fatal indecision or emotional and impulsive action with personal breakdown. . . . Leadership requires not only a sense of responsibility, but a high degree of morality and the ability to cope with the conflicting demands of those moralities (or values). (1975, p. 42)

The successful executive or leader must be able to resolve value conflict while personally supporting a highly sophisticated pattern of values and to act so that none are violated. Violations would undermine his or her leadership.

Barnard (1966) and Vickers (1965) tell us how successful leaders resolve value conflict. Barnard calls it the process of "determination." The first method is to analyze the environment to accurately determine the strategic or limiting factor, an analysis which may lead to the discovery of that "correct" action which violates no codes; examples of this include contractual, personal and organizational changes. The second is "to adopt a new detailed purpose consistent with general objectives," that is, to change the objective or strategy of the organizations or both. The third and most challenging approach is by changing culture, that is, the mutual expectations and self-expectations of (the organization's) members.

Smith explores what Barnard called the "distinguishing mark" of executive responsibility, the creating of (new) culture and values for others. Culture is established in two ways:

> The first constitutes the process of inculcating points of view, fundamental attitudes and loyalties to the organization; the second is a judicial function which implies the substitution of a new action to avoid conflict or providing a moral justification for exception or compromise (the exceptional case). (1975, p. 44)

Essentially, the leader facilitates change not so much by solving problems as by exploiting problems, especially those that are exceptions, and occasionally by creating turbulence. Indeed, exceptions are most important because they mark *the way things will be done* and signal the passing of the old ways, the old culture and old values. Exceptions are the opportunities for change and creativity and, as Barnard puts it, "leadership is the indispensible fulminator of its forces."

Smith extols the importance of this leadership function:

> Creating values becomes then "the highest exemplification of responsibility" for the executive. It demands conviction on the part of the leaders—"conviction that what they do for the good of organization they *personally* believe to be right." This creative function, according to Barnard, "is the essence of leadership." It is in fact "the highest test of executive responsibility, because it requires for successful accomplishment that element of 'conviction' that means identification of personal codes (values) and organization codes (values) in the view of the leader." (1975, p. 44)

Ultimately, these new values will be reflected in the organization's sense of an ideal state (of relating with its environment) and in new ideal standards of performance (Zaleznick, 1977; Henderson, 1979).

LEADERSHIP AND IDEALS

Indeed, ideals and leadership go hand in hand: The critical skill in maintaining a creative tension between continuity and change is social, and the ideal facilitates communication and is motivating.

Ideals are objectives set high. Leaders, to cite Machiavelli's *The Prince* (circa 1514),

> . . . behave like those archers who, if they are skillful, when the target seems too distant, know the capabilities of their bow and aim a good deal higher than their objective, not in order to shoot so high but so that by aiming high they can reach the target. (1961, p. 49)

Exceptions provide the opportunity to promote new ideals. There are objectives which we must reach quickly to survive and those we can defer. What is important and what is not is unclear to most people until a choice is needed and made. Thus, management by example is an important component of leadership, and exceptions focus the organization's attention on its new objectives.

Values are usually transmitted by leadership action, by example, by letting people see "this is the way we do it." By revising the ideals and exploiting exceptions, leaders use success to motivate the organization, examples to point the way, and failures as learning experience for all. The leader has to maintain a productive relationship with the organization, not overcoming resistance so much as using it to help him or her gauge the rate at which the organization's members can change their concept of the organization and performance.

LEADERSHIP AND RESISTANCE

Leaders develop an appreciation of these factors, especially resistance, because they have used their own lives as instruments of learning. They move with the times and their followers, the existing organization, adapting now for the future, preserving and creating what is needed for survival and success (Selznick, 1957). It is not an easy task and never has been. Machiavelli wrote,

> It should be borne in mind that there is nothing more difficult to arrange, more doubtful of success, and more dangerous to carry through than initiating changes in a state's constitution. The innovator makes enemies of all those who prospered under the old order, and only lukewarm support is forthcoming from those who would prosper under the new. Their support is lukewarm partly from fear of their adversaries, who have the existing laws on their side, and partly because men are generally incredulous never really trusting new things unless they have tested them by experience. (1961, p. 51)

This passage is a warning to any potential leader of powerful social forces against change. Resistance is natural, only overcome by the leader's ability to maintain and expand the base of organizational support for his or her program of change. Moreover, Machiavelli suggests one of the key differences between leaders and managers: leaders act on a vision of the future, managers on results or experience. Only in exceptional circumstances, when an organization is in crisis or its leader is very secure, or both, is rapid change possible.

LEADER AND MANAGERS

Giving us some additional insight into the leadership process, Zaleznick (1977) says leaders use themselves as instruments of learning, shaping ideas to influence the way people think about what is possible, desirable, and necessary. Exceptions provide one set of opportunities for shaping ideas. By using ideas and projecting those ideas into images that excite people, and by then developing choices, tangible objectives and strategies that give the projected images substance, the leader changes the focus of the organization and its sense of performance.

Managers, Zaleznick says, rely on trial and error and logical techniques and on constant analysis to accumulate experience and results which point the way to the future. They frame objectives passively and impersonally and focus on necessities rather than desires. Managers try to balance interests, judiciously eliminating choices as they go to maintain cooperative effort. Leaders synthesize the future from skeletal data and choose a way. Managers wait until they have enough information to decide, or at least to decide to proceed (Pascale, 1978).

A manager is a steward who conserves value and keeps things running. A leader, in contrast, is entrepreneurial and concerned with value creation and the future integrity and well-being of the organization.

CHANGE AND CONTINUITY

The critical role of leadership is to direct change. Leaders have to adapt their organizations to changing environments in a timely manner while maintaining the dynamic stability of their operating systems. This is nothing less than using the resources accumulated to create more value. Note, most unique integrated and synergistic strategies are "associated with single powerful leaders" (Mintzberg, 1978). Mintzberg explains,

> Perhaps the sophisticated integration called for in gestalt strategy requires innovative thinking rooted in synthesis rather than analysis, based on the "intuitive" or inexplicit processes that have been associated with the brain's right hemisphere. (p. 944)

Let us emphasize change and continuity and the mediating role of the leader. Failure can occur if the balance between inside and out is not developed and held in a productive and dynamic state of equilibrium. Mintzberg warns:

> A strategy is not a fixed plan, nor does it change systematically at prearranged times solely at the will of management. The dichotomy between strategy formulation and strategy implementation is a false one under certain common conditions, because it ignores the learning that must often follow the conception of an intended strategy. (p. 947)

Note, too, that Mintzberg said a strategy is not a fixed plan nor is will sufficient to affect change. Finally, note his warning that organizations have to learn and, remember, organizational learning consumes time.

Time is needed because for most people success depends upon the ability to operate productively in the context of an ongoing organization. Cataclysmic change occurs infrequently, and the need for major strategic change arises irregularly. Hence, to survive and prosper in the organization, people need first to understand the strategy and objectives of their organization at their own and other levels of responsibility; to interpret orders, directives, and requests; and to implement them successfully.

Yet, when continuity and incremental change are not enough to ensure the survival of the organization and leadership is needed, it is the managers on the spot who must share in that leadership as leading followers. Henry Mintzberg (1975) may have summed up managerial work when he wrote:

> The executives I was observing—all very competent by any standard—are fundamentally indistinguishable from their counterparts of a hundred years ago (or a thousand years ago, for that matter). (p. 54)

We agree wholeheartedly and have tried to support this point with quotations from the Bible, Sun Tzu, and classic as well as contemporary writers on management issues.

Strategic change demands leadership. And leadership demands informed understanding of the organization and its environment. Only if these are present can the conflicting demands of continuity and change be synthesized so that the organization is served and its members given an opportunity to prosper.

chapter 22

Epilogue

Herbert Simon (1964) emphasized the dual nature of objectives, noting that they can be used in two ways: as targets that we work from to develop strategies, or as bench marks or constraints against which we measure the potential or actual performance of a prospective strategy. Objectives can help us generate alternatives or test them. Simon warned that the strategies ultimately selected would likely depend on which objectives were used as constraints and which as targets, pointing out that the choice is inevitably personal and so a source of differences between the strategies of organizations with different management groups.

Although we, too, subscribe to the idea that there may not be only a single path for a corporation, we believe the choice is not unlimited. There is a feasible zone and several likely paths within it. Analysis helps us define the feasible zone. Personal experience and values influence us toward specific choices within that feasible zone.

Nevertheless, although there may be no one way to achieve many strategic and administrative objectives, and although a number of strategies may lead to satisfactory results, strategists have to choose. Once committed to their choice, strategists face a situation where no guarantees exist. Managers cannot guarantee a specific result. At best, they can underwrite specific performance with their jobs, act in the light of results, and change their subsequent actions to achieve their objectives.

In the context of a world where results count, what is the role of strategic analysis and planning? One executive responded this way: The basic issue of strategy is to get consistent, comprehensive, and longer-term thinking into current decision making. Strategy enables a manager to test results against plan and ask, "why?"

This book presents many different approaches to strategic analysis. Each one is a lens through which you can view an organization and its actions. Sometimes one lens will suffice. On other occasions, two or even more may be necessary before you see the path to the future to which you are prepared to commit.

In an optometrist's chair, the patient is asked to view the wall chart through a series of lenses. One is rarely enough. Some blur the chart, others clear it. The optometrist, however, uses the lenses and results in sequence to analyze the patient's vision problem. The analysis complete, an appropriate lens can be synthesized from all the lenses on the basis of the results achieved.

Analysis is followed by synthesis and then prescription. So, too, strategic analysis is a first step to strategy formulation and action. As your experience builds, you can choose the approach more skillfully and increase your efficiency by omitting some of the steps. Sometimes, however, you'll need to work slowly through the fundamentals, one by one.

Each method presented here relies on a model of purposeful action, but emphasizes different parts of the strategic problem. Simon pointed out that whether we use goal or constraint, we are taking different views of the same world. Similarly, ''strategy,'' ''operations,'' ''resource,'' ''structure,'' ''industry,'' and ''stakeholder'' are all words which help us analyze and communicate ideas. They are themselves nothing more or less than convenient linguistic models of a reality.

Strategists need many models in their armory. Use those you find helpful. Try to develop your own ways to address the problems you'll confront en route to the future.

The essence of strategic management is analysis followed by action, and action by analysis of the results earned. Managers add value in many ways, but one of the most powerful is to conceive a vision of a better future, a concept of what can be and how it can be achieved, and to use it to focus and coordinate action. Experience and framework are combined to find the way to a prosperous future.

Action requires continuity, and the future often requires change. Balancing the two and monitoring the rate of change so that there is a controlled and dynamic equilibrium is the way most organizations move through the present to their future. Continuity is resource management; change is, too. Strategies are needed to exploit the environment, use and husband the corporation's resources, satisfy its stakeholders and so serve the best interests of all.

References

Chapter 1

ABELL, DEREK, F., "Strategic Windows," *Journal of Marketing,* 42, no. 3 (July 1978), 21–26.

ANDREWS, KENNETH R., *The Concept of Corporate Strategy,* revised edition. Homewood, IL: Richard D. Irwin, 1980. First published, 1971.

ARGYRIS, CHRIS, "Double Loop Learning in Organizations," *Harvard Business Review,* 55, no. 5 (September–October 1977), 115–125.

BARNARD, CHESTER L., *The Functions of the Executive.* Cambridge, MA: Harvard University Press, 1966. First printed, 1938.

DRUCKER, PETER F., *Management.* New York: Harper and Row, 1973.

FAYOL, HENRI, *General and Industrial Management,* trans. Constance Storrs. New York: Pitman Publishing 1972. First French edition, 1916.

OHMAE, KENICHI, *The Mind of the Strategist: The Art of Japanese Business.* New York: McGraw-Hill, 1982.

QUINN, JAMES BRIAN, *Strategies for Change, Logical Incrementalism.* Homewood, IL: Richard D. Irwin, 1980.

SALANCIK, GERALD R., and JEFFREY PFEFFER, "Who Gets Power—And How They Hold on to It: A Strategic Contingency Model of Power," *Organizational Dynamics,* Winter 1977, 3–21.

SELZNICK, PHILIP, *Leadership in Administration,* New York: Harper & Row, 1957.

SUN TZU, *The Art of War,* trans. Samuel B. Griffith. New York: Oxford University Press, 1963.

Chapter 2

ANSOFF, H. I., *Corporate Strategy.* New York: McGraw-Hill, 1965.

ARGYRIS, CHRIS, "Double Loop Learning in Organizations," *Harvard Business Review,* 55, no. 5 (September–October 1977), 115–125.

BRAYBROOKE, DAVID, and CHARLES E. LINDBLOOM, *A Strategy of Decision: Policy Evaluation as a Social Process.* New York: The Free Press, 1970.

BOURGEOIS, L. J. III, "Performance and Consensus," *Strategic Management Journal,* 1 (1980), 227–248.

CYERT, R., and J. MARCH, *A Behavioral Theory of the Firm.* Englewood Cliffs, NJ: Prentice Hall, 1963.

EMSHOFF, JAMES R., IAN L. MITROFF, and RALPH H. KILMAN, "The Role of Idealization in Long Range Planning: An Essay on the Logical and Socio Emotional Aspects of Planning," *Technological Forecasting and Social Change,* 11 (1978), 335–348.

FAYOL, HENRI, *General and Industrial Management,* trans. Constance Storrs. New York: Pitman Publishing, 1972. First French edition, 1916.

GILMORE, FRANK F., *Formulation & Advocacy of Business Policy,* revised edition. Ithaca, NY: Cornell University Press, 1970.

GILMORE, FRANK F., "Formulating a Strategy in Small Companies," *Harvard Business Review,* May–June 1971, 71–81.

HENDERSON, BRUCE D., *Henderson on Corporate Strategy.* Cambridge, MA: Abt Books, 1979.

LEVITT, T., "Marketing Myopia," *Harvard Business Review,* 53, no. 5 (September–October 1960), 26.

OHMAE, KENICHI, *The Mind of the Strategist: The Japanese Business.* New York: McGraw-Hill Book Company, 1982.

QUINN, JAMES BRIAN, *Strategies for Change: Logical Incrementalism,* Homewood, IL: Richard D. Irwin, 1980.

SCHOEN, DONALD R., "Managing Technological Innovation," *Harvard Business Review,* 47, no. 3 (May–June 1969), 156–165.

STEVENSON, HOWARD H., "Defining Corporate Strengths and Weaknesses," *Sloan Management Review,* Spring 1976, 51–68.

WOLF, WILLIAM B., *Management and Consulting, An Introduction to James O. McKinsey.* Ithaca, NY: Cornell University Press, 1978.

Chapter 3

ANDREWS, KENNETH R., *The Concept of Corporate Strategy,* revised edition. Homewood, IL: Richard D. Irwin, 1980. First published in 1971.

LEVITT, T., "Marketing Myopia," *Harvard Business Review,* 53, no. 5 (September–October 1975), 26.

MCCARTHY, E. JEROME, *Basic Marketing: A Managerial Approach.* Homewood, IL: Richard D. Irwin, 1960.

MINTZBERG, HENRY, "Patterns in Strategy Formulation," *Management Science,* 24, no. 9 (May 1978), 934–948.

RUMELT, R. P., *Strategy, Structure, and Economic Performance.* Boston, MA: Division of Research, Harvard Business School, 1974.

RUMELT, R. P., "Diversification Strategy and Profitability," *Strategic Management Journal,* 3, no. 4 (October–December 1982), 359–370.

SALTER, MALCOM S., *Diversification Through Acquisition: Strategies for Creating Economic Value.* New York: The Free Press, 1979.

SALTER, MALCOM S., and WOLF A. WEINHOLD, "Diversification via Acquisition: Creating Value," *Harvard Business Review,* 56, no. 4 (July–August 1978), 166–176.

Chapter 4

BARNARD, CHESTER L., *The Functions of the Executive.* Cambridge, MA: Harvard University Press, 1966. First printed in 1938.

VICKERS, SIR GEOFFREY, *The Art of Judgment, A Study of Policy Making.* New York: Basic Books, 1965.

Chapter 5

ACKOFF, RUSSELL L., and JAMES R. EMSHOFF, "Advertising Research at Anheuser-Busch, Inc. (1963–68)," *Sloan Management Review,* Winter 1975, 1–15.

ACKOFF, RUSSELL L., and JAMES R. EMSHOFF, "Advertising Research at Anheuser-Busch, Inc. (1968–74)," *Sloan Management Review,* Spring 1975, 1–15.

BARNARD, CHESTER L., *The Functions of the Executive*. Cambridge: Harvard University Press, 1966. First printed 1938.

CLEMENTS, W. W., quoted by Richard B. Schmitt, "Dr Pepper Co. Prods Peppers to Drink More," *Wall Street Journal,* Thursday, January 13, 1983.

HAYES, R. H., and S. C. WHEELWRIGHT, "Dynamics of Process-Product Life-Cycles," *Harvard Business Review,* 57, no. 2 (March–April 1979), 127–136.

HUSSEY, DAVID E., "The Corporate Appraisal, Assessing Company Strengths and Weaknesses," *Long Range Planning,* 1 (December 1968), 19–25.

JENNINGS, EUGENE E., "Managing Excellence, The Maze Bright Manager: Skills of Exceptional Executives." Presented at a *Business Week* Strategic Planning Conference on Business Unit Planning, New Orleans, LA, May 1–2, 1980.

MAJARO, SIMON, "Market Share: Deception or Diagnosis," *Marketing,* March 1977, 44–47.

OHMAE, KENICHI, *The Mind of the Strategist: The Art of Japanese Business*. New York: McGraw-Hill, 1982.

SKINNER, WICKHAM, "The Focused Factory," *Harvard Business Review,* 52, no. 3 (May–June 1974), 113.

STEVENSON, HOWARD H., "Defining Corporate Strengths and Weaknesses," *Sloan Management Review,* Spring 1976, 51–68.

SUN TZU, *The Art of War,* trans. Samuel B. Griffith. New York: Oxford University Press, 1963.

UTTERBACK, JAMES M., and WILLIAM J. ABERNATHY, "A Dynamic Model of Process and Product Innovation," *OMEGA, The International Journal of Management Science,* 3, no. 6 (1975), 639–656.

WEBSTER, FREDERICK E. JR., *Industrial Marketing Strategy*. New York: John Wiley & Sons, 1979.

Chapter 6

ABELL, DEREK F. and JOHN S. HAMMOND, *Strategic Market Planning: Problems and Analytical Approaches*. Englewood Cliffs, NJ: Prentice-Hall, 1979.

ABERNATHY, WILLIAM J., and KENNETH WAYNE, "Limits of the Learning Curve," *Harvard Business Review,* 52, no. 5 (September–October 1974), 109.

ALCHIAN, ARMEN, "Costs and Outputs," in M. Abramowitz, ed., *The Allocation of Economic Resources: Essays in Honor of B. F. Haley*. Stanford, CA: Stanford University Press, 1959.

ANDRESS, FRANK J., "The Learning Curve as a Production Tool," *Harvard Business Review,* 32, no. 1 (January–February 1954), 87–95.

BIGGADIKE, RALPH, "Scott-Air Corporation (B)." Working Paper, Colgate Darden School, University of Virginia, 1977.

BOSTON CONSULTING GROUP, *Perspectives on Experience*. Boston, MA: The Boston Consulting Group, 1972.

CHEVALIER, MICHEL, "The Strategy Spectre Behind Your Market Share," *European Business,* Summer 1972, 63–72.

CONWAY, R. W., and ANDREW SCHULTZ, JR., "The Manufacturing Progress Function," *Journal of Industrial Engineering,* 10, no. 1 (January–February 1959), 39–54.

DAY, GEORGE and DAVID B. MONTGOMERY, "Diagnosing the Experience Curve," *Journal of Marketing,* 47, no. 2 (Spring 1983), 44–85.

FRUHAN, WILLIAM E., JR., "Pyrrhic Victories in Fights for Market Share," *Harvard Business Review,* 50, no. 5 (September–October 1972), 100–107.

GHEMAWAT, PANKAJ, "Building Strategy on the Experience Curve," *Harvard Business Review,* 63, no. 2 (March–April 1985), 143–149.

HAX, ARNOLDO and NICOLAS S. MAJLEEF, *Strategic Management: An Integrated Perspective,* Englewood Cliffs, NJ: Prentice-Hall, 1984.

HIRSCHMANN, WINFRED B., "Profit from the Learning Curve," *Harvard Business Review,* 42, no. 1 (January–February 1964), 125.

HIRSCHLEIFER, JACK, "The Firm's Cost Function: A Successful Reconstruction," *Journal of Business,* 35, no. 3 (July 1962), 235–255.

KIECHEL, WALTER III, "The Decline of the Experience Curve," *Fortune,* October 5, 1981, 139–146.

LEVITT, T., "Marketing Myopia," *Harvard Business Review,* 53, no. 5 (September–October 1975), 26.

MCKINSEY, JAMES O., "Adjusting Policies to Meet Changing Conditions," General Management Series, no. 116, New York: American Management Association, 1932.

RAPPING, LEONARD, "Learning and World War II Production Functions," *Review of Economics and Statistics,* 47, no. 1 (1965), 81–86.

STOBAUGH, ROBERT B. and PHILLIP L. TOWNSEND, "Price Forecasting and Strategic Planning: The Case of Petrochemicals," *Journal of Marketing Research,* 12, February 1975, 19–29.

SULTAN, RALPH, *Pricing in the Electrical Oligopoly,* Volumes I and II. Boston, MA: Division of Research, Graduate School of Business Administration, Harvard University, 1975.

WRIGHT, T. P., "Factors Affecting the Cost of Airplanes," *Journal of Aeronautical Sciences,* 3, no. 4 (February 1936), 122–28.

Chapter 7

ABERCROMBIE, M. L. JOHNSON, *The Anatomy of Judgement* London: Hutchinson, 1967.

ABERNATHY, WILLIAM J., and JAMES M. UTTERBACK, "Patterns of Industrial Innovation," *Technology Review,* 80, no. 7 (June–July 1978), 1–9.

BASS, FRANK M., "A New Product Growth Model for Consumer Durables," *Management Science Theory,* 15, no. 5 (January 1969), 215–27.

BUZZELL, ROBERT D., BRADLEY GALE, and RALPH G. M. SULTAN, "Market Share—A Key to Profitability," *Harvard Business Review,* 53, no. 1 (January–February 1975), 97–106.

CHRISTENSEN, C. R., NORMAN BERG, and MALCOLM S. SALTER, *Policy Formulation and Administration,* 8th edition. Homewood, IL: Richard D. Irwin, 1980.

CHUDLEY, JOHN A., *LETRASET, A lesson in Growth.* London: Business Books Unlimited, 1974.

COX, WILLIAM E. JR., "Product Life Cycles as Marketing Models," *Journal of Business,* 40, no. 4 (October 1967), 375–384.

EMSHOFF, JAMES R., and R. EDWARD FREEMAN, "Who's Butting into Your Business?" *The Wharton Magazine,* Fall 1979, 44–59.

ENIS, BEN M., RAYMOND LAGARCE, and ARTHUR E. PRELL, "Extending the Product Life Cycle," *Business Horizons,* 20, no. 3 (June 1977), 46–56.

FAYOL, HENRI, *General and Industrial Management,* trans. Constance Storrs. New York: Pitman Publishing, 1972. First French edition, 1916.

FISHER, J. C., and R. H. PRY, "A Simple Model of Technological Change," *Technological Forecasting & Social Change,* 3 (1971), 75–88.

FREEMAN, EDWARD R., "Strategic Management: A Stakeholder Approach." Mimeograph for publication in *Latest Advances in Strategic Management,* November 1981, 1–47.

GALE, BRADLEY T., "Market Share and Rate of Return," *Review of Economics and Statistics,* 54, no. 4 (November 1972), 412–423.

GASTON, FRANK J., "Growth Patterns in Industry: A Reexamination." National Industrial Conference Board, Inc., New York, no. 75, 1961.

GOLD, BELA, "Industry Growth Patterns: Theory & Empirical Results," *Journal of Industrial Economics,* 13, no. 1 (1964), 53–73.

HATTEN, KENNETH J., and MARY LOUISE HATTEN, "Some Empirical Insights for Strategic Marketers: The Case of Beer,'' in H. Thomas and D. Gardner, eds., *Strategic Marketing and Management*. London: John Wiley and Sons, 1985.

HAYES, R. H., and S. C. WHEELWRIGHT, ''Dynamics of Process-Product Life-Cycles,'' *Harvard Business Review,* 57, no. 2 (March–April 1979), 127–136.

KROC, RAY, with ROBERT ANDERSON, *Grinding it Out: The Making of McDonalds*. New York: Berkley, 1977.

LENZ, RALPH C. JR., and H. W. LANFORD, ''The Substitution Phenomenon,'' *Business Horizons,* 15, no. 1 (February 1972), 63–68.

LEVITT, THEODORE, ''Exploit the Product Life Cycle,'' *Harvard Business Review,* November–December 1965, 81–94.

LEVITT, THEODORE, ''Marketing Myopia,'' *Harvard Business Review,* 53, no. 5 (September–October 1975), 26.

MCKINSEY, JAMES O., ''Adjusting Policies to Meet Changing Conditions,'' General Management Series, No. 116. New York: American Management Association, 1932.

MCLEAN, JOHN G., and ROBERT W. HAIGH, *The Growth of Integrated Oil Companies*. Boston, MA: Division of Research, Graduate School of Business Administration, Harvard University, 1954.

NEVERS, JOHN V., ''Further Applications of the Bass New Product Growth Model,'' Institute Paper No. 283. Institute for Research in the Behavioral, Economic, and Management Sciences, Purdue University, 1970.

PFEFFER, JEFFREY, and GERALD R. SALANCIK, *The External Control of Organizations, A Resource Dependence Perspective*. New York: Harper and Row, 1978.

POLLI, R., and V. J. COOK, ''Validity of the Product Life Cycle,'' *Journal of Business,* 42, no. 4 (October 1969), 385–400.

PORTER, MICHAEL E., *Competitive Strategy, Techniques for Analyzing Industries and Competitors*. New York: The Free Press, 1980.

RUMELT, R. P., and ROBIN WENSLEY, ''In Search of the Market Share Effect,'' *Proceedings of the Academy of Management,* 1981, 2–6.

SCHERER, F. M., *Industrial Market Structure and Economic Performance*. Chicago: Rand McNally, 1970.

SCHOEFFLER, SIDNEY, ROBERT D. BUZZELL, and DONALD F. HEANY, ''Impact of Strategic Planning on Profit Performance,'' *Harvard Business Review,* 52, no. 2 (March–April 1974), 137–145.

STIPP, DAVID and G. CHRISTIAN HILL, ''Texas Instruments' Problems Show Pitfalls of Home-Computer Market,'' *Wall Street Journal,* June 17, 1983, p. 29.

UTTERBACK, JAMES M., and WILLIAM J. ABERNATHY, ''A Dynamic Model of Process and Product Innovation,'' *OMEGA, The International Journal of Management Science,* 3, no. 6 (1975), 639–656.

UYTERHOEVEN, HUGO E. JR., ROBERT E. ACKERMAN, and JOHN W. ROSENBLUM, *Strategy and Organization*. Homewood, IL: Richard D. Irwin, 1977.

WILLIAMSON, OLIVER E., *Markets and Hierarchies: Analysis and Antitrust Implications*. New York: The Free Press, 1975.

WOO, CAROLYN Y., ''Evaluation of the Strategies and Performance of Low ROI Market Share Leaders,'' *Strategic Management Journal,* 4 (1983), 123–135.

YALE, JORDON P., *Modern Textiles Magazine,* February 1964, 33.

Chapter 8

ABELL, DEREK F., ''Strategic Windows,'' *Journal of Marketing,* 42, no. 3 (July 1978), 21–26.

BAIN, JOE S., *Barriers to New Competition,* Cambridge, MA: Harvard University Press, 1956.

BASS, FRANK M., PHILLIPPE J. CATTIN, and DICK R. WITTINK, ''Market Structure and Industry

Influence on Profitability,'' in Hans B. Thorelli, ed., *Strategy + Structure = Performance.* Bloomington, IN: Indiana University Press, 1977.

BAUMOL, WILLIAM J., ''Contestable Markets: An Uprising in the Theory of Industrial Structure,'' *American Economic Review,* 72, no. 1 (March 1982), 97–106.

BOSTON CONSULTING GROUP, *Perspectives on Experience.* Boston, MA: Boston Consulting Group, 1968 and 1972.

BUZZELL, ROBERT D., BRADLEY GALE, and RALPH G. M. SULTAN, ''Market Share—A Key to Profitability,'' *Harvard Business Review,* 53, no. 1 (January–February 1975), 97–106.

CAVES, RICHARD, *American Industry: Structure, Conduct, Performance.* Englewood Cliffs, NJ: Prentice-Hall, 1964.

COOKE, ERNEST F., ''Market Share Measures of Rivalry,'' unpublished Doctoral Dissertation, Case Western Reserve University, 1974.

COX, WILLIAM E., JR., ''Product Portfolio Strategy, Market Structure, and Performance,'' in Hans B. Thorelli, ed., *Strategy + Structure = Performance.* Bloomington, IN: Indiana University Press, 1977.

HATTEN, KENNETH J., and MARY LOUISE HATTEN, ''Some Empirical Insights for Strategic Marketers: The Case of Beer,'' in H. Thomas and D. Gardner, eds., *Strategic Marketing and Management.* London: John Wiley and Sons, 1985.

HATTEN, KENNETH J., DAN E. SCHENDEL, and ARNOLD C. COOPER, ''A Strategic Model of the US Brewing Industry: 1952–1971,'' *Academy of Management Journal,* 21, no. 2 (1978), 592–610.

HATTEN, KENNETH J., and DAN E. SCHENDEL, ''Heterogeneity Within An Industry,'' *Journal of Industrial Economics,* 26, no. 2 (December 1977), 97–113.

HENDERSON, BRUCE D., ''Brinkmanship in Business,'' *Harvard Business Review,* 45, no. 2 (March–April 1967), 49–55.

HENDERSON, BRUCE D., *Henderson on Corporate Strategy.* Cambridge, MA: Abt Books, 1979.

HIRSCHMANN, WINFRED B., ''Profit from the Learning Curve,'' *Harvard Business Review,* 42, no. 1 (January–February 1964), 125.

HUNT, MICHAEL S., ''Competition in the Major Home Appliance Industry,'' unpublished Doctoral Dissertation, Harvard University, 1973.

MCGEE, JOHN, ''Strategic Groups: Review and Prospects.'' Presented at Strategic Marketing Workshop, University of Illinois, May 10–11, 1982.

MILLER, JOSEPH C., ''Comments on the Essay by William E. Cox, Jr.,'' in Hans B. Thorelli, ed., *Strategy + Structure = Performance.* Bloomington, IN: Indiana University Press, 1977.

NEWMAN, HOWARD H., ''Strategic Groups and the Structure Performance Relationship,'' *The Review of Economics and Statistics,* 60, no. 3 (August 1978), 417–427.

PORTER, MICHAEL E., ''Consumer Behavior, Retailer Power, and Market Performance in Consumer Goods Industries,'' *The Review of Economics and Statistics,* 56, no. 4 (November 1974), 419–436.

PORTER, MICHAEL E., ''How Competitive Forces Shape Strategy,'' *Harvard Business Review,* 57, no. 2 (March–April 1979), 137–145.

SCHENDEL, DAN E. and G. RICHARD PATTON, ''A Simultaneous Equation Model of Corporate Strategy,'' *Management Science,* 24, no. 75 (November 1978), 1611–21.

SCHOEFFLER, SIDNEY, ROBERT D. BUZZELL, and DONALD F. HEANY, ''Impact of Strategic Planning on Profit Performance,'' *Harvard Business Review,* 52, no. 2 (March–April 1974), 137–45.

WENSLEY, ROBIN, ''Pims and BCG: New Horizons or False Dawn,'' *Strategic Management Journal,* 3 (1982), 147–58.

Chapter 9

ACKERMAN, ROBERT W., *The Social Challenge to Business.* Cambridge, MA: Harvard University Press, 1975.

ANDREWS, KENNETH R., *The Concept of Corporate Strategy,* revised edition. Homewood, IL: Richard D. Irwin, 1980.

ANSOFF, H. IGOR, *Corporate Strategy.* New York: McGraw-Hill, 1965.

BARNARD, CHESTER L., *The Functions of the Executive.* Cambridge, MA: Harvard University Press, 1966. First printed, 1938.

BOWER, MARVIN, *The Will to Manage.* New York: McGraw-Hill, 1966.

BOURGEOIS, L. J. III, ''Performance and Consensus,'' *Strategic Management Journal,* 1 (1980), 227–248.

COHEN, HERB, *You Can Negotiate Anything.* New York: Bantam Books, 1982.

CYERT R., and J. MARCH, *A Behavioral Theory of a Firm.* Englewood Cliffs, NJ: Prentice Hall, 1963.

DALTON, DAN R., and RICHARD A. COSIER, ''The Four Faces of Social Responsibility,'' *Business Horizons,* 25, no 3 (May–June 1982), 19–27.

DILL, W., ''Strategic Management in a Kibitzer's World,'' in I. R. Ansoff, J. Declerk, and R. Hayes, eds., *Planning to Strategic Management.* New York: John Wiley and Sons, 1976.

EMSHOFF, JAMES R., and R. EDWARD FREEMAN, ''Who's Butting into Your Business?'' *The Wharton Magazine,* Fall 1979, 44–59.

FREEMAN, EDWARD R., ''Strategic Management: A Stakeholder Approach.'' Mimeograph for publication in *Latest Advances in Strategic Management,* November 1981, 1–47.

FRIEDMAN, MILTON, *Capitalism & Freedom.* Chicago: The University of Chicago Press, 1962.

GREFE, EDWARD A., *Fighting to Win: Business Political Power.* New York: Law and Business Inc./Harcourt Brace Javonovich Publishers, 1982.

KAMI, MICHAEL J., ''Gap Analysis: Key to Super Growth,'' *Long Range Planning,* 1, no. 4 (June 1969), 44–47.

MILLER, ARJAY, ''Manager's Journal: A Director's Questions,'' *Wall Street Journal,* August 18, 1980.

MURRAY, EDWIN A. JR., ''Strategic Choice as a Negotiated Outcome,'' *Management Science,* 24, no. 9 (May 1978), 960–972.

POST, JAMES E., *Corporate Behavior & Social Change.* Reston, VA: Reston Publishing Company, 1978.

POST, JAMES E., ''The Internal Management of Social Responsiveness: The Role of the Public Affairs Department.'' Presented at ''The Corporation and Society: Planning and Management of Corporate Responsibility,'' Seminar, University of Santa Clara, October 31–November 2, 1979.

POST, JAMES E., *Risk and Response: Management and Social Change in the American Insurance Industry.* Lexington, MA: D. C. Heath, 1976.

ROGERS, CARL R., *Carl Rogers on Personal Power.* New York: Delacorte Press, 1977.

SCHWARTZ, JULES J., *Corporate Policy.* Englewood Cliffs, NJ: Prentice Hall, 1978.

SELZNICK, PHILIP, *Leadership in Administration: A Sociological Interpretation.* New York: Harper and Row, 1957.

SELZNICK, PHILIP, ''Private Government and Corporate Conscience.'' Mimeograph prepared for Symposium of Business Policy, April 8–11, 1963. Graduate School of Business Administration, Harvard University, 1964.

SIMON, HERBERT A., ''On the Concept of Organizational Goal,'' *Administrative Science Quarterly,* 9, no. 1 (June 1964), 1–22.

SIMON, HERBERT A., *Administrative Behavior: A Study of Decision Making Processes in Administrative Organizations,* third edition. New York: The Free Press, 1976.

SUN TZU, *The Art of War,* trans. Samuel B. Griffith. New York: Oxford University Press, 1963.

VICKERS, SIR GEOFFREY, *The Art of Judgment, A Study of Policy Making*. New York: Basic Books, 1965.

Chapter 10

ANDREWS, KENNETH R., *The Concept of Corporate Strategy,* revised edition. Homewood, IL: Richard D. Irwin, 1980.

ANSOFF, H. I., *Corporate Strategy*. New York: McGraw-Hill, 1965.

CRAWFORD, C. MERLE, "The Trajectory Theory of Goal Setting for New Products," *Journal of Marketing Research,* 3, no. 2 (May 1966), 117–125.

HENDERSON, BRUCE D., *Henderson on Corporate Strategy*. Cambridge, MA: Abt Books, 1979.

KAMI, MICHAEL J., "Planning: Realities vs. Theory," *Management Thinking,* January 1968.

KAMI, MICHAEL J., "Gap Analysis: Key to Super Growth," *Long Range Planning,* 1, no. 4 (June 1969), 44–47.

LUCE, R. DUNCAN, and HOWARD RAIFFA, *Games & Decisions*. New York: John Wiley, 1957.

MINTZBERG, HENRY, *The Nature of Managerial Work*. New York: Harper and Row, 1973.

MUSASHI, MIYAMOTO, *A Book of Five Rings,* trans. Victor Harris. Woodstock, NY: The Overlook Press, 1974. First published, 1645.

PFEFFER, JEFFREY, and GERALD R. SALANCIK, *The External Control of Organizations, A Resource Dependence Perspective*. New York: Harper and Row, 1978.

SIMON, HERBERT A., *Administrative Behavior,* 3rd edition. New York: The Free Press, 1976.

SWALM, RALPH O., "Utility Theory—Insights into Risk Taking," *Harvard Business Review,* 44, no. 6 (November–December 1966), 123–130.

TILLES, SEYMOUR, "How to Evaluate Corporate Strategy," *Harvard Business Review,* 41, no. 3 (July–August 1963), 111–121.

WILLIAMSON, OLIVER E., *Markets and Hierarchies: Analysis and Antitrust Implications*. New York: The Free Press, 1975.

ZAMMUTO, RAYMOND F., *Assessing Organizational Effectiveness,* Albany, NY: State University of New York Press, 1982.

Chapter 11

ANDREWS, KENNETH R., *The Concept of Corporate Strategy,* revised edition. Homewood, IL: Richard D. Irwin, 1980.

ANSOFF, H. I., "Managerial Problem Solving," *Journal of Business Policy,* 2, no. 1 (Autumn 1971), 3–20.

ARGYRIS, CHRIS, "Double Loop Learning in Organizations," *Harvard Business Review,* 55, no. 5 (September–October 1977), 115–125.

BOWER, JOSEPH L., "Strategy as a Problem Solving Theory of Business Planning." Mimeograph, Harvard Graduate School of Business Administration, Presidents and Fellows of Harvard College, 1967.

BOWER, JOSEPH L., "Solving the Problems of Business Planning," *The Journal of Business Strategy,* 2, no. 3 (1982), 32–44.

BOWER, JOSEPH L., *Managing the Resource Allocation Process; A Study of Corporate Planning and Investment*. Boston: Harvard University Division of Research, Graduate School of Business Administration, 1970.

BRAYBROOKE, DAVID, and CHARLES E. LINDBLOOM, *A Strategy of Decision: Policy Evaluation as a Social Process*. New York: The Free Press, 1970.

COOPER, ARNOLD C., and DAN SCHENDEL, "Strategic Responses to Technological Threats," *Business Horizons,* 19, no. 1 (February 1976), 61–69.

DEBONO, EDWARD, *New Think: The Use of Lateral Thinking in the Generation of New Ideas.* New York: Buni Books, 1968.

DEBONO, EDWARD. "Why Opportunities are Often Missed," *International Management,* 32, no. 9 (September 1977), 57–63.

EMSHOFF, JAMES R., IAN I. MITROFF, and RALPH H. KILMAN, "The Role of Idealization in Long Range Planning: An Essay on the Logical and Socio Emotional Aspects of Planning," *Technological Forecasting and Social Change,* 11, 1978, 335–348.

GALBRAITH, CRAIG, and DAN E. SCHENDEL, "An Empirical Analysis of Strategic Types," *Strategic Management Journal,* 4 (1983), 153–173.

HENDERSON, BRUCE D., *Henderson on Corporate Strategy.* Cambridge, MA: Abt Books, 1979.

JANIS, IRVING L., and LEON MANN, *Decision Making.* New York: The Free Press, 1977.

LEVITT, T., "Marketing Myopia," *Harvard Business Review,* 53, no. 5 (September–October 1975), 26.

LEVITT. T., "Innovative Imitation," *Harvard Business Review,* 44, no. 5 (September–October 1966), 63–70.

MCLEAN, JOHN G., and ROBERT WM. HAIGH, *The Growth of Integrated Oil Companies.* Boston: Division of Research, Graduate School of Business Administration, Harvard University, 1954.

MITROFF, IAN I., and JAMES R. EMSHOFF, "On Strategic Assumption-Making: A Dialectic Approach to Policy and Planning," *Academy of Management Review,* 4, no. 1 (1979), 1–12.

OHMAE, KENICHI, *The Mind of the Strategist: The Art of Japanese Business.* New York: McGraw-Hill, 1982.

PORTER, MICHAEL E., *Competitive Strategy, Techniques for Analyzing Industries and Competitors.* New York: The Free Press, 1980.

QUINN, JAMES BRIAN, *Strategies for Change, Logical Incrementalism.* Homewood, IL: Richard D. Irwin, 1980.

UTTERBACK, JAMES M., and WILLIAM J. ABERNATHY, "A Dynamic Model of Process and Product Innovation, *OMEGA, The International Journal of Management Science,* 3, no. 6 (1975), 639–656.

UYTERHOEVEN, HUGO E. JR., "General Managers in the Middle," *Harvard Business Review,* 50, no. 2 (March–April 1972), 72–85.

UYTERHOEVEN, HUGO E. JR., ROBERT E. ACKERMAN, and JOHN W. ROSENBLUM. *Strategy and Organization.* Homewood, IL: Richard D. Irwin, 1977.

WILLIAMSON, OLIVER E., *Markets and Hierarchies: Analysis and Antitrust Implications.* New York: The Free Press, 1975.

Chapter 12

BOURGEOIS, L. J. III, "Performance and Consensus," *Strategic Management Journal,* 1 (1980), 227–248.

DEBONO, EDWARD, *New Think: The Use of Lateral Thinking in the Generation of New Ideas.* New York: Buni Books, 1968.

HENDERSON, BRUCE D., *Henderson on Corporate Strategy,* Cambridge, MA: Abt Books, 1979.

HIRSCHMAN, ALBERT, *Development Projects Observed.* Washington, DC: Brookings Institute, 1967.

JANIS, IRVING L., and LEON MANN, *Decision Making.* New York: The Free Press, 1977.

MYERSON, ADAM, and SUSAN CAREY, "Fletcher Byrom Doesn't Want to Hold Your Hand," *Wall Street Journal,* June 1, 1982, p. 26.

PRICE, ROBERT M., "Uncertainty and Strategic Opportunity," *The Journal of Business Strategy,* 2, no. 3 (Winter 1982), 3–8.

SCHOEN, DONALD R., "Managing Technological Innovation," *Harvard Business Review,* 47, no. 3 (May–June 1969), 156–163.

VICKERS, SIR GEOFFREY, *The Art of Judgment, A Study of Policy Making*. New York: Basic Books, 1965.

Chapter 13

BOWER, MARVIN, *The Will to Manage*. New York: McGraw-Hill, 1966.

DEAL, TERRENCE E., and ALLAN A. KENNEDY, *Corporate Cultures: The Rites and Rituals of Corporate Life*. Reading, MA: Addison-Wesley, 1982.

FORD, C. S., *Cross-Cultural Approaches: Readings in Comparative Research*. New Haven, CT: HRAF Press, 1967.

KLUCKHOLN, CLYDE, *Mirror For Man: The Relation of Anthropology to Modern Life*. New York: Whittlesey House, 1949.

PARSONS, TALCOTT, "Suggestions for a Sociological Approach to the Theory of Organizations—I," *Administrative Science Quarterly,* 1, no. 1 (June 1956), 63–85.

SCHWARTZ, HOWARD, and STANLEY M. DAVIS, "Matching Corporate Culture and Business Strategy," *Organizational Dynamics,* 10, no. 1 (Summer 1981), 30–48.

UYTERHOEVEN, HUGO E. JR., "General Managers in the Middle," *Harvard Business Review,* 50, no. 3 (March–April 1972), 75–85.

WEST, MORRIS, *The Clowns of God,* New York: Bantam Books, 1981.

Chapter 14

ANDREWS, KENNETH R., *The Concept of Corporate Strategy,* revised edition. Homewood, IL: Richard D. Irwin, 1980.

BARNARD, CHESTER L., *The Functions of the Executive*. Cambridge: Harvard University Press, 1966. First printed, 1938.

BARNES, LOUIS B. and SIMON A. HERSHON, "Trnasferring Power in the Family Business," *Harvard Business Review,* 54, no. 4 (July–August 1976), 105–114.

CHANDLER, ALFRED D. JR., *Strategy and Structure: Chapters in the History of the American Industrial Enterprise*. Cambridge, MA: MIT Press, 1962.

CHANDLER, ALFRED D. JR., *The Visible Hand, The Managerial Revolution in American Business*. Cambridge, MA: Harvard University Press, 1977.

CLIFFORD, DONALD K. JR., "Growth Pains of the Threshold Company," *Harvard Business Review,* 51, no. 5 (September–October 1973), 143–154.

DAVIS, STANLEY M., and PAUL R. LAWRENCE, *Matrix*. Reading, MA: Addison-Wesley, 1977.

ERICKSON, ERIC, *Childhood & Society,* 2nd edition. New York: W. W. Norton, 1963.

FAYOL, HENRI, *General and Industrial Management,* trans. Constance Storrs. New York: Pitman Publishing 1972. First French edition, 1916.

GREINER, LARRY E., "Evolution and Revolution as Organizations Grow," *Harvard Business Review,* 50, no. 4 (July–August 1972), 37–46.

HIRSCHMAN, ALBERT, *Development Projects Observed*. Washington, DC: Brookings Institute, 1967.

HUNT, J. W., *The Restless Organization*. Sydney: John Wiley and Sons, Australasia Pty. Ltd., 1972.

JENNINGS, EUGENE E., "Managing The Maze Bright Manager: Skills of Exceptional Executives."

Presented at a *Business Week* Startegic Planning Conference on Business Unit Planning, New Orleans, LA, May 1–2, 1980.

KOTTER, JOHN P., *Power in Management: How to Understand, Acquire, and Use It.* New York: Amacom, 1979.

KOTTER, JOHN P., *The General Managers.* New York: The Free Press, 1982.

LIPPITT, GORDON L., and WARREN H. SCHMIDT, "Crisis in a Developing Organization," *Harvard Business Review,* 45, no. 6 (November–December 1967), 102–112.

MCCASKEY, MICHAEL B., *The Executive Challenge: Managing Change and Ambiguity.* Boston: Pittman, 1982.

MCGREGOR, DOUGLAS, *The Human Side of Enterprise.* New York: McGraw-Hill Book Company, 1960.

MINTZBERG, HENRY, "Patterns in Strategy Formulation," *Management Science,* 24, no. 9 (May 1978), 934–948.

OUCHI, WILLIAM, *Theory Z. How American Business Should Meet the Japanese Challenge.* Reading, MA: Addison-Wesley, 1981.

OUCHI, WILLIAM and JERRY B. JOHNSON, "Types of Organizational Control and Their Relationship to Emotional Well-Being." *Administrative Science Quarterly,* 23 (1978), 293–317.

QUINN, JAMES BRIAN, *Strategies for Change: Logical Incrementalism.* Homewood, IL: Richard D. Irwin, 1980.

SALTER, MALCOLM S., "Stages of Corporate Development," *Journal of Business Policy,* 1, no. 1 (1970), 23–37.

SCOTT, BRUCE R., "Stages of Corporate Development, Part I." Cambridge, MA: President and Fellows of Harvard College, 1971 (ICCH Case # 9-371-294).

SUN TZU, *The Art of War,* trans. Samuel B. Griffith. New York: Oxford University Press, 1963.

THOMPSON, JAMES D., *Organizations in Action.* New York: McGraw-Hill, 1967.

WILLIAMSON, OLIVER E., *Markets and Hierarchies: Analysis and Antitrust Implications.* New York: The Free Press, 1975.

Chapter 15

BARNARD, CHESTER L., *The Functions of the Executive.* Cambridge: Harvard University Press, 1966. First printed, 1938.

BARNES, LOUIS B., "Managing the Paradox of Organizational Trust," *Harvard Business Review,* March–April 1981, 107–116.

BARNES, LOUIS B., and SIMON A. HERSHON, "Transferring Power in the Family Business," *Harvard Business Review,* 54, no. 4 (July–August 1976), 105–114.

BLANCHARD, KENNETH, and SPENCER JOHNSON, *The One Minute Manager.* New York: William Morrow, 1982.

BOWER, MARVIN, *The Will to Manage.* New York: McGraw-Hill, 1966.

DEUTSCH, CLAUDIA H., "Guidance Counselors: The Art and the Dangers of Having or Being a Mentor," *TWA Ambassador,* September 1983, 12–14.

GERSTEIN, MARC, and HEATHER REISMAN, "Strategic Selection: Matching Executives to Business Conditions," *Sloan Management Review,* 24, no. 2 (Winter 1983), 33–49.

GOVINDARGAN, V., and ANIL K. GUPTA, "Business Unit Strategy, Control Systems and Business Unit Performance." Research Paper funded by the Graduate School, Boston University and the Graduate School of Business, Harvard University, November 1981.

KOTTER, JOHN P., *The General Managers.* New York: The Free Press, 1982.

LIVINGSTON, J. STERLING, "Pygmalion in Management," *Harvard Business Review,* 47, no. 4 (July–August 1969), 81–89.

McGregor, Douglas, *The Human Side of Enterprise.* New York: McGraw-Hill, 1960.

Peters, Thomas J., and Robert H. Waterman, Jr., *In Search of Excellence, Lessons from America's Best-Run Companies.* New York: Harper and Row, 1982.

Salter, Malcolm, "What is Fair Pay for the Executive?" *Harvard Business Review,* 52, no. 3 (May–June, 1972), 5–13.

Selznick, Philip, *Leadership in Administration, A Sociological Interpretation.* New York: Harper and Row, 1957.

Sloan, Alfred P., *My Years with General Motors.* New York: Doubleday, 1963.

Stata, Ray, and Modesto A. Maidique, "Bonus System for Balanced Strategy," *Harvard Business Review,* 58, no. 6 (November–December, 1980), 156–163.

Stonich, Paul J., "Using Rewards in Implementing Strategy," *Strategic Management Journal,* 2 (1981), 345–352.

Stybel, Laurence J., "Linking Strategic Planning and Management Manpower Planning," *California Management Review,* 25, no. 1 (Fall 1982), 48–56.

Sun Tzu, *The Art of War,* trans. Samuel B. Griffith. New York: Oxford University Press, 1963. Circa 500 B.C.

Towl, A., "Patterns of Executive Compensation," *Harvard Business Review,* 29, no. 4 (July 1951), 25.

Vancil, Richard F., *Decentralization: Managerial Ambiguity by Design.* Homewood, IL: Dow Jones-Irwin, 1979.

Zaleznick, Abraham, "Managers and Leaders: Are They Different?" *Harvard Business Review,* 55, no. 3 (May-June 1977), 67–78.

Chapter 16

Ackoff, Russell L., *A Concept of Corporate Planning.* New York: Wiley-Interscience, 1970.

Ansoff, H. I., "Managerial Problem Solving," *Journal of Business Policy,* 2, no. 1 (Autumn 1971), 3–20.

Ansoff, H. Igor, Jay Avner, Richard G. Brandenburg, Fred E. Portner, and Raymond Radosevich, "Does Planning Pay? The Effect of Planning on Success of Acquisitions in American Firms? *Long Range Planning,* 3, no. 2 (December 1970), 2–7.

Argyris, Chris, "Double Loop Learning in Organizations," *Harvard Business Review,* 55, no. 5 (September-October 1977), 115–125.

Armstrong, J. Scott, "The Value of Formal Planning for Strategic Decisions: Review of Empirical Research," *Strategic Management Journal,* 3 (1982), 197–211.

Bales, Carter F., "Strategic Control: The President's Paradox," *Business Horizons,* 20, no. 4 (August 1977), 17–28.

Bourgeois, L. J. III, "Performance and Consensus," *Strategic Management Journal,* 1 (1980), 227–248.

Bower, Joseph L., *Managing the Resource Allocation Process: A Study of Corporate Planning and Investment.* Boston: Graduate School of Business Administration, Harvard University, 1970.

Bower, Joseph L., "Strategy as a Problem Solving Theory of Business Planning." Mimeograph, Harvard Graduate School of Business Administration, Presidents and Fellows of Harvard College, 1967.

Bower, Joseph L., "Solving the Problems of Business Planning," *The Journal of Business Strategy,* 2, no. 3 (1982), 32–44.

Bower, Marvin, *The Will to Manage.* New York: McGraw-Hill, 1966.

Cosier, Richard A., "Dialectical Inquiry in Strategic Planning: A Case of Premature Acceptance?" *Academy of Management Review,* 6, no. 4 (1981), 643–648.

COSIER, RICHARD A., "Further Thoughts on Dialectical Inquiry: A Rejoinder to Mitroff and Mason," *Academy of Management Review,* 6, no. 4 (1981a), 653–654.

COSIER, RICHARD A., and JOHN C. APLIN, "A Critical View of Dialectical Inquiry as a Tool in Strategic Planning," *Strategic Management Journal,* 7 (1980), 343–356.

DEBONO, EDWARD, *New Think: The Use of Lateral Thinking in the Generation of New Ideas.* New York: Buni Books, 1968.

DEWEY, JOHN, *How We Think.* Boston: D. C. Heath, 1933.

EMSHOFF, JAMES R., and ARTHUR FINNEL, "Defining Corporate Strategy: A Case Study Using Strategic Assumptions Analysis," *Sloan Management Review,* Spring 1979, 41–52.

EMSHOFF, JAMES R., IAN I. MITROFF, and RALPH H. KILMAN, "The Role of Idealization in Long Range Planning: An Essay on the Logical and Socio Emotional Aspects of Planning," *Technological Forecasting and Social Change,* 11 (1978), 335–348.

FAYOL, HENRI., *General and Industrial Management,* trans. Constance Storrs. New York: Pitman Publishing, 1972. First French edition, 1916.

HENRY, HAROLD W., "Formal Planning in Major U.S. Corporations," *Long Range Planning,* 10 (October 1977), 40–45.

HEROLD, DAVID M., "Long-Range Planning and Organizational Performance: A Cross-Valuation Study," *Academy of Management Journal,* 15, no. 1 (March 1972), 92–102.

HUNSICKER, J. QUINCY, "The Malaise of Strategic Planning," *The Management Review,* 69, no. 3 (March 1980), 8–14.

KAMI, MICHAEL J., "Planning: Realities vs. Theory," *Management Thinking,* January 1968, 1–4.

KIDDER, TRACY, *The Soul of a New Machine.* Boston, MA: Little Brown, 1981.

LORANGE, PETER, and RICHARD F. VANCIL, "How to Design a Strategic Planning System," *Harvard Business Review,* 54, no. 5 (September–October 1976), 75–81.

LYLES, MARJORIE A., and R. T. LENZ, "Managing the Planning Process: A Field Study of the Human Side of Planning," *Strategic Planning Journal,* 3 (1982), 105–118.

MASON, RICHARD O., and IAN I. MITROFF, "Assumptions of Majestic Metals: Strategy Through Dialectics," *California Management Review,* 22, no. 2 (Winter 1979), 80–88.

MCKINSEY, JAMES O., "Adjusting Policies to Meet Changing Conditions," General Management Series, No. 116. New York: American Management Association, 1932.

MINTZBERG, HENRY, "Planning on the Left Side and Managing on the Right," *Harvard Business Review,* 54, no. 4 (July–August 1976), 49–58.

MITROFF, IAN I., and JAMES R. EMSHOFF, "On Strategic Assumption-Making: A Dialectic Approach to Polict and Planning," *Academy of Management Review,* 4, no. 1 (1979), 1–12.

MITROFF, IAN I., JAMES R. EMSHOFF, and RALPH H. KILMANN, "Assumptional Analysis: A Methodology for Strategic Problem Solving," *Management Science,* 25, no. 6 (June 1979), 583–593.

MITROFF, IAN I., and RICHARD O. MASON, "Structuring Ill-Structured Policy Issues: Further Explorations in a Methodology for Messy Problems," *Strategic Management Journal,* 1 (1980), 331–342.

MITROFF, IAN I., and RICHARD O. MASON, "The Metaphysics of Policy and Planning: A Reply to Cosier," *The Academy of Management Review,* 6, no. 4 (1981), 649–651.

NAYLOR, THOMAS H., and HORST SCHAULAND, "A Survey of Users of Corporate Planning Models," *Management Science,* 22, no. 9 (May 1976), 927–937.

PASCALE, RICHARD TANNER, and ANTHONY G. ATHOS, *The Art of Japanese Management, Applications for American Executives.* New York: Simon and Schuster, 1981.

PENNINGTON, MALCOLM W., "Why Has Planning Failed?" *Long Range Planning,* 5, no. 1 (March 1972), 2–9.

PETERS, THOMAS J., and ROBERT H. WATERMAN, JR., *In Search of Excellence, Lessons from America's Best-Run Companies.* New York: Harper and Row, 1982.

REICHMAN, W., and M. LEVY, "Psychological Restraints on Effective Planning," *Management Review,* 64, no. 10 (1975), 37–42.

SHANK, JOHN K., EDWARD G. NIBLOCK, and WILLIAM T. SANDALLS, JR., "Balance, 'Creativity' and 'Practicality' in Formal Planning," *Harvard Business Review,* 51, no. 1 (January–February 1973), 87–94.

SLOAN, ALFRED P., JR., *My Years at General Motors,* New York: Doubleday, 1963.

STEINER, GEORGE A., "Top Management's Role in Planning" *Long Range Planning,* 2, June 1969, 2–8.

THOMPSON, JAMES D., *Organizations in Action.* New York: McGraw-Hill, 1967.

THUNE, STANLEY S., and ROBERT J. HOUSE, "Where Long Range Planning Pays Off: Findings of a Survey of Formal, Informal Plans," *Business Horizons,* 13, no. 4 (August 1970), 81–87.

WELCH, JOHN F., "Where Is Marketing Now That We Really Need It?" Presented to The Conference Board's Marketing Conference, 1981.

WOLF, WILLIAM B., *Management and Consulting, An Introduction to James O. McKinsey.* Ithaca, NY: Cornell University Press, 1978.

WRAPP, H. EDWARD, "Good Managers Don't Make Policy Decisions," *Harvard Business Review,* 45, no. 5 (September–October 1967), 91–99.

Chapter 17

ANSOFF, H. I., *Corporate Strategy,* New York: McGraw-Hill, 1965.

BASS, FRANK M., PHILLIPPE J. CATTIN, and DICK R. WITTINK, "Market Structure and Industry Influence on Profitability," in H. Thorelli (ed.), *Strategy + Structure = Performance.* Bloomington, IN: Indiana University Press 1977.

BAUMOL, WILLIAM J., *Business Behavior, Value, and Growth,* New York: Harcourt, Brace and World, 1967.

BEAVER, WILLIAM, and DALE MORSE, "What Determines Price-Earnings Ratios?" *Financial Analysts Journal,* 34, no. 4 (July–August 1978), 65–76.

BETTIS, RICHARD A., and WILLIAM K. HALL, "Risks and Industry Effects in Large Diversified Firms." Proceedings of the Academy of Management National Meeting, 1981.

CHANDLER, ALFRED D., *Strategy and Structure, Chapters in the History of the American Industrial Enterprise,* Cambridge, MA: MIT Press, 1962.

CHANNON, DEREK F., *The Strategy & Structure of British Enterprise,* Boston, MA: Division of Research, Harvard Business School, 1973.

CHRISTENSEN, H. KURT, and CYNTHIA A. MONTGOMERY, "Corporate Economic Performance: Diversification Strategy Versus Market Structure." *Strategic Management Journal,* 2 (1981) 327–343.

DRUCKER, PETER F., "The Five Rules of Successful Acquisition," *The Wall Street Journal,* 28, no. 3 (October 15, 1981), 31.

DUNDAS, K. M., and P. R. RICHARDSON, "Implementing the Unrelated Product Strategy," *Journal of Strategic Management,* 3 (1982), 287–301.

DYAS, GARETH POOLEY, "The Strategy & Structure of French Industrial Enterprise," unpublished Doctoral Dissertation, Harvard Business School, 1972.

HARRINGTON, DIANA R., "Stock Prices, Beta, and Strategic Planning, *Harvard Business Review,* 61, no. 3 (May–June 1983), 157–164.

KATTEN, KENNETH J., and DAN E. SCHENDEL, "Strategy's Role in Policy Research," *Journal of Economics and Business,* 28, no. 3 (Spring–Summer 1976), 195–202.

HATTEN, KENNETH J., and DAN E. SCHENDEL, "Heterogeneity Within an Industry: Firm Conduct in the U.S. Brewing Industry 1952–1971," *Journal of Industrial Economics,* 26, no. 2 (December 1977), 97–113.

HATTEN, KENNETH J., DAN E. SCHENDEL, and ARNOLD C. COOPER, "A Strategic Model of the U.S. Brewing Industry, 1952–1971," *Academy of Management Journal,* 21, no. 4 (December 1978), 592–610.

HATTEN, KENNETH J., and MARY LOUISE HATTEN, "Some Empirical Insights for Strategic Marketers: The Case of Beer," in H. Thomas and D. Gardner, eds., *Strategic Marketing and Management.* London: John Wiley and Sons, 1985.

HENDERSON, BRUCE, *Henderson on Corporate Strategy,* Cambridge, MA: Abt Books, 1979.

KITCHING, JOHN, "Why do Mergers Miscarry?" *Harvard Business Review,* 45, no. 6 (November–December 1967), 84–101.

KITCHING, JOHN, "Winning and Losing with European Acquisitions," *Harvard Business Review,* 52, no. 2 (March–April 1974), 124–136.

LEWELLEN, WILBUR G., "A Pure Financial Rationale for the Conglomerate Merger," *The Journal of Finance,* 26, no. 2 (May 1971).

MADER, CHRIS, and ROBERT HAGIN, *Common Stocks,* Homewood, IL: Dow Jones-Irwin, 1976.

MARRIS, ROBIN, *The Economic Theory of "Managerial" Capitalism,* London: MacMillan, 1964.

MCLEAN, JOHN G., and ROBERT WM. HAIGH, *The Growth of Integrated Oil Companies.* Boston, MA: Division of Research, Graduate School of Business Administration, Harvard University, 1954.

MULLINS, DAVID W., JR., "Does the Capital Asset Pricing Model Work?" *Harvard Business Review,* 60, no. 1 (January–February 1982), 105–111.

PAVAN, ROBERT J., "The Strategy and Structure of Italian Enterprise," unpublished Doctoral Dissertation, Harvard Business School, 1972.

RUMELT, RICHARD P., *Strategy, Structural and Economic Performance,* Boston, MA: Division of Research, Harvard Business School, 1974.

RUMELT, RICHARD P., "Diversification Strategy and Profitability," *Strategic Management Journal,* 3, no. 4 (October–December 1982), 359–370.

SALTER, MALCOLM S., and WOLF A. WEINHOLD, "Diversification via Acquisition: Creating Value," *Harvard Business Review,* 56, no. 4 (July–August 1978), 166–176.

SCOTT, BRUCE R., "The Industrial State: Old Myths and New Realities," *Harvard Business Review,* 51, no. 2 (March–April 1973), 133–143.

THANHEISER, HEINZ T., "Strategy & Structure of German Industrial Enterprise," unpublished Doctoral Dissertation, Harvard Business School, 1972.

WRIGLEY, LEONARD, "Divisional Autonomy and Diversification," unpublished Doctoral Dissertation, Harvard Business School, 1970.

Chapter 18

ABELL, DEREK F., and JOHN S. HAMMOND, *Strategic Market Planning, Problems, and Analytical Approches.* Englewood Cliffs, NJ: Prentice Hall, 1979.

ANDERSON, CARL R., and FRANK T. PAINE, "PIMS: A Re-examination." Presentation to Academy of Management, Orlando FL, August 1977.

ANSOFF, H. I., and JAMES LEONTIADES, "Strategic Portfolio Management," *Journal of General Management,* 4, no. 1 (1976), 13–29.

BARNES, LOUIS B., and SIMON A. HERSHON, "Transferring Power in the Family Business," *Harvard Business Review,* 54, no. 4 (July–August 1976), 105–114.

BEAVER, WILLIAM AND DALE MORSE, "What Determines Price-Earnings Ratios?" *Financial Analysts Journal,* 34, no. 4 (July–August 1978), 65–76.

BETTIS, RICHARD A., and WILLIAM K. HALL, Strategic Portfolio Management in the Multibusiness Firm, *California Management Review,* 24, no. 1 (Fall 1981), 23–38.

BIGGADIKE, RALPH, "Drawing Portfolio Charts." Mimeograph UVA-M-187, Darden Graduate School of Business Administration, University of Virginia, May 1978.

CHEVALIER, MICHEL, "The Strategy Spectre Behind Your Market Share," *European Business*, Summer 1972, 63–72.

CHRISTENSEN, H. KURT, ARNOLD C. COOPER, and CORNELIS A. DEKLUYVER, "The Dog Business: A Re-Examination," *Business Horizons*, 25, no. 6 (November–December 1982), 12–18.

DAY, GEORGE S., "Diagnosing the Product Portfolio," *Journal of Marketing*, 41, no. 2 (April 1977), 29–38.

FRUHAN, WILLIAM E., JR., "Pyrrhic Victories in Fights for Market Share," *Harvard Business Review*, 50, no. 5 (September–October 1972), 100–110.

HALL, WILLIAM K., "Survival Strategies in a Hostile Environment," *Harvard Business Review*, 58, no. 5 (September–October 1980), 75–85.

HAMBRICK, DONALD C., and IAN C. MACMILLAN, "The Product Portfolio and Man's Best Friend," *California Management Review*, 25, no. 1 (Fall 1982), 84–95.

HASPESLAGH, PHILIPPE, "Portfolio Planning: Uses and Limits," *Harvard Business Review*, 60, no. 1 (January–February 1982), 58–67.

HATTEN, KENNETH J. and DAN E. SCHENDEL, "Strategy's Role in Policy Research," *Journal of Economics and Business*, 28, no. 3 (Spring–Summer 1976), 195–202.

HEDLEY, BARRY, "Strategy and the Business Portfolio," *Long Range Planning*, 10 (1977), 9–15.

HENDERSON, BRUCE D., *Henderson on Corporate Strategy*, Cambridge, MA: Abt Books, 1979.

HUSSEY, D. E., "Portfolio Analysis: Practical Experience with the Directional Policy Matrix," *Long Range Planning*, 11 (1978), 2–8.

LOOMIS, WORTH, "Strategic Planning in Uncertain Times," *Chief Executive*, 1980, 7–12.

MACMILLAN, IAN C., DONALD C. HAMBRICK, and DIANA L. DAY, "The Product Portfolio and Profitability—A PIMS-Based Analysis of Industrial-Product Businesses," *Academy of Management Journal*, 25, no. 4 (December 1982), 733–755.

MARAKON ASSOCIATES, *The Marakon Profitability Matrix*. San Francisco: Marakon Associates, 1981.

PORTER, MICHAEL E., *Competitive Strategy: Techniques for Analyzing Industries and Competitors*, New York: Free Press, 1980.

VERITY, C. WILLIAMS JR., "Why a Portfolio of Businesses?" *Chief Executive*, c. 1975, 54.

WENSLEY, ROBIN, "Strategic Marketing: Betas, Boxes or Basics?" *Journal of Marketing*, 45, no. 3 (1981), 173–182.

Chapter 19

ANSOFF, H. I., *Corporate Strategy*, New York: McGraw-Hill, 1965.

Chapter 20

BURNS, TOM, and D. M. STALKER, *The Management of Innovation*. London: Tavistock, 1959.

COOPER, ARNOLD C., and DAN E. SCHENDEL, "Strategic Responses to Technological Threats," *Business Horizons*, 19, no. 1 (February 1976), 61–69.

HENDERSON, BRUCE D., "Brinkmanship in Business," *Harvard Business Review*, 45, no. 2 (March–April 1967), 49–55.

HOUT, THOMAS, MICHAEL E. PORTER, and EILEEN RUDDEN, "How Global Companies Win Out," *Harvard Business Review*, 60, no. 5 (September–October 1982), 98–108.

LEVITT, THEODORE, "The Globalization of Markets," *Harvard Business Review*, 61, no. 3 (May–June 1983), 92–102.

SCHON, DONALD A., *Technology and Change*, New York: Delacorte Press, 1967.

SLOAN, ALFRED P., JR., *My Years at General Motors.* New York: Doubleday, 1964.

WILLIAMSON, OLIVER E., *Markets and Hierarchies: Analysis and Antitrust Implications.* New York: The Free Press, 1975.

Chapter 21

BARNARD, CHESTER L., *The Functions of the Executive.* Cambridge, MA: Harvard University Press, 1966. First printed, 1938.

HENDERSON, BRUCE D., *Henderson on Corporate Strategy.* Cambridge, MA: Abt Books, 1979.

HIRSCHMAN, ALBERT, *Development Projects Observed.* Washington, DC: Brookings Institute, 1967.

HOMANS, GEORGE C., *The Human Group.* New York: Harcourt, Brace & World, 1950.

KATZ, ROBERT L., "Skills of an Effective Administrator," *Harvard Business Review,* 52, no. 5 (September–October 1974), 90–99.

LAWRENCE, PAUL R., "How to Deal with Resistance to Change," *Harvard Business Review,* 47, no. 1 (January–February 1969), 4–13.

LIEBERSON, STANLEY, and JAMES F. O'CONNOR, "Leadership and Organizational Performance: A Study of Large Corporations," *American Sociological Review,* 37, no. 2 (1972), 117–130.

LITZINGER, WILLIAM and THOMAS SCHAEFER, "Leadership Through Followship," *Business Horizons,* 25, no. 5 (September–October 1982), 78–81.

LOMBARDI, VINCE, "Leadership and Teamwork in Management," AMA Personnel Conference.

MACHIAVELLI, NICCOLO, *The Prince,* trans. George Bull, Harmondsworth, England: Penguin Books, 1961.

MINTZBERG, HENRY, "The Manager's Job: Folklore and Fact," *Harvard Business Review,* 53, no. 3 (July–August 1975), 49–61.

MINTZBERG, HENRY, "Patterns in Strategy Formulation," *Management Science,* 24, no. 9 (1978), 934–948.

PASCALE, RICHARD TANNER, "Zen and the Art of Management," *Harvard Business Review,* 56, no. 2 (March–April 1978), 153–162.

SALANCIK, GERALD R., B. J. CALDER, K. M. ROWLAND, H. LEBLEBICI, and M. CONWAY, "Leadership is an Outcome of Social Structure and Process: A Multidimensional Analysis," in J. G. Hunt and L. L. Larson, eds., *Leadership Frontiers.* Kent, OH: Kent State University Press, 1975.

SCHULLER, ROBERT H., *Tough Times Never Last, But Tough People Do!,* Nashville, TN: Thomas Nelson, 1983.

SELZNICK, PHILIP, *Leadership in Administration: A Sociological Interpretation,* New York: Harper and Row, 1957.

SMITH, EDWARD BOLAND, "Chester Barnard's Concept of Leadership," *Education Administration Quarterly,* 11, no. 3 (Autumn 1975), 37–48.

SMITH, BRIAN P., "Leadership in Management: the Elusive Element," *Journal of Business Policy,* 2, no. 3 (Spring 1972), 3–14.

SUN TZU, *The Art of War,* trans, Samuel B. Griffith. New York: Oxford University Press, 1963.

VICKERS, SIR GEOFFREY, *The Art of Judgment, A Study on Policy Making,* New York: Basic Books, 1965.

ZALEZNICK, ABRAHAM, "Managers and Leaders: Are They Different?" *Harvard Business Review,* 55, no. 3 (May–June 1977), 67–78.

Chapter 22

SIMON, HERBERT A., "On the Concept of Organizational Goal," *Administrative Science Quarterly,* 9, no. 1 (June 1964), 1–22.

Suggestions for Reading, Preparing, and Discussing a Case

SOME SIMPLE RULES

1 You must work effectively and efficiently. Quickly establish a purpose, then work selectively.

ESTABLISHING THE PURPOSE

2 Read the introductory section and decide what the case is about.
Write down:
a What you think the principal issues or problems are;
b What the significant trends are; and
c What you'd like to know, or need to know before deciding what to do.

This list should be the agenda for your subsequent work. Note: Trust your feelings and intuition; they are your experience at work. Use any preparation questions or assignments you may be given to focus your thinking. Use every clue.

MAINTAINING EFFICIENCY

3 *Next,* read the headings and subheadings and anticipate the content of each section. What should be there? Read the last section carefully and completely. Use this information to modify your initial agenda (See 2). Try to stick to one page. You'll be more effective if you are focused on the most important issues. Later, you can seek out surprises, unexpected omissions, and inconsistencies.

4 Next, scan the exhibits, tables, pictures, and maps:
  - **a** Why are they included?
  - **b** Which of your agenda items do they bear upon? Keep a record of where the data are (that is, write the page numbers next to your agenda items).
  - **c** What do the data mean?
  - **d** What questions do they raise?
  - **e** What choices or alternatives seem viable?

5 Try to stick to one or two pages. Reformulate your working hypotheses and determine what you *now* need to know—essentially, *synthesize* your work to date and set the agenda for your research.

WORKING SELECTIVELY LEADS TO EFFECTIVENESS

6 Return to the beginning again, this time *seeking data relevant* to your revised agenda:
  - **a** Section by section, focus on key sentences, but let your eyes wander;
  - **b** Make brief marginal notes on the case and maybe on your agenda sheet, recording relevant opinions, emphasizing facts, events, and inconsistencies as well as recording questions that you would like resolved.

Note: You're seeking not just facts, but *linkages* that point you towards the resolution of your personal case agenda. Hence, make marginal notes on the case to record your thinking so that you can recall it later—simple underlining will not help in this regard.

7 Collect the data relevant to critical items on your agenda. Use the analytical concepts and frameworks you know or are introduced to during the course to organize the data and to sharpen your understanding of the organization you are studying. At the same time you'll be testing the frameworks and concepts you know and your understanding of them.

REVIEW YOUR POSITION

8 Next, spend some time synthesizing your work again. What is your position on what the organization should do? What are the sources of doubt, uncertainty, or ambiguity?

9 If there is time, study the relevant sections and exhibits in detail to determine what you think about every issue you see as important. Focus on the most important issues. Take the time to specify your position in writing on the key issues, noting why. Take this final sheet to class or to your team or group or syndicate meeting.

GROUP WORK

10 In your group meeting, remember that not everyone will see the same patterns, and not everyone will see them at the same time. Except where the group has committed to a formal presentation of a group position, the purpose of the group is not to reach consensus (it is rarely possible to develop a consensus in an hour or so anyhow).

Focus first on the facts, on what they mean, on what the issues are—not on future actions. The group's purpose is to help each individual sharpen his or her perceptions and understanding of the case. Exposure to other people's thinking should widen your perspective. It should help you expand your inventory of analytical frameworks and develop new perspectives on business problems. The group is an opportunity to learn what helps others see things differently and allows you to test the relevance of your past experience to the matters at hand.

In particular, if you are the group discussion leader, you might consider the wisdom of summarizing the group discussion too finally or too quickly—it may inhibit further thinking in the group, and later in class. Use the group to develop ideas. Be aware that the group may not be effective if people use the group to defend their positions, if they don't listen to each other, or if the group moves to a solution too quickly.

CLASS WORK

11 In class, contribute to everyone's understanding of the situation by:

- **a** Presenting case data organized with some purpose in mind;
- **b** Probing the assumptions underlying someone else's analysis;
- **c** Offering specific proposals for action buttressed by considered evaluation;
- **d** Contributing relevant personal experience to help further the analysis;
- **e** Linking the issues at hand to earlier cases or readings and thereby contributing to the value of the course as a whole;
- **f** Thoughtfully playing the role of a case protagonist to heighten the administrative aspects of the case.

Remember, not every problem is worth solving. Focus on those that contribute to strategy implementation and the achievement of your (or the company's) objectives.

FOOD FOR THOUGHT

12 Essentially, case-based education and executive development depends on your desire *to get something out of it.* You have to decide what you want. For example, one critical administrative talent to which case studies contribute is the ability to ask the right questions and the flexibility to reformulate them so that someone less experienced can resolve them—if that is necessary or desirable.

13 To use more of the information available to you in your professional life and, thereby, lift the quality of your analysis, you have to face the need for change in yourself. Experience shows that people define problems quickly and narrowly, especially when they're under pressure. They tend to ignore what doesn't fit with the patterns they expected or are familiar with.

14 Can you use these cases to determine how you think and why, and where your blind spots are? Most people know when they have reached an impasse—they feel blocked. Use the cases to learn what blocks you—or, in other words, how you block yourself. Usually, people block when they define a problem too narrowly. Try to see things broadly. Be flexible.

15 Can you relinquish the security of your own well-defined (yet maybe unconscious) ways of addressing business situations and develop a new approach that works for you—thinking which allows for a greater recognition and acceptance of ambiguity, uncertainty, and choice—in which you will be responsible, not for wise decisions, but for results?

YELLOWTAIL MARINE, INC. (A)

"I wouldn't offer you a job like this unless I thought you had the ability to run the company and the guts to buy me out within seven years. You know how I've always made my money: turning rundown companies around by providing an opportunity to a talented manager who's wasting away inside some over-organized large corporation.

"Robyn, you've been with Sportscraft, Inc. for almost four years and you're years away from a top management job. This is a chance to do your own thing and end up with your own business—come aboard, eh?"

HOW THE SITUATION DEVELOPED

It was March 25, 1976. Charles Boswell, an alumnus of the same famous Californian business school attended by Robyn Gilcrist was trying to convince her to take a job as chief operating executive of Yellowtail Marine, a company Boswell had just bought. Boswell was president of CBG, Inc., a privately held venture capital firm which he had founded in 1964. Boswell's fortune was based on his ownership of the West Coast distributorship of a major earthmoving equipment company and he had prospered: first on highway construction and land boom in Southern California and more recently from his involvement with Alaskan oil development. However, he maintained that the challenge in his life was new ventures and turnarounds.

Boswell first met Robyn Gilcrist in 1967 when, as President of the American Water Skiing Association, he presented her with the national championship. As they became acquainted, Boswell learned that Robyn had graduated in the top 5% of her MBA class. During the next three years as Robyn continued to win national events, he had kept in touch with her and over the last few years he had followed her career at Sportscraft. She had started in the marine division in promotions and marketing where she had increased total sales by 70% in just two years. Her next assignment was as marketing director of the Winter Sports division (Boswell wondered whether Sportscraft knew the difference between "sea and ski"). More recently she had been Assistant to the President of Sportscraft and when Boswell had spoken with her in San Francisco, she had mentioned that she felt she was at a dead end and needed a more challenging position.

Boswell had offered her a job which would leave her as President of Yellowtail by May, 1977. Boswell had acquired Yellowtail from old Olaf Gunerson. Olaf himself was something of a legend in San Diego where his inboard and outboard boats with their distinctive yellow sterns could always be seen zipping about the harbor or bobbing up and down at their moorings looking as if they were raring to go.

As was his practice, Boswell had negotiated a deal which left the owner in place for twelve months while he took Board control. As always, he intended to bring a new professional manager in to work with the retiring owner and he had thought of Robyn

This case was prepared by Assistant Professor Kenneth J. Hatten as a basis for class discussion rather than to illustrate either effective or ineffective handling of an administrative situation.

Gilcrist. She had extensive marketing experience in the water sports industry and Boswell felt that Yellowtail would respond quickly if the company were made ''market''-oriented.

Thinking back on it, Robyn realized that what had swung the deal was Boswell's willingness to allow her to buy into the business: $65,000 plus a few generous fringe benefits and the rights to acquire up to 20% of the business over the next seven years, followed by the chance to increase her ownership to a controlling interest in year 10 if things worked out. It had seemed too good to be true.

Boswell had shown her Yellowtail's 1975 financial statements, *Exhibit 1,* and told her that the company needed work. He said that sales had slipped from just over $10 million in 1973 to about $8.4 million in 1975. The oil crisis and the 1974 recession had cut the boat industry's sales deeply. Although Gunerson was active, he was not, at seventy-three, up to turning the company around himself and wanted to retire. Boswell said he had already talked Gunerson into hiring a new advertising agency to beef up the company's sales in the 1976 summer. Happily, when Robyn accepted Boswell's offer, Gunerson and his wife had invited her to their home for a weekend and had held a dinner for her at the Green Dolphin Club where Olaf introduced her to most of Yellowtail's managers as his new Executive Vice President and heir-apparent.

Robyn had agreed to start work with Yellowtail on May 4, but on April 12, 1976 she had a telephone call from Boswell telling her that Gunerson had died of a heart attack. He had been out in his favorite Yellowtail ''Corsair,'' a high-speed game fishing boat, when he had collapsed. Boswell wondered whether she could start earlier. After a call to Sportcraft's president she agreed to start on April 14.

Boswell thanked her and said that he would appreciate it if she could get to the plant, deal with whatever needed doing, fly to San Francisco for a Board meeting that same afternoon and then return with him and his wife to Olaf's funeral on April 15. Boswell mentioned that after the funeral he would be flying to the Middle East for about ten days. He said that if she could manage it he would like to see some kind of preliminary strategic plan for Yellowtail before he left. That way she could have about fourteen days to work on it and develop a budget for Board approval.

YELLOWTAIL MARINE

Yellowtail Marine was founded in 1926 by Olaf Gunerson when he acquired the White Bay Boatyard. Gunerson, who had been trained as a naval architect initially offered a two-model line: a cabin cruiser and a game fishing boat. His choice was fortunate. First because he met with almost instant success, secondly because his boats appealed to the small segment of the West Coast population who had money to spend through the 1930s; and finally, because a special version of his game fishing boat was used by police departments, the IRS and customs agents, and the military.

When the U.S. entered the war in 1941, Yellowtail Marine was one of the firms selected to produce offshore patrol boats, naval launches and a few other small craft. Because of its strategic task, Yellowtail Marine was able to maintain its place as a small boat builder and in fact the company's products became widely known. Many servicemen had used Yellowtails by the war's end.

During the 1950s, Gunerson sought materials that would allow some measure of automation in the boat building industry. He was one of the first to use fiberglass in pleasure craft and a pioneer in extensively using foam to improve the flotation, a characteristic of Yellowtails which later became an important selling point.

In 1975, the company was predominantly serving the West Coast and the Rocky Mountain region and offered a wide range of fiberglass and wooden craft beginning at 14 feet and ending at 40 feet long. The smaller boats up to 26 feet in length were primarily outboard boats which retailed at $100 to $275 per foot, placing them in the medium- to high-priced segments of the market, as *Exhibit 2* indicates. About 64% of the boats the company produced were outboards. About 35% were inboard/outboard boats selling for about $8,500 and the rest were customized or special-order craft between 26 and 40 feet long selling for between $800 and $1,400 per foot. These boats were primarily game fishing boats, the "Corsair," or an adaptation of the Corsair design for police or military use. Gunerson had deliberately fought to preserve a niche in these last two markets because he felt they had saved the company through the Depression and World War II. In 1975, he stated that the game and police boats were the only products that had increased sales since 1973. Yellowtail sold about 1,600 boats and employed 235 people in 1975.

Yellowtail was simply organized on a functional basis by Olaf Gunerson after World War II. The major functional areas in April, 1976, were: Boatyard, the production center, under the leadership of Robert McPhail, who was fifty-seven years old and who had been with the company for twenty-three years; Financial Control and Personnel, Mark Lopez, a CPA who was fifty-nine years old and who had fifteen years with Yellowtail; and Marketing under Paul Lees, who had been with the firm four years. He was thirty-six years old and had been the sales manager of one of Yellowtail's dealers before he joined the company.

WALKING IN AS PRESIDENT

When Robyn Gilcrist got to Yellowtail's boatyard, where the company's office was located, she realized that it was already 8:15 a.m. and her plane to San Francisco left at 11:30 a.m. She had only 2 hours or perhaps a little more before she would have to leave.

She entered Gunerson's office, picked up his in-basket and took it into the office Olaf had set up for her. She felt it would be better to leave Olaf's office free until his personal effects had been returned to his wife. Then she went to work.

THE PLEASURE BOAT INDUSTRY

The pleasure boat industry[1] serves almost one quarter of the U.S. population. There are the yacht owners who are insulated from the effects of the economic cycle and who cheerfully pay $150,000 to $300,000 and more for cabin cruisers and racing yachts; the

[1]Frost and Sullivan, *The Pleasure Boat and Boat Equipment Market,* (New York: Frost and Sullivan, Inc., June 1974) is a useful reference on this industry.

$40,000-a-year middle-income families who aspire to the same fare but feel the pinch of hard times; and those with less who enjoy boating but probably feel the pinch most of the time.

The industry is large with 1975 sales estimated at $4.8 billion encompassing new and used equipment, services, insurance, mooring and launching fees, repairs and boat club memberships. Across the country, *Boating Industry* claims almost 50 million participated in recreational boating more than once or twice during 1975. Twelve million people went water skiing, 34 million went fishing, 4 million went skin- and scuba-diving and almost 10 million pleasure craft of all types and sizes plied U.S. waters. Sixteen thousand boating dealers and 6,000 marinas, boatyards and yacht clubs served the needs of boating families. Retail sales increased from about $2.6 billion in 1964 to almost $4.8 billion in 1975.[2]

Although the industry's dollar sales increased, 1974 and 1975 were marred by a turndown in units sold (across the board). Inflation was a major factor in the industry's dollar growth as builders and manufacturers passed on their costs in an effort to maintain profit levels. Fortunately for the industry, used boat sales were brisk and used boat prices benefited from the increased cost of new equipment.

> The continued high sales value of used boats, dealers agree, has loosened bankers' attitudes towards boat financing. "The collateral," one dealer notes, "is good." So apparently are the repayment habits of weekend sailors. Says a boat financing specialist for Seattle's Washington Mutual Savings Bank, which now advertises 10½% loans to boat buyers. "We have never had a repossessed boat and have hardly ever had a delinquency."[3]

The pleasure boat industry has historically been a craft industry, regionally-based because of the high cost of transporting boats overland, and cyclical. At least until now it has been an easy business to enter because of its traditional labor-intensive nature.[4]

The industry is changing, however, partly because of the development of new materials, which lend themselves to semi-automated and automated production processes—e.g. aluminum and fiberglass—and partly because of the investments of larger well-capitalized corporations in the industry.[5] In the late 1960s and early 1970s a number of well-known boat firms were acquired by or merged with larger companies. *Exhibit 3* suggests the extent to which the industry has changed. Only five of the twenty largest firms are independent.

The merger and acquisition activity was prompted by the industry's steady growth

[2]*Boating Industry,* January, 1976.

[3]*Business Week,* July 28, 1975, p. 17.

[4]In 1973/74 it was estimated that there were about 1,600 boat builders and manufacturers in the U.S. Eighty-two percent had less than 20 employees and more than 900 had between 1 and 4 employees. *Chemical Market Reporter,* July 20, 1974.

[5]Some large corporations, e.g. Chris-Craft, have set up regionally-based plants around and across the country.

through the 1960s and early 1970s. But the oil crisis in 1973 and the recession of 1974 and 1975 led to a shakeout. *Exhibit 4* shows how some raw materials prices changed over the period. Large and small firms were all affected but it seems likely that many small firms will not survive. It has been estimated that outboard boat sales fell by almost 40% between 1973 and 1975. Boat trailer sales fell by about 25% in the same period and outboard motor sales fell by almost 20%.

In 1976, it is expected that the industry will begin to grow again (*Exhibit 5*). It may be in a different direction, however. The energy crisis gave an impetus to sailing over power boating. In fact, in 1975 only sailboats[6] and boats costing more than $45,000 gained sales. This has led some experts to predict that the sailing segment of the boating industry will grow at a rate between 15% and 20% through the remainder of the 1970s. However, they see much of this growth coming in the low-priced end of the market which is dominated by Snark with its foam sailers.

Other changes are affecting the sailboat market as the following quote suggests:

> If you're a sailor, you can listen open-mouthed to some of the cruise adventures young couples have these days: bumbling breathlessly and laughingly about getting underway while the "blue blazers" gape; stopping in the most improbable places . . . . To a traditional cruiser it all sounds a bit superficial and over-romanticized.
>
> But if you're a sailing dealer and you expect to reach the new, young buying couples—the folks with money in their jeans and willingness to spend it on the outdoor life, the "freedom" sports—you better try to dig it.

Dealers seem to be recognizing a non-traditional, non-nautical market of non-expert but affluent sailors who are more interested in comfort, wall-to-wall stereo, and gourmet galleys than in sailing performance. These people are not interested in the organized club life of the yacht club but want hassle-free cruising. One type of sailboat that seems to appeal to this market is the trailer sailer.

Trailer sailers are normally 20 to 26 feet long and allow almost continental mobility–something few other liveable boats offer. They cut maintenance costs considerably because the boat can be kept out of the water when not in use and as *Exhibit 6* suggests, day-to-day storage costs can be substantial. Sales of trailerable boats slipped during the energy crisis but are expected to pick up in the last half of the 1970s.

The power boat segment of the industry is expected to resume growth as its historical rate or, perhaps, a little better. The experts are more confident of their predictions that among the companies which will survive will be the more adequately capitalized firms which have the ability to widen their distribution systems and sustain volume production. At present this suggests that the power boat segment of the industry will be split into two quite different businesses. Boats larger than 26 feet will be at least partially hand-built and virtually customized. Boats below 26 feet will be semi-automatically or automatically produced.

[6]The four most popular product classes have about equal dollar sales. Foam sailers sell for between $100 and $150; multiple hulls generally sell in the $1000 to $3000 range; sailboats range from $1400 to $7500 or more; and day sailers run up to $5000 or $6000. Shipped value, 1975, was about $44 million.

In the under-26 feet segment, manufacturers will have to continue to fight for uniqueness because new designs can be easily imitated. It may be that, like the auto industry, annual model changes will be more widely adopted—as a defensive as well as an aggressive strategy.

Males are thought to dominate most boat purchase decisions, certainly in the traditional markets. Surveys suggest that the typical male boat user is afloat at least twice the time the typical female boat user is. The outboard market is described in *Exhibits 7* and *8*. The sailing market seems to be different if the profile of the typical reader of *Yachting* and similar magazines is coincident with the profile of the typical sailboat buyer: mostly college-educated and in the growing 25–44 age bracket. However, there is a substantial readership in the 55–65 age bracket. Most readers are interested in sailing as a recreational activity and, consistent with this theme, it is reported that most boat sales are made on weekends between 10 a.m. and 3 p.m.

Aside from sales and manufacturing problems, the boating industry has other problems. Its executives often feel beset by governmental regulations. The Boat Safety Act of 1971 requires boat manufacturers to keep records of their compliance efforts. The EPA and OSHA have had an effect. Motor boat noise levels are being reduced under government pressure. The Clean Water legislation impacts boat sanitation systems, and the chemicals used in boat manufacturing have been found harmful to workers.

Among the problems facing the industry in 1976 was a shortage of marinas and service centers. To be successful, a marina has to be located in a heavily populated area. In these areas real estate values are high, especially when beach frontage is involved. One response has been the ''dry land'' marina, but many boat owners have to have waterside service. Brand turnover is rising as dealers and original equipment manufacturers (OEM's) jockey for relative bargaining power and return on investment. As the industry entered its major selling season in 1976 dealers were conservative about the industry's sales prospects and OEM orders were slow. In the case of boat sales, dealer conservatism could be due to the problems of trade-ins. In 1975, about 46% of all new boat sales involved a trade-in. Concerning service, *Exhibit 9* details the types of service provided by a number of Massachusetts marinas.

AT THE PRESIDENT'S DESK

Robyn Gilcrist was eager to confirm Mr. Boswell's high opinion of her. She had to deal with what Olaf had left, whatever had come up since, and the tasks Boswell had given her.

Because she was acting under a time constraint, Robyn decided to be specific and write the letters she needed to write, to make notes to herself and others as necessary. She liked to plan every action and clarify its purpose: What was to be done, by whom and when? There might be other factors which seemed important, if so she would be specific with respect to them. She decided to even write out the substance of any phone calls she made, and to plan her movements if she had to leave San Diego.

IN-BASKET

April 13, 1975

Ms. Gilcrist
President

Dear Ms. Gilcrist:

Normally we plan our show dates about 12 months ahead. This year we are running late. Which shows do you want us to participate in? I have attached a list of major shows from February through September.

Sincerely,

Paul Lees
Marketing Manager

PL/wm

Attachment: Boat Show Calendar

* * * * * *

Boat Show Calendar

1977

FEBRUARY 27 TO MARCH 7, MONTREAL, QUEBEC, CANADA—Salon Nautique '76. Place Bonaventure; 12 Noon to 10:30 p.m. Daily; sponsored by Allied Boating Association of Canada; produced by P. R. Charette, Inc.; managed by P. R. Charette. 5890 Monkland Avenue, Suite 306, Montreal, Quebec, Canada; (514) 489- 8671.
FEBRUARY 27 TO MARCH 7, STOCKHOLM, SWEDEN—Stockholm International Boat Show, Stockholm International Fairs & Activity Centre, Alvsjo, Stockholm; Weekdays 12 Noon to 9 p.m.; Weekends 10 a.m. to 8 p.m.; sponsored by Swedish Boating Industries Associations (SWE-BOAT); produced by AB S:t Eriks-Massan; managed by Bengt R. Hult, AB S:t Eriks-Massan, S-106, 80 Stockholm, Sweden; (08) 99-01-00.
FEBRUARY 27 TO MARCH 7, MINNEAPOLIS, MINNESOTA—Northtown Boat Show, Northtown Shopping Center; Daily 10 a.m. to 9:30 p.m., Saturday 9:30 a.m. to 6 p.m., Sunday 12 Noon to 5 p.m.; sponsored by Northtown Merchants Association; managed by Gayle Niendorf, 398 Northtown Drive, Minneapolis, MN; (612) 786-9704.
FEBRUARY 27 TO MARCH 7, VANCOUVER, BRITISH COLUMBIA, CANADA—Vancouver Boat & Sport Show, Exhibition Park; Dealer Day February 23 9 a.m. to 2 p.m., Public Days: opening Friday 6 p.m. to 10 p.m., Saturdays 2 p.m. to 10 p.m., Sundays 2 p.m. to 6 p.m., Weekdays 2 p.m. to 10 p.m.; sponsored by Marine Trades Association of British Columbia; produced by Harmon O Loughlin Enterprises, Ltd.; managed by Robert O Loughlin, P.O. Box 69067, Vancouver, B.C. Canada V5K 4W3; (604) 291-6651.
FEBRUARY 28 to MARCH 7, BERLIN, GERMANY—Boat, Sports & Recreation Exhibition Berlin, Berlin Exhibition Grounds at Radio Tower; Daily from 10 a.m. to 7 p.m.; produced by AMK Berlin, Company for Exhibitions, Fairs & Congresses, D 1000 Berlin 19, Messedamm 2, Berlin, Germany; (030) 3038-1.
MARCH 2 TO 7, DENVER, COLORADO—19Th Annual Colorado Sport, Boat & Travel Show. Denver Coliseum Complex; Weekdays 6 p.m. to 11 p.m., Saturday 12 Noon to 11 p.m.; Sunday 12 Noon to 6 p.m., produced by Industrial Expositions, Inc.; managed by Dick Haughton, P.O. Box 12297. Denver, CO 80212; (303) 477- 5994.
MARCH 3 TO MARCH 7, NEW HAVEN, CONNECTICUT—New Haven Boat Show, Goffe Street Armory; Weekdays 2 p.m. to 10 p.m., Saturday 10 a.m. to 10 p.m., Sunday 12 Noon to 7 p.m.; produced by New Haven Boat Show, Inc.; managed by Arthur Vreeland, 148 Cove Street, New Haven, CT 06512; (203) 467-6505.
MARCH 3 TO 7, ROCK ISLAND, ILLINOIS—Quad Cities Boat, Sports & Travel Show, Rock Island Armory; Weekdays 5 p.m. to 11 p.m., Saturday 12 Noon to 11 p.m., Sunday 12 Noon to 8 p.m.; produced by Cenaiko Productions, Inc.; managed by Dean Sherman, 1212 98th Lane, N.W., Minneapolis, MN 55433, (612) 427-4850.
MARCH 5 TO 14, ARLINGTON HEIGHTS, ILLINOIS—Midwest Boat Show, Arlington Heights Exhibition Center; Weekdays 6 p.m. to 10 p.m., Saturdays 12 Noon to 10 p.m., Sundays 12 Noon to 7 p.m.; managed by Edward P. Hansen, Box 426, McHenry, IL 60050; (815) 385-1560.
MARCH 6 TO 14, ANAHEIM, CALIFORNIA—Western National Boat Show & Marine Show, Anaheim Convention Center, Weekdays 3 p.m. to 10 p.m., Saturdays 12 Noon to 10:30 p.m., Sundays 12 Noon to 7:30 p.m.; produced by H. Werner Buck Enterprises; managed by H. Werner Buck, 1050 Georgia Street, Los Angeles, CA 90015; (213) 749-9331.
MARCH 6 TO 14, NIAGARA FALLS, NEW YORK—Western New York Boat Show, Niagara Falls International Convention Center, sponsored by The Marine Trades Association of Western New York; produced by Creative Mall Promotions, Inc.; managed by Jay Silberman, 800 Kings Highway North, Cherry Hill, NJ 08034; (609) 667-9110.
MARCH 7 TO 10, BOISE, IDAHO—Idaho State Boat, Sport, Recreational Vehicle Show, West Idaho Fairgrounds; 2 p.m. to 10 p.m. Daily, produced by Spectra Productions; managed by Doug Fitzgerald, P.O. Box 1308. Boise, ID 83701; (208) 345-0146.
MARCH 7 TO 14, DALLAS, TEXAS—Southwest Sports, Boat, Camping & Vacation Show, Dallas Memorial Auditorium & Convention Center; Weekdays 6 p.m. to 10:30 p.m., Saturday 12 Noon to 10:30 p.m., Sunday 12 Noon to 7 p.m.; sponsored by The Dallas Morning News; managed by William H. Brown, Suite 166. 11424 Woodmeadow Parkway, Dallas, TX 75228; (214) 270-5129.
MARCH 9 TO 14, SALT LAKE CITY, UTAH—Utah Boat, Sports & Travel Show, Salt Palace; Weekdays 5 p.m. to 10:30 p.m., Weekends 12 Noon to 10:30 p.m.; produced by Edward Greenband Enterprises, 6868 North 7th Avenue, Phoenix, AZ 85013; (602) 277-4748.
MARCH 12 TO 21, AMSTERDAM, THE NETHERLANDS—International Boat Show HISWA '76, RAI Exhibition Centre opening hours 10 a.m. to 5 p.m. & 7 p.m. to 10 p.m., Saturday and Sunday 10 a.m. to 5 p.m.; sponsored by HISWA; produced by RAI Gebouw B.V.; managed by J. H. Sijdzes. RAI Gebouw B.V., Europaplein 8, Amsterdam, Telephone 020- 5411411; Telex 16017.
MARCH 10 TO 14, SAN DIEGO, CALIFORNIA—National Marine Distributors Association Annual Convention, Hotel Del Coronado; sponsored by NMDA; managed by Ms. Elizabeth A. Kelly, NMDA, 2017 Walnut Street, Philadelphia, PA 19103; (215) LO 9-3650.
MARCH 10 TO 14, EDMONTON, ALBERTA, CANADA—Edmonton Boat, Trailer & Sport Show, Coliseum & Gardens; Wednesday & Thursday 6 p.m. to 10:30 p.m., Friday & Saturday 1 p.m. to 10:30 p.m., Sunday 1 p.m. to 6 p.m.; sponsored by Marine Trades Association of Alberta, produced by Harmon O'Loughlin Enterprises, Ltd.; managed by Robert O'Loughlin, P.O. Box 69067, Vancouver, British Columbia V5K 4W3; (604) 291-6651.
MARCH 10 TO 14, MORRISTOWN, NEW JERSEY—Central New Jersey Sports, Boat & Camping Show, Armory; Daily 1 p.m. to 10 p.m. except Sunday 12 Noon to 6 p.m.; produced by Pocono Promotions; managed by Walter E. Murray, 102 Miner St., Hudson, PA; (717) 824-6008.
MARCH 11 TO 14, ROCHESTER, NEW YORK—Finger Lakes Boat Show, Dome Arena; Weekdays 3 p.m. to 10 p.m., Saturday 12 Noon to 10 p.m., Sunday 12 Noon to 9 p.m.; sponsored by Finger Lakes Marine Dealers; produced by S & S Productions; managed by C. Marshall Seager, City Pier, Canadaigua, NY 14424; (315) 3941372.
MARCH 13 TO 21, BRUSSELS, BELGIUM—Salon Des Vacances; Palais Du Centenaire-Heysel; 10 a.m. to 7 p.m. daily; produced by Salon Des Vacances, 345 Avenue Charles Quint, Keizer Karellaan, 345 Bruxelles 1080, Brussels, Belgium; (02) 466-1514.
MARCH 12 TO 21, MILWAUKEE, WISCONSIN—Milwaukee Sentinel Sports, Travel & Boat Show, Mecca Convention Center & Auditorium; Friday 6 p.m. to 11 p.m., Daily 1 p.m. to 11 p.m., Sunday 1 p.m. to 6 p.m.; produced by The Milwaukee Sentinel; managed by George Schansberg, 914 North 4th Street, Milwaukee, WI 53201; (414) 224-2427.
MARCH 17 TO 21, NEWPORT BEACH, CALIFORNIA—Newport Harbor Sailboat Show, Lido Village Marina; Opening day 11 a.m. to 2 p.m. trade, public 2 p.m. to 7 p.m.; Thursday 11 a.m. to 7 p.m.; Friday & Saturday 11 a.m. to 7 p.m.; Sunday 11 a.m. to 6 p.m.; produced by Dnncan McIntosh Co.; managed by Duncan McIntosh, 3424 Via Oporto, Suite 202, Newport Beach, CA 92663; (714) 673-4231.
MARCH 19 TO 21, WHITE PLAINS, NEW YORK—Westchester Boat, Sport & Camping Show, Westchester County Center; Friday 1 p.m. to 11 p.m., Saturday 11 a.m. to 11 p.m., Sunday 12 Noon to 9 p.m.; produced by Annual Enterprises, Inc.; managed by Edward L. Ceccolini, Box 122, Eastchester, NY 10709; (914) SC 5-3371.
MARCH 19 TO 28, CLEVELAND, OHIO—American & Canadian Sportsmen's Vacation & Boat Show, Cleveland Public Hall, East Sixth & Lakeside, Saturdays 11 a.m. to 11 p.m., Sunday 11 a.m. to 10:30 p.m. (closing Sunday 11 a.m. to 8:30 p.m.). Opening Friday 4 p.m. to 11 p.m., Wednesday and Thursday 1 p.m. to 11 p.m. all other days 4 p.m. to 11 p.m.; produced by Expositions, Inc.; managed by David M. Fassnacht & Betty Friedlander, 314 Lincoln Building, Cleveland, OH; (216) 771-3677.
MARCH 19 TO 28, TORONTO, CANADA—Canadian National Sportsmen's Show. Coliseum-Exhibition Place; Weekdays 12 Noon to 11 p.m., Saturdays 10 a.m. to 11 p.m., Sunday 1 p.m. to 9 p.m.; sponsored by Toronto Anglers & Hunters Association; produced by Canadian National Sportsmen's Show; managed by Harold D. Shield, Box 168, Toronto-Dominion Centre, Toronto M5K 1H8, Ontario, Canada; (416) 366-6518.
MARCH 23 TO MARCH 28, DES MOINES, IOWA—Iowa Sports, Boat, Camping & Vacation Show, Veterans Memorial Auditorium; Tuesday through Thursday 4 p.m. to 11 p.m., Friday 12 Noon to 11 p.m., Saturday 10 a.m. to 11 p.m., Sunday 11 a.m. to 6:30 p.m.; sponsored by The Desmoines Register & Tribune; produced by United Sports & Vacation Shows; managed by Ms. Joan Kelly, First National Bank Building, St. Paul, MN 55101; (612) 222-8695.
MARCH 24 TO 28, TOLEDO, OHIO—Boat Show, Southwyck Mall; Daily 10 a.m. to 9 p.m.; sponsored and produced by Toledo Marine Dealers Association, P.O. Box 8315. Toledo, OH 43605.
MARCH 24 TO 28, NEWPORT BEACH, CALIFORNIA—Newport Harbor Powerboat Show, Lido Village Marina; Opening day 11 a.m. to 2 p.m., trade, public 2 p.m. to 7 p.m., Thursday 11 a.m. to 7 p.m., Friday & Saturday 11 a.m. to 9 p.m., Sunday 11 a.m. to 6 p.m.; produced by Duncan McIntosh Co.; managed by Duncan McIntosh, 3424 Via Oporto, Suite 202, Newport Beach, CA 92663; (714) 673-4231.
MARCH 25 to 28, SIOUX FALLS, SOUTH DAKOTA—Sioux Empire Boat, Sports, Camping & Vacation Show, Sioux Falls Arena, Weekdays 5 p.m., to 11 p.m., Saturday 12 Noon to 11 p.m., Sunday 12 Noon to 8 p.m.; sponsored by Sioux Falls Cosmopolitan Club, produced by Cenaiko Productions, Inc.; managed by Dean Sherman, 1212 98th Lane N.W., Minneapolis, NN 55433; (612) 427-4850.
MARCH 26 TO 28, EVANSVILLE, INDIANA—Tri State Boat & Sport Show, Roberts Municipal Stadium; Friday 6 p.m. to 10 p.m., Saturday & Sunday 12 Noon to 10 p.m.; sponsored by the Outboard Boating Club of Evansville; managed by Dixie Herendeen, P.O. Box 471, Evansville, IN 47703; (812) 477-6177.
MARCH 26 TO 28, WILMINGTON, NORTH CAROLINA—Second Annual Lower Cape Fear Boat Show, Long Leaf Shopping Mall; Friday & Saturday 12 Noon to 9 p.m., Sunday 12 Noon to 6 p.m.; sponsored by the Azalea Coast Marine Dealers Association; managed by Norman Phillips. Route 4, Box 496 M, Wilmington, NC 28401; (919) 686-0070.
MARCH 26 TO APRIL 4, MINNEAPOLIS, MINNESOTA—Northwest Sports Show, Auditorium & Convention Hall; Opening Friday 6 p.m. to 11 p.m.,

Calendar (*Cont.*)

Weekdays 1 p.m. to 11 p.m., Saturday 12 Noon to 8 p.m., Sunday 12 Noon to 8 p.m.; sponsored by North Central Marine Association; produced by General Sports Shows, Inc.; managed by Philip D. Perkins, 3539 Hennepin Avenue South, Minneapolis, MN 55408; (612) 827-5833.

MARCH 26 TO APRIL 4, OSLO, NORWAY—The Sea For All, The Sjolyst Centre & Harbor at Frognerstranda; Opening day 12 Noon to 9 p.m., Saturday 10 a.m. to 8 p.m., Sunday 1 p.m. to 9 p.m., other days 12 noon to 9 p.m.; produced by The Norwegian International Boat & Engine Exhibition; managed by Gerhard Wiese; Sjoen For Alle, Informasjonst Jenesten, Boks 130, Skoyen, Oslo 2, Norway; (02) 55-37-90; Telex 18748 Messe N.

MARCH 31 TO APRIL 4, WINNIPEG, MANITOBA, CANADA—Winnipeg Boat & Sport Show, Winnipeg Convention Centre; Wednesday & Thursday 6 p.m. to 10:30 p.m., Friday & Saturday 1 p.m. to 10:30 p.m., Sunday 1 p.m. to 6 p.m.; produced by Harmon O'Loughlin Enterprises, Ltd., P.O. Box 101, St. James Postal Station, Winnipeg, Manitoba, Canada R3J OH4; (204) 774-7406.

APRIL 1 TO 4, GRAND FORKS, NORTH DAKOTA—Grand Forks Boat, Sports, Camping & Vacation Show, University Field House; Weekdays 5 p.m. to 11 p.m., Saturdays 12 Noon to 11 p.m., Sundays 12 Noon to 8 p.m.; sponsored by Grand Forks Kiwanis Club, produced by Cenaiko Productions, Inc.; managed by Nick Cenaiko; 1212 98th Lane, N.W., Minneapolis, MN 55433; (612) 427-4850.

APRIL 7 TO 11, MADISON, WISCONSIN—Madison Sports, Boat & Home Shows, Dane County Exposition Center, Weekdays 4 p.m. to 11 p.m., Saturday 1 p.m. to 11 p.m., Sunday 1 p.m. to 6 p.m.; produced by Shows Plus 3, Inc.; managed by Tom Johnson, 2825 North Mayfair Road, Milwaukee, WI 53222; (414) 258-6350.

APRIL 8 TO 11, FARGO, NORTH DAKOTA—Red River Boat, Sports, Camping & Vacation Show, University Field House, Weekdays 5 p.m. to 11 p.m., Saturday 12 Noon to 11 p.m., Sundays 12 Noon to 8 p.m.; sponsored by Lake Agassiz Kiwanis Club, produced by Cenaiko Productions, Inc., managed by Dean Sherman, 1212 98th Lane, N.W., Minneapolis, MN 55433; (612) 427-4850.

APRL 27 TO 30, LONDON, ENGLAND—International Marine Exhibition (IMEX). Earls Court, London; 10 a.m. to 6 p.m. Daily; sponsored by The British Marine Equipment Council, produced by Brintex Exhibitions, Ltd.; managed by Capt. Frank Harrison, 178-202 Great Portland St., London W1N 6NH, England; (01) 637-2400.

APRIL 29 TO MAY 2, BALTIMORE, MARYLAND—Baltimore Inner Harbor Boat Show, Baltimore Inner Harbor; 12 Noon to 9 p.m. Daily; produced by Exhibitors, Inc.; managed by James K. Donahue, 2 E. Read St., Suite 407, Baltimore, MD 21202; (301) 837-8388.

APRIL 30 TO MAY 2, GALESVILLE, MARYLAND—Chesapeake Bay Yacht Bazaar, West River Marina; 10 a.m. to 6 p.m.; produced by Yankee Boat Peddlers; managed by Don C. Glassie, 259 Water St., Warren, RI 02885; (401) 245-6188.

APRIL 30 TO MAY 2, POINT PLEASANT, NEW JERSEY—Marine Expo '76, King's Grant Inn; 12 Noon to 7 p.m. Daily; sponsored and produced by Marine Trades Association of New Jersey; managed by Michael Redpath, P.O. Box 210, Island Heights, NJ 08732; (201) 244-4440.

MAY 21 TO 31, SAN JOSE, CALIFORNIA—California Recreational Vehicle & Boat Show, Santa Clara County Fairgrounds; Weekdays 5 p.m. to 11 p.m., Saturdays 12 Noon to 11 p.m., Sundays 12 Noon to 9 p.m., Memorial Day 12 Noon to 9 p.m.; produced by George Colouris Productions; managed by George Colouris c/o Santa Clara County Fairgrounds, 344 Tully Rd., San Jose, CA 95112; (408) 286-8330.

JUNE 4 TO 6, NEWPORT, RHODE ISLAND—The Newport Yacht Bazaar, The Treadway Inn on Newport Waterfront; 10 a.m. to 6 p.m. Daily; produced by Yankee Boat Peddlers, managed by Don C. Glassie, 259 Water St. Warren, RI 02885; (401) 245-6188.

JUNE 5 TO 7, NEWPORT, RHODE ISLAND—Newport Yacht Bazaar, Newport Harbor Treadway Inn; Daily 10 a.m. to 6 p.m.; sponsored and produced by Yankee Boat Peddlers; managed by Don C. Glassie, Jr., 9 Riverside Drive, Barrington, RI 02806; (401) 245-1054.

JUNE 15 TO 19, HILTON HEAD ISLAND, SOUTH CAROLINA—Boating Industry Association Summer Symposium, Hilton Head Inn; sponsored by Boating Industry Associations; managed by Matt Kaufman, 401 North Michigan Ave., Chicago, IL 60611; (312) 329-0590.

JULY 9 TO 11, MADISON, WISCONSIN—Madison Dealers Boat Show, Dane County Exposition Center, Sunday 4 p.m. to 11 p.m., Monday 11 a.m. to 11 p.m., Tuesday 11 a.m. to 6 p.m.; sponsored by Madison Marine Dealers Association; produced by Tom Johnson, Inc., managed by Tom Johnson, 2825 N. Mayfair Rd., Milwaukee, WI 53222; (414) 258-6350.

JULY 30 TO AUGUST 1, DALLAS, TEXAS—AFTMA Annual Trade Show, Dallas Convention Center; 9 a.m. to 5 p.m. Daily; sponsored and produced by the American Fishing Tackle Manufacturers Association, 20 North Wacker Drive, Chicago, IL 60606; (312) 236-0565.

SEPTEMBER 15 TO 19, GLOUCESTER, MASSACHUSETTS—The New England In The Water Sail & Power Boat Show, Cape Ann Marina; Trade Day September 15 12 Noon to 5 p.m., September 16 to 19 10 a.m. to 7 p.m. Daily; produced by Boating Expositions, managed by Gerald A. Milden, 325 Harvard St., Brookline, MA 02146; (617) 734-6972.

SEPTEMBER 16 TO 19, TORONTO, ONTARIO, CANADA—Dockside '76, Ontario Place; 11 a.m. to 9 p.m. Daily; sponsored by Allied Boating Association of Canada; produced by Canadian National Sportsmen's Show; managed by Harold D. Shield, Box 168, Toronto-Dominion Centre, Toronto, Canada; (416) 366-6518.

SEPTEMBER 22 TO 26, OAKLAND, CALIFORNIA—Boat Show '76, Oakland Alameda Coliseum; Weekdays 2 p.m. to 11 p.m., Weekends 10 a.m. to 11 p.m.; sponsored and produced by the Northern California Marine Association; managed by Neil Turner, 16032 Hesperian Blvd., San Lorenzo, CA 94580; (415) 278-2558.

SEPTEMBER 22 TO 26, PHILADELPHIA, PENNSYLVANIA—America's International In-Water Boat Show, Penn's Landing; produced by Leisure Expositions; managed by Paul Rimmeir, 108 Market St., Philadelphia, PA 19106; (215) MA7- 4412.

SEPTEMBER 23 TO 26, NEWPORT, RHODE ISLAND—Newport International Sailboat Show, Fort Adams State Park; Thursday (trade day) 10 a.m. to 6 p.m., Friday & Saturday 10 a.m. to 7 p.m., Sunday 10 a.m., to 6p.m.; produced by Newport International Sailboat Show, Inc.; managed by Paul Dodson, 431 Thames St., Newport, RI 02840; (401) 846-1600.

SEPTEMBER 29 TO OCTOBER 3, STAMFORD, CONNECTICUT—North Atlantic Boat Show, Yacht Haven West; September 29 (trade day) 10 a.m. to 6 p.m., September 30 to October 3 10 a.m. to 7 p.m.; produced by The In The Water Boat Shows, P.O. Box 1631, Annapolis, MD 21404; (301) 268-8828.

SEPTEMBER 30 TO OCTOBER 3, CHICAGO, ILLINOIS—Marine Trades Exhibit & Conference, McCormick Place; Weekdays 10 a.m. to 6 p.m.; Weekdays 9 a.m. to 6 p.m.; sponsored by Boating Industry Associations; produced by International Marine Expositions, Inc.; managed by John Dobbertin, 401 North Michigan Ave., Chicago, IL 60611; (312) 644-9000.

April 13, 1976

Ms. Gilcrist
President
Yellowtail, Inc.

Dear Ms. Gilcrist,

Mrs. Naumes, who was Mr. Gunderson's secretary, is very upset and will not be in for a few days. I'll try to help out where I can.

Cordially,

Sarah Clarke

Sarah Clarke

April 13, 1976

Ms. Robyn Gilcrist
President
Robyn:

Welcome to Yellowtail. Sorry you have to start without Olaf.

Finish off the stuff Olaf left and fly to Miami to meet Stewart Marschal. He is a large dealer for Chris Craft in Florida. He is unhappy with the way they are dealing with him and may switch to us. Forget San Francisco but get back to San Diego for the funeral.

Let me have your ideas on Yellowtail's strategy before the funeral. We can go over it then and you'll have plenty of time to get set for the Board meeting on April 29.

Good luck,

Boz

Charles Boswell

CB:lhd

* * * * * *

YELLOWTAIL MARINE, INC.

April 14, 1976
8:27 a.m.

NOTE: Telephone call. Charlie Douglas, Yard Foreman.

. . . real glad I'm here . . . met at Gunerson's club and . . . plant . . . problem in the yard. Mr. McPhail (the yard manager) on vacation one more week . . . can't afford to wait . . . trouble . . . Outboard plant where space between the inner and outer skins filled . . . two foam injection units . . . one acting up . . . odd . . . new high pressure unit . . . first time trouble. Usually old one . . . problem hard to pin down . . . getting nine times normal number of air pockets in the hulls . . . only way to fix them . . . by hand. . . drill through the fiberglass skins and fill hole, then patch and smooth skin. Normally, one part-time man but now . . . have to stop production to fix boats already made . . . not sure whether it's injectors or men causing problem . . . McPhail fired Bob Lewis . . . with us 8 years. Last week *his* brother, Mike . . . works on foam injection was complaining . . . saying he would show us a thing or two one day . . . thinks men upset about Bob Lewis . . . knows he and McPhail . . . sharp words . . . number of occasions (lately) . . . never had sabotage here Mike Lawson, Personnel Manager, said . . . that's what he thinks. Jack Patterson . . . shop steward, says men aren't doing it . . . doesn't want to push . . . always been straight but election soon . . . Lawson suspects trouble. Kendall, the organizer of the Boatyard Carpenters and Painters . . . here on Thursday, April 15 . . . lives in San Diego . . . always stops here on the third Thursday of the month on way back from Los Angeles . . . thought might have been the new foam, but both injectors using it . . . old one not having any trouble . . . not sure what to do next . . . needs help.

* * * * * *

ANDREWS, PETERS AND FINCH
Attorneys at Law

April 8, 1976

Re: EPA letter of April 5, 1976

Dear Mr. Gunerson:

As your legal advisor we believe that the law on your particular case is such that it would take years to force the company to comply with the "clean water" regulations. Even then, the annual costs for continued non-compliance would be about $12,000 if successful legal action were taken.

Cordially,

Patrick Finch

PF/tjb

* * * * * *

April 12, 1976

Mr. Gunerson
President
Yellowtail Marine, Inc.

Mr. Gunerson:

I could not find the exact information you asked for, but I have collected what I could.

The Boat Manufacturers Association prints estimated unit sales of outboard motors by city and state and I have found estimates of the numbers of motors owned as of December 31, 1975. I think the Coast Guard Report Map may be more useful.

I'm sorry that the hull material report is only up to 1971, but the librarian said that government statistics are usually a year or two behind. It takes a year or two to work them out I guess.

Sincerely,

Robert J. Blake
Marketing Department

RJB/jt

Enclosures

Registered Craft Totals by Hull Material as of December 31, Each Year

	Wood		*Steel*		*Aluminum*		*Fiberglass*	
As of Dec. 31	*Inboard*	*Outboard*	*Inboard*	*Outboard*	*Inboard*	*Outboard*	*Inboard*	*Outboard*
1965	350,087	1,530,054	13,861	124,203	9,119	891,651	51,923	943,523
1966	326,388	1,389,627	13,286	118,127	9,420	957,591	68,566	980,865
1967	331,484	1,361,657	14,770	97,232	14,956	1,159,504	129,012	1,132,360
1968	331,452	1,278,079	16,061	105,164	27,551	1,297,822	168,152	1,284,437
1969	322,181	1,180,910	16,624	100,755	29,654	1,373,626	201,511	1,398,797
1970	318,194	1,140,156	15,654	104,085	27,385	1,492,069	239,386	1,531,956
1971	319,927	1,070,753	16,387	103,449	33,010	1,681,222	303,588	1,704,331

Source: U.S. Coast Guard Report, *Boating Statistics,* CG-359 (May 1972)

1971 Registered Craft Totals by Hull Material and By Length

	Wood		*Steel*		*Aluminum*		*Fiberglass*	
Length	*Inboard*	*Outboard*	*Inboard*	*Outboard*	*Inboard*	*Outboard*	*Inboard*	*Outboard*
Under 16′	23,617	729,846	2,395	49,569	11,639	1,415,321	27,008	1,108,325
16′ less than 26′	175,328	333,954	4,614	45,164	18,194	260,513	248,064	591,014
26′ less than 40′	109,485	6,485	6,986	7,696	2,817	5,178	25,723	4,655
40′–65′	11,070	422	2,222	970	347	179	2,758	277
Over 65′	427	46	170	50	13	31	35	60
	319,927	1,070,753	16,387	109,449	33,010	1,681,222	303,588	1,704,331

Source: U.S. Coast Guard Report, *Boating Statistics,* CG-359 (May 1972)

Distribution of 5,510,092 Numbered Boats by State

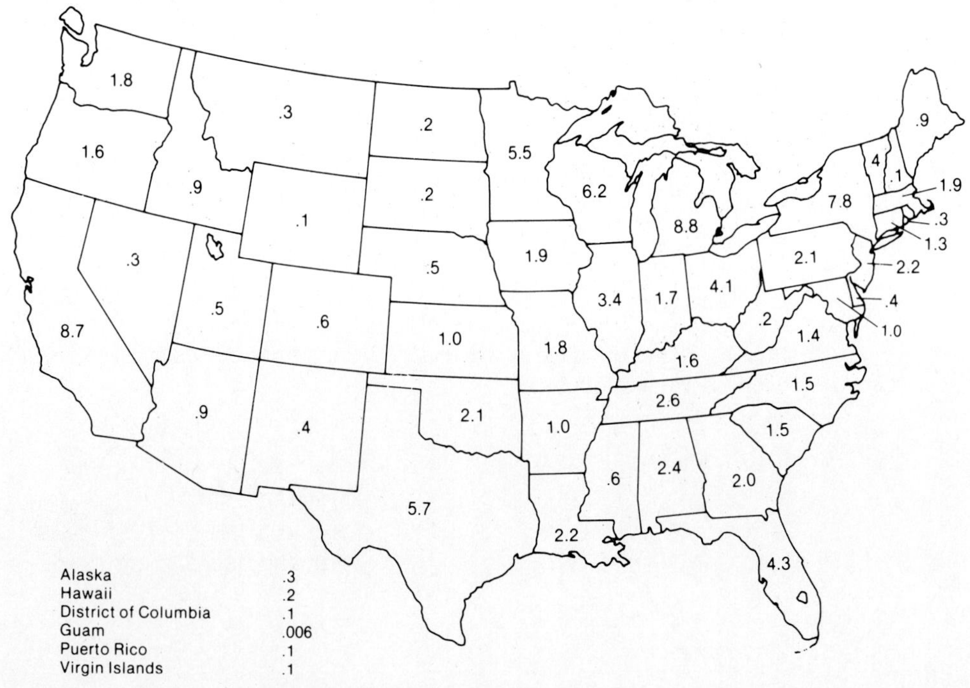

 Source: U.S. Coast Guard Report, *Boating Statistics,* CG-359 (May 1972)

Leading Metropolitan Markets for Outboard Motors in 1974 and 1975

Central City	*Estimated Unit Sales* 1973	1974	1975	*Estimated Motors Owned - 12/31/75*
Minneapolis-St. Paul, MN	16,000	14,300	11,200	211,000
Nassau-Suffolk, NY	13,800	11,000	9,500	169,000
Chicago, IL	12,800	11,200	9,300	167,000
Houston, TX	8,500	6,700	8,100	110,000
Detroit, MI	10,400	8,000	7,800	145,000
Milwaukee, WI	9,800	8,100	6,700	128,000
Dallas-Ft. Worth, TX	8,200	8,100	6,400	119,000
Tampa-St. Petersburg, FL	6,800	8,200	5,600	96,000
Seattle-Everett, WA	5,900	5,400	5,300	83,000
Baltimore, MD	4,900	3,500	4,500	70,000
New Orleans, LA	5,400	5,100	4,400	80,000
Miami, FL	4,600	5,400	4,300	83,000
New York, NY	5,700	4,700	4,100	90,000
Philadelphia, PA	4,900	4,700	4,100	67,000
Boston, MA	5,400	5,600	3,900	86,000
Los Angeles, Long Beach, CA	5,500	4,600	3,700	86,000
Jacksonville, FL	3,200	4,300	3,700	46,000
Washington, D.C.	4,500	3,700	3,600	50,000
St. Louis, MO	5,100	4,100	3,500	71,000
San Francisco-Oakland, CA	3,000	2,800	3,200	59,000
Baton Rouge, LA	4,100	3,000	2,800	43,000
Kansas City, MO	3,700	2,800	2,700	49,000
Tulsa, OK	2,500	2,400	2,600	36,000
Atlanta, GA	3,500	2,900	2,500	44,000
Indianapolis, IN	3,200	2,200	2,500	39,000
Buffalo, NY	3,200	2,700	2,500	40,000
Memphis, TN	3,900	3,100	2,500	47,000
Phoenix, AZ	2,200	2,400	2,400	32,000
Shreveport, LA	2,800	3,000	2,400	38,000
Charlestown, SC	2,300	2,100	2,400	31,000
Orlando, FL	2,700	4,000	2,200	45,000
Duluth-Superior, MN	3,200	2,700	2,200	42,000
Denver-Boulder, CO	—	1,700	2,100	27,000
Pittsburgh, PA	1,900	2,700	2,100	32,000
Norfolk-Va. Bch-Portsmouth, VA	2,600	2,600	2,100	30,000
Ft. Lauderdale-Hollywood, FL	2,500	3,000	2,000	44,000
Ft. Meyers, FL	2,100	3,000	2,000	26,000
Cleveland, OH	2,700	2,700	2,000	39,000
Oklahoma City, OK	—	1,700	2,000	31,000
Portland, OR	3,000	2,700	2,000	45,000
Sacramento, CA	2,700	2,100	1,900	28,000
West Palm Bch.-Boca Raton, FL	2,100	2,500	1,900	29,000

Data obtained from the Marketing Department of Marex, the National Association of Engine and Boat Manufacturers, and *Boating Industry*, January 1976

State Distribution of Outboard Motors

State	Estimated Unit Sales 1973	1974	1975	Estimated Motors Owned - 12/31/75
Alabama	13,200	15,000	7,100	161,000
Arizona	4,700	3,500	3,500	50,000
Arkansas	10,900	11,200	7,300	133,000
California	22,400	20,400	19,000	385,000
Colorado	2,700	2,700	3,100	41,000
Connecticut	7,100	5,100	4,800	84,000
Delaware	1,900	1,600	1,500	25,000
Dist. of Columbia	600	300	500	7,000
Florida	44,000	51,500	36,100	590,000
Georgia	15,000	9,900	9,100	154,000
Idaho	2,700	2,900	1,600	46,000
Illinois	23,400	21,100	16,800	289,000
Indiana	17,000	12,400	12,100	200,000
Iowa	9,500	9,300	7,500	116,000
Kansas	5,800	3,800	3,300	74,000
Kentucky	7,800	7,400	6,000	102,000
Louisiana	25,600	24,000	19,100	308,000
Maine	7,100	7,400	4,100	89,000
Maryland	9,400	8,100	7,900	129,000
Massachusetts	11,200	11,800	8,300	165,000
Michigan	34,600	28,400	23,100	516,000
Minnesota	35,000	33,500	24,500	480,000
Mississippi	5,900	8,200	4,800	75,000
Missouri	14,600	11,600	9,400	183,000
Montana	1,600	1,500	1,000	21,000
Nebraska	3,000	3,400	3,000	42,000
Nevada	900	900	900	18,000
New Hampshire	2,900	2,400	2,000	38,000
New Jersey	11,100	11,600	9,900	166,000
New Mexico	2,800	2,000	1,600	24,000
New York	34,900	16,200	9,400	150,000
North Carolina	14,800	27,600	24,400	478,000
North Dakota	1,500	3,200	2,200	28,000
Ohio	19,200	18,700	14,700	274,000
Oklahoma	9,100	6,800	7,900	128,000
Oregon	6,500	5,100	4,400	114,000
Pennsylvania	12,600	14,300	12,700	186,000
Rhode Island	2,100	1,400	1,700	26,000
South Carolina	9,600	10,600	8,500	142,000
South Dakota	2,900	1,900	1,800	22,000
Tennessee	17,200	12,200	9,200	179,000
Texas	38,100	36,700	30,000	490,000
Utah	2,000	1,600	2,100	31,000
Vermont	900	600	700	24,000
Virginia	10,800	10,100	8,800	135,000
Washington	13,200	13,400	11,900	173,000
West Virginia	1,600	1,600	1,400	28,000
Wisconsin	33,200	29,100	24,100	392,000
Wyoming	400	1,000	200	10,000
TOTAL	585,000	545,000	435,000	7,649,000

Data obtained from the Marketing Department of Marex, the National Associationn of Engine and Boat Manufacturers, and *Boating Industry*, January 1976

8:37 A.M.

Ms. Clarke knocks and brings a letter into office saying as she comes in that Mr. Arch Towne of OSHA and two men are in the foyer. Mr. Towne wants a representative of management and shop steward to tour plant with him and he asked for the President.

OCCUPATIONAL SAFETY AND HEALTH ADMINISTRATION
Department of Labor
Government Center
San Diego Office
California

April 12, 1976

Mr. Olaf Gunerson
President
Yellowtail Marine, Inc.
San Diego, California

Dear Mr. Gunerson:

Your company has been selected for an in-depth investigation by our inspectors. As one of San Diego's leading marine businesses you are doubtlessly aware of the threats to worker safety commonly encountered in the boat building industry and we look forward to your cooperation during the inspections.

A team of inspectors under the supervision of Mr. Arch Towne will arrive on the morning of Wednesday, April 14 to give your boatyard a thorough going-over. This letter will serve to introduce Mr. Towne the Senior Inspector.

Sincerely,

Marvin E. Sharppe
Marvin E. Sharppe
Regional Director

MS:dl

* * * * * *

MOUTON, LAMBE and WOLFE
Investment Bankers & Venture Capitalists
111 North LaSalle Street
Chicago, Illinois 60607

April 9, 1976

Mr. Olaf Gunerson
President
Yellowtail Marine, Inc.
San Diego, California

Dear Mr. Gunerson:

As I mentioned on the telephone on April 8, Saggitarius Inflatable Boats, Inc. is for sale at an attractive price. We would be delighted to meet your Executive Vice President whenever it is convenient for her.

Saggitarius is a new entry into the Inflatable Boat market, which is estimated to be growing at 20% per annum. The company had sales of $501,000 in 1975, its first full year of operations, and had a profit of $12,000 after meeting a number of start up expenses. The company has a good distribution network in the Great Lakes area and a small leased plant which is an old boatyard in Waukegan, near Chicago.

Our advisors think that the company needs an additional investment of $375,000 if it is to improve the quality of its products and ensure dealer reorders. However, our investigations show that the dealers are anxious to have the Saggitarius line.

Saggitarius makes eight outboard runabouts taking up to 100 horsepower, four dinghies, two lifeboats and whitewater rafts which are distributed mainly on the East Coast. The company's products sell for between $450 and $850.

We approached you initially to seek potential buyers with whom you were familiar and when you said that Yellowtail might be interested itself we were delighted. The ask price is $250,000. Management will continue if needed.

My partners and I are ready to assist you at your convenience.

Sincerely,

Roger Lambe

Roger Lambe

RL/ky

* * * * * *

ENVIRONMENTAL PROTECTION AGENCY
Southern California Office
San Diego

April 5, 1976

Mr. Olaf G. Gunerson
President
Yellowtail Marine, Inc.

Dear Mr. Gunerson:

On a recent inspection of the San Diego harbor our inspectors found high levels of cyanide and other chemicals in the bay off your boatyard. A closer inspection revealed that paint and other waste materials were being flushed out of your plant into the Bay.

Our inspector, Mr. Andrew Tozallowzki, will call on you on April 19 at 9 a.m. if that is convenient, to discuss your plans for complying with the Clean Air and Water Act of 1971.

Sincerely,

George Davidson
District Supervisor

GD/m

* * * * * *

GRAND ADS
283 Sunset Boulevard
Los Angeles, California

April 5, 1976

Mr. Olaf Gunerson
President
Yellowtail Marine, Inc.
San Diego, California

Dear Olaf:

I'm glad that Boswell introduced us, because I know I can really help your company. I am looking forward to talking with you on the 15th.

I'm particularly excited about the idea of a girl in a yellow bikini with the message, "Let Your Yellowtail Dealer Show You More" across her chest. Just the kind of thing boat buyers want.

I can't wait to see your reaction. I'll bring the slides with me on the 15th.

Regards,

Murray Grandee
President

MG/shg

EXHIBIT 1

YELLOWTAIL MARINE, INC.
Balance Sheet
July 31, 1975

Assets		
Current Assets		
Cash	$ 8,000	
Accounts Receivable	842,000	
Inventory	1,251,000	
Other	22,000	
Current Assets		$2,123,000
Fixed Assets		
Plant and Equipment	2,511,000	
Less Accumulated Depreciation	989,000	
Net Fixed Assets		1,522,000
Other Assets at Cost	152,000	
Less Amortization	22,000	
Other Assets Net		130,000
Total Assets		$3,775,000
Liabilities and Stockholders' Equity		
Current Liabilities		
Accounts Payable	$665,000	
Short Term Note	212,000	
Accrued Liabilities (Salaries, Rents, Property Taxes, etc.)	78,000	
Current Portion Long Term Debt	39,000	
Current Liabilities		$ 994,000
Long Term Obligations		
Bank of San Diego	52,000	
Mortgages	399,000	
C.B.G. Inc. (10 yr. subordinate loan)	1,200,000	
Long Term Liabilities		1,651,000
Stockholders' Equity		
Common Stock (no par value)	782,000	
Retained Earnings	348,000	
Stockholders' Equity		1,130,000
Total Liabilities and Stockholders' Equity		$3,775,000

YELLOWTAIL MARINE, INC.
Income Statement
August 1, 1974 to July 31, 1975

Revenue		
Gross Sales		$8,376,000
Less: Discounts, Returns and Allowances		36,000
Net Sales		8,340,000
Cost of Goods Sold		6,662,000
Gross Profit		1,678,000
Operating Expenses		
Selling and Advertising	$710,000	
General and Administrative	528,000	
Miscellaneous	21,000	
Total Operating Expenses		1,259,000
Operating Income		419,000
Financial Payments		
Bank Interest	8,000	
Mortgage Interest	32,000	
Lease Payment	9,000	
Interest on C.B.G. Loan	114,000	
Total Financial Payments		163,000
Income Before Tax		256,000
Taxes Paid		88,000
Profit After Tax		$ 168,000

EXHIBIT 2 **Sales of New Outboard Boats, Inboard/Outboard Boats, and Outboard Motors**

	1972	*1973*	*1974*	*1975*
Outboard Boats				
Units Sold	375,000	448,000	425,000	328,000
Average Price Per Unit	$714.00	$726.00	$730.00	$801.00
Total Dollars Spent	$267,800,000	$325,200,000	$310,200,000	$262,700,000
Inboard/Outdboard Boats				
Units Sold	63,000	78,000	70,000	70,000
Average Price Per Unit	$4,885	$5,261	$5,524	$6,000
Total Dollars Spent	$307,800,000	$410,400,000	$386,700,000	$420,000,000
Outboard Motors				
Units Sold	535,000	585,000	545,000	435,000
Average Price Per Unit	$808.00	$857.00	$850.00	$945.00
Total Dollars Spent	$432,300,000	$501,300,000	$463,300,000	$411,100,000

Source: *Boating Industry*, January 1976.

EXHIBIT 3 **Examples of Non-Independent Boat Manufacturers in the Top Forty Highest Sellers**

Manufacturer	*Parent Company*
Chrysler Marine	Chrysler Corporation
Duo Boats	Bangor Punta
Jensen Marine	
The Luhrs Company	
O'Day Boat Company	
Starcraft Company	
Alcort	AMF
Crestliner	
Hatteras	
Slickcraft	
Boston Whaler, Inc.	CML
Ericson Yacht	
Columbia/Corando	Whittaker
Trojan Yachts	

EXHIBIT 4 **Current Prices of Chemicals**

	December			
	1972	*1973*	*1974*	*1975*
Styrene, monomer (lb.)	.066–.0675	.09–.095	.1925–.22	.19
Polyester resin, unsaturated (lb.)	—	.185–.20	.39	.36

Figures from *Chemical Marketing Reporter*, December issues.

EXHIBIT 5 **Boating Industry Investment and Sales**

Manufacture				*Expectations (millions)*			
Plant Expansion		*New Machinery and Equipment*		*Marine Dealer Inventory—Avg. Daily*		*Renovation and Repair (older boats)*	
1976	$19.40	1976	$18.70	1976	$241.00	1976	$246.00
1975	16.90	1975	16.90	1975	204.55	1975	210.00
1974	15.00	1974	15.30	1974	223.84	1974	202.40
1973	14.10	1973	14.40	1973	193.23	1973	190.60
1972	17.10	1972	17.20	1972	180.74	1972	169.47
1971	8.20	1971	9.45	1971	156.90	1971	158.00
1970	8.61	1970	10.11	1970	150.30	1970	147.39
1969	10.30	1969	12.98	1969	160.30	1969	141.06
1968	8.53	1968	9.47	1968	145.39	1968	132.31
1967	8.14	1967	9.24	1967	142.53	1967	127.68
1966	7.40	1966	8.90	1966	139.60	1966	124.47
1965	8.13	1965	8.74	1965	135.70	1965	120.38

Peter B. B. Andrews, "What's Going To Happen In '76"; *Boating Industry*, January 1976, p. 54

EXHIBIT 6 1973 Rental Charges for Summer Berthing—Surveyed Establishments (Charge per Season in Dollars*)

	Flat Charge		*Charge per Foot*	
Type of Berthing	*Range*	*Average*	*Range*	*Average*
Moorings	$ 5–300	$129	$ 2– 8	$ 4.67
Breasted on Docks	100–500	253	6–30	15.60
Slips	75–920	273	8–30	13.03
Tie-Offs	90–400	297	5–10	7.50
Dry-Stack	300–325	313	12–15	12.75

*Typical Season = 6 months
Source: David A. Storey, *The Massachusetts Marina Boatyard Industry 1972–1973*, October 1974/Bulletin #612. Massachusetts Agricultural Experimental Station. College of Food and Natural Resources, University of Massachusetts at Amherst

EXHIBIT 7 Why Customers Buy Outboard Boats and Motors

	*% of Buyers Mentioning**					
	1970	*1971*	*1972*	*1973*	*1974*	*1975*
Outboard Motors						
Cruising	36.5	32.6	32.1	31.1	32.7	40.0
Fishing	55.4	47.0	36.1	36.4	33.0	42.3
Hunting	32.0	30.2	30.0	28.8	31.4	26.1
Skiing	54.1	50.4	49.2	49.3	47.7	40.2
All Other	7.0	7.0	6.8	6.8	7.6	11.6
Outboard Boats						
Cruising	41.4	37.2	36.9	40.5	37.9	38.8
Fishing	53.1	44.0	39.7	42.2	35.5	40.6
Hunting	37.7	35.8	29.9	36.9	32.9	25.9
Skiing	45.7	48.5	48.5	44.6	50.5	33.3
All Other	6.1	6.5	5.9	5.9	6.7	9.9

*Percentages add to more than 100% because of multiple responses
Source: Boating Industry, January 1976

EXHIBIT 8

Top Market for Outboard Boats and Motors Is the Skilled Worker

	Outboard Boats						Outboard Motors					
Occupation of Purchaser	*1970*	*1971*	*1972*	*1973*	*1974*	*1975*	*1970*	*1971*	*1972*	*1973*	*1974*	*1975*
Skilled Worker	24.2	21.6	21.6	21.8	22.2	22.4	24.5	22.6	24.3	22.4	22.3	22.6
Clerical Workers, Salesmen	17.9	20.3	21.4	15.8	14.0	15.8	17.2	19.4	19.7	15.4	13.4	15.6
Managers, Proprietors	15.9	13.7	11.3	15.4	19.3	19.8	14.3	12.9	11.8	14.5	19.3	19.1
Professional	17.0	18.1	15.9	24.7	20.5	16.7	17.6	18.8	18.2	25.7	22.3	18.5
Semi-Skilled Workers	12.9	11.1	13.9	7.3	10.3	12.6	13.9	14.6	13.3	6.7	10.1	12.2
Farmers and Farm Labor	2.4	2.4	2.2	2.2	2.6	3.1	2.6	2.6	2.5	2.4	2.8	2.9
Protective and Service Workers	7.9	7.8	7.4	9.2	9.0	8.7	7.9	7.1	7.3	9.1	8.5	8.1
Factory Labor	1.8	2.0	3.3	3.6	1.6	0.9	2.0	2.0	2.9	3.8	1.3	1.0
Total	100%	100%	100%	100%	100%	100%	100%	100%	100%	100%	100%	100%

Source: Boating Industry, January 1976

EXHIBIT 9 Type of Repair Activities Engaged in by Surveyed Establishments

Type of Repair	*Establishments*	
Activities	*Number*	*Percent*
Wooden Boats	81	69
Fiberglass Boats	79	67
Inboard Engines	81	69
Outboard Engines	62	53

Source: David A. Storey, *The Massachusetts Marina Boatyard Industry 1972–1973*, October 1974/Bulletin #612. Massachusetts Agricultural Experimental Station. College of Food and Natural Resources, University of Massachusetts at Amherst

ROBIN HOOD

I like being in charge and I don't think I could ever work for anyone again. Naturally, I've had a lot of problems but it's been fun.

Speaking was Al Adams who, immediately upon graduating from Harvard Business School in June 1976, took over as President of Robin Hood, a wholesaler and manufacturer of archery equipment, which was a subsidiary of CML.

One thing about running a company is that you carry it in your gut all the time. You might be lying on the beach with your family on Sunday, but you're still thinking about the company. And in my situation, there's no one I can talk to about even basic things, like cash flow; I'm really on my own.

I'm overwhelmed by detail and really have little information. I think the Business School makes you feel you need more information than you can get, at least in a small company. But I like having a lot of problems to work on rather than being tied to a desk concentrating on one problem.

With all these details and operating problems, it's difficult to find time to make strategy. Sometimes you make what seems to be a simple operational decision only to realize that it will have an impact on your strategy for a long time. It's the old chicken and egg problem—you need a strategy so you have a context for your operational decisions, but you have to make your operational decisions while you're trying to find time to develop a strategy. CML's criticism of my predecessor was that he wasn't a planner. I can sympathize with his problem—it's hard to find the time to plan.

When they took me on, CML told me to leave things alone for awhile and just develop an understanding of the business. But you can't do that. People knock at your door all day long. I feel that I've developed a good enough understanding now so that I can sit down and make some of the decisions that my predecessor never made and which, if I'm not careful, I'll be making by default.

PERSONAL BACKGROUND

Before entering Harvard Business School, Adams had been a Navy pilot for six years. He eventually became an aircraft division officer, a key management job which involved responsibility for approximately a hundred men.

I had to get involved in everything. I felt that if I was going to lead men who are mechanics, I'd better understand their job from their point of view, so I'd pitch in with the ground crew on repair and maintenance. And I got involved with the men's personal problems as well as their Navy duties. Basically, I was in the middle of

This case was prepared by Mark T. Teagan, Research Assistant, under the direction of Assistant Professor Kenneth J. Hatten, as a basis for class discussion rather than to illustrate either effective or ineffective handling of an administrative situation.

everything and that's the way I like it, rather than being on the fringe, like a consultant, for instance.

Adams left the Navy to avoid the frequent transfers which would disrupt his family, particularly since the oldest of his four children was getting ready to attend school. Being older than most of his contemporaries at the Business School (thirty-three when he graduated), he felt a sense of urgency to make up for starting late. At the same time, he found many of the cases and his company visits presenting situations which didn't appeal to him. In the large companies, it seemed everyone had a little corner and that was all they were concerned about.

Between his first and second years at the Business School, Adams worked for the CML group, a Boston-based, diversified company, whose ten wholly owned subsidiaries' products were recreation-oriented. Adams joined CML's lean staff of six people as an assistant to the vice president for finance. He got along well with the CML people who, he felt, liked him because he could go into a small business and not turn people off by posing as a business school expert. Adams also shared CML's enthusiasm for recreation and the feeling that business is an important part of life but not the only thing.

TAKING THE JOB

During his second year at the Business School, Adams conducted a job search which included interviewing with big companies as well as with small ones. His main criterion was that the position be one of operational responsibility. Although he received attractive offers from some large companies, he still harbored reservations about taking on a job which would have a narrow focus and which would leave him somewhere else than in the center of activity. Adams became interested in a position as vice president at CML's Ericson Yacht subsidiary. At the same time, CML became interested in having him take over as president of Robin Hood, CML's smallest holding and a profitable but no-growth company.

Initially, Adams had preferred to work at Ericson Yacht because boating appealed to him whereas archery—"Well, I'd never thought much about it." However, he eventually decided that being the president of a company would provide much better experience than being the number-two man at another, even if apparently more glamorous, company. He could later transfer his developed managerial skills to a product in which he had more interest. He felt the Robin Hood position offered him a chance to be in the middle of the action as he had been in the Navy.

In fact, after he finally made the decision to take the Robin Hood job, he felt euphoric about the prospect of using his business and personal skills to run a company. However, when he visited the company before completing school, he found it was in chaos. He became apprehensive, thinking that perhaps the company was too fragmented for him to handle.

Also giving rise to second thoughts were his reservations about his ability to get excited about selling archery equipment, and the tendency of the name and concept of Robin Hood to provoke hilarity among his Business School friends.

I was never concerned about prestige. I think some people from Harvard, particularly those who go to Wall Street, wear Harvard on their sleeve. I don't go along with that routine. Even so, I have to admit that people's reactions to Robin Hood concerned me. For a while, at school, I'd even say I was going to work for CML rather than mention Robin Hood. People would laugh and say all the ridiculous things like, "Where's Maid Marian," or "My name's Little John." (You won't believe this, but we actually have a guy on our sales force named Little John.) But I think that sort of thing is more prevalent at Harvard than anywhere else.

THE COMPANY

Robin Hood comprised three main operations. The major one was wholesaling a full line of archery equipment and accessories. Adams's Montclair, NJ, office handled the storage and shipment of the equipment and what little paperwork accompanied the operation. Within three blocks, Robin Hood had its own pro shop which was small but profitable. In Sailorsburg, Pennsylvania, 150 miles away, Robin Hood had seven people manufacturing arrows in a leased house. The company employed a sales force of six people which had been established in March 1974. Before that, Robin Hood had sold only through a dealer catalog.

GOING TO WORK

After evaluating Robin Hood in light of his personal and professional goals, Adams decided to take the job. He went to New Jersey, found the homes in the towns immediately surrounding Montclair out of his price range, and finally settled on a home in western New Jersey, about an hour's ride from work. CML provided the down payment which Adams would pay back from his bonus,[1] thus not reducing his regular personal cash flow.

CML's only direction was that Adams, after learning the business, should determine a strategy which would provide "quality earnings," i.e., good steady margins and reliable customers. Because Robin Hood's historic return on assets was low, CML was not intent upon growth there, at least in the short run.

During his first two weeks, Adams worked under Robin Hood's then president, Wolfgang Zinzius, whom CML chose not to inform that Adams would soon take over. Adams soon learned that Zinzius had established no goals or strategy, and was overwhelmed with detail because he was unable to delegate responsibility. Zinzius handled everything informally, keeping few records on purchases, sales, or inventory. He was also prone to defer to the assertive people in the company, thus allowing the formation of enclaves of informal leaders as well as groups of those who preferred to shirk responsibility. Although he was having the benefit of a two-week breaking-in period, Adams felt that he would have great difficulty presiding over this chaotic, yet functioning, company when he finally took over.

[1]Adams was paid a salary plus a percentage of pretax profits over a certain amount.

BECOMING PRESIDENT

Zinzius was informed that Adams would take over as president and that he would have to return to international marketing which provided 25% of the company's sales and which, having developed it himself, Zinzius liked very much. He had started in the company as a stock clerk and worked his way into marketing. He apparently knew he was weak in finance, felt overwhelmed by the top position, and suspected that he would eventually be replaced; he seemed merely surprised that CML had taken so long. He went on a two-week vacation when Adams took over.

Adams received expressions of support from the thirteen people in his office, most of whom were middle-aged women performing clerical work. The difficulty of trying to impose some order on the company was aggravated by the staff's constantly asking him routine questions which would interrupt Adams' train of thought on more substantial matters. An example was the bookkeeper who had asserted herself into a position of power under Zinzius. She knocked on Adams's door ''thirty times a day to ask routine questions like in what ledger to enter a purchase or sale.''

Within two hours of his first day as president, Adams learned that one salesman was blithely preparing two price lists; he couldn't understand why Adams said such a practice was illegal. (It was price discrimination.) Adams chose the price list to be used.

During the first week, the bookeeper informed Adams that everyone in the company was due for a raise.

> I had no idea what to say; that was one problem I'd never had in the Navy. And the Business School had never specifically addressed how you determine how much you need to pay to keep people, especially clerical help.

Adams learned that Zinzius had given a blanket 8% raise each year and Adams noted that the people whom he considered more aggressive had the highest salaries. He decided to give everyone a 6% cost-of-living increase, and to those he thought deserved it, an extra 2% increase in pay plus an increase in the company's contributions to their life and medical insurance policies.

Another problem which came up soon after Adams became president concerned the United Parcel Service, which Robin Hood used to deliver its orders. The UPS workers went on strike and the local post office said it couldn't accept any more than twenty parcels a day. Adams had warehouse personnel mail twenty parcels from each post office in the adjoining towns as well as from Montclair.

AUTHORITY

In terms of his authority, Adams's biggest problem was the sales manager. Mr. Amos, an imposing-looking thirty-seven-year-old man who wore his hair in a long ponytail, seemed to have wrested considerable power from Zinzius. Amos immediately tried to gain an upper hand over Adams by assuming authority which Adams was intent on keeping for himself. One example was Amos's reaction to an order from Vermont for $7,000, a large order in the archery business. Amos was set to accept the order and ship it immediately. Adams, however, insisted on making an informal credit check during which he learned that the order had come from an aggressive discounter who could threaten the sales of a nearby Robin Hood outlet of long standing. Feeling that the large archery equipment manufacturers could beat Robin Hood on price and therefore appeal to discounters, and that Robin Hoods' major sales strengths were service and delivery to dealers, Adams decided against accepting the order. His intention was to retain the loyalty of the company's Vermont dealer and to serve notice that Robin Hood would emphasize service to its network of small dealers. The sales manager and other personnel thought Adams was, as it were, a little green:

> It was a major decision, really. It set a course for the company. I was worried that I might be being misled about the discounter's operation or that I was naive. That sort of decision comes up every day: you have to decide on a course of action with little information, sometimes with little confidence, and without having defined the company's strategy.

Adams found it difficult to evaluate the advice given him by company personnel because of his lack of familiarity with archery and the archery industry, and because he did not know what personal motives might be prompting a given line of reasoning. He felt that if he appeared weak, people would take advantage of him; if he appeared indecisive, people would make decisions for him.

> At first, it's easy to be defensive when someone strongly recommends something; it's easy to ask yourself what their real motives are. Don't get me wrong—it's not a feeling that "they" are out to get you. I think it's feeling that when a new president comes on, people naturally want to have him make decisions they like. And I found it too easy to react favorably to a, let's say, brown noser, because he was supportive; he can make you feel comfortable in an uncertain situation. But even if you react favorably to him, you know that you don't want yes-men helping you make decisions. You want someone who's willing to give you a good argument so you can look at a problem from all sides. Of course, to do that, you have to know what you're talking about yourself. So I decided that, before I asked for any advice or input, I'd research the problem myself. Research takes time and it is a major reason for my hectic pace and long hours.'

CONTROL

In addition to asserting his authority, Adams's initial daily problems centered around imposing controls on the company's operations. Adams felt a lack of control was indicated by an inventory turnover of 1½ times a year and by there being no perpetual inventory. In the past, inventory control had consisted only of a semiannual physical audit. Being unfamiliar with purchasing and wanting to get out from under it, Adams delegated responsibility for it to a young man who, with Zinzius's help, had recently immigrated to the United States. Adams felt that the man, who seemed to feel a sense of debt to Zinzius, had been somewhat self-effacing and had not had an opportunity to demonstrate his abilities. Adams felt he had considerable native ability and gave him responsibility for purchasing. Adams set up a perpetual inventory system which the young man quickly understood and implemented; Adams then gave him a raise and responsibility for an open-to-buy of $2,500.[2]

While at the Business School, Adams had paid lip-service to the importance of cash flow, but its importance became concrete during his second week as president when he was faced with a payroll to meet, $300,000 of Accounts Receivable due, and $0 Cash. This situation was caused in part by the poor control systems at Robin Hood, but also by the nature of its business: most archery equipment was normally sold during the fall hunting season and dated 120 days, whereas Robin Hood had to purchase equipment in the spring. Financial statements for August 1975, January 1976, and August 1976 appear in *Exhibit 1*. Adams had to borrow the money from CML.

Overall, however, Adams found lack of information to be his biggest problem in getting control over the company. There was no information on when and where the different products sold, on inventory levels, or on margins. Adams didn't have the time to get the information himself but hoped that the systems he had installed would provide it once they had been in operation for a while.

MARKETING AND SALES

Within a week of taking over, Adams had to consider the installation of a WATS line. His competition had toll-free phone numbers which dealers could call, and some dealers had requested Robin Hood to provide the same service. Adams felt a WATS line afforded his competition an advantage insofar as it was an aspect of the service which he felt should be Robin Hood's main strength. However, a WATS line (incoming only) would cost $245 a month.

> I had to do a B-School analysis, figuring what incremental sales would be necessary to justify the extra expense. So I divided the $245, no zeros omitted, by our estimated contribution figure. It seemed a bit silly after dealing with the big numbers you do at business school, but you can two-hundred-forty-five-dollar yourself to death in a small company.

Again, Adams felt he was confronted with a strategic decision while solving an operational problem. He decided to install the WATS line, informed his customers, and was pleased that, after a month or two, the WATS line seemed to be giving rise to the needed incremental sales, even considering Adams's estimate of cannibalization of sales which normally would have been made by mail or regular phone calls. Adams then learned that the company had reserved space in some archery magazines and that he would have to work with the women in charge of advertising to create copy before the deadline for copy submission—the next day. "I'd like to plan our advertising a little more than that," said Adams.

The sales force, the company's biggest single expense, was of major concern to

[2]An authority to buy goods for resale to the amount of $2,500.

Adams who felt it might even be unnecessary. Its six members, all friends of Amos, received $150 a week draw against a 6% commission on all sales in their assigned territories.

In the 2½ years of its existence, the sales force had increased sales a total of $400,000 over what they would otherwise have been, and had increased direct expenses by about $160,000. Adams determined that, with the average margin being 32%, the increase in expenses (which did not include associate office overhead) wiped out any additional profit the extra sales may have provided. A problem was that Robin Hood had previously had steady sales of $1.3 million a year while selling to dealers only through its catalog. When the sales force came on board, it received commissions on these assured sales as well as on additional sales. Adams's calculations indicated that one salesman's calls cost an average of $218 each; another's averaged $32.[3]

Adams had considered placing the salesmen on commission only for those sales they personally wrote. However, he feared such a system might encourage the salesmen to push for orders, thereby antagonizing and straining Robin Hood's small but loyal customers. He also felt that because Robin Hood was known in the trade any new dealer would want some of its products.

Another possibility was to disband the sales force and conduct an aggressive telephone campaign. His warehouse manager, Ken Prelopsky, had assumed responsibility for taking calls on the WATS line and had increased his already excellent rapport with the dealers. Prelopsky had found that, not only had phone calls increased, but that he was able to sell more over the phone than by mail:

> During hunting season, I've been getting a phone call every three or four minutes. And when dealers order something we don't have in stock, I can suggest a substitute item which they more than likely will accept. I can also remind them to order other items; I might say, "By the way, you have enough Little John bows? The hunters'll be looking for them." And they might say, "As a matter of fact, I only have one left; better send me a few." You can't do these sort of things by mail; you don't get that spontaneous reaction. And I know these guys; they trust me. I know they often don't think ahead and I can help them. I also think that I could convince them to order things earlier and help our cash flow problem.

One of Adams's nagging concerns was the preparation of the company catalog which was scheduled to be ready within four months of the day he took over.

> The catalog is a major undertaking. It goes to press in September and comes out in February. It's what we send to all our dealers. It's what they buy from. Essentially, it *is* the company and we're stuck with it for a year. So I have to make product decisions which will commit us to a certain line and to our manufacturers while I'm still trying to learn what archery is all about. The problem is aggravated by fads in the market. This year one type of arrowhead may be the big seller, only to give way to another type next year. Sales are affected by the large manufacturers.

[3]The January 1976 issue of *Sales and Marketing Management* stated that the average cost per call of account representatives, including those in the wholesale industry, was $20 in urban areas and $39 in rural areas. A noted sales management authority estimated the average cost per call for industrial salesmen was $75.

He decided to delay publication of the catalog, feeling that, though a delay would lead to the catalog's being issued after the national archery trade show, its importance dictated that it be as productive as possible.

Simultaneously, Adams would have to decide when he would purchase his products because CML wanted a cash flow forecast. Whereas Zinzius had purchased large batches of items at one time, Adams wanted to purchase in a series of smaller lots to reduce his cash flow problems and his inventory carrying costs. Therefore, he had to determine the flexibility of his vendors. Adams contemplated establishing a product committee of about five people to discuss each product category; he thought such a device would help him make his decisions with more information and would give committee members a feeling of participating in making company policy.

At one time the catalog had been 250 pages; Adams felt that was much too long—it presented the small dealer with an overwhelming number of choices, and the company with a severe inventory problem. He initially considered cutting it down to 90 pages, but then decided that, in line with his full-service concept, its length should be somewhere in the middle to provide dealers with a sufficient assortment. Sample pages of the 1976 catalog are provided in *Exhibit 2*.

Feeling that Robin Hood did not have the resources to advertise extensively, Adams felt there was probably little brand awareness of Robin Hood products among final consumers. He, therefore, decided to downplay Robin Hood branded products in the catalog in favor of products of those companies which, having greater resources, advertised more. As with many of his other decisions, he had to make this one with little moral support from the people in the company. They did not understand his line of reasoning and seemed to think that he was crazy to downplay the brand name of his own company. However, Adams decided to continue publishing the company's monthly newsletter, which was distributed as part of an effort to sustain the feeling of being part of a family among the dealers. Amos prepared the newsletter and wrote it in a style the dealers understood and liked. A sample newsletter appears in *Exhibit 3*.

RETAILING AND MANUFACTURING

In addition to the problems arising in Robin Hood's main business of wholesaling, Adams had to deal with the pro shop and the arrow manufacturing operations. The pro shop had long been a sore point with CML's management who thought it was unprofitable. Adams's initial analysis indicated that it was profitable even if not a big money-maker. However, he found it difficult to allocate the time and effort to day-to-day retail problems such as advertising, and was having difficulty devising a system for measuring and motivating Mr. Tucker who ran the shop. At the time, Tucker was receiving a base salary plus a percentage of the shop's profits.

Presenting even more difficult problems was the arrow division. Because it was so far away, Adams could exert little control over it. The division, newly created in November 1975, was run by Amos's wife, employed six of their female friends, and was located in a house leased from one of Amos's acquaintances.

The atmosphere at the division was not that of a conventional manufacturer's operation. The women often brought in their children and were sometimes absent for a few days. Adams's initial analysis indicated that the division was not getting the 32% margin he wanted it to. Although the division's capacity was constrained in its present location and although it needed a larger volume to make Robin Hood competitive in arrow manufacturing, Adams had turned down Amos's request to rent the house next door. (Adams did grant Amos a requested $1,000 for expanding the arrow division's storage space.) Adams did not want to increase his break-even and he had doubts about keeping the division at all. He calculated that materials costs for the arrows totaled approximately $11 a dozen. Initially, overhead had been approximately $3.12. After start-up, production had increased to what seemed to be a capacity of 2,000 dozen arrows a month. At that output, Adams figured his overhead was more like $2.25 a dozen. The price to retailers for the cheapest and most popular arrow was $15.95. Adams had received an offer from an arrow manufacturer to supply arrows for $15.50 a dozen. Although that amounted to an effective overhead rate of $4.50 a dozen, he figured his $3.12 figure did not include Amos's two days a week at the division, his travel expenses, inventory carrying costs, associated risks, and "grief." While analyzing the problem, Adams noted that Amos received a salary of about $15,000 a year and about $3,000 in travel expenses.

> Although I've been thinking of disbanding the division, I gave him the $1,000 because maybe the extra space would save labor costs involved in moving the product around the present constrained facilities. I guess I also figured I should give the operation a chance to prove itself since I have to admit one of my biggest reservations about it is my not being able to control it because of its distance from Montclair. One risk of disbanding it is that arrows can be a faddish item—in coloring and differing type heads—which can help us get in the door. However, I figure even if this $15.50 contract doesn't work out, I could reestablish an arrow division within three months, in a location under my control, and with less overhead to deal with.

MAKING CONTACTS

Soon after taking over the company, Adams contacted its founder, Mr. Jackson, who, at seventy, had not been actively involved in the business for some time. However, Jackson was well known and respected throughout the industry. Through Jackson, Adams met some of the industry's better known personalities including the principals of the larger manufacturing firms, the 1976 Olympic archery team coach, and a number of famous bow hunters. Jackson also introduced Adams to many of Robin Hood's dealers who, Adams learned, were often in the business because they loved archery rather than to satisfy simple economic motives. For many, their archery dealerships were home- or garage-based businesses which they operated after hours and on weekends.

Adams's contacts with CML's other subsidiary presidents were personally and professionally satisfying. At a company meeting, Adams was pleased that he was immediately treated as one of the family; he also discovered the other presidents had many of the same problems he did. Adams was gratified that he had defined the issues in much the same way as the other presidents, and that he was able to make positive contributions to defining and analyzing common problems.

> That first president's meeting was great. It was the first time I had someone to talk to face to face about my problems, and I liked them personally—we'd go jogging or swimming together. A big thing was that quite often you can feel that you are forgetting something, that you aren't considering something you should be—but I came out of that meeting feeling that I had at least touched all the major bases.

THE ARCHERY MARKET

From what little published information was available and from his own contacts, Adams pieced together a view of the archery market. Manufacturing sales amounted to approximately \$45 million. Although Bear Archery had 40% of the wholesale market, and Martin Archery had about 11%, Robin Hood was still a major factor with its 4% market share because the industry was so fragmented—in many cases like a cottage industry. The US market was growing at about 15% a year. In 1974 there were over 16 million licensed hunters of whom about one million were bow hunters. Arrow dollar sales were almost equal to bow dollar sales. Adams determined that Robin Hood's sales were distributed as follows: Pennsylvania, 23.2%; Michigan, 16.4%; New York, 11.7%; Maine, 6.8%; and Ohio, 6.4%. The rest of Robin Hood's sales were spread nationally but with concentration in the eastern United States. Industry markups were approximately: manufacturers, 25%; wholesalers, 33%; and dealers, 40%. Large companies like Bear Archery often sold to large sports specialists like the Hermann's sporting goods chain. Bear had an aggressive eighteen-man sales force, sold a large volume at discount prices, and had introduced into a rather sleepy industry modern marketing techniques such as the use of blister packs.

Robin Hood was constrained from expanding its sales because large accounts like Hermann's could get better prices by buying directly from large manufacturers like Bear. Believing that Robin Hood could not compete on price with these larger companies, Adams thought it should stay with its conventional, small outlets, and that it should emphasize being a full-service company, providing quick delivery, good credit terms, and liberal take-back policies for the small dealers.

Adams had determined that Robin Hood had a mailing list of about 1400 dealers; approximately 1200 were active accounts. The average order size was \$197.00. Ken Prelopsky, the warehouse manager, claimed that the small dealers did not mind paying a little extra to Robin Hood because they needed and appreciated its service. Robin Hood occasionally had seminars to inform dealers of the specifications and advantages of new equipment. The company also carried many parts which the manufacturers chose not to carry because they were slow movers. Robin Hood repaired equipment for the price of parts and a small labor charge whereas many manufacturers granted no warranties or would take a long time to repair and return equipment. Prelopsky recalled several dealers telling him that, even after having placed large orders with manufacturers, they were treated as strangers when they called the companies. On the other hand, Prelopsky knew the dealers personally, discussed their problems with them and, equally important, treated them with respect. Although he had reservations about keeping the sales force, Adams felt that having one as part of his full-service concept might make sense. Instead of disbanding it, perhaps he could use the sales staff more effectively.

Adams noted that archery addressed two major markets, hunters and target shooters. Target shooting had suffered a serious decline in the United States to the point where it represented only about 15% of the market. But, several states had passed laws providing for two hunting seasons, one for firearms and one for archery. These laws were encouraging many firearms hunters to take up archery so they could extend the time during which they were allowed to hunt. The politically powerful gun industry felt such laws cut into its sales and was lobbying to repeal them.

With a recent innovation—the compound bow—archery could be a highly technical sport.[4] Because most archers were enthusiasts, and the equipment could be expensive ($75–$300 for a bow), Adams felt they would attach great importance to their purchase and therefore tend to seek information and want to handle the equipment before purchasing it. He believed such consumer behavior would bode well for the small pro shops and was surprised when mass merchandisers, who typically provided little information, were able to sell so much archery equipment, particularly since the industry advertised so little.

Adams felt Robin Hood was vulnerable as a small wholesaler because manufacturers could go around this middle link in the distribution chain and sell directly to small dealers, just as the larger manufacturers were doing with their larger accounts. The power of the manufacturers was illustrated by Bear Archery's being able to insist on its approving dealers before allowing Robin Hood to sell its equipment to them. There was also the possibility of mass merchandisers taking sales away from the traditional pro shops. A more immediate threat was the current establishment of many archery shops in converted bowling alleys and warehouses where customers could shoot as well as purchase equipment. As yet, Robin Hood had no formal contact with such operations.

DECISION POINTS

Adams felt he had done well in imposing at least a semblance of order on Robin Hood, but knew he had a long way to go. He still had been unable to set aside time for the sole purpose of creating a strategy. He was aware of some strategic alternatives and of some major operational problems which he was facing.

Adams wondered if it might be possible to expand the market for target archery by having salesmen encourage high schools to introduce it into their recreational curricula. Because archery became an Olympic event in 1972 after a forty-eight-year absence, and because the U.S. won gold medals in the 1976 Olympics, he believed there could be a better chance of creating such interest than there had been before.

Adams also had to decide what to do about his sales force and about Amos. Adams felt Amos often tried to assume authority which should be Adams's alone. On a case-by-case basis, however, Amos always seemed to follow Adams's directions once it was established that Adams was the one making the decision. Adams felt that perhaps he had been too defensive about Amos, whose aggressiveness, which seemed threatening while

[4]A compound bow works through a pulley mechanism which enables an archer to pull back the bowstring at, say, a pressure of 45 pounds and hold it at 15 pounds; however, when the bowstring is released, during its last few inches of return to the straight position, it would assume a pressure of, say, 60 pounds. Such an innovation is particularly useful in hunting insofar as it enables archers to shoot more accurately and with greater force than with conventional bows. An example of a compound bow appears in *Exhibit 4*.

Adams was getting established, now showed a dedication to the job and a strong point of view which would serve as useful input to future decision making. Adams recalled an occasion on which he had inadvertently crossed Amos. Robin Hood had had a policy of charging a $5 service charge on orders under $20.00. But when Adams determined what the average order was, he decided to eliminate the charge. He had once taken a call from a dealer and told him he would not have to pay the extra $5 on a recent order. However, Amos had handled the original order and, in line with the company policy then in effect, had already charged the $5. Perhaps such situations contributed to the conflicts Adams sensed.

If Adams fired Amos, Amos's friends on the sales force, his friends at the arrow division, and his wife might all leave as well. Of course, this might be desirable, but even if it were, Adams was unsure about the timing—should he wait until he had a more firm grasp on the company and its operations?

Zinzius had signed what Adams viewed as expensive leases for the arrow division, the main office, and a malfunctioning copier. Adams said he would like to get out of some of these leases so that he could reduce his fixed costs and improve his cash flow. But he felt it was unlikely he could renegotiate the leases downward, and if he were able to get out of the leases altogether, where would he move the company? He was considering moving to Pennsylvania where labor was plentiful and cheap and where welfare benefits were not as competitive with wages as they were in New Jersey. In New Jersey the minimum wage was $3.30; in Pennsylvania it was $2.35 per hour. If the whole operation were to be in Pennsylvania, he could assert more control over the arrow operation and use workers interchangeably between the arrow manufacturing and the warehouse season by season. One drawback might be difficulty in getting some of the present key employees to move with the company.

Adams also felt that the company was overstaffed; at the same time, he wanted to delegate many of the routine decisions which Zinzius had made himself. Adams wanted the clerical staff to take responsibility for the relatively minor decisions their jobs involved, but he was having difficulty in motivating them to do so. He had been successful at creating an urgency about filling orders which, in line with his intent to provide excellent service, were now more promptly filled. He now had to develop the same sort of commitment to job responsibility and decision making.

Adams also wondered if he should refuse to see people about simple problems, such as the bookkeeper with her questions about ledger accounts. A more closed-door policy would give him more time to plan strategy but at the same time might isolate him from important information, especially when he was still new and needed it.

His surprise at mass merchandisers like Hermann's doing so well in the industry led Adams to question his analysis of the consumer behavior involved in buying archery equipment. Perhaps archers did not seek as much information as he thought they did. Or perhaps they sought the information at pro shops, but bought the equipment at the less expensive outlets. Perhaps pro shops would become obsolete and Robin Hood would have to try to gain an entree to the mass merchandisers, but how could it do this when the manufacturers could go to these outlets themselves?

Given these possible trends, on which there was little or no published information, Adams wondered if Robin Hood should integrate backward and get into manufacturing, perhaps through an acquisition. If he were to integrate backward, decisions such as not selling to the Vermont discounter might have to be revised. Perhaps Robin Hood should integrate forward and get involved in converting buildings to pro shops and target ranges. Such an operation might even be franchised.

A major concern was the product decisions which had to be made for the catalog. Although Adams was developing an understanding of archery and archers, he knew he would have to rely to a great extent on company personnel for input. He wondered how best to structure the product committee's work and how to run the meetings.

And there was the nagging problem of cash flow. Buying in the spring and selling in the fall imposed severe problems on Robin Hood, especially because, in line with its dealer service concept, it allowed its small vulnerable dealers liberal credit. It dated small orders on a 2/10/30 basis and allowed 120 days on orders of over $1,000. One dealer had mentioned he would prefer a stepped dating schedule allowing for bigger discounts with earlier payments, e.g., 5% off for payments within 30 days, 2% off for payment within 60 days and no discount after 60 days. Perhaps such a schedule would encourage Robin Hood's dealers, who probably were not that concerned about the time value of money, to pay earlier and thus help alleviate the company's cash flow problems.

As he considered his many problems, Adams said:

> There is plenty to think about. Living an hour from work, I leave home at 7 in the morning and return between 8 and 9 in the evening. My family is almost in shock; they've never seen so little of me. It's particularly tough on the older kids because they had made friends in Cambridge and now have to adjust to a new home and to going to a new school. I bring in a sleeping bag and sleep in the office two nights a week so I can get my work done and return home at 4 the next afternoon to be with the kids. Fortunately, my wife is understanding; she's bothered only by my being a bit tense sometimes—I think it's because I have no peers at work I can talk to. She once said that she thought the sacrifices we both made to get me through B-School were temporary and would lead to much better things. Now she finds I'm still working long hours. And with our mortgage and school debts we really have little discretionary income—we hardly ever eat out—even though I'm being paid well. My description of the company may have been somewhat disjointed but that's the way it seems when you walk into something like that. I guess what I have to do now is continue wading through the daily problems, set some priorities and establish a strategy. I feel up to it too; it's amazing how I've become so confident so fast.

EXHIBIT 1

ROBIN HOOD
Balance Sheet
($000)

	August 1975	*January 1976*	*August 1976*
Assets			
Cash	$ 54	$ 21	$ 37
A/R	213	101	370
Inventory	492	529	703
Other Current	15	8	1
	$774	$659	$1,111
Plant & Equipment	40	52	58
Less Accum. Dep.	(11)	(13)	(17)
Net P & E	29	39	41
Other	1	2	3
Goodwill	53	52	50
CML Cash Acct.	(54)	4	(349)
	$803	$756	$856
Liabilities			
A/P	$ 73	$ 74	$150
Accrued Liabilities	41	9	22
Accrued Taxes	24	3	7
Total Current	$138	$ 86	$179
Capital Stock	1	1	1
Paid-in Surplus	548	548	548
Retained Earnings	116	121	128
	$803	$756	$856

Income Statement
(for month)

	August 1975	January 1976	August 1976
Sales	$174	$ 70	$287
Less COGS	117	47	195
Gross Margin	$ 57	$ 23	$ 92
S & A	12	11	19
Shipping & Warehouse	7	7	9
G & A	11	17	18
Total	$ 30	$ 35	$ 46
Operating Income	$ 27	$(12)	$ 46
Interest			
PBT	27	(12)	46
Taxes (credit)	14	(6)	24
Net Income	$ 13	$ (6)	$ 22

EXHIBIT 2 Robin Hood

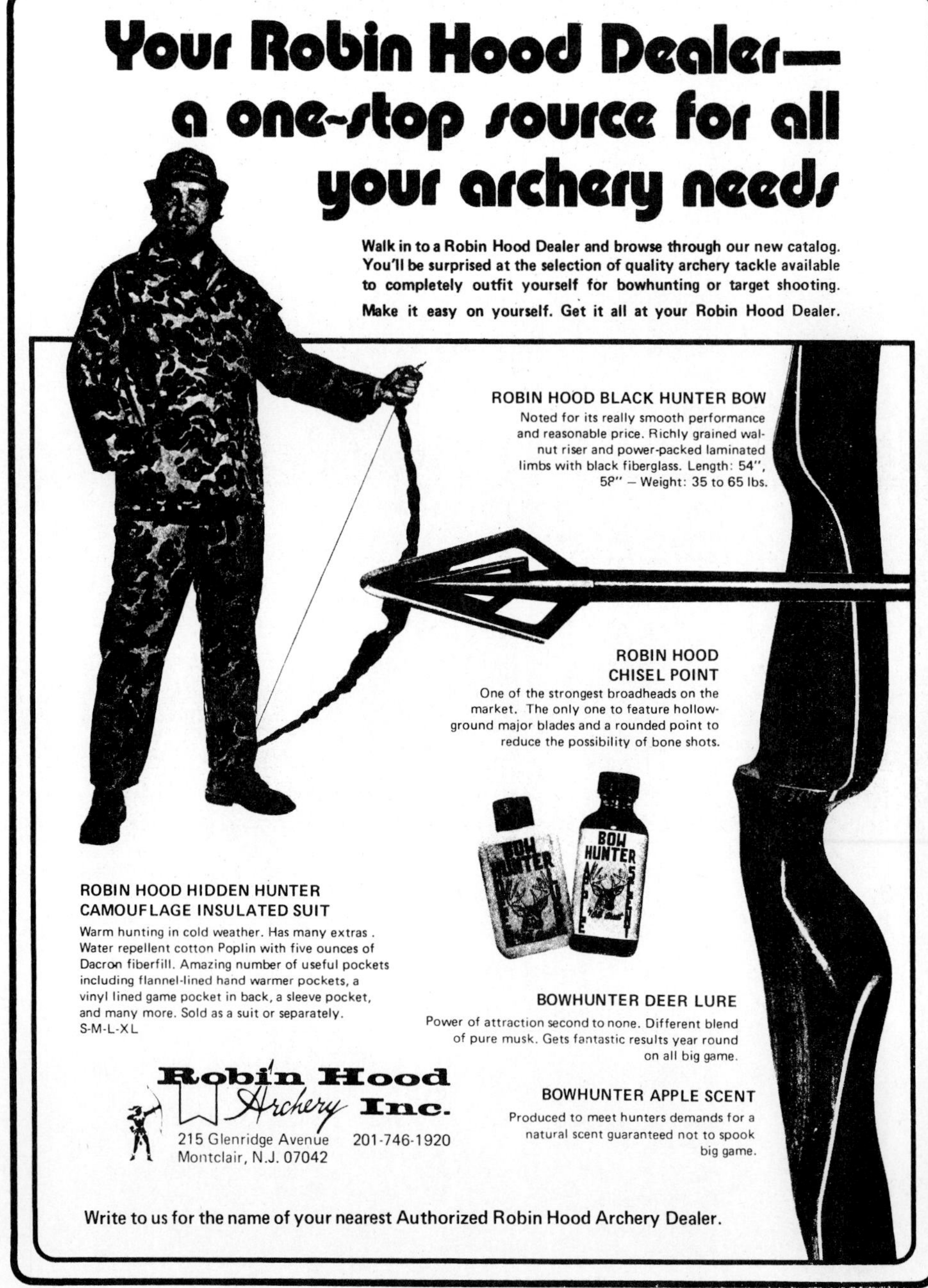

EXHIBIT 3 Robin Hood

DEALER NEWSLETTER—July 1976

1 It's July already and we have some very significant announcements to make that will substantially reinforce our service program for your immediate benefit.

2 As of Monday, July 12th, we will be installing a "toll-free" phone service for your convenience in placing orders.
ROBIN HOOD FASTCOM—800-631-1252 (All states *Except New Jersey*)

- **a** We are installing this new dealer service on a three month trial basis in an attempt to speed up our order service to you.
- **b** The phone lines will be staffed during our normal working hours of 8 to 5 Eastern time. I would prefer to have a 24 hour service, but we couldn't possibly staff it with qualified people. So it will be 8 to 5 Eastern, 7 to 4 Central, 6 to 3 Mountain, and 5 to 2 Pacific time.
- **c** This is something I have been thinking about for a long time and I am very excited about finally being able to make this announcement.

3 My second announcement is to let you know that Al Adams has assumed the President's position at Robin Hood Archery. Al brings us a heavy management background that will give us the versatility that we have only thought about until now. He's an "outdoors" person, married, four kids, 34 years old, and the first day we worked together he gained my complete confidence in his ability to relate to what Robin Hood is all about. If you want to talk to the President, call and ask for Al. If you use the "toll free" line, I'll expect you to give him a big stock order.

Wolf will be concentrating his efforts on our export business. This is a market area that has been growing each year and one we have not had the time to devote our efforts to. With Al joining the company, Wolf will be able to expand our foreign market as only he is qualified to do.

4 We are attempting to set-up and use a mechanical addressing system. This new system will allow us more complete coverage in our newsletter mailings and make our overall postal communications more efficient. Before instituting this system I have one request: Please check your most recent invoice or statement from us and if there are any corrections in your *business name or address,* please mail these in to me as soon as possible.

5 I am enclosing a new price list supplement with this issue of the newsletter. This is primarily an update and will pick-up all of the new items that have been added since February.

6 I made the announcement of our new Economy Gamegetters and Economy Glass Hunting arrows last month and you have responded very well indeed. We have very good raw material stocks on this arrow style and our manufacturing capability is now in excess of 2,000 dozen per month. I don't anticipate any problems in being able to supply right up to the deadline. I requested that your orders be in 12 dozen lots. This has generally been followed but where it isn't you will be charged extra for additional service. This is a necessity as my price work-up is too low to offer any "no charge" frills.

- **a** Less than 12 dozen quantities will result in a $.40 per dozen boxing charge.
- **b** Requests for cutting and installing SAP inserts will be $.60 per dozen additional cost.
- **c** Marking arrows with your store name at $.50 per dozen.

7 Once again there are no XX75 Orange shafts available in hunting sizes. I now have

EXHIBIT 3 (*Cont.*)

28,440 Orange shafts on back order with Easton and no scheduled delivery information.

8 We are tooling up at present to supply all arrows (except wood arrows) as "compound arrows" with nocks offset enough to provide optimum fletch clearance for right handed shooters. These arrows will still function out of conventional bows. I anticipate that our conversion will be complete by August 1st and all production after that time will be in the new style. Our current production is on a straight fletch basis and provides adequate vane clearance for most compound shooters.

9 In our last newsletter we provided a size chart on Easton shafts by grade. Please add 2213 in XX75 grade as one that I missed. Sorry about the omission.

10 We are starting to utilize Marco vanes in arrow production to reduce costs. I cannot offer these for sale as I haven't yet been able to get enough for general stock and arrow production too. I mentioned these new vanes for two reasons, one to let you know what we are doing and to give you a little information on various vane weights on the market.

Item (based on 3 fletch)	*Weight in Grains*
Pro Fletch (PF500)	43.2
Flex Fletch (FFP-500)	34.5
Bohning (5″ vane)-New	36.0
Bear Weathers-New	39.8
Marco Fletch (MF500)-New	29.2
5″ Trueshape Diecut Feathers	7.8

With everyone concerned about arrow speed, this might be an interesting comparison for feathers. Another note: Marco Fletch has the same cut or shape as a diecut feather.

11 Last month I mentioned how well my son Wally was doing with his "Little John" (detuned) peaked at 38 lbs. Some speed comparison data follows that is pretty graphic and should help you in your compound sales to kids and women that can't bow hunt now. One very interesting fact is that if my son could draw and hold a 42 lb. recurve (which he can't) his arrow speed from the conventional stick would be 150 fps as opposed to 161 fps with the compound. I am also including some Carbonglas data comparisons against aluminum arrows.

	Bow and Set-Up	*Arrow Data*	*Speed (fps)*
Little John Compound	Peak 59 lb.	2117 at 29″	
	Hold 27 lb.	3 fletch (PF400)	
		125 grain FP	178.8
Little John Compound	Peak 38.5 lb.	1816 at 26″	
	Hold 20 lb.	3 fletch (PF400)	
		125 grain FP	161.0
Black Hunter Recurve	49 lb. at 29″	2117 at 29″	155.9
	42 lb. at 26″	1816 at 26″	149.9

All shots of above were hand shot.

EXHIBIT 3 (Cont.)

	Bow and Set-Up	Arrow	Arrow Weight	Speed (fps)
Little John Compound	Peak 59 lb. Hold 27 lb.	Carbonglas X17 at 29″ 3 fletch (MF400) 150 grain FP	505 grain	192.2
		2117 at 29″ 3 fletch (PF400) 125 grain FP	542 grain	181.4
		2020 at 29″ 3 fletch (MF400) 150 grain FP	583 grain	175.5

Above test run with all arrows machine shot.

12 It is pretty obvious to me at this time that we are not going to get any delivery on Carbonglas this year. I am not going to continue to embarrass myself by making any further delivery promises.

13 Hidden Hunter Insulated Camo Suits: After a little supplier negotiation, I have a "fill-in" order to supplement our general stock on this item. In addition to our standard sizing I have been able to add two *new* sizes to the line. These are XXL (48–52) and XXXL (52–56) for the "bigger bowhunter" (like me). Since it takes more material to fold around the bigger guy, the new sizes will naturally cost more: HHS-$39.90-dealer, $66.50-retail, HHJ-$22.95-dealer, $38.25-retail, HHP-$16.95-dealer, $28.25-retail. It's a shame that you can't get the Large Economy Size in clothes too!! We expect delivery by August 1st.

EXHIBIT 4 Robin Hood

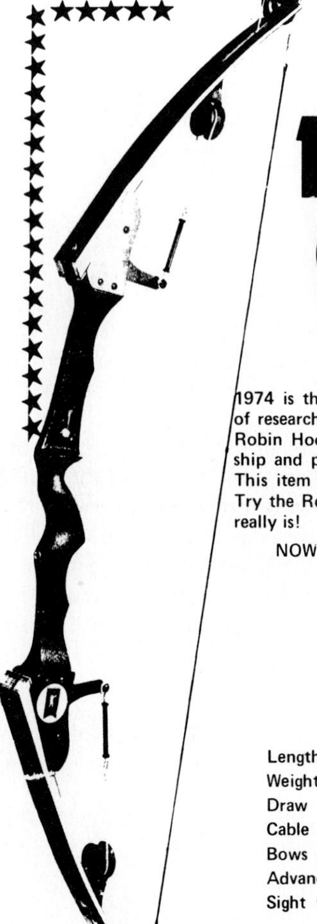

Robin Hood Compound

mfg. by Precision Shooting Equipment - licensed under Allen Patent #3-486-495

1974 is the year of the Compound at Robin Hood Archery. After two years of research and testing, Precision Shooting has come up with a compound for Robin Hood Archery that fully meets our standards for quality of craftsmanship and performance. It is our pleasure to make this bow available to you. This item will be a valuable addition to your inventory of superior products. Try the Robin Hood Compound and see for yourself what customer response really is!

NOW FEATURES SPEED BRACKETS AT NO EXTRA CHARGE!

Hunting Model: $250.00	Black handle with Black limbs and Black side plates. 40 – 50 lbs. and 45 – 60 lbs.
Target Model: $250.00	Black handle with White limbs and Gold color side plates. 25 – 35 lbs. and 35 – 45 lbs.

Length: 52 inches
Weight: 4½ pounds
Draw Length: 23 – 34½ inches
Cable adjustment simplified
Bows come with custom cushion plunger & stabilizer adapter
Advanced magnesium handle design
Sight window cut 3/8 inch beyond center

Bow Case $17.95 Seven Arrow Bow Quiver $14.95

REPLACEMENT PARTS

Limbs (2)	$110.00	Super PSE String (1)	$ 3.95
Handle (1)	$110.00	S-Hooks (2)	$ 1.40
Side Plates (4)	$ 7.75	Stabilizer Inserts (1)	$ 2.65
Eccentric Wheels (2)	$ 16.00	Dealer Repair Kit (Necessary tools & repair parts for dealer service)	$93.50
Idler Wheels (2)	$ 18.10		
Turnbuckle Assembly (2)	$ 7.75	Half-round Pads (2)	$ .65
Cables (2)	$ 10.00	String Changer (1)	$ 3.95
Limb bolt Assembly (2)	$ 4.00	Needle Bearings	$16.50
Axles (2)	$ 5.75	Stabilizer (1) (30", 32", 34" 36")	$11.37
E-rings (4)	$ .60		
8/32 Allen Screws (12)	$ 1.65	Drill & Tap for Chek-it	$ 2.37

ZACHARY ROBERTS

Late in the spring of his second year in the MBA program, Zachary Roberts was waiting for an offer from the B.J. Gunness Construction Company, a small company based in Tucson, Arizona, with 1976 billings of about $14 million.

Zachary had been introduced to Frank Gunness, Executive Vice President of the B.J. Gunness Construction Company, by one of his Business School professors who knew of Zachery's career plans. Frank Gunness, 38, was a participant in the Small Company Management Program (SCMP) at the time he and Zachary were first introduced.

Their initial meeting occurred in February. Three months of telephone conversations, letter exchanges, and a visit at company expense to Tucson during Zachary's spring break subsequently followed. The objective of the visit was to have Zachary meet with Frank's father, B.J. Gunness (the founder, President and Chairman of the company), Frank's brother Charles, and other key employees of the company.

Now, however, several weeks had passed since his visit to Tucson and Zachary wondered whether he would get an offer. In the back of his mind there was a question: Could he have done anything else to have improved his chances of a position with Gunness?

ZACHARY ROBERTS

Following graduation from high school in 1963, Zachary was selected as a member of the U.S. Olympic boxing team. Shortly after the Games, Zachary turned professional. Though an outstanding student, he believed the upward potential of professional sports was considerably greater than that which could have been attained had he gone to college. However, it took less than one year as a professional for him to become aware of the downward risk associated with his decision.

Leaving professional sports behind, Zachary turned his attention and energies to business. He became involved in several small start-up situations, some of which were successful. However, he frequently found himself unable to take advantage of "real" opportunities as he did not have the requisite "credibility." Furstrated at being turned away so frequently, Zachary finally decided to go to college. He applied for and was granted admission to Dartmouth College in New Hampshire. Two years after graduation, he entered the MBA program at Harvard.

Shortly after his graduation from the MBA program, Zachary would turn 31 and he felt that he was too old to give serious consideration to an entry-level position in a large corporation. In Zachary's view:

> I've worked in a large company only once in my life and that was enough. I met some outstanding people and I had a lot of fun but there is little else I can say favorable about that experience. The tragedy with working in large business is that you're too frequently a cog in a wheel and nobody really cares what you do or how you do it. As

This case was prepared by Professors Kenneth Hatten and Neil Churchill as a basis for class discussion rather than to illustrate either effective or ineffective handling of an administrative situation.

> long as you put in your eight hours a day, that's all that's expected of you. I guess I don't care to invest three years of my life in some entry-level position with little or no real responsibility, waiting for the slight chance of being able to rise—oh, so gradually—through the ranks. The best I can ever see for myself in a large company is one day being awarded the innocuous position of Senior Vice President—Public Relations.

Zachary saw much greater opportunity for development and advancement in small business. Small businesses, he knew, could not afford the luxury of paying someone who was unproductive. In addition, he believed that many of the skills he had developed through his concentration in marketing in the MBA program and during his two years in commercial banking between college and graduate school would be of great value to many small businesses.

INITIAL MEETING WITH FRANK GUNNESS

During his initial meeting with Frank Gunness, Zachary was able to get a pretty good understanding of Gunness Construction and its problems. What was even more important to Zachary, however, was his feeling that the chemistry between Frank and himself was genuine. According to Zachary:

> It really meant a lot to me that my background and my being black were no big deal. Frank's primary interest, all the while, seemed to be my capabilities as a professional manager and my accompanying ability to help him with the problems facing his company.

During their discussion, Frank indicated that the company was coming off the worst year in its 40-year history. Frank further suggested that, as chief operating officer for the company, he had need for someone to assist him with marketing and new business development. "The meeting ended with Frank stating he needed someone like me to help him in the business and would like to discuss the matter further," Zachary explained.

FIRST LETTER TO FRANK

Collecting his thoughts on his meeting with Frank, Zachary could see two primary problems at Gunness Construction. The first problem was the relationship between Frank Gunness and his father, B.J. Gunness. B.J. had founded the business and still exercised considerable control over its direction. However, B.J. was not actively involved, and apparently often claimed that he "would like to get out." In spite of this, it was impractical to recommend that Frank raise money and buy out his father because his father's personal statement was needed to maintain the firm's existing bonding capacity—B.J.'s wealth partly indemnified for the bonding company.

A second problem in the company was that Frank had been spreading himself thin. The volume of business which the company enjoyed had long since passed the point where one person could handle all phases effectively. Frank, as chief operating officer, was attempting to coordinate projects in several parts of the state, bring a new branch office on-line in Phoenix, manage the home office in Tucson, prepare bids, and sell construction services. It seemed too much for one person to handle.

In his first letter to Frank (*Exhibit 1*), Zachary highlighted these problems and went into some depth as to the reasons for the company's poor performance during the most recent fiscal year. Zachary ended the letter with a series of corrective strategic suggestions to which Frank might wish to give some consideration and a statement of his sincere interest in the position which he and Frank had discussed.

Looking at the situation, Zachary had thought to himself, "The company is coming off its worst year ever. If I can contribute to the company's return to profitability, my potential reward could be significant. As far as I'm concerned my task is somewhat easy as I really don't believe there is anywhere else that the business can go except for up. I believe in this so much, and in my ability, that I am willing to guarantee 'performance to Frank's satisfaction' or will give him his money back!"

SUBSEQUENT COMMUNICATIONS

Following several conversations by telephone, Frank forwarded to Zachary, at the latter's request, Gunness's most recent financials and the promotional materials it used to sell various construction services.

The financials showed that company's net worth during the fiscal year ended May 31, 1976, had shrunk to half its value in the previous year. During that period, the cyclical construction market had contracted. With limited new construction, existing firms found themselves bidding on whatever business was available. For example, Frank had indicated that for two projects of the same type, which were separated by a year, on the first project there were two bidders while on the latter there were 17.

Between 1974 and 1976, margins had declined precipitously. Zachary noted that for each one-point margin decline, approximately $100,000 to $150,000 in contribution was involved. He also noted that if he separated revenues into public (bid) and private (negotiated), the public percentage of revenue was always greater—but contribution to overhead and profit was always greater for private work.

The promotional materials were at best bland and Zachary felt they did little or nothing to tell the story of the company or to help sell various construction services.

During the course of several of these conversations with Frank, Zachary detected what he believed to be a certain "cooling." He wondered whether B.J.'s lack of enthusiasm for a black professional in the company was the trouble. The reason B.J. gave, however, was his concern as to whether the company could "afford" Zachary's services.

THE TUCSON VISIT

It was at this point that Zachary suggested a visit to Tucson to meet with Frank, his father, and Frank's brother Charles.

On the plane, Zachary used the time to prepare a written report on the company's position. He highlighted the financial problems as well as several marketing problems, foremost of which was that (as he saw it) the company performed no systematic marketing whatsoever. The root of this problem was that B.J. had been a resident of Tucson since 1928 and had been active in a variety of civic organizations. For several years he had been Vice-Mayor of Tucson and he had expressed his opinion that since everyone knew him and the quality work Gunness did, there was no need to sell.

Zachary's report concluded with a two-phased recommendation. The first he titled "Short-term Survival." His position was that he did not doubt that the company could get as much 3% contribution margin business as it desired (which was what B.J. believed—a belief which led him to see no problems for the business at all). However, Zachary suggested that the attendant risks of relying on this type of business were too great; any unforeseen delay or problem could wipe out the entire profit on the job and even result in a loss. Zachary recommended a short-term objective for the company: to build up its traditional business by focusing on negotiated work.

The second phase of Zachary Robert's recommendation dealt with the long-term growth prospects of the business. Here he suggested using any excess cash the business generated more productively. Rather than be persuaded to put excess cash into things they did not understand (as had been the case in the past—the Gunness family had invested in a project headed by a professor from the University of Arizona to develop a revolutionary carburetor scheme and had lost money), they should invest only in projects they could control. Zachary suggested that his tack raised for consideration speculative real estate projects of a turnkey type, where Gunness could be both general contractor and developer. These investments could be "inventoried," and Zachary believed they would not in any way adversely affect the company's working capital position or bonding capacity.

Upon arrival, Zachary presented his report to Frank. Frank was immediately impressed and had the report typed to be presented to B.J. and Charles.

MEETING WITH B.J. AND CHARLES

Zachary recalled, "Frank had described B.J. as 'an ornery and cantankerous old cuss'—your classic stubborn, hard-nosed entrepreneur as I imagined Alfred Schumpeter, the conservative economist of the 1930s, would have described him." Zachary found him to be eccentric, but this was not too surprising as B.J. was "74 years young." What was most surprising for Zachary, however, was that B.J. was extremely polite and receptive to everything he said about the business. Zachary was caught quite off guard and could only think to himself, "I'm either extremely convincing or I've most certainly blown it. I don't know if all this is either good or bad!"

Between Frank and his brother Charles, Zachary detected what appeared to be a classic relationship between brothers in a small business context. Charles, 27, was the younger of the two and was looked upon by Frank as being inexperienced and unable to take on additional responsibility. Characteristically, Charles seemed somewhat insecure and aligned himself with B.J. when disagreements occurred. B.J. insulated him from Frank. Zachary felt he had to be very careful to do nothing, either in word or action, to directly or indirectly threaten Charles.

Nonetheless, Zachary left Tucson feeling pretty optimistic. The meetings with B.J., Charles, and business associates of Frank had gone, in his opinion, "extremely well." Frank indicated he would be getting back to Zachary within a few days. As the plane headed east into the twilight, Zachary thought he would receive an offer from Gunness and could begin work in either Phoenix or Tucson sometime in June.

THE PRESENT

Several weeks had passed since his visit and Zachary had not yet received an offer. Zachary wondered what could have gone wrong, what he could have done better, and when, if at all, an offer would be forthcoming. He wondered what he should do next.

EXHIBIT 1

February 22, 1977

Mr. Frank Gunness
B. J. Gunness Construction Co.
Tucson, Arizona

Dear Frank:

I especially enjoyed meeting and speaking with you during your trip here for the SCMP. Since our conversation, I've given considerable thought to the position we discussed as well as to your particular situation. It seems to me the position which we talked about can be subdivided into three distinct tasks: New business development generation; construction management services (project control); and strategic market planning.

Let me discuss how I view each of these tasks. I recall that you indicated one of your prime objectives is to grow "as fast as you can." With your billings in the vicinity of $14 million, your sales growth objective suggests exponential rather than arithmetic growth. To illustrate this graphically, your task could be described as follows:

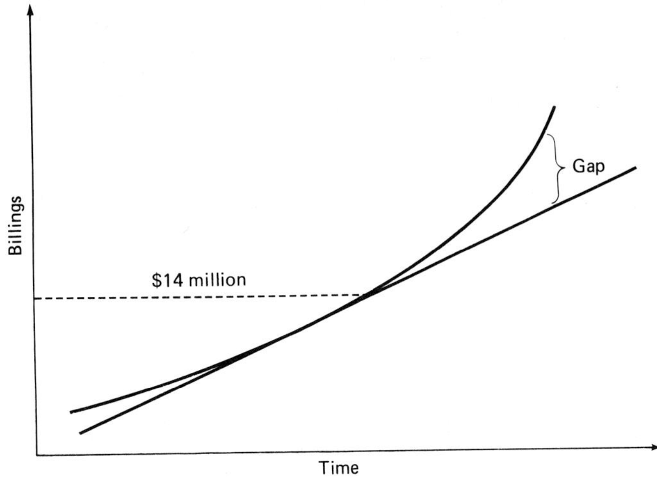

To transcend the gap in order to realize your desired rate of growth, you're going to have to be creative and very aggressive in your pursuit of new business. Only in this way will you be able to overcome the gap between your *historical* and your desired billings projected trend line.

New business development activities will, of course, include concerted efforts to promote construction and engineering projects in your traditional lines. However, aggressive and all-out attempts should be made to establish yourself in new areas such as construction management services and, possibly, subject to further investigation, even real property development projects.

You indicated that on a recent project in Phoenix, you had some problems which resulted in cost overruns. My familiarity with PERT and Critical Path Methods of analysis can help you to better stay abreast of costs and project progress in your traditional businesses as well as in the feasibility analysis and control of projects in new business areas.

The last critical task associated with the job which we discussed is perhaps the most important to the B. J. Gunness Construction Company. Everything I have discussed up to this point, as well as everything you should be doing to achieve your desired growth and profit objectives, lies inextricably tied to it. This task is the strategic planning function. From our conversation it was evident you've clearly given considerable thought to this critical issue. To be certain, the time and expense invested to formulate a strategic corporate plan by appraising your current performance and assessing the long term needs and prospects of your business will be well justified.

The thoughts I've had since I talked to you have preoccupied my mind and would permit me to write on almost without end. But as time and space are limited, allow me to close by stating I am *especially* interested in pursuing this matter further. I know well my capabilities as well as my limitations. What I can tell you for sure is that each of the tasks discussed in this letter I could perform very well. I can assure you, in fact, I can generate enough new business and cost savings for B. J. Gunness Construction Company in my first year to have earned my pay. Further, without hesitation, I *guarantee* results and your personal satisfaction or will give you your money back.

The position with its attendant responsibilities represents a real opportunity. Personally, my objective is to be able to earn a low six figure salary within the next five years. You can see I am obliged to work very hard if I am to achieve this goal.

I am extremely enthusiastic over the prospect of joining B. J. Gunness Construction Company. In fact, I doubt seriously if you could find anyone who wants the opportunity more or who would work as hard or who could be as successful in the position as I.

I would like to begin work on the presentation which we discussed as soon as possible. In order to do so, I must first get from you copies of your most recent financials (three years), types of projects in which you have been involved (by project description and by dollar amount), and any information—general or specific—as to the operations of your competitors.

I can be reached at the address shown on the above letterhead or by phone if you should wish to call. I look forward to hearing from you soon.

Very truly yours,

B. J. GUNNESS CONSTRUCTION COMPANY

''I would like to get off the hook to the bonding company but I don't know if I can do it,'' said Benjamin J. Gunness, President and founder of the B. J. Gunness Construction Company. ''The bonding company insists that every officer of the construction company they bond put his personal financial statements behind the bond. If I pull out of the company, it could cut our bonding capacity and our ability to bid for new work. If I stay, all that my wife and I have worked for can be wiped out by one or two really bad jobs. I like the business; it is at least half of what I own, and I don't want to jeopardize it since it is going to my boys, Frank and Charles. But while they do most of the work, I still like to be involved, and people in this town know me and like to do business with me. Besides, I really don't have any other interests. Yet at my age, I would like to know that my wife and I have financial security.

HISTORY OF GUNNESS CONSTRUCTION

B. J. Gunness moved to Arizona in 1922. Although he came from a construction family, B.J. was interested in banking and worked in it in Tucson and then Phoenix until the banks closed at the start of the Depression. With jobs in banking essentially nonexistent, B.J. moved back to Tucson with his new wife ''doing most anything I could, including repairing and remodeling repossessed houses using the skills I picked up working with my father. My wife also worked as a secretary/bookkeeper in a number of offices.'' When the economy turned up a bit, B.J. began to manage properties for mortgage and insurance companies which had repossessed the properties back ''when their owners couldn't make the payment and simply walked away.''

His property management work led B.J. to start a small house-building operation with his wife and one or two employees in the late 1930s. When the war came along, and building materials could be obtained only with government allocations, Gunness kept his business afloat by bidding on small government contracts and working in a Tucson aircraft factory. ''My wife did the payroll and kept the books. I was out at the job early in the morning and at the plant from 4:00 P.M. until midnight. I kept this up during the war until 1945 when I finally got a medical discharge from the factory.''

With the war over, B.J. began building houses and small commercial buildings, one or two at a time. He increased his equity capital to buying old houses, fixing them up and selling them on a contract basis. He then moved into school construction and ''just grew with Tucson,'' becoming a city council member and then vice-mayor in the late 1950s. In addition to construction, he developed some desert land for cotton outside of Tucson and then in Mexico—flying back and forth between Tucson and Hermosillio, and, in his words, ''keeping pretty busy.'' By the late 1950s, Gunness Construction was doing

This case was prepared by Professor Neil C. Churchill as a basis for class discussion rather than to illustrate either effective or ineffective handling of an administrative situation.

$2 million to $3 million a year in business and had moved out of housing into heavier construction, employing engineers and supervisors capable of building hospitals, schools, and industrial buildings.

In 1960, B.J.'s oldest son, Frank, entered the business full time—although he had worked in all its different aspects part time and in summers during his school years. Frank left the company in 1963 to work for Rhyne & Murdoch, a large construction company in San Francisco. He returned in 1965 to become General Manager, the position he has held ever since.

During the 1960s Gunness Construction took on increasingly larger jobs, including a community college project for $3.5 million ("$8 million to $10 million at 1977 prices," remarked B.J. Gunness), expanded the sphere of its operations to communities up to 150 miles from Tucson, and developed the capability to do more complex engineering jobs. In 1968, B.J.'s other son, Charles, entered the company from college. At that time, Frank was 30 and B.J. was 64.

THE COMPANY AND ITS ENVIRONMENT

Gunness Construction, as a general contractor, has two main sources of business. In the first, it submits competitive bids to governmental organizations or private businesses for construction work, usually against very detailed specifications. For the second type of work, it "negotiates" contracts with organizations in situations where Gunness helps develop the specifications, as well as construct the building. The profit margin on negotiable contracts is usually higher than on competitively bid jobs. In either case, Gunness subcontracts some 80% of the job and performs the other 20% with its own employees. Gunness, however, guarantees the satisfactory completion of the building. If one of its subcontractors goes out of business or does the job poorly, Gunness has to finish the job, "a situation that can cost us a lot unless the subs are bonded," B.J. noted.

To perform its work properly, Gunness has engineers and estimators evaluate what the job requires, develop a detailed plan to do the job, and "take off the costs of the specifications" to determine the bid price. Besides the bids themselves, a key factor in contract profitability is the job superintendent who manages the jobs and sees that the subcontractors do their work properly. Gunness also tries to keep a nucleus of good carpenters and laborers employed all year long so they can be spread out among those hired from the union when new jobs come along.

To give a financial assurance for performance, all major contracts require that Gunness take out a construction bond for the value of the contract. The bonding company is then liable for the building being completed properly. It in turn has recourse against Gunness Construction and, as mentioned before, the personal assets of its owner/managers.

Bonding companies limit the extent of their liability by restricting the dollar amount that they will go "on risk" to a construction company. This "bonding capacity" of the construction company is based on the perceived strength of the management, its track record, its financial strength, and its owners' financial assets. The bonding capacity is usually stated as a multiple of the construction company's "net surety allowed," which is defined as : 1) current assets—not including prepaid expenses, deposits, inventory, and receivables from officers—less 2) current liabilities plus one year's interest on all debt. Gunness nominally has had a multiple of 20:1 of its net surety allowed but has had exceptions regularly made on a contract-by-contract basis. Gunness has also found that it can plan to "sell" about 130% of its bonding capacity a year, since the amount of the bond required on each job is for the uncompleted construction, which decreases as the job proceeds.

There is a third type of business which Gunness and other large contractors are involved in called "construction management." In construction management, the contractor assumes a role similar to that of an agent for the organization which wants a building constructed. As such, Gunness works with the designers, architects and contractors, "managing" the process and ensuring that what is constructed is what the owners want in design, quality and done at a relevant price. They do not, however, do any construction work. It is, in Frank Gunness' words, "a more technically and managerially challenging type of business, with less risk. It also does not use up very much, if any, of our bonding capacity."

THE CURRENT SITUATION

During the late 1960s and early 1970s, Gunness Construction grew and prospered. It built a number of schools, hospitals, and public and private buildings in and around Tucson. In 1975 it established a branch in Phoenix, acquiring an office building and incurring, for the first time in the company's history, some long-term debt. As B.J. put it, "Perhaps because I worked in a bank, or maybe because of what I saw during the Depression, I have always tried to keep our debt down. All the equipment we bought was for cash, the Tucson building was paid for in cash, and, until the Phoenix acquisition, I hadn't borrowed a dime from the bank in 10 years."

Gunness Construction not only constructed buildings on its own, but also entered into joint venture arrangements with Rhyne & Murdoch on several larger projects in Arizona. Profits were good in the late 1960s and early 1970s, and Gunness shared them with its employees through profit-sharing and pension fund plans that gave 25% of each year's profits to the employees. "The reason for this," said B. J. Gunness, "is that there is a very uneven profit cycle in the construction business. When the company makes money, the people who produced it should share in it; when it doesn't, you don't want these payments locked into high wages. The IRS challenged me for going over 15%, but they gave in, since we had been allocating 25% for so many years."

Besides substantial bonuses, Gunness Construction also provided transportation and entertainment allowances to its top employees and had entered into two or three tax saving ventures in the last few years. The result was a growth in sales, growth in profits, but little or no growth in working capital. To paraphrase a representative of the bonding company, "We could not tell if B.J.'s intent was to grow the company or to gradually liquidate it."

In 1973, the economy in Tucson turned down and building contractors "started to hurt badly." Gunness, however, had several large jobs in process and so did not feel the effects until late 1974. Its May 31, 1975 statements showed an operating loss (see *Exhibits 1* and *2*). The recession worsened and became, for the building industry in Tucson, "the worst since the Depression of the '30s. Competition grew very severe." In 1975 and 1976

Gunness increased its volume, due in part to $4 million in sales from its Phoenix office. The sales, however, produced little profit due to severe competitive pressures, increased activity by open shop contractors, and the increasing use of non-union subcontractors by union shop construction firms. The summer and fall of 1976 found Gunness unable to successfully bid for any contract under $500,000 in size. "We would bid along with twenty others and be the lowest of all the union shop bidders and maybe four or five down from the top of the ten open shop people," said Frank Gunness. "We could never get as low as the others and we would lose the bid." Gunness, however, did obtain two or three negotiated contracts and a number of smaller jobs in the latter part of 1976. In early 1977, business began to pick up and Gary Thompson, the controller, estimated that Gunness Construction would end the 1977 fiscal year with a sales volume of $8 million and continue at that level through the first six months of fiscal 1978. Profits, however, would probably reflect the extreme competitiveness in Tucson and a negative adjustment of over $100,000 on two jobs in Phoenix. These jobs produced a $40,000 loss, but Gunness Construction had, through its construction in-process accounting system, recognized profits of $60,000 on them in the 1976 statements.

THE UNION SITUATION

Gunness Construction is a closed shop, that is, a union shop bound by its contract from hiring nonunion labor. Every third year, it signs a contract with five craft unions,[1] as do most of the large contractors in Arizona. In recent years, quite a few contractors have moved to an "open shop" or nonunion operation, and several have begun to operate two companies, one open and one union shop. In addition, a number of other contractors have begun using nonunion subcontractors on their jobs. The advantage of a closed shop is the greater availability of trained people to take on large projects or those under time pressure. "On the airport facility we built last year, we had thirty-five electricians working at one time," said B.J. Gunness. "That was a six-month, $2-million-plus job and we couldn't do that any way except as a union shop." The disadvantages of a union shop are higher labor costs per hour—one estimate has the effective cost some 60% higher—and less flexibility in work rules and work assignments.

"To meet competition, we used a nonunion electrical subcontractor for the first time," said Charles Gunness. "We can only do that for the unions which are not signatories on our labor contracts, such as electricians and plumbers, and we may get into trouble with union subcontractors on later bids. But we can only wait and see. Maybe we should try to have two companies, one union and one non-union. Some contractors have done it successfully and some have had trouble. The law may change on union picketing and make this all unworkable, but, until then, it is sure something we have to consider. Otherwise, I don't see how we can compete, at least on the smaller jobs, in the competitive bid market."

[1]Laborers, cement finishers, carpenters, operating engineers, and teamsters.

BONDING

Gunness Construction Company had done business for many years with one bonding company, a subsidiary of MMF, Inc. Then, in 1974, MMF and a number of other bonding companies experienced a series of losses nationwide. While most bonding companies cut back their exposure and their bonding limits, MMF closed down its bonding operations entirely and Gunness Construction moved to Acme Bonding.

Acme Bonding has a firm policy of having those responsible for activities of the construction companies they bond "stand behind what they ask of the bonding company with their personal assets," according to Woody Jones, Gunness' account representative from Acme. "This keeps them from walking away from any problem jobs. They work on them, save most of them, and we are all better off."

Besides requiring personal indemnification, Jones was concerned that Gunness demonstrate that it could make a profit. "We don't want Gunness Construction to be a well for B.J. to drop his money into; we want it to be a viable company." He stated that Acme's commitment to Gunness Construction had been reduced to $6 million in bonding capacity because of Gunness' financial trend, and that this limit was subject to:

1 Gunness making at least $25,000 in profit in the first six months of the 1978 fiscal year (June through November 1977) and showing a positive profit trend thereafter;
2 Increases or decreases in bonding capacity in subsequent periods based on twenty times the "net surety allowed" at the beginning of each six-month period.

In discussing B.J.'s involvement on the bond, Woody Jones re-emphasized Acme's policy of personal commitment of those involved in the business. When asked what would happen should B.J. have to suddenly leave the business because of ill health, he replied, "The bonding limit would depend on Frank's ability to manage the company when such an event occurs." He added, "If there were no problems with the financial position of the company due, say, to inheritance taxes, and there were profits and management continuity, I would see no problems in bonding Gunness." Jones then reminded Frank, Charles, and B.J. that a bonding capacity of $6 million would require a surety capital of $300,000 by November 30 and that he would like to see some money stay in, or even enter, the company "instead of being withdrawn."

FRANK GUNNESS

When asked to comment on his position in Gunness Construction and how he sees its current problems, Frank Gunness said: "My present role is general manager of operations and new business development," (see the organization chart, *Exhibit 3*). "I make the assignments as far as project management is concerned. I select the projects we want to bid, and I hire and fire personnel, although, as far as the engineering personnel are concerned, I don't get out into the field. The field superintendents do their own hiring and firing but I hire and fire the superintendents and it is up to me in the final analysis to see that we maintain control.

"I think over the last couple of years I have had to assume more responsibility for financial control and planning. I had more or less left these up to my dad in the past—setting policy, collecting money, and distributing funds—but in the past couple of years I have had to do more of this. That is why I went to the SCMP[2] program—to get a little more in-depth understanding of financial principles, accounting, and control, since I see myself getting more intensely involved in this in the next few years. This was why I hired a CPA with some experience early this year, to provide us the information we, as top managers, need to make decisions in both the long run and the short run. Gary has been with us only a short time, but he has been very helpful.

"What we need now is more negotiated contract work, design and build work, and construction management work. We have been fortunate because our joint venture experiences with Rhyne and Murdoch have given us the capability to handle the large jobs this work involves. We have the people, and we have the in-house expertise to do projects up to $5 million in size. We have the joint venture capability for larger projects; we could even be the sponsor on joint ventures up to $10 million. The competitive bid market is not so hot these days, and these are the areas we should be looking at.

"Now one problem we have is that I don't really have enough time to do as much in sales as I would like. I think I should put more of my time in operations—we have had some cost overruns that we can't afford to repeat. We moved into Phoenix too rapidly without the necessary staff. The hardest thing in expanding into a new market is having the proper experienced and knowledgeable people behind the operation. We didn't and we paid for it. Phoenix is a good market but it will require some time to run it well, and it will take time for someone to build up a selling effort. When I was back at Harvard for the second SCMP unit, I talked with an MBA who will be graduating this June, Zachary Roberts, who seemed interested in moving out to the Southwest and getting involved with a small company. He doesn't know construction, but he has been involved in real estate with a Boston bank. He is coming out to visit us next week, we can take a closer look at each other. I had thought about moving to Phoenix myself last year, but now with the bonding company problem I think I should stay here. We could move with a marketing man there; it could really pay off to hire one. We have a good project manager in Phoenix now, and they could be the team we need. That way I could stay in Tucson where our estimating will be done. We are selling our office building in Phoenix and will rent a smaller facility.

"Charles, my younger brother, is still in the process of learning the management ropes. He knows field work and is coming along with his new responsibilities, but he is not ready for a general management job just yet. If we grow larger—particularly if we develop the Phoenix market—there will be work for both of us, and we will need, in addition, more professional people.

"Right now, however, the priority should be getting more negotiated contracts and more contract management business. I think we need a well-thought-through marketing effort and that's what I am looking for in Zack Roberts. I also think that his background at Harvard will help all of us at Gunness. One of the things he can do is to help professionalize the firm. I hope I can figure out how to afford him if he is interested and if he fits.

[2]Smaller Company Management Program at Harvard Business School.

"It is also clear to me that we will have to change our way of thinking about this corporation and get it out in front, instead of thinking primarily about our own private interests. We are going to have to build up working capital and cut down on the distribution of earnings to the shareholders. If we want to grow, we will have fewer officer perks and maybe substitute stock options for cash bonuses. This is all going to take planning. This year we are getting, for the first time in the history of the company, an operating budget. Gary Thompson is preparing a budget for fiscal 1978, and we can compare costs against it on an item-by-item basis. I think Roberts could work with Gary in this area as well.

"With the market the way it is, we may have to get into non-traditional construction areas even beyond the negotiated contracts we are used to. There are other contractors doing 'design and build' projects, turnkey projects, real estate development, and the like. Here too, Zack Roberts could be of help. All this means working capital, however, and I think B.J., Charles, and I are going to have to look a little bit more at equity growth than cash payout. We also have to worry about Dad's financial commitment on our bonding contract and start phasing out his exposure and getting the company on its own two feet.

"As an alternative, we could cut back to $3 to $4 million a year, start over, and go back up. We have the experience, the record of successful projects, but we would have to let almost all our personnel go. Charles and I have talked about it, and neither of us like it.

"We have a devil of a problem with this open shop competition, but building trends are up. The bonding company has us between two edges of a scissors—we have to live with a reduced bond but we also have to turn a profit. We know we have to raise working capital, so we are selling our Phoenix office building and taking out a bank loan to borrow the $250,000, the bank manager asked him why he needed the money since we had $148,000 in our operating account and $140,000 in a savings account. All we are going to do is put the money in Certificates of Deposit (CD's) through the bank—and that is pretty good business for them.

"We know we have to make profits so we've worked out a plan to reduce overhead. We let an engineer go last week, a payroll clerk will go by Friday, and we are letting an estimator go in Phoenix at the end of the month. Gary worked up an operating budget with B.J., Charles, and me [*Exhibit 4*] which cuts our overhead from $500,000 to $328,000. We cut the rent we pay Dad on the building by half, I'm going to sell the Maserati, and we all are cutting personal charges. It will take us April and May to get there, but that is what we will live with next year. I hope it is enough."

GARY THOMPSON

Following his interview with Frank, the casewriter discussed the financial projections with Gary Thompson. Gary stated that his best estimate was that Gunness Construction would lose, after tax refunds, $55,000 in 1977 and have surety working capital on May 31, 1977, of approximately $120,000. The company had taken out a 5-year installment loan on its construction equipment and machinery with the bank for $250,000 at 1½% over prime. This would add about $180,000 to the net surety allowed—since the first year's principal payments of $50,000 and interest of about $20,000 would have to be subtracted from the proceeds. Gary also believed that the sale of the Phoenix property would yield $80,000, giving them $380,000 surety at the start of the fiscal year.

In looking toward 1978, Gary stated, "We are working at a rate of about $675,000 a month, and that is 135% of a $6 million bonding capacity; 130% is about what we have managed historically. Our gross profit figures have ranged between 3½% and 5%, and, if I would project our current market mix, I would use 4% based on the recent past. We have enough contracts to give us a $25,000 to $30,000 operating profit by November, and since we will put the borrowed money in CD's, our net interest expenses won't be very much.

"As I see it, we have to move faster to be competitive. We haven't moved with the times in bidding, in using nonunion subs, or in moving into negotiated work. This means we have to have some type of a marketing program. If it costs more, we will just have to take the money from somewhere else. We need a strong marketing man, particularly in Phoenix, the potential there for negotiated business is outstanding. Maybe this Zachary Roberts is our man and maybe he isn't, but we can't afford to wait too long. We have six months to mount a marketing effort that gets us the jobs we need to produce a profit in the six months following our November statements. These are the ones that are critical to the bonding company."

Gary and the casewriter discussed the financial projections beyond November 30, 1977. When Gary stated that the market beyond November was so unsettled that he was hesitant to make a forecast, the casewriter suggested, and Gary agreed, that it would be useful to have a forecast prepared. The forecast should use three different estimated rates of return on contract revenues—4%, 4½%, and 5%—with sales (contract revenues) calculated in each case at the maximum allowed under Gunness's bonding agreement. The 4% rate forecast represented a good level of profits that could be expected from business that was predominantly competitively bid. The 5% rate forecast represented a reasonable level of profits expected from negotiated contracts, and the 4½% rate has a level that would be the maximum Gunness could aspire to without a substantial change in market direction. It was also agreed to build into the costs an extra $50,000 a year needed to obtain a high percentage of negotiated contracts, $25,000 a year for the 4½% forecast, and no extra expenses at the 4% profit level. Gary said he could have a three-year forecast for the planning meeting scheduled the next morning.

THE PLANNING MEETING

The planning meeting, attended by B. J. Gunness, Frank Gunness, Gary Thompson, and the casewriter, began with Gary distributing his operating projections (*Exhibits 4* and *5*) and explaining what assumptions lay behind the numbers.

"The November 30, 1977 figures are pretty solid; we have almost all the contracts in the house, with enough progress on the bigger ones to estimate our six-month profit. The bonding company will let us have $6 million capacity, so with construction revenues at 1.3 times bonding capacity, I estimate six-month sales at $4,050,000 and a gross profit of $202,500. Our budgeted operating expenses are estimated to be $327,810 a year (*Exhibit 3*). But I think we will be a bit slow getting there, so I estimated $175,000. This gives us a profit of $27,500. We will make $25,000 in installment payments to the bank, so this leaves us with a $2,500 addition to working capital. If we begin with the $380,000

I told you about earlier, we will have a bonding capacity of $7,650,000 for use in the six months following November 30. I assume that this will take effect in the middle of the period, so I took an average and got a $6,825,000 average bonding capacity. At a 130% utilization for one half year, that is contract revenue of $4,436,000 for the last six months of our next fiscal year.

"Now, in the six months ended May 31, 1978, I assumed three different gross profit margins and three different levels of operating expenses. For operations that produce a 5% gross profit, I added one-half of $50,000 extra marketing expenditures a year to our budget operating expenses; at 4½%, one-half of $25,000; and at 4%, I just took the budgeted figures. To cover a minimum level of inflation, I added $25,000 a year after 1978 in two $12,500 steps. Any questions?"

While the profit planning worksheet was being read and discussed with Gary, the casewriter drew up a graph of profits that Gary forecasted. This graph, *Exhibit 6,* was then shown to the group. "You will notice," said the casewriter, "that the bonding capacity holds you down on the one side so that you can't spread high overhead over a lot of low-profit contracts. On the other hand, overhead, inflation, and debt repayment holds down your working capital, and hence your bonding capacity. There is a phrase that comes to mind—'between a rock and a hard place!'"

B. J. Gunness: Well, I hear the numbers and I see the picture. What do we do, Gary?

Gary: If we could cut our operating expenses back to $250,000 a year, we can survive handsomely at 4%. If we can't, then we had better get the 5% business. If that is not possible, then we had better bite the bullet as soon as possible and shrink the company and its overhead.

B.J.: Well, if we can get away from competitive bidding the 5% margin is no problem. But we can't get it if we have to bid—at least not as we are—and I don't know if we could do it successfully on an open shop basis.

On the other hand, how can we, with these numbers and with our present overhead, afford to go out and spend another $50,000 to open up another market with the limited bonding capacity we have to work with? And how can someone who doesn't know contracting, and doesn't know Tucson or Phoenix, do it in time to help us? This is the thing in my mind, and I wish someone could answer it.

Frank Gunness: We would have to gamble and take on the overhead before we would see any results, and there would be a learning period in front of that. I don't think that $50,000 is the right cost, however. I think that salary, fringes, automobile, and T&E wouldn't run over $35,000 a year.

Gary: But how can we continue in the markets we are in and make the profits the analysis shows we need?

Frank: I don't think a 1% difference in price is going to really make that much difference as to whether we get a job or not. The difference between a low bidder and the second low bidder is greater than a 1% spread—usually 2% to 2½%.

B.J.: I agree with that, Frank, and the economy is turning around now. This has been a really bad year in Tucson. All the architects in town have laid off people and that doesn't happen here very often. I think the picture is changing. I think next year will see a lot of jobs up for bid, and we have always gotten our share. I really don't think we have to get excited and go out after new business—at least as long as our pipeline is full.

Gary: Well, whatever we decide, it has to be done quickly. We have April and May to make a plan; four months to implement it; and two months to react one way or another before November 30 when the bonding company looks at our situation. We aren't really pressed, but we don't have that much breathing-room either.

Frank: One thing I learned at SCMP is that any plan we put together has to fit our interests and the realities of the business market. It has to be coordinated—all the pieces put together under the same assumptions.

Casewriter: That's right, Frank. As I see it you have two simultaneous sets of decisions to make. The first is, what should be the business strategy of Gunness Construction. What do you want the company to be and how do you plan to get it there—competitive bids, negotiable contracts, open shop, open subcontractors, marketing, Zack Roberts, or what?

The second is, what do you want your role in Gunness Construction to be, Frank, and yours, B.J.? What do you personally want from the company, and what do you want to put into it—time, energy, money? And most importantly, how does the second set of factors fit in with the first? If you want to remain active in the company for personal reasons, B.J.,—and you have said that you would rather do that than play golf or gin—then that has an implication not only on your financial exposure, but on the bond size and even on the way the bonding company will view you, Frank, and the company. I think the idea of developing a corporate plan is a good idea, but, it seems to me, you have some personal planning to do at the same time.

EXHIBIT 1
B. J. GUNNESS CONSTRUCTION COMPANY
Statement of Income and Retained Earnings
(Thousands of dollars)

	Year Ended May 31			6 Months Ended Nov. 30	Projected Year Ended
	1974	1975	1976	1976	5-31-77
Contract Income	7385.9	6186.0	13669.7	4924.9	8100
Cost of Contract Income	6849.4	5821.9	13154.8	4830.8	7800
Gross Profit	536.5	364.1	514.9	94.1	300
Cost of Contract Guarantee				(7.2)	
Joint Venture Income, rentals, etc.	154.5	62.2	(11.9)	(3.8)	-0-
Gross Profit from Contracting Operations	691.0	426.3	503.0	83.1	300
Operating Expenses	400.3	512.2	497.6	249.1	500
Operating Income	290.7	(85.9)	5.4	(166.0)	(200)
Interest and other Income (expenses)	44.5	(36.0)	7.7	4.5	5
Profit (loss) before Taxes	335.2	(121.9)	13.1	(161.5)	(195)
Taxes (including Reduction in Deferred amounts and Tax carry-backs)	169.5	(92.3)	(12.3)	(140.0)	(140)
Net Profit after Tax Considerations and adjustments	165.7	(29.6)	25.4	(21.5)	(55)
Retained Earnings - Beginning of Period	167.8	333.5	303.9	329.3	308
Retained Earnings - End of Period	33.5	303.9	329.3	307.8	253
Gross Profit Percentages	7.3%	5.9%	3.8%	1.9%	3.7%

EXHIBIT 2
B. J. GUNNESS CONSTRUCTION COMPANY
Comparative Balance Sheets
(Thousands of Dollars)

Assets	May 31 1974	May 31 1975	May 31 1976	Nov. 30 1976
Current Assets				
Cash and Certificates of Deposit	493.7	246.9	241.6	68.9
Contract Receivables	—			
Current	907.2	639.9	1452.8	1104.9
Retention	462.6	382.6	696.3	397.3
Receivables from Federal & State Tax Refunds	—	—	—	41.4
Officers Notes & Accrued Interest	75.2	221.6	51.3	30.5
Other Receivables	17.2	6.3	7.8	8.8
Costs & Estimated Earnings in Excess of Billings on Uncompleted Orders	4.8	27.5	15.0	4.3
Prepaid Expenses, Deposits, and Cash Value of Life Insurance	23.6	34.6	42.7	38.7
Investment and Advances to Joint Venture	118.9	63.5	29.0	8.0
Total	2103.2	1622.9	2536.5	1702.8
Property, Plant & Equipment				
Land	—	37.6	38.9	33.7
Buildings & Improvements	—	90.3	95.3	92.3
Transportation Equipment	92.1	111.9	138.0	138.0
Construction Equipment & Machinery	137.4	133.3	144.0	146.8
Office Furniture and Equipment	27.2	26.9	28.9	34.0
Leasehold Improvements	19.5	22.5	22.5	22.5
	276.2	422.5	467.6	467.3
Less Accumulated Depreciation	161.4	177.8	216.4	232.0
Net Property, Plant & Equipment	114.8	244.7	251.2	235.3
TOTAL ASSETS	2218.0	1867.6	2787.7	1938.1
Equities				
Current Liabilities				
Subcontracts Payable				
Current	880.4	550.1	1204.6	940.0
Retention	268.3	276.2	500.6	275.5
Current Portion of Mortgage Payable	—	18.2	2.5	2.7
Billings in Excess of Cost & Estimated Earnings on Uncompleted Contracts	331.0	245.7	457.2	187.1
Accrued Liabilities	59.3	208.7	69.2	39.2
Taxes Payable	278.3	144.5	107.6	70.6
Total	1817.3	1443.4	2341.7	1515.1
Long Term Liabilities				
Mortgage Payable (Net of Current Portion)	—	53.1	49.5	48.0
Deferred Taxes	48.7	48.7	48.7	48.7
Total Liabilities	1866.0	1545.2	2439.9	1611.8
Stockholders Equity				
Common Stock	18.5	18.5	18.5	18.5
Retained Earnings	333.5	303.9	329.3	307.8
Total	352.0	322.4	347.8	326.3
TOTAL EQUITY	2218.0	1867.6	2787.7	1938.1

EXHIBIT 3

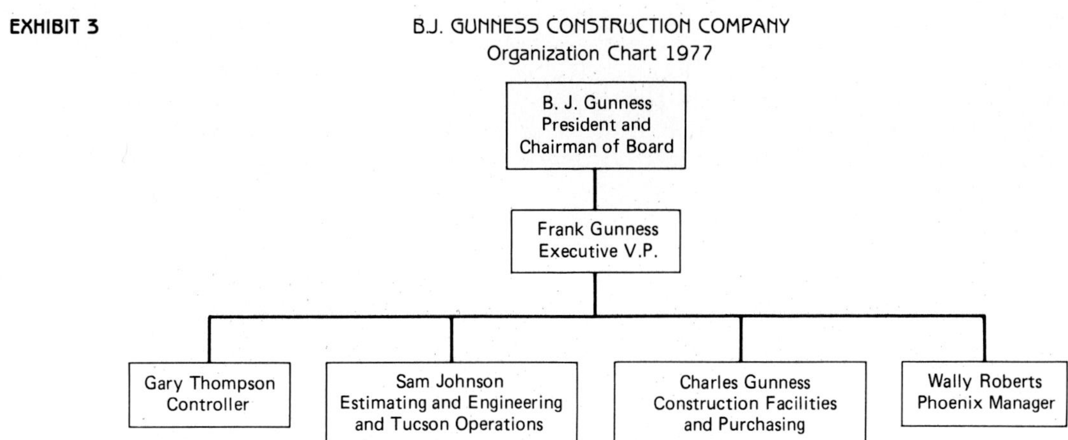

EXHIBIT 4 Gunness Construction Company Overhead Account

Budget Category	*Current Operating Expenses*	*Proposed Reductions*	*Projected Operating Expenses*
Salaries & Payroll Taxes	285,960	(76,942)	209,018
Depreciation	47,550	(22,444)	25,106
Equip. Repair & Maint.	27,500	(5,000)	22,500
Legal & Accounting	25,000	(15,000)	10,000
Pension and Profit Sharing	25,000	(25,000)	—
Rent	19,500	(9,500)	10,000
Telephone	19,000	(8,000)	11,000
Insurance	28,570	(2,194)	26,376
Office Expense	18,750	(8,000)	10,750
Travel & Entertainment	17,500	(11,500)	6,000
Training & Recruiting	16,000	(13,500)	2,500
Property Tax	10,000	—	10,000
Utilities	8,000	—	8,000
Gas & Oil	7,160	(2,160)	5,000
Advertising	6,640	(4,140)	2,500
Interest	4,450	6,500	10,950
Vehicle Licenses	5,370	(2,970)	2,400
Data Processing	4,500	(1,500)	3,000
Building Maintenance	4,400	—	4,400
Group Insurance	3,300	(690)	2,610
Radio	3,470	(2,520)	950
Shop Supplies	3,480	(1,230)	2,250
Dues & Subscriptions	3,340	(840)	2,500
Other	1,000	(1,000)	—
Total Operating Expenses	595,440	(207,630)	387,810
Allocations to Job Cost			
Equipment	(65,024)	(20,024)	(45,000)
Insurance	(20,916)	(5,916)	(15,000)
Net Operating Expenses	509,500	181,690	327,810

EXHIBIT 5
B. J. GUNNESS CONSTRUCTION COMPANY
Profit Planning Worksheet
Six-Month Periods Ending
(Thousands of Dollars)

Date	*November 30 1977*	*March 31, 1978*			*November 30, 1978*			*March 31, 1979*		
Forecast gross profit percentage	*NA*	*5%*	*4½%*	*4%*	*5%*	*4½%*	*4%*	*5%*	*4½%*	*4%*
Bonding capacity—start of period (annual)	6000	6000.	6000	6000	7650	7650		7808	7614	7421
Bonding capacity—end of period (annual)	6000	7650	7650	7650	7808	7614	7421	8332	7828	7339
Average	6000	6825	6825	6825	7729	7632		8070	7721	7380
Annual sales rate (1.3 times average)	Not applicable	8872	8872	8872	10048	9922		10491	10037	9594
Sales available in six months' period	4050	4436	4436	4436	5023	4960	4898	5246	5019	4799
Gross profit	202.5	221.8	199.6	177.4	251.2	223.2		262.3	225.8	191.9
Operating expenses	175.0	188.9[1]	176.4[2]	163.9[3]	200.0	187.5		212.5	200.0	187.5
Income before taxes	27.5	32.9	23.2	13.5	51.2	35.7		47.8	25.8	4.4
Taxes to be paid	—	—	—	—	—	—	—	(13.1)	(6.8)	(1.1)
Bank loan payment	(25.0)	(25.0)	(25.0)	(25.0)	(25.0)	(25.0)	(25.0)	(25.0)	25.0)	(25.0)
Working capital addition	2.5	7.9	(1.8)	(11.5)	26.2	10.7		11.7	(6.0)	(21.7)
Net surety allowed at beginning of period	380.0	382.5	382.5	382.5	390.4	380.7		416.6	391.4	366.9
Net surety allowed at end of period	382.5	390.4	380.7	371.0	416.6	391.4		428.3	385.4	345.2
Bonding capacity at 20:1 (annualized) available for next six months	7650.0	7808	7614	7421	8332	7828	7339	8566	7708	6904

Date	November 30, 1979			March 31, 1980			November 30, 1980		
Gross Profit Percentage	5%	4½%	4%	5%	4½%	4%	5%	4½%	4%
Bonding capacity—start of period (annual)	8332	7828	7339	8566	7708	6904	8956	7600	6370
Bonding capacity—end of period (annual)	8566	7708	6904	8956	7600	6370	9312	7264	5329
Average	8449	7768	7122	8761	7654	6637	9134	7432	5850
Annual sales rate (1.3 times average)	10938	10098	9528	11389	9950	8628	11874	9662	7604
Sales available in six months' period	5492	5049	4629	5695	4975	4314	5937	4831	3802
Gross profit	274.6	227.2	185.2	284.7	223.9	172.6	296.9	217.4	152.1
Operating expenses	212.5	200.0	187.5	225.0	212.5	200.0	225.0	212.5	200.0
Income before taxes	62.1	27.2	(2.3)	59.7	11.4	(27.4)	71.9	4.9	(47.9)
Taxes to be paid	(17.6)	(7.6)	.7	(16.9)	(3.2)	.4	(21.6)	(1.5)	—
Bank loan payment	(25.0)	(25.0)	(25.0)	(25.0)	(25.0)	(25.0)	(25.0)	(25.0)	(2.15.0)
Working capital addition	19.5	(5.4)	(26.7)	17.8	(16.8)	(52.0)	25.3	(21.6)	(72.9)
Net surety allowed at beginning of period	428.3	385.4	345.2	447.8	380.0	318.5	465.6	363.2	266.5
Net surety allowed at end of period	447.8	380.0	318.5	465.6	363.2	266.5	490.9	341.6	193.6
Bonding capacity at 20:1 (annualized) available for next six months	8956	7600	6370	9312	7264	5329	9819	6832	2904[4]

1. ½ 327,810 + 25,000
2. ½ 327,810 + 12,500
3. ½ 327,810
4. Multiple lowered to 15:1

EXHIBIT 6 Planning Projections, 22 March 1977

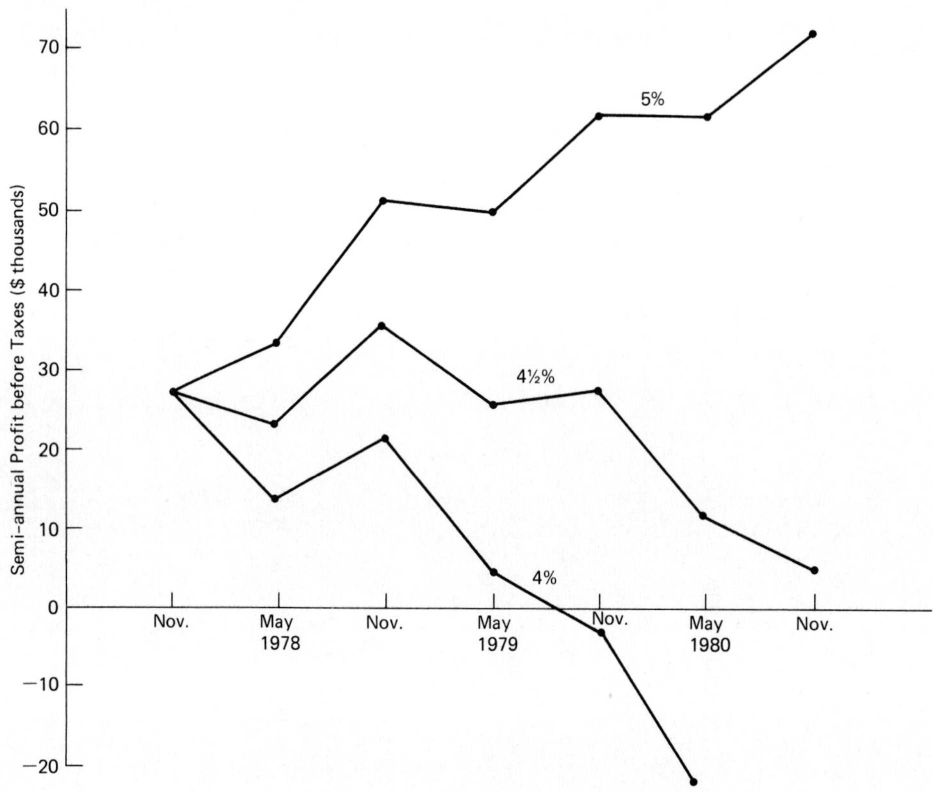

THE BREWING INDUSTRY

The U.S. brewing industry is the world's largest beer producer, (see *Exhibit 1*—sales volume in barrels over time) and its leaders, both historic and current, probably include some of the most colorful companies and personalities in U.S. business. For instance, Alvin Griesedieck, past Chairman of Falstaff and son of its founder, writes of the activities of the Goetz Brewing Company of St. Joseph, Missouri during Prohibition:

> The Goetz Brewing Company of St. Joseph, Missouri had the good fortune of having the public discover that their particular product, Country Club, would spike. By that it was meant that pure alcohol could be added to the beverage in the bottle and the two would blend harmoniously so that the resultant product would taste very much like real beer with no noticeable flavor or odor of the alcohol itself.[1]

Griesedieck reports that the public caught on very quickly and without advertising. The demand for Country Club boomed, so much so that Goetz had to enlarge their brewery to satisfy the demand—this during Prohibition.

August Busch III, current Chairman and Chief Executive of Anheuser Busch, the nation's largest brewery, drank beer before mother's milk: his father had arranged with the doctor that he be given a few drops of Budweiser soon after his birth.[2] Although the boss's son, Busch's entry into the business in 1957 was as a Teamster member shoveling odorous malt and he recalls, "When you finished a shift there, you knew you were a man."[3]

John Murphy, the chain-smoking President of Miller, a Philip Morris subsidiary, is credited by many with changing the rules of the industry in the 70's. Discussing how he could move so successfully from executive positions in the cigarette industry to beer, he says, "After all, we're not in the brain-surgery business." And at a recent wholesalers meeting, to show his distributors how seriously he wanted to make Miller the industry leader, he ran a movie of the famous Anheuser-Busch Clydesdales being overtaken by a speeding Miller truck.

Most of the major breweries, including Anheuser-Busch, Schlitz, Pabst and Coors, remain family-controlled, but publicly-owned, frequently with founding family names very visible in the management and the Board. In recent years, the industry's concentration (*Exhibit 2*) has increased markedly and many small breweries have discontinued operations. A common complaint is that they have been unable to compete with the aggressive advertising and capital investment strategies of the national brewers. In an attempt to gain financial resources, a number of brewing companies have been acquired

This note was prepared from public sources by Dr. Kenneth J. Hatten as a basis for class discussion rather than to illustrate either effective or ineffective handling of an administrative situation.

[1]Griesedieck, A., *The Falstaff Story*. St. Louis: Falstaff Brewing Corp., 1952.

[2]*Esquire*, July 18, 1978.

[3]*Fortune*, January 15, 1979.

by large diversified corporations. Miller Brewing Company is controlled by Philip Morris, Rheingold by the Pepsi Corporation, and until late 1973, Hamm was owned by Heublein. Unsuccessful merger overtures were also reported in 1978 as R.J. Reynolds approached Schlitz. Pabst seemed to have successfully rebuffed the advance of a small conglomerate (APL), also in 1978.

Industry experts claim the best way to differentiate among the various brewing companies is by the size of their market: national, regional and local. Thus, Anheuser-Busch, Schlitz, Miller and Pabst are national brewers. Semi-national brewers and well-known brands such as Carling and Falstaff sold their beer in more than 30 states in their heydays, although their futures are uncertain. Carling O'Keefe sold its U.S. brewing operations to the British-based tobacco company, Rothman's, in December 1977[4] apparently at a loss of $11.5 million. Falstaff, after a series of losses, was acquired by Paul Kalmarovitz. Coors is an extraordinarily far-reaching regional brewer selling the bulk of its beer in 16 western states, including California, the nation's largest beer market. The regionals serve markets of varying size and include Heileman in the Midwest and Northwest, Schaefer serving the major metropolitan markets of New York, and Olympia which has recently extended its reach from Washington, its home state, into the Midwest and Texas with its acquisitions of the Hamm brands and the Lone Star Brewery. Local breweries, small and often family-owned, represent brewers with the least extensive markets. A researcher using regression analysis to model the effects of various strategies on profitability (ROE) in the industry from 1952 to 1971 claims to have statistically confirmed the uniqueness and validity of these categories and suggested that firms in different categories should pursue different strategies (see *Exhibit 3*).

Many current trends and characteristics of the industry—for example, the industry's increasing concentration and its present market structure—have roots in the history of brewing in America. The next section of this note explores the history of the brewing industry in some detail.

HISTORY OF THE BEER INDUSTRY

Pre-Prohibition

Lager beer first became popular in the United States in the 1840s and 50s, when German immigration began in earnest. It was in this period that many of the well known brewing companies of today were founded; in 1850, there were 431 brewers in the U.S. and that number swelled to over 1200 by 1860. In Milwaukee, the Blatz Brewing Company was founded in 1851, Miller in 1855 and Schlitz in 1856, and in St. Louis, Anheuser-Busch was founded in 1857. The prosperity of the Milwaukee brewers was founded on the Chicago Fire of 1871 when all the Chicago breweries were lost and the potential market for Milwaukee beer expanded virtually overnight. This successful expansion out of their local market may have marked the first step in the evolution of today's national brewers.

In the later years of the 19th century, a number of technical advances in the

[4]*Wall Street Journal,* December 17, 1977.

production process and the rail system gave additional impetus to the expansion of the more outward-looking brewing companies, often those who could not dominate their immediate or home market.

One of the most important was the commercialization of mechanical refrigeration. Temperature is extremely important to the brewing process: lager beer must be fermented at low temperatures and aged or "lagered" in a cool environment for a long period of time. Increasing sales made it necessary to brew all year round, not just in winter. This was first accomplished by storing natural ice (one of the major reasons the brewers found the colder northern states hospitable) in cool underground caves.[5] The introduction of mechanical ice machines in 1869, perfected by 1880, made large-scale year-round brewing a reality. In addition, it opened large-scale brewing to many of the Southern cities. Anheuser-Busch's production increased ten-fold during the first ten years after it adopted its first refrigerated plant.

Another important event was the research of Louis Pasteur on the fermentation process of beer. The pasteurization process, which was originally proposed to preserve beer and wine, not milk, allowed beer to be stored more easily and for longer periods of time. The yeast was killed by steam heating the beer, leaving it in more stable form. Another equally important discovery, yet less well known, was the work of the Danish researcher Hansen who isolated two pure strains of brewing yeast, "top-fermenting" and "bottom-fermenting" yeast, from hundreds of wild yeasts. The use of Hansen's pure cultured yeast could assure a uniform product. It was quickly adopted by the Schlitz and Pabst breweries, soon followed by others.

Bottling beer gained popularity in the 1870s and again in the 1890s because of improvements in the packing process and the increasing demand for beer. Pasteurization and rigorous cleanliness in breweries assured the stability of the bottled beer. In 1892, the "crown" replaced corks as the stopper on most bottled products. The brewers did not do their own bottling but set up concessions for agents to do it, primarily because tax laws required that bottling not take place in the brewery or warehouse.

Pasteurization, bottling and refrigeration made the shipment of beer feasible and innovations in the transportation system, such as the development of a coordinated rail system and refrigerated rail cars, made it practical by extending the reach of the interested brewing companies. These developments combined to allow large-scale processing, and off-the-premises consumption of beer. They also enabled brewers to expand production well beyond their local markets. Some of the early shipping brewers were Schlitz, Miller and Anheuser-Busch and, because initially their patrons willingly paid the costs of transportation, they obtained a premium price over local beers—price differentials which seem likely to continue.

As the more aggressive brewers turned to shipping in the 1880s and 90s, national beer consumption grew and the number of brewers in the US declined. This period marked the beginning of registered brands and trademarks, and advertising in the industry. The structure of the wholesaler distribution system also dates from this period: early wholesalers were referred to as "branches."

[5]The storage caves were frequently large, deep and uncharted, which occasionally resulted in problems. Drilling during the 1860 Pennsylvania oil rush produced one such problem when what the drillers thought was an oil well turned out to be a well drilled directly over the storage vault of a brewery.

Prohibition

Prohibition, brought on with the passage of the Volstead Act in 1919, was an example of a law that was expensive and difficult to enforce as it was unpopular with the general public. It was passed because the prohibitionists, although they had been around for about one hundred years, became well financed by such people as John D. Rockefeller and S.S. Kresge, and very adept at organizing and applying political pressure. The anti-prohibitionists were not well organized and, indeed, the brewers' anti-prohibition efforts came under attack as the work of a pro-German group. As a result, legal brewing of malt beverages came to an end in 1919. Many brewers closed their doors permanently.

The more enterprising brewers turned to other products during Prohibition.

Falstaff produced smoked ham and bacon in St. Louis, using their cellars for smoking chambers. Schlitz sold candy. Pabst sold cheese and soft drinks while Blatz produced industrialized alcohol. Anheuser-Busch sold a malt syrup and near beer called "Bevo." Indeed, nearly all brewers produced near beers which could be spiked but, because they could not legally advocate such doctoring in their advertisements, their short-run success was limited. They were, however, fortunate in the long run, for their breweries were operational and ready to produce beer after Repeal. Griesedieck writes:

> Under our permit to sell near beer, we first had to make a normal alcoholic beer—then de-alcoholize it. So all we had to do was turn off the de-alcoholizing unit [at Repeal].[6]

In April, 1933, Prohibition ended. Falstaff obtained the first license and began operations immediately. By June 31st, brewers were in operation and within a year there were 756. Many people felt that the new industry would be an excellent source of profit and some breweries were built with little consideration for location and market potential. These firms quickly failed, and their failure quickly re-established a trend which has persisted from 1880 until the present: An annual decline in the number of active breweries.

Prohibition had a lasting effect on the industry. In 1911 per capita consumption in the US reached 21 gallons. While in the years before Prohibition it had gradually declined (there were 25 dry states in 1917, for example), in 1934 it was only 7.9 gallons per capita, partly due to shortages of supply but also because of the serious competition of soft drinks. It was not until the war years that consumption increased to 18 gallons per person. During the 1950s and early 1960s, demand began to decline again and dropped as low as 14.9 gallons in 1961. By 1971 demand had climbed to 18.6 gallons per capita. Per capita consumption was 20.6 gallons in 1974 (see *Exhibit 4*—per capita consumption over time).

Changes After Repeal

While the effects of Prohibition may have constrained consumption until the 1960s, it was during the first years after Repeal in 1933 that the character of the industry itself changed as brewers tried to adapt to new conditions. Prohibition had broken the working man's

[6] Griesedieck, A., *The Falstaff Story*. St. Louis: Falstaff Brewing Corp., 1952.

habit of dropping into the local tavern for a drink on the way home, and as refrigerators became generally available to Americans during the 1930s, home storage of packaged beer became practical.

In 1935 Pabst announced that its beer would be canned and a month later Heileman and other brewers followed suit. Cans offered important advantages to the brewers. They made the packaged beer more compact and so easier to store and, in addition, the cans were impervious to light and required less pasteurization time. The glass companies quickly introduced a no-deposit, no-return bottle to compete with the cans. As the leaders of the industry took advantage of the changes in both technologies, they began to stress the sale of packaged beer. While, in 1933, package sales were 31.6% of all sales, by 1940 52.7% of sales were packaged. In 1951 packaged sales amounted to 74.4% and by 1971 the proportion had reached 86.4% of all sales. The trend has continued and the advantages of marketing packaged beer seem clear:

1 The distribution was wider because beer could be sold in groceries; and
2 It provided for better merchandising because the brewer's trademark was clearly visible.

For some companies, however, the picture was not so rosy. When the bulk of beer sales were draught sales, transport costs gave the local brewers a potential 200 mile monopoly.[7] As packaged sales gained strength and passed the 70% level, the local brewers were increasingly at a disadvantage. Larger firms emphasizing packaged sales could sell at 600 to 700 miles from their breweries—Coors's average shipping distance in 1975 was 1000 miles.

Packaging made invasion of the local markets easier for the larger and aggressive brewers, since cans could be more cheaply shipped than draught beer. Old strengths and advantages were superseded by new merchandising skills, and the small brewers' ability to compete was eroded. The costs of competition, of advertising and packaging, tended to reduce the margin per barrel sold. For the small brewer with a limited distribution system, there was no way of quickly increasing revenues.

Thus, one of the most interesting trends in the brewing industry and one which has gained strength is the general decline in the number of brewers and the increasing concentration of market share with a few large companies. *Exhibit 5* illustrates the decline in the number of active brewing companies from 1952 to 1978; this decline occurred even though total sales of the industry increased by almost 47 million barrels during this period. (In 1977, the share of the nation's four largest brewers increased from 24.2% to 48.5%, and *Exhibit 5* illustrates this concentration.)

Prohibition, the decline of the tavern, and the brewers' later emphasis on package sales combined to introduce beer to women. Beer's availability in grocery stores and later supermarkets gave women an important role as beer buyers. It has been speculated that the current trend toward lighter, more carbonated beers has been accelerated by women's tastes and preferences. The larger breweries appear to have exploited the trends toward home drinking, convenience packaging, supermarket distribution and lighter beers suitable for 'family' tastes.

[7]*Forbes*, November 1, 1967.

The 1940s

By the 1940s beer sales had reached their pre-Prohibition levels although per capita consumption was still down. Six brewers were selling over a million barrels per year. High federal taxes (six dollars per barrel) decreased profit margins and raised the consumer's price, which may have held down consumption. In addition, war-time production was difficult due to shortages of men and material.

After World War II, production capacity and the expansion of the larger firms continued. In the past it had been possible to gradually add capacity in small units by enlarging current plants. Now, because enlargement was not the most efficient way to make major capacity additions, it became necessary to acquire additional plants or build new and more efficient ones.

In the merger movement prior to World War I it was not technically feasible to manufacture the same brand in different locations and separate labels were kept for each plant. After World War II, understanding of the brewing process was sufficiently sophisticated to insure identical products, and the operation of subsidiary plants in various areas of the country became common. By 1960 in fact, P. Ballantine & Sons Brewing was the only one of the then top ten brewers operating from a single plant.

Falstaff was one of the first to employ a multiple plant strategy to guide it through the 50's.[8] As the following statement made by Falstaff management in 1949 suggests, it was only one part of a more complex strategy which integrated:

> **1** Decentralization of beer production and distribution to major consumption areas, so as to achieve maximum operating efficiency and minimum transportation expenses;
> **2** Sale of top-quality beer at regular market prices instead of attempting to realize premium rates. In such manner a sound competitive position is maintained in relation to equal quality beers;
> **3** Large appropriations for advertising and sales promotion, so as to establish growing consumer brand demand;
> **4** Merchandizing almost 95% of sales via bottle or can packaged beer, so as to widen markets and to derive larger profit margins; and
> **5** Expansion of capacity at a low cost by purchasing medium size breweries at bargain prices, and then enlarging and modernizing the units. The total capacity is enlarged in ratio to the increased demand developed and at low competitive costs.

Hemphill, Noyes, Research Department commented in 1949 that "Falstaff has been one of the progressive leaders in modernization and as a consequence is one of the lowest cost producers."[9]

[8]Falstaff was also the first to establish identical plant environments to insure uniform taste and character in its brews from different plants. This uniformity was first developed by the simple expedient of destroying all the old "taste polluted" wooden lagering vats in acquired breweries (Griesedieck, 1951). This development made the multiple plant strategy feasible.

[9]*Fortune*, October 1964.

The 1950s and 1960s

During the 1950s and 1960s, the growth of the brewing industry slowed and the premium brands' share of the market stabilized at about 23%. Indeed, it was not until 1959 that sales exceeded the 1947 figure.

A significant event in this period contributing to this slowing of sales was a major strike of the Milwaukee brewers in 1953, lasting 76 days. During this strike St. Louis-based Anheuser-Busch ran out of capacity. It could not satisfy demand and the popular-priced regional brewers like Hamm and Carling found beer-thirsty wholesalers ready to promote their brews. Their sales soared.

After the strike, the premium brewers passed their higher wage bill on to their customers in the form of higher prices but found many of their wholesalers less cooperative than in the old days. In response to this change and the resurgence of the popular-priced regional brands, Pabst, a former premium-priced brand, in an effort to stimulate profits, cut prices by 15¢ to 20¢ a six-pack in 1962. Its sales jumped 1½ million barrels and its profits rose 60% by 1963. Anheuser-Busch brought out Busch Bavarian in the popular-price range and began to compete more aggressively in local markets (*Exhibit 6*). Schlitz for a time did nothing and lost its position as the nation's leading brewer in 1958.

This period also marks a time of much merger activity in the brewing industry, including the acquisitions of brewing companies by non-brewers. The acquisition of Hamm by Heublein in 1966 falls into this category, as does the acquisition of Miller by W.R. Grace in 1966. These acquisitions have tended to experience less opposition from the Federal Trade Commission and the Justice Department than mergers between brewers since Antitrust activity is directed:

> . . . toward the identification and prevention of those mergers which alter market structure in ways likely now or eventually to encourage or permit noncompetitive conduct.[10]

Justice Department Policy

Whether a particular merger will be challenged depends to some extent on the degree of concentration of market share in the industry at the time of merger, current movements in industry concentration, and the market shares of the merging companies. *Exhibit 7* provides more guidelines as to the specifics of the antitrust policy. The Justice Department also indicated that if the market share of the two largest companies has increased by 7% or more in the preceding five to ten years, the evaluation of proposed mergers will be more critical.

On Friday, December 29, 1978, however, David Ignatius of the *Wall Street Journal* reported that John Shenefield, Assistant Attorney General for Antitrust, said he hoped President Carter would approve new antitrust legislation that would:

[10]"Merger Guidelines," Justice Department. May 30, 1968.

1 Ban any merger that would combine $2 billion or more in annual sales or assets, where each concern had at least $100 million in sales or assets.
2 Ban any merger in which a company with $1 billion or more in sales or assets proposed to acquire a company with a 20% or greater share of a concentrated market, where that market totaled at least $100 million in annual sales.

Mr. Shenefield explained that the underlying premise of the proposal was that bigness is bad in corporate life. Shenefield said Senator Edward Kennedy (D., Mass.) was drafting a similar legislative proposal and continued by pointing out that ". . . if you feel the pulse of the people . . . there's a predominant sense that big business is getting too big."

These prohibitions would be waived only where companies could show that mergers would produce "significant competitive benefits." As a hypothetical example of mergers that might meet such a test, Mr. Shenefield suggested an acquisition by Exxon Corporation of "floundering American Motors Corporation."

The Brewers versus the Justice Department

Anheuser-Busch was the first company to run into trouble with the Justice Department and also the first to resolve its difficulties. After running out of capacity during the 1953 strike, Anheuser-Busch in 1958 purchased the Miami, Florida brewery of American Brewing Company. After the final judgement against Anheuser-Busch (U.S. vs. Anheuser-Busch, 1960, CCH Trade Cases), Anheuser-Busch agreed to sell the Miami brewery and refrain from buying any other for the next five years. Some years later, Anheuser-Busch's President Richard Meyer said:

> We got into trouble several years ago when we had to sell a Miami brewery. As a result of that experience, we felt that it was impossible for us to acquire so we built.[11]

Thus, Busch built new plants earlier than its rivals, spending its capital on aggressive marketing and capital projects rather than acquisitions.

The Pabst-Blatz merger, which was also arranged in 1958, lifted Pabst from the tenth biggest brewer to the fifth and, by 1961, to the third largest brewer in the country. In a protracted antitrust suit which extended from 1959 to 1969, Pabst lost and had to divest Blatz. Pabst sold the brand to Heileman in 1969 but was, as late as mid-1974, still attempting to sell the Blatz plant. Pabst claimed in its defense that it was heading to ruin before the merger with Blatz, but the court held that the failing firm defense applies to the acquired firm, not the acquiring firm.[12]

Schlitz, too, ran into trouble with the Justice Department when it bought a 40% and controlling interest in John Labatt Limited in 1964. Not only was the Labatt merger challenged but, because Labatt controlled Lucky Lager, a California brewery, Schlitz's

[11]*Magazine of Wall Street,* October 1, 1966, p. 93.

[12]The Department regards as failing only those firms with no reasonable prospect by remaining viable; it does not regard a firm as failing merely because the firm has been unprofitable for a period of time, has lost market position or has failed to maintain its competitive position in some respect, has poor management or has not fully explored the possibility of overcoming its difficulties through self help (Justice Department, "Merger Guidelines," Section 9, page 11).

1961 merger with Burgermeister, another California company, was also disputed. Schlitz in 1966 had to divest itself of its Labatt shares and of Burgermeister at a substantial financial loss.

Falstaff, between 1948 and 1967, acquired six firms with brewing capacities ranging from 129 thousand barrels to 1.2 million barrels per year. However, the firms acquired tended to be underutilizing their capacity and were experiencing declining sales at the time of acquisition. In 1965, Falstaff acquired Narragansett, a merger which was opposed by the Federal Trade Commission unsuccessfully. Subsequently, in 1972 Falstaff announced its proposal to acquire Ballantine's, a large New York brewing company which once again was experiencing sales declines.

Associated Breweries, a firm which has divested itself from the brewing business,[13] was itself a product of a series of mergers culminating with the merger of Associated Breweries and Drewry's. Drewry's had acquired five other firms between 1951 and 1962. Associated was the product of an earlier merger between Pfeiffer and E & B Brewing Company. Associated in 1964 acquired Sterling with a capacity of 750,000 barrels per year and sales of 650,000 barrels per year. However, from 1964 until its divestment from the industry, Associated's sales declined continuously. Heileman, a company which now ranks in the top ten, has benefitted from the divestments of Blatz by Pabst and of Associated Breweries, from whom it acquired five brands. Heileman has since acquired Grain Belt Breweries of St. Paul, Minn. (1975) and the Rainier Brewery of Seattle, Wash. (1977).

One outcome of the Justice Department's and the Federal Trade Commission's activity to restrict mergers and acquisitions is that many brewers have been forced to diversify, but the scope of their diversification has been limited and, in general, has met with little success. Pabst, for example, sold Hoffman, a soft drink company, in 1961 when it had sales of $12.1 million, about 7% of Pabst's total sales. Anheuser-Busch's corn products division has the second market share position in that industry, but, notwithstanding, the profitability of Anheuser-Busch's diversified investments, although increasing in importance, has been low and often negative.

Perhaps because of the Justice Department's administration of the antitrust laws, the competitive effort of the largest companies has been directed towards internal growth, with large amounts of money and effort being spent on new plants, advertising and marketing, and on the firm's distribution system.

Multiple Plants

The multiple plant strategy has been implemented in two ways, Falstaff, Hamm and Pabst tried to extend their markets into new areas, by merging with other brewers or purchasing established breweries. Anheuser-Busch and Schlitz built new plants, especially during the 1965–1970 period.

Before World War II, Hamm was a regional brewer operating in five states with sales of about 1 million barrels per annum. In 1945, management decided that the days of regional brewers were numbered and moved into Chicago, the west coast and Baltimore by acquisition of four breweries. In 15 years, Hamm spent $47 million for expansion.

[13]*Business Week,* February 25, 1973, p. 20.

Hamm believed it needed three or four more breweries to take it to capacity of 12 million barrels, to allow it to compete with the market leaders by 1970. It planned a major expansion every three years. In 1961, new breweries cost about $25 to $35 per annual barrel capacity, while older established breweries could be bought for $6 to $10 per annual barrel. The strategy of geographic expansion looked right and so did the means chosen to implement it, but "A mere desire to be leader does not make it so."[14]

By 1961, the sales growth the company had experienced during the 1950s had slowed and there were weaknesses in distribution. Although 80% were exclusive, Hamm's distributors tended to be small and under-financed. The family sold Hamm to Heublein in 1966 for $62.2 million. It was divested by Heublein in 1973 for $6 million after nine years of deteriorating gross margins in spite of Heublein's efforts to reorganize Hamm's distribution system, to enter new markets and to revitalize its advertising.

Anheuser-Busch, in 1951, started another trend by building a new plant in Newark from the bottom up and a second one in Los Angeles in 1954. The Los Angeles plant was likely a response to its lack of desired capacity during the 1953 Milwaukee strike. The strategy used by Anheuser-Busch was to enter a new market with sales supported from an established plant. If that market developed, then and only then was a new plant considered. These plants tended to be relatively large, with a 2 to 4 million barrel capacity.

Carling built a plant in Fort Worth at a cost of about $10 million in 1964 before its sales ability in that area was proven, and the plant never reached full production. Carling's sales could not support it. This plant, which incorporated a major innovation in brewing, continuous brewing as opposed to batch brewing, was claimed to be the most modern in the world. It was sold by Carling at a loss of $7 million to Miller in 1968. Miller demolished the continuous brewing section and replaced it with a more traditional process.

It is interesting to note the extent to which the major brewers adopted this multiple plant strategy and the speed with which they implemented it. In 1955, the top ten operated ten plants. In 1961 they operated 40 plants and by 1968 they had 48 plants. After Carling's unsuccessful plant construction in Texas, entry into new markets is now made before building new plants. Miller, the last of the nationals to adopt the multiplant strategy, has followed this sequence consistently.

Plant Size: Scale

Plant size seems to be a key competitive factor. In 1969, Roy E. Krumm, President of Heileman, claimed the nationals produce a case of beer for 80% of the costs of the small operator. The regionals make $.50 a case, while the nationals make $2.00 or more.[15] The difference can be attributed to the nationals' premium prices and their scale advantages. Anheuser-Busch, Schlitz and Pabst lifted capacity by 27% from 1968 to 1970, 42 million to 53 million barrels.[16] The large brewers gain major advantages from their new plants and widened distribution system:

[14]*Advertising Age,* January, 1961.
[15]*Business Week,* September 13, 1969, p. 139.
[16]*Wall Street Transcripts,* p. 16488, April 28, 1969.

1 Unit cost savings from high volume production;
2 Financial ability to adopt new large and efficient machines as they become available, such as in-house canning, filtering, etc.; and
3 Benefits of nationwide advertising and distribution.

Schlitz, for example, when it operates at full capacity, produces beer with about one quarter the labor costs of firms such as Rheingold. And because its modern plants incorporate in-house can manufacturing, Schlitz is achieving container cost reductions of about 15–20%. This is not insignificant since the container cost is about 50% of total product cost.[17]

Schlitz's beer is produced at its newer plants using accelerated batch processing, a new technology which pares the brewing cycle from 30 to about 17 days and extends shelf life.[18] Thus, the Schlitz brewing cycle is about half as long as Anheuser-Busch's. Anheuser-Busch, however, has steadfastly maintained the traditional brewing cycle although its margin is narrowing under pressure from rising materials and labor costs. The company apparently considers the quality of brew produced by the new processes inferior, although it is said that the new process and changes in raw materials quality could cut production costs by 50%.[19] It has been reported, for example, that Anheuser-Busch's oldest plant in St. Louis experiences labor costs five times the labor costs at Schlitz's newest plants. In May, 1974, *Barron's*[20] reported that Busch had modified its process to reduce the brewing time by two days—a modification which would enable the company to increase output by 3 million barrels per year.

The minimum size of a competitive plant was estimated in 1976 at 1.5 million barrels per year,[21] since two breweries of 1.2 million barrel annual capacity were closed in the 1968 to 1971 period. Furthermore, a modern can line operating at 1200 to 1400 cans per minute would require a 1.5 million capacity for "full" utilization. If the 1.5 million barrels capacity estimate is right, about 50% of the plants operated by the fifth to fourteenth largest companies are obsolete and only those companies which invested in large modern plants since 1965 are operating at the most efficient level (see *Exhibit 8*).

As the nationals increased plant efficiency, their use of labor also became more efficient. Both Milwaukee and St. Louis brewers were hit with strikes frequently in the 1970s, and the older brewers' unions have lost a number of representation elections to the Teamsters, especially in the new plants. Average hourly earnings in the brewing industry were $3.51 in 1964 and $6.48 in 1974, compared with $2.37 and $4.15 for all other food manufacturers.

Quality of product is also said to vary among national brewers. Anheuser-Busch has the longest brewing cycle, as noted earlier, about 42 days, and uses more expensive rice rather than corn or artificial ingredients. Schlitz and Miller have approximately 20-day brewing cycles, and Miller has strongly opposed an Anheuser-Busch move which would require members of the National Brewers Association to have ingredient labelling. For the

[17]*Wall Street Transcripts*, pl. 35572.
[18]*Forbes*, December 15, 1972, p. 36.
[19]*Business Week*, March 24, 1973, p. 42.
[20]*Barron's*, Margaret D. Pacey, "End of the Drought," May 27, 1974.
[21]*Wall Street Week*, March 24, 1973, p. 42.

brewers who rely on natural ingredients, raw materials costs rose tremendously in 1973: corn rose 40% over the previous year, barley, the source of hops, rose 30% and prices for whole rice climbed 50% in six months (see *Exhibits 9* and *10*).

Advertising

Between 1947 and 1965, average industry advertising expense per barrel trebled from $.86 to $2.52; it declined until Philip Morris acquired Miller in 1971. It has been rising again since. Advertising seems to be viewed by the brewing industry as a useful competitive tool—Schlitz increased expenditures when its leading position was taken by Anheuser-Busch, for example. Not all agree, however. For example, Falstaff Executive Vice President Robert Colson said:

> We have to correct or alter people's beliefs about the product. Advertising can be used to alter those beliefs. But I do not believe advertising sells one damn thing. We are an unorthodox company. We do not measure sales against advertising.[22]

Coors has historically ignored the rules and has been a low user of measured advertising, perhaps preferring retail promotion and personal sales attention to advertising as means to stimulate demand.

A positive relationship of advertising to market share growth is taken for granted in most businesses, but the effect of advertising on profitability is not so clear. Many observers feel the entry of Philip Morris into the industry is leading brewers to sacrifice profitability unwisely by overspending on advertising. Indeed, two researchers working for Anheuser-Busch suggest that overspending on advertising may be the norm in the industry.

Russell Ackoff and James Emshoff provided an unusual insight into Anheuser-Busch's advertising campaigns in the Winter of 1975.[23] Apparently working from stimulus response theory, they designed experiments for Anheuser-Busch to explore the effectiveness of the company's advertising expenditures. They report that while the company's market share rose from 8.1% to 12.9% between 1963 and 1968, it was able to cut its advertising per barrel from $1.89 to $0.80, partly because of their work.

Ackoff and Emshoff report that on a market by market basis they discovered the Sales/Advertising relationship shown in *Exhibit 11*. The research led Busch to investigate the usefulness of "pulse" advertising (on/off), varying timing and media mix. Research showed that some patterns worked better with high expenditure levels and some with low. Time and media pulsing seemed equally efficient but, Ackoff and Emshoff point out, media pulsing was easier to administer.

Later research showed media effectiveness in stimulating beer sales fell into this order: national TV (most effective), local TV, radio, newspapers and, finally, billboards. Busch discontinued virtually all billboard advertising in this period. It was once 20% of the ad budget.

In a later paper, Ackoff and Emshoff reported on their work for Busch between 1968

[22]St. Louis, March 14, 1972, quoted in *Advertising Age,* March 20, 1972, p. 25.

[23]Russell L. Ackoff and James R. Emshoff, "Advertising Research at Anheuser-Busch, Inc. (1963–1968)," *Sloan Management Review,* Winter 1975.

and 1974,[24] which sought to explain drinking behavior. Although for obvious reasons the paper does not specify segments and their sizes, it offers some clues which are summarized in *Exhibit 12*.

Ackoff and Emshoff claim that their research substantiates the accuracy and validity of their drinker classification scheme. Furthermore, they claim that people who drink certain brands fall into certain clusters (B - 1 to 4 in *Exhibit 12*). They note that rarely did they find brand advertising using the right personality types and situations for the drinkers. Their research also allowed them to determine that different media reach different segments more effectively: separatives via TV, indulgents by radio, and oceanics by magazines like *Playboy*—while objectives could be reached best by radio.

Perhaps one of the key factors in stimulating competitive escalation of advertising and promotion in the 1950s was the postwar introduction and growth of television. Anheuser-Busch in 1952 reported that in areas using television advertising, sales increased at twice the rate of the non-TV areas. It seems likely that television also increased the attraction of home entertainment over the neighborhood tavern, giving additional impetus to the trend from draught to package beer and the success of the nationals.

Today, brewers' advertising expenditures are heavy, especially for TV. In addition the target market for brewers' advertising has changed. Formerly, 18- to 34-year-olds were thought to be the best market for beer, and ads stressed youth; but with the decline in the birth rate and the aging of the population (*Appendix 2*) this appeared to be a less promising long-run strategy than before. While beer is now consumed in two out of three American homes and over half of U.S. men and women consider themselves "beer drinkers," industry leaders frequently cite as the most important consumer statistic the fact that 30% of all beer drinkers consume 80% of U.S. beer production. Current advertising strategy is heavily aimed at the heavy beer drinker. John Murphy, Miller's President, says "our ads identify with the American work ethic. We see the work and workers of America as heroic and that's how we present them in our TV advertising."

Pricing

Consumers' response to pricing is currently very different than the tremendous increase in market share which greeted the price cutting brewers in the 1950s and 1960s.

Consumer tests have shown that price is significantly related to modern quality perceptions. McConnell[25] reports on an experiment in which consumers were offered the choice to purchase any of three "brands" of beer, each at a different price; the brands were really identical. Consumers rated the brands as follows:

Price	$1.30	$1.20	$.90
Favorable Rating	93%	73%	57%
Unfavorable Rating	71	82	101

The cells are significantly different at the .005 level, so the researchers concluded that consumers appear to use price as a surrogate for product quality.

[24]Russell L. Ackoff and James R. Emshoff, "Advertising Research at Anheuser-Busch, Inc. (1968–1974)," *Sloan Management Review*, Spring 1975.

[25]*Journal of Business*, October 1968.

Consumers were apparently favorably impressed by the quality of high-priced beers in 1977 and 1978 since premiums and even super premium-priced beers are high sellers and profit makers for the brewers. Super premiums include Anheuser-Busch's Michelob with 75% of that market, Pabst's Andeker, and Miller's U.S.-brewed Lowenbrau. Budweiser, Schlitz and Miller High Life are all premium-priced, and Anheuser-Busch has even reformulated Busch beer as Busch Premium with encouraging sales results. Beers selling at "popular" prices and below come from regional and small local brewers.

Distribution

Busch's post-1958 resurgence, which has extended into the late 1970s, has been attributed to that company's efforts to achieve the best possible "communications" with its wholesalers throughout the country. In 1956, the Chairman, Augustus Busch II, visited the company's once exclusive distribution system to check the inroads Carling, Falstaff and Hamm had made. He was successful in his personal approach, and the company used a number of devices to insure that his success was cemented. Anheuser-Busch acquired or financed trucks and warehouses to reduce the cost pressures on the wholesalers; 25% of Busch's 960 wholesalers in 1967 were exclusive and had equity interests in Busch.

In 1977, Anheuser-Busch once again turned to its 950 wholesalers in its hour of need. As in the 1950s, other brewers had made inroads into Busch's market, this time while Anheuser-Busch was struck for three months beginning March 1, 1976. Busch lost market, its share falling from 23.7% in 1975 to 19.4% in 1976.

The *Wall Street Journal* (June 28, 1977) reported on Anheuser-Busch's fight to regain its market:

> To the delight of quaffers, the growing competition in beer has brought unusual bargains, mostly in the form of special promotions in selected markets where the competition is hottest or where a brewer seeks to bolster its market share. Discounting by a major brewer is often met by similar cuts by competitors. Budweiser has been sold at discounts of 10 cents to 40 cents per six-pack recently, for the first time in many years in some cities.
>
> "The last time we discounted Bud was the Dark Ages, something like 1962," says Howard Hallom, a Dallas wholesaler.

Yet, the company's volume did not rebound quickly as it had after strikes in other years. The company itself wasn't sure why. However, the strike, prolonged by a dispute over grievance procedures, dragged on longer than those of previous years, and so the company's products were off the market—and out of mind—longer. Moreover, in some key cities, such as St. Louis, the beer distributors as well as the brewery were struck, and so it took even longer in some places to get beer delivered to retail outlets.

Moreover, with Miller marketing aggressively, the smaller brewers were probably trying to keep their plants operating at full capacity and doubtlessly met Busch's discounts with price cuts of their own. Although Anheuser-Busch's market share had climbed to about 22% by March 1977, Anheuser-Busch executives were reported to be stunned by the failure of Budweiser to recover strongly.

The company made a number of moves. It revamped the Budweiser advertising program to "elevate beer drinkers' self-image, to convince them that only the King of Beers is good enough." In addition, the black market (about 15%) was given special effort. The company's price cuts worked; for example, in Dallas sales rose 26% in March during the promotions but fell 20% in April when the discount was ended. Mr. Busch stressed that the price cuts are short-lived and "simply a way to get drinkers to re-sample our beer."

Busch appeared to be trying to protect Anheuser-Busch profit margins through better utilization of capacity and general cost reductions. "There are more ways to get to a better bottom line besides price," he said, noting, for example, the recent leveling-off of packaging and ingredient cost increases. The company apparently discovered still another way to a better bottom line in January, when it raised its prices generally by 1% but strongly suggested that wholesalers swallow the increase.

The wholesalers, in fact, were supposed to play a major role in the company's recovery plan. Anheuser-Busch held eight regional meetings with its 950 wholesalers, who were urged to ride delivery trucks and court their retail accounts (a "back to basics" message).

"We're out to give the wholesaler every possible tool to help increase volume," Busch said. The company concedes that in the past it may have been slow in developing new products and packaging because of its sellout position at the time. Then, another executive says, wholesalers may have felt shortchanged because they didn't have a light beer and a variety of packaging sizes.

In response, it has introduced nationwide the seven-ounce Michelob and the seven-ounce Budweiser, with the latter promoted as "the greatest little beer." And it has reintroduced a quarter-barrel Budweiser, which had been popular at colleges and for party use.

Early in 1977, the company finally came out with its entry in the light beer sweepstakes, Natural Light. Anheuser also tested an 8-ounce can and, according to August A. Busch, III, President and Chief Executive, it may come out with still another brand within a year. "We're very aggressive," he said, almost defensively. "We'll be probing and testing the market—if there's a void we'll find it."

Historically, beer has been a three-tier business—manufacturer, distributor, and retailer. Now that the big guns are committing enormous investments to increase capacity, more and more pressure is being put on wholesalers to fulfill ambitious marketing goals. Miller seems eager to own distributorships in major markets, which is analogous to General Motors' buying its most prosperous dealerships. That kind of integration, if it continues, could threaten the established structure of the industry.

For its part, *Fortune* reports (January 15, 1979) Anheuser-Busch wants no part of this integration. Nor do such distributors as Robert Lewis, president of Foothills Beverage Co. in Pomona, California, who is probably earning twice as much as August Busch's $335,000-a-year compensation. Lewis began 22 years ago with two trucks and a couple of helpers. His beer-distributing operation now grosses some $35 million a year, more than is brought in by his colleague to the south, Frank Sinatra, who owns the Long Beach agency. With a lock on a big slice of the California market, the nation's biggest, Lewis could well be grossing $75 million a year within a decade.

Late 1978 at Anheuser-Busch[26]

To even hint to August Busch III that Anheuser-Busch, the world's largest brewer, should make beer by any method other than the time-consuming way devised by his great-grandfather Adolphus is tantamount to hinting to a dedicated Belfast Orangeman that he might consider doffing his bowler hat to a bishop. "Never, never," is Busch's gritty response, "You have to have the best. Sooner or later the customer will recognize quality."

Busch believes there is a reward for maintaining quality. Over the long haul, Anheuser-Busch has increased its share of market. Budweiser remains the world's best-selling beer, although it sells at a premium price. And Michelob, which sells in an even higher price range, commands fully 75 percent of its market segment.

Since 1970, Anheuser-Busch's volume has increased from 22.2 million barrels to 41 million, an average annual growth of 8%. It now has 24 percent of the market, compared with Miller's 19 percent. A study ordered by August Busch in 1977 to justify a capital-expenditure program of more than $250 million a year predicts that the St. Louis company will maintain its superiority.[27] That study shows that Miller will increase its volume to 46 million barrels by 1982 (24% of the market) while Anheuser-Busch's will swell to 59 million barrels, or 31%.

What makes Busch so confident is that beer drinkers have switched by the millions from drinking popular beers—i.e., the lower-priced brands—to those that command a premium price. With Budweiser, Anheuser-Busch leads the premium market by miles. In the even higher-priced super premium category it outsells everyone with Michelob. In the light-beer market Miller leads with over 60%, but Anheuser-Busch is closing the gap.

A rule of thumb in the industry is that a new product must sell at least one million barrels a year to break even. Natural Light did that and more. It is now being consumed at the rate of 2.5 million barrels a year and sales are growing at about 15%. It has edged out Miller's Lite, introduced 3 years earlier in several regional markets. To increase market share in the light segment, Anheuser-Busch introduced Michelob Light in 1978 and within 6 months was selling it successfully in 34 states.

But Anheuser-Busch had employed still another tactic to counteract Miller. Busch Bavarian was reformulated in 1978, so that the sweeter taste appealed to the younger drinkers. Then it was presented, in a new package, as a high-priced brew. In less than 8 months, Busch Premium accounted for 8% of the market in six New England states and is being hurriedly introduced throughout the Southeast. "A lot of people think Miller outsmarted us with Lite beer," says Dennis Long. "But that was one successful product out of eight brands introduced or acquired. We've clicked on three out of three."

The major brewers, laments William Coors, chairman of his family's Colorado firm, have "gone berserk with advertising expenditures." Anheuser-Busch's budget, zoomed from $49 million in 1976 to $115 million in 1978, an increase of more than 134%. Because most of this advertising is concentrated on TV sports and special-interest programs, the "noise level," as August Busch refers to the clutter, is piercing. TV

[26]This section draws heavily on Thomas O'Hanlon's "August Busch Brews up a New Spirit in St. Louis," *Fortune*, January 15, 1979.

[27]Anheuser-Busch makes about 40% of the cans it uses.

advertising is a solid seller's market; the brewers find the ever-rising cost rather unpleasant.

However awesome those advertising costs may appear, brewers consider them justified. For Anheuser-Busch, the 1978 budget represents an average advertising cost of \$2.70 per barrel, or about 5% of revenues. "The introduction of new brands has pushed the figure up fast," says August Busch. In order to attract customers to a new brew, the industry lavishes as much as \$15 a barrel on advertising. But expenditures for established brands have been soaring, too. As an example, industry volume increased about 3% in the first nine months of 1978, but advertising costs were up by 25%.

If the tear-away race for market share continues to be conducted by escalating advertising budgets, profits could suffer. Since 1975, Anheuser-Busch has managed to increase revenue per barrel from \$42.25 to \$50, partly through price increases, partly because of spectacular growth in premium-priced brands. With production and other overhead mounting, however, every additional cent spent on advertising eats into the bottom line. August Busch doesn't like having his profits gnawed away. "We know advertising works," he says, "but at what level those dollars become non-productive, nobody really knows."

Nonetheless, Anheuser-Busch intends to bracket every other brewer with a variety of high-profit brands. It intends to unveil yet another super-premium brand shortly. And for the past year it has experimented with new packaging for an imported beer, Wurzburger, that will compete with Miller's Lowenbrau. Wurzburger may be shipped from Germany in refrigerated tanks, then bottled in the U.S. Lowenbrau, by contrast, is brewed in the U.S., although the Federal Trade Commission is probing charges that the packaging and advertising hint ever so subtly that it's an import. Imported beers represent less than 2% of the U.S. market, but sales of the foreign brands are now growing at a 30% clip—not a market to ignore.

The effect of this marketing activity is dramatic. The *New York Times* (August 7, 1977), reports that:

> According to an industry newsletter published by Herry Steinman of West Nyack, N.Y., Miller captured 30% and Anheuser 20% of the total industry's sales gains in May, 1977 in 27 states with more than half the national population.
>
> At that time, some analysts wondered what Anheuser's fast rebound, fueled by extensive discounting, may be doing to its margins, which are already lower than Miller's. When asked about the company's profitability, Mr. Busch replied, "We're not necessarily out to have the highest unit margins in this industry, and we think that says something to the consumer."

EXHIBIT 1
Calendar Year Beer Sales*
(31 gallon barrels)

	Packaged	*Draft*	*Total*	*Percent of Packaged Beer*
1977	138,737,345	18,240,884	156,948,229	88.6
1976	132,169,746	18,256,112	150,425,858	87.9
1975	130,161,490	18,405,730	148,567,220	87.6
1974	127,227,768	18,227,375	145,464,143	87.5
1973	120,339,245	18,110,021	138,449,266	86.9
1972	114,222,674	17,589,082	131,811,756	86.5
1971	110,009,619	17,365,378	127,374,997	86.1
1970	104,581,536	17,250,000	121,861,000	85.7
1969	98,991,856	17,279,464	116,271,320	83.4
1968	94,007,714	17,407,714	111,415,455	83.4
1967	89,579,442	17,394,921	106,974,363	83.5
1966	86,531,861	17,730,638	104,262,499	83.0
1965	82,618,211	17,792,874	100,411,085	82.5
1964	80,277,500	18,222,500	98,643,644	81.5
1963	76,347,185	17,446,818	93,794,003	81.4
1962	74,128,498	17,068,694	91,197,192	81.3
1961	71,910,648	17,117,728	89,028,376	80.8
1960	70,955,558	16,957,289	87,912,847	80.7
1959	70,308,462	17,313,897	87,622,359	80.2
1958	67,168,341	17,256,368	84,424,709	79.6
1957	66,982,200	17,388,825	84,371,025	79.4
1956	67,087,002	17,921,154	85,008,156	78.9
1955	66,179,019	18,798,255	84,977,274	77.9
1954	63,927,035	19,377,986	83,305,021	76.7
1953	65,830,505	20,214,611	86,045,116	76.5
1952	63,359,469	21,477,011	84,836,480	74.7
1951	61,706,743	22,166,893	83,823,636	73.6
1950	59,487,521	23,342,616	82,830,137	71.8
1949	59,443,805	25,113,802	84,557,607	70.3
1948	58,699,355	26,367,959	85,067,314	69.0
1947	58,899,447	28,272,887	87,172,334	67.6
1946	53,010,253	26,530,243	79,540,496	66.6
1945	52,664,148	27,177,247	81,841,395	64.3
1944	49,543,252	29,970,952	79,514,204	62.3
1943	44,248,184	28,444,754	72,692,938	60.9
1942	37,917,179	26,666,939	64,584,118	58.7
1941	32,199,010	25,204,862	57,403,372	56.1
1940	26,761,946	25,049,151	51,811,097	51.7
1939	26,043,002	26,744,031	52,787,033	49.3
1938	23,734,562	27,668,571	51,403,133	46.2
1937	24,431,399	31,300,794	55,732,193	43.8
1936	20,218,406	32,791,610	53,010,016	38.1
1935	13,311,837	31,831,195	45,143,032	29.5
1934	10,024,344	30,012,563	40,034,907	25.0
1933	6,467,400	14,002,241	20,469,641	31.6

*Compiled and copyrighted in this order by Modern Brewery Age 1978. U.S. Treasury Dept. Figures.

EXHIBIT 2 **U.S. Market Shares in Percents**

	1977	1976	1975	1974	1973	1972	1971	1970	1969
Anheuser-Busch	24.0	19.3	23.7	23.4	21.6	20.1	19.2	18.5	16.3
Miller	15.4	12.2	8.6	6.2	5.0	4.0	4.0	4.1	4.2
Schlitz	14.1	16.1	15.7	15.6	15.4	14.3	13.2	12.4	11.7
Pabst	10.3	11.3	10.5	9.8	9.5	9.6	9.3	8.4	7.9
Coors	8.1	9.0	8.0	8.5	7.9	7.4	6.7	6.0	5.4
Sum	71.9	67.9	66.5	63.5	59.4	55.4	52.4	49.4	45.5

Major Media Advertising Cost/Barrel in Dollars*

	1976	1975	1974	1973	1972	1971	1970	1969
Anheuser-Busch	0.98	0.78	0.52	0.69	0.98	0.98	0.84	0.86
Miller	1.58	1.65	1.50	1.58	2.07	2.59	2.12	1.83
Schlitz	1.41	1.14	0.92	0.92	1.09	1.03	1.10	1.20
Pabst	0.57	0.61	0.59	0.55	0.51	0.56	0.61	0.51
Coors	0.15	0.10	0.13	0.13	0.19	0.22	0.24	0.16

*6 major media, i.e., general magazines, sport and network TV, spot radio, newspapers and outdoor. These figures are not complete records of expenditure (1971 excludes newspapers).

Source: Advertising Age, September 26, 1977, and November 3, 1975.

EXHIBIT 3
Independent Variables, Abbreviations, and Expected Signs

Variable	Abbreviation	Expected Sign	Measurement	Scale
Manufacturing Strategy				
Number of plants	NP	±	Count of Operating Plants	10^{-2}
Average capacity	AC	+	Total Rated Capacity/Number of Plants	10^{-3}
Newness of plants	NWP	+	Net Book Value of Fixed Assets Dollars / Gross Book Value of Fixed Assets Dollars	1
Length of production cycle	LPC	−	$\frac{\text{Inventory Dollars}}{\text{Sales Dollars}} \times 365$ days	10^{-3}
Capital intensity	CI	−	Invested Capital Dollars/Sales Dollars	1
Financial Strategy				
Debt	D	+	Total Debt Dollars/Invested Capital Dollars	10^{-1}
Mergers and acquisition	MA	−	1 = Occurrence in Year, 0 = Nonoccurrence in Year	10^{-2}
Market Strategy				
Number of brands	NB	−	Count	10^{-3}
Price	P	+	Annual Net Beer Sales Dollars/Barrels Sold	10^{-2}
Distribution:				
Receivables/Sales Dollars	RS	−	Receivables Dollars/Sales Dollars	
Marketing expenditure	ME	−	Estimated Total Market Expenditure Dollars/Barrels Sold	10^{-3}
Market share	MS	−	Barrels/Sold Industry Barrels Sold	1
Size	LA	−	1/log Assets	1
Environmental Variables				
Eight firm Concentration	C	±	Total Market Share of Top Eight Companies	10^{-1}
Industry advertising intensity	IA	−	Total Industry Advertising Dollars / Total Industry Sales in Barrels	10^{-3}
Strike days in industry	SD	±	Beverage Industry Man Work Days Lost	10^{-8}

$$\text{Performance}^{*} = f\left(\begin{array}{c}\text{Controlled} \\ \text{or Strategic} \\ \text{Variables}\end{array};\ \begin{array}{c}\text{Noncontrollable} \\ \text{or Environmental} \\ \text{Variables}\end{array}\right) \quad (1)$$

*Performance = Return on Equity

Results

	Manufacturing Strategy					Financial Strategy		Marketing Strategy					Environmental Variables					
	NP	*AC*	*NWP*	*LPC*	*CI*	*D*	*MA*	*NB*	*P*	*RS*	*ME*	*MS*	*C*	*IA*	*SD*	*LA*	R^2	*F*
Industry Estimates																		
Equation 1																		
coefficient	−2.364	−.043	.202	−1.483	−.206	.498	4.143	−6.375	−.165	−.619	3.416	1.323	.591	−11.370	−2.584	.063	.704	32.210
significance	.000	.000	.000	.002	.002	.191	.000	.002	.118	.000	.043	.000	.280	.561	.207	.002		(16,217)
Group Estimates																		
Equation 2 *Anheuser-Busch—Schlitz*																		
coefficient	.486	.000	.119	−1.080	−.167	.013	−.165	−7.569	−.401	−.600	−6.593	−.745	−1.180	2.349	−3.352	.135	.996	276.849
significance	.038	.929	.011	.006	.000	.557	.544	.006	.014	.000	.120	.003	.035	.828	.000	.000		(16,19)
Equation 3 *Associated Breweries—Falstaff*																		
coefficient	.423	−.052	.277	−.174	−.326	−2.390	.453	−4.572	−1.011	−.713	.320	−2.594	−.009	23.840	−1.841	.148	.958	33.167
significance	.616	.379	.010	.858	.000	.001	.630	.302	.100	.078	.882	.291	.962	.571	.291	.132		(16,23)
Equation 4 *Heileman—Grain Belt—Lone Star—Olympia*																		
coefficient	−4.596	−.082	.377	−1.193	−.181	2.490	1.815	10.051	.077	.220	−1.052	5.848	−1.190	38.480	3.336	.032	.803	16.019
significance	.009	.002	.006	.319	.023	.000	.159	.026	.765	.701	.838	.052	.420	.331	.134	.622		(16,63)
Equation 5 *Iroquois Industries—Lucky Breweries*																		
coefficient	−5.534	−21.090	.396	−.633	−.150	.309	1.632	−6.569	1.646	−.762	15.400	.704	−.888	−100.000	−9.427	.183	.959	11.605
significance	.074	.194	.061	.769	.293	.766	.656	.655	.062	.083	.240	.916	.057	.341	.268	.164		(16,8)
Equation 6 *Pittsburgh Breweries—Rainier*																		
coefficient	8.136	.062	.178	−1.218	.147	2.390	2.885	−19.010	−.375	.061	11.190	30.595	4.250	191.000	−3.714	−.092	.946	17.426
significance	.319	.676	.404	.297	.477	.012	.374	.057	.800	.904	.641	.269	.263	.067	.270	.524		(16,17)
Equation 7 *Heileman—Grain Belt—Lone Star—Olympia and Pabst*																		
coefficient	−3.498	−.026	.404	−.177	−.263	1.130	2.034	9.745	−.469	−.582	5.362	.181	.529	−3.563	.079	.056	.811	22.200
significance	.005	.135	.000	.851	.000	.034	.123	.077	.017	.227	.124	.807	.623	.912	.968	.297		(16,83)

Source: Hatten, Schendel and Cooper, "A Strategic Model of the U.S. Brewing Industry: 1952–1971," *Academy of Management Journal,* 21, No. 4, December 1978.

EXHIBIT 4 U.S. Consumption of Malt Beverages

Year	Million Barrels	Gallons Per Person
1935	45.23	10.3
1940	54.23	12.5
1945	86.60	18.6
1950	88.81	17.2
1955	89.79	15.9
1960	94.55	15.4
1965	108.02	16.0
1970	134.65	18.7
1974	153.05	20.9

EXHIBIT 5 Number of Brewers

Year	Number of Companies
1952	357
1957	264
1962	220
1967	176
1971	148
1978	97

Source: *Brewers Almanac*, 1964, 1972 and *Modern Brewery Age Blue Book*, 1978.

EXHIBIT 6 Market Share Response to Price Cuts Anheuser-Busch, 1953–1955

	Anheuser-Busch Price Differential per Case			
	December 1953	June 1954	March 1955	July 1955
	+58¢	+33¢	0	+30¢
	Shares of St. Louis Market			
Anheuser-Busch	12.5	16.6	39.3	21.0
Griesedieck Brothers	14.4	12.6	4.8	7.4
Falstaff	29.4	32.0	29.1	36.6
Griesedieck Western	38.9	33.0	23.1	27.8
Others	4.8	5.8	3.9	7.2

Source: Adapted from W. Adams, *The Structure of American Industry*, 4th ed. (New York: Macmillan, 1971) p. 193. Taken from Federal Trade Commission vs. Anheuser-Busch 363 U.S. 536 at 541. Adams noted that factors in addition to price appeared to account for the Griesedieck Brothers drop in market share.

EXHIBIT 7 Guidelines for Justice Department Antitrust Challenge of Acquisitions

*Industry Concentration**	*Acquiring Firm*	*Acquired Firm*
75% or more	4	4 or more
	10	2 or more
	15 or more	1 or more
less than 75%	5	5 or more
	10	4 or more
	15	3 or more
	20	2 or more
	more than 25	1 or more

*Market Share of Four Largest Firms - %.
Source: Justice Department, "Merger Guidelines," Sections 5 and 6, May 30, 1968.

EXHIBIT 8 "Top 5" Plant Locations & Capacity, 1978 (million barrels) (1978 Estimated Industry Capacity = 190 million barrels)

Anheuser-Busch (44.3)			
Fairfield, CA	3.4	Merrimack, NH	2.7
Los Angeles, CA	3.6	Newark, NJ	4.7
Jacksonville, FL	5.9	Columbus, OH	6.0
Tampa, FL	1.6	Houston, TX	2.6
St. Louis, MO	10.7	Williamsburg, VA	3.1
Miller (28)			
Azusa, CA	2.2	Irwindale, CA*	5.0
Fulton, NY	8.2	Eden, N.C.	3.0
Fort Worth, TX	7.0	expanding to	8.8
Milwaukee, WI	9.0	Albany, GA**	10.0
Schlitz (32)			
Van Nuys, CA	3.1	Baldwinsville, NY	4.4
Tampa, FL	1.4	Winston Salem, NC	5.5
Honolulu, HI	0.4	Memphis, TN	6.2
Longview, TX	4.5	Milwaukee, WI	6.5
Pabst (19)			
Los Angeles, CA	1.3	Milwaukee, WI	6.0
Pabst, GA	6.0		
Peoria Heights, IL	3.2		
Newark, NJ	2.5		
Coors (15)			
Golden, CO	15.0		

*To replace Azusa, CA under construction $170 million, *Wall Street Journal,* April 12, 1978.
**$247 million, *The Wall Street Journal,* April 12, 1978.
Source: Modern Brewery Age Blue Book, 1978.

EXHIBIT 9 Wholesale Grain Prices

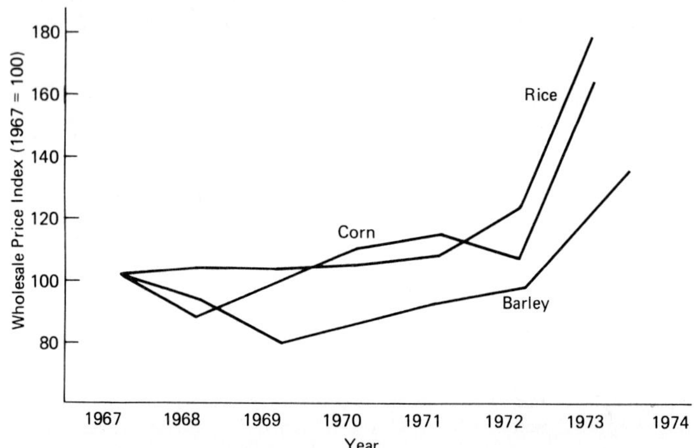

Source: Standard and Poor's, 1974.

EXHIBIT 10 Brewers' Malt and Corn Grits—Monthly Prices 1972–1976

	Malt (per 34 lb. bushel FOB Chicago)				
Month	*1972*	*1973*	*1974*	*1975*	*1976*
Jan	$1.77	$1.83	$3.06	$5.18	$4.43
Feb	1.77	1.91	3.21	5.10	4.37
Mar	1.77	1.97	3.27	5.00	4.37
Apr	1.77	2.03	3.57	5.00	
May	1.77	2.03	3.83	5.00	
Jun	1.77	2.03	3.83	5.00	
Jul	1.77	2.03	3.99	5.00	
Aug	1.77	2.17	4.15	4.96	
Sept	1.77	2.62	4.15	4.82	
Oct	1.77	2.83	4.45	4.82	
Nov	1.77	3.01	4.65	4.62	
Dec	1.77	3.06	4.85	4.62	

	Corn Grits (per cwt)				
Month	1972	1973	1974	1975	1976
Jan	$3.51	$4.13	$7.12	$8.27	$6.95
Feb	3.58	4.42	7.71	8.25	7.21
Mar	3.64	4.61	7.43	8.01	7.59
Apr	3.65	4.77	6.88	7.88	
May	3.70	5.46	6.92	8.07	
Jun	3.71	6.20	7.57	8.27	
Jul	3.78	7.10	8.59	8.25	
Aug	3.82	7.62	8.62	8.94	
Sept	3.90	6.79	9.02	8.32	
Oct	3.84	6.82	9.46	7.61	
Nov	3.71	6.55	8.65	7.11	
Dec	3.99	6.63	8.92	7.09	

Source: Allan Kaplan, "Outlook for the Brewing Industry," Goldman Sachs, May 10, 1976.

EXHIBIT 11 Advertising at Anheuser Busch

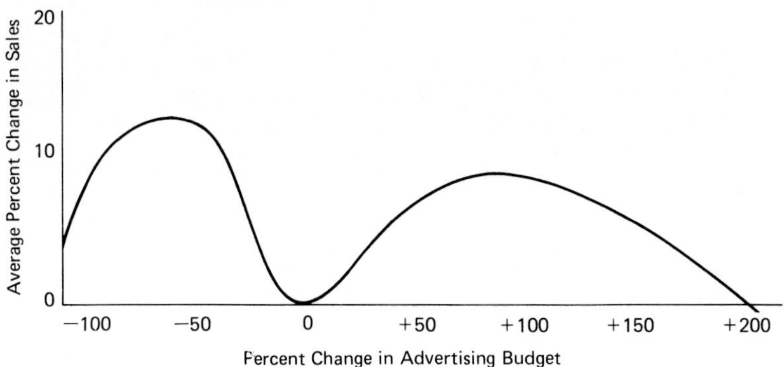

Where the zero point is "budgeted advertising" and last year's sales.

Source: Russell L. Ackoff and James Emshoff, "Advertising Research at Anheuser-Busch, Inc. (1963–1968)," *Sloan Management Review,* Winter 1975.

EXHIBIT 12 Personality Types* and Drinking Behavior

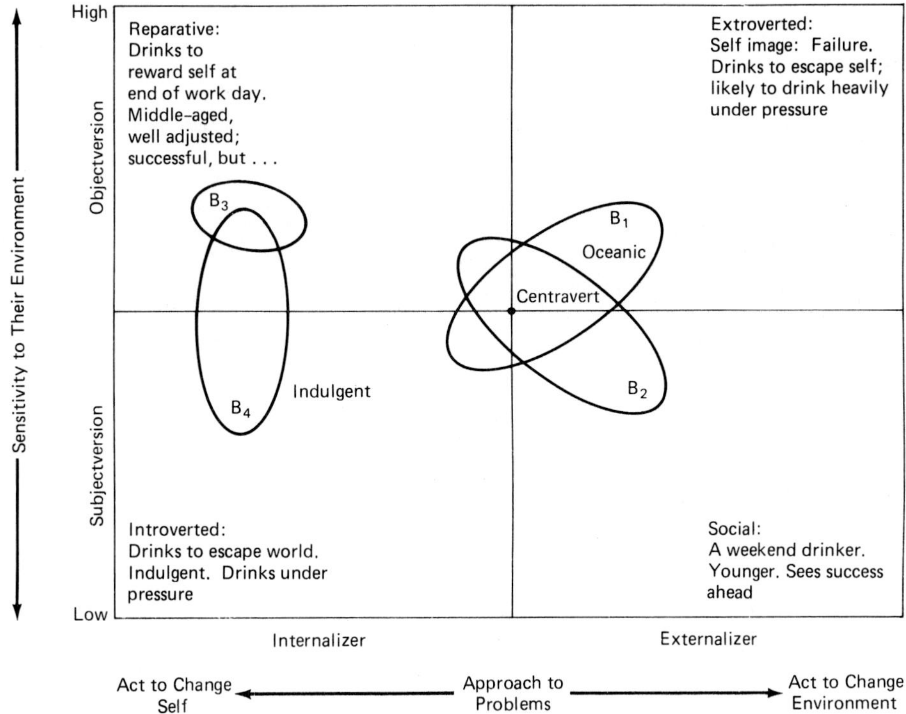

*The researchers point out most people fall into mixed classes, not the extremes. Most are in the reparative or social drinker categories.

Source: Adapted from Russell Ackoff and James Emshoff "Advertising Research at Anheuser-Busch Inc. (1968–1974)," *Sloan Management Review,* Spring 1975.

APPENDIX 1
ENVIRONMENTAL ISSUES*

A possible ban on the use of nonreturnable containers is probably the greatest threat to the industry. Just as creative packaging has aided industry growth over the past decade, the absence of cans and one-way bottles could reduce demand. Although the Environmental Protection Agency (EPA) gained ground last November by issuing guidelines that would require deposits on all beverage containers sold on federal facilities, it does not appear likely that Congress will be able to put through national legislation banning nonreturnable containers in the foreseeable future. There are too many industries connected with the manufacture of cans and bottles to allow its passage without severe pressure from labor, can producers, and steel and aluminum producers. These factions received some new ammunition from a recently released Commerce Department study that concludes that a shift to 100% returnables would result in the loss of about 80,000 manufacturing jobs. But 100,000 stockroom jobs in handling the returnables would be created. The study also indicated that the shift would reduce highway litter by only 10%–12%, even if 90% of the bottles were returned. Even if national legislation did pass, the effective date would probably be after some span of time—perhaps five years—to give the industry time to adjust. (However, the effect on the price of the brewing and soft drink stocks would be immediate.)

*Source: Allan Kaplan, ''Outlook for the Brewing Industry,'' Goldman Sachs, May 10, 1976

APPENDIX 2
Demographic Factors

Estimated Weekly Beer Consumption by Age Group, Summer of 1961

Age Group	*Estimated Per Capita Consumption (12-oz units)*	*Population (millions)*	*Total Consumption (mil. units)*
20–24	5.0	11.5	57.5
25–34	8.3	22.7	188.1
35–44	7.5	24.4	182.5
45–54	5.8	20.9	121.9
55 and over	2.8	33.0	92.3
Total	5.7	112.5	642.3

Source: American Can Company.

U.S. Population by Age Group in Five-Year Intervals, 1960–1990E* (millions)

Age Group	*1960*	*1965*	*1970*	*1975*	*1980E*	*1985E*	*1990E*
20–24	11.1	13.7	17.2	19.4	21.1	20.4	17.8
25–34	22.9	22.3	25.3	31.1	37.0	40.8	41.8
35–44	24.2	24.4	23.1	22.7	25.4	31.2	36.9
45–54	20.6	22.0	23.3	23.6	22.4	22.0	24.6
55 and over	32.3	35.1	38.7	42.0	45.1	47.3	48.1

Compound Annual Growth Rate by Age Group for Five-Year Periods Ending 1965–1990E

Age Group	*1965*	*1970*	*1975*	*1980E*	*1985E*	*1990E*
20–24	4.3%	4.7%	2.4%	1.7%	(0.8)%	(2.8)%
25–34	(0.5)	2.6	4.2	3.5	2.0	0.5
35–44	0.2	(1.2)	(0.3)	2.3	4.2	3.4
45–54	1.2	1.1	0.2	(1.0)	(0.4)	2.3
55 and over	1.7	2.0	1.7	1.5	1.0	0.3
Total population	1.5	1.1	0.8	0.8	0.8	0.7

Weekly Beer Consumption by Age Group as Calculated from Tables 5 and 6 in Five-Year Intervals, 1960–1990E (million 12-oz units)

Age Group	*1960*	*1965*	*1970*	*1975*	*1980E*	*1985E*	*1990E*
20–24	55.5	68.5	86.0	97.0	105.5	102.0	89.0
25–34	190.0	185.0	210.0	258.1	307.1	338.6	346.9
35–44	181.5	183.0	173.3	170.7	190.5	234.0	276.8
45–54	119.5	127.6	135.1	136.9	129.9	127.6	142.7
55 and over	90.4	98.3	108.4	117.6	126.3	132.4	134.7
Total	636.9	662.4	712.8	780.3	859.3	934.6	990.1

*E = estimated.

Source: Allan Kaplan, "Outlook for the Brewing Industry" Goldman Sachs, May 10, 1976.

APPENDIX 3
Per-Share and Financial Data for Anheuser-Busch, Schlitz, Pabst, and Coors, 1965–1976E

Year	Earnings Per Share	Price Range	P/E Ratio Range	Dividend Data: Amount	Dividend Data: Payout Ratio	Dividend Data: Yield	Long-Term Debt as % of Total Capital	Return on Average Net Worth	Return on Average Total Capital
				Anheuser-Busch					
1965	0.61	12– 8	19.7–13.1	0.22	36.1	2.2	20.5	13.6	11.0
1966	0.76	15–12	19.7–15.8	0.25	32.9	1.9	30.0	15.5	12.1
1967	0.82	21–15	25.6–18.3	0.30	36.6	1.6	36.7	15.2	10.7
1968	1.00	38–20	38.0–20.0	0.36	36.3	1.3	33.3	16.5	11.7
1969	1.02	37–29	36.3–28.4	0.40	39.2	1.2	30.0	15.1	11.2
1970	1.40	39–27	27.9–19.3	0.42	30.4	1.3	26.3	18.6	14.1
1971	1.60	56–37	35.0–23.1	0.53	33.1	1.1	22.0	18.5	14.7
1972	1.70	69–51	40.6–30.0	0.58	34.1	1.0	17.7	17.4	14.6
1973	1.46	56–29	38.4–19.9	0.60	41.1	1.4	15.7	13.6	11.8
1974	1.42	38–21	26.8–14.8	0.60	42.3	2.0	26.4	12.3	10.6
1975	1.88	40–25	21.3–13.3	0.68	36.2	2.1	36.6	15.0	11.5
1976E	1.90	31[a]		0.68					
				Schlitz					
1965	0.56	10– 8	17.9–14.3	0.258	46.1	2.9	—	10.1	10.0
1966	0.60	10– 6	16.7–10.0	0.292	48.7	3.6	—	10.3	10.3
1967	0.67	13– 7	19.4–10.4	0.325	48.5	3.3	2.2	11.0	11.0
1968	0.73	21–12	28.8–16.4	0.383	52.5	2.3	3.6	11.5	11.3
1969	0.86	27–17	31.4–19.8	0.45	52.3	2.0	13.7	13.0	12.2
1970	1.04	28–18	26.9–17.3	0.467	44.9	2.0	23.2	15.0	13.0
1971	1.22	33–22	27.0–18.0	0.517	42.4	1.9	23.6	16.1	13.3
1972	1.58	64–32	40.5–20.3	0.553	35.0	1.1	20.4	19.0	15.7
1973	1.90	68–49	35.8–25.8	0.608	32.0	1.0	17.8	20.5	17.5
1974	1.69	57–14	33.7– 8.3	0.67	39.6	1.9	31.3	16.3	13.1
1975[a]	1.06	30–15	24.0–12.0	0.68	54.4	3.0	39.4	9.6	7.6
1976E	1.90	26[a]		0.68					
				Pabst					
1965	1.31	21–16	16.0–12.2	0.25	26.3	1.4	10.0	12.9	11.9
1966	1.61	21–15	13.0– 9.3	0.375	23.3	2.1	4.3	14.4	13.7
1967	1.91	32–19	16.8–10.0	0.50	26.2	2.0	—	15.3	15.0
1968	2.14	51–30	23.8–14.0	0.50	23.4	1.2	—	15.3	15.4
1969	1.90	51–34	26.8–17.9	0.575	29.5	1.4	—	12.1	12.2
1970	2.44	53–35	21.7–14.3	0.65	26.6	1.5	—	14.0	14.0
1971	2.66	75–47	28.2–17.7	0.80	30.1	1.3	—	13.8	13.8
1972	2.99	100–71	33.4–23.8	0.83	27.8	1.0	—	14.0	14.0
1973	2.51	75–19	29.9– 7.6	0.86	34.3	1.8	—	10.9	10.9
1974	2.02	25–11	12.4– 5.5	0.91	45.0	5.1	—	8.1	8.2
1975	2.42	32–17	13.2– 7.0	1.04	43.0	4.2	—	9.0	9.1
1976E	3.30	26[a]		1.04					
				Coors					
1970	0.77			0.02	2.5	—	—	NA	NA
1971	1.05			0.03	2.8	—	—	17.4	NA
1972	1.35			0.04	2.8	—	—	18.7	NA
1973	1.34			0.04	2.8	—	—	16.4	NA
1974	1.16			0.05	4.1	—	—	12.8	13.1
1975	1.68	35–22	19.8–12.4	0.06	3.4	0.2	—	16.0	16.3
1976E	2.00	26[a]		0.06					

[a]As of May 7, 1976.

Source: Allan Kaplan, "Outlook for the Brewing Industry," Goldman Sachs, May 10, 1976.

APPENDIX 4
AD COSTS FOR BEER, ALE, MALT LIQUOR

Brewer	*1976*	*1975*	*1974*	*1973*
Anheuser-Busch Inc. (Budweiser, Budweiser malt liquor, Michelob, Busch Bavarian)				
1,000 bbls. sold	29,060	35,200	34,100	29,887
Ad investment	$28,535,300	$27,354,000	$17,839,935	$20,522,602
Ad cost per bbl.	98¢	78¢	52¢	69¢
Add cost per case	7¢	5¢	4¢	5¢
Jos. Schlitz Brewing Co. (Schlitz, Schlitz malt liquor, Old Milwaukee, Primo, Schlitz Light)				
1,000 bbls. sold	24,162	23,279	22,661	21,343
Ad investment	$34,131,400	$26,530,000	$20,910,940	$19,722,864
Ad cost per bbl.	$1.41	$1.14	92¢	92¢
Ad cost per case	10¢	8¢	6¢	6¢
Miller Brewing Co. (Miller High Life, Miller malt liquor, Miller Lite, Lowenbrau)				
1,000 bbls. sold	18,403	12,862	9,066	6,919
Ad investment	$29,114,700	$21,252,000	$13,556,133	$10,914,623
Ad cost per bbl.	$1.58	$1.65	$1.50	$1.58
Ad cost per case	11¢	12¢	11¢	11¢
Pabst Brewing Co. (Pabst Blue Ribbon, Andeker of America)				
1,000 bbls. sold	17,087	15,669	14,297	13,128
Ad investment	$ 9,727,900	$ 9,622,000	$ 8,449,274	$ 7,219,051
Ad cost per bbl.	57¢	61¢	59¢	55¢
Ad cost per case	4¢	4¢	4¢	4¢
Adolph Coors Co. (Coors)				
1,000 bbls. sold	13,600	11,950	12,400	10,950
Ad investment	$ 2,016,200	$ 1,243,000	$ 1,611,931	$ 1,374,929
Ad cost per bbl.	15¢	10¢	13¢	13¢
Ad cost per case	1¢	7¢	9¢	9¢
Olympia Brewing Co. (Olympia, Hamm's, Lone Star)				
1,000 bbls. sold	6,367	5,557	4,300	3,636
Ad investment	$ 5,659,800	$ 5,774,600	$ 3,892,676	$ 3,258,529
Ad cost per bbl.	89¢	$1.04	90¢	90¢
Ad cost per case	6¢	7¢	6¢	6¢

Source: *Advertising Age*, September 26, 1977. Copyright 1977 by Crain Communications Inc.

APPENDIX 5
Approximate Size & Growth of the Premium Beer Segment

	Million Barrels	*10 Year Growth Rate*	*Premium % of Beer Market*
1973	46	10.7%	33.0%
1974	52	11.3	35.7
1975	56	11.2	38.1
1976	60	10.6	40.0
1977	75	11.2	48.1

Source: Philip Morris Annual Reports.

APPENDIX 6
Regional Structure of U.S. Beer Market (1976)

New England	Massachusetts, Connecticut, Maine, New Hampshire, Rhode Island, Vermont
Mid-Atlantic	New York, Pennsylvania, New Jersey
East North Central	Illinois, Ohio, Michigan, Wisconsin, Indiana
West North Central	Missouri, Minnesota, Iowa, Kansas, Nebraska, North Dakota, South Dakota
South Atlantic	Florida, Virginia, Maryland, North Carolina, Georgia, South Carolina, West Virginia, Delaware, Washington, D.C.
East South Central	Tennessee, Kentucky, Alabama, Mississippi
West South Central	Texas, Louisiana, Oklahoma, Arkansas
Mountain	Colorado, Arizona, New Mexico, Idaho, Montana, Nevada, Utah, Wyoming
Pacific	California, Washington, Oregon, Alaska, Hawaii

Source: Emanuel Goldman, "The Brewing Industry," Sanford C. Berstein & Co., Inc., Critical Variable Update, May 26, 1977.

APPENDIX 6 (Cont.)

Estimated Increase in Barrelage by Brewer & Region from 1974 to 1976* (millions of barrels)

Region	Anheuser	Schlitz	Miller	Pabst	Coors	Total Top 5	All Other	Total All Brewers
New England	(0.3)	(0.1)	0.9	0.1	—	0.6*	(0.5)	0.1
Mid-Atlantic	(1.5)	0.3	1.1	0.7	—	0.6	(1.0)	(0.4)
Total Northeast	(1.8)	0.2	2.0	0.8	—	1.2	(1.5)	(0.3)
East North Central	(0.8)	(0.1)	1.6	0.5	—	1.2	(0.1)	1.1
West North Central	(0.3)	—	0.4	0.9	0.1	1.1	(0.7)	0.4
Total North Central	(1.1)	(0.1)	2.0	1.4	0.1	2.3	(0.8)	1.5
South Atlantic	(1.6)	0.3	2.4	0.1	—	1.0	(0.3)	0.7
East South Central	(0.4)	—	1.0	0.1	—	0.7	(0.4)	0.3
West South Central	(0.5)	—	1.2	—	1.3	2.0	(1.1)	0.9
Total South	(2.5)	0.3	4.6	0.2	1.3	3.7	(1.8)	1.9
Mountain	(0.1)	0.3	0.3	0.1	0.3	0.9	(0.3)	0.6
Pacific	0.5	0.8	0.5	0.4	(0.3)	1.9	(0.7)	1.2
Total West	0.4	1.1	0.8	0.5	—	2.8	(1.0)	1.8
Total All Regions	(5.0)	1.5	9.3	2.7	1.2	9.7	(4.8)	4.9

*Errors due to rounding.

Estimated Market Share by Region & Brewer for 1976* (% of region)

Region	Anheuser	Schlitz	Miller	Pabst	Coors	Total Top 5	All Other	Total All Brewers
New England	21.3%	23.6%	16.9%	11.3%	—	67.4%	32.6%	100.0%
Mid-Atlantic	22.2	7.3	12.5	8.1	—	50.0	50.0	100.0
Total Northeast	22.0%	11.6%	13.6%	7.4%	—	54.6%	45.4%	100.0%
East North Central	12.5%	10.6%	10.9%	24.1%	—	58.1%	41.9%	100.0%
West North Central	17.9	16.2	7.7	15.4	7.7	65.0	35.0	100.0
Total North Central	14.0%	12.1%	10.0%	21.7%	7.7%	60.0%	40.0%	100.0%
South Atlantic	26.6%	24.8%	19.3%	15.6%	—	86.2%	13.8%	100.0%
East South Central	25.3	30.7	20.0	12.0	—	88.0	12.0	100.0
West South Central	15.2	29.1	12.7	1.3	23.4%	81.6	18.4	100.0
Total South	22.4%	27.3%	17.1%	10.0%	8.2%	84.9%	15.1%	100.0%
Mountain	18.3%	11.0%	6.1%	2.4%	37.8%	75.6%	24.4%	100.0%
Pacific	19.6	9.3	6.5	3.3	27.1	65.9	34.1	100.0
Total West	19.3%	9.8%	6.4%	3.0%	30.1%	68.6%	31.4%	100.0%
Total All Regions	19.3%	16.1%	12.2%	11.3%	9.0%	68.0%	32.0%	100.0%

*Errors due to rounding.

Sources: Beer Statistics Monthly, Beer Marketer's Insights, Inc.; U.S. Brewer's Association; corporate reports and Bernstein estimates. Emanuel Goldman, "The Brewing Industry" Sanford C. Bernstein & Co., Inc., Critical Variable Update, May 26, 1977

APPENDIX 6 (Cont.)

Competitive Positions in 50 States 1978

	Rank					
	#1	#2	#3	#4	#5	#6
Anheuser-Busch	14	17	12	7	1	—
Miller	3	12	13	12	11	—
Schlitz	4	8	12	13	14	—
Pabst	3	6	3	14	14	11
Coors	10	1	—	—	—	3

Source: R. S. Weinberg & Associates, St. Louis, in *Beverage World,* May 1978.

APPENDIX 7
Estimated Pricing Requirements and Earnings Sensitivity for Changes in Selected Variables

Beer Price Change (%) Necessary to Cover 1% Change in Listed Variable

	Anheuser	*Schlitz*	*Miller*	*Pabst*	*Coors*
Cans	0.27%	0.27%	0.18%	0.30%	0.26%
Non-Ret. Bottles	0.06	0.06	0.15	0.07	0.06
Malt	0.08	0.09	0.08	0.10	0.10
Corn	*	0.03	0.02	0.03	*
Rice	0.02	*	*	*	0.02
Wage Rate	0.12	0.12	0.13	0.18	0.08
SG&A	0.09	0.15	0.09	0.08	0.09

Source: Emanuel Goldman, "The Brewing Industry," Sanford C. Bernstein & Co., Inc., Critical Variable Update, May 26, 1977.

FERMENT IN THE BEER INDUSTRY: SCHLITZ/MILLER

THE JOS. SCHLITZ BREWING COMPANY

1977 was Daniel F. (Jack) McKeithan's first year as chairman of Jos. Schlitz Brewing Company. It began with falling sales (see *Exhibits 1–4*). Then came an explosive annual meeting at which members of the Uihlein family, which owned about 75% of the stock, traded angry charges and countercharges with the company's management. Sales continued to fall and so did earnings, forcing the resignation of the company's President, Eugene B. Peters, in October, 1977, after eleven months in office. By the time the year ended, Schlitz had lost its number two sales position in the industry, behind Anheuser-Busch, to Philip Morris's fast-growing Miller Brewing. The company's dismal showing prompted exploratory merger talks with R. J. Reynolds. *Fortune* commented that nothing came of the talks, but the very fact that they occurred shows how much the once-proud brewer had declined.

In late 1978, Schlitz was caught between Anheuser-Busch and Miller in a fierce battle for market share. Its two major brands, premium-priced Schlitz and popular-priced Old Milwaukee, had both lost ground. The company had no product in the fast-growing and highly profitable "super-premium" category, which included such brands as Anheuser-Busch, Michelob, Miller's new brewed-in-America Lowenbrau, and Pabst's Andeker. Schlitz was the second major brewer, after Miller, to enter the light-beer market—which was the fastest-growing segment of all—but its entry, Schlitz Light, trailed Anheuser-Busch's Natural Light, introduced in 1977. Miller Lite was number one in 1978. Only in the malt-liquor segments, which accounted for about 3% of total industry sales, did Schlitz lead. The issue for management was why, and what to do about the company's market share decline.

Corporate History

Schlitz was not founded by an Uihlein (pronounced Ee-line) or even a Schlitz, but by a Bavarian-born immigrant named August Krug. His widow married Joseph Schlitz, the firm's bookkeeper. Both Krug and Schlitz were childless, so when Schlitz perished in a shipwreck in 1865, control passed to Krug's nephew, August Uihlein. During August's long reign, giants emerged in the U.S. brewing industry, among them Schlitz, Pabst, Miller and Blatz in Milwaukee, and Anheuser-Busch in St. Louis. These were the "shipping brewers," marketing their beer over broad and expanding areas.

As one of the great shipping brewers, Schlitz thrived and grew until Prohibition intervened. The company bottled soft drinks during the beer-less years and quickly got back to brewing after Repeal in 1933. A two-man team managed the post-Repeal Schlitz: August Uihlein's youngest son Erwin, and a remarkably durable employee named Sol

This case was prepared from public sources by Dr. Kenneth J. Hatten as a basis for class discussion rather than to illustrate either effective or ineffective handling of an administrative situation.

Abrams, who went to work for the company at seventeen and retired at eighty-seven. Erwin was President and oversaw production; Sol was General Manager and oversaw almost everything else. He had two dozen men reporting to him and he made the decisions for all of them. Under Erwin and Sol, Schlitz became the U.S.'s number one beermaker, setting in 1952 a new world production record of 6,347,000 barrels.

The company's shipments didn't reach the 1952 level again for another ten years. The basic trouble was that the market for beer stopped growing. It was an established beer-business fact that people in their twenties and thirties drank a lot more beer on the average than people past forty. During the 1950s, and indeed into the early 1960s, the number of Americans in these younger age groups failed to increase even though population was growing. Brewers, however, continued to add to capacity, and the result was severe pressure on profits. Premium brewers were jolted especially hard.

Erwin's nephew, Robert Uihlein, urged him to take the company into the popular-price market by purchasing some existing brand. Erwin rejected that idea, but he did come to see that Schlitz needed a second brand of beer. He decided to revive Old Milwaukee, a popular-price beer that Schlitz had brought out in the 1930s and had abandoned during World War II when the federal government imposed grain rationing.

Introduced in Michigan in early 1959, Old Milwaukee failed to win consumer acceptance. Instead of getting a lift from the entry into the popular-price market, the company's total sales kept drifting downward, and the board gradually came to the conclusion that it was time for a change of management. In early 1961, Sol Abrams retired. Shortly afterward, the board elected forty-four-year-old Robert Uihlein, Jr. President, and Erwin Chairman of the Board. The new President, the board made clear, was to be the Chief Executive Officer.

Schlitz was one of the biggest firms still under family control in the U.S. in 1978. The Uihleins had controlled the company, and generally managed it, since 1875. During the 1950s, because of a timorous management, Schlitz went downhill steadily. But the family produced its own remedy in Robert. He reshaped management, recruiting outsiders and promising that his executives would have the latitude to make their own decisions. His policies turned the company around, and the people he hired made it grow. Even before becoming President, for example, he brought into the company a director of marketing, Fred R. Haviland, from Anheuser-Busch. Haviland shaped new advertising and marketing strategies, and spent heavily to put them into practice. He was also a hearty, inspirational leader who built up a confident and aggressive sales team. He fired the company's wholesalers with enthusiasm.

Haviland's first job was to salvage Old Milwaukee, and as a result of his prodding the beer was soon lightened and put into brown bottles. In 1962, new ads proclaimed Old Milwaukee to be "America's light beer . . . brewed for that wonderful world of leisure."

"There has been a liberation of this company. The joint is charged and rocking." In October, 1964, with these heady words, a top executive of the Jos. Schlitz Brewing Company summed up the changes that had taken place since February, 1961. Uihlein felt that decision making had been slow and overcentralized at Schlitz. "The first thing I'm going to do," he said, "is give some of the men around here a chance to make a mistake."

With his own marketing department just getting organized, Uihlein put the Schlitz image problem up to Chicago's Leo Burnett ad agency. Looking for a word that would express the liveliness it wanted to get into the new Schlitz ads, the agency considered and rejected hundreds of words before hitting on "gusto," a "vessel" word into which everybody pours his own meaning. Asked to say what gusto meant to them, people gave such diverse answers as "flavor," "fun," "life," "refreshment," "zest," and even "guts." The meanings were always positive. Burnett's Schlitz campaign was built on gusto, "Real gusto in a great light beer."

In 1961 Schlitz purchased Burgermeister, a California beer with sales of $22 million. Early in 1964, Schlitz acquired Primo, a Hawaiian brand. In addition, Uihlein took Schlitz international into Turkey and Spain. All these ventures proved unsuccessful.

Faced with the task of marketing several brands that to some extent competed with one another, Haviland organized separate brand teams, one each for Schlitz, Old Milwaukee, Burgermeister, Primo and the new Schlitz Malt Liquor. Each team handled planning, advertising, and merchandising for its brand with undivided devotion, as if the other brands did not exist. "It's the Procter and Gamble way," Haviland said in 1964. "We're Procter and Gamblizing the beer business." The sales force was separate, serving all brands.

With sales of the other brands added to expanding sales of Schlitz, the Jos. Schlitz Brewing Company began to gain on Anheuser-Busch. In 1960, Schlitz had lagged 2,783,000 barrels behind. In 1963, Anheuser-Busch led by only 1,563,000 barrels—9,397,000 to Schlitz's 7,834,000. Schlitz executives talked about catching up and re-establishing Schlitz as the number one brewing company.

It was inevitable that Schlitz's acquisitions would draw the attention of the Justice Department. Schlitz's acquisition of 39% of John Labatt Ltd., Canada's third-largest brewer, was the trigger event. Through its controlling interest in Labatt, Schlitz could influence California's General Brewing, the makers of Lucky Lager. Schlitz, Lucky and Burgermeister held 25% of the California market in 1964.

In spite of Schlitz's protests that it had no interest in Lucky Lager, the court was unimpressed. It ordered Schlitz to divest itself of Labatt and advised that Justice could challenge the 1961 Burgermeister acquisition, which it did successfully. Schlitz' acquisition had been seen as unfriendly by Labatt's management and the court seemed unconvinced by Schlitz's apparent lack of interest in introducing Labatt to the United States market. It concluded that Schlitz's acquisitions eliminated potential competitors and lessened competition.

Schlitz subsequently—and, perhaps, consequently—turned to new plant construction but, by this time, Anheuser-Busch already had its construction program underway. The results of Schlitz's expansion program are listed in *Exhibit 5*.

Operations, 1968 to 1976

1968 In 1968, the company disposed of its controlling interest in its Spanish breweries after a series of losses, retaining about a 25% interest. This move made consolidation of the Spanish results with Schlitz's unnecessary. Schlitz then acquired a small Belgian brewery.

Domestically, the company announced the establishment of a new operations area, Distribution, under the control of a Vice President, one of seven new vice presidential posts which reinforced Schlitz's functional organization. The company began testing a ''premium-plus'' beer, Encore, and initiated a plant expansion program at its five established plants. A new brewery at Winston-Salem, North Carolina, with an initial capacity of 3.3 million barrels per year, got underway.

1969 In 1969, Schlitz's market share was almost 12% and the company's expansion program began to heat up. Winston-Salem was heralded as the ''largest brewery built in modern times,'' with a present capacity of 4.4 million barrels. In April, 1969, another 4.4-million-barrel brewery was announced, this time for Memphis, Tennessee. Schlitz planned expansions of its capacity in Hawaii (for Primo) and in Los Angeles.

The company finally was able to comply with the court order to sell Burgermeister (to Hamm) and its San Francisco brewery (to Miller Brewing Company). It took a loss of $840,000. Also in 1969, the company liquidated its Puerto Rico brewing company, writing off $3,160,000.

In spite of these setbacks, however, Schlitz's management was optimistic. The new advertising campaign for Schlitz was underway and apparently well-received. The campaign, prepared by Leo Burnett, featured ''Men at Sea'' and the theme:

> *You only go around once in life.*
> *So grab for all the gusto you can.*
> *Even in the beer you drink.*
> *Why settle for less?*
>
> *When you're out of Schlitz, you're out of beer.*

1970 In 1970, the Belgian brewery acquired in 1968 went into voluntary liquidation. Schlitz retained an ecological consultant to help the company deal with the growing environmental pressures on the industry—including the prospect of legislation banning the nonreturnable can.

The annual report featured photographs of young people enjoying Schlitz and the beach. The company attributed its success to:

1 Continued emphasis on product quality at every level.
2 Market research designed to assure maximum use of marketing dollars.
3 The company's multiple-brand strategy, which facilitated participation in all competitive markets and coverage of all important product categories during the year.

In fact, Schlitz had five brands at the time: Schlitz (premium-priced), Old Milwaukee (popular), Schlitz Malt Liquor (a specialty product), Primo in Hawaii and Encore (premium-plus) in test.

The company sold three branches to independent wholesalers, leaving only the Milwaukee branch in Schlitz's hands. The company issued $50 million in debentures and obtained a $35 million credit line during the year. The annual report noted that prices were relatively unchanged, despite sharply higher costs.

1971 By 1971, 45% of Schlitz's capacity was less than six years old. The Memphis plant was on stream and expected to reach full capacity by 1973. The company announced its intention to close its 1,000,000 barrel Brooklyn, New York, plant ''because of its limited expansion potential and lack of rail shipment facilities.'' The involved unions took the matter to arbitration; it was ruled the plant could not be closed.

The company added to its list of success factors its ''constant efforts to develop and maintain the industry's most effective wholesale network'' and boasted that Old Milwaukee was the fastest-growing national brand.

On April 14, 1971, *Ad Age* added some detail about Schlitz's advertising campaign, reporting an address by Joseph T. Plummer, Manager of Copy and Creative Research for Leo Burnett Company:

> An informal bit of research by a Leo Burnett Co. creative director, conducted while touring Chicago taverns, formed the core of the current Schlitz ad campaign.
>
> "The heavy beer drinker is the man who belongs to that 20% of the population that drinks 80% of the beer," Mr. Plummer said. "A man who drinks a case a weekend, or even a case a day. He is the guy who is not making it and probably never will. He is a dreamer, a wisher, a limited edition of Walter Mitty. He is a sports nut because he is a hero worshipper. He goes to the tavern and has six or seven beers with the boys. If we are to talk to this man where he lives, in terms he respects and can identify with, we must find for him a believable kind of hero he inwardly admires."
>
> These conclusions led to a new Schlitz campaign . . . using the theme, "You only go around once in life, so you have to grab for all the gusto you can."
>
> The creative man's informal survey was supported by more formal life style research, which pinpointed the heavy beer drinker as young, blue-collar, middle-class, and with a high school education. He seems to be more "hedonistic and pleasure-seeking" than the non-drinker, Mr. Plummer said; he has less regard for responsibilities of family and job, tends to prefer a physical, male-oriented existence, and has an inclination to fantasize.
>
> "We concluded from the life style portrait of the heavy beer drinker that the 'gusto man and gusto life' approach would strongly appeal to this heavy beer drinker's sense of masculinity, hedonism and fantasy," Mr. Plummer said.

1972 In 1972, Schlitz and Old Milwaukee received awards for the creative excellence of their advertising programs. Schlitz's market share went over 14% and the company decided to expand its new Memphis plant to 6.2 million barrels at a cost of $17 million. The plan was to complete the project by 1974. By 1972, Schlitz manufactured 60% of the cans it used in Milwaukee and began construction of a can plant in Tampa, Florida. It closed its Brooklyn plant, displacing 400 people and suffering an extraordinary charge of $8.3 million.

1973 In 1973, Schlitz announced a $300 million expansion program, including the construction of a new brewery near Syracuse, New York, to supply the northeastern states. It was scheduled to have a capacity of 5.8 million barrels and slated for completion in 1976. Other plants were to be expanded, too:

- Memphis, from 6.2 to 8.3 million barrels
- Longview, Texas, from 2.8 to 4.5 million barrels
- Winston-Salem, from 4.4 to 5.5 million barrels
- Los Angeles, from 2.0 to 3.8 million barrels.

The company's 700,000-barrel Kansas City plant was closed. The company explained its plant location strategy: to build large efficient plants at locations carefully selected for water quality and ease of distribution.

Encore was withdrawn from the market.

1974 Sales passed $1 billion in 1974 but the company's earnings declined 11.3% ". . . due to unprecedented increases in costs which were not fully offset by increased beer selling prices and corporate cost reduction measures." (In 1976, William Blair & Company of Chicago reported that unlike Anheuser-Busch which used rice and Coors which used refined corn starch, Pabst used corn grits and Schlitz used corn syrup which were piped straight into the brewing kettle.)[1] Apparently, the 10.18% price increase approved in 1973 plus cost-efficiency measures were insufficient to offset cost increases; (e.g., brewing materials rose 70% and packaging materials 30% according to the annual report for 1974)[2] and the ravages of competition.

Schlitz revised its plant expansion plans, slowing completion timetables; Syracuse was put back twelve months—to 1977. The company announced two $75-million debt instruments, one being debentures, the other ten-year notes.

Apparently the drive for efficiency in 1974 had other deleterious effects:

> Primo, top selling beer in Hawaii in 1970 with 70% of the market, slid to a 20% market share in 1974, following a disastrous decision to produce the basic mixture in Los Angeles and ship a dehydrated mixture to Hawaii for fermentation and bottling. Primo was locked into a taste, and it was a taste the customers didn't like.
>
> After two agency switches, the company moved the brewing process back to Hawaii in November, 1974, and began a long, slow process of wooing back the market.[3]

Schlitz announced plans to step up its manufacture of cans by building plants in Los Angeles and at Winston-Salem. Even so, the company was already 35% self-sufficient. Management projected spending 55% of its capital budget on brewing capacity and 20% on can manufacturing facilities over the next few years.

Perhaps to help keep capacity utilization up, Schlitz took Old Milwaukee national (making it available to 40% of the population). Prices rose 15%.

1975 In the 1975 Annual Report there was a new emphasis: quality. "Quality is a tradition at Schlitz." Again, management noted a difficult year, explaining yet another earnings decline. Again, agricultural products and packaging costs were the villains: costs increased 25% and 15% respectively whereas beer prices rose only 10%.

The company stressed its dedication to quality: "Long ago it was determined that none would brew beers better than Schlitz" . . . "Quality is an attitude." The annual report stressed that only the best ingredients were used, explaining how corn and rice were added to barley malts to produce starches which in turn produced sugars and, ultimately, the alcohol in beer. "Taste is the ultimate test." Schlitz's plants were equipped with Accurate Balanced Fermentation (ABF) equipment to help ensure quality and uniformity of the brew.[4]

[1]William Blair & Co., The Brewing Industry, Basic Report, January 22, 1976.

[2]According to the annual report for 1974, brewing materials rose 70% (corn 125%, malt 40%) and packaging materials 30% (cans 30%, bottles 20%).

[3]*Ad Age*, August 18, 1975.

[4]Basically ABF uses agitators in each fermentation tank to keep the yeast evenly dispersed and working uniformly throughout the fermenting brew for a specific time.

1976 In 1976 Schlitz Light was taken national after a limited (four months') test-marketing effort in late 1975. The theme was "It took Schlitz to bring the taste to light." *Modern Brewery Age* discussed the label on April 12:

> The design incorporates the familiar Schlitz Globe along with another symbol strongly referred by interviewees, the sun. This new symbol was selected because of its universal appeal and expression of pleasure, cheerfulness, happiness, vitality, activity, fun, joy, life and health . . . all positive characteristics associated with the contemporary life style of the target consumers.

Although the introduction expenses for Schlitz Light were large (about $10 million; see *Exhibit 6*), Schlitz seemed to be meeting with success as early sales figures came in. Again quoting *Modern Brewery Age:*

> Old Milwaukee Planning Manager, Tom Siefkes, said, "Initial response has surpassed all of the brand's goals which were pretty substantial going in. Because of this, we should be able to expand much faster than anticipated into other key areas of the country, into the predetermined bigger light markets."
>
> . . . . Who was drinking the product? Virtually all types, including light, medium and heavy drinkers; young adults, white-collar workers, females (a major factor); married and singles in mid- as well as upper-income brackets.

Schlitz also had a new image: "When it's right, you know it!"

But this apparent success was marred by signs of trouble. As *Business Week* reported on September 6, 1976:

> In the five-page news release, Chairman and President Robert A. Uihlein Jr. revealed that the company was postponing its debenture offering and placing four top marketing executives on an indefinite leave of absence.

One observer explained:

> For decades, brewers simply made the best beer they knew how, and they got their markets any way they could—legally or not. When a new saloon opened, the beer company that put in the beer pipes, or did the lighting, or paid a straight cash bribe to the proprietor, was the one whose beer was sold over the bar. Payoffs went to the lowliest and the mightiest. It's no coincidence, for example, that baseball and football stadiums commonly feature only one beer, and that the beer company often sponsors the team's games on television.

A former sales executive of a major brewery told *The Wall Street Journal* (June 10, 1976):

> The name of the game was sales, pure and simple. You did what you had to do to get the business. A lot of it was small stuff, like an occasional free keg of beer or a case of glasses for a guy who had a bar, but it got a lot bigger, too. If what you were doing was wrong, well, at least you knew you had a lot of company.

The company's marketing department was reorganized on a functional basis. Then, on November 12, 1976, Robert Uihlein died of leukemia. The company's board selected Jack McKeithan as Chairman. The next section of this case describes the management team Robert Uihlein had built.

Top Management

In 1969 Robert Uihlein began to groom his Executive Vice President and General Manager, Roy C. Satchell, for the Presidency. Satchell was a highly respected financial executive who had worked in several industries before joining Schlitz in 1967, as Treasurer. A year later he was named Vice President for finance, but left to head a small construction-equipment company. He returned to Schlitz in 1969, was made President in 1973, and then—after only six weeks—resigned once again. Satchell's only public explanation was that with Schlitz running "like a fine Swiss watch," he didn't see what he could contribute. In 1978 as a senior vice president at American Standard in New York, Satchell said he left because he concluded he would never be free to run the company as he felt it should be run. "There were not many family members in management," he said, "but the family did influence the company behind the scenes."[5]

Apparently responding to a question about family factions within Schlitz's board, Daniel McKeithan, Chairman and Chief Executive Officer, said:

> The board is not behaving factionally. They're really addressing themselves to the things that management takes into the meetings.[6]

It no doubt helped that in recent months two new outside directors had been added (for a total of five)—Gerald J. Slade, Chairman and President of Western Publishing, and I. Andrew Rader, Chairman of Allen-Bradley Company.

Upon Satchell's departure from the company, Uihlein elevated Eugene B. Peters, who had succeeded Satchell as Vice President for finance, to Executive Vice President. In 1976, Peters became President and after Uihlein's death he served as CEO for elevan months.

Shortly after Peters was made Executive Vice President, Haviland left. His departure affected Schlitz profoundly. As the person in top management who was most sensitive to what was happening at lower levels in the managerial ranks, he was an important link between Uihlein and the rest of the company—and the company's wholesalers. After his departure, they began to complain that the Schlitz sales staff was "dictatorial and arrogant." In earlier years, the wholesalers had been able to bring their complaints and suggestions to the gregarious Haviland, but with him gone they found nobody in authority to talk to.

When Miller introduced its seven-ounce bottles in 1972, for example, the com-

[5]Some 500 family members owned 75% of Schlitz's stock. Even at the recent depressed price of about $12 a share, those holdings were worth roughly $270 million. At 68 cents per share, the family collected $15 million annually in dividends. Uihleins and their in-laws held 11 of the 16 board seats. Three of the family-connected directors ran small privately-held businesses; the others included a retired Schlitz executive, a retired neurosurgeon, an IBM program manager, and 2 men who devoted their time to managing their own investments.

[6]*Fortune*, August 24, 1978.

pany's wholesalers tried to get Milwaukee to respond. "But trying to talk to anybody there was like trying to force spaghetti through a keyhole," said Neal W. Kaye, Sr., of New Orleans, one of Schlitz's most successful distributors. In just two years in the business, Kaye had raised Schlitz from a fourth-place tie with Budweiser to top seller in his market. "It took more than two years," he said, for Schlitz to come up with its own seven-ounce containers. "Miller was selling 100,000 cases a month before I got my first one, and they just gobbled us up." In 1978 Miller was in first place in New Orleans and Schlitz was second.

Nonetheless, in a *Fortune* article (August 24, 1978), it was claimed that "The consensus of Schlitz's wholesalers today is that relations with the company have never been better." Apparently, repair work began even before the advent of the new leadership. For example, a wholesalers' council was created early in 1977 to meet regularly with top management, including the Chairman and President, to air complaints and suggestions. The council also had access to directors: the Schlitz board scheduled meetings at plants in such places as Syracuse and Tampa so that wholesalers could come in, tour the premises, and talk personally with the directors.

Setbacks and Legal Problems

Mr. McKeithan summarized the company's 1977 performance and outlined its current situation in his letter to the shareholders of March 15, 1978. He wrote:

> For the first time since 1961, sales were lower than in the previous year. Peaks and valleys are not unusual in business, of course; but a decline is all the more disappointing after fifteen years of record sales.
>
> Gross sales for 1977 were $1,134,079,000, down about seven percent from the previous year. Beer shipments were 22,130,000 barrels in 1977, down about eight percent. Net earnings for 1977 were $19,765,000 or 68 cents per share compared with $49,947,000 or $1.72 per share in 1976.
>
> Lower shipments volume accounted for half of the year's earnings reduction. Other contributing factors included beer prices which did not increase as fast as production costs in 1977, substantial unused brewery capacity, higher marketing expenditures, a one-month strike at four of our can manufacturing plants, and a provision for estimated losses on the disposal of certain assets. The losses were related primarily to the disposition of equipment previously acquired for brewery capacity expansion.
>
> Despite setbacks in the marketplace, our financial position improved in 1977. Long-term debt was reduced $27 million and working capital increased $12 million.
>
> Completion of a major plant construction and improvement program resulted in a reduction of capital expenditures to $3 million in 1977 compared with $111 million in 1976. In the five years through 1977, nearly one-half billion dollars was spent for new brewery and can manufacturing capacity.[7] Most of our production facilities are relatively new and highly efficient, and sufficient capacity exists for substantial volume growth (32 million barrels for 1978). Capital expenditures are expected to be about $20 million in each of the next several years. Cash flow from operations is

[7]Schlitz manufactured about 80% of its can requirements.

expected to be adequate to cover the projected needs of the company and permit further reductions in long-term debt.

Legal problems arising primarily out of past marketing practices continue to be a source of concern to the company and its management. Over the course of many months, counsel for the company met frequently with the United States Attorney in Milwaukee who was in charge of the federal grand jury investigation looking into past marketing practices of the company, as well as with attorneys of the Department of Justice in Washington, exploring every possible means to settle these matters under investigation by the grand jury. A resolution satisfactory to the company and the United States Attorney was reached, but was overruled by the Department of Justice in Washington. Accordingly, on March 15, 1978, the company was indicted for three felony tax fraud counts, one misdemeanor conspiracy count, allegedly to violate the Federal Alcohol Administration Act (FAAA), and approximately 700 individual misdemeanor counts alleging violations of the FAAA. The company intends to vigorously defend these charges in court.

Our recognized line of outstanding malt beverage products provides a strong marketing base for future growth. We will continue to aggressively support our four national brands. The Schlitz brand in 1978 will emphasize quality and its appeal to all beer drinkers. Schlitz Light Beer will continue to be presented as the low-calorie beer for people who want true beer taste. Schlitz Malt Liquor, the number-one-selling malt liquor, will receive added emphasis in beer markets where malt liquor has a small percentage of beer industry sales. Old Milwaukee, which is marketed nationally, will continue to be presented as the quality beer in the popular price segment. We are committed to providing superior advertising and merchandising support which tells the story of our fine products. As an example, we have made the largest individual sports purchase in television history with a four-year, multi-million dollar commitment for NBC National Football League telecasts.

We are also exploring the introduction of new brands. In 1978, we plan to test-market new malt beverage products with a possibility for nationwide introduction by early 1979.

The competitive nature of the industry has increased significantly in recent years. Analyzing the industry and the changes taking place in it is a prerequisite to arriving at sound decisions on present and future programs.

For Schlitz, the legal and management problems couldn't have come at a worse time. *Newsweek* commented on September 4, 1978:

> For one thing, its beer had come under heavy fire for uneven quality. Apparently, the company had cut back on the amount of barley malt used in the brewing process because grain prices were high, and that—plus an effort to shorten the brewing cycle—had caused serious taste problems.

For another, Schlitz's advertising, once about the best in the industry, lost its edge. In 1977, in an attempt to revive it, the company brought out a television campaign built around a series of presumably formidable beer drinkers—boxers and the like—who were supposedly responding to a suggestion that they abandon Schlitz for another beer. Glowering into the camera, they demanded: "You want to take away my gusto?" Intended to be slyly humorous, the ads struck most viewers as menacing, and the campaign became known in the industry as the "drink Schlitz or I'll kill you" approach before it was yanked off the air. (While a new campaign was prepared, Schlitz reverted to an earlier "gusto" theme.)

In 1978 Schlitz was attempting to turn its fortunes around. The company had fired Leo Burnett, the Chicago ad agency that produced the gusto debacle, and moved quickly to correct its brewing process. In February, it announced a price increase to wholesalers. Schlitz Light lost its second-place position to Anheuser-Busch's Natural. The company began to develop a super-premium beer to compete with Michelob and Lowenbrau.[8]

The Future at Schlitz

McKeithan and Frank J. Sellinger, President, were reported to be making their presence felt throughout the whole of the company, down to the field salespeople who dealt with the wholesalers and the hourly workers on the bottle-shop floors. The two were doing their job with evident enthusiasm—with gusto, one might say—that extended to after-hours pub-crawling in the line of duty.

McKeithan, then forty-two, was a geologist by training. Until he was made Schlitz's Chairman, he headed Tamarack Petroleum, an oil exploration company in which the Uihleins were interested. McKeithan joined Tamarack in 1959, several years after marrying Gillian Uihlein, the daughter of Joseph Uihlein, Jr., a Schlitz director. McKeithan got his first taste of the beer business in 1973, when he was appointed to the Schlitz board. His marriage ended in divorce in 1974.

McKeithan's choice of Frank J. Sellinger, then sixty-three, for President may be revealing. Sellinger's career in the beer business spanned some forty years, thirteen of them at Anheuser-Busch, mostly in production. He had most recently been Executive Vice President for management and industry affairs, and right-hand man to the Chairman and President, August A. Busch III. Sellinger was an earthy and plainspoken man with an encyclopedic knowledge of the business and a practical sense of what made a management function. He could, it was said, walk into a boardroom or onto a brewery floor and be at ease with anyone he met, and he was adept at challenging people to do their best.

In Sellinger's view, "There aren't many big things in a company—what makes it run are a lot of little things." When he found a little thing gone awry, he called the people responsible immediately to account. "If I'm looking over their shoulders," he said, "they're going to do a better job. There are good people here, but they are not completely experienced—they haven't been asked to make the hard decisions." Added McKeithan, "We want our people to know that they have the authority to go out and do the job that falls in their area—and also to know that they will be held responsible and accountable for it. We don't expect any miracle cures. It is a long-range effort."

PHILIP MORRIS INCORPORATED

In April, 1971, Philip Morris Incorporated was riding the crest of 17 years of uninterrupted growth in sales and net earnings. In 1970, Philip Morris's sales ($1.5 billion) and

[8]*Advertising Age*, July 3, 1978, reported that Schlitz had reverted to its traditional brand management structure, abandoned in 1976. Marketing was headed by an ex-Vice President of Coca Cola.

earnings ($77 million) were 296% and 369%, respectively, of the 1960 results. The company's earnings per share had grown at a compound annual rate of 13% since 1960 and 23% since 1965. In addition, Philip Morris had increased its share of the U.S. cigarette market from 9% to 16% in the decade of the 1960s. In the international market (free world only), the company's market share had spurted from 1% in 1960 to 6% in 1970. Philip Morris was the third-largest privately owned cigarette manufacturer in the world market, ranking behind the British-American Tobacco Company and R.J. Reynolds Industries, the leading U.S. manufacturer.

The rapid acceptance of filter-tip brands introduced by competitors and the corresponding threat to the non-filter Philip Morris brand led to the 1954 purchase for $22 million of Benson & Hedges, makers of Parliament filter cigarettes. The next year Philip Morris introduced a filter brand: Marlboro. The product was unique in that it came in a flip-top box. Marlboro was an immediate success, so much so that Philip Morris agreed to purchase the next two years' production of the patented packaging machinery from the manufacturer.

Mr. George Weissman, then President of Philip Morris, outlined some of the policies that guided the company's marketing policy:

> We have not often been first with a new cigarette. For example, others introduced king-sized, filters, menthols, and even 100-millimeter brands before we did. Yet we have been successful in making our products unique. Marlboro came out in a flip-top box. We put a plastic package around Multi-Filter, our charcoal-filter brand. Virginia Slims was a "first" for us, since it was the first cigarette to be directed specifically at women. We were also unique in taking a corporate name, Benson & Hedges, and putting it on a premium cigarette, Benson & Hedges 100s. We want to give the consumer a high-quality cigarette that is distinctive.
>
> Another essential element in our success is our ability to react rapidly to changes in market or competitive conditions. We have a corporate products committee which regularly reviews the progress on individual brands. The Chairman and I are personally involved with the formulation of marketing policy for our major brands. Moreover, if we have a good product idea, we can get top-management commitment in a hurry.

Mr. Ross Millhiser, then President of Philip Morris USA and former Marlboro brand manager, explained certain further dimensions of the marketing task:

> We want our products to have charisma, and this requires attention to packaging and advertising. When we think we have the optimal combination of product quality and consumer appeal for a certain segment of the market, we test the brand for several months. If it gets 1% of the market, we consider launching it nationwide. I don't really need market surveys to tell me how a new brand is doing. We can get some idea in a few weeks from the repurchase pattern whether it is taking hold.

Philip Morris spent roughly 80% of its $60 million 1970 advertising budget on broadcast media. The company had been highly successful in the use of creative advertising for its products. The campaigns for Marlboro and Benson & Hedges 100s had been widely acclaimed in advertising circles for their sophisticated consumer appeal. In April, 1971, company officials were assessing the impact of losing the opportunity to advertise cigarettes on television because of government regulations.

The more remarkable aspect of Philip Morris's advance in recent years was that the cigarette industry had not been a dynamic area. From 1966 to 1976, the average annual increase in cigarette industry unit had been a scant 1.7%—meaning, of course, that Philip Morris had won market share at the expense of other major manufacturers. Its share of the available market action soared from 10.3% in 1963 to 22.5% in 1974. Moreover, in 1975 this gifted marketer had a rate of growth which was twice as large as that of the industry as a whole. There were a few blemishes on the company's record, notably a less than outstanding diversification into razor blades and shaving supplies, through the purchase in 1960 of the Personna brand. More recent financial results of Philip Morris (and Miller) are contained in *Exhibits 7–9*.

Acquisition of the Miller Brewing Company

The saga of Philip Morris and Miller began in 1969 with a statement of acquisition criteria by Philip Morris:

> Inevitably our domestic cigarette business will level off as our market share increases and growth in consumption stabilizes around one–two percent per year. Our cash flow will increase dramatically at that time and we need growth businesses in which to invest this cash flow. . . . [However] it's hard to find another business that is as good as this one. . . . Beer probably comes closest to matching our skills with a market opportunity.

Thus, in mid-1969, Philip Morris purchased 53 percent of Miller's stock from the W. R. Grace Company and one year later completed the transaction by acquiring the remaining 47 percent from the DeRance Foundation. The total purchase price was $227 million, of which $150 million was in excess of estimated book value.

The announcement of the acquisition to Philip Morris stockholders emphasized:

1. Miller High Life as one of the three nationally distributed premium beers, with the premium segment of the beer market growing almost three times as fast as the total market (8.7% as opposed to 3.17%);[9]
2. modern production capacity in the Midwest, West and Southwest, with feasibility studies for a fourth brewery in the East underway; and
3. a network of 750 independent beer wholesalers serving all 50 states.

By 1970, when the acquisition was completed, Philip Morris said:

> We believe the long-range potential of Miller will be best served by increasing its share of the growing premium beer market rather than by emphasizing short-term profit goals.

[9]Premium sales in 1965 were 22.2 million barrels; by 1970 they were 33.7 million barrels.

1970 In 1970, the Fort Worth brewery was enlarged by 300,000 barrels and a site was purchased in Newark, Delaware, for the future construction of an eastern brewery. A new advertising agency was hired, and the Miller sales organization was overhauled. Sales rose slightly (to $198 million), market share was constant (at 4.3 percent), and operating income declined (to $11 million).

For a year, Philip Morris's George Weissman had refrained from making any big changes at Miller. It was a year in which it became increasingly clear that the brewer's old-line management was neither hard-working nor responsive enough to be able to carry through the changes that New York headquarters wished to make.

1971 The solution in 1971 was a wholesale clean-out of the incumbent managers, an unusual step in an industry dominated by old brewing dynasties. It was even more shocking when the Philip Morris people injected a whole top cadre of ex-cigarette managers to turn Miller around. Weissman remembered the common reactions at the time: "The brewing industry had just been in a debacle at Hamms, which had been acquired by Heublein's. Heublein couldn't solve those problems, but they at least knew their business. What were these cigarette jerks gonna do with beer?"

The strategy shift for Miller was in full gear. The Executive Vice President of Philip Morris International was named as Miller's Chief Executive Officer, and he brought in a new management team from Philip Morris's international cigarette operation led by John A. Murphy, who later became Miller's President.

Miller's new managers discovered that around the U.S. there were large inventories of stale beer on supermarket shelves, which were driving away old habitues and turning off new customers. Old beer worth approximately $1 million was therefore destroyed.[10] The company eliminated the previous practice of price promotions. The basis for this decision was "that anyone who chose beer on price alone wasn't going to stick with us, and was going to go after the next price promoter," Weissman said.

As the 45% capacity expansion in Texas and management shifts proceeded, Miller announced:

1 Miller Malt Liquor—the first new product in Miller's history, positioned to compete in a market segment growing at 10% per year;
2 A new advertising campaign featuring youth at play and blue-collar workers in "manly exploits"—clearly directed at two growth segments of the beer market.

Miller High Life had been known as "the champagne of beers," a slogan that seemed to appeal to a more effete group of consumers than the six-pack-a-day crowd the company wanted to win. Miller's new slogan: "If you've got the time, we've got the beer" was a great success. "They wanted to appeal to blue-collar workers, and they came up with a campaign that said, 'Hey, you're doing a great job and you deserve a reward,' " said Andres J. Melnick, an industry analyst for Drexel Burnham Lambert.

Miller also announced the conversion to aluminum cans in the Texas and California breweries. Sales grew 2.8%, while operating income declined from $11.4 million to $1.3 million.

[10] Today every Miller label or can is dated by month and year. When the beer "expires," distributors are supposed to turn it back to the brewer.

1972 The downward profitability trend continued through 1972. Although sales increased 3%, operating income declined to $228,000. The organizational shifts in marketing and sales continued, resulting in the acquisition of the trade names and distribution network of Meister Brau, Inc., the introduction of two more new products—Milwaukee Ale and Miller Ale—and several innovative packages, including a seven-ounce bottle sold in eight-packs. "If you've got the time, we've got the beer," continued as the advertising theme.

1973 By 1973, Miller was operating in the red, and some industry observers openly predicted that another debacle, like Hamm's, was just around the corner. Increased capacity helped boost barrel sales by 29% and dollar sales by 30% (to $276 million). Still, an operating loss of $2.4 million was incurred.

In the midst of these losses, Miller announced a $200 million capital expenditure program (at certain times during the year, Miller lacked capacity to meet demand):

1. Capacity expansion in Milwaukee (from 4 million to 7 million barrels) and Texas (from 2 million to 5 million barrels).
2. Facility modernization and new packaging equipment in Milwaukee and Texas.
3. A new $16-million aluminum can plant in Milwaukee, along with a new warehouse and shipping depot.
4. A new $70-million brewery in New York State, with an initial capacity of 2 million barrels and ultimate capacity of 6 million barrels (a $20-million aluminum can plant was subsequently announced, with a capacity of 500 million cans per year at the Fulton, New York site).

1974 By 1974 Philip Morris management began to see the results of the Miller strategy shift initiated in 1970. Its 1974 Annual Report noted:

> Our extensive program to realign Miller is meeting expectations. The company has begun to achieve economies of large volume production while increasing the utilization of modern, efficient and competitive equipment. . . . The momentum of Miller High Life's growth has permitted a proportionate reduction in marketing costs per barrel.

Despite a 46% sales gain (to $404 million) and a more than proportional profit gain (to $6.3 million), the facility expansion plan continued—a new can plant was planned for Fort Worth.

1975 The growth trajectory for Miller accelerated in 1975 (sales were up 42%). With 15 million barrels of capacity in place, sales rose to capacity, and all products were on allocation during most of the year. Dollar revenues increased 63% (to $658 million) and operating income rose almost 400% (to $29 million). Miller's was clearly entrenched as the fourth-largest U.S. brewer with a market share of 8.6% (24% of the premium segment).

Two major new product moves were made:

1. Lite was introduced on a national basis, complete with a major $10 million promotional campaign after testing in 1974;
2. Miller assumed exclusive U.S. distribution rights for Lowenbrau, a premium German beer.

1976 In 1976, Miller announced another round of capacity expansion in Fulton—from 3.3 million to 4 million and eventually (in 1978) to 8 million barrels. The expansion would give Miller 21 million barrels of capacity, surpassing Pabst and placing the brewer only slightly behind the number two, Schlitz (with 25 million barrels of capacity).

Philip Morris's Chairman commented modestly: "Your beer drinker and cigarette smoker are often the same guy." Other industry analysts were not so restrained. Commented one: "What Philip Morris did was turn a manufacturing company into a marketing company."

1977 Philip Morris announced that over one-half of planned investment in the following five years would be in Miller Brewing Company. Miller's operating profit represented a 23.3% return on its average operating assets (excluding construction in progress) in 1977, and the after-tax return on Philip Morris's investment in Miller increased to 13%. Miller was steadily generating a larger proportion of funds required for its growth. (Miller's estimated costs for 1976–1977 are given in *Exhibit 10.*)

Introduction of Lite

In 1978 Miller controlled about 60% of the light beer market. But it was not the first to introduce a light beer. Rheingold Brewing Company, New York, had introduced a low-calorie beer called Gablingers in 1968, and marketed it as a dietary drink—"One of the most incredibly poor advertising jobs I've ever seen in my life," said one industry source.

Rheingold put a picture of the beer's inventor on one side of the can, and on the other side, emphasized the low-carbohydrate contents. Beauty queens and fashion models were used to promote the beer's low-calorie virtues in television commercials and magazine ads.

Despite the Gablingers fiasco, a Chicago brewery, Peter Hand Brewing Company, came out in the early 1970s with another light beer, named Meister Brau Lite. It did not do very well, either, and Peter Hand went broke. But after Miller acquired the Lite brand, along with several others from Meister Brau, they were impressed with Meister Brau's market research on Lite. It showed a lot more consumer interest in a low-calorie beer, even among heavy beer drinkers, than sales had reflected.

In particular, Miller executives were intrigued by how Lite was accepted in Anderson, Indiana, an industrial town where many brawny beer drinkers actually preferred Meister Brau's Lite to regular brands. Murphy, Miller's president, recalled summoning his brewmaster and telling him to come up with a light beer that had something that Lite at that time lacked: a beery taste.[11] The aim was to come up with a full-strength beer (over 3.2% alcohol) that had one-third fewer calories and could taste-test well against Coors, then the fastest-growing beer in the country.

After many months of trials, one brew was deemed worthy enough to test-market.

[11]Joseph Ortlieb is president of the Henry F. Ortlieb Brewing Co.—founded by his grandfather 109 years ago. Along with Schmidt's, Ortlieb's is one of just two breweries in Philadelphia. A new ad campaign features Ortlieb casually touting his product ("Drink Joe's beer"). He has also added some additional brands including McSorley's Ale, but has staunchly refused to market a light beer. "If you take 3 ice cubes and an 8-ounce glass and pour our beer in, you get the same effect," he says.

Walter Landor, the San Francisco graphic designer who had previously created the Marlboro, Virginia Slims and Benson & Hedges packages for Philip Morris, got the job of designing the Lite logo and containers.

The new Lite was tried out in four cities in the late summer of 1973 and proved a success. In January, 1975, the beer was marketed nationally. Miller oiled the launch liberally with strong advertising support—about $12 million the first year alone, almost all for television.

The Lite account was something advertising people dream about. It went to McCann-Erickson by default. A few years earlier, McCann had bought Mathisson & Company, Miller's longtime agency. McCann kept Miller's management happy with what they were doing with Miller premium beer, which was selling more than ever. So the agency got Lite, too. "We were skilled in selling packaged goods," recalled account manager Bob Holmen. "That's where the real competition is."

Beer and sports go together, but an obscure federal regulation prohibited using active ballplayers in beer commercials. Using ex-ballplayers was a stroke of genius. Their glories were past, frozen in time and perhaps magnified a bit—just like the time you hit the one over the wall, or hit the winning jump shot in the school yard. How could Miller find better spokesmen for a beer made for sissies who were worried about their waistlines?

Almost all the Lite ads were shot in saloons, not on the ski slopes or on a yacht. When Joe Frazier, Buck Buchanan or Bubba Smith strolled into the bar and ordered Lite, the customers knew they could get away with it, too.

The Lite spokesmen's age was important, too. Most were in their mid-thirties to early fifties. While traditionally the prime market for beer drinkers had been among eighteen- to thirty-four-year-olds, their numbers were shrinking. Post-war babies were in their thirties.

The success of the Lite ads and their effect on sales was spectacular. In 1978, it was expected that 10% of all beer sold would be in the light category. Virtually every brewer in the country had introduced a light beer. But many of these were simply "light versions" of the basic brands (e.g., Schlitz Light, Coors Light, Pabst Light) which could be expected to cannibalize their own markets to some degree.

In response to Miller's challenge, Busch brought out Natural Light in 1977, and within eight months it had zoomed into second place among low-calorie beers. Busch then added Michelob Light and a wholly new product: a low-alcohol fruit drink called Chelsea.

The Beer Market

By 1981, Anheuser-Busch plans to expand its production capacity to 51 million barrels a year—well ahead of Miller's expected 35 million. And this year it will spend an estimated $80 million on advertising, $20 million more than Miller.

Under Philip Morris' guidance, Miller has moved from seventh place in 1972, with sales of 5.3 million barrels, to second in 1977, with sales of 24.2 million barrels. Philip Morris has poured about $600 million into new breweries and other plants, and has earmarked $1 billion for expansion over the next five years. In 1978, Miller is spending an estimated $60 million on advertising alone. The aim is clear: to displace Anheuser-Busch, the industry leader since 1957. "Ours is a simple objective," says Murphy, 48, whose desk sits atop a red and white rug bearing the Anheuser-Busch seal. "It's to become number one." The Miller team has even fixed a target date for toppling the king—but will not reveal what it is.

August A. Busch III, the 41-year-old president of Anheuser-Busch, is ready to meet the challenge. "Miller is aggressive. They're fine marketers. We compliment them," he says. Then, speaking very slowly, he adds with an icy stare: "But we will remain number one."

EXHIBIT 1

JOS. SCHLITZ BREWING COMPANY
Statements of Consolidated Earnings

	1977	*1976*
Sales	$1,134,079,000	$1,214,662,000
Less—Excise taxes	196,655,000	214,666,000
Net sales	937,424,000	999,996,000
Cost and Expenses:		
Cost of goods sold	726,445,000	755,712,000
Marketing, administrative and general expenses	150,124,000	131,639,000
	876,569,000	887,351,000
Earnings from operations	60,855,000	112,645,000
Other Income (Expense)		
Interest and dividend income	1,861,000	1,791,000
Interest expense	(16,724,000)	(17,220,000)
Loss on disposal of assets	(8,325,000)	(194,000)
Settlement of lawsuit	(2,600,000)	—
Miscellaneous, net	(53,000)	(298,000)
	(25,841,000)	(15,921,000)
Earnings Before Income Taxes	35,014,000	96,724,000
Provision for Income Taxes	15,249,000	46,777,000
Net Earnings	$ 19,765,000	$ 49,947,000
Per Share of Common Stock	$.68	$1.72

Source: Company annual report, 1977.

EXHIBIT 2

JOS. SCHLITZ BREWING COMPANY
Consolidated Balance Sheets

Assets	*1977*	*1976*
Current Assets		
Cash	$ 8,348,000	$ 15,153,000
Marketable securities, at lower of cost or market	13,756,000	14,414,000
Accounts receivable, less reserves of $678,000 in 1977 and $899,000 in 1976	30,441,000	25,440,000
Refundable income taxes	12,770,000	5,760,000
Inventories, at lower of cost or market	58,404,000	62,192,000
Prepaid expenses	10,620,000	5,099,000
Total current assets	134,339,000	128,058,000
Investments and Other Assets		
Notes receivable and other noncurrent assets	5,166,000	6,419,000
Investments	16,871,000	17,581,000
Land and equipment held for sale, less reserve	5,766,000	—
	27,803,000	24,000,000
Plant and Equipment at Cost (Note 4)	855,279,000	840,027,000
Less—Accumulated depreciation and unamortized investment tax credit	290,659,000	254,242,000
	564,620,000	585,785,000
	$726,762,000	$737,843,000

Liabilities	*1977*	*1976*
Current Liabilities		
Notes payable	$ 768,000	$ 6,373,000
Accounts payable	44,229,000	41,166,000
Dividend payable	4,941,000	4,941,000
Accrued liabilities	32,712,000	30,573,000
Federal and state income taxes	3,995,000	8,935,000
Total current liabilities	86,645,000	91,988,000
Long-Term Debt (Note 5)	196,506,000	223,195,000
Deferred Income Taxes	86,906,000	65,957,000
Shareholders' Investment		
Common stock, par value $2.50 per share, authorized 30,000,000 shares, issued 29,373,654 shares (Note 6)	73,434,000	73,434,000
Capital in excess of par value	2,921,000	2,921,000
Retained earnings	286,978,000	286,976,000
	363,333,000	363,331,000
Less—Cost of 310,672 shares of treasury stock	6,628,000	6,628,000
Total shareholders' investment	356,705,000	356,703,000
	$726,762,000	$737,843,000

EXHIBIT 3

JOS. SCHLITZ BREWING COMPANY
Statements of Changes in Consolidated Financial Position

	1977	1976
Working Capital Was Provided from		
Operations:		
Net earnings for the year	$19,765,000	$ 49,947,000
Add—Expenses not requiring outlay of working capital in current period—		
Depreciation of plant and equipment	41,127,000	35,685,000
Amortization of investment tax credit	(4,743,000)	(3,765,000)
Deferred income taxes	20,949,000	19,117,000
Loss on disposal of assets	8,325,000	194,000
Working Capital Provided from Operations	85,423,000	101,178,000
Issuance of long-term debt	—	45,000,000
Retirement of plant and equipment	2,877,000	911,000
Investment tax credit	3,483,000	15,707,000
Decrease in other noncurrent assets	1,963,000	5,818,000
Total Working Capital Provided	93,746,000	168,614,000
Working Capital Was Used for		
Additions to plant and equipment	35,670,000	111,234,000
Cash dividends declared	19,763,000	19,763,000
Reduction in long-term debt	26,689,000	34,522,000
Total Working Capital Used	82,122,000	165,519,000
Increase in Working Capital	$11,624,000	$ 3,095,000
Changes in Components of Working Capital		
Increase (decrease) in current assets:		
Cash	$(6,805,000)	$ 2,582,000
Marketable securities	(658,000)	2,933,000
Accounts receivable	5,001,000	(5,613,000)
Refundable income taxes	7,010,000	5,760,000
Inventories	(3,788,000)	5,671,000
Prepaid expenses	5,521,000	(409,000)
Increase in Current Assets	6,281,000	10,924,000
Increase (decrease) in current liabilities:		
Notes payable	(5,605,000)	4,679,000
Accounts payable	3,063,000	(3,177,000)
Accrued liabilities	2,139,000	582,000
Federal and state income taxes	(4,940,000)	5,745,000
Increase (Decrease) in Current Liabilities	(5,343,000)	7,829,000
Increase in Working Capital	$11,624,000	$ 3,095,000

Source: Company annual report, 1977.

EXHIBIT 4
JOS. SCHLITZ BREWING COMPANY
Ten-Year Financial Summary

	1977	1976	1975	1974	1973	1972	1971	1970	1969	1968
Statements of Consolidated Earnings (000 omitted)										
Sales	$1,134,079	$1,214,662	$1,130,439	$1,015,978	$892,745	$779,359	$669,178	$594,437	$537,185	$449,194
Less—Excise taxes	196,655	214,666	207,452	201,454	189,703	168,082	147,084	132,072	118,399	100,053
Net Sales	937,424	999,996	922,987	814,524	703,042	611,277	522,094	462,365	418,786	349,141
Cost and Expenses:										
Cost of Goods Sold	726,445	755,712	728,861	619,949	498,901	422,490	360,819	312,430	278,653	226,575
Marketing, Administrative and General Expenses	150,124	131,639	110,641	100,932	94,371	95,462	86,570	83,028	82,226	71,461
	876,569	887,351	839,502	720,881	593,272	517,952	447,389	395,458	360,879	298,036
Earnings from Operations	60,855	112,645	83,485	93,643	109,770	93,325	74,705	66,907	57,907	51,105
Interest Expense	(16,724)	(17,220)	(14,526)	(7,857)	(6,071)	(5,747)	(5,910)	(4,066)	(1,341)	(9)
Other Income (Expense), Net	(9,117)	1,299	(8,044)	8,013	5,752	2,179	1,252	1,246	1,507	1,911
Earnings from Continuing Operations before Income Taxes and Extraordinary Items	35,014	96,724	60,915	93,799	109,451	89,757	70,047	64,087	58,073	53,007
Provision for Income Taxes	15,249	46,777	30,019	44,817	54,241	43,918	34,798	32,636	31,252	28,600
Earnings from Continuing Operations before Extraordinary Items	19,765	49,947	30,896	48,982	55,210	45,839	35,249	31,451	26,821	24,407
Operating Losses of Former Subsidiaries	—	—	—	—	—	—	—	(1,300)	(1,947)	(3,210)
Earnings before Extraordinary Items	19,765	49,947	30,896	48,982	55,210	45,839	35,249	30,151	24,874	21,197
Extraordinary Items	—	—	—	—	(1,535)	(8,300)	—	(1,100)	(4,000)	(4,501)
Net Earnings	$ 19,765	$ 49,947	$ 30,896	$ 48,982	$ 53,675	$ 37,539	$ 35,249	$ 29,051	$ 20,874	$ 16,696
*Per Common Share**										
Earnings before Extraordinary Items	$.68	$1.72	$1.06	$1.69	$1.90	$1.58	$1.22	$1.04	$.86	$.73
Extraordinary Items	—	—	—	—	(.05)	(.29)	—	(.03)	(.14)	(.15)
Net Earnings	$.68	$1.72	$1.06	$1.69	$1.85	$1.29	$1.22	$1.01	$.72	$.58
Dividends	$.68	$ .68	$ .68	$ .67	$ .60 4/5	$ .55 1/3	$ .51 2/3	$ .46 2/3	$.45	$.38 1/3
Balance Sheet Statistics (000 omitted)										
Working Capital	$ 47,694	$ 36,070	$ 32,975	$ 57,296	$ 66,355	$ 68,638	$ 48,549	$ 40,797	$ 38,751	$ 40,290
Current Ratio	1.6 to 1	1.4 to 1	1.4 to 1	1.8 to 1	1.8 to 1	1.8 to 1	1.9 to 1	1.7 to 1	1.7 to 1	1.9 to 1
Plant and Equipment, Net	564,620	585,785	523,283	400,363	276,976	240,015	236,361	207,948	159,132	125,431
Long-Term Debt	196,506	223,195	212,717	143,828	62,026	64,800	70,879	63,386	31,032	—
Shareholders' Investment	356,705	356,703	326,519	315,260	285,478	252,500	229,213	206,920	193,454	185,586
Per Share*	12.27	12.27	11.24	10.85	9.82	8.71	7.93	7.16	6.69	6.43
Other Statistics (000 omitted)										
Depreciation	41,127	35,685	27,697	23,361	20,027	17,855	14,392	11,684	9,954	8,705
Amortization of Investment Tax Credit	(4,743)	(3,765)	(2,396)	(1,669)	(1,391)	(1,201)	(896)	(619)	(444)	(294)
Cash Flow (Net earnings and noncash charges)	85,423	101,178	73,884	76,124	79,080	65,858	54,857	48,811	41,040	33,338
Cash Dividends Declared	19,763	19,763	19,760	19,466	17,677	16,056	14,940	13,484	13,016	11,068
Capital Expenditures	35,670	111,234	165,417	150,500	64,105	28,923	48,223	62,930	56,333	35,358
Plant Capacity in Barrels	29,500	27,000	25,300	24,000	21,700	20,500	18,000	16,600	14,250	12,165
Barrels of Beer Sold	22,130	24,162	23,279	22,661	21,343	18,906	16,708	15,129	13,709	11,576

*Based on average number of shares outstanding during the year

Source: Company annual report, 1977

EXHIBIT 5 Schlitz Sales, Capacity & Employment

Year	*Barrels Sold (000's)*	*Capacity (000's bls)*	*# Employees*
1961	5,767	8,130	4,550
1963	7,833	9,100	5,033
1965	8,607	9,440	5,172
1967	10,382	11,920	6,225
1969	13,709	14,250	6,208
1971	16,708	18,000	
1973	21,343	24,000	
1974	22,661	24,000	6,600
1975	23,279	25,300	
1976	24,162	27,000	
1977	22,130	29,500	

Source: Jos. Schlitz Brewing Company Annual Reports.

EXHIBIT 6
Advertising Expenditures 1973–1977 ($000's)

	Schlitz					*Anheuser-Busch*				
	1977	*1976*	*1975*	*1974*	*1973*	*1977*	*1976*	*1975*	*1974*	*1973*
Newspapers	1,142	—	—	—	—	2,027	—	—	147	271
Magazines	731	349	103	508	88	2,964	2,518	2,447	939	545
Spot TV	6,197	4,668	5,285	11,000	9,916	10,237	8,833	6,619	3,888	5,782
Network TV	33,847	28,551	17,690	6,678	6,602	32,165	14,617	9,603	7,281	6,553
Spot Radio	1,955	1,216	2,902	2,774	3,000	8,573	8,352	7,298	5,391	7,352
Network Radio	—	—	—	—	—	1,842	1,983	1,245	676	—
Outdoor	58	140	176	695	9	879	491	141	116	386
Total Measured Media	43,929	34,953	26,156	21,160	19,742	58,687	36,794	27,354	18,438	20,889
Total Unmeasured Media	15,200	16,000	16,505	14,040	14,758	16,750	12,227	15,646	15,562	15,631
Estimated Total	59,129[1]	50,950	42,500	35,200	34,500	75,437[2]	49,021	43,000	32,000	36,520

[1]Schlitz Light $12,546,000 in 1977, up from $9,346,700 in 1976. Mostly network TV. Miller allocated $12,493,000 to High Life in 1976 and $14,785,000 to Lite. In 1977 it spent $14,595,000 on High Life and $16,218,000 on Lite, mostly for network and spot TV.
[2]Natural Light $9,211,000; Michelob $9,969,000; Budweiser $22,727.
Source: "Top 100 Advertisers," *Advertising Age,* August 1974, 1975, 1976, 1977.

EXHIBIT 7
PHILIP MORRIS, INC.
Five-Year Financial Highlights
(dollar amounts except per-share amounts expressed in thousands)

	1977	*1976*	*1975*	*1974*	*1973*
Operating Revenues	$5,201,977	$4,293,782	$3,642,414	$3,010,961	$2,602,498
Net Earnings	334,926	265,675	211,638	175,516	148,632
Earnings Per Common Share:					
Primary	5.60	4.47	3.62	3.15	2.71
Fully Diluted	5.60	4.47	3.62	3.07	2.61
Dividends Declared Per Common Share	1.563	1.150	.925	.775	.674
Percent Increase Over Prior Year					
Operating Revenues	21.2%	17.9%	21.0%	15.7%	22.1%
Net Earnings	26.1%	25.5%	20.6%	18.1%	19.4%
Earnings Per Common Share:					
Primary	25.3%	23.5%	14.9%	16.2%	15.8%
Fully Diluted	25.3%	23.5%	17.9%	17.6%	19.7%
Operating Companies Revenues					
Philip Morris U.S.A.	$2,160,362	$1,963,144	$1,721,549	$1,502,267	$1,303,629
Philip Morris International	1,349,280	1,083,970	1,040,002	887,077	822,907
Miller Brewing company	1,327,619	982,810	658,268	403,551	275,860
Philip Morris Industrial	216,699	169,096	151,960	155,390	132,126
Mission Viejo Company	148,017	94,762	70,635	62,676	67,976
Consolidated Operating Revenues	$5,201,977	$4,293,782	$3,642,414	$3,010,961	$2,602,498
Operating Companies Income					
Philip Morris U.S.A.	$ 474,400	$ 401,426	$ 337,314	$ 286,225	$ 227,282
Philip Morris International	153,791	130,104	112,975	94,017	92,150
Miller Brewing Company	106,456	76,056	28,628	6,291	(2,371)
Philip Morris Industrial	14,860	10,620	8,052	12,280	8,300
Mission Viejo Company	33,225	16,333	5,875	4,772	4,122
Consolidated Operating Income	$ 782,732	$ 634,539	$ 492,844	$ 403,585	$ 329,483

Source: Company annual report, 1977.

EXHIBIT 8
PHILLIP MORRIS, INC.
Five-Year Financial Review

	1977	*1976*	*1975*	*1974*	*1973*
Summary of Operations					
Operating Revenues	$ 5,201,977	4,293,782	3,642,414	3,010,961	2,602,498
Cost of Sales					
Cost of Products Sold	2,401,680	1,966,871	1,656,839	1,290,319	1,060,777
Federal Excise Taxes	862,115	778,161	686,276	619,504	558,947
Foreign Excise Taxes	490,372	381,125	392,127	349,363	334,512
Operating Income	782,732	634,539	492,844	403,585	329,483
Interest Expense	101,584	102,834	99,045	82,741	50,993
Earnings Before Income Taxes	625,516	471,928	360,810	297,502	255,609
Pre-Tax Profit Margins	12.0%	11.0%	9.9%	9.9%	9.8%
Provision for Income Taxes	290,590	206,253	149,172	121,986	106,977
Net Earnings	334,926	265,675	211,638	175,516	148,632
Primary Earnings Per Common Share	5.60	4.47	3.62	3.15	2.71
Fully Diluted Earnings Per Common Share	5.60	4.47	3.62	3.07	2.61
Dividends Declared Per Common Share	1.563	1.150	.925	.775	.674
Weighted Average Shares—Primary	59,822,487	59,408,484	58,442,362	55,649,417	54,804,174
Weighted Average Shares—Fully Diluted	59,822,487	59,408,484	58,442,362	57,339,255	57,315,784
Capital Expenditures	$ 279,818	220,173	244,477	215,770	174,665
Annual Depreciation	78,466	64,856	49,853	38,006	30,245
Property, Plant & Equipment (Gross)	1,594,910	1,323,923	1,129,838	899,810	728,726
Property, Plant & Equipment (Net)	1,202,432	993,879	851,103	659,520	510,286
Inventories	1,817,561	1,657,504	1,448,428	1,269,212	1,009,414
Current Assets	2,221,020	2,005,745	1,788,085	1,557,908	1,245,934
Working Capital	1,415,867	1,202,224	890,797	725,000	515,347
Total Assets	4,048,039	3,582,209	3,134,326	2,653,263	2,108,403
Total Debt	1,563,498	1,525,638	1,443,270	1,239,312	947,364
Stockholders Equity	1,690,066	1,429,982	1,227,781	974,673	815,028
Net Earnings Reinvested	253,661	197,195	157,102	131,890	111,376
Common Dividends Declared as % of Net Earnings	27.9%	25.7%	25.7%	24.8%	25.0%
Book Value Per Common Share	$ 28.16	23.99	20.63	16.97	14.66
Market Price of Common Share High-Low	64⅞-51½	63¼-49¾	59¼-40⅞	61⅜-34⅛	68⅜-48¾
Closing Price Year-End	61⅞	61¾	53	48	57⅜
Price/Earnings Ratio	11	13	14	15	21
No. of Common Shares—Actual Year-End	59,919,917	59,487,393	59,357,236	57,264,586	55,378,434

Source: Company annual report, 1977.

EXHIBIT 9

PHILIP MORRIS, INC.
Data by Product Line 1977

	Consolidated
Operating Revenues	
Tobacco	$3,493,443,000
Beer	1,327,619,000
Other Products	380,915,000
	$5,201,977,000
Operating Profit	
Tobacco	$ 615,253,000
Beer	106,456,000
Other Products	49,329,000
	771,038,000
Equity in net earnings of unconsolidated foreign subsidiaries and affiliates	11,694,000
Operating Income of Operating Companies	$ 782,732,000
Depreciation Expense	
Tobacco	$ 42,442,000
Beer	27,299,000
Identifiable Assets	
Tobacco	$2,509,878,000
Beer	819,413,000
Other Products	406,837,000
	3,736,128,000
Investments in and advances to unconsolidated foreign subsidiaries and affiliates	229,508,000
Corporate Assets	82,403,000
Total Assets	$4,048,039,000
Capital Expenditures	
Tobacco	$ 77,568,000
Beer	182,899,000

Note: Operating income has been calculated before any allocation of interest or any corporate expenses.
Source: Company annual report, 1977.

EXHIBIT 10 Miller's Estimated 1976–1977 Costs (In millions)

	Actual			*% Change*	*Possible*
	1974	*1975*	*1976*	*'76 vs. '75*	*1977*
Barrels (shipped) (000)	9,066	12,900	18,400	40%	23,500
Total revenues	$403.6	$658.3	$982.8	49	$1,280.0
Excise taxes	81.6	116.1	165.5	43	211.5
Containers & packaging	136.0	203.0	303.5	50	411.0
Freight	45.3	64.5	87.0	35	106.0
Raw materials	43.1	71.0	89.0	25	117.5
Labor	39.0	58.0	75.5	30	90.5
Depreciation	11.3	19.5	27.5	41	35.0
SG&A	40.0	60.0	80.0	33	100.0
Other expenses	0.8	37.6	78.8	110	108.5
Operating earnings	$ 6.3	$ 28.6	$ 76.0	166%	100.0
Per Barrel Operating Data*					
Revenues	$ 44.52	$ 51.03	$ 53.41	5%	$ 54.50
Excise taxes	9.00	9.00	9.00	0	9.00
Containers & packaging	15.00	15.75	16.50	5	17.50
Freight	5.00	5.00	4.75	(5)	4.50
Raw materials	4.75	5.50	4.85	(12)	5.00
Labor	4.30	4.50	4.10	(9)	3.85
Depreciation	1.25	1.50	1.50	—	1.50
SG&A	4.41	4.65	4.35	(6)	4.26
Other expenses	0.09	2.91	4.28	47	4.62
Operating profit	$ 0.70	$ 2.22	$ 4.13	86%	$ 4.26

*Totals may not add precisely due to rounding.

Note: Miller had 2000 employed in 1970 shortly after Philip Morris acquired it, and its sales were 5.1 million barrels. In 1977, it had 8000, about 100 more wholesalers.

Source: Philip Morris, Inc. (Interim Report) Wainwright Securities, Inc., May 26, 1977.

CRAY RESEARCH, INC.

PRELIMINARY PROSPECTUS DATED JANUARY 28, 1976

PROSPECTUS

A registration statement relating to these securities has been filed with the Securities and Exchange Commission but has not yet become effective. Information contained herein is subject to completion or amendment. These securities may not be sold nor may offers to buy be accepted prior to the time the registration statement becomes effective. This prospectus shall not constitute an offer to sell or the solicitation of an offer to buy nor shall there by any sale of these securities in any State in which such offer, solicitation or sale would be unlawful prior to registration or qualification under the securities laws of any such State.

600,000 *SHARES*

COMMON STOCK

($1.00 Par Value)

Prior to this offering the Company has been engaged in the development of the CRAY-1 computer and has had no sales or earnings. There has been no public market for the Common Stock of the Company. The offering price has been determined by negotiation between the Company and the Underwriters and bears no relationship to earnings, assets or book value. It is currently estimated that the initial public offering price may range from $15 to $17 per share. (See *Pricing of the Offering.*) This offering involves pricing arrangements in accordance with certain provisions of the By-Laws of the National Association of Securities Dealers, Inc. (See *Underwriting.*) This offering also involves special risks concerning the Company and an immediate dilution of the investment of purchasers. (See *Introductory Statement.*)

THESE SECURITIES INVOLVE A HIGH DEGREE OF RISK

THESE SECURITIES HAVE NOT BEEN APPROVED OR DISAPPROVED BY THE SECURITIES AND EXCHANGE COMMISSION NOR HAS THE COMMISSION PASSED UPON THE ACCURACY OR ADEQUACY OF THIS PROSPECTUS. ANY REPRESENTATION TO THE CONTRARY IS A CRIMINAL OFFENSE.

	Offering Price to Public	Underwriting Discounts and Commissions	Proceeds to Company (1)
Per Share	$	$	$
Total (2)			
Minimum	$	$	$
Maximum	$	$	$

(1) Before deducting expenses estimated at $ payable by the Company.

(2) In order to cover over-allotments, if any, the Company has granted to the Underwriters an option to purchase up to an additional 60,000 shares. In the foregoing table, the minimum amounts assume that the option will not be exercised and the maximum amounts assume that the option will be exercised in full. (See *Underwriting.*)

C. E. UNTERBERG, TOWBIN CO.

PIPER, JAFFRAY & HOPWOOD INCORPORATED

NEW COURT SECURITIES CORPORATION

The date of this Prospectus is , 1976.

CRAY-1 COMPUTER

IN CONNECTION WITH THIS OFFERING, THE UNDERWRITERS MAY OVER-ALLOT OR EFFECT TRANSACTIONS WHICH STABILIZE OR MAINTAIN THE MARKET PRICE OF THE COMPANY'S COMMON STOCK AT LEVELS ABOVE THOSE WHICH MIGHT OTHERWISE PREVAIL IN THE OPEN MARKET. SUCH STABILIZING, IF COMMENCED, MAY BE DISCONTINUED AT ANY TIME.

SUMMARY OF PROSPECTUS

The following is a summary of certain information contained in this Prospectus. More complete information is contained in the remainder of this Prospectus.

The Offering

Common Stock offered by Cray Research, Inc. .... 600,000 Shares*
Common Stock to be outstanding after the offering .... 1,307,006 Shares*

---

* Does not include up to 60,000 shares which may be sold pursuant to the Underwriters' over-allotment option.

Business

Cray Research, Inc. (the Company) was incorporated in 1972 to design, develop, manufacture and market large capacity, high speed computers intended for scientific applications. The Company believes that its initial computer model, the CRAY-1, incorporates a number of improvements over existing scientific computers. These include advanced vector capabilities, a large internal bipolar memory, and significantly reduced physical size made possible by an advanced freon cooling system. As a result of these improvements, the Company believes that the CRAY-1 provides significantly increased computational speed and capacity. The initial CRAY-1 has been constructed, is undergoing testing and is being used in connection with marketing efforts and software development. (See *The Company* and *Business.*)

Risk Factors

The Company has had no sales or earnings to date and investors should carefully consider the risk factors which will affect the business of the Company. (See *Introductory Statement.*)

Use of Proceeds

The proceeds of this offering will be used for production of CRAY-1 computers, hardware and software development, operating expenses and working capital. (See *1976 Operating Plan* and *Use of Proceeds.*)

Financial Information

The Company has been engaged in development of the CRAY-1 computer since its formation and has had no sales or earnings to date. The following tables set forth certain financial information with respect to the Company.

	April 6, 1972 to Dec. 31, 1972	Year Ended December 31, 1973	1974	1975	Cumulative to Dec. 31, 1975
Interest and other nonoperating income	$ 58,327	$147,724	$ 217,699	$ 84,621	$ 508,371
Total expenses	130,685	674,459	1,161,349	971,155	2,937,648
Net loss	$(72,358)	$(526,735)	$(943,650)	$(886,534)	$(2,429,277)
Loss per share	$ (.27)	$ (1.38)	$ (1.48)	$ (1.33)	

	December 31, 1975
Working capital	$5,756,288
Total assets	6,242,942
Long term debt	2,720,000
Accumulated deficit	(2,429,277)
Stockholders' equity	3,434,410

THE COMPANY

Cray Research, Inc. was organized to design, develop, manufacture and market large capacity, high speed computers intended for scientific applications. The first model produced by the Company, the CRAY-1 computer, has been designed and developed under the direction of Seymour R. Cray, who has been a pioneer in the design and development of a number of large scale computer systems. The CRAY-1 computer has an internal bipolar memory capacity of up to one million 64-bit words and operates on the solution of many complex scientific problems at speeds that the Company believes are significantly faster than those obtained by any other existing computer. Based on its high computation speed and large internal memory, management believes the CRAY-1 to be the most advanced computer available for complex research applications. It is expected to be particularly adaptable to a class of problems involving the analysis and prediction of physical phenomena. These problems are encountered in fields such as weather forecasting, aircraft design, nuclear research, geophysical research and seismic analysis.

The CRAY-1 computer incorporates major improvements over existing large scale computers including advanced vector capabilities, a large internal bipolar memory, and significantly reduced physical size made possible by an advanced freon cooling system.

The initial CRAY-1 computer has been constructed, is undergoing testing and is being used in connection with marketing efforts and software development. However, no on site user testing has been performed. Construction of an additional unit has commenced. The Company proposes to offer three versions of the CRAY-1 computer with one-quarter million, one-half million and one million 64-bit word memories. These versions of the CRAY-1 will be offered for sale at prices, excluding peripheral equipment, of $4,500,000, $5,500,000 and $7,500,000 or for lease at monthly payments of $120,000, $145,000 and $195,000. No sales or leases of the CRAY-1 have been made to date.

The Company was incorporated as a Delaware corporation on April 6, 1972. Its executive offices are located at 7850 Metro Parkway, Suite 213, Minneapolis, Minnesota 55420, and its telephone number is (612) 854-7472.

INTRODUCTORY STATEMENT

Risk Factors

The securities being offered by this Prospectus are speculative in nature. Prospective investors should consider carefully the risks which will affect the business of the Company before purchasing any of the shares offered hereby.

1. *No Sales or Earnings.* The Company has had no sales or earnings to date, has an accumulated deficit in the amount of $2,429,277 as of December 31, 1975, and anticipates a substantial loss in 1976.

2. *Development Status of the Computer.* The Company has constructed only one unit of the CRAY-1 computer. This unit has a memory of one-half million 64-bit words. Although the unit has undergone testing by the Company, no on site user testing has been performed to date, and there has been no extended use which would establish its reliability or customer acceptability.

3. *Lack of Orders.* Although the Company is presently discussing prospective installations with several potential customers, no orders have been received to date. Nevertheless, the Company has partially completed a second unit and production of two additional units has been

scheduled to commence in the second half of 1976. A portion of the proceeds of this offering will be used to complete the second unit and to commence the production of the additional units. There can be no assurance that the Company will receive orders for such units.

4. *Development of Fortran Compiler.* The ability of the Company to market the CRAY-1 computer is dependent upon the development of an efficient Fortran compiler for the CRAY-1. While the compiler has been under development since 1973 and the Company anticipates the availability of an initial version by mid-1976, failure of the compiler to attain its design objective or substantial delay in its availability would adversely affect the marketability of the CRAY-1. (See *Business—Software.*)

5. *Competition.* The manufacturers with which the Company will compete in the market for large scientific computers, while small in number, have significantly greater financial and other resources than the Company. There are at least three large scale scientific computers currently being offered which will compete directly with the CRAY-1. One manufacturer has indicated publicly that it is conducting development work to further advance its large scale scientific computers. Other computer manufacturers may also be engaged in the development of large scale scientific computers. Moreover, the Company believes that to secure and maintain a competitive position in the market for large computers for scientific use, it will be necessary to continue the development of advanced models. (See *Business—Competition.*)

6. *Limited Market.* The CRAY-1 computer is an expensive, advanced computer which will be marketed to a relatively small number of potential customers. The nature of the scientific computer business involves lengthy and uncertain procurement processes and negotiations. These factors, together with the potential for delays in or cancellation of government procurements, make the scheduling of production and deliveries extremely difficult to establish and control, and will have a material effect on the cash flow and profitability of the Company.

7. *Need for Additional Financing.* The development, construction and marketing of large scale computers requires the expenditure of significant sums of money with no certainty that revenues will result. The Company's need for financing can be affected substantially by the decisions of customers to lease or purchase machines, by the timing of shipments and by required investments in inventory to expand production.

In the event that the Company expends its funds to the full extent of its 1976 operating plan, and unless it has received orders for purchase on which payments are made in early 1977, the Company will have expended the proceeds from the sale of stock offered hereby and will require additional debt or equity financing at that time. The Company presently believes that there is a substantial likelihood that initial shipments will be based on leases rather than outright sales, and accordingly expects that either additional debt or equity financing will be required during 1977 or the production schedule for the third and fourth units would have to be delayed. At present, however, the Company is unable to estimate with any certainty the amounts of such additional financing which may be required and is unable to assure investors that such financing will be available. (See *1976 Operating Plan* and *Use of Proceeds.*)

8. *Dependence on Founder.* Seymour R. Cray, the President of the Company, has been essential to the design and development of the CRAY-1 computer. Should Mr. Cray's services and reputation no longer be available to the Company, the operations of the Company and the design

and development of future products of the Company would be adversely affected. (See *Management.*)

9. *Reliance on Certain Suppliers.* Integrated memory circuits, a critical component of the CRAY-1 computer, are currently available in production quantities from only one supplier. Other components are being purchased from single suppliers. Should the supply of any of these components become unavailable, the Company may incur delays which would affect its ability to produce and deliver computer units. (See *Business--Suppliers.*)

Dilution

The aggregate tangible book value of the Common Stock of the Company at December 31, 1975 was $3,382,044 or $4.78 per share. Giving effect to the offering, but without regard to any shares which may be issued as a result of the Underwriters' over-allotment option, the tangible book value of the Company at December 31, 1975 would have been $ or $ per share. The increase of $ in book value would be due solely to the purchase of shares by the investors in this offering and an immediate dilution of $ per share will be incurred by them.

The following table illustrates the dilution of a new investor's equity in a share of Common Stock:

Public offering price (1)	$
Net tangible book value before offering (2)	$ 4.78
Increase attributable to payments by new investors	$
Net tangible book value after offering	$
Dilution to new investors (3)	$

The following table sets forth, as of December 31, 1975, a comparison of the respective investments and equity holdings of the investors purchasing shares of Common Stock in this offering and of the founders and other previous investors in the Company:

	Average Amount Paid Per Share of Common Stock	Percent of Equity Purchased	Total Capital Invested
New investors (600,000 shares) (4)	$ (1)	45.91%(4)	$ (4)
Present stockholders:			
Shares sold during 1972	$ 6.67	29.26%	$2,550,000
Shares sold upon exercise of employee stock options granted in 1972	$ 6.67	.41%	$ 36,000
Shares sold during 1974	$10.00	20.47%	$2,675,025
Shares sold to a component supplier in 1975	$12.44	3.95%	$ 641,942
Average or total for present stockholders	$ 8.35	54.09%	$5,902,967
Differential	$		

(1) Offering price before deduction of Underwriters' commissions and offering expenses.

(2) "Tangible Book Value" is determined by dividing the number of shares of Common Stock outstanding into the tangible net worth of the Company (tangible assets less liabilities).

(3) "Dilution" is determined by subtracting tangible book value per share after the offering from the amount of cash paid by an investor for a share of stock.

(4) Excludes any shares issued as a consequence of the Underwriters' over-allotment option.

As of December 31, 1975 the Company had outstanding $2,720,000 of 8% Convertible Subordinated Notes which are convertible into 204,033 shares of Common Stock at a price of $13.33 per share. In the event of sale of any shares by the Company prior to June 30, 1977 at a price below $13.33 per share, the conversion price is reduced directly to such sale price (but not below $6.67 per share). In the event of a sale after June 30, 1977 at a price below $13.33 per share, the conversion price is reduced proportionately in accordance with an anti-dilution formula.

Options were also outstanding as of December 31, 1975 to purchase 52,350 shares of the Company's Common Stock at prices ranging from $6.67 to $12.44 per share under the Company's Qualified Stock Option Plans. (See *Management—Qualified Stock Option Plans.*) An additional 23,397 shares are expected to be issued pursuant to an arrangement with Fairchild Camera and Instrument Corporation, a supplier to the Company, under which the Company pays for integrated memory circuits with equivalent amounts of cash and stock valued at a stated price of $12.44 per share. (See *Management—Certain Transactions.*) The number of shares issuable upon exercise of stock options, upon purchase of stock by Fairchild and upon conversion of the Convertible Notes, and the purchase price per share, are subject to adjustment in the event of stock splits or dividends.

If all options, conversion rights and purchase rights were exercised, the net tangible book value after the offering would increase. However, the purchasers of the shares offered hereby may incur further dilution of the book value of their shares and a reduction of their equity interest in the Company to the extent that certain of such options or rights are exercised. The existence of such options and rights could also have an adverse impact on the ability of the Company to obtain equity financing in the future and the holders of such options or rights may be expected to exercise them at a time when the price of any needed equity that the Company may obtain would be on terms more favorable to the Company than those provided with respect to such options or rights.

Shares Available for Sale

Persons who own the 707,006 shares of Common Stock outstanding, and persons who may own, assuming the exercise of option, conversion or purchase rights, an additional 279,780 shares of Common Stock possess certain rights to require the Company to register their stock for sale. (See *Description of Common Stock.*) An aggregate of 636,503 shares may also be eligible for sale beginning 90 days after the date of this Prospectus pursuant to Rule 144 under the Securities Act of 1933. However, stockholders who would be eligible to exercise such registration rights, or otherwise be entitled to sell shares in the Company pursuant to Rule 144, have agreed not to offer for sale or sell any shares of Common Stock for a period of six months after the date of this Prospectus without prior consent of the Representatives of the Underwriters. In addition, all of the directors and officers of the Company, who hold an aggregate of 201,000 shares, have agreed not to offer for sale or sell their Common Stock without the prior written consent of the Representatives of the Underwriters until after the Company has marketed three units of the CRAY-1 computer, at least one of which has been purchased, or has marketed four units of the CRAY-1 on a lease basis. Stockholders may elect to exercise their rights to sell their shares when they become able to do so, and any such sales may adversely affect the market price of the Common Stock.

1976 OPERATING PLAN

The Company's 1976 operating plan anticipates the installation on a trial basis of the first CRAY-1 computer at a customer's site during 1976. The plan also contemplates the completion of the second unit by the end of the year. The Company has deferred further production work on this second unit pending receipt of the proceeds of this offering. Production of the third and fourth units is scheduled to begin midway through 1976 with both units expected to be completed in 1977. While the Company has no firm commitments from customers at this time, it believes it has identified several prospective users for these units. The Company, however, does not propose to begin construction of the fourth unit without a suitable commitment for acquisition of one of the first three units.

Based on its production and installation schedule, the Company does not expect to realize any significant revenues from operations in 1976. (See *Use of Proceeds.*)

The Company anticipates that its expenditures during 1976 will be approximately as follows:

Production of CRAY-1 computers	$6,850,000
Hardware development	300,000
Software development	250,000
Marketing, sales and applications support	500,000
Installation and maintenance	550,000
Furniture, fixtures and equipment	200,000
Administration	350,000
Interest	218,000
	$9,218,000

Hardware development will be limited primarily to continuation engineering on the CRAY-1 computer and initial design work on the Company's anticipated next computer model.

Completion of a Fortran compiler will be the main activity in software development in 1976. A preliminary version is expected to be available for user testing by mid-year. The first operating version is expected to be available to users in the third quarter of 1976.

In 1976 the Company plans an increase in marketing, sales and support personnel whose efforts will be specifically directed toward a limited number of prospects which the Company has identified.

The Company does not anticipate any significant acquisition of new plant or facilities in 1976 but does anticipate making plans for additional facilities to be secured in 1977.

Based on the foregoing operating plan, during 1976 the Company expects to increase its number of employees from 45 to approximately 97, including an addition of 14 persons in the hardware engineering and production area, 5 in software development, 17 in marketing, sales and customer support, 14 in field maintenance and 2 in administration. These employees do not include assembly labor which is employed on a subcontract basis. (See *Business—Production.*)

USE OF PROCEEDS

The estimated net proceeds of the offering in the amount of $, plus any proceeds received as a consequence of the exercise of the Underwriters' over-allotment option, will be used as set forth in the following table. Pending application of the proceeds, such funds would be invested in marketable interest-bearing securities.

Application	Amount
Production of CRAY-1 computers	$
Hardware development	
Software development	
Marketing, sales and applications support	
Installation and maintenance	
Administration	
Interest	
Working Capital	(1)
	$

---

(1) Plus any proceeds of the exercise of the Underwriters' over-allotment option.

The Company anticipates that these proceeds will be expended during 1976 and in future fiscal periods. (See *1976 Operating Plan.*) In the event the Company's anticipated production schedule is delayed, some funds designated for production may be used to cover other operating expenses.

In the event that the Company expends its funds to the full extent of its 1976 operating plan, and unless it has received orders for purchase on which payments are made in early 1977, the Company will have expended the proceeds from the sale of its stock offered hereby and will require additional debt or equity financing at that time. Moreover, based on discussions to date with potential customers and on general experience in the computer industry, the Company believes that significant revenues may not be generated from its first unit for a number of months after its installation. After installation of the unit, several months may elapse during a test and evaluation period, following which the customer may determine to lease the unit for a year or more before any ultimate decision to purchase is made. These factors may further affect the need for additional debt or equity financing. The Company presently believes that there is a substantial likelihood that initial shipments will be based on leases rather than outright sales and accordingly expects that either additional debt or equity financing will be required during 1977 or the production schedule for the third and fourth units would have to be delayed.

CAPITALIZATION

The following table sets forth the capitalization of the Company as of December 31, 1975 and as adjusted to reflect the sale of the 600,000 shares of Common Stock offered hereby.

	December 31, 1975	As Adjusted(1)
Long Term Debt:		
8% Convertible Subordinated Notes, due March 31, 1982	$2,720,000	$2,720,000
Stockholders' Equity:		
Common Stock $1.00 par value:		
Authorized 5,000,000 shares; issued 707,006 shares (1,307,006 as adjusted) (2)	$ 707,006	$1,307,006
Additional paid-in capital	5,156,681	
Deficit accumulated during the development stage	(2,429,277)	(2,429,277)
TOTAL STOCKHOLDERS' EQUITY	$3,434,410	$

(1) Does not reflect the issuance of any shares as a result of the exercise of the Underwriters' ove~-allotment option.

(2) In addition, 60,600 shares are reserved for issuance upon exercise of options granted or which may be granted under the Company's two Qualified Stock Option Plans, 204,033 shares are reserved for issuance upon conversion of the 8% Convertible Subordinated Notes of the Company and 23,397 shares are reserved for issuance in connection with a stock purchase agreement with a major supplier of the Company. See notes 5, 7 and 8 to financial statements.

(3) See note 9 to financial statements for information concerning lease obligation.

(4) The Company has made arrangements for a discretionary credit line from a bank which provides for secured loans of up to $1,100,000 at an interest rate of 3% over the bank's prime rate. See note 10 to financial statements.

DIVIDEND POLICY

The Company has not paid any cash dividends and does not expect to pay any cash dividends in the foreseeable future. The Company expects to retain any earnings it may receive in the foreseeable future to support continued production, marketing and development activities.

CRAY RESEARCH, INC.

STATEMENTS OF OPERATIONS

The following statements of operations of Cray Research, Inc. have been examined by Peat, Marwick, Mitchell & Co., independent certified public accountants, as set forth in their report (which is qualified with respect to recoverability of inventories) appearing elsewhere in this Prospectus. The following statements should be read in conjunction with the other financial statements and related notes thereto included elsewhere in this Prospectus.

	April 6, 1972 (date of organization) to December 31, 1972	Year ended December 31, 1973	1974	1975	Cumulative to December 31, 1975
Income:					
Interest	$ 57,067	$ 147,724	$ 217,699	$ 81,113	$ 503,603
Other	1,260	—	—	3,508	4,768
Total income	58,327	147,724	217,699	84,621	508,371
Expenses:					
Product development (note B)	69,221	536,155	912,884	308,365	1,826,625
Marketing	15,714	47,877	96,806	320,437	480,834
General and administrative	45,750	90,427	151,659	219,015	506,851
Interest on subordinated notes	—	—	—	123,338	123,338
Total expenses	130,685	674,459	1,161,349	971,155	2,937,648
Net loss (note 6)	$(72,358)	$(526,735)	$(943,650)	$(886,534)	$(2,429,277)
Weighted average number of shares outstanding (note 7)	265,926	383,043	639,321	665,424	
Loss per share (note A)	$ (.27)	$ (1.38)	$ (1.48)	$ (1.33)	

Numerical note references are to notes to financial statements included elsewhere in this Prospectus.

See following notes to statements of operations.

NOTES TO STATEMENTS OF OPERATIONS

A. *Loss Per Share*

The net loss per share is computed by dividing the net loss by the weighted average number of common shares outstanding during the period. The effect on loss per share would be anti-dilutive (the loss per share would be reduced) had common equivalent shares consisting of shares issuable upon exercise of outstanding stock options and pursuant to a stock purchase agreement with a major supplier been included. The convertible subordinated notes are not common stock equivalents; inclusion of shares issuable upon conversion of such notes would also be anti-dilutive.

All share and per share figures have been retroactively adjusted to give effect to the stock dividend as described in note 7 to financial statements.

B. *Product Development Costs*

Product development costs are charged to expense as incurred. See note 2 to financial statements for further description.

C. *Supplemental Income Statement Information*

	April 6, 1972 to December 31, 1972	Year ended December 31,		
		1973	1974	1975
Maintenance and repairs	$ 787	$ 1,603	$ 3,034	$ 12,496
Depreciation and amortization of furniture, fixtures and equipment	3,309	15,216	43,250	92,961
Amortization of deferred charges	1,169	1,754	1,754	7,619
Taxes, other than income taxes:				
Payroll taxes	4,854	10,025	18,634	31,664
Real estate and personal property	—	4,965	9,819	14,989
Miscellaneous	1,636	2,464	5,234	5,142
Rents	10,947	24,377	26,062	37,069
Product development	69,221	536,155	912,884	308,365
	$91,923	$596,559	$1,020,671	$510,305

MANAGEMENT'S DISCUSSION AND ANALYSIS OF THE STATEMENTS OF OPERATIONS

Since its inception in 1972, the Company has been engaged primarily in design and production activities related to its CRAY-1 computer. As a result, no sales or earnings have been generated. The Company has expensed product development costs as incurred.

During the period from April 6, 1972 through December 31, 1975, product development costs increased from $69,221 for the period ended December 31, 1972 to $536,155 in 1973 and reached a peak of $912,884 in 1974. Thereafter, product development costs in 1975 decreased to $308,365, reflecting the substantial completion of the development effort on the CRAY-1.

During these same periods, marketing expenses, including software support and computer maintenance, increased in each period from $15,714 in 1972 to $47,877 in 1973, $96,806 in 1974 and $320,437 in 1975. The largest part of the increases in 1975 resulted from the expansion of marketing facilities, the addition of a number of software support personnel and the addition of customer engineers who will be responsible for the maintenance of the initial unit of the CRAY-1.

General and administrative expenses have increased in each of the periods, primarily because of additions to personnel and increased fees for professional services.

Interest income increased in each of the periods through 1974 due primarily to the temporary investment of cash balances resulting from the sale of common stock, and then declined in 1975 as the Company expended substantial funds on the construction of the first unit of the CRAY-1 computer.

In 1975, the Company incurred its first interest expense following issuance of $2,720,000 of 8% Convertible Subordinated Notes.

BUSINESS

Background

The Company was founded by Seymour R. Cray and others to design, develop, manufacture and market large capacity, high speed computers intended for scientific applications. Mr. Cray was a pioneer in the design and development of large scale scientific computer systems. Between 1957 and 1970, he was a principal architect of and led the design and development of the Control Data 1604, 6600 and 7600 computer lines. The 1604 was one of the first commercially available transistorized computers, and the 6600 and 7600 have been leading scientific computers from 1964 to the present. The market for such scientific computers consists of approximately 100 government agencies, corporations and educational institutions in the United States and abroad which are primarily engaged in scientific research.

The CRAY-1 Computer

The CRAY-1 computer is intended to solve complex scientific problems at speeds that the Company believes are significantly faster than those obtained by any other existing computer, depending on the nature of the problem. The Company believes that this increased problem solving speed will enable users to solve problems more complex than would otherwise be attempted. The principal features of the CRAY-1 which contribute to its advanced performance are its vector processing capability, its large internal bipolar memory and its compact design.

A key design feature of the CRAY-1 computer is its ability to process vector operations in addition to its high speed scalar processing ability. Vector processing in a computer is the performance of an operation, such as addition or multiplication, on a set of numbers with a single instruction. In contrast, scalar processing requires the execution of a separate instruction for each number in such a set. The CRAY-1 is also designed to permit a substantial amount of "chaining" which allows operations to be performed on several sets of data concurrently rather than requiring each set to be completely processed before beginning on the next.

The CRAY-1 computer has an internal memory capacity of up to 64 million bits with a cycle time of 50 nanoseconds (50 billionths of a second). Cycle time is the time required to remove or insert an element of data in the memory. The Company knows of no other computer which has as large an internal memory coupled with a comparable cycle time.

In a computer which performs calculations as rapidly as the CRAY-1, the time required to send data along connecting wires constitutes a significant portion of the time required to solve a problem. Therefore, a key design objective is to make the computer compact in order to reduce wire lengths. The principal difficulty encountered in reducing computer size is the resulting concentration of heat which must be dissipated. The CRAY-1 incorporates an advanced freon cooling system for this purpose. As a result, the overall wire lengths within the CRAY-1 are reduced significantly from what they would have been if conventional cooling techniques had been used.

The CRAY-1 computer is expected to be particularly useful in solving problems requiring the analysis and prediction of the behavior of physical phenomena through computer simulation. The fields of weather forecasting, aircraft design, nuclear research, geophysical research and seismic analysis involve this process. For example, the movements of global air masses for weather forecasting, air flows over wing and airframe surfaces for aircraft design, and the movements of particles for nuclear physics research, all lend themselves to such simulations. In each scientific field, the equations are known, but the solutions require extensive computations involving large quantities of data. The quality of a solution is heavily dependent on the number of data points that can be considered and the number of computations that can be performed. The CRAY-1 is expected to permit substantial increases with respect to both the number of data points and computations.

Software

The Company intends to engage in the development of three types of software in connection with the CRAY-1 computer: operating systems, compilers and applications software.

Initially, the Company intends to provide a simple operating system for the CRAY-1 computer. An operating system is a program which controls the resources within a computer installation and supervises the running of other programs. The initial operating system to be provided will allow the processing of Fortran programs only on a serial basis. The Company believes that this system will be adequate for a period of time. In order to expand the range of applications for the CRAY-1, more sophisticated operating systems software will be required. The initial operating system has been in development for over a year, and the Company intends to expand its operating systems development as future installations of the CRAY-1 are made.

During the development of the CRAY-1 computer, the Company has also been developing a Fortran compiler. Compilers are programs which convert computer instructions written in a source language such as Fortran into machine code which can be executed directly by the computer. Most of the scientific computer facilities that are prospective users of the CRAY-1 do a considerable amount of their own applications programming in the Fortran language. As a result, such scientific computer facilities require that a Fortran compiler be provided with any computer which they acquire. Furthermore, to the extent that a new computer provides a new capability, such as vector processing, users expect to be able to utilize that new capability through the Fortran compiler. The first version of this compiler has been designed to utilize the vector capabilities of the CRAY-1 but has not been completed. The Company expects that it will be ready for testing by mid-1976 and that it will be available to users in the third quarter of 1976. There can be no assurance, however, that this schedule can be met. If it is not met, there will be an adverse effect on the Company's ability to market the CRAY-1 computer. The Company does not expect the first version of the Fortran compiler to make the most efficient use of the inherent capabilities of the CRAY-1. Continuing compiler development is planned in conjunction with experience at user installations.

Applications software consists of specific programs, usually written in a source language such as Fortran, which solve particular user problems. Most potential customers for the CRAY-1 computer have the capability to develop the specialized applications software required to meet their own computational needs. The Company, therefore, does not anticipate that it will be necessary initially to develop extensive applications software programs. The Company does, however, anticipate providing software specialists to assist customers in the development of specific applications programs.

Marketing and Sales

Most of the scientific institutions which are potential customers for the CRAY-1 computer already have substantial computational facilities that have been developed over many years. The Company believes that the procurement of the CRAY-1 will result from the interest of the scientific community in finding solutions to problems which existing equipment can not feasibly solve at present. To meet this type of market demand, new computers generally must provide a several fold expansion in performance capability over previously installed computers and must be extensions of existing systems. For that reason, the Company has designed the CRAY-1 not only with increased computational capability, but also to be integrated into existing systems rather than to replace customer equipment. Such integration will also permit use of existing communications networks and peripheral equipment by the CRAY-1.

A special characteristic of this market is that most of such institutions, whether public or private, are United States government funded. Consequently, procurement processes of such potential users are usually dictated by federal government policy. Procurements tend to take a considerable length of time (12 to 24 months), involve many people or agencies within the government, and are subject to numerous uncertainties including general funding priorities within the government's budget. Unexpected delays and complications may occur requiring the Company to expend an indeterminate amount of financial and personnel resources during the procurement process. (See *Government Regulation and Renegotiation.*) Further, because the federal government can not make financial commitments beyond its current fiscal year, it may be necessary to ship CRAY-1 computers based on only a short term lease even when ultimate purchase is anticipated.

Primarily to meet the budget constraints of potential users and to provide marketing flexibility, the Company proposes to offer three versions of the CRAY-1 computer with one-quarter million, one-half million and one million 64-bit word memories. The prices of these versions, excluding peripheral equipment, are $4,500,000, $5,500,000 and $7,500,000, respectively. The initial unit of the CRAY-1 has been constructed with a memory of one-half million 64-bit words. Maintenance services and peripheral equipment will be charged for separately. (See *Maintenance Services.*)

The Company also proposes to offer the CRAY-1 computer on a lease basis for $120,000, $145,000 and $195,000 per month depending on memory size. Maintenance service charges will be in addition to basic lease payments. It is anticipated that these leases would be for a maximum of 12 months since most of the Company's prospective customers are United States government funded and cannot be committed to leases that extend beyond the current government fiscal year. The Company's lease policy will provide for a purchase option in which the user will be given credit for 60% of its lease payments toward the purchase price of the equipment.

Software specialists may also be provided for each installation to assist customers with the development of specific applications. These services may be provided as part of the purchase or lease or may be charged for separately.

The main sales office of the Company is located in Minneapolis, Minnesota and is presently staffed with a small group of experienced sales and technical support people. The Company engages a part-time marketing consultant in Livermore, California, and employs a full-time marketing representative in the Washington, D. C. area. Additional sales offices will be established as appropriate.

The initial CRAY-1 computer with a one-half million 64-bit word memory has been constructed and is undergoing testing. The Company is discussing its installation for evaluation with interested institutions. While the Company believes that the initial computer and future units can be sold or leased, there can be no assurance that the CRAY-1 can be marketed.

Competition

The manufacturers which will compete with the Company in the market for large scientific computers, while small in number, have significantly greater financial and other resources than the Company. There are at least three large scale scientific computer lines currently being offered which compete directly with the CRAY-1. These computers are Control Data Corporation's 7600 and STAR and Texas Instruments Incorporated's ASC. Control Data Corporation has publicly indicated that it is conducting development work to further advance its large scale computers.

In addition, IBM and Burroughs Corporation have previously marketed large scale computers to the scientific community and have the resources to re-enter this market at any time. Other computer manufacturers may also be engaged in the development of advanced models of large scale computers and there can be no assurance that any computers produced by the Company will have competitive advantages over any such advanced models. Moreover, the Company believes that to secure and maintain a competitive position in the market for large scientific computers, it will be necessary to continue the development of advanced models.

Hardware and Software Development

During the fiscal years ended December 31, 1974 and December 31, 1975, the Company's product development costs amounted to approximately $913,000 and $308,000, respectively. From its formation to December 31, 1975, product development costs have aggregated $1,827,000. In addition to the necessity to continue the development of advanced models, further software development must also be continued for the CRAY-1 computer. The Company anticipates that approximately $550,000 will be spent in both hardware and software development in 1976. (See *1976 Operating Plan.*) The Company expects future product development expenditures to grow significantly above this level in the development of both hardware and software systems. (See *Business—Software.*)

Production

The production of a CRAY-1 computer involves a significant lead time to acquire and test the required quantity of certain components, the assembly of these and other components to construct the computer, and extensive testing of the completed computer. Assembly and testing of each of the initial computers is expected to require approximately 12 to 15 months, of which the greater portion is spent in the testing phase. Production of each CRAY-1 computer requires limited space and a limited number of production personnel. The personnel required for the testing phase of production must be highly skilled.

The Company has obtained most of its assembly labor on a subcontract basis and intends to continue this practice in the foreseeable future. Chip-Tronics, Inc. of Chippewa Falls, Wisconsin, presently supplies the Company's assembly labor which has included up to 40 persons. (See *Management—Certain Transactions.*)

Production of the initial units of the CRAY-1 computer will be concentrated at the Company's Chippewa Falls, Wisconsin facilities. Based on its present operating plan, the Company anticipates that it will be required to establish additional production facilities during 1977. (See *1976 Operating Plan.*)

Suppliers

The components used by the Company in the production of the CRAY-1 are purchased from outside sources. The Company will be dependent upon the availability of outside suppliers and assemblers meeting high standards of quality and reliability.

Many of the components required by the Company have been designed for the Company and are supplied pursuant to specific purchase orders. These components do not, however, represent significant departures from existing technology. Important components required by the Company include integrated circuits for use in the memory and logic portions of the CRAY-1 computer. Logic circuits have been purchased in approximately equal quantities from Fairchild Camera and Instrument Corporation and Motorola, Inc. All memory circuits to date have been purchased from Fairchild, although sample quantities have been supplied by Motorola. The Company knows of no other sources for memory circuits and production quantities currently are available only from Fairchild. Certain other components are presently being purchased from single suppliers. Should the supply of any of these components become unavailable for any reason, the Company may incur delays which would affect its production capabilities. Fairchild is a stockholder and noteholder of the Company. (See *Management—Certain Transactions* and *Principal Holders of Securities.*)

No material difficulties in obtaining supplies have been encountered but component shortages have occurred in the past in the computer industry, and any such shortages or increased component requirements by the Company could result in delays in delivery which would adversely affect sales of the CRAY-1 computer.

Maintenance Services

The Company intends to provide several resident maintenance engineers to support each CRAY-1 computer. The Company expects to follow the industry practice of performing maintenance services on a contractual basis. The maintenance agreement will specify certain performance criteria which must be met, and require a monthly fee to be paid by the user. The Company will be obligated to ensure that its computer meets these performance requirements even if expenditures in excess of the fee payments are required. Further, if the Company experiences difficulty with these performance requirements, an adverse impact on future sales of the CRAY-1 could result. To meet its commitments in this regard, the Company expects to maintain a substantial spare parts inventory equivalent to approximately 10% of the parts complement of each machine installed.

Properties

The Company currently leases executive and other offices at 7850 and 7851 Metro Parkway, Minneapolis, Minnesota consisting of 3,585 square feet leased for $23,340 per year for a renewable one year term.

The Company's development and production facility is located in a 9,168 square foot building in Chippewa Falls, Wisconsin constructed in 1972 by Mr. Cray. The facility is leased to the Company by Mr. Cray until September 1977 at $20,900 per year plus maintenance, taxes and insurance on a net lease basis with an option to renew the lease for an additional five years. The Company believes that the terms of the lease are fair and competitive with terms for similar facilities in the area. The Company considers this facility to be primarily a product development laboratory but anticipates that it will be adequate for the production of the initial units of the CRAY-1 computer. Thereafter, the Company expects to secure additional facilities.

The Company also leases 3,000 square feet for its operations in a building in Chippewa Falls on a year to year basis at $3,600 per year plus utilities.

Patents

The Company has no patents and, at present, does not plan to file any patent applications. While the Company may apply for patents as it develops products and processes which it believes to be patentable, the Company believes that its success depends principally upon its skills in the areas of design, engineering and marketing, and the quality of its products, rather than its ability to secure patents.

Government Regulation and Renegotiation

Substantially all of the initial group of potential customers for the CRAY-1 computer are United States government funded institutions to which the laws and regulations relating to procurement and renegotiation of government contracts would apply.

Under United States government procurement regulations, initial pricing of products sold to government funded agencies must be justified by one of three methods: cost disclosure, substantial commercial sales at the same or higher price or competitive performance. These regulations could restrict revenues from sales or leases to government funded institutions.

Renegotiation on a retroactive basis under the Renegotiation Act of 1951, as amended, could require the Company to refund profits from sales or leases to government funded institutions. Under the Act, the Company may be required to justify profits derived by the Company from such sales or leases. Factors taken into consideration by the government in evaluating profit levels include capital employed, extent of risk assumed, efficiency and economy in use of materials, facilities and manpower, the character and complexity of the business and contribution to the national defense effort.

Employees

As of December 31, 1975, the Company had 45 full-time employees, including 35 technical personnel, 5 marketing personnel and 5 administrative and clerical personnel. The Company presently obtains its assembly labor on a subcontract basis. (See *Business—Production.*) The Company will be required to hire additional employees to the extent that needs increase. (See *1976 Operating Plan.*) The future of the Company will depend in part upon its ability to attract and retain such employees.

The Company has two qualified stock option plans for key employees and also has group health, life and disability insurance plans. (See *Management—Qualified Stock Option Plans.*) None of the Company's employees are represented by a labor union and the Company has had no work stoppages. The Company believes that its employee relations are excellent.

All key employees of the Company have signed agreements with the Company to treat certain information gained in the course of their employment as confidential and not to use such information should they leave the employ of the Company. While the enforceability of such agreements cannot be assured, the Company believes that they provide a deterrent to the use of information which may be proprietary to the Company.

MANAGEMENT

Officers and Directors

The executive officers and directors of the Company are as follows:

Name	Age	Title
Seymour R. Cray	50	President, Chief Executive Officer and Director
Frank C. Mullaney	53	Chairman of the Board
Lester T. Davis	45	Vice President
George S. Hanson	58	Vice President and Director
John A. Rollwagen	35	Vice President
Noel T. Stone	55	Treasurer and Director
Marshall A. Wiley	63	Secretary
Irvin E. Engebretson	37	Controller
Francis X. Driscoll	47	Director
R. Patrick Durch	48	Director
Thomas A. Longo	49	Director
Andrew Scott	47	Director
Robert F. Zicarelli	51	Director

All officers listed above joined the Company when it was founded in 1972 except Mr. Rollwagen, who joined the Company in 1975.

Mr. Cray has been a leading architect of large scientific computers for more than twenty years. From 1957 to 1968, he served as a director of Control Data Corporation (CDC) and was a Senior Vice President at the time of his resignation in early 1972. Previously he was employed at the Univac Division of Sperry Rand Corporation (Univac) and its predecessor companies, Engineering Research Associates (ERA) and Remington Rand. Mr. Cray holds a Bachelor of Electrical Engineering degree and a Masters degree in Mathematics from the University of Minnesota. Mr. Cray has been the principal designer and developer of the CRAY-1 computer and it is anticipated that future products developed by the Company will depend, to a large part, on his expertise. The Company has in force a $3,500,000 term life insurance policy covering Mr. Cray in which the Company is named beneficiary and has agreed to keep this policy in force for at least two years from the date of this Prospectus.

Mr. Mullaney is a private investor and consultant to businesses in the computer industry. He was a founder of Control Data Corporation and was a Vice President and Director until his resignation in February 1966. He serves as a director of a number of corporations, including Data Products Corporation and DeLuxe Check Printers, Inc. Mr. Mullaney has been a director of the Company since its formation.

Mr. Davis was General Manager of CDC's Chippewa Falls Laboratory from 1962 to 1972, when he resigned to join the Company. He had been with CDC since 1959. From 1955 to 1959, Mr. Davis was with Univac.

Mr. Hanson was associated with CDC from 1959 to 1967 and was Vice President-Marketing when he left in 1967 to pursue a number of personal business interests. Mr. Hanson holds a Bachelor of Electrical Engineering degree from the University of Minnesota and a Bachelor of Science degree in Mathematics and Physics from Hamline University.

Mr. Rollwagen was formerly a Vice President of International Timesharing Corporation, and was associated with that company from 1968 to 1975. He holds a Bachelor of Electrical Engineering degree from Massachusetts Institute of Technology and a Master of Business Administration degree from the Harvard Graduate School of Business Administration.

Mr. Stone was a Vice President of CDC from 1966 to 1970, after which he pursued private business interests until formation of the Company. He holds a Bachelor of Electrical Engineering degree from the University of Minnesota.

Mr. Wiley is the Senior Partner in the law firm of Wiley and Frasch in Chippewa Falls, Wisconsin. Mr. Wiley has been the Secretary of the Company since its formation.

Mr. Engebretson was the manager of accounting at CDC's Chippewa Falls Laboratory from 1967 until joining the Company in 1972. Mr. Engebretson holds a Bachelor's degree in Business Administration from Bemidji State University.

Mr. Driscoll is a Senior Vice President of New Court Securities Corporation, New York, New York, whose managed accounts are stockholders and noteholders of the Company, and is also a Senior Vice President of New Court Private Equity Fund, Inc., one of such managed accounts. Mr. Driscoll has been a director of the Company since 1974.

Mr. Durch is President of Tschopp-Durch-Camastral Company, Inc., general contractors, of Chippewa Falls, Wisconsin. He is also Vice President and General Manager of Chip-Tronics, Inc. of Chippewa Falls, an electronics company which assembles electronics components. He has been a director of the Company since its formation.

Dr. Longo is Vice President and Chief Technical Officer of Fairchild Camera and Instrument Corporation, and holds a Ph.D. in Physics. Fairchild is a stockholder and noteholder of the Company. Dr. Longo has been a director of the Company since 1975.

Mr. Scott is a Partner in the law firm of Doherty, Rumble & Butler in Minneapolis, Minnesota. Mr. Scott has been counsel to the Company since its formation and has been a director of the Company since 1973.

Mr. Zicarelli is President of Northwest Growth Fund, Inc., Minneapolis, Minnesota. Northwest Growth Fund is a stockholder and noteholder of the Company. He has been a director of the Company since 1975.

All officers and directors are elected for a term of one year and until their successors are elected and qualified.

Remuneration

The following table shows the aggregate direct remuneration during the year ended December 31, 1975 for the only director or officer of the Company whose remuneration from the Company exceeded $40,000, and for all directors and officers as a group.

Name and Capacity	Remuneration
Seymour R. Cray, President	$ 40,002
All Directors and Officers as a group (7 persons)	$162,765

The salary of Mr. Cray is presently established at a rate of $45,000 per annum and the total salaries of all directors and officers are presently established by the Board of Directors at a rate of $202,200 per annum.

Qualified Stock Option Plans

The Company has two Qualified Stock Option Plans for key employees. The 1972 Plan authorized options for 36,000 shares. All of such options have been granted at an option price of $6.67 per share. Options for 23,850 shares expire on July 18, 1977 and options for 6,750 shares expire on August 15, 1977. Options for 5,400 shares have been exercised. The 1974 Plan authorized options for 30,000 shares, of which options for 21,750 shares have been granted. Of the options granted, options for 6,000 shares were granted at $10.00 per share and expire on January 17, 1979, and options for 15,750 shares were granted at $12.44 per share of which options for 8,250 shares expire on April 29, 1980 and options for 7,500 shares expire on August 3, 1980. Options under the Plans are intended to constitute "qualified stock options" within the meaning of Section 422 of the Internal Revenue Code. Options are exercisable in cumulative annual installments of 25% of the shares subject to option commencing one year after the date of grant. Options expire five years after grant or earlier in the event of termination of employment or death.

As of December 31, 1975, options for the purchase of 30,600 shares were outstanding under the 1972 Plan (options for 5,400 shares having been exercised) and options for the 21,750 shares granted were outstanding under the 1974 Plan. Options for 8,250 shares remained available for future grant under the 1974 Plan. No directors have been granted options. As of December 31, 1975 options granted to three officers of the Company were outstanding for 7,500 shares at an option price of $6.67 per share expiring July 18, 1977, 6,000 shares at $6.67 per share expiring August 15, 1977 and 7,500 shares at $12.44 per share expiring August 3, 1980.

Certain Transactions

The Company leases its research and plant facilities from Seymour R. Cray, its President and director. (See *Business—Properties.*)

Fairchild Camera and Instrument Corporation, of which Dr. Thomas A. Longo, a director of the Company, is Group Vice President, is a supplier of memory circuits, logic circuits and other components to the Company. During 1973, 1974 and 1975, aggregate payments by the Company to Fairchild amounted to $25,000, $685,020 and $1,202,167, respectively. In January 1975, the Company entered into arrangements to issue up to 75,000 shares of its Common Stock to Fairchild pursuant to an arrangement under which the Company pays for integrated memory circuits with equivalent amounts of cash and stock valued at a stated price of $12.44 per share. If the Company does not order an agreed upon number of memory circuits, Fairchild has the right to purchase the balance of the shares at that price. Fairchild currently supplies these integrated memory circuits to the Company on a sole source basis. At December 31, 1975, 51,603 shares had been issued to Fairchild under these arrangements.

Chip-Tronics, Inc., of which Mr. R. Patrick Durch, a director of the Company, is Vice President, has supplied substantially all of the assembly labor used by the Company. During 1973, 1974 and 1975, aggregate payments by the Company to Chip-Tronics amounted to $70,057, $235,034 and $211,665, respectively.

In 1975 the Company purchased peripheral equipment for $87,200 from Control Data Corporation, the parent of Commercial Credit Capital Corp. which holds 10.25% of the Company's Common Stock.

The law firm of Doherty, Rumble & Butler of which Andrew Scott, a founder and director of the Company, is a Partner, has received fees for legal services aggregating $15,120 in 1973, $26,700 in 1974 and $50,400 in 1975.

PRINCIPAL HOLDERS OF SECURITIES

The following table sets forth as of December 31, 1975, the ownership of Common Stock of the Company held by each person who owned of record or was known by the Company to own beneficially more than 10% of the outstanding shares of Common Stock and by all directors and officers as a group. All shares owned by the persons named are owned of record and beneficially. The table also sets forth the percentage of the outstanding shares of Common Stock to be owned by each such person and group assuming full exercise of conversion rights on the Company's Convertible Notes, employee stock options and other rights to purchase Common Stock, and as adjusted for the issuance of the shares of Common Stock offered hereby.

	Common Stock Owned December 31, 1975		Shares Issuable Upon Exercise of Conversion and Purchase Rights	Percentage to be Owned	
				Assuming Full Exercise of Conversion and Purchase Rights	Assuming Full Exercise of Conversion and Purchase Rights and As Adjusted for this Offering (1)
	Shares	%	Shares	%	%
Seymour R. Cray	75,000	10.61	12,378	8.85	5.51
New Court Private Equity Fund, Inc. and Arrow Capital N.V. (2)	75,000	10.61	22,505	9.88	6.14
Commercial Credit Capital Corp. (a subsidiary of Control Data Corporation)	72,501	10.25	—	7.35	4.57
All Directors and Officers as a group (10 persons)	201,000	28.43	60,665	26.52	16.49

(1) Excluding shares issuable pursuant to the Underwriters over-allotment option.

(2) New Court Securities Corporation, one of the representatives of the Underwriters, acts as investment advisor to New Court Private Equity Fund, Inc. and Arrow Capital N.V. New Court Securities Corporation and an affiliate have direct beneficial interests in New Court Private Equity Fund, Inc. Mr. Francis X. Driscoll, a director of the Company, is a Senior Vice President of New Court Securities Corporation and of New Court Private Equity Fund, Inc. In addition, New Court Securities Corporation holds as agent $3,000 principal amount of the Company's Convertible Notes, convertible into 225 shares of Common Stock, for two individuals who are officers of New Court Securities Corporation and an affiliate thereof, respectively.

The directors and officers of the Company, as a group, own $528,800 principal amount of the Company's Convertible Notes, representing 19.44% of the Notes outstanding. These Notes are convertible into an aggregate of 39,665 shares of Common Stock.

Northwest Growth Fund, Inc., of which Mr. Robert F. Zicarelli, a director of the Company, is President, owns 30,000 shares of Common Stock and $250,000 principal amount of the Company's 8% Convertible Subordinated Notes, which are convertible into 18,754 shares of Common Stock. Fairchild Camera and Instrument Corporation, a supplier to the Company and of which Dr. Thomas A. Longo, a director of the Company, is Vice President and Chief Technical Officer, owns 51,603 shares of the Company's Common Stock (7.30%) and is entitled to purchase 23,397 additional shares at a price of $12.44 per share. (See *Management—Certain Transactions.*) It also holds a $150,000 8% Convertible Note of the Company, which is convertible into 11,252 shares of Common Stock.

The Company believes that Messrs. Cray, Mullaney, Hanson, Stone and Scott may be considered founders of the Company. The following table sets forth the amount and purchase price of securities of the Company held by each of them:

	Common Stock			8% Subordinated Notes Convertible at $13.33 Per Share	
	Shares	Price Per Share	Date of Purchase	Amount	Date of Purchase
Seymour R. Cray	75,000	$ 6.67	April to June 1972	$165,000	April and May 1975
Frank C. Mullaney	30,000	$ 6.67	April to June 1972	$100,000	April 1975
George S. Hanson	37,500	$ 6.67	April to June 1972	$ 50,000	April 1975
Noel T. Stone	30,000	$ 6.67	April to June 1972	—	—
Andrew Scott	7,500	$ 6.67	May and June 1972	$150,000	July and October 1975

DESCRIPTION OF COMMON STOCK

The Company's authorized capital consists of 5,000,000 shares of Common Stock, $1.00 par value. Holders of shares of Common Stock have one vote for each share. There is no cumulative voting, and, consequently, stockholders having more than 50% of the combined voting power are able to elect all of the directors of the Company. Stockholders are entitled to receive such dividends as may be declared from time to time by the Board of Directors out of funds legally available therefor and to share pro rata in any other distribution to stockholders. Stockholders have no preemptive or other rights to subscribe for additional shares, except as described below. Outstanding shares of Common Stock are, and those offered hereby will be upon their issuance, fully paid and nonassessable.

The Company furnishes its stockholders with unaudited quarterly statements of earnings and annual reports containing audited financial statements.

First Trust Company of Saint Paul is Transfer Agent and Registrar for the Common Stock. Manufacturers Hanover Trust Company, 4 New York Plaza, New York, N.Y. 10015 will act as agent for the Transfer Agent and Registrar in New York City.

The Company has outstanding options for the purchase of 52,350 shares of Common Stock. (See *Management—Qualified Stock Option Plans.*) In addition, the Company has outstanding $2,720,000 of Convertible Notes which may be converted into an aggregate of 204,033 shares of Common Stock at a price of $13.33 per share. Such conversion rights expire if the Notes are redeemed by the Company, which it may require after March 31, 1978, or if the conversion rights are not exercised by March 31, 1982, the date on which the Convertible Notes mature. The number of shares issuable upon exercise of the stock options and upon conversion of the Notes, and the purchase price per share, are subject to adjustment in certain events. (See *Introductory Statement—Dilution.*) The agreements relating to the Notes also contain restrictions on merger and on the sale of substantially all of the assets of the Company and other customary covenants and default provisions.

If the Company plans to issue additional shares of capital stock or any warrants, securities convertible into capital stock of the Company or other rights to subscribe for or to purchase any capital stock of the Company, and if after such issuance the Company would not be required to file reports pursuant to Section 13 of the Securities Exchange Act of 1934, stockholders holding shares of Common Stock prior to this offering would have prior rights to participate in the purchase proportionate to their interests in the outstanding stock of the Company. The Company anticipates that it will be required to file reports pursuant to Section 13 of the Securities Exchange Act of 1934 after the completion of the offering made by this Prospectus.

The holders of shares of Common Stock originally issued to the founders and private investors in the Company, or which may be issued upon the exercise of employee stock options, upon the conversion of the Company's Convertible Notes or to Fairchild Camera and Instrument Corporation, have rights, under certain circumstances, to require the Company to register their shares with the Securities and Exchange Commission or to include their shares in registrations of other shares which may be filed with the Commission by the Company. The expense of such registrations would be borne by the Company. The exercise of such registration rights could adversely affect the ability of the Company to raise capital through the sale of equity securities.

The stockholders of the Company have agreed not to offer for sale or sell their Common Stock for a period of six months after the date of this Prospectus without the prior written consent of the Representatives of the Underwriters. All of the directors and officers of the Company, who hold an aggregate 201,000 shares, have agreed not to offer for sale or sell their Common Stock without the prior written consent of the Representatives of the Underwriters or until after the Company has marketed three units of the CRAY-1 computer, at least one of which has been purchased, or has marketed four units of the CRAY-1 on a lease basis.

Increase in Authorized Stock; Stock Dividend

All shares and per share figures in this Prospectus give effect to the increase in authorized shares of the Company from 1,000,000 shares, $1.00 par value, to 5,000,000 shares, $1.00 par value and the 50% stock dividend authorized on December 17, 1975.

UNDERWRITING

The Underwriters named below have severally agreed to purchase the number of shares of Common Stock of the Company set opposite their respective names:

Underwriters	Number of Shares
C. E. Unterberg, Towbin Co.	
Piper, Jaffray & Hopwood Incorporated	
New Court Securities Corporation	
Total	600,000

The Purchase Agreement between the Company and the Underwriters provides that the obligations of the Underwriters are subject to certain conditions precedent and that the Underwriters will be obligated to purchase all shares offered if any are purchased.

The Company has been advised by C. E. Unterberg, Towbin Co., Piper, Jaffray & Hopwood Incorporated and New Court Securities Corporation as Representatives of the Underwriters that the Underwriters propose initially to offer the shares to the public at the public offering price set forth on the cover page; that the Underwriters may allow a concession to selected dealers who are members of the National Association of Securities Dealers, Inc., and to certain foreign dealers, of not exceeding $ per share; that the Underwriters may allow, and such dealers may reallow, to members of the National Association of Securities Dealers, Inc., and to certain foreign dealers, a concession of not exceeding $ per share; and that after the initial public offering, the public offering price and concessions may be changed.

If the Underwriters exercise their option referred to on the cover page of this Prospectus to purchase up to 60,000 additional shares to cover over-allotments, each of the Underwriters will have a firm commitment subject to certain conditions to purchase his pro rata portion of the additional shares purchased. The Underwriters may exercise the option only to cover over-allotments made in connection with the sale of the 600,000 shares. The over-allotment option will expire 30 days from the date of this Prospectus.

The shares are offered by the several Underwriters when, as and if accepted by the Underwriters and subject to their right to reject offers in whole or in part. It is expected that the shares will be ready for delivery in New York, N.Y. on or about , 1976.

The Company has agreed to indemnify the Underwriters against certain civil liabilities, including liabilities under the Securities Act of 1933 as amended.

The Underwriters do not intend to confirm sales to any accounts over which they exercise discretionary authority.

Mr. Francis X. Driscoll, a director of the Company, is a Senior Vice President of New Court Securities Corporation, one of the Representatives of the Underwriters.

A corporation and a fund for which New Court Securities Corporation acts as investment advisor own over 10% of the outstanding common stock of the Company. (See *Principal Holders of Securities.*) Since the corporation and the fund may be deemed to be affiliates of New Court Securities Corporation for purposes of the By-Laws of the National Association of Securities Dealers, Inc. ("NASD"), the Company may be deemed to be an affiliate of New Court Securities Corporation under such By-Laws. The NASD By-Laws permit a member of the NASD to underwrite or participate in the distribution of securities of an affiliate under certain conditions, including the requirement that the public offering price be no higher than that recommended by two "qualified independent underwriters." The public offering price is no higher than that recommended by C. E. Unterberg, Towbin Co. and Piper, Jaffray & Hopwood Incorporated, which are "qualified independent underwriters" as defined in such By-Laws.

PRICING OF THE OFFERING

There has been no prior market for the Common Stock of the Company. Consequently, the offering price has been determined by negotiation between the Company and the Representatives of the Underwriters. Among the factors considered in such negotiations were the prices paid by purchasers of securities of the Company since its formation, estimates of the business potential of the Company and the present state of the Company's development. The estimated offering price set forth on the cover page of this Preliminary Prospectus should not, however, be considered an indication of the actual value of the Company. Such price is subject to change as a result of market conditions and other factors.

LEGAL OPINIONS

The validity of the shares of Common Stock being offered hereby will be passed upon for the Company by Messrs. Doherty, Rumble & Butler, Minneapolis, Minnesota and for the Underwriters by Messrs. Faegre & Benson, Minneapolis, Minnesota. Andrew Scott, a Partner in the law firm of Doherty, Rumble & Butler, is a founder and director of the Company. (See *Principal Holders of Securities.*)

EXPERTS

The financial statements and schedules included herein and elsewhere in the Registration Statement have been included in reliance upon the reports of Peat, Marwick, Mitchell & Co., independent certified public accountants, and upon the authority of said firm as experts in accounting and auditing. The report of Peat, Marwick, Mitchell & Co., covering the December 31, 1975 financial statements is qualified with respect to the recoverability of inventories.

ADDITIONAL INFORMATION

The Company has filed with the Securities and Exchange Commission in Washington, D.C. a Registration Statement under the Securities Act of 1933 with respect to the shares of Common Stock offered by this Prospectus. For further information about the Company, reference is made to the Registration Statement and the exhibits thereto which may be inspected at the office of the Commission without charge and copies of which may be obtained from the Commission upon the payment of copying charges in accordance with its regular schedule therefor.

REPORT OF INDEPENDENT CERTIFIED PUBLIC ACCOUNTANTS

The Board of Directors
Cray Research, Inc.:

We have examined the balance sheet of Cray Research, Inc. as of December 31, 1975 and the related statements of operations, stockholders' equity and changes in financial position for the period from April 6, 1972 (date of organization) to December 31, 1975. Our examination was made in accordance with generally accepted auditing standards, and accordingly included such tests of the accounting records and such other auditing procedures as we considered necessary in the circumstances.

As more fully explained in note 1 to the financial statements, the Company is in the development stage and has not generated any sales or earnings from operations. The accompanying balance sheet includes inventories with a carrying value of $5,266,431. The recoverability of this inventory is dependent upon future events, including the ability of the Company to market the CRAY-1 computer and to raise needed capital. The outcome of these matters cannot be determined at this time.

In our opinion, subject to the effects, if any, on the financial statements of the matter discussed in the preceding paragraph, the aforementioned financial statements present fairly the financial position of Cray Research, Inc. at December 31, 1975 and the results of its operations and changes in its financial position for the period from April 6, 1972 to December 31, 1975, in conformity with generally accepted accounting principles consistently applied during the period after restatement for the changes, with which we concur, in the method of accounting for product development costs and in financial statement presentation made pursuant to Statements No. 2 and 7 of the Financial Accounting Standards Board, as described in note 2 to the financial statements.

PEAT, MARWICK, MITCHELL & CO.

Saint Paul, Minnesota
January 12, 1976

CRAY RESEARCH, INC.

Balance Sheet

December 31, 1975

ASSETS

Current assets:		
Cash and cash items:		
Demand deposits	$ 23,901	
Time deposits	515,000	$ 538,901
Accounts receivable		6,554
Inventories (note 3):		
Work-in-process	4,122,069	
Components and subassemblies	1,144,362	5,266,431
Prepaid expenses		32,934
Total current assets		5,844,820
Furniture, fixtures and equipment (note 4)	492,113	
Less accumulated depreciation and amortization	146,357	345,756
Deferred debt and organization expense	64,662	
Less accumulated amortization	12,296	52,366
		$6,242,942

LIABILITIES AND STOCKHOLDERS' EQUITY

Current liabilities:		
Accounts payable		$ 44,753
Accrued expenses:		
Property and other taxes	$ 20,790	
Other expenses	22,989	43,779
Total current liabilities		88,532
8% convertible subordinated notes (note 5)		2,720,000
Stockholders' equity:		
Common stock of $1 par value per share. Authorized 5,000,000 shares; issued 707,006 shares (notes 5, 7 and 8)	707,006	
Additional paid-in capital	5,156,681	
Deficit accumulated during the development stage	(2,429,277)	3,434,410
Lease commitment (note 9)		
		$6,242,942

See accompanying notes to financial statements.

CRAY RESEARCH, INC.

Statement of Stockholders' Equity

For the period from April 6, 1972 (date of organization) to December 31, 1975

	Common stock		Additional paid-in capital	Deficit accumulated during the development stage	Total stockholders' equity
	Shares	Amount			
Shares issued for cash:					
Pursuant to stock subscription agreements:					
Issued in 1972 at $6.67 per share	382,500	$382,500	$2,167,500	—	$2,550,000
Issued in 1974 at $10.00 per share, less stock issuance expenses of $33,280	267,503	267,503	2,374,242	—	2,641,745
Pursuant to exercise of employee stock options at $6.67 per share (note 8)					
Issued in 1973	1,500	1,500	8,500	—	10,000
Issued in 1974	750	750	4,250	—	5,000
Issued in 1975	3,150	3,150	17,850	—	21,000
Shares issued pursuant to purchase agreement with major supplier at $12.44 per share, less issuance expenses of $6,000 (note 7)	51,603	51,603	584,339	—	635,942
Deficit accumulated for the period from April 6, 1972 (date of organization) to December 31, 1975	—	—	—	$(2,429,277)	(2,429,277)
	707,006	$707,006	$5,156,681	$(2,429,277)	$3,434,410

See accompanying notes to financial statements.

CRAY RESEARCH, INC.
Statements of Changes in Financial Position

	April 6, 1972 (date of organization) to December 31, 1972	Year ended December 31, 1973	1974	1975	Cumulative to December 31, 1975
Sources of working capital:					
Proceeds from sale of common stock	$2,550,000	—	$2,675,025	—	$5,225,025
Proceeds from exercise of employee stock options (note 8)	—	$ 10,000	5,000	$ 21,000	36,000
Shares issued to major supplier (note 7)	—	—	—	641,942	641,942
Issuance of subordinated notes (note 5)	—	—	—	2,720,000	2,720,000
	$2,550,000	$ 10,000	$2,680,025	$3,382,942	$8,622,967
Uses of working capital:					
Net loss	$ 72,358	$ 526,735	$ 943,650	$ 886,534	$2,429,277
Items which do not use working capital:					
Depreciation and amortization of furniture, fixtures and equipment	(3,309)	(15,216)	(43,250)	(92,961)	(154,736)
Other amortization	(1,169)	(1,754)	(1,754)	(7,619)	(12,296)
Working capital used in operations	67,880	509,765	898,646	785,954	2,262,245
Stock issuance expenses	—	27,650	5,630	6,000	39,280
Additions to furniture, fixtures and equipment	98,238	64,433	244,951	92,870	500,492
Deferred debt and organization expense	8,770	—	2,000	53,892	64,662
Increase (decrease) in working capital	2,375,112	(591,848)	1,528,798	2,444,226	5,756,288
	$2,550,000	$ 10,000	2,680,025	3,382,942	$8,622,967
Changes in components of working capital:					
Increase (decrease) in current assets:					
Cash and time deposits	$2,101,222	$(609,639)	$(538,239)	$(414,443)	$ 538,901
Short-term commercial obligations	202,439	(152,439)	150,000	(200,000)	—
Accounts receivable	13,977	(485)	36,750	(43,688)	6,554
Inventories	59,201	249,025	1,961,087	2,997,118	5,266,431
Prepaid expenses	1,841	5,940	7,815	17,338	32,934
	2,378,680	(507,598)	1,617,413	2,356,325	5,844,820
Increase (decrease) in current liabilities:					
Accounts payable	1,943	51,753	92,270	(101,213)	44,753
Accrued expenses	1,625	32,497	(3,655)	13,312	43,779
	3,568	84,250	88,615	(87,901)	88,532
Increase (decrease) in working capital	$2,375,112	$(591,848)	$1,528,798	$2,444,226	$5,756,288

See accompanying notes to financial statements.

CRAY RESEARCH, INC.
Notes to Financial Statements

(1) Organization and Business

The Company was incorporated on April 6, 1972, in Delaware as a general business corporation. Since its formation, the Company has been engaged in the design, development and manufacture of a large scale scientific computer referred to under *The Company* and *Business* elsewhere in the Prospectus.

The Company is in the development stage and has had no sales or earnings to date and anticipates a substantial loss in 1976. The initial CRAY-1 computer has been constructed, is undergoing testing and is being used in connection with marketing efforts and software development. However, no orders have been received to date and there has been no on site user testing which would establish reliability or customer acceptability. Additionally, the ability of the Company to market the CRAY-1 computer is dependent upon the development of an efficient Fortran compiler. (See *Introductory Statement—Risk Factors.*)

It is not practicable, at this stage of the Company's development, to determine the recoverability of inventories. Such recoverability is dependent on future events, including the ability of the Company to market the CRAY-1 computer and to raise needed capital. The outcome of these matters cannot be determined at this time.

(2) Summary of Significant Accounting Policies

(a) Basis of Presentation

The accompanying financial statements have been prepared in accordance with Statement No. 7 of the Financial Accounting Standards Board entitled "Accounting and Reporting by Development Stage Enterprises". Accordingly, the financial statements are presented in conformity with generally accepted accounting principles applicable to operating enterprises. Previously, the Company followed the special financial reporting practices permitted for development stage enterprises. The financial statements included a statement of cash receipts and disbursements rather than statements of operations and changes in financial position.

(b) Inventories

Inventories are stated at cost, which approximates current replacement cost, not in excess of anticipated selling price less a profit margin. No adjustment is made, however, for the lower replacement cost of certain components resulting from volume orders.

(c) Product Development Costs

Statement No. 2 of the Financial Accounting Standards Board requires that product development costs be charged to expense as incurred. This statement became effective for fiscal periods beginning on or after January 1, 1975, and required restatement of prior period financial statements. The Company previously followed the practice of deferring such costs.

Accordingly, in the accompanying financial statements, costs not specifically applicable to components approved for inclusion in the initial computer are charged to expense in the year incurred as product development costs.

CRAY RESEARCH, INC.

Notes to Financial Statements, Continued

(2) Summary of Significant Accounting Policies, Continued

(d) Furniture, Fixtures and Equipment

Furniture, fixtures and equipment are carried at cost less accumulated depreciation.

Depreciation has been computed principally on the straight-line method; however, the double-declining balance method is used for certain machinery and equipment. The rates used are based on estimated useful lives of 3 to 8 years for machinery and equipment, and 8 years for office furniture and equipment. Costs of improvements to leased property are being amortized on the straight-line method over terms of the related lease.

Maintenance, repairs and minor renewals are charged to expense when incurred and betterments and major renewals are capitalized. Upon retirement or disposal of assets, cost and accumulated depreciation are eliminated from the asset and the allowance for depreciation accounts and the related gain or loss is credited or charged to income.

(e) Deferred Debt and Organization Expenses

Expenses related to issuance of the subordinated notes have been deferred and are being amortized over the term of the related debt. Costs incurred in connection with the organization of the Company have been deferred and are being amortized over 5 years.

(3) Inventories

Work-in-process consists principally of amounts related to production of the initial CRAY-1 computer. Costs incurred in connection with the second unit are included primarily in components and subassemblies. The Company has deferred further production work on the second unit.

The Company purchased certain components, peripheral equipment and substantially all assembly labor from two companies, officers of which are directors of the Company (including the major supplier referred to in note 7) and one principal stockholder. Such purchases aggregated approximately $95,000 in 1973, $920,000 in 1974 and $1,500,000 in 1975. (See *Management—Certain Transactions.*)

The initial CRAY-1 computer has been constructed, is undergoing testing and is being used in connection with software development (including development of Fortran compiler). Such software development costs are charged to expense as incurred.

(4) Furniture, Fixtures and Equipment

A summary of furniture, fixtures and equipment follows:

Machinery and equipment	$389,757
Office furniture and equipment	47,041
Leasehold improvements	55,315
	$492,113

CRAY RESEARCH, INC.

Notes to Financial Statements, Continued

(5) 8% Convertible Subordinated Notes

During 1975, the Company issued 8% subordinated notes which are convertible at any time into 204,033 shares of common stock at the rate of $13.33 per share. In the event of sale of common stock prior to June 30, 1977, at a price below $13.33 per share, the conversion price is reduced to such sales price (but not below $6.67). Subsequent to June 30, 1977, a sale at less than $13.33 per share will require adjustment of the conversion price in accordance with the agreement.

The Company may, at its option, redeem the notes in whole or in part, without premium, at any time after March 31, 1978. The notes are due on March 31, 1982.

(6) Tax Loss Carryforward

At December 31, 1975, the Company had unused operating loss carryforwards for Federal income tax purposes of approximately $560,000 of which $10,000 will expire if not used before 1979 and $550,000 in 1980. The deficit accumulated during the development stage includes $1,826,625 of product development costs which the Company has deferred for tax purposes and $44,300 of life insurance premiums which are not deductible for tax purposes.

The Company also has unused investment tax credits of approximately $25,000 at December 31, 1975, which are available as credits against future Federal income taxes.

(7) Common Stock

(a) Stock Dividend

On December 17, 1975, the stockholders of the Company adopted an amendment to the articles of incorporation increasing the authorized common stock from 1,000,000 shares to 5,000,000 shares with the par value remaining at $1.00 per share. Concurrently, the Board of Directors approved a stock split effected in the form of a stock dividend by issuance of an additional one share of stock for each two shares held, payable January 19, 1976. To account for these changes, the common stock account was increased by a transfer of $235,669 from additional paid-in capital. All share and per share figures in the accompanying financial statements have been retroactively adjusted to give effect to such changes.

(b) Purchase Agreement

In January 1975, the Company entered into an agreement with a major supplier whereby the Company will purchase memory circuits required for the computer at a contract price of $1,866,000. The agreement provides for 50% of the contract price ($933,000) to be paid in cash and the remaining 50% to be paid by the issuance of 75,000 shares of common stock valued at $12.44 per share. If the agreement is cancelled with cause by the supplier or without cause by the Company, the supplier has an option to purchase, for $12.44 per share, any shares not previously delivered under the agreement up to a maximum of 75,000 shares in total. This option is exercisable within 90 days of the effective date of cancellation.

CRAY RESEARCH, INC.

Notes to Financial Statements, Continued

(8) Stock Options and Other Reservations of Common Stock

At December 31, 1975, 60,600 shares of authorized but unissued common stock are reserved for issuance under stock option plans at not less than the fair market value at dates granted. Option shares granted become exercisable over a period of four years and must be fully exercised within five years from date of grant. (See *Management—Qualified Stock Option Plans.*)

A summary of transactions under the stock option plans follows:

	1972	1973	1974	1975
Options granted:				
Number of shares	36,000	—	6,000	15,750
Option price per share (a)	$ 6.67	—	$ 10.00	$ 12.44
Aggregate option price	$240,000	—	$ 60,000	$195,930
Options which became exercisable:				
Number of shares	—	9,000	9,000	10,500
Option price per share (a)	—	$ 6.67	$ 6.67	$ 6.67 to $10.00
Aggregate option price	—	$ 60,000	$ 60,000	$ 75,000
Options exercised:				
Number of shares	—	1,500	750	3,150
Option price per share (a)	—	$ 6.67	$ 6.67	$ 6.67
Aggregate option price	—	$ 10,000	$ 5,000	$ 21,000
Unexercised options at end of year:				
Number of shares	36,000	34,500	39,750	52,350
Option price per share (a)	$ 6.67	$ 6.67	$ 6.67 to $10.00	$ 6.67 to $12.44
Aggregate option price	$240,000	$230,000	$285,000	$459,930
Shares reserved for additional options which may be granted	—	—	24,000	8,250

(a) Estimated fair value on date granted.

Of the unexercised options at December 31, 1975, options for 23,100 shares were exercisable and the balance will become exercisable at various dates through 1980. Upon exercise of options, the proceeds are credited to common stock and additional paid-in capital and no charges are made to operations.

Additional shares of unissued common stock were reserved at December 31, 1975, as follows:

	Number of shares reserved
Conversion of 8% subordinated notes into shares of common stock at an initial conversion price of $13.33 per share (conversion price is subject to adjustment in certain cases—see note 5)	204,033
Shares unissued in connection with stock purchase agreement with major supplier at $12.44 per share	23,397
	227,430

CRAY RESEARCH, INC.

Notes to Financial Statements, Continued

(9) Lease Commitment

The Company leases certain office space and manufacturing facilities under a five year lease arrangement with its President. The annual rental under terms of the lease expiring in 1977, excluding taxes, insurance and maintenance costs payable by the Company, is $20,900. The Company has an option to renew the lease for an additional five years at the same rental.

(10) Credit Arrangement

The Company has a discretionary credit arrangement to borrow, with interest at 3% in excess of the then prime rate, up to an aggregate of $1,100,000 from a bank. No funds have been borrowed under this arrangement. Any borrowing by the Company pursuant to this arrangement is expected to be secured by inventories and accounts receivable and it is not anticipated that any compensating balances will be required.

Printed circuit board module with integrated circuits installed.

Integrated circuits used in the CRAY-1 computer.

CRAY-1 computer shown with installed banks of printed circuit board modules.

Section of the CRAY-1 computer showing installation of printed circuit board modules.

Data station (equipment not manufactured by the Company) used in the operation of the CRAY-1.

No dealer, salesman or other person has been authorized in connection with this offering to give any information or to make any representations not contained in this Prospectus and, if given or made, such information or representations must not be relied upon as having been authorized by the Company or any Underwriter. This Prospectus does not constitute an offer or solicitation by anyone in any State in which such offer or solicitation is not authorized or in which the person making such offer or solicitation is not qualified to do so, or to any person to whom it is unlawful to make such offer or solicitation. Neither the delivery of this Prospectus nor any sales made hereunder shall, under any circumstances, create any implication that there has been no change in the affairs of the Company since the date of this Prospectus.

TABLE OF CONTENTS

Until , 1976 (90 days after the date of this Prospectus), all dealers effecting transactions in the registered securities, whether or not participating in this distribution, may be required to deliver a Prospectus. This is in addition to the obligation of dealers to deliver a Prospectus when acting as Underwriters and with respect to their unsold allotments or subscriptions.

600,000 SHARES

COMMON STOCK
($1.00 Par Value)

PROSPECTUS

C. E. UNTERBERG, TOWBIN CO.

PIPER, JAFFRAY & HOPWOOD
INCORPORATED

NEW COURT SECURITIES CORPORATION

MORGAN SHOE MANUFACTURING COMPANY

I was in Fond du Lac, Wisconsin, in the office of Jon Morgan, the founder and President of the Morgan Shoe Company, a manufacturer of girls' shoes.

"Yes, the company has grown," Morgan said. "When we opened for business in 1965 we had a potential capacity of 450 pairs per day. Now, we're trying for 6,000 pairs per day, and we'll do it."

"You might be interested in our sales figures," he said, reaching into a large file cabinet. "Here they are."

Morgan Shoe Manufacturing Company

Year	*$ Sales Millions*
1968	1.7
1969	1.9
1970	2.4
1971	3.1
1972	3.5
1973	4.0
1974	4.7
1975	5.6
1976	7.2
1977	7.6

Morgan's compounded rate of growth over this nine-year period was 18.1%. This success contrasts with the fate of the U.S. shoe industry in general (see *Exhibit 1*), and in Wisconsin in particular (*Exhibit 2*). The shoe industry has been hit severely by imports, as *Exhibit 1* illustrates, and by inflation. For example, *Exhibit 2* shows how hide and leather prices and wages have moved since 1966. Part of the movement of leather prices appears to be explained by a shortage of hides caused by disruptions to the flow of Argentine hides to the U.S. (*Exhibit 3*).

I asked Mr. Morgan how he had been able to grow in what many people think is a declining industry. He replied,

"Our goal is not to increase volume for its own sake. You see, we don't produce all the shoes we could sell. We use the most advanced technology in this country in the production of our shoes. For example, we had one of the first successful lasting-room conveyors in the U.S., and Morgan was one of the first companies to develop an in-house capacity to manufacture molded unit soles."

I interrupted, "Then you're production-oriented . . . ."

"I wouldn't say we are a production-oriented company," Mr. Morgan replied, "Our strength lies in marketing."

"But Jon," I challenged, "if you're a marketing company, why don't you get out and chase volume?"

He continued: "We pick our customers; we don't sell to the giant retailers, for example. We see ourselves as being suppliers to the small chains who have to compete with the giants. Contrary to the practice of most unbranded shoe manufacturers,[1] we don't have just 25 customers for our product, we have 200. In spite of this, we have no sales staff in the normal sense, although we all go out on the road and sell for a couple of weeks a year. We have only one full-time salesman. He is in California—he handles west of the Rockies—that's just too far from Fond du Lac.

"Many of our customers ask for more than we can supply and they would really like to be able to reorder our good sellers—but we have no inventory. We pride ourselves on the fashionable product we offer our customers, and we give them good value for the price.

Providing them with a stylish image is really our business. Why, we start thinking of styles in April, and we're ready for the National Shoe Fair with samples on June 5. Those shoes are in production in October for the Christmas season. That's one of the fastest design-to-production cycles in the business, where unit soles are used."

"Jon, I'm confused," I persisted. "You say you're a marketing company but you talk production. You say you're marketing but you have no salesforce. . . . I think you had better explain how Morgan was founded and how it has grown to be a $7.6 million company."

A HISTORY OF THE COMPANY

Early Days at Pierpont

"You've got to be crazy." Jon Morgan describes his friends' perception of his decision to join his father and his two uncles at Pierpont Shoe in Chicago, IL, after he graduated from the Stanford Business School in 1964. He explained, "I was never at the top of the class at school, and the shoe industry was depressed. But, I had worked at Pierpont in the women's shoe manufacturing business all my life. I thought I could do a little better with shoes than with IBM or something like that. . . . The competition looked attractive in those days.

"Pierpont made low-grade women's shoes. They didn't sell to the big stores or chains because they couldn't; their shoes weren't good enough. But the company had made money over the years and my father and uncles had a nice income.

"One of the things I wanted to do was to get them to sit down and talk about what they were going to do in the future. I felt that the tax and labor situation meant Illinois was becoming a difficult place to make shoes and they agreed. Since I had set up a little factory in Fort Wayne before I went to business school, my job as assistant superintendent of the plant, with a sales territory, was expanded. I began a search for new plant locations. The idea was that Pierpont would set up a factory elsewhere, then move the business out of Illinois.

"I came up with three really good possibilities in towns eager for new industry. However, in every instance the family turned it down. And then the reasons dawned on me: my uncles, and my father too, just didn't want to move from Chicago. Their children were grown and not involved in the business, and, at that time in their lives, they didn't

[1]An unbranded shoe manufacturer makes private brand shoes for retailers.

view expansion as critical. I could already see that they and Pierpont and I were going to die in Chicago. I didn't see that in my future. So I founded Morgan.''

Pierpont Fathers Morgan: Relationships Help

''In many ways the founding and growth of Morgan was due to a series of lucky events. Of course, our relationship with Pierpont was close and that closeness turned out to be very important, but Morgan was totally separate from Pierpont. Pierpont's reputation with suppliers in the industry seemed to carry over to Morgan, and the contacts I had gained while at Pierpont helped.

''For instance, I knew Myron Segal through my sales for Pierpont in New York. Myron was a gentleman, one of my uncle's old cronies. He was what we called a 'Brooklyn partner'—you have six people who are partners in a factory in Brooklyn, and on Monday you wondered who the partners were because somebody would have gone on Friday and they'd pick up a new one on Monday—kind of a revolving door partnership. Anyway, Myron was in the children's shoe business—he made girls' and boys' shoes—and I used his office in New York City whenever I went down there on a selling trip. Finally he sold the business.

''So, Myron was kicking around, when I got the idea to step out of Pierpont. Myron said he'd join us and he brought along maybe ten accounts, all large discount chains. I knew we could make misses' shoes for Pierpont cheaper than direct cost there in Chicago, because they were making them in a women's factory which is as inefficient as hell. They needed additional misses' shoes, and with Myron's help I thought we could market children's shoes on our own.[2]

''I talked to my uncles about the idea. They thought it was good; so we got $25,000 together from various relatives, $5,000 there, $1,000 here, and I went to Fond du Lac, Wisconsin, to set up a business.

''It's interesting how we actually got into the girls' business. We had agreed not to compete with Pierpont. We knew that although there were many price points in the girls' market, there were two fundamental concepts for designing the shoes. For example, if Pierpont had a women's style and wanted a misses' to go with it, we would make a misses' shoe to match it. The alternative would be to make a misses' shoe predicated off our children's shoe. We found that if we offered Pierpont the misses' styles we had copied from our children's lines, they did not sell. In fact, they couldn't sell them because it was out of their price point. We were making those shoes almost as good as our own, but their customers, although they knew the source was Morgan, couldn't accept the fact that they were so good—after all, they 'came from Pierpont.' Reputations are hard to beat in the shoe industry.

''Nonetheless, I felt Morgan could sell them and we did, once we had Pierpont's permission. We sold that better grade of shoe and they sold the lower-priced grade right until the end. They liquidated Pierpont finally in late 1970 and that freed us to operate independently in our markets. We dropped the lower grade shoe.

'Well, to get back to the founding of Morgan, Fond du Lac was one of the towns I had visited in my search for Pierpont's new plant. It was an old shoe town and there was

[2]Children's shoes are sizes 8½ to 12; misses' sizes are 12½ to 4.

experienced labor available there—unemployment was over 10%. You could rent space for less than 40 cents per square foot and lease most of the machinery and equipment you needed; so there was only a small capital investment required for fixed assets. And, at that particular time, everything was stocked here in Fond du Lac. Suppliers would come in every week with thread and leather— it was like going to a supermarket. You had to carry only a few days inventory. The advantages of Fond du Lac were just incredible for someone without any money.

"I had asked my father if I could take one man with me, Brian Hawkins, who is now Vice President of Manufacturing. My father recognized the handwriting on the wall down there in Chicago—Dad was pretty smart—and he said he would be only too happy to have him come. Brian said yes.

"We worked together, we were our own foremen and did everything on a shoe string, but it was exciting. Brian and I are both engineers, and we're really on the same wavelength. For example, when Brian and I are talking about something, we don't need to finish a sentence. Nobody else can understand, but he and I do.

"Although Morgan was totally separate from Pierpont, being linked with Pierpont in people's minds really helped us. Suppliers would ship to us on regular terms. Normally, if you were starting out in the shoe industry, you'd have to pay cash. But those suppliers were probably right: if we'd gone bust, knowing my uncles, they might have paid the bills—they had that kind of reputation in the industry. But they might have bounced me out of the family.

"Leather suppliers treated us like Pierpont, too. About 25% of your costs are leather, and it's still a negotiated item. Leather prices fluctuate [*Exhibit 2*] but you could buy the same material for 50¢ or 60¢ depending on your negotiating strength. Pierpont bought a lot of leather, and, being in the business for a long time, they bought it well. Back in those days, price was probably the most important part of the leather business. It isn't as important today because of fashion. We bought at Pierpont prices. Pierpont at that time was about a $5-million company; we had started with $25,000 capital and 50 employees and were able to buy at their prices."

"Was that the only capital you had?" I asked.

"No, we had debt capital," Mr. Morgan replied, "although we no longer rely on debt to the same extent we had to in the beginning. It was another piece of luck.

"I went to one of our local banks to see about a loan, when we were starting out, and I came out with $200,000 worth of the state's money. I had no idea that this would happen, although our banker later told me what had happened.

"The bank was not growing, and it was trying to figure out how to make more industrial loans. The biggest manufacturing industries in Wisconsin are well known, but many of them raise their capital in the large financial centers. The shoe industry, though, was a small industry, with many individually-owned companies. The bank realized they had no customers in the shoe industry. On Tuesday at its board meeting, the bank decided it was going out after the shoe business. I walked into this guy's office on Wednesday. That's luckier than smart. He bent over backwards for us, whereas a week earlier he might have thrown us out."

"But it can't have been that simple or Morgan must be a very lucky company," I commented.

Jon Morgan continued, "I took out credit insurance before I even went to the bank to prove to them that Morgan was not as risky as it looked at first glance. My plan was, I told them, not to make anything unless we had an order. If we make it it's sold, and once it's shipped we've got credit insurance that the buyer will pay. 'Besides,' I said, 'our loan needs will be seasonal, so Morgan's not as risky as it appears.' ''

''Then, Jon, your plan was built on your choice of a particular market.''

''That's right,'' Morgan said.

WHAT IS MORGAN'S MARKET?

''It all goes back to marketing. We picked out a segment of the market: female footwear, girls only. None of our competitors or even those on the fringe of our business make only girls' footwear. They either make girls' and boys', or they are big conglomerates who make everything. We view ourselves as carrying a full line of shoes for the retailer in our segment of the market. We do our homework, and the shoes we put together are the right ones for the chain store in that specific part of the market. We all do it as a group—Brian Hawkins, our Manufacturing VP, is an important member of that group—we have no outside designers. You see, when we offer our shoes for sale, we're also providing a service; we are saying, 'This is what we think is going to happen in girls' shoes.' We do our homework, and we'd better not be wrong twice in a row or we're going to find ourselves in trouble.

''But I'm jumping ahead and talking about today. In the beginning we made misses' shoes for Pierpont while we went after a different market—a better-grade market. We got some initial orders from Myron and from the people I knew, my father's and uncles' customers. We made misses' shoes for Pierpont and smaller girls' shoes for ourselves. We sold to Pierpont at prices with sales expense thrown out, so our shoes and Pierpont's carried equal costs. The first season, of course, a customer might order a couple of cases to see what the shoes were like, if you have a reputation like the one we carried over from Myron and Pierpont. Luckily, the shoes, I guess, were alright. Customers reorder only if they're good.

''Before our second season, U.S. Shoe bought the Freeman Shoe Company, which made men's shoes, and the H.O. Toor Company, which made children's shoes, and decided to merge them and make men's shoes in the H.O. Toor factories. Anyway, after one season, our customers knew our shoes were pretty good when all of a sudden one of their major sources of children's shoes disappeared. Toor's demise gave us a big boost in volume.''

I said, ''Jon, I understand why you made misses' shoes: Pierpont was an outlet for you, they needed shoes and they had a market. But why did you go into little girls' shoes?

''Well, although we're technically oriented, it was a marketing decision. We had some technical resources and they matched the needs of the children's markets. Let me explain.

''Inexpensive rubber and leather shoes get holes in them when they wear. A kid will go through a conventional bottom in two months, where it will take you two years. However, PVC, or vinyl, is perfect for kids' shoes because every three months they're in another size, and a PVC sole will wear longer than that. It had a natural place in children's shoes.

"The better-wearing rubber soles were too expensive, and I believed that the children's shoe market was more price-conscious than the adult market: people know that kids are going to grow out of their shoes.

"From our viewpoint, though, the manufacturing process is the same to make a children's shoe as to make a woman's shoe. Material content is different, but material at most is only 45% of the cost of the shoe. Mothers have always felt that the final prices for children's and misses' shoes should be significantly lower than women's, but labor and overhead costs don't change much."

"Hence your 'quality for the price' policy?"

"In part, yes." Morgan continued, "We went into the children's market because we saw there was an opportunity for a cost effective producer there. We felt that molded unit soles would enable us to compete on a cost basis and that molded PVC soles would be most readily accepted in the children's market.

"What about market resistance to PVC unit soles?" I asked.

Morgan replied, "There was buyer resistance to nonrubber soles, since people were used to the rubber unit soles which preceded the plastic. One of the big things that helped us over this was the fact that Sears got involved with Genesco, giving PVC unit soles heavy promotional support and guaranteeing that the bottom would outwear the upper. That was a big thing. People expected the sole of the shoe to wear out. The problem with PVC-soled shoes was that mothers got mad when the uppers wore out—they figured the shoes were not good quality. Sears's promotions really helped change this perception."

"Then, Jon, you were cost conscious so that you could be price competitive in your markets."

"The interdependence of price and buyers' perceptions of the relative quality of shoes which incorporate PVC has always been important in our markets," Jon explained. "The markets which we served at that time were basically the big self-service discounters. Ninety percent of the business was in leased departments (for example, in a store like Zayre's the shoe departments were leased to a chain operator) and 70% of this type of chain was headquartered in Chicago, which was an easy market for us to reach. PVC was acceptable in those markets, while it was not acceptable in the Stride Rite market segment where buyers felt that leather soles were better. However, Morgan was also selling to some of the small, service-oriented regional shoe chains, many with stores in malls. We were probably supplying their lowest-priced girls' shoes since they carried a higher-priced shoe as well.

INNOVATION

"We had two things going for us. One, our experiences at Pierpont influenced our adoption of the molded sole. Pierpont was one of the initiators of that technology, so, although it was a new process, Brian and I knew an awful lot about it. Two, we had a close contact in the up-and-coming injection molding department of United Shoe Machinery, who kept us abreast of developments in this field. Most of our competitors were stitch-down manufacturers like Myron had been, and we just felt that molded unit soles were the wave of the future and could give us a competitive cost advantage.

''Anyhow, the Mears Division of USM wanted to get into the PVC sole business, and it wanted to find out if this process was economically feasible. Mears wanted to get some molds working. It might as well make them for us, right? So that got us started.

''We realized what the cost savings could be if we used unit soles. We had lasting-room conveyor lines from the beginning, and we were probably one of the first to do that in the US. Anyway, for small people trying to do what we were doing, we thought unit soles really offered flexibility. The machinery people were trying to push direct sole-attaching, rather than unit soles, in those days, saying that the unit soles were more expensive. But direct attaching involves other operations during production.

''In our cost comparisons we found that additional handling costs in direct sole-attaching almost wiped out the cost savings you got by eliminating the cementing and sole-laying operations which are necessary in unit sole usage. And the continuous switching and resetting of injection molds needed in direct sole-attaching seemed inefficient to us. In a small plant, unit soles were the attractive technology.''

''Jon, I'm sorry to interrupt but could you explain that for me?'' I asked.

''We thought the direct attaching method was for the big companies. The flexibility of the unit sole made it suitable for small people, especially for a small company which had a lasting-room conveyor running 1200 pairs of shoes per shift, with 18 sizes necessary to fill an order. If you use unit soles, as the shoes come down the conveyor you can just take one of those unit soles out of the box and slap it on. But if you are direct attaching—at that time we had a machine with 12 stations (that's six sizes)—it means you're only going to have six sizes on the machine. As those shoes come through you have to take them off the machine and then change the mold and make another six sizes—you have to do that three times to get a full size run of shoes. For small companies trying to do what we were doing, we thought unit soles were more flexible.

''Well, there were no machines to make unit soles in those days; so we had to buy some machines and jury-rig them to do the job. Oddly enough, although we had learned a lot about what to look for from USM, and although USM was trying to sell us their machinery, we ended up buying a Desma Machine. It's considered the Cadillac of the industry—you can't wear it out. We made a big capital investment at that time, $75,000. Only big companies like Genesco and Interco had the money to adopt this technology then. Small companies were the ones we really competed with and they didn't put their money into new technology.

''So, we made our own unit soles, and we started to enjoy a price advantage over our competitors. What happened later was that non-shoe manufacturers started making unit soles, companies like Compo Industries, the big rubber companies like Goodyear—people with money. I've always said that we are really in the sole business but we make a shoe to make a profit on the sole. In other words, we don't make a double profit, as a sole manufacturer and a shoe manufacturer each would.''

''Jon, you said earlier that the shoe industry had not been particularly innovative in the years before you founded Morgan; yet you went into the market with a new material and innovative manufacturing technology in an old shoe town. You never had any trouble. Why?''

''We've never had the operator resistance to new technology that many companies have had in the older shoe plants, probably because of the way we dealt with the issue from the beginning. I had a background in the shoe industry, and I'd seen the effects of negativism towards new ideas. We didn't want just anyone working in this business; we wanted only people who were naturally open-minded.

''We had them try out with the lasting-room conveyor when we first started. We put an ad in the paper saying, 'Assemblers, tryouts at Morgan Shoe, 8:00 A.M., Monday; Side Lasters, tryouts, 9:00 A.M., Monday. . . .'

''People came and they tried out. I'll never forget one fellow came in, looked at the conveyor and said, 'That will never work,' I said, 'Fine, forget it.' 'Aren't you going to give me a chance to try out?' 'No, forget it,' I said. 'If you think that's not going to work, we don't want you.'

''Right from that point that's the way we did it; so we ended up getting a different class of workers from the usual. Fond du Lac was a women's shoe town and people were used to working like hell for nine months then getting furloughed for the rest of the year—the women employees liked that arrangement. It was a real change when they discovered they were expected to work for 50 weeks a year at Morgan. We have about 100% turnover, with most of the turnover in the least skilled jobs, and we have a terrible time getting people for the third shift which we need to run some of our machines. But none of that is unusual in this industry. We probably end up training most of our people, but those we train become believers in modern shoe technology.''

''Jon, what kinds of compensation systems do you have?'' I asked. ''I've heard it said that a company best expresses its priorities through its compensation system.''

''Our pay schedule is different from what I think the industry norm is. Many of our operators are on piece work like the rest of the industry, but in our lasting room we have a group incentive program, not individual piece work. For our foremen, supervisors, and executives we have a corporate bonus system which distributes a very significant part of our corporate profits to them as a group in both cash and retirement benefits.''

A CHANGE IN THE ENVIRONMENT: OPPORTUNITY AND DECISIONS

''A turning point for our company was a crisis for a lot of small shoe manufacturers,'' Morgan continued. ''The leather market took a tremendous jump in 1966 [see *Exhibit 2*]. That was the time when everybody started thinking of synthetic uppers. At this time 75% of our customers were in the self-service discount business we spoke about, and they all advised us to go with the synthetic uppers so that we could survive. They said that they would not be able to buy from us if we stuck with leather uppers because we would be out of their price point.

''It was at this time that we recognized that we were already in another market, the small chain store market. We already had a foot in the door. We decided to go with our quality product. We knew that if we were to keep producing shoes with vinyl bottoms and leather uppers, we would have to almost completely change our target market from the self-service discount chains to the small regional chains—from rack retailers to box chains.

''Within two years, we had gotten almost completely out of the self-service business and completely into the chains. You see, the small regional chains were faced with the same problem that we had. They were selling a better grade shoe than ours, and we were probably their bottom-priced line, but the companies making shoes with leather uppers and soles just priced themselves right out of the market. The small chains had to rely more heavily on us because, at the same time, most of our former direct competitors went to vinyl uppers. We were the only ones left to fill the market in the price gap that had opened.

"We were the only ones who had the vinyl unit soles with leather uppers and, while our prices went up slightly, higher priced branded and private-labelled shoes became much more expensive. Our former direct competitors held their old price point only by really cutting quality. An all-vinyl shoe is perceived as a totally different product to a leather-upper shoe: it has no mystique. The result of the change was that Morgan was about the only company in the middle-priced girls' shoe market.

"We felt safe in relying on the small chain store market. We did some market research, and we saw there was an opportunity for us to move away from the rack jobber. We spent $5,000 for that research. We went to our retail customers and they agreed to give us the names of their store managers so that we could get a grass-roots feel for the needs of the market and the sizes of the different segments. This kind of research was unusual at that time in the shoe industry, especially among smaller companies. The research indicated that our expectations were well-founded."

ANOTHER MARKETING DECISION

"In 1972, we saw something that again surprised us. We were looking at the sales figures for a mall in Akron. This mall had a large independent store and a Sears as its anchors, and three family shoe stores which were owned by national chains. We figured what each did in children's shoes; the average family shoe store does about 10 to 11% of its business in children's shoes. We estimated the children's shoe business in that mall at about $150,000 a year, except for one store which was exclusively devoted to high-grade children's shoes. Its volume alone was $250,000. The specialty store did more business than the other five all together. 'Whoa!' I thought to myself, 'The potential of specialists for us is incredible.'

"Until that time, we had felt that someone had to have 10 to 15 stores to buy from us; in other words, they had to order 180 pairs of one shoe for us to make it for them. Now we believed a children's specialist with 5 stores might be able to buy our shoes. We had never gone out after that business, and they didn't look for us because many of these chains regularly attended only regional shows, while we only went to the national shoe fairs. Furthermore, most of them sold branded shoes: they had never gone out looking for unbranded shoes. Nonetheless, we recognized that the business opportunity was there, and we started going out after it, identifying the chains, contacting their principals or buyers by mail, explaining our product line, and inviting them to visit us at the shoe fair. Luckily for us, the fair had just switched to open booth exhibits—it used to be separate hotel rooms—and they could check us out with little extra effort. It really helped. Because leather prices were rising rapidly, the major children's manufacturers were raising their prices, which meant that these people needed our grade of shoes.

"We don't have full-time salesmen, except for the person in California. The rest of our sales effort is done out of Fond du Lac. Each seller has another job—the fellow who buys the materials, the fellow who buys the leather, the pattern man, the mold design man, are also on the road selling. I sell. We all have small territories, so we're not gone very often, or for very long. We call on only 25 customers, but we sell about 200. Most unbranded manufacturers have only 25 accounts and those big companies keep them in business. We want to avoid that kind of dependency, so we sell to 200 smaller retailers. Generally, our customers see us at the national shoe fair or they don't buy from us at all. A few come up to see us, but that is probably only because they're spending a weekend in Wisconsin anyhow.

"Because we don't have a travelling sales force, our basic philosophy has been that we have to make the shoes so right that they have to buy. Again, being an unbranded shoe manufacturer, we do not have a controlled distribution system: either you control distribution or you make the product so attractive that they have to buy it. We've always taken the position that we're not going to make enough shoes for all our potential customers. To date, we have always had a backlog of customers who want to buy. This allows us to select our customers. That way we're controlling our rate of growth so that we maintain an economically sound operating capacity.

"Morgan's growth is also governed by what I feel we can do with our manpower. Technically, we're different from the average shoe company: we have people who want to try new things, people who get excited about new things. It takes a while for them to get experience so that they can be promoted and we can bring in somebody else to replace them without losing that sense of excitement. We prefer to promote from within, although in specific instances we have hired outside."

"Is technology the key to your success then?" I asked.

"No, while we are advanced technically, I'd say marketing is the key to our success. We picked a segment of the market, female footwear, focused exclusively on girls, because of my early experience with Pierpont and our association with it. 'Quality for price' is our motto. We try to offer a full line of girls' shoes, as we perceive it. We have never made the full range of children's shoes, both boys' and girls'. We've made only girls'.

"None of our competitors exactly duplicates our offerings. We have a niche of our own. We recognize that for the small retailer, with five, ten or fifteen stores, kids are only 10% of his business and more than half of that is boys. They're tougher on shoes. We give him three choices of any one type of girls' shoe, say a party shoe, he picks one, and his buying is simplified. It's worth his taking time to buy women's shoes but not girls'. That is the service component of our marketing effort.

"With eighteen sizes in girls' shoes, retailers have to carry a shallow line; with low unit volume they just can't carry many styles in their inventory. The idea is that if we can capture the look, we're all right, even if we're not exact, because kids are not as discerning as adults. A kid can't tell that our molded vinyl sole is not Malaysian crepe, but a twenty-four-year-old woman can. So we try to imitate all the important fashion trends with the construction processes that we have mastered. You can do that in girls', but I guarantee that you can't do it in women's.

"We can provide the look girls want very quickly compared with the rest of the industry. For instance, we go out to all the big cities in North America and Europe in early April and come back April 15 with our ideas on the shoes that will be big. For the rest of April and May we put these shoes together, adapting the styles to our technology to get the look. And on June 5 we're ready with samples for the National Shoe Fair. The skill with our technology, of course, is to minimize the number of bottoms and lasts while varying the number of styles.

"We test, mostly when we're getting into a new program. When you design, though, you try to work off a standard back part of the last. If you keep the same back part of the last the fit remains the same, and your customers get used to your fit. You can change looks a lot with different fronts, different foreparts. This is fine unless you are after a different market segment.

"For example, we've introduced ethnic programs to make shoes for the downtown Baltimore and Washington markets and for the Hispanic markets in Florida and on the West Coast. These kids use more shoes than the suburban customer, black or white. And in terms of styles, it's a much faster market. We had to be very careful to change the fit of these shoes from our standard lasts.

"Fashion is important to our customers. Girls follow teenagers, so we're chasing teenagers, and teenagers are the most difficult customers in the world. Teenagers are fickle. We offer more fashion to our customers than Stride Rite or Buster Brown, and that's our pitch to the retailers. 'Buy your staple shoes from Stride Rite and Buster Brown, the Mama and Papa shoes, but buy your promotional shoes from us.'

"We carry no inventory. Our customers, of course, want our prices and styling, but they also want us to carry an inventory. They ask us why we can't give them what Stride Rite does in terms of inventory availability. But Stride Rite's doing an enormous volume. We can't be like them. We tell our customers that since we're serving the fashion segment of their business, 'Don't worry about reorder! Sell 'em at Back-to-School and bring in new styles at Christmas!"

THE TECHNOLOGY—MARKETING MIX: THE MARKETING IMPERATIVE

"A little while ago, Jon, you said, 'You can't imitate "looks" in young women's shoes; you must be authentic, particularly in better-grade shoes.' That was the reason you gave for not going into the women's business. Doesn't that mean that you really are a technology company? You're constrained by your technology."

"That's probably true of every company in the shoe industry," Morgan countered. "Each company has strengths and skills that make it distinctive. Because we're small and informally organized, our technology doesn't dictate what we adopt, though. It forces us to do a lot of work for a big look that we have to get. Take athletic shoes, for example. The kids are buying them. How can we make them in molded unit shoes? We have to figure out how to do it to provide the customer service we have committed ourselves to providing. We've said 'We are going to offer you whatever you need in girls' shoes.' That's what we must do.

"So, as an example of our attitude to technology, we are not experimenting with urethanes just because they've got a better wear. That's not important to what we're trying to do, since kids grow out of their shoes so fast. We are experimenting with urethanes based on the fact that there might be something coming in the market that only urethanes can provide. We'd better be ready to make it for the kids if it becomes necessary.

"We're not hampered now by a lack of capital in our adoption of technology. This company is financially one of the more successful in the industry. Based on what we view as our customer service needs, we purchase just about all our machines. We borrow at the prime rate from the local bank and, usually, that gives us a better return than a lease. We have a good cash flow from our own operations. We depreciate everything as rapidly as we possibly can, and we take advantage of the investment tax credits available.

"If we don't see a need for a new technology in our product, if it won't make it better, if it's not automatically a high-yield product, if it's not economically sound, we won't adopt it."

"Jon, one more question: has Morgan been affected by imports?"

"Yes. We have to be sharper because of imports. And the trends show that it's going to get tougher in the children's markets."

Exhibits 4 and 5 show just how far imports have intruded into the U.S. market. *Exhibit 6* shows how quickly the foreign manufacturers are moving up through the price segments. *Exhibits 7 and 8* show how the imported shoes are rising in price under the pressure of inflation in the exporting countries themselves, even as American shoe prices are rising.

Mr. Morgan continued, "We have been relatively insulated from the pressure of imports to date, because our market is small compared to the men's or women's markets and because the imports' labor cost advantage is not as great in this smaller segment. But it's going to be tough to hold them at bay."

THE FUTURE

"Some time ago now, our bank came to me and said, 'Listen, you're the only guy we know at Morgan, and that's our biggest risk. We know you, but you have no ownership, zero.' So I gained control of the company. I bought shares in the company from my relatives, but not all the shares. I gave them $40,000 for an original investment of $5,000 and now I have a majority of the stock.

"We treat Morgan like a public corporation. I pay dividends, even though it's ridiculous for a company our size,[3] but that's because I still have outside stockholders. I take a salary. I ask for advice of the board of directors when we get together. No one from the bank is on the board or ever will be.

"The demographics of a declining birth rate mean that my market is limited." (See *Exhibit 13*.) "Producing girls' shoes has a lid on it. Over the last few years, the unisex trend has meant that a lot of girls have worn boys' shoes. Girls are now dressing up and we're going to get some of that market back again.

"We have an informal organization, and, although I don't serve as a foreman anymore, I'm still involved in every aspect of the company. Our controller is a CPA and he is just around the corner from my office. Our designers' offices are across the hall. They are key sales people: one handles the main line, the other handles athletic footwear. Our manufacturing VP, Brian Hawkins, is in the next office. We're all physically together. You can see the production line from my doorway. You can see it from everyone's

[3]*Exhibits 9 through 12* provide general financial and operating data on shoe manufacturers in general. They are included to help the reader develop a financial picture of the Morgan Shoe Manufacturing Company.

doorway. We all have to walk through the packing room to get to the bathroom, so we're always inspecting shoes. None of us has a private secretary; we share a receptionist and two typists. I don't know how to run a formal organization, but we're getting pretty big.

"I could sell and let someone take over Morgan, but that worries me. One of the reasons we've been so successful with the new technology is that our profit sharing systems provide a much better incentive to learn a new technology than the normal industry compensation schemes. I'm not sure that another company would have the flexibility to allow us to do it our way.

"I could wait for another opportunity, hoping we can keep up with trends well enough to keep the company moving ahead in the meantime. Pierpont's fate is not attractive to me.

"We realize that we're coming up against a time limit, and that we will soon have to make a major decision about the future direction of this company. If we don't move at the right time our options will begin to shrink.

"We may move into another market segment, boys' shoes, for example, although boys' and girls' shoes use different materials, and that presents some problems. We may integrate backwards and produce molds or unit soles for other companies. We are independent in both these areas now, probably one of the few shoe companies in the industry with this strength.

"Whatever we do, it will depend on how the market looks to us, on how well we think we can match our technological strengths and marketing skills to that market, and on the adequacy of our human and financial resources in that market. We will only take on risks we can manage where we have the resources to succeed."

EXHIBIT 1 Nonrubber Footwear Supply Per Capita 1947–1976

Year	Millions of Pairs				Resident Population in Millions	Per Capita Consumption (number of pairs)
	Domestic Production	Exports	Imports	Market Supply		
1947	479.8	6.6	1.7	474.9	144.1	3.3
1948	479.6	5.8	2.5	476.3	146.7	3.2
1949	474.3	5.1	3.2	472.4	149.3	3.2
1950	522.5	3.7	6.1	524.9	151.9	3.5
1951	481.9	4.2	5.4	483.1	154.0	3.1
1952	533.2	4.8	5.3	533.7	156.4	3.4
1953	532.0	5.2	6.9	533.7	159.0	3.4
1954	530.4	4.7	5.6	531.3	161.9	3.3
1955	585.4	4.6	7.8	588.6	165.1	3.6
1956	591.8	4.5	10.0	597.3	168.1	3.6
1957	597.6	4.4	11.0	604.2	171.2	3.5
1958	587.1	4.2	23.6	606.5	174.1	3.5
1959	637.4	3.6	22.3	656.1	177.1	3.7
1960	600.0	3.2	26.6	623.4	180.0	3.5
1961	592.9	3.0	36.7	626.6	183.0	3.4
1962	633.2	2.9	63.0	693.3	185.8	3.7
1963	604.3	2.8	62.8	664.3	188.5	3.5
1964	612.8	2.8	75.4	685.4	191.1	3.6
1965	626.2	2.5	87.6	711.3	193.5	3.7
1966	641.7	2.7	96.1	735.1	195.6	3.8
1967	600.0	2.2	129.1	726.9	197.5	3.7
1968	642.4	2.4	175.3	815.3	199.4	4.1
1969	577.0	2.3	202.0	776.7	201.4	3.9
1970	562.3	2.1	241.6	801.8	203.8	3.9
1971	535.8	2.1	268.6	802.3	206.2	3.9
1972	526.7	2.3	296.7	821.1	208.2	3.9
1973	490.0	3.6	307.5	793.9	209.8	3.8
1974	453.0	4.0	266.4	715.4	211.4	3.4
1975(r)	413.1	4.6	286.4	694.9	213.5*	3.3
1976(p)	422.5	6.0	369.8	786.3	215.1*	3.7

Notes: (r) = Revised.
(p) = Preliminary.
* = Including armed forces overseas.

Source: U.S. Department of Commerce, Bureau of the Census, and American Footwear Industries Associations.

EXHIBIT 2
Selected Trends in the U.S. Shoe Industry

	Juvenile Market (under 10)				*Wholesale Price Indices*						*Wholesale Price Index Nonrubber Footwear*			*Consumer Price Index*	
	Market (million pairs)	*Population (million)*	*Per Capita*	*Expenditure on Footwear as % of Total Personal Consumption*	*High*	*Hides and Skins Monthly Average*	*Low*	*Leather*	*Average Weekly Earnings of Production Workers in Leather Industries (Wisconsin)*	*Footwear Production Wisconsin (000 pairs)*	*Men's, Youths' & Boys'*	*Women's and Misses*	*Children's and Infants'*	*All Commodities*	*Footwear*
1966				1.27	173.0	149.5	115.9	109.8	$ 85.49	$14,695	97.0	96.8	96.6	97.2	95.3
1967	127.3	39.0	3.26	1.26	114.4	100.0	92.1	100.0	90.87	13,859	100.0	100.0	100.0	100.0	100.0
1968	135.1	38.3	3.53	1.29	113.6	106.1	93.7	102.1	97.54	14,250	103.6	105.3	107.4	104.2	105.3
1969	132.9	37.5	3.54	1.33	136.6	124.1	115.6	108.7	103.58	14,303	108.1	110.1	112.9	109.8	111.8
1970	130.9	37.1	3.53	1.24	109.2	104.3	96.4	107.8	105.17	15,527	111.4	113.7	117.0	116.3	117.7
1971	133.1	36.6	3.64	1.23	128.6	115.1	98.9	112.5	111.20	14,577	115.7	117.2	119.8	121.3	121.5
1972	138.3	35.9	3.85	1.21	287.0	213.9	136.0	140.3	119.51	15,078	125.9	123.3	126.1	125.3	124.9
1973	126.1	35.0	3.60	1.23	274.0	253.9	227.3	160.1	122.75	14,779	137.9	125.4	130.2	133.1	130.2
1974	112.4	33.8	3.33	1.14	220.0	195.9	136.7	154.3	131.26	N/A	150.4	132.8	138.5	147.7	138.1
1975	107.9	33.3	3.24	1.10	209.1	174.5	122.3	151.5	142.60	N/A	159.3	140.2	143.7	161.2	144.2
1976	140.8	29.9	4.28	1.07	292.1	258.1	224.9	188.1	154.28	N/A	174.4	147.9	149.4	170.5	149.9

N/A: Not available since 1974

Source: Various tables in *Footwear Manual, 1977* prepared by Mr. Sundar A. Shelty, Manager, Bureau of Statistical Services, American Footwear Industries Association, Arlington, VA, 1977.

EXHIBIT 3
Analysis of the Hide Situation 1968–1976 (in million pieces)

	1968	1969	1970	1971	1972	1973	1974	1975	1976
I. *A Measure of Supply*									
U.S. hide supply (est. slaughter)	35.0	35.2	35.0	25.6	35.8	33.7	36.8	40.9	42.7
Argentine exports	8.3	8.3	7.5	3.4	1.3	0.5	0.5	0.5	0.5 (est.)
U.S. hide supply + Argentine exports	43.3	43.5	42.5	39.0	37.1	34.2	37.3	41.4	43.2
II. *A Measure of Demand*									
Domestic leather production	24.0	22.0	20.4	20.5	20.1	17.8	17.1	18.8	20.2
U.S. net hide exports	12.4	14.5	14.8	15.7	17.7	16.2	17.9	20.3	24.3
Production + exports	36.4	36.5	35.2	36.2	37.8	34.0	35.0	39.1	44.5
III. *A Measure of Supply in Relation to Demand*									
Total I minus total II	+6.9	+7.0	+7.3	+2.8	−0.7	+0.2	+2.3	+2.3	−0.7
IV. Composite hide prices* (cents per lb.)	12¢	15¢	13¢	14¢	30¢	32¢	23¢	23¢	34¢

*Composite of three common types: Heavy native steer, light native cow, butt branded steer.

Source: Footwear Manual, 1977, prepared by Sundar A. Shelty, Manager, Bureau of Statistical Services, American Footwear Industries Association, Arlington, VA. 1977.

EXHIBIT 4
Total Nonrubber Footwear Supply by Types (Domestic Production Plus Imports) 1966–1976 (millions of pairs)

Year	*Men's*	*Youths' and Boys'*	*Women's*	*Misses'*	*Children's*	*Infants' and Babies'*	*Athletic*	*Slippers*	*Other*	*Total*
1966	142.8	26.8	347.9	38.3	36.8	35.5	8.5	97.4	3.9	737.8
1967	143.3	28.3	348.5	30.8	35.4	32.8	8.3	98.7	2.9	729.1
1968	152.4	27.1	408.6	38.3	38.4	31.3	10.0	108.3	4.2	817.8
1969	153.7	27.6	373.3	35.1	38.8	31.4	11.5	103.0	4.5	779.0
1970	164.7	28.8	390.2	30.2	37.9	34.0	13.2	98.1	6.8	803.9
1971	171.2	27.6	382.1	33.4	37.9	34.2	13.9	99.9	4.2	804.4
1972	185.6	29.3	381.7	33.7	40.0	35.3	14.9	100.0	2.9	823.3
1973	178.1[1]	28.6	381.2[1]	26.9	37.8	32.8	15.9	92.7	3.4	797.4[1]
1974	158.3[1]	25.0	340.5[1]	24.0	32.8	30.6	18.2	86.9	3.2	719.5[1]
1975(r)	155.9[1]	26.5	335.8[1]	20.6	29.7	31.1	24.7	71.1	4.0	699.5[1]
1976(p)	177.1[1]	39.1	361.1[1]	29.3	36.8	35.6	44.8	65.5	3.1	792.3[1]

Notes: Details may not add up to totals due to independent rounding.
(r) - Revised.
(p) - Preliminary.
[1] - Excluding disposable footwear.

Source: U.S. Department of Commerce and AFIA.

EXHIBIT 5
Imports as a Percentage of Market Supply by Types 1966–1976

Year	Men's	Youths' and Boys'	Women's	Misses'	Children's	Infants' and Babies'	Athletic	Slippers	Other	Total
1966	11.1	8.2	18.3	6.3	8.7	8.6	14.1	3.7	25.6	13.0
1967	13.7	10.6	25.9	10.4	13.3	8.5	16.9	3.1	31.0	17.7
1968	17.1	13.3	30.5	13.8	18.2	8.3	17.0	2.7	50.0	21.4
1969	23.8	16.3	36.2	17.1	27.1	12.7	21.7	2.0	20.0	25.9
1970	27.3	17.4	41.0	23.2	31.7	14.7	31.8	1.9	20.6	30.0
1971	31.3	19.9	45.8	24.0	33.0	17.5	39.6	1.7	21.4	33.4
1972	31.8	20.5	49.4	25.2	42.5	25.5	41.6	1.7	27.6	36.0
1973	33.3	22.7	53.0	35.3	37.0	23.2	39.0	1.6	26.5	38.6
1974	30.5	28.0	51.0	34.2	37.2	22.2	45.6	1.6	21.1	37.0
1975	32.2	41.5	54.1	36.4	37.4	22.2	68.0	0.8	15.0	40.9
1976	38.2	52.4	56.8	46.8	42.9	30.1	77.5	0.9	32.3	46.7

Source: U.S. Department of Commerce and AFIA.

EXHIBIT 6
Nonrubber Footwear: Percentage Distribution of Domestic and Imported Footwear, by Types and by Price Ranges, 1974

Type and Price Range	Percent of Domestic Production	Percent of Imports	Type and Price Range	Percent of Domestic Production	Percent of Imports
Misses' shoes			Children's shoes (inc. little boys')		
Less than $3.00	23	62	Less than $3.00	20[1]	54
$3.01–$5.00	33	33	$3.01–$5.00	40	29
$5.01–$7.00	23	3	$5.01–$7.00	22	4
$7.01–$9.00	15	1	$7.01–$9.00	16	9
Greater than $9.00	6	0.3	Greater than $9.00	2	3
Total	100	100	Total	100	100

Nonrubber Footwear: Percentage Distribution of Domestic and Imported Footwear, by Types and by Price Ranges, 1975

Type and Price Range	Percent of Domestic Production	Percent of Imports	Type and Price Range	Percent of Domestic Production	Percent of Imports
Misses' shoes			Children's shoes (inc. little boys')		
Less than $3.00	15	45	Less than $3.00	15	41
$3.01–$5.00	33	30	$4.01–$5.00	38	46
$5.01–$7.00	22	6	$5.01–$7.00	25	3
$7.01–$9.00	21	8	$7.01–$9.00	18	3
Greater than $9.00	9	11	Greater than $9.00	4	7
Total	100	100	Total	100	100

[1]25 to 40 percent of this item is estimated. Because of rounding, figures may not add to the totals shown.

Source: Domestic data compiled from official statistics of the U.S. Department of Commerce; import data compiled by U.S. International Trade Commission from data submitted in response to importers' questionnaires.

EXHIBIT 7 Estimated Average Factory Values of Nonrubber Footwear by Major Types 1965–1973 (dollars per pair)

Year	Nonrubber Footwear	*Establishments Exclusively Producing* Men's, Youths' and Boys'	Women's, Misses' Children's and Infants'	House Slippers	All Other
1965	3.99	5.91	3.78	1.51	4.08
1966	4.34	6.60	4.04	1.50	4.45
1967	4.58	6.93	4.37	1.58	4.82
1968	4.71	7.05	4.57	1.57	4.90
1969	4.94	7.38	4.90	1.70	5.02
1970	5.14	7.62	5.11	1.66	5.30
1971	5.25	7.76	5.13	1.69	5.65
1972	5.56	8.21	5.37	1.67	6.12
1973	6.24	9.09	5.82	1.77	6.80

Note: These data are not revised by the government on an annual basis. The data extracted from the monthly "Current Industrial Reports" (CIR) are not available since 1974.
Source: U.S. Department of Commerce.

EXHIBIT 8

U.S. Imports of Footwear (Except Rubber) Average Price Per Pair by Type 1966–1976 (dollars per pair)

Type of Footwear	*1966*	*1967*	*1968*	*1969*	*1970*	*1971*	*1972*	*1973*	*1974*	*1975*	*1976*
Leather Footwear	$2.72	$2.86	$3.07	$3.56	$3.57	$3.91	$4.44	$5.12	$5.52	$ 5.75	$ 5.82
Men's and boys' (including athletic)[1]	3.90	4.01	4.00	4.40	4.53	4.99	5.93	6.87	7.01	6.65	6.06
Women's and misses' (including athletic)	2.12	2.39	2.71	3.27	3.33	3.58	3.97	4.47	4.90	5.37	5.85
Infants' and children's	1.37	1.43	1.46	1.59	1.51	1.62	1.96	2.28	2.56	2.54	2.53
Moccasins	1.07	1.12	1.11	1.21	1.15	1.30	1.57	2.31	2.29	1.85	2.50
Other leather not specified by sex*	9.37	7.77	5.73	6.10	4.17	5.07	5.20	6.08	6.92	13.12	11.67
Slippers	1.88	2.08	1.98	2.15	2.58	2.67	2.88	2.90	3.83	3.30	3.39
Vinyl Footwear	$0.55	$0.60	$0.70	$0.83	$1.00	$1.24	$1.29	$1.52	$1.95	$ 1.95	$ 2.10
Men's and boys'	0.89	0.92	1.00	1.26	1.33	1.43	1.66	2.16	2.94	2.83	3.04
Women's and misses'	0.51	0.56	0.68	0.79	0.95	1.20	1.22	1.40	1.86	1.85	1.96
Children's and infants'	0.55	0.63	0.65	0.71	0.82	0.92	1.00	1.00	1.31	1.32	1.41
Soft sole	0.27	0.49	0.51	0.53	0.71	0.72	0.76	1.19	1.12	0.87	1.27
Vinyl, 90% upper rubber/plastic	—	—	—	0.97	1.72	1.70	1.56	1.89	2.48[2]	2.21[2]	2.24[2]
Other Nonrubber Types	$0.68	$0.78	$0.82	$1.17	$1.46	$0.96	$1.25	$1.64[3]	$2.11[3]	$ 2.39[3]	2.02[3]
Wood	—	1.29	2.11	2.49	2.56	2.68	3.03	3.18	3.35	3.97	3.96
Fabric and other uppers**	0.66	0.75	0.76	0.87	0.91	0.79	0.83	1.05[3]	1.60[3]	1.72[3]	1.58[3]
Total All	$1.60	$1.68	$1.87	$2.14	$2.32	$2.53	$2.81	$3.17[3]	$3.68[3]	$ 3.95[3]	$ 3.92[3]

Note: Figures may not add to totals due to independent rounding.

*Includes welt footwear, (other than work welt) footwear with molded soles laced to uppers, McKay sewed footwear, huaraches, ski boots not shown by sex.

**Includes footwear leather sole, fiber upper, footwear made of wool felt, textiles, and vegetable fiber.

[1]Including work welt.

[2]Included with the respective age-sex categories beginning with 1974.

[3]Excluding disposable footwear.

Source: Compiled from official statistics of the U.S. Department of Commerce. Estimates are AFIA's.

EXHIBIT 9
General Statistics for the Footwear Industry 1964–1974
Shoes, Except Rubber (SIC 3141)

Industry and Census Year	Total Establishments	All Employees		Production Workers			Value Added by Manufacture ($000)	Cost of Materials, Fuels, etc. ($000)	Value of Shipments ($000)	Capital Expenditures ($000)	End of Year Inventories ($000)
		Number	Payroll ($000)	Number	Man-Hours (000)	Wages ($000)					
1964	n.a.	201,424	750,913	182,891	342,405	620,892	1,319,909	1,069,821	2,365,904	20,320	286,300
1965	n.a.	205,350	780,844	186,317	346,375	639,309	1,343,338	1,125,654	2,461,289	21,842	301,600
1966	n.a.	206,020	817,565	186,838	348,833	671,583	1,446,054	1,229,260	2,650,092	27,310	344,900
1967	951	198,500	835,300	180,000	333,700	680,800	1,525,700	1,241,700	2,770,500	25,200	336,200
1968	n.a.	203,400	923,700	184,400	344,400	755,700	1,724,800	1,337,900	3,030,500	43,400	382,700
1969	n.a.	198,700	932,300	179,200	327,300	756,900	1,696,700	1,311,700	2,956,800	30,800	406,900
1970	n.a.	180,500	895,700	162,200	297,100	724,800	1,663,300	1,304,300	2,966,600	29,900	391,800
1971	n.a.	166,500	871,200	149,100	273,300	700,600	1,616,900	1,268,500	2,892,100	29,700	384,500
1972	826	167,600	924,600	150,000	281,700	748,000	1,710,600	1,422,600	3,120,900	35,500	410,200
1973	n.a.	161,300	920,300	144,100	265,900	743,400	1,766,400	1,489,200	3,227,000	42,700	464,700
1974	n.a.	153,600	910,500	136,100	245,600	32,500	1,757,600	1,508,800	3,258,100	43,900	461,200

Note: n.a. - Not available.
Source: Annual Survey of Manufacturers, Census of Manufacturers (CM) of U.S. Department of Commerce.

EXHIBIT 10

Ratios of Shoe Manufacturing (Except Slippers) (median ratios) 1965–1975

		1965	*1966*	*1967*	*1968*	*1969*	*1970*	*1971*	*1972*	*1973*	*1974*	*1975*
Current assets to current debt	(times)	2.19	2.05	2.24	2.19	2.41	2.33	2.68	2.20	2.34	2.36	2.70
Net profits on net sales	(%)	2.00	2.62	2.17	2.94	2.04	1.50	1.73	1.80	1.66	1.55	3.12
Net profits on tangible net worth	(%)	9.85	10.79	8.94	11.35	8.89	6.27	7.38	8.82	6.36	6.16	8.83
Net profits on net working capital	(%)	12.59	15.01	12.95	15.03	10.73	7.40	9.75	11.15	7.35	6.64	9.76
Net sales to tangible net worth	(times)	4.12	4.34	4.17	4.24	4.26	4.03	3.78	4.03	4.02	4.10	3.73
Net sales to net working capital	(times)	5.54	5.55	4.98	4.98	4.99	5.30	4.48	4.65	4.58	4.93	3.95
Collection period	(days)	48	45	48	48	51	55	51	52	59	53	49
Net sales to inventory	(times)	5.6	4.9	5.8	5.4	5.5	6.0	5.6	5.5	5.3	5.1	5.7
Fixed assets to tangible net worth	(%)	20.1	22.7	21.0	22.7	25.0	23.9	23.7	22.8	27.9	27.0	17.3
Current debt to tangible net worth	(%)	68.2	71.5	63.0	62.4	59.0	59.1	57.4	65.1	73.4	64.5	55.9
Total debt to tangible net worth	(%)	108.9	108.9	105.6	95.8	101.9	108.4	108.4	111.4	122.0	103.2	87.9
Inventory to net working capital	(%)	96.7	105.1	84.8	97.4	91.7	87.2	83.8	92.8	93.3	95:1	85.7
Current debt to inventory	(%)	88.0	81.9	87.6	89.1	79.9	90.2	82.5	96.9	102.2	95.8	82.7
Funded debts to net working capital	(%)	27.8	27.2	28.3	21.2	25.4	21.9	27.2	25.7	24.2	30.5	20.5
Total Number of Reporting		115	117	119	115	109	111	99	99	82	82	56

Source: Dun & Bradstreet.

EXHIBIT 11

Profit-and-Loss Experience of Producers of Footwear Except Protective-Type and Canvas, on Footwear Operations Only, 1970–1974

Size-of-Output Group and Year	*Net Sales*	*Cost of Sales*	*Gross Profit*	*Selling, Administrative, and General Expenses*	*Net Operating Profit*	*Other (Expense), Net*	*Net Profit or (Loss) before Taxes*	*Ratio of Net Operating Profit to Net Sales*
	1,000 dollars	*1,000 dollars*	*1,000 dollars*	*1,000 dollars*	*1,000 dollars*	*1,000 dollars*	*1,000 dollars*	*Percent*
Less than 200,000 pairs								
1970	38,652	29,796	8,856	7,862	994	(653)	341	2.6
1971	41,223	31,086	10,137	9,227	910	(707)	203	2.2
1972	43,020	32,594	10,426	8,978	1,448	(481)	967	3.4
1973	47,143	35,357	11,786	10,288	1,498	(413)	1,085	3.2
1974	54,608	41,683	12,925	12,098	827	(645)	182	1.5
200,000 to 499,999 pairs								
1970	200,504	164,531	35,973	32,443	3,530	(2,920)	610	1.8
1971	193,947	153,033	40,914	33,072	7,842	(1,654)	6,188	4.0
1972	213,195	169,502	43,693	35,932	7,761	(1,284)	6,477	3.6
1973	229,104	187,161	41,943	37,833	4,110	(2,340)	1,770	1.8
1974	268,780	213,904	54,876	43,111	11,765	(2,051)	9,714	4.4
500,000 to 999,999 pairs								
1970	207,397	164,086	43,311	34,817	8,494	(1,635)	6,859	4.1
1971	246,404	196,323	50,081	37,320	12,761	(824)	11,937	5.2
1972	280,717	224,323	56,394	42,695	13,699	(876)	12,823	4.9
1973	305,986	241,618	64,368	49,759	14,609	(1,079)	13,530	4.8
1974	335,876	264,404	71,472	56,633	14,839	(555)	14,284	4.4
1,000,000 to 1,999,999 pairs								
1970	413,977	329,167	84,810	57,578	27,232	(3,759)	23,473	6.6
1971	448,455	351,130	97,325	72,813	24,512	(4,580)	19,932	5.5
1972	455,661	372,122	83,539	75,362	8,177	(3,189)	4,988	1.8
1973	509,311	421,136	88,175	79,830	8,345	(6,010)	2,335	1.6
1974	510,987	420,878	90,109	82,983	7,126	(7,892)	(766)	1.4
2,000,000 to 3,999,999 pairs								
1970	471,060	351,459	119,601	86,813	32,788	(8,880)	23,908	7.0
1971	479,963	358,130	121,833	91,504	30,329	(5,920)	24,409	6.3
1972	539,248	406,062	133,186	97,802	35,384	(5,743)	29,641	6.6
1973	598,026	454,851	143,175	112,561	30,614	(7,767)	22,847	5.1
1974	616,855	463,085	153,770	123,779	29,991	(13,792)	16,199	4.9
More than 4,000,000 pairs								
1970	1,474,660	1,106,889	367,771	251,635	116,136	(7,911)	108,225	7.9
1971	1,568,850	1,175,923	392,927	272,004	120,923	(4,628)	116,295	7.7
1972	1,755,280	1,342,372	412,908	292,919	119,989	(4,727)	115,262	6.8
1973	1,818,462	1,380,415	438,047	314,329	123,718	(6,798)	116,920	6.8
1974	1,854,918	1,396,619	453,299	336,639	121,660	(13,209)	108,451	6.6

Source: Compiled from data submitted to the U.S. International Trade Commission by the domestic producers.

EXHIBIT 12
Percent Utilization of Capacity by Types of Nonrubber Footwear 1966–1976

Type of Footwear	*1966*	*1967*	*1968*	*1969*	*1970*	*1971*	*1972*	*1973*	*1974*	*1975 (r)*	*1976 (p)*
Men's	86.5	84.4	86.1	84.6	87.8	87.6	89.3	82.8	77.0	74.1	83.7
Youths' and Boys'	83.4	83.6	77.6	76.3	84.6	78.7	82.2	77.9	63.4	55.7	79.5
Women's	85.8	78.1	85.8	75.5	72.9	71.3	73.4	73.2	77.0	75.2	80.8
Misses'	83.1	63.8	76.3	75.1	59.7	82.5	88.3	61.1	55.3	52.8	76.0
Children's	83.5	76.4	78.1	76.6	72.3	71.0	80.3	83.0	80.3	72.4	78.1
Infants' and Babies'	75.5	72.5	69.3	79.0	83.7	83.7	77.3	76.9	72.5	78.3	76.9
Athletic	57.7	79.2	88.8	86.8	87.8	82.7	84.5	85.2	87.4	70.0	81.3
Slippers	78.3	79.7	80.7	76.4	73.6	79.1	75.7	70.2	65.9	56.5	66.4
Other	nc	49.8	51.4	83.3	65.8	40.6	25.2	47.9	72.4	66.9	65.3
Total Production	80.2	78.4	82.7	77.8	76.1	77.0	78.2	75.0	73.1	69.1	78.1
Totals (000 pairs)											
Effective Capacity	782,952	765,156	776,412	741,948	738,576	695,760	673,044	653,376	619,428	598,176	568,404
Census Production	641,696	599,964	642,427	576,961	562,318	535,777	526,655	490,033	452,955	413,080	444,087

Notes: nc - Not comparable due to change in definition.
(r) - Revised.
(p) - Preliminary.

Total effective capacity is the sum of the monthly production peaks for each type of footwear over a 36-month period ending December 31st of the year involved.

Source: American Footwear Institute of America.

EXHIBIT 13 Estimated and Projected Population, Under 13, 1950–2000

	Total		*Male*		*Female*	
Year	*Under 5*	*5–13*	*Under 5*	*5–13*	*Under 5*	*5–13*
1950	16,410	22,423	8,362	11,415	8,048	11,008
1960	20,341	32,965	10,339	16,762	10,002	16,203
1970	17,148	36,636	8,742	18,667	8,406	17,969
1975	15,882	33,440	8,115	17,047	7,767	16,393
1980	16,020	30,197	8,201	15,418	7,819	14,779
1985	18,803	29,098	9,632	14,888	9,171	14,210
1990	19,437	32,568	9,963	16,685	9,474	15,883
2000	17,852	35,080	9,153	17,981	8,699	17,099

The base date for the projections is 1976. These projections were prepared using the "cohort-component" method. This series assumes a slight improvement in mortality, an annual net immigration of 400,000, and completed cohort fertility rates (i.e., average number of lifetime births per 1,000 women) that move toward the 2100 level.

Source: Statistical Abstracts of the U.S., 1976.

TOWNSEND CAMPINAS

At its June, 1974, meeting, the board of directors of Townsend Manufacturing Company, a consumer hard goods producer, discussed the company investment in its Brazilian subsidiary, Townsend Campinas. Townsend had been active in foreign markets for many years; in fact, some of its products were better accepted abroad than domestically in product lines where the company was a latecomer in the United States.

TOWNSEND CAMPINAS

Townsend Campinas was organized in 1965 to assemble and distribute refrigerators in Brazil. The country had a growing market that was large enough to make it feasible to set up a plant there. It was felt that the local citizens would accept the product more readily if it were produced in their own country. The government of Brazil was anxious to avail itself of the income and employment generating benefits of local production, and had offered Townsend attractive tax and investment credits when the plant was established.

Townsend's size, technological dynamism, access to credit sources and asset concentration allowed it market dominance in Brazil. Townsend's subsidiary was in a position to condition the environment in which it operated, while its local competitors tended to expand passively in response to the growth of their markets. As a consequence of these advantages inherent in foreign investment, and massive inflows of foreign capital, Brazil's manufacturing industry has exhibited large growth rates (see *Exhibit 1*).

Although sales in Brazil had increased substantially each year (see *Exhibit 2*), the market had grown only in conjunction with the availability of consumer credit. Townsend had experienced a similar association of the growth of consumer credit and advancing consumer hard goods sales in other countries, including the United States.

Liberal credit terms were, however, of extraordinary importance to inflation-conscious Brazilian consumers, who insisted on incurring indebtedness to turn price-rise to their advantage. Management was forced to extend instalment purchase terms from twelve to twenty-four months to assure sales. In the past, management had followed a pricing formula to ensure that payment received would equal replacement cost plus overhead and a normal profit on day of receipt (see *Exhibit 3*). However, in 1973 the Interministerial Council on Prices (CIP) was created as an instrument for the application of price controls. The company was forced to discontinue its inflation-indexed pricing, as may be seen in the erosion of its profit margin (*Exhibit 2*).

THE ECONOMIC AND POLITICAL CLIMATE IN BRAZIL, 1974

CIP's powers appeared to be widening, and it was attempting to set margins on a wide variety of manufactured products. Although this had not yet been applied in Townsend's case, there appeared to be a strong possibility of this occuring in the near future. In order to get price increases authorized, Townsend had to submit detailed cost data to the commission justifying the increase. In the past, Townsend had found that CIP used stalling tactics to delay putting new prices into effect. Although the time set for the decision to be made was forty-five days, late in the examination period CIP would ask the company for additional information, notifying Townsend that a new forty-five day period had begun. In order to protect itself against a cost-price squeeze, Townsend had started the practice of asking CIP for more than was really needed. It also started to use its discount policies as a cushion against too severe action by CIP, decreasing its discount to buyers whenever CIP failed to come through with price hikes that were sufficient to make up for cost increases.

In addition to prospects of increased price control, the political climate in Brazil appeared to be changing. Brazil's politically stable government, with policies that actively solicited foreign investment, had played a substantial role in Townsend's decision to build an assembly plant there. However, a deteriorating structure of income distribution and the declining standard of living for the poor had resulted in the government party losing almost 50% of the popular vote in the recent elections. Brazil's foreign investment policy traditionally did not have a high emotional content. Recently, however, foreign ownership of industry climbed to about 20% of total net worth and undercurrents of nationalism had become stronger.

PLANNING FOR THE FUTURE

To Townsend, however, Brazil was still a profitable growing market, and it forecast rapidly growing sales. To finance the refrigerator sales forecast for the next fiscal year, on the extended credit terms, Townsend Campinas would need $5,137,000 to support its inventory and accounts receivable. Other fund needs would be met from Campinas's internal sources.

The board of directors met to decide whether the firm's Brazilian subsidiary ought to try and realize its sales forecast, and, if so, how its financing needs should be met.

Elliot Robinson, International Treasurer for Townsend, questioned the wisdom of making any funds available to the subsidiary. "In an inflationary climate, sound corporate financial management requires that liquid assets such as cash and accounts receivable are kept as low as possible," he said. "This avoids an erosion of their value as a result of inflation. However, due to the long-term credit nature of its sales, the subsidiary's net exposure (the difference between its exposed assets and exposed liabilities) is substantial. It therefore presents a large purchasing power risk to the firm."

"It is unfortunate that we were forced to discontinue our past indexed pricing policy," Mr. Senturia, Managing Director of Townsend Campinas, said. "We are attempting to offset the adverse inflationary effects on our current asset account by delaying to settle our accounts payable for as long as possible. Delays of up to six months are not uncommon in Brazil. It is, however, unwise for us to decrease our accounts receivable as the cost in lost sales would be extremely large."

"Townsend Campinas faces other problems," Mr. Robinson pointed out. "It depends upon domestically produced components in its manufacture of refrigerators. With the recent return of 30% inflation, we may find ourselves in a position where the CIP may permit the subsidiary's cost of goods sold to rise while its sales price increases are refused or delayed.'' He also noted that, in the past, delays in the authorization of dividend remittances had actually devalued dividends because of Brazil's inflationary climate.

''Finally,'' Mr. Robinson said, addressing the board of directors, ''We must recognize the fact that certain technical parts used in the refrigerators are imported. This has not been a problem in the past as the Brazilian government has traditionally followed a liberal import policy. However, today it is attempting to control inflation by restricting imports through high duties and deposit requirements. When we import our parts today we are required to deposit 20% of the total import value of the items with a bank. Although the deposit is remitted after ninety days, its cost is high in terms of capital tied up. The percentage requirement may go up; as it is, the practice has been adding to our subsidiary's cost of sales and intensified the need for working capital. In view of these developments, I recommend that the subsidiary either find a means of internally generating the funds it needs, or finance itself through local borrowing. Brazil's continued inflation, repeated currency devaluations, price controls and future economic prospects have made further investment too risky.''

Mr. Senturia, however, disagreed. ''Over the past nine years the firm has seen an exceptionally large return on its investment in Brazil,'' he said (see Exhibits 4 and 5). ''We all recognize that large rates of return are accompanied by some degree of risk. Townsend now holds a dominant position in the Brazilian market; it will not continue to do so if we do not expand operations. We are in a sector of the economy that is growing faster than any other and it is vital that we continue to increase sales.''

''Our firm has a policy of not investing more than 25% of total capital in any one subsidiary,'' the Chairman of the board pointed out. ''What other methods of meeting Townsend Campinas's financing needs may be considered?''

''Although local borrowing would minimize the currency risk, it may not be the best solution,'' Mr. Senturia said. ''Following the government's introduction of indexed principal and interest payments, short-term credit and term loans are more available; however credit supply has not kept pace with credit needs and finding adequate sources of credit is still a problem. In the past, we have found it necessary to use twenty to thirty banks at one time to finance working capital needs. In addition to this problem, local borrowing is costly: indexed interest and repayments have cost us 30 to 40% in the past. The effective cost of the credit may be higher than if foreign funds had been used, and currency losses as a result of devaluations had been incurred.''

''There are hedging policies that may be used to provide funds,'' Mr. Robinson mentioned. ''They would protect us from currency risk, and may also be expanded to give the subsidiary protection against inflationary erosion of its accounts receivable. However, such policies are expensive: in the past they have cost us almost $1 million in a bad year. I therefore have strong reservations about using them in this case.''

''One of our major advantages as a foreign subsidiary has been our access to external sources of credit,'' Mr. Senturia pointed out. ''A well-thought-out hedging strategy would continue to allow us this advantage and minimize our currency risk. The parent company may purchase a forward exchange contract, calling for delivery, at a specified future date, of a specified amount of one currency against another currency. The rate of exchange would be fixed at the time of the contract. This approach has the advantage of having fixed costs and so may be used to minimize asset exposure. As it would not increase cash availability, I would suggest that it be used together with a policy of discounting company receivables at Brazilian commercial banks to provide finance for future operations.''

''The solution could prove to be extremely expensive,'' Mr. Robinson said. ''The seller's expectations of future inflation and currency depreciation in Brazil would be incorporated in the contract price. Given Brazil's recent economic down-turn, the price tag will certainly be high.''

''There is yet another strategy that would increase cash availability to the subsidiary, while decreasing net exposure,'' said Mr. Senturia. ''We could use international interest arbitrage loan transactions. The parent company could borrow money from a market where money was relatively abundant, and transfer it to Brazil. Simultaneously it could purchase a forward exchange contract bearing the same maturity as the loan itself. This is the alternative that I feel to be most attractive. It reduces currency risk, and allows us to keep the advantage inherent in the use of external financing.''

''The advantage you mention is only true if the financing obtained is cheaper than that which is available to you within Brazil,'' Mr. Robinson claimed. ''Another method of obtaining funds through local borrowing would involve the capital market in Brazil. Although the indexed principal and interest payments make this an expensive venture, it may be comparable in cost to the other strategies we have discussed.''

''You must keep in mind that, following an encouraging initial start, the money market in Brazil is weak,'' Mr. Senturia said. ''It is unwise to rely heavily on it for future financing needs.''

With the background information collected, and the alternative financing methods identified, the board now had to make its decision. The members recognized that in large measure the appropriate financing methods would depend on future economic and political development in Brazil. More particularly, since the alternatives varied in the amount of funds exposed to inflation and currency exchange risk, expectations about the pace of inflation and the resultant deterioration of exchange rates would of necessity play a major role in the policy choice.

EXHIBIT 1 Annual Growth Rates—Manufacturing Industry, 1966–1973

	Growth Rates	
Industrial Sectors	*1966–69*	*1970–73*
Capital Goods	7.5	27.2
Consumer Durables	16.2	18.4
Non-Durable Consumer Goods	8.4	7.2
Intermediate Goods	9.5	11.4

EXHIBIT 2 **Townsend Campinas S. A. Income Statements (in millions of cruzerios)**

	1970	*1971*	*1972*	*1973*	*1974*
Sales	7650	8965	10020	11976	13007
Cost of Sales	3006	3409	3675	5688	9009
Gross Profit	4644	5556	6345	6288	3998
Expenses:					
Selling, Administrative and Operating	1287	1530	1559	1600	2007
Profit before Taxes	3357	4026	4786	4688	1991
Income Tax (30%)	1007	1207	1436	1406	590
Net Income	2350	2819	3350	3282	1401

EXHIBIT 3 **Townsend's Pricing Formula—35% Inflation**

January 1	
Cost of assembling refrigerator	1,000
April 1	
Sells item for payment at year end:	
(a) Replacment cost on April	1,090
(b) 25% sales mark-up	272
Sale value	1,362
Plus estimated tax on inflationary profit	160
Contract price	1,522
December 31	
Bills customer:	
(a) Contract price	1,522
(b) Price adjustment for 9 months on Cr. 1,362 (3% monthly)	368
Total collected	1,890
January 1	
Townsend replaces item	1,384

EXHIBIT 4 **Townsend Campinas S. A. Comparative Balance Sheets (figures in millions of cruzieros)**

	1970	*1971*	*1972*	*1973*	*1974*
Assets					
Cash	116	108	125	123	115
Accounts Receivable	6989	7731	9214	10722	11711
Inventory	3060	3586	4416	4790	5203
Total Current Assets	10165	11425	13755	15635	17029
Plant and Equipment	3581	3239	3896	3987	3763
Total Assets	13746	14664	17651	19622	20792
Liabilities					
Accounts Payable	5328	5987	6875	7995	9839
Due Banks	1040	1590	1889	2798	3005
Total Current Liabilities	6396	7577	8764	10793	12844
Capital Stock	5000	5000	5000	5000	5000
Retained Earnings	2350	2087	3887	3829	2948
Total C/L and Capital	13746	14664	17651	19622	20792

EXHIBIT 5 Cost of Living Increase

1965	45%
1966	41%
1967	24%
1968	24%
1969	24%
1970	21%
1971	18%
1972	14%
1973	13%
1974	34%

Devaluation of the Cruzerio in the Year 1974

Date	*Buying $*	*Selling $*	*% Change*
1/31	6.300	6.340	1.92
2/20	6.145	6.455	1.81
4/16	6.515	6.555	1.55
6/5	6.640	6.680	1.91
6/25	6.775	6.815	2.02
7/9	6.845	6.885	1.03
8/15	6.980	7.020	1.26
9/18	7.090	7.130	1.57
10/28	7.180	7.220	1.26
11/19	7.285	7.325	1.45
12/19	7.395	7.435	1.50

NOTE TO TOWNSEND CAMPINAS—INFLATION, INDEXING, AND DEVELOPMENT IN BRAZIL

BACKGROUND—BRAZIL BEFORE INDEXING: 1947–64

Brazil is the largest and wealthiest country in South America; its main resources consist of coffee, cacao, cotton, sugar and iron. Its economic growth figures are impressive: from 1947 to 1961 real Gross Domestic Product increased at an annual rate of 6%; between 1962 and 1965 this dropped to 3.4%, rising to 5.5% from 1966 to 1968. Since 1968, Brazil has had one of the highest real growth rates among Less Developed Countries (LDCs), a rate of about 10% a year. This growth rate has taken place despite a very high rate of inflation.

From 1947 to 1964, rapid industrialization occurred in Brazil through the use of inflation as a device for development, and a strategy of import substitution was followed. The government merely ''created'' money and sent it to the industrial sectors it wished to develop, levying an inflation ''tax'' on the other sectors. Imports were severely restricted, as the government wished to make Brazil economically self-sufficient.

TABLE 1 Inflation in Brazil

Period	*Annual %*
1947–49	12%
1950–58	17%
1959	45%
1960–61	25–30%
1962	50–60%
1963	80%
1964	80%
1965–66	40%
1967	28%
1968	24%
1969	21%
1970	22%
1971	20%
1972	18%
1973	15.5%
1974	34.6%

However, by 1962 it had become clear that inflation was no longer an effective means of development. This was reflected in the fact that GDP declined in 1965, while inflation was as high as 91% in 1964 and was the cause of considerable distortion in the economy (see *Table 1*).

1964-1974—A PRAGMATIC APPROACH TO DEVELOPMENT

Between 1964 and 1974, the Brazilian government altered its policies, and a flexible, pragmatic approach to economic development was adopted. The government's goal was not to eradicate inflation over the short term, but to compromise with declining rates that would be compatible with the accelerated growth of GDP. With this in mind, stabilization policies followed were concerned mainly with applying mechanisms to counteract those effects of inflation that create disequilibrium within the economy. Periodic devaluations of the exchange rate and a wide use of generalized monetary adjustments (indexing) were used, together with a wage and price control policy. The government showed itself willing to tolerate an "acceptable" rate of inflation.

In the same time period, Brazil altered the direction of its growth model, turning it outwards. An active policy to attract foreign capital was followed, and investment in any area of economic activity, with the sole exception of the petroleum industry, was welcome. The country came to depend increasingly on the external sector as a source of capital for current and long-term financing. Foreign capital was attracted by the possibilities for exceptionally high rates of return (see *Table 7*), a large market and the availability of cheap labor.

A more liberal import policy was adopted aimed at avoiding production bottlenecks and increasing the growth rate of the economy. *Table 2* shows the increasing inflow of capital in its two main forms: financing of imports (supplier's credit) and money loans. As a result, Brazil's external debt increased at an annual rate of 25% from 1967 to 1973.

TABLE 2 Situation of External Debt—(millions of $)

Type	1970	%	1971	%	1972	%	1973	%
Compensatory Loans	381	12.4	300	4.4	240	2.5	203	1.6
Financing Imports	1709	32	2201	33	2783	29	3486	27.8
Money Loans	2284	43	3193	48	5528	58	7848	62.5
Other	919	17	926	14	968	10	1032	8.1

INDEXING AS A DEVICE FOR DEVELOPMENT

Ample use was made of indexing as a device for neutralizing the effects of inflation. Its application was a corner-stone of Brazil's entire financial policy, and it was a powerful tool used to reform the financial system. It may therefore have been directly related to Brazil's economic growth during this period, as the financial system was considered to be one of the factors that facilitated this growth.

Prior to the reforms of 1964, it was almost impossible to obtain long-term financing due to the high inflation. Commercial banks, which represented a majority of the financial intermediaries, traditionally lent only short-term because the majority of their liabilities were in the form of demand deposits (*Table 3*). As the interest rate was relatively low, and did not take into account the erosion of value as a result of inflation, banks had to deal with an excessive demand for funds that they could not satisfy. During the period of great inflation (1959–64), banks rarely lent for more than 120 days. This was a severe constraint on development, as funds were unavailable for the financing of working capital and long-term investment.

In order to increase the availability and duration of loans, the principal as well as the interest payments on financial assets were index-linked to rises in the consumer price index. This was introduced in 1964 in the form of indexed government bonds, but expanded to other financial instruments such as savings deposits, housing bonds and index-tied debentures issued by commercial firms.

When large, unanticipated inflation occurs, and the real interest rate on financial

TABLE 3 Time and Savings Deposits (millions of crucieros)

Year	Commercial Banks	Investment Banks	Federal and State Banks	Housing	Saving and Loan
1964	52		6		
1965	88		30		
1966	57	2	33		
1967	257	83	105	9	
1968	438	324	96	41	96
1969	545	690	245	23	43
1970	634	1709	1476	74	88
1971	1936	2947	1549	146	65
1972	2709	4607	3129	584	355

TABLE 4 Percent Interest Rates on Loans Deflated by the Price Index

Year	*Commercial Banks*	*Central Bank*	*Bills of Exchange*	*Other*
1964	−30.0	−37.5	−4.9	
1965	−14.0	−21.7	14.1	
1966	−2.3	−9.1	24.2	
1967	4.5	−5.1	16.1	9.3
1968	7.6	8.4	17.7	28.9
1969	8.4	—	19.3	11.1
1970	—	—	19.9	8.6

instruments is not positive, people have little incentive to invest in these assets; money flows instead into items such as consumer durables that may be used to make a speculative profit from the inflation. However, in Brazil, as the interest rate moved with the inflation rate, and the real interest earned was positive, financial instruments became attractive assets to hold (*Table 4*).

As their supply of funds increased, financial institutions were able to meet the current financing needs of enterprises. The supply of credit also became more responsive and flexible in meeting the demands of the dynamic sectors of the economy. Until 1967, the interest payments and principal of the loan outstanding were not indexed; the government therefore subsidized the banks as their costs were greater than their income. However, in 1967 this practice was discontinued, and both the interest and the loan principal were indexed to reflect the true cost of borrowing.

Some economists believe that the positive real interest rate contributed to Brazil's economic growth. When the real rate was negative, banks were faced with excessive loan demand, and rationed the funds available in an arbitrary manner. However, after reform, the interest rate itself acted as an allocative mechanism, excluding uneconomical investments with low rates of return. With a negative real cost of borrowing, investments that would not ordinarily be feasible were attractive.

INDEXING—THE WAGE POLICY

Wages in Brazil were indexed to keep pace with the cost of living. The rise in wages was calculated using a formula that resulted in average real wages equivalent to the average for the preceding twenty-four months, augmented by a percentage representative of the increase in productivity, and a percentage to account for projected future inflation. Although future inflation was considered, the amount was continually underestimated, and real wages steadily decreased (*Table 5*).

There are many problems that must be solved in order to effectively index wages; these include the choice of an appropriate index, and the fact that when past inflation data is used there is always a lag before wage increases catch up to the cost of living. In Brazil, however, there was in fact no effort made to ensure that wages kept pace with inflation. Instead, they were deliberately less than the increase in prices, and this wage policy was of decisive importance in the gradual reduction of the rate of inflation.

Wage policy had a depressive effect on the basic wages in the economy, favoring a redistribution of income which benefited the upper-middle and upper income strata, in

TABLE 5 Changes in Legal Minimum Wage and the Cost of Living

Year	*% Increase in Cost of Living*	*Real Wage Index*
1964	91.7	105
1965	65.9	100
1966	41.3	93
1967	30.6	89
1968	22.3	89
1969	22.1	87
1970	22.7	85
1971	20.2	85
1972	16.5	88

TABLE 6 Income Distribution Among the Economically Active Population

	1960	*1970*
Poorest 40 percent	11.56	10.01
Next 40 percent	34.09	27.75
Richest 20 percent	54.35	62.24

Percentage Increase in Real Per Capita Income 1960–70

Poorest 40 percent	16.0
Next 40 percent	9.1
Richest 20 percent	53.5

whose hands the dynamic purchasing power of the system lay (*Table 6*). Therefore, real private consumption in the economy expanded at an average annual rate of 12.1% during the period when the real minimum wage—the standard of pay for a large proportion of the economically active population—was diminishing.

The rise in consumption together with the falling rate of inflation (until 1973) contributed a great deal to Brazilian growth. This economic growth, however, took place at the cost of a drop in the standard of living for the majority of Brazil's population.

THE EXPANSION OF INDEXING

Indexing was originally introduced in conjunction with the use of financial instruments, but rapidly spread to public utility tariffs, rentals, balance sheets of enterprises, and taxes. It helped to reduce the volume of speculative operations, consequently weakening one of the causes of inflationary pressures.

TABLE 7 Rates of Return in Industry by Branches of Activity (%)

Branch of Activity	*1967*	*1968*	*1970*	*1972*
Consumer Goods	14.9	15.6	11.7	16.6
Intermediate Goods (chemicals, etc.)	13.5	14.7	17.5	17.5
Capital Goods (metals, etc.)	9.4	16.9	16.1	20.8
Miscellaneous	7.9	16.0	16.5	17.8
Total	12.6	16.0	16.5	17.8

In addition to this, the exchange rate in Brazil became directly related to inflation; periodic devaluations reflected the inflationary situation within the country. As these devaluations were relatively small and took place frequently, speculative movements of capital were discouraged.

Prices in the economy were not indexed, and price increases had to be approved by the Interministerial Price Commission. Price changes had to be justified by equivalent increases in the costs of the operation. The price controls appeared to have been fair and realistic, without unfavorable repercussions on the industrial sector, as may be seen in *Table 7*.

These exceptionally high rates of return explain why, despite the problems of inflation, an indexed economy, price control and substantial exchange rate risks, foreign companies were still willing to invest millions of dollars in Brazil.

Although periodic devaluations and indexing mitigated some of the effects of inflation, and permitted a sort of compromise with it, in a certain sense they also tended to institutionalize it.

Indexing seems to have exercised a pervasive influence on the behavior of agents in the economic process, encouraging a propensity to expect price increases as a matter of course. The importance of this is inverse to the rate of inflation. In cases of galloping inflation (30–40%), deep-rooted causes exist which detract from the relative importance of price expectations. For example, Brazil saw the return of 35–40% inflation due to external factors outside its control; the role played by the expectation of price increases was not major. On the other hand, when the rate of inflation falls to 10 or 15%, the inertia caused by indexing may become a serious hindrance to combatting inflation.

THE RETURN OF INFLATION

Between 1972 and 1973 the rate of inflation regained momentum, reaching 34.6% at the end of 1973. This inflation, however, was directly linked to the external sector. In the first place, the economy was affected by the repercussions of the world petroleum crises and inflation in the industrialized nations. This was felt through price increases of imported goods. For example, from January to June of 1974, imports increased in value by 112.5% while the increase in quantity was only 14.7%. Since 1964 Brazil's imports had risen substantially (see *Table 2*) and in 1973 it was importing inflation through these imports.

International price increases also contributed to inflation by affecting the prices of products exported by Brazil. As the external prices of some products rose, supply was diverted from the national to the international market, causing problems in domestic supply and consequent rise in prices.

The price curve of basic materials appeared to be pointing downward; this also included petroleum, if account was taken of its terms of trade vis-à-vis the rise in industrial prices. Thus the one advantageous aspect of the imported inflation—the rising prices and expansion of exports—came to an end. However, the prices of imports (consisting mainly of industrialized goods) continued to rise.

Consequently, the effect of the rise in import prices continued to be felt. In addition to this, any slowing down of the inflationary process, as a result of the slackening in the rise of export prices and the channeling of some of the export commodities to the domestic market, would also mean a deterioration in the balance of payments, and in the growth of important sectors of production.

CHAMPAIGN CONCRETE BLOCK COMPANY

WORRIES

As David Cullen fastened himself into the DC 10's first class seat on the return trip from Naples, Florida, to Champaign, Illinois, his thoughts shifted from the good times he had been having fishing with his retired friends to his concrete block manufacturing business. Until the last few years, these return trips brought on good feelings, nervous energy and excited anticipation—a feeling of "I can't wait to get back to work and sink my teeth into the problems and challenges of my business." The last two or three years, though, had been different. Those good feelings had been replaced by mild depression and a reluctance to get involved, a desire to avoid conflicts and ignore problems.

Dave felt he would be justified in retiring to enjoy the fruits of his labor. After all, he had built his business from scratch and had been managing it for twenty-two years. And some shrewd real estate investments had built his personal net worth in excess of $2 million, not including the value of the business. Yet Dave wanted to hang on for another three or four years until his son, John, was out of graduate school so he could take over the business. "It seems like a long time to wait," he thought as he finished his salad.

Dave knew that John had worked in the business during college vacations and said he wanted to take over. But there was no guarantee John would still be interested after receiving his MBA, or, for that matter, that John really had what it takes to manage a small business.

Dave was worried. Although his start-up had been difficult, the stability of a Midwestern college town and his conservative management had led to fifteen years of steady profitable growth. However, changes had begun four years ago. Dave had seen his sales growth flatten, and then begin to decline; the company would end the year with a substantial loss.

Dave first realized what was happening through talking with his friends and business associates at Rotary functions. Some national trends had finally started to take hold in Champaign. He believed he was losing the foundation market he had nurtured for many years to two "redimix" producers new to town. One of the "redimix" producers was a well-financed subsidiary of a large Chicago firm which had provided forms and training for a dozen or so new concrete-forming contractors in Champaign.

Another more recent change in the market was competition from steel studs. There were a lot of architect-designed buildings, but, because Champaign was a university town, they had always been either face brick over a block wall, or had used architectural blocks such as split rib. Recently, however, several buildings had been built with face brick and steel studs. Dave had also heard several architects complain that single-width block walls were too difficult to keep watertight and to insulate.

Considering all this, it was clear to Dave that if he was going to have a company to turn over to John in three or four years, he would have to dig in and work hard to improve his market position. He wasn't sure he was ready to do the job.

Dave wondered if his company could survive several years of losses while he attempted to buck the market trends. What kind of company would he turn over to his son if he was unsuccessful? Dave felt time was closing in on him. He did not like losing money, but he had no clear plan to do something about it. As he thought about his company, he compared his manufacturing costs to the industry's. His numbers looked good. He knew his equipment was state-of-the-art.

PERFORMANCE

Financially, Dave's company was strong. His business had built up a considerable net worth over the years and the company was liquid. He could finance any reasonable investment in new equipment.

However, Dave felt somewhat uncomfortable with marketing. He had always relied heavily on Bob Jamison in sales. Bob had worked for Dave for sixteen years and had built up a smooth-running department. As a result, Dave really let Bob handle all sales and marketing decisions. About the only thing they conferred on were the prices—and Dave usually rubber-stamped Bob's recommendations.

Bob had set up his department with two employees, Susan Samson and Jacob Paulson. Jake stayed on the road five days a week and called on contractors and dealers. Suzy worked inside on the phone providing quotes, scheduling trucking and expediting orders.

Bob had spent an average of two days a week in the office making sure the sales department was running smoothly and the rest of his time calling on the larger home builders and architects in the area. But since Bob's death in 1981, Dave had felt increasingly uneasy. On one hand, sales kept rolling in with Suzy and Jake pinch-hitting to fill the void left by Bob. Suzy had taken over administrative duties, correspondence and the like. Jake said he was getting around to seeing most of the people Bob used to call on. On the other hand, Bob used to go to a lot of trade shows and belong to a lot of associations, and these were not getting covered. It had seemed to Dave that Bob was always going to some dinner or lunch meeting. Now, particularly considering the profit problems, these were expenses Dave felt he could do without.

HELP

"Please fasten your seat belts. Return your trays to their stowed position and your seat backs to their upright position." The stewardess's harsh voice jarred Dave. That was it, no more daydreaming. He was going to call Ralph Connely first thing when he got to the office, even though he rarely asked for outside advice. (His accountant reviewed the books and prepared his taxes; his lawyer drew up his will. It all cost more money than Dave thought it should.)

Ralph Connely taught Small Business and Marketing at the University of Illinois and had a successful consulting practice on the side. He served several *Fortune* 500 companies such as 3M Corporation and Johns Manville and Dave had met him at a Rotary meeting. Ralph had told him he was interested in developing some local consulting customers to keep him in touch with the world of small business.

MOVING ALONG

The next day, Dave called Ralph and explained his situation. Ralph said he would see what relevant information was available and call Dave in a week, after he had a better feel for the situation and what his work might entail. In the meantime, he asked Dave to send him whatever historical financial information he might have going back four or five years. Dave sent him the income statement and balance sheet the accountants had prepared at the end of last year (*Exhibits 1* and *2*).

Next, Dave asked Jake in. He reviewed his concerns about the "redimix" manufacturers and the several buildings which had recently been built with steel studs and face brick. He casually mentioned that he was bringing in a consultant from the University. Jake reacted strongly. Dave was taken by surprise. Jake had always been easy-going.

Jake yelled "What are you wasting money on some pipe-smoking professor for? He ain't going to understand the block business! The only thing I need is a little help! I've been working my ass off for three years trying to do the job of two men and all the thanks I get is some professor to come in and criticize what I've been doing. Let him try and make six or seven calls a day, every stinkin' day. Then he'll understand the block business, and not until! All I can say, Dave, is, if you go through with this, don't expect me to do any more unless you get me some help!

"As a matter of fact, while we're on the subject, what about hiring that buddy of mine I told you about? He knows the masonry business inside and out. He's been a bricky for twenty years and he's got a real way with people. He's a hard worker; he just can't lay blocks anymore because his back is shot. I could break him into sales and teach him how to do it right. If you want to spend some money, that's what you oughta spend it on."

Jake stood up awkwardly, hesitated, then looked at Dave. "I feel strongly about this. Let me know if you want to talk to my buddy." He walked to the door, stopped. "I've got to get going. I'm already late for my first call—I usually meet Joe Salvucci for breakfast at 8:00 on Monday mornings. Bye."

Dave was concerned. Maybe he'd made a wrong decision. Maybe Ralph Connely couldn't understand the problems of a small business. Jake probably just needed a vacation. He had been working pretty hard lately, Dave thought. A few years ago he might have been tempted to hit Jake in the mouth . . . but no . . . that wasn't his style. What did Jake's behavior mean?

RESULTS?

Several days later, a packet of information, along with a $400.00 invoice for research services (*Exhibit 3*), came in the mail from Connely. Ralph sure had been busy. He had assembled a substantial amount of information in a very short time. But the invoice seemed steep. The cover letter had suggested that Dave and Ralph get together next Monday for lunch to discuss Dave's concerns and scope out his objectives. Ralph indicated his belief that Champaign Concrete Block had a viable future if Dave could put his energy and money into the business.

Dave thought again about Jake's reaction and then about whether Connely's advice was going to be worth the price. He wavered but then decided to go ahead with the lunch and instructed his secretary to confirm the appointment.

EXHIBIT 1

CHAMPAIGN CONCRETE BLOCK COMPANY
Balance Sheet
December 31, 1983

ASSETS			
Current Assets			
Cash	$323,000		
Accounts Receivable	$209,000		
Inventories	$262,000		
Total Current Assets		$794,000	
Property Plant and Equipment			
Machinery and Equipment		$412,000	
Furniture and Fixtures		$ 65,000	
Total Assets			$1,271,000
LIABILITIES AND EQUITY			
Current Liabilities			
Current Portion Long Term Debt	$ 15,000		
Accounts Payable	$ 94,000		
Salaries and Wages Payable	$ 6,000		
Accrued Expenses	$ 43,000		
Total Current Liabilities		$ 158,000	
Long Term Debt		$ 60,000	
Total Liabilities		$ 218,000	
Stockholders Equity			
Common Stock	$ 50,000		
Retained Earnings	$1,003,000		
Total Equity		$1,053,000	
Total Liabilities and Equity			$1,271,000

EXHIBIT 2

CHAMPAIGN CONCRETE BLOCK COMPANY
Income Statement

	1979	*1980*	*1981*	*1982*	*1983*
Sales					
Manufactured Goods	1,370	1,101	1,222	1,182	1,119
Accessories	450	389	323	303	273
Total Sales	1,820	1,490	1,445	1,485	1,392
Cost of Goods Sold	(1,110)	(894)	(881)	(910)	(863)
Delivery Expense	(225)	(211)	(202)	(210)	(195)
Gross Profit	455	385	362	365	334
Operating Expenses					
Selling Expense	122	125	85	88	87
General & Administration*	201	204	215	217	215
Total Operating Expenses	323	329	300	305	302
Income Before Taxes	132	56	62	60	32
Provision for Taxes	(40)	(17)	(19)	(18)	(9)
Net Income	92	39	43	42	23

*G & A includes owner's salary.

EXHIBIT 3

RALPH D. CONNELY
720 Acacia Road
Champaign, Illinois 61820

February 15, 1985

Mr. David Cullen
President
Champaign Concrete Block Company
Champaign, Illinois 61820

Dear Dave:

Enclosed is some valuable information (see Brief Note on the Masonry Industry) my research has turned up. My fee for professional services rendered to date is:

4 hours @ $100.00 per hour. $400.00

Let's get together for lunch to go over this material and discuss the scope of the project going forward.

Sincerely,

Ralph D. Connely

Ralph D. Connely, Ph.D.

RDC:ch
Enclosure

APPENDIX
A BRIEF NOTE ON THE MASONRY INDUSTRY

The masonry industry is in decline. Is it suffering from the decline in construction generally, or is it a victim of ineffective marketing in the face of aggressive competition from other materials?

As *Table 1* shows, construction has essentially held its own over the past five years in terms of current dollars. The bite has occurred because of inflation. In constant 1977 dollars, the construction industry has been declining at 4.7% annually.

Historically, concrete block shipments have been about 1% of total building expenditures, but, during the past few years, this figure has been declining as the industry has lost its share of the nonresidential sector.

In 1982, the in-place cost of masonry, clay brick, and concrete block was estimated at $8.6 billion, as *Table 2* shows. Of that total, 51% came from the nonresidential sector, while the residential sector was responsible for about 44% (*Table 3*). Additionally, note

TABLE 1 New Building Construction Put in Place, by Sector, 1978–1982 (millions of current and constant 1977 dollars)

	Residential		*Nonresidential*		*Total*	
Year	*Current*	*Constant*	*Current*	*Constant*	*Current*	*Constant*
1978	93,424	81,226	51,534	45,774	144,958	127,000
1979	99,030	75,958	62,856	47,959	161,886	123,917
1980	87,261	60,911	70,951	47,984	158,212	108,895
1981	86,566	55,893	78,610	50,871	165,176	106,764
1982	74,810	47,230	82,131	52,775	156,941	100,005
Average Annual Growth Rates		(10.3%)		2.9%		(4.7%)

Source: U.S. Department of Commerce, Construction Review.

TABLE 2 Overview of Masonry Industry Costs, 1982 (millions of dollars)

			Contractor			
Type	*Material*[1]	*Labor*[2]	*Margin*[3]	*Other*[4]	*Total*	*Percent*
Brick	500	1,260	500	340	2,600	30
Concrete Block	1,500	2,625	1,025	850	6,000	70
Total	$2,000	$3,885	$1,525	$1,190	$8,600	100%

[1]Value, FOB plant.
[2]Wages plus fringe benefits.
[3]Overhead plus profit
[4]Transportation, distribution costs, mortar, etc.
Source: Battelle estimate based on *1982 Masonry Cost Guide*, Masonry Advisory Council, and masonry market data.

TABLE 3 Value of Masonry Industry Output, by Sector, 1982 (millions of dollars)

Type	*Residential*	*Nonresidential*	*Other*	*Total*
Brick	$1,690	$ 780	$130	$2,600
Concrete Block	2,100	3,600	300	6,000
Totals	$3,790 (44%)	$4,380 (51%)	$430 (5%)	$8,600

Source: Battelle and industry estimates.

that 70% of the in-place value of masonry construction was attributable to the concrete block industry. Concrete blocks dominate masonry.

MARKETING

The concrete block industry tends to be defensive rather than aggressive, trying to stop the penetration of competitive materials into the industry. One observer, Roland Guy of the Battelle Institute, suggested that this response could be attributed to the fragmented nature of the industry and a production, rather than a marketing, orientation.

TABLE 4 New Nonresidential Wall Area by Type of Construction 1981

Building Type	Total Wall Area	Opaque Wall Area	Percent of Opaque Wall Area
Offices and banks	145	100	18%
Other commercial	265	200	36
Manufacturing	114	98	18
Educational	48	38	7
Hospital	26	19	3
Public	10	8	2
Religious	21	18	3
Recreational	34	27	5
Miscellaneous Nonresidential	32	28	5
Non-housekeeping Residential	26	18	3
Total:	721	554	100%

Based upon 1980 floor area, 1,260 million square feet. Continental United States data. Alaska and Hawaii excluded.

TABLE 5 The Total Opportunity in Nonresidential Construction

New	350 million square feet
Remodeling retrofit	100 million square feet
Total	450 million square feet

Who Is the Market?

Statistics indicate that during the 1980s, approximately 80% of new building construction was low-rise, containing 15,000 square feet or less space. These buildings, primarily built by owner-developers and contractors, rarely use the services of large independent architectural firms. Architects directly influence the choice of material in only 20% of construction value put in place each year. *Table 4* shows wall area in various building types, and *Table 5* illustrates new and retrofit nonresidential construction.

THE PRODUCT

Typical applications of masonry block construction include exterior walls, back-up walls for various facade materials, stairwells, partitions, and elevator shafts. Most block is used in new construction; little is used in rehabilitations of existing buildings.

Block has been slowly losing market share in these applications to other materials, such as metal panels, tilt-up concrete panels, poured concrete and pre-engineered metal building systems (*Table 6*). These systems are replacing concrete block in most of its back-up applications. In the residential sector, concrete block basement walls are being replaced by poured concrete and wooden foundations. Above-grade, concrete block load-bearing wall systems are losing share to wood-framing systems.

Why? The reason for this change is the inability of the small, local block manufac-

TABLE 6 Types of Wall Construction Nonresidential (millions of square feet)

Building Category	1981 Total Opaque Wall	Concrete Block	Brick Block	Concrete	Precast and Metal Curtain-Wall	Other
Offices and banks	100	19	32	4	27	18
Other Commercial	200	36	74	6	49	35
Manufacturing	98	18	17	4	51	8
Educational	38	5	15	—	10	8
Hospital	19	3	7	1	7	1
Public	8	1	4	1	2	—
Religious	18	2	5	1	3	7
Recreational	27	8	6	—	5	8
Miscellaneous Nonresidential	28	7	11	—	4	6
Non-housekeeping Residential	18	5	7	—	2	4
Total:	554	104	178	17	160	95
(Percent)	(100)	(19)	(32)	(3)	(29)	(17)

turer to counter the national-scale promotions of the alternative construction systems. Yet, the concrete block is fire-proof, maintenance-free, durable, has good acoustical properties, and can function as a heat-sink, making it extremely attractive in cold-winter climates. Moreover, concrete block prices have tended to be relatively stable compared with wood, a feature which should make blocks attractive to the small contractor bidding for work.

PRODUCT DEVELOPMENT

User surveys indicate that lighter-weight blocks might be more attractive to contractors, and that through-wall units—insulated and finished on both faces—could compete effectively with alternative wall systems were they panelized. Finally, new block-laying techniques which would cut labor costs and boost strength could have appeal to contractors, although it may be some time before union labor is prepared to participate in the increased productivity possible following such an innovation.

USER NEEDS

In the construction industry, if a product cannot be delivered as scheduled, people are hesitant to specify the product and the market will decline. Concrete block is readily available, very often from multiple local sources.

Similarly, faster erection saves money, and no-mortar block systems can reduce in-place costs and stimulate the market for blocks.

PATIO TIME, INC.

Matthew Whitlam is a board member and 25% owner of Patio Time, Inc., a California-based patio furniture manufacturer with 1977 sales of $5.5 million. Back in 1966, at the invitation of David Cooper (the company's founder, chairman, and president), Whitlam put up $25,000 to match Cooper's investment to get operations under way. Although over the years he has been committed to the full-time management of his own company, Whitlam has always been an active board member and Cooper's confidant. Now, as he prepares for his retirement, he wants to get his money out. There's only one problem: the value of his investment is in question because of trouble between Cooper and the head of Patio Time's subsidiary, which is located 3,000 miles away. As the case opens, Whitlam is about to learn that events have taken a turn for the worse, which will require some fast thinking and a decision on his part.

THE PROBLEM

It was 8:30 P.M. on November 19, 1977. Matt Whitlam had just opened his front door to Dave Cooper. Cooper said he had a problem. Will Madden, the president of Patio Time's Virginia subsidiary, Virginia Padding, Inc., had refused to cooperate with the parent company by coordinating his marketing efforts with California's or by merging the two companies. The trouble was that Patio Time held only 50% of the Virginia company's stock and did not control its board. Cooper handed Whitlam a letter he had received from Madden that afternoon:

Dear Dave,

I haven't been able to dismiss our last conversation from my mind. I have to tell you what I feel.

First, there is no need for a fifth director. Originally, our fifth director was your man, but our agreement clearly spelled out that either he would resign or a sixth director from Virginia would be chosen when Patio Time was paid back its original investment. The choice was not necessary because your man resigned from your company and from Virginia Padding. The original debt was repaid within a year.

Now, suddenly, when Virginia is financially independent, you decide you want me to merge with you. We owe you $21,400. Every invoice older than October 1 is being paid today. Last year we bought merchandise worth $392,000 from you. Also, I promised you that I would not extend our payments beyond 60 days next season when you explained that Patio Time could not finance it. Furthermore, Patio Time has not had to "execute guarantees" for us. It isn't necessary now.

Why are you pressuring me to merge with California? I hate to come right out and say no because I feel we will be driven apart. Yet, I do not share your opinion of

This case was prepared by Assistant Professor Kenneth J. Hatten as a basis for class discussion rather than to illustrate either effective or ineffective handling of an administrative situation.

how great the combination of the two companies might be. Nor do I see how this union you're proposing can be better for me. I enjoy what I am doing now so much and business here is so promising that I do not want to risk changing things. Whether you agree with me or not, those are my feelings.

You have been pressuring me for months. Don't try to convince me to sell out my interest in Virginia and merge. I won't do it. I don't know what more I can tell you other than I want our relationship to continue as it has for the past four years. Virginia isn't failing. Can't you see we are succeeding totally?

The last guy in the world I want on the opposite side of the fence is you. But all of your recent exchanges have been loaded with, "Do this or else." You never call without mentioning how naive I am. That's no compliment. The whole essence of your conversation has been loaded with veiled threats. In your office, your marketing manager said that if it were necessary to open an eastern plant, you would do it and compete with me. You heard him. You didn't contradict him.

What do you want out of me? I will be happy to continue on our present basis for as long as we find it profitable. I don't want any other basis.

After Whitlam had finished the letter, Cooper said, "I can't deal effectively with Madden anymore. Sleep on it, Matt, and see what you can come up with for the board meeting tomorrow."

Whitlam, who wanted to liquidate his investment in Patio Time in preparation for his retirement, wondered, "How did Dave let the situation get out of hand?" Only a few days earlier, at Whitlam's request, Cooper had agreed to meet the representatives of a large eastern company that was listed on the New York Stock Exchange and interested in acquiring a substantial interest in Patio Time. "It's a pity this has happened," he thought. "When I introduced Cooper to Eastco's executives, it was clear that their interest in buying my share of Patio Time was based on its being trouble-free."

As he watched Cooper's car leave, Whitlam thought to himself, "I've been counting on a substantial sum for my share of the company. What is the real problem, and what should I do about it? How can I best protect my interests, and how active a role should I take in resolving Cooper's and Madden's differences?"

EARLY YEARS

Cooper, 59, had been affiliated with the outdoor furniture business for more than 40 years. During the past 11 years, he had developed his own company to the point where its sales were over $5.5 million and its equity more than $850,000 (see *Exhibit 1*).

From a factory he leased in San Rafael, Cooper initially produced padded chaise lounges and webbed aluminum patio furniture for the West Coast markets. Because of his astute management, Patio Time was able to operate with little inventory other than in-process goods. With an ample supply of low cost, unskilled labor, it was able to readily market its products and take advantage of the population growth and outdoor lifestyle of the West Coast. In 1970, at the request of some of his larger customers, Cooper decided to widen Patio Time's product line and to move to a larger plant nearby.

With the move, Cooper hired a number of experienced executives to reinforce his organization. He brought in an experienced retail merchandiser as marketing manager and a manufacturing executive with over twenty-five years experience in the production of leisure furniture. This man reduced manufacturing costs and substantially increased the production capacity of the new plant.

With extra capacity, however, the need for additional orders became apparent, and the overall strategic pressure on the company shifted from manufacturing to marketing. Although the company was ultimately able to sell all it produced, the necessary change of emphasis had been astutely appreciated by Cooper, who had also hired a sales manager and two well-qualified executives to head purchasing and accounting.

By 1973, Cooper had brought the company to a point where it was poised for another leap forward in growth and profitability. Over the years, it had developed a reputation for having good products and timely deliveries, and it had begun to make substantial sales to national chains such as Sears, Montgomery Ward, and K mart. These sales brought a new opportunity into reach: selling nationally. With the lure of profitable growth in front of him, Cooper decided to spread the company's wings and set up a manufacturing plant in the East.

First expansion attempt: Early in 1973, after some research, Cooper decided to locate his eastern operations in a small town hear Harrisburg, Pennsylvania. Anxious for new industry, the town's officials agreed to build a manufacturing plant and lease it to Patio Time on very reasonable terms. They also implied that there would be no labor organization attempts.

A plant manager was hired locally and trained in California, and, once constructed, the plant was equipped with machinery from California. The opening ceremonies were inspiring, but, when production started, things did not go very well. The plant manager proved to be less than competent. Cooper found himself really up in the air: nursing along a sick operation on one coast and maintaining the health of his growing enterprise on the other, he was spending half his time flying back and forth between the two.

After six months of increasing ineffectiveness and growing frustration, the final blow came. A local labor union decided that the 100 employees of the Pennsylvania plant could be organized. The organization attempt was brief and never proceeded to an election, but shortly afterward Cooper told the town officials they had broken their bond with him and that he no longer felt ethically bound to operate in their plant. He summarily closed the plant, pulled all the equipment out, and turned his full attention to San Rafael.

The Harrisburg venture was extremely costly, but it had enriched Patio Time's management through hard experience. Cooper felt that he had learned two all-important lessons about expansion: that there must be an adequate supply of capable personnel, and that he could be in only one place at a time.

A second opportunity: In 1974, Patio Time needed additional capacity to manufacture tubular aluminum furniture. Since manufacturing lounge pads required minimal technical knowledge, equipment, capital or skilled personnel, it seemed logical to relocate the pad operation and to devote the San Rafael facilities to aluminum furniture.

Mindful of his Harrisburg troubles, Cooper wanted an experienced manager for the new operation. To this end, he contacted an old friend, William Madden, who lived in Virginia and had worked for many years in the leisure furniture industry. Madden was receptive to the general idea of becoming manager of Patio Time's lounge pad division, but he wanted no part of California.

Instead, he told Cooper that there was a new 40,000-square-foot factory in Fayetteville, an attractive small town about 100 miles from his present home. Madden was sure it would suit Patio Time's needs and that it could be leased or bought on attractive terms. He said he would be delighted to move to Fayetteville if Cooper decided to go ahead. Cooper immediately saw an opportunity to create a springboard to the Eastern markets.

VIRGINIA PADDING, INC.

With perhaps more enthusiasm than planning, Virginia Padding was incorporated in October 1974, with 50% of its stock going to Madden as its president and 50% to Patio Time, which invested $15,000 and high hopes in the venture. Madden put in no money for his 50% share but committed himself to operating the new venture to the best of his ability.

The articles of incorporation for Virginia Padding called for the board to have five directors and for the parent company to control three of their positions until any indebtedness from Virginia to the parent company was paid off. This requirement was considered important because Cooper anticipated that Patio Time might have to extend credit to Virginia for quite a while.

Business is business and more: Madden started operations with tremendous enthusiasm and personal effort and with the strong support of Patio Time. He enjoyed the freedom of being his own boss, and he was determined to justify the confidence his friend had placed in him.

Madden also relished life as president of the largest employer in Fayetteville. The company employed over 100 of the town's 3,000 residents, and he was accorded the tribute one might expect of his lofty position whenever he attended a local function. He joined the town's country club, bought a new Eldorado, lunched with the town's leading bankers, counseled the mayor on the redevelopment of the town center, kept in touch with local politics, and generally found himself in the role of the "compleat man" for the first time in his life.

Within a short time, Madden added a number of new customers for his chaise lounge pads, among them some of Patio Time's competitors. Cooper made no fuss at the time because he wanted to get the fledgling company off the ground. Virginia's sales increased, but, except for Patio Time's umbrella frames, Madden paid little attention to the wider product line that California offered. He would buy aluminum patio umbrella frames from Patio Time, sew a covering onto them, and sell the finished product wherever he could. His marketing organization was loosely controlled, being himself and six independent manufacturers' representatives.

Madden's first full year of operations, 1975, ended with only a small profit, but in 1976 sales increased to $1.5 million and aftertax profits to $21,000. In fact, the company was able to clear itself of debt for a few days and completely pay off Patio Time. This development negated the two-to-three ratio on the board of directors in favor of the parent.

Madden then had the right to reconstitute the board on a fifty-fifty basis with California. As a practical matter, Cooper suggested that, rather than relying on California, Madden should fill the board seats with people of his choice. After all, since there was a potential impasse with a fifty-fifty membership, it would be to everyone's advantage to have a harmonious, working board with the good interest of Virginia Padding at heart.

In 1977, Virginia's sales more than doubled to $2.9 million, and aftertax net income increased to $100,000 (see *Exhibit 2*). Madden projected earnings of nearly $150,000 for fiscal 1978 and felt that the future would bring increased profits.

While Cooper was also optimistic about Virginia, he suspected "a little opium" in Madden's 1978 projection. Furthermore, he privately wondered whether Madden would continue to be an effective manager if Virginia's rate of growth persisted. Cooper felt that the rapid growth of his subsidiary in Virginia could increase the need for organizational and financial support from California.

More important, he was becoming increasingly concerned about Madden's growing independence. Cooper's dreams were for national product distribution; Madden did not exactly have this in mind. It wasn't that Madden was deliberately trying to be difficult; he was simply enjoying the fruits of his labor.

The phone call: On November 16, Cooper's marketing manager burst into his office complaining that Virginia had just underpriced the parent company on a major order for patio umbrellas to one of the company's national customers. He demanded that Cooper do something about it. After some reflection, Cooper telephoned Madden and explained that it was impossible for Virginia to continue to operate independently. Cooper said that independent operations were preventing the optimization of sales and earnings for both companies.

For example, he pointed out, nearly half of Virginia's sales were to competitors of Patio Time. He explained that whenever Virginia sold $100,000 worth of pads to one of Patio Time's competitors, Virginia was helping the competitor sell patio furniture worth about $500,000. He said that Virginia's haphazard marketing was leading to serious problems and cited the recent quotes made by Virginia's representatives in direct competition with Patio Time's. Furthermore, Cooper expressed his concern that Virginia's independent representatives handled other lines competing with Patio Time's and were not exclusively serving Patio Time.

When challenged that Virginia would lose sales if it changed its business practices, Cooper admitted that some of Madden's sales to other manufacturers would have to be dropped if Madden were to market the full California line. But Cooper said he believed that any loss would be more than recovered by Virginia's new retail sales and larger profit margins.

To encourage a complete commonality of spirit and interest, Cooper suggested that Madden change his 50% ownership of Virginia Padding for an equitable share in the combined operations of the two companies. Cooper explained that the existing stock ownership pattern was a problem, because effort was not being followed by an equitable reward for all concerned.

For example, he said, California's marketing manager had spent nearly a year working to help Madden penetrate the eastern markets. Cooper himself had spent countless days helping Madden in many ways. California provided many services free of charge. "This can't continue indefinitely. It's time for everybody to be on the same team," said Cooper. "We'll all be better off, Will."

Madden responded, "With my splendid Profit and Loss Statement, what do you expect—blood? Count your money and be happy. You never had it so good. I'm increasing sales and profits at a faster rate than you are, and for your paltry $15,000 investment, you get half of all these blessings."

WHITLAM'S CHOICE

Matt Whitlam had been very disturbed by these events. He wondered whether Madden was trying to bluff Cooper and simply negotiate for a larger share of the combined companies. Although Whitlam was not a member of Virginia Padding's board, he knew Madden as a manager educated in the "school of hard knocks." Madden was aware,

Whitlam also knew, that he was retiring and ready to sell out. He wondered whether Cooper had told Madden of the meeting with Eastco.

Whitlam attempted to list his alternatives. He could simply wait and see, but that strategy could prove expensive—buyers like Eastco were not easy to seduce. Could the companies exist independently? Could Patio Time buy out Virginia? Who had the bargaining power—Cooper or Madden? Whitlam felt that, if he could come up with his own definition of the problem, he might be able to solve it and get the pugnacious presidents working together. "Who's the cat and who's the mouse in this game?" he wondered. "The trouble is, they're spoiling my cheese!"

EXHIBIT 1 Patio Time's Balance Sheets and Income Statements (years ending September 30)

	1977	*1976*
Assets		
Current assets		
Cash and certificates of deposit	$ 203,325	$ 303,552
Accounts receivable, net	173,733	119,099
Due from 50%-owned company	46,857	29,443
Inventories	269,456	233,946
Other	42,970	21,507
Total current assets	$ 736,341	$ 707,547
Investment in 50%-owned company, at equity	$ 70,617	$ 20,528
Equipment and improvements, at cost, net of accumulated depreciation	186,628	221,792
Other	73,600	90,791
	$1,067,186	$1,040,658
Liabilities and stockholders' equity		
Current liabilities		
Accounts payable, trade	$ 115,160	$ 103,180
Federal and state income taxes	60,661	376,628
Accrued liabilities	39,804	37,028
Total current liabilities	$ 215,625	$ 516,836
Stockholders' equity	851,561	523,822
	$1,067,186	$1,040,658

Exhibit 1 (Cont.)

	1977		1976	
Net sales	$5,529,944	100.00%	$5,199,969	100.00%
Cost of goods sold	4,587,631	82.96	4,242,947	81.60
Gross profit	$ 942,313	17.04%	$ 957,022	18.40%
Operating expenses	379,442	6.86	345,466	6.64
Operating income	$ 562,871	10.18%	$ 611,556	11.76%
Other income (expense), net	5,037	0.09	(30,404)	(0.58)
Income before income taxes and equity in earnings of 50%-owned company	$ 567,908	10.27%	$ 581,152	11.18%
Income taxes or credits	290,258	5.25	299,264	5.76
Income (or loss) before equity in earnings of 50%-owned company	$ 277,650	5.02%	$ 281,888	5.42%
Equity in earnings of 50%-owned company	50,089	0.91	10,624	0.20
Net income (or loss)	$ 327,739	5.93%	$ 292,512	5.62%

EXHIBIT 2 **Virginia Padding's Balance Sheets and Income Statements (years ending September 30)**

	1977	1976
Assets		
Current assets		
Cash	$ 112	$ 781
Receivables	351,447	39,877
Inventories	193,116	72,930
Prepayments	4,716	5,680
Total current assets	$ 549,391	$ 119,268
Property and equipment, at cost, net of accumulated depreciation	$ 58,638	$ 49,078
Other assets	5,801	5,895
Total assets	$613,830	$174,241
Liabilities and stockholders' equity		
Current liabilities		
Bank overdraft	$ 3,641	
Accounts payable and accrued expenses	357,725	$109,293
Federal and state taxes payable	102,610	11,270
Long-term debt due within one year	4,333	4,001
Total current liabilities	$468,309	$124,564
Long-term debt due after one year	4,287	8,621
Stockholders' equity	141,234	41,056
Total liabilities and stockholders' equity	$613,830	$174,241

Exhibit 2 (Cont.)

	1977		1976	
Net sales	$2,925,978	100.00%	$1,447,338	100.00%
Cost of goods sold	2,471,287	84.46	1,266,093	87.48
Gross profit	$ 454,691	15.54%	$ 181,245	12.52%
Operating expenses	227,150	7.76	136,742	9.45
Operating income	$ 227,541	7.78%	$ 44,503	3.07%
Other deductions	22,863	0.78	12,755	0.88
Income before taxes on income	$ 204,678	7.00%	$ 31,748	2.19%
Taxes on income	104,500	3.58	10,500	0.72
Net income	$ 100,178	3.42%	$ 21,248	1.47%

THE UNITED WAY OF HEATON

It was Friday afternoon, 5:47 p.m., June 17, 1977. Chuck Marschall, the Executive Director of the United Way of Heaton, and David Hendricks, the President and a substantial shareholder of Electro-Chemical Systems, Inc., Heaton's largest company and second-largest employer, were in Marschall's office. Hendricks was slated to be campaign chairman for the 1978 campaign and, although he was actively working on the fall 1977 campaign, he was already thinking about his role in the United Way in '78.

"You know, Chuck," Hendricks said, "as a board, we're pretty complacent. I've been attending board meetings for five years now and although I've heard over and over again that our strength as a fund raising organization stems from our 'monopoly' access to the corporations of the city, buttressed by our linkages with almost every influential member of Heaton society, I can't remember the last time any board member suggested that we had a problem."

"But Dave, our organization is strong. I'd be worried about my job if the board thought we had problems."

"I won't deny that the United Way is strong here. What worries me is that I can't see where it's weak. One of the board members, Jon Alwyn, commented to me last week that the real reason he now misses half our meetings is because he knows he won't miss anything important. His view seemed to be that because Sid Simons and his predecessors in the chair have managed the agenda so deliberately, there are never any surprises. He says, and I may agree with him, that a few rough spots—a little conflict—would enliven the meetings and us. He says that the United Way is operating so smoothly that our meetings are 'bored' rather than board."

"Jon says that, Dave. But he's behind the campaign. His company is one of our best performers in employee giving. I'm not too worried about Jon."

"What worries me, Chuck, is that when we hired you Jon was one of our most active members. As you rebuilt the United Way in Heaton by cementing its relationship with business and government, you've reduced the need for guys like Jon and me to really work. Success could be our enemy in Heaton."

Recognizing that Hendricks was in a reflective mood, Marschall nodded and leaned back in his chair encouraging Hendricks to continue. Hendricks said, "I want to do more than run a successful campaign next year. I want to revitalize our whole organization and I'd like your advice and help. I'm worried that we are so safe from catastrophe. Short of a press revelation that you and Peter Hammond [the President of the Heaton National Bank, the United Way's bank] had systematically embezzled the Fund, I can't think of anything which could wipe us off the map in Heaton. But I wonder whether the United Way is like

This case was prepared by Assistant Professor Kenneth J. Hatten, assisted by Mr. Mark T. Teagan, Research Assistant, with the cooperation of a number of executives associated directly and indirectly with the United Way of Massachusetts Bay, and from published sources. No resemblance to any particular existing United Way is intended nor should any be inferred.

The case was prepared as a basis for class discussion rather than to illustrate either effective or ineffective handling of an administrative situation.

'old soldiers who never die.' We may not suffer a heart attack but how do we know we haven't got hardening of the arteries?

"We have a monopoly position to raise money inside business," Hendricks continued. "We're secure, stable and our operations are smooth. As a board member, I think I'm accurate in saying that the closest we've ever come to 'conflict' was when we cut the Salvation Army's allocation,[1]—but that was a storm in a tea cup. It never amounted to anything.

"The United Way is almost untested by competition because it has a monopoly to raise money inside businesses. Because of that I can't be sure that things are as good as they appear. I believe in the United Way and its role in the community. What concerns me is, how can I fulfill my responsibility to the community to ensure that the United Way as an organization is adaptive and vital, so that as the community's needs for health care and social services change—and, more importantly, if the role of private philanthropy itself changes—Heaton will be a better place than it is today?

"I'd value your counsel, Chuck," Hendricks said. "How do we ensure that the United Way will be relevant and valued in Heaton ten years from now? What should I do and what should you do? How can we separate the real problems in our future from the trivial stuff that comes up day by day? The United Way occasionally receives some criticism, but we tend to discount it as 'sloganeering'. I hope we can use some of that criticism to sharpen our mettle. I'd like your thoughts on the United Way's long-term future: What we should be worrying about and what we might do to make sure we can handle it?"

"What would you like to do, Dave? Would you like to get together on this again?" Marschall asked.

"I'll drop by next week," Hendricks replied. "Maybe then you could let me have some data showing how we have been performing as an organization."

That night, as he settled down in the living room after dinner with his wife, Chuck Marschall's mind turned to Hendricks's ideas. He wondered where to start and where Hendrick's quiet but persistent enthusiasm would take the United Way.

HEATON AND THE UNITED WAY

Heaton was the capital of the state of West Aloe. It had a population of about 2.1 million and was growing at a rate of about 1% annually. The city was located near some of the country's most beautiful areas for both summer and winter recreation. It was a "clean" city and even its large employers, like Electro-Chemical Systems, Inc., had relatively modern plants which were almost non-polluting. City fathers were inclined to think that Heaton and West Aloe (and, maybe, themselves) were close to God's heart. Two nationally reputable universities were located close to the city center, one a private institution and the other state-financed.

The United Way of Heaton evolved from a much older group of Community Chests. In the late 1950s, William Heaton, a member of the city's founding family and, at the time, the retiring State Governor, called the city's leadership together in an effort to

[1]The Salvation Army was a United Way agency in Heaton.

streamline philanthropic fund-raising in the city. The result was the consolidation of a number of Community Chests into the United Way of Heaton.

Over the years, the United Way of Heaton absorbed most of the earlier Community Chests; however, its geographic reach did not keep pace with suburban growth during the 1960s. The result was that, outside the city's ring freeway, some suburbs had no United Way while others were served by small local organizations. In all, about 80% of the metro-region's population fell under the aegis of the United Way of Heaton.

In 1971, the former Executive Director of the United Way retired and Chuck Marschall took the job. At the time, Heaton's campaign organization was rather ineffective. It had raised less than $10 million in 1970. Between 1971 and 1977, however, the organization responded to Marschall's direction and the enthusiastic involvement of a few dedicated community leaders. Working together, they developed and cemented the United Way's relationships with both business and government to such an extent that in 1977 the United Way had virtual monopoly access to "employees at work." In 1976, the United Way of Heaton raised a total of $18 million.

Exhibit 1 lists some of the key population and employment characteristics of Heaton and of other cities with large United Way organizations. It also allows a comparison of Heaton's campaign record with those of the other cities, all of which fall into the United Way category "Metro 1."

A WEEK ON THE JOB WITH CHUCK MARSCHALL

Monday, June 20, 1977

Monday seemed likely to be a fairly routine day as it began. Bob Hines, the Campaign Director, had left a message which said that Mr. Michael Johnson, a resident of Fairlight, one of Heaton's outer suburbs, had called him over the weekend wanting to know how to set up a United Way in Fairlight. Looking at the map on his office wall, Marschall noted that although Fairlight was outside Heaton's perimeter, it was not represented in any United Way. Johnson, a senior research engineer at Analog Instruments, Inc. on Route 485, was concerned that Fairlight's social service organizations were under-funded and therefore unable to deliver services effectively. Marschall decided to handle the matter himself. Fairlight abutted Heaton's territory on the south and east and the territory of the Aloe River Valley United Way on the west and north. Aloe River covered a semi-urban/semi-rural territory which was relatively autonomous from the city of Heaton for most day-to-day human care services.

Marschall's thoughts were interrupted by the telephone. Dan Lewis, Director of Allocations, was on the line.

"Hi, Chuck. Have a good weekend? Did you see that report of the Archbishop's dinner in the *Evening Star?* I wondered whether it had been cleared by you."

"No, Dan, I've always let you handle the agencies' supplementary fund-raising activities."

"Well, in that case, it was never cleared. I'd better call the organizers and see what's been going on. They raised $73,000, I understand. I'm sure you'll get a call from Toby Heaton at the Red Cross. Ever since we cut their allocation he's been keen to see an *even* application of the rules."

Marschall's thoughts drifted back to Fairlight as he put down the phone. He wondered whether he should try to absorb Fairlight into the Heaton United Way. He decided to file the matter for a few days and see what doors he could open to learn more about Michael Johnson. Marschall's appointment book showed that Peter Sloan, the Chairman, and Ethan Merrett, the Executive Director of the Family Counselling Service of Heaton (FCS) were due in a few minutes.

Marschall's secretary knocked to announce their arrival, and then, with Marschall's consent, showed them in.

"Good morning, Chuck. I think you know our chairman, Peter Sloan," Ethan Merrett said as he held out his hand.

"We came by for a particular reason, Chuck. As you know we've been trying to cope with the busing issue by defusing rumors, by keeping our center open for longer hours, and with our neighborhood recreation programs. But it's costing money. We've applied for government funding but it's going to be too little, too late! Can you help?"

"You know that your application would have to go to the appropriations committee and then the board, Ethan," Marschall said.

"I know that," Sloan interrupted, "but my board and I are concerned that the United Way has not come out and made a statement on the busing issue. If you people really want to be community leaders you have to lead. And to lead you have to take a position." Sloan continued, "People see your reticence as an abdication of responsibility."

"Our responsibilities are to the whole community," Marschall replied. "The busing issue is difficult for all of us and, personally I think what you're trying to do is valuable. But what is of greatest concern to our board is the success of the campaign. If we can't raise the money needed, there'll be more than one agency in trouble. We have to balance the needs of particular agencies against the long-term good of the United Way. In addition, the United Way has never taken an advocacy position . . ."

"Before I retired from the active management of the Sloan Street Bank and Trust," Sloan interjected, "I used to tell our clients and my colleagues in business that it isn't always the amount that counts, it's the *quality* of the money that's important. Quality is what comes with the dollars. What we are looking for is support as much as money," Sloan said, and Merrett nodded his agreement.

"We're not serving just the black community in this case," Merrett said. "They're an important part of Heaton and if they're in trouble, so is the city. But you should know that we're getting more calls for help from white neighborhoods than black."

As the meeting continued, Marschall appreciated the legitimacy of Merrett's and Sloan's request, but he knew the busing issue was controversial, if not political dynamite. He supposed there might be a way for the United Way to split an allocation to separate agencies serving either the black or white communities, but he sensed that such an action might not be enough for Sloan and Merrett. They appeared annoyed as they left Marschall's office with only his promise to place their request before the special allocations committee.

Two hours later, Marschall was walking across the city square to a luncheon meeting with Bernard O'Rourke, President of Marcheon Industries, an electronic components manufacturer. With its 1976 sales of $650 million, Marcheon was a major employer to the north of Heaton in Jefferson County. O'Rourke, as its President, was an influential community leader. Marschall had invited O'Rourke to lunch to enlist his support in

Marschall's efforts to "salve the wounds" of the northern districts before the '77 campaign kicked off. In 1976, the Jefferson Girl Scouts Council had suffered a cut in its "traditional" United Way support. The cut had caused quite a fuss in Jefferson County.

"Hello, Bernie," Marschall said as he sat down in the dining room of the Aloean Club. After some minor pleasantries, Marschall got down to business.

"As you know, Bernie, I've been concerned about the hue and cry in Jefferson County since we cut the allocation of the Girl Scouts in your area from $22 to $12 per girl. We were merely correcting a long-standing anomoly: the average allocation to the Girl Scouts in the Heaton United Way is $12 per girl."

"I understand, Chuck, but you have to remember that we always have a battle in Jefferson County. We're well outside the city limits and there are plenty of people who never come into Heaton. We're always wrestling with the problem of what the northern lake area owes to the city core. People are involved in their immediate community. Most of them don't see what they get out of the United Way. To many of them it looks like an inner-city subsidization program. That's why the cut hurt. It looked like a blow against the north. I'll think about what we might do, Chuck, and get back to you," O'Rourke said as the meal ended.

Back in his office that afternoon, Marschall realized that Monday was setting a pretty good pace for the week. Next on his calendar was a performance review meeting with his Director of Communication and Public Relations, Bob Andrews. Marschall had hired him from Meagan, Scott and Towl, Heaton's most successful advertising agency, on the recommendation of a number of board members. But Andrews hadn't worked out as well as Marschall had hoped. He seemed to be enthusiastic but there was something about him that was increasingly annoying Marschall.

When Andrews came into Marschall's office he didn't act like someone who was being reviewed. Instead he said to Marschall: "Chief, I don't know whether you realize it, but you're like an old fire horse or a circus dog. You keep going back to your old haunts. . . . There's more to this business than the campaign![2] This is the first chance I've had to get your *undivided* attention for almost a month. I have two things I'd like to discuss with you."

Andrews continued, "First, as you know, the world's changing. For example, the percentage of women in the workforce is increasing and our campaign advertising and promotion have never acknowledged the fact. I've had a couple of people out on the street in the office district asking women if they give to the United Way. About one quarter of them say, 'My husband gives at his office.' That means we're losing dollars. I could design a series of TV slots directed at working women to really hit home that it's everyone's responsibility. We should have a message for each significant segment of the population.

"The second thing," Andrews said, "is that my people are finding that our traditional image is *too* family-oriented. We should jazz up our image. There's an ad they used in Boston that really makes a point: "Without United Way, you might be asked to buy an awful lot of cookies." I can see it now—two enormous stacks of cookies. . . . I'd like to

[2]Prior to joining the Heaton United Way as Executive Director, Marschall had been Campaign Director in another Metro 1 city. Andrews believed that 'Chief', as he called Marschall, spent too much time working with Bob Hines, the Heaton Campaign Director.

come up with something along those lines. I think it would virtually guarantee the 10% increase in funds-raised that you're after.''

''Bob, I'll think about all this later and get back to you,'' Marschall said. ''Right now we're supposed to be reviewing your performance. It's already mid-June and I still haven't seen the campaign film.

''You're outside too much!'' Marschall continued forcefully. ''The way to get a good campaign running is to ensure that the inside organization is operating smoothly with every item needed, ready on time. You're focusing on the outside too much! I read your memo on segmented advertising. I think it would be too expensive and too confusing if we tried to run ads for every element of the community. Bob Hines and I will worry about getting the dollars in—you know that Simons and his team are enthusiastic and hard working.

''The message you have to communicate is simple,'' Marschall said. ''Inflation hits human care services hard and Heaton is growing. Expanding the community's present services and introducing new services will cost money. We need 10% to stay even. We're an efficient fund-raiser; 88% of every dollar raised goes to the agencies it's intended for. But not everyone is giving their fair share.''

Marschall continued speaking for some time and concluded by telling Andrews that if his creativity was directed to embellishing the campaign message that had worked for the past six years, he (Marschall) would be happy. He concluded by stressing the need for timely performance and for a less flamboyantly decorated office, pointing out that ''BULL—'' in six-inch-high letters on the wall was out of keeping with the image of the United Way in Heaton.

Feeling somewhat exhausted by this experience, Marschall asked his secretary to take any calls and began to read the minutes of the last board meeting. Then, recalling Hendrick's report of Jon Alwyn's attendance, Marschall began to track a few people to see what their attendance records were like. It appeared that a 50% record was about the norm. A few stalwarts were always present, but at most thirty to thirty-five of the board of fifty were there.

At a charity dinner that night at Heaton's world-renowned St. Jacques Hotel, Marschall happened to be seated next to Jeff Fox, whom he knew well. For some years, Fox had been a substantial personal donor to the United Way but he had never allowed any employee solicitation inside his company (which now employed 1500 people). Yet, Fox was active on the board of a local charity and had recently chaired a Governor's Task Force on the State's health services and welfare budget.

''Hello, Jeff; one of these days I'm going to get you onto the United Way board,'' Marschall said with a grin as he sat down.

As the evening wore on, Fox explained why he was a United Way supporter, but a non-participant. ''Before I founded my own business, Chuck, the company I was with had a President who was really keen on the United Way. Every year he would hold a meeting of the executives and say 'Giving is a private matter. What you decide to give is your decision and it will never reflect on your job.' Then he would get a list of payroll deductions and call, 'I hope we haven't missed you!' It really stuck in my craw. When I started this company I vowed to never unofficially tax my employees. I never have and I never will!''

Overhearing the conversation, one of Fox's friends, James McGregor of McGregor

Constructions, Inc., joined the two men, saying, "There are better reasons than that for not participating in the United Way."

McGregor continued and explained that it was neither the "tax" nor "peer pressure" which kept him from joining the United Way. He simply believed that the "real costs" of the United Way to the community were much higher than the typical expenses reported by the United Way: 9% to 12% of funds raised.

"You have 180 nominating members," McGregor said, "A 50-person board, working committees of almost 200 people, 85 loaned executives for 3 months and 40,000 volunteers, plus your permanent organization working to raise $18 million in one year.[3] As you know, I was on the health service and welfare Task Force for the Governor this year. We have a volunteer committee of 10 and we are dealing with a total budget of $1 billion. Already, the first quarter's results alone show we saved the State $41 million. By the end of this year we will have saved the State $250 million, and $180 million of that saving will continue year after year. These are results I can get excited about. As time goes on, the United Way's role in the community is going to shrink because people expect government to do it. Unless you can find a new role for the United Way, its days as a major community force in this city are numbered."

Tuesday, June 21, 1977

As he rode into the city the next morning, Marschall pondered McGregor's comments of the previous evening. Critics were always making remarks like "a dollar cost for a dollar raised" but the United Way had an outstanding record for controlling its expenses. Not only that, but Marschall knew that agency heads valued the United Way dollars highly. Only last week the head of one agency showed Marschall that administering United Way allocations was costing the agency about one-third the cost of administering government contracts simply because of the kind of reporting required by each source of funds.[4]

Back in his office, Marschall consulted his copy of the *Statistical Abstract of the United States* to check government spending on welfare programs (*Exhibit 2*). Of course, he knew that government involvement in health and welfare services was substantial and growing, but what did it mean for the United Way?

His first caller that morning was a board member who was concerned about what he

[3]Using a page from his pocket notebook, McGregor estimated the "costs" of Heaton's United Way Campaign in 1976. He claimed he was being conservative.

Group Involved	*Number of Executives*	*Effective Days Given (Average)*	*Reasonable Daily Rate ($'s)*	*Total Value $(000's)*
Nominating committee	180	.5	500	45
Board	50	6.0	500	150
Working committees	200	12.0	250	600
Loaned executives	85	65.0	80	442
Campaign volunteers	40,000	1.0	60	2400
	Value of volunteer time			$3637
	Plus United Way expenses (10%)			1800
			Total Cost	$5437

[4]The United Way grants were given for the general purposes of the agency. Government contracts were for explicit services to individuals and were reported on an individual service basis, not on an agency basis.

called "advocacy agencies hiding under the skirts of traditional family agencies." As Marschall was aware, the YMCA allowed its meeting facilities to be used by an anti-gun group and by a pro-abortion women's group. The focus of the board member's concern was a circular from the National Rifle Association advising its members that the United Way funds were being used to support an anti-gun campaign. The circular suggested that this was outside the function of the United Way, indicating that the United Way was not supervising its spending and hinting that the best way to get action was to "cut giving this year."

Marschall's response was that the two strong features of Heaton's United Way allocation process were its stability (*Exhibit 3*) and its focus on end results. Marschall had always advocated that the United Way focus on results and not the details of agency operations; yet, many members of his board from time to time advocated tighter "controls."

What worried Marschall about "controls" was their ultimate impact on the agencies themselves. He believed that if the United Way were too rigid and too detail-oriented, there would be only "one game in town" and only one charitable board worth serving on: the United Way's. It would lead to a situation where the attractiveness of the delivery agencies' boards, to concerned executives and community leaders, would be diminished. As one corporate president said, "At my age, why play in the Little League?"

Dan Lewis interrupted Marschall by knocking and walking into the room. As Director of Allocations, Lewis handled agency relations.

"Yes, Dan," Marschall said, "What is it?"

"I'm concerned that so many of our agencies will not display the United Way logo and inform their clients that they're a United Way agency," Lewis said.

"I've just come back from Fidelity House out in Aloedale. There's not one sign that they're supported by the United Way. What bothers me is that I've written, argued and tried to explain to their Director, that they'll benefit from letting people know they're a United Way agency, but, although they promise to do something, they never do. I was wondering if you could discuss it with someone on their board. I think it's important. We allocated over $95,000 to them last year, about 18% of their budget."

"Okay, Dan, I think I know who to call. This is an important matter and I know you've been working on it. With the '77 campaign only a few months away, I'd appreciate it if you'd push the agencies to help us. Let me know if there are any holdouts."

Next, a computer service bureau salesman dropped in some material on COFRS, a computer program for philanthropic agencies designed to report on the "Costs of Funds Raised and Spent."

The rest of the day was consumed by scheduled meetings, preparations for some working committees and a farewell dinner for the divisional Vice President of one of the city's largest employers, an active United Way supporter, who had been transferred out of Heaton to the company's headquarters in Chicago.

Wednesday, June 22, 1977

The most notable event of the day was a visit from a delegation of small agency managers inquiring as to how the United Way could help them promote their services. The spokeswoman for the group explained that the agencies felt they were unable to reach all of their potential clientele through conventional channels. She complained that the United Way did little to help the small agencies develop the community presence which the United Way, itself, viewed as being so important. She concluded by saying that the small agencies she represented hoped that the United Way, next year, might approve significant budget allocations for promotion and, perhaps, provide the agencies with its expert advice.

Thursday, June 23, 1977

Thursday opened quietly but ended more dramatically when Monsignor Peters, Director of the Catholic Charities Bureau, came in to discuss his new plans. Apparently at the Archbishop's dinner on Saturday, June 18, a group of priests and businessmen had put their heads together and had come up with a plan which would enable businessmen to directly allocate their contributions to specific charities in their local communities. Monsignor Peters smiled and said to Marschall, "The Archbishop wants to call it the 'Adopt an Agency Program.'" The consensus of the group, Monsignor Peters reported, was that each corporation could also loan one or two executives directly to the agencies to help improve the efficiency and effectiveness of the services they provided the community. One of the businessmen had stated that his company always got four times the mileage from its donations to the local high schools and arts councils as from its much larger donation to the United Way. He said, "The most important community for my firm is the one surrounding my plant."

Friday, June 24, 1977

"How are things, Chuck?" Hendricks greeted Marschall. He had arranged to drive Marschall home that night.

Marschall said, "It's been a hectic week. I've been thinking about our conversation last Friday. What I'd like to do is take a few days off and spend some uninterrupted time thinking about the long-term future of the United Way, but I feel that unless I'm here something crucial to the '77 campaign won't be done. We're late with the campaign film as it is."

"I suspect Andrews is going all out for you, Chuck. He's a meticulous guy with some really great ideas. I was talking to him while I waited in the foyer. He's talking about a scientifically-designed promotional strategy based on market segmentation. I've had great results with segmented promotions at Electro-Chem, you know," Hendricks said.

As they walked to the car, Hendricks continued, "I've just realized that the United Way has always followed a segmentation strategy. I did a little research during the week and I was surprised to learn that of the almost $30 billion philanthropic dollars received by private non-profit organizations, corporations gave only $1.35 billion, about 4.6% of the total. What was more surprising was that 2% of all corporations were responsible for 50% of all corporate giving.

"Now, I've related this to the United Way and it's surprising. I'll certainly have to revise my ideas about our monopoly. In rough figures it looks like this." He handed Marschall a sheet of paper, which read:

All giving	\$30 billion
United Way	\$ 1 billion
United Way share	3.3%
All Corporate giving	\$ 1.35 billion
Corporate giving to United Way	\$300 billion
United Way share	22.2%
All public giving	\$23.6 billion
Employee giving to United Way	\$650 million
General public giving to United Way	\$ 50 million
United Way share of general giving	.2%

"The numbers are surprising to me on two counts. One, just how much of the corporate giving we hold—I suspect that the national figures more or less hold for Heaton. What this means is that we can't expect to substantially increase our share of the corporate philanthropic dollar. Perhaps our best hope is to push employee giving. I've heard that Xerox and Rohm & Hass and a few other companies have really pushed employee giving in the past year. Maybe that's what we should do. AT&T increased their employee giving 91% last year—that's a hell of a record, but I want to know how they did it and why it was possible.

"The second surprise was our minute share of general giving by the public, only 0.2%. In Heaton last year, I know we raised only 4.7% of our dollars from the general public [*Exhibit 1*]. There must be some way to do better here without increasing costs too much," Hendricks concluded.

Once in his car, Hendricks gave Marschall a folder with a few tables in it and said, "We can talk about these as we drive home.

"Look at this table [*Exhibit 4*]. Imagine the impact the aging of the population is going to have on the country and Heaton," he said. "It's not just the percentages but the total numbers that are overwhelming. Of course, what we have to consider is how other social changes which are occurring now will affect us."

"Well, for one, inflation," Marschall replied. "Look at this graph from the United Way of America [*Exhibit 5*]. It looks like we've been losing ground instead of growing when you value the dollars raised at 1967 prices. And, lately, we've been losing ground to the 'Nationals' [*Exhibit 6*].

"Another is government," Marschall added. "They're taking responsibility for a larger and larger proportion of all basic health and welfare services. Although I'm sure they'll never take it all, the changing role of government could force us to change our role as a support agency in the community.

"Of course," Marschall continued, "if you want to blue sky a little, there are some major social trends that affect Heaton where we might consider special allocations. There's violent crime on the increase, and black infant mortality which is still almost twice the white rate. And there are plenty of other issues which should be of concern in this community. The problem is to identify those we should be concerned with now and in the future.

"However, one thing that came up during the week sticks in my mind. Out on the West Coast, consumerism is more aggressive than here in Heaton. One of the United Way's out there now has equal representation by donors, agencies and consumers of social services. Last week I met with the heads of six small agencies who asked for board representation by professional staff members. They want us to let them elect agency managers to the board. I explained that we already had people on our board who were also on agency boards but, they said, that wasn't what they wanted. They wanted to elect their professional staff to the United Way board.

"They say that with professional staff representation on the board, the United Way could take a more innovative role in the development of new agencies and new social services. They claim that we are too conservative, too wedded to our existing clientele, and too slow to let 'embryonic' agencies into the United Way."

Hendricks answered, "Of course, I'm not sure that pioneering or exploring is the United Way's appropriate role, Chuck. The United Way is like the Dow Jones. It's not volatile, it's secure—or at least relatively so. I'm not sure that we should get into R&D in the human care field. By focusing on stable agencies whose long histories demonstrate that they're needed, we can ensure our donors that the money we raise is well spent. That way, too, we can better balance the emotional appeal of the popular agency against the real needs of the community.

"The representation issue is an interesting one. Sometimes I think we have a few too many board members whose involvement is titular. As a whole, we place too much of the burden on the professional staff and you, Chuck. Maybe a few agency representatives would be a good idea," Hendricks concluded as his car pulled up in front of Marschall's home. "By the way," he added, "did you hear of the 'Whose Fair Share Are You Carrying?' seminar over at the State University tomorrow evening?[5] It was advertised in the local papers."

As Marschall's wife opened the front door, he said to her, "What a week! It was one issue after another starting Monday and ending with Dave Hendricks outside the door. I've spent so much time fighting fires and attending to everyday matters that I've hardly thought about the long run." Hendricks wants to work on the United Way's future—how we make sure it's relevant and vital ten years from now. I'm not sure quite where to start or how to make time to start at all."

[5]The seminar was being offered by a group of academicians who were actively campaigning against United Way fund raising. One major element of their platform centered on "big business" controlling community services via its control of United Way boards.

EXHIBIT 1
Metro 1 Campaign Performance

	Population		Firms with 5,000 or More Employees		1976 Campaign Result		Per Capita Giving		Giving as % Effective Buying Income		Sources of Funds Raised, 1975		"100 Largest Employers—1975"		
City Names	1975 Millions	Annual Growth Rate 1971/75 %	#	% Community Work Force	$ Raised Millions	Annual Growth Rate 1971/76 %	1975 $/Head	Annual Growth Rate 1971/75 %	%	Annual Growth Rate %	Corporate %	Employee %	Campaign Result %	Corporate Gift per Employee $/Person	Employee Gift $/Person
Atlanta	1.7	5.0	10	10.9	13.1	8.3	7.2	3.8	.15	−3.0	.6	68.1	56.7	10.1	23.8
Baltimore	2.1	0.0	10	11.1	15.0	8.7	6.6	8.4	.14	0.0	27.1	67.1	60.0	12.5	26.7
Boston	2.5	0.0	13	8.4	17.0	4.3	6.3	3.6	.12	−4.3	30.5	52.2	49.8	11.8	19.9
Buffalo	1.1	0.0	3	5.5	9.9	2.4	8.9	2.4	.19	−4.2	26.8	66.8	59.2	15.9	34.5
Chicago	6.0	0.4	23	7.7	44.1	7.9	6.8	7.3	.12	−0.4	33.3	61.3	47.8	17.1	27.5
Cincinnati	1.3	0.0	6	10.5	14.5	7.3	9.9	5.5	.21	1.9	30.8	61.9	60.5	17.7	32.6
Cleveland	1.9	0.0	5	7.9	27.6	6.4	13.7	6.1	.29	−2.1	29.4	59.6	52.5	21.5	38.1
Dallas	1.4	0.0	4	4.9	12.5	7.3	8.1	6.0	.15	−3.2	32.3	62.6	52.5	12.8	23.5
Detroit	3.9	0.0	13	25.5	37.9	4.0	8.9	2.8	.16	−5.4	18.4	75.8	73.5	8.0	41.2
Heaton	2.1	1.1	5	9.0	18.1	7.2	8.3	7.1	.15	−2.1	28.2	67.1	42.1	11.6	27.8
Houston	1.9	1.4	6	6.2	16.0	9.4	7.6	8.1	.15	−2.1	27.3	64.5	58.0	13.9	33.9
Kansas City	1.0	0.0	3	4.2	9.7	4.7	9.0	4.3	.16	−6.0	21.4	73.5	46.4	7.8	30.0
Los Angeles	6.9	0.0	18	9.4	32.2	4.1	3.9	1.0	.07	−5.0	29.9	60.8	29.1	7.5	10.5
Miami	1.4	1.9	3	8.1	9.9	9.5	6.5	7.7	.13	−2.2	28.2	65.5	47.1	7.7	25.6
Milwaukee	1.2	0.0	4	5.0	12.8	4.9	9.8	4.4	.20	−3.1	31.9	62.2	61.7	18.9	33.3
Minneapolis	1.2	2.2	3	4.9	12.5	8.8	9.5	9.9	.19	2.3	32.6	60.2	54.7	20.9	31.0
New York	7.9	0.0	31	NR	30.1	9.5	3.5	9.5	.07	3.9	49.7	50.3	36.8	10.8	11.0
Philadelphia	2.9	−0.8	9	7.2	22.9	3.8	7.6	4.5	.15	−3.7	33.9	52.6	46.3	15.9	19.4
Pittsburgh	1.6	0.0	4	10.5	19.5	6.0	11.6	6.3	.23	−2.2	28.7	59.6	69.6	20.7	42.4
Rochester	0.9	6.5	2	19.6	15.1	7.3	16.1	1.2	.32	−2.6	28.9	58.9	74.6	28.4	49.0
San Francisco															
Seattle	3.1	0.0	18	17.9	19.6	5.4	6.1	6.0	.10	−5.0	28.3	68.9	63.5	9.1	22.5
St. Louis	1.1	0.0	4	12.8	11.2	8.6	9.2	9.5	.16	−0.9	26.5	67.6	65.0	11.6	31.5
Toronto	1.7	0.0	6	8.9	17.5	5.3	9.5	4.1	.19	−3.5	21.9	60.8	55.4	15.2	34.8
Washington,	2.1	0.0	7	6.6	15.6	4.4	7.4	5.1	.15	−3.1	40.4	46.1	39.9	17.1	13.6
D.C.	3.0	0.9	7	4.1	11.2	−4.6	5.4	2.2	.08	−9.8	17.2	81.6	29.1	9.9	19.1

Source: 1976 Metro 1, United Way of America.

EXHIBIT 2

Social Welfare Expenditures Under Public Programs: 1950 to 1973

Year	Total Social Welfare	Social Insurance	Public Aid	Health and Medical Programs	Veterans Programs	Education	Housing	Other Social Welfare	All Health and Medical Care	Total Social Welfare as Percent of	
										Gross National Product	Total Government Expenditures
TOTAL (millions)											
1950	23,508	4,947	2,496	2,064	6,866	6,674	15	448	3,065	8.9%	37.6%
1960	52,293	19,307	4,101	4,464	5,479	17,626	177	1,139	6,395	10.6	38.0
1970	145,894	54,676	16,488	9,753	9,018	50,848	701	4,408	25,232	15.3	47.8
1973 (prel.)	215,228	85,892	28,327	14,603	12,953	65,247	1,922	6,284	37,544	17.6	55.0

Source: *Statistical Abstract of the United States, 1974*, U.S. Department of Commerce, Bureau of the Census.

EXHIBIT 3

United Way of Heaton Allocation History: Funding of 15 Randomly Selected Agencies ($000)*

Agency	1970	1971	1972	1973	1974	1975	1976	1977	Percent of Agency's Budget, 1974	Percent of Agency's Budget, 1976
Heaton Boys' Club	$48.0	$47.6	$49.0	$49.2	$47.1	$66.4	$67.5	$73.9	20.4%	25.2%
	3.5	34.1	34.5	34.5	34.5	40.4	47.6	51.3		
Arthritis Foundation, Aloe Chapter				180.0	132.0	170.0	150.0	169.1	23.3	20.5
		150.1	141.2	132.2	132.2	102.2	98.9	104.9[a]		
North Heaton Council, B.S.A.	29.3	32.4	32.5	38.3	42.4	36.6	19.4	26.0	14.2	20.3
	17.0	16.4	17.0	13.0	13.0	7.0	13.0	19.0		
Hispanic Community Center				28.3	28.5	43.5	49.6	44.4	11.6	15.2
			25.0	25.0	25.0	35.0	40.0	44.3		
Ecumenical Social Action Committee				43.6	124.9	33.0	66.8	60.5	5.6	19.1
			14.0	14.0	14.0	33.0	40.5	51.5		
Family Services of Melham	37.0	39.9	38.9	38.9	37.3	26.7	45.9	51.5	35.3	33.3
	22.0	22.7	23.6	29.6	29.6	31.7	34.6	36.2		
Youth Social Development Center	9.1	8.4	10.9	9.0	7.3	13.6	10.7	11.0	9.5	6.9
	6.2	6.1	5.5	5.0	5.0	5.0	5.0	8.0		
Greater Heaton Girl Scouts	62.9	48.2	47.3	47.9	75.7	49.2	50.0	62.5	40.5	22.6
	30.7	30.7	30.7	30.7	30.7	35.7	39.0	42.5		
Intercommunity Homemaker Services				22.7	12.0	15.0	12.0	20.0	5.3	5.0
	5.0	5.0	11.4	12.0	12.0	12.0	12.0	17.0		
Heaton Valley Council, B.S.A.	7.4	7.9	9.6	9.7	9.0	9.2	9.6	9.9	1.7	1.7
	3.7	3.6	3.0	3.0	3.0	3.0	3.3	4.8		
Heaton-Matler VNA					94.6	82.1	92.8	40.0	13.4	6.4
					32.4	37.5	30.0	22.5		
North Meagan Street Industrial School	74.6	82.9	92.6	111.1	106.7	97.7	79.7	69.5	10.7	11.5
	41.7	40.9	30.0	30.0	30.0	30.0	35.0	42.5		
West Side Committee on Alcoholism			10.0	25.0	30.0	44.0	85.0	64.0	2.7	2.5
		7.6	10.0	17.0	17.0	29.0	59.0	29.0		
Central Heaton VNA			8.7	8.1	9.2	10.7	20.9	14.3	10.6	6.0
		5.4	5.4	5.4	5.4	5.4	15.4[b]	5.4		
West Heaton Community Center	57.2	81.2	77.3	90.0	89.5	67.3	60.0	72.1	58.4	40.8
	33.5	32.7	35.0	50.0	40.0	45.0	37.5	45.0		

*Top figure is requested support; bottom figure is United Way allocation.

[a]*Arthritis Foundation* - The recommended increase is for basic operating expenses of an organization that has made significant progress in strengthening its management capability over the past year. The committee is particularly pleased to see the efforts to develop consumer action education groups which will work to improve the quality of care provided to arthritis sufferers. The committee notes that the research component of its budget was largely directed at clinical research which directly involves patient care - the delivery of a service to a resident of the UW service area.

[b]Extra $10,000 contingent on merger.

EXHIBIT 4 Estimated and Projected* Population Structure by Age, 1960 to 2000 (%)

	Total Population (millions)	*25–29 Years*	*30–44 Years*	*45–64 Years*	*65–75 Years*	*75 Years and Over*
1960	180.7	6.1%	20.0%	20.0%	6.1%	3.1%
1970	204.9	6.7	17.0	20.5	6.1	3.8
1980	222.0	8.6	18.9	19.3	6.2	4.2
1990	238.9	8.2	23.4	18.3	6.6	4.6
2000	251.1	6.8	22.3	22.1	6.3	5.0

*Series X, which would reach zero growth around the middle of the twenty-first century at 277 million, is one of the many possible approaches to zero growth. The immediate cessation of net immigration, combined with replacement level fertility would not lead to immediate zero growth because the U.S. has a relatively young age structure (due to the post-World War II baby boom) which provides momentum for continued growth. Zero growth in 1974 (assuming no dramatic change in mortality) required an annual total fertility rate of about 1,000 with net immigration at the current level, or about 1,200 with no net immigration. The total fertility rate in 1973 was about 1,900.

Source: Statistical Abstract of the United States, 1974, U.S. Department of Commerce, Bureau of the Census.

EXHIBIT 5 U.W. Giving from All Sources . . . (Funding Goal Component Projections)

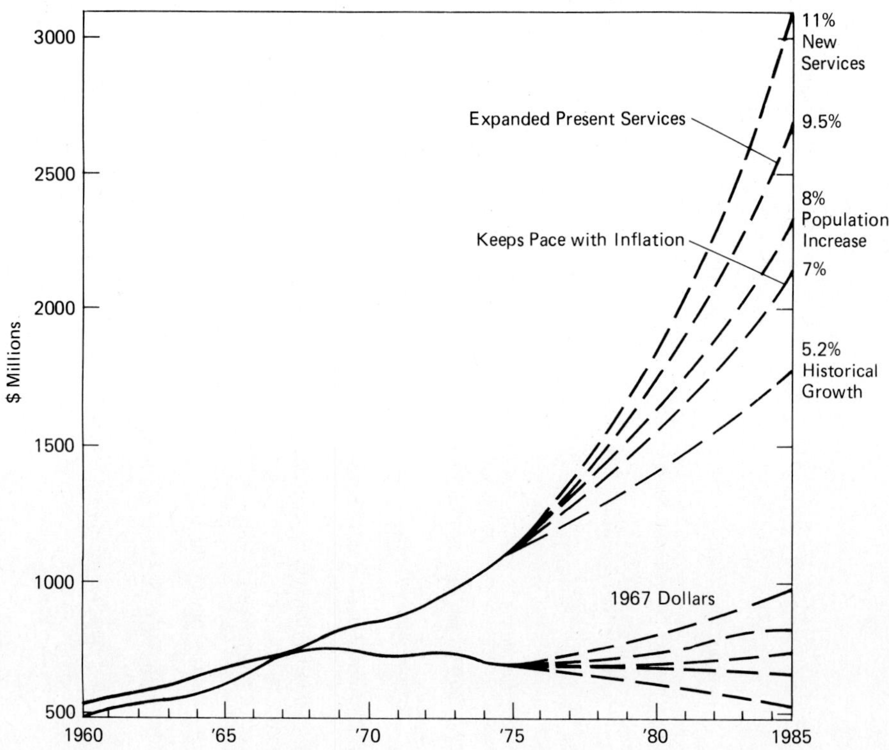

EXHIBIT 6
Campaign Performance of Major U.S. Charities

Campaign Dates	Organization	*Funds Raised ($ millions)* 1965	1969	*Increase of 1969 over 1965 (%)*	*Funds Raised ($ millions) 1974*	*Increase of 1974 over 1970 (%)*	*Percent Allocation to research (1974)*
April	American Cancer Society	36.9	45.3	+23%	73.2	+46%	24%
February	American Heart Association	25.5	31.9	+25	43.1	+32	26
Nov. 12-Dec. 31	American Lung Association				37.6	+7	3
May	The Arthritis Foundation	4.7	6.5	+40	8.8	+28	24
May-June (1974) Oct.-Dec. (1970)	Muscular Dystrophy Association of America	6.8	8.1	+20	22.1	+148	24
May	National Association for Mental Health	8.6	10.4	+21	12.5	+28	1
November	National Association for Retarded Children	6.0	6.1	+2			
	National Association for Retarded Citizens				2.7	$142	7
Feb. 24-March 30 (1974)	National Easter Seal Society for Crippled Children & Adults	20.5	16.0	+28	27.0	+29	1
January	The National Foundation	21.6	22.1	−2	46.1	+97	7
April & October	National Fund for Medical Education	2.1	1.0	−52			
May 11-June 15 (1974)	National Multiple Sclerosis Society	6.8	4.0	+69	11.1	+55	23
Nov. 10-Dec. 31 (1970)	National Tuberculosis and Respiratory Disease Association	33.0	28.8	+15			
	Planned Parenthood Federation of America	8.1	15.0	+86	18.5	+35	1
January	United Cerebral Palsy Assoc.	11.6	13.2	+13	19.5	+41	3
Total:13	Nat'l Health Agencies 1969	180.6	219.9	+22			16
Total:12	Nat'l Health Agencies 1974 (above)				322.2	+44	13
Fall/March	American National Red Cross (June)	90.5	102.6	+13	133.5	+7	1
Fall	Local United Funds & Community Chests in U.S.A. (1965 & 1969). Since 1970, Local United Way Campaigns in U.S.A.	556.3	764.0	+37	976.6	+24	

Source: National Information Bureau, Inc., 419 Park Avenue South, New York, NY 10016.

CONTINENTAL ILLINOIS NATIONAL BANK AND TRUST COMPANY (A)

In June, 1975, Mr. Roger Anderson, Chairman of Continental Illinois National Bank and Trust Company, was trying to decide how Continental could best improve its business with multinational companies. Continental's problems with these customers were essentially twofold: First, its US-based multinational customers were not as profitable accounts as Continental management thought they could be; and, second, it had relatively few customers among foreign-headquartered multinational companies. Though numerous banks competed in the multinational market, Mr. Anderson considered First National City Bank of New York (Citibank) and Morgan Guaranty Trust Company to be Continental's chief competitors. These banks approached the multinational market in markedly different manners, and Mr. Anderson was trying to decide whether Continental should follow one of their models or take an entirely different approach.

COMPANY HISTORY

Continental was Chicago's oldest bank. It traced its origins to the Merchants' Savings, Loan and Trust Company, which was established in 1857 and which quickly gained a reputation as a conservative bank in an era of "wildcat" banking. The bank changed its location, as well as its name, several times as it and Chicago's business center grew. When the bank's building was destroyed in the great Chicago fire on October 9, 1871, Mr. Solomon A. Smith, the President of the bank, set up temporary quarters in his home. Though all the bank's records were destroyed, no depositor lost a penny. Cash and securities survived, and bank officials decided to honor the word of their depositors as a guide in paying out funds.

During the first two decades of the 1900s, Continental grew steadily and merged with several other Illinois banks. The present institution, Continental Illinois National Bank and Trust Company of Chicago, was issued a national charter in 1932. Though the bank operated a full-service commercial banking and trust business serving individuals, businesses, financial institutions, and government agencies, its primary area of expertise came to be servicing large U.S. companies, especially those headquartered in the Midwest. One reason for Continental's focus on corporate customers was that Illinois's banking law limited commercial banks to only two branch offices, both of which had to be within 3,500 yards of headquarters. With such a restriction, it was very difficult to be an aggressive retail bank, so Continental, like other leading Illinois banks, looked to corporate accounts for major growth opportunities.

In 1950 Continental was widely considered to be the major financial institution in

This case was prepared by Nancy J. Davis, Research Associate, under the direction of Assistant Professor Dan R. E. Thomas and Associate Professor Fred K. Foulkes, as the basis for class discussion rather than to illustrate either effective or ineffective handling of an administrative situation. Confidential company data have been disguised, and while useful for purposes of case analysis, they are not useful for research purposes.

the Midwest; it was especially strong in industries such as energy and mineral resources. In 1961, in an attempt to diversify its customer base, it merged with City National Bank and Trust Company which was well-known for serving small and growing companies.

On April 1, 1969, Continental became the wholly owned subsidiary of a one-bank holding company created to allow diversification into other financially related service areas. By the end of 1974, the bank had total assets of over $19 billion and total deposits of about $13.5 billion. In terms of assets it was the eighth largest bank in the U.S. It was fourth among the twenty largest U.S. banks in five-year Earnings per Share (E.P.S.) growth. It employed 9,880 people. (See *Exhibit 1* for income statements and balance sheets, 1970–1974.)

CONTINENTAL'S ORGANIZATION

In June, 1975, Continental's organization consisted of four staff service areas and six line units. The staff areas and their functions were as follows:

1 Corporate Personnel Services—had responsibility for all organizational structure and development programs.
2 Corporate Counsel—coordinated Continental's relations with its various publics through its legal department and public affairs division.
3 Corporate Financial Services—consisted of the treasurer's office, and the control, auditing, and economic research divisions.
4 Operations and Management Services—handled facilities management, date processing, methods engineering, marketing services, strategic planning, and area development.

The line units and their functions were:

1 Trust and Investment Services—managed customer estates, corporate pension and profit-sharing plans, investment programs, and funds of businesses, charitable institutions, and governmental bodies. Also handled corporate fiduciary services.
2 Bond and Money Market Services—financed all bank operations, including the management of its investment portfolio.
3 Real Estate Services—provided short- and long-term financing throughout the world.
4 Personal Banking Services—provided a complete range of consumer banking services.
5 Commercial Banking Services—provided deposit and loan facilities and other financial services to individuals, partnerships, associations, corporations, banks, and other financial institutions within the U.S.
6 International Services—responsible for all of Continental's foreign business.

CINB's top management operated as an executive office. The Chairman and President each had several functions reporting to them. The units that would be most affected by a change in CINB's approach to multinational customers were Commercial Banking Services and International Services. Both of these units reported to Mr. Roger Anderson. (See *Exhibit 2* for a corporate organization chart and *Exhibit 3* for biographical data regarding key executives in Commercial Banking and International Services, plus the President and Chairman of the Board.)

Continental serviced multinational corporations through Commercial Banking Services and International Services. Commercial Services handled all business of corporations that operated solely in the U.S. and domestic business of US-based multinationals. International Services was responsible for foreign business of US-based and foreign-based multinationals and all business of foreign companies which were not multinationals. These two operations were separate profit centers, and Commercial Services was considered to be markedly the more successful. While Commercial contributed about 65% of the bank's operating income, it contributed about 96% of the operating earnings in 1974. (See *Exhibit 4*.)

COMMERCIAL BANKING SERVICES

Commercial Banking Services, under the direction of Executive Vice President Eugene Holland, Jr., consisted of three staff and three operating units. The operating units were the National Division, the Metropolitan Division, and the Special Industries Division. (See *Exhibit 5* for an organization chart of Commercial Banking Services.)

I. National Division

The National Division, headed by Mr. Donald Myers, Senior Vice President, was responsible for all of Continental's domestic corporate business outside the greater Chicago metropolitan area. It had about 700 to 800 corporate customers, most of whom were among *Fortune* magazine's top 1,000 U.S. companies. It offered some 182 different services to these customers. In addition, this Division was responsible for about 2,500 correspondent banks throughout the U.S. It provided them with computer services, bond services, capital, and lines of credit. Many of the correspondent banks were very small. They were not particularly profitable accounts, but they were considered good training ground for new account managers.[1] An account manager could handle 75 to 100 of these accounts, whereas he might handle anywhere from 15 to 30 corporate accounts, depending on his experience and the complexity of the account.

The National Division had staff of about 125 (including account managers and their supervisors), plus about 50 support personnel. The Division's account managers ranged in age from 25 to 40, with the average being about 32. The average length of time these account managers had been with the bank was about 5 years.

The tasks involved in servicing a National Division client differed from one customer to another. The account manager had to understand thoroughly each client's business and to identify those needs which Continental could satisfy. While his first contact was usually with a client's financial Vice President, he might also have to deal with the company's Chairman, President, Assistant Treasurer, or any number of other officials. "There are as many different decision-making processes as there are corporations," commented Mr. Hollis Rademacher, Vice President of the Western and Central groups of the National Division. "Our people have to develop a separate strategy for each custom-

[1]Throughout this case "account manager" will be used to refer to officers with primary responsibility for calling on clients.

er.'' The account managers usually spent about one week a month on the road visiting customers and the other three doing follow-up and analytical work.

II. The Metropolitan Division

The Metropolitan Division, headed by Senior Vice President John E. Jones, served corporate customers headquartered in the greater Chicago area. This division had undergone a substantial reorganization in 1973. Its smaller clients—companies with sales of $500,000 or less—were placed into one unit, as were its very large clients—companies with sales of $100,000,000 or more. All other clients—i.e., those with sales between $500,000 and $100,000,000—were divided into units according to whether they were heavy manufacturing companies, light manufacturing, or professional and financial services.

Jones stated that the lead relationships[2] and account managers in his five units broke down as follows:

Units	*Percent of Account Managers*	*Percent of Lead Relationships*
I. Companies with sales of $500,000 or less	22%	35%
II. Companies with sales of $100,000,000 or more	17	2
III. Heavy manufacturing companies*	19	8
IV. Light manufacturing companies*	20	11
V. Professional or financial services*	22	44
	100%	100%

*Sales of $500,000 to $100,000,000.

In addition, some administrative officers carried a few accounts. The division's employees, including support personnel, totaled about 100 people.

III. The Special Industries Division

Commercial Services' Special Industries Division was the largest department in the Commercial Division in terms of loan volume. Headed by Mr. Gerald Bergman, it was responsible for domestic business of companies which, for several reasons, lent themselves to organization by industry rather than by size of company or geographical location. For example, the companies were generally well-developed and operated in mature markets; regular trade meetings were held; people moved freely from one company to another; and their financing followed a pattern distinct to each industry.

In June 1975, this Division consisted of four units:

1. Energy and Mineral Resources—oil, gas, mining, and utilities.
2. Surface Transportation—leasing companies, railroads, and trucking companies.

[2]Jones used the term ''lead relationships'' to refer to all the contacts which his account managers had to maintain to service any given client adequately. Therefore, there might be several lead relationships for a single corporate customer.

3 Securities, Commodities, and Agribusiness—investment banking, brokerage firms, commodities, agricultural customers up to the first processing stage.

4 Continental Illinois Leasing Corporation—miscellaneous leasing functions, especially leasing equipment to energy companies.

Bergman stated that the forty account managers in his division were "pretty similar" to any commercial banking officers except that several had technical training in energy and mineral resources. He said that, in dealing with some of his larger customers, multilevel contacts were necessary, and several people from the bank might get involved in the transaction.

The customers handled by the Special Industries Division broke out as follows:

Size of Company	*Percent of Customers in Energy and Mineral Resources*	*Percent of Customers in Surface Transportation*	*Percent of Customers in Securities, Commodities, and Agribusiness*
Over $100 million sales	16%	5%	4%
Under $100 million sales	19	14	42
Percent of total Special Industries Customers	35%	19%	46%

International Services

International Services was headed by Executive Vice President George R. Baker. Baker was officially responsible for overseeing the operations of both the International Department and Continental Illinois Ltd., a merchant bank[3] which Continental had recently established. However, because of unusual difficulties with the latter organization, most of Baker's time had been devoted to it in recent months.

Mr. Alfred Miossi, Executive Vice President, headed the International Banking Department, the organization responsible for the vast majority of Continental's international business. Miossi's department consisted of six geographical divisions, sixteen offshore branch management offices, twelve subsidiaries, fifteen representative offices, and thirty-one affiliates.[4] (See *Exhibit 6* for an organizational chart of International Services.)

Most of the International Department's branch offices were staffed by eighteen to

[3]Merchant banks were banks incorporated outside the U.S. and designed originally to finance international trade between the country of incorporation and other countries. In the case of a merchant banking subsidiary of a U.S. bank, the subsidiary could engage in financial activities which were prohibited for the U.S. parent by U.S. banking laws.

[4]Branches were legally part of the parent corporation. Subsidiaries were wholly owned by the parent corporation but were separate operations, whereas affiliates were separate operations which were only partly owned by the parent. Representative offices, on the other hand, were only sales offices and had very few legal ties to the parent. Branches, subsidiaries, and affiliates provided whatever services of the parent bank were customary in a given country, whereas representative offices offered only a limited line of services and most of their transactions had to be approved by the Chicago office.

twenty-five people, one to three of whom were from the US while the remainder were foreign nationals. Some of the branch managers were Americans, while others were foreign nationals. They all, however, had some experience working in Continental's Chicago headquarters. Each of Continental's branches was a separate profit center, and the branch manager was responsible for the total operations of his office. Two important aspects of his job were maintaining good relationships with the government of the country in which the branch was located and socializing with key members of client firms. He worked within two major constraints set by Continental headquarters. First, a committee[5] at Continental's headquarters established a limit for the bank's exposure in different countries. Second, there was a bank policy that all loans over a specified amount had to be approved through the Chicago office.

Each branch had one officer in charge of lending—who could be the branch manager—and several account managers reporting to him. These people made most of the calls on clients, most of whom were foreign nationals. Some account managers were experienced officers whom Continental hired from other banks, some had worked in Commercial Services, and others had been hired right after they graduated from a university. Most of them were between thirty and thirty-five, and, as a group, they were described as "slightly less experienced than Commercial Services' account managers."

The customers serviced by the International Department included foreign national and foreign-based multinational companies, foreign subsidiaries of American multinational companies, foreign banks, and other financial institutions. Mr. Gerard M. Keeley, Senior Vice President, International Banking Division, stated that foreign nationals were especially profitable customers:

> Banking is a cartel in most foreign countries, so customers can't shop around for better interest rates the way companies do in the U.S. The result is that foreign-owned companies are willing to pay higher rates, simply because they have no choice, whereas a foreign subsidiary of, say, Ford, would request rates comparable to what Ford is getting in the U.S. On the whole, the margins on business with foreign companies are larger than those on foreign-based subsidiaries of U.S. companies, so our account officers can lend to them more profitably without any extra risk.

It was widely agreed throughout the bank that International Services had a number of problems. As was the case with any bank that operated in different countries, its foreign units were subject to expropriation, non-repatriation, and inconvertibility of assets. Furthermore, policies of foreign governments sometimes impaired the financial condition of companies which were otherwise credit-worthy according to traditional criteria. In addition to these general problems connected with international banking, Continental had some particular problems. First, it entered the international financial market relatively late. Its first foreign branch was opened in London in 1963 (as compared to Citibank's entry in 1902 and Morgan's entry in 1897). Thus, it simply was not as well-established as

[5]The committee consisted of Baker, Miossi, Mr. Leo deGrijs, Mr. Gerard Keeley, Mr. Joseph Anderson, and Mr. Richard Peterson. DeGrijs, Keely and Anderson were all Senior Vice Presidents in International Services, and Peterson was the bank's economist.

were other banks. Second, because Illinois laws prohibited branch banking, Continental's first experience operating branches was in the international market. Finally, most of Continental's account managers were fairly young, and they were dealing with foreign businesspeople who were ''gray hair and title conscious.'' Hence, the account managers had to work very hard to establish credibility with their clients.

THE MULTINATIONAL BANKING MARKET[6]

Customers

Since the late 1960s, multinational corporations had received considerable attention in business and government circles as they became distinct from the national corporate business sector. By the early 1970s, about 25% of all U.S. corporate profits after taxes came from investments abroad. Many of the largest U.S. corporations such as Mobil, IBM, and ITT earned over half their profits abroad.

Continental management interviewed several of the bank's large multinational customers, as well as some multinational corporations that were not Continental customers, in an attempt to determine exactly what these customers looked for in a bank. The companies indicated that their top priority was for the bank to have a comprehensive view of their total worldwide operations. Moreover, they said they wanted their relationship with the bank to be managed by one key lending officer who could get things done anywhere in the world. They said their major criteria for selecting and/or retaining a bank were the quality of its account officers and its ability to deliver services across geographic lines. (See *Exhibit 7* for details of concerns expressed by Continental customers and noncustomers.)

Competition

In the area of multinational banking, Continental competed with about ten major U.S. banks and numerous foreign banks. However, Continental executives considered Citibank and Morgan to be their chief competitors. Though the banks differed in many respects, both were known to have high-quality account executives, an outstanding ability to deliver services, and considerable product expertise.

Citibank had been active in international banking since 1902, when it opened branches in London and five Asian countries. By 1973, it had 242 overseas branches, 320 affiliate offices, and 69 banking subsidiaries located in 95 countries. These various offices accounted for about 40% of all foreign installations of U.S. banks, and in 1974 they contributed 62% of Citicorp's net operating income.[7]

Early in 1974, Citibank created a major new organizational unit, the World Corporation Group, to handle its multinational customers. Accounts for this division were

[6]Information regarding the multinational banking market and Citicorp in particular is drawn from Stanley M. Davis, *First National City Bank, Multinational Corporate Banking (A)*, ICCH #9-476-079, Harvard Graduate School of Business Administration, Intercollegiate Case Clearing House, Soldiers Field, Boston, MA 02163.

[7]''The Swinging Days are Over Overseas,'' *Business Week*, April 21, 1975, p. 99.

drawn from three divisions: the Commercial Banking Group, the International Banking Group, and the Corporate Banking Group. Discussion of a World Corporation Group had begun in 1971 when a committee was created to compile data on multinational customers on a worldwide basis, to inform people throughout the bank about the multinational market, and to get the support of the Corporate, Commercial, and International groups. In its attempts to be all things to all people, the committee managed to irritate everyone, and conflicts which normally would have occurred among the International, Commercial, and Corporate divisions were lessened as all three attacked the committee. However, over the next couple of years, the committee and other key staff organizations generated considerable discussion regarding reorganizing to better serve multinational companies, so that the need to reorganize gradually came to be accepted, not only by key corporate executives, but also by members of the three divisions which would be most affected by the change.[8]

Within Citibank's World Corporation Group were two account management roles, and a manager might at any time play both roles. Each of the 457 customers in the World Corporation Group had a global account manager and several field account managers. The global account managers were responsible for marketing Citicorp's total banking and nonbanking product line to the client corporation and for the global profitability of that account. Field account managers were responsible for the foreign subsidiaries of a World Corporate client that were located in their country of domicile.

Regarding Citibank's reorganization, one industry analyst commented as follows:

> Citibank has a lot of people and is very competitive internally. There was disruption with some of its clients during the restructuring, but apparently the World Corporate Group is working well enough to keep customers happy now, in spite of continued high turnover among the bank's account managers.

Morgan Guaranty had a very different system for handling multinational clients. It had a group of global financial specialists who went to a client as a team with the account manager, but the customer also had an independent line of communication with the specialists. If he wanted to know what was happening in the world financial market, he would call one of these specialists rather than the account manager or someone in international banking.

One industry analyst stated that Morgan used ''Continental's style'' but that ''somehow it works better for them. They've been in business a long time and have an informal, efficient system of exchanging information and managing tradeoffs among divisions.'' He thought that the key to Morgan's success was its account managers. ''A Morgan account manager is a king,'' he said. ''There are all kinds of rules and rituals that grow up around his job, and there are many rewards that make the position an attractive long-term career. Staying on-line there has much prestige.'' He went on to say that he thought Morgan's success was due largely to its ability to instill a sense of loyalty to the total corporation among its people. Continental and Citibank had not been quite as successful in this regard. Division loyalties tended to run high in the latter two companies.

[8]The problems this committee encountered are discussed in detail in Stanley M. Davis, *First National City Bank, Multinational Corporate Banking (A),* ICCH #9-476-079, Harvard Graduate School of Business Administration, Intercollegiate Case Clearing House, Soldiers Field, Boston, MA 02163.

CONTINENTAL'S POSITION REGARDING MULTINATIONAL CUSTOMERS, JUNE, 1975

In June, 1975, Continental had some exposure[9] with 72% of the companies on *Fortune* magazine's list of 500 leading U.S. corporations and with 36% of *Fortune*'s list of 300 leading foreign companies. This amounted to about $8.8 billion of exposure, about $3.6 billion of which was in loans. U.S. and foreign multinational[10] corporate customers used only 16% of these funds, but they contributed 29% of the branches' net interest margin.

Continental management felt there were significant opportunities to improve the bank's multinational business. They pointed out that, of Continental's US-based multinational customers, 28% had no international exposure with Continental, and 66% had under $5 million exposure. They further stated that multinational customers were not using key services such as foreign exchange and sales finance adequately, and that Continental's penetration of foreign-based multinationals was low in both number and size. Finally, they said, US-based multinational customers headquartered outside the Midwest had substantially less international exposure with Continental than did those based in the Midwest.

Improved penetration of the multinational corporate market could be extremely profitable for Continental. For example, if the bank made an additional $1 billion of overseas loans to multinational corporations and earned a 1.8% return (the average overseas return on worldwide corporate loans), its increased contribution would be $18 million. Furthermore, if Continental's exposure with its current U.S.-based multinational customers increased to at least $10 million for companies with sales between $100 million and $200 million, and $20 million for companies with sales over $200 million, incremental exposure would be $2.5 billion. If 40% of this exposure were used and earned a 3.13% return (the average return earned by U.S. companies), the resulting contribution would be almost $31 million.

Many Continental executives felt that pursuing the multinational market more aggressively neither should nor would interfere with their current business. "It's not that the multinational market is any more profitable or easier to deal with than the markets where we're performing best," commented one executive. "We think we could just do better in this segment than we're currently doing. We also feel that other banks—Citibank and Morgan, specifically—are doing a better job there than we are, and they could constitute a threat sometime in the future."

Continental executives felt that the major source of their failure to service multinational customers as well as they would like was the interaction—or lack thereof—between Commercial Banking Services and International Services. They said that over the years a "two-bank mentality" had developed at Continental and that there had been more rivalry than cooperation between the two organizations. The origins of this rivalry were obscure, but one executive speculated that it went back to the founding of International Services.

[9]Exposure equalled all credit lines and commitments (foreign exchange lines at 10%) and any outstanding transaction credits.

[10]Continental management defined multinational customers as those which had assets, liabilities, and financial decision makers in multiple countries.

> I think the international organization may have been viewed as a young—and expensive—upstart. I can imagine the irritation someone in Commercial must have felt when he telephoned his counterpart in International only to find that he was off evaluating the economic situation of Europe. Word soon got around that the people in International were never around when you needed them.

A second executive had a different analysis:

> There were three scarce resources which, historically, have been split between Commercial and International. The first one, capital, found each department with a fixed allocation. When Commercial asked International to lend to a nondomestic subsidiary of one of their U.S. companies, International tended to decline because it would have to use some portion of their capital to further Commercial's objectives rather than International's objective.
>
> A similar situation arose with country limits. If a country limit of $150 million was set for Italy, then International, which considered that $150 million theirs because they were responsible for loans in Italy, preferred to protect that $150 million for their own customers rather than using up any of it for Commercial's customers.
>
> The third problem area has been in people allocation. Commercial wanted International to call on subsidiaries of their customers offshore, but International preferred to have their people call on International's customers.

Whatever the source of the two-bank mentality, executives differed in their assessments of why it still existed. Many felt it was primarily a "people problem," while others argued that it was a problem with incentive and management information systems.

Continental's major personnel problem was that it did not have a large number of corporate bankers with international skills. Relatively few people ever transferred from Commercial to International Services, or vice versa, especially at higher management levels. The result was that, not only were there few people who knew both businesses, but also that members of one division often actually distrusted those of the other. Furthermore, though the position of account manager was extremely important, it did not carry the status of a career job. Consequently, account managers often showed a strong desire to move up the organization chart.

Those executives who thought that Continental's structure was its major problem with multinational customers stated that the current structure certainly perpetuated, if in fact it did not actually create, Continental's two-bank mentality. "Our structure virtually assures that a multinational client's total banking needs will not be satisfied," commented Baker. He gave the following example to illustrate his point.

> Suppose Caterpillar executives at their headquarters decide they need financing for a new venture in Brazil. Chances are they will call their account manager in Commercial because he handles a lot of domestic financing for them. However, since the dollars will be going into a foreign country, the transaction will be handled by International Services. So, the Commercial account manager will go to someone in International *and* request that he put up, say, $1 million for Caterpillar's new venture. That particular venture might yield very little profit to Continental, but it will strengthen our relationship with a blue-chip customer. However, the person in International will refuse the loan, pointing out that his division simply cannot sustain an unprofitable $1 million transaction.

Many Continental executives felt the company's problems with multinational customers stemmed from its systems of collecting and disseminating information, compensating employees, and approving loans. Some managers characterized the management information function as "chaotic." First of all, each International branch developed its own account analysis systems, and seldom was one branch's system compatible with that of another. Second, the account hierarchy and cross-reference reports[11] of International and Commercial Services were inconsistent, so it was impossible to determine the relative profitability of different accounts on a worldwide basis. Even if somehow this information were obtained, no one could be sure that it would be transmitted to all the people with responsibility for the specific customers.

Continental's compensation system consisted of a salary alone. The bank's personnel were among the highest paid in the industry, but there were no management bonus plans. Furthermore, a person's performance was evaluated only by how well he handled the business of the specific division, department, or branch for which he worked. This meant that Commercial personnel concentrated on developing a client's domestic business, and International personnel concentrated on lucrative foreign national accounts. There were no incentives for anyone to think about subsidiaries of either U.S.- or foreign-based multinationals.

The bank's system of approving loans was also counter-productive to maximizing service to multinational customers. The present overseas credit approval limits were quite low. This was not a problem in dealing with single-country foreign companies whose loan requests were usually sufficiently small so that the International branch manager could approve them. However, if a subsidiary of a major American firm requested a loan from one of Continental's International officers, the amount of the transaction was often so large that it had to be approved through a cumbersome system in Chicago, and the reaction time was often quite long. If the transaction involved several countries, a Continental representative in each would be involved, thus further slowing the transaction. A problem closely related to this was that if International Services had reached its exposure limit in a given country and a branch officer felt that further funds could be used profitably there, he had to submit his request to the committee in Chicago which set country exposure limits, and it sometimes took a while for the committee to act on the request.

PROPOSALS FOR IMPROVING CONTINENTAL'S MULTINATIONAL BUSINESS

There was considerable discussion among Continental executives as to whether Continental should follow either the Citibank or the Morgan model in dealing with multinational corporations, or perhaps create an entirely different model. In essence, following the Morgan model would mean upgrading Continental's people and systems, while following the Citibank model would necessitate a radical change in the bank's entire structure.

[11]These reports were supposed to contain client names and identification numbers, the relationship of the client to the parent entity, the country of exposure, total exposure, account officers and so forth.

People

Mr. Eugene R. Croisant, Senior Vice President of the Personnel Division, felt that Continental could improve the overall level of its employees by developing intensive training seminars to teach skills regarding products, calling on customers, and managing and evaluating the bank's relationships with specific customers. Moreover, he thought personnel transfers between International and Commercial Services should be increased dramatically and that more positive attitudes regarding regular cross-department assignments should be created. Finally, he thought the bank should create longer-term career opportunities in account management so people would not view this position as a steppingstone to higher-level jobs. One way to do this, he said, was by giving account managers considerably more credit authority.

Systems

Everyone agreed that Continental was going to have to alter its system of collecting and disseminating information about multinational clients if it were to serve them better. One executive listed the following reports which he felt should be generated as soon as possible:

Report	*Specific Information Contained in Report*
1. Net interest contribution family of reports.	Exposure, average credit usage, average below-market deposits, all income received from the client (fees, interest, and net balance equivalents after activity, interest if any, and reserve reductions) less funds charged at a standard rate.
2. External pricing reports (US).	Credit and noncredit products requiring deposit balances (or fee equivalent) against actual deposit balances maintained.
3. Account hierarchy and cross-reference report.	Identification numbers, client name, relationship to parent entity, country of exposure, total exposure, account officer assignments, memo relationship (if any), feeder system, and account numbers.
4. External account and worldwide relationship reports.	Exposure, average credit usage, average below-market deposits for past year and projected into future.
5. Credit data and other customer information.	Credit data, key points of customer contact, industry information, customer information, cross-selling information, etc.
6. Flash reports	Information where the timing is critical for either action or for customer services purposes.
7. Market reports.	Market trends, size of market, interest trends, opportunities, etc.

He estimated that the lead time for fully implementing this information system was two to three years.

Regarding credit policies, it was generally agreed that senior bank management should continue to allocate funds by market and/or customer segments. However, several people felt that field officers who dealt with branches of major multinationals should have considerably more authority to approve a loan. Some pointed out that such authority would assist greatly in developing overseas lending officers.

Structure

Those executives who argued for the Citibank model did so in part because they felt merely upgrading people and systems would not be enough and that doing so would take too much time. "If we don't move fast, we're going to be in big trouble," commented Joseph Anderson.

> Anything short of a dramatic restructuring will be too little. By 1980 we want to be among the top three leading factors in the multinational business. Now we probably rank about fifth or sixth with multinational customers head-quartered in the U.S., but we're lower among foreign multinationals. Overall, we're probably somewhere between seventh and tenth in multinational volume right now.

Anderson and the other executives who argued for restructuring thought that Continental should create a new Multinational Banking Division comparable to Citibank's World Corporation Group. This division would create a "worldwide relationship management process" that incorporated global account planning, centrally directed execution, and direct communication among all people who had dealings with any given multinational customer. This process would enable the bank to match its capabilities with customer needs on a worldwide basis, and it would increase the knowledge throughout the bank of the bank's objectives and overall relationship with specific multinational customers. Moreover, it would enable the bank to make tradeoffs among opportunities to serve a single customer in different markets and different customers in a single market.

To create a new department and install this "worldwide relationship management process" successfully, the executives thought they had to define the process in detail, set up a supporting worldwide information system, modify credit policies, and communicate the new process formally to customers. They felt that the people who became multinational account managers should be responsible for between five and ten accounts. In addition to these account managers, they said, the bank would need a centrally directed team to mobilize its global resources to serve the customer's needs.

IMPACT ON THE NATIONAL DIVISION

If Continental adopted this new structure, the impact on the National Division of Commercial Services would be substantial. About 180 of its customers—Gulf + Western, Pillsbury, General Mills, Raytheon, etc.—would be transferred into the Multinational

Banking Department. Rademacher, speaking on behalf of the National Division, commented on this as follows:

> There will be a significant psychological impact on our people. Even if the total business for which an individual or unit is responsible remains about the same, each will experience a sense of psychological loss in terms of identification with the larger, more prestigious, market leader names as the transfer of those relationships to the Multinational Department is accomplished. [On the other hand] there is a certain excitement and personal involvement in dealing with smaller companies. An account manager feels that what he does matters a lot to his clients. There may be more status involved in knowing the treasurer of International Harvester, but the creative job is greater with the smaller companies. Our people get a lot of satisfaction from solving their clients' problems.

He further stated that the account manager who handled several small customers in Minneapolis might generate more profit for the bank than the one who handled a couple of major multinational companies.

Regarding the two models Continental was considering, Rademacher said:

> All of us see the advantages of the Morgan culture. We'd really like to establish the notion that the account manager position is a career job, and that you don't have to manage other people to be considered a success.

He went on to say that many Continental executives did not consider the bank's structure to be its main problem. "We need to change the attitudes of our managers," he said, "and changing the structure may or may not do that."

IMPACT ON THE METROPOLITAN DIVISION

In the Metropolitan Division, all but two clients who would be classed as multinationals were in the unit containing companies with sales of $100 million or more. The division had about ninety-three clients and seven prospects in this category. Jones commented on this unit as follows:

> These companies handle everything from peanuts to steel. They have access to both public and private capital markets, and we compete with anywhere from fifteen to a hundred banks for their business.

He went on to say that this unit was staffed by "a fair number of people who have worked in International Services and who know the international market well." Jones himself had worked for twelve years in International Services. As a result of their experience in the international business and their contacts with International Services personnel, account managers in this unit often communicated directly with people in Continental's foreign branches regarding the needs of multinational clients.

> This works pretty well for Metro, but it does create a schizophrenic situation for people in International. If our requests conflict with the directives of their division, they will understandably go with their division. Nevertheless, I think we're doing a lot to overcome the two-bank mentality.

Regarding the possible creation of a multinational banking group, Jones said that about forty accounts and all fourteen account managers in the large company unit would be affected. He stressed that his account managers were already moving toward serving a customer's total worldwide needs, and that they could easily move into a multinational group. He continued as follows:

> There's no question about the competence of our people in the international area. Our real concern is how to maintain customer relationships if we tear apart Division II. For example, the same account manager handles Beatrice Foods, and A&P; the former is a multinational and the latter is not. If we create a multinational division and this account manager moves into it—which, given his skills, he is likely to do—what happens to A&P?

Impact on the Special Industries Division

In all, about eighteen of the Special Industries Division's customers, most of whom were energy and mineral resource companies or securities, commodities, and agribusiness companies, met Continental's definition of multinational. If these companies were placed in a newly created Multinational Banking Division, the loss to Special Industries would be substantial. Bergman argued that it "makes far more sense to grant the Special Industries Division a global charter." He pointed out that the special industries' concept had evolved over time to meet special needs of the marketplace, and that it had not been superimposed on companies that did not fit it naturally. Furthermore, he said, this particular grouping made it clear to certain companies that Continental had made a commitment to their industry. He went on to express his doubts about creating a new division:

> I'm skeptical about changing a structure that's already handling multinational business pretty well. Those of us in Commercial Services feel that our track record has been very good, and any shortcomings, if they do in fact exist, are in the way International Services is structured and handles its business. I'm reluctant to take the whole organization through a traumatic change.

Bergman did acknowledge that Continental's two-bank mentality had caused some problems. He thought the problems were inevitable, however, as long as Commercial and International were separate profit centers. He said that people tended to look at what was best for their division instead of taking a broader view of what was best for the bank as a whole.

> We do need to change attitudes, and it may take something cathartic to do that. But if we do reorganize, we have to manage it very carefully so that it will cause minimal disruption among our personnel and between our personnel and our clients.

IMPACT ON THE INTERNATIONAL DEPARTMENT

Keeley stated that, in the International Department, the European area would be most affected by the creation of a Multinational Banking Division. He said that about 25% of the customers and 35% of the prospects would be transferred from International to Multinational along with approximately 25% of the International officers.

Keeley thought that the greatest short-term risk in creating a new division was that there would be a lot of disruption internally and with customers. ''If we don't manage the change very well, we'll lose a lot of our people as well as our customers,'' he said. He was also concerned about the impact of the change on the International Division's off-shore organization. ''How will we measure the performance of a branch manager when he doesn't have total control of his operations? Will he just become an office manager?'' he asked. A third concern Keeley voiced was that a Multinational Banking Division might become an elite organization that received a disproportionate amount of the bank's attention, people and dollars. He stated further that the change would mean that larger customers would be pulled out of both International and Commercial and that these departments would have to reorient themselves to the medium and small clients. Finally, Keeley said that the greatest long-term risk was that the whole premise was wrong—that multinational customers would not necessarily be served better by a multinational division.

> This would be an awfully hard egg to unscramble. If we make the move, we can't back off from it. Chase tried and the difficulties were enormous. Also, things will get unhinged if we don't have a commitment from the top of the house. If we try this and it doesn't work, morale here will go to hell.

CONCLUSION

As Roger Anderson contemplated the possible paths Continental might take regarding its multinational business, he was keenly aware of the advantages and disadvantages of each, as well as of the opinions which various Continental executives held. He noted that Continental had been doing increasingly well with multinationals over the last few years, and he was reluctant to tamper with what seemed to be working fairly well. Furthermore, he felt that there was a tremendous value in maintaining continuity between Continental and its clients, and he knew that creating a Multinational Banking Division would be disruptive. ''If we go through a wholesale reassignment of clients, how many will we drop between the cracks?'' he wondered. A third major problem he saw with creating a new multinational division was that such a structure would require more qualified international bankers than Continental then had, and he was not sure that the bank could develop or recruit people fast enough.

On the other hand, Anderson thought a Multinational Banking Department might serve multinational companies better in the long run because it would encourage bank personnel to develop a broader mentality. ''Our people have got to start looking beyond the concerns of their immediate divisions,'' he said. ''Adopting a new structure might in fact force them to have a wider perspective.''

EXHIBIT 1

CONTINENTAL ILLINOIS NATIONAL BANK AND TRUST COMPANY

Consolidated Operating Statements of Continental Illinois Corporation and Subsidiaries, 1970–1974

($ in thousands)

	1974	*1973*	*1972*	*1971*	*1970*
Operating Income					
Interest and Fees on Loans	$1,258,868	$ 720,527	$359,486	$319,271	$373,238
Interest and Dividends on Investment Securities:					
United States Treasury Securities	$ 31,209	$ 27,359	$ 29,474	$ 47,620	$ 33,788
State, County and Municipal Securities	44,438	48,826	43,845	39,805	34,385
Other Securities	42,607	23,156	15,821	15,439	8,049
Total Interest and Dividends on Investment Securities	$ 118,254	$ 99,341	$ 89,140	$102,864	$ 76,222
Trading Account Income:					
Profits and Commissions	$ 12,673	$ 8,863	$ 2,277	$ 4,299	—
Interest on Trading Account Securities	19,839	10,950	6,437	10,604	—
Total Trading Account Income	$ 32,512	$ 19,813	$ 8,714	$ 14,903	$ 34,236
Interest on Funds Sold	$ 229,048	$ 152,144	$ 63,284	$ 15,750	$ 2,395
Trust Department Income	31,465	31,404	29,773	27,824	22,732
All Other Income	73,818	63,481	35,214	28,117	17,563
Total Operating Income	$1,743,965	$1,086,710	$585,611	$508,729	$526,386
Operating Expense					
Interest Expense:					
Interest on Deposits	$ 915,323	$ 538,834	$243,052	$208,939	$198,962
Interest on Funds Borrowed	412,948	221,525	59,533	47,087	99,047
Interest on Long-Term Notes	9,135	6,652	6,357	—	—
Total Interest Expense	$1,337,406	$ 767,011	$308,942	$256,026	$298,009

Salaries and Wages	$ 105,924	$ 89,618	$ 77,574	$ 66,766	$ 60,927
Pension, Profit Sharing and Other Employee Benefits	24,099	20,401	17,669	15,936	13,934
Net Occupancy Expense	21,009	17,679	15,940	13,276	10,457
Equipment Rentals, Depreciation and Maintenance	10,749	8,652	6,886	6,491	5,461
Provision for Loan Losses	32,900	15,300	12,353	15,262	14,221
Other Expense	61,484	48,125	38,823	35,681	29,638
Total Operating Expense	$1,593,571	$ 966,786	$478,187	$409,438	$432,647
Income before Income Taxes and Security Gains or Losses	$ 150,394	$ 119,924	$107,424	$ 99,291	$ 93,739
Less Applicable Income Taxes	54,488	33,619	29,294	29,493	29,394
Income before Security Gains or Losses	$ 95,906	$ 86,305	$ 78,130	$69,798	$ 64,345
Security Gains or (Losses)-less related income tax effect	(226)	(835)	265	576	(6,815)
Net Income	$ 95,680	$ 85,470	$ 78,395	$ 70,374	$ 57,530
Income before Security Gains or Losses	$ 5.53	$ 4.99	$ 4.54	$ 4.07	$ 3.78
Net Income	5.51	4.94	4.55	4.11	3.38
Cash Dividends Declared	2.20	1.93	1.84	1.76	1.64
Average Book Value	40.92	38.61	35.69	33.10	31.45
Market Value—Closing Quotations					
High	59	60¾	67⅜	45	39¼
Low	23½	41	38⅛	34¾	29½
Year End	26⅝	51⅞	54½	38⅝	38
Year-End Price/Earnings Ratio	4.8×	10.4×	12.0×	9.5×	10.1×
Average Shares Outstanding	17,358,108	17,291,566	17,226,293	17,132,086	17,015,612

(continued)

EXHIBIT 1 (Cont.)

CONTINENTAL ILLINOIS NATIONAL BANK AND TRUST COMPANY

Consolidated Balance Sheets of Continental Illinois Corporation and Subsidiaries, 1970–1974

($ in thousands)

	1974		1973		1972		1971		1970	
	Amount	*% of Total*	*Amount*	*% of Total*	*Amount*	*% of Total*	*Amount*	*% of Total*	*Amount*	*% of Total*
Assets										
Cash and Due from Banks	$ 2,532,413	13.3	$ 1,964,131	13.5	$ 1,662,045	15.4	$2,191,820	22.8	$1,900,739	22.2
Funds Sold:										
Domestic	$ 206,944	1.1	$ 216,331	1.5	$ 158,387	1.5	$ 84,224	0.9	$ 32,171	0.4
Overseas	1,905,066	10.0	1,564,651	10.7	1,048,876	9.7	158,506	1.6	41,503	0.5
Total Funds Sold	$ 2,112,010	11.1	$ 1,780,982	12.2	$ 1,207,263	11.2	$ 242,730	2.5	$ 73,674	0.9
Investment Securities:										
United States Treasury Securities	$ 405,397	2.1	$ 344,499	2.4	$ 435,105	4.0	$ 713,180	7.4	$ 473,909	5.5
State, County and Municipal Securities	905,932	4.8	1,048,663	7.2	1,004,837	9.3	873,303	9.1	762,961	8.9
Other Securities	587,204	3.1	316,999	2.2	225,787	2.1	241,428	2.5	134,950	1.6
Total Investment Securities	$ 1,898,533	10.0	$ 1,712,161	11.8	$ 1,665,729	15.4	$1,827,911	19.0	$1,371,820	16.0
Trading Account Securities	$ 336,204	1.7	$ 237,635	1.6	$ 166,980	1.5	$ 237,981	2.5	$ 248,811	2.9
Loans and Discounts:										
Domestic	$ 9,243,707	48.5	$ 6,878,608	47.3	$ 4,701,287	43.6	$3,962,456	41.2	$4,057,928	47.5
Overseas	2,245,774	11.8	1,522,601	10.5	1,020,526	9.5	723,521	7.5	470,470	5.5
Total Loans and Discounts	$11,489,481	60.3	$ 8,401,209	57.8	$ 5,721,813	53.1	$4,685,977	48.7	$4,528,398	53.0
Premises and Equipment	$ 52,607	0.3	$ 47,216	0.3	$ 44,799	0.4	$ 34,024	0.4	$ 29,781	0.4
Customers' Liability on Acceptances	128,737	0.7	96,310	0.7	144,422	1.3	157,766	1.6	163,167	1.9
Other Assets	487,096	2.6	303,587	2.1	173,925	1.7	243,746	2.5	233,551	2.7
Total Assets	$19,037,081	100.0	$14,543,231	100.0	$10,786,956	100.0	$9,621,955	100.0	$8,549,941	100.0

Liabilities, Reserves, and Shareholders' Equity										
Deposits										
Head Office—Demand	$ 3,203,922	16.8	$ 2,959,871	20.4	$ 2,860,824	26.5	$2,842,759	29.5	$2,660,463	31.1
Savings	1,577,044	8.3	1,371,926	9.4	1,247,884	11.6	998,082	10.4	789,965	9.2
Other Time	3,823,692	20.1	2,886,763	19.8	1,719,672	15.9	1,449,613	15.1	766,046	9.0
Overseas Branches and Subsidiaries	4,919,516	25.9	3,459,858	23.8	2,531,531	23.5	2,330,821	24.2	2,050,801	24.0
Total Deposits	$13,524,174	71.1	$10,678,418	73.4	$ 8,359,911	77.5	$7,621,275	79.2	$6,267,275	73.3
Funds Borrowed	$ 3,964,322	20.9	$ 2,541,685	17.5	$ 1,249,195	11.6	$1,005,130	10.4	$1,338,399	15.6
Acceptances Outstanding	130,681	0.7	100,669	0.7	148,416	1.4	160,474	1.7	164,589	1.9
Other Liabilities	406,063	2.1	318,317	2.2	186,973	1.7	136,703	1.4	116,780	1.4
Notes Due 1979 (6⅝%)	100,000	0.5	100,000	0.7	95,699	0.9	—	—	—	—
Notes Due 1989 (Variable Rate)	24,667	0.1	—	—	—	—	—	—	—	—
Reserves on Loans	$ 176,949	0.9	$ 136,431	0.9	$ 132,030	1.2	$ 131,222	1.4	$ 127,697	1.5
Shareholders' Equity										
Preferred Stock	$ 186	—	$ 186	—	$ 186	—	$ 188	—	$ 167	—
Common Stock	173,531	0.9	172,901	1.2	172,149	1.6	171,321	1.8	170,157	2.0
Capital Surplus	424,429	2.2	395,560	2.7	350,272	3.2	316,612	3.3	285,544	3.3
Retained Earnings	112,079	0.6	99,064	0.7	92,125	0.9	79,030	0.8	79,333	1.0
Total Shareholders' Equity	$ 710,225	3.7	$ 667,711	4.6	$ 614,732	5.7	$ 567,151	5.9	$ 535,201	6.3
Total Liabilities, Reserves, and Shareholders' Equity	$19,037,081	100.0	$14,543,231	100.0	$10,786,956	100.0	$9,621,955	100.0	$8,549,941	100.0

EXHIBIT 2

CONTINENTAL ILLINOIS NATIONAL BANK AND TRUST COMPANY
Corporate Office Organization Chart, June 1975

BOARD OF DIRECTORS

EXECUTIVE OFFICE
CHAIRMAN OF THE BOARD OF DIRECTORS
Roger E. Anderson
PRESIDENT
John H. Perkins

STAFF UNITS

CORPORATE PERSONNEL SERVICES C
Eugene R. Croisant
Senior Vice President

CORPORATE COUNSEL C
Ray F. Myers
Executive Vice President, Corporate Counsel and Secretary

CORPORATE FINANCIAL SERVICES P
Donald C. Miller
Executive Vice President and Treasurer

OPERATIONS AND MANAGEMENT SERVICES P
Gail M. Melick
Executive Vice President

LINE UNITS

COMMERCIAL BANKING SERVICES C
Eugene Holland, Jr.
Executive Vice President

INTERNATIONAL SERVICES C
George R. Baker
Executive Vice President

TRUST AND INVESTMENT SERVICES C
Charles R. Hall
Executive Vice President

BOND AND MONEY MARKET SERVICES P
David G. Taylor
Executive Vice President

PERSONAL BANKING SERVICES P
William D. Plechaty
Senior Vice President

REAL ESTATE SERVICES P
James D. Harper, Jr.
Executive Vice President

C–Reports to the Chairman
P–Reports to the President

EXHIBIT 3 CONTINENTAL ILLINOIS NATIONAL BANK AND TRUST COMPANY

Biographical Data of Key Executives in Commercial Banking Services and International Services, Plus the President and Chairman of the Board

- *Roger E. Anderson*, 54, chairman of the board of directors, Continental Illinois Corporation and Continental Bank. Joined Continental's Commercial Banking Department, 1946; assigned to International Banking, 1949, becoming department head, 1959; named senior vice president, 1965; executive vice president and director with responsibility for the Commercial Banking and Real Estate Departments, 1968; and International Banking the following year; elected vice chairman of the board of directors, 1971, and to his present position, 1973.
- *John H. Perkins*, 54, president, Continental Illinois Corporation and Continental Bank. Began career with Continental in 1946, as member of the Commercial Banking Department; later assigned to Bond Department, eventually becoming its chief officer; elected senior vice president, 1965, and assumed broader administrative duties the following year; elected executive vice president and director, 1968; elected vice chairman of the board of directors, 1971, and to his present position, 1973.
- *George R. Baker*, 45, executive vice president, International Services, Continental Illinois Corporation and Continental Bank. Joined Continental as member of Metropolitan Division, Commercial Banking Department, 1951; later assigned to National Division, becoming a vice president; returned to Metropolitan Division as senior vice president, 1969; elected executive vice president for Metropolitan and Special Industries Divisions, 1972, and to his present position, 1974.
- *Eugene Holland, Jr.*, 52, executive vice president, Commercial Banking Services. Began association with Continental, 1946, in Commercial Banking Department; became head of Energy and Mineral Resources Division, and subsequently named head of Eastern Division; elected senior vice president of National Divisions, 1969; appointed executive vice president and head of Metropolitan Divisions, 1971; named head of the Commercial Banking Department and executive vice president of Continental Illinois Corporation, 1973.
- *Alfred F. Miossi*, 53, executive vice president, International Banking Department, Continental Bank. After experience with Bank of America in the Far East and with International Harvester Export Company, began 22-year association with Continental's overseas expansion, 1953, starting in Foreign Division of Commercial Banking Department; became vice president of International Banking Department, 1960; appointed executive vice president, 1971, and named to board of directors of Continental Illinois Limited, London merchant banking subsidiary, 1975.
- *J. Joseph Anderson*, 37, senior vice president, International Services. Began career with Continental as member of Methods Research Division, 1963, after previous experience as accountant for UARCO Business Forms, Inc.; following posts in Electronics Installation and Technical Planning Divisions, elected auditor of Continental Bank, 1972; named vice president of holding company and bank, 1974, and to present position later that year.
- *Gerald K. Bergman*, 41, senior vice president and head of Special Industries Divisions, Commercial Banking Department. Joined Continental Commercial Banking Department, 1957; elected vice president and a group head in Metropolitan Divisions, 1969; appointed president of Continental Leasing Corporation, 1972, and to his present position, 1974; apponted a director of Continental's London merchant banking subsidiary, 1975.

- *Eugene R. Croisant*, 38, senior vice president, Personnel Division. Began career with bank, 1959; held various posts in Central Proof and Methods Research; became manager of Bookkeeping Computer Installation Division, 1964; elected electronics officer, 1966, second vice president, 1967, and vice president, 1970; assigned to Personnel Division, 1972, and appointed senior vice president for bank and holding company, 1974.
- *Leo C. deGrijs*, 49, senior vice president, International Banking Department. Joined Continental's London Branch, 1963, after previous experience in the Netherlands and Far East; elected second vice president in charge of bank's Tokyo and Osaka branches; became head of Far East Group, International Banking Department, 1968; assigned to Continental Development Bank, Beirut, Lebanon, 1970; returned to Chicago, 1973; assumed present responsibilities, 1974.
- *John E. Jones*, 41, senior vice president and division head, Metropolitan Division of Commercial Banking Department. Joined Continental International Banking Department, 1957; named vice president, 1966; transferred to Commercial Banking Department, 1970; appointed vice president and assistant division head of Metropolitan and Special Industries Divisions, 1973, and became senior vice president the same year; named to present position, 1974.
- *Gerard M. Keeley*, 44, senior vice president, International Banking Department. Joined Continental's Commercial Banking Department, 1956; appointed assistant manager of bank's London West End branch, 1964; became vice president for both London branches, 1967; returned to Chicago as member of International Banking Department, 1970; elected senior vice president, 1973; and named a director of Continental Illinois Limited, London, 1975.
- *Donald H. Myers*, 40, senior vice president and head of National Divisions, Commercial Banking Department. Began career with Continental's Commercial Banking Department, 1958; appointed second vice president, National Divisions, 1966; elected vice president, 1968, and head of New York Office, 1969; named a group head, National Divisions, 1970; elected senior vice president, 1972, and became head of National Divisions, 1974.

EXHIBIT 4 Operating Income and Income Before Security Transactions Derived from Domestic and International Operations[1]

	1974		1973		1972		1971	
	$[2]	%	$	%	$	%	$	%
	Continental Illinois National Bank							
Operating Revenue								
Domestic	1,133	65	713	66	400	68	386	76
International	611	35	374	34	186	32	123	24
Total	1,744	100	1,087	100	586	100	509	100
Operating Earnings								
Domestic	92	96	69	80	65	83	68	97
International	4	4	17	20	13	17	2	3
Total	96	100	86	100	78	100	70	100
	J. P. Morgan and Company							
Operating Revenue								
Domestic	900	45	582	46	397	53	411	57
International	1,100	55	676	54	358	47	305	43
Total	2,000	100	1,258	100	755	100	716	100
Operating Earnings								
Domestic	100	56	79	54	78	65	78	71
International	79	44	68	46	42	35	32	29
Total	179	100	147	100	120	100	110	100
	Citicorp							
Operating Revenue								
Domestic	1,899	38	1,268	41	821	42	841	47
International	3,089	62	1,824	59	1,134	58	948	53
Total	4,988	100	3,092	100	1,955	100	1,789	100
Operating Earnings								
Domestic	120	38	102	40	92	46	97	57
International	193	62	153	60	110	54	72	43
Total	313	100	255	100	202	100	169	100

[1]Note that each company has its own internal system of allocation of revenues and earnings to domestic and international operations. Therefore the data in this exhibit should not be used for exact comparisons.
[2]All dollar figures are in millions.
Source: Company Annual Reports and Forms 10-K.

EXHIBIT 5

CONTINENTAL ILLINOIS NATIONAL BANK AND TRUST COMPANY
Commercial Banking Service Organization Chart, June 1975

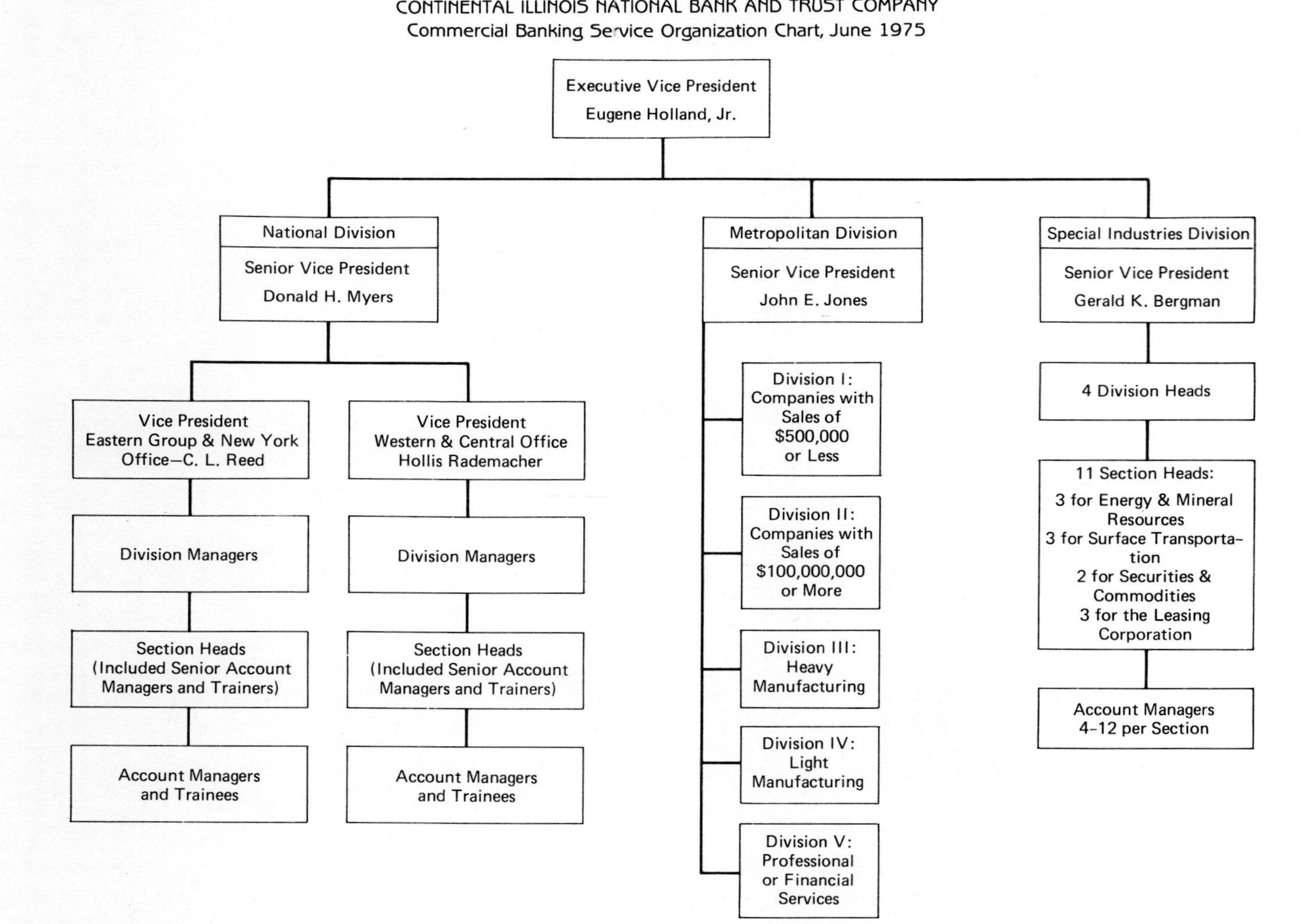

EXHIBIT 6 CONTINTENTAL ILLINOIS NATIONAL BANK AND TRUST COMPANY
International Services Organization Chart, June 1975

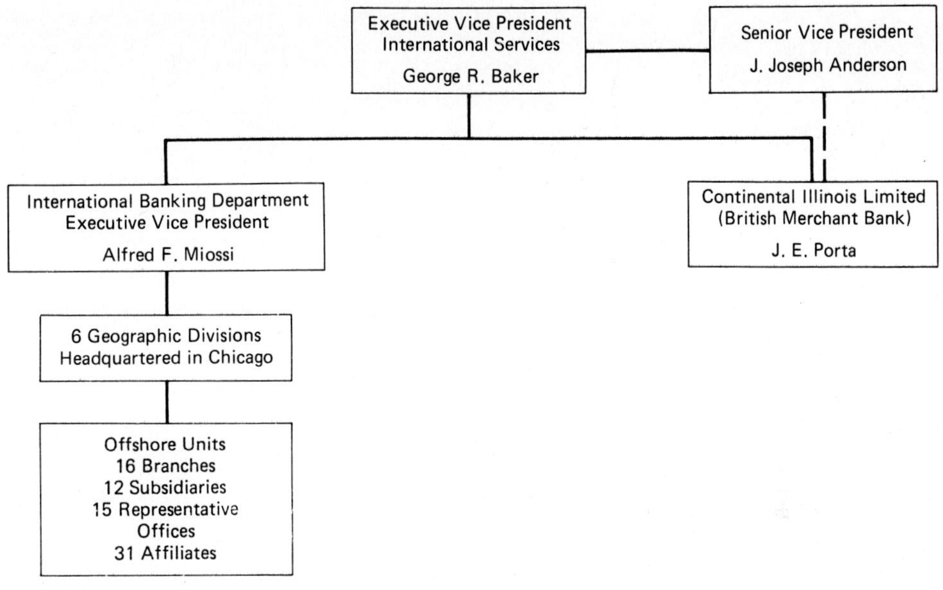

EXHIBIT 7 CONTINENTAL ILLINOIS NATIONAL BANK AND TRUST COMPANY
Worldwide Customers' Requirements of Relationship Management

		Relationship Management Process	
		Global View*	One Key Contact with Continuity
CINB Customers	Dayton Drug Company	Very Important	Very Important
	Atlas Automotive Supplies	Important	Very Important
	Investment Management, LTD	Very Important	Very Important
	Parker Paper Company	Very Important	Very Important
	Universal Farm Equipment	Very Important	Very Important
	Capital Chemical Company	Important	Important
	Everready Oil	Very Important	Very Important
	Earthmovers, Int.	Very Important	Very Important
	Edison Communications	Not Important	Not Important
	Wong Electronics, Inc.	Important	Important
	Amalgamated, Ltd.	Important	Very Important
Noncustomers	Food Unlimited	Important	Very Important
	Bordeaux, Int.	Important	Very Important
	Copugraphic, Int.	Not Important	Very Important
	International Multiproducts	Important	Important
	Shinoda Corporation	Not Important	Very Important
	Wittinzeller, Int.	Important	Important

*Affiliates to be treated as part of worldwide relationship.

Very Important Important Not Important

Source: Company records. Names of multinational companies have been changed.

EXHIBIT 7 (Cont.)

MAJOR CRITERIA USED BY WORLDWIDE COMPANIES FOR BANK SELECTION

CINB Customers	Quality of Account Officers	Bank Size and Resources	Geographic Network	Special Market Expertise	Special Product Expertise	Competitive Pricing	Ability to Deliver Products/ Services
Dayton Drug Company	Very Important	Not Mentioned	Important	Not Mentioned	Important	Important	Very Important
Atlas Automotive Supplies	Important	Not Mentioned	Not Mentioned	Not Mentioned	Important	Very Important	Important
Investment Management, LTD	Very Important	Important	Very Important	Not Mentioned	Not Mentioned	Important	Important
Parker Paper Company	Very Important	Important	Not Mentioned	Not Mentioned	Not Mentioned	Important	Very Important
Universal Farm Equipment	Very Important	Important	Important	Important	Very Important	Not Mentioned	Important
Capital Chemical Company	Very Important	Not Mentioned	Important	Not Mentioned	Not Mentioned	Not Mentioned	Important
Everready Oil	Very Important	Very Important	Important	Important	Very Important	Important	Important
Earthmovers, Int.	Very Important	Important	Important	Important	Important	Important	Very Important
Edison Communications	Very Important	Not Mentioned	Not Mentioned	Very Important	Important	Very Important	Important
Wong Electronics, Inc.	Important	Very Important	Important	Not Mentioned	Not Mentioned	Important	Very Important
Amalgamated, Ltd.	Very Important	Not Mentioned	Not Mentioned	Important	Important	Important	Very Important

Noncustomers	Quality of Account Officers	Bank Size and Resources	Geographic Network	Special Market Expertise	Special Product Expertise	Competitive Pricing	Ability to Deliver Products/ Services
Food Unlimited	Very Important	Not Mentioned	Important	Not Mentioned	Not Mentioned	Not Mentioned	Important
Bordeaux, Int.	Very Important	Important	Important	Important	Not Mentioned	Important	Very Important
Copugraphic, Int.	Very Important	Not Mentioned	Not Mentioned	Not Mentioned	Very Important	Important	Very Important
International Multiproducts	Not Mentioned	Important	Important	Not Mentioned	Important	Not Mentioned	Not Mentioned
Shinoda Corporation	Important	Not Mentioned	Not Mentioned	Important	Important	Very Important	Important
Wittinzeller, Int.	Not Mentioned	Important	Very Important	Not Mentioned	Important	Important	Important

Legend: Very Important (dotted) · Important (hatched) · Not Mentioned (blank)

Source: Company records.

MAMMOTH PAPER

Both industry leaders and conservationists testified at a public hearing considering future antipollution legislation. Below is an excerpt from the presentation of Richard Bennington, President of Mammoth Paper, at public hearings for the repeal of the Water Act Requirements of Zero Pollution by 1985.

During the late 1950s and early 1960s, the American public recognized the serious problems of pollution. Social conscience was set into motion and, as a result, the Clean Air Act of 1967 and the amended Clean Water Act (see *Exhibit 1*) were enacted into law. In these acts, restraints were put on the firm as to what pollutants were to be allowed in the production process. In short, the production process was to be drastically changed or modified in many industries so as to meet the environmental standards.

Since these acts were passed, the paper industry has spent 30 to 40% of its annual capital investment to reduce pollution in the production process. These expenditures do not create greater capacity or any financial return. Going one step further, since environmental expenditures reap no return on investment, they serve only to raise operating expenses. As a result, prices must be raised and passed on to the consumer. Firm performance has already been severely hampered and, as we get closer to the zero pollution goal in 1985, the problems of the industry will worsen. We are, therefore, seeking amendments to abolish the mandatory time period allowed for pollution standard compliance, as an aide to both the paper industry and the consumers of its products, the general public.

As I have already stated, environmental expenditures in the past five years have been between 30 to 40% of total production expenditures in the paper industry. Thus, as an industry, since 1967 environmental expenditures were close to $3 billion; to the firm this represents unproductive, wasteful expenditures which do not increase production. All this means lack of expansionary power in the industry, loss of jobs, supply shortages, increased long-term debt, increased cost, and built-in inflationary pressure.

For Mammoth Paper, environmental expenditures totalled $308,934,080 between 1972 and 1976, adding no productive capacity to the firm or to the United States economy. Also, such increased costs limit Mammoth as to what expenditures can be made outside the firm. In the past, Mammoth Paper played a large part in community affairs and local organizations. In the future, such expenditures might not be financially possible.

The firm today is operating in uncharted territory. Management has to be more efficient and responsive to change than ever before. Costs are increasing at an alarming rate. Let me cite some examples (*Exhibit 2*). The costs per acre of prime Southern woodlands has increased 750% since 1965. Cost of fiber delivered to the mills, up 100%; oil per BTU, up 300%; construction costs for a plant to produce 600 tons per day fine paper, up 200%; hourly wages, up 100%. Such a list of increased costs could go on to cover almost every related production cost in the industry. Add to this the increase in long-term debt from $1,500,000 in 1965 to $389,800,000 in 1970 and $530,700,000 in 1974. Over that same period of time, current liabilities have increased from $131,400,000 to $347,500,000. Cost of products sold has gone from $663,600,000 in 1965 to $1,553,400,000 in 1974. The increase from 1973 to 1974 alone was $340,900,000. Further burdening the cost of products sold are heavy environmental expenditures. I think you can understand, from all this, the catastrophic possibilities facing the industry and the paper consumer.

There are those who would point to all I've said as industry propaganda in light of the fine year Mammoth had in 1974. But even this must be re-examined (*Exhibits* 3 and 4). In 1974, sales reached an all-time high of over $2.2 billion and net income was also a record of $192 million. There are several reasons for this prosperous year. First, the removal of price controls and accompanying high demand enabled the company to recover increasing materials costs. Second, the volume of production of pulp, paper and paper products was at an all-time high, and operating efficiency improves with longer production runs. Third, better margins were realized in international sales. Fourth, improved liquidity earned higher interest income. And fifth, raw material shortages and labor stoppages were minimized. Such positive industry forces cannot be relied upon in the future. A more realistic demand schedule will probably be realized in coming years, and we shall face continued labor problems and material shortages.

Such problems are beginning to plague us again. As you can see from *Exhibit 2*, net earnings have decreased in 1975 by $32,900,000 from 1974, even though sales increased by $28,400,000 in the same time. Long-term debt has also gone up sharply and working capital has substantially decreased. Taking the inflation rate into account, our net earnings show no real growth (that is, growth greater than the inflation rate) from 1968 to 1975. In addition, today's rates of return are calculated by the antiquated means of using formerly low-cost figures to evaluate timberland and plant and equipment costs; such low costs no longer exist in production today.

To get a clearer picture of the effects of environmental standards not only on Mammoth Paper but for the industry as a whole, I refer to an Arthur D. Little study, "The Economic Impact of Anticipated Paper Industry Pollution-Abatement Costs," made to the Council on Environmental Quality, showing that 1977 water pollution requirements will close 30 to 34 mills. The study finds that the "Zero Pollution" 1985 goal would close up to 110 mills and cost up to 68,000 jobs. Regions to be hardest hit are small communities in Massachusetts, Connecticut, Wisconsin and New York. These states and their neighbors will incur 85% of the paper industry unemployment, according to the Arthur D. Little report. Again, the impact felt from unemployment will be heightened by the inflation that is caused when industry passes on the environmental costs in higher consumer prices.

In addition, rebuilding closed mills will not provide the necessary new jobs to absorb the unemployed labor force in those areas hardest hit. The Arthur D. Little study estimates that:

> Production capacity lost through marginal mill closures will be made up by mill construction or expansions principally in the South and West and to a lesser extent in Maine and Minnesota. Such expansion should more than compensate for pollution-related jobs lost in the South and West; however, they will do little to relieve the unemployment in other regions. These expansions not only will involve long-distance moves by the unemployed mill workers in the other regions but also, because of economies of scale, will offer fewer jobs than those eliminated by the closures.[1]

[1]Arthur D. Little, Inc., "Economic Impact of Anticipated Paper Industry Pollution-Abatement Costs, Part 1: Executive Summary." Report to the Council on Environmental Quality, November, 1971, C-73977.

The long-term effects of the closings will be high unemployment in already depressed regions of the country, with expansion simply adding to already high employment in growing areas of the country, boosting already growing labor costs in those areas (*Exhibit 5*).

The predictions of the Little report have already begun to be realized. In January, 1973, Weyerhaeuser Company announced the closing of its sulfite mill in Everett, Washington, although the Everett mill reported a $1 million pre-tax profit in the previous year, and that year was one of the worst for market pulp. In closing the mill, three hundred jobs were lost—as well as tax revenue for the city and State. The reason given for the closing was $10 million in environmental expenditures which would be necessary to meet State environment standards. No new mill is being planned.

In 1969 the paper industry produced 576 pounds of paper for every person in the US. Thus, the long-term effects of the Zero Pollution legislation are frightening for both the industry and the consumers. Giant corporations like Mammoth Paper or Weyerhauser can afford to close a mill if they feel it necessary and still produce paper. But small firms must take on the burden of environmental cost, for closing a mill might force them out of business. And complying with the necessary environmental costs might also put them out of business. They face bankruptcy either way. With high environmental expenditures necessary, entry costs to the industry rise, and the industry become more concentrated with firms which wield greater market power and have greater control over price. As both the surviving large and small firms cut back their production in the face of rising costs, it is indeed the consumer who pays the price for the luxury of Zero Pollution legislation.

International Paper has been a leader in compliance with antipollution legislation. Nevertheless, J. Stanford Smith, Chairman and Chief Executive Officer of International Paper, wrote on October 31, 1975, in International Paper's 1975 Annual Report:

> What is needed are realistic pollution control policies by the Federal and state governments, balanced policies which will protect health, recreation and the quality of life instead of intemperate absolutes which cannot be attained economically or technically within the time frame presently specified by environmental regulations. Congress needs to eliminate disincentives to capital formation, such as tax depreciation lives longer than the economic life of the property. Also, Congress should adopt several of the recently proposed incentives to capital investment, such as full depreciation of pollution control equipment in the year of installation since it earns no return. Such an approach would increase capital formation and advance environmental improvement.

I agree with Mr. Smith. Absolutes, such as Zero Pollution by 1985, are not constructive approaches to saving the environment. Tax incentives appealing to the needs of the firm and its responsibilities to its shareholders are necessary if, indeed, the quality of our environment, American productive capacity, and the consumer's standard of living are to improve to the levels which we all desire and which, working together, we can all achieve.

Responding to Mr. Bennington's presentation, Benjamin Spencer, noted environmentalist and President of Spencer Investigations of Noncompliance (SIN), a public interest consulting group, stated:

Russel Train, head of the Environmental Protection Agency, compares the necessity for environmental expenditures with the necessity of expenditures for national defense and law enforcement. As a concerned conservationist, and chief investigator of SIN, I reiterate Russel Train's thoughts that massive environmental expenditures *are* necessary. I wholeheartedly support the Zero Pollution by 1985 legislation and ask you to ignore requests for its repeal such as the one you have just heard.

It is time that industry develops a social responsibility, not only toward their shareholders but also toward those who ultimately support them, namely the consumer. This responsibility should take the form of industry bearing the cost of environmental cleanup, for it was their shortsighted planning and high profits which caused the deterioration of our land and water and the death of our wildlife. It was industry which has taken our most valuable natural resources and turned them into sewage disposals.

In 1967, the paper industry used 2.1 trillion gallons of water in the production process. They returned 1.9 trillion gallons to our waterways laden with sludge-forming solids, bleaching and paper-coating chemicals, and other discoloring matter. In 1967 it was common for mills not even to have secondary pollution treatment. When we examine the 50s and 60s, the years that made companies like Mammoth Paper what they are today, we see tremendous profits. Why, then, is it unfair to now expect them to incur the cost of cleaning up what they nearly permanently ruined? The fact of the matter is that it is not unfair, but simply just.

When we recall the devastation the paper industry has caused, we can feel no other way. For example, International Paper operated a mill at Ticonderoga, New York, for 88 years. That's 88 years of discharge floating into Lake Champlain. A Ralph Nader Report estimates there is now a 300-acre sludge residing on the bottom of the lake. Not only does this sludge kill the aquatic life in the lake, but parts of the sludge sometimes break off and move to another part of the lake so that further destruction can occur where no production mill exists. While it is true that International, responding to the recent environmental legislation, had to close the Ticonderoga mill and build another one, International is not required to clean up the sludge in Lake Champlain, nor are they likely to do so on their own volition. Incidentally, the new mill has an increased capacity of 94,000 tons annually, in direct contradiction to Mr. Bennington's statement that environmental expenditures do not increase a firm's productive capacity.

Mammoth Paper also said its profits will not stay as high as they are now, and would have you believe that the environmental costs are the main reason for this. Yet environmental expenditures are only about 10% of their capital expenditures and only about 1 1/2% of their sales. Mr. Bennington pointed out that profits have dropped substantially in 1975 from their high 1974 level. Nevertheless, I wish to remind you that Mammoth and other large paper companies have an important component of their sales dependent on the construction industry. If you think profits are high in 1974 or in 1975, just wait until the housing industry, which has been depressed for these two years of already high profits, recovers within the next two years. Under a close scrutiny of its balance sheets, the industry simply cannot be believed as it pleads poverty and asks for extensions for compliance with environmental legislation or repeal of the Zero Pollution by 1985 law.

In the past five years the paper industry has gone into the production of "snow." They quote big numbers which, in fact, have little meaning when looked at in the context of their total operations. Ask a paper industry executive, for example:

- How many pollution expenditures were funneled into projects that made huge profits?
- What is the net cost after tax write offs and depreciation allowances? *Exhibit 6* gives my estimates of Mammoth Paper's antipollution equipment expenditures and tax advantage on capital gains.
- How much should have been spent to clean up the environment but wasn't because of the firm's legal delay tactics to subvert the spirit of recent environmental legislation?

In addition, Mr. Bennington referred to the Little Report and cited sections which suited his purposes. He neglected to quote the Little Report's finding that demand in the paper industry is price inelastic, so that the increased costs can be easily passed on to the consumers and actually raise revenues in the industry. Thus we believe that price controls must accompany future pollution regulations, so that we can be sure the public does not absorb the costs of repairing the industry's past abuse of the earth.

The industry tells us how many jobs will be lost due to mill closings because of environmental expenditures. What about the jobs created in the production of antipollution equipment and the mills that are increased in size to replace the closed mills and take advantage of modern economies of scale? And what about the fact that public concern about the environment has meant high demand for recycled products? For Mammoth, recycled (converted) paper products now make up nearly 31% of their production and nearly 34% of their sales revenues (*Exhibit 7*).

We must get the public united still more strongly against the polluters. The paper industry's past neglect can be viewed as a loan the public granted them. But now we want it paid back. And the only way to do this is to force them. With voluntary compliance in 1969, the paper industry spent .69% of its gross revenue for environmental expenditures. Voluntarism is not enough. Leo Weaver of Enviro-Chem Systems, Inc., states, "We are living in a fool's paradise if we think industry will do anything until it is forced to." It is time to apply that force.

EXHIBIT I Federal Water Pollution Control Act of Amendments of 1972*

Title I—Research and Related Programs

Declaration of Goals and Policy

Sec. 101. [125] (a) The objective of this Act is to restore and maintain the chemical, physical, and biological integrity of the Nation's waters. In order to achieve this objective it is hereby declared that, consistent with the provisions of this Act—

1 it is the national goal that the discharge of pollutants into the navigable waters be eliminated by 1985;

2 it is the national goal that wherever attainable, an interim goal of water quality which provides for the protection and propagation of fish, shellfish, and wildlife and provides for recreation in and on the water be achieved by July 1, 1983;

*Section numbers in brackets refer to title 33 of U.S.C.A. Some sections of the Act have been omitted.

3 it is the national policy that the discharge of toxic pollutants in toxic amounts be prohibited;
4 it is the national policy that Federal financial assistance be provided to construct publicly owned waste treatment works;
5 it is the national policy that area-wide waste treatment management planning processes be developed and implemented to assure adequate control of sources of pollutants in each State; and
6 it is the national policy that a major research and demonstration effort be made to develop technology necessary to eliminate the discharge of pollutants into the navigable waters, waters of the contiguous zone, and the oceans.

EXHIBIT 2 Cost Trends (1971 = 100) in US Paper Industry

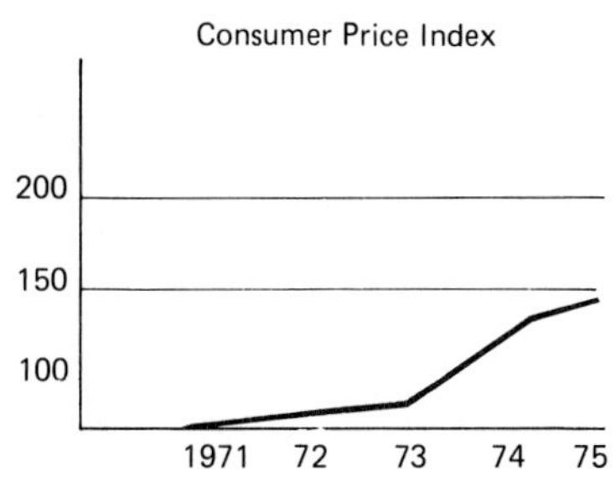

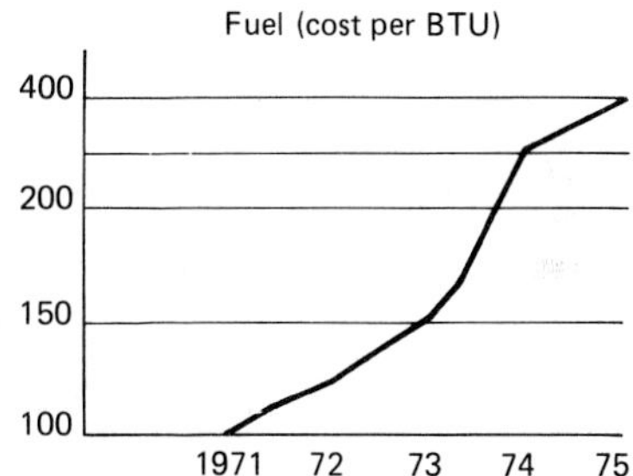

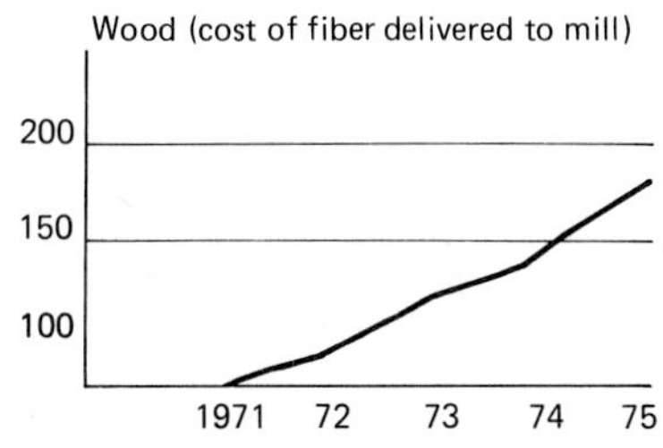

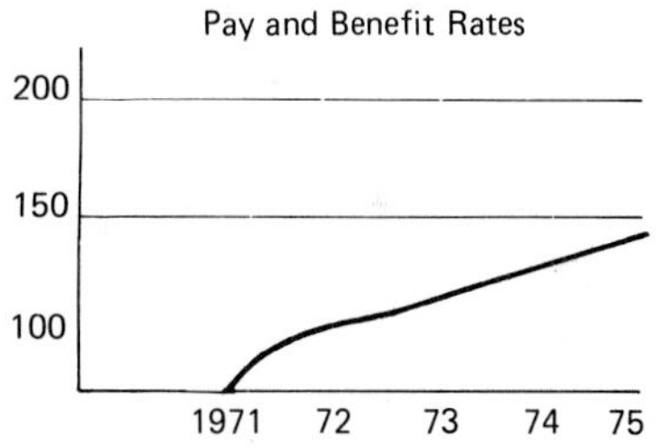

COSTS FOR NEW CAPACITY 1955-1975

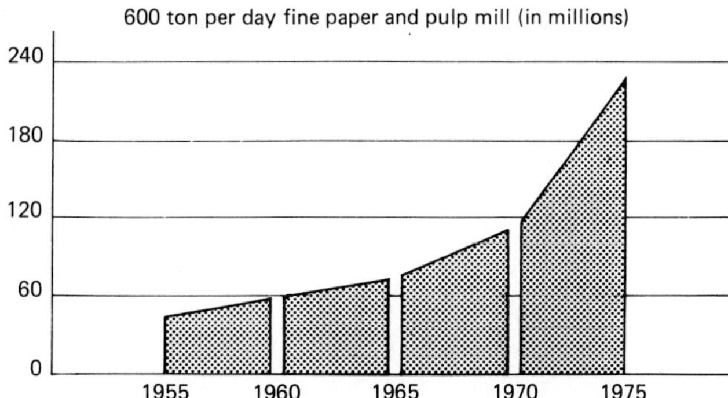

Source: International Paper, Annual Report, 1975.

EXHIBIT 3
MAMMOTH PAPER
Financial Summary, 1965–1975
($ millions)

	1975	*1974*	*1973*	*1972*	*1971*	*1970*	*1969*	*1968*	*1967*	*1966*	*1965*
Sales	2249.1	2220.7	1689.2	1527.9	1438.1	1343.9	1297.2	1149.0	1037.3	1062.2	955.6
Other income, net	15.2	38.7	29.9	15.3	12.4	12.4	16.1	13.9	9.5	12.4	14.6
Cost of products sold	1557.8	1553.4	1212.5	1105.2	1045.4	965.8	909.6	814.	750.4	740.2	663.6
Distribution, selling & administrative expenses	240.2	240.2	208.1	211.7	216.8	202.9	184.0	157.7	140.2	136.5	129.2
Depreciation	86.9	78.8	75.9	71.5	70.8	65.	57.7	56.9	54.0	49.6	55.5
Cost of timber harvested	15.2	19.7	13.1	10.2	10.2	7.3	6.6	5.1	2.2	8.8	9.5
Interest expense	60.2	32.9	29.9	27.7	29.9	28.5	19.	12.4	6.6	1.5	.73
Income taxes	111.7	142.4	62.8	41.6	27.0	27.0	53.3	45.3	32.1	61.3	46.7
Earnings before extraordinary items	159.1	192.0	116.8	75.2	50.4	59.9	83.2	71.5	61.3	76.7	65.0
Extraordinary items	—	—	—	—	(11.)	(28.5)	—	—	—	—	—
Net earnings	159.1	192.0	116.8	75.2	39.4	31.4	83.2	71.5	61.3	76.7	65.0
Cash dividends	65.0	56.2	56.9	48.9	48.9	48.9	48.2	44.5	43.1	39.4	40.2
Financial Position											
Current assets	683.3	742.4	538.7	492.0	415.4	443.1	417.6	392.7	330.7	337.3	316.1
Current liabilities	363.5	347.5	202.9	183.2	165.0	202.2	228.5	164.3	156.2	131.4	131.4
Working capital	319.7	394.9	335.9	308.8	250.4	240.9	189.1	228.5	174.5	205.9	184.7
Plants & properties—net	1272.4	776.0	722.0	751.9	773.8	773.8	713.9	634.4	582.5	476.7	420.5
Timberlands—net	319.0	271.6	133.6	120.5	121.2	124.8	112.4	111.7	113.9	101.5	70.1
Long-term debt	829.9	530.7	425.6	421.9	411.7	389.8	272.3	262.1	132.1	57.7	1.5
Reserves & deferred liabilities	148.9	116.1	114.6	94.2	116.8	100.7	57.7	42.3	30.7	23.4	16.8
Share owners equity—common stock	1091.1	993.5	856.3	807.4	780.4	789.1	806.7	779.6	756.3	741.7	705.2

EXHIBIT 4
MAMMOTH PAPER
Five Year Summaries

	1975	*1974*	*1973*	*1972*	*1971*	*1970*
			(in millions)			
Changes in Net Earnings						
Net earnings reported	159.1	192	116.8	75.2	39.4	31.4
Increase (decrease) from prior year	(32.9)	75.2	41.6	35.8	(8.0)	(51.8)
Changes in Components of Earnings						
Income						
Net sales	28.4	531.5	161.3	89.8	94.2	46.7
Equity in earnings of affiliates	(9.4)	5.0	5.7	.8	.1	.5
Interest income	(14.6)	10.8	8.3	2.7	2.0	.1
Other	6.9	(7.1)	.1	(.1)	(2.3)	(3.9)
	11.6	540.2	175.4	93.2	94.0	43.4
Cost and Expenses						
Cost of products sold	4.4	430.9	107.3	59.8	79.6	56.2
Distribution expenses	(10.1)	21.8	(.4)	5.8	6.9	5.0
Selling & administrative expenses	10.2	9.9	(3.4)	(11.3)	7.7	13.8
Depreciation & cost of timber harvested	9.0	9.6	6.9	1.4	8.4	7.9
Interest	27.9	3.0	2.2	(2.2)	1.4	9.5
	74.3	385.2	112.6	53.5	104.	92.4
Total pre-tax changes	(63.0)	154.7	62.9	40.2	(10.5)	(49.2)
Provision for income taxes	(30.7)	79.6	21.1	15.1	(.6)	(26.1)
Net Change	(32.3)	75.1	41.7	25.1	9.9	(23.1)
Total	2249.	2220.8	1689.3	1528.1	1437.8	1343.7
Sales by Products						
Paperboard, pulp, & paper	1188.7	1235.0	873.7	798.7	743.1	749.5
Converted paper products	730.1	752.3	572.5	502.4	465.5	435.4
Plywood & lumber	49.6	57.1	58.7	48.8	44.2	32.3
Other wood products	139.6	128.6	136.9	113.7	89.6	65.8
Other products	61.2	47.8	47.5	64.5	95.4	60.7
Oil & natural gas	79.8	—	—	—	—	—
Production by Products	*1975*	*1974*	*1973*	*1972*	*1971*	*1970*
			(in thousands of tons)			
Paperboard, Paper, & Pulp						
Paperboard						
Container	1189.9	1566.6	1488.5	1524.2	1465.8	1383.4
Bleached board	858.5	984.0	876.0	785.5	727.1	711.0
Total paperboard	2048.4	2550.6	2364.5	2309.7	2192.9	2094.4
Printing, writing, & other bleached paper	556.3	810.3	795.0	760.7	695.7	642.4
Newsprint	981.1	984.8	811.8	915.4	838.8	931.5
Industrial & miscellaneous paper	304.4	477.4	489.1	486.2	499.3	465.7
Market pulp	589.1	805.2	735.1	776.0	842.4	952.7
	4479.3	5628.3	5195.5	5248.0	5069.1	5086.7
Converted Paper Products	1503.8	1726.5	1528.6	1439.6	1323.5	1241.7
Plywood and Lumber			(in millions)			
Plywood (sq. ft.-3/8")	193.5	313.2	360.6	345.3	327.0	233.6
Lumber (board feet)	229.2	195.6	177.4	180.3	178.1	159.1
Crude oil (barrels)	28.2					
Natural gas	24.5					

EXHIBIT 5

U.S. Projected Capacity Increases and Capital Expenditures—By Regions

Region*	Capacity Increase 1973–1975**				Reported Expenditure in P&P Survey			
	Paper/Board	Pulp (000s tons)	Total	% of U.S. Total	Production	% of Total	Environment	% of Total
New England	197	170	367	4.2%	$ 188,289,000	11.9%	$ 91,329,000	8.5%
Mid-Atlantic	604	211	815	9.3	60,796,700	3.8	44,898,750	4.2
East North Central	1,061	143	1,204	13.7	113,450,000	7.2	90,202,200	8.4
West North Central	69	31	100	1.1	55,593,000	3.5	37,836,000	3.5
South Atlantic	1,004	702	1,706	19.4	355,349,485	22.4	384,800,000	35.9
East South Central	795	533	1,328	15.1	180,675,000	11.4	97,361,000	9.1
West South Central	1,071	798	1,869	21.2	379,100,000	23.9	64,918,000	6.0
Mountain & Pacific	1,008	404	1,412	16.0	251,027,900	15.8	261,205,382	24.4
U.S. total	5,809	2,992	8,801	100.0%	1,584,281,085	99.9%	$1,072,550,332	100.0%

*Regions are as follows: New England (Me., Vt., N.H., Conn., R.I., Mass.); Mid-Atlantic (N.Y., N.J., Pa.); East North Central (Wis., Mich., Ill., Ind., Ohio); West North Central (N.D., S.D., Neb., Kans., Minn., Iowa, Mo.); South Atlantic (Del, Md., W. Va., Va., N.C., S.C., Ga., Fla.); East South Central (Ky., Tenn., Miss., Ala.); West South Central (Okla., Tex., Ark., La.); Mountain & Pacific (Wash., Ore., Calif., Alaska, Ida., Nev., Mont., Wyo., Utah, Ariz., Colo., N.M.).

**Source: American Paper Institute, Capacity Survey 1972–75.

United States—Reported Capital Expenditures for 1975–77 by Regions, and by Type of Facility

Region	Pulping/Fiber	New Machines	Machine Modifications	Plant and Miscellaneous	Production Total	Environment		
						Water	Air	Total
New England	$ 395,730,000	$ 93,500,000	$ 23,378,000	$ 152,768,000	$ 665,376,000	$162,900,000	$ 56,050,000	$ 218,950,000
Mid-Atlantic	8,500,000	25,000,000	5,152,000	14,397,000	53,049,000	22,146,000	20,145,000	42,291,000
E. No. Central	18,417,000	59,000,000	41,359,000	88,012,000	206,788,000	103,837,000	71,185,000	175,022,000
W. No. Central	86,139,000	20,000,000	1,345,000	27,674,000	87,158,000	4,966,000	1,672,000	6,638,000
So. Atlantic	204,568,000	75,000,000	62,286,000	240,905,000	582,759,000	61,675,000	242,943,000	304,618,000
E. So. Central	486,000,000	145,500,000	11,410,000	155,696,000	798,606,000	92,112,000	178,396,000	270,508,000
W. So. Central	183,715,000	145,000,000	45,600,000	354,124,000	728,439,000	55,621,000	76,654,000	132,275,000
Mount./Pacific	126,181,000	35,000,000	65,414,000	61,347,000	287,942,000	122,324,000	68,722,500	191,046,500
Totals	$1,461,250,000	$598,000,000	$255,944,000	$1,094,923,000	$3,410,117,000	$625,581,000	$715,767,500	$1,341,348,500

(Expenditures of approximately $900,000,000, not specified for location, omitted from above data)

Source: *Pulp and Paper Magazine*, 1975.

EXHIBIT 6 Mammoth Paper's Effective Tax Rate*

1975	41.3%
1974	42.7%
1973	35%
1972	35.8%

*Calculated from base 48% corporate tax rate with reductions for investment tax credits and income taxes at capital gains rate.

EXHIBIT 7 Percent of Converted (i.e., recycled) Paper Products Compared to Total Paperboard, Paper, and Pulp

	Production	*Sales*
1970	24.4%	32.99%
1971	26.27%	32.37%
1972	27.43%	32.87%
1973	29.42%	33.88%
1974	30.67%	33.87%

Source: Mammoth Paper, Annual Report, 1974.

MIDWESTERN MORTGAGE INVESTORS: A REIT IN 1975

In September, 1975, John Colt, a vice president of Third National Bank of New York, was faced with a problem. One of the bank's debtors, Midwestern Mortgage Investors, a real estate investment trust (REIT), was in serious trouble and wanted to reorganize.

John Colt was thirty-three years old and had been with Third National for eleven years. He had started at the bank as a management trainee shortly after his graduation from a local college with a B.A. in political science. Colt's first assignment was as a teller in a central city branch. He then became a loan officer at a busy downtown office for five years, before moving to the corporate banking area as an assistant vice president. Two years later he moved into the real estate field. In February, 1975, he was promoted to vice president and put in charge of the bank's REIT loan committee.

Third National is one of the nation's leading financial institutions with total assets in 1974 of just over $16 billion and shareholders' equity of $559 million. Some months earlier the bank had been forced to postpone a proposed debenture sale because of investor concern over problem loans in its real estate portfolio, particularly its loans to REITs.

Third National had originally committed $200 million in direct loans to real estate investment trusts. The bank had also furnished these trusts with a backup line of credit of $150 million to facilitate the REITs' sales of their own commercial paper. Initially, the backup lines were very profitable since, besides charging commitment fees, many banks required the REITs to carry compensating balances of 10% of the unused amount of the line, and 20% of any borrowings actually drawn down. Thus when the prime rate was 6%, loans to the REITs yielded in excess of 8%. In addition to its REIT loans Third National had real estate loans amounting to $250 million in its portfolio.

Early in 1974, when a combination of tight money and overbuilding caused a wave of real estate bankruptcies, investors declined to reinvest in commercial paper. The banks, however, were forced to honor their REIT commitments. By September, 1975, Third National had $350 million in REIT loans on its books. Colt knew that his bank was not alone in its commitments to the REITs, or in the problems it was experiencing (*Exhibit 2*).

REITS: INDUSTRY BACKGROUND

A Real Estate Investment Trust (REIT) is a business trust, organized to invest in real estate. To preserve its trust status, a REIT must distribute virtually all of its income in the year earned. REITs were created by Congressional legislation in 1960 and treasury regulations set out in 1962 (see *Appendix 1*). They are fundamentally financial intermediaries.

In 1960, to attract small investors and their money to the real estate industry, Congress set up REITs as investment vehicles analogous to mutual funds—small inves-

This case was prepared as a basis for class discussion rather than to illustrate either effective or ineffective handling of an administrative situation.

tors, large diversified professionally managed portfolios. The incentive provided was to remove the penalty of corporate double taxation by giving conduit treatment to all income distributed in the year earned as long as the income distributed exceeded 90% of the trust's taxable income. The form of income, ordinary or capital gains, remains the same with the beneficiary as with the trust. Losses, however, cannot be passed through. With regard to income retained, the trust is taxed like a corporation.

REITs can also be used as conduits of untaxed earnings to institutions which would otherwise be taxed. For example, while a pension fund could invest directly in unlevered real property, it would be taxed on income derived from property purchased with financial leverage. However, a pension fund is not taxed on dividend income (as of 1975). Hence as a financial intermediary, the REIT form allows passage of income, as dividends, tax-free to the pension fund. Curiously only a few trusts were set up this way, Property Capital Trust and Realty Income Trust being two examples.

In the first years of the trust legislation many real estate holding companies found it advantageous to utilize this new legal form. These trusts were generally not aggressive investors and used only moderate leverage in their property acquisitions. However, while the objective of the REIT legislation was to attract equity to real estate, the regulations did not distinguish rent from interest income.

Therefore, in 1962, two trusts were formed which focused on relatively short-term interest-bearing mortgages (i.e. construction and development loans)—First Mortgage Investors and Continental Mortgage Investors. These trusts grew rapidly as the result of frequent equity and debt offerings and by 1969 they had portfolios in excess of $500 million each. The promoters of this type of trust saw it as a vehicle for developing a large and profitable management company. Many others attempted to follow their lead, eschewing equity investments for short-term and lucrative construction lending. By borrowing short-term at prime rate plus 1% and lending at an effective rate of prime plus 5%, they reaped large profits which, in turn, yielded good stock market performance.

During the 1970 credit squeeze, many traditional participants in the construction and development loan market withdrew, thereby creating an opportunity for the REITs. Yield spreads widened further under the pressure of demand from the development industry. This in turn allowed the trusts to increase their earnings substantially, a success which attracted Wall Street's interest to the REIT form.

Higher earnings encouraged Wall Street to bid up the prices of the short-term construction and development trusts, and made new equity issues feasible and attractive. Many issues were placed at well over book value, prompting some investment banking firms to approach a large number of likely sponsors of REITs with the view of participating in the equity placements. By 1974 there were some two hundred REITs in existence with a total capital of about $21 billion, $5 billion being equity and the rest debt. In all, a total of $18 billion was put into the industry between late 1969 and late 1973. In addition, commercial bank mortgages increased from $66.7 billion to $113.6 billion over the same period.

While *Exhibit 2* provides a glimpse into some of the twenty largest banks' investment portfolios, it also suggests that it was the largest banks which made nearly two-thirds of the almost $12 billion bank commitment to the REIT industry. This situation developed in part because the banks saw in the REITs profitable opportunity. In many cases, they actually competed to make loans available to the trusts.

With their new capital to place and with competition from the commercial banks, the REITs were under pressure to make loans. In the competition for investment opportunities, some overlooked traditionally sound underwriting practice. Some aggravated matters by rewarding their loan officers with bonuses based on the money they lent out. As a result, virtually any real estate deal that looked good on paper got funded by someone, regardless of its real economic viability. The result was overbuilding in most markets, especially of condominiums and recreational land developments.

When interest rates began to rise in 1974 and money became tight, many developers were caught in the squeeze between higher financial costs and falling demand. Many once ''economic'' projects became uneconomic and a number of developers defaulted. As the tight money, inflation, and unemployment worsened, demand for many classes of real estate, especially overbuilt condominiums and recreational land projects, fell off. Concurrently, most REITs found it difficult to turn over their own liability structure, i.e. convert short-term debt to longer-term capital. New equity was unavailable. The original idea of most REIT promoters—to limit the use of short-term debt and to quickly replace it with equity—proved unworkable. In even worse shape were the trusts that had loaned on a fixed-rate basis, borrowing at variable rates. They especially felt the squeeze. Mortgage money then became unavailable at almost any price, causing many more defaults by developers. As the economy as a whole turned down, the real estate industry ground to a halt and with it payments on the subordinated loans held by many REITs. *Exhibit 3* shows how the prime rate has varied since 1969 and, in addition, how housing starts have varied over the same period. *Exhibit 4* shows a balance sheet for the REIT industry and gives some idea of both its capital structure and its loan portfolio at the end of 1974.

REIT MANAGEMENT

Typically, the REIT's advisor, its independent professional management, might receive 1% to 1.2% of the gross assets per year up to about $100 million, and a little less thereafter. Many trusts make incentive payments to encourage the acquisition of a quality portfolio; perhaps 10% of all income, ordinary and capital gains, would be paid to the advisor subject to an overall ceiling payment of 1.3% or 1.5% times assets. Some agreements also provided for a maximum fee based on earnings. In early 1975, to comply with their agreements, many advisors should have made substantial ''reimbursements'' to the trusts but most were unable to pay because of increased expenses, primarily due to the cost of monitoring problem loans.

REITS: A MIXED BAG

Colt, who had been transferred to the real estate department in 1972, was well aware of the REITs' problems in 1975. Not that all trusts had major problems. About $25 million of Third National's REIT loans were to equity trusts and these were all current. Pure equity trusts primarily purchased completed, income-producing properties, and usually passed the net cash flow (rental income less operating expenses and debt service) through to shareholders. Other trusts operated in effect as equity trusts by gearing their return to property rentals, while legally still maintaining a debt position. Some equity trusts had problems, but almost all were current on their loans and, in fact, paying dividends.

About 28% of the portfolio consisted of loans to hybrid trusts. Hybrids often had a large portion of their assets in conventional self-liquidating mortgages, and many also owned real estate. Typically, hybrids had been sponsored by major insurance companies and usually had conservative lending practices. However, some had experienced problems with their construction and development loans. Third National had only one problem loan to a hybrid trust, amounting to $1.2 million out of the $100 million it had lent to this group of REITs.

The short-term construction and development trusts were another matter. Third National had some $225 million in loans to this class of REIT, of which $175 million were in default of the original loan covenants or paying below market rates. So far, however, only two major construction trusts had taken the Chapter 11 Bankruptcy route to gain the protection of the bankruptcy laws: Fidelity Mortgage Trust and Associated Mortgage Trust. Third National had made small loans to Associated but it had loans outstanding to other construction REITs which were threatening to declare bankruptcy.

PROBLEMS, THREATS, AND BANKRUPTCIES

Colt had first learned of his promotion and new job in February, 1975, when Charles Young, head of the real estate area, asked him into his office one morning to talk about the future of the REITs.

Young reviewed the bank's position in the REIT industry and told Colt of the unofficial stance that the Federal Reserve Board had taken, showing him a portion of a clipping from *Forbes*,[1] which suggested how and why the Fed acted.

> But Burns [Chairman of the Federal Reserve] was listening. "He was receptive," says Courshon, chief executive of First Mortgage Investors, which was threatening bankruptcy. Within weeks, in its quiet way, the Fed began urging the major banks to back the REITs—not just FMI, but all of the walking wounded. And, in turn, the powerful city banks began pressuring the frightened country banks to go along too.
>
> Why did the Fed step in? Basically because the REITs are pivotal financial middlemen who borrow from the pin-striped bankers and lend to muddy-shoed builders. There was no way for them to collapse without hurting banking, the tottering building business and a lot of little people. The Fed had just buried Franklin National Bank; it didn't want any more funerals right then.

Young also talked of the difficulties Third National and the other major banks occasionally had with smaller members of the REIT credit line. Young reminisced about a bank in Wheeling, West Virginia, which had sued to get back its $1.8 million participation in a loan to Delta Mortgage Investors, a trust in which Third National had the lead position.

At the time, the major banks were replacing their traditionally informal loan ar-

[1] "Horror Story: How shaky are the billions the big banks have lent to the REITs? Bluntly put, the answer is: *Very.*" *Forbes*, February 1, 1975, p. 27.

rangements with contractual loans called revolvers. These loans provided the trusts with working capital to fund commitments, as well as to pay interest on their public debt. Typically a revolver would last for about a year, locking all participating banks into the same terms: any returns of principal to be shared pro rata by all the banks so no one would be repaid before any other. The bank in Wheeling had declined to participate in the rearrangement and wanted out, going so far as to sue Delta to get its money back.

The chairman of Third National called Wheeling and pointed out that although the lead position was an informal role and without obligation to other participants (who had little legal redress to the senior lender), Third National hoped Wheeling would participate in this and many future profitable transactions. After another call from a Federal Reserve officer, Young chuckled, "the Wheeling bank called off the suit and joined the revolver."

Colt had his own opinions and had not been reluctant to make them known. He felt that many short-term REITs were an incredible boondoggle. Essentially, since many REITs were bank-sponsored and most were run by ex-bankers, it appeared natural for them to concentrate on the same types of construction loans they had been making as bankers. However, because the REITs had to charge higher rates than commercial banks, the better loans still went to the banks. The REITs got the riskier construction projects. Then, when the economy slumped in 1974, the construction REITs were hit hardest because many of the properties securing their loans were basically unsound.

Colt recalled one story printed by *Forbes* in February 1975:

> When FMI got stuck with a foreclosure, for example, it would sometimes lend a friendly builder extra money against one of his properties and then induce him to put up some of those dollars as a sort of "down payment" on one of the trust's lemons. If the project carried, say, a $4 million loan and the builder put up $500,000, FMI called it a $4.5 million sale, booked a $500,000 profit. But how was the new owner going to pay interest on the loan when the previous one couldn't? The loan was renegotiated to include a couple of years' interest. And after that? Perhaps inflation and better times would bail everybody out.

Colt felt that, while the concept of a specialized financial intermediary to make short-term construction loans was sound, the way the construction REITs went at it was not.

Towards the end of the conversation Young asked if Colt would like to head up a special group the bank was creating to monitor the REIT industry. The new group was to prepare a weekly status report on the bank's REIT loans for its executive committee. The purpose of the group, Young seemed to say, was to effect an orderly liquidation of the bank's loans without resorting to the bankruptcy laws, i.e. Chapter 10 or Chapter 11 proceedings.

Under Chapter 11 proceedings the debtor voluntarily seeks the protection of the court against creditor suits and remains in control of its affairs while it tries to work out a way to pay its debts. Once its Chapter 11 status is approved, interest payments stop and only the debtor can propose reorganization terms.

Under Chapter 10 proceedings, the court at the request of a firm's creditors appoints a trustee to investigate the debtor's affairs and to attempt to completely reorganize it. If necessary, the trustee may sell some or all the debtor's assets to raise money to pay the creditors. From his commercial lending experience Colt knew that putting a court-appointed trustee between the creditors and debtors always complicated and bureaucratized matters. In addition, interest payments would be stopped immediately by the court.

Colt felt that Chapter 10 would be worse than Chapter 11 from the bank's point of view because he believed the bank was much better qualified to decide when and how to liquidate a trust than someone appointed by the court, who would be in it for the fees. The bank would not have the same rights to veto the reorganization under Chapter 10 as it would under Chapter 11. Besides, Chapter 10 cost more in fees and involved more red tape than Chapter 11 proceedings.

On one point Young was emphatic. "Let us do everything possible," he stated, "to postpone or delay any possible bankruptcy proceeding by the trusts."

With an apple-sized lump in his throat, Colt agreed to take on the job, aware of the potential and pitfalls it offered. If the REITs folded up entirely and the bank had to take huge losses, then no matter how noble his endeavor was, he would be a pariah at the bank. If he was successful, Young seemed to imply that a senior vice presidency would be his.

BEFORE THE STORM

The first month at the new job proceeded smoothly. Work consisted mainly of talking—first, to other bankers about their attitudes towards the various trusts, to insure they cooperated; and second, to various trusts to renegotiate interest rates on their debt (downward), and to alter various restrictive covenants which a trust could not meet and hope to survive through 1975.

Colt did not like the apparently worsening situation of many larger trusts. As the few good loans the trusts had were paid off, the percentage of nonaccruing loans in their total portfolios grew rapidly. This meant that the cash flows the REITs generated decreased. Yet, none of the other bankers Colt talked to wanted to face this problem head on. They preferred to deal with problems on a piecemeal basis, fighting each fire as it flamed.

The accounting profession was not making Colt's life easier. It was forcing the REITs to use a present value approach in their financial reporting, to discount the face amounts of problem loans by the cost of carrying them. Colt feared what would happen when some of the larger trusts suddenly ended up with a negative net worth as a result of newly created reserves. He was concerned that the accountants would try to force the banks to adopt similar measures on their loans to REITs. That was quite a ways off, Colt thought, since he knew there would be substantial delays in processing any change through the many regulatory bodies involved in setting bank accounting standards. In September, 1975, the Financial Accounting Standards Board (FASB), in fact, had declined to make the new accounting standards official. The American Institute of Certified Public Accountants (AICPA), however, continued to require the trusts to use the preliminary standards.

AN INVITATION TO LUNCH

One day, Thomas Bain, the President of Midwestern Mortgage Investors, came by for lunch. Bain had been number-two man in the real estate department of Midwestern National Bank and ran the bank's REIT. Third National had a $25 million loan outstanding to Midwestern and was lead bank on its line of credit, currently a revolving term loan. *Exhibit 5* contains Midwestern Mortgage's Income Statements and Balance Sheets for 1974 and 1973.

Midwestern, long in the real estate lending business, used its REIT to make loans that the bank normally would not touch. In its portfolio the trust had loans to recreational land developers, loans on resort condominiums, and some construction loans without a permanent mortgage takeout commitment. Such loans paid a higher than average interest rate—four to five percentage points over prime—but, obviously, they were riskier.

Colt knew that REITs could not compete with banks in making high-quality construction loans to first-class well-financed developers. The REITs' cost of capital was much higher. Whereas a bank could give a construction loan with a committed takeout to a favored client at one point over prime, a soundly managed REIT's cost of capital was one to two points over prime—even before management fees.

Midwestern, like many banks and insurance companies, initially used the same people to manage both the bank's real estate lending activities and its trusts. In some cases, the existence of a separate list of REIT officers and trustees was essentially a fiction that could leave these banks open to conflict of interest charges.

Midwestern's board was sensitive to the conflict of interest question. Midwestern Mortgage's trustees were equally if not more concerned, because they had potentially extensive individual liability and there were several shareholder suits pending, naming the trustees individually—including Bain. The suits alleged civil liability, because of conflicts of interest, and criminal liability under the Securities Act of 1933. Eventually, at the bank board's insistence, Bain had left the bank to manage the trust on a full-time basis.

Midwestern's Annual Report for 1975 was not available. Colt knew, however, that Midwestern's loan loss reserve stood at about $40 million. He also knew Midwestern had drawn down its backup bank lines under its revolving credit agreements with its banks and paid off its commercial paper. He knew the trust had about 65% of its portfolio not accruing interest but he thought it likely that 70% or more were not paying interest. Midwestern put its loans on a nonaccruing basis when ninety days had passed without payment of interest due or when there was substantial evidence that the property securing the loan could not support the accruing interest payments. Midwestern reported to its holders of beneficial interest on an accrual basis but used a cash basis for tax purposes. Colt felt sure that no dividend would be distributed for 1975.

While the trust had foreclosed on only one small property so far, Colt expected more foreclosures in 1975 to 1976. Ownership would increase the trust's "Investments in Real Estate" and it would reduce the trust's income since depreciation would have to be taken and the trust would be responsible for property taxes, operating expenses and any senior debt. Some properties could show losses. The implications of a large number of foreclosures by the trust could be serious for the bank. Also, as the cash needed to sustain the trust increased, the bank's efforts to keep the trust alive and out of the Bankruptcy Court could be threatened.

Colt and Bain, who was thirty-five years old, had first met at a Mortgage Bankers convention and had become friends. Both were relatively young and had advanced rapidly in their respective banks. Shortly before he expected Bain to arrive for lunch, Colt reflected upon their last conversation six months ago. Third National had a construction loan on an office building in Houston, Texas, and the developer, Julius Granger, had a standby commitment for a permanent takeout by Midwestern Mortgage.[2] The developer filed for Chapter 11 protection before completing the property. When Colt and Bain met last, the building was still totally vacant, although it had been completed by the company bonding the contractor.

Colt, in his former role as a real estate officer, had talked to Bain about Midwestern Mortgage's honoring its standby commitment, thus taking Third National out of a problem loan. Bain had said, "No dice. First, because of the developer's bankruptcy, Midwestern's obligation is vague, giving enough outs that we think we could win a court fight if Granger tried to force the issue. Second, we do not have the money to make the loan and we would have to ask you, as our lead lender, to get the other banks to increase our revolver if we did have to fund." Colt was afraid that Midwestern had gone downhill from that point. The bank's records were not terribly enlightening, however.

Colt and Bain went to lunch at a local restaurant, preferring the food there to the drab cuisine usually served at the bank's panelled private dining rooms. Over lunch, Bain explained that 65% of Midwestern Mortgage's total portfolio of close to $300 million was not accruing interest although the trust's average lending rate in 1975 had been about 12%. Bain said that he expected the 1975 balance sheet to show total assets of about $292 million and he suggested that 1975's earnings, before interest charges, would be about 3.17% on assets; a figure that could improve to close to 5% next year if the real estate industry and the economy improved.

Colt knew that the trust's revolving credit agreement set interest charges at 120% of prime, or about 10% for 1975. Interest on the subordinate debt would be the same as in 1974.

REALITY

After lunch Bain commented on the extra window in Colt's new office and then got down to the real reason he had come to town. He took out a thick report and put it on Colt's desk. "John," he said, "you are our lead lender so I have brought this to you first. We have always tried to be honorable in our dealings with you. If we are not to file for bankruptcy the only way we are going to work out of the hole we are in, and survive, is to refinance our existing senior debt.

"As we see it there is only one alternative. If all the banks go along, we will obviously be a much smaller trust. We would have much less debt, but we should be able to survive as on operating entity.

"We want to 'auction' all loans to the banks. They would pay by putting up some portion in cash and tendering debt for the rest. The advantage of this proposal is that participating banks could get out or stay in as they chose. There would be few problems in deciding who gets what. Our major creditors and the trust would be in a better and more stable condition. Remember, the trust still has outstanding commitments to fund and cash

[2]A standby is a commitment by a lender to place a permanent mortgage at agreed-upon terms. The developer essentially has purchased an option and hopes to get better terms when the project is completed and rented. Typically, the developer needs the standby to get construction financing. The standby lender receives a couple of points either on a one-time or an annual basis. The interest rate in the standby is usually set to insure against the necessity of funding the loan. In 1975, however, many calls were made to fund standbys.

is hard to come by. Disappointed borrowers could create as many problems as recalcitrant small banks if the trust does not honor the commitments it made in better times.''

Bain concluded by saying, ''I will leave this proposal with you and let you study it at length. I would appreciate your comments, though, since you are our lead bank. We have to decide what to propose and how to negotiate with the other banks in our line.'' *Appendix 2* outlines the details of Bain's proposal.

INDIGESTION

After Midwestern Mortgage Investor's official left, Colt started leafing through the report. He knew that taking over someone else's loans would put additional pressure on Third National's already sorely tested real estate group. Third National had recently taken over another small bank that went under primarily because of its bad real estate loans, and those loans had yet to be resolved.

There were good and bad situations among the loans that Midwestern Mortgage proposed swapping. There was a current loan on a completed apartment project in Houston, Texas, which would pay 8% on the $3.5 million in the deal when 93% occupied. The apartments were renting up nicely, being 87% rented and providing a 6.8% yield.

A second loan was for $2 million on a proposed industrial park outside of Cleveland, Ohio. The developer was one of the nation's largest and, according to all reports, still financially sound. However, attached to this loan was a future commitment for an additional $5 million to complete the project.

Another was a $1.8 million loan on a condominium project in southern Florida where the developer was being kept alive by the original lender, although there was virtually no sales activity. Colt had heard that even in June, 1975, after a twelve-month financially imposed ''moratorium'' on new construction, southern Florida was blessed with nearly 44,000 unsold condominiums—about 7 or 8 years' supply at the absorption rate of the early 1970s.

There was also a $1.7 million land development loan made to a newly bankrupt recreational homebuilder. The land was on one of the offshore Georgia islands and all development activity had been suspended. Another $4 million in funding would be needed to get work started again. In reviewing the other real estate loans the trust proposed trading off to its lenders, Colt saw that they were very similar to the first four. As lead lender in Midwestern Mortgage's line, which involved thirty-eight banks in all, Colt knew he had some clout in the matter. Although Third National did not have an in-house REIT, many of the banks it dealt with daily did. Colt felt that Third National would have more flexibility than the other banks and could take a hard line in the negotiations which would assuredly follow. Right now and for the next few months, Third National could do more for them than vice versa.

Colt wondered just what Midwestern's 1975 balance sheet and income statement would look like. He was worried that the 1975 results, including reserves for losses, would effectively wipe out the remaining equity of the trust, thereby placing the trust in violation of the covenants attached to its subordinate debt and revolving credit agreements. If this happened, Colt would have to come up with a creative solution to the trust's and his bank's problems.

Colt was worried that bankruptcy might be unavoidable. Nonetheless, he was concerned that he and the bank were being forced to take an active role in managing Midwestern. Just what were the legal implications of the role, he did not know. He wondered if the bank and its directors could be accused of managing the trust for the bank's and not the shareholders' benefit. He wondered whether actions taken by the trust could be attacked as "voidable preferences." He also speculated on the personal options he had. His career with the bank was at stake.

Thinking more and more about the alternatives he had, Colt fell deeper and deeper into a midafternoon depression. "I shouldn't have had that second drink. Maybe we should have had lunch upstairs. At least they don't serve drinks there."

EXHIBIT 1 THIRD NATIONAL BANK OF NEW YORK
Selected Financial Information (000,000's)

	1974 $	*1973* $
Loans	9,600	9,942
Securities	1,282	1,193
Total assets	16,003	13,440
Deposits	12,510	10,190
Shareholders' equity	559	538

EXHIBIT 2
Help from Big Banks for Six Troubled Trusts ($ millions)

	Chase Manhattan Mortgage & Realty Trust 41 Banks	*Continental Mortgage Investors 83 Banks*	*First Mortgage Investors 100 Banks*	*Citizens & Southern Realty Investors 33 Banks*	*Builders Investment Group 49 Banks*	*Great American Mortgage Investors 71 Banks*	*Total*
Chase Manhattan	150.0	18.9	14.5	12.1	16.8	15.0	227.3
Bankers Trust	33.9	52.7	27.5	32.6	21.0	10.0	177.7
First National of Chicago	38.3	22.1	33.5	6.0	39.6	27.5	167.0
First National City	42.7		28.5	24.1	28.0	23.2	146.5
Continental Illinois Natl.	43.9	28.3	33.5	18.1		15.0	138.8
Chemical	27.7	42.7	34.8	12.1	7.0	10.0	134.3
Manufactures Hanover	28.9	39.9	6.0	18.1	21.0		113.9
Bank of America	27.7	10.5	8.0	18.1	21.0	25.0	110.3
Morgan Guaranty	27.7	16.8	5.0	24.1	8.4	10.0	92.0
Total, nine banks	420.8	231.9	191.3	165.3	162.8	135.7	1,307.8
Other banks	279.2	299.9	208.7	164.3	147.8	137.3	1,237.2
Total	700.0	531.8	400.0	329.6	310.6	273.0	2,545.0

Nine major banks agreed to provide 51% of the $2.5 billion in credits negotiated under the largest REIT revolving-loan agreements. (The total of banks participating appears at the top of each column.) That $150-million commitment from the Chase Manhattan Bank to the trust that bears its name was close to the maximum Chase could legally lend to any one borrower. Other bankers insisted that Chase back its trust to the hilt. Under the terms of Citizens & Southern Realty Investors' credit agreement, the C.&S. National Bank agreed to lend $16 million, and to purchase $30 million worth of assets if the trust became strapped for cash before the revolver matured.

Source: Wyndham Robertson, "How the Banks Got Trapped in the REIT Disaster," *Fortune,* March 1975, p. 113.

EXHIBIT 3 Midwestern Mortgage Investors

Short-Term Interest Rates

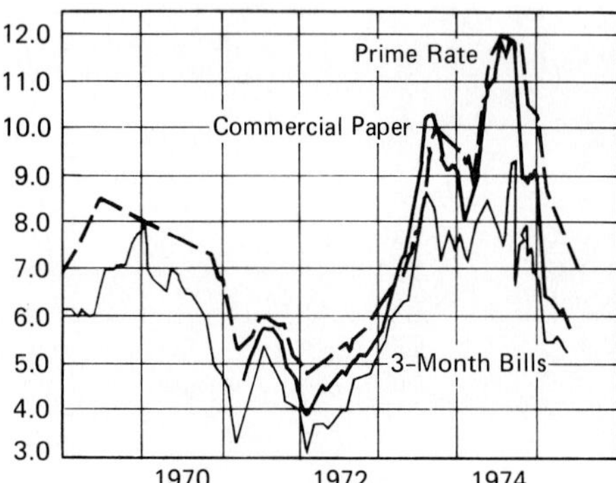

Source: See *Federal Reserve Bulletin.*

Changes in the Prime Rate Since 1969*

Start of 1969	6.75		
01/07/69	7.00	08/28/73	9.75
03/17/69	7.50	09/18/73	10.00
06/09/69	8.50	10/24/73	9.75
03/25/70	8.00	01/29/74	9.50
09/21/70	7.50	02/11/74	9.25
11/12/70	7.25	02/19/74	9.00
11/23/70	7.00	02/25/74	8.75
12/22/70	6.75	03/22/74	9.00
01/06/71	6.50	03/29/74	9.25
01/15/71	6.25	04/03/74	9.50
01/18/71	6.00	04/05/74	9.75
02/16/71	5.75	04/11/74	10.00
03/11/71	5.25	04/19/74	10.25
05/11/71	5.50	04/25/74	10.50
07/06/71	6.00	05/02/74	10.75
10/20/71	5.75	05/06/74	11.00
11/04/71	5.50	05/10/74	11.25
12/31/71	5.25	05/17/74	11.50
01/24/72	5.00	06/26/74	11.75
01/31/72	4.75	07/05/74	12.00
04/05/72	5.00	07/10/74	11.75
06/26/72	5.25	21/10/74	11.50
08/03/72	5.50	28/10/74	11.25
08/07/72	5.25	04/11/74	11.00
08/29/72	5.50	14/11/74	10.75
10/04/72	5.75	25/11/74	10.50
12/27/72	6.00	01/09/75	10.25
01/27/73	6.25	01/15/75	10.00
03/26/73	6.50	01/20/75	9.75
04/18/73	6.75	01/28/75	9.50
05/07/73	7.00	02/03/75	9.25
05/25/73	7.25	02/10/75	9.00
06/08/73	7.50	02/18/75	8.75
06/25/73	7.75	02/24/75	8.50
07/03/73	8.00	03/05/75	8.25
07/09/73	8.25	03/10/75	8.00
07/18/73	8.50	03/18/75	7.75
07/30/73	8.75	03/24/75	7.50
08/06/73	9.00	05/20/75	7.25
08/13/73	9.25	06/09/75	7.00
08/22/73	9.50		

*Predominant rate as noted in the *Federal Reserve Bulletin.*

Long-Term Interest Rates

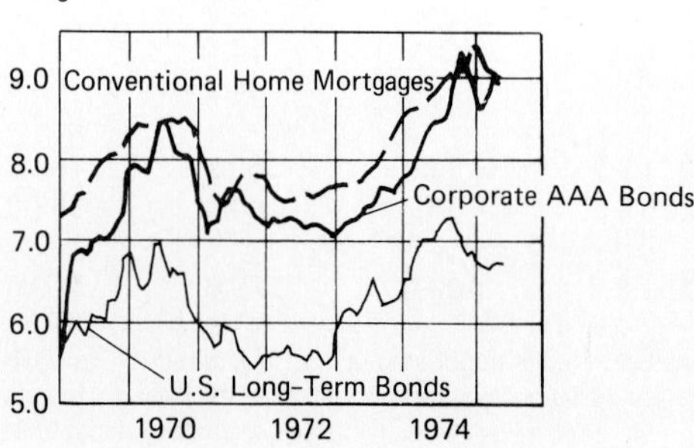

Source: See *Federal Reserve Bulletins.* (April)

New Privately Owned Housing Starts

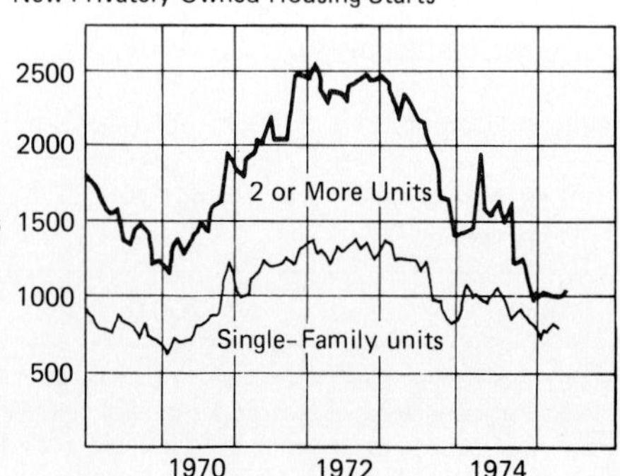

*Seasonally-adjusted annual rate.
Source: U.S. Department of Commerce. Bureau of the Census.

EXHIBIT 4
REIT Industry Balance Sheet ($ millions)

	4th Qtr. 1974	*3rd Qtr. 1974*		*4th Qtr. 1974*	*3rd Qtr. 1974*
First mortgages			Commercial paper	$ 709.8	$ 895.0
Land loans	$ 896.4	$ 983.1	Bank term loans & revolving credits in use	5,784,7	4,122.6
Development	2,343.8	2,355.4			
Construction	7,754.3	7,828.4			
Completed properties			Bank lines in use	5,290.2	6,764.0
0–10 years	1,511.9	1,521.9	Senior non-convertible debt	376.4	338.1
10+ years	1,949.1	1,889.4	Sub. non-convertible debt	1,013.5	1,043.9
Junior mortgages:					
			Convertible debt	677.0	661.2
Land, dev., & construction	387.2	302.0	Mortgages on property owned	1,649.2	1,582.5
Completed properties	1,054.0	1,035.3			
Loan loss reserves	(612.4)	(431.7)	Other Liabilities	472.9	475.8
Land leasebacks	541.7	533.3		$15,973.7	$15,883.2
Property owned	3,719.9	3,546.6	Shareholders' equity	5,206.6	5,535.8
Cash & other assets	1,634.4	1,855.3		$21,180.3	$21,419.0
	$21,180.3	$21,419.0			

The NAREIT quarterly statistics are as of each trust's reporting period closest to the quarter end date. Thus the fourth quarter 1974 statistics in this table contain data from REITs for November, December and January depending upon each trust's reporting period. The quarterly statistics include data from all REITs of which NAREIT has any record excluding those trusts which are not filing as REITs for tax purposes. The fourth quarter data is for 208 trusts, while the third quarter data is for 211 trusts. All data are subject to minor revisions as new information becomes available. "Property owned" includes REIT participations in joint ventures and partnerships at the amounts reported on REIT balance sheets. Property acquired by foreclosure is also included in this category.

Source: REIT Statistics compiled by Research Department of National Association of Real Estate Investment Trusts, Washington, D.C. (1974:IV) July 1975.

EXHIBIT 5

MIDWESTERN MORTGAGE INVESTORS
Balance Sheet and Income Statement
(000's)

	September 30	
	1974	*1973*
Assets		
Cash (includes time deposits of $7,984,006 in 1974 and $720,000 in 1973)	$ 15,732	$ 8,350
Commercial paper—at cost which approximates market	4,967	
Mortgage loans		
Construction:		
Condominiums	74,694	18,840
Commercial	65,879	47,055
Apartments	50,773	42,575
Total	191,346	108,470
Land	62,432	39,626
Standing	19,689	1,864
Long-term	14,919	10,907
Other	12,762	14,314
Total	301,148	175,181
Less allowance for possible loan loses	953	613
Total	300,195	174,568
Investments in real estate:		
Land purchase leasebacks—at cost	3,904	3,464
Partnerships and joint ventures—at equity	1,523	1,094
Accrued interest receivable	5,341	1,975
Other—principally unammortized debt expenses in '74	867	120
Total	$332,530	$189,571
Liabilities and Shareholders' Equity		
Liabilities:		
Short-term debt:		
Commercial paper	$143,340	$112,098
Notes payable—banks	69,904	24,439
Total	213,246	136,537
Notes payable—revolving credit agreement	32,000	
Dividends payable	2,508	1,886
Accrued interest payable	2,190	127
Other liabilities	935	497
6-3/4% subordinated debentures due 1978 (less unamortized original issue discount of $2,208,100)	21,791	
Total	272,670	139,047
Shareholders' equity:		
Shares of beneficial interest, $1 par value, authorized, 10,000,000 shares; issued and outstanding 3,055,000 shares in 1974 and 2,719,000 shares in 1973	3,055	2,719
Additional paid-in capital:		
Shares of beneficial interest	54,168	47,791
Series A warrants	2,564	
Undistributed net income	73	14
Total	59,860	50,524
Total	$332,530	$189,571

(continued)

EXHIBIT 5 (Cont.)

	September 30	
	1974	*1973*
Income		
Mortgage loan interest	$27,365	$12,374
Rental income	808	587
Loan fees	847	714
Interest on commercial paper	435	8
Other	38	28
Total	$ 29,492	$ 13,711
Expenses		
Interest:		
Notes payable and commercial paper	$ 13,956	$ 4,342
Subordinated debentures	1,620	
Investment advisory fees	2,921	1,647
Addition to allowance for loan losses	603	451
Expenses of real estate operation	446	474
Amortization of original issue discount on subordinated debentures	354	
Trustees' fees	69	57
Other expenses	333	152
Total	$ 20,302	$ 7,123
Net income	$ 9,190	$ 6,588
Primary EPS	$ 3.10	$ 2.60
Fully diluted	$ 2.84	$ 2.32

APPENDIX 1
REQUIREMENTS FOR REIT STATUS

One unique feature of REITs is their form of management. The legal theory of the REIT is that the members of the trust transfer cash and other valuable assets to the trustees, who manage and control the trust's properties in the interest of the beneficiaries. In practice, the management responsibilities are often divided between the trustees and a professional management advisory company which is hired for a fee. This is more the case for REITs which specialize in mortgage investments than those which emphasize equity investments. Typically, the advisor handles the daily operations, reviews the proposed investments and advises the trustees on economic and financial matters. At all times, the trustees retain the basic responsibility for every investment decision. The trustees and the advisory company agree on the operational mechanics for providing a flow of recommended investments to the trustees.

The definition of what constitutes a qualified REIT is very clearly laid out in Section 856-858 of the Internal Revenue Code as amended in September, 1960. The qualifications can be broken down into three categories: 1) income qualifications; 2) asset or investment qualifications; and 3) conduct qualifications.

The *income qualifications* restrict the acceptable sources of income:

1.1 At least 75% of gross income must be derived from property rents, interest on obligations secured by a mortgage on real property, property tax refunds and abatements, gain from the sale or other disposition of real property interests, and gain from the sale of shares in other qualified REITs.

1.2 An additional 15% must come from these sources plus dividends and interest or gain from the sale or other disposition of stock or securities.

1.3 Less than 30% of the gross income must be in the form of short-term capital gains which are defined here as including gain on the sale or other disposition of stock held for less than six months and real property held for less than four years.

The effect of these restrictions is that 10% of the gross income can come from sources which are tainted. Many REITs use this provision to cover income which comes from commitment fees, discounts paid out of loan proceeds and technically usurious interest.

The *asset or investment qualifications* restrict the form and amount of acceptable investments:

2.1 At least 75% of an REIT's assets must be invested in real estate interests, government securities, cash or cash items;

2.2 Out of the remaining 25% not more than 5% of the trust assets can be invested in the securities of any one issuer;

2.3 A REIT may not hold more than 10% of the outstanding voting stock or any one issuer.

A third set of restrictions applies to the *conduct of an REIT:*

3.1 A REIT must pay out at least 90% of its income in the year earned;

3.2 A REIT must issue certificates of beneficial interest and have at least one hundred beneficiaries for 335 days of the taxable year;

3.3 A REIT should remain "passive", which means that it should not acquire property as a broker/dealer.

It should be noted that in December, 1974, however, Congress—on the tail of an act "to amend the Tariff schedules of the United States to permit the importation of upholstery regulators, upholsterer's regulating needles, and upholsterer's pins free of duty"—amended Section 856 with respect to foreclosures. The amendment allowed a REIT to foreclose a property after default to protect its interests, and to hold and operate the property for up to two years, subject to extensions with IRS permission, without jeopardizing its REIT status. (Income from foreclosed property is taxed at corporate rates.)

APPENDIX 2
BANK CREDIT ASSET EXCHANGE PROPOSAL, SEPTEMBER 1975

Midwestern Mortgage Investors (MMI) proposes a Bank Credit Asset Exchange (swap) whereby MMI may make to holders of its senior notes asset payments with respect to any portion of any notes if the holders thereof agree to accept the same. The objectives of the program are to A) improve earnings and maximize cash flow; B) dispose of those assets which for a variety of reasons will not contribute to MMI's ongoing viability; C) provide

MMI's banks and other senior lenders with a way to eliminate or reduce their commitments to MMI, thereby reducing its leverage and the size of the lending group.

Great care was used in selecting the assets to be offered for swap. Predominant among the factors considered were those characteristics which would make an asset unattractive from MMI's point of view, but not necessarily unattractive from a lender's point of view, e.g. the amount of additional funds required for completion and the permanent financing available. Generally the quality of loans offered for swap is, from MMI's point of view, lower than those to be retained. However, it must be emphasized that the fact that an asset is being offered for swap should not be interpreted as either a positive or negative evaluation of that asset. MMI makes no representations or warranties with respect to the merits of any asset offered for swap. MMI will, however, make available for inspection, by any interested lender, its books and records pertaining to any asset on the exchange list.

PROCEDURE FOR BIDDING

A) Any lender desiring to submit a bid or bids with respect to any asset in the catalog must submit such bids to the trust's accountant, Elder, Hartig & Danley (EHD), Chicago, Illinois. All bids must be received on or before September 30, 1975, in order to be considered.

B) Each lender may bid on any assets in the catalog. Each lender is limited, however, to three bids in order of priority per asset. Each bid must be in a separate sealed envelope with the loan number and name of the asset being bid on typed on the outside of the envelope. A clear letter of instructions as to the order and priority of consideration of a lender's bids must accompany the bids. In order that Midwestern can insure that bids sent have been received by EHD, we request that a copy of the transmittal letter sent to EHD by a lender also be sent to Midwestern. The letter of instructions should clearly indicate the sequence and conditions under which the bids are to be considered.

EXAMPLE Assume a lender is willing to bid on three assets: Asset X, Asset Y and Asset Z. Assume also that it is most desirous of obtaining Asset X, least desirous of Asset Z, and has submitted three bids on Asset X and one each on Asset Y and Z. Its letter of instruction should clearly indicate that the primary bid on Asset X should be considered first. If no other lender bid on Asset X, or if the lender's primary bid was the highest of those submitted on X, then the lender may indicate that its remaining bids on Assets Y and Z should not be considered, unless it desires to purchase additional assets, in which case its instruction letter should so state. If a second lender bids on Asset X and overbids the first lender, the letter of instruction should indicate that the secondary bid should be considered. If the secondary bid of the first lender is unsuccessful, the instruction would indicate that the third (and last allowable) for Asset X should be considered. If this is successful, then the sequence will stop unless, again, the lender desires to bid on Y and Z. If the lender is unsuccessful in its three bids on Asset X then the letter of instructions would indicate that its bid on Asset Y be considered, and if unsuccessful, its bid on Asset Z. (Although not indicated in this example, a lender could, of course, have had three bids on Assets Y and Z as well as Asset X.) The sequence of consideration must be in the order in which a lender desires to obtain the assets in question. No bids may be conditioned upon losing a later bid.

C) In the event of a tie (that is, two or more high bids on an asset are exactly the same as to amount of debt reduction and amount of cash to be paid) the next higher priority bid on that asset by all lenders bidding on that asset will be considered. In the event that the tie is on the third bid on that asset, or no other lender matches the tie in its third or subsequent bid if the tie is on an earlier priority bid, the parties involved will be notified immediately to submit an additional bid on that asset. The tie breaking bids should be made by telegram to within 24 hours of receiving notification of the tie from EHD. This is to enable the bidding to proceed in a timely manner.

D) MMI has placed a minimum price as of September 30, 1975 on each asset in the catalog. This consists of a minimum amount of debt reduction and, in certain cases, a minimum amount of cash. MMI must accept the highest bid which meets or exceeds the minimum price. Should a bid meet the total minimum, but not meet either MMI's minimum debt reduction or minimum cash requirement for the asset (as for example, if MMI's total minimum price for an asset is $5,000,000 broken down into the following components: $3,500,000 minimum debt reduction and $1,500,000 minimum cash, and the bid is for $5,000,000 total but offers less cash and more debt reduction or more cash and less debt reduction), MMI is not obligated to accept that bid. Alternatively, if two bids are the same as to total price and the minimums are met or exceeded with respect to debt reduction and cash payments, the bid with the most cash will be accepted. The minimum total price placed on each asset at least equals and in some cases may exceed the book value of that asset. Book value for these purposes means principal plus accrued and booked interest. MMI, in accordance with the terms of the amendments to its credit agreements, *is not allowed* to accept any bid which is less than the book value for that asset. However, to the extent that a bid may be below MMI's minimum price but equal to or in excess of the book value of the asset being bid on, and such bid is the only, or the highest bid for that asset, MMI may, but is not obligated to accept such bid. As indicated above, the minimum price has been stated as of September 30, 1975. However, certain of the loans in the catalog are still accruing interest and will continue to do so during the term of the swap program, which interest is being recorded on the books of MMI. In addition, MMI may make additional fundings pursuant to the terms of certain loans or in order to preserve the value of certain assets, between September 30, and the time such assets might be swapped pursuant to the program. To the extent that interest is still being accrued and fundings made on certain assets, or both during this time period, the amounts will automatically be added to the reduction of debt portion of MMI's minimum price for those assets. All bids thus will be considered to be made with the understanding that the offer includes such additional amounts, if any, to the reduction of debt portion of the minimum price for the asset being bid on and will be accepted on that basis.

E) Syndicated bids will be acceptable. The bid must indicate each member of the syndicate, and its respective share (debt reduction, etc.).

F) Bids will be opened by EHD on or about October 17, 1975 in the presence of representatives of MMI and representatives of the agent bank under MMI's bank credit agreements. Bidding will be deemed completed when all letters of instructions have been fulfilled and all ties, if any have been broken. Successful bids must be accepted by the trustees of MMI, and for certain purposes, explained below, the day on which that occurs shall be the "acceptance date." Acceptance of each successful bid is subject to satisfactory documentation and otherwise obtaining necessary borrower consents (if required) and is, of course, after review of the Asset Swap Information Certificate ultimately subject to the consent of MMI's lenders. If so approved, implementation of the swap must be completed by November 30, 1975. The transfer of any asset will be effected on a non-recourse basis (except for warranties as to title). Upon the transfer of any asset or assets pursuant to the swap the lender receiving such asset or assets will make an appropriate notation on MMI's note that it holds indicating the amount of indebtedness being satisfied by the swap. After the acceptance date, MMI shall hold for the benefit of the successful bidder until such time as the transfer is effectuated, or until November 30, 1975, and the requisite consent is not in hand, any cash payments or other benefits paid on the asset by the borrower. Unpaid interest on that portion of Midwestern's debt to the lender being reduced by a swap, calculated to the date the swap is effected, will be paid on February 1, 1976, *except* that contingent interest on any such debt (as provided for in Credit Agreements with its banks) will be forgiven.

GENERAL DEVELOPMENT CORPORATION

In September, 1975, Louis E. Fischer was attempting to evaluate the future directions to be taken by General Development Corporation (GDV), a Miami-based community developer. He had been elected President of GDV in April 1974. Prior to that he had been Vice-Chairman of the Larwin Group, INV., and prior to joining Larwin in 1972, he had been President of ITT Levitt and Sons. GDV was developing seven planned communities in Florida, encompassing almost 236,000 acres. (*Exhibit 1*.)

The company's operations included homesite and shelter development and sales, mortgage financing, utilities operations and resort and community operations such as major shopping centers and recreational facilities (for example, golf clubs). GDV employed approximately 3,800 people and marketed its products nationally and internationally. GDV was traded on the New York Stock Exchange and was 59% owned by City Investing Company. In March 1975, in his letter to shareholders in the company's annual report for 1974, Mr. Fischer said:

> Net income increased 5% to $11.0 million from 1973's record level of $10.5 million. Higher profit was primarily attributable to increased shelter profitability, other land sales and reduced operating expenses. . . . Total revenues were $152.0 million, a 12% decline from $172.7 million in 1973, reflecting lower unit homesite sales and reduced shelter closings.

The significance of these results was unclear, in part because of the state of the US economy in general and the real estate industry in particular, and in part because shelter sales were profitable for the first time in many years while homesite (lot) sales had declined for the second year running, as *Exhibit 2* shows.

The sustained decline in lot sales was a problem because it threatened one of GDV's real strengths, its interest income from its contracts receivable. Because GDV was an installment land sales company, a drop in current lot sales would affect the company's income for the next ten years. Fischer had to decide whether this decline was a temporary phenomenon or the forerunner of a permanent change in the Florida land sales business. His conclusion would be important because the corporation was developing its plans for 1975 and beyond. The plans would be the basis of GDV's investment decisions for the next ten years. However, aside from the long-run problem, Fischer had to find an immediate way to stop the company's sales decline.

In 1975, most of GDV's senior management team were new to the firm but experienced in other companies, as *Exhibit 3* shows. Because of this Fischer felt that conditions in the company were amenable to a change of strategy.

Mr. Fischer had strong views about the potential of GDV, but he saw that the road ahead was not an easy one. "Unlike Levitt, which built its communities on the edge of major cities like New York and Washington," he recalled, "the Florida land developers

This case was prepared as a basis for class discussion rather than to illustrate either effective or ineffective handling of an administrative situation.

have sold developed or 'to be developed' lots in relatively remote areas. But whatever their motives, our homesite buyers seem likely to be our best potential customers for home sales.''

''Look at the projected family growth in the U.S. over the next fifteen years in *Exhibit 4,* and consider the potential for growth in our Florida communities, *Exhibit 5.* The key to harvesting the potential for population growth is probably employment.

''Employable people are moving to Florida on a state-wide basis, as *Exhibit 6* shows. Sixteen percent of our homesite buyers have indicated that they would move to Florida today if jobs were available.[1] Jobs will attract people and employable people will attract industry.

''GDV has products that people want. Twenty-two percent of our buyers said they might retire to Florida—they too would create additional job opportunities. There's no question that a viable market exists for Florida homesites and homes. Moreover, if we can increase home sales a number of new possibilities could open up for GDV. In a few years we could be significant mortgage bankers and ultimately GDV could become a significant utility.''

''City Investing's interests and those of GDV's minority shareholders have to be considered in any change of corporate direction, but GDV is a stable and successful company. Look at our balance sheet and income statements for 1972 and 1974, *Exhibit 7.* We have the resources to wait out the present recession and to prepare for profitable growth during the recovery which is coming.''

NOTE ON NEW AICPA RULES

Traditionally, installment land sellers like GDV have used two sets of books, one for financial reporting and one for tax purposes. Financial reporting was typically based on a simple accrual system, while reporting for tax purposes was based on an installment system. On July 1, 1973, however, the American Institute of Certified Public Accountants (AICPA) published a new set of rules on ''Accounting for Profit Recognition on Sales of Real Estate'' (and a separate guide, ''Accounting for Retail Land Sales''). One industry observer noted, ''Tax people don't see it the same way as the accountants. In essence, the accountants are being conservative and saying, 'If there's any doubt about collectability of profits, don't book them,' while the IRS is being liberal and saying 'If there's any possibility of collecting taxes on profits, we want them.' ''

Continued involvement in a piece of land sold may seriously affect a developer's financial statement. The following excerpt from *House & Home*, January, 1974, which documents the sale of land by a private developer for cash, demonstrates this.[2]

Private Development Company buys a parcel of land for $85,000, completes certain engineering work at a cost of $15,000 and then sells the property to Profit Savings and Loan Association for $200,000 cash.

[1]Data from a 1973 telephone survey of 2,000 homesite buyers, half pre-1970 and half post-1970. The survey had a 55% response rate.

[2]N. Gerardi, ''Those New Accounting Rules,'' *House & Home*, January 1974, p. 127.

Economic Profit

Sales price		$200,000
Cost of sales		
Land	$85,000	
Engineering	15,000	100,000
Gross profit		100,000
Tax liability on profit		50,000
Net economic profit contribution		$ 50,000

If the transaction did not contain any continuing involvement by the seller, the economic profit shown above would equal the seller's financial profit. But in this case the seller has also agreed to complete the site development work at a price of $300,000. The cost to the developer based upon firm contracts will be $270,000.

This contract, added to the land sale, indicates that the seller remains involved with the property after the sale and under the new rules in the guide an allocation of total income based upon costs incurred to total estimated costs is required. The financial income is calculated as follows:

Financial Income

1. Total income

	Sale of Land	*Site Development*	*Total*
Income	$200,000	$300,000	$500,000
Costs	100,000	270,000	370,000
Gross profit	$100,000	$ 30,000	$130,000

2. Income reportable upon the disposition of the land

$$\frac{\text{(Cost of land) } \$100{,}000}{\text{(Cost of land) } \$100{,}000 + \text{(Cost of site development) } \$270{,}000} \times$$

(Total gross profit) $130,000

= Reportable gross profit of $35,126

The $35,126 would have a *financial* statement tax of $17,563, resulting in a net profit constribution of $17,563.

Thus, although the developer had an economic increase in net worth of $50,000 after paying income taxes of $50,000, his financial statements will only reflect $17,563 because he had involvement with the property after sale.

The new accounting guide will have a drastic effect on Private Development Company's financial statements, which could result in limiting its financing capability. Therefore, the privately held company must consider these rules when structuring transactions.

For public companies the effect of the new rules was significant—for example, GDV's earnings per share (E.P.S.) for 1970 and 1971 under the old system was $1.70 and $2.03. Under the new rules these results had to be restated as $0.66 and $0.90 respectively.

The "Summary of Significant Accounting Policies" (*Exhibit 7*) throws additional light on the effect of the rules on GDV. However, it is apparent that, for GDV, the effect is more complicated than for the private company in the excerpt table from *House & Home*. GDV homesite sales are installment sales, not cash sales, and GDV has a liability to complete its development for estimable but still uncertain costs.

Mr. Fischer said that over the next ten years his objectives were to restore GDV's historical growth rate, and preferably exceed it, while at least maintaining the company's earnings rate. Mr. Fischer wanted a strategy that would excite management to help him attract and retain good people in top management positions at GDV. Moreover, he wanted a strategy based on a thorough and accurate assessment of the risks and opportunities open to GDV, and on the corporation's ability to exploit them.

GDV's most apparent skills were land development, installment land sales, and homebuilding. However, land sales were the primary source of the company's earnings and reputation. In part, this was a legacy of the past, as GDV had pioneered installment lot sales in Florida, but it was also a reflection of success in the marketplace. On a number of occasions in the past, GDV's management had unsuccessfully attempted to increase the company's involvement in homebuilding and to break its dependence on sustained lot sales.

Mr. Fischer believed that this was because management had failed to identify the unique characteristics of the land and homebuilding businesses and, importantly, because it had not understood how the two businesses could be interrelated through GDV. Installment land sales and homebuilding were subject to different environmental pressures and had different economics. Because of this they had different requirements for success. Lot sales were declining and a house sale had a greater current effect on earnings than an equal dollar volume of lot sales. Was this the time to step up the corporate effort in home sales? What other profitable opportunities could GDV exploit? What choices were open to it? What could the company do to increase its current sales?

OPERATIONS

This section of the case is concerned with GDV's operations. It is substantially extracted from the company's 1974 Report on Form 10K to the Securities and Exchange Commission.

GDV has been a community developer since its initial formation in 1956. It acquires large tracts of unimproved land for development. *Exhibit 8* describes the company's land inventory in its major Florida communities as of December 31, 1974.

Exhibit 9 sets forth, as of December 31, 1974, information as to sales prices and payments received, estimated cost of improvements and expenditures made by GDV with respect to its major development communities.

In early 1975, management estimated that GDV's current inventory of Florida land was sufficient to continue its sales of homesites at 1974 levels for approximately five years. Since a period of two to three years is normally required from the date of acquisition of an unplatted tract until individual homesites can be offered for sale, management then believed it would be necessary to make at least one major land acquisition during the next several years to allow homesite sales to continue at 1973–1974 levels.

With the exception of other land sales in 1974, and about $2 million from Shelter, virtually all GDV's aggregate net income during the period referred to above was attributable to homesite sales and interest income on outstanding homesite contracts receivable.

Homesite Sales

GDV's sales of homesite lots are generally made on an installment basis with a small downpayment ranging from 5% to 25% of the purchase price (currently averaging approximately 9%), with the balance payment in monthly installments over approximately ten years. Interest is payable by the purchaser on the unpaid balance at rates currently ranging from 8% to 9% per annum, depending on the amount of the downpayment. The average rate on installment contracts outstanding at December 31, 1974, was 7.1% per annum. GDV does not investigate the credit of its homesite customers, and its homesite sales contracts do not impose personal liability. However, extensive efforts are made to encourage customers to keep all installment payments current. The company normally cancels sales contracts on which no payment has been received for approximately six months. In case of cancellation, all contracts provided for retention of any prior payments by GDV as liquidated damages. The homesite becomes available for resale. At December 31, 1974, approximately 92% of the contracts receivable balance was current or prepaid. A contract is classified as ''current'' if all payments due at the end of the preceding month (as required by the contract or pursuant to arrangements whereby GDV has extended the terms of the contract) had been received. *Exhibit 10* shows estimated collections of principal, 1975 to 1979.

In its homesite installment contracts, GDV undertakes to provide the basic improvements by the end of the year of the customer's scheduled final installment payment. The improvements which GDV undertakes for standard homesites consist of a paved street in front of the homesite, provision for surface drainage, and, when required for such drainage, clearing, filling and grading of the land. In certain areas, particularly more recently platted subdivisions, the company also undertakes to install central water and sewer lines to serve each homesite lot. In addition, where the homesite is located on a waterway or in other special locations, the completion of additional improvements may be required. If a customer prepays his contract before the necessary improvements have been completed, most contracts grant him the option to transfer his payments to the purchase of a homesite in a developed area and, where the contracts do not so provide, GDV afforded customers this option.

GDV is often required to develop a substantial number of homesite areas before the related homesite installment contracts matured. GDV attempts to effect development of all homesites in an area at the time of the first maturing installment contract within the area, but occasionally homesites have not been developed in the year in which the company had a contractual obligation so to do. GDV believes such delays have been minimal in relation to its overall development obligations. GDV estimates its total obligation at December 31, 1974 to be approximately $148.5 million to complete the improvements in respect of all areas from which homesites have been and are presently being offered for sale.[3] The company records as ''Estimated homesite improvement cost'' in its balance sheet only that portion of the estimated cost of improvements relating to recorded homesite sales. At December 31, 1974 such ''estimated homesite improvement cost'' was approximately $76 million. The remaining $72 million relates to development of home-

[3]The difference between the figures for homesite improvements here and the estimates in *Exhibit 9* is due to the exclusion of improvement costs in ''other land areas'' from estimated homesite improvement cost.

sites in areas which are offered for sale. These estimates are based on engineering studies of the quantities of work to be performed and estimated costs at the time the work will be performed. For purposes of these estimates, GDV applied an assumed annual compound inflation rate of approximately 6%. (See *Appendix 1* for additional information on construction costs.)

GDV retains possession of the title to each homesite sold until the date scheduled for payment of the entire purchase price. At such time and when the entire purchase price is paid, a deed to the property together with a certificate of title insurance is furnished to the purchaser.[4] Prior to deeding of the homesite, GDV is obligated to pay all real estate taxes and assessments on the property, but in certain recent sales the purchasers are obligated to reimburse GDV for real estate taxes incurred from the contract date.

GDV's sales of homesites originate from company-owned sales offices in major northern markets, such as New York City, Chicago, Boston, Cleveland and Detroit; in Florida communities; and in major Florida tourist areas. Seven independent sales agencies located in the eastern United States and in certain overseas areas also contributed to sales. During the years ended December 31, 1973 and 1974, the proportions of sales originated by GDV sales offices (as compared with independent sales agencies) were 67% and 75%, respectively.

GDV's employee salesmen generally received commissions ranging from 4% to 10% on homesite sales, depending upon the location of the sales office where they are employed and other factors. Such salesmen generally receive 75% of customers' payments until their commissions are paid in full. In addition to these standard sales commissions GDV has a variety of override agreements with its sales management personnel. The company employs approximately 1,100 salesmen at any one time, most of whom are compensated solely by commissions. Statistics indicated that about 90% of GDV's sales force work part-time and receive less than $5,000 commission/year.

GDV's seven independent sales agencies are compensated by commissions on homesite sales ranging from 19% to 30% of the sales price. On such sales, the agencies are generally paid 100% of the downpayment received and 100% of the first three monthly payments. Thereafter the agencies receive 60% of the monthly payments until the commission is paid in full. Aggregate commissions on all homesite sales average approximately 16.6%.

Other Land Sales

In connection with community development, GDV also markets land for commercial and other uses. Such other uses included multi-family residential, industrial and special purpose properties such as sites for schools, churches, utilities and other community facilities. In 1974 the marketing of such special purpose properties became an increasingly significant portion of GDV's land sales. In January 1974, GDV sold a 736-acre tract of land in Martin County, Florida, for commercial and multi-family use at a price of

[4]Late in 1975, legislation which would have required a deed to be passed to the buyer at the outset, and the use of a mortgage to pay for the land rather than a "contract for deed," based on simple monthly payments, was introduced to the House in New York State. However, the bill was defeated. It would have added closing costs to the cost of the land sold in New York State, one of GDV's principal markets, and would have added substantially to the difficulty of recovery of the land by a seller in the event of buyer default.

$2,869,000 (net of prepaid interest of $445,000), for $844,000 cash and notes secured by purchase money mortgages aggregating $2,470,000. In 1974 GDV recorded the entire gross profit on the transaction of $2,302,000. GDV also closed the sale in 1974 of certain platted and unplatted land at a price of $764,000, and recorded a gross profit thereon of $279,000.

In recognition of the increasing importance of commercial properties to GDV's business, a new Commercial Properties Division was organized in August 1974, with responsibility for all phases of the marketing of properties for multi-family residential, industrial and special purposes. A total of up to 87,000 acres in all communities is allocated to this Division (including recorded tracts and raw land).

Shelter Sales

GDV currently offers a selection of single-family houses at basic prices ranging from approximately $24,000 to $75,000, condominium apartments ranging from approximately $25,000 to $37,500, and mobile home packages ranging from approximately $16,400 to $30,000. All prices include the land. GDV's homes normally range in size from 900 to 2,200 square feet. Mobile homes accounted for 11% of Shelter revenue in 1974, condominiums 4%, and single-family homes 85%.

Sales of shelter units and all related costs and expenses are recorded in full at the time of the closing of the completed unit. The cost of construction of shelter units sold is determined by specific identification. Payments received from buyers prior to closing are recorded as deposits.

Historically, the construction of sale of shelter units by GDV has been marginally unprofitable. Until late in 1973, GDV acted as the contractor in the construction of its shelter units and in most cases performed all the construction functions. Construction workers in various trades were employed directly by GDV. Commencing in early 1974, GDV's shelter operation was restructured so that GDV contracts with building contractors rather than utilizing its own construction forces. The company's management believes that this change in method of shelter construction will enable GDV to maintain better control of its shelter construction costs and enable it to conduct shelter activities on a profitable basis. However, due to the financial difficulties of certain contractors, GDV has incurred and provided for additional expenses in connection with construction operations and anticipates that it may be required to make payments to certain subcontractors and suppliers of such contractors.

GDV constructs single-family houses within its communities in designated housing areas pursuant to sales contracts which include both the house and land, and in "suburban" or homesite areas either on the customer's own homesite or a homesite conveyed to the customer in exchange for his original homesite. In either situation, the completion of construction and the closing of the home sale transactions generally take place from four to ten months after the execution of the home sales contract.

GDV currently finances the construction of shelter units by means of existing bank lines of credit. Sales contracts normally requiring a down-payment of approximately 15% of the entire purchase price with the balance payable at closing. The purchaser generally obtains financing of his shelter unit purchase from conventional mortgage lenders located in or near the GDV communities.[5]

GDV compensates its various sales sources on shelter sales at commission rates ranging from 3% to 8%, depending upon whether the sale is made by an employee salesman or by a sales agency. Aggregate commissions on shelter sales currently average approximately 6% of the selling price.

In July 1974, GDV formed a wholly owned subsidiary, GDV Financial Corporation, to provide mortgage banking services for its shelter customers and others.

OTHER OPERATIONS

Utility Operations

GDV provides water, sewerage and propane gas service to residents of GDV's community and subdivision developments. It owns and operates eight water systems, eight sewerage systems and four propane gas systems which during 1974 served, respectively, approximately 17,700, 13,000 and 7,900 customers. Gross operating revenues from such utility operations in 1974 were $2.9 million. To date, utility operations have required substantial capital investment, but have yielded only a nominal profit.[6]

Approximately 98% of the occupied houses in GDV's communities are served by the company's water systems and approximately 80% and 50% are served by its sewerage and gas systems, respectively. Water and sewerage services are available to substantially all purchasers of houses in GDV's designated housing areas. In general, such services are not currently available in suburban housing areas. It is expected, however, that these services will be extended as warranted by future shelter construction and homesite sales and to the extent that the concentration of homeowners desiring utility services makes such extension economically feasible. In certain recently marketed areas GDV is obligated to extend water and sewer lines when a purchaser with a deeded homesite has obtained a building permit and has given GDV advance notice of that fact.

GDV's utility operations are subject to rate and service regulation by various state and local governmental agencies, depending upon the location of the area served. Operations are generally conducted under non-exclusive 20- to 30-year franchises. The Securities and Exchange Commission has granted GDV an exemption from the provisions of the Public Utility Holding Company Act.

Community Operations

GDV has developed on a section of its Port St. Lucie community, Sandpiper Bay, a vacation resort consisting of a 280-room hotel, 2 18-hole championship golf courses and a par 3 course, 8 tennis courts, boating and other recreational facilities, and a 225-seat luxury restaurant. Extensive convention facilities are also available. GDV builds and

[5]In many years, over 50% of GDV's home sales have been for cash.
[6]Many communities insist that the developer pays for these installations.

owns the principal shopping centers in its communities and leased space to a wide variety of businesses. At the present time the company owns 6 shopping centers, of which 4 are neighborhood centers, and 2 are larger shopping centers located in Port Charlotte. It owns and operates a number of other community facilities including the 102-room Port Charlotte Ramada Inn, two Home Port Inns (which are family-style restaurants), community centers, small yacht clubs, marinas, beaches, fishing piers, golf courses and bowling centers. To date these community operations have required substantial capital investment and have operated at a loss.

COMPETITION

The community development business is highly competitive, particularly with respect to property located in Florida. GDV competed with many other companies currently operating in the United States and abroad, a number of which sell homesites on payment terms similar to those offered by GDV. Many national corporations with substantial financial resources have entered the community development business.

Among GDV's larger competitors are such well-known companies as GAC, Deltona and Amrep. *Exhibit 11* shows the 1974 sales of the eight largest land sales companies operating in Florida.

The shelter construction business in most areas of Florida in which GDV's communities are located is also highly competitive, particularly at Port Charlotte, where a number of firms are engaged in selling shelter units of similar quality and style to GDV's at prices lower than those charged by GDV. These price disadvantages offset to some degree by GDV's shelter sales programs including: 1) offers to existing homesite purchasers of inspection trips to its Florida communities in which the customer's expenses are defrayed by the company if a shelter unit is purchased from GDV; 2) the allowance of a credit by GDV to a homesite customer against the purchase of a shelter unit equivalent to the principal payments made under the original homesite contract plus part of any appreciation in the sales price of the original homesite, as determined by GDV's current sales price for an equivalent homesite; and 3) the crediting of bonus certificates held by existing homesite purchasers in amounts ranging from $500 to $700 which can be applied as a discount to the purchase of a shelter unit.

OPERATING PROBLEMS AND THE FUTURE

An informal record of a discussion between the casewriter (C) and a number of operating managers (OM) at GDV in September, 1975, produced the following comments:

C.: What are the major operating problems confronting GDV as a whole?

O.M.: The economy is slow, so are sales. But we have to make our investment decisions for the next ten years now. We will just have to live with inflation and deal with the risk of uncertain costs it adds to development. We will also have to cope with new legislation affecting our business. (See *Appendix 2*.) The new environmental laws, for example.

Look at GDV. Its principal strength is its cash flow, which is reliable, predictable and relatively large. It makes GDV an almost unique developer in 1975. Our financial strength has allowed us to raise debt capital even in these hard times. Right now we are strong and can negotiate from strength. It's nice to have cash when you need it.

C.: Will GDV have to change?

O.M.: This company will change, but we're concerned that we might misunderstand the source of financial stability or imagine that it will always be that way. We wonder whether our major strength is eroding.

Right now we want to decentralize, but we have to keep control of the key areas. A major mistake on one project could affect every other project and the whole company. Other land developers have made one mistake and gone belly-up.

C.: What kind of mistake?

O.M.: Geographic expansion is a common trap. It looks attractive but real estate is capital-intensive and becoming more so. People overlook start-up problems and forget the long years of negative cash flow. While we remain a Florida company we can switch men and equipment about quickly and top management can get to any site within two hours.

If we expand geographically we couldn't do this. We would need a different management structure and have to carry a higher overhead. We would need new people, but in this business the best people are entrepreneurs but no one knows how to keep entrepreneurs in a large organization.

Geographic expansion could be okay nonetheless, but we would like to know what negative cash flows we'd be exposed to, and for how long. Risk in this business can be measured in terms of the negative cash flows involved. Of course, we could cut our risks by letting small entrepreneurs test new markets and then move in where they are successful. We would have the same people problems but more market information. A small operator can go into a market and test it at low cost. When a company like GDV moves into a market, its costs are high. Because we are much bigger we can't afford to operate on a small scale.

C.: Is there any other operating problem?

O.M.: Control has to extend down to the salesforce. If a salesman misrepresents the land, you've got trouble. Management has to keep the pressure on but must judge its effect on the salesforce accurately. Pressure to produce sales has to be controlled so that the company is not exposed to risk. This is a hard-sell business and while we get few complaints they have to be dealt with quickly and adjusted. The FTC, the Interstate Land Sales Board, the Florida Land Sales Board and the licensing agents of every state we are active in, get in the middle of this business.[7]

C.: Can you sum up from an administrative point of view?

O.M.: Our major problem is not to be lulled by the status quo into thinking there's no downside risk for GDV. We have good management at the top. They've been tested.

[7]See *Appendix 2*.

Lower down—I haven't been here too long and I haven't seen them under heavy fire—they probably have to learn to take a wider view. Right now they are narrowly focused, sometimes frantically trying to maximize on one dimension but ignoring other key factors. Nonetheless, we have people with a wide range of skills in the development field. Besides our traditional markets, homesite and shelters, we could look out for turnaround situations in the real estate business; we could ''cherry-pick'' as equity participants or as managers, for example.

GDV's problem extended beyond making a choice of a new product emphasis and new markets however. Although strategic choices could be made quickly there was the problem of bringing the operating organization into line. Strategy and operations have to be consistent and matched through people available to the company.

Homesite Marketing

C.: What about the Homesite Marketing area?

O.M.: Right now GDV has an almost monolothic product line, 80′ × 125′ lots with no real prospect of new waterfront lots because of the environmental laws, and only a few country-club or green-belt lots to break the monotony. We have ''all Chevys and some Impalas.'' In a market like 1975, this doesn't seem enough. Our present marketing approach may be obsolete. It is mass-oriented and was pretty much consistent with our product line, but while it worked in the economic upswing throughout the sixties, it doesn't seem so good today. Results in the last two years suggest we have a problem. Maybe its price. Maybe its the lots we sell. Or perhaps its our marketing approach.

C.: What could be done?

O.M.: One approach would be to tailor-make new types of lots for particular markets—a rifle approach, not the shotgun approach we use now, with different products and prices for different markets. Our developments need a theme. ''Florida,'' by itself may not be enough to sustain sales without waterfront access. Other companies have found that theme communities linked to the environment work. However, it will be difficult to come up with cheaper lots while inflation is with us.

C.: What about the sales force?

O.M.: Whether homesites and shelter sales can proceed independently is a problem. Right now they have to. The sales force for each product needs to be different. Think of the money involved and the seriousness of the purchase decisions. With land sales, the sales are mostly off-site and you are selling not realty so much as a long-term financial plan. You need a formal costume (business suit) but not too sophisticated a sales force.

With home sales its different. It isn't a simple ten-year payout. It's usually for twenty-five or thirty years if it's a mortgage. If it's for cash, it's the buyer's life savings.

And of course, unless we make shelter sales and get a visible community underway, it may seem to many buyers that the company has no commitment to the project. This makes lot sales difficult to make. This is in spite of the fact that only 10% of our lot buyers see the communities before they buy.

C.: Do many people buy more than one lot?

O.M.: How many people bought multiple lots? I don't know what the figures are for GDV, but it probably isn't too many. You might be interested in another set of figures, however. At a land developer's conference in January, 1975, a speaker from one of the northern universities said that, on an industry level, about 25% buy two lots, 10% buy three and four or 5% buy four lots or more. These figures seem on the high side for our company, however. We have an interesting buyer. (See *Exhibit 13*.)

C.: We've covered the product, the sales force and the buyers, what about selling costs?

O.M.: The cost of selling is a problem. We have to establish the real cost of a sale and the cost effectiveness of our advertising. Too much emphasis has been placed on number of leads, not on their quality. I'd like to see our conversion rate go up (i.e., of leads to sales), but right now we are just beginning to collect information.

You see, not all of the problem is lead generation. The real cost effectiveness of our sales offices is unclear—the same applies to our salesmen and supervisors. Why, the commission scheme is biased toward number of sales. The credit of the buyers is not even checked. Salesmen may come out ahead of the company if a contract is cancelled. The commission on a $5,000 lot is 75% of the downpayment and 75% of the payments until the commission is fully paid.

C.: We talked about price, but has the company tried to change the terms of its contracts?

O.M.: We have tried to broaden our market by offering longer payout periods (i.e., greater than ten years) but it doesn't work. The interest amounts, which we have to disclose, look too big. We know interest payments are tax deductible but we don't want to be tax counsellors. Our major task is to sell. We need to identify our best market prospects and learn how to reach them. Some mailing lists seem attractive and we are exploring their use now.

Shelter

C.: The other major operating area at GDV is Shelter. What are its problems?

O.M.: The division has two major problems. One is to develop an effective marketing organization and lower marketing costs. The second is to lower the breakdown volume of the company's building operations. The two problems are not totally independent.

C.: What's most important?

O.M.: Our first priority is to get buyers into our homes soon. The GDV communities are viable and self-sustaining. Every year they become more attractive places to live. In fact, one of our strongest selling points is that the communities *really* exist. Another factor in our favor is that we know almost 270,000 people who like Florida, our homesite buyers.

C.: What are you doing to sell more houses?

O.M.: Only last week we hired a new man at the vice-president level to take charge of shelter marketing. However, we have already taken some steps to stimulate demand. First, we offer an incentive to encourage lot owners to build. GDV will reacquire the original homesite and allow a credit towards the purchase of a shelter package equivalent to the principal payments made under the original homesite contract plus a portion of any appreciation in the sale price of the original lot, based on the company's current price for an equivalent lot.

At present we allow about 70% of the appreciated value whether the home buyers want a house in a tract development or on their original lot. From our point of view, it's either a tract house or a scattered and isolated house. We are considering changing this to favor the tract houses because there are real cost savings possible in tract development. Even now we charge more for a scattered house.

C.: Is it working out well for the company?

O.M.: Right now, with our breakeven point high, we would probably be better if we increased the advantages of the tract house. Our marketing expenses are high, about 12% of sales. An efficient developer would spend 4%. A reasonable figure would be 6% of sales. We pay a 6% commission, 2% for general administrative costs and 4% is the appreciation "lock in."

C.: Is that the only thing you do?

O.M.: In another effort to stimulate demand we have begun questioning our lot buyers through our in-house quarterly magazine, "New Vistas." (*Exhibit 14.*) We are trying to find out who will move to Florida if a job is available. An earlier survey of 2,000 buyers suggested that 16% of lot buyers would move to a GDV community if jobs were available for them. On the other end of the chain, we are seeking industry for our communities. We have hired a senior consultant on a long-term basis. She is an expert in industrial promotions. With data on employers and employees we hope she can generate some primary demand pull in our housing market.

C.: You mentioned breakeven earlier. Can you explain how the present situation developed?

O.M.: Tract building is a bit of an art. To market homes effectively, you need an inventory. Therefore, you have to build ahead of demand to maintain efficient building operations and to be able to deliver a home to a buyer when it's first wanted or with as little delay as possible.

Inventory in the business means substantial costs and a substantial risk of obsolescence. If the model line doesn't move, you have a real problem. You can take it slow, hold prices down and with luck inflation will bail you out—but you can't bet on inflation, especially when it's combined with recession. Right now, GDV has a large inventory of unsold homes which are moving slowly.

We would like to introduce a new model line. The recession has flattened sales and we can't discount the homes. Recent buyers would be too upset, so we have to wait it out. It is the problem of moving a line of homes when you've built ahead and you have a new line in mind.

Home building in this company has been only marginally profitable at the best of times. The former management had gone to a highly integrated construction organization, even moving into the materials supply business. There are still two major warehouses crammed with building materials. We make our subcontractors use them and, eventually, we will use or sell them all, but we'll be stuck with two warehouses. I can rent them out but it's impossible to sell them in this market at a reasonable price. In the development business you want to limit the risks you take to those where you have skill.

C.: But what about breakeven?

O.M.: GDV became too capital-intensive, unnecessarily. It's easy to get long-term contracts for materials in Florida when you are as big as GDV and have its reputation. We don't have to take materials inventory risks and add that risk to the other risks we carry. We can free up a lot of capital and this will lift our profitability. We are trying to get our breakeven volume down to between 450 and 550 homes a year. But this won't be possible while we have a large raw materials inventory and those warehouses.

Real estate and home building is a cyclical business, especially the second home and recreational land business.[8] We have to pitch ourselves at a level where we can service the basic market and survive, and develop the ability to gear up temporarily for the boom periods . . . to "cream" the market.

We can't let this operation get too big, or too comprehensive. We have to be tract developers. Not customer builders. We want custom builders in our area. Even with a wide model line you can get monotony if you keep it all. Custom builders can add variety and do a more efficient job on the "unique" home than we could.

CORPORATE HISTORY

Mr. Fischer had to improve GDV's performance but the organization he had to lead is not the result of a single consistent strategy. Rather it is the product of a series of decisions and actions by different owners and managers attempting to build the company and its value. The history, which follows, suggests that these decisions have led to a set of beliefs and resources which may be conditioning the company's strategic posture and its strategic choices.

Early Days

General Development Corporation merged into Florida Canada Corporation on April 21, 1958. The surviving concern took the name General Development Corporation. The original General Development Corporation had been owned by Florida Canada, a company controlled by the flamboyant Canadian entrepreneur, Louis A. Chesler, and half by the Mackle Company, Inc.

The half interest owned by the Mackle Company, a 50-year-old Miami home-building firm that ranked as Florida's largest, was converted into 200,000 shares of common stock in GDV. Mr. Chesler became Chairman, Frank E. Mackle, Jr., President, and Elliot and Robert Mackle took board positions in the new company.

[8]The second home market in the U.S. was strong through the late 1960s and early 1970s. In 1967, for example, about 2.9% of households owned a second home. By 1970 the percentage had increased to 4.6%. Construction of new second homes since World War II has averaged: in the 1940s, 40,000; 1950s, 50,000; 1960s, 60,000; and in the 1970s about 70,000 until the recession hit the industry. In 1975 the U.S. population was estimated at 213 million and the number of households at 69.7 million.

What prompted the corporate reorganization was Chesler's and the Mackles' reactions to an almost frantic Florida land-buying spree in the late 1950s. Early in 1957, Chesler, through GDC, placed a single ad in a national magazine offering lots for "$10 down and $10 a month." The ad drew 17,000 responses. The demand for Florida land was stimulated to such an extent that small companies could not manage the paperwork it required, acquire and develop sufficient land to satisfy it, or obtain the capital needed to finance it. As part of the merger agreement, the Mackle Company contracted to supervise construction work and other development services for GDV at a rate of 2.67% of the sales price of each vacant lot. The payments were to be in equal installments from the first thirty-six payments received in installment sales and as a lump sum in the case of cash sales. In the event of default on a purchase contract, the Mackle Company was to receive no further payments on the contract. GDV also agreed to pay the Mackle Company 5% of the cost of each residence or other building constructed during the term of the contract, together with incurred construction, development, and overhead costs.

In September 1958, GDV took a second major step when it acquired nearly 6,000 acres of land near Fort Pierce from interests headed by Gardner Cowles, publisher of *Look Magazine*. As part of the $4.9 million transaction, Mr. Cowles took 156,533 shares of GDV stock, became a company Director, and late in 1959 took over as Chairman. The Cowles land became the core of the Port St. Lucie development.

Over the next two or three years, sales held up and GDV's debt capital increased dramatically as the company increased its land holdings from 87,000 to nearly 185,000 acres. GDV's 1958 annual report waxed enthusiastic upon the future of Port St. Lucie where nearly 3,000 lots had been sold in less than 1 year. Management's goal for Port St. Lucie in 1959 was 25,000 homesites and 1,000 homes; sales of 91,000 homesites and 9,000 homes were projected in the next few years. At Port Charlotte, 34,000 homesites were sold in 1958—non-waterfront lots, 80′ × 125′, for $895, waterfront lots for $2,650 to $12,000. GDV offered 24 different home models with FHA financing available and terms as low as $210 down and $46 a month (including principal, interest, taxes and insurance).

Frank E. Mackle, then president of GDV, identified the company's principal market and highlighted management's belief in the future during his address at the company's annual meeting in June 1960.

> No one is going to invent a better product. For good land in a good location, there is no substitute. And there is only so much of it. Your company has the best land in the best state, with the greatest potential for fast growth, both near- and long-term. . . .
>
> Study after study had pointed to the rising number of retired persons and their ever-growing need for good housing at moderate and low cost. And there is every indication that a large proportion of those retirees intend to make their homes in Florida.
>
> Besides that vast and virtually untapped market, we have a great potential demand for homes among the people who already own homesites in our communities. A recent sampling of 3,000 of our lot owners disclosed that 78% plan to build homes on their lots within the next ten years.
>
> These, then, are some of the economics of investing in land and community development. They go far beyond how many lots we plan to sell in 1960 or 1970 or

1980. They go beyond whether we can, within the next 5 or 6 years, build and sell homes at the rate of 25,000 a year—which I fully expect we will do.

The company set up a new promotional drive, the "Build on Your Lot" campaign, to convert its 46,000 homesite owners into home owners. Management speculated that by 1973 the company would have 93,000 households and maybe 300,000 people living in its developments. It was even looking beyond Florida to other parts of the country and areas outside the United States where a combination of favorable natural surroundings and modern social and economic trends made for "similarly intriguing potential"—parts of California and the Southwest, for instance, and the islands to the east of Florida.

However, 1960s results suggested that the new home sales program was affecting lot sales. The extensive efforts involved in retooling the company's sales organization to emphasize home sales had diverted effort from its more traditional homesite sales program. Lot sales declined from 49,933 in 1959 to 33,250 units in 1960—a decline which, management believed, more than offset the gains in home sales.

A Change of Management

In 1961 there was a turnover of ownership and management, possibly a result of the changing balance between homesite and homesales. Frank Mackle and his brothers left GDV and Mr. H. A. Yoars, a trustee of the Bowery Bank of New York and a mortgage financing expert, who had joined GDV as Financial Vice-President in 1960, agreed to become President on a temporary basis. Mr. Cowles remained Chairman.

At a meeting of the New York Society of Security Analysts on October 10, 1961, Mr. Yoars reviewed change in management.

> It was a direct result of the growth of the business. This growth has been so great that it confronted Frank Mackle and his brothers with a choice: Would they concentrate on the job of managing General Development's increasingly complex activities? Or would they concentrate on carrying forward the family business in the highly complicated field of construction? They chose—understandably—to follow the trail their father had blazed in the construction business.

The Mackles, however, apparently had a different impression as a 1968 *Business Week* article reported:

> "We came to the conclusion," elaborates Mackle, "that to build a successful community we had to do three things: Limit its size, bear down hard on home sales, and pre-plan the entire 15,000 acres."
>
> In addition . . . the Mackles pressed for higher down payments and larger monthly payments to eliminate some of the cash flow problems that plagued GDV's developments. . . . They reasoned that buyers with more equity in the property are not so likely to cancel.[9]

[9]In five years, the Mackles sold 30,000 lots out of the 32,000 lots available at Deltona. More than 2,100 homes were built, giving the Mackles a 1-in-15 ratio of home-to-homesite sales during a period when anything better than a 1-in-20 was considered "wholesome."

New Policies at GDV

With the change of management, the Mackles' contract, which had been scheduled to run until December 31, 1962, was terminated. The company announced a new strategy for the home building side of the business:

> . . . to concentrate on the sale of homes and homesites and turn over the development of the land and the building of the communities to top-flight subcontractors.

It was expected that self-contained operations would allow GDV greater flexibility in product design and give it a more competitive position in the home building market.

Termination of the old contract (which Cowles financed by acquiring the Mackles' stock) was expected to materially improve the company's profit picture because it eliminated contractor's fees which had totalled approximately $1.7 million in 1961. The company retained consultants to supervise its development operations at a price amounting to only one-fifth of its 1961 payments to the Mackle Company.

This cost reduction lent credence to another policy change: To watch GDV's finances more carefully.

> It is time to concentrate on putting our financial house completely in order. This is our most important single goal for 1962.
>
> The key to the situation is our cash flow. For years, General Development had been spending more cash than it took in . . . we had to borrow to make up the difference. This year we are dedicated to changing that pattern. We are trying to turn a $12 million operating cash outgo into a balanced cash flow.[10,11]

Another step in this direction was a major refinancing which involved the sale of $20 million of 6% promissory notes, payable $2,500,000 annually, commencing in 1964, to the Prudential Insurance Company of America and the Ford Foundation—two unusual financial backers for a land development company in the late 1950s and early 1960s. The note agreements gave the two institutions the right to demand repayment in the event of substantial management changes, and partial repayments if the quality of GDV's receivables fell. GDV was restricted in a number of other ways as well:

1 dividends and stock and debenture acquisitions were restricted;
2 the company agreed to maintain its liquid assets at an amount equal to 150% of specified liabilities and it agreed to increase this cover to 300% after 1965; and
3 land purchases and advance improvements beyond a pro rata collection of principal plus $500,000 were prohibited.

Mr. Yoars also announced that a survey of GDV's lot buyers indicated a rosy future for the company. Seventh-five percent of those surveyed planned to build on their lots in

[10]H. A. Yoars, President of GDV, Annual Meeting Miamia, Florida, May 15, 1962.

[11]One of the most significant operating problems of any company engaged in land development is its cash requirements. Particularly in the early stages, developers are faced with a cash drain occasioned by selling and administrative expenses, and by the need for cash outlays to carry out scheduled development work in advance of installment collections from their customers.

the future. Management believed that "current homesite contracts are an indication of our future in the community building business."

In 1962, however, GDV had a bad year. Sales declined dramatically and the company suffered extraordinary losses through contract cancellations. Management attributed the company's poor performance to factors outside its control: a decline in stock prices in spring, 1962; the Cuban crisis; and an unusual cold spell in Florida.

However, there was a light in the company's hour of trouble. GDV "turned the corner" from the standpoint of balancing cash income and expenditures, and, for the first time in the company's history, there was a net debt retirement of $3,650,000. Furthermore, Mr. Yoars pointed out to shareholders that, although contract cancellations had increased, they were not a serious problem.

> We can afford to be lenient in our policies toward installment buyers. It's good public relations, and it costs us nothing. Actually, a cancellation can even benefit GDV in one way. The homesite isn't a perishable item. We take it back into inventory and resell it—often at a higher price.

Management looked to a better year in 1963, referring to: 1) replacement of the old contractor; 2) the company's efforts to increase home sales—reasoning that, unlike most homesite sales from which cash income was deferred for some years, home sales were a cash item; 3) accelerated cash income from homesite sales, where down payments were averaging $40 compared to $15 in 1962; and 4) increasing interest income from past sales.

In spite of these rosy prospects, however, 1963 seemed to be even worse than 1962. The explanation was not simple. Although sales had declined severely (*Exhibit 2*), part of the reported loss of $5.3 million was due to the fact that the new president, Charles H. Kellstadt, who had just retired as Chairman of Sears Roebuck, had decided to write off some doubtful investments, which were "holdovers" from the Chesler era, and identify bad debts (non-active accounts receivable). In addition GDV made substantial additions to its reserves for bad debt to bring the company's operations to a realistic financial position.

Charles H. Kellstadt

Almost ten years later, in an interview with *Nation's Business* in June 1971, Mr. Kellstadt, who had joined GDV's board in 1962 at the invitation of his friend Gardner Cowles, discussed why he took the job:

> I had the idea that I would go into banking. because finance had always intrigued me and I'd made an avocation out of it—all kinds of financing and financial structures and so forth . . . but General Development came up and it is just as exciting.

Mr. Kellstadt believed in conservative financial management and disliked high leverage. (Many people in GDV believe that Mr. Kellstadt's reputation as a responsible manager may have been an important factor in GDV's institutional backers' decisions to continue to support the company.) Kellstadt believed that corporations should be good citizens and conduct business with integrity. This had been his way at Sears and it would be the way at GDV. In fact, in some ways GDV was reorganized and managed like Sears.

For example, in spite of the fact that in 1962 the company had found that "research shows independent franchised agents more productive than company-owned branches," and although it has shut all company branches to cut overhead in 1962, GDV reopened them in 1962. Mr. Kellstadt believed that the selling task was so sensitive that it had to be company-controlled. He therefore reversed the 1962 policy and switched to company branches. Merchandising efforts were intensified. Under Mr. Kellstadt, GDV also became a more integrated home construction company, building warehouses to stockpile building materials and hiring its own construction crews.

When GDV's 1964 results were released, they suggested that the company had been turned around. Earnings were 21¢ per share, compared with a net loss in 1963 of 80¢ per share. Total sales for 1964 were only slightly higher than in 1963 although dollar sales of homesites had increased by 24.3%. In spite of considerable management effort, sales of homes had declined again. GDV, however, had a positive cash flow for the third year in succession and the excess of revenues over expenditures was, as in the two previous years, applied to the retirement of indebtedness. By 1966, long-term debt had been reduced by $22,316,195, $6 million in 1966 alone. The next years passed without major changes in policy as the company continued to reduce its reliance on debt capital.

Enter City Investing

Early in 1966, Louis Chesler sold his 16½% holdings to City Investing Company, a financial conglomerate. City believed GDV's 190,000 shares offered an ideal product—low-cost land for prospective "Social Security Recipients"—and hoped that one of City's subsidiaries would produce a suitable low-cost factory-built house to harvest the anticipated demand for housing. City, like GDV, reasoned that many of the $10-down sales were maturing and the paid-off lots would be built on. This was where the "gravy" would be; after all, GDV had made only 7,119 homes sales in the 9 years between 1957 and 1965. In addition GDV was planning some new products in the home sales market in 1967, for example condominiums and 90 cluster homes at Port Charlotte. In 1967 City Investing Company increased its ownership of GDV from 16.5% to 49%, exchanging 416,000 shares of City stock for 2,500,000 shares of GDV's.

Problems

In mid-1971, however, GDV's stock price collapsed. A controversy about accounting practices in the land development business hit the stock prices of all land developers hard. To make GDV's stock prices even more vulnerable, land sales slowed 4%. Conservationists managed to block development of 9,000 acres owned by GDV at Port St. Lucie and the government of Florida began forcing land developers to install central sewage systems in their developments. And one analyst noted that GDV's contract cancellation reserves dropped from 15% to 13% of receivables in 6 months. Mr. Kellstadt retorted that he did not do that to buttress earnings: "We dropped the reserve only in relation to our experience of cancellations. We have not done a damn thing to bolster earnings. If anyone says we do, I'd like to make him come down here and pound his head in."

However, a more serious matter for GDV was the American Institute of Certified Public Accountants' proposal that land sale companies record sales only after 10% of the payment had been collected, and the AICPA's suggestion that perhaps 20% more be kept off the books until the raw land was ready for houses.

Some analysts argued that this would benefit GDV since, when accounts were restated for past years, Mr. Kellstadt would be able to lower revenues and earnings in earlier years and carry the figures forward to bolster current and future profits. However, others thought it would not work that way because the SEC would prohibit any restatement of *past* earnings by land sale companies. ''If that happens, we would go half a year without showing any profits,'' Mr. Kellstadt said. ''There's nothing wrong with the way we sell land.'' His attitude was: ''This too, shall pass. . . . We'll be the second biggest U.S. housebuilder.''[12]

And he had some support on Wall Street. In *Barrons,* May 15, 1972, an analyst commented:

> None of the proposals suggested by the Accounting Principles Board would affect General Development's earnings by more than 5% at worst because General Development is a relatively mature company.
>
> One area of concern to the accounting profession is the handling of long-term receivables, which, in the land development industry, are booked as current sales and flowed through to earnings after deducting reserves for cancellations, deferred development costs and actual cash outlays. The APB wants to discount these receivables to present value, because the average interest rate charged against the paper is below the real market rate. This would build up deferred income, which would flow back through the P&L in future years. For a mature company like General Development, restatement would create a large amount of deferred income which would offset current deferrals, so the net effect would be minimal. This would not be true for a company new to the land development business.
>
> Another problem area is deferred development costs, and here too the company is in good shape. General Development had been accelerating its development expenditures during the past few years; which means that deferred outlays in this area will be relatively low in relation to both sales and receivables. In certain respects, this is the best company in the business, and I think one day its stock will sell at 25 times earnings.
>
> I don't see any problems for General Development. It has a high-quality marketing organization, and its name rarely appears in FTC complaints.
>
> The government might tell the industry when it can book a sale, but I don't believe for a minute that it's going to tell a General Development what kind of down payment it ought to receive.

City Takes Charge

With GDV's stock price low, City moved to take control of the company in an unsuccessful merger attempt. However, in June and July 1973, City increased its ownership to 53% with a cash offer of about $9.00 a share. Then GDV offered to purchase up to 500,000 shares of its stock at $7 a share. In fact, the company acquired over 943,000 shares, leaving City with 59% of the outstanding shares in GDV. Then, late in 1973, City again unsuccessfully attempted to merge GDV into City.

[12]*Forbes,* November 15, 1972.

On August 6, 1973 Charles E. Kellstadt retired as Chairman and Chief Executive Officer in accordance with his employment contract, written in 1968, although he continued as a Director, Chairman of the executive committee and as a company consultant. In the 1973 Annual Report, Peter C. R. Huang, GDV's new Chairman and City's Executive Vice President, announced that General Development had been reorganized to achieve a more efficient organization with clear internal communications, improved controls and more precise setting of goals and objectives. There were now four profit centers: Marketing, Shelter, Land Development and Communities. Furthermore, Mr. Huang announced that, instead of employing its own construction crews for all phases of house construction, the Shelter division would assume a role similar to that of a general contractor and let out most physical construction to independent contractors. In addition, he said that a major redesign of housing lines was being prepared to increase consumer appeal.

In his first months as Chairman, Mr. Huang attempted to bring overhead in line with revenues by cutting back on employment. Mr. Fischer, when elected President, continued the process. For the first time in many years personnel had been laid off.

Fischer's Position

Mr. Fischer was aware of the company's history when he took charge. However, he was not certain that the lessons of the past would be directly applicable to the months ahead. The company had gone through a major sales decline between 1961–1962 and 1966–1967. Was the current sales decline similar to this earlier one? Would similar responses to the problem work again? Mr. Fischer needed a strategy which would increase the company's current sales and serve as the springboard for renewed profitable growth in the future.

EXHIBIT 1 General Development Locations in Florida

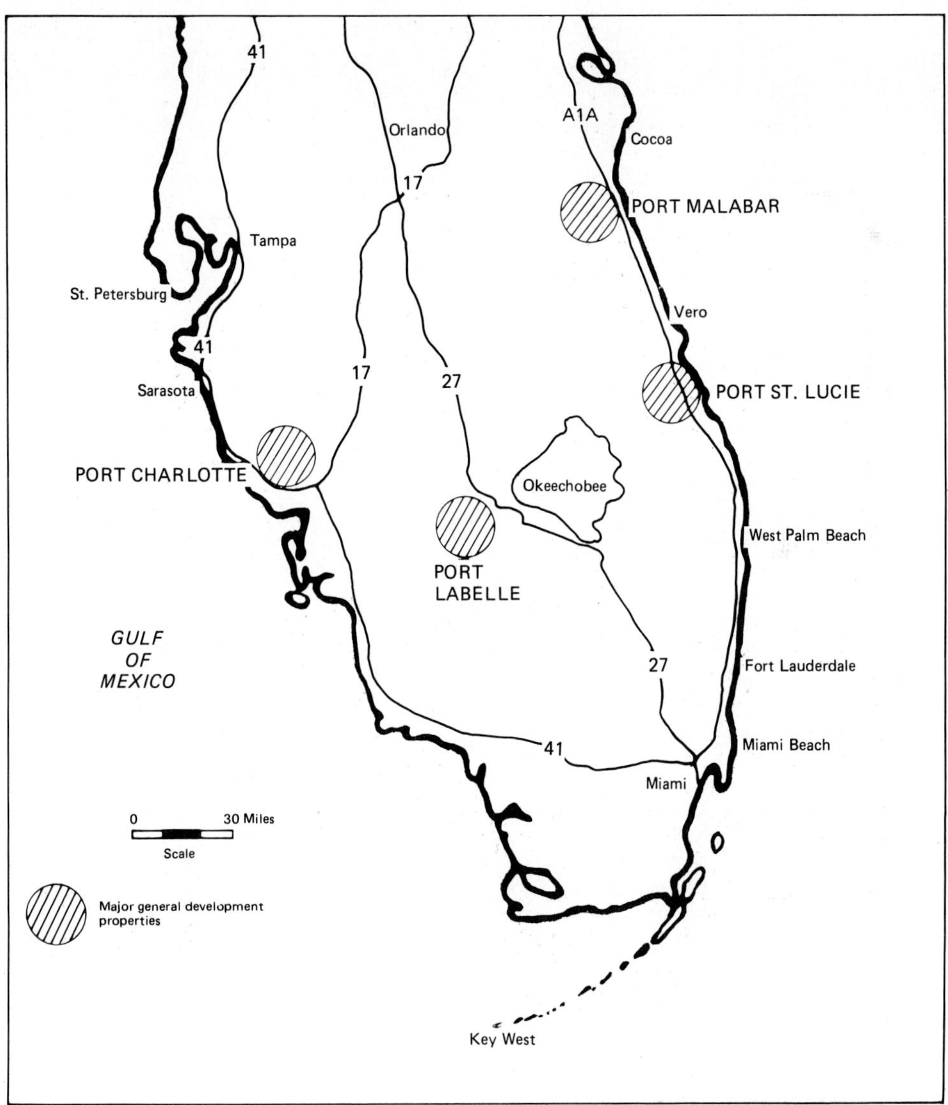

EXHIBIT 2 Lot and Home Sales 1957–1974

	Lot Sales			Home Sales		
Year	$000's	# Lots	Avg. Price $	$000's	# Homes	Avg. Price $
1957	12,734	20,203	630	6,757	985	6,860
1958	30,893	33,224	930	7,544	706	10,686
1959	56,679	49,933	1,135	10,559	904	11,680
1960	40,479	33,250	1,217	15,673	1,252	12,512
1961	49,366	37,862	1,304	19,035	1,538	12,370
1962	40,035	29,077	1,377	14,211	1,123	12,655
1963	18,833	9,809	1,920	10,597	799	13,263
1964	23,413	12,088	1,881	6,317	436	14,489
1965	24,781	12,405	2,370	4,620	280	16,500
1966	33,087	12,760	2,593	4,742	na	na
1967	44,362	17,625	2,517	5,865	na	na
1968	67,166	26,590	2,526	9,276	na	na
1969	85,528	32,397	2,640	11,344	na	na
1970	74,795	26,905	2,780	16,038	702	22,846
1971	97,358	29,385	3,391	17,358	763	22,750
1972	107,404	30,235	3,552	31,481	1,413	22,279
1973	94,888	23,746	3,996	53,357	1,962	28,215
1974	74,325	15,469	4,805	46,846	1,446	32,397

EXHIBIT 3
Executive Officers of GDV (March 1975)

Name	Office	Age 3/75	Officer Since
Peter C. R. Huang	Chairman of the Board	39	August, 1973
Louis Fischer	President and Chief Executive Officer and Director	45	April, 1974
William Avella	Senior Vice President—Finance and Administration	39	May, 1974
Charles J. Clark, Jr.	Senior Vice President—Marketing Division	40	May, 1972
C. C. Crump	Senior Vice President—Homesite Development Division	57	May, 1972
David A. Doheny	Senior Vice President, General Counsel and Secretary	43	March, 1966
———	Senior Vice President—Shelter Division	Vacant since August 1975	
George V. Flagg	Vice President and Controller	33	February, 1971
Cyrus E. Hornsby, III	Vice President and Treasurer	32	October, 1974
Harold E. Schmidt	Vice President—Communities Division	49	May, 1973
Jack D. Suiter	Vice President—Commercial Properties	48	September, 1974

From 1966 until 1972, Mr. Huang served as Vice President—Corporate Development of City Investing Company and since 1972 has served as Executive Vice President of City Investing. From 1973 until his election as President and Chief Executive Officer of General, Mr. Fischer served as Vice Chairman of the Larwin Group, Inc., a subsidiary of CNA Financial Corporation; prior to joining Larwin in 1972, he was President of Levitt and Sons, Inc. Mr. Avella was Vice President–Planning and Administration of Levitt and Sons, Inc., from 1969 until 1973, when he joined The Larwin Group, Inc., as Vice President–Finance and Administration. Mr. Clark has served in various capacities related to sales and marketing since joining General in 1967. Mr. Crump joined General as a staff engineer in 1968 and since that time has had executive responsibilities for General's planning and development of community properties. Mr. Doheny joined General in 1965 and in 1966 became General Counsel and Secretary and in 1973 a Senior Vice President. Prior to joining General in 1971 and undertaking responsibilities for the gathering, recording and reporting of all corporate and financial data, Mr. Flagg had been associated for six years with Lybrand, Ross Bros., and Montgomery (now Coopers & Lybrand) in New York. From 1970 to 1974 Mr. Hornsby was President of Rutenberg Corp., a housing and land development holding company; prior to 1970 he was successively in Atlanta an associate of the law firm Jones, Byrd & Howell and an investment banker with Robinson-Humphrey Co. Since joining General in 1958 until 1973, Mr. Schmidt held various positions in connection with General's utilities operations. Mr. Suiter was director of General's commercial and industrial sales from 1969 until 1974.

EXHIBIT 4 Population of U.S. Households 1965–1990[1]

		Number of Households in Millions[2]					
Age	Rent v. Own %[3]	1965	1970	1975	1980	1985	1990
Under 25	79–21	3.7	4.4	5.3	6.0	6.0	5.4
25–34	60–40 (25–29)	10.0	11.5	14.8	18.2	20.5	21.6
35–44	40–60 (30–34)	12.0	11.8	11.6	12.9	16.2	19.4
45–54	31–69	11.4	12.2	12.4	11.9	11.7	13.0
55–64	25–75	9.8	10.8	11.6	12.4	13.0	12.2
Over 64	27–73	10.9	12.2	14.0	15.7	16.9	18.4
Total	29–71	57.8	62.9	69.7	77.1	84.3	90.0

Note 1 - U.S. Department of Commerce, Bureau of the Census. *Current Population Reports,* "Population Estimates and Projections," Series P-25, No. 476, February 1972, page 25.

Note 2 - A household is defined as any person or group of persons, related or not, occupying a permanent and distinct living unit. Not included are hotels, dormitories, or institutions.

Note 3 - U.S. Department of Commerce, Bureau of the Census. Current Population Reports, "Household Ownership," Series P-65, No. 40, May 1972, page 7.

EXHIBIT 5 Population, GDV Communities

	Potential	Actual, 1974
Port Charlotte	267,550	35,000
Port St. Lucie	84,790	8,000
Port Malabar	66,800	7,500
Port St. John Sebastian Highlands Vero Beach Port La Belle	44,960	3,000

Source: Company estimates.

EXHIBIT 6 Florida Non-Agricultural Employees: Annual Averages (000's)

	1960	1965	1970	1973
Employees	1,321	1,619	2,152	2,708
Population	5,004	5,954	6,848	7,688
% Employees	26.4%	27.2%	31.4%	35.2%

Source: U.S. Bureau of the Census, *Statistical Abstract of the United States, 1974* (95th Edition), Washington, D.C., 1974.

EXHIBIT 7
GENERAL DEVELOPMENT CORPORATION AND SUBSIDIARIES
Consolidated Balance Sheets
(in thousands of dollars)

December 31	*1974*	*1973*	*1972*
Assets			
Cash	$ 9,294	$ 9,313	$ 9,729
Contracts receivable on homesite sales	306,300	302,659	278,424
Less deferred profit	(120,150)	(120,827)	(128,639)
	186,150	181,832	149,785
Other receivables, net	8,785	4,022	3,526
Land improvements and shelter units for sale, at cost	81,492	78,145	68,853
Property, plant and equipment, at cost	85,630	75,195	60,623
Less accumulated depreciation	19,625)	(18.071)	(15,500)
	66,005	57,124	45,123
Deferred selling expenses	6,595	8,149	10,798
Equity in and advances to wholly-owned subsidiary	2,660	—	—
Other assets	5,133	7,046	4,613
	$366,114	$345,631	$292,427
Liabilities			
Accounts payable and accrued liabilities	$ 13,923	$ 15,260	$ 14,590
Customers' deposits	12,799	20,855	21,515
Estimated homesite improvement cost	76,105	70,112	47,200
Deferred and current income taxes (current $3,000 in 1974)*	67,933	57,168	46,700
Mortgages payable	28,946	27,283	30,468
Notes payable	67,705	60,260	47,772
	267,411	250,938	208,245
Contingency			
Stockholders' Equity			
Common stock, $1.00 par value. Authorized 15,000,000 shares issued 10,173,419 shares	10,173	10,173	10,173
Capital contributed in excess of par value	52,607	52,607	52,607
Retained earnings	42,898	31,913	21,402
Less treasury stock (943,163 shares) at cost	(6,975)	—	—
	98,703	94,693	84,182
	$366,114	$345,631	$292,427

EXHIBIT 7 (Cont.)
GENERAL DEVELOPMENT CORPORATION AND SUBSIDIARIES
Five Year Summary of Operations
Five Years Ended December 31, 1974
(in thousands of dollars)

	1974	*1973*	*1972*	*1971*	*1970*
Revenues					
Homesite sales	$ 74,325	$ 94,888	$107,404	$ 97,358	$ 74,795
Other land sales	4,029	865	517	975	441
Shelter sales	46,846	55,357	31,481	17,358	16,038
Other revenue, principally from amenities and utilities	12,517	11,550	9,392	7,423	6,071
Interest income on contracts receivable	21,670	20,645	18,062	14,659	11,635
Profit deferred on homesite sales	(25,450)	(35,580)	(45,347)	(44,175)	(31,513)
Deferred profit recognized on homesite sales	18,076	24,965	16,426	15,111	11,927
	152,013	172,690	137,935	108,709	89,394
Cost and Expenses					
Cost of sales:					
Homesites	22,423	27,149	25,669	23,111	18,533
Other land	1,307	430	92	509	240
Shelters	36,937	49,651	27,359	13,637	13,298
Other, principally amenities and utilities	13,177	11,448	9,289	7,719	5,983
	73,844	88,678	62,409	44,976	38,054
Commissions, advertising and other selling	32,938	37,553	39,053	30,539	35,855
General and administrative	11,644	13,001	10,356	11,297	9,015
Loss on cancellation of contracts receivable on homesite sales	4,999	7,771	2,792	1,818	1,004
Interest on mortgages and notes net of amounts capitalized	7,132	5,097	2,854	2,544	2,328
Other interest, net	(402)	78	(357)	(198)	(226)
Other, net	(382)	(759)	838	(99)	277
	129,773	151,419	117,945	90,877	76,307
Income before provision for income taxes	22,240	21,271	19,990	17,832	13,087
Provision for Income Taxes					
Current	3,000	—	—	—	—
Deferred	8,255	10,760	10,100	8,550	6,275
	11,255	10,760	10,100	8,550	6,275
Net Income	$ 10,985	$ 10,511	$ 9,890	$ 9,282	$ 6,812
Net income per share and equivalent share (same as fully diluted)	$ 1.18	$ 1.03	$ 96	$ 90	$ 66
Number of shares used in computation of net income per share and equivalent share	9,345,000	10,234,000	10,347,000	10,329,000	10,268,000
Stock prices for GDV — *High*	7 5/8	14 1/4	35 3/8	33 3/4	32 1/14
Common stock par $1 — *Low*	2 1/8	4	12 1/4	23 3/4	14 1/2

(continued)

EXHIBIT 7 (Cont.)
GENERAL DEVELOPMENT CORPORATION AND SUBSIDIARIES
Consolidated Statements of Sources and Uses of Cash
Years Ended December 31, 1974 and 1973
(in thousands of dollars)

	1974	*1973*
Operating cash receipts		
Collections on homesite contracts (down payments, principal and interest)	$ 76,563	$ 75,096
Proceeds from shelter sales	31,538	55,156
Other, principally amenities and utilities	14,477	11,873
	122,578	142,125
Operating cash expenditures		
Land improvements	13,671	12,184
Shelter construction	28,856	56,411
Commissions, advertising and other selling expenses	27,766	34,156
General and administrative expenses	11,154	12,233
Property taxes	2,262	702
Payments on purchase money mortgages and down payments on land purchases	2,752	5,730
Interest	8,386	5,599
Other, principally amenities and utilities	13,241	10,046
	108,088	137,061
Cash generated from operations	14,490	5,064
Other sources and (uses) of cash		
Proceeds from mortgages and notes issued, excluding purchase money mortgages	7,500	13,038
Purchases of property, plant and equipment, net	(14,091)	(16,788)
Repayments of mortgages and notes payable, excluding purchase money mortgages	(489)	(1,446)
Purchase of treasury stock	(6,975)	—
Other	(454)	(284)
	(14,509)	(5,480)
(Decrease) in cash	($ 19)	($ 416)

SUMMARY OF SIGNIFICANT ACCOUNTING POLICIES

Homesite Sales—Installment Method The Company sells land principally under installment contracts (nonrecourse) which require payments over an average period of ten years. Under the installment method, the Company records homesite sales when aggregate payments (including interest) equivalent to 10% of the contract price have been received. Costs and direct selling expenses (including commissions) related to a homesite sale are recorded at the time the sale is recognized. Costs include the cost of unimproved land (including interest on purchase money mortgages), estimated real estate taxes, estimated closing costs and estimated cost of improvements, such as roads and drainage. Land cost and capitalized interest for each project is allocated to homesites sold based on the total number of homesites which the project is expected to yield. All other costs, which are estimated in total, are allocated to homesites sold based upon the relationship of their sales price to the aggregate estimated sales price of all platted homesites in the project.

The gross profit less direct selling expenses relating to recorded homesite sales is recognized in income on a pro rata basis as payments of principal under the installment contracts are received.

Interest on installment contracts which have been recorded as sales is included in income when it is received.

Upon cancellation of a contract receivable relating to prior years' sales, the excess of the unpaid balance over recovered costs (land and estimated homesite improvements) and deferred profit is charged to income. Land is restored to inventory at cost and the estimated homesite improvement liability established when the sale was recorded is reversed. The Company's policy generally is to cancel a contract when, after appropriate notification to the customer, no payment is received for approximately six months.

When a purchaser of a homesite subsequently buys a shelter unit and lot package, the Company will reacquire the original homesite and allow a credit toward the purchase of the shelter package equivalent to the principal payments made under the original homesite contract plus a portion of any appreciation in the sales price of the original homesite, as determined by a formula which considers the Company's current sales price for an equivalent homesite.

The Company accounts for this exchange by returning the original homesite to inventory at an amount equal to the original homesite cost and previously recognized gross profit reduced by recovered selling expenses, or at net realizable value, if lower. Unrecovered selling expenses are charged to income. Any discount given related to the appreciation in sales price of the original homesite is considered an expense of the sale and charged to income.

Deposits Until a homesite contract is recorded as a sale, all payments received (including interest) are treated as deposits. Direct selling expenses applicable to such contracts which are expected to be recorded as sales are also deferred and charged to expense when the related sale is recorded.

Income Recognition—Shelter Sales Sales of shelter units including houses, mobile homes, condominium apartments, the related underlying land and all related costs and expenses, are recorded at the time of the closings. The costs of construction of shelter units sold are determined by specific identification. Payments received from buyers prior to closing are recorded as deposits.

Income Recognition—Other Land Other land sales are recorded in accordance with "Accounting for Profit Recognition on Sales of Real Estate," an industry accounting guide. Profit is not recognized on sales unless prescribed down-payment rates and other terms of sale meet the requirements of the guide.

Land and Shelter Inventory Land and improvements are carried at average cost which includes capitalized carrying costs consisting of real estate taxes and interest on purchase money mortgages. Shelter units are carried at the lower of specifically identified cost or net realizable value.

Depreciation Depreciation is provided on the straight-line method primarily through charges to income, land improvements, estimated homesite improvement cost or construction in progress.

The following tabulation indicates the principal estimated useful lives upon which depreciation charges are based:

	Years
Land improvements	10–33
Land development machinery and equipment	4–12
Buildings	10–40
Fixtures and equipment	3–10
Utility equipment and facilities	15–50

Maintenance and repair costs customarily are charged, as incurred, to income, land improvements or estimated homesite improvement cost. Renewals and betterments to owned properties are capitalized. Betterments to leased properties are capitalized and amortized over the shorter of the terms of the leases or the lives of the betterments.

Accumulated depreciation is charged with the amount of accumulated depreciation at the time properties are retired or otherwise disposed of, the profit or loss being credited or charged to income.

Estimated Homesite Improvement Cost Sales of homesites are generally made in advance of the completion of land improvements. The cost of such improvements to be completed in the future is accrued as an estimated liability when the homesite sale is recorded. The estimated homesite improvement cost is re-evaluated at least annually. The remaining deferred profit on sales previously recorded is adjusted for the retroactive effect of any changes in these estimates. Under the terms of the Company's installment sales contracts, the required improvements must be completed no later than the end of the year of the customer's scheduled final installment payment.

The Company has also agreed to provide water and sewer service in areas in which homesites have been sold. The cost of the required utility facilities will be capitalized as construction progresses.

Income Taxes Income taxes are provided on the basis of rates currently in effect at the time of recording. Deferred income taxes arise principally because income from homesite sales is reported on a basis for tax purposes which differs from the method used for financial reporting purposes which is described above. Investment tax credits are accounted for on the flow-through method.

Capitalized Interest The Company capitalizes all interest on purchase money mortgages as part of the cost of the related land in conformity with the provisions of the industry accounting guide "Accounting for Retail Land Sales." Capitalized interest is subsequently charged to expense primarily through the installment method of accounting used for homesite sales. Capitalization of this interest had the effect of increasing net income by $453,000 and $341,000 in 1974 and 1973, respectively.

Consolidation The consolidated financial statements include the accounts of the Company and all significant subsidiaries. All significant inter-company transactions have been eliminated.

In July, 1974, the Company formed a wholly-owned unconsolidated subsidiary. GDV Financial Corporation, to provide mortgage banking services for its shelter customers and others. The Company accounts for this investment on the equity method. At December 31, 1974, GDV Financial Corporation's total assets and total liabilities were $2,787,000 and $127,000 (net of amounts payable to the Company), respectively. The Company has agreed with the lender, to purchase on demand individual mortgages and notes securing advances made under the subsidiary's $2,000,000 bank line of credit. The net loss of the subsidiary was not significant.

EXHIBIT 8
Florida Communities Land Inventory[1]

Community	Date Sales Commenced	Total Land Area (acres)	Land Sold (acres)[3]	Unsold Land Remaining (acres)	Unsold Land Platted as Homesites (acres)	Unsold Land Platted as Homesites (lots)	Other Unsold Land (acres)
Port Charlotte	1956	100,327	64,070	36,257	10,179	28,589	26,078
Port St. Lucie	1959	48,538	29,365	19,173	2,968	7,657	16,205
Port Malabar	1960	43,194	22,679	20,515	2,495	7,310	18,020
Port LaBelle	1973	31,528	2,602	28,926	5,582	9,992	23,344
Other communities[2]	1956	12,178	7,089	5,089	1,531	4,425	3,558
Totals		235,765	125,805	109,960	22,755	57,973	87,205

[1]In addition, GDV owned as of December 31, 1974, approximately 9,000 acres in DeSoto County contiguous to Port Charlotte, 4,600 acres at Julington Creek near Jacksonville, Florida, and approximately 21,000 acres located 75 miles west of Knoxville, in the Cumberland Region of Tennessee.
[2]Includes Port St. John, Sebastian Highlands and Vero Shores/Vero Beach Highlands.
[3]Includes land deeded or subject to contracts of sale.

EXHIBIT 9 (000's)

Community	Aggregate Sales Price of Homesites Net of Cancellations and Other Land Sold	Payments (of Sales Price) Received	Estimated Cost of Improvements	Amount Spent on Improvements in Homesite and Other Land Areas
Port Charlotte	$343,862	$215,640	$ 91,647	$ 50,146
Port St. Lucie	169,997	91,908	35,087	20,718
Port Malabar	171,012	97,941	36,682	16,781
Port LaBelle	19,158	3,462	4,305	982
Other communities	38,505	24,344	11,037	13,986
Total	$742,534	$433,295	$178,758	$102,613

EXHIBIT 10 Estimated Collections of Principal on Contracts Receivable (after giving effect to anticipated cancellations) (000's)

1975	$45,000
1976	42,000
1977	39,000
1978	35,000
1979	31,000

EXHIBIT 11 Florida Land Sales 1974

Rank	*Sales (million)*	*Company*
1	$152.0	General Development
2	128.4	GAC
3	108.0	Deltona
4	89.4	Amrep
5	83.3	Horizon
6	53.6	ITT Community Development Corp.
7	37.0	Royal Palm Beach
8	25.9	Punta Gorda Isles
	$677.6	

However, as already noted, the full scope of the interstate land sales industry is much larger, as *Exhibit 12* shows:

EXHIBIT 12 U.S. Registered Land Holdings—Interstate Land Sales

Geographic Area	*Number of Acres Registered in Filings Through 1974* (000's acres)*	*Sold Acreage Through 1974 Eight Largest Florida Developers (000's acres)*
United States	7,146	
Florida	1,942	891
New Mexico	1,030	—
Subtotal	2,972	891
Texas	876	
Colorado	825	
California	622	
Arizona	467	
Total	5,762	891

**Source*: Richard Ragatz Associates Inc., "An Analysis of the Markets for Privately Owned Recreational Lots and Leisure Homes," Eugene, Oregon. May 1974.

EXHIBIT 13 Who Buys General Development Land[1]

	U.S. 1960	*GDV Customers, pre-1970*	*U.S. 1970*	*GDV Customers, post-1970*	*U.S. 1973*
	%	%	%	%	%
Age					
Less than 25 (18-24)	13.6	12	17.8	10	18.6
25–34	19.8	24	18.7	29	20.1
35–44	21.0	29	17.3	22	16.0
45–54	17.8	25	17.4	24	16.7
More than 54	28.0	10	28.9	15	28.5
	U.S.—25 yrs. and over, 1960	*GDV Customers, pre-1970*	*U.S.—25 yrs. and over, 1970*	*GDV Customers post-1970*	*U.S.—25 yrs. and over, 1973*
Education[2]					
Completed Grade School	17.6	3	12.3	2	10.1
Some High School	19.3	7	15.6	8	14.4
Completed High School	24.7	40	31.1	38	31.7
Some College	8.8	23	9.3	22	10.1
Completed College	7.7	21	10.1	25	11.2
	U.S. Family Income, 1960	*GDV Customers, pre-1970*	*U.S. Family Income, 1970*	*GDV Customers, post-1970*	*U.S. Family Income, 1972*
	%	%	%	%	%
Income					
Less than $10,000	85.7	25	51.0	15	43.6
$10,000–$15,000	10.6	—	26.8	—	26.1
$10,000–$20,000	—	45	—	61	—
More than $20,000	—	9	—	14	—
$15,000–$25,000	} 3.7	—	} 22.2		23.0
More than $25,000		—			7.3

[1]Based on a random sample of 2,000 buyers by telephone interview with a 55% response rate. In GDV customer series, incomplete or "no" responses account for the fact that columns do not total 100%. The survey was made by Bates Associates for GDV.

[2]U.S. Figures based on population 25 years and over.

Source: U.S. Bureau of the Census, *Statistical Abstract of the United States, 1974,* (95th Edition), Washington, D.C., 1974.

Exhibit 14 **THIS SHORT SURVEY MAY LEAD TO ONE OF THE WISEST MOVES YOU'VE EVER MADE!**

If you've been dreaming of moving your family into a pleasant new mode of living in Florida, but you've been held back by the uncertainty of earning a livelihood once you get there, here's an easy way to do something about it.

Simply tell General Development a little bit about yourself, your plans and your career aspirations. That way our company, which already has developed more than 5,000 jobs in its Florida communities, can continue bringing in more of the right kinds of industry.

Our concern—and our challenge—is to help make dreams come true by providing jobs for those who want them.

That's it. Pure and simple.

All you have to do is take a few moments to answer the quick questions on the postage-paid card at the right.* General Development will take over from there.

So reply today! Putting your dreams down on paper may get you and your family to Florida way ahead of schedule.

COMMUNITY JOB OPPORTUNITY SURVEY

1. Please indicate your age classification:
[1]( ) Below 25 [3]( ) 35–44 [5]( ) 55–64
[2]( ) 25–34 [4]( ) 45–54 [6]( ) 65 and over

2. Please indicate your sex:
[1]( ) Female [2]( ) Male

3. Please indicate the community in which you own property:
[1]( ) Charlotte [3]( ) Malabar [5]( ) St. Lucie
[2]( ) LaBelle [4]( ) Sebastian/St. John [6]( ) Vero

4. Please indicate why you would consider moving to Florida in the near future (check one):
[1]( ) Retirement [3]( ) Relocate Family
[2]( ) Semi-retirement [4]( ) Recreation
Specify Other:________________

5. Please indicate if available employment opportunities in your field would be a factor in your decision to move to Florida:
[1]( ) Maybe [2]( ) No [3]( ) Yes

6. Please indicate the type of work in which you now are engaged:
[1]( ) Agriculture [6]( ) Mining
[2]( ) Construction [7]( ) Personal/Domestic Services
[3]( ) Education [8]( ) Professional/Technical Services
[4]( ) Government [9]( ) Public Utilities/Transportation
[5]( ) Manufacturing Specify Other____________

*In Canada, address replies to Can-Am Real Estate Ltd., 1000 Finch Ave. W., Downsview, Ont. M3J2V5. Ontario residents require a work permit.

7. Please indicate the category which best describes your occupation:

1( ) Accounting/Bookkeeping	5( ) Owner/Partner
2( ) Corporate Director/Officer	6( ) Sales
3( ) Industrial/Trade/Craft	7( ) Secretarial/Clerical/Office
4( ) Manager/Supervisor	Specify Other__________

8. Please indicate the salary range you would consider acceptable for a challenging position in Florida equal in responsibility to your present job:

1( ) Below $8,000	5( ) $16,000–$19,999
2( ) $8,000–$9,999	6( ) $20,000–$24,999
3( ) $10,000–$12,999	7( ) $25,000–$29,999
4( ) $13,000–$15,999	8( ) $30,000 and above

9. Please indicate ideas or suggestions which would be useful in developing the types of employment opportunities which best meet your specific needs:______

____

____

APPENDIX 1
Assorted Indexes Based on 1967 = 100

Year	*General Construction Index*	*Price Index New One-Family House*	*Construction Materials*	*Consumer Price Index*	*Wage Rate, Building Trade*	*Middle Management Salaries*	*Wages, Manufacturing Workers*	*Capital Invested per Manufacturing Worker ($'s)*
1955	61.1	na	na	80.2	60.0	na	65.9	na
1960	76.9	na	95.5	88.7	75.4	76.4	78.1	na
1965	90.7	93.1	95.8	94.5	90.9	92.1	93.6	na
1967	100.0	100.0	100.0	100.0	100.0	100.0	100.0	$27,800
1968	107.8	105.1	na	101.2	106.6	105.1	106.6	$30,300
1969	118.9	113.6	na	109.8	115.4	110.7	112.7	$33,900
1970	128.9	117.4	112.5	116.3	128.8	117.2	116.4	$38,300
1971	146.8	123.2	na	121.3	144.0	124.0	123.6	na
1972	162.9	131.0	126.6	125.3	153.2	130.3	134.6	na
1973	176.6	144.8	138.5	133.1	160.8	137.4	144.2	na
Rate of Increase 1965–1973	8.69%	5.68%	4.72%	4.37%	7.39%	4.62%	5.55%	na

na . . . not available
Source: U.S. Bureau of the Census, *Statistical Abstract of the United States,* Washington, D.C., 1970 and 1974. Middle management salaries: corporate sources.

APPENDIX 2*
REGULATORY AGENCIES AND GDV

LAND SALES REGULATION

GDV's business, like that of all persons engaged in the interstate sale of real estate, is subject to substantial regulation by the cities or counties in which the company's communities are located, by the State of Florida, by many states where GDV's properties are sold, and by the Federal government. GDV's installment sales are also subject to the Federal Consumer Credit Protection ("Truth in Lending") Act. In addition, GDV's business is also subject to Federal, state and local regulation with respect to environmental matters.

In most of the areas in which GDV's communities are located, approval by local governmental authorities of the layout of the development, the nature and extent of improvements, zoning provisions and related matters is required. Normally a developer must conform to certain minimum standards respecting lot sizes and other matters prior to obtaining approval of a subdivision plan and must thereafter pave and dedicate the streets, and because complete primary wells and sewerage disposal through septic tanks are either not available or not permitted, provision for community water and sewerage facilities will be required. Guarantees are generally required to assure the completion of improvements such as streets and drainage facilities.

The Florida Land Sales Act requires GDV and all other persons selling subdivided land on a comparable basis to file a registration statement with the Land Sales Division of the Florida Board of Business Regulation as to the land being offered for sale and to file with the Division numerous supporting documents and to deliver to the purchaser a property report approved by the Division prior to the execution of the sales contract, the purpose of which is to make a full and fair disclosure of all relevant facts with respect to such land. The Florida Land Sales Act also requires registrants to file for prior approval all advertising to be published and all promotional material, wherever circulated, together with supporting data to show that such information is neither false nor misleading. The Florida Land Sales Act requires that all governmental approvals necessary for the development of subdivided lands be obtained prior to the registration of such land with the Division. Florida law gives to any person who, in reliance upon any false or misleading information or information which does not make a full and fair disclosure, purchases real estate located in Florida, the right to rescind the contract or to recover damages. GDV has had and expects to have no material difficulty in complying with the Florida land sales laws, although recent laws, regulations and policies have increased the time and expense necessary to effect compliance.

The laws of many states impose requirements similar to those of Florida, including the furnishing of an offering statement or property report to purchasers or prospective purchasers. These laws must be complied with by GDV or its agents in order to sell real estate to persons within such states and GDV has had, and may have in the future,

*Source: General Development Corporation's 1974 Annual Report on Form 10K to the Securities and Exchange Commission.

difficulties in complying with the requirements of a few states, particularly those states which treat installment land sales as "securities" so as to make such sales subject to regulation under the state securities law. GDV has agreed to offer refunds to several hundred homesite purchasers in the States of Missouri and Ohio as a result of GDV's difficulty in registering and marketing homesites as "securities" in those States during 1969 and 1974, respectively. Assuming all persons to whom such refunds are offered elect to accept, GDV's maximum aggregate cash refund obligation is estimated to be $1,400,000. Additional laws and regulations are continually being adopted by various states and GDV cannot predict the effect of any specific laws or regulations.

The Office of Interstate Land Sales Registration of the United States Department of Housing and Urban Development (OILSR) has jurisdiction over the interstate sales of subdivided land. Under the Federal Land Sales Full Disclosure Act, a registration statement must be filed with respect to all GDV's subdivided land offered for sale in interstate commerce and a Property Report approved by OILSR must be delivered to each purchaser of a homesite prior to the execution of a sales contract. In the event that the purchaser has not received the Property Report at least 48 hours prior to the execution of the sales contract, he may rescind the contract up to three business days after the execution of the sales contract. OILSR has by regulation permitted registration statements which have become effective under the Florida Land Sales Act to be accepted in satisfaction of the Federal registration requirement. Accordingly, to date GDV has had no material difficulty in complying with the Federal act. However, OILSR has proposed that the acceptance of Florida-approved registration statements will take a substantially greater time and will be substantially more expensive.

Under the Truth in Lending Act, GDV is required to disclose all relevant credit terms to its purchasers prior to the execution of a sales contract. As currently interpreted by the Federal Reserve Board and the Federal Trade Commission, that Act permits a homesite purchaser to rescind a sales contract within three business days of the execution of the sales contract by delivery of written notice to the seller. To date GDV has had no material difficulty in complying with the Truth in Lending Act.

The Federal Trade Commission has also asserted jurisdiction over GDV's sales practices under the Federal Trade Commission Act.[1]

ENVIRONMENTAL MATTERS

Federal, state and local laws, regulations and policies relating to the protection of the environment and having impact on GDV and its business have become increasingly restrictive in recent years. In reliance on previously applicable laws, regulations and policies, GDV has platted, offered and sold certain homesites, particularly in waterfront areas and in areas where digging of canals is planned, which have not yet been developed and which under current laws, regulations and policies may be difficult or impossible to

[1]In January 1975, GDV received an inquiry from the Miami office of the Securities and Exchange Commission ("the SEC") which indicated that on the basis of certain available information, GDV might be involved in the unregistered offering of a "security" through certain of its shelter sales practices. GDV does not believe this to be the case and has so advised the SEC's Miami office.

develop in the manner previously contemplated. To the extent that such improvements may not be completed, GDV has voluntarily refunded and may in the future be required to refund payments to purchasers of homesites in the areas affected. GDV believes that the majority of these areas will ultimately be improved in a manner which will satisfy or substantially satisfy its contractual commitments, although modifications in improvement methods may be required. GDV has not recorded any income with respect to these homesite sales and has treated all payments of such contracts as deposits.

In addition, all future land development work must be planned and performed in accordance with these new and more restrictive laws, regulations and policies. GDV is not able to predict at this time what effect the new laws, regulations and policies may have upon its capital expenditures, earnings and competitive position and whether any effect will be material to such expenditures, earnings or competitive position.

The Florida Water Resources Act of 1972 and the Florida Environmental Land and Water Management Act of 1972, impose substantial additional regulation by regional water management districts and state and local land planning agencies and for the first time these acts will subject GDV's overall development plan to control by state planning agencies (although normally not applicable to subdivision plans previously approved by the Florida Land Sales Division) considering the overall statewide and regional impact of the development. GDV does not anticipate undue difficulty in complying with regulations adopted under these laws. In addition, amendments to the Federal Water Pollution Control Act which recently became effective will place substantial regulatory authority as to the issues of water quality (including construction of canals and waterways) in the U.S. Environmental Protection Agency. Since this act has only recently been adopted, GDV cannot predict its effect.

ASSUMING CONTROL AT ALTEX AVIATION (A)

> We closed on Altex Aviation in the late evening of December 29, 1971. I wrote a check for $100,000, which represented all the cash we had, gave it to Bill Dickerson, who no longer owned the company, and said, "Would you give this to Sarah and have her deposit it." He said, "Fine." Frank flew back to Los Angeles that night and I went up to Dallas to pick up some papers and to resign from McKenzie & Boze. The next day, I went down to M & B, resigned, and then about lunch time, after saying goodbye to folks, I picked up the phone and called Sarah. With the $100,000 we gave her, Altex had $102,000 in the bank. I said, "Hello, Sarah, this is Ted Edwards." "Oh, Mr. Edwards," she said, "I am so glad you called. When will you be in?" I said, "I will be in shortly." She said, "Oh, good, I have a few checks for you to sign." I said, "That's wonderful. What are the checks for?" She said, "I have written checks *only* for our most pressing bills. I tried very hard to make sure that only those that are most important be paid." I said, "That's fine. What's the total of the checks you have written?" She said, "$92,000." I said, "We'll discuss it."
>
> I drove very calmly down to Altex Aviation to have my first confrontation with Sarah Arthur. I had envisioned, as every business school graduate does, that when I bought my company, I would walk in the front door, everyone would bow down, and there would be a brass band. Instead, I'm walking in through the back door (a) realizing that I have a crisis on my hands; (b) hoping no one is going to see me so I can deal with this crisis; and (c) of course, I don't really know how I am going to deal with it. What I did was, I said to Sarah, "We are *not* going to pay these bills." And she said, "Oh, you *must*." And I said, "No, I will decide what bills we are going to pay." She said, "Okay." And then sat back to watch this idiot make a fool of himself. That was my first day.

Thus did Ted Edwards describe the beginning of his and Frank Richards's ownership of Altex Aviation.

THE PURCHASE

Theodore Edwards and Frank Richards met in 1968 as graduate students at the Harvard Business School. Although planning on going to work for large companies, they decided that they eventually wanted to own their own business. Upon graduation in 1970, Frank took a job in the corporate finance department with an electronics firm in Los Angeles and Ted went with a New York consulting firm's Dallas office, doing market planning.

After six months, Frank transferred to the marketing support group for the Southwest operations and Ted and Frank saw each other frequently. It was on these occasions

This case was prepared by Professors Neil C. Churchill of Southern Methodist University, Edmund M. Goodhue of the Massachusetts Institute of Technology, and Kenneth A. Merchant of the Harvard Business School as a basis for class discussion rather than to illustrate either effective or ineffective handling of an administrative situation.

that they developed further the idea of going into business together. ''In good business-school fashion,'' said Frank, ''we established some criteria, which were:

1 The company couldn't cost anything since we didn't have any money.
2 The company had to need what we had to offer—which we thought at that time were managerial skills.
3 The industry had to be fragmented and non-oligopolistic. We didn't want to be small fish in a big pond.
4 We needed to be able to see our way clear to have the company grow at a rate of 20% per year the first five-year period.''

Ted and Frank looked at a number of businesses over the next year and a half. In early fall of 1971, they located a ''fixed-base operation''[1] at San Miguel Airport in Texas that was losing money and looking for a purchaser. After four months of negotiation, on December 29, 1971, Ted, aged 26, and Frank, aged 28, purchased the stock of the company for $10,000 each, took on the lease on the building, assumed all the assets and liabilities, and were in business.

The lease on the facilities had a purchase option at a price considerably less than the market value. By exercising the option and then selling and leasing back the building, Ted and Frank were able to raise the $100,000 for working capital referred to above.

Ted and Frank had discussed the organizational structure at Altex and agreed to decentralize its operations by making each operating activity a profit center and grouping the activities by departments. Each departmental manager would be given authority over his operations, including credit granting, purchasing to a predetermined limit, policy, and collection of receivables. He would also be held responsible for its results. Frank was concerned, however:

> I agree with our decision to decentralize this authority, but I am concerned whether now is the time to do it. We will have a tough time when we first walk in the door and I don't know if the departmental managers can be taught some of these management techniques fast enough. After all, some have never finished high school. Maybe we should begin by making all these decisions ourselves for a month or two. Even though we don't know the aviation business yet and neither of us has been a line manager, maybe we can learn the aviation business faster than some of our managers can learn formal management skills. Either way, we're putting the company on the line and the two-minute warning whistle has already blown.

During the four months they were negotiating the deal, Frank and Ted spent virtually every weekend together. Of this period, Ted commented:

> We spent something on the order of ten hours a week—maybe two or three hours on trying to understand Sarah Arthur's accounting system and accounting statements, another two or three on discussing pro forma financial projections, and the rest on

[1]Fixed-base operations (FBOs) are companies located at an airport that service the non-airline aviation market. They generally buy, sell, fuel and maintain aircraft as well as provide flight instruction and charter services. These companies can range from family operations to multiple-location companies with sales exceeding $100 million.

what we would do when we acquired the company. Frank basically did the financial projections and I designed the accounting system. Actually I dreamt it up one afternoon at McKenzie & Boze. I sat down at their IBM composer and did it, using their artwork and all. Frank's projections, by profit center for the next ten years, showed that things were really tight. Even with the $100,000 from the sale and leaseback of the facilities, Frank projected that we were going to run out of money near the end of the first year. We knew this when we were negotiating for the company, and it made us a bit nervous. Well, three days before the closing, Frank came to me, white as a sheet, and confessed that we had made, not an arithmetical error, but a structural error in the projections. He was computing accounts payable on the wrong basis and we were going to run out of money in three months. We had a little discussion as to whether we should blow the whole deal out of the water right there. He basically turned to me and said, "I will do whatever you want to do." I said, "Let's do it anyway. Who cares?" So we did it but I have to say we were a bit shaken. We knew it would be an impossible job no matter how we sliced it but we were prepared to do it and I must say we leaned on each other for support a great deal in the first few months.

ALTEX AVIATION PRIOR TO PURCHASE

Altex Aviation was one of eight fixed-base operations at San Miguel Airport, which served Center County, Texas, one of the most rapidly growing communities in the nation. Altex had a loss of $100,000 on sales of $2,000,000 in fiscal year 1971 (see *Exhibit 1*). The company conducted activities through six informal departments (see *Exhibit 2*). Altex's location at the airport is shown in *Exhibit 3A*.

Fuel (Line) Activity

This activity employed some twelve unskilled fueling people who had an average tenure with the company of eight months, and three dispatchers who coordinated their activities via two-way radio. It was managed by Will Leonard, a man in his middle thirties, who had been the construction foreman for Bill Dickerson when Bill was a real estate developer. When Dickerson bought Altex in 1964, he brought Will Leonard with him to manage the "line crew." Will was enthusiastic about his job, extremely loyal to Dickerson, and well-liked by his employees. Although lacking in any theory of management (he had a high school diploma and some junior college credits), Will was a good first line manager who was instinctively people-conscious while holding them in line.

The fuel activity encompassed four operations:

- *Fueling*—A Phillips Petroleum franchise of underground storage of 60,000 gallons of jet fuel, 20,000 gallons of "AV-Gas," and five fuel trucks to serve aircraft. Sales were of two types: retail to locally-based and transient aircraft, wholesale to Tex Air, an airline company connecting San Miguel with other cities in Texas, Louisiana, Arkansas and Oklahoma.
- *Fuel Hauling*—An over-the-road fuel truck and a Texas Public Utilities permit to haul fuel on public roads. The truck, in essence, served Phillips, at a price, by delivering its fuel to Altex.
- *Rental Cars*—An agency of a local automobile rental company. Basically this was a service to transient pilots.

- *Tie-Downs*—Storage of transient and San Miguel-based aircraft in six hangars and fifty open tie-downs.[2]

The fuel activity was open 18 hours a day, 7 days a week, 365 days a year.

Service and Parts

The *service activity* repaired, maintained, and overhauled piston-engine aircraft. It employed six mechanics and a departmental secretary. The *parts activity,* a separate accounting entity, employed one person and was managed by the head of service (sales went almost entirely to the service activity). The manager of these operations was Carl Green, a man in his sixties, who had been chief mechanic for Dove Aircraft at Love Field in Dallas prior to moving out to Center County. Before that, he was the mechanic/co-pilot for a Dallas oil executive. Carl had a high school diploma, aircraft and power-plant license, and multi-engine and commercial pilot certificates. He knew airplanes, engines, and aircraft mechanics. He was, in Ted's words, ''not a self-starter, had a bit of retirement mentality, and avoided conflict except when it came to quality. You would never worry about anything that he rolled out of his shop.''

Flight Training

This activity was managed by Roy Douglas, whose pilot's license was signed by one of the Wright brothers. Roy had held several world's records in aviation's early days and was highly respected by the aviation community. He spent a lot of time ''hangar flying'' with old cronies. While he didn't manage the department in any real day-to-day sense, he hired the instructor pilots, gave check rides[3] to students prior to their Federal Aviation Administration flight examination, and set safety policies. He and his chief dispatcher, who now had been with him for over ten years, were intensely loyal to both Altex Aviation and the flying community. They had, however, ''seen everything and were surprised by nothing'' and were very resistant to change—be it new aircraft technology, aviation teaching methodology, or accounting systems.

Flight Training had two types of operations:

- *Flight School*—Flight training in eighteen single-engine light aircraft from eight flight instructors coordinated by three dispatchers. Flight ratings were offered from private pilot through air transport ratings.
- *Pilot Shop*—Sales of flight supplies, such as logbooks, navigational charts, and personal and training flight supplies. Sales were made from three display counters by the flight school dispatchers.

Flight training lost money each year.

[2]A tie-down is an area of asphalt or concrete with ropes where an aircraft is parked by tying it down to prevent it from rolling away or from sustaining wind damage. It is the aviation equivalent of a parking lot.

[3]FAA regulations require a certified instructor to check each student's competence prior to recommendation for the FAA flight examination.

AVIONICS

A single-person activity conducted by Leon Praxis. Leon was a college-trained electronics technician whose interests were in repairing radios and electronic navigational equipment from 8 A.M. to 5 P.M.—when he left promptly for his non-job-related activities.

Aircraft Sales

Altex had been a Piper Aircraft dealer until two months before its sale. Bill Dickerson, unable to finance the number of aircraft Piper required to be carried in inventory, had lost the franchise. He fired his two salespeople and closed the department down.

Accounting

The Accounting Department was central to the company in two ways. First, it was located in a glass enclosed office in the center of the building [*Exhibit 3B*] where it could be seen by everyone and hence everyone could be seen.[4] The second part of its centrality was the role that its manager, Sarah Arthur, played in Altex. Sarah had worked for Bill Dickerson for some twenty years. Indeed, during his absences, which were frequent, Sarah managed the company. While her title was accountant, she had no accounting training of any kind and her idea of running the company was to be the central repository of all information. She received and opened all the mail—not just accounting-type mail—and she distributed it to the department heads as she saw fit. What she distributed, in Ted's words, ''was typically nothing. Bills would come and she would keep them; checks would appear and she would keep them; and at the end of the day, she would collect cash from all the departments and keep it.'' Sarah managed all the receivables and all the payables. All accounting information was hers and nothing left her office. The department managers knew nothing about the profitability of their operations. All they knew was that airplanes would fly and that Sarah Arthur would come around at the end of each day and collect their money. Then, occasionally, she would berate department managers for their high receivables. Of course, they had no idea how big their receivables were or who they represented; they would just ''be beaten over the head.'' Other times, mysteriously, suppliers would put the company C.O.D. and somebody would go to Sarah and say, ''I want C.O.D. money. I can't get janitorial supplies'' or ''I need cash because I can't get aircraft parts'' and she would say, ''Okay,'' and mysteriously, a week later they would go off C.O.D. As Ted described it:

> The management system that was in place when we bought the company was one woman who magically kept everything in her head. There was a limited and almost incomprehensible formal system. There were basic financial statements and a set of reports that were produced for Piper Aircraft and according to their specifications each month—but they helped Piper, not the management. We may have negotiated with Bill Dickerson but we were going to take over the management of the company from Sarah Arthur.

[4]By contrast, the Aircraft Sales Department was located, according to Ted, ''in an old dark office far away from the action.''

ASSUMING MANAGEMENT

The Roles of Ted and Frank

Frank and Ted took over the business not only as full and equal partners but as fast friends who understood one another. Frank assumed the Chairmanship, and turned his attention to specific and critical projects, the first being the re-establishment of aircraft sales—potentially a major profit area. Ted took the title of President and Chief Operating Officer and began to manage the rest of the business. As Ted said later:

> I knew Frank wouldn't be at my right side at every decision but I made sure that four times a day I could walk into his office and say, "Frank, I don't really know what I am doing," and he would pat me on the back—symbolically—and put my head in order.

Frank, in turn, depended on Ted for operational inputs and intellectual support. They both worked twelve-hour days, five days a week, with Ted, a bachelor, putting in ten to twelve hours each day on weekends, and Frank, a family man, three or four hours on Saturdays and often on Sundays as well.

Management and Control

Beyond the immediate cash crisis, Ted viewed his three most important tasks as:

1 Revamping the management of Altex Aviation;
2 Installing a control system that would
  a support the management,
  b provide information needed in order to make decisions (although the company wasn't large, it was rather complicated in terms of the businesses it was in),
3 Wresting *de facto* control of the company from Sarah Arthur promptly.

Frank and Ted believed that it was very important to provide an environment where the departmental managers could make correct decisions on their own. They themselves could not make all the decisions—they had neither the time nor the technical knowledge. As Ted put it:

> One of the things I was very concerned about was how to manage by providing an environment that encouraged the managers to make decisions the way I would want them made. That was very, very important to me. I wanted to provide a framework that didn't limit their actions but provided very fast feedback as to how they were doing and made it personally worthwhile to them to do the right thing. I spent a lot of time thinking about how to do that and it occurred to me that there were really two ways to do that. I recognize that there has to be the black hat and the white hat in any of these situations and so I decided to make the control system represent reality; my personal role would then be that of an emotional leader, as opposed to a task leader. I would let the control system be the task leader and then I could exert a more avuncular personal leadership.
>
> I also realized that I didn't have the time to train everyone in the management

approach we wanted to use at Altex. Nor did I have the guts to fire everyone and bring in new talent—and that wouldn't have been a good idea anyway. I also realized that unless the basic attitudes in the company were changed, we would never survive. To change attitudes, we needed to do a lot of educating and that would be my personal role. But if I was going to do that successfully, I couldn't at the same time be berating them about the receivables. It was necessary to take the nitty gritty daily tasks of banging people over the head and put them somewhere else. I didn't really feel that Frank should do that. So to provide this environment for them was very, very important.

To provide the environment for decentralized decision making, Ted began to implement a management control structure incorporating the following policies:

1 Profit centers would be established for each major activity. These profit centers would be combined where appropriate into departments.
2 Revenues and expenses would be identified by profit center and communicated to the profit center manager.
3 Departmental managers would be responsible for their profit centers and receive a bonus of 10% of their profit center profits after administrative allocation.
4 The profit center managers would have pricing authority for their products or services, both internally and externally. The Fuel Department manager could, and did, charge the Flight School the retail price for the fuel it used, whereas he charged the Service Department his cost for the oil it needed.
5 The profit center managers could buy products externally rather than internally if it was in their best interests to do so. The Flight School manager could, and did, have his aircraft repaired outside of Altex's shop when it was unable to fulfill his service needs.
6 The profit center managers could buy needed capital equipment and operating supplies on their own authority within established purchase order limits.
7 The profit center managers had the authority to hire, fire and administer the salary schedule in their departments quite independent of the rest of the company.

Ted recalled one of the first times decentralized authority was tested. It involved the purchase of capital equipment.

When we bought the company it had a mimeograph machine and an old, rotten, obsolete copier. They were under the control of Sarah Arthur and everyone who wanted a copy of anything had to go to Sarah, the Witch of the North, and plead—which was really an awful thing to do. I remember one day Will Leonard, the manager of the Fuel Department, said, "Can I get a Xerox machine?" I said, "Will, you can do anything you want within purchase order limitations." So he acquired the smallest Xerox machine made and let everyone in the company make copies, charging them 10¢ a copy. At the end of the month, he would present bills to every department for the copies they had made. He made money on his Xerox machine because everyone was scared to death to walk into the Accounting Department and face the Witch of the North. Here was a classic entrepreneurial example and it became almost a *cause celebre.* People were saying, "How did he get a Xerox machine? What right does he have to charge me for the Xerox machine?" I would say, "If you want a Xerox machine, you go get one." But there was one here at 10¢ a copy, and they realized they couldn't really afford a machine themselves. So they grumbled that Leonard had stolen the march on them.

Cash Management

CASH AND ACCOUNTS PAYABLE When Ted arrived at Altex on the first day of his ownership, he gathered up the checks Sarah had written and the accounts payable ledger cards, called in his departmental managers one by one and asked, "Who are your most important suppliers?" Then he looked at the ledger cards to see how old the balances were and called up each of the suppliers, saying, "I'm the new owner of Altex Aviation and I would like to come down and talk to you about our credit arrangements." Ted stated:

> Over the next six months, I got on good terms with the suppliers. I talked to them, took them out to lunch, and let them take me out to lunch. We paid them a little bit here and a little bit there and we stayed out of serious trouble.

A direct result of Ted's decision about accounts payable was that Sarah Arthur began to view her stay at Altex Aviation as being limited to the four-month transition period agreed upon in the purchase agreement. As it became clear that Ted was not going to let her make management decisions any more, her attitude changed. As Ted put it:

> She effectively said, "I will work from 11:00 A.M. to 2:00 P.M. every day. I will answer your questions and that is all." That was fine with me. I hired a new accounting clerk to be Sarah's assistant. She worked from eight in the morning until seven at night. I hired her; she worked for *me*; and when Sarah Arthur quietly packed up and left, after four months, the departure was easy.

CASH AND ACCOUNTS RECEIVABLE With the accounts payable crisis on the road to a solution, Ted turned his attention to cash inflow. In his words:

> My biggest worry was how to control cash. How was I going to provide a system that would motivate the departments to manage cash? The solution I came up with was to take the receivables and give them back to the departments. That was very controversial. Everybody in the whole company fought me on that. Frank didn't like it—I was totally alone. The reason they didn't like it had several aspects to it. First of all, the managers didn't understand it. They had never seen receivables, they didn't know what they were. They felt as though they were playing with dynamite. "Here they are but what am I to do with them?" Frank, on the other hand, was concerned that things would get totally out of control because our most important asset—our incoming cash flow—had suddenly been handed out to amateurs. Sarah Arthur may not have been perfect but she had a lot of experience.
>
> In the Fuel Department, I handed the receivables to the dispatcher, a twenty-year-old surfer who had dropped out of college after two years. In the Flight School, I also gave them to the dispatcher, a fifty-five-year-old, loyal employee. These were the only two departments with significant accounts receivable. In Service and Avionics, I gave them to the managers.
>
> Literally, one Saturday morning, I went to a stationery store and bought one of those opening metal folders and some ledger cards and I sat down in the accounting office while Sarah was not there. I transferred all the balances over to these ledger cards and physically presented them to the two dispatchers—the *de facto* departmental heads. Then I sat down and showed them how to use the forms for the correct week. So we started to collect data on the accounts receivable.

To motivate the department heads to manage their accounts receivable, Ted gave them credit-granting authority and the responsibility for collections. Since they were on a profit bonus, he also established the following charges against their departmental profits:

Receivables	60 days old or less	1% of the balance
Receivables	60–90 days old	3% of the balance
Receivables	90–120 days old	6% of the balance
Receivables	over 120 days old	Charged the unpaid balance to the profit center

CASH AND THE BANKS When Frank and Ted acquired Altex, they also acquired short-term bank notes payable of $60,000 from the Center National Bank, which had been outstanding for several years. Ted was concerned; if Center National Bank called the notes, it would put the company into bankruptcy. As Ted recalled:

> One of the first people I called after we bought the company was Harold Lattimer, the manager of the branch we did business with. I took him out to dinner and over dinner and a glass of wine, I told him about myself, what I was doing, my thoughts, and I said, "We have this problem of the $60,000 I owe you." He replied, "What do you want to do with it?" I said, "I would love to convert it to a 24-month note to get it out of the short-term category so as to increase our working capital to make us more attractive to our suppliers. That way we can get better terms from them." He looked at me and said, "Fine, I'll do it."
>
> Now at that point, he had made a gut decision based upon some vibrations. And I was so shocked, since I was prepared to negotiate with him, that I said to myself, "The basis upon which business is done, at least with this man, is total candor and honesty." So I started this program of giving the bank our internal financial reports every month along with a cover letter summarizing what I was doing. Hal's reaction was superb. He thought it was the greatest thing he'd seen. No customer had ever done that to him before, ever! The result was that whenever I went to him and said, "Hal, it looks as if I'm going to need $100,000 for 60 days," he would say, "Yes, I've been following it, I've been watching your receivables growing because of your extra business. I know a growing business needs money from time to time. It's no problem and I'll put the money in your account this afternoon." And we paid the loan off ahead of time.

The Accounting System

By the end of the second month, Altex was producing a profit and loss statement on the activities of each department. *Appendix A* shows the Profit Center Reports for the Fuel Department. Each department kept account of its own sales, receivables, inventories, expenses and, through the purchase order system, expenses initiated by the department.

In order to provide a predictable and simple method of cost allocation which still would be understood and "managed" by the department heads, Ted established an Administration Profit Center which paid taxes, borrowed money, and paid interest, utilities, bills and other general administrative expenses. The Administrative Department in turn levied a series of monthly charges to each department, as follows:

- Social Security taxes, health insurance, and other fringe benefits were charged to departments as a predetermined percentage of wages. Thus, when a manager took on a new employee, he or she knew that it would cost the department, say, 125% of the wage.
- Accounts receivable—a monthly charge based on the amount and age of the receivables (see above).
- Operating assets, including the Parts Department inventory and the Service Department's shop equipment, were charged to the departments using them on a predetermined percent of the asset's costs.
- Rent, fire and occupancy insurance, building maintenance and depreciation and other occupancy costs were charged as predetermined rental per square foot of floor or ramp space occupied.
- A predetermined percentage of sales which represented the cost of Ted's office and the Accounting Department.

As all the charges were predetermined, calculated and announced twice a year, the managers would control their expenses by managing their receivable balances, conserving on equipment purchases, and varying the square footage they occupied. There were never any unanticipated expenses and the charging rates were set for breakeven. As Ted put it:

> There was an interesting example of the effects of this system. Altex had a total of 5.2 acres of land, of which about 3 acres were tie-downs that accommodated approximately 60 aircraft. The Fuel Department always wanted more space because it meant that they could accommodate more transient aircraft. The Flight School always wanted more space to make it easier to manage their comings and goings. The Shop always wanted more space as a service and convenience to customers leaving or dropping off aircraft to be serviced.
>
> Before the departments were charged for the area they occupied, there was no way to intelligently resolve this conflict. Bill Dickerson or Sarah would have to make what was essentially an arbitrary decision. When we showed up, however, there was a definite price to be paid for demanding more space—and with the manager's bonus system, 10% of that price came right out of the manager's pocket.
>
> The result was that we had very few of these discussions that did not reach a "natural" compromise. And when, over time, each department truly needed more space and was more and more willing to pay the rent, we raised the rent until demand equaled supply. It was wonderful to see a free market in action!

The monthly financial statements given the Altex department managers are shown in *Exhibits 4* to *8*. These are the same reports Ted gave his banker. Although there is provision for including budget figures, no budgets were projected.

The Task Guidance System

As an aid towards educating departmental managers in the management of their operations, and to keep them aware of their activities, responsibilities, and results, Frank and Ted instituted a Daily Department Report (DDR). This required the departments to submit internally consistent operating and accounting information. Each department kept the customer ledger cards; Central Accounting kept only receivables control accounts which would balance to each department's detail. The managers would account for their daily activity in units and in dollars. As an example, the DDR for the Flight School is shown in *Exhibit 9*.

Flight School's DDR is prepared each morning by 11:00 A.M. and reports the activity of the preceding day. The first set of entries on the report details the sales made by the Flight Department by type of sale. The total represents all the revenue that should be credited to *SALES* [1].

The second set of numbers categorizes the flow of funds into the Flight Department by type—cash, credit-card slips, reductions in block accounts, or leaseback payments due.[5] The total of these funds is indicated by ''2'' on the DRR.

The final group of items details the direct costs incurred in the production of revenue. These were:

- The expenses incurred in utilizing leased training aircraft. These were, by contract, a fixed amount per actual hour of aircraft use.
- The wages due the flight instructors. These instructors were paid a contractual amount for each hour of instruction. If the flight student was charged $12.00 per instructional hour by Altex, Altex would then owe the instructor $8.00 for that hour.
- Cost of supplies—the direct cost of the items sold in the Pilot Shop.

The total [3] represented the direct costs of the Flight Department for that day.

Cash received in the mail and cash collected by the departments was deposited daily. Photocopies of the checks were given to the departments for identification of source and inclusion on their DDR's. Ted commented:

> We would deposit the check and send the photocopies around to the departments. Sometimes a check would come into Altex Aviation from someone and no one would know who it was. Sometimes it would take two or three weeks to find out what it was for. It was passed around the various departments but, in the meantime, we had the money. We couldn't account for it so we put it in a little suspense account. And interestingly enough, sometimes no-one accounted for it and it became administrative profit.
>
> The detail of charge slips, photocopies of checks, and physical currency would be attached to the DDR and by 11:00 A.M. each department would turn them into Accounting—with sales balanced against receipts, inventory against fuel flows, and receivables proven-out. There were still errors but they got corrected at the department level—and at least one department had to hire an additional person to do the DDR. The system left Accounting with a simple task. They had DDR's from each department but only one sales figure from each. Thus their postings were trivial. All they had to do was to post the DDR's and then worry about other corporate issues—taxes and that sort of thing. Thus we only needed one person in Accounting. And the detail was where it should be: in the departments where it could be used.

[5]A block account represents prepaid flying lessons or aircraft rental. Cash is received in advance and recorded as an accounts payable by Altex. The customer's flying activities are charged to this account as they occur. Altex leases most of its instructional aircraft from private owners. Altex contracts to pay them so much per hour of use of the aircraft. Some leases are ''wet'' and the aircraft owner furnishes the fuel; others are ''dry'' and Altex pays for the fuel it uses.

Similar systems were put in place for the Flight School, Service Department and Parts Department. In the latter, a physical card was maintained for each part in inventory. To purchase, the Parts Department would issue a PO. When the parts and invoice arrived, the inventory would be increased by its cost and a copy of the invoice sent to the Parts Department. They would update their card files with the units and the costs. Similarly, they would decrease them for sales made. At the end of each month, Accounting would balance its control account against the sum of the parts cards. In addition, each department would submit an aging of its accounts receivable and Accounting would compare it against their control. Ted commented:

> We balanced the aging provided by the department against the books in central accounting down to the penny. That gave us our basic control.

Aircraft Sales

While Ted was implementing the control system, educating the managers, dealing with the creditors, and establishing a better relationship with the bank, Frank was dealing with aircraft sales.

Frank began by re-establishing Altex's relationship with the Piper Aircraft Corporation. He convinced them that Altex was on its way to financial stability and could not only sell but could also inventory the requisite number of aircraft to maintain dealer status. Frank negotiated the terms with Piper, involving Ted only with Piper's reporting requirements.

A few years before, Altex had been the largest Piper dealer in the territory, so Piper was interested in the potential of the new management. Things went well until Piper brought up the subject of their standard accounting reports. Frank and Ted were willing to commit to purchase five aircraft in the first six months but balked at the standardized reporting requirements which Ted characterized as "factory-oriented." He stated:

> Basically, I wanted to be independent. The reports weren't all that onerous. It may have been childish, but it was partly the feeling, "I own this place and no one is going to tell me what to do." It was also partly a feeling that I wanted to establish an equal relationship with Piper. I did not want to come to them as a supplicant. For the past several years, Altex had always been begging Daddy Piper for handouts. I wanted to establish a relationship with them that was one of equals. "We have different jobs to do. You help me. I help you." So it was psychological, but also I didn't want to waste the time of my people on something that I did not think would be productive. I told Piper that they could have access to any of our reports that they wanted. I said, "Here are our forms. If there is any information that you would like that is not here, we would be happy to supply it, and if you want to transfer this information to a Piper form, enjoy. But we think all the information is here." They didn't like it but they bought it. I think Frank worked pretty hard on that one.

After obtaining the Piper franchise, Frank rehired the old salesmen but personally shepherded the first aircraft sales through. The first one was, in Frank's word, "memorable." He said:

> Our first sale was to a local Chevrolet dealer. He wanted to buy the aircraft but he wouldn't pay for it until it arrived at San Miguel. "In my business," he said, "you don't pay for a car until you see it." Now we had to pay for it when we picked it up at the factory so I asked Ted how we stood. He said, "We have enough money, although, if he doesn't pay for it, we won't make the next payroll. And we will be out $40,000 for however long it takes to get the airplane from Vero Beach to here. But I'm willing to do it. Go do whatever you have to do." So we did. I engaged the son of the aircraft salesman to fly the airplane. Unfortunately, there was horrible weather and that grounded him in Tuscaloosa, Alabama, for a week—thunderstorms and everything. I nearly lost my mind. I had committed every last cent the company had and it was sitting in Tuscaloosa. That's how tight things were.

PERSONAL MANAGEMENT

Facial Hair

In the second month of Ted and Frank's ownership, Will Leonard, the manager of the Fuel Department, resigned. There were two reasons. First, a local newpaper had written up Altex Aviation and the new ''boy-wonder owners'' in a way that seemed to disparage the former owner, a close friend of Will's. The second reason for Will's resignation had to do with Ted and Frank's philosophy of management. As Ted related it:

> One of the fuel drivers came to us about two weeks after we bought the company and said, "The former owner never let us wear mustaches or beards or anything like that. How do you guys feel about mustaches or beards?"
>
> Now there was a lot of feeling about facial hair and long hair during that period and the fuel drivers were in contact with the public. Frank and I wanted to say, "We agree with the former owners." But we were consistent Harvard Business School people and we said, "As long as it does not affect your work performance, you can do anything you want." As a result, beards start cropping up all over the place and the manager of the Fuel Department rightly felt that he had been undercut and he quit. We really blew that. We were dumb—just from pure inexperience, naivete. He was not that valuable but that is not the way to get rid of a man—forcing him to quit in a huff.

Management Style

In running the company, Ted took an active role both through long hours of planning and managing and also through learning and doing. He learned to fly and got a multi-engine commercial license, changed the oil in the shop, and worked on the engine. It was, as Ted said,

> . . . a part of the process of being an avuncular, emotional leader. In the first couple of years, I deliberately set out to make my role that of a teacher. The first thing I did in my office was to put up a blackboard and arrange the furniture so that there was a sofa facing the blackboard and a side chair canted towards the blackboard. My desk was at right angles to the blackboard—all of us could see it. When departmental managers would come to me with problems, rather than focusing on the problem, we would talk

about the process. I would say, "Where are your accounting data? Where are your profit center reports? What do your profit center reports tell you about this problem? What thought processes did you go through to extract information from the profit center reports that would help you solve this problem? What alternatives did you consider?" And I did this in a typical Socratic teaching process. Through Frank's and my personal involvement in the company, and through this teaching approach, we could not only obviate bankruptcy in three months (Frank's forecast), but we could rely on our managers and build for the future.

EXHIBIT 1
ALTEX AVIATION
Balance Sheets
(000's)

Assets	*8/26/71*[a]	*1/1/72*[b]	*Liabilities and Net Worth*	*8/26/71*	*1/1/72*
Cash and marketable securities	$ 8	$ 88	Accounts payable—trade	$ 62	$ 50
Accounts receivable	25	49	Accounts payable—Phillips Oil	112	116
Contracts receivable—current	51[c]	15	Contracts payable—current	31	33
Financing commissions due	20	20	Customer deposits	—	2
Receivables from officers & employees	68	—	Notes payable	88	31
Other receivables	14	—	Accrued expenses	32	35
Inventory			Deferred block time	5	4
Aircraft	33	103	Other current liabilities	2	2
Parts and flight supplies	50	45	Total current liabilities	332	273
Fuel	13	25	Contracts payable—long-term	41	90
Work in process	7	2	Long-term debt	424	34
Prepaid expenses	7	30	Total liabilities	797	397
Total current assets	296	377	Net worth	(17)	62
Fixed assets (net)	437	27	Total liabilities and net worth	$780	$459
Contracts receivable—long-term	—	26			
Investments	29	29			
Other	18	—			
Total assets	$780	$459			

[a]Fiscal year-end before purchase
[b]Just after purchase
[c]Not split out between current and long-term; no room on Piper aircraft form to do so.

EXHIBIT 2

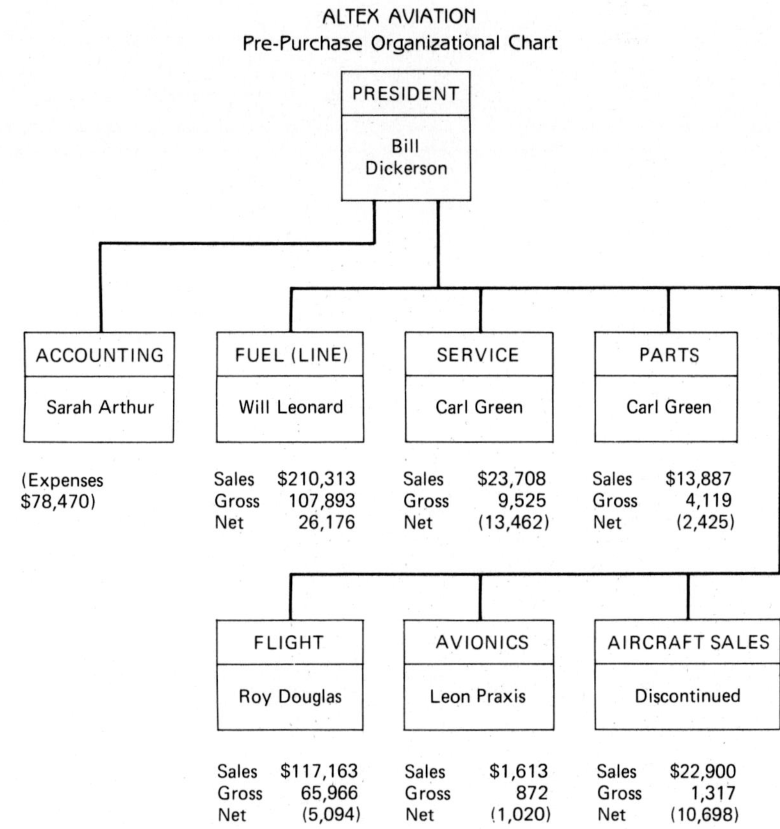

Sales, Gross Profit Margin, and Net Income were for the four months preceding purchase—September–December, 1971. Profit was calculated from the extant accounting system which fully allocated administrative costs. Comparable figures for the August 31, 1970, fiscal year were Sales $2,073,000, Gross $657,000, Net ($109,000).

EXHIBIT 3A

ALTEX AVIATION
Physical Facilities, 12/29/71.

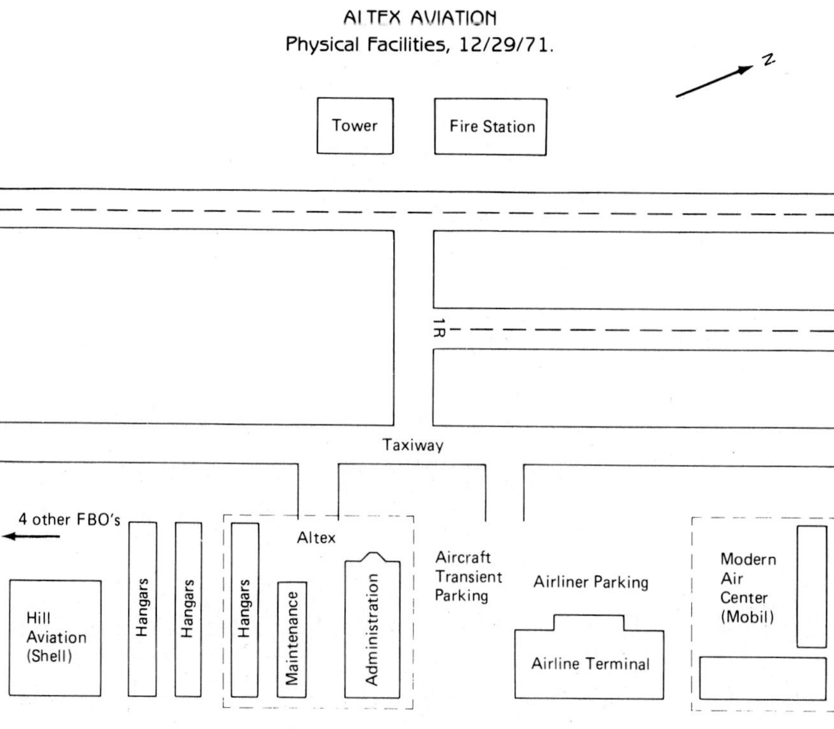

EXHIBIT 3B

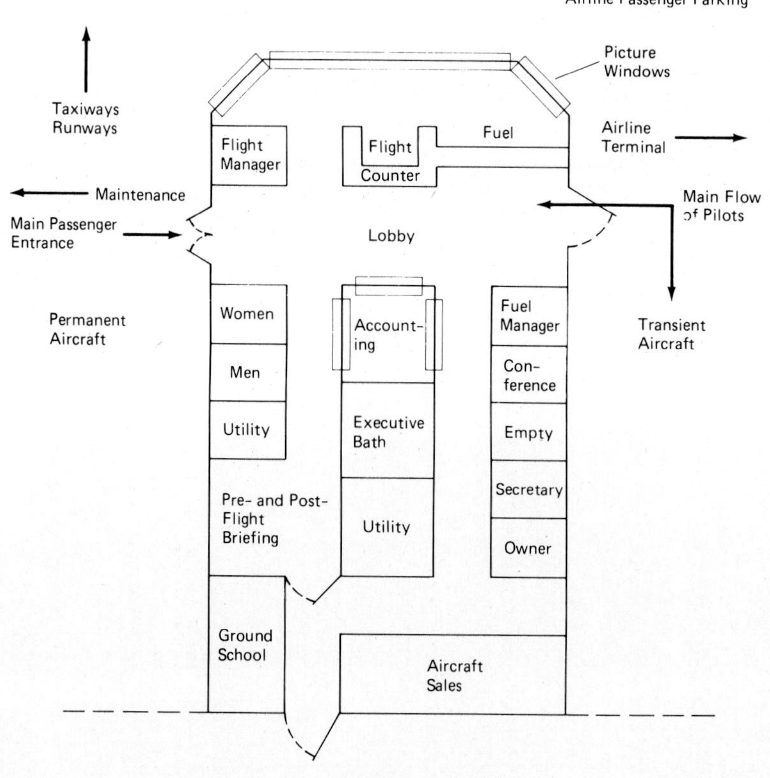

EXHIBIT 4

ALTEX AVIATION

Summary Balance Sheets (at end of month indicated)

(000's)

Assets	*Feb. 1972*	*May 1972*	*Aug. 1972*	*Liabilities and Net Worth*	*Feb. 1972*	*May 1972*	*Aug. 1972*
Cash and marketable securities	$ 67	$112	$129	Accounts payable—trade	$ 39	$ 38	$ 47
Accounts receivable	52	73	91	Accounts payable—Phillips Oil	103	102	52
Contracts receivable—current	35	4	4	Contracts payable—current	34	33	46
Finance accounts receivable	12	12	12	Customer deposits	1	4	1
Inventory				Notes payable	29	28	27
Aircraft	103	144	183	Accrued expenses	30	35	14
Parts	52	52	53	Deferred block time	14	21	20
Fuel	20	19	15	Total current liabilities	250	261	207
Work in process and other	0	2	8	Contracts payable—long-term	85	85	104
Prepaid expenses	30	32	39	Long-term debt	34	104	104
Total current assets	371	450	534	Total liabilities	369	450	415
Contracts receivable—long-term	5	4	3	Net worth	64	63	187
Fixed assets (net)	28	27	28	Total liabilities and net worth	$433	$513	$602
Investments and other	29	32	37				
Total assets	$433	$513	$602				

EXHIBIT 5

ALTEX AVIATION
Summary Monthly Income and Operating Statements (for period indicated)
(000's)

Corporate Summary	*Jan.–Feb. 1972*	*May 1972*	*August 1972*
Sales	$181	$164	$162
Cost of sales	146	133	113
Gross margin	35	31	49
Total expenses	24	28	29
Operating profit (Loss)	$ 11	$ 3	$ 20
Profit (Loss) by activity			
Parts	$ (1)	$ (2)	$ 1
Radio	(2)	—	—
Service	0	(2)	4
Flight school	3	4	3
Flight supplies	1	(1)	0
Tie-downs and hangars	(1)	0	0
Fuel hauling	(1)	1	2
Retail avgas	{ 0	(2)	2
Retail jet fuel		4	3
Wholesale fuel	4	7	11
Aircraft sales	3	(4)	(6)
Car rentals	(1)	—	—
Charter	—	0	2
Unrecovered administrative costs (+ = gain)	6	(2)	(2)
Total operating profit	$ 11	$ 3	$ 20
Other income	0	1	1
Extraordinary items	(22)	(8)	(2)
Total Income	$(11)	$ (4)	$ 19

[a]Merged with Service Dpt. in March 1972

EXHIBIT 6

ALTEX AVIATION

Summary Income Statements by Activity—January-February 1972

($000's)

	Parts	*Radio*	*Service*	*Flight School*	*Flight Supplies*	*Tie-Downs & Hangars*	*Fuel Hauling*	*Retail Fuel**	*Wholesale Fuel*	*Aircraft Sales*	*Car Rentals***
Sales	4.7	-0-	11.0	23.4	1.7	3.8	2.7	50.0	5.4	87.9	.7
Cost of product	3.4	1.4	2.3	10.4	***	1.2	1.6	37.5		76.4	.6
Salaries & commissions	.5		3.0	5.7	.3	.6	.6	5.8	.5	.5	.3
Payroll-related expenses	.1		.6	1.1		.3	.1	.6			
	4.0	1.4	5.9	17.2	.3	2.1	2.3	43.9	.5	76.9	.9
Gross margin	.7	(1.4)	5.1	6.2	1.4	1.7	.4	6.1	4.9	11.0	(.2)
Other expenses	1.6	.1	5.2	3.7	.8	2.7	1.6	6.0	.5	7.9	.2
Operating profit	(.9)	(1.5)	(.1)	2.5	.6	(1.0)	(1.2)	.1	4.4	3.1	(.4)

*Avgas and jet fuel

**Discontinued in April

***Could not be captured in January-February because inventory control system not yet in place

EXHIBIT 7

ALTEX AVIATION

Summary Income Statements by Activity—May 1972

($000's)

	Parts	Service	Flight School	Flight Supplies	Tie-Downs & Hangars	Fuel Hauling	Retail Avgas	Retail Jet Fuel	Wholesale Fuel	Aircraft Sales	Charter*
Sales	4.8	8.2	39.4	2.0	4.4	3.8	26.4	18.9	9.6	45.1	1.6
Cost of product	3.8	.1	20.5	1.4	1.3	.8	18.0	13.2		42.9**	1.4
Direct payroll	.7	4.3	8.9	.4	.4	.8	4.8	1.3	1.0		
Commissions							1.0				
Payroll-related expenses	.1	.7	1.1		.2	.6	.8	.2	.1		
	4.6	5.1	30.5	1.8	1.9	2.2	24.6	14.7	1.1	42.9	1.4
Gross margin	.2	3.1	8.9	.2	2.5	1.6	1.8	4.2	8.5	2.2	.2
Other expenses	1.7	4.8	5.8	.8	2.7	.5	4.4	.6	1.6	6.2	.1
Operating profit	(1.5)	(1.7)	4.1	(.6)	(.2)	1.1	(2.6)	3.6	6.9	(4.0)	.1

*Charter activity started in May

**Costs not broken out after March

EXHIBIT 8

ALTEX AVIATION

Summary Income Statements by Activity—August 1972

($000's)

	Parts	Service	Flight School	Flight Supplies	Tie-Downs & Hangars	Fuel Hauling	Retail Avgas	Retail Jet Fuel	Wholesale Fuel	Aircraft Sales	Charter
Sales	10.1	16.4	33.4	2.0	4.9	4.3	28.6	13.7	14.0	22.3	12.3
Cost of product	6.3	3.0	17.4	1.2	1.0	.8	20.2	11.7		19.9	6.8
Salaries & commissions	.6	4.0	7.5	.3	.6	.7	4.6	.8	1.0		.6
Payroll-related expenses	.1	.8	.8	.1	.2	.7	1.8				
	7.0	7.8	25.7	1.6	1.8	2.2	26.6	12.5	1.0	19.9	7.4
Gross margin	3.1	8.6	7.7	.4	3.1	2.1	2.0	1.2	13.0	2.4	4.9
Other expenses	2.0	4.7	5.2	.8	2.8	.4	(.2)*	(1.7)*	1.5	8.6	2.5
Operating profit	1.1	3.9	2.5	(.4)	.3	1.7	2.2	2.9	11.5	(6.2)	2.4

*Includes Inventory Adjustment (end of year)

EXHIBIT 9 Flight Department Daily Report

DATE:________

SALES

Primary Ground School	________	
Flight Instruction (Wait, Ground Training, Pre-Post)	________	
Leaseback Owner's Rental + Employees Rental .... (________) + Cost of Sales	________	
Rental (Solo)	________	
Flight Supplies and Over-Counter Sales (Retail Sales)	________	
Sales Tax Collected	________	
Check Rides	________	
Waiver	________	
Mexican Insurance	________	
Car Wash and Aircraft Wash + Tie-downs	________	
Student Tuition Refund Fee	________	
Enrollment Fee + X-C Dues	________	
Interest Service Charges	________	
TOTAL	$ ________	{1}

RECEIPTS

Cash or Checks	________	
Credit Card Payment...... (Phillips______)...... (AX______)	________	
Block Accounts and Block Account Supplies	________	
Altex Charges and Altex Charge Supplies	________	
Altex Charge and Visa	________	
Leaseback Refunds	________	
TOTAL	$ ________	{2}

DIRECT COST OF SALES

Leaseback Expenses	________	
Instructor Wages	________	
Cost of Supplies Sold Today	________	
TOTAL	$ ________	{3}

APPENDIX A
PROFIT CENTER REPORTS
Fuel Department
August 31, 1972

Profit Center Report, Fuel Hauling, August 1972

	This Month			2/1/72 to Date		
	Actual	*Budget*	*Variance*	*Actual*	*Budget*	*Variance*
Sales	4335	3700	635	24994		
Direct Payroll	736			5037		
Commissions						
Overtime & Vacations	568			2286		
Fringe at %	52			307		
Payroll Taxes	67			568		
Cost of Product	775			6470		
GROSS MARGIN	2137	1600	537	10326		
EXPENSES						
Supervisory Payroll						
Commissions						
Fringe at %						
Payroll Taxes						
Administrative	173			1197		
Use of Assets						
Advertising						
Demo. Flights[1]						
Bad Debts						
Telephone, etc.						
Donations, Dues, etc.						
Freight, Postage, etc.				397		
Insurance				35		
Inventory Adjustment						
Maintenance	139			1339		
Professional Services						
Rent	80			559		
Supplies				711		
Tie-Downs[6]						
Travel, Entertainment						
Utilities						
Vehicles						
Warranty						
Adjustments						

(continued)

APPENDIX A (Cont.)

Profit Center Report, Retail Avgas

	This Month			5/1/72 to Date		
	Actual	*Budget*	*Variance*	*Actual*	*Budget*	*Variance*
Cash O/S				45		
Misc.						
TOTAL EXPENSES	392	700	308	4283		
TOTAL PROFIT (LOSS)	1745	900	845	6043		
COST OF PRODUCT DETAIL						
Primary Cost[2]						
Freight, Delivery[3]						
Taxes[4]						
Other Costs						
______						
______						
______						
______						
LESS BREAKDOWN[5]						
______						
______						
______						
Sales	28623	N/A	N/A	105132		
Direct Payroll	4605			18610		
Commissions	910			3596		
Overtime & Vacations	229			481		
Fringe at %	252			921		
Payroll Taxes	403			1814		
Cost of Product	20234			72142		
GROSS MARGIN	1990			7568		
EXPENSES						
Supervisory Payroll	340			1813		
Commissions						
Fringe at %	10			55		
Payroll Taxes						
Administrative	1145			4971		
Use of Assets	376			1562		
Advertising						
Demo. Flights[1]						
Bad Debts						

(continued)

APPENDIX A (Cont.)

Profit Center Report, Retail Jet

	This Month			5/1/72 to Date		
	Actual	*Budget*	*Variance*	*Actual*	*Budget*	*Variance*
Telephone, etc. Donations, Dues, etc. Freight, Postage, etc.				 13		
Insurance Inventory Adjustment Maintenance	200 (3935) 278			401 (2042) 1064		
Professional Services Rent Supplies	 239 182			 596 977		
Tie-Downs[6] Travel, Entertainment Utilities						
Vehicles Warranty Adjustments	865			3999		
Cash O/S Misc. TOTAL EXPENSES	 68 (232)			 96 13505		
TOTAL PROFIT (LOSS)	2222			(5937)		
COST OF PRODUCT DETAIL Primary Cost[2] Freight, Delivery[3] Taxes[4]						
Other Costs ________ ________						
________ ________						
LESS BREAKDOWN[5] ________ ________ ________						
Sales	13,686			69,527		

(continued)

APPENDIX A (Cont.)

Profit Center Report, Retail Jet

	This Month			5/1/72 to Date		
	Actual	*Budget*	*Variance*	*Actual*	*Budget*	*Variance*
Direct Payroll	797			4,502		
Commissions		N/A				
Overtime & Vacations						
Fringe at %	12			160		
Payroll Taxes				290		
Cost of Product	11,688			51,659		
GROSS MARGIN	1,189			12,916		
EXPENSES						
Supervisory Payroll	341			1,796		
Commissions						
Fringe at %	10			54		
Payroll Taxes						
Administrative	547			3,339		
Use of Assets	41			41		
Advertising						
Demo. Flights[1]						
Bad Debts						
Telephone, etc.						
Donations, Dues, etc.						
Freight, Postage, etc.						
Insurance						
Inventory Adjustment	(3,079)			(5,125)		
Maintenance						
Professional Services						
Rent	200			800		
Supplies						
Tie-Downs[6]						
Travel, Entertainment						
Utilities						
Vehicles	215			360		
Warranty						
Adjustments						
Cash O/S				20		
Misc.	7			7		
TOTAL EXPENSES	(1,718)			1,702		

(continued)

APPENDIX A (Cont.)

Profit Center Report, Retail Jet

	This Month			5/1/72 to Date		
	Actual	*Budget*	*Variance*	*Actual*	*Budget*	*Variance*
TOTAL PROFIT (LOSS)	2,907			11,124		
COST OF PRODUCT DETAIL Primary Cost[2] Freight, Delivery[3] Taxes[4]						
Other Costs __________ __________						
__________ __________						
LESS BREAKDOWN[5] __________ __________ __________						
Sales	4923	4800	(123)	31984		
Direct Payroll Commissions Overtime & Vacations	649 134			3220 964		
Fringe at % Payroll Taxes Cost of Product	31 26 1000			175 297 8259		
GROSS MARGIN EXPENSES Supervisory Payroll Commissions Fringe at %	3083 85 3	3000	83	19,069 534 17		
Payroll Taxes Administrative Use of Assets	 197 			 1,587 		
Advertising Demo. Flights[1] Bad Debts						
Telephone, etc. Donations, Dues, etc. Freight, Postage, etc.						

(continued)

APPENDIX A (Cont.)

Profit Center Report, Tie-Downs and Hangars, August 1972

	This Month			2/1/72 to Date		
	Actual	*Budget*	*Variance*	*Actual*	*Budget*	*Variance*
Insurance						
Inventory Adjustment						
Maintenance						
Professional Services						
Rent	2467			17,269		
Supplies						
Tie-Downs[6]						
Travel, Entertainment						
Utilities						
Vehicles						
Warranty						
Adjustments						
Cash O/S						
Misc.						
TOTAL EXPENSES	2752	2800	48	19,407		
TOTAL PROFIT (LOSS)	331	200	131	(338)		
COST OF PRODUCT DETAIL						
Primary Cost[2]						
Freight, Delivery[3]						
Taxes[4]						
Other Costs						
LESS BREAKDOWN[5]						
Sales	13977	8200	(5777)	66746		
Direct Payroll	981			6716		
Commissions						
Overtime & Vacations						

(continued)

APPENDIX A (Cont.)

Profit Center Report, Wholesale Fuel, August 1972

•	This Month			2/1/72 to Date		
	Actual	*Budget*	*Variance*	*Actual*	*Budget*	*Variance*
Fringe at %	39			275		
Payroll Taxes						
Cost of Product				173		
GROSS MARGIN	12957	6900	6057	59582		
EXPENSES						
Supervisory Payroll	84			882		
Commissions						
Fringe at %	3			28		
Payroll Taxes						
Administrative	559			3278		
Use of Assets	124			622		
Advertising						
Demo. Flights[1]						
Bad Debts						
Telephone, etc.						
Donations, Dues, etc.						
Freight, Postage, etc.						
Insurance						
Inventory Adjustment				(231)		
Maintenance						
Professional Services						
Rent	159			1113		
Supplies						
Tie-Downs[6]						
Travel, Entertainment						
Utilities						
Vehicles	575			2875		
Warranty						
Adjustments						
Cash O/S						
Misc.						
TOTAL EXPENSES	1504	1500	(4)	(8567)		
TOTAL PROFIT (LOSS)	11453	5400	6053	51015		

(*continued*)

APPENDIX A (Cont.)

Profit Center Report, Wholesale Fuel, August 1972

	This Month			2/1/72 to Date		
	Actual	Budget	Variance	Actual	Budget	Variance
COST OF PRODUCT DETAIL Primary Cost[2] Freight, Delivery[3] Taxes[4]						
Other Costs ________ ________						
________ ________						
LESS BREAKDOWN[5] ________ ________ ________						

Breakdown of Administrative Charges, Wholesale Fuel August 1972

		Rate	Charge
Total Direct Payroll (incl. comm., overtime etc.)	$______ ×	______ % =	$ ________
Total Supervisory Payroll	$______ ×	______ % =	$ ________
	TOTAL.		$ ________

Breakdown of Charges for Use of Assets

Item	Amount	Rate	Charge
Accounts Receivable (less than 60 days)	$ ______	× 1.0% =	$ ________
Accounts Receivable (60–90 days)	$ ______	× 3.0% =	$ ________
Accounts Receivable (over 90 days)	$ ______	× 6.0% =	$ ________
Inventory	$ 8257	× 1.5% =	$ 124
Market Value of Physical Assets Used			
________	$ ______	× 1.5% =	$ ________
________	$ ______	× 1.5% =	$ ________
________	$ ______	× 1.5% =	$ ________
________	$ ______	× 1.5% =	$ ________
________	$ ______	× 1.5% =	$ ________
________	$ ______	× 1.5% =	$ ________
TOTAL			$ ________

1. For use by any department that uses flight school planes for demonstration or promotional purposes. This amount is the same as if a customer rented one of our aircraft and is credited to flight school sales.
2. Primary cost is:
   Parts: Invoice cost of parts sold
   Service: Transfer cost of parts used or installed
   Flight: Cost of leasebacks
   Fuel: Cost of fuel and oil
   Sales: Cost of aircraft
3. All freight and delivery charges are added to the inventory cost of products and become an expense when the product is sold. For the fuel dept., PUC rates are used.
4. This includes all taxes that we must pay for the products used, primarily excise taxes. These taxes are carried in inventory and are expensed when the product is sold.
5. Each department head can specify how he wants his sales broken down. This subcategory should be used for different activities that are not sufficiently separable to warrant becoming a separate profit center. For example, service might be subdivided into flat rate sales versus time and material sales. The flight school department might wish to separate instruction from charter.
6. This is a charge for aircraft under your control that used tie-down space and appears as part of the revenue of the tie-down department.

Breakdown of Administrative Charges, Retail Avgas August 1972

		Rate		Charge
Total Direct Payroll (incl. comm., overtime etc.)	$______	× ______	% =	$ ______
Total Supervisory Payroll	$______	× ______	% =	$ ______
	TOTAL.			$ ______

Breakdown of Charges for Use of Assets

Item	Amount	Rate	Charge
Accounts Receivable (less than 60 days)	$ 6111	× 1.0% =	$ 61
Accounts Receivable (60–90 days)	$ 1903	× 3.0% =	$ 57
Accounts Receivable (over 90 days)	$ 1032	× 6.0% =	$ 62
Inventory	$ 9187	× 1.5% =	$ 138
Market Value of Physical Assets Used			
______	$ 3902	× 1.5% =	$ 58
______	$ ______	× 1.5% =	$ ______
______	$ ______	× 1.5% =	$ ______
______	$ ______	× 1.5% =	$ ______
______	$ ______	× 1.5% =	$ ______
______	$ ______	× 1.5% =	$ ______
TOTAL			$ 376

1. For use by any department that uses flight school planes for demonstration or promotional purposes. This amount is the same as if a customer rented one of our aircraft and is credited to flight school sales.
2. Primary cost is:
   Parts: Invoice cost of parts sold
   Service: Transfer cost of parts used or installed
   Flight: Cost of leasebacks
   Fuel: Cost of fuel and oil
   Sales: Cost of aircraft
3. All freight and delivery charges are added to the inventory cost of products and become an expense when the product is sold. For the fuel dept., PUC rates are used.
4. This includes all taxes that we must pay for the products used, primarily excise taxes. These taxes are carried in inventory and are expensed when the product is sold.
5. Each department head can specify how he wants his sales broken down. This subcategory should be used for different activities that are not sufficiently separable to warrant becoming a separate profit center. For example, service might be subdivided into flat rate sales versus time and material sales. The flight school department might wish to separate instruction from charter.
6. This is a charge for aircraft under your control that used tie-down space and appears as part of the revenue of the tie-down department.

Breakdown of Administrative Charges, Retail Jet August 1972

			Rate		*Charge*
Total Direct Payroll (incl. comm., overtime etc.)	$______	×	______ %	=	$ ______
Total Supervisory Payroll	$______	×	______ %	=	$ ______
	TOTAL.				$ ______

Breakdown of Charges for Use of Assets

Item	*Amount*	*Rate*	*Charge*
Accounts Receivable (less than 60 days)	$ ______	× 1.0% =	$ ______
Accounts Receivable (60–90 days)	$ ______	× 3.0% =	$ ______
Accounts Receivable (over 90 days)	$ ______	× 6.0% =	$ ______
Inventory	$ 2752	× 1.5% =	$ 41
Market Value of Physical Assets Used			
______	$ ______	× 1.5% =	$ ______
______	$ ______	× 1.5% =	$ ______
______	$ ______	× 1.5% =	$ ______
______	$ ______	× 1.5% =	$ ______
______	$ ______	× 1.5% =	$ ______
______	$ ______	× 1.5% =	$ ______
TOTAL			$ 41

1. For use by any department that uses flight school planes for demonstration or promotional purposes. This amount is the same as if a customer rented one of our aircraft and is credited to flight school sales.
2. Primary cost is:
   Parts: Invoice cost of parts sold
   Service: Transfer cost of parts used or installed
   Flight: Cost of leasebacks
   Fuel: Cost of fuel and oil
   Sales: Cost of aircraft
3. All freight and delivery charges are added to the inventory cost of products and become an expense when the product is sold. For the fuel dept., PUC rates are used.
4. This includes all taxes that we must pay for the products used, primarily excise taxes. These taxes are carried in inventory and are expensed when the product is sold.
5. Each department head can specify how he wants his sales broken down. This subcategory should be used for different activities that are not sufficiently separable to warrant becoming a separate profit center. For example, service might be subdivided into flat rate sales versus time and material sales. The flight school department might wish to separate instruction from charter.
6. This is a charge for aircraft under your control that used tie-down space and appears as part of the revenue of the tie-down department.

MARK WHITCOMB

Mark Whitcomb had been at Harkon Inc. for six months as a senior executive with substantial organizational and fiduciary responsibilities. Today Mr. Whitcomb had a visitor, Mr. Greylock.

Greylock's visit had been a matter of some concern for Whitcomb for the ten days since the appointment had been made, but things seemed to be going smoothly.

"I know other areas of the organization have personnel problems, but I have my finger on it here," Whitcomb said. "I really know my people and what bothers them."

As Whitcomb and Greylock entered the foyer they passed an older, distinguished-looking man, Harry Winslow, who had been with Harkon for many years.

"Hello Harry! How's the wife?" Whitcomb called out in a friendly way.

"Still dead, sir," was Harry's reply.

This case was prepared by Assistant Professor Kenneth J. Hatten as a basis for class discussion rather than to illustrate either effective or ineffective handling of an administrative situation.

HASKET COMPUTER SERVICES

On May 14, 1976, Brian F. Hasket, President of Hasket Computer Services, a Boston-based company, and Tarkington Meagan, President of Building Corporate Growth, Inc., well-known management consultants, walked into Hasket's office. Mr. Hasket hurriedly made a few requests of his secretary.

"Would you move back my four afternoon appointments by an hour and tell Bob [Mr. Robert Michaels, Director of Personnel and Communications, Hasket Computer Services] I'd like to talk to him at about 1:30. I'd also like to see the past quarter's files on Region II. And, oh yes, would you call Mather [Mr. Mather Heaton, a director of the company] to get his initial reaction to our Detroit problem. Sorry, Jane, looks like it's going to be a busy day."

"Routine stuff," thought Jane as she started dialing the number of Hasket's first appointment, but not without taking notice of what had long been a trademark, Meagan's purple tie, this one being made of a Thai silk he had personally chosen in Bangkok.

"If you'll just pardon me a moment, Tark, while I glance through this mail," said Hasket while sitting at his round desk and motioning for Meagan to take a seat. "Certainly . . ." replied Meagan, who was cut off by Jane's calling from the outside office, "Urgent call from Detroit, Mr. Hasket!"

Tarkington Meagan enjoyed the view of Boston's recently rehabilitated wharf area as Hasket pushed the flashing button on his phone and continued reading some of the correspondence in his in-box while cradling the phone between his shoulder and ear.

"Hi Fred, how's it going? . . . I'm sorry to hear that, Fred. I know you and Charlie had some problems out there but I'm disappointed that we haven't had a chance to work them out before your decision. I really think you should reconsider. What's that?"

Fred Snurl, co-manager of Hasket's Detroit branch, had just announced that he and the other co-manager, Charlie Anders, were leaving Hasket to start their own company. He had asked Hasket if he had received "Alan's letter." As it turned out, Brian Hasket had just unfolded a letter from Alan Bamford, the Vice President in charge of Region II, when Fred Snurl called. Hasket was taken aback to see that the first paragraph said that Alan, too, was resigning. Having read the letter, Hasket handed it to Mr. Meagan. (See letter on page 696.)

A RECURRING PROBLEM

Brian Hasket was becoming used to having some of his best managers leave his company. In the last six weeks, four key men had left: Hal Linden, formerly Executive V. P., an old friend, and Brian Hasket's "right hand" in the company, and now Snurl, Anders and

This case was prepared by Mark T. Teagan, Research Assistant and Kenneth J. Hatten, Assistant Professor, as a basis for class discussion rather than to illustrate either effective or ineffective handling of an administrative situation.

ALAN A. BAMFORD
84 CHESTNUT DRIVE, BEVERLY, MASSACHUSETTS

May 14, 1976

Mr. Brian F. Hasket, President
Hasket Computer Services, Inc.
21 Wharf Street
Boston, Massachusetts 02108

Dear Brian:

It is with both excitement and regret that I submit my resignation; excitement for the new opportunities that await me and regret I could not satisfy my personal and financial goals at Hasket Computer Services.

The reasons are simple:

First, the financial rewards promised me in my earliest years at Hasket never materialized. The saying, "Those that make Hasket successful will be successful," has been qualified, restated and misrepresented over the years.

Earlier this year, you and I reviewed the matter and you clearly stated your position, that Hasket gave me no more nor any less than any other corporation. In my mind, an equal exchange system has never existed for me or anyone else at Hasket. I and many others have made you a millionaire and in return you gave me a job. I generated over $750,000 in profits, with Hasket providing little more than capital for start-up.

Secondly, your style of "one-man" management does not provide an environment which is conducive to personal growth. If ideas or decisions fail to match your own, if priorities set fail to match your priorities, you become uncooperative and impatient with others, feeling that you alone can save the company. Much of what you are trying to correct, you have created.

Thirdly, I'm tired of a lack of candor where problems in Services are openly discussed and criticized while failures in the President's office are casually ignored.

In summary, the causes of my concerns are your management style and the day-to-day decisions you have every right to make. It's your company and you can do what you damn well please. I understand that and I'm mature enough to know that I can't change it.

I would like to leave in the best of spirit and, before I go, resolve or turn over to my successor those key items pending in my branches. This should take two weeks at most. I look to May 31 as a last employment date and for reimbursement for three weeks of outstanding vacation.

I wish you well in your future endeavors and hope that you wish me well in mine.

Very truly yours,

Alan A. Bamford

Alan A. Bamford

Alan Bamford. In fact, Hasket had called Meagan, whose consulting company enjoyed an excellent international reputation, to get help on just this problem. Tark had been a classmate of Brian's at business school and offered to take on the task himself. When Brian had expressed his appreciation, Tarkington had replied, "What's a friend for? You helped me through the 'numbers' at school, Brian, and I have a debt to repay."

The Detroit phone call prompted Hasket to define his problem: "I saw these problems coming a few years ago. As a small company grows, and pressures increase, personnel problems inevitably come up. In addition, some people see themselves as contributing a lot to the company, and since this is a service company selling people's talent and knowledge, they figure why not go it alone and take the full profit. They overlook the corporate support for their activities. Another part of it is that some of these guys are thirty-five or forty-five and having to adjust for the first time to the fact that their options in life are limited.

"I may have mishandled some of these problems, but I'd like to know what to do now because I see Hasket Computer Services growing for the next few years. Additional growth could lead to another organizational shakeup. If I can learn what I did right and what I did wrong, I should have a better batting average next time."

"I see . . ." replied Meagan.

After lightly tapping his pen on Hasket's desk, Meagan continued, "Brian, let me tell you what I'd like to do. When you called you said, 'Pull no punches.' I intend to comply. What you just said is your story. I want to hear from some other witnesses. There are three groups of people I'd like to meet: some who have stayed, some who have left, and a couple of members of your board. That should do for an initial cut. I'm interested in the company's top management. Can you suggest some names?"

The names Mr. Hasket suggested are listed in *Exhibit 1.*

THE COMPANY

Hasket was a computer services company providing software services to commercial, financial, industrial, and municipal clients. Before founding the business, Brian Hasket had been in marketing with IBM's Data Processing Division for six years; prior to that he had been employed as a staff consultant by Arthur D. Little. Having long desired his own business and preferring to remain in New England, he founded the business in December 1965, with "an office and a telephone." IBM had just announced its Model 360 computer.

Hasket had felt that users of the new computer would need assistance in applying it to their specific needs. According to one Hasket executive:

> Brian marketed, then hired people to do the job while he marketed some more so he could hire still more people. The people Hasket hired normally had one to three years in the data processing (DP) business. They were technicians who were "personable" and able to sell. People came to Hasket because the growing small company excited them and because they could get more exposure to DP there than at one user's DP center. Also, "Good people attracted good people."

By the time Hasket incorporated in 1970, the company had 4 offices in the 3 southern New England states, 114 professional employees and approximately 125 clients, the largest 5 of which accounted for approximately 44% of revenues. In 1970, substantially all of Hasket's clients were in New England, 70% in the Greater Boston area.

During Hasket Services' twelve-year life, user organizations had expanded their in-house capability so that, to remain viable, Hasket had to develop new capabilities and applications for its skills, as well as maintain its old capabilities. Among the services which Hasket had developed was a user-controlled time-shared data base system whereby, rather than having separate and often duplicate data bases for different functions or divisions, a client could have large central files of data, any item of which could be accessed almost immediately. Currently, Brian Hasket was particularly interested in developing new applications for a concept known as ''Productivity Management,'' initially developed in response to his own company's problems and his belief that many of his clients were using their computer resource at only 60 to 80% capacity. Productivity management comprised six basic operating rules for project management. Steps in the process included 1) job specification; 2) the evaluation and selection of personnel; 3) rules for precise cost estimating; 4) progress measurement; and 5) provisions for project modification.

An important part of productivity management was the ''Eighty-Hour Rule,'' laid down by Mr. Hasket, to curtail time and cost overruns due to misestimates of the status of programming in development projects—the most common cause of system implementation delays. Essentially, the rule stated that every task in a project could be broken down to a work unit requiring no more than eighty hours to complete. Every week in the course of a project, each task was reported as either done or not done, thereby elimating subjective judgments of the percentage completion. The rule not only facilitated precise week-by-week progress reporting, but it assured management that each small subunit of work was properly sequenced from the outset. Mr. Hasket felt that productivity management represented a new way of controlling the total performance of an information system at every level in an organization.

Facilities management was another service Hasket provided. Under contract, Hasket would manage the day-to-day operations of a client's computer system.

The increasing importance and costs of the services Hasket and its competitors provided had led client companies to apply more stringent criteria when selecting a computer services contractor. Users were increasingly insisting on fixed-schedule fixed-price bids, demanding evidence of relevant past experience and proof of staffing depth; there was often a *de facto* prerequisite of a prior working relationship with the vendor. Fortunately, throughout its history, about 70% of Hasket's revenues were repeat business, and much of the rest came from the references these satisfied customers provided. To maintain these relationships, several officers and employees had primary marketing responsibilities. Hasket did not advertise.

As Hasket's reputation had grown, it had landed joint venture contracts with mainframe suppliers including, in 1972, an unprecedented contract with IBM to develop an on-line teleprocessing system for a large Midwestern account. These and other contracts led Hasket to expand its services, then its facilities, beyond New England. By 1973, over

one-half of its revenues came from outside Massachusetts; by 1976, it had ten offices

including those located in New York, Philadelphia and Detroit. Among its more than 150 clients were Aetna, Boise-Casacade, Dunkin' Donuts, Exxon, General Dynamics, S. S. Kresge, the State of Rhode Island, State Street Bank and Warner-Lambert.

In 1976, Brian Hasket was actively seeking acquisitions but, although the company had considered several candidates over the years, it had consummated only two—*Unidata* (1970), an EDP consultant to universities; and *Medical Information Systems* (MIS), (1974), a New York supplier of hospital information services. MIS represented a further expansion into health care by Hasket, which was becoming a large factor in that business in the Northeast.

Brian Hasket explained why Hasket Services had been able to survive while many of its competitors had failed:

> We have always done what we said we'd do. Companies with their own computers contract us because of Hasket's experience. We've been there before; we've lived through the same problems with other clients. A top-flight user might develop five different information systems in a year whereas we're involved in close to a hundred.
>
> Essentially, I guess you would say, that, for the services we provide, we're further down the experience curve. Therefore, it's less expensive for clients to pay us our costs plus a profit than it is for them to do the job themselves.
>
> Hasket Services has to know more about the operations and use of computers than the clients it seeks to serve. Of course, in-house staffs are constantly becoming more sophisticated and we have to be at least one step ahead of them. There's no way around it; this is a tough business.

Exhibit 2 contains Hasket's financial statements.

ORGANIZATION

Hasket Services had developed in five stages (see *Exhibit 3*).

1. During the early years, the people Brian Hasket hired reported directly to him.
2. As the company grew, Hasket hired a respected friend, Hal Linden, to supervise the firm's marketing and to oversee the managers of the newly-created branches.
3. As the branches grew larger and became too complex for one person to manage, a new position, systems manager, was created to split the responsibilities of branch management. The branch manager was responsible for marketing and the administration of the branch office, while the systems manager handled all projects.
4. As the number of branches expanded, the corporate headquarters' responsibility for overseeing their operations had been split into two regions. Hal Linden was in charge of Region I and Alan Bamford, whom Linden had hired earlier as a branch manager, was in charge of Region II.
5. Ed Johnson, the new Vice President in charge of Services, was in the process of implementing a new area management concept. The branches were grouped into three areas, each of which would be presided over by an area manager who reported to Johnson. Under Johnson's scheme, a successful branch could evolve into a new area.

MARKETING

Marketing consisted of maintaining contacts with present and former clients and seeking new business, particularly at new locations, through referrals and cold calling. One branch manager described the process:

> On the first call you tell them who you are and try to establish credibility. You try to get a feel for their needs. The most important thing is to arrange for a call-back or a visit—to get your foot in the proverbial door.
>
> The follow-up can vary. Sometimes a company might be ready to buy some DP services when you arrive on the scene. In other cases, it is a long selling process—six months to a year—which necessitates extensive social contact. That's the major advantage of the branch structure; Hasket people become part of the community.

Hasket's managers had to be sensitive to market trends. Trend-setters were IBM, a few big clients, professional journals, and the government. The government was considered innovative since it had both the resources to pay for the development of new techniques and the need for them.

PERSONNEL

A major problem for service companies like Hasket was keeping its people as productive as possible. Hasket planned on 80% billing of available man-hours. The other 20% was consumed by unassigned time, holidays, overruns, and items such as educational programs. Brian Hasket considered 80% a respectable average in the context of the industry's norms, and he was proud that only once, in late 1971, had business conditions caused him to lay people off. Mr. Hasket felt it was bad business and morally irresponsible to hire people for just one job and lay them off when the job was completed.

Hasket's manpower planning was based on a six- to eight-week rolling forecast and a one-year plan. It was an iterative process insofar as forecast and plan were revised as market conditions evolved. It was, by its nature, never totally successful. In the words of one manager, "You always need something—business or people."

The management of individual projects varied. On routine two- or three-man projects, the personnel were merely dispatched. On nonroutine or larger projects, branch management would appoint a project manager. The project manager would be the firm's surrogate on the job. The branch manager would oversee the project; he and the project manager would work out its design and plan its implementation. (Corporate management would get involved in particularly large and important projects.) The people on the team were usually specialists, and task-oriented. They rarely knew the overall "concept" behind the project.

There was no dollar threshold over which a project had to be approved by corporate headquarters, although all fixed price contracts had to be signed by Vice President Johnson. Fixed price contracts were considered one of Hasket's major marketing tools; they accounted for approximately 50% of the company's revenues. Most companies emphasized "time and materials" contracts.

Mr. Robert Michaels, Director of Personnel and Communications, described the career paths employees might aspire to:

> A person might come in as a programmer for one to three years. Then he might become a systems designer for one or two years. He then has a critical decision—to pursue a management position or to develop further expertise as a technician in, say, a given application or industry area. At that point it is hard to straddle the line. If he chooses management he will aspire to become a project manager. After doing that for some time, he might become a marketing manager or a systems manager. A problem, until now, with the area manager concept, was that there was really nothing feasible after that step—you could continue to be a marketing or systems manager or go elsewhere. An organization should offer its people a view of at least two steps up, but we had difficulty providing these middle managers even one.

FIELD WORK

While driving his metallic grey Mercedes 600SEL along Massachusetts Avenue past the Massachusetts Institute of Technology in Cambridge, Meagan recalled that he had spent little time in this part of town during his undergraduate days. "Just as well," he thought to himself as he dodged a pothole in Central Square. However, Meagan was enjoying himself. It was a welcome respite to being in the office or on the road. He parked near MIT's Sloan School of Management and walked into Computex, Inc.

Meagan asked for Mr. Segreto, who, before joining Computex, had been a branch manager at Hasket's.

Bernie Segreto was personable and appeared to be in his thirties. He had prepared an outline of some of the salient points he had thought of in relation to Hasket Services. Meagan opened his thin cordovan-colored leather briefcase. The following conversation ensued.

Tarkington Meagan: What do you think are the basic causes of the problems at Hasket?

Bernie Segreto: Many of the problems—the turnover, the flat revenues and profits—are due to a classic case of entrepreneurial ego. Past a certain stage a manager has to delegate, but Brian couldn't do it.

Brian is controls-oriented; he'd be perfect for a large organization in that respect. But, because *he thought* he had the company so well controlled, he thought people were dispensable. The truth is, despite the controls, he doesn't delegate well. He can theorize and he is articulate, but he's weak in selecting people and in day-to-day management.

T. M.: Why is that?

B. S.: His liking for abstraction may interfere with his understanding of people. Most people thought Hal was weak at organization and numbers—which is part of the reason Brian's confidence in him declined—but great with people. I don't know about the first part but the second part's true. And it was Hal who brought in Bamford, who was good at numbers and organization and who, therefore, served as an excellent complement to Hal.

I think Brian is risk-averse, or put another way, tight as hell, a classic Yankee. That's another reason he doesn't invest internally. His own record in acquisition isn't good; he's acquired few companies and they haven't performed well. MIS hadn't made its first big sale when I left and we'd had it for about a year. But I have to admit I'm a bit biased there; I wanted to manage MIS—it could have been exciting.

T. M.: Do you think some of these problems have been rectified? Brian hired Ed Johnson.

B. S.: I haven't met Ed Johnson, but from what I've heard, the things he's doing now were recommended over a year ago. It sounds like he has influence with Brian, now, and that Brian is giving him leeway. But I'm afraid that the people who've tended to remain at Hasket are 'yes' men. Johnson may be different; the chemistry may be right. It will be interesting to see what leverage he has with Brian a year from now.

T. M.: What was the ''atmosphere'' at Hasket before you left?

B. S.: People in the field felt the success of the branch operations was entirely due to them. The clients buy individuals as well as the company—though the bigger the job, the more important the company image is.

Just about everyone who's left has made out better in money. However, I must add that I think every one of them would admit that Brian Hasket taught them a lot about business and control systems; he just overdid the controls. In six months some of those who left have had twenty people working for them.

T. M.: What caused the turnover?

B. S.: The turnover involved people who'd been there a long time. Bamford left in frustration over not getting his bonus plan across. The saying, ''Those who make Hasket successful will be successful'' was not true. I hope for Brian's sake he doesn't use it again.

Of course it depends on how you define success. Some people, particularly Bamford, were angry when Brian became a multimillionaire. No one else came even close to that. When you go from nothing to great success you should take someone with you.

People in the field feel that they are paid OK but they think they can do better elsewhere. Hasket paid himself $40,000 which meant there was a ceiling for the rest of us. That stuck in our craws. He's not as concerned with money as most people and he overlooks other people's concern for it.

T. M.: Did it make any difference when Hasket went public?[1]

B. S.: That had a lot to do with its compensation policy. Before going public, Brian began to cut compensation to make profits look better. For instance, he rammed through a more restrictive stock and bonus plan. Of course, it's tough running a publicly-held service company. Perhaps that's why accounting and law firms are partnerships. Brian is concerned about his shareholders first—I think he feels concerned about the stock's performance—and his employment second. I feel that if he took care of his employees, the rest would take care of itself.

[1]Hasket went public at $10.50 in 1970. In May, 1976, it was selling at about $3.25. During 1974, the stock had sold for a few cents less than $1.00 on some occasions.

T. M.: Are you bitter about your experience at Hasket?

B. S.: I'm more disappointed than bitter. I put some good years into that company; it could have been a good career situation. I wish him well but I think he's got problems which the current boom in the DP business is masking.

T. M.: Would you elaborate on that?

B. S.: Sure. In the DP industry, independent vendors like Hasket can sell to client DP managers or to final users. DP managers want "power" and so use outside services for menial tasks, keeping feasibility studies and major systems analysis and design for themselves.

Final users, on the other hand, like to use outside firms for feasibility and systems studies, design and implementation. This business requires a sales force with background business as well as DP; so you have up-front costs, expensive people and a longer selling process. But it's like a capital investment.

Performing routine jobs for DP managers is a low-margin proposition. For example, a DP manager might send out a proposal to five firms which he thinks are qualified. The deciding factor will be price. It's a classic application of Economics I theory: Selling an undifferentiated product in a competitive market means small profit margins.

Contrast that to selling a new system to a final user, a line manager, for example. It's like defining the specs for a government contract and then getting the contract because, having defined the specs, you're obviously the only one qualified to implement them. This is differentiated stuff and it's where the profit margins are. Hasket has been going after the routine stuff and it shows in his low and flat profits over the past few years. I wrote a memo about a year ago describing all this. Of course, it went unheeded.

T. M.: Has Hasket always been in the low-margin end of the business?

B. S.: No. When Hasket was primarily a New England firm, it had an Industrial and Technical Support Group. This consisted of experts in various industry groups like manufacturing and engineering, and experts in computers. The group solved business problems for users. It was creative and landed lucrative contracts. But, as Hasket expanded, many of these people were promoted to branch managers. Unfortunately, Brian didn't replace them and the group ceased to exist.

Another example is data base systems. Hasket had a strong position in that market, probably the best in the United States around 1970. Even now it's among the very best, but Brian won't capitalize on it. He never advertised it or pushed it. Again, he won't risk up-front funds to get some high-margin things going.

Facilities management is another case. Hasket had one of the first facilities management contracts in the country in 1970, with a company called Nobel Shoes. It had great potential for leverage but it got in trouble. Brian put in his worst people rather than investing in high-powered people to make the thing fly.

At one point Hasket was dominant in Boston; there wasn't even a distant second. But that's not true anymore for the reasons I mentioned above.

T. M.: How did this policy affect you in the branches?

B. S.: By the time I left, the branch managers couldn't breathe. For example, we couldn't hire a hot-shot who might cost quite a bit but who might be quite capable of producing lucrative contracts within six months. There was an intense pressure to meet budget—that was another reason we sold to DP managers rather than final users. The problem was, Brian wanted to keep his quarterly statements looking good. This led to some risk aversion in the branches as well. For instance, why should a branch manager risk the up-front costs of pursuing a complex data base contract when the costs would show on his expenses and might lead to his falling short of his profit goal—especially since there was no extra bonus for the extra profit the contract might generate?[2]

One last example of the whole complex of products Brian has failed to push is productivity management. It's a great idea, but Brian isn't leveraging it; he's not letting people know he has it through advertising or extensive education programs. Everyone in the business says they're qualified, concerned, etc.. But with something like productivity management or the data base thing, you can differentiate yourself.

THE SECOND INTERVIEW: MATHER HEATON, A DIRECTOR

Hoping to get a balanced overview of the company's top management, Mr. Meagan next arranged to visit one of its directors, Mather Heaton, a partner in one of the city's leading law firms. From his car phone, Meagan called his office to check on a new contract he hoped this company would land with a leading oil company. It had. He parked and proceeded directly to Heaton's office which was across the street from his own in Boston's financial district.

Heaton greeted Meagan and they got down to business.

Tarkington Meagan: How would you characterize Brian's management style?

Mather Heaton: Brian's is a personal style. He's deeply concerned about people and what motivates them. He feels it on a one-to-one basis. He's more of a modern man than I; he feels that love makes the world go 'round and that people respond to it. He tries to force them to look at their own hearts. I don't think this philosophy reflects reality. For instance, his concern with people sometimes makes him unwilling to do what must be done: fire people, make adjustments and all that.

He's a peculiar blend of hard-sell salesman and sentimentalist. He could do much better if he were a pure capitalist chasing money. He's too concerned with people and spends too long massaging a problem rather than just doing it—like installing this new bonus system. He hasn't got the killer instinct with human problems—he doesn't go for the jugular. He's also not as concerned with money and power as most people. He prefers to ski and be with his kids and all that. Overall, I'd say Brian is the most underpaid entrepreneur I know.

T. M.: How did Hal Linden fit into the company?

M. H.: Linden's joining the company very early led to his being in top management whereas he should have been, say, a branch manager. In top management he was out of his league in temperament and, perhaps, in management ability. He also got stale. In a sense he was in competition with Brian but it was Brian's company. I don't really know

[2]Until May 1976, Hasket paid its branch managers a fixed $5,000 bonus when they met or exceeded budget.

about Bamford and the other managers, but if Brian hadn't been so hung up on Linden, he could have done better with the other management problems he's had.

T. M.: Do you think the firm's staff turnover problem is related to its compensation policy?

M. H.: It's partly the industry—it has a high turnover anyway—and partly Hasket. Those who complained about the discrepancy in compensation between Brian and themselves—well, it's appropriate that they go; there's only one entrepreneur in a company. It's true that many service companies are partnerships, but a company like Hasket is fragile. Hasket's word must stick and the "partners" would feel lousy about it.

This whole compensation issue has been treated as being more complex than it is. You should merely reward people for a good job and fire them for a consistently bad one. People at Hasket are good at what they do, which makes them feel smarter than they really are. And when they stay with the company they gain seniority and pay without necessarily increasing their contribution to profit.

With Johnson's new pay scheme, perhaps these men can earn a $10,000 bonus and make $30,000 to $40,000. But it really isn't that much, especially compared to what a hot-shot out of business school who goes to Wall Street should be able to make within five years—$100,000 or more. My point is, these men, smart as they are, don't have really big aspirations; $50,000 would probably be enough for them and, of course, that's small money for really ambitious people.

These guys at the branches are salesmen and DP experts but it's a low-paying industry. It's true that the combination of technical and sales skills is a rare combination in an individual but there are a lot of these people here.

T. M.: How do you react to the statement that Hasket is a body shop and that is why it's had flat earnings?

M. H.: All these computer service companies claim to offer quality service; it's a matter of merchandising. You have to convince the buyer that you are the one that should provide it. This business about the body shop—I don't know. I don't think it's Hasket's job to be at the forefront of the industry. His job is to make money. This business about being at the forefront and offering a creative service is good PR both for the employees and for clients, but that's all. The recent flat earnings are probably due to the nature of business in general during recent years. Brian's agonizing over the Linden thing probably hurt as well.

THE THIRD MAN: THE PERSONNEL DIRECTOR

Upon entering Hasket Services' building, Tarkington Meagan was shown to the office of Robert Michaels, Director of Personnel.[3] After exchanging some minor pleasantries,

[3]Michaels had joined Hasket Computer Services in March, 1969, as a member of Management Services, a ten-man consulting group which he built and which designed computer systems. In 1972, he took charge of the group and, in 1975, became Corporate Systems Manager. He became Director of Personnel shortly after Linden resigned in March 1976.

Meagan proceeded to ask his basic questions. While the issues seemed to be fundamental, the difficulty was in melding several points of view into ''not truth necessarily, but the closest approximation to it one can get.'' As Alfred North Whitehead once said, ''There are no whole truths; just half-truths.''

T. M.: Were you surprised that Bamford left?

R. M.: No. He was bitter that Brian had become a millionaire while he was still getting a salary, a reasonably good one, but nothing like Brian's total compensation.

T. M.: And Hal?

R. M.: We were shocked when Hal left. People had always thought of Hasket and Linden as synonymous. It was like the divorce of a happily married couple. Hal's reasons for leaving weren't as clear. It probably was due to the change in the company. Hal's strength was personal, one-to-one; he was charismatic. But, profits have been flat for three or four years; it's hard to say whether Linden and Bamford were responsible (each managed half the branches), or whether it was the economy.

There had been a lot of tension during the past year and the high turnover reflected it,[4] especially in Services which is the heart of the company. They felt the pressure when they fell below target. When you can't grow and you have to scramble to keep what you have, each person's problems feed the other's.

T. M.: Were there other reasons for it?

R. M.: Part of it was that everyone in the company was intelligent and able to understand the business. They were aggressive people who were convinced that the company's growth would benefit them. But when revenues and earnings went flat, many felt it was the end. However, many of these guys come in looking for experience; companies like Hasket offer them broad exposure. I bet 90% of our current staff have no intention of retiring from Hasket, and that 20% to 30% of them haven't met Brian.

The cast of characters who made Hasket a $5-million company may have been best for that job, but not for making the $5-million company into a $20-million organization. People here are given numbers—consecutively—when they're hired. And there used to be a subtle pride in having a low number, in being number six for example. But now probably only ten of the first hundred people are left.

People at Hasket get feedback from clients and internal management similar to the feedback an entrepreneur gets. This encourages some of them to go out on their own. Those who've started their own companies, and for whom the results are in, are doing OK in money and prestige. One is bordering on $1 million and others have eight or ten people working for them. And if they fail, they can get another job easily; it's much easier than, say, banking—just look at the ''help wanteds.''

Another factor is that many of these branch managers built large branch teams which were split when another branch was opened. They had to start all over again. To many people, this doesn't look like progress. Success is usually associated with size—with creating a 200-person operation rather than making an 8-man operation into a 20-man operation 10 times.

[4]Trade journals indicated that industry turnover averaged 30%–40%. Hasket had been at, or below, that range until late 1975 to early 1976, when turnover increased to around 60%.

Many people below branch-manager-level leave when the branch managers leave because they identify more with the branch than with the company. Sometimes they are invited to join their former boss in his new company. This branch identity has been quite strong since branches have been responsible for their own profit and loss and hiring. A while ago, we found that bidding, proposals, documentation and classifications for jobs were different at different branches; each manager saw himself as an entrepreneur with his own company and had his own system.

Another reason many guys left was that Hasket is a marketing-oriented company. The end of the line, as technical people saw it, was systems manager at a branch. We hate to see good people leave but the company takes it in stride now; we used to take it personally. You can't provide career growth for everyone unless you grow exponentially.

T. M.: Do you think you could have avoided this turnover?

R. M.: It's hard to say. I feel people are compensated well here—in dollars and stroking. But people in a small company often expect to participate financially and managerially in its growth in return for foregoing the perks of a large company. A large company buffers you against the environment whereas a small company doesn't. So these guys want a piece of the action.

We didn't give a premium for growth. A guy would get the same bonus if he beat his goals by $1 or by $50,000. Our new plan to pay a "percentage of profit over goal" remedies that shortcoming. The lack of a pension plan hasn't been a major factor—most of our people are under 40. For people like myself—there's only about 20 of us over 40—the pension question will become more important.

T. M.: Does Brian delegate effectively?

R. M.: It's probably tough for Brian to relinquish control. During good times he has given everyone a lot of rope but when unfavorable variances occur he gets back in. He works through the people who formally report to him and goes lower only if he's not satisfied; he doesn't bypass managers.

A FEW DAYS LATER: ONE MISS AND ONE HIT

Meagan next called Alan Bamford, the former Vice President who had resigned the day he was in Hasket's office. Although Hasket was suing Bamford for recruiting some of Hasket's employees, Bamford was courteous and said that he would be delighted to talk with Meagan. A day later, however, he called back, saying that his lawyer advised against it until the legal action was settled.

Meagan then visited John Waters, a director of the company and a senior lecturer at MIT's Sloan School. While driving along Memorial Drive toward the MIT turnoff, Meagan enjoyed the balmy day and was reminded, by the sailboats on the Charles River that, although his Pearson had been in the water for over three weeks at his family's summer home in Newport, RI, he hadn't made the time to use it. Having parked his car in the same pay lot he had used while visiting Computex, he walked through the MIT campus. His three-piece Saville Row suit and purple silk tie contrasted sharply with the denim which, he noted, seemed to be *de rigeur* among MIT students.

Meagan and Waters exchanged greetings and got down to business, Meagan leading off with a question about Hasket's management style. Waters replied:

John Waters: Hasket is bright, aggressive and analytical. He works on the numbers in planning and in control. He really analyzes variances that come up in reports. I think his recent problems are due partly to his compensation package. He hasn't thought the whole thing through. He doesn't have a feel for how important pay and bonuses are to his employees.

The branch managers see themselves as entrepreneurs. In this light, a salary plus fixed bonus isn't sufficient motivation. I thought Brian should have changed the pay scale. He claimed that for their abilities, his people were getting paid enough. I've told him, "Then you need better people." From my experience, firms similar to Hasket pay their top people more. Brian feels that if he paid more, say a $15,000 bonus potential, the costs would outweigh the benefits.

T. M.: How did Brian and Hal work together?

J. W.: Hal was an able guy and particularly personable. But he was not into planning and organization, which is one reason the company's market strategy has become more reactive than proactive. Hal was a good complement to Brian in the early days when things could be done on a one-to-one basis. But that style became less effective as the company became larger and more organized.

The rift between Hal and Brian didn't occur suddenly. It developed over two or three years. During that time, morale suffered. It was a tough problem for Brian. Hal had been a good friend. And, what do you do with a guy who helped you make the company but who no longer fits? All of us, Brian and the board, were slow in addressing the problem.

T. M.: Hasket replaced Hal with Ed Johnson. How does he fit?

J. W.: Johnson is close to Hasket in style. He's analytical and a planner who believes in a hands-off style. Johnson will be more gutsy in hiring and firing people. Hal saw the operation as a team. Ed sees it as a team with him as captain.

A FIFTH INTERVIEW

The next Monday morning, having parked his Turbo Carrera by Lewis Wharf, Meagan enjoyed the ambience of the harborfront area as he walked toward Hasket's corporate headquarters to meet Ed Johnson.[5] After exchanging greetings, the men walked to Johnson's office where Meagan immediately began asking about Hasket's recent and present problems. Johnson answered:

Ed Johnson: Of course, I wasn't here when the major turnover took place, but I've heard quite a bit about it. I had about fifty hours of interviews with Hasket before I took this job and I've heard a lot since then.

[5]Johnson, hired to take charge of Hasket Services Division, was a large man in his 40's. He came to Hasket after serving as Director of Marketing for Computer Corporation of America. Prior to that, he had been in charge of a $3.5 million operation at Services Bureau Corporation while it was still owned by IBM.

It seems that Linden—and Bamford, once he was promoted to corporate headquarters from a branch where he'd done well—reached the limit of their abilities in this organization. Sometimes a person can go to another company and do the same job he's had difficulty with and do it well. I think a lot of this is a matter of perceptions which get built up through long-term interpersonal relationships. A person might have a problem and see himself, and feel he's seen, as incompetent.

It seems certain that Linden and Hasket came to distrust each other professionally. Hasket felt Linden was sitting on problems and not letting him know. Naturally, Hasket found out when the problem became critical—like a phone call from an angry client yelling about the job the company was doing. This led to Hasket giving Linden fewer responsibilities, which made Linden up-tight. Over time, two years or more, they became locked into their view of each other. Sometimes a showdown can be avoided, but here, the problem had been brewing too long.

T. M.: Why has the company survived?

E. J.: Part of Hasket's success is being able to stand behind its work. Continuing contracts give us stability. A lot of our competitors have been up and down in revenues and profits; the fluctuations we've had have been moderate. And, our branch structure helps. The branch structure is unique in the industry. Most similar firms work from a central location. The major strength of having branches is that their members can become part of the local business community, and people tend to give business to people they know particularly with a service business.

On the other side, the branch structure makes it difficult for us to perform large jobs. Although we have 300 employees, we have only 20 to 30 at any branch. We don't have large numbers of people to put on any new job. For instance, there's a \$3 million conversion job going on in Boston now. We weren't invited to bid on it because we lack a "national image." We couldn't do it anyway. We typically do one- to three-man projects.

T. M.: How do you see your job, Ed?

E. J.: My job is to give the company a strategic direction and to balance operations. I think this area manager concept I've introduced will help. In addition to providing new positions people can aspire to, the area concept will enable us to take on larger jobs by using people from contiguous branches.

Another weakness I'm trying to offset is the tendency of people at the branches to identify more with the branches than with the company. One thing I've done is to standardize methods of business. I'm also increasing our public relations effort, for example, getting articles on Hasket into *Computerworld*. Internally, I'm doing things like having a company newsletter.

For the company to grow it will have to change. Brian has to stay away from daily operations. He should be looking at acquisitions, public relations and high-level selling. Brian's good at selling, particularly to presidents of other organizations.

T. M.: What does the company need now?

E. J.: Structure. In the past we had entrepreneurial management and no systems. Then the company reached a stage which many service companies go through—traumatic change. This sort of transition will probably happen again at about $20 million because an area manager can handle about $2.5 million and an individual can handle only about six to eight people reporting to him. I can handle about eight area managers who could each handle about $2.5 million, i.e., $20 million. At that time we'll need restructuring again. When you restructure, people have to change or be replaced. That causes problems like the ones Hasket's just been through. We hope it will be less traumatic next time.

AT MEAGAN'S OFFICE: THE SIXTH INTERVIEW

While working on the last in a series of notes on ''Building Corporate Growth,'' to be used for promotional purposes, Meagan was notified by his secretary that Hal Linden had arrived. Linden, having other business in the same building, had decided to visit Meagan at this office. Meagan entered the oak panelled foyer where Mr. Linden was admiring his collection of French impressionist originals.

Linden turned and, after exchanging greetings, said, ''I'm particularly intrigued by this Degas. It's very different from his normal style, yet . . .''

''Yet it is a quintessential Degas,'' Meagan said, pleased that Linden had noticed. ''His themes are more of style and process than of content, and this painting, though little known, is one of his most successful efforts,'' he added.

As they entered Meagan's office, his secretary, Eve, a very sensible woman selected by Meagan's father, the founder of the firm, some years before his retirement, shook her head as though to express some dubiety. Once settled, Tarkington Meagan proceeded to ask Linden his version of recent events at Hasket.

Linden began:

Hal Linden: As a small company grows, the ego running it must change—from the ''I'' to ''we.'' Brian hasn't done this. Brian's spontaneous with his own ideas but needs documentation to react to others'. It's to the point that the people around him now won't get involved. For instance, productivity management is a good thing but the only reason it has support is because it is Brian's.

T. M.: What has this attitude done to the business?

H. L.: Hasket has excellent controls and probably does more planning than most small companies but we really haven't looked at the long term. We're not worried about what's happening in the market and we're deficient in some state-of-the-art things like minicomputers. As a result, the company is a body shop—well, not entirely, but it's doing mostly contract programming.

One reason is that many of the branch managers don't have the foresight to hire guys at $22,000 or $25,000 to get into new businesses. The company needs different levels of capability, that is, some higher billing rates—not margins. We have always worked on the same margins, but, of course, if you're billing a $25,000 guy and a $15,000 guy at the same percentage margin, the $25,000 guy will provide a bigger dollar contribution.

T. M.: How much effort did Brian put into operations when you were with Hasket?

H. L.: Quite a bit. The plus was that when he became involved, he became totally involved and less critical; the minus was that he'd sometimes create problems because he can be insensitive.

Brian hasn't been close to his employees recently. At one time I would have said he knew what motivated his people but now I don't think he does. You see, he's a complex thinker but a poor listener. Many people told me before I left that Brian would say that he wanted to discuss business with them, but that he would end up telling them about problems occurring because ''people'' had let him down.

T. M.: Hal, what was your real strength at Hasket?

H. L.: Operations, not staff work—that's not my forte. In fact, when Brian and I got together ten years ago he said he liked to make systems and then move on to something else; whereas I was good at marketing and operations. He thought we'd complement each other and make a good team. If we'd had controls staff, someone to enforce standards and plan, et cetera, it would have freed me up for operations.

T. M.: Were you comfortable with staff?

H. L.: It wasn't a matter of being comfortable. After all, I'd hired most of the people at the branches and had ramrodded Hasket's move to the branch structure. It wasn't a complicated thing to run and I felt I could run it better than anyone I knew. Part of the difference between Brian and me involved control. He worked through numbers. I worked through people. At the size the company is now, you need control systems, but I still feel it's a people business and you can't run it just by numbers. A turnover of even 30% is unacceptable.

T. M.: What really caused the rift between you and Brian?

H. L.: There probably was a bit of my not telling Brian about problems, but even as late as the spring of '75 he was saying, ''Hey, you worry about that.'' I felt it was my job to concentrate on operations, and Brian's to concentrate on the direction of the company.

Some problems should have been discussed with him, but, on the other hand, I solved a lot of problems without going through him. My intent was to solve problems, not hide them.

T. M.: What was the essence of your conflict with Brian?

H. L.: Well, like many others, I was becoming unhappy with the leadership of the business, with the direction it was taking. I was displeased by Brian's not fulfilling commitments to his top people. It became a philosophical difference—I honestly didn't agree with the way the company was being run and I no longer enjoyed the working relationship.

Some of the other people were bothered by Brian's philosophy about the branches and their size. He felt that they should be no larger than twenty to twenty-five people and over that they should be split. He felt at that size they'd be manageable and, over that, it'd be hard to motivate people through them. I disagreed with the policy; it didn't give branch managers anything to look forward to.

Brian didn't want these guys seeing themselves as managers. He saw them as salesmen. It seemed a negative rather than a positive view. And it became a de-motivator, especially when he fixed bonuses at $5,000. I don't know why he fixed the bonus—perhaps he was concerned they'd make too much. That was a key reason why the people in Detroit left. I think a different approach would have been able to lock these guys into Hasket—to motivate them to stay with the company.

T. M.: What's the answer?

H. L.: The problem is to figure what's going to keep good people in the company. It's a people-intensive business, so finding the right compensation packages need not be at the expense of profit. A highly turned-on company can be more profitable than any non-turned-on company.

Setting Up the Final Interview

Having talked to many of the principles involved in Hasket's recent problems, Meagan now wished to test Brian Hasket's initial reactions to some central issues. He, therefore, telephoned Hasket.

''Hello Brian,'' he said. ''I'm ready to get together on this.'' Hasket asked, ''What have you found out?'' Meagan laughed, and answered, ''You know consultants don't answer questions; we just ask them. Would you like to discuss it over dinner Tuesday night?'' ''Sounds fine.''

A MEETING OVER DINNER

Tark and Brian met at one of the city's finest restaurants where Brian ordered a Beaulieu Vineyard George de Latour wine. Upon testing it, Tarkington was pleasantly surprised.

''I've always had respect for this collection,'' he said, ''But I guess in the past I've mistaken its straightforward honesty for mere simplicity.''

''I've always liked it,'' said Brian, who then steered the conversation toward the subject of his company.

T. M.: I'd like you to respond to some of the issues that have come up. It will serve as feedback to you and will help me round out the several perspectives I've obtained. Do you want to make a statement ''in your defense'' before we begin?

B. H.: Naturally, Tarkington, I've made mistakes but the enthusiasm of being a small company has carried us through. I've had days, though, when I thought just one more thing gone wrong would do me in.

My biggest mistake has been not facing up to the management problems we've had in Services—the management there had reached its limits. Just look at their performance. [Mr. Hasket's notes have been summarized in *Exhibit 4*.]

T. M.: What is your management style, Brian?

B. H.: As problems developed, my image in the company and my day-to-day activity changed. I didn't like my style of management—pointing out faults rather than motivating. My preferred style is more positive. I used to tell people to work smarter rather than harder. But I've been tough lately.

T. M.: Are you tight in allocating time and money to new product ideas?

B. H.: I don't think so. The problem has been that people talk about new ideas but will not specifically commit themselves to implementing them.

Take data base, for instance. That was just one guy, Peter Denver, and he couldn't delegate. There's more than enough genius in the world; the problem is to reproduce its products in mass—that's the task of management. I think the higher you go in an organization, the more cerebral the thinking should be. Facilities management, productivity management, and industries groups were all my ideas but that's not because I won't accept other peoples'—the problem is that at lower levels they weren't cerebral enough. All these ideas should have flown, too, and probably would have, if I'd straightened out Services three years ago.

The problem was Hal, who had done an excellent job until then. He was great on a one-to-one basis but couldn't administer as things grew. Yet he wanted to retain all his authority. When I decided to divide Services into two regions with Hal and Alan Bamford each in charge of one region, Hal insisted that Alan report to him. I let it go the first year, but then I told Alan to report directly to me.

I really learned what was going on in August, 1973, when Hal went on vacation. It was then that I learned that we had several cost overruns giving us a loss exposure of $350,000. Naturally, I wanted a complete analysis of the overruns so that nothing of that magnitude could happen again. I said, "Hal, someone got killed on the highway and my purpose is not to be critical but to make sure you wear seat belts in the future." Hal was angry at Alan for telling me about the problems. He became secretive after that. Hal hadn't gotten the guys in the field to review projects, so he didn't know the nature of the problems himself.

My major disappointment with guys in the field is their lack of curiosity. When I visit a client and see a new piece of machinery, I always ask about it, where they got it, why they purchased it rather than a competitor's, what it does, et cetera. I feel we should try to learn from clients, as well as teach them. The guys in the field don't have this curiosity. They just want a package to market.

T. M.: Has your turnover been very high?

B. H.: Turnover in the DP business is high, tending to be higher in good times and less in bad times. In our early years, our turnover was less than the industry average and it's been about the same recently. Last year, the cause of the higher turnover was that our managers were becoming introspective—they had their own problems so they didn't stroke their people.

Much of the turnover we had last year was a result of the small difference between love and hate. A small company is a love affair. When things start going wrong, in some cases, the love is quickly transformed to hate.

T. M.: Brian, is the statement "Those who make Hasket successful will be successful," true?

B. H.: There's no doubt about it, that statement backfired. It is something I've said from the outset. In our second year we distributed 20% of the pretax profits. After we went public, things slowed down. What it takes to make someone "successful" is in the eyes of the beholder.

Bamford, for instance, knew that I owned about 66% of the company. He felt that he deserved to have a nest egg of some $250,000 to $500,000 because he had contributed profits. However, even before corporate overhead, he hadn't contributed anything like the $250,000 to $500,000 he felt he should have laid away. They say, "When I was at the _____ branch, I contributed $200,000," and I say, "It should have been $275,000 and what about corporate overhead. You haven't made a quarter-million dollar profit." And they say to themselves, "I can do this on my own." But when they try it, they learn it doesn't work out so well. They may be good center-fielders, but can they start a whole new team? I don't see the numbers on the balance sheet as mine, to do with what I want; I feel a responsibility to the shareholders and employees to use the assets those numbers describe in the best interests of the company.

T. M.: Compensation comes up again and again.

B. H.: Compensation wouldn't have been so important if we'd kept growing. Some of those who've left say that, having been as successful as I've been, I should have taken someone with me. I just point out that many of these guys who've complained about lack of compensation started at Hasket at $8,000 and left with compensation packages of $40,000 after only 6 or 7 years.

Tark, look at the performance and the salary histories of two of my branch managers. They're just the first two in the file and I think they're not exceptional. Aren't they personally successful? [The data Mr. Hasket referred to have been summarized in *Exhibit* 5.]

T. M.: How do their salaries compare with the industry's, Brian?

B. H.: "The figures say, OK, Tark. [See *Exhibit 6,* courtesy of Mr. Hasket.] Remember, when they leave, I've been able to hire their replacements for the same salary or less; we're doing OK according to the market."

T. M.: What about your fixed performance bonus?

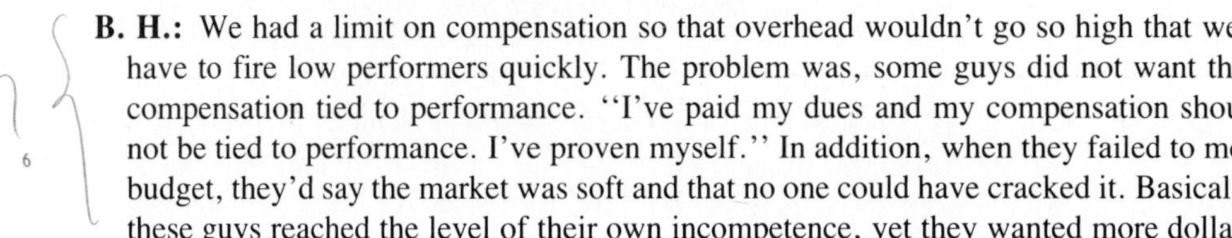

B. H.: We had a limit on compensation so that overhead wouldn't go so high that we'd have to fire low performers quickly. The problem was, some guys did not want their compensation tied to performance. "I've paid my dues and my compensation should not be tied to performance. I've proven myself." In addition, when they failed to meet budget, they'd say the market was soft and that no one could have cracked it. Basically, these guys reached the level of their own incompetence, yet they wanted more dollars.

T. M.: Could you separate personal performance from market performance?

B. H.: I could get a handle on whether it was the market or not by checking things like sales calls they made and the time sheets they submitted, usually late. When it came right down to it, some of them admitted it was them by saying, "Yeah, I've lost enthusiasm." The problem is, no one wants to admit they or their friends aren't successful or that they're being out-performed by a "kid who came in four years ago." This can be really tough for a thirty-five or forty-year-old guy who is reaching his limits.

T. M.: Do you deliver what you promise?

B. H.: I've been careful not to promise anything specific unless I know I can do it. I took 50,000 shares of my own stock and gave it to the 8 top managers. I was going to give them another 50,000 shares but I got only grief from my first donation.

Let me tell you what it was like, just how hard it was to link compensation to performance. Hal came in during 1972–73 asking me to approve 120% bonus for performance at 79% of budget. He said the guys were loyal and worked hard. His psychology was that a guy can't lose. I said that you have to forgo some security if you want to ''Shoot for the Roses''—roses have thorns. And, these guys weren't taking risks or forgoing perks by going with a small company. We have one of the best life insurance programs around. And, if Hasket folds, they can just get another job. What are they risking? The ''risks and lost perks'' argument is a rationalization.

I say, show me a company anywhere in the world where all the managers come out with $100,000 a year, plus a nest egg. I've made mistakes in my compensation policies, particularly in the fixed bonus area, but we're changing that. Overall, our compensation has been competitive.

This whole thing's been like having pimples; it's been a rite-of-passage into a larger company. If I had to do it over again, I'd emphasize performance. I'd say promotion doesn't guarantee success. I wouldn't say, ''Those who make Hasket successful will be successful.'' I would have a concrete compensation plan from day one.

T. M.: Delegation?

B. H.: I've delegated extensively. In the early days, we had no standards and little structure. As we grew, we found that guys in the field were making errors in things like pricing policy. We then started having someone at corporate headquarters sign all contracts; there was resentment about that but as you grow you need a different psychology and management style. Overall, I feel I've been *super-sensitive,* trying not to be the entrepreneur who can't delegate.''

T. M.: Why did you limit the number of people at a branch to twenty-five?

B. H.: Because I found that, over that size, facts and figures showed a deterioration in the performance. Just why, I'm not certain; perhaps people can't identify with an organizational unit when it gets larger than that. I agree that this branch-size policy frustrated our branch managers. I think this new area-manager structure will solve both problems. If a guy at a branch can say ''I want to hire a salesman and do more business than twenty-five men can take care of,'' we'll now make him a branch manager with the old branch and a small new branch under him. If he does this a third time he will become an area manager. So we will soon have a system under which both the branch-size and branch-manager motivation problems will be solved.

T. M.: Is Hasket a ''body shop''?

B. H.: We try to be distinctive in the marketplace and we don't want to be a body shop; this is important for our employees' self-image and for the marketing effort. Our greater-than-average use of fixed price contracts is part of our distinction. Doing what we'll say we'll do is another. In the early days, we did a lot of probing—facilities management, data base, that sort of thing—but none of these elevated us out of the body-shop category. To go beyond a body shop you need guys with pride in doing well, guys who'd rather be a Corporal in a commando unit than a Second Lieutenant in the regular army. There's a style, an aura to being part of a commando unit.

T. M.: Wouldn't that image be easier to create if you pushed higher-margin services?

B. H.: Our margins are good. Those who talk about getting higher margins overlook the fact that while you might be able to do so on the unique services and jobs for a short period, you have to look at the costs of subsequent unbilled time. We can create needs for our services only to a very limited extent. We are in a responding mode a good deal of the time, so it's hard to plan further than a year out.

Our strategy consists of doing business locally, in being part of the community. We're still the dominant factor in Boston and about 75% of our business is from former clients. We have never tried to be an industry leader. We respond to our client's needs with current technology.

T. M.: What keeps this company functioning?

B. H.: Two things. A need in the market place and—pardon me if this sounds a bit purple—a need in the hearts of young men. There are a lot of guys out there who want to make an imprint. In today's world, everything is larger than the individual, but at a small company like Hasket, someone is really counting on you. The reason some of these people left during this past year is that they weren't being taken care of—their managers were worried about their own problems.

Until last year, no one in the management ranks could say who their successor might be. The area concept will take care of that. Hal and the others weren't good managers in that sense.

WHAT IS A MANAGEMENT CONSULTANT PAID FOR?

While returning to his Louisburg Square townhouse, Tarkington Meagan thought about the report he would write for Hasket. "Children and fools speak true," John Lyly once said. Mused Tarkington, "I suppose it's appropriate that consultants be categorized with them." Tarkington felt that his people-oriented cases were always the most difficult. "It's like listening to a good debate; each side sounds convincing—until the other side speaks."

Having parked his Mercedes, Tarkington walked the cobblestone street to the brick sidewalk, his beige raincoat becoming visible under the turn-of-the-century-style streetlight, then melting into the darkness. The only sound was the muffled tones of his shoes on the damp bricks. A slight fog shrouded his lone figure as he turned toward his residence. He was thinking, "A good part of the answer lies, I think, in accurately defining the strategic significance of Hasket's compensation scheme and, more important, his overall attitude toward his managers. It's interesting that those who've left should have been so helpful."

EXHIBIT 1

HASKET COMPUTER SERVICES

Names of People Suggested for Mr. Meagan to Interview

Bernie Segreto	Former branch manager; left the company in early 1976.
Mather Heaton	A director of the company.
Robert Michaels	Director of Personnel and Communications.
Alan Bamford	Vice President, Region II; recently resigned.
John Waters	A director of the company.
Ed Johnson	Newly hired Vice President in charge of the Services Division.
Hal Linden	The former Executive Vice President and Hasket's number two man. Also a personal friend.

EXHIBIT 2

HASKET COMPUTER SERVICES

Financial Highlights

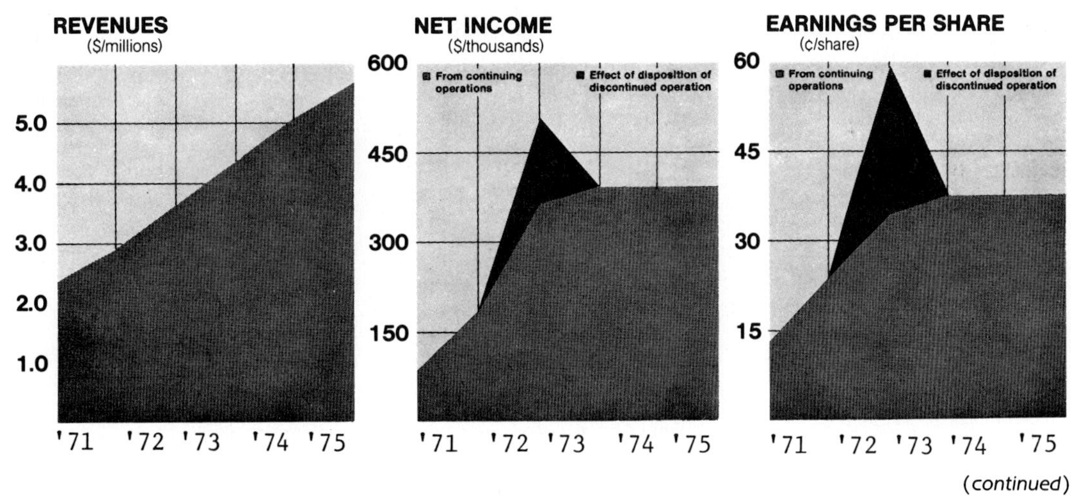

(continued)

EXHIBIT 2 (Cont.)

	1975	1974
Operations		
Revenues	$5,673,000	$5,149,000
Net income	355,000	357,000
Earnings per share	0.42	0.43
Financial		
Cash and investments	2,174,000	2,193,000
Accounts receivable	1,294,000	1,254,000
Current ratio	3.2-1	3.0-1
Total assets	4,639,000	4,550,000
Total liabilities	1,160,000	1,301,000
Retained earnings	2,349,000	2,095,000
Stockholders' equity	3,479,000	3,249,000
Other		
Book value per common share	4.16	3.87
Number of equivalent shares outstanding	839,000	839,000
Number of shareholders	475	517
Number of employees	250	210
Number of clients	170	159

Dividends	*1975*	*1974*
Per Share		
First Quarter	$.04	Special annual
Second Quarter	.04	dividends
Third Quarter	.04	of $.10
Fourth Quarter	—	per share
	$.12	$.10

Stock Prices	*1975*		*1974*	
Quarter	*High*	*Low*	*High*	*Low*
First	$3.75	$2.13	$2.50	$1.00
Second	3.50	3.00	3.25	1.88
Third	3.00	2.13	2.50	1.75
Fourth	3.13	2.13	3.00	1.75

Traded
Boston Stock Exchange

MANAGEMENT'S ANALYSIS OF SUMMARY OF OPERATIONS

1975 vs. 1974

A full-year operation of IIT Division in 1975 versus nine months of 1974 reflected an overall increase in revenues of 10%.

Directly related expenses increased 5%. Effective utilization of manpower during the major part of the year contributed to this moderate increase in related expenses.

Continuing inflation in all aspects of operation and cost of maintaining a qualified staff are major contributors to a 16% increase in general and administrative expenses.

Other income/expense primarily consists of interest income. A lower average investment base in 1975 and a decrease of short-term rates at the end of 1974 which continued throughout 1975 reflected lower interest income.

Higher effective tax rate of 41% in 1975 versus 36% in 1974 reflects less investment tax credit available in 1975.

1974 vs. 1973

Revenue increased 17% reflecting an increasing demand for the Company's services. The growth in our newer offices and the acquisition of innovations in Technology (IIT), a New York based company specializing in providing computer capability to small and medium size hospitals, contributed to this growth.

Directly related expenses increased 25%. In addition to normal inflation and proportionate increases due to volume, a decision was made to retain qualified technical personnel in the first quarter for increased business activity during the rest of the year.

General and administrative expenses increased 22% primarily due to inflation and maintaining qualified management personnel to support a higher revenue.

Other income/expense primarily consists of interest income. Increases in short-term investment base and interest rates accounted for increase in income.

Provision for income taxes in 1974 resulted in an effective tax rate of 36% versus 49% in 1973. Major contributions to this favorable percentage in 1974 were in the increase of nontaxable interest and investment tax credits.

Five-year Financial Review (all dollar figures in thousands except amounts per share)

	1975	*1974*	*1973*	*1972*	*1971*
Revenues	$5,673	$5,149	$4,401	$3,736	$2,835
Directly Related Expense	3,013	2,882	2,306	1,956	1,508
General and Administrative Expense	2,184	1,884	1,544	1,154	977
Other Income/Expense, Net	126	174	157	72	78
Income Before Provision for Income Taxes	602	557	708	698	428
Provision for Income Taxes	247	200	347	348	210
Income from Continuing Operations	355	357	361	350	218
Discontinued Operations and Related Gain	—	—	—	194	(32)
NET INCOME	$ 355	$ 357	$ 361	$ 544	$ 186
Earnings per Common and Common Equivalent Share					
Continuing Operations	.42	.43	.43	.42	.26
Discontinued Operations and Related Gain				.23	(.04
NET INCOME	$ .42	$ .43	$ .43	$ .65	$ .22

EXHIBIT 2 (Cont.)

Balance Sheet, December 31, 1975 and 1974

ASSETS

	1975	1974
Current		
Cash	$ 44,636	$ 60,845
Short-term investments, at cost (which approximates market) plus accrued interest	2,129,061	2,132,318
Accounts receivable:		
Trade	1,266,774	1,171,180
Other	27,796	82,692
Current portion of notes receivable	80,000	376,925
Prepaid expenses	51,293	52,270
Total current assets	3,599,560	3,876,230
Property and Equipment, at Cost		
Building	43,879	43,879
Equipment and furniture	689,226	421,508
Leasehold improvements	75,975	71,410
	809,080	536,797
Less accumulated depreciation and amortization	156,315	101,577
	652,765	435,220
Purchased software at cost, net of amortization of $67,383 and $28,881, respectively	125,128	163,630
Note receivable	98,728	—
Other assets at cost, net of amortization of $35,581 and $11,974, respectively	162,823	75,274
	$4,639,004	$4,550,354

LIABILITIES

	1975	1974
Current		
Accounts payable	$ 296,811	$ 140,095
Accrued expenses and other liabilities	94,755	153,269
Notes payable	47,111	195,067
Federal and state income taxes payable	69,687	81,653
Deferred federal and state income taxes	613,955	710,955
Total current liabilities	1,122,319	1,281,039
Deferred federal and state income taxes	38,000	20,000
Commitments		
STOCKHOLDERS' EQUITY		
Common stock, par value 10¢, authorized 2,500,000 shares, issued 851,124 in 1975 and 846,114 in 1974	85,112	84,611
Additional paid-in capital	1,087,817	1,075,839
Retained earnings	2,348,563	2,094,553
Less treasury stock at cost, 14,361 shares in 1975 and 4,511 in 1974	(42,807)	(5,688)
Total stockholders' equity	3,478,685	3,249,315
	$4,639,004	$4,550,354

(*continued*)

EXHIBIT 2 (Cont.)

Statement of Income and Retained Earnings for the Years Ended December 31

INCOME

	1975	1974
Revenue from services	$5,673,074	$5,149,495
Salaries, wages and other direct costs	3,013,029	2,882,222
General and administrative expenses	2,183,601	1,884,268
Total costs and expenses	5,196,630	4,766,490
Income from operations	476,444	383,005
Interest on temporary investments	126,018	161,552
Other income (expense), net	(744)	12,069
Income before provision for income taxes	601,718	556,626
Provision for income taxes		
State	63,000	47,000
Federal	184,000	153,000
	247,000	200,000
Net income	354,718	356,626
Retained earnings at beginning of year	2,094,553	1,821,486
Dividends paid ($.12 and $.10 per share, respectively)	(100,708)	(83,559)
Retained earnings at end of year	$2,348,563	$2,094,553
Net income per share	$.42	$.43

Statement of Additional Paid-In Capital for the Years Ended December 31

ADDITIONAL PAID-IN CAPITAL

	1975	1974
Balance at beginning of year	$1,075,839	$1,068,079
Excess of proceeds over par value from sale of stock under Employee Stock Purchase Plan	11,978	7,760
	$1,087,817	$1,075,839

Statement of Changes in Financial Position for the Years Ended December 31

CHANGES IN FINANCIAL POSITION

	1975	1974
Sources of Working Capital		
Net Income	$ 354,718	$ 356,626
Charges not requiring working capital:		
Depreciation	85,742	42,557
Amortization	62,109	53,277
Equity in loss of affiliated company	21,000	—
Deferred taxes	18,000	(85,000)
Provided from operations	541,569	367,460
Disposition of property	12,234	4,068
Stock sold pursuant to Employee Stock Purchase Plan	12,479	8,147
Issuance of treasury stock	2,378	8,949
Notes receivable from sale of computer equipment, long-term	—	341,509
Total	568,660	730,133
Uses of Working Capital		
Dividends	100,708	83,559
Investment in affiliated company	122,258	—
Purchase of computer software	—	192,511
Purchase of fixed assets	315,521	366,100
Notes receivable	98,728	—
Purchase of treasury stock	39,497	5,455
Cash surrender value and other assets	9,898	71,026
	686,610	718,651
(Decrease) Increase in working capital	$(117,950)	$ 11,482
Changes in Working Capital		
Cash	$ (16,209)	$ 10,573
Short-term investments	(3,257)	462,194
Accounts receivable, trade and other	40,698	(141,570)
Notes receivable	(296,925)	(31,610)
Prepaid expenses	(977)	43,084
Accounts payable	(156,716)	(115,885)
Accrued expenses and other liabilities	58,514	(76,543)
Notes payable	147,956	(195,067)
Federal and state income taxes	11,966	78,619
Deferred federal and state income taxes	97,000	(22,313)
(Decrease) Increase in working capital	$(117,950)	$ 11,482

EXHIBIT 3 Organizational Developments at Hasket Computer Services, Inc. (*Service Division*)

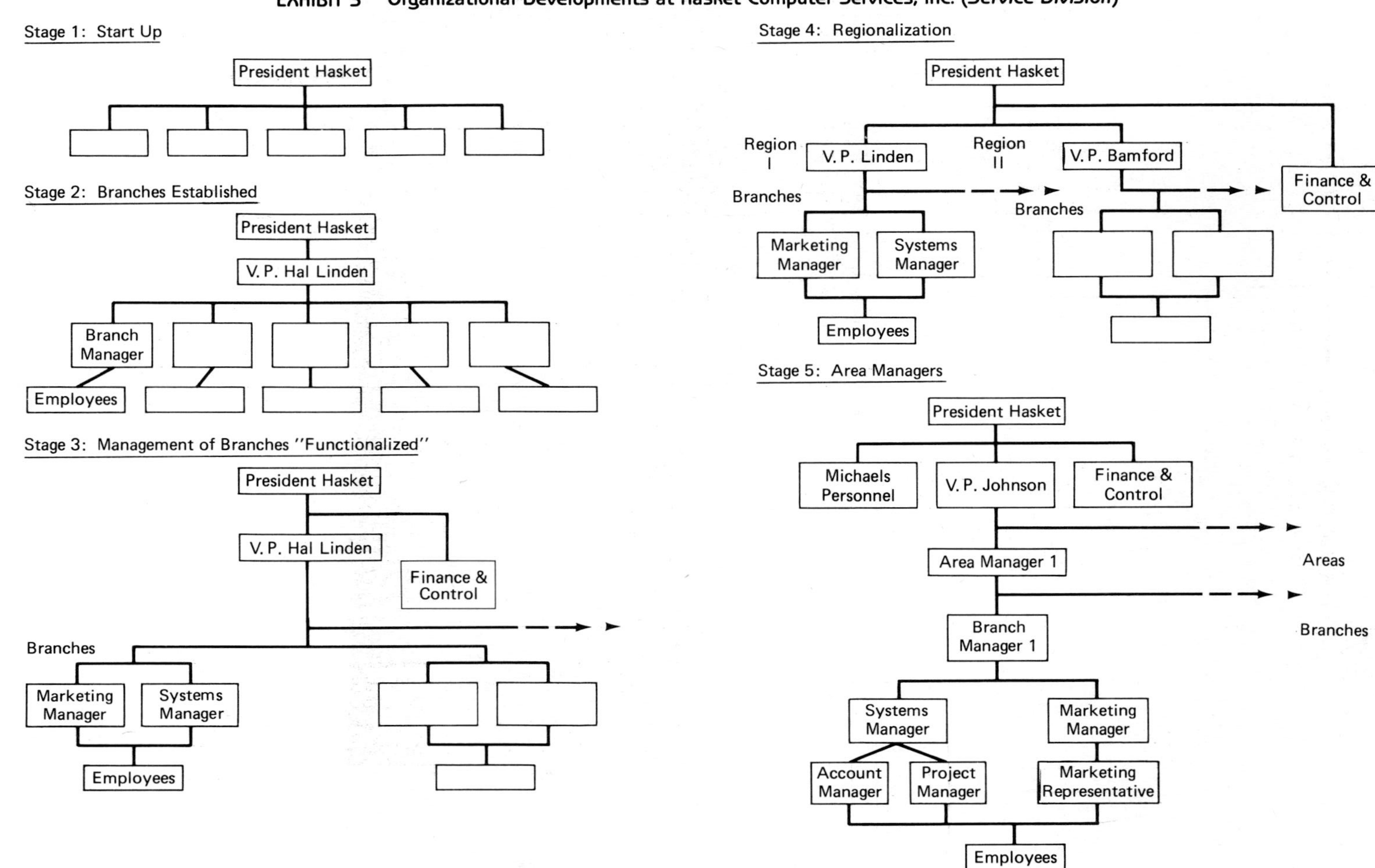

EXHIBIT 4

HASKET COMPUTER SERVICE
Variance from Budget of Selected Items for Services Division

	Variance from Budget		
	1973	*1974*	*1975*
Total Net Revenue	(2.2%)	(15.7%)	(6.9%)
Direct Related Expenses	4.1%	(7.8%)	(5.2%)
Branch Administration*	9.7%	(12.9%)	37.6%
Total Contribution	(16.7%)	(30.2%)	(18.0%)

*Includes recruiting expenses which were as follows: 1973, $108,000; 1974, $55,000; 1975, $202,000.

EXHIBIT 5

HASKET COMPUTER SERVICE
Variance from Budgeted Goals and Salary Histories for Two Branch Managers

	Branch Manager A—Variance from Budget				
	1971	*1972*	*1973*	*1974*	*1975 (9 months)*
Total Revenue	(13.0%) (under)	(1.0%)	(79.0%)	(1.0%)	(44.0%)
Total Contribution	(28.0%) (under)	(20.0%)	(253.0%)	(79.0%)	(73.0%)
Salary	$18,000	$23,500	$26,000	$30,000	$31,000

	Branch Manager B—Variance from Budget			
	1972	*1973*	*1974*	*1975*
Total Net Revenue	(12.0%)	2.4%	(24.0%)	(11.0%)
Total Contribution	(10.0%)	17.6%	(28.0%)	(12.0%)
Salary (not including bonuses)	$25,000	$27,500	$29,000	$32,000

EXHIBIT 6 **Compensation: At Hasket and National Averages**

HASKET COMPUTER SERVICES

Compensation for managers, including a non-recoverable draw to be applied toward bonuses:

- Marketing Manager—ranged from about $20,000 to the high $30,000 range, the average being a bit under $30,000.
- Systems Manager—same range as above with the average being in the mid-$20's.
- Area Managers—in the mid-$30's.

NATIONAL AVERAGES

Compensation for personnel working at fixed installations:

Corporate or Department Management (with all functions reporting)

	1st Quartile	*Average*	*3rd Quartile*
Manager	$25,000	$32,396	$37,180
Assistant Manager	21,268	27,352	31,304
Division Manager	21,684	26,364	30,000
Technical Assistant	20,176	24,440	27,820

Organizations Reporting Through Separate Managers—DP "Operations" Management

Manager	$18,512	$23,452	$27,300
Assistant Manager	15,444	18,460	20,540
Technical Assistant	14,196	18,148	21,268

Source: EDP, November 1975.

CYBERSYN SYSTEMS, INC.

It was 9:25 P.M. on Friday, December 21, 1969, and it was raining. Jay R. Wahlrig, President of Cybersyn Systems, Inc., a small high-technology firm located in Pasadena, California, was at his office desk, not sure whether the emotion slowly taking over his mind was frustration or anger. Perhaps it was a little of each. Wahlrig had just completed his review of sales and profit forecasts submitted by his three divisional Vice-Presidents. (*Exhibits 1, 2* and *3*).

In spite of his memorandum of November 15, 1969, which had specified that the firm's objective was "to double sales in 3 years, and simultaneously achieve a 10% return on net worth after tax," the plans seemed to fall far short of Wahlrig's objectives, as *Exhibit 4* shows. Worse, his divisional Vice-Presidents had asked for only $250,000 of the $550,000 he was certain he could make available for investment (see *Exhibit 5*). Wahlrig had felt certain that his ambitious growth objective would have stimulated his Vice-Presidents to be more aggressive and venturesome. Yet, only one, John Richards, in Control, had given him any notion of what his division's sales would be over the next 5 years. And, he seemed to have no proposals to substantially increase sales to provide Control's share of the company's target growth.

Wahlrig wasn't sure what to do. Were his divisional vice-presidents simply unable or unwilling to make the effort, or had they misunderstood his instructions? Was it something else, perhaps his management? Wahlrig had to do something to get Cybersyn moving. At its last meeting, the Board strongly criticized the company's failure to emphasize growth and profits. They wanted action. "Although I am president," he had told them, "there are definite limits as to how much I can personally do to effect changes at CSI. It seems almost as if I am allowed to make a certain number of innovations each year, but no more. If I come up with too many new ideas, whether they are for new products or for administrative changes, everybody begins to become uneasy and tremendous resistance builds up." But they weren't convinced. As a 30% owner of CSI, Wahlrig knew that he needed Board confidence to maintain a supply of capital to the firm. How was he going to satisfy their demands for growth and profit if he couldn't get his managers to plan?

COMPANY HISTORY

Cybersyn Systems, Incorporated, was founded in 1955 by a group of engineers, none of whom had business experience, to capitalize on their specialized competence in inertial

This case is based on an earlier case (9-370-100 and supplements) of the same name prepared under the supervision of Professor Francis J. Aguilar. This revision has substantially shortened the older cases. It was prepared by Assistant Professor Kenneth J. Hatten as a basis for class discussion rather than to illustrate either effective or ineffective handling of an administrative situation. All company data and much industry data have been disguised.

guidance systems. They had all formerly worked at the Jet Propulsion Laboratory in Pasadena, California.

CSI's initial activity was to provide engineering services in the analysis and design of inertial guidance and navigation systems. Soon after its founding, the company began designing and producing rotary shaft encoders. These were highly sophisticated devices used to make precise measurements of the speed and position of rotating shafts and were often used in the guidance systems of missiles. Virtually all of CSI's work during the first few years was performed for the Army, the Air Force, and the National Aeronautics and Space Administration (NASA).

The company grew slowly at first, reaching a sales level of about $300,000 by 1959. Its operations during this period were financed by the initial equity capital—a $100 contribution from each of the 6 founders—plus the incremental cash generated by its early contracts. By 1959, management saw a need for additional funds to finance work on a large encoder contract and was able to obtain an unsecured short-term loan of $15,000 from a local bank.

The early 1960s was a period of rapid growth for CSI. For example, in 1962 the company expanded its product line with the acquisition of W. F. Merton Laboratories, one of CSI's major suppliers, a company specializing in the production of precise patterns on metal and glass. It had been supplying CSI with precision glass discs for its encoders. This firm became the Exactex division of CSI.

As the government increased its expenditures for space and military projects, CSI's sales grew, reaching almost $4.5 million by 1965. But almost all sales were to the government, for the design and production of rotary encoders, and for the analysis and design of inertial guidance and navigation systems. CSI financed this period of rapid growth through a combination of retained earnings, short-term debt, and privately placed equity.

In December 1965, CSI went public in a favorable stock market, motivated in part by the desire of several owners to dispose of part of their holdings. Of the 150,000 shares offered, 102,000 were secondary offerings by stockholders in the company. Jay Wahlrig did not sell any of his 32,000 shares; this left him the largest single holder of CSI stock.

The second half of the 1960s saw CSI expand its product lines and make a serious attempt to enter the industrial market. For the industrial market, CSI designed and built encoders and related devices for computer peripheral equipment and numerically-controlled machine tools. On the government side of its business, management was determined to develop "total systems capability" in the area of inertial guidance and navigation. Under this concept, CSI began to design and build a small computer, as well as other instruments related to the inertial field. Many of these new products, however, failed. A few met with limited success, but the net result was a decided pause in the company's growth, particularly during 1966 and 1967.

During this period, the company relied solely on short-term bank loans to finance its capital needs.[1] In 1968, CSI completed a new plant in Pasadena, California, about ten miles away from its original facilities in Monrovia. The new plant housed the offices of

[1]The company received three-month, unsecured loans with an effective interest rate of about 12% as of the end of 1969. The interest on such loans was a non-reimbursable expense on government contracts of the type commonly negotiated by CSI.

the Control division, the Accounting and Personnel departments, and the President, senior Vice-President and Treasurer. The Exactex and Transmation divisions remained in Monrovia awaiting completion of another building adjacent to the new plant.

By early 1969, the company had increased its bank borrowing to $1.1 million, according to Wahlrig, an amount about 25% above the bank's normal loan limit for this type of situation. The bank was ''very nervous,'' he recalled, prompting him to give a high priority to reducing these loans. In mid 1969, CSI began a program to decrease inventories and accounts receivable, so that by the end of the year the loan had been reduced to $520,000, considerably easing CSI's need for more equity.

Exhibits 6 and *7* show comparative financial statements for selected years. *Exhibit 8* shows CSI's sales breakdown by divisions and by product lines for 1969. *Exhibit 9* shows the proportions of government and commercial sales for the period 1961 to 1968.

COMPANY ORGANIZATION

CSI was organized along divisional lines. Each divisional Vice-President had responsibility for marketing, production, engineering, and research functions in his division, but all financial and accounting functions were centralized. *Exhibit 8* also contains an abbreviated organization chart and shows each division's major products, sales organization, and number of employees.

The divisional structure had evolved between 1965 and 1968, as the company broadened its products and services. It was also a response to a series of crises that eventually resulted in the departure of three of the founders, leaving only Jay Wahlrig, William Spellman, and Bill Grossman from the original group. Management conflicts persisted however. In particular, there was friction between the Transmutation and Exactex divisions over the latter's internal (transfer) prices and external sales.

Controls Division

The Controls division provided engineering services in the inertial guidance and navigation fields, similar to those originally provided by CSI. In 1968 and 1969, the Controls division had also designed and produced a small number of hardware[2] products related to its consulting work. Because of the highly technical nature of this business, most of the division's staff were engineers and almost all management personnel had a technical background.

Virtually all of the division's work was done for military and space programs, mostly as the prime contractor. The division's service contracts were typically CPFF (cost-plus-fixed-fee) (*Exhibit 10*); hardware items were generally supplied under a fixed price contract. Controls had no manufacturing; the only production-like activities were the processing of computer programs (done by technicians), and the assembly of electronic systems (done by engineers).

The division had four product departments; Analysis, Engineering Data Analysis

[2]Hardware refers to equipment and other ''hard'' physical items; whereas software refers to computer programs, engineering reports and other ''soft'' items.

and Reporting Systems (EDARS), Equipment Design, and Systems Design. The Marketing department, Contracts department and Computer Center supported all four product groups. The product groups operated virtually independently from one another, except for Equipment Design and Systems Design, which, until recently, had been a single unit. The two groups still worked closely together. Controls division, as a whole, had very little interaction with the other two divisions in the company.

CONTROLS DIVISION: ANALYSIS DEPARTMENT This group had specialized in the field of inertial guidance and navigation, but was trying to broaden the scope of its capabilities to include the study of optimal missile trajectories. Most of the work done by the department involved the application of advanced mathematical and statistical techniques to the analysis of inertial systems. This work included the development of mathematical models and computer programs to simulate such systems in order to evaluate their performance and accuracy, and the design and specification of "optimum" systems configurations.

The Analysis department had performed contract work on some most important military and space contracts, including the Minuteman Guidance System, the Apollo Program, the Pershing Missile Guidance System, and the Saturn V Missile. Many of the contracts were for an independent evaluation of systems being produced by a large prime contractor such as Litton or Honeywell. CSI, therefore, not only had to maintain a technical competence in the application of advanced guidance and navigational techniques, but it also had to maintain familiarity with the capabilities of hardware built by other companies.

Analysis handled contracts ranging from $10,000 to about $400,000.[3] The group generally worked concurrently on from 2 to 4 contracts. However, many contracts were of a follow-on nature, that is, they resulted from work already done by the group. For example, CSI had been working on one system for nearly 10 years, analyzing the effects of proposed mission changes and making recommendations for performance improvements.

According to its chief, the atmosphere in Analysis was close to what might be found in a university. "People receive recognition for doing good analyses, and in my opinion, they can be more honest than they could be if they worked for a large contractor. We encourage them to write technical papers and to further their education."

CONTROLS DIVISION: ENGINEERING DATA ANALYSIS AND REPORTING SYSTEMS (EDARS) DEPARTMENT Developed by CSI, EDARS was a computer software system used for the collection, storage, retrieval, and analysis of data from complex technical systems. It was designed to support technical managers by providing concise analyses of technical data to help them make design and management decisions.

EDARS had been developed originally for the Pershing inertial guidance system. Later it had been used on the Apollo and Minuteman missiles. Although its use had been exclusively for inertial guidance systems, the department's managers generally agreed that EDARS could be gainfully applied to any complex technical system.

Like Analysis, the EDARS Department was generally contracted by a government

[3]The total value of work on any one project might be much larger, but these are maximum amounts for a one-year period.

agency to monitor contractors in charge of producing and installing hardware. Whereas Analysis specialized in very advanced mathematical design work, EDARS was concerned with processing and converting existing data into a form which would be helpful to the sponsoring agency in making its complex design and logistics decisions.

The EDARS system was sold on the basis of cost reductions which could be effected through its use. In a typical application, CSI would analyze the customer's needs, design appropriate programs and computer files, train personnel, maintain and process the data, and produce management reports on a periodic basis. The group generally had about 2 to 4 contracts at one time, ranging from $20,000 to $500,000 per year. They were all of a long-term nature, generally lasting for the duration of a missile program.

CSI's main competitors in this field, as in the analysis area, were the prime contractors themselves. The government's desire to have an independent outsider evaluate the prime contractor's work, however, had given the company a competitive edge against the large firms. Other competition came from small firms, some of which were offshoots of CSI.

Controls Division: The Equipment and Systems Design Departments Equipment Design designed and built instruments for inertial guidance and navigation systems. These included a small digital computer and a sonar coupler. In contrast, Systems Design designed and constructed inertial guidance and navigation systems using both CSI instruments and some produced by other manufacturers.

Until 1969, the two groups operated as one unit. They were divided when the head of the group resigned and two equally qualified "number two" men were left. The situation was resolved by putting each in charge of a separate group.

The original, combined department had been created in 1967 to develop a capability not only to analyze and design a system, but to produce it. To provide its potential customers with evidence of the firm's competence in this area, CSI had set out to design and build a small digital computer for inertial guidance systems.

The group eventually succeeded in producing this new product, but, although the computer was soundly designed, by mid-1969 management concluded that it was a failure—its market niche was too small. No other new product had been significantly profitable and one had resulted in substantial losses. These failures had led CSI to abandon its strategy of developing "total systems capability." Jay Wahlrig explained, "The former head of the division did a very poor job—both of planning and executing a strategy and of relating personally to the people in his organization."

Control Division: Other Departments The three other departments in the Controls division—Marketing, Contracts, and Computer Center—provided support functions for the four product departments.

The Marketing group consisted of three men, each a specialist in a different product area. According to John Richards, the head of the Controls division, Marketing was primarily responsible for finding interested customers and checking out leads. "In this kind of business, although engineers have to make sales, salesmen are needed to maintain customer contacts. Most of our business comes from unsolicited technical proposals made by our engineers after a salesman has alerted us to an interested customer."

The Contracts group coordinated the administration of government contracts, maintained relations with sponsoring agencies, and made sure that the contracts were fulfilled.

The Computer Center, organizationally located in the Controls division, was a service organization for the whole company and was operating at close to full capacity.

Controls Division: Product Policy In attempting to achieve Wahlrig's target of doubling sales in three years, John Richards had been searching for answers to three key questions regarding the division's products:

1. Should high priority be placed on expanding sales in the "bread and butter" business of Analysis and EDARS? If so, how could this be accomplished?

Richards said: "In EDARS, I decided, for the time being, to seek more contracts on existing government programs in the inertial control field. While this job will keep one salesman busy, the preparation of proposals is relatively simple and does not involve much time or effort. For the longer term, I feel CSI will have to move out of the inertial field and into other areas having similar technical requirements. One good possibility for EDARS is the jet engine field, where it is necessary to maintain records on performance, reliability, and logistics similar to those kept for inertial equipment.

"To serve the jet engine users (or to enter into any similar market), I figure that CSI would have to hire 2 men who are knowledgeable and experienced in the field. It would probably take them about 6 months to develop a concept of what kind of system the company should offer, and then another 12 to 18 months to secure the first contract. This means that about $100,000 would have to be invested over a 2-year period. I feel that such an effort would almost certainly result in at least one contract for $500,000 per year (which would contribute about $300,000 to overhead and profit, or about $30,000 to pre-tax profit); and there would be a good chance of reaching a volume of $1.5 million per year within 2 years of receiving the first contract.

"In the analysis area, it is more difficult to enter new fields because of the difficulty of acquiring top-flight technical expertise and customer contacts. Close personal contacts are imperative since few contracts are competitively bid. Again, CSI would have to hire at least two people to enter any new field and it would probably take about two years before any substantial contracts could be obtained. It is unlikely that profitable contracts could be obtained as fast as for EDARS."

2. What can the Equipment and Systems Design groups contribute to growth?

Richards commented, "These groups are operating unprofitably, doing any work that comes in. They're not pushing any specific product line.

"They have had several new product ideas, but Wahlrig has stated that to develop any one would require that the *division* not invest in any other areas for, probably, a two-year period. I don't agree with his assessment, and I would prefer to maintain the division's hardware capability."

3. Could CSI use the division's Computer Center personnel to enter the computer services field?

Richards said, "I don't have any specific ideas here but there are many possibilities. The investment required should be reasonably small."

The Second Division: Transmation

The Transmation division produced tachometers, rotary and linear optical incremental encoders, and special military subassemblies. The encoders were highly sophisticated devices used to measure incremental rotary (angle) and linear movements respectively. They were sold to both governmental and commercial users for a variety of applications, at prices ranging from $150 to $250 per unit for industrial sales unit, $500 to $2,000 for military units, with the most expensive ones going as high as $25,000. According to the head of the division, Joseph Coyle, CSI was as large as any of its competitors in the optical incremental segment of the market, although there were other companies selling a larger total volume of all types of encoders. The division was organized on a functional basis, with about 80% of its personnel employed by the Engineering, Manufacturing and Quality Assurance departments.

TRANSMATION: THE GOVERNMENT MARKET The government market for the division's product broke down into the following areas:

1 Rotary encoders for special high-security programs produced for prime defense contractors. To serve these customers, the division maintained a large staff of engineers with the capability of performing advanced design work. In 1969, the division had one cost-plus contract for about $1 million of business per year.
2 Rotary encoders for other defense and space applications were generally "specials" specified by the customer. Some sales were also made of CSI's line of standard encoders. Coyle estimated this market was about $3.5 million dollars per year.

TRANSMATION: INDUSTRIAL MARKET Although encoders had occasionally been sold for use on automatic machine tools, magnetic tape drives, and other continuous process applications, no serious attempt to push industrial sales had been made until 1966, when a major selling effort was launched. Design engineers went into the field to promote sales. Military sales declined and were not fully replaced by increased industrial sales. As a result, the division operated at a loss during the second half of 1966 and through early 1967.

In 1967, CSI designed a new linear encoder for the industrial market. This product, which translated physical linear displacement into electrical impulses, was designed for a wide variety of applications where precise position measurement was necessary. A market research report (by a consultant) had identified the numerically-controlled machine tool industry as the largest single market for the CSI system. The rapid growth of the total non-government market for linear measuring devices ($2.1 million in 1964 and a forecast of $6.1 million in 1970), and the high margins expected from the new system, had led CSI's management to expect the linear measuring system to make a very significant contribution to the company's sales and profits.

In October, 1967, the linear encoder was officially introduced to the market. Unfortunately, a series of problems were encountered in changing from prototype production to volume manufacturing (for example, a difficulty in producing glass scales of the accuracy required), and problems in using the system in the harsh environment of a machine shop, since it had not been designed with an enclosure to protect it from dust and oil. The company was forced to restrict sales to applications not involving metal cutting, and several large orders received in late 1967 and early 1968 were canceled because of these continuing problems. As a result, sales were disappointing in 1968, reaching only about $100,000 as against a forecast of $800,000. Sales for 1969 were about $150,000 as against a forecast of $600,000, because, as Wahlrig explained, "Unfortunately, in 1969 several competitive products were introduced to the market, the machine tool industry was in a slump, and, due to a tight money situation, machine tool manufacturers were proceeding slowly with the incorporation of linear measuring systems into their numerically-controlled units. However, we now have a standard commercial product line and we are the sole supplier of rotary encoders for Giddings and Lewis, one of the nation's largest producers of numerically-controlled machine tools.''

Transmation: Divisional Strategy Coyle, who had been the head of Transmation for less than one year, felt that the company had done a very poor job of exploiting the resources available in the Transmation and Exactex divisions. He noted, ''CSI has, in Exactex, one of the three state-of-the-art pattern-generating facilities in the industry. But, instead of exploiting it, we've been selling this capability to our competitors. The company also has good engineering capabilities but has done a terrible job of marketing them. The only reason CSI has done as well as it has is that everybody in the encoder business has approached the business all wrong. If a company ever came along and did a good job in this business, they'd wrap it up for themselves.'' Coyle said that CSI's competitors included many small firms as well as divisions of large companies such as Litton, Itek, Conrac, and Bausch and Lomb.

''No company has been particularly successful in this business because they are all too involved in government research contracts. You can't make money on contracts to sell engineering capability. You need volume production. Everyone in the business faces this same problem. This is *the* problem of this company. It's always fun to work on technical projects, but the only way you can make money is to exploit the *results* of good engineering in commercial, high-volume business.''

In line with this thinking, Coyle had begun a program to simultaneously develop three products which had the possibility of achieving volume sales in the commercial market:

1. A low-cost rotary encoder to be used as an optical tachometer on magnetic tape drives.

Prototypes had been developed, and CSI was working with the producers to develop a product suitable to their needs for this application. Management estimated the total market for magnetic tape drives was about 35,000 units in 1969. It also figured that the division would need a volume of 5,000 units per year to break even.

2. A low-resolution version of the linear encoder for use on magnetic disc units (another data storage device for computer systems).

The encoder would replace the hydraulic and mechanical system for controlling the positioning of the reading heads over the proper data tracks on the discs. It would have to compete with other new techniques for positioning the heads, including a voice coil device developed by General Electric and Farrand Controls. CSI had built several prototypes which it had given to computer peripheral manufacturers—including IBM, other major companies, and smaller firms—for testing. The company had received a lot of feedback about the design and was modifying it to meet the needs of these manufacturers. The device would sell for about $75, a price which could be met if volume was 1,000 units per year or more. The total market for these control devices was growing rapidly and was forecast to reach about 50,000 units by 1970.

3. An altimeter for use in commercial aircraft.

It appeared likely that new government regulations would force commercial airlines to improve their navigation equipment, and a precision altimeter would be one important requirement. A precision altimeter based on an optical absolute rotary encoder could be produced quite economically. Although the product was quite different from CSI's incremental encoders, Coyle felt that the large volume of sales that might develop (around 50,000 units was his estimate of the total requirement to recondition all commercial aircraft) made the product an attractive possibility. He said that the division was trying to obtain a $25,000 preliminary development contract from the government to build a prototype.

"I'm interested in the machine tool market," Coyle said, "but I feel that the rapidly changing computer peripheral market is more exciting and for that reason I am concentrating my efforts there. I don't expect any of the new products I've told you about to reach volume production before 1971."

According to Coyle, the change in emphasis from the governmental to the industrial market had tremendous organizational implications. To be successful in marketing commercial products, he believed that CSI would have to improve its production and control systems, make engineering more responsive to the market, and learn a lot about markets with which it was not familiar. Said Coyle, "This is going to be a different ball game. We'll have to invest a lot of money and the whole organization will have to change to take advantage of the long-range opportunities offered by the industrial market."

Division Three: Exactex

Exactex produced very precise patterns or lines on glass and metal surfaces. According to management, it was a leader in its ability to produce patterns to very tight tolerances. Typical of its products were precision measuring scales, measuring reticles for microscopes and telescopes, microcircuit masks, and optical pickups for computer peripheral equipment. The technologies involved in the production of these parts included precision photography, metal evaporation, etching, electroforming, and glass cutting and cementing. Some of Exactex's products and processes are illustrated in *Exhibit 11*.

Most of Exactex's sales were custom orders; the division had no inventory of finished products. The number of orders varied widely from month to month, and planning was difficult because there was usually little advance notice of a new order.

Exactex's customers included a wide variety of industrial firms, including most of the large technology-oriented firms in the U.S., as well as many small companies. Its most important products were code discs.

Code discs were used in the encoders produced by Transmation and were also sold to outside customers, some of whom were competitors of Transmation. Business generated by Controls consumed about 25% to 30% of Exactex's direct labor.

The major portion of outside disc sales had originally gone to major military contractors, but this market had dried up somewhat as the companies developed their own capabilities to make code discs. On the other hand, the market for discs in the computer peripheral area had grown rapidly. Management estimated that Exactex produced close to half the code discs made in the U.S. in 1969.

Exactex competed against two types of companies. The first were small jobs shops; the second were larger firms whose custom business was of secondary importance to their standard product lines. According to Phillip Barnard, Vice-President for Exactex, the most important ingredients for success in the custom-made precision patterns business were (1) company reputation, (2) delivery, and (3) price. Most important by far was reputation, based on past performance. Since a precision pattern was generally a small part of an end-product's total cost, the customer was more interested in getting a high-quality job "than in saving nickels and dimes." Another aspect of reputation, in Barnard's opinion, was a firm's ability to analyze a customer's problems and to help specify its exact product needs. Exactex did not have such capabilities.

The division's sales in 1969 totaled $675,000 against a budgeted figure of $1,000,000. The division had two salesmen, one the head of Marketing and the other an independent sales representative on the East Coast. Barnard felt that more reps should be added, but this would involve training them and providing engineering support. Without such support, the reps would generate a flood of orders, most of which would not be profitable.

A new line of proprietary products was being developed. The most advanced was a metal mesh for use in image storage tubes for computer terminals. The division hoped to begin selling this product in quantity by mid-1970. Most manufacturers of image storage tubes produced this mesh themselves and Exactex's largest competitor was currently the only independent supplier. Nonetheless, Barnard felt that Exactex could capture a significant share of the market with a product having superior transmission properties and pattern fidelity, important characteristics for image storage applications.

COMPANY ATMOSPHERE

Jay Wahlrig was very concerned about producing the right atmosphere in the firm. He often spoke of trying to create an environment in which there was "open communication" among all groups, especially management.

His concern stemmed in part from the high rate of management turnover at CSI. He attributed this problem to a failure of CSI to provide a stimulating atmosphere for talented managers and to a lack of feedback from top management as to where people stood in the organization, how they were being evaluated, and how they fit into the company's future.

During 1969, the former head of the Controls division and the former Treasurer, each of whom had been hired from outside shortly before, left the company. According to Wahlrig, the first had not only failed to create a viable business strategy for Controls, but had been a failure in his relations with other people in the organization. Said Wahlrig, "I don't like to work with anyone who isn't open, and this guy was closed like a book." The Treasurer had "fallen flat on his face" in his job of setting up an adequate budgeting and control system.

In addition to the high management turnover, Wahlrig saw a lack of communication among managers of the different divisions, and even within divisions, as a major problem. His belief was confirmed by other people in the organization, who added that some people hardly spoke to anyone.

In an effort to improve the situation, Wahlrig had been stressing atmosphere. He had also been encouraging more staff meetings to increase communication. In addition, he had hired an industrial psychologist to spend two days a week in the plant. This man worked with the division managers in resolving specific personnel problems, and was also developing a program of "work planning" for lower-level supervisors as the beginning of a management development effort. The psychologist had also helped Wahlrig improve his relationships with the other managers in the organization, and had helped him develop the company's philosophy with respect to its people (see *Exhibit 12*).

PLANNING AT CSI

Jay Wahlrig first felt the need for long-range planning at CSI in 1962, when he decided he was too involved in day-to-day operations and that he should spend his time planning and monitoring operations. A promising new man was promoted to manage operations, and Wahlrig moved his office across the street. He soon found, however, that he was losing touch with what was going on in the company and, after a series of crises which occurred at least in part because of his absence, he returned to his original pattern of management. The new man was dismissed.

By 1966, Wahlrig had prepared many memoranda for planning purposes, but found these efforts "had absolutely no effect on operations." He recalled, "I resolved to approach planning in new ways and with renewed vigor. I began working with the divisional Vice-Presidents, but I found that while some were enthusiastic about planning, others failed to understand the concept or felt that they had more urgent things to do."

Wahlrig, therefore, adopted a different approach to planning in each division. For example, there were differences among divisions as to the time periods used for planning. According to the circumstances, plans covered periods from two weeks to one year. They were usually formulated in informal conversations between a division manager and Wahlrig. Follow-up was also on an informal basis.

In Exactex, he worked directly with Phillip Barnard to develop plans. Barnard in turn used his department heads to assist him. He was enthusiastic about planning, and Wahlrig felt he was doing a good job. In Controls, Wahlrig worked with the divisional Vice-President and his Marketing manager. So far, each attempt to develop long-range plans had "degenerated into a crash sales program." However, Wahlrig sensed that a better understanding of planning was developing. In Transmation, he worked with a consultant who had been helping the division with its product planning. According to Wahlrig, the head of Transmation had resisted the planning idea on the grounds that there were more immediate problems to deal with. Wahlrig did not want to force the issue, as he was busy planning with the other two divisions, but he was not content with the progress he had made.

Jay Wahlrig wanted each divisional manager to do his own planning with the help of his own subordinates. He felt that planning only progressed in CSI when he actively pushed it himself. When he let up, nothing happened. Wahlrig stated, "I would like to have a system in which the divisional managers plan and budget, and I approve the plans. I could then monitor the managers throughout the year on the basis of the plans. This approach has been impractical so far, because the firm's accounting system is inadequate and because the divisional Vice-Presidents lack experience. At present, I feel planning is really a management development tool." Wahlrig added that it also served as a convenient way for him to keep informed of the latest thinking in the divisions.

Wahlrig, however, was enthusiastic about the progress that had been made in explicitly defining the objectives and philosophy of the company. He said, "It's amazing how this has developed. I re-worked my original statement of the objectives, strategy and philosophy of CSI several times in the last year, and it's still being refined and made more action oriented." (See *Exhibit 13*.)

THE FUTURE OF CSI

Jay Wahlrig was optimistic about the future of CSI. He felt that the company had a strong technical base on which to build and that progress was being made to correct the major weaknesses which had slowed the firm's growth. He recognized that the firm still had many problems, however. "The company needs to develop its personnel and especially its managers. I have trouble getting them to think about anything outside their traditional product lines, and it seems difficult to convince them that the company can grow as fast as I believe it should."

Thinking about the future of CSI, Wahlrig said, "I envision an independent, multi-divisional firm, but I expect that the divisions will remain relatively independent. We could create new divisions, either through internal development or acquisitions." Wahlrig felt the company would adjust its commitments to the military, space, and industrial markets, with the latter gradually increasing, he hoped, to about half the company's total sales.

"I am faced with the task of generating a record level of sales and profits and of deciding where to invest our available funds. In the past, I have basically allowed each division to retain its contribution to profits. This policy is a product of the restrictions placed on the company's financial flexibility by its CPFF contracts; and in part from my desire to achieve a balanced growth in all divisions. Since the Board wants the company to invest in new activities, however, my task has become far more complicated. What's so frustrating is the poor results my planning efforts have produced."

EXHIBIT 1

CYBERSYN SYSTEMS INCORPORATED
CONTROLS DIVISION
Preliminary 1970 Profit Plan

During 1969, there was considerable pressure from Congress and the public to reduce defense spending. This pressure, when added to President Nixon's anti-inflationary efforts, promises to have a significant impact on defense outlays over the next five years. However, the effect of cuts on procurement and research expenditures, and hence on aerospace contractors, is still not certain.

Current Contracts and Proposals Table 1 provides data on the contracts held by the Controls division as of the end of 1969. Table 2 shows data on outstanding proposals. All contracts are of one-year duration; some are of a follow-on nature, while others are one-shot.

Cost of Obtaining Contracts As an illustration of the effort expended in obtaining a new contract, I estimate that approximately $40,000 was expended over a 15-month period to obtain contract #4 in Table 1. This was an EDARS contract, very similar to ones that had already been executed, but for a different government agency.

TABLE 1 Contracts as of December, 1969

Contract Number	1969 Dollar Amount ($000)	Years of Previous Work for This Contracting Office	Expected Number of Additional Years of Work (after 1970)
1	$500	8–10	2–3 } depending on political climate
2	500	8–10	2–3
3	250	10	2–3
4	500	1	5
5	100	6	0

TABLE 2 Contract Proposals Outstanding as of December, 1969

Proposal Number	Annual Dollar Amount	Estimated Duration	Probability of Securing Contract
1	$500	1 year	>.9 Waiting only for government agency budget review
2	200	1 year	>.9
3	400	1 year	>.9
4	200	1 year may lead to follow-on contracts	>.9
5	500	1 year	.5
6	500	1 year	.1

BUDGET FOR 1970[1] Table 3 shows the Controls division's preliminary budget for 1970 (in $000's).

TABLE 3 Preliminary Budget for 1970

	Last Year 1968	1969 Original Plan	1969 Outlook as of Nov. 1969	1970 Plan
Net Sales	$2,106	$3,144	$3,135	$3,175
Cost of Sales	1,790	2,714	2,684	2,546
Gross Margin	316	430	451	629
Selling Expense	215	220	219	244
Div. Contribution	101	210	232	385
Corp. G & A	162	280	276	300
Net Income from Operations[2]	(61)	(70)	(44)	85

[1]*Costs of Professional Staff.* In 1969, the average salary at CSI for an engineer in a non-supervisory capacity with a bachelor's degree and 5 years experience was $13,000. In a supervisory position, the average was $15,000. The cost of finding and hiring an electronics engineer was about 20% of the man's annual salary. In costing projects, overhead was charged at 120%, but G & A, fee and special charges raised the effective burden to about 200%. Thus, a team of 4 engineers would typically be capable of supporting a project of about $162,000, excluding costs of materials.

[2]In the aerospace industry, according to SEC reports, Net Profit *after tax* as a percent of sales was 3.2% in 1965, 3.0% in 1966, 2.7% in 1967, and 3.1% in 1968. Net Profit after taxes as a percent of stockholder's equity was 12.8% in 1967, and 14.2% in 1968.

EXHIBIT 2

CYBERSYN, INC.
Transmation Division Prospects for 1970

A. ORDER BACKLOG As of November 1, 1969, the Transmation division had the following total backlog of orders:

Fixed Price Orders	
Linear measuring systems	$ 70,891
Standard rotary encoders	328,996
Special programs	395,490
Cost Type Orders	
Special programs	$2,671,274
Total	$3,466,651

B. BUDGET FOR 1970 *Table 1* shows the Transmation division's preliminary budget for 1970. We expect the revised sales figure to be about $500,000 lower, and profits to be slightly higher.

TABLE 1 Preliminary 1970 Profit Plan Comparative Income Statement

		1969		
	Last Year 1968	*Original Plan*	*Outlook as of Nov. 1969*	*1970 Plan*
Net Sales	2,548	2,543	2,415	2,643
Cost of Sales	2,037	1,887	1,859	2,100
Gross Margin	511	656	556	543
Selling Expense	184	286	272	291
Division Contribution	327	370	284	252
Corporate General & Administrative	293	194	196	248
Net Income from Operations	34	176	88	4

Shipments of digital-shaft encoders in 1967 totalled an estimated $44 million. The composition of this market is described by *Table 2*. Note that the growth of the market is occurring in the inductive segment and in inertial guidance applications.

TABLE 2 The U.S. Encoder Market, 1967 ($ million)

Uses	Government			Government Market Growth	Non-Government Market Sales	Total Industry Sales by Type of Encoder
	Avionics	Inertial Guidance	Tracking & Data Acquisition			
Encoder Types						
Optical	3.0	1.5	4.5	6%	3.0	12.0
Contract	13.8	—	1.2	−3%	5.0	20.0
Magnetic	0.5	—	0.5	0%	1.0	2.0
Inductive with A/D	4.5	3.1	1.4	17%	1.0	10.0
Total sales by use of Encoder	$21.8	$4.6	$7.6		$10.0	$44.0*
Use Growth Rates %	6%	12%	4%			

*Being $38 million absolute, $6 million incremental. In the government market for optical encoders, $3.0 million are incremental and $6 million are absolute encoders.

Notwithstanding these trends, there have been no indications of marked shifts in market share among our competitors. CSI's share was 14.1%, about the same as last year (see *Table 3*).

TABLE 3 1967 Optical Encoder Sales

	$ Millions	Market Share (%)
Wayne-George	2.3	19.2
Baldwin Electronics	1.9	15.8
CSI	1.7	14.1
Dynamics Research	1.5	12.5
Datex	0.8	6.7
Gurley	0.8	6.7
Litton	0.8	6.7
Sequential	0.6	5.0
Norden	0.3	2.5
Others	1.3	10.8
	12.0	100.0

However, CSI is working in a relatively small part of the encoder market. CSI is a specialist in "incremental" encoders. In the government market for optical encoders, $6 million in total sales are of the absolute type while $3 million are of incremental encoders. CSI's sales are predominantly governmental (in the total digital encoder market of $44 million, $6 million are incremental sales). Technological innovations are making the A/D converter smaller, more reliable, and cheaper. Ultimately, the A/D converter will become a formidable competitor in our avionics and guidance markets.

In the *Numerical Control (N/C) and Machine Tool Market*, anaiog resolvers, as opposed to encoders, dominate the market. The analog systems are mature, debugged, and extremely trouble-free. Machine tools manufacturers are not eager to change their current systems—in any event twenty-two out of the top thirty suppliers of N/C machine tools buy their controls from Bendix, G. E., Bunker Ramo, and Westinghouse. Of the eight who make their own controls, only two are committed to digital systems: Pratt & Whitney and Giddings and Lewis.

Next year, 1968, the unit volume for rotary encoders should reach 1800 units. By 1970, we expect the unit volume will be 2,600 and by 1972 it should reach 4,300. This forecast is based on the growth of N/C drills and lathes, not on increased penetration by rotary encoders.

The *Computer Peripheral* market is large and one of the fastest-growing segments in the electronics industry. Most non-captive peripheral equipment requires some speedy position sensing and control components. There appear to be twenty to thirty potential customers for CSI's optical encoding devices in this market.

The total peripheral market in 1967 used 5500 units—about $285,000. Almost 90% of these requirements were satisfied by encoder discs ($112,000); the remainder by complete encoders. We expect by 1971 that this market will consume about 8000 units—about $160,000 to $200,000 in sales. Note that IBM holds a dominant position in the peripheral market and influences the technologies used and, therefore, the size of the encoder market. The remainder of the industry is widely dispersed geographically and primarily made up of small companies, which continue to enter and depart rapidly. Design practice is constantly evaluating new technological approaches.

EXHIBIT 3

CYBERSYN, INC.
Exactex's Prospects for 1970

As of November 1, 1969, Exactex had a total order backlog of $146,501. The division's preliminary budget for 1970 is shown in *Table 1*.

TABLE 1 Preliminary 1970 Profit Plan Comparative Income Statement

		1969		
	Last Year 1968	*Original Plan*	*Outlook as of Nov. 1969*	*1970 Plan*
Net sales	658	660	930	660
Cost of sales	537	505	614	480
Gross margin	121	155	316	180
Selling expense	48	38	79	55
Division Contribution	73	117	237	125
Corporate General & Administrative	35	51	73	49
Net income from Operations	38	66	164	76

Table 2 shows my rough estimates of the incremental costs and revenues that could be obtained by an additional five or six sales representatives. I am attempting to reorganize the division to provide the necessary support for a few additional representatives without having to hire additional people.

TABLE 2 **Incremental Costs and Benefits of Adding Sales Representatives* (all figures in thousands of dollars)**

	Current Level	Additional Costs and Benefits During First Year	Additional Costs and Benefits During Second Year
Sales	$660	$120	$300
Costs			
Labor & Materials	238	54	120
Commisions	9	35**	55**
	247	89	175
Contribution	413	31	125
Fixed overhead	338	38***	71***
Income (loss) before taxes and corporate charges	75	(7)	54

*Calculated on the basis of adding 5 or 6 reps at the beginning of the first year.
**Including some commissions on current business which would be turned over to the representatives.
***Corresponds to salaries of additional personnel required within the division.

However, I want to point out that each new independent sales representative will probably generate a six-inch stack of orders, of which one-half inch will be worth quoting on. Then we'll have to explain to the reps why we can't work on each of the remaining five and a half inches of orders. To avoid this problem, we will have to assign someone within the division to work with them on a continuing basis. In addition, because the representatives could be expected to generate many orders for jobs having special production requirements, additional technical personnel will be required in the manufacturing department.

The Markets for Exactex's Products[1]

Probably the most significant aspect of optical encoding is that it is capable of providing greater precision of shaft speed measurement and greater resolution of shaft angular position than any other available system. But it is also the most costly. As a result, optical encoder and glass disc manufacturers have developed a particular character, namely an orientation to small quantities, high prices, and a limitation to applications requiring the unique precision, resolution, long life, high speed, and low inertia provided by optical encoding.

1 Sales of digital encoders of all types have been predominantly (90%) governmental. The government market is sophisticated, requires only small quantities, and commands high prices.
2 Sales of optically-based digital encoders have also been predominantly (85%) governmental. Sales of optically-based types for governmental use are expected to grow faster than inductive and magnetic types, doubling between 1964 and 1970.
3 Numerically-controlled machine tools were believed to be the largest non-governmental end-use of rotary encoders of all types in 1964. However, this is clearly a small and fragmented market, and the growth prospects for optical techniques are consid-

[1]Some of the following data are taken from a consulting report, presented to Exactex in December 1967. Encoder discs represent approximately 30% of Exactex's sales in 1969.

ered unfavorable. Most machine tool builders are using inductive rather than optical units, and there is a trend away from use of rotary encoding of any type for position measurement in the machine tool business. Total use by 1970 should be about 2,500 units.

4 The largest identifiable use of code discs, in 1964, other than in encoders, was in magnetic tape transports. The estimated market in 1964 was 1,900 units, worth a total of $67,000. Optical systems are apparently being displaced by other technologies in line printers and disc file drives.

5 A wide variety of possible applications for optical encoders was noted, including: digital measuring equipment, X-Y plotters and recorders, precision counting and measuring, speed control, process control, transfer machines, weighing and batching, and laboratory and test equipment.

In many instances, optical encoding was too good for the application. The fundamental reason in each case was the same: optical encoding has inherent precision, resolution, and speed control capabilities which are in excess of the mechanisms being controlled.

It is apparent that both economics and lack of familiarity have tended to inhibit the use of optical encoders.

EXHIBIT 4 **A Comparison of the Divisional Plans with Cybersyn System's Sales Objective ($000's)**

	1970	*1971*	*1972*	*1973*
Control Division				
Current Contracts[1]	$1,850	$1,750	$ 1,125	$ 500
Proposals[2]	1,470	100	100	100
Total	$3,320	$1,850	$ 1,225	$ 600
Transmation				
1970 Budget[3]	$2,643			
Carryover Backlog		$ 823		
Total	$2,643	$ 823		
Exactex				
"Current Level"[4]	$ 930	$ 930	$ 930	$ 930
Extra Sales Force[5]		120	300	300
Total	$ 930	$1,050	$ 1,230	$ 1,230
Company Total Sales	$6,893	$3,723	$ 2,455	$ 1,800
Company Sales Objective[6]	$6,893	$8,685	$10,942	$13,786
"Strategic Gap" Between Objective and Ongoing Performance (deficiency)	$ 0	($4,962)	($ 8,487)	($11,986)

[1]Based on Table 1 of Exhibit 1 assuming proposals 1 to 2 run out $500, 1970; $500, 1971; and $250, 1972.

[2]Assuming each proposal has expected sales of "$ amount by probability of success."

[3]Based on Exhibit 2.

[4]Assuming "current" sales would continue until 1973.

[5]Assumes extra sales force impact is as specified by Exhibit 3 and continues until 1973.

[6]Assumes 1970 budget from each division is maximum realizable sales potential for 1970. Objective is to double by 1973; implicit rate of growth is 25.99% per annum.

EXHIBIT 5 **R&D Requests 1969/70**

Controls Division	$145,000
Transmation Division	97,000
Exactex Division	8,000
	$250,000

EXHIBIT 6

CYBERSYN SYSTEMS INCORPORATED
Comparative Balance Sheets: (1965–1968)

Item	*1965*	*1966*	*1967*	*1968*
Assets				
Cash	173,592	325,240	51,507	43,770
Accounts Receivable	851,299	639,776	979,195	1,116,815
Refundable prior year income taxes	—	—	73,184	31,614
Received from employees' stock purchase	—	—	29,421	79,365
Unbilled expenditures & fees (CPFF)	155,122	64,643	159,161	250,227
Inventories (FIFO)	437,159	309,559	490,425	673,925
Prepaid Expenses	21,390	23,439	35,901	58,216
Total Current Assets	1,638,562	1,362,657	1,818,794	2,253,932
Land	9,570	9,570	9,570	9,570
Building	70,180	70,180	70,180	70,180
Equipment	540,711	639,965	818,158	1,005,016
Building & Leasehold Improvements	231,431	250,944	279,299	205,573
	851,892	970,659	1,177,207	1,290,339
Less Accumulated Depreciation & Amortization	356,409	471,625	633,775	693,718
	495,483	499,034	543,432	596,621
	2,134,045	1,861,691	2,362,226	2,850,553
Liabilities				
Notes Payable	11,000	11,000	449,900	660,000
Accounts Payable	117,245	115,572	184,116	348,680
Accrued Expenses:				
Payroll & Vacation Pay	62,512	56,487	86,884	100,828
Taxes (Other than Federal)	22,148	9,651	16,413	20,090
Other	46,254	24,289	42,270	79,244
Accrued Federal Income Taxes	212,146	56,336	25,799	6,497
Total Current Liabilities	471,305	273,335	805,382	1,215,339
Real Estate Mortgage	22,000	11,000	—	16,500
Deferred Federal Income Taxes	—	—	—	—
Deferred Investment Tax Credit	—	—	30,716	36,778
Common Stock (342,430 shares out)	342,430	342,430	342,430	342,430
Capital in Excess of Par	429,311	429,311	407,198	437,133
Retained Earnings	868,999	915,615	856,843	865,237
	1,640,740	1,687,356	1,606,491	1,644,800
Less Shares in Treasury at Cost	—	110,000	80,363	62,864
	1,640,740	1,577,356	1,526,128	1,581,936
	2,134,045	1,861,691	2,362,226	2,850,553

EXHIBIT 7

CYBERSYN SYSTEMS INCORPORATED

Ten-Year Comparative Income Statements: 1960–1969

	1960	*1961*	*1962*	*1963*	*1964*	*1965*	*1966*	*1967*	*1968*	*1969**
Product Sales and Contract	$990,267	$1,308,728	$2,551,307	$3,688,925	$4,153,200	$4,486,700	$4,088,327	$4,330,340	$5,421,925	$6,209,500
Costs and Expenses										
Cost of goods sold	596,990	681,500	1,691,112	2,574,281	3,143,234	3,259,237	3,285,143	3,705,857	4,465,418	5,047,900
Selling, general and administrative	236,306	382,166	495,052	646,900	672,852	733,160	735,594	759,884	941,754	1,051,600
Profit sharing plan contribution	16,500	27,500	115,500	126,500	—	—	—	—	—	—
	$849,796	$1,091,166	$2,301,664	$3,347,681	$3,816,086	$3,992,397	$4,020,737	$4,465,741	$5,407,172	$6,099,500
Operating income (loss)	$140,471	$ 217,562	$ 249,643	$ 341,244	$ 337,114	$ 494,303	$ 67,590	$ (135,401)	$ 14,753	$ 110,000
Other Income (Expense)										
Interest expense	(655)	—	(1,365)	(4,443)	(18,061)	(2,839)	8,726	(6,254)	(23,736)	(66,000)
Other (net)	1,575	1,714	2,831	3,758	9,584			15,247	21,227	
Income (loss) before taxes	$141,391	$ 219,276	$ 251,109	$ 340,559	$ 328,637	$ 491,464	$ 76,316	$ (126,408)	$ 12,244	$ 44,000
Provision (Credit) for Taxes	$ 68,750	110,000	124,850	171,600	154,000	244,200	29,700	(67,636)	3,850	20,900
Net income (loss)	$ 72,641	$ 109,276	$ 126,259	$ 168,959	$ 174,637	$ 247,264	$ 46,616	$ (58,772)	$ 8,394	$ 23,100
Number of Shares										
Outstanding at Year End	261,360	261,382	294,030	294,074	294,140	342,430	342,430	342,430	342,430	342,430
Net Income (Loss) per Share	$ .28	$ .42	$ .43	$ .57	$ .59	$ .72	$ .14	$(.17)	$ .03	$ .07

*Estimate

EXHIBIT 8
CYBERSYN SYSTEMS INCORPORATED
Organization Chart

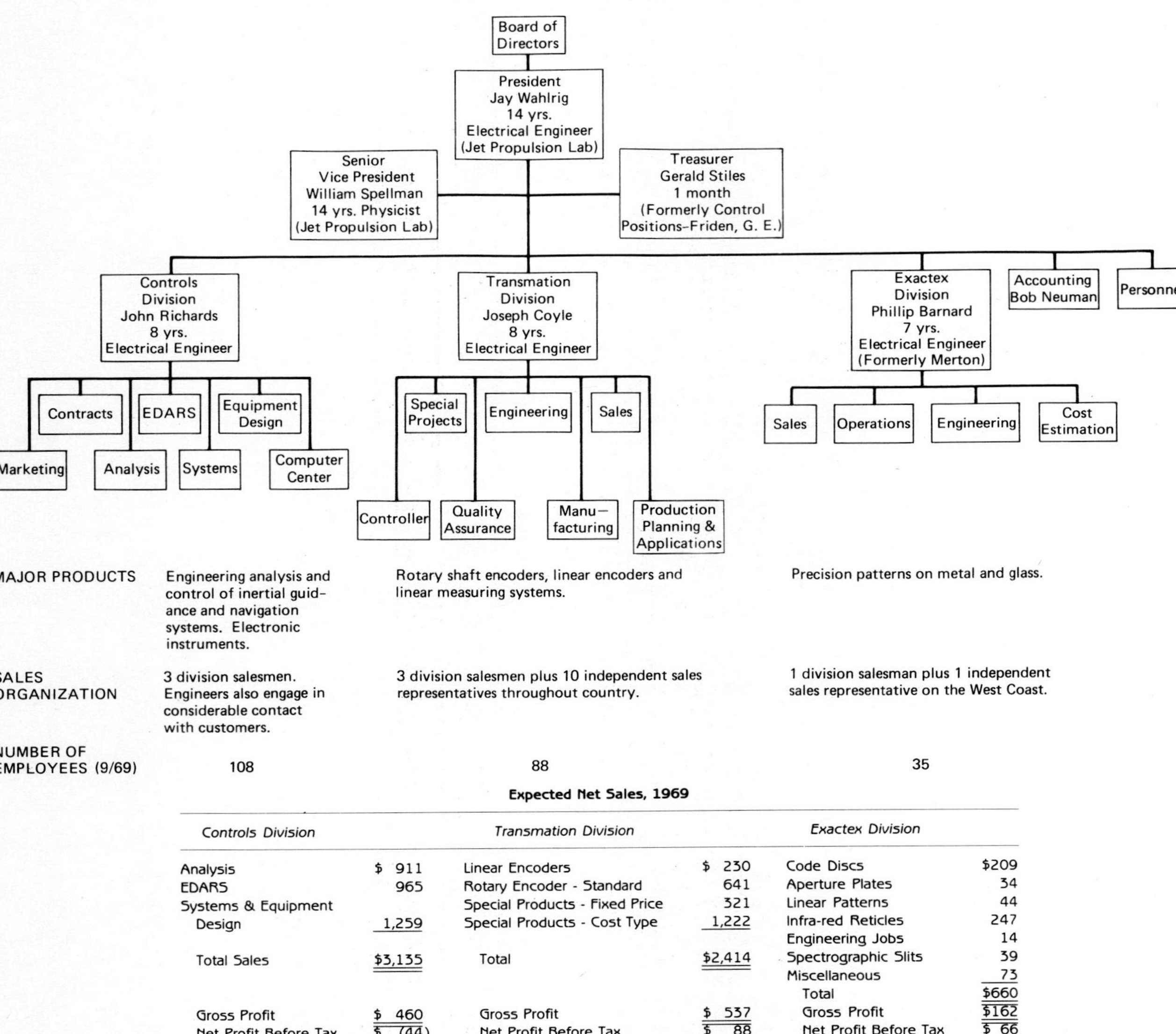

	Controls Division	Transmation Division	Exactex Division
MAJOR PRODUCTS	Engineering analysis and control of inertial guidance and navigation systems. Electronic instruments.	Rotary shaft encoders, linear encoders and linear measuring systems.	Precision patterns on metal and glass.
SALES ORGANIZATION	3 division salesmen. Engineers also engage in considerable contact with customers.	3 division salesmen plus 10 independent sales representatives throughout country.	1 division salesman plus 1 independent sales representative on the West Coast.
NUMBER OF EMPLOYEES (9/69)	108	88	35

Expected Net Sales, 1969

Controls Division		*Transmation Division*		*Exactex Division*	
Analysis	$ 911	Linear Encoders	$ 230	Code Discs	$209
EDARS	965	Rotary Encoder - Standard	641	Aperture Plates	34
Systems & Equipment Design	1,259	Special Products - Fixed Price	321	Linear Patterns	44
		Special Products - Cost Type	1,222	Infra-red Reticles	247
				Engineering Jobs	14
Total Sales	$3,135	Total	$2,414	Spectrographic Slits	39
				Miscellaneous	73
				Total	$660
Gross Profit	$ 460	Gross Profit	$ 537	Gross Profit	$162
Net Profit Before Tax	$ (44)	Net Profit Before Tax	$ 88	Net Profit Before Tax	$ 66

EXHIBIT 9

CYBERSYN SYSTEMS INCORPORATED

Percentage Breakdown of Company Sales by Government vs. Commercial, and by Contract Type

Market	*1961*	*1962*	*1963*	*1964*	*1965*	*1966*	*1967*	*1968*
Government	95%	93%	90%	91%	90%	85%	81%	78%
Commercial	5%	7	10	9	10	15	19	22
Total	100%	100%	100%	100%	100%	100%	100%	100%
Contract								
Fixed Price	61%	67%	61%	63%	62%	60%	52%	44%
Cost Type	39	33	39	29	30	35	47	50
Time and Material	0	0	0	8	8	5	1	6
Total	100%	100%	100%	100%	100%	100%	100%	100%

EXHIBIT 10 **CPFF Contracts**

Cost-plus-fixed-fee (CPFF) contracts are the most prevalent type of cost-reimbursement contract. Under this type of contract, the contractor has a right to be reimbursed for all costs determined to be allowable, reasonable, and allocable. He is also paid a fixed-dollar profit or fee for his services, with the dollar amount of the fee established before work begins. Cost-plus-fixed-fee contracts provide the contractor very little incentive to manage his costs effectively. He may even find it advisable to increase his direct costs. By so doing, he may be able to charge more of his overhead or indirect costs to the contract. He may also be able to justify high estimates on future contracts.

Cost-plus-fixed-fee contracts can be written in one of two forms: completion or term. The completion contract describes the scope of work and a definite goal or target, and normally requires delivery of a specific weapon system. The term contract describes the scope of the work in general terms and obligates the contractor to maintain a specified level of effort for a stated period of time to the research and development program. Because the completion contract requires that the contractor assume more obligations than the term contract, the form is generally preferred by the Government.[1]

CPFF contracts were extensively employed by the Defense Department during the 1950s and early 1960s. As the following figures show, the actual fee, although fixed in amount, varies as a percentage of cost with the contractor's performance:

	Negotiated Contract	*Cost Below Target*	*Cost Overrun*
Estimated Cost	$100,000	$50,000	$200,000
Fixed Fee	8,000	8,000	8,000
Price	$108,000	$58,000	$208,000
Actual Fee as a Percentage of Cost	8%	16%	4%

[1]J. Ronald Fox, *Arming America: How the U.S. Buys Weapons,* Division of Research, Graduate School of Business Administration, Harvard University, Boston, 1974.

Because the size of the fixed payment the contractor receives is *almost* independent of the contractor's performance, the CPFF contract provides little incentive for contractor efficiency. For this reason, during the latter 1960s the use of CPFF contracts was being discouraged. Perhaps as part of this government drive for efficiency, the NASA "authorized" fees on CPFF contracts are lower than those authorized in 1940 by Congress for Department of Defense contracts.

Maximum Fees of Fixed Fee Contracts

Service Provided	*DOD*	*NASA*
R&D	15%	10%
Architecture and Engineering (Public Works and Utilities)	6%	6%
Other	10%	7%

The normal fee for most R&D contracts in the late 1960s was about 8% of "estimated" cost. Cost-plus-percentage contracts are illegal.

As the quotation from Fox's book notes, a CPFF contract is a reimbursement contract. This means that a cost allocation is an important item. For Cybersyn, a company attempting to diversify out of the defense contracting business, allocation has even greater importance than for a company which is content with its product market mix as the following extracts from Gilbert A. Cuneo's *Government Contracts Handbook* suggest:[2]

Standards for Allowability

The comprehensive cost principles set forth tests for determining the allowability of costs. The factors to be considered in deciding the allowability of individual items of cost include (1) reasonableness, (2) allocability, (3) application of those generally accepted accounting principles and practices appropriate to the particular circumstances, and (4) any limitations or exclusions set forth in the applicable cost principles or otherwise included in the contract as to types or amounts of cost items.

REASONABLENESS A cost is reasonable if, in its nature or amount, it does not exceed that which would be incurred by an ordinarily prudent person in the conduct of competitive business. In determining reasonableness, consideration is to be given to: (1) whether the cost is of a type generally recognized as ordinary and necessary for the conduct of the contractor's business or the performance of the contract; (2) the restraints or requirements imposed by such factors as generally accepted sound business practices, arm's-length bargaining, federal and state laws and regulations, and contract terms and specifications; (3) the action that a prudent businessman would take in the circumstances, considering his responsibilities to the owners of the business, his employees, his customers, the government, and the public at large; and (4) significant deviations from the established practices of the contractor which may unjustifiably increase the contract costs.

[2]Gilbert A. Cuneo, *Government Contracts Handbook,* Machinery and Allied Products Institute and Council for Technological Advancement, Washington, D.C., 1962, pp. 157–58, 164, 168. Reprinted by permission.

Allocability A cost is allocable to a government contract if it: (1) is incurred specifically for the contract; (2) benefits both the contract and other work, or both government work and other work, and can be distributed between them in reasonable proportion to the benefits received; or (3) is necessary to the over-all operation of the business, although a direct relationship to any particular cost objective cannot be shown. . . .

Indirect costs [These are costs] which are incurred for the general purpose of the contractor and are not in the first instance charged directly and finally to the contract, but are first charged to departments, burden centers, or other overhead units, and through those units allocated to the work which they have benefited. The allocation is accomplished by establishing rates or bases which may differ with the class of indirect cost being distributed. Such rates are established by relating the total of the indirect costs to be allocated for a certain representative period of time to a selected base for that period. Normally, the base period will be the contractor's fiscal year. The use of a shorter period may be appropriate in case of (1) contracts whose performance involves only a minor portion of the fiscal year, or (2) where it is general practice in the industry to use a shorter period. . . .

Selling and distribution costs which are not related to a contract are unallowable indirect costs. Advertising solely for recruitment of personnel for a contract, for the procurement of scarce items for the contract or for the disposal of scrap or surplus materials acquired for the contract is an allowable indirect cost.[3]

Bad debts are unallowable costs, as are contributions and donations. Depreciation on idle or excess facilities (not those maintained for standby purposes) is not an allowable cost.

Interest on borrowings (however represented), bond discounts, costs of financing and refinancing operations, legal and professional fees paid in connection with the preparation of prospectuses, costs of preparation and issuance of stock rights, and costs related thereto, are unallowable except for interest assessed by state or local taxing authorities under certain [specified] conditions. . . .

A contractor's independent *research and development* is that research and development which is not sponsored by a contract, grant, or other arrangement. . . . [These costs] are allowable as indirect costs provided that they are allocated to all work of the contractor. Costs of the contractor's independent development are allowable to the extent that such development is related to the product lines for which the government has contracts, provided the costs are reasonable in amount and are allocated as indirect costs to all work of the contractor on such product lines. Where a contractor's normal business does not involve production business, the cost of independent development is allowable to the extent that such development is related and allocated as an indirect cost to the field of effort of government research and development contracts.

Independent research and development costs are to include an amount for the absorption of their appropriate share of indirect and administrative costs, unless the contractor, in accordance with his accounting practices consistently applied, treats such costs otherwise.

Research and development costs (including amounts capitalized) regardless of their nature, which were incurred in accounting periods prior to the award of a particular contract, are unallowable except as pre-contract costs.[4]

[3]This paragraph and the one following it are paraphrased from Cuneo.
[4]Footnote omitted.

The reasonableness of expenditures for independent research and development should be determined in light of all pertinent considerations such as previous contractor research and development activity, cost of past programs, and changes in science and technology. Such expenditures are to be pursuant to a broad planned program which is reasonable in scope and well managed. Advance agreements are particularly important with regard to these costs.

EXHIBIT 11 CYBERSYN SYSTEMS INCORPORATED
Exactex Products and Processes

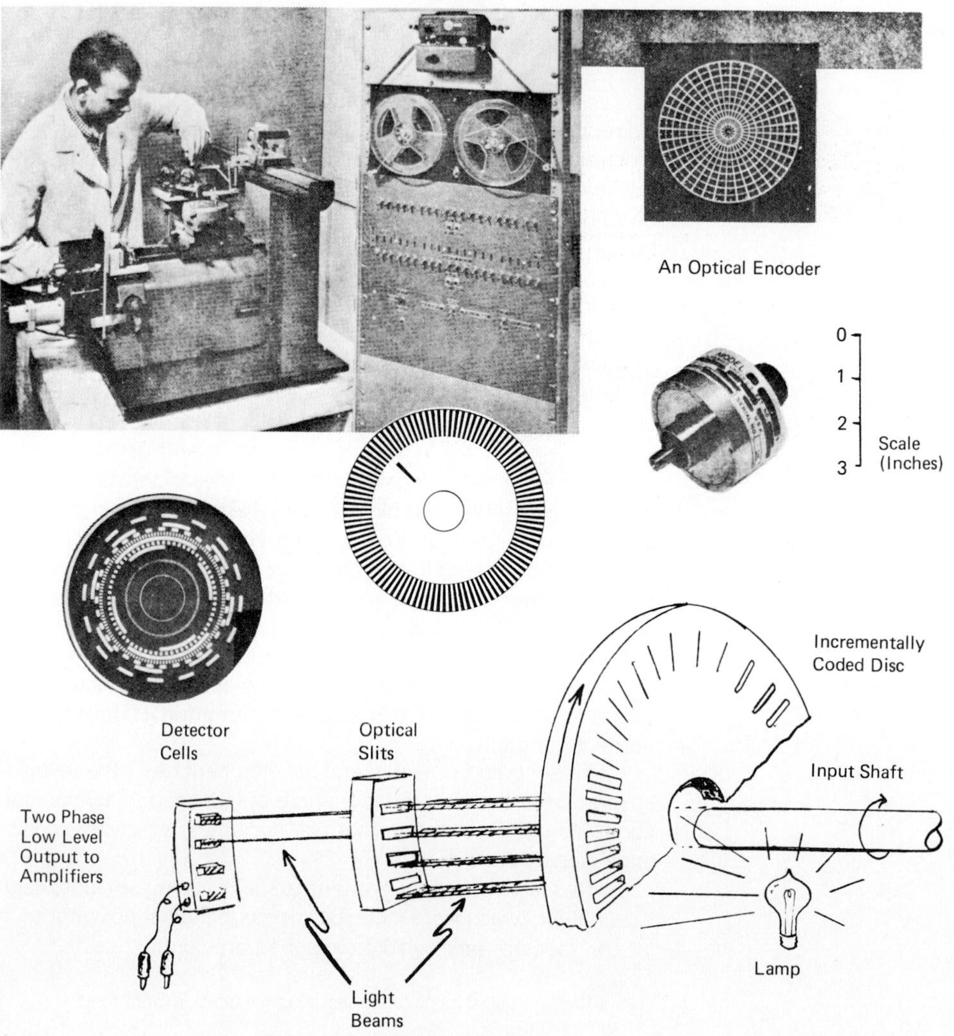

EXHIBIT 12

CYBERSYN SYSTEMS INCORPORATED
Statement of Philosophy Concerning Corporate Internal Environment

4/9/69
JRW
Amended 12/2/69

1 The environment inside the company should be open, fact-based, and result-oriented so that: decisions are thought through on the basis of facts, objectively considered; people are evaluated on the basis of their performance; people understand what is expected of them and the criteria for successful performance.
2 An effort should be made to communicate to people what is going on, where the company is going, and how they fit in so that they can understand and appreciate their importance to the company.
3 There should be a concern for increasing the technical and managerial competence of individuals and teams within the company.
4 There should be an awareness and sensitivity to the needs and problems of individual people in all parts of the company, so that appropriate assistance is made available when needed.
5 Work should involve a sense of urgency, include careful planning, and give the individual a sense of accomplishment.
6 Individuals at every level should be encouraged to listen for customer needs and to take the responsibility for getting them adequately explored.
7 We should expect high ethical standards in external and internal relationships.

EXHIBIT 13 Statement of Company Objectives and Strategy

Cybersyn Systems Incorporated
November 15, 1969

To All Divisional Vice-Presidents:

As a result of the discussion last week, I have rewritten the company's objectives and strategy with the aim of making them more specific and action-oriented. Broadly, what I am saying here is: exploit the present situations to the utmost and broaden them. In the process we will be building a base from which to really move.

Objectives

Growth	Double in three years.
Profitability	10% return on net worth after tax.
Capital	Have capital available to finance profitable growth.
Balancing Objectives	Plan the use of resources to achieve specified results.
Personnel	Achieve an operating environment that holds highly qualified people.

Strategy

1 Take damn good care of the present business. Recognize what we are good in and what we are not good in. Take what we are good in and match it with growth opportunities.
2 When the present business is really taken care of in all areas—engineering, management, marketing, production—then identify new areas in which we can function. These must be growth areas (5 to 15% natural market growth) and must be contiguous to present operations.
3 When these are accomplished, we will have a sound, established base with different capabilities than now. Again, we equate these capabilities against the markets we see and move forward, perhaps by developing an acquisition program.

Jay R. Wahlrig

Jay R. Wahlrig
President

MYSTIC ELECTRONICS, INC. (C)

"I took on MacBurney in March, 1974, two and a half years ago, to take care of the day-to-day operations so I would be freed up to get involved with the firm's strategy and to look around for acquisitions," said Tod Armstrong, President and 90% owner of Mystic Electronics of Mystic, Connecticut.

Armstrong leaned back in his swivel chair behind his paper-laden desk as the presses downstairs, belonging to Elonics Corporation, the company from which Armstrong had bought his capacitor lines, continued to hammer away like slightly muffled pile drivers. Hanging from the sometimes vibrating beige walls were some old charts of the Mystic area and a set of British Admiralty lithographs depicting ships of the time in Newport harbor of the 1750s. Armstrong continued, "MacBurney is a good complement to me. He digs in and gets to the bottom of a problem—my interest span is rather short, his appears to be longer. Naturally, we have our conflicts. He wants me to be involved in the company more than I have been, and I want to pursue outside interests like acquisitions. Lately, I've been busy with my new house and my lobster boat; my divorce has taken a lot of time.

"I feel that he's come on board to take care of the daily operations and that I shouldn't have to be concerned with them—though sometimes I question some things he has done and give him a hard time about some of his decisions.

"But these conflicts between MacBurney and me—and they are relatively minor—are really pretty normal in a small business. I'm more concerned about Ned Troy. He did a great job in sales before the recession, but he has retreated into a shell since sales have dropped. I just can't seem to communicate with him and it's all the more frustrating since he was my only confidant in the company when I first took over. Another problem I have to contend with concerns Abe Steiner. He's doing a great job at production and inventory control, but he's a one-man show. You can't understudy him. And he's sixty-two. He could easily become ill or retire and leave us with a problem—it'll be hard to replace his forty years of experience. That's why I'd like to see his operations become more documented and formalized."

Armstrong leaned forward. "But what I'm most concerned about now is getting these foreign ventures working. I've just come back from India and the Far East. We have a lot of big U.S. contracts on the line which could provide us with an extra $1 million or more in sales if we could only be assured of receiving a supply from abroad."

Armstrong was discussing the fortunes of Mystic Electronics since he had brought on Alex MacBurney to be V.P. operations in March 1974. Operations in the Mystic plant had improved considerably (see *Exhibits 1, 2* and *3* for financial statements), and the company's reputation as a reliable source of supply was provoking the interest of some of the largest manufacturing companies in consumer electronics. However, Mystic was

This case was prepared by Mark T. Teagan, Research Assistant, under the direction of Assistant Professor Kenneth J. Hatten as a basis for class discussion rather than to illustrate either effective or ineffective handling of an administrative situation.

having major difficulties in obtaining a consistent supply from the foreign sources with which it had contracted. This was jeopardizing its chances of entering the large mass markets which were, for the first time, opening to it.

STARTING THE COMPANY

After graduating from Harvard Business School, Armstrong had worked both as an entrepreneur and as an employee in a large company, USM. After a stint with a fellow Business School graduate in a small manufacturing company, he went to work for Elonics Corporation, one of the three full-line capacitor manufacturers in the U.S. After Armstrong had been with the company for two years, Elonics announced that it was going to write off its paper, film and mica capacitor lines. Armstrong felt they could be turned around, made an offer to buy them and was finally able to purchase the lines; to do so, he assumed $90,000 of debt, $75,000 of which was insured or guaranteed by THE Insurance Company for a one-time fee of 1% of the appraisal value of the firm's assets and 2% annually of the outstanding loan guarantee.

As part of the deal with Elonics, Armstrong agreed to lease 25,000 square feet in the rear portion of the old 446,000-square-foot Elonics plant, a former textile mill in Mystic, Connecticut, at a modest figure. The space was more than sufficient for the existing operation which then employed 100 hourly and supervisory personnel. Upon taking over the company, Armstrong assembled a management team primarily by contacting former managers who had been laid off by the divesting Elonics company and by keeping on those who were still working on the lines he had purchased. Production began on April 12, 1972.

PRODUCTS AND COMPETITION

After stagnating for several years, the noncaptive market for discrete capacitors took off in 1973 and 1974, and then slumped back again during 1975 as the recession took its toll (*Exhibit 4*). Within the market, tantalum and especially ceramic capacitors had demonstrated the greatest growth potential (*Exhibit 4*). The overall slow market growth of the previous decade had been caused in part by advances in integrated circuits which contained within one package the capability of numerous discrete electronic components. However, Mystic's management believed that, over any reasonable long-term planning horizon, there would be a need for discrete capacitors and that integrated circuits did not threaten to eliminate their market. Furthermore, the lack of rapid growth in the capacitor market had led many firms, including large ones like General Instrument, to leave it, creating turmoil—and opportunity—for those remaining.

Behind the largest producers like Sprague Electric and Cornell-Dubilier were another fifty to seventy firms, normally with more specialized product lines than Mystic and with sales generally less than $2 million. Armstrong noted that Mystic, with its inherited product line and customer base, remained unique among the small firms in having a shot at competing on even terms with the large companies. In part this was because Mystic was able to rely on Elonics for the critical impregnating step[1] required on about 20% of output (a service Elonics had agreed to provide at cost), which required large-scale expensive equipment. Nevertheless, being a small company, Mystic was almost always a second source of supply to large buyers.

Mystic's markets had changed only slightly during its four and a half years of existence. Its five main markets were:

- *Telephone equipment manufacturers,* such as Western Electric, Stromberg Carlson, GT&E, Northern Electric and ITT, accounted for approximately 20% of Mystic's sales. This business was especially welcome because demand was relatively stable, foreign competition was limited, there was little pressure on prices and the average price per unit was typically somewhat higher than in other market segments.
- *Industrial electronics manufacturers* accounted for between 30 and 40% of sales. This market required strict adherence to specifications, in contrast to the consumer market, because end uses included such items as test equipment and welders. Foreign competition was limited in the industrial market.
- *Aerospace and Defense* accounted for approximately 20% of sales. Most of the final applications were in ground networks, especially communications systems, though some of Mystic's capacitors were used in missiles.
- *Computer manufacturers* accounted for about 10% of sales, often ordering large quantities of low-priced, small-size units. Ned Troy felt sales in this market would be much larger if Mystic could gain an entree to IBM. However, IBM's earlier experience with Elonics, Mystic's former parent company, had been unsatisfactory and Mystic was still working on living down Elonics's reputation.
- *Distributors* accounted for about 10% of Mystic's sales and sold to the same markets as Mystic's manufacturers' reps, though reps were paid a commission on all sales made in their areas, including those to distributors.

Essentially, Mystic sold to commercial and industrial markets which were characterized by more stable demand and less price pressure than the large, lower price-per-unit consumer and automotive markets.

DISTRIBUTION AND SALES

Like most companies in the industry, Mystic sold primarily through manufacturers' representatives who normally sold a broad range of electronic components. Each of Mystic's twenty-one rep organizations had five or more salesmen, and received a 5% commission on all sales in their exclusive territories, including those by Mystic to distributors. ''Although most capacitor manufacturers offer reps a 7% commission, Mystic has been able to attract reps with its 5% because it is one of the few independent sources offering a broad line of paper, film and mica capacitors, and because there are more reps seeking capacitor lines than there are capacitor manufacturers.'' In addition, Ned Troy,

[1]Certain capacitors, typically those made of paper, were impregnated with wax, oil or resin to reduce moisture in the device which would otherwise destroy their electrical properties.

the sales manager, estimated that, of the fifty to seventy capacitor manufacturers, Mystic was in reputation, if not in sales, among the top ten or twenty.

Mystic's network of reps, viewed as one of the company's primary assets, was a major factor in Mystic's success with the lines Elonics had been prepared to write off. Mystic simply stepped into the gap left by Elonics. The reps had been reassured because so many familiar faces were at Mystic—especially one, Ned Troy's.

The selling process included the reps' discussing problems with engineers, and offering solutions which would often favor use of Mystic's product line or capabilities. When a rep made a sale to a purchasing agent, the groundwork for the sale had often been laid six months to a year in advance in the engineering department, which told the purchasing agent what it wanted. Capacitors being a low-price and, within specific categories, homogenous product, service and delivery were key selling points. A good rep provided the service and a good capacitor company provided both.

The importance of the Mystic line to its reps varied. It provided $1 million in sales to the New England rep, who was a close friend of Ned Troy's, but was an almost negligible part of the line carried by reps in the Western states.

Troy handled virtually all the customer contacts himself and much of his time was spent working directly with the reps and major Original Equipment Manufacturer (OEM) accounts. Although not technically trained, Troy felt he had learned enough about capacitors to solve many of the simpler product problems in the field and to know what questions to ask should the difficulty be more complex.

ORGANIZATIONAL DEVELOPMENT 1973–1976

In 1973, Mystic had been plagued by its inability to get enough product out. Often the cause was materials shortages, even though accounts payable to materials suppliers increased dramatically. The job shop nature of the work made ordering difficult, especially since each order had unique materials requirements. For instance, mica capacitors could require many different widths and lengths of mica, so the problem was far more complex than merely having "mica" on stock. John Lysenko, who was in charge of materials control through early 1974, seemed unable to match purchasing to production needs and put out blanket orders for materials without relation to price or near-term sales.

Armstrong had been concerned to find new opportunities to expand the business, and he was anxious to get these operational problems under control. He became convinced that he needed a manager of operations who would be responsible for all phases of the firm's activities except sales and marketing. He decided to hire Alex MacBurney, a fellow graduate of the Harvard Business School and former co-worker at USM.

MacBurney joined Mystic in March, 1974, and immediately attacked the problems of materials control. He concurred with Armstrong's analysis that Lysenko, the materials control manager, was over-ordering in an attempt to cover every contingency. The excess inventory aggravated the company's cash flow problems stemming from its growth. MacBurney also discovered that Lysenko had a poor working relationship with his people and was getting little support from them. He, therefore, decided to test Lysenko by giving him a specific task: to reduce inventory to a lower percentage of sales. When Lysenko failed to meet the goal, MacBurney fired him.

MacBurney then instituted an organizational change whereby Abe Steiner assumed Lysenko's duties in addition to those he already had in production management. However, Steiner relinquished control of the assembly operations in his paper and film lines to Paul McCosh, who retained his mica line.

Unfortunately, this change did not work out. Each month, production was scheduled in advance; each line was programmed to produce a given output measured in sales dollars. Performance was measured throughout the month against the scheduled output. If it became apparent a line was falling short of its schedule, the foremen had a tendency to grab the big dollar items to ensure they would finish the month on target. Of course, this practice led to delayed shipments on smaller orders and poor customer relations.

MacBurney felt that the root of the problem was McCosh who, though organized and efficient, lacked a sense of urgency. He often tended to agree with the workers that a given output could not be met, thus leading the workers to let up. By contrast, Steiner was a driver and a man whose forty years' experience lent him authority when he insisted a given output could be achieved. McCosh's comparatively lax methods led to negative labor variances. Labor[2] was programmed at a given percentage of sales output; if output fell below expectations or if output was met only by taking on extra workers, a variance occurred.

Therefore, with reluctance, MacBurney made another organizational change in the summer of 1975. Steiner reassumed control of the film and paper lines in addition to materials control. McCosh was left with engineering and the mica line. MacBurney tried to minimize the traumatic nature of the change, which was intensified because it entailed a corresponding change in support personnel such as line foremen, by explaining to McCosh that Mystic's increasing diversity necessitated it.

The new organization worked effectively. Output became more predictable, and Steiner, with his intimate knowledge of the operations, was able to keep inventory to a minimum.

MANAGEMENT DURING THE RECESSION

Having reorganized Mystic so that inventory and labor variances were under control, MacBurney was pleased that cash flow and profits improved. However, in November, 1974, the economic downturn started to affect the capacitor industry as orders decreased and cancellations increased. The structure of the capacitor industry and Mystic's role as a small company and back-up supplier aggravated the problem. Large companies which made expensive telephone or industrial products wanted to insure there would be no production bottlenecks because of delays in the shipments of comparatively inexpensive parts such as capacitors. Therefore, their purchasing agents would order supplies from another large company and order the same supplies from a back-up producer like Mystic to minimize the risk of delay. When the economy was good, these companies could absorb the extra parts. When the economy went bad, their orders, especially back-up orders, were often cancelled; thus the double ordering helped small companies like Mystic

[2]Workers were paid an hourly wage plus a bonus if output exceeded the standard established by an industrial engineering time study. Almost all the workers earned bonuses.

in good times but severely hurt them in bad times. In addition, the recession forced many rep organizations to lay people off, resulting in a reduced coverage of the market.

Despite cancellations, Mystic entered the recession with a backlog large enough to keep it above breakeven but, although management saw the recession coming, it did not cut back sufficiently to maintain healthy profits. Looking back on the situation, MacBurney said, "Perhaps each management team needs to go through a recession before it knows how to react. We knew it was coming; we just didn't know how long and how deep it would be so we were slow in cutting back; for example, we hired an extra engineer in mid-1974 and kept him on the payroll until mid-1975. We simply hoped the slump would end and we would be able to afford him."

The recession affected cash flow in many ways. For instance, whereas Raytheon used to accept entire shipments of capacitors as soon as Mystic had them ready, it now insisted on accepting them only as needed, leaving Mystic holding the inventory. Similarly, ESI, a small company in New Jersey, put in a rush order for $43,000 worth of capacitors. However, by the time Mystic had them ready, ESI was suffering cash flow problems itself, and having just cut back from 140 to 40 people, said it wouldn't need the entire order as soon as it had thought. Although ESI was sympathetic to Mystic's problems, during bad times each company had to attend to its own survival.

Mystic was able to cancel orders with large companies on standard items; however, it often had to accept deliveries from small companies and on orders which were nonstandard. And, because of the shortages, Steiner had to order some materials without customer orders to avoid being caught without them when he needed them. Fortunately, Mystic had brought its inventory under control so it could weather the recession and look ahead.

In the depths of the recession during 1975, even Steiner had difficulty keeping inventory down. Many materials became difficult to obtain so, as Steiner said: "If someone offered 1,000 pounds of material to be delivered in 3 months, you would take it because it would take you 9 months to get it by routine ordering. This happens in most recessions. And it's also a function of Mystic's size. Our $10,000 order was easy for suppliers to overlook when they had several $100,000 orders."

PRODUCTION CONTROL

As the economy improved, the raw materials shortages occurred less frequently. Steiner would order material upon receipt of a customer's order, but only if the material needed was not already in stock. Although inventory control cards on each material were maintained, Steiner operated, for the most part, with his own "undocumented system." This system basically involved ordering materials only if they were not in storage or on the floor. The inventory control cards kept record of materials in stock, but not the materials on the floor.

On-the-floor inventory existed because when an order was being produced, one or more parts were often left over as a result of lower than expected yields earlier in the production process. This led to surplus of the rest of the materials involved in the order. These materials would be kept by the workers at their machines for use on another order. Through his intimate knowledge of the system and of the people, Steiner was able to keep track of these hold-over materials. In addition, though he ordered materials only upon receipt of a customer's order, the minimum order quantities often exceeded the material needed to produce a customer's order. This often led to there being material in the plant which could be used for a new order. Steiner was also able to control inventory purchases through "deviating"—adapting material intended for one application to another.

Twice a year, Steiner supervised plant-wide inventory checks which involved physically counting the quantity of each material in storage and on the floor. These checks were used to compare the amount of materials purchased to the amount used, so that the material component of cost of goods sold could be verified and variances accurately quantified.

Steiner stated that Mystic did not calculate a materials cost for each order but did so for overall output. Although such a system could lead to Mystic's making unprofitable items, Steiner said that Mystic made cost estimates for doubtful products and monitored costs by such cross-references as noting when additional material was requested for given orders.

Steiner said he would not advise the use of such a system for most operations but that he could use it because he and the workers knew what they were doing. He also said that another recession would require "crystal balling" needs again. And if sales were to increase by 50%, Mystic would have to start using the more formal inventory control system which was in place.

MacBurney noted that some large buyers like Wescom were starting to send orders for a year's needs, asking Mystic to keep 10% on stock. But although such orders aided in Mystic's scheduling and purchasing, they amounted to only a small part of total sales.

A NEW CONTROLLER

Having come on as Vice President, Operations, MacBurney was initially involved in daily operations in manufacturing and in financial control. He soon became Executive Vice President and hired a former associate at USM, Paul Benedict, to be controller and to deal with billing, collecting receivables and with other financial responsibilities so that he could assume responsibility for Mystic's operations and for its foreign ventures.

In addition to his daily financial responsibilities, Benedict became concerned with creating a formal control system for inventory and production. Benedict felt that, though Steiner was controlling inventory and production in a particularly able manner, a system would enable others to assume the sixty-two-year-old Steiner's responsibilities were he to become ill or retire. In addition, it would better prepare Mystic for a larger sales volume, which Steiner admitted would make his undocumented system ineffective. Most importantly, a system would enable more workers to become involved and push decision making to a lower level, giving more people the opportunity to develop themselves while working at Mystic. Benedict felt that Steiner's total control of inventory and production placed Mystic in a precarious position.

Benedict felt that scheduling by the availability of people and machines would be preferable to the present system of scheduling by sales dollar and unit output. Such a system would encourage long-term maximum output rather than short-term meeting of monthly goals. Benedict was aware of the complexity of the task insofar as Mystic was a job shop, had little ability to forecast due to the nature of its market, and used no materials for which future demand was guaranteed. End users tended to predict needs of their big dollar items but not of inexpensive items like capacitors. Normally they ordered capacitors on short notice. Yet he felt there were computer software packages which could well apply to Mystic's scheduling situation.

He felt that he himself would have to learn the intricacies of the operation before suggesting a change because Steiner's strong will could easily rebel against modification of his system. Benedict stated, "I'm aware a formal system may be impractical, that it may be an example of spending $20,000 to save $2,000. But I believe it's worth looking into because, if it can work, it would make the system operate more smoothly, develop people's skills, and prepare us for rapid growth or another recession."

MacBurney felt that the job-shop nature of the business made the implementation of a computer-based system difficult if not impractical. However, he had recently hired an experienced engineer who, he expected, would be able to quantify the tradeoffs between cost and margin versus product quality and performance in specific functions.

FOREIGN VENTURES

India

By 1976, Mystic had been negotiating with a number of foreign suppliers for three years. Mystic's involvement in foreign ventures started in 1973 when Armstrong received a letter from a family in Calcutta, India, suggesting the possibility of their manufacturing low-priced dipped mica capacitors for Mystic. Armstrong made some initial contacts with the family but the deal fell through.

He then received another letter from a company in Bombay, India, which offered to pay for Mystic's sending a person there to establish the groundwork for a potential deal. Wanting to follow this possibility up, Armstrong arranged to go to India. Troy, however, suggested he first talk to one of Troy's friends, George Cooper, who had been to India and who might be able to inform Armstrong about Indian business practices. Upon hearing Armstrong's plans, Cooper became excited, saying that his boss, John Weston, an influential Boston businessman and a board member of one of the world's largest corporations, already had many contacts in India, including a business involvement with Baracin Electronics, Ltd., a company which was set up to supply mica. Mystic could teach them to partially assemble mica capacitors. Cooper called Weston immediately, and within two hours, he, Armstrong and Troy were in Weston's Boston office.

Weston offered to pay to send a member of Mystic's management to talk with his Indian colleagues. It was decided that Troy should make the initial contact. Three months later, the manager of the Indian operation, Gupta, came to Mystic for a month during which Mystic personnel taught him the details of their dipped mica operation. Soon afterward, Armstrong visited India to close the deal.

As agreed to in December, 1973, the deal called for Gupta to partially assemble mica capacitors which would be sold to an offshore trading company for resale to Mystic. Mystic would perform the final dipping and packaging operations, and market the capacitors to high-volume users in the U.S. Mystic would be 50% owner of the Bermuda-based offshore trading company; John Weston would own 15% in addition to his partial ownership of the Indian company; another foreign corporation would own the remainder.[3] This arrangement would enable Mystic to take advantage of India's plentiful mica supplies and low labor costs (12½¢ per hour), and to defer taxes on profits made by the Bermuda company until the money was brought into the U.S. Gupta would start out making 10,000 units a day and increase output to 50,000 a day within 6 months; Mystic would buy almost the entire output and sell the capacitors under its name.

Unfortunately, the venture soon ran into trouble; the recession in the United States made it impossible for Mystic to market the number of capacitors Gupta was set to produce. Like many small Indian companies, Gupta's was highly levered with high interest rate debt, making it vulnerable to economic cycles. In addition, the first big order Gupta sent to Mystic was late and only 50% of the capacitors met specifications. The buyer canceled. The samples Gupta sent Mystic also failed to meet specifications, making it impossible for Mystic to get new orders. Gupta was angry with Mystic for not buying enough capacitors even though he knew the recession caused the problem. And Mystic was frustrated with Gupta for his late deliveries and poor quality product.

John Weston then got a prominent and wealthy Indian family, the Ramichans, to buy a major interest in the Indian company, leaving Gupta in charge of operations. Under the new ownership, some of the mutual suspicions diminished though Gupta became adamant about having assured orders before manufacturing capacitors for Mystic. Some major accounts, such as one with Digital Equipment, were cancelled because of Mystic's inability to get from Gupta timely deliveries of capacitors which met specifications.

Taiwan

In early 1974, Armstrong received a letter from Aodin Electron of Taiwan suggesting the possibility of Aodin's providing Mystic with low-cost aluminum electrolytic capacitors which were enjoying a large market in the U.S. Although Taiwan's labor costs were four times those in India, Armstrong was optimistic about the market for aluminum electrolytic capacitors. Aluminum electrolytic capacitors would be a new product for Mystic and, though they had many applications in Mystic's industrial and commercial markets, they would also be marketable to the mass market which Mystic had yet to enter.

Armstrong decided to visit Taiwan while returning home from a visit to India. Upon arriving at the airport, he was surprised to be greeted by a boyish-looking man holding aloft a sign saying, "Mr. Armstrong." Lacking a company car, the man, Alan Li, used a taxi to escort Armstrong to his plant where Armstrong was pleased to find a small but efficient ongoing operation. After a few months of correspondence, Armstrong closed the deal in September 1974; it was agreed that Li would provide Mystic with assembled aluminum electrolytic capacitors for Mystic to market in the U.S. under its own name.

Armstrong was pleased that the Taiwan venture had proceeded with few problems. Even though it commenced just as the recession was reducing Mystic's market, Mystic's orders were not so large a part of Li's output as to make a significant impact by their absence, and Li was pleased to get the additional business when it did come.

[3]Americans were allowed no more than 50% voting control of an offshore trading company. Mystic had a 50% beneficial interest and had 35% of the voting rights in the company.

Korea

In late 1974, Armstrong also received a letter from Kyung Pak of Korea, who was interested in supplying Mystic with low-cost film capacitors. Pak said that some members of his management team would soon be in the U.S. and would like to visit Mystic. Armstrong agreed, only to find that he had to leave on a trip to India on the day the Koreans arrived. He, therefore, arranged to meet them at the airport with MacBurney. After Armstrong had left, MacBurney escorted the Koreans to Mystic to look at the plant. MacBurney negotiated and closed a deal in March, 1975, whereby the Koreans agreed to provide Mystic with film capacitors to be marketed under Mystic's name in the U.S. To help Pak meet Mystic's needs, Mystic sold the Koreans some fully depreciated machinery for $15,000 to be paid in the form of a 10% discount on all orders from Korea until the $15,000 was paid off. Armstrong was enthusiastic about the arrangement because Pak's low-cost capacitors had many applications in the consumer and automotive markets and would help Mystic break into them.

After some initial difficulties in obtaining requested samples and orders from Korea, Armstrong visited Pak while returning from another trip to India during which he had tried to rectify the problems Mystic was having there. Armstrong found his relationship with Pak frustrating. Pak always said "yes" to any request Armstrong made, with profuse assurances that he would fill Mystic's orders. Yet, the capacitors never came. And, while in Korea, Armstrong had requested a weekly Telex to notify him of progress on his orders. Pak assured him he would send the Telex, yet they never came.

Armstrong noted that Pak was a wealthy and highly regarded man in Korean society. His wife ran a private high school for 2,600 girls,[4] and he had set up his capacitor factory to provide the girls with a means of making income to support themselves during their schooling. The factory's output was large, and Mystic's orders were small by comparison to orders such as those of a capacitor company supplying Zenith with much of its needs.

Although Armstrong consummated the arrangements of Mystic's foreign ventures, MacBurney took charge of day-to-day operations, overseeing the drafting of letters of credit (see *Appendix*), correspondence and the placing of orders.

DOMESTIC EXPANSION

Having been long aware of the many market opportunities for tantalum capacitors, Armstrong wished to enter that market. Knowing that he did not have the in-house capability to manufacture tantalum capacitors, he was on the lookout for an acquisition opportunity. A small company, Vanguard Electronics, located in Middleton, Connecticut was brought to his attention, and in May, 1975, Mystic paid $30,000 as a downpayment and gave the principal owner, Anthony Alaimo, a note for $70,000, an employment contract and 5% of Mystic's stock. Although Vanguard Electronics had shown little profit on its income statements, Armstrong learned that Alaimo had been taking out a good deal of the profit in perquisites. And, with apparently little marketing effort, the company had

[4] 96% of Korean high school students attended private schools.

sales of about $300,000. Immediately upon acquiring Vanguard, Mystic received a $150,000 order from Motorola.

Initially, operations continued in Middleton, but coordination became a ''nightmare.'' To solve this problem, Vanguard's equipment was moved to Mystic in two trailer trucks. Alaimo and some of his workers moved with it, but Alaimo's chief assistant, Virginia Bronte, wanted to remain in Middleton so she visited the Mystic plant only occasionally.

The manufacture of tantalum capacitors differed considerably from the manufacture of Mystic's traditional lines in that it involved an electro-chemical process rather than Mystic's normal electro-mechanical processes. The initial step involved tantalum powder held in a polyester binder being placed in a sulfuric acid bath and being charged with electricity, which caused the tantalum to react with the acid. The voltage, bath consistency and bath temperature had to adhere to strict specifications. The resultant tantalum sulfate was dipped in a silver paste, then in solder and finally in an epoxy. The complex and rigid process left little room for error and thus required considerable expertise to get good yields.

It soon became evident that Alaimo, though he had an engineering background and had been the principal of Vanguard, was unwilling to control the operation. It also became evident that Virginia Bronte had been the one who had made the process work for Vanguard, but, unfortunately, she spent too little time at Mystic to convey her knowledge to others. Thus, Mystic had to compete on price with companies like Union Carbide which had 95% yields while Mystic was getting a 25% yield. Production and delivery problems created rep and customer bad will in addition to losses of $10,000 a month. In November, 1975, Armstrong fired Alaimo and then, in May, 1976, when the first note installment ($25,000) was due, Mystic got Alaimo to agree to cancel the $70,000 note in exchange for the tantalum assets and inventory. It was agreed that Alaimo would become a contract manufacturer and that Mystic would become his sole outlet; Mystic repurchased his stock.

Although Alaimo had refused to ship tantalum capacitors from Mystic unless they met rigid quality control standards, as a contract manufacturer, he shipped capacitors to Mystic which were of low quality, leading Mystic to cancel the new contract within a month. Alaimo sued Mystic for $18,000 of his employment contract; Mystic retaliated by suing for $250,000, claiming that Alaimo had misrepresented his operation and his balance sheet and had not performed under his employment contract.

PROBLEMS AND OPPORTUNITIES

Armstrong and MacBurney, though aware of some problems remaining at the Mystic plant, were pleased that their changes in the operation had led to its being profitable and to Mystic's gaining a good reputation in the industry.

There was considerable frustration over their foreign ventures and their tantalum experience. Reviewing Mystic's poor batting average in its outside ventures, MacBurney said that Mystic had most likely been trying to do too many things without researching them well enough. Perhaps the reason Mystic had had problems with the Indian operation was that Mystic was too big a factor in its fortunes, so when Mystic could not provide

Gupta with orders, he was in deep trouble. And perhaps the opposite was true in Korea: Mystic's being such a small factor in its output made the Koreans less sensitive to its needs. A happy middle ground existed in Taiwan where Mystic was a good customer, neither too big nor too small.

Armstrong speculated that perhaps the reason had more to do with the people involved. In India and Korea, the owners were wealthy and influential families, whereas in Taiwan, Li was from a working family background and was now anxious to succeed and therefore to serve his customers well.

The problems in India included personal problems in communication—not in the physical process of relaying messages, but in understanding. Gupta was obviously sore about losing control of his company and about Mystic's not having supplied a reliable outlet for him. Although he claimed to understand that the recession had caused the problem rather than ill will on Mystic's part, he still felt resentment and demanded long-term commitments whereas the industry imposed a need for short-term, fast reaction. In Korea, Armstrong recognized that Mystic's orders were small in relation to Pak's output, and that, with a non-profit operation, Pak probably did not feel the pressures of the market place as much as Mystic might wish.

The tantalum venture had been a people problem. Mystic had misjudged Alaimo. Although MacBurney had sent McCosh and a foreman to Middleton, and although they reported that Virginia Bronte was the key to the operation, Mystic had already committed itself to the deal. MacBurney said that Mystic had obviously not done its homework on that acquisition. The certainty of a good market had led Mystic to see the capabilities of Alaimo and his operation through rose-colored glasses.

MacBurney felt that Mystic might have a tendency to grab at deals without thinking them through, to grab opportunities and then work out how to make money from them. Yet, he said, this was not an unnatural thing for a small, enthusiastic and hungry company. They had not wanted to miss opportunities. Both he and Armstrong felt that it was only too easy to err on the other side of things—that one could become overly cautious and analytical and miss opportunities. While at USM both men had seen lawyers, who had recently fought a major antitrust suit, slow down many acquisitions, causing USM to miss some excellent deals.

Another problem at Mystic was the deteriorating relationship between Ned Troy and Armstrong. Whereas Troy had been close to Armstrong during the early months of Mystic's operations, he was now distant and seemingly intent on insulating himself from the rest of the company. Armstrong and MacBurney noted that Troy would say that he would not push Mystic's foreign-sourced capacitors until "you straighten out the problems in getting assured supply." Although Troy was the sales manager and had no operational responsibility for the foreign operations, he also expressed no interest in them, merely stating that Armstrong and MacBurney had performed inadequately in making the foreign operations work.

Troy's lack of interest in the rest of the company, despite his 5% ownership, affected his performance. He would not submit proposed brochures even after MacBurney repeatedly reminded him of their due dates. And, perhaps worst of all, because there were no firm orders for the foreign-sourced capacitors, it was impossible for Mystic to provide Gupta with firm orders. Armstrong had thought of terminating Troy but felt he had to consider the effect of Troy's leaving on the rep organization which was so essential to Mystic's success. Besides, Troy had helped him found Mystic.

Regarding the foreign ventures, Armstrong and MacBurney hoped the difficulties could be ironed out. Upon first entering these ventures, Armstrong thought they would enable him to increase sales, but he had soon found that the low-cost capacitors most often provoked interest among automotive companies and manufacturers of consumer products, different markets than the industrial and commercial market Mystic had been supplying. This consumer and industrial market often involved different purchasing agents and buying criteria, even within the same company. And whereas an order could often be salvaged despite late delivery in the industrial market, a late delivery usually led to immediate cancellation in the automotive and consumer markets.

Mystic had been able to make some initial forays into the high-volume market with comparatively little difficulty on the marketing side. In fact, the rep in the New Jersey region had been employed by Western Electric which he had interested in the prospect of Mystic's becoming a back-up supplier for dipped mica capacitors. Western's annual needs were 60 million units a year at approximately 15¢ apiece. Mystic could start with between 5% and 10% of that business and might even aim for getting 25% of it eventually. Mystic's original samples satisfied Western Electric. Western was interested enough to consider providing financial assistance for the necessary equipment, most likely through temporarily higher margins, and to offer making a commitment for a minimum dollar amount. Mystic's problem was that, to make the dipped mica capacitors economically, it would have to rely on getting a sub-assembly from India. However, the problems with Gupta continued and Mystic had reservations about its ability to fulfill Western Electric's order unless it got its own supply problems straightened out.

In addition, Mystic was being considered by other large users like Digital Equipment and General Electric. Digital had already had one order from Mystic arrive late, but would most likely give them but one more chance. And GE would need assurances of Mystic's ability to deliver.

Armstrong had hopes many of his problems could be solved by another company in India, run by the Nahani family. Nahani had visited Mystic and expressed enthusiasm for supplying Mystic with mica capacitors. Having vast wealth and already being one of the largest capacitor manufacturers in India, Nahani might easily adjust to Mystic's needs. During his second trip to India, Armstrong visited Nahani and found the enthusiasm still there. In September, 1976, Nahani was overdue for a visit to Mystic to arrange for production for the Western Electric contract. Yet, Armstrong had reservations insofar as Mystic would have to go through the process of teaching Nahani to make capacitors to its specifications just as it had so laboriously done with Gupta. He still felt some responsibility toward Gupta. He hoped that he might be able to keep Gupta making the smaller capacitors with which he had become familiar, and have Nahani make larger-sized capacitors. Such an arrangement would spread his supply risk. However, Armstrong thought that both companies would most likely want all or none of the business.

To capitalize on the opportunities of supplying large customers such as GE and Digital, Armstrong would have to have a sure supply of low-cost film capacitors. Although he hoped he could obtain such a supply from Korea, Armstrong had initiated contacts with two other film capacitor companies—CTR of India and Plessy of Italy. CTR would provide cost advantages on small orders by taking advantage of India's low labor costs; Plessy would be advantageous on large orders because it was highly automated. Armstrong and MacBurney were considering placing trial orders with both companies to get an indication of which might be more reliable. MacBurney felt that, based on their experiences, he and Armstrong should write a list of questions relevant to any such future ventures.

LOOKING AHEAD

As Tod Armstrong thought about the past several months, he could not help feeling frustrated about many things, for example his foreign ventures and Ned Troy. These problems made it more difficult for him to decide how he and MacBurney should divide their responsibilities. And they also made it more difficult for him to devote time to locating possible acquisitions.

''I guess a problem, too, is that the capacitor business is not particularly glamorous. Of late, I haven't felt the same excitement I did when I bought the company,'' said Armstrong. ''I want MacBurney to accept more of the responsibility for operations and decision making within Mystic, yet I want to keep on top of the entire operation.''

As Armstrong weighed Mystic's problems and lucrative possibilities, he wondered how best to proceed and what Mystic's priorities should be.

EXHIBIT 1

MYSTIC ELECTRONICS, INC. **(C)**
Sales and Income
Years Ending February 28
1973–1976
(000's omitted)

	1973	*1974*	*1975*	*1976*
Sales	$1,299.5	$2,494.1	$2,948.5	$2,068.5
Net Income After Tax	$ 23.8	$ 112.3	$ 73.2	$ 46.8

EXHIBIT 2

MYSTIC ELECTRONICS, INC. **(C)**
Balance Sheet - Consolidated
February 29, 1976 and February 28, 1975

	Consolidated	
Assets	*1976*	*1975*
Current Assets		
Cash	$ 2,337	$ 69,453
Accounts receivable (less allowance for doubtful accounts)	298,781	268,524
Intercompany accounts receivable and payable		
Inventory - at lower of cost or market	210,177	206,310
Investments in subsidiaries at equity		
Net income tax overpayment	7,674	12,955
Total current assets	518,969	557,242
Property and Equipment (at cost)		
Manufacturing machinery and equipment	114,751	116,351
Office furniture and equipment	11,858	11,077
Automotive equipment	15,105	13,605
Total	141,714	141,033
Less accumulated depreciation	68,202	46,077
Net property and equipment	73,512	94,956
Other Assets		
Deferred charges	42,150	
Prepaid expenses	21,329	16,239
Total other assets	63,479	16,239
TOTAL ASSETS	$655,960	$668,437
Liabilities and Stockholders' Equity		
Current Liabilities		
Current portion of bank note	$ 18,749	$ 18,749
Accounts payable	183,486	243,510
Accrued payroll and expenses	80,975	95,658
State income taxes payable		2,498
Total current liabilities	283,210	360,415
Long-Term Debt		
9.15% bank note	23,436	42,185
Advances from officers	68,600	31,962
Total long-term debt	92,036	74,147
TOTAL LIABILITIES	375,246	434,562
Minority Interest in Capital Stock	150	(1,789)
Stockholders' Equity		
Common stock - no par; authorized 7,500 shares, issued and outstanding 1,110 shares	24,400	
Retained earnings (deficit)	256,164	211,264
Total stockholders' equity (deficiency)	280,564	235,664
TOTAL LIABILITIES AND STOCKHOLDERS' EQUITY	$655,960	$668,437

EXHIBIT 3

MYSTIC ELECTRONICS, INC. **(C)**
Statement of Income and Retained Earnings (Deficit) Consolidated
For the Years Ended February 29, 1976 and February 28, 1975

	Consolidated	
	1976	*1975*
Net Sales	$2,068,537	$2,948,552
Cost of Goods Sold		
Inventory, Beginning of year	206,310	146,207
Purchases - net	406,432	827,216
Direct labor	606,525	825,105
Manufacturing expenses	553,904	713,765
Total	1,773,171	2,512,293
Less inventory, End of year	(210,177)	(206,310)
Total cost of goods sold	1,562,994	2,305,983
Gross Profit	505,543	642,569
Selling Expenses	134,910	184,947
General and Administrative Expenses	299,007	310,817
Total selling and general and administrative expenses	433,917	495,764
Income from Operations	71,626	146,805
Other Income (Expense)		
Dividends	(11,390)	(8,612)
Interest - net	(11,390)	(8,612)
Moving expense	(5,231)	
Miscellaneous	6,834	
Increase in equity of subsidiary		
Net other income (expense)	(9,787)	(8,612)
Income before Provision for Income Taxes	61,839	138,193
Provision for Federal and State Income Taxes	15,000	65,000
Net Income ($42 and $70 per share in 1976 and 1975, respectively	46,839	73,193
Retained Earnings (Deficit) - Beginning of Year	211,264	136,132
Dividends Paid		
Minority Interest in Subsidiary	(1,939)	1,939
Retained Earnings (Deficit) - End of Year	$ 256,164	$ 211,264

EXHIBIT 4

MYSTIC ELECTRONICS, INC. **(C)**
Industry Sales and Market Share
Integrated Circuit and Capacitor Sales
(in millions of dollars)

	1971	*1972*	*1973*	*1974*	*1975*
Integrated Circuits	534	718	NA	NA	NA
Capacitors	435	438	612	676	470
Percent of Capacitor Sales by type:					
Paper and film dielectric	35.0%	23.6%	22.5%	20.5%	19.9%
Tantalum electrolytic	18.8	20.8	22.1	23.9	23.1
Aluminum electrolytic	17.8	20.0	19.2	20.3	17.7
Mica dielectric	5.1	5.0	5.0	5.1	4.6
Ceramic dielectric, fixed	18.9	24.2	25.1	25.6	29.5
All other, fixed	1.7	2.0	1.8	1.9	2.2
Variable	2.7	4.4	4.3	2.7	3.0

Share of Capacitor Market
(percentage of dollar sales by type)

	1971 to 1972 Percentage Change in			*1974 to 1975 Percentage Change in*		
	Price	*Volume*	*$Sales*	*Price*	*Volume*	*$Sales*
Paper and film dielectric	(22.0%)	(13.0%)	(32.1%)	0.6%	(33.0%)	(32.6%)
Tantalum electrolytic	(16.0)	33.6	12.2	14.4	(41.3)	(32.9)
Aluminum electrolytic	0.6	12.4	13.0	16.4	(48.0)	(39.4)
Mica dielectric	(17.5)	20.1	(0.9)	18.3	(46.6)	(36.8)
Ceramic dielectric, fixed	3.8	23.7	28.5	5.2	(23.9)	(19.9)
All other, fixed	(9.0)	29.5	17.8	42.4	(42.0)	(17.3)
Variable	26.4	29.5	63.6	(19.0)	(7.0)	(25.3)
Total Industry Change	(13.9)	17.0	0.7	.68	(31.0)	(30.5)

TWENTIETH CENTURY-FOX

On October 27, 1976, Ms. Judith Frank drove along an old New York street. After being waved on by a uniformed guard, she turned a corner and parked her car under the hot Los Angeles sun. On her left, men in olive drab Army fatigues milled around a snack wagon. On the right, a tow truck loaded with dock pilings passed a twenty-two-foot-long submarine as Ms. Frank walked toward the executive office building of Twentieth Century-Fox. After climbing to the second floor, she walked along a hallway on both sides of which hung photographs from Fox films such as *The French Connection, The Sound of Music,* and *Gentleman's Agreement.* Ms. Frank, Fox Vice-President for Realty and Development, walked into her office, where her secretary informed her that Mr. Rubenstein, the company's consultant on local government relations, had asked her to call him.

"Hello, Allen. . . . I'm not surprised they've come out with a new plan, but your tone of voice suggests I should ask how bad it is. How bad is it? . . . That's ridiculous, Allen!" Animated words emanating from the phone indicated that Mr. Rubenstein agreed. And with good reason: the Los Angeles Planning Department had just recommended severe new zoning restrictions. Ms. Frank feared that, in accordance with SEC regulations, Fox might have to alter its balance sheet by writing down the value of the affected land if the recommendations became law. Her immediate concern, however, was to determine the effect such recommendations might have on her plans for the seventy-six acres of land owned by Fox in West Los Angeles.

Some of Fox's executives felt the land's location in the most prestigious and commercially active part of Los Angeles made it too valuable to use for film production and low-intensity office space. Said Ms. Frank:

> Our corporate staff is housed in two- and three-story buildings spread over seventy-six acres on two sites separated by Olympic Boulevard and surrounded by forty-plus-story towers. We don't want to stack people into a high-rise like an insurance company—but we want to use this valuable land more economically and to consolidate our unwieldy offices.
>
> Basically, we have three major decisions to make: 1) sell the land, or not; 2) build a new corporate headquarters building, or not; and 3) fight Los Angeles on these new restrictions, or not. These decisions seem straightforward enough at first glance, but they're highly interdependent and there are many factors to consider. In any event, I have to recommend what Fox should do with this site.

THE LAND

The value of Fox's seventy-six-acre site in Los Angeles was difficult to determine. That depended, among other things, upon its zoning and future development adjacent to it.

This case was prepared by Mr. Mark Teagan, Research Assistant, under the direction of Assistant Professor Kenneth J. Hatten as a basis for class discussion rather than to illustrate either effective or ineffective handling of an administrative situation.

However, it was clear that its location on the edge of Beverly Hills and Century City, and its proximity to the prestigious Westwood area, made it a highly desirable property.

Alcoa Corporation had recognized its value as early as 1961 when Fox became one of the first studios to sell off back-lot facilities as a result of its interpretation of industry trends. Alcoa purchased Fox's entire studio site, then 260 acres, for $43,000,000, leasing back the 76 acres Fox now occupied. The leased part contained all the studio's permanent structures, such as sound stages; the part taken by Alcoa consisted primarily of exterior sets.

On the site, Alcoa developed Century City, a mixed-use development of international reputation. Details of the development, its tenants, and its occupancy rates, appear in *Exhibit 1*. Fox continued operating on the remaining 76 acres and, in November 1973, repurchased its leasehold for $21,000,000.

Although Fox became the fee owner of the entire 76 acres, a 17.3-acre strip along Avenue of the Stars, between Pico and Olympic Boulevards, was optioned to Alcoa for a ten-year period beginning November 3, 1973, the date of sale. Alcoa had the right to purchase designated portions or the entire parcel at any time during the next ten years. Ms. Frank felt that the purpose of the option was to assure Alcoa that no other development could compete with Century City.

Alcoa's option price alternatives are given in *Exhibit 2*. Assuming that this price structure represented a reasonable proxy for the value of the entire 76 acres, Fox's site had a value of between $12.41 and $28.13 a square foot—and those figures were set in 1973, before the rampant inflation of 1974 and 1975 and the completion of much of Alcoa's Century City development. Sales in the immediate area substantiated these prices. However, the site's value could be reduced considerably if the Planning Department's restrictive recommendations became law.

The Planning Department's proposal would limit Fox to 350,000 square feet of development on its first city-approved increment, compared to the 1,275,000 square feet allowed under the ordinance then in effect. For further development, Fox would have to obtain new city permission for each 100,000-square-foot increment[1] in floor space—compared to the 1,275,000-square-foot increments then in effect. The need to return repeatedly to the city for approval, up to as many as 40 times compared to the 4 times required under the approved plan, would be time-consuming and expensive. It would also be a very uncertain process. The major provisions of the plan and some of Fox's objections appear in *Exhibit 3*.

Although Fox would be free to develop its corporate headquarters, Ms. Frank felt that such development, because of its high cost, was contingent on Fox's being able to dispose of the rest of the land profitably. *Exhibit 4* provides some statistics which Ms. Frank felt might be used by potential purchasers. She feared that the value of the land could have already been reduced because of the extensive governmental attention the site had received. Potential purchasers rarely welcome the uncertainties and encumbrances which confrontations with government tend to produce.

[1]Fox would be allowed 500,000 square feet for its corporate headquarters building separately from the requirements of other development; this was considered a reflection of the city's desire to keep Fox in Los Angeles.

PLANS: PRO AND CON

Top management had approved a plan to sell and/or develop most of the seventy-six acres and build a corporate headquarters on part of the parcel. The new headquarters would house corporate staff, independent producers, and post-production facilities. It would not include production facilities which, it was projected, would be rented from independent operators or other studios when the need arose. Many members of the top management group felt that production facilities were not needed because an insufficient number of films was being made to justify the overhead they entailed and because industry trends rendered them of secondary importance. One industry observer claimed, "These facilities were designed for the great days of Hollywood which are no more; 'gone with the wind,' if you like."

During the late 1960s, Fox had produced more films than usual, partly as a direct attempt to spread production facilities' overhead over more product. However, many of the films did poorly at the box office and Fox slid to near-bankruptcy. Since that time, the company had tried to alleviate the overhead burden by renting production facilities to independent producers and directors. Opinions differed as to how successful this program had been.

There were some in the company, however, who were against the sale of the corporation's production facilities. They felt it made little sense, even in the short run, and that it would place Fox at a competitive disadvantage when the programming needs of innovations such as cable television added to the demand for the already strained (and diminishing) production facilities of the industry.

In addition, because Fox's top management was also considering diversifying into more stable businesses, while remaining in the leisure-entertainment field (*Exhibits 5* and *6*), management did not want to commit to the \$40–\$50 million headquarters project—"a lot for a volatile company like this"(*Exhibit 7*)—unless cash from the sale of the rest of the land could offset much of its expense. Fox's chairman, Dennis Stanfill, who had worked at Lehman Brothers and then at Times-Mirror Company, before coming to Fox, had observed too many corporate disasters in real estate. He did not want to add avoidable and unfamiliar real estate risks to the risks Fox was managing in its principal business.[2]

Knowing that Fox's land-use plans would strongly affect its strategy, and knowing that, even during its short history, the film business had been affected by several basic social and technological changes, Ms. Frank had decided long ago that a history of the picture business and of Twentieth Century-Fox might help her place her current problems in a useful context.

THE INDUSTRY

During the early 1900s, scores of entrepreneurs opened penny arcade houses based on the moving picture invention of Thomas Edison.[3] Some of these men—most of them immi-

[2]Although it was quite common to spend \$4 or \$5 million on a film, the upside potential on films like "The Omen" and "The Sound of Music" was "unlimited." Stanfill felt that it would be difficult to justify risking a corresponding amount of equity (assuming a non-recourse loan) in real estate where the upside potential was considerably less.

[3]Actually, Edison relinquished most of the task to his assistant, William Dickson, who presented his boss with a moving picture device (with sound!) in 1889.

grants, such as Adolph Zukor, William Fox, Samuel Goldwyn, and Louis B. Mayer—saw opportunity in this unsophisticated form of entertainment. Despite vacancy signs saying, "No dogs or actors allowed," many of them moved to Southern California where year-round sunshine and a proximity to ocean, desert, and mountains permitted comparatively trouble-free and variegated filming.[4]

One-minute penny-arcade films gave way to longer silent films screened in nickelodeons and, eventually, in movie theatres. The success of these ventures led to the building of scenery and backdrops some distance from Los Angeles in a sleepy village called Hollywood which became the generic name for the American commercial film industry, even though many of the major film companies located at other, though nearby, places.

It wasn't until 1914 when D. W. Griffith, a failed playwright, directed *Birth of a Nation,* that films regularly used such devices as cross-cutting (cutting back and forth between two dramatically related scenes) and assumed their now-familiar extended narrative form. Sound was introduced in 1927 and color of varying quality at about the same time. From the 1920s through the 1940s, Hollywood enjoyed its greatest financial success,[5] established an aura of glamor, and garnered its most pervasive social influence. Each major studio had under full-time contract its own gallery of stars, writers, directors, and other creative personnel.

During the early 1950s, however, two major events occurred which fundamentally altered Hollywood's market and social power. One was a consent judgment requiring film producers—that is, the major studios—to divest their theater holdings, which were considered to be in restraint of trade. This loss of controlled (guaranteed) outlets, important as it was, paled in significance, however, compared to the second event: the introduction of television to the mass market.

Whereas film-goers had been used to leaving their homes and paying admission to a movie, they could now be entertained in their own homes for free—or at least for no incremental cost. Taking notice of this drastic change, Samuel Goldwyn said, "Who wants to go out and see a bad movie when they can stay at home and see a bad one for free on television?" Attendance figures reflected the massive change in attitudes. In 1947, approximately 90 million people attended movies each week; by 1975 the figure was just under 20 million, despite a national population increase during the same period from about 150 million to 210 million.

During the 1960s, these trends, in conjunction with overbudgeted and often poor films, created financial difficulties for many major studios. In addition, Cinemobiles[6] made on-location work more feasible, and filming at studios less necessary.

In view of their financial woes and the decreasing use of their production facilities, some major studios sold off large portions of their back-lots and many of their props because they believed the costs could be justified only by the volume of pictures made during Hollywood's heyday. The most famous sale was in 1970, when auctioneers for

[4]Hollywood's relative proximity to the Mexican border was also useful to those who used bootlegged cameras and who therefore had to avoid the agents of the Motion Picture Patents Company, a trust of producers and distributors which controlled the industry from 1909 to 1912. Edison became a member and his agents were avid in seeking out, suing, and (it is said) sometimes beating up those using illegal equipment. The Trust, though long disregarded, was declared illegal in 1917.

[5]By 1927 Joseph P. Kennedy could introduce his fellow film magnates to a Harvard Business School audience as the leaders of the nation's fourth largest industry.

[6]Cinemobiles are medium-sized vans carrying light, compact filming equipment. They were first used consistently by the producers of the popular television series, "I Spy."

MGM sold items such as Rhett Butler's top hat and the ruby slippers ($15,000) which had helped Judy Garland down the yellow brick road in *The Wizard of Oz*. Sets were razed and real estate development soon followed. Studios changed their function, becoming packaging, financing, and distribution houses rather than full-time production facilities with creative talent on their full-time payrolls.

While the movie companies were trying to fight television with devices such as Fox's successful CinemaScope (1953), some securities analysts believed that only one company, Music Corporation of America (MCA), seemed to have understood the implications of television for the film industry.

MCA, which had been solely a talent agency, acquired the Universal lot in 1959. It then devoted most of its energy to producing for television, something which other film companies became involved in only belatedly. Universal constantly provided television with new ideas, such as "Movie of the Week" and the serialized novel—for example, "Rich Man, Poor Man." By 1976, Universal was supplying 14 hours of prime-time programming weekly, while its closest competitor provided 4. As a result, television production covered much of the studio's overhead. Universal was able to keep its entire back-lot (200 acres, 34 sound stages), the only back-lot in the business large enough to attract hordes of paying tourists—approximately 3 million in 1976.

THE COMPANY: TWENTIETH CENTURY-FOX[7]

The history of Twentieth Century-Fox closely parallelled that of the film industry as a whole. In 1907, twenty-nine-year-old William Fox, who had arrived in America from Hungary when he was nine months old, abandoned his successful cloth sponging business to set up a nickelodeon chain in Brooklyn, New York. Quickly establishing fifteen cinemas and his own film exchange, he finally entered film production in 1912. In 1915 he established the Fox Film Corporation. The small company flourished and, in 1929, Fox tried to take over Loew's Incorporated, then the parent company of MGM. His bid failed partly because the stock market crashed, while he himself was injured in a car accident. The bid's failure and his ill health led to the dapper and wealthy Fox being kicked out of his own company in 1931. (As a postscript, in 1936 William Fox filed for bankruptcy, and in 1942 went to jail for a year after being convicted of trying to bribe a Federal judge.)

While William Fox was building his business, Nebraska-born Darryl F. Zanuck served in World War I, and then worked a series of odd jobs before becoming a screenwriter for Warner Brothers. By 1929, Zanuck was head of production at Warner's. After a dispute, he left Warners to form Twentieth Century Company in 1933, a year in which many found it difficult to make a living, much less form a corporation. However, his partner, Joseph Schenck, had access to money and Zanuck had developed the expertise to make it work in the motion picture industry. In 1935, Twentieth Century acquired the ailing Fox Film Corporation whose chain of theatres and Hollywood production facilities made the new corporation, Twentieth Century-Fox, one of the top four movie companies.

Zanuck flourished; as V.P. in charge of production and as the company's largest

[7]All historical references under the heading "The Company: Twentieth Century-Fox" were developed through independent research by the casewriter. They were not furnished by Fox or its executives.

shareholder, he presided over Twentieth Century-Fox's productions from initial hiring of scriptwriters to final publicity and bookings. His method of operation was epitomized by his famous remark, "For God's sake, don't say yes until I've finished talking!" Zanuck's productions ranged from the saccharine and foolish to some of Hollywood's more serious undertakings, such as *The Grapes of Wrath* and *Gentleman's Agreement.*

Zanuck left the company in 1956 and travelled to Paris where he became an independent film producer working through Fox. He returned in 1962 to take over the Chairmanship of the company from the aging Spyros Skouras.

Dennis Stanfill suceeded Zanuck as Chairman and Chief Operating Officer and later became President, following the resignation of Gordon Stulberg in late 1974. Fox described its business in its 1975 10-K as follows:

> Certain of the feature films released or distributed have been produced by the Company and others by independent producers. When the Company obtains distribution rights to a film produced by an independent producer, the Company frequently provides financing for the production. There is no fixed pattern of agreement for the financing of independent productions. Sometimes the Company, if it does not purchase the film outright from the producer, receives a distribution fee, is reimbursed for its financing out of the proceeds of the film, and thereafter shares in the earnings of the film either through ownership of a percentage of the film or through a right to receive a percentage of profits from the film. At other times, the gross receipts are shared by the parties in agreed percentages based on specified formulae. With respect to certain films, the independent producer arranges his own financing and the Company, which obtains distribution rights, may under certain circumstances become responsible to the lender for part or all of such borrowings.

Ms. Frank said that during the mid-1970s, of the films produced and financed by Fox, an average of only three or four a year had been shot on the Fox premises. During the previous ten years, Fox had "released" for theater exhibition in the United States (but had not necessarily produced or financed the production of) the following numbers of feature films:

Fox Feature Films, 1966–1975

Year	*#*	*Year*	*#*
1966	26	1971	15
1967	19	1972	18
1968	21	1973	16
1969	23	1974	19
1970	14	1975	15

"I think the many changes the film business has gone through suggests that we should consider even the most seemingly outlandish future possibility as being thoroughly realistic," said Ms. Frank. "But what is further complicating my problem with our seventy-six acres is Fox's relationship with the local community. Zoning is a local decision and it can affect the value of the land which, in turn, can affect our view of how the land should be used. Of course, this affects company strategy, and, as you might expect, problems we face in implementing strategy can in turn create pressure for zoning changes. In any event, you have to understand the influence of the local community when you look at my problem.''

LOS ANGELES

A city of over 3 million people, Los Angeles is located near the coast in Southern California. The city is physically fragmented and sprawled out over 460 square miles connected by a massive freeway system. One observer described it as ''a collection of suburbs in search of a city.''[8]

During the early 1900s, the Progressive political movement took firm root in Los Angeles, ultimately leading to the adoption of a City Charter creating many public service departments with considerable power, and a Mayor with less power than that usually accorded a city chief executive. The board and commissions presiding over different aspects of city policy were staffed primarily by civil service personnel, a fact which rendered them independent of political control; departmental chief executives usually came from the ranks and were thus loyal primarily to their departments.

Proponents of Los Angeles noted its excellent weather, easy access to nearly year-round water sports, almost equally easy access to mountains and skiing, increasing cultural activity, and an informal life style unencumbered by what many Californians considered ''the artificial social barriers of many Eastern cities.'' Its detractors cited its smog and its dependence on the automobile, and claimed that its informal life style often led to a culture which was either bland or so eclectic as to provide no sense of purpose or roots.

Proponents and detractors alike, however, agreed that, in many respects, Los Angeles' way of life could well be a harbinger of things to come in the rest of the United States. And even avid proponents admitted that, although Los Angeles's freeway and road system usually provided easy and quick access to most parts of the city, rush-hour traffic could be among the worst to be found anywhere in the United States.

So far, two major problems had prevented the construction of a mass transit system: 1) the city's sheer physical size, which made such construction a potentially massive undertaking; and 2) the area's location in an earthquake zone, which made *underground* networks either hazardous or extremely expensive, and would necessitate extra expense to assure the safety of *above ground* construction. Perhaps most important was the integral place the automobile had in the Southern Californian lifestyle.

To help prevent aggravation of its traffic, smog, and urban sprawl problems, Los Angeles adopted a Citywide Plan and Concept in 1974. This city plan had the force of law and codified the official general objectives, policies, and programs for the development of the city as a whole for the next twenty years. The City Council also adopted district plans, including the West Los Angeles District Plan, as portions of the general plan.

The plans specified thirty-seven centers of high-intensity urban development within the city. A major objective was to preserve single-family neighborhoods which, according

[8]Werner Z. Hirsch, *Los Angeles: Viability and Prospects for Metropolitan Leadership*. New York: Praeger Publishers, 1971, p. 4.

to Ms. Frank, were "God, mother, and country in Los Angeles." The principal centers included the downtown area, Hollywood Center, Westwood Center and Century City. Although the centers would vary in size, shape and intensity, all future high-intensity high-rise commercial development would be in these centers, as would all future high-density residential development. Established residential areas throughout Los Angeles would thus be protected from further intrusion by more intensive development. The urban centers would also include recreational, cultural, educational, and other public facilities. Eventually, it was hoped, these centers would become the sites of mass transit stations.

The major participants in the process of creating and administering Los Angeles's plans were:

- *Planning Department*—a staff to the Planning Director. Conducted research and made recommendations. Ms. Frank stated that many of its members were young and aggressive, and had been trained in urban planning at major universities.
- *Planning Director*—appointed by the Mayor and approved by the City Council. He had considerable autonomy.
- *Planning Commission*—five part-time members also appointed by the Mayor and approved by the City Council. The Planning Commission had no final decision-making authority; its work consisted primarily in advising the City Council.
- *City Council*—fifteen members elected from specific areas of the city. In zoning matters, eight votes in the City Council were required to pass an ordinance approved by the Planning Commission. If the commission had not approved the proposed zone change, ten votes were required. If the Mayor vetoed a commission-approved matter, it took ten votes to override the veto; if the Mayor vetoed a matter which had been disapproved at the commission level, it took twelve votes to override him.
- *The Mayor*—in 1976, Thomas Bradley. Although accused in some quarters of not being as "activist" as his campaign promises had suggested, he was widely considered a safe bet for re-election in the fall of 1977.

FOX AND LOCAL GOVERNMENT

Fox had been and remained an enthusiastic supporter of the Los Angeles centers concept and had supported bond issues for the public transportation facilities called for by the plan. For more than three years, while developing its own preliminary plans for its seventy-six acres, Fox had worked closely with the city to ensure that its plans conformed to the spirit and legal detail of the city plan. Fox had even voluntarily imposed upon itself a moratorium on development while the city finalized its own plans (*Exhibit 8*).

The plan (referred to as Twentieth Century-Fox Specific Plan)[9] which Fox and the city finally agreed on, was for a planned community of 2,489 residential units on 56 acres with the remaining 20 acres zoned for 4.9 million square feet of commercial space. Fox, and the city planners with whom it worked, felt that the heavy emphasis on residential development would establish a balanced environment in Century City and would meet the

[9]The City Plan and Concept created a hierarchy of plans as follows: The City Plan; District Plans, e.g., the West Los Angeles Plan; Specific Plans, e.g., the Century City Center Specific Plan, which would have to integrate into the two above plans. In this context, the Twentieth Century-Fox Specific Plan would come immediately under the Century City Center Specific Plan.

strong demand for upper-income housing on the highly desirable Westside of Los Angeles.

Whatever management's eventual decision about selling or not selling the entire seventy-six acres, it had been ''virtually decided'' that thirteen acres (see ''Subject Site'' in *Exhibit 1*) would be developed into a townhouse condominium project. Having paid for four favorable independent market research studies on the project, Ms. Frank had been anxious to proceed with it. However, the City of Beverly Hills had delayed the project with a suit against Los Angeles as defendant and Fox as the ''party in real interest.'' Beverly Hills claimed that the Fox Specific Plan violated Los Angeles's own General Plan and its West Los Angeles Plan, and that the proposed development would have a negative impact on Beverly Hills.

Since Beverly Hills was challenging Los Angeles's entire plan and planning process, Los Angeles, particularly its Planning Director, joined Fox in aggressively fighting the suit. In the heat of the hearings, the issue had been raised as to whether the Supreme Court might have to decide whether one city could affect the plans of another. However, when the dust settled, all issues had been decided by the superior court of Los Angeles in favor of Fox and Los Angeles. The action then became subject to appeal.

The Beverly Hills suit had until then been a delaying tactic, effectively preventing development of the 13 acres for 1½ years. In addition to the arguments in the suit, particularly those concerning traffic, Ms. Frank felt a major if unstated reason for it might be Beverly Hills's fear of losing retail sales to Century City outlets which might increase in number if the Fox Specific Plan were *fully* implemented. With only 0.5% of the population of Los Angeles County, (35,000 of 7 million) Beverly Hills accounted for 8% of the county's sales tax revenues, of which it was remanded 1%. This source of income enabled Beverly Hills to keep its property tax among the lowest in the United States. Prior to Alcoa's development of Century City, Beverly Hills had been the only ''upscale'' shopping district in the entire area, and most observers agreed that there had been almost no traffic congestion. The city now wanted no more competition or traffic. Because of this, Ms. Frank was not surprised that Beverly Hills appealed within the required 60 days, an action which would further delay Fox's plans.

Later in the course of events, the city of Los Angeles brought suit against Beverly Hills. The suit concerned Beverly Hills's granting separate spot zonings to two large, prestigious retailers, Neiman-Marcus and Bullocks Wilshire. An increase in traffic had been one of Beverly Hills's major complaints against the Fox plan; Los Angeles now claimed that Beverly Hills was intent on inviting within its city limits two department stores, the largest traffic-generating land use next to hospitals. Thus, Los Angeles could claim that Beverly Hills's complaint about Fox's planned development's generating traffic was specious and motivated solely by commercial self-interest. Ms. Frank pointed out that Fox had no ax to grind with either of the department stores or their parent companies.

CONFLICTS WITHIN THE COMPANY

In addition to her need to tread a path between the two conflicting cities, Ms. Frank had to contend with what she considered reasonable differences of opinion within the company. The major issue was whether Fox would retain production facilities. The tentative plans, which had been informally approved by top management, called for Fox's selling off most of the seventy-six acres and building a corporate headquarters on part of the parcel. Plans provided for the headquarters to house:

1. Corporate management and staff;
2. Post-production facilities—e.g., editing rooms, dubbing facilities and screening rooms;
3. Producers and directors who stayed for a specified number of pictures, then moved on. Since these people operated like senior staff or management, yet were transient, they were referred to by Ms. Frank as ''hybrids.''

Another possibility was leasing similar space in a building like the nearby Century City Alcoa Towers, in which case the entire seventy-six acres would be sold. Initial calculations showed the total space operating costs (including finance or lease payments) before taxes to be the same, about $7 million, for either choice. Complicating the ''to build'' decision was initial research showing that an optimal site along the prestigious Avenue of the Stars would include some of the land under option to Alcoa. In addition, the holder of the mortgage to the property[10] could force a refinancing if any part of the parcel were sold.

Burt Morrison, Vice-President, Finance and Administration, in the Feature Film Division, described the problems of analyzing the studio operation and the various ways in which Fox had tried to deal with them. In 1972, after the disasters of the late 1960s, Fox attempted to operate the studio as a separate business, as a profit center. Outside producers and Fox's own films were charged rates for using different facilities, equipment, props, and costumes. After a while, Fox found that its rates were driving some producers to other lots and to on-location work, so it lowered its rates for outsiders. This policy led to internal problems—for example, the Television Department complained that it was charged more than its competitors by its own studio. In addition, the policy did not increase studio revenue.

Therefore, during 1973 and 1974, Fox moved away from the profit center concept and judged its studio's performance on its contribution to corporate overhead, net of shared carrying costs. Under this policy, feature films were charged 12% of their direct production costs for overhead. Half of this allocation was credited to the production department and half to the studio. Under this system, the studio was viewed as making a positive contribution to corporate overhead; however, the 6% allocation was charged to films shot on location as well as to those on the lot, causing more problems in operating philosophies.

From 1974 through 1976, Fox charged $2,000 a day for access to all facilities and equipment, whether they were used or not. But, even though Fox had been trying to analyze the different studio departments (e.g., wardrobe) as mini-profit centers since 1972, the revenues under this $2,000-a-day package were not allocated to any particular profit center.

For 1977, Morrison was going to implement a new plan whereby revenues could be more easily allocated. The $2,000 daily charge would be considerably reduced but users would pay extra for the use of additional facilities beyond an agreed-upon minimum—''a

[10]Equitable Life Assurance Society held a $12.5 million mortgage at 6% on the 76 acres.

European plan rather than a tour package.'' Morrison pointed out that use of the lot by outsiders as well as by Fox created scheduling problems in the use of some facilities. There was also a lack of office space for outsiders.

Depending on the method used to allocate expenses and revenues, the studio production facilities appeared to be making a negative contribution of between \$200,000 and \$2 million. Mr. Edward Bowen, Vice-President, Administration and Finance, felt that if the studio's negative contribution were \$200,000 it would not be worth the effort to get rid of it on that basis alone; if the loss were \$2 million, it would be. He felt Fox needed more convincing numbers to determine precisely what the studio's performance was. And, he pointed out, Fox had no numbers at all concerning the net difference between the cost of maintaining its ownership of the studio facilities and the cost of leasing such facilities as needed.

Some of the company's top managers, however, claimed that Fox had to retain some production facilities if it were to remain in the film business. Mr. Bernard Barron, Studio Operations Vice-President, pointed out that during the industry's peak TV production time, October through January, production facilities in town were strained.[11] He noted that during the current production season, Universal Studios, the company with the largest remaining studio facilities, was actually renting space elsewhere because it had run out of space on its own lot. He claimed he had producers ''begging to get on the Fox lot''; twenty-one of its twenty-two sound stages were in use.

Expanding on his description of the situation, Barron claimed that the studio could not be profitable while providing both office and production space; if it were just a production facility, it could be profitable because of the demand he knew was there. The office space was nonproductive from the studio's point of view—and since 1972, when the corporate offices had been moved from New York to Los Angeles, additional studio space had been allocated to office use. He also noted that the decision to move from the studio had already been made, at least implicitly, as shown by the company's repeated decisions not to spend money updating it.

Barron felt that if a greater commitment had been made to renting facilities, the studio could have generated considerable profit. For instance, if Fox had built an office tower (as Universal had) to house corporate staff and outsiders, it could have made more economical use of the production facilities. And Fox would not have had to turn away outsiders for lack of office space.

Barron claimed that television production required studio facilities because the cost and time constraints of television production did not permit extensive on-site work. He pointed out that no major film company without a film studio had successfully competed in the television market. This was partly because the networks required a producer to have guaranteed access to facilities over a period of (usually) two or three years. For example, when one network contracted for the pilot to the television series ''Mod Squad'' with Spelling-Goldberg Productions, Spelling-Goldberg had to leave the Paramount studio because Paramount could not guarantee that its facilities would be available for at least

[11]The television production cycle worked approximately as follows: March–May: production was at a minimum as networks were busy purchasing new ideas for programming. April–June: producers were given the go-ahead by networks, and hired writers for thirteen episodes. June: earliest shooting date. July–January: heavy production schedules, particularly October–January.

three years. Since the network would not contract with Spelling-Goldberg unless they could guarantee ability to produce for three years (in the event that ''Mod Squad'' became a successful series), Spelling-Goldberg moved to another studio which could provide a guarantee—in this case, Twentieth Century-Fox.

Barron disputed the numbers which had been used to evaluate the studio facility's economic performance (*Exhibit 8*) claiming some of the allocations were arbitrary. He claimed that there were two factors which dictated that Fox retain studio facilities. One was the return of the ''escape film.'' After the realism which had been popular in films during the latter 1960s and early 1970s, audiences in 1976 and 1977 were interested in escapist entertainment like *King Kong,* and Fox's own *The Towering Inferno*. For many of their scenes, such films required the control and versatility available only on a sound stage or back-lot.

A second factor noted by Barron was the development of videodisk and pay television.[12] A major commercial breakthrough with either technology, he speculated, would create the need for many more films. And filmmakers could address much smaller audiences than those economically demanded by the production-distribution system in effect in 1976.

A rule of thumb in the motion picture business was that a film had to generate between two-and-a-half and three times its basic production cost to break even. This was true because of the costs of distribution, advertising and promotion, prints, and the theater owner's profit. According to Barron, people in the industry believed that the pay TV approach, which would access filmed material by dialing a number on a phone, would eliminate much of this extra marketing expense so that films would not have to generate as much revenue to break even. This change would allow the production of films previously considered commercially marginal. Naturally, many of these additional films would be shot on location—but many would need studio facilities.

Barron also noted the possibility of other film companies selling off their studio facilities, as MGM and Paramount had done. Paramount's facilities had been sold to EIE, from which Paramount leased them back. There was always the chance that EIE would redevelop that site. Thus, Barron saw an increasing demand for studio facilities in an already strained market, along with the threat of a decreasing supply (*Exhibit 9*). Fox could find itself paying its competitors ''monopoly'' rents, or finding studios unavailable, if it sold its production facilities.

Barron felt the 76-acre site was too valuable to be used as a studio and he felt that, someday, the company would have to come to grips with the need for alternative production facilities. He noted that Warner Brothers and Columbia Studios had joined in sharing the use—and expenses—of Warner Brothers' studio (now the Burbank Studio); perhaps Fox could do something similar with another company, possibly CBS or MGM. Or perhaps Fox could build separate production studios on cheaper land outside the Los Angeles urban area while keeping its corporate headquarters in Los Angeles. Barron had estimated the replacement cost of a sound stage was approximately $1.5 million. Ms. Frank said that all structures were appraised for replacement cost purposes at $85 million.

[12]In addition, many advertisers, concerned about the natural constraints on network advertising time, were advocating the establishment of a fourth network.

LATER THE SAME DAY

Returning from a meeting at which she played a major part in finalizing allocation of Fox's existing office facilities among corporate staff and production people, Ms. Frank again considered the interrelated decisions the company had to make. "I am really surprised by the severity of the Planning Department's proposed restrictions. The problem is that this is the last parcel in the 'hottest' part of town, so it's being looked at under a microscope."

Ms. Frank felt that to maintain the value of Fox's land as well as to clarify its zoning status she would have to develop a strategy to counter Los Angeles's opposition. She knew that she could argue that Fox injected $84 million into the Los Angeles economy and provided 1,240 full-time jobs (5,990 part-time jobs) and that both numbers would be more substantial when increased by a multiplier effect (*Exhibit 10*).

Fox could also point out that additional tax dollars and jobs would be provided by developing its seventy-six acres. And it could threaten to pull all its operations out of Los Angeles in favor of some nearby "reasonable" community. However, all these arguments might not be effective. The City Council members were elected from specific areas of the city; the councilman representing Fox and its neighbors could easily be blamed for increased traffic congestion, but it would be more difficult to blame him for the loss of jobs and tax dollars. Opponents to development could say that the jobs and tax dollars lost in Century City would be picked up elsewhere in Los Angeles. But, of course, this would not be true if Fox or potential buyers of its land settled in another city such as neighboring Santa Monica, or in Orange County. Los Angeles would lose one of the comparatively few corporations headquartered there, and an important member of the industry which had lent the city much of its tradition and ambience.

The opponents of development were primarily local homeowners, most of whom were affluent, active, and politically liberal. The homeowners' group included many attorneys with the time and inclination to pursue their political objectives. Ms. Frank felt that the local city councilman might be reluctant to support the original Fox plan after the recent action of the city's Planning Department. Perhaps the Fox and Alcoa parcels could be treated separately for planning purposes. Or Fox could hope that, although the City Council usually voted along with the councilman representing the particular area affected by a proposal, it might not do so in this case because of the tax dollars and jobs involved.

The proposed plan affected Alcoa as well as Fox, so it too had a stake. Ms. Frank had learned that, previously, Alcoa had chosen not to work on lower bureaucratic levels. It had gone to the top—in a case like this to the Mayor—and hit hard with the jobs and taxes issues. Ms. Frank wondered if it was a poor gamble to bet everything on the outcome of one lobbying effort. She also wondered if the Mayor and his advisors might be more likely to decide in favor of development if several people in the lower echelons, the people with whom the Mayor had to work, were to express their convictions in support of development. If so, it would be worthwhile to continue working with these people. On the other hand, the Mayor couldn't help but be aware of the problems of cities like New York, which were in financial straits because of loss of jobs and tax bases. Some observers noted similar trends beginning in Los Angeles. Ms. Frank wondered just how to go about lobbying the Mayor.

She stated, "The problem is that sometimes we have so little control. Because of new city decisions, we can never assume that previous plans will remain in effect. Even the previous 25% incremental 'approvals' introduced considerable additional uncertainty to the development process—never mind the new proposal.''

Ms. Frank knew that the final decision on how to deal with Fox's real estate would have a major effect on corporate strategy for a long time. She also knew that zoning laws could affect the viability of any plans. Therefore, the question of how to deal with city authorities and the probability of success on each approach would have to be defined. She and her colleagues had ''been doing some soul-searching about the nature and needs of Fox's business'' and knew that they would have to make some hard decisions soon.

EXHIBIT 1 Existing Century City Development

	Gross Area	Floor Area	Leasable Area	Vacant Leasable Area
		(square feet in 000s)		
Offices				
Gateway West	314.0	297.9	260.0	57.2
1901 Building	488.6	452.8	406.5	36.5
Gateway East	314.0	296.9	260.0	10.0
1900 Building	635.6	572.0	491.4	128.2
Century City North	657.6	589.6	527.0	120.0
Century Park Plaza	422.5	380.3	320.0	32.0
Northrop Building	291.4	262.2	244.0	17.8
Security Builders	360.0	324.0	270.0	4.8
Shareholders	550.0	522.5	485.0	83.8
Century Plaza Towers	2450.8	2169.2	1943.7	1550.0
ABC Entertainment Center	232.0	208.8	180.0	11.7
National Cash Register	62.5	59.4	59.4	—
Southern California Auto Club	32.5	30.9	30.9	—
Pacific Telephone	66.4	63.1	63.1	—
Prudential Savings	54.0	51.3	48.6	29.7
Welton Becket & Associates	115.0	103.0	98.0	49.0
Century City Medical	254.0	241.3	228.6	22.0
Total Offices	7300.9	6625.2	5916.2	2152.7
Special Function Buildings				
ABC Entertainment Center Theater	166.9	158.5*	158.5*	—
Century Plaza Hotel	750.4	712.8*	712.8*	—
Century City Hospital	191.0	181.5*	181.5*	—
Total Special Function	1108.3	1052.8	1052.8	—
Retail				
ABC Entertainment Center	220.1	199.9	180.0	85.0
Century Square Shopping Center	710.0	674.0	674.0	—
Century Plaza Towers	33.9	32.2	29.5	14.5
Total Retail	964.0	906.1	883.5	99.5
*Low-Density Development***				
Senior Pico Restaurant	20.0	20.0	20.0	—
First Los Angeles Bank	15.0	15.0	15.0	—
Total Low-Density Development	35.0	35.0	35.0	—
GRAND TOTAL	9480.2	8619.1	7887.5	2252.2

*Gruen Associates estimate, November 1976.

**The restaurant site is 2.77 acres. The bank site is 2.66 acres.

Source: Alcoa, November 1976.

EXHIBIT 2 Alcoa Option Price Alternatives†

Zoning at Time of Purchase*	Total Price if Entire Option Parcel Purchased at Once	Price per Square Foot if Portion Exercised
Commercial Property (13.6 Acres)		
1. Office + retail stores with density at six times buildable area	\$16,665,339	\$28.13
2. Less intensive commercial than No. 1	\$13,703,137–\$16,665,339**	\$23.13–\$28.13***
Residential Property (3.45 Acres)		
1. Residential allowing 40+ dwelling units per acre	\$ 2,619,888	\$17.41
2. Less intensive residential than No. 1	\$ 1,867,482–\$ 2,619,888	\$12.41–\$17.41

*Range of total purchase price, depending on conditions shown in chart:

Commercial	\$13,703,137–\$16,665,339
Residential	\$ 1,867,482–\$ 2,619,888
TOTAL	\$15,570,619–\$19,285,227

**Assume dedication of right-of-way for public street.

***MAI appraiser to make exact determination at time of purchase.

†Naturally, Fox wanted to retain the most favorable zoning for the land so Alcoa would have to pay the highest price if it chose to purchase.

EXHIBIT 3 Significant Changes in the Century City Specific Plan[1]

TRAFFIC REQUIREMENT FOR INCREMENT APPROVAL

In order to permit an increment, the Planning Commission must find that the average travel speed on Santa Monica, Olympic and Pico Boulevards during the most congested peak hour is more than 15 mph, *or* the "intersection capacity utilization" does not exceed 1.00. This compares to the TCF Specific Plan requirement that "approval to permit additional floor area in each increment shall be based upon a finding that the level of service in the circulation and transportation system has been improved to justify said increment of development."

The change is prompted by the planning staff's desire to replace subjective criteria with an objective standard. There is a pragmatic advantage for a reasonable impartial objective measure that replaces the subjective opinion with an objective test, if one could be found. However, since the technical tests would be binding, they should be simple, unbiased, not subject to manipulation and represent a reasonable indication of the existing traffic conditions. The decision level should also allow the maximum freedom of development consistent with the urban conditions. There is insufficient information, at this time, to determine whether the proposed criteria will be acceptable.

HEIGHT LIMITS

A height limit of 1-VL (45 ft. or 3 stories maximum) is imposed for a 300 ft. strip on the easterly and westerly sides of Century City. This is at variance with the W.L.A. District Plan and the TCF Specific Plan.

COMMENTARY

The Planning Department does not indicate or justify why the subsequent increments are 1 million s.f. less 90% of the vacant office space and the unused development rights. Initial

[1]Source: Twentieth Century-Fox

calculations indicate that TCF would receive the minimum allocation of 100,000 s.f. from the second and subsequent increments, assuming the most probable range of development. This conceivably could require in excess of 40 incremental approvals prior to utilizing the entire potential of the TCF commercial acreage, requiring an almost continuous series of applications for traffic studies, EIR, hearings, and allocations. This extraordinary and expensive process, with the attendant uncertainty of approvals, seriously hinders reasonable planning for the properties. . . .

The formula also encourages the parcelization and sale of commercial property rather than the retention of property, because of the ramifications of the minimum allotment provision. This is because small vacant properties can be allocated the same development rights as properties 10 to 20 times in size under the most probable developmental assumptions. . . .

Another way to look at it is that the second allocation to TCF is 8% of that permitted in the current plan. . . .

There is an inherent inequity in the entire incremental approval process, in that, as traffic deteriorates, only the Century City property owners are restricted, while no other part of the City is subjected to such restrictions. This provides even greater reason why the traffic "trigger levels" must be established at clear and indisputable levels of extreme congestion. . . .

For two years since the passage of the TCF plan, the potential of high-rise commercial and residential buildings has clearly existed and been publicized. There is no evidence that the value of any property has been diminished, or made less desirable. Thus the 1-VL limitation is capricious, arbitrary and unjustified. . . .

EXHIBIT 4 Summary of Rents, Free and Clear Income, and Construction Costs per Square Foot for Apartment, Office and Retail Space in Los Angeles, and the United States, 1970–1976.

Los Angeles

	Apartments[1]		*Office Space*[2]		*Retail Space*[3]	
	Rent	*F&C*	*Rent*	*F&C*	*Rent*	*F&C*
1976			$9.00	$4.50		
1975					$2.66	$1.72
1974	$2.14	$1.11				
1973	2.22	1.15	7.50	3–4		
1972	1.90	.97			2.38	1.53
1971	1.74	.89				
1970						

United States

	Apartments[1]		*Office Space*[2]		*Retail Space*[3]	
	Rent	*F&C*	*Rent*	*F&C*	*Rent*	*F&C*
1976						
1975						
1974	$2.64	$1.23			$2.47	1.91
1973	2.48	1.19				
1972	2.41	1.14	$5.28	$1.39		
1971	2.23	.96	5.14	1.32	2.32	1.90
1970	2.13	1.05	4.98	1.46		

(continued)

EXHIBIT 4 (Cont.)

Construction Costs[4]

	Construction Index	*Office Space*	*Retail Space*
1976	223	$50.00 ± $5.00	$50.00
1975	206		
1974	188		
1973	177		
1972	164		
1971			
1970			
	(1967=100)		

[1]Institute of Real Estate Management, Experience Exchange Committee, *A Statistical Compilation and Analysis of Actual Income and Expenses Experienced in Apartment, Condominium and Cooperative Building Operation.*
[2]Coldwell Banker, Inc. Figures are for Century City.
[3]Dollars and Cents of Shopping Center.
[4]*Engineering News-Record.*

Prime Rate: 1974–1976[1]

1974	Nov.	1	11.25%	1975	Oct.	31	7.75%
		15	11.0		Nov.	14	7.5
		29	10.25			28	7.5
	Dec.	13	10.25		Dec.	12	7.25
		27	10.25			26	7.25
	Jan.	10	10.25	1976	Jan.	9	7.25
		24	10.0			23	6.75
	Feb.	7	9.0		Feb.	6	6.5
		21	8.75			20	6.5
	Mar.	7	8.25		Mar.	5	6.75
		21	7.75			19	6.75
	Apr.	4	7.5		Apr.	2	6.75
		16	7.5			16	6.75
	May	2	7.5			30	6.75
		16	7.5		May	14	6.5
		30	7.25			28	7.0
	Jun.	13	7.0		Jun.	11	7.25
		27	7.0			25	7.25
	Jul.	11	7.0		Jul.	9	7.25
		25	7.25			23	7.25
	Aug.	8	7.0		Aug.	6	7.25
		22	7.75			20	7.0
	Sept	5	7.75		Sept	3	7.0
		19	8.0			17	7.0
	Oct.	3	8.0		Oct.	1	6.75
		17	8.0			15	6.75

[1]*Source:* Federal Reserve Bank of Saint Louis and the *New York Times*

EXHIBIT 5 Twentieth Century-Fox Businesses Other Than Film Production

A film-processing lab in Los Angeles serving the needs of Fox and other film producers.

Forty percent of Precision Film Laboratories, Inc. of New York, a film-processing lab serving customers in the New York area.

Keith Cole Photography, headquartered in Redwood City, California, a processor of professional color film in the fields of portrait, commercial aerial and industrial work for a nationwide market.

Twentieth Century Records, producer of phonograph records and music publisher.

United Television Inc., which owns VHF television stations located in Salt Lake City, Utah; San Antonio, Texas; and Minneapolis, Minnesota.

International Theaters Division, which owns and operates or has interests in 131 movie theaters in Australia, New Zealand and Europe. Fox also had interests in the food and soft drink catering facilities used in conjunction with its theater operations.

Marineland of the Pacific, an aquatic amusement park leased by the company with an option to buy.

EXHIBIT 6
Five-Year Summary of Product Line Data

	Year Ended				
	Dec. 27, 1975	*Dec. 28, 1974*	*Dec. 29, 1973*	*Dec. 30, 1972*	*Dec. 25, 1971*
			(in thousands)		
Revenues					
Filmed entertainment:					
Feature films	$210,800	$159,735	$152,647	$118,750	$143,157
Television programs	31,263	26,954	27,392	25,903	28,267
International theatre admissions and related income	44,322	43,057	34,568	25,427	20,753
Film processing	26,330	23,931	19,956	20,214	23,154
Record and music publishing	17,927	16,092	7,653	2,098	2,022
Television Stations	9,947	6,998	6,634	5,881	5,040
Operating revenues	340,589	276,767	248,850	198,273	222,392
Interest and non-operating income	2,141	3,369	1,579	398	124
Total revenues	$342,730	$280,136	$250,429	$198,671	$222,517
Earnings from Continuing Operations					
Filmed entertainment	$ 28,850	$ 12,932	$ 12,141	$ 8,055	$ 12,434
International theatres	4,879	6,754	5,603	3,300	2,278
Film processing	1,856	3,097	2,926	2,479	180
Record and music publishing	595	1,441	335	457	1,166
Television stations	3,579	2,737	2,726	2,462	1,927
	39,759	26,961	23,731	16,753	17,985
Interest and non-operating income	2,141	3,369	1,579	398	124
Corporate, general and administrative expense*	(5,476)	(5,607)	(3,800)	—	—
Interest expense	(4,239)	(3,619)	(2,968)	(3,001)	(5,596)
Earnings from continuing operations before income taxes and extraordinary items	$ 32,185	$ 21,110	$ 18,542	$ 14,150	$ 12,513

*Corporate, general and administrative expense was not separately classified prior to 1973.

EXHIBIT 7

TWENTIETH CENTURY-FOX FILM CORPORATION AND SUBSIDIARIES
Summary of Consolidated Earnings
Five Years Ended December 27, 1975

	Year Ended				
	Dec. 27, 1975	*Dec. 28, 1974*	*Dec. 29, 1973*	*Dec. 30, 1972*	*Dec. 25, 1971*
			(in thousands)		
Revenues					
Operating revenues	$340,589	$276,767	$248,850	$198,273	$222,393
Interest	1,707	2,591	1,579	398	124
Non-operating income	434	778	—	—	—
	342,730	280,136	250,429	198,671	222,517
Costs and Expenses					
Costs relating to operating revenues	248,699	206,532	188,327	143,853	169,310
Selling, general and administrative expenses	57,607	48,875	40,592	37,667	35,098
Interest expense	4,239	3,619	2,968	3,001	5,596
	310,545	259,026	231,887	184,521	210,004
Earnings from continuing operations before income taxes and extraordinary items	32,185	21,110	18,542	14,150	12,513
Income taxes	14,805	10,529	9,881	7,054	6,274
Earnings from continuing operations	17,380	10,581	8,661	7,096	6,239
Earnings (loss) from discontinued operations, less applicable tax effect	—	(4,491)	(983)	(355)	324
Earnings before extraordinary items	17,380	6,090	7,678	6,741	6,563
Extraordinary items	5,300	4,862	3,071	1,067	3,160
Net earnings	$ 22,680	$ 10,952	$ 10,749	$ 7,808	$ 9,723

Consolidated Balance Sheets
December 27, 1975

Assets	*1975* (in thousands)
Current Assets	
Cash and Treasury notes	$ 19,246
Receivables, net of an allowance for doubtful accounts of $5,535,000 in 1975 and $5,685,000 in 1974	59,507
Inventories	62,901
Prepaid expenses	3,159
Deferred tax charges	12,377
Total current assets	157,190
Inventories—non-current	55,440
Investments and Long-Term Receivables	
Receivables from television network agreements	7,769
Investments, at equity in net assets	4,415
Other	2,588
Property and equipment, at cost, less accumulated depreciation and amortization	76,503

(*continued*)

EXHIBIT 7 (Cont.)

Assets	1975 (in thousands)
Other Assets	
Excess of cost over net assets acquired	1,016
Music copyrights	1,903
Television station licenses, contracts, and network affiliation agreements	12,344
Other	3,826
Total assets	$322,994
Liabilities and Stockholders' Equity	
Current Liabilities	
Contractual obligations	$ 7,624
Participants' share payable	22,309
Accounts payable	31,703
Accrued liabilities	14,443
Advance film rentals	20,250
Accrued domestic and foreign taxes	23,534
Guarantees of producers' borrowings	4,578
Total current liabilities	124,441
Long-Term Liabilities	
Loans payable to banks	8,000
Contractual obligations	16,778
Convertible debentures	26,134
Mortgages payable	19,014
Guarantees of producers' borrowings	12,668
Stockholders' Equity	
Preferred stock, without par value; authorized and unissued 2,000,000 shares	—
Common stock $1 par value; authorized 15,000,000 shares, issued 8,561,815 shares	8,562
Capital in excess of par value	82,223
Retained earnings	34,422
	125,207
Less cost of 1,013,363 shares in treasury (1,029,706 shares in 1974)	9,248
Total stockholders' equity	115,959
Contingent liabilities, commitments and subsequent events	
Total Liabilities	$322,994

EXHIBIT 8 Summary of Proposed 1977 Studio Facilities Charges

GENERAL POLICY

The Facilities Division will no longer be considered a profit center. All charge outs will be considered a rational way to absorb the overhead cost of the Division. Since the Division will still be dealing with outsiders (Spelling, and others that may rent space on the lot), it is still necessary to have a formal structure for charging out specific functions. This structure also accomplishes our objective of charging individual features and television series in an appropriate way.

The performance of the Division will no longer be judged on the basis of profit or "contribution," but rather on service and how closely costs are controlled and relate to budgets.

The individual service departments may be judged on the basis of "contribution" since all free allowances, under the new arrangement, will be eliminated, and we can, therefore, judge whether these departments are paying their own way. If any department is marginal or operates at a loss on the new basis, it will become a candidate for elimination.

Deal With Aaron Spelling

Attached as *Exhibit 8A* is the new arrangement with Aaron Spelling. This will become effective for any pilots that Spelling is currently producing and for series with the commencement of production for the 1977–78 season. It will cover not only any new shows that Spelling develops, but also new seasons of old shows ("Starsky & Hutch," "Family," etc.).

The deal with Spelling will provide that he has a minimum commitment of 500 shooting days over a three-year period (with a minimum of 100 days per year). There is also no provision for a surcharge except a continuation of the $150 an episode handling charge in the current arrangement.

Office space has been increased from the current 10¢ per square foot to 20¢ per square foot per week. This is lower than the 30¢ per square foot to which we will increase all other Divisions, and is based on the fact that the space occupied by Spelling is generally inferior space to that occupied by Features, Corporate, or the TV Division. It was determined that all space comparable to the space occupied by Spelling would be charged at the 20¢ per square foot rate.

Deal With TV Division

The TV Division will continue to be charged under their current arrangement through May 31st (for existing series as well as charges to television overhead departments). Any new series would come under the same deal as has been given to Spelling; also any new episodes of "MASH" started subsequent to May 31st will come under the Spelling deal.

After May 31st, the TV Division will have exactly the same deal as Spelling does except for office space paid in the Executive and Administrative areas, for which they would be charged 30¢ per square foot.

The minimum guarantee with Spelling will apply to the TV Division.

All Other Outsiders

In any deals with other outside renters, we will use the Spelling deal as a standard, and endeavor to achieve generally higher rates than are included in that arrangement. It should be pointed out that since the Facilities Division is no longer considered a profit center, service to existing tenants, (Spelling, Fox and the Fox TV Division), are to be considered the primary objectives to the Division and any other tenants are to be taken on only when it will not interfere with the service to these existing tenants.

Feature Division

The deal with the Feature Division is essentially the same as the Spelling deal except for slightly higher rates for electrical and grip equipment per day, because features use more of this equipment than TV series. For this Division there will be no handling charge, but the Division will continue the 12% overhead charge. This will be done on a contractual basis as well as on the books. A portion of the 12% will be considered absorption of Facilities Division overhead.

Budgeting under the new basis will commence for features starting in 1977. Charges to features which were started under the old basis will continue on the old basis with appropriate adjustment in our accounts.

Corporate Departments

Exhibit 8B shows the justification for charging Corporate departments (as well as overhead departments of other divisions) at 30¢ per square foot. While some of the breakdowns between office activity and production activity are somewhat arbitrary, the 30¢ per square foot compares reasonably with space in nearby office locations and is, therefore, considered an appropriate charge for all office space except inferior space occupied by Spelling and any other departments located in comparable facilities.

It also shows on an estimated (pre-budget) basis how the Facilities Division would fare under this new arrangement, *Exhibit 8C*.

EXHIBIT 8A **Proposed Rate Schedule for Television Tenants in which Free Allowances Are Eliminated and All Services Are Charged Out on the Basis of Market Value**

Proposed New Rates

	Per Day
Wardrobe	$ 60
Grip	55
Sound Channel	65
Electrical Equipment	120
Props and Set Dressings	180
Stages (up to 2)	500
Fringe Benefits	Charged at Fox Standard Rates
Camera	Actual
D. C. Power	Actual
Post-production Sound	No Free Allowance
Projection Facilities	No Free Allowance
Offices	No Free Allowance
Dressing Rooms	No Free Allowance
Cutting Rooms	No Free Allowance
Generator Operator & First Aid	No Free Allowance

This proposed new rate schedule will be structured in such a way that *all* future union increases will be passed on in the form of appropriate rate increases.
Nothing in the proposed future arrangement will obligate Fox to continue to provide the services of any given department.
All other charges to remain as per existing agreement.

EXHIBIT 8B **Facilities Division Analysis of Office Related Expenses (000's omitted)**

	Amount	*Office Space Related*	*Production Activities Related*	
Studio Operations:				
Salaries & fringe	$ 214	$ 199	$ 15	7%
Depreciation	136	119	17	13
Repairs & maintenance	444	310	134	30
Utilities (net of chargeouts)	325	255	70	22
Janitorial, trash, etc.	542	525	17	3
Costs applicable to basic facilities	290	80	210	72
Office expenses	45	25	20	44
Transportation - company equipment	41	34	7	17
Other	23	20	3	13
Insurance	205	150	55	27
Accounting	339	—	339	100
Communications	470	352	118	25
First Aid	66	—	66	100
Plant protection	477	358	119	25
Purchasing	207	52	155	75
Air conditioning & maintenance	164	110	54	33
Electrical	257	104	153	60
Research	37	—	37	100
Office services	178	178	—	0
Total Facilities - General & Admin.	$4,460	$2,871*	$1,589	36%
Weekly Rental 166,000* square feet (estimate) at .33/sq. ft.				

*Does not include approximately 10,000 square feet added for Legal Department. Added costs as a result of additional space have not been considered—effect minor.

EXHIBIT 8C Effect of Office Rental and Production Activities (in millions)

Overhead Costs	*Office Space*	*Other Activities*	*Total*
General & administrative expense (Note A)	$ 2.9	$ 1.6	$ 4.5
Allocations	—	.6	.6
Total Overhead Costs	2.9	2.2	5.1
Income			
1. Revenue from Fox Features (Note B) (Under new pricing arrangement)	—	.1	.1
2. Revenue from outside tenants	—	.8	.8
3. Revenue from Fox TV	—	.2	.2
4. Net income from service departments	—	1.0	1.0
5. Office rent (30¢ sq. ft./week)			
Fox Corporate	.6	—	.6
Fox Feature Division	1.0	—	1.0
Fox Television Division	.4	—	.4
Fox Studio Facilities	.2	—	.2
Outside tenants	.4	—	.4
Total Income	2.6	2.1	4.7
Net Contribution (loss) - Studio Facilities	$ (.3)	$ (.1)	$ (.4)

Note A: Excludes studio carrying costs.
Note B: Before allocation of any portion of 12% overhead charged to features.

EXHIBIT 9 Hollywood Sound Stage Inventory

Company	*# Sound Stages*	*Company*	*# Sound Stages*
Burbank Studios	33	MGM	27
CBS Studio Center	17	Paramount	31
Culver City Studios	11	Producer's Studio	7
Disney	4	20th Century-Fox	22
General Service Studios	9	Universal	34
Goldwyn	10		

EXHIBIT 10 Economic Impact Study L.A. City Income Multiplier

TC-F Direct Spending	*Multiplier*	*Annual Dollar Impact of TC-F Spending*
$84,038,993	1.1	92,442,892
	1.2	100,846,792
	1.5	126,058,490
	1.8	151,270,187
	2.0*	168,077,986
	2.5	210,097,483
	3.57**	300,019,205

*Income Multiplier used by the Department of Planning and Development, State of Hawaii for Film and Television Dollars; also used by Urbanomics Research Associates as the regional income multiplier for the Southern California economy in a study done on Kaiser Steel Corporation, Fontana Plant.
**Regional Income Multiplier used by the State of Louisiana. This multiplier is claimed to be a reasonable multiplier for many states.

TC-F Primary Jobs									
Full-time	*Part-time*	×	*Multiplier*	*Full-time*	+	*Part-time*	=	*Total Employment*
1,241	5,990		1.12*	1,390	+	6,709	=	8,099
			1.2	1,489	+	7,188	=	8,677
			1.5	1,862	+	8,985	=	10,847
			2.0	2,482	+	11,980	=	14,412
			2.5	3,103	+	14,975	=	18,078
			2.8**	3,475	+	16,772	=	20,247

*Source: *Markets for California Products*, State of California Economic Development Agency, a study by Hansen, Robson and Tiebout, 1959, p. 59. Was used as the Service Industry Group employment multiplier for the State of California.
**Source: *Impact of the Space Shuttle Program on the California Economy*, Rockwell International, a study by Larry Kimbell, December 1974, p. 11. It was used as the employment multiplier for the aerospace industry of California.

WOLFE INDUSTRIES, INC.

"Not go public!" The thought was anathema to Fritz Wolfe, president of Wolfe Industries of Lima, Ohio. It was nine years since his father had died and he had taken over as CEO of the family company. During that time, he had patiently and persistently been preparing the company for a public offering. Now, in October, 1976, when he was about to make an acquisition which would add to the momentum of Wolfe's sales and profit growth, some of his directors were saying "No!"

Their argument was simple. They believed that the addition of Midwestern Health Care, Inc. (MHC), a nursing-home operator, to Wolfe's diversified portfolio could only hurt the company's image. One irascible director, an outsider and a professor at Mr. Wolfe's alma mater, said the move would be a mistake: 1) because the $4 million-plus price was too high; 2) because the acquisition would increase the company's dependence on Ohio and one state's health-care reimbursement policies; 3) because the nursing-home industry was nationally known for its fraud scandals.

He went so far as to say that if Wolfe went ahead with the acquisition, Fritz might as well give up the idea of going public. The director added: "That might not hurt, however. If we dropped the 'go public' idea we could set about making some real money!"

FREDERIC WOLFE

Fritz Wolfe graduated from business school in 1955 and returned to Lima, Ohio, where his father controlled an integrated building company, the Lima Lumber Co., which later became Wolfe Industries. Mr. Wolfe, Sr., a successful Toledo lawyer, had purchased the company in 1944. Later, he had acquired a stone quarry and started a construction company and a number of related businesses.

Fritz's role at Lima Lumber was as a stabilizing influence on his father who tended to enter new business ventures without a great deal of prior planning. Fritz found he had to develop many organizational and managerial skills quickly; in particular, he took upon himself the role of the firm's controller because he found that financial and accounting information gave him an effective lever to check his father's entrepreneurial bent.

When Mr. Wolfe, Sr., died in mid-1967, he left his estate to his family using two eparate trusts: a marital trust with Fritz's mother as beneficiary, and a residual trust benefiting Fritz and his three sisters. Fritz and one of his brothers-in-law, Bob James, were appointed trustees under the terms of the will. In practice, this gave Fritz management control of the Wolfe family's assets for ten years, so long as he paid a dividend of $0.04 per share each year.

Fritz had taken over the business when its sales were less than $5 million. Now, in October 1976, in the company's fiscal 1977, Wolfe's sales were expected to top $30

This case was prepared by Assistant Professor Kenneth J. Hatten as a basis for class discussion rather than to illustrate either effective or ineffective handling of an administrative situation.

million and its dividend payment would be $0.14 per share. As *Exhibit 1* shows, Fritz had more than met the conditions of the trusts. In addition, although one of the trusts would end in 1977, Fritz and Bob James would still have effective control of the company. James sat on Wolfe Industries' Board and was the firm's investment banker.

HEALTH CARE FUND

Mr. James's firm had already raised $1.5 million for Health Care Fund, which had been founded in 1970 and which operated as a Real Estate Investment Trust (REIT) under Sections 856–858 of the Internal Revenue Code of 1954. In addition, Mr. James's firm was underwriting a public offering of 250,000 shares in the trust at a price of $21.

The prospectus for the offering, at the SEC's prompting, treated Wolfe Industries as an affiliate of the trust by reason of the two organizations' business ties, which are described in the following extract from the trust's prospectus:

> Investment opportunities have been originated for the Fund by Wolfe acting in its capacity as a developer. Sales people employed by Wolfe call on operators of existing nursing homes in an attempt to locate prospects who would be interested in constructing a new facility. Many of these operators have insufficient credit to borrow the financing needed for construction. As a result, a leasing program is offered and if the operator qualifies for such a program, and the proposed investment meets Wolfe's investment standards, a construction contract is entered into by Wolfe with the operator. As a condition of the leasing program, the operator must provide suitable land, free and clear of all liens, upon which the nursing home can be constructed. The construction contract contains the customer's undertaking to enter into a twenty-year lease with Wolfe or its nominee, which nominee is usually the Fund or Wolfe Investment Company. On several occasions the nominees have been third parties. It is the current policy of the Fund to grant the operator an option to purchase the property at any time after five years from the execution of the lease agreement, at a price usually equal to the Fund's original cost with no credit or deduction on account of lease payments. The lessee must also discharge the Fund of any liability under any mortgage lien on the property. The lease payments are designed to provide the Fund with an annual cash flow of approximately 12–13%.
>
> The operator is required to deed the property on which the nursing home is to be built to the Fund. For convenience, the Fund has become the record owner at the outset by contracts with Wolfe (the developer) to hold the property merely as nominee for the developer during the development stage. The Fund then extends a construction loan to the developer, taking back a mortgage. If the Fund purchases the nursing home upon completion, the construction loan is paid off by application of a portion of the purchase price and at the same time the construction mortgage is released. If the Fund does not elect to buy the nursing home, the Fund reconveys the record title upon instruction of the developer and Wolfe purchases the project or it is sold to a third party and the construction loan repaid to the Fund.

Exhibit 2, which has been extracted from Health Care Fund's prospectus, lists a number of completed and proposed transactions between Wolfe Industries and Health Care Fund.

Mr. Wolfe and Wolfe Industries' secretary, Mr. Bruce Thompson, were two of the trust's seven trustees. In addition, they owned the trust's management company, First Toledo Corporation (50% each). *Exhibit 3* shows the fees paid to the manager by the Fund since it commenced operations.

CORPORATE OBJECTIVES

The fact that Wolfe Industries had access to the public capital market through Mr. James and the Real Estate Investment Trust had prompted some of the Wolfe directors to question the wisdom of Fritz Wolfe's present objective to take the firm public. In 1967, after he had taken control of the firm, Fritz had felt that when sales reached $25 million, the company would be big enough to attract public interest. However, with the weak capital markets of 1974 and 1975, it had become obvious to Mr. Wolfe and Mr. James that the firm would have to be substantially bigger before it could attract public interest. However, it wasn't clear to some of the directors whether even $100 million in sales would make the firm, as it was presently constituted, attractive in the market.

Yet, Mr. Wolfe was loath to let go of this objective. For the past five years, he had consistently reported Wolfe Industries' earnings to maximize profit and, in spite of the protests of his outside directors who pointed out that he was paying somewhat higher taxes than he would otherwise need to pay and passing up opportunities to shelter income, Mr. Wolfe had felt justified in pursuing his goal in this way. An example of the seriousness of Mr. Wolfe's intention to go public was his publication of an annual report which he distributed widely, although the firm was privately held. Another example of his persistence was his ongoing search for a related "Stock Exchange Listed" company, a company large enough to attract a real market for its stock and short of management which Mr. Wolfe thought his company could provide.

WOLFE INDUSTRIES

Between 1967 and 1970 the companies under Mr. Wolfe's control grew, and in 1970, he decided to reorganize them. The Lima Lumber Company was renamed Wolfe Industries, and two new companies were formed: Lima Lumber, Inc., to control the retail lumber business, and Wolfe Industries Construction Co. "This was more than a name change," Fritz said. "It amounted to a change of strategy because it changed the way our managers thought about the company. We became something more than a retail lumber yard."

By 1976, Wolfe Industries was composed of fourteen companies organized into five operating groups: building materials, construction, financing and leasing, truck sales and service, and nursing-home operations. The company operated in the states of Ohio, Indiana, West Virginia and Kentucky. Mr. Wolfe felt that diversification of locality and businesses would give Wolfe Industries a more consistent earnings pattern. He also believed that the symbiotic relationship between the various companies strengthened Wolfe. As he put it, "The financing and leasing provided by Wolfe Investment Company helps the marketing of our Construction Company which, in turn, purchases materials from Lima Lumber, Inc." Wolfe's policy was to reinvest over 80% of its earnings in the company. The following section, which is extracted from Wolfe Industries' 1976 Annual Report, reviews the operations of the five groups.

A REVIEW OF GROUP OPERATIONS

Building Materials Group

One segment of this group includes the retail lumber and building supply yards of Lima Lumber, Inc., located in Lima, Auglaize Lumber Company of Wapakoneta, and Putnam Lumber Company in Ottawa. Sales increased 8% over fiscal 1975 and profits were up 21%. Approximately 37% of such sales were to Wolfe Industries Construction Company for nursing homes, up from 25% in 1975.

Another segment is Cole Lumber and Supply Company, Inc., the largest retail yard in Paducah, Kentucky, which was acquired in fiscal 1976. William H. Merritt is President of both Cole and Lima Lumber. The yard includes 9 acres of land, a modern office and store building, many large storage warehouses and a well-equipped mill and truss manufacturing plant. Cole added sales of $5.6 million and very good profits in fiscal 1976.

The third segment involves quarrying operations in Lima, carried on by the Western Ohio Stone Company, a division of Western Ohio Corporation. The stone company suffered a disappointing year in 1976 after enjoying a record year in 1975. Sales of crushed limestone, readi-mix concrete, and asphaltic concrete were down 33% from the previous year and profits were off 84%.

The building materials group contributed about 58% of Wolfe Consolidated earnings in 1976 compared with 39% in 1975. Increased sales and profits are projected in all three companies for 1977.

A new panelization program is being introduced by Lima Panelized Homes Company, a division of Lima Lumber, Inc. The panel is manufactured in Wapakoneta, and features a post-and-beam frame, polystyrene foam insulation, and glue-bonded skins of plywood or plasterboard. Called the "Smith Insulated Panel," it is used in roofs and floors as well as side walls. This panel, together with Lima Lumber's roof trusses, is being marketed through appointed builder-dealers, one to a county. To date, the response has been encouraging, and a substantial increase in panelized homes sales is expected in 1977.

Construction and Development Group

The Construction Group, comprising the nursing-home and commercial construction operations of Wolfe Industries Construction Company and Lima Lumber's house-building program, had a record year. This group produced 35% of Wolfe Industries' consolidated earnings, up from 14% the year before. Sales increased 61% and net income over 200% for the past year.

Nursing-home development is the major thrust of the Construction Group. Ten nursing-home projects were completed and fourteen more started (an all-time high) reflecting the excellent demand for health-care facilities and the availability of long-term financing. (Ground was broken for only five new projects in calendar 1974 because of the tight money market.) Commercial construction sales consisting of Butler pre-engineered projects were less than the previous year and no land sales were made at the sixty-five-acre Bible Road Industrial Park, a joint venture project in Lima, Ohio. The Construction Division recently moved its office and warehouse to the industrial park, Lima's first such development.

The house-building program of Lima Lumber, Inc., in Wapakoneta and Lima, produced ten house sales and five additional lot sales in fiscal 1976. This compares to eleven house sales and three additional lot sales in the previous year. There were four completed houses and five under construction in the inventory as of March 31, 1976, plus ninety-seven completed lots. The losses in this area were offset by the nursing-home contribution during the year.

Finance Group

The group is composed of Wolfe Investment Company, which owns and leases nursing-home and other commercial properties, and Wolfe Financial, Inc., which finances trucks and nursing-home equipment. The revenues, assets and liabilities of this group are not consolidated into the Wolfe Industries, Inc. totals as they are dissimilar in character to the other operations. Instead, they are reported on the equity basis in the balance sheet and income statement.

In fiscal 1975 Wolfe Investment Company added only 2 leased properties to its portfolio, but 5 lessees of existing properties exercised their purchase options, creating record capital gains exceeding $350,000. Capital gains result from depreciation, which has been charged on the building during the lease, and the realization of the profit margin from the construction of the project. (The carrying value of the buildings is less than the option prices by approximately $684,000 after tax.) In fiscal 1976 only 2 lease options were exercised and capital gains were cut in half. Four new leases were added to the portfolio, including Heartland of Perrysburg, a 136-bed nursing home developed by another corporation and costing almost $1,800,000. Lease income did increase slightly in fiscal 1976, but net after-tax income dropped over 50%. There were 13 leased properties in the portfolio as of March 31, 1976, including 10 nursing homes.

There have been three options exercised already in fiscal 1977 with a chance of more to come. Three projects which were started last year will be completed during the year, and we expect to start three additional projects this year, including a psychiatric clinic near Indianapolis.

Wolfe Investment Company will embark on a new activity starting this fall. The furniture and equipment required to operate a new nursing home will be purchased by Wolfe Investment and leased to the operator on a seven-year contract. This will lower the operator's monthly payment for these assets, and it will provide Wolfe Investment Company with a desirable earning asset and an investment tax credit. We are planning three contracts for this year and expecting this business to increase in the future.

Wolfe Financial, Inc. experienced its first full year of operations in fiscal 1976. Outstanding loans increased during the year from $273,000 to $1,412,000 with very little loss experience. Income is booked by the rule of 78's and income for the month of March, 1976, just about equaled expenses. However, the company experienced a small loss during the year while the loan portfolio was building up. The loan volume in 1976 was down due to depressed truck sales. Mr. Kruse[1] and his staff helped our truck dealerships with their collection problems, which were aggravated by the gener-

[1]General Manager of the Truck Group and President of Wolfe Financial, Inc.

al business recession. A small profit has been projected for fiscal 1977 and outstanding loans should grow to over $2,500,000.

The finance group produced 14% of consolidated Wolfe Industries profits in fiscal 1976, down from 42% in 1975. A substantial increase in volume is anticipated in the current year resulting from the option exercises in Wolfe Investment Company.

Truck Group

Fiscal 1976 was a recession year for the truck industry, and our three dealerships did not escape the effects of the depressed conditions. Western Ohio Truck Company in Lima, our original dealership, suffered a 42% truck sales decline but operated at a breakeven level. Parts and service sales did not decline appreciably and margins from those two excellent departments covered the overhead and offset losses on truck sales.

The failure of the Diamond-Reo Truck Company continued to dampen dealership operations in Perrysburg during fiscal 1976, as related truck and parts inventories left on hand had to be worked down. Sales declined by 43%, but losses were held in check as overhead was substantially trimmed. The name was changed from Northwest Ohio Truck Company to Wolfe Kenworth, Inc., in order to better identify with the trade mark of our manufacturer and to create a new image.

Wolfe Truck Sales, Inc., Ft. Wayne, experienced a good year. Total sales declined 30%, but parts and service sales increased by 19% and the margins from those two departments increased by $21,000, a noteworthy achievement. Profits declined 44% for the year, but they still remained respectable, demonstrating how well an ably managed truck dealership can do in a bad year.

Western Ohio Transportation Company, which brokers dump trucks for the delivery of crushed stone in Lima, suffered a sales and earnings decline from fiscal 1975 due to the depressed sales at Western Ohio Stone Company.

The truck group showed a $28,000 loss in 1976, up from a $15,000 group loss in fiscal 1975. The Perrysburg dealership continued to more than offset the profits in the other companies. Considering the 39% decline in sales and depressed industry conditions, the result is not too surprising.

Bill Kruse, President of Wolfe Financial, Inc., was put in charge of the truck group, with the three dealership managers reporting to him. He has had the responsibility of building new management teams at each dealership.

A four-truck bay addition to the Perrysburg building will be constructed this year and it will include a paint booth. An expansion of truck body-work is planned at Wolfe Kenworth in order to improve service and parts sales. Full-service truck-leasing is planned to begin in Lima during the current year.

Health-Care Operations Group

This group started fiscal 1976 with one 60-bed nursing home and 45 employees; it ended the year with 336 beds in 3 homes, employing 227 persons. We had made a good start toward developing an operating chain. A 40-bed addition was completed at Indian Lake Manor in September, 1975, and the home is presently operating near its capacity of 100 beds. Dick Aldrich was appointed Administrator, replacing Bill Hurles who was transferred to Bucyrus to start up that facility.

In December 1975, Wolfe Nursing Homes, Inc. was merged into Wolfe Industries, Inc., and a new trade style, Heartland Health Care Company, was adopted. This company will be operated as a division of Wolfe Industries, Inc.

Also in December, Wolfe Investment Company acquired a 136-bed home in Perrysburg from Rembrandt Enterprises, Inc. of Edina, Minnesota. Heartland purchased the supplies, furniture, and equipment, leased the building from Wolfe Investment Company, and took over the operations and care of patients. The staff, numbering over 100 employees, was put on the Heartland payroll, and the name was changed to Heartland of Perrysburg. The transition was accomplished with a minimum of problems, and the facility has been profitable from inception. The building is somewhat more elaborate than our standard models, the total investment exceeding $2 million.

In February, Wolfe Industries Construction Company completed a 100-bed home in Bucyrus for Wolfe Investment Company. Heartland, the lessee, purchased the furniture and equipment with financing from Wolfe Financial, Inc. Bill Hurles assembled a competent staff and started admitting patients in March. The rent-up has been somewhat slower than anticipated, as there has been a delay in certification for Medicare/Medicaid.

Wolfe Industries Construction Company is planning to start 3 new projects for Heartland this fall, and they should go on-stream in 1977. They include a 100-bed home in Kettering, a 120-bed facility in Clarksburg, West Virginia (to be financed with industrial revenue bonds), and a 60-bed home in Rainelle, West Virginia.

A $42,000 loss was incurred in fiscal 1976, but a profit is expected in 1977. Indian Lake and Perrysburg are full and profitable, and Bucyrus is expected to break even by year-end.

Other Operations & Financial Statements

Wolfe also owns and manages a 96-unit apartment complex in Lima, Ohio, and owns approximately 160 acres of undeveloped land for future development. *Exhibit 4* contains the consolidated financial statements for Wolfe Industries for the years ending March 31, 1975 and 1976, and the company's profit and loss statement for the 6 months ending September 30, 1976.

THE GROWTH STRATEGY

Wolfe Industry's growth strategy had developed slowly between 1967 and 1970. It was based on Fritz Wolfe's belief that the nursing-home business was a growth industry, on the firm's experience in coping with the cyclical nature of the construction industry, and on the limitations of the firm's primary market in western Ohio. Also of importance was the fact that the businesses in which the company operated were fundamentally local in character.[2]

Lima Lumber built its first nursing home in 1963. It was a larger project than the company had previously attempted but Fritz and his father were able to finance it. Fritz said,

[2]A rule of thumb in the nursing-home industry stated that over 75% of the patients came from within 20 miles, with between 15% and 20% coming from within the 20- to 50-mile radius.

My father established the pattern. The terms we set were the key. The operators had to own the land and deed it to us. Then we'd finance the project and lease it back to them with an option to buy after five years. After our second project, I realized that nursing homes were great business—once they rent up, they stay up. I told my father that I'd finance anything he could build.

Further experience and research led Fritz to the realization that there was a real need for nursing homes. Government regulations, backed up by Medicaid and Medicare payments, were forcing the rate of replacement of obsolete and unsafe facilities (Bruce Thompson estimated, in 1976, that there were 8,000 nursing homes in Ohio and adjacent states, only 2,000 of which satisfied the latest standards). In addition, the segment of the U.S. population aged 65 or older was growing significantly, as *Exhibit 5* shows. In 1974, one analyst wrote:

The market served by the nursing-home industry is largely composed of the elderly. Due to better care, increasing pension benefits, and government health care programs, this group is growing in numbers and better able to afford health services. A survey made by the Federal Housing Authority of patients in nursing homes showed that only 5% of the patients were under 60 years of age. The median age of residents was 79.1 years. This segment is large and growing. Over 10% of the U.S. population is 65 years of age or older and this percentage will rise slowly. However, currently, the growth rate of this population segment is 2½ times that of the population as a whole.

Wolfe's strategy for exploiting this market was quite simple. Ideally the company would identify a market need[3] for nursing homes over an extended region and then acquire a local lumber or building-materials company to serve as a base for construction-operations management and as a source of sales and earnings. In essence, Fritz wanted to replicate the company's Lima experience. Fritz said:

We tend to locate in smaller communities where our financing techniques give us a competitive advantage. I think small communities are where nursing homes belong. The people in those towns need jobs and they're very responsive to our patients' needs. In bigger centers, nursing-home operators have other sources of financing and they don't need us. Of course, they have expensive land, construction unions, and high staff costs and competition to contend with.

We look for retail lumber yards because they're part of our history and we know how to run them. They give us a base of operations within a 200-mile radius and a local image which helps us develop working relationships with local S & L's.

In the late 1960s, financing this strategy was not a problem. It was a matter of finding an operator with the capital to operate a home. Mortgage money was usually available from nearby S & L's and, although the loans were relatively large (for the S & L's), Wolfe's financial strength and its successful track record seemed to inspire confidence. Wolfe's policy was to move cautiously, imposing rigid quality standards on the operator-lessees:

[3]Wolfe Industries was both helped and hindered in this regard by various local and state regulations concerning land use, zoning, and the "need" for nursing homes.

1 The operator-lessee had to own the land (which was deeded to Wolfe) and have sufficient working capital to tide the home over any rent-up period. Experience suggested that as much as 18 months was required to achieve a breakeven month on a new nursing home. During this period, losses might climb to $100,000 or more for a 100-bed home.
2 Wolfe would deal only with its own construction company.
3 It would not finance ''strangers'' in any community.
4 Wolfe built only homes which it would be happy to operate and own in event of default.

Wolfe felt that ''quality'' contributed to sustained repeat business in a region. Complementing these standards was Wolfe's ''in event of default'' policy. When something went wrong, Wolfe was prepared to give management advice to the operator at no charge or to arrange a buyout by a more successful operator. The company was not eager to foreclose—to date it never had—and no lessee had ever lost his original investment in a Wolfe-financed nursing home.

By 1970, however, the total debt carried by Wolfe Industries had become so large that Fritz was finding it difficult to get new mortgage finance, although the company had customers. This was when the REIT, Health Care Fund, was organized.

The trust was designed to allow Wolfe access to sources of local Ohio capital, other than the S & L's, to finance its construction activity. Simultaneously, the trust allowed Fritz to manage Wolfe Industries' capital structure and to report higher profits. To manage the conflict of interest built into this arrangement, all prices in transactions between Wolfe Industries and the trust were negotiated with third parties (the unaffiliated lessees) and supported by an independent professional appraisal. One of Wolfe's managers said the net result was that Wolfe could make sensible deals happen sooner than its competitors.

THE BUSINESS PRESS

In February and March 1976, the press saw a revival of the New York nursing-home scandal when a special commission appointed by New York's Governor pointed an accusing finger at Vice-President Nelson Rockefeller. *The Economist* reported:

> Moreover, Mr. Rockefeller failed to act on the repeated requests from his own health department for more audits of nursing-home accounts. He also turned a blind eye to reports charging glaring neglect of aged patients. The pattern, as detailed by Mr. Abram, was one of peddling government influence in return for political support. . . . Nursing-home operators garnered millions in profits.[4]

To many observers it was simply another page in the history of an industry long beset with problems. For example, the near failure of Four Seasons Nursing Homes had culminated in the sentencing of its president to jail and heavy fines for some partners in the Wall Street firm which had underwritten the company. In spite of these problems, Fritz Wolfe believed that the nursing-home industry was economically exciting and that the way his company competed was totally ethical. He said,

[4]*The Economist,* March 6, 1976, p. 42.

I believe that, one day, health care will enjoy the status of a growth industry. Already, proprietary hospital companies like Humana have P/E's of 15 or thereabouts and their financial results are no better than ours. You see, this is a sensitive business, full of human interest and ripe for sensational reporting.

There will always be scandals like Four Seasons but 95% of the firms in this business do a great job. It's an efficient health-care delivery system. We can provide a bed, the services of an RN, laundry, social activities, meals, and a nice place to live for between $20 and $25 a day. A hospital bed costs $80 to $150 or more.

Fritz recalled a recent board meeting when an outside director quoted *Financial World,* and recited the fate of another, larger company which had committed itself to the nursing-home field:

"We're not in the business to build up our stock price," says ARA's president and chief operating officer William S. Fishman. "Through the years the company's growth strategy has been to continue to increase its share of existing service markets, to penetrate new markets for present services, and to add new services which can be sold to existing and potential clients. We've been in the medical-care market for over thirty years, so it [owning and operating 110 extended-care facilities throughout the Southwest] was just a natural transition."

"But the market apparently hasn't seen it that way. ARA's stock, at 57, is now trading near the low end of its eight-year trading range and its P/E is down to 11," as White, Weld analyst John A. Jensen, Jr., points out. "Of course, its move into nursing homes has impacted the stock. Just look at its low multiple."[5]

Of course, not every analyst saw such a bleak future for ARA. Many thought the market had overreacted to ARA's involvement in the nursing-home field. They predicted future profits. Philip Clark, Vice-President at Drexel Burnham was quoted as saying that ARA had been the first company to make a long-term commitment to nursing homes. The same article emphasized Fishman's (ARA's CEO) plans that when real estate and money-market conditions permit, ''we plan on selling [our owned nursing homes] on a lease-back basis.''[6]

The director of ARA suggested that Fishman and Clark seemed to see things differently and said, in effect, ''It's what the market thinks that's important. Look at the figures [*Exhibit 6*] and then decide whether nursing homes should be our business!''

THE PROPOSED ACQUISITION

Midwestern Health Care, Inc. (MHC) was a private company which operated a number of nursing homes in Ohio. It was based in Mt. Vernon, Ohio, about a hundred miles from Lima. Fritz had met the principals of the company at a Health Care Fund trustees' meeting and he had felt, at the time, that the company could readily fit into Wolfe. Not only would it boost Wolfe's sales and profits, but it would add tested management to Wolfe's team.

[5]*Financial World,* February 5, 1975.
[6]*Ibid.*

Bob Bargmann, Wolfe's treasurer and controller, at Fritz's request, had projected MHC's income for the years ending October 31, 1976, 1977, and 1978. He also projected its balance sheet. The 1976 figures were based on fairly accurate figures through August 1, 1976, which MHC provided. Fritz said: "As you can see [*Exhibits* 7 and 8], MHC is coming off a super year. Their operating results are good and they also have a capital gain on the sale of one sixty-bed home. My projections show less profit per home in 1977 and 1978, due to an anticipated lowering of the Medicaid reimbursement formula. The 1977 figures are conservative because of rent-up losses in Fremont, Delaware and Hillsboro. The 1978 figures show what MHC's system could do without rent-up losses.

"MHC's cash position is quite strong. They executed an option on Sherwood this year, without bothering to get a long-term loan. They could have borrowed $600,000 on this nursing home; they have a line of credit at Lowes National Bank for $300,000 with less than $50,000 outstanding at the present time. They also have two nursing homes under construction which are being leased and built by another contractor at what I think are extremely favorable terms—almost $75,000 less than our own prices."

At this point, a director asked "How much?"

"I think we'll have to offer $4 million," Fritz answered.

"How would we pay?"

"It depends on the terms. If they go with an installment sale, we could offer $4,430,000, taking 29% of their common stock in the year of sale for $1,284,700 and the balance over 15 to 20 years at 8% interest. We have $1 million available and we could borrow against their Sherwood home for the balance of the $1,287,700.

"An alternative would be to offer a tax-free exchange using 8% Wolfe Industries Preferred (payable quarterly). We could make a market for this preferred stock by investing about a quarter of our profit-sharing retirement monies in it. On an informal basis, I would have to promise them that they could 'put' $300,000 in any given year—that is, sell $300,000 to Wolfe.

"The installment sale would be subject to capital gains versus the preferred stock which would give them tax-free transfer privileges. Of course, if they sold the preferred, they would have to pay capital gains tax. We would probably have to provide them with a tax ruling to this effect, but Bruce has researched this for me and he is fairly certain that exemptions are available under an 'A' reorganization and merger."

"Fritz, are you going to make the preferred convertible?"

"No, not unless they make an issue of it. We could consider conversion into common stock for, say, $25 per share. If we invest 25% of our annual profit sharing investment, that would only provide a market for $25–50,000. We would have to provide the balance out of Wolfe Industries' treasury."

"That's all very well, Fritz, but how did you come up with $4 million?" another director asked.

Fritz replied, "By capitalizing their after-tax income at about 10. Since we *are* paying for the company with 8% preferred, the purchase will be made out of MHC's anticipated income. Ten is a high cap rate, but they will not sell for less. They feel that their value is at least $12,000 per bed."

"It's costing us $12,000 per bed to build a home and get it operating," Pier Borra said. "We paid $14,750 per bed in Perrysburg."

"That's true," Fritz said. "If we use $12,000, after deducting debentures, preferred stock and debt, the company might be worth $4.8–4.9 million, and that's conservative because I've made no allowance for the two homes under construction.''

''I'm not sure that that figure's right,'' the bad-mouthing director said with a smile.

Fritz showed him *Exhibits 9* and *10,* which, for some reason, failed to convince him.

''What will it do to our EPS?'' he pressed, with something that Fritz could have considered glee, as he threw Fritz's favorite criterion back at him.

Fritz pulled out *Exhibit 11,* demonstrating that he had anticipated the question. Fritz said, ''These are the advantages of the acquisition:

1 If they take our preferred stock, it will establish our preferred as an acquisition vehicle.
2 They have a good management team and a good reporting system, which is compatible with ours. They use the Lowes National Bank computer, too.
3 They could move into the old Wolfe Industries' Construction building.
4 They probably won't want a lot of cash, although I could offer up to $1.5 million. I think they'd prefer a tax-free exchange. If they do, we would have an excellent cash position to cover our dividend payout and to make other acquisitions.''

''I don't care about that!'' the director interrupted. ''I think you would be paying too much, but what's more important is the size of the commitment you would be making to the nursing-home operations business. Is this going to do as much for Wolfe Industries as additional investments in construction or building materials supplies? How is it going to affect our long-term growth, and what about the potential multiplier for a public offering of common stock? Is this the best strategy for structuring ourselves for a public offering?''

AFTERMATH: SOME HARD THINKING TO DO

The next morning Fritz drove the seventy miles to Lima from his home in Perrysburg, a southern suburb of Toledo.[9] He was concerned. Going public was important, he believed, because over time the number of stock holders in the company would increase by gift and inheritance. Currently sales of Wolfe stock were restricted but one day market values could be important for estate planning purposes. ''None of us should be locked in,'' he thought. ''Besides, a public market would help me attract talented and experienced managers.''

In May, 1976, he had attempted to hire an MBA from a major business school to head the new division he was forming to operate nursing homes. ''However,'' he thought to himself, ''they all seem to want to go to either New York or Chicago or to stay in Boston. A few want to go to the Rocky Mountains or the Northwest, but mention the Midwest and you'd think you were asking them to go back down on the farm. Boston may not be Paris, but it sure affects a lot of people that way.''

Even the prospects of obtaining an equity interest in Wolfe had little appeal. That

[7]Fritz usually stayed in Lima one or two nights a week, primarily to clear his desk, free of interruptions. He and his wife had lived in Lima while their children were small, but had moved to Toledo five years ago to be closer to Bowling Green University where Mrs. Wolfe was on the faculty, and to send their children to the private country day school which Fritz had attended thirty years before.

would change with a public market. Besides, my key managers have a stock interest. They joined me partly because I promised them equity.'' (*Exhibit 12* gives some biographical data on the officers and directors of Wolfe Industries.)

As his car pulled into the parking space reserved for him outside Lima Lumber's hardware store and his office, Fritz thought, ''Am I being realistic about the firm's objectives and the way I'm pursuing them? Should I go ahead with the MHC acquisition in spite of the board's objections?''

EXHIBIT 1
WOLFE INDUSTRIES, INC.
7-Year Financial Highlights
(in thousands)

	1976	1975	1974	1973	1972	1971	1970
Revenues	$24,598	$20,361	$18,293	$14,386	$10,805	$7,281	$7,010
Net income (a)	$ 935	$ 713	813	$ 621	$ 499	$ 214	$ 294
Per share (b)	89¢	69¢	81¢	62¢	50¢	22¢	30¢
Dividendends paid	$ 126	$ 103	$ 81	$ 60	$ 49	$ 39	$ 39
Per share (b)	12¢	10¢	8¢	6¢	5¢	4¢	4¢
Return on investment (d)	19%	17%	24%	23%	23%	11%	18%
Total shareholders' equity	$ 5,263	$ 4,433	$ 3,805	$ 2,987	$ 2,423	$1,968	$1,771
Per share	$ 4.96	$ 4.25	$ 3.71	$ 3.00	$ 2.44	$ 2.00	$ 1.83
Total assets (c)	$13,553	$10,449	$11,781	$ 7,765	$ 6,874	$5,483	$4,498
Number of shares outstanding (b)	$ 1,060	1,042	1,026	996	995	983	968
Unrealized gain on Wolfe Investment properties less applicable taxes	$ 684	$ 635	$ 821	$ 876	$ 717	$ 669	$ 530
Adjusted shareholders' equity	$ 5,947	$ 4,996	$ 4,626	$ 3,863	$ 3,140	$2,736	$2,301
Per share	$ 5.61	$ 4.79	$ 4.51	$ 3.88	$ 3.16	$ 2.68	$ 2.38

(a) includes extraordinary item net of applicable taxes for 1970, 1971, and 1972 in the amount of $20,500, $7,200, and $83,980 respectively.
(b) Adjusted for 10 for 1 stock split.
(c) Years prior to 1973 adjusted for change in method of accounting for investment in Wolfe investment Company.
(d) Percentage of income to average stockholders' equity.

EXHIBIT 2
Health Care Fund's Equity Investment

A summary of the existing equity investments as of December 31, 1975 is set forth below. All of these investments have been acquired from Wolfe, and with the exception of two (Upper Sandusky and Lakeview), have been leased to unaffiliated persons. The homes have a 92–98% occupancy rate.[1]

Location	*# Beds*	*Date of Acquisition*	*Cost*	*Mortgages*		*Lease Exp. Date*[2]	*Current Annual Rent*	*Total Square Feet*
				Interest Rate	*Maturity*			
Upper Sandusky, Ohio	100	5/71	$699,886	Prime + ¾%	11/94	1994	$ 81,782	29,800
Edgerton, Ohio	100	5/71	$659,956	8¼%	1/87	1991	$ 85,629	31,880
Fairborn, Ohio	100	10/72	$671,265	8%	6/93	1992	$ 85,351	24,500
Albany, Indiana	100	3/73	$713,426	9%	5/95	1995	$ 90,868	27,680
Elwood, Indiana	94	7/73	$690,025	8–9¼%	9/94	1994	$ 88,639	26,750
Columbus, Ohio	100	9/73	$624,741	9%	4/94	1993	$ 77,930	24,800
Lakeview, Ohio	100	10/74	$737,020	10½%	9/94	1995	$ 92,127	26,300
Lancaster, Ohio	100	5/74	$679,331	10½%	7/94	1994	$ 83,150	24,800
Salem, Ohio	50	11/74	$500,400	10¼%	7/96	1994	$ 61,200	15,800
Fremont, Ohio	100	8/75	$860,265	10%	8/2000	1995	$111,841	24,200
							$858,517	

[1]Rate excludes amortization of "points" and other related costs incurred in connection with mortgage loans. All mortgages are prepayable; in some cases, however, prepayment within the first 5 years would entail penalties up to 3% of the loan.
[2]The option to acquire the leased property after 5 years and before 20 years is given in each lease instrument.

EXHIBIT 2 (Cont.)

Health Care Fund's Construction Loans

The following nursing-home construction loans were being made by the Fund as of December 31, 1975. Advances are generally made over a 12-month period.

Location	# Beds	Total Amt. of Loan	Interest Rate	Date of Funding (12 mo.)	Permanent Financing
Canal Winchester, Ohio	100	$ 545,000	Prime + 2%	1/75	Pending
Newark, Ohio	50	$ 411,000	11%	8/75	Obtained
Greenville, Ohio	50	$ 409,000	11½%	6/75	Obtained
Miamisburg, Ohio	100	$ 760,000	Prime + 2%	11/75	Pending
Bryan, Ohio	100	$ 637,500	11¼%	9/75	Obtained
Zanesville, Ohio	100	$ 670,000	Prime + 2%	9/75	Pending
		$3,432,500			

In addition, the manager has been authorized (as of December 31, 1975) to make the following construction loans to Wolfe.[1] The money to fund such loans will be obtained from the proceeds of this offering and from loans from institutional lenders. One or more of such loans may not be funded in the manager's discretion should they not meet the Fund's investment standards.

Location	# Beds	Total Amt. of Loan	Interest Rate	Date of Funding (12 mo.)	Permanent Financing
Salem, Ohio	50	$ 325,000	11¾%	2/76	Obtained
Lancaster, Ohio	100	$ 725,000	Prime + 2%	6/76	None
Ravenna, Ohio	100	$ 725,000	Prime + 2%	7/76	None
		$1,775,000			

[1]The Fund charges an additional 1½ points as extra interest on the construction loans to the developer.

Health Care Fund's Projected Equity Investments

A summary of projected equity investments as of December 31, 1975, is set forth below. All of these projects are being, or will be, developed by Wolfe. One or more of these investments may not be made in the Trustees' discretion. All must be offered first to the Fund and rejected before Wolfe, as developer, can offer such investments to others.

			Anticipated			
Location	# Beds	Purchase Price	Loans Payable	Net-Equity Investment	Est. Time of Funding	Annual Lease Rate
Canal Winchester, Ohio	100	$ 700,000	$ 525,000	$ 175,000	2/76	12%
Newark, Ohio	50	$ 525,000	$ 400,000	$ 125,000	3/76	13%
Greenville, Ohio	50	$ 510,000	$ 375,000	$ 135,000	4/76	13%
Salem, Ohio	51	$ 425,000	$ 325,000	$ 100,000	5/76	12½%
Zanesville, Ohio	100	$ 865,000	$ 650,000	$ 215,000	8/76	13%
Bryan, Ohio	100	$ 835,000	$ 631,000	$ 204,000	8/76	13%
Miamisburg, Ohio	100	$ 950,000	$ 710,000	$ 240,000	9/76	13%
Lancaster, Ohio	100	$1,000,000	0	$1,000,000	4/77	13%
Ravenna, Ohio	100	$ 975,000	0	$ 975,000	4/77	13%
		$6,785,000	$3,616,000	$3,169,000		

EXHIBIT 3 **Management Fees Paid by Health Care Fund to First Toledo Corporation (for the years ended December 31)**

	1971	1972	1973	1974	1975
Management fee paid by the fund[1]	$2,948	$9,737	$17,252	$24,630	$28,546
Incentive fee	0	0	0	0	4,751[2]
Commitment forfeitures	0	0	0	0	0

[1]The manager pays all charges, including salaries, wages, payroll taxes, costs of employee benefit plans and charges for incidental help, attributable to its own operations. The manager also pays its own accounting fees and related expenses, legal fees, insurance, rent, telephone, utilities and travel expenses of its officers and employees.
[2]Waived through June 30, 1975.

EXHIBIT 4

WOLFE INDUSTRIES, INC.
Consolidated Balance Sheet
(March 31, 1976 and 1975)

Assets	1976	1975
Current Assets		
Cash	$ 403,733	$ 330,730
Trade accounts and notes receivable, less allowances for doubtful accounts and discounts of	2,200,355	1,197,170
Inventories (partially pledged)		
Lumber, hardware, and building supplies	$ 1,284,278	$ 593,735
Trucks, parts, and accessories	1,057,719	1,040,808
Real estate developments in progress	686,568	803,371
Crushed stone, sand, and supplies	199,670	145,668
	$ 3,228,235	$ 2,583,582
Accumulated costs and profits of construction contracts in process in excess of related billings (partially pledged)	2,243,129	1,583,706
Prepaid and deferred expenses	161,843	146,810
Total Current Assets	$ 8,237,295	$ 5,841,998
Other Assets		
Investments in unconsolidated subsidiaries—Note D	$ 1,216,560	$ 1,194,918
Investment in joint venture	55,230	53,789
Other investments	12,500	12,500
Notes receivable—due after one year	63,456	73,960
Land for future development or sale	200,904	213,557
Sundry other assets and deferred expenses	244,914	91,061
	$ 1,793,564	$ 1,639,785
Property, Plant and Equipment (partially pledged)		
Operating properties:		
Land and land improvements	$ 306,427	$ 258,824
Buildings	1,388,733	902,120
Machinery and equipment	3,554,264	2,878,138
Allowances for depreciation and depletion (deduction)	(3,044,462)	(2,417,255)
	$ 2,204,962	$ 1,621,827
Rental properties:		
Land and land improvements	$ 154,828	$ 152,414
Buildings and equipment	1,416,691	1,390,126
Furniture and fixtures	67,477	67,242
Allowances for depreciation (deduction)	(321,591)	(264,511)
	$ 1,317,405	$ 1,345,271
	$ 3,522,367	$ 2,967,098
	$13,553,226	$10,448,881

See notes to consolidated financial statements.

EXHIBIT 4 (Cont.)

Liabilities and Shareholders' Equity	*1976*	*1975*
Current Liabilities		
Notes payable:		
Collateralized by:		
Construction contracts	$ 1,233,535	$ 1,055,860
Trucks, parts, and accessories	682,805	677,761
Real estate developments in progress	462,600	571,175
Notes receivable		10,300
Unsecured	180,000	440,000
	$ 2,558,940	$ 2,755,096
Trade accounts payable	1,550,699	659,819
Employee compensation, local taxes, and accrued expenses	551,321	413,504
Income taxes:		
Currently payable	247,674	249,239
Deferred	226,000	157,100
Current portion of long-term debt	320,951	83,582
Total Current Liabilities	$ 5,455,585	$ 4,318,340
Long-Term Debt (less current portion)—Note E	2,437,859	1,290,533
Deferred Federal Income Taxes	100,500	105,000
Minority Interest in Subsidiary	296,322	302,439
Shareholders' Equity		
Preferred Stock, without par value:		
Authorized—50,000 shares		
Issued—none		
Common Stock, par value $1.00 a share—Notes F, G, and H:		
Authorized—1,250,000 shares		
Issued and outstanding—1,060,075 shares in 1976 and 1,042,395 shares in 1975, deducting 2,000 shares held in treasury in each year	$ 1,060,075	$ 1,042,395
Additional capital	94,386	90,224
Retained earnings—Note E	4,108,499	3,299,950
	$ 5,262,960	$ 4,432,569
Contingent Liabilities—Note I	$13,553,226	$10,448,881

See notes to consolidated financial statements.

WOLFE INDUSTRIES, INC. AND SUBSIDIARIES
Statement of Consolidated Income
Year Ended March 31, 1976 and 1975

	1976	*1975*
Sales and Revenues		
Net sales of products and merchandise	$14,843,841	$14,432,572
Construction and contract revenues	8,600,834	5,425,961
Nursing home revenue	822,203	167,511
Sales of land	105,900	123,350
Rental income	225,643	211,689
	$24,598,422	$20,361,083

(*continued*)

EXHIBIT 4 (Cont.)

	1976	1975
Cost of Sales and Revenues		
Cost of products and merchandise sold	$13,398,045	$13,265,566
Construction and contract costs	6,900,149	4,506,290
Nursing home expenses	844,418	161,972
Cost of land sold	66,871	84,430
Rental expenses	144,242	124,012
	$21,353,725	$18,142,270
	$ 3,244,696	$ 2,218,813
Selling, Administrative, and General Expenses	$ 1,721,804	$ 1,456,825
Interest Expense	276,819	179,846
	$ 1,998,623	$ 1,636,671
	$ 1,246,073	$ 582,142
Other Income, including Management Fees from Affiliates	327,161	254,881
Income Before Income Taxes and Other Charges and Credits	$ 1,573,234	$ 837,023
Income Taxes		
Federal—current	$ 547,800	$ 518,100
State and municipal—current	99,900	66,205
Deferred—(credit)	119,300	(174,800)
	$ 767,000	409,505
Income Before Other Charges and Credits	$ 806,234	$ 427,518
Equity in Net Income of Unconsolidated Subsidiaries	141,642	312,630
	$ 947,876	$ 740,148
Minority Interest in Net Income of Consolidated Subsidiary	13,085	26,733
Net Income	$ 934,791	$ 713,415
Earnings Per Common Share	$ 0.89	$ 0.69

Extracts From Notes

Investments in Unconsolidated Subsidiaries

The Company has two wholly-owned subsidiaries which are carried on the equity basis:

	Carrying Amount	
	Mar. 31, 1976	*Mar. 31, 1975*
Wolfe Investment Company	$1,139,264	$1,101,225
Wolfe Financial, Inc.	77,296	93,693
Totals	$1,216,560	$1,194,918

Wolfe Investment company is the owner-lessor of nursing home facilities under leases which are generally for a term of 20 years during which the lessee has the option to purchase the leased property. The financial statements of the subsidiary are summarized below:

(continued)

EXHIBIT 4 (Cont.)

Balance Sheet	March 31 1976	March 31 1975
Rental properties		
Cost	$8,596,353	$5,304,623
Allowance for depreciation	401,951	371,531
	$8,194,402	$4,933,092
Other assets	123,977	302,107
	$8,318,379	$5,235,199
Real estate mortgages	$5,511,860	$3,698,524
Lease payable	1,188,836	
Other liabilities	478,419	435,450
Shareholder's equity	1,139,264	1,101,225
	$8,318,379	$5,235,199

Statement of Income	Year Ended March 31 1976	Year Ended March 31 1975
Rental income	$ 730,518	$ 626,795
Gain from sale of properties	159,347	351,038
	$ 889,865	$ 977,833
Provision for depreciation	153,378	124,770
Interest	432,219	320,968
Income taxes	106,000	210,000
Other—net	40,228	3,158
	$ 731,825	$ 658,896
Net income	$ 158,040	$ 318,937

Wolfe Financial, Inc. makes installment loans on sales (principally trucks) by affiliated companies. Business commenced on January 27, 1975, when Common Stock was issued for $100,000. The financial statements of the subsidiary are summarized below:

Balance Sheet	March 31 1976	March 31 1975
Installment loans receivable, less loans rediscounted	$ 50,944	$ 73,362
Other assets	125,274	51,794
	$ 176,218	$ 125,156
Liabilities and deferred income	$ 98,922	$ 31,463
Shareholder's equity	77,296	93,693
	$ 176,218	$ 125,156

(continued)

EXHIBIT 4 (Cont.)

Statement of Income		Year Ended Mar. 31, 1976		Jan. 27, 1975 to Mar. 31, 1975
Interest income	$	30,645	$	1,110
Other income		5,957		316
	$	36,602	$	1,426
Expenses		53,000		7,733
Net loss	$	(16,398)	$	(6,307)

Transactions with Related Parties

The following tabulation summarizes transactions with related parties. The principal related parties are Wolfe Investment Company and Wolfe Financial, Inc. (see Note D) and Health Care Fund (real estate investment trust). Two of Health Care Fund's seven trustees, F. D. Wolfe and B. G. Thompson, are president and secretary, respectively, of the Company.

	March 31	
	1976	1975
Assets		
Accounts receivable from unconsolidated subsidiary	$ 358,229	$ 189,216
Liabilities		
Notes payable to:		
Unconsolidated subsidiary	$ 323,019	$ 185,000
Real estate investment trust	1,233,585	570,033
	$1,556,604	$ 755,033
Accounts payable to:		
Unconsolidated subsidiary	$ 17,317	$ 15,818
Real estate investment trust	13,851	4,937
	$ 31,168	$ 20,755

	Year Ended March 31	
	1976	1975
Revenues		
Sale of nursing homes to:		
Unconsolidated subsidiary	$2,730,758	$2,143,789
Real estate investment trust	4,140,486	1,750,655
	$6,871,244	$3,894,444
Management fees from affiliates	$ 78,330	$ 67,600
Expenses		
Nursing home rent to:		
Unconsolidated subsidiary	$ 71,258	$
Real estate investment trust	74,440	19,533
	$ 145,698	$ 19,533
Interest to unconsolidated subsidiary	$ 7,553	$ 9,953

(continued)

EXHIBIT 4 (Cont.)

Statement of Consolidated Income

	Six Months Ended September 30	
	1976	*1975*
Sales and revenues		
Net sales of products and merchandise	$10,579,997	$ 7,422,824
Construction and contract revenues	4,122,272	3,259,393
Nursing home revenue	1,047,643	199,738
Sales of land	10,200	52,000
Rental income	117,522	108,266
	$15,877,634	$11,042,221
Cost of sales and revenues		
Cost of products and merchandise sold	$ 9,545,817	$ 6,754,684
Construction	3,075,934	2,600,328
Nursing home expenses	1,023,667	203,980
Cost of land sales	8,359	31,949
Rental expenses	68,014	75,110
	$13,721,791	$ 9,666,051
	$ 2,155,843	$ 1,376,170
Selling, administrative, and general expenses	$ 1,011,841	$ 811,262
Interest expense	128,157	127,287
	$ 1,139,998	$ 938,549
	$ 1,015,845	$ 437,621
Other income	272,205	211,522
Income before income taxes and other charges and credits	$ 1,288,050	$ 649,143
Income taxes		
Federal—current	$ 455,800	$ 212,100
State and municipal—current	81,375	37,290
Deferred	77,500	77,500
	$ 614,675	326,890
Income before other charges and credits	$ 673,375	$ 322,253
Equity in net income of unconsolidated subsidiaries	223,797	73,974
	$ 897,172	$ 396,227
Minority interest in net income of consolidated subsidiary	6,794	9,536
Net income	$ 890,378	$ 386,691
Earnings per common share	$ 0.84	$ 0.37

EXHIBIT 5 Estimated and Projected* Population by Age, 1960 to 2000

Year	*Total All Ages*	*25–29 Years*	*30–34 Years*	*35–39 Years*	*40–44 Years*	*45–54 Years*	*55–64 Years*	*65–74 Years*	*75 Years and Over*
1960	180,671	10,939	11,979	12,532	11,680	20,573	15,627	11,055	5,624
1970	204,879	13,687	11,570	11,174	11,982	23,287	18,651	12,482	7,695
1972	208,837	15,045	12,308	11,125	11,648	23,591	19,104	12,845	8,104
1980	222,043	19,117	17,019	13,540	11,355	22,158	20,953	14,641	9,364
1990	238,910	19,626	20,398	18,810	16,636	23,831	19,959	16,605	10,961
2000	251,056	17,042	16,807	19,333	19,967	34,000	21,618	15,908	12,429

*Series X, which would reach zero growth around the middle of 21st century at 277 million, is one of the many possible approaches to zero growth. The immediate cessation of net immigration, combined with replacement-level fertility would not lead to immediate zero growth because the U.S. has a relatively young age structure (due to the post-World War II baby boom) which provides momentum for continued growth. In 1974 zero growth (assuming no dramatic change in mortality) required an annual total fertility rate of about 1,000 with net immigration at the current level, or about 1,200 with no net immigration. The total fertility rate in 1973 was about 1,900.

Source: Statistical Abstract of the United States, 1974, U.S. Dept. of Commerce, Bureau of the Census.

EXHIBIT 6 ARA Services (Years Ended September 30)

Year	*Sales ($ Millions)*	*Earnings Per Share*	*Dividends Per Share*	*P/E Ratio High—Low*
1976	$1,315	$4.05	$1.10	15—12
1975	1,198	3.25	.99	19—10
1974	1,120	3.65	.90	18— 8
1973*	992	3.41	.83	30—16
1972	873	3.09	.79	40—27
1971	767	2.63	.73	40—30
1970	687	2.41	.66	33—20
1969	623	2.20	.58	37—30

*Year ARA entered the health-care industry. By the end of 1973, about 11% of the company's sales were in health care. The company's second health-care acquisition was completed in 1974. Since that time, the company has entered a number of unrelated industries by acquisition.

EXHIBIT 7

MHC, INC. AND SUBSIDIARIES
Projected Balance Sheet
October 31

		Projected		
Assets	*Actual 1975*	*1976*	*1977*	*1978*
Current Assets	$ 437,956	$ 524,613	$ 635,099	$1,508,542
Other Assets (largely lease deposits)	$ 148,554	$ 228,826	$ 248,316	$ 226,650
Property, Plant, & Equipment				
Land	$ 144,597	$ 125,911	$ 80,911	$ 80,911
Buildings and improvements	2,437,151	2,723,437	2,723,437	2,723,437
Equipment	676,158	862,795	1,082,795	1,082,795
Allowance for depreciation	(370,956)	(405,705)	(559,772)	(728,172)
	$2,886,950	$3,306,438	$3,327,371	$3,158,971
Intangibles				
Goodwill	241,058	171,958	165,858	159,758
	$3,714,518	$4,231,835	$4,376,644	$5,053,921
Liabilities				
Current Liabilities				
Payables, taxes & payroll	$ 461,051	$ 522,500	$ 465,500	$ 813,500
Current portion of long-term debt	153,874	318,860	250,982	242,342
Total Current Liabilities	$ 614,925	$ 840,860	$ 716,482	$1,055,842
Long-Term Debt	$2,592,654	$2,337,697	$2,289,300	$2,046,958
Shareholders' Equity				
Preferred stock	$ 148,350	$ 135,975	$ 128,775	$ 122,250
Common stock	188,000	188,000	188,000	188,000
Retained earnings	170,589	729,303	1,054,078	1,640,871
	$ 506,939	$1,053,278	$1,370,862	$1,951,121
	$3,714,518	$4,231,835	$4,376,644	$5,053,931

EXHIBIT 8
MHC Inc. and Subsidiaries—Income Details
(Years ended October 31, 1974 through 1976 and projection for 1977 and 1978)

	10/31/74	10/31/75	10/31/76	10/31/77	10/31/78
Mt. Vernon	$ 65,365	$ 88,111	$142,585	$125,000	$ 130,000
Cairo	37,880	86,022	148,497	130,000	135,000
Sherwood	59,270	59,873	146,229	128,000	133,000
Johnstown	4,702	17,534	1,834	—	—
Zanesville	8,504	62,137	99,043	80,000	85,000
Circleville	9,765	119,666	146,136	128,000	133,000
Portsmouth	(11,005)	(368)	102,552	80,000	85,000
London	(75,361)	5,855	89,515	100,000	120,000
Louisville		(101,597)	88,321	100,000	120,000
Greenwich			(66,855)	50,000	100,000
Freemont				(75,000)	75,000
Delaware				(100,000)	75,000
Hillsboro				(40,000)	—
Equipping Company		17,045	18,875	20,000	20,000
Central Office			3,762	—	—
Eliminations	(7,005)	(6,092)	(6,100)	(6,100)	(6,100)
Income Before Taxes	$ 92,115	$348,186	$914,394	$719,900	$1,204,900
Taxes on Income					
State	$ 7,750	$ 21,000	$ 70,000	$ 52,000	$ 90,000
Federal	26,500	166,900	400,000	325,000	510,000
	$ 34,250	$187,900	$470,000	$377,000	$ 600,000
Income Before Special Item	$ 57,865	$160,286	$444,394	$342,900	$ 604,900
Gain on sale of Johnstown Retirement Center less applicable taxes ($98,000) and goodwill ($63,000)			$133,453		
Net Income	$ 57,865	$160,286	$577,847	$342,900	$ 604,900

EXHIBIT 9 MHC, Inc. and Subsidiaries—Nursing Home Incumbrances (October 31, 1976)

Location[1]	*Real Estate Lease Option Price*	*Real Estate Mortgage*	*Equipment Loan*	*Equipment Lease Payable*	*Total*
Mt. Vernon	$	$ 631,375	$	$ 662	$ 631,997
Cairo		562,718			562,718
Sherwood				501	501
London	664,149		55,668	622	720,439
Louisville	786,387		91,854	501	878,742
Circleville		401,897			401,897
Zanesville		544,055	20,000	1,637	565,692
Portsmouth	654,253		28,194	622	683,069
Greenwich	882,885		72,850		955,735
Freemont	925,000		130,000		1,055,000
Totals	$3,912,674	$2,140,045	$398,566	$4,505	$6,455,790

[1]Each nursing home had 100 beds.

EXHIBIT 10 MHC, Inc. and Subsidiaries—Valuation (October 31, 1976)

		Rate	*Total*
Mt. Vernon, Cairo, Sherwood, London, Louisville, Circlesville, Zanesville	100 beds	$ 12,000	$ 8,400,000
Portsmouth, Greenwich, Fremont	100 beds	$ 11,000	3,300,000
			$11,700,000
Less Debt Outstanding			
Debentures		$ 140,000	
Preferred stock		136,000	
Encumbrances per schedule		6,455,790	$ 6,731,790
			$ 4,968,210

EXHIBIT 11 Effect on Wolfe Industries Earnings of MHC, Inc. Acquisition

		10/31/77	*10/31/78*
Net income		$ 342,900	$ 604,900
Less amortization of additional goodwill			
Price	$4,000,000		
Book value of assets 10/31/76	1,053,278		
	$2,946,722 × 2½%	73,668	73,668
M.H.C. contribution to earnings		$ 269,232	$ 531,232
Less preferred dividends			
Wolfe $4,000,000 @ 8%		$ 320,000	$ 320,000
Minority preferred in HCF		16,236	15,453
		$ 336,236	$ 335,453
Contribution to Wolfe earnings		(67,004)	$ 195,779
Contribution per Wolfe share			
Wolfe shares projected		1,094,435	1,111,615
Per share—no conversion			17¢
Per share of conversion of preferred to 160,000 Wolfe common			41¢

EXHIBIT 12

WOLFE INDUSTRIES, INC.
Corporate Directory

Directors	*Officers*
R. E. Bargmann	F. D. Wolfe President
P. C. Borra	W. H. Merritt Vice-President
R. A. James	P. C. Borra Vice-President
W. H. Merritt	B. G. Thompson Secretary
H. H. Stevenson	R. E. Bargmann Treasurer & Controller
B. G. Thompson	H. A. Shaw Assistant Controller
F. D. Wolfe	

- *Frederic D. Wolfe*—B.S. Yale U., M.B.A. Harvard U.; Director, Tower National Bank of Lima; Co-founder, Secretary and Trustee of Health Care Fund; member Young Presidents' Organization (YPO).
- *William H. Merritt*—B.S. Miami U.; served as Air Force Major; joined Lima Lumber 1946; General Manager 1952; President 1968; President of Cole Lumber & Supply Co., Inc.; President of South Side Savings & Loan Association, Lima. Civic affiliations: Allen County Soil & Water Conservation District, Lima Area Chamber of Commerce, United Way.
- *Pier C. Borra*—B.S. Illinois Institute of Technology, M.B.A. University of Chicago; 1963–68, staff of construction division of General American Transportation Corp.; 1968–72, management consultant with Donald R. Booz & Associates; Director of Marketing, H. F. Campbell Co.; joined Wolfe Industries, Inc., 1972, as President, Wolfe Industries Construction Co.
- *Bruce G. Thompson*—Yale U. and Virginia Law School graduate; 1958–67, practiced law with Messrs. Shearman and Sterling, New York; 1967–69, U.S. Government Investment Banking Consultant to government of Pakistan; joined Wolfe Industries, Inc. 1969; President, Wolfe Investment Co.; co-founder, Chief Executive, Health Care Fund.
- *Robert E. Bargmann*—B.S. University of Toledo; C.P.A.; Ernst & Ernst, Tax Department, Toledo office; 1961, Manager, Lima office; 1972, joined Wolfe Industries, Inc. to serve as Treasurer and Controller. Activities and affiliations: United Way, Kiwanis Club, American Institute of C.P.A.'s.
- *Howard Stevenson*—B.S. Stanford; M.B.A. and D.B.A. Harvard Business School; Professor, Harvard Business School, Real Property Investment and Management Program. Member: Urban Land Institute, National Association of Real Estate Boards, National Association of Corporate Real Estate Executives, Articles and Papers published on real estate.
- *Robert A. James*—Harvard U. graduate; 1952, brokerage business; 1963, organized, founded the securities firm, Raymond, James & Associates, Inc.; Trustee, McCormock Mortgage Investors, Inc.; Advisory Board, Growth Properties, Inc. Member: Business Conduct Committee, National Association of Securities Dealers.

FLORAFAX INTERNATIONAL, INC.

"When we put together the syndicate to acquire the wire service in 1970, it had sales of $8.5 million, and I thought Jim Schmidt and I would be able to expand it substantially. Our goal was $40 million in gross wire service sending by 1975. In 1976, we hit $22.9 million." The speaker was Dick Hughes, the Chairman and CEO of Florafax International, Inc., a Tulsa-based flowers-by-wire service.

It was November, 1976, two weeks before Florafax's strategic planning meeting for 1977, and Hughes wanted to lay out some ground rules for discussion. Not that he wanted to constrain the creativity of his managers—he simply wanted to make sure that there were some strong reference points to keep the discussion focused.

In the past three years, Mr. Hughes had hired three newly-graduated MBA's from two prestigious business schools. Hughes knew that these younger managers would recommend that the company convert the wire service into a cash cow, a source of funds for investment in new product lines. The product-portfolio strategy they would advocate was based on the product life cycle, the idea being to cut investment in mature products and use the cash thrown off from their profits to move the firm into new, high-growth product markets, particularly those where the firm could win a dominant market share.

Hughes and Florafax's President, Jim Schmidt, understood the product life cycle concept and product-portfolio management, but they were reluctant to take capital from the wire service. In fact, they were privately considering the possibility of expanding it by acquiring or merging with one of Florafax's five competitors. As of November, however, they had not decided which company would be their target. Hughes and Schmidt wondered how the MBA's would react to this idea.

"Jim Schmidt and I would like this company to hit $100 million in sales by 1980," Hughes said. "If we were that big, we could try for a Big Board listing and we could afford to add experienced managers to our team. That would free up my time and let me focus on some of my personal goals. When we set our goals in 1970, we assumed the industry would grow at 10% or better and that we would be able to capture at least 30% of the growth. It wasn't that easy. Our principal competitors, FTD and Teleflora, are big and well established [*Exhibit 1*], and there was the 1974–1975 recession. It took us a lot of time to get the wire service into shape—for example, to weed out the weak accounts and build a more effective sales organization. Then, our acquisitions took a lot of time. Our financial results [*Exhibits 2* and *3*] show that our work has paid off.

"I like the idea of exploiting the product life cycle, but I think that it would be impetuous to cut investment in the wire service now." Hughes stopped abruptly, punched a button on his phone, and asked his secretary to bring in some recent annual reports. He then continued, "There are two catches to using the wire service as a cash cow. First, I'm not sure that our market position in the wire service business is secure enough to allow us to take cash out yet. The second problem relates to diversification. In 1974 we adopted 'a

This case was prepared by Assistant Professor Kenneth J. Hatten as a basis of class discussion rather than to illustrate either effective or ineffective handling of an administrative situation.

focus on flowers' as the theme of what I call our concentric diversification strategy.'' Hughes' secretary entered and placed the reports on his desk. He quickly thumbed through them and said, ''Here it is; in 1974 I wrote:

> Florafax International intends to enter further into the mainstream of the floral industry by vertically integrating throughout its distribution channels. This maneuver is designed to capitalize on the industry's high margins, and is expected to result in a concentric diversification program. With Florafax, Inc., the wire service, at the strategic center, the company is planning to branch out into all pertinent and profitable floral product/market areas.

''In essence, I believe that the wire service's selling organization and the relationship it has with its clients make it an ideal platform for establishing the company in enterprises complementary to both distribution and the wire service itself. In 1974, I had hoped to take advantage of the fragmented, unorganized state of the floral business by becoming a major supplier and distributor to retail flower shops. Ultimately, I expected to expand into floral-related product/market areas other than just those along the immediate channels of flower distribution.''

Hughes continued, ''So far, we've bought two plant growers, a wholesale supplier, an insurance agency, and an underwriting company. Jim Schmidt still asks me what an insurance underwriter has to do with flowers. He says we should focus our efforts on one sector of the floriculture industry and make a major commitment there. But unfortunately, he's not firmly committed to any particular sector—growing, wire services, wholesaling, or retailing. Growth opportunities exist but we're worried about ROI and our ability to get a solid and defensible market position. You can see my problem. I'm CEO and when push comes to shove I'll have to decide what to do.''

THE INDUSTRY

The floriculture industry in 1976 had an apparently simple structure: flowers were grown, both domestically and abroad, by professionals on floriculture farms and in greenhouses. The crops were sold to wholesalers, who in turn sold to retailers. The wire services worked for the retailers and substantially facilitated their ability to satisfy the ultimate consumer by financing interstore sales.

In 1976, typical markups on cost at each stage in the distribution chain were: growers, 60%; wholesalers, 30%; retailers, 80–100%. Prices were volatile and fluctuated seasonally—for example, the price of a cut flower, say a carnation, might range from 3¢ to 25¢ per stem during the year, and vary from state to state. Year to year, however, wholesale prices had been relatively stable since the late 1950s.[1]

The industry was characterized by frantic activity at holiday seasons. At Christmas poinsettias were in heavy demand; at Easter it was lilies. Coordinating supply with this

[1]Between 1957 and 1968, carnations sold wholesale for from 6.3¢ per bloom to as high as 7.3¢ in 1966. In 1957, the price was 6.7¢ and in 1968 it was 6.9¢ per bloom. (USDA, Crop Reporting Board, *Flowers and Foliage Plants*.)

peaked demand was still part science and part art, as one large company discovered in 1975 when, despite careful planning and scientific management, it had 60,000 unsold Easter lilies bloom in unison 2 days late.

In 1975, the industry's retail sales were over $2 billion, according to industry sources, but when every facet of the industry was considered—wholesalers, accessory manufacturers and pesticide producers—the total sales of the industry reached $6 billion. Between 1965 and 1975, the industry's sales growth had been between 8 and 10% per annum and sometimes higher.

Hughes felt this growth had been caused primarily by the following trends:

1 A greater emphasis on the quality of life and increased consumer awareness of the beauty of flowers and plants, a trend complementing a national concern over ecology and pollution.
2 Improved product quality and greater reliability of delivery to retail outlets.
3 Increased interest by lower-price sellers, such as supermarkets and variety stores, in floral products as an important source of profits. For example, Stratford of Texas, a major green plant grower, made 50% of its $40 million floriculture sales to chains like K-Mart.
4 An expanding demand for foliage plants in offices, plants, schools, and public buildings.
5 Increased consumer discretionary income, of which, however, only a negligible fraction was being spent on flowers and plants (about one-half the European rate).
6 More aggressive consumer-oriented marketing activities, for example, educational programs in flower use, stimulated in part by recent corporate entries—such as many supermarkets, and companies like Pillsbury and D&B, and United Brands in Florida—into commercial floriculture.
7 The discovery by emerging nations, particularly in South America, that flowers were a lucrative export product, used inexpensive land, and were labor-intensive. (In Colombia, 10 acres of carnations employed 300 people.) Product shipment was economic if a national airline was available to haul the cargo. Some tropical countries were encouraging investment by offering cheap land and other benefits to experienced growers from developed countries.

Dick Hughes and Jim Schmidt felt that the whole industry was moving from a highly fragmented, uncoordinated network of small individual units to a more concentrated structure. Consequently, they felt that ultimately there would be a need for a logistics system to provide efficient procurement and assembly of floriculture products from domestic and foreign sources, and to distribute these products to retail buyers throughout the United States. They believed that, despite technological advances in air freight and refrigerated truck transportation, the cost and reliability of transport was still a major problem in the industry.[2]

PLANT GROWING

Available evidence suggested that growers using traditional production methods had suffered a significant cost-price squeeze during the 1960s. Cost of labor, materials, and

[2]A major technological development on the horizon, but one which had not reached prototype stage yet, was "near vacuum" storage. Carnations currently had a 9-day cut life. With the new technology, if commercially practical, their cut life would be extended to 300 days.

other inputs had risen faster than sales prices, a trend which was slowly pushing smaller growers out of the industry, as *Exhibit 4* suggests. This squeeze on margins was confirmed by special surveys conducted since 1968 by the Florida Cooperative Extension Service of the University of Florida. In contrast to the general cost-price squeeze in the industry, however, some companies' margins were increasing.

One example of a successful new entrant to the industry was Stratford of Texas. Formerly a cattle feeder largely financed by syndicated limited partnerships, through the 1970s it had been actively divesting from the cattle business and moving into plant growing and distribution. Stratford was specializing in foliage and tropical plants which required little maintenance, low light, and limited care. The company's 10K showed an impressive track record in the floriculture industry (*Exhibit 5*).

Mr. Hughes felt that Stratford was primarily a producer buttressed by distribution and marketing. The company had acquired 14 or 15 regional distribution centers which performed grow out,[3] soil packaging, and distribution functions outside the nation's major cities, and it was leasing 4 or 5 others. Of the company's sales, 77% were door-to-door (i.e. from distribution point to the florist's store door) and the company claimed 19,000 customers. To a certain extent, Stratford had already contributed to the displacement of some traditional terminal wholesalers.

Florafax's managers believed that by developing efficient truck routings, better scheduling, and more efficient staffing the industry's traditionally high distribution costs might be cut by up to 30%. Their investigations suggested that an efficient wholesaler-distributor could make between $1.5 million and $2 million in revenues and show a net profit in excess of $150,000 on an investment of $500,000.

WHOLESALING AND DISTRIBUTION

In the floriculture industry, wholesalers have traditionally located near major urban markets, in the city centers or on the city outskirts. Those on the outskirts were often both wholesalers and grow out operators. The typical wholesaler made 90% or more of sales on credit. However, during the late 1960s and early 1970s many wholesalers in the largest terminal markets were forced to relocate by the fixed costs of operations, and by the competitive activities of the largest growers. These difficulties were aggravated by the pressure from growers to have wholesalers assume inventory risks rather than sell on consignment as they had traditionally done—this at a time when highway speeds had been cut to 55 mph, extending truck delivery times and increasing the risk of spoilage en route.

As *Exhibit 6* suggests, most wholesalers did not have a large margin. Many of them were small family businesses operated by unskilled managers, and offered a poor product mix. The wholesale product mix varied across regions and by size of firm. Generally speaking, the larger firms sold a larger proportion of nonperishables, had lower margins on sales but higher returns on assets and on equity investment. The 1970 Goodrich study also showed that although only 18.5% of the sampled wholesale florists' sales originated beyond fifty miles, the percentage varied from 8.2% in the Northeast to 36% in the West,

[3]Grow out refers to the practice of buying seedlings and small plants and moving them to near-city nurseries to grow until they bloom.

about 23.2% in the South, and 25.6% in the Midwest. In the West a large percentage of the ''long-distance'' sales were made to other wholesalers, but sales of perishables were very limited.

RETAIL

In 1976, there were more than 25,000 retail florists, mostly small shops with sales under $50,000. Substantially less than 1% of florists (maybe 50 to 80) had sales exceeding the $1,000,000 level. About 30% of florists—those selling from $50,000 to $300,000 annually—accounted for nearly 60% of the total floral sales dollars in the U.S. Only about 25% of the industry's sales were in cash, principally because three-quarters of the orders were telephoned in and were therefore charged to house accounts or to major credit cards.

Retailing was changing, however. In 1940, florists accounted for more than 80% of retail flower sales, but in the 1960s and 1970s their share had dwindled. Flower consumers were not easy to identify, but there were some common traits that helped define them. To begin with, purchase patterns were largely dictated by disposable income—the more discretionary income, the more flowers purchased. The American Florists Marketing Council (AFMC) report, ''A Psychographic Study of the Market for Flowers,'' determined that approximately 77,000,000 people purchased flowers at least once in 1972; over half (54%) were women. Almost three-quarters of these people purchased their flowers from florists; the remainder bought them from ''other'' sources, including supermarkets. Of those who went to florists for their flowers, 68% planned their purchase ahead of time; 52% of those who bought from ''other'' sources picked their items on impulse. The industry expected that florist shops would continue to dominate the planned purchase market, where consumers have distinct service needs, such as for beautifully arranged bouquets of cut flowers for special occasions (*Exhibit 7*). In 1976, florist-goers spent about $13 for their average purchase, the others, $8—up from $11.00 and $6.00 respectively in 1972. Per capita, U.S. flower sales equalled approximately half the European rate.

WIRE SERVICE

The wire services offered technical, marketing and management expertise to their member retail florists through seminars, meetings, design contests, and conventions. Florafax's 1976 convention was aboard the luxury liner Angelina Laura on a seven-day work-play cruise from Fort Lauderdale to San Juan, St. Thomas and Montego Bay. Nearly one thousand Florafax subscribers joined the company's marketing executives and a number of special lecturers to gain new insights and fresh perspectives on their work. Management believed this gala convention generated enthusiasm and a sense of family among its subscribers and company staff.

As Paul Goodman, Vice-President and general manager of the wire service explained, ''The mechanics of a wire service are fairly simple. If you want to send flowers from Chicago to New York, you go to your local florist in Chicago; and he calls a florist in New York, placing the order. As soon as this conversation has taken place, two problems immediately arise. The florist in Chicago has to trust the florist in New York to deliver a full value of the order, and the florist in New York has to trust the florist in Chicago to pay him once the order has been delivered. With florists sending orders all over the country every month to different florists, this is too much 'trust.' Hence, a wire service steps in the middle and asks florists to join their service. The wire service then guarantees quality and payment to the respective florists. The procedure is still the same in that the florist in Chicago calls the florist in New York, except he calls the florist in New York who belongs to the same wire service as he does and locates that florist through a directory provided by the wire service. The florist in New York then reports on a reporting form in the mail that he received the order from the florist in Chicago. This order is processed through a computer with all the other orders placed through the system during the month. Each florist at the end of the month receives a statement indicating that he sent 'x' number of orders and owes Florafax 80% of that amount. In addition, the statement indicates that he received 'x' number of orders and Florafax owes him 75% of that amount. The two amounts are netted, miscellaneous charges are added, and then either Florafax sends the florist a check or the florist sends Florafax a check. Consequently, a third service performed by the wire service is that of accounting. The florists get one statement listing their volume for the month rather than having to send individual bills or checks to the individual florists they dealt with." As *Exhibit 8* shows, the actual charges made by the competing wire services varied over time as they jockeyed for market share.

As *Exhibit 1* shows, there were five flowers-by-wire services in the U.S.; FTD, Teleflora and Florafax were the three largest. However, because Teleflora was a very small part of Dun and Bradstreet's corporate activities, and because FTD was a not-for-profit cooperative, there was only a limited amount of public information on each company. Although *Exhibit 1* presents some key data, it was impossible to determine how many exclusive members each had (the USDA stated in 1966 that approximately 21% of all florists were members of more than one network).

Multiple memberships were common in the industry since the more services an individual florist subscribed to, the more comprehensive the network of florists he or she could deal with and the greater the exposure to incoming orders. Since each wire service "controlled" part of the total flowers-by-wire business, multiple memberships were one way florists would increase their share of flowers-by-wire sales in their trade area. Of course, with multiple memberships, they had the problem of allocating their business among the competing networks—a series of decisions complicated by the industry's tradition of reciprocity. Florists were expected to reciprocate to other wire service members on a dollar-for-dollar basis whenever possible but, since location often hindered a particular store's ability to respond, most wire services took location into account when they evaluated a member's status.

To become a member of the Florafax wire service, the florist was typically invited to apply to join the service by a company representative. Once an application was filed, Florafax performed an extensive check on the florist's product quality and credit rating. If this proved favorable, the florist's name was added to the wire service directory and, as a member of the system, he or she became eligible to send and receive orders from any of the service's subscribers.

Every month, each Florafax member received *Florafacts,* the wire service's business education journal, which contained a calendar of coming events. Seven times a year a

Florafax member also received the directory of subscribers, a telephone directory-type book, which was the florist's guide to all members who were currently acceptable to receive an order for delivery of flowers (these publications were produced by Florafax's Publishing Division). Because of its guarantee obligations to its members, Florafax constantly monitored the status of its receivables. If member florists were delinquent in their payments, their names were removed from the directory until they could meet their obligations and provide evidence that they would continue to do so.

FLORAFAX, 1961–1969

FTD, the largest flowers-by-wire service, was also the oldest. Until 1959, its membership policy was simple—all for one and one for all. However, in that year, the Justice Department obtained a consent decree from FTD which opened the way for competition. Teleflora and Florafax both commenced business in 1961. Florafax was founded by Mr. Kenneth Short in a small town in Arkansas.

Florafax's distinctive feature so far as its subscribers were concerned had been its draft system: florists who received an order through Florafax could draw a draft on the company immediately by writing themselves a Florafax check. Mr. Short had appreciated the ever-present need for cash which afflicted small florists and had worked with the Federal Reserve Board to design a draft system which could be processed as a cash item. Over the years, Florafax never had a fraudulent draft.

As *Exhibit 9* shows, Florafax grew quickly, although primarily by attracting smaller florists in non-metropolitan areas. However, in 1968, Florafax's management had become concerned that the company's growth might slow. Reasoning that florists joined the wire service primarily to receive orders rather than to send them, Florafax's managers felt that the one way to stimulate growth would be to make the sender's choice of Florafax less costly in terms of time. Mr. Short altered Florafax's reporting procedures so that the sender would have no paper work at all.

Until then, each florist had filled out a weekly report of the orders sent through the system. This report, and a check for 85% of the retail value of the orders, was forwarded to Florafax. Under the new procedures, the weekly report was eliminated and accounts receivable information was taken from the bank drafts returned to the company by its banks. The receiving florist recorded the sender's name on the draft, and it was from this data that the sender was billed, twice monthly, at 85% of the retail value of the orders sent.

Previously, the company had often received the sender's payment before the receiving florist's draft was debited against the corporate bank account. Under the new system, the payment was delayed. The draft had to be in Florafax's hands before the sender could be billed. It was usually an additional week before the average bill was mailed. The changes necessitated, therefore, a large amount of capital to finance Florafax's accounts receivable. This capital was obtained through a bank loan at 10%.[4]

In 1969, when interest rates began to climb, the company's bank grew apprehen-

[4]Florafax itself charged interest on its outstanding accounts receivable.

sive. Under state usury laws it couldn't charge more than 10%, including service charges, fees, and so on. The only way around this law was to use compensating balances, but Florafax couldn't support interest charges and compensating balances without new capital. In addition, the bank requested that Florafax pledge another $480,000 as collateral to offset the company's $50 refundable deposit to each of its subscribers. Then, late in 1969, an acquisition finder introduced Mr. Short to Dick Hughes.

DICK HUGHES: PERSONAL BACKGROUND

Dick Hughes had controlled a number of businesses. When he left business school in 1959, Hughes and two fellow students formed a company to acquire and develop small industrial concerns. Their first acquisition was a small company which made satellite tracking antennas. After losing eighty-five consecutive contract bids, Hughes and his colleagues decided to change the company's product line—a decision which ultimately allowed them to sell out without heavy losses.

Next, Hughes bought the Tulsa Bottling Co., a Pepsi distributor. Over the next 8 years, 1960–1968, the bottling company's sales increased from $1.8 million to $10 million—partly because of several acquisitions the company made.

By 1968, however, Hughes had become disenchanted with his company and realized that his personal goals had changed. He set his mind on a political career as either an appointed or an elected government official, preferably at the federal level, and concluded that the best way to realize his ambition was to develop a large publicly-held company as his base. To this end, he sold his stock in the bottling company and set about looking for a new business venture. At the same time, he began to take a more active role in political and civic affairs in Tulsa.

Early in 1969, Hughes, as the leader of a syndicate of Tulsa investors, incorporated Franchise Management Services, Inc., to franchise successful restaurants. He was successful in obtaining the franchise rights for two different restaurants, a burger chain and a higher-priced restaurant, by exchanging stock in Franchise Management for the franchise rights to the restaurants.

Six months later, however, it became apparent to Hughes that food franchising was out of favor in the stock market (*Exhibit 10*), and that there was no hope for an early recovery of market enthusiasm for new issues in the fast-food industry. This affected Franchise Management in two ways. First, it made the realization of Hughes' long-term personal goal unlikely; second, it became difficult to use the company's stock to create a deal to attract restauranteurs to Franchise Management. Hughes said:

> It was more than a matter of timing. The whole franchising business had changed. First, the Accounting Principles Board had issued new standards for reporting earnings. Whereas earlier a company could report its franchise fee income as received, henceforth it had to be spread over the life of the franchise agreement. Second, a large franchiser, Minnie Pearl, had folded and made everyone cautious about new companies. Banks and realty owners wanted corporate guarantees for every franchise point and buyers wanted guarantees too. It was a tougher hill to climb than I wanted.

Hughes therefore decided to divest from the franchise business and negotiated an amicable parting of the ways with his restauranteur collaborators.

By late 1969, when Florafax was brought to Hughes' attention, it was already the third-largest entrant in the flowers-by-wire industry. Hughes felt that with additional capital the company could become the growth vehicle he was seeking, so Franchise Management acquired it. Mr. Short stayed on as a board member and Franchise Management's name was changed to Florafax International. In April, 1970, Jim Schmidt joined Hughes at Florafax as Financial Vice-President and after a few weeks was made President and Chief Operating Officer.

Shortly afterward, in early 1970, Florafax merged with a small publicly-held company, Spotts International, Inc., a supplier of promotional premiums to a wide range of companies. Subsequently, Spotts Florafax Corporation was incorporated in Delaware as the successor to Spotts International.

JIM SCHMIDT

''Some of my friends look on me as a deal-swinger,'' Dick Hughes said as he recounted how he and Jim Schmidt got together. ''When I decided that Franchise Management should try for Florafax, I recognized that I needed a right hand to keep me out of trouble. Florafax was a bank of sorts, and I wanted someone I could count on to ensure there would be no 'surprises'; that the money we needed would always be there.''

Schmidt, like Hughes, had an entrepreneurial background. In 1966, he had been with a Big Eight accounting firm for six years, specializing in small business troubleshooting. He had reached the position where a managing partnership was available for him—but not in Tulsa. At that point, he decided that he was tired of life as a consultant-adviser and was curious as to whether he could be an effective manager. He joined forces with an investor and founded an aerospace and plastics company. In 1969, he sold his interest in the firm and founded three new manufacturing enterprises.

At that point, he offered a job to one of Hughes employees, Bob Surrett. Surrett asked Hughes's advice, prompting Hughes to phone Schmidt and say ''Hell! If you're going to steal my men you at least owe me a lunch.''

Over lunch, the two realized they were kindred spirits with similar goals, surplus funds for investment, and what they thought were complementary management skills. When the Florafax deal came along, Schmidt, who had invested in Franchise Management, was a natural choice. Hughes felt Schmidt would say ''no'' often enough to keep him ''back in reality'' but was entrepreneurially motivated and so would work to make any new venture a success.[5]

THE NEXT FEW YEARS: ACQUISITIONS

Over the next few years, the company made a number of acquisitions and divestments which are outlined in *Exhibit 11*. Schmidt commented, ''When we originally got involved

[5]In 1976, Mr. Surrett held an executive position with Florafax International as head of its Financial Services division.

we looked on Florafax as a good turnaround situation and Dick and I had a three-year agreement to work together. But then we realized that we had a company which could ultimately make the Big Board.

"At first we had to clean up the wire service and that took time. In addition, we both felt that selected acquisitions could strengthen the company and get us to our goal quicker."

Hughes added, "We've never bought on a P/E basis—that's how we'll get out when we succeed. Our acquisitions have all been mutually negotiated deals. We can't compete head-on with the major acquirers. We tailor-make our deals to satisfy the seller.

"When we took Spotts, we were looking to make a corporate currency so that we could acquire with stock, but Spotts gave us a few surprises. Our financial statements show the write-offs we made. Spotts was even losing money in Australia, if you can believe that.

"Florafax itself took time to straighten out. We weren't sure whether the sales force controlled our customer base. Money was tight and interest rates climbed, slowing our growth. We had to make every change carefully. Let me give you an example of the problems we've had to work with: In 1970, 90% of our receivables were ninety days or older. In 1976, 80% are sixty days old, but in the same time our interest rate has gone from 1.5% over prime to 3.5% over."

THE INSURANCE BUSINESS

Hughes met energetic opposition only once—when he took control of Liberty. "The story is interesting," he said. "For a number of years, Florafax had offered its member florists insurance through a group policy sold by an agency operated by A. B. Johnson in Arkansas. The policies covered life, health, and accident insurance for the florist and his employees. One day in March 1972, about 2 years after we took control of Florafax, Johnson walked into my office and said, 'I'm 56. I don't need more money and my family is well provided for. Would you like to buy my business?' " At the time, Johnson was writing about $500,000 in annual premium business with florists and both Hughes and Schmidt felt that they should acquire the business to protect Florafax's service capability.

In mid-1973, Hughes learned that an underwriting company, Liberty Investors Life Insurance Co. of Oklahoma City, was in trouble and he decided to attempt to take control of it, reasoning that since Florafax was already in the insurance business it might as well get the underwriting commissions as well. An additional consideration was Liberty's investment portfolio, worth about $8.5 million, and the personal challenge of turning the company around.

At the time, the factor about the insurance business which had disturbed Schmidt more than any other was its low ROI and the proportion of Hughes's time it would consume. Schmidt believed that time had proven him right. The series of transactions needed to consumate the deal and satisfy Oklahoma's insurance commissioner that policy holders' interests were fully protected was extensive, and there was still the problem of managing the on-going business to distract Hughes from Florafax's other businesses. In fact, Hughes admitted to spending at least fifteen hours per week on the insurance company's affairs—only ten less than he devoted to Florafax's other business. The rest of his sixty- to eighty-hour week was spent on personal business and in political and community affairs.

An additional problem associated with the insurance companies had arisen only in the past few months when the company and its underwriter were preparing a registration statement to be filed with the SEC as part of the documentation for a $2,500,000, 11% convertible subordinated debenture issue (the conversion price was $3.33 per share, the stock was trading at $1⅜ : $1⅞ in November 1976). To satisfy its auditors, Florafax had "put" (sold according to a "prior" agreement) a substantial portion of its insurance investment to a private company controlled by Mr. Hughes. Schmidt, although chagrined by the delay the auditor's anxieties had caused, said to Hughes, "I told you so!"

FLORAFAX'S ORGANIZATION

Florafax was organized into profit centers late in 1974 as part of the company's effort to implement its concentric diversification strategy. By 1976 the profit centers were as shown in *Exhibit 12*. The exhibit also provides a few biographical details about the executives managing each division. With its 10,500 member florists, Hughes felt that Florafax's flowers-by-wire service was the mainstay of the company and the wellspring from which the other operations drew their customers. However, it was the other operations which were at the cutting edge of the company's diversified growth.

THE OTHER OPERATING DIVISIONS

The company's Growing Division was under the control of a single general manager, Wally Gammel, the founder of Leaf, Inc., which had been acquired by Florafax in October, 1973. Leaf, Inc. grew foliage plants on almost eighteen acres of land in Florida, while its fiberglass operation embraced a complete line of modern, durable, and attractive planters and landscapers. These glass-reinforced polyester products were many times stronger than those made of concrete. They were used commercially, and also for residential and interior office decor. The smaller planters were utilized predominantly by interior decorators, architects, and green plant rental firms serving shopping malls, hotels, banks and office buildings.

Another part of the growing division, Island Orchids, grew orchids and anthuriums on sixteen acres in Hilo, Hawaii. Relative to competing growers, Island Orchids was a major force in the industry. Its operations included greenhouses and packing facilities, plus additional raw land for production at a future date. The flowers grown in Hawaii were cut and sent air freight to the United States mainland for sale to wholesalers. Early in November, 1974, Island Orchids had planted two more acres of anthuriums in a new anthurium building which represented a totally innovative design. (The design proved so successful that it was duplicated by many other Hawaiian anthurium growers and by the State of Hawaii's Department of Agriculture.)

Although Island Orchids accounted for only a minor part of the company's revenues, Hughes said its true significance lay in the experience Florafax was gaining and in the long-run competitive advantage the growing operations gave the firm. In addition, Jim

Schmidt was working on a program to use the enterprise as the company's first base for limited partnership ventures in plant growing, to take advantage of the high front-end costs during the four years it took before the anthuriums came into full production. Schmidt felt that Leaf had been one of Florafax's successes; he cited the data in *Exhibits 13* and *14* to support his conclusion.

The Publishing Division prepared the wire service's regular publications and promotional materials and was effectively an in-house publishing company. Advance Printing and Office Supplies, Inc. serviced Florafax's own printing needs and had been acquired to take advantage of what appeared to be real printing opportunities in the floral industry. In 1976, however, Advanced's customer mix was pretty much as it had been in 1970—85% Florafax and 15% others. Mr. Hughes hoped to shift the mix to something more like 50-50 as soon as he could find a new manager for the division.

The Distribution Division had been created to explore the possibilities of wholesale operations as one means of capitalizing on the industry's high margins. Immediately after the company's books were closed for 1975, Florafax International acquired Vestal Wholesale Florist, Inc. This company wholesaled florist supplies ranging from ribbons and vases to dried, plastic, and fresh cut flowers. It operated in Tennessee, Arkansas, and 9 other states, and had 1975 sales of $2,300,000. Vestal's President and former owner had joined Florafax as President of this division. To date the division had lost money, as *Exhibit 14* shows.

Aside from its needs for staffing, and for financial and inventory control, Hughes and Schmidt felt that if Florafax pushed distribution, there were two fundamental decisions to make. First, should they be full-line or specialists in nonperishables? Second, should they overlay the existing industry structure by opening centers in major metropolitan markets, or should they establish a new national grid of six or seven giant distribution centers? The choices implied different strategies, different timing, and different risks. No clear consensus nor any strong advocate for any choice had emerged.

REORGANIZING THE WIRE SERVICE SALESFORCE

When Paul Goodman joined Florafax, Inc. as Western regional sales manager in July, 1974, he fully expected to return to California, his home state, from Boston, where he had been working since completing his MBA. "I was supposed to have nine months to learn the industry and live on the West Coast," he said. "After two weeks I was promoted to Vice-President and transferred to Tulsa. My job was to increase sales and cut selling costs."

Goodman started by gathering information on the sales task and on the salesforce itself. In 1974, Florafax's twelve-person salesforce received an average salary of $25,000 and the use of a company car (costing the company about $2,400 per person each year). Reps were expected to cover their own expenses—e.g., meals, hotels and gas—out of their salaries.

Goodman found sales performance varying highly from territory to territory, yet the compensation range was very limited. He therefore sought and obtained Jim Schmidt's approval to alter the basis of the salesforce compensation plan from a high basic salary to a moderate salary with high production-oriented commissions.

Goodman's first step was to take control of expenses. He guaranteed incomes before implementing the change and asked each sales person to estimate his or her annual expenses. The low producer reported $2,400; the second highest producer, $7,200 (the average in 1976 was $5,500).

Next, he realigned territories, added eight new salesmen and promoted two men to regional manager (for the East and West respectively)—new positions in the firm. One of these men, formerly the company's high producer, had helped Goodman complete his sales data base, particularly on expenses and on ways to stimulate sales.

In 1976, a "to-budget" producer would receive between $16,000 and $18,000 per year depending on years of service. A good producer would get about $20,000, while a super salesman would make $25,000, plus a car and expenses. This compensation was based on a $6,000 to $8,000 salary and on commissions for increased orders sent from a territory, new accounts added and new advertising revenue. Goodman said that only 4 members remained of the initial 12-man salesforce he had taken over. Total direct cost, including cars, was $450,000.

RECENT CHANGES IN THE WIRE SERVICE BUSINESS

As *Exhibit 8* shows, Florafax had moved to "free sending" in September 1974. Reasoning that "no florist ever turned down an order," management altered Florafax's pricing policies so that the sender paid nothing and the receiving florist paid 5% on each order received.[6] Before the change, the company had estimated that it needed a 38% increase in orders-sent to break even. Nonetheless, although revenue increased by 48%, management felt the increase should have been bigger. Schmidt and Goodman's explanation was that many florists made their business decisions on an emotional rather than an economic basis and were unaffected.

In another effort to increase sales, Florafax had been experimenting for about six months with what Hughes called the "Third Market"—the impulse buyer who did not have ready access to florist shops. With the cooperation of the Airline Passengers Association, Florafax had mailed a small card the size of a credit card to the Association's members. The card carried the name Flowers Express and a toll-free telephone number to Florafax's Tulsa office. Florafax would take an order, quote a price, arrange for delivery, and debit the customer's national credit card. The results looked promising. *Exhibit 15* shows Florafax's track record.

Concurrently, but in two separate moves, Paul Goodman, who had become the wire service's general manager, had been working with the salesforce to introduce a certification program and to increase advertising revenues from the wire service directory (included in miscellaneous revenues). He explained the certification program:

> In the last six months, every Florafax subscriber was inspected by our area directors. If the shop passed, they were invited to sign an agreement between them and Florafax guaranteeing that any flowers delivered would be fresh for at least twenty-four hours. This guarantee was to be given to the final customer in writing.

[6] Plus a 1% promotional charge.

> If the florist then signed the agreement, we would publish a little "CPFF" for "Certified Professional Florafax Florist" next to his identification number in the Directory.
>
> No CPFF may mean a florist didn't pass the inspection, or it may mean he passed but didn't want to agree to the rules of the certification agreement. It might mean we dropped the CPFF because he was not fulfilling all the conditions of the agreement.
>
> In areas where one florist has CPFF and his competitor doesn't, there has been a switch of business in favor of the CPFF store.

Goodman was also trying to increase advertising revenue from the Florafax Directory. Florists could have a simple entry as in a telephone directory or have advertisements of one, two or three column-inches like those in the Yellow Pages. To date, receivings were correlated positively with ad size. Goodman then described the next step in the wire service's marketing plan:

> As soon as the CPFF program is fully implemented, we will launch a major effort to strengthen our membership in the larger metropolitan markets. Historically we have always had metropolitan representation but it has not had the depth of our competitors'. We'll probably use our jet extensively. It's an Aero Commander. It costs about $75,000 a year to operate, but I think it will attract business. It will let those big city florists know that this Oklahoma outfit has arrived.

NEEDED DECISIONS

With 1976's results in, and with his knowledge of the industry, Hughes was concerned that his two-year-old concentric diversification strategy might be obsolete. He felt the floral industry was changing, probably faster than most people realized. In addition, Hughes was concerned that his major business, the wire service, was vulnerable to technological substitution. Already, IBM had the technological capability to provide online banking—the checkless society. The only obstacles to its adoption were political and cultural. If banks offered their florist customers automatic debiting and crediting on a national network via a mini-terminal or perhaps by phone, Hughes believed that the flowers-by-wire business could be seriously affected.

Jim Schmidt felt that the growth of companies like Stratford suggested that Florafax's long-run profitability could be threatened by the ultimate market power of large corporate buyers and the large integrated agribusiness and floriculture firms. Opportunities not seized now might be lost.

Hughes stated:

> The wire service could more than double its business without incurring extra fixed costs. Our computer and accounting systems could easily cope with the additional volume. Our salesforce and promotional expenses are our major variable costs these days.
>
> In making our past decisions, we considered the future rewards of increased market share worth a short-term profit sacrifice. But now I wonder whether the payoff

from extensive marketing is still worth the effort. Maybe we should acquire one of our competitors and then convert the wire service into a cash cow.

This was the strategy advocated by Florafax's younger managers. They, however, were recommending that Florafax integrate vertically at once by investing heavily in wholesale distribution or retailing, or integrate backward into the growing business. They wanted to dump Florafax's diversification strategy and focus the company's investment. Hughes knew they would have Jim Schmidt's support at least with respect to the insurance companies but, beyond that, he wasn't sure. The floral industry offered a number of attractive opportunities—but which were right for Florafax?

EXHIBIT 1 U.S. Flowers-by-Wire[1]

Company	*Estimated Members, Nov. 1976*	*1969 Sales (million)*	*1975 Sales (million)*
FTD[2]	13,600	$125	$192
Teleflora[3]	13,600	$ 20*	$ 35–50*
Florafax	11,000	$ 10.8	$ 19.2
American Floral Services (AFS)	5,000	na	$ 5–10*
Florist Clearing Network (FCN)	800	na	$ 1–3*
	Total	$160*	$257 to $279*
Floral Industry Retail Sales		$1.2 billion*	$2.0 billion*

[1]Many of the country's 25,000 or more retail florists were members of more than one wire service.
[2]FTD, the oldest of the wire services, was a cooperative organization owned by participating florists and managed by an elected board. FTD paid no income tax on operating margins of patronage pools to the extent that patronage distributions were declared and paid within the period prescribed by the IRS.
[3]Teleflora Inc. was a subsidiary of Dunn & Bradstreet.
*Estimated figures.

EXHIBIT 2

FLORAFAX INTERNATIONAL, INC.
Consolidated Balance Sheets
August 31
Assets

	1976	1975	1974	1973
Current Assets				
Cash	$ 164,244	$ 162,785	$ 71,989	$ 209,654
Accounts and notes receivable less allowance for doubtful accounts	2,568,026	2,096,260	1,845,944	1,591,716
Current portion of long-term notes receivable	164,910	162,427	160,133	—
Inventories	1,483,691	583,322	468,895	57,106
Prepaid expenses	105,195	52,690	66,349	53,376
Prepaid income taxes	40,177	45,477	51,477	65,477
Total current assets	$ 4,526,963	$ 3,102,961	$2,664,787	$1,977,329
Investments				
Long-term notes receivable, less current portion	$ 1,683,540	$ 1,786,262	$1,948,690	$ —
Investments in affiliates at cost adjusted for equity in earnings since acquisition	—	499,596	—	—
Investments in and advances to discontinued operations	—	—	—	189,613
Other investments, at cost	1,466,327	1,042,000	474,075	33,637
Total Investments	$ 3,149,867	$ 3,327,858	$2,422,765	$ 223,250
Property and Equipment				
Land	$ 496,280	$ 477,898	$ 240,078	$ 59,730
Buildings and improvements	890,950	660,696	582,826	336,785
Machinery, equipment and other	702,279	530,784	613,959	422,341
Orchid and anthurium plants	218,970	218,970	218,970	218,970
Less - Accumulated depreciation and amortization	(453,779)	(307,131)	(279,561)	(147,875)
Total property and equipment	$ 1,854,700	$ 1,581,217	$1,376,272	$ 889,951
Other Assets				
Excess of cost over net assets of acquired businesses	$ 2,513,359	$ 2,283,665	$2,134,983	$2,116,088
Other	85,412	73,371	106,555	104,880
Total other assets	$ 2,598,771	$ 2,357,036	$2,241,538	$2,220,968
	$12,130,301	$10,369,072	$8,705,362	$5,311,498

(*continued*)

EXHIBIT 2 (Cont.)

FLORAFAX INTERNATIONAL, INC.
Consolidated Balance Sheets
August 31
Liabilities and Stockholders' Investment

	1976	*1975*	*1974*	*1973*
Current Liabilities				
Current maturities of long-term debt	$ 317,910	$ 292,602	$ 232,114	$ 120,606
Short-term notes payable	400,000	112,500	258,000	—
Accounts payable	892,760	590,187	268,981	92,883
Accrued liabilities	347,992	449,272	312,546	124,200
Other	25,308	35,081	44,167	55,844
Accrued Federal and State tax	48,785	160,627	201,475	147,347
Total current liabilities	$2,032,755	$1,640,269	$1,317,283	$ 540,880
Subscription deposits	$ 652,123	$ 558,943	$ 447,843	$ 425,443
Deferred income taxes	$ 155,902	$ 131,862	$ 117,862	23,800
Long-term debt,[1] less current maturities above	$4,304,972	$3,232,107	$2,306,238	$ 908,870
Unearned gain on sale of discontinued operations	$1,086,664	$1,185,425	$1,271,174	—
Stockholders' Investment				
Preferred stock, Series A, $10 par value	$ 70,000	$ 70,000	—	—
Convertible preferred stock, Series B, $10 par value	1,073,990	1,173,990	1,273,990	1,373,990
Common Stock, $.10 par value	141,763	137,319	137,319	137,319
Additional paid-in capital	1,597,076	1,537,939	1,412,464	1,416,989
Retained earnings	1,505,174	1,191,336	859,189	484,207
Treasury stock, at cost	(490,118)	(490,118)	(438,000)	—
Total stockholders' investment	$ 3,897,885	$ 3,620,466	$3,244,962	$3,412,505
	$12,130,301	$10,369,072	$8,705,362	$5,311,498

[1]Including (revolving) bank lines of credit amounting to:	1,628,890	968,098	725,990	545,901

EXHIBIT 3
FLORAFAX INTERNATIONAL, INC.
Consolidated Statements of Income
Years Ended August 31, 1973–1975

	1976	1975	1974	1973
Revenues				
Gross revenues from floral orders	$18,295,097	$15,359,937	$10,936,477	$10,740,149
Merchandise sales	4,165,986	1,711,281	1,532,332	202,774
Floral service and misc. revenues	2,740,829	2,297,265	1,399,649	1,231,109
Total revenues	$25,201,912	$19,368,483	$13,868,458	$12,174,032
Costs and Expenses				
Amount paid member florists on orders	$17,162,602	$14,281,554	$ 9,678,344	$ 9,501,806
Cost of merchandise sold	2,541,445	952,319	821,649	111,307
Operating expenses	966,673	544,961	416,775	386,577
Selling, general and administrative expenses*	3,692,904	2,835,288	2,289,954	1,658,226
Interest expense	332,311	282,578	243,331	132,366
Total costs and expenses	$24,695,935	$18,896,700	$13,450,053	$11,790,282
Income from continuing operations before provision for income taxes	$ 505,977	$ 471,783	$ 418,405	$ 383,750
Provision for income taxes	199,200	206,700	202,000	187,500
Income from continuing operations	$ 306,777	$ 265,083	$ 216,405	$ 196,250
Income from Discontinued Operations				
Income (loss) from operations of premium promotion subsidiaries after federal income tax effect of $16,700, 1974; and $43,500, 1973.	$ —	$ —	$ (7,192)	$ 11,040
Income from installment sale of discontinued operations, net of income tax of $73,762, 1974; and $30,359, 1975.	67,168	67,064	165,769	—
Total income from discontinued operations	$ 67,168	$ 67,064	$ 158,577	$ 11,040
Extraordinary item—Taxes eliminated by carry forward of prior year operating losses	$ —	$ —	$ —	$ 20,178
Net Income	$ 373,945	$ 332,147	$ 374,982	$ 227,468
Earnings per Share				
Primary—				
Income from continuing operations	$ .21	$ .19	$ .16	$ .14
Income from discontinued operations	.05	.06	.12	.01
Extraordinary item	—	—	—	—
	$ .26	$ .25	$ .28	$ .16
Fully diluted—				
Income from continuing operations	$ .20	$ .19	$ .16	$ .13
Income from discontinued operations	.05	.05	.11	.01
Extraordinary item	—	—	—	.01
Net income	$ .25	$ .24	$ .27	$ .15

*Includes interest cost for receivables financing.

EXHIBIT 4 Number of Growers, Production and Wholesale Value of Potted Plants, 1966/1972

	1966	*1972*
Number of Growers		
Potted Mums	1,545	1,359
Foliage Plants	1,039	898
Production (mil.)		
Potted Mums (pots)	11.8	19.6
Foliage Plants (sq. ft.)	32.4	38.8
Wholesale Value (mil. $)		
Potted Mums	$15.9	$30.2
Foliage Plants*	24.0	48.1
Total	$39.9	$78.3

*Gross value of sales less cost of plant material purchased from other growers for growing-on.

Source: USDA, Crop Reporting Board, *Flowers and Foliage Plants—Production and Sales in Selected States,* Annual Issues April 1969, 1970, 1971, 1972, and 1973.

EXHIBIT 5 Stratford of Texas Horticulture Business

Year	Sales ($000's)	Pre-Tax Income ($000's)	Property and Equipment at Cost	Inventories Average (Whole-gross)
1970	1,380	225	na	na
1971	9,499	404	na	na
1972	11,880	531	4,043	4,043
1973	15,849	1,534	5,795	5,795
1974	25,531	3,226	12,341	10,014
1975	40,774	4,447	13,852	12,349

EXHIBIT 6 Estimated Profit After Tax on Sales For "Average Wholesaler," by Region, 136 Wholesale Florists, 1970

	Percent of Firms				
Profit on Sales (percent)	*Northeast*	*Midwest*	*South*	*West*	*Total*
3 or less (generally larger business)	41	52	23	50	42
4–6	21	34	27	23	25
7–9	2	7	36	5	9
10 or more (generally smaller business)	17	—	5	5	9
No answer	19	7	9	18	15
Total	100	100	100	100	100

Note: Florist supply firms were not included unless their sales of *perishables* were 50% of gross income. The 136 firms represent a selected sample of *unspecified size.*

Source: D. C. Goodrich, G. H. Sullivan, and J. V. Powell, *Selected Terminal Wholesale Markets for Flowers,* U.S. Department of Agriculture, Economic Research Service, Marketing Research Report No. 1005, Washington, DC, June 1973.

EXHIBIT 7 Distribution of Florist's Sales Dollar by Customers' Use of Purchases

Funerals and Memorials	46%
Hospitals	19
Home Use	10
Weddings	9
Churches	5
Conventions and Business Openings	4
Others	7
	100%

Source: United States Department of Agriculture (Survey 1964–1965)

EXHIBIT 8
Flowers-by-Wire Industry
Major Competitors' Prices and Price Behavior 1970–1976

Wire Service	*Date*	*Initial Subscription Charge*[1]	*Regular Dues*	*Billing*[2] *to Sending Florist*	*Pay Receiving Florist*	*Other Charges*
Florafax	1/1970	$120.00	$3.00	85%	75%	
	9/1974	$175.00	$6.00/mo.	80%	75%	1% Promotional Fund charged to receiving florist
	9/1976	$175.00	$6.25/mo.	80%	75%	1% Promotional Fund charged to receiving florist
FTD	1/1970	($25–$50/yr. national) (Up to $15/yr. local)		82.5%	76.5%	
	8/1975	($35–$70/yr. national) (Up to $25/yr. local)				
	10/1975	$400.00		80%	75%	
Teleflora	1/1970			80% plus 20¢/order	78% minus 30¢/order	
	4/1975	$400.00	$6.00/mo.	80%	75%	$4/mo. Sending Fee

[1]As an example of how the subscription fee was used, Florafax in October 1974 went to a $175,000 membership fee: $100 was a refundable bond, $30.00 was for a credit check and $45.00 was the company's set up charge ($30.00 of this was a sales commission).
[2]80% is free sending.

EXHIBIT 9 Wire Service Growth to 1970

Year	*Number of Subscribers to Wire Service (March)*
1961	180
1962	450
1963	1,832
1964	3,575
1965	3,214
1966	5,423
1967	6,367
1968	7,528
1969	8,444
1970	8,984

EXHIBIT 10 P/E Ratios Restaurants 1965–1970 (Composite Figures)

	Restaurant Companies		*Restaurant Company P/E's as a % of the Industrial P/E*	
	High	*Low*	*High*	*Low*
1970	27	17	142	121
1969	39	31	205	194
1968	40	27	211	180
1967	30	18	158	120
1966	27	15	159	115
1965	24	19	133	119

Source: Standard & Poors Industry Analyses, Supermarkets, Restaurants, Food Service, December 18, 1975, Section 2.

EXHIBIT 11 Florafax Acquisitions and Divestments, 1970 to 1976

Date & Company	*Terms*
March 31, 1970	
Florafax Delivery Inc. Prior Years Sales: $7,053,000 Earnings: 50,000	350,000 shares of convertible preferred $6 par, $0.60 noncumulative dividend preference (intended to check cash takeout) 6% convertible/annum. At vendor's option, 20,000 to be redeemed at par each year beginning May 1, 1971. Salaries (vendor and wife for 10 years) $35,000 and $25,000. One executive. Paid $60,000 for option on Advanced Printing at $250,000. Of working capital, $120,000 transferred to wire service.
Spotts International, Inc. Prior years Sales: $2,500,000 Earnings: $250,000 pre-tax	Spotts acquired Florafax Delivery Inc. A new parent company, Spotts Florafax Corporation was created. Two new (Delaware) corporations, operating subsidiaries, set up. Control of the new company was held by the Hughes-Schmidt investor group.
December 1970	
Advanced Printing & Office Supplies	Exercised option initially acquired (with Florafax) on March 31, 1970 for $60,000 by paying $240,000 in cash.
March 1972	
A.B. Johnson Insurance Co.	Purchase of assets $60,000 in cash plus a $150,000 contingent note payable at $1250 per month plus interest at 8% from May 1, 1972, to May 1, 1982. The contingent liability is subject to total of all payments not exceeding 50% of earnings to May 1, 1982. If 50% of commissions and fees are not sufficient to liquidate indebtedness by May, 1982, amount unpaid will be forgiven. Fair market value of assets: $55,000.
October 1972	
Island Orchids, Inc. Prior Years Sales: $200,000 Earnings: Breakeven	Acquired assets for cash and debentures ($325,000) assumption of certain liabilities ($79,000) and other costs ($22,500). The company is obligated to issue up to 18,750 shares of common stock to vendors based on average after-tax income of the acquired business for 5 years, 1 share per dollar earned. Fair market value of assets, $565,000.
October 1973	
Leaf Incorporated Prior Years Sales: $800,000 Earnings: $50,000	100% of common stock. Initial payment $312,500 pursuant to an earn out agreement; will make additional annual payments of one and one-half times the after-tax earnings of Leaf for a period of 6 years with a maximum total payment of $1,250,000 (refinancing on assets restricted until payout).
October 1973	
United Investors, Inc., Oklahoma City Major asset Control of Investors Life Insurance Company	Purchased majority of B class stock for $395,000, $244,000 in cash. Balance by debt instruments with various terms. Finder's fee of $30,000. Gives rights to elect 6 or 11 members of board of directors of United Investors, but does not represent a significant equity interest due to number of A shares outstanding. United Investors owns 75% of Investors Life Insurance Company of Oklahoma City.

(continued)

EXHIBIT 11 (Cont.)

Date & Company	*Terms*
July 1, 1974 Divestment	Florafax exchanged all its issued and outstanding stock in Spotts International, Inc. for 190,000 shares of Florafax stock held by Donald L. Spotts and Onnolee M. Spotts. The company agreed to sell the Spotts building in New Brighton, Minnesota, for $2,125,000 pursuant to two notes: Note A for $800,000 @ 8%, monthly payments $7,455; Note B, $1,325,000 @ 8%, annual payments $132,500. In 1973, Spotts accounted for 24% of gross revenue and 13% of net income before tax. In 1972, it accounted for 21% of gross and operated at a loss.
January & February 1975 *Liberty Investors Life Insurance Company* Major assets $350,000 annual premium income $1,500,000 cash $2,500,000 other assets Earnings: $46,000	Purchased 2,471,173 shares of Liberty Investors Life Insurance Company for cash $137,738 (38% of company). In addition Florafax issued 7,000 shares of Series A preferred and 6% debentures with an aggregate principal amount of $100,000 and received a 5% convertible surplus debenture from Liberty in the principal amount of $695,000. The debenture is redeemable 20 years from date of issue and interest is due only in the years in which the company pays the full $6.00 dividend on its Series A preferred stock. The convertible debenture may be redeemed only from surplus funds of Liberty in excess of $250,000 and converted at rate on 1 Liberty common for every 5¢ of indebtedness at option of holder. The debenture has an estimate market value of $300,000. Excess of price paid over underlying net book value was $3450.
August 31, 1975 *Investors Life Insurance Company* Major assets No cash $5,500,000 assets $1,000,000 premium income Loss	Liberty obtained all the insurance in force and substantially all the assets and liabilities of Investors Life Insurance Company under the terms of a bulk reinsurance agreement and issued 9,152,369 shares of Liberty common stock. As a result, Florafax's ownership of Liberty was reduced to approximately 16%. However, upon conversion of the convertible surplus debenture, Florafax would own 55% of the issued and outstanding common stock of Liberty.
August 31, 1975 *Vestal Companies* Prior years Sales: $2,000,000 Earnings: None	Purchased assets and assumed certain liabilities for a total of $515,410, of which $505,410 is payable over 5 years in 5 equal installments.

EXHIBIT 12 Florafax—Organization Structure (1976)

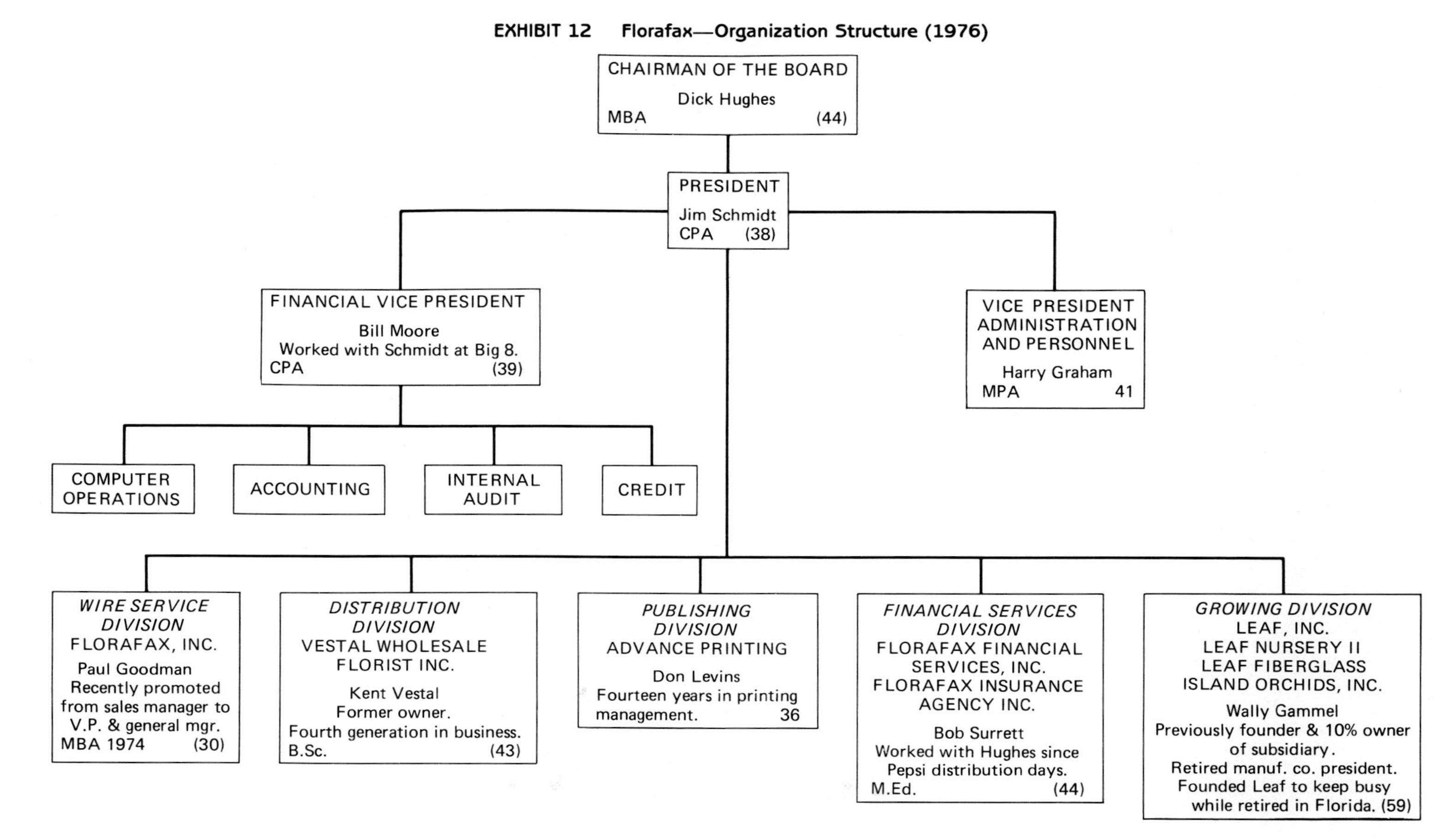

EXHIBIT 13

Year	Leaf Sales	Comment
1971–1972	$ 432,000	Negotiations began
1973	660,000	Closed deal when sales were $580,000 for year to date
1974	960,000	
1975	1,032,000	
1976	1,193,000	

EXHIBIT 14 **Revenues from Lines of Business Years Ended August 31**

	1972	1973	1974	1975	1976
Total Revenue					
Flowers-by-Wire	100%	98%	89%	91%	83%
Growing	0	2%	11%	9%	7%
Wholesale	0	0	0	0	10%
Income Before Taxes					
Flowers-by-Wire	100%	105%	60%	74%	74%
Growing	0	(5)%	40%	26%	35%
Wholesale	0	0	0	0	(9)%

EXHIBIT 15

FLORAFAX INTERNATIONAL, INC.
(and antecedent Corporations)
Revenue

		Revenue ($000's)	
Year	Subscribers to Wire Service	Company	Wire Service
March, 1968	7,500	$ 8,053	$ 8,053
March, 1969	8,400	10,242	10,242
August, 1970	7,500	10,805	10,805
August, 1971	8,000	10,000	8,453
August, 1972	8,100	11,227	11,227
August, 1973	8,500	12,174	11,931
August, 1974	8,600	13,868	10,134
August, 1975	10,000	19,369	17,626
August, 1976	10,500	25,202	20,917

MIDLAND SPARK PLUG COMPANY (C)

It was 10:00 P.M. on Friday, May 17, 1974 and Jeff Kincaid, President, and a major stockholder, of Midland Spark Plug, was sitting in his office with C. R. Reaske, Midland's Executive V.P., waiting for a call from the Polish Home. At 2:00 P.M., Midland's representatives had agreed on a new three-year contract with the company's union, Local 080 of the International Brotherhood of the Manufacturing-Workers of America (AFL-CIO); each member of the union committee indicated that he or she would personally recommend ratification by the rank and file at a meeting to be held at 7:30 that evening at the Polish Home in Midland, Michigan.

Br-r-r-ing . . . Br-r-r-ing . . .

"There it is!" Reaske said. "Will I take it, Mr. Kincaid?"

"No, Chuck. The union likes to keep it formal." Kincaid smiled tiredly as he reached for the phone.

The negotiations had been smooth and even the five-day time-limit had caused no problems. The company's representatives were complaining that Kincaid had been too generous; the union representatives, when they left the plant that afternoon, were sure that the contract would be ratified.

"Mr. Kincale?"

"Kincaid speaking."

"At 12:00 midnight the IBM-W will be on strike!" Jack Beaty, Local 080's business agent, told him.

"But why? What happened?" Kincaid asked, as Reaske sat up alert and perplexed.

"What's happening, Mr. Kincaid?" Reaske queried, but Kincaid was listening in disbelief to Beaty.

"Nothing I can do with this wild bunch," Beaty said. "I'm going back to Cleveland, Kincale. I'll be back in Midland next week." He hung up.

Kincaid held the phone dumbfounded. "Chuck," he said, "We've been struck."

BACKGROUND

Originally founded in 1910, Midland Spark Plug was one of the largest producers of specialty igniters used to trigger industrial oil and gas heaters, agricultural grain and cotton dryers, commercial jet engines, automobiles, lawn mowers and chain saws. The company also manufactured liquid-level control electrodes for use in the beverage, drug, and chemical industries. Other products included electric feed-throughs and motor terminals used in heavy transformer and motor applications, and observation posts used in steam boilers and gas generators. Approximately 10% of Midland's sales were exported.

The company was controlled by two small business investment companies (SBICs)

This case was prepared by Assistant Professor Kenneth J. Hatten as a basis for class discussion rather than to illustrate either effective or ineffective handling of an administrative situation.

which had acquired it in 1961. The two owner-investors, aside from attendance at occasional board meetings (to save time, most board business was done by phone), let Mr. Kincaid manage the company his way. Kincaid held 25% of the outstanding stock; other senior employees held a total of 20%.

In the fourteen years he had been President, Kincaid had never experienced a strike. Reaske, who had been with Midland since 1937, said it was the first time anything like that had happened. When Kincaid called Sam Barnes, Midland's labor attorney, Barnes was flabbergasted. He couldn't understand what had gone wrong. But when Kincaid could offer no reason for the strike other than ''not ratified,'' Barnes said, ''You'll have to wait for the union to make a move to tell you what it wants. My guess is that you'll be struck for at least two weeks—the IBM-W will need at least that amount of time, even if only to justify the strike. My recommendation is for you to go to work on Monday and call your salaried and office staff together to tell them what's going on and keep them informed.''

The company had been unionized under its former owner. He had actually invited the IBM-W to unionize the plant. Apparently, he had felt the union lent the company prestige and he signed a profit-sharing plan with it. He had managed the company in typical ''family'' fashion with his wife and children on the payroll and two holiday homes on the expense account. The union's share of the residuals was limited and when they realized that the owner had netted $600,000 (on a $1,000,000 cash sale) and they had nothing, they decided to really bite hard the next chance they got. So in 1962, only 5 months after Kincaid had taken over as President, the union decided to claim its ''debt.''

Thirty days before the 1959 contract expired, Kincaid received a registered letter demanding everything—retroactive pensions for the old and dollars for the young (medical benefits didn't matter much then). Kincaid remembered, ''The only thing they didn't want was severance pay—they were too worried about our moving. They asked for 50¢ per hour for a 12-month contract. I wanted to liquidate—I had a $1,000,000 debt and $6000 cash.

''My lawyer told me never say 'no' so I offered 1¢ and I thought that was that. Well, we had a federal mediator on the case—they have to maintain absolute impartiality and they do—and he took me aside and said I'd have to do better. I checked the numbers and almost wept tears of blood as I offered 3¢/3¢/3¢ for a three-year contract. They balked. Finally, the mediator in passing asked me if I knew what the bargaining committee made. I said I didn't and he said to find out.

''Well, I offered them an extra 4¢ for the first year and they took it. The mediator said it was the cheapest settlement he'd seen that year—$35,000 total cost to the company.''

A WEEKEND TO REFLECT

Over the weekend, Kincaid wondered what to do. Midland had just received a major contract from AC Spark Plugs for a special jet igniter. AC had sold Midland its full inventory and a number of specialty tools for producing the product, making Midland AC's sole source. AC was owned by General Motors and was a volume producer with a capacity of millions of spark plugs per day. Midland could produce even single items economically although it was equipped to make up to 10,000 per day on a simple standardized design—for example, a lawn mower spark plug.

Kincaid was worried. Midland was a specialist in producing what the big companies found uneconomical to make, but its market security was founded on product reliability and performance, and on timely deliveries. Kincaid commented, ''This is a 'how they're sold' business, not 'how they're made.' '' If Midland was out for any length of time, companies like AC, the jet engine manufacturers, and the airlines for whom Midland was sole source might start looking elsewhere. Kincaid felt that they might even go so far as to fund a competitive source.

He tried to determine what had gone wrong and what had caused the strike. After all, he had been negotiating with the union since 1962, only a few months after he joined Midland. And he felt that the offer he had made them on Friday was fair and even generous (*Exhibit 1*).

One article in Friday's local paper caught his eye:

> Prices rose 11.5% in first quarter, worse than previous estimates, the government reported today. The rate of inflation—solidly in the double-digit category—was the worst since a 13% inflation rate in the first quarter of 1951. . . . The new figures, based on more complete information, showed the nation's economic problems were worse than expected. . . . The Commerce Department also reported today that the nation's corporations recorded a 12% increase in after-tax profits in the first quarter, increasing $8.6 billion to $80.2 billion at an annual rate.

Maybe this had something to do with the strike; 1974 had been a severe strike year nationwide. Maybe Midland was simply another victim of the nation's economic problem. Kincaid summarized his earlier agreements (*Exhibit 2*). He felt that he had always been fair and this agreement did not seem out of line to him.

Kincaid didn't like Beaty, Local 080's business agent. ''Of course,'' he reminded himself, ''I didn't like Mike Potelli who preceded him[1] and I was glad when he was promoted last year.'' Beaty seemed easy-going and fond of a drink.

Kincaid had learned a lot about union negotiations as time passed. Typically, the business agent did all the talking for the union and the lawyer for the company. ''Never'' and ''no'' were words rarely used. Kincaid remembered the Spartan motel room Midland always used as its quarters through the bargaining period. In the past, the union had the best suite and an ample supply of cool water and soft drinks. ''Each time the union and the company met, the union would have to caucus and then come and get us. We'd sit there in a stark room. My lawyer does crossword puzzles throughout the whole negotiation, which drives me mad. They would come to our room, knock, look in and take us back to luxury.'' This time Kincaid had noticed the odd ''empty'' in the waste bin. As in the past, the ratification meeting was at the Polish Club; Mrs. Kincaid said she knew there was an open bar this time.

Reviewing the situation, Kincaid noted that the number of union employees had increased from 80 to 114 (50 male and 64 female) within the previous 6 months. Most of

[1]Potelli had once told Kincaid that his job as business agent was to get a contract that left company and union equally unhappy.

the new hires were second wage-earners in their families, starting their first job or coming off unemployment (usually welfare) which was about 6.5% of the local labor market. All were unskilled. In addition, with the product mix changing and sales increasing, new jobs (for which no contract classification existed) were being created continuously. To avoid what Kincaid called an unwanted and costly musical-chairs effect—moving 3 or 4 people to fill 1 new job, with all the associated retraining costs—the starting rate was deliberately kept low. The upper rate was high enough to keep the trained employee and thereby effectively limit lateral transfer via bidding.

The company had been running its assembly operations on a continuous one-hour-per-day overtime for the past four months on a voluntary basis. The workers had never seemed unhappy on any of his weekly walks through the plant.

The AC contract was really worrying him. How could he be sure Midland would be able to meet AC's requirements? What about his accounts payable? Midland was heavy with in-process inventory for a variety of reasons, ranging from erratic supplier deliveries to deliberate hedge-buying of automotive spark plug insulators in anticipation of a change of ownership of Midland's main ceramics source under a Justice Department divestment order.

He, Barnes, and Beaty had declined the services of a federal mediator. There had seemed no need. Even when Barnes and Beaty found that their business schedules restricted negotiations to a five-day period prior to contract expiration, they had seen no reason for alarm. When Kincaid had joined the company's representatives for the last two negotiation sessions, he had sensed no problem. But there it was—a strike.

MANAGING THROUGH THE STRIKE

On Monday, May 20, the thirty-one non-striking employees—the guards, office workers, supervisors and engineers—all turned up as usual, to find a picket line at the plant gate and Kincaid at the plant door telling them to come in. The picket line parted and in they went. The non-strikers seemed surprised.

Kincaid explained the contract offer to them and announced that it would apply to them immediately.[2] Some of the salaried personnel felt threatened by the strike, knowing that Midland's customers might react by cutting their relationships with the company. One normally mild man who worked in the office wanted to fight the pickets. Kincaid, however, outlawed all violence, instructing everyone to ignore the pickets. He then told all salaried personnel to come to work each day, saying that they would make small assembly runs to maintain deliveries to key accounts—for example, the high-dollar OEM (Original Equipment Manufacturer) accounts—in anticipation of a major shipment during or just after the strike. Kincaid arranged for all incoming phone calls to be directed to himself, Mr. Reaske or to Mr. King. (King, the chief engineer, was a ten-year employee with twenty years' experience at AC, who had joined Midland partly because he felt his way blocked at AC and partly because of the salary Kincaid offered him.)

[2]Salaried payroll personnel at Midland were paid on a sliding scale based on the hourly payroll rates. However, the benefits the company offered applied to both hourly and salaried personnel.

With these two and Mr. David Hershell, the personnel officer, who had been with Midland for thirty-seven years, Kincaid began to plan for raw materials deliveries and dispatches of finished goods.

Meanwhile, the union organized its members into shifts for a twenty-four-hour picket line (six four-hour shifts). The women were scheduled to picket in the day and the men at night. Because the local had little money, and because the International's strike benefits would not start until the fifteenth day of the strike, fines were levied for not picketing—in lieu of payment for picketing. The picket lines were well attended.

The union local, in spite of its inexperience with strikes, arranged for its members to collectively and individually file for benefits, welfare, and food stamps so that once the eligibility period had passed they could be paid. Before leaving town, Mr. Beaty took Local 080's president, Bob Kovich (a two-year employee aged twenty-seven), to the Teamsters regional headquarters to ensure their support for the strike.

Although a few trucks arrived at the plant on the first day of the strike, UPS and other delivery services—including the unionized Post Office drivers—refused to cross the picket lines or even come near the plant. Rather than press the matter, Kincaid arranged with a neighbor who had a trucking business to store all incoming deliveries for the duration of the strike. For the first time, he read the union's constitution.

Success stimulated the pickets to stop everyone and everything going into and out of the plant, including visitors, trash, and service men working on office and vending machines. They made a big thing of their right to stop and search and, when "challenged," were able to quickly assemble thirty to fifty members.

Some picketers appeared to enjoy the role and volunteered for extra duty. The local newspaper photographed them and added to their fame—or notoriety, depending on whose view one took. There was no violence, however; simply abusive language, especially from a few of the assembly workers.

Kincaid decided to tell as few customers as possible that the company was out. The office workers and supervisors were able to assemble enough items to ensure that no customer suffered because a critical item was not available. Each afternoon, led by Kincaid, the whole staff would leave with their briefcases, pockets, satchels—in the case of one lady "enthusiast," her underwear—packed with parcels for shipment from local post offices and truck depots and the Emery Freight depot. One customer picked up its plugs daily at nearby freeway exits.

The strike nonetheless caused considerable concern at AC and unwelcome pressure from their Flint headquarters—a problem solved when Mr. King essentially offered to ship back to AC, by air, all tooling and work in process to let GM resume production at AC. GM declined. But Midland spent half of each subsequent day on AC's orders.

While the company made no secret of its being on strike, neither did it send a general notice to its customers. However, all suppliers with May and June delivery dates were advised by blanket TWX to continue to manufacture but to hold up shipments until further notice. To Kincaid's surprise, Midland's cash position rose as payments to suppliers were suspended. In addition the company had an unused $100,000 written credit line with its bank of record at ¼% above prime.

Inside the plant, every light burned and every machine ran; the place was a veritable beehive. Some of the pickets were sure Midland had hired replacement workers because of all the noise and the large number of cartons being readied for dispatch (many were in fact empty and were stacked in sheltered areas visible to the pickets to discourage the strikers).

At the end of the first week, the company offered to pay its striking employees their previous week's pay at a neutral location to avoid any need to cross the picket lines. With the pay was enclosed a straightforward reminder of the pending expiration of life insurance and medical benefits (*Exhibit 3*).

PRESS COVERAGE

Throughout the strike, the local press kept a close eye on the situation, but whereas on the first day it was page-one news with the headlines ''Hearing Aid Turned Up at Midland'' and ''Tunnel Dark in Spark Plug Strike,'' within a week it was on page four. This was partly because no proposals or counterproposals were released; by mutual consent, each side had agreed to keep quiet.

Monday's paper presented the union's position and Midland's:

> Bob Kovich, Local 080's president, said the employees basically are asking for "an honest day's pay for an honest day's work." He said the employees feel wages have not kept up with the increase in the cost of living.
>
> Kincaid said he thinks the employees are "frustrated" by generally bad economic conditions affecting the country as a whole. "It's a choice of beat your wife, kick your dog, or strike your company," he said. He said the company wants no hard feelings and plans no "muscle-flexing."
>
> "They have a right to strike," Kincaid said, adding that the company had no plans today to contact the union, but had "the hearing aid turned up" and was waiting to be approached by the union business agent. Union representatives also said they were ready to bargain but had no plans to get the bargaining process started again.

On Tuesday the paper reported: '' 'We can't negotiate with a picket line,' Kincaid said, adding that the Midland manufacturing firm had received no word from Jack Beaty, business agent for the union.

On Wednesday, May 22, the paper brought news from the union:

> "We are willing to go right back in and talk," Kovich said, "but must wait for the company to issue an invitation and come up with a new offer." Kovich called the employees' position on the offer which had been made earlier "quite firm." He said the employees have a certain minimum wage increase and benefit improvement in mind and they are very serious about the strike.
>
> To illustrate the union's feelings, Kovich cited one old employee who, in an unusually long speech for him, said, "I worry that those of us who have kept this place going will get nothing. After thirty years, what do I get? I should get something. Even if they took some of it out of my pay it would build up and I'd be better off. They ought to know that the company is going to lose some of its best younger ones because they can't build up any security. Sometimes we wonder, you know, whether management even knows who we are. When you never see them on the floor you wonder if you're a

> block of wood. You'd be surprised how seeing them on the floor and saying hello makes us feel good."

Kincaid said in May 28's paper that the company ''still does not know what was wrong with the contract offer.'' The report continued:

> Kincaid said today . . . the company is ready and willing to get the strike settled as soon as possible, but cannot negotiate unless contacted by official representatives of the union. Referring to the Mayor's offer last week to Kincaid to aid in any way possible in settling the strike, Kovich said, "I wish the Mayor would call me and ask me if I need help."

THE TWO SIDES MEET

On June 4, 1974, the company met with the union at a local motel in the presence of the same federal mediator they had worked with since 1962. Kincaid said: ''At this meeting union spirits were up. The siege mentality was at high tide, the strike still had novelty, and the reflected attitude was that the company should make a 'new proposal' as the former one was 'inadequate' as evidenced by the strike. This latter suggestion was formally declined by the company as impractical. I saw it as the road to an offer-of-the-day or week.

''At this point, the federal mediator advised the committee to knock it off and come up with a specific counter-proposal. What do you know, on the spot, presumably under Mr. Beaty's shrewd but not smart guidance, the additional 'demands' were:

a) Cost of living index subject to some kind of cap. We were expected to know how and what but, actually, we were in the dark.
b) Pension past service benefits going back to original date of employment (in 60% of the cases to the former company).
c) Job evaluation subject to arbitration.

All in all, it was a catchall package with something for everyone to provide a way to maintain their present style of living, take care of their old age, and provide instant job mobility. The mediator indicated the committee was in no mood to receive any type of company reply except a composite 'yes.'

''So that was what I was left with; I had no idea of what it would cost and I didn't like the vagueness of the whole thing—the committee didn't seem to have anything specific in mind.''

BACK AT THE PLANT

''We went back to the plant late that afternoon and as I went in I met one of the foremen who said he was getting sick of us sitting inside with them outside marching up and down. He said, 'Why don't you do something!'

"Well, I was feeling isolated—about the only people in town who would talk to me were the Mayor and the police who were quarreling over the use of CB radios. Each wanted publicity. The pickets had us under siege and I felt that we needed to do something to boost morale, break the monotony and generate some revenue. I decided to try to make a shipment. I thought I had only one alternative.

"The routine would entail a rented truck (with a payload easily calculated by the pickets) driven by company personnel with a police escort to a transfer location, which would be subject to ambulatory picketing under state law. Then the shipment would go with over-the-road truckers. There was a risk of possible violence and escalating the strike to a higher level of hostility, however."

IF YOU CAN'T GET THROUGH THEM, HOP OVER THEM

"I was talking to the shipping dock supervisor who said, 'It's a pity we can't fly over the fence.' That gave me an idea. I called Chuck's assistant, Alan Swinborn, who I knew had a pilot's license, and asked him if he thought we could get a helicopter into the back of the plant. He agreed we could and I asked him to try to find a charter pilot. Eventually he got the name of a guy with a jet helicopter in a trailer park about 150 miles away, up near the lake. At first no one knew him, but Alan turned over a few rocks and took me up to meet him and we had a deal: $250 per hour with a minimum of $1000; $250 on arrival and the rest in cash at the beginning of each trip at each end—no questions asked. We told him where we were and he told us the name of a private airfield just out of town. None of us even knew it was there.

"I agreed to his terms and went back to the plant with Alan Swinborn. We never told anyone what we were up to, but by the night of June 7 I had organized trucks to shift our incoming supplies out of my neighbor's warehouse to the airport and organized transhipment and drop points for three outgoing truck loads.

"That night I told Chuck to be ready to make a shipment and to receive a delivery in the morning—nothing more. I telephoned the chopper pilot and went home to bed. The next morning, once everyone was at work, I went out for the day with 3 men armed with $1000 in $100 and $50 bills while Chuck, similarly armed, stayed inside forewarned to expect a helicopter. He said I was crazy. One of the foremen put his hands over his face and muttered, 'I don't want to know! I don't want to know!'

"Unknown to me, the company out the back was showing off its new plant to some security analysts and was flying them into town in 3 small planes from the Detroit International Airport 175 miles away. And to top it off they had a helicopter to bring them from the airport right into the plant.

"Chuck saw a helicopter coming in and nearly died when it landed on the other side of our fence. He couldn't believe his eyes. The pickets were all watching and everyone in the plant too.

"Finally a second chopper appeared and hopped in over the back fence. There were helicopters everywhere. The pickets apparently thought it was next door so took little notice. Our guys ran out of the plant carrying boxes. It was just like "MASH." The pilot got out, held out his hand for $100 bills and said nothing but 'Put it here,' or 'Not that one,' as the chopper was loaded. He told them that on the next trip he could take more as he would have used up fuel. Then, he took off. He had a pistol strapped to his leg, a half-beard and dark glasses. Alan said the pistol was part of his standard equipment because he was some kind of auxiliary to the state police. I never asked. The chopper was black and its identification numbers had been painted over.

"Back and forth he went four times, each time with his paw out for $100 bills. He used regular gas. Each time he took off he flew in a different direction until he was out of town and then he would fly at tree height or lower until he hit the field. The union didn't know what to do—they couldn't stop him inside the plant and they couldn't find us outside." *Exhibit 4* shows what Midland shipped that day.

"The total time we used was 4.3 hours with the engine never off. Altogether, with some fly-in changes, it cost me $1200. It sure helped my morale and, besides, we got about 2000 lbs. of raw material back in. One of Midland's foremen said, 'It was fantastic. I was encouraged to see that we could go that far. I could hardly believe it. It made the workers think twice—we got out the gate!' "

Kincaid continued, "So now I have the problem of what to do. To keep pressing the union, I've asked for a meeting on June 14. This is a calculated risk. On the plus side, we have made the shipments with the helicopter and I think it has put a damper on the strikers' morale and boosted our own. I also want to force the International to pay 2 weeks of strike benefits (approximately $2600 per week) to match the first 2, supposedly borne by the Local. Finally, the day of hospitalization and insurance expiration is moving closer and this will probably worry the union committee. On the minus side, June 14 is only 3 weeks away from general state unemployment eligibility (up to $95 per week for 39 weeks). It is also only 5 weeks away from accrued (under the old contract) vacation pay (from zero to 3 weeks) due on July 19.

"If we continue to ship at our present 'brief-case' rate, by June 14 we should have shipped products worth about $80,000, plus what we got out by chopper" (*Exhibit 5*).

KINCAID'S FEELINGS

"The stress is on me and on the senior management who, in addition to everything else, have had to prevent an erosion of customer confidence by everything from juggling daily production schedules up to and including 'conning' some of our sole source accounts. The pressure has been continuous and its effects will be with us for a long time.

"When the dust settles, if we can get a contract, the lame, the loud, and the malcontents will all return to work. However, I know I've already lost seven good male employees: one a skilled tool grinder, and six set-up men, all of whom worked on the AC contract in Engineered Products, all trained from scratch for one to two years, all snapped up overnight by local industry. A perfect pocket-sized example of the non-relationship between 'unemployment rates' and any one with a skill for hire.

"Unrelated losses include a skilled female machine operator who joined the Navy as she had planned, but earlier, and a senior screw machinist who had a heart attack the day of the strike and is unlikely to ever return to work.

"The only benefit I can see is that we've seen some of our hourly hands under pressure and they are really good. They seem to have good attitudes of responsibility to their fellow workers and the company. When the opportunity arises I may promote them. I like to develop our own people.

"On the economic plane, the mathematics of welfare, food stamps, unemployment compensation are too close to the average wage level for relatively unskilled workers. No individual or company group health and hospitalization plan can approach Medicaid. And self-respect, the work ethic, or 'example' for children are outmoded cliches.

"After the strike, if we can settle it, I will probably have to ask for extended terms from our major suppliers to avoid being forced to borrow at historically high short-term rates. It will be the first time I've done that. I think nobody wins in a strike. The real cost of this strike to the company and all employees will not be known for at least a year after it ends."

THE ALTERNATIVES

"I'm not sure how long we can go on. There's only a very limited amount of assembly work left. We aren't equipped to do basic machining, and we are running out of raw materials. I would consider replacing the work force but that would mean crossing the picket lines and there aren't many people in this town who will do it. Besides, I'm not sure that I could get 100 people whom we could train. Usually it takes 3 weeks to get a new employee up to speed but that's with the other workers helping. A recall movement is risky and could only be tried once. To accede to further financial burdens and organizational handicaps could place the company in a position where liquidation might be the alternative in best interest of the stockholders. [The company's financial position is given in *Exhibits 6* and *7*.]

"I have to develop a sensible and affordable offer for the union and I know I'll feel more comfortable if I have a contingency plan up my sleeve just in case I can't get a contract."

EXHIBIT 1 Company Offer Accepted by Union Committee but Rejected by General Membership

Friday, May 17, 1974

1 Increase to 11 (from 10) paid holidays; liberalization of vacation eligibility based on seniority.
2 Increase of life insurance (by 20%) from $4000 to $5000.
3 Increase of annual pension benefit (by 66%) from $36 per year of service to $60.
4 Liberalization (almost to the point of elimination) of $100 deductible for health and hospitalization benefits. Unlimited Major Medical co-insurance. Increase of semi-private rate to $95 per day.[1]
5 Annual wage increase of 8%, 8%, 8% (not compounded). With an average wage of $3.09/hr., this totaled 92.7¢/hr. over three years.

[1]Kincaid had known that hospitalization benefits had been a constant irritant during the previous contract and at his request Reaske had gone to great lengths to work out a completely new plan with a new carrier. Kincaid said that in 1974 the cost of this insurance was almost beyond prediction as no carrier would provide guaranteed rates for three years. A new benefit plan normally needs four to five months to design, cost and settle with an insurance company.

EXHIBIT 2

Contract Date	Wage Increases	Total Over 3-Year Contract
May 1971	15¢/10¢/7¢ and 4¢[1]+20¢[1]	56¢
May 1968[2]	15¢/10¢/10¢	35¢
May 1965[3]	10¢/5¢/5¢ and 4¢[4]	24¢
May 1962	7¢/3¢/3¢	13¢

[1]Given by company above contract in 1973.
[2]The 1968 contract added pension venefits and major medical insurance. Kincaid felt Midland needed these to attract and hold staff.
[3]The union took cash in lieu of a pension plan in 1965.
[4]Given by company above contract in 1967. Kincaid had felt the contract was too tight and it would not keep the "faith" of the union since the company had the funds available.

EXHIBIT 3 Salesmen's and Interdepartment Correspondence

From: Jeffery D. Kincaid — Date: May 24, 1974
To: Members of Local 080 IBM-W — Subject: Insurance Coverage

Kindly be advised that your existing life insurance coverage under Prudential Group Policy A-06298 is effective through 6/17/74. Your existing hospital/accident/medical coverage under Hartford Group Policy GXK-014868-P is effective through 6/25/74. Under the terms of both policies you will have up to thirty days from the above-named dates to convert to a personal policy if so desired.

Prudential Contact:
(either address)

Prudential Life Insurance Co.
80 North Street
Trenton, Michigan 64021

Prudential Life Insurance Co.
109 S. Warren Street
Livonia, Michigan 65111

Hartford Contact:
(either address)

Adams & Son, Inc.
44 South Street
Trenton, Michigan 54021

The Hartford Insurance Co.
100 Madison Street
Livonia, Michigan 65111

As a matter of legal record this notice is being included with and distributed on an individual basis on this date with the final pay for the week ending 5/17/74. Extra copies of this same notice will be available upon request at the company offices at 198 King Street, Midland, Michigan.

EXHIBIT 4 Shipments by Helicopter, June 8, 1974

Product Type	by Dollars	by Weight
Spark Plugs	Zero	Zero
Engineered Products[1]	42,781	3711
Screw Machine Products	9,766	1790
Total	$52,547	5501 lbs.

[1]Includes AC igniters.

EXHIBIT 5 **Estimated "Brief Case" Shipments, 5/20/74–6/14/74**

Product Type	*Total Dollars*
Spark Plugs	$ 413
Engineered Products[1]	66,037
Screw Machine Products	13,985
Total	$80,435

[1]Includes AC igniters.

EXHIBIT 6

MIDLAND SPARK PLUG COMPANY, INC.
Balance Sheet
December 31, 1973 and 1972

Assets	*1973*	*1972*
Current Assets		
Cash	$ 7,954	$ 8,298
U.S. Treasury Notes, at cost (approximates market)	79,449	89,453
Accounts receivable—trade, less allowance for doubtful accounts, $3,500 each year	205,355	158,057
Inventories[1]	709,918	581,054
Prepaid expenses	11,407	11,597
Total current assets	1,014,083	848,459
Cash surrender value—life insurance	83,333	78,380
Property, Plant, and Equipment, at Cost		
Land and buildings	91,210	88,545
Machinery and equipment	380,217	366,034
Furniture and fixtures	11,471	10,440
Automobiles and trucks	1,825	1,825
	484,723	466,844
Less: Accumulated depreciation[2]	351,276	330,265
Property, plant, and equipment—net	133,447	136,579
Other assets	425	725
	$1,231,288	$1,064,143

Liabilities and Stockholders' Equity		
Current Liabilities		
Notes payable—Midland Bank—Central	$ 1,000	$ 5,000
Accounts payable—trade	109,672	75,203
Payroll taxes withheld and payable	10,328	7,443
Federal and state income taxes	30,207	29,440
Accrued expenses	33,825	19,676
Total current liabilities	185,032	136,762
Stockholders' Equity		
Common stock—no par value; Authorized, 200 shares; Issued and outstanding, 1973—116 shares; 1972—115 shares	74,000	72,500
Paid in capital	50,000	50,000
Retained earnings	922,256	804,881
Total stockholders' equity	1,046,256	927,381
	$1,231,288	$1,064,143

(*continued*)

EXHIBIT 6 (Cont.) Statement of Income and Retained Earnings
Years Ended December 31, 1973 and 1972

	1973	*1972*
Gross sales	$2,364,302	$2,154,020
Less: Returns and allowances	11,590	14,469
Net sales	2,352,712	2,139,551
Cost of goods sold	1,815,903	1,633,142
Gross profit	536,809	506,409
Selling and administrative expenses	225,236	232,352
Operating income	311,573	274,057
Other income		
Purchase discounts	4,793	4,274
Life insurance premiums—net	1,163	3,457
Interest	5,570	3,274
Bad debt recoveries—net	486	188
Total other income	12,012	11,193
	323,585	285,250
Other expenses		
Interest	270	451
Sales discounts	21,553	21,739
Total other expenses	21,823	22,190
Income before federal and state income taxes	301,762	263,060
Federal income taxes	123,594	104,343
Michigan State franchise tax	26,865	23,002
Total taxes	150,459	127,345
Net Income	151,303	135,715
Retained earnings, January 1	804,881	688,716
Retained earnings pre dividend, December 31	956,184	824,431
Cash dividends per share, 1973—$292.48; 1972—$170.00	33,928	19,550
Retained Earnings, December 31	$ 922,256	$ 804,881
Earnings per share	$ 1,304	$ 1,180

(*continued*)

EXHIBIT 6 (Cont.)

Statement of Changes in Financial Position
Years Ended December 31, 1973 and 1972

	1973	1972
Source of funds		
Operations:		
Net income	$ 151,303	$ 135,715
Expenses charged to operations not requiring outlay of working capital:		
Depreciation	21,011	18,817
	172,314	154,532
Sale of common stock	1,500	1,500
Decrease in other assets	300	
	74,114	156,032
Application of funds		
Dividends	33,928	19,550
Purchases of property, plant and equipment	17,879	42,636
Increase in cash value—life insurance	4,953	8,135
	56,760	70,321
Increase in working capital	117,354	85,711
Working capital—January 1	711,697	625,986
Working capital—December 31	$ 829,051	$ 711,697
The changes in working capital consisted of		
Increase (decrease) in current assets:		
Cash	($ 344)	($ 3,805)
U.S. Treasury Notes	(10,004)	19,840
Accounts receivable	47,298	(2,309)
Inventory	128,864	50,043
Prepaid expenses	(190)	(986)
(Increase) decrease in current liabilities:		
Notes payable	4,000	10,000
Federal and state income taxes	(767)	24,079
Accounts payable and other	(51,503)	(11,151)
Increase in working capital	$ 117,354	$ 85,711

(continued)

EXHIBIT 6 (Cont.) Cost of Goods Sold
Years Ended December 31, 1973 and 1972

	1973	*1972*
Raw materials consumed		
Inventory—January 1	$ 171,883	$ 178,141
Purchases	850,506	725,218
	1,022,389	903,359
Inventory—December 31	362,661	171,883
Raw materials consumed	659,728	731,476
Direct labor	348,241	294,351
Manufacturing expenses		
Indirect labor	166,158	138,744
Service department labor	147,086	132,702
Engineering labor	64,007	54,373
Tools and supplies	64,128	50,272
Insurance	53,134	51,293
Repairs and maintenance—machinery and equipment	17,858	19,031
Depreciation	19,833	18,219
Payroll taxes	60,920	46,506
Repairs and maintenance—buildings	49,381	54,139
Heat, light, power and water	20,945	19,012
Outside services	18,207	16,989
Freight	27,946	26,923
Oil and grease	3,649	2,811
Real estate taxes	11,466	11,074
Employees' welfare fund	4,364	3,770
Employees' pension expense	15,485	15,818
Engineering expense	1,453	1,940
Total manufacturing expenses	746,020	663,616
Work in process and finished goods inventories—January 1	409,171	352,870
	2,163,160	2,042,313
Work in process and finished goods inventories—December 31	347,257	409,171
Cost of goods sold	$1,815,903	$1,633,142

(*continued*)

EXHIBIT 6 (Cont.) Selling and Administrative Expenses
Years Ended December 31, 1973 and 1972

	1973	1972
Selling expenses		
Commissions	$ 16,945	$ 18,944
Travel and entertainment	4,105	4,572
Advertising	2,494	4,751
Salesmen's salaries	1,339	17,018
Total selling expenses	24,883	45,285
Administrative expenses		
Officers' salaries	124,356	112,177
Office salaries	39,690	38,042
Professional services	3,789	4,279
Office expense	9,320	11,313
Telephone and telegraph	6,762	5,775
Payroll taxes	7,419	5,703
Depreciation	1,178	598
Dues and subscriptions	978	1,012
Automobile expense	100	549
Sales and use tax	3,861	4,719
Contributions	1,100	1,100
Employees' pension expense	1,800	1,800
Total administrative expenses	200,353	187,067
Total selling and administrative expenses	$225,236	$232,352

[1]Inventories are valued at the lower cost (first-in; first-out basis).
[2]It is the policy of the company to provide for depreciation of property, plant and equipment over their estimated useful lives on a straight-line basis.

EXHIBIT 7 **Sales Comparison Summary 1973/1974 ($000)**

	Apr. 1973	Apr. 1974	Percent Change	Year-to-Date 1973	Year-to-Date 1974	Percent Change
Screw Machine Products	43	39	(− 9%)	167	140	(−16%)
Spark Plugs	68	82	(+21%)	217	307	(+41%)
Engineered Products	115	120	(+ 4%)	390	475	(+22%)
Misc. (Incl. Scrap)	13	—	—	26	21*	(−19%)
Totals	239	241	(+ 1%)	800	943	(+18%)

*Includes $3500/sale of capital assets.

Notes:

a) Monthly breakeven point for 1973 in terms of sales: $149,000.

b) Projected monthly breakeven point for 1974 in terms of sales: $175,000.

c) As a rule of thumb, IBT (Income Before Taxes) equals total sales (monthly or cumulative) less breakeven-point sales divided by two. However, the further away actual sales are (either way) from breakeven-point sales, the more the relationship changes from arithmetic to geometric.

MIDLAND SPARK PLUG COMPANY (E)

Louis Cushman was seventy-six on December 7, 1975. He had been retired for eleven years but he had not gone to seed. Cushman kept himself fully employed as the Chairman of Great Lakes Capital Corporation in Milwaukee, the small business investment company (SBIC) he had founded in 1961, before he left Conglomco. Conglomco was the Fortune 500 conglomerate Cushman had developed from a small business he had founded in 1928 with a borrowed $10,000. Cushman said:

> I remember the Depression when I had no capital and I had to struggle to get financial backing. I was determined that when I retired I would devote my time to helping promising business ventures. The thing I get a kick out of doing is giving management a piece of the action. It's better than anything my friends have come up with—I've seen them: when they had no plans and no purpose and nothing to work at, they just went to seed.

Cushman's lowest day was in 1952 when he reported a $4.5 million loss on Conglomco's sales of $103 million. At his last annual meeting in 1965, however, Cushman was able to report earnings of $44 million on sales of $1.14 billion and the company's seventy-fifth acquisition since 1952. Cushman's success at Conglomco had been repeated on a smaller scale at Great Lakes. Between 1961 and 1975, the SBIC's portfolio companies' sales had increased from an initial $6 million to $456 million and Cushman had seen his equity investment of $500,000 grow to $16 million.

Today—Tuesday, February 24, 1976—Cushman was waiting for Graham McMillan, principal shareholder and Chairman of Mid-Continent Capital Corporation, another SBIC. The two men were friends and fellow investors: their venture capital companies had acquired the Midland Spark Plug Company of Midland, Michigan, in 1961. Cushman recalled that in 1974 the company had been the scene of an unexpected strike.

A few days earlier, on February 17, 1976, Jeffery Kincaid, Midland's President, had called Cushman (who sat as Midland's chairman) to tell him that David Hershell, the company's Personnel Officer, had shot himself to death on the company's loading dock. Kincaid related that, while examining the company's personnel records, he had noticed an unfamiliar name. Upon investigation he had found a series of bogus employees on the payroll for several periods of four to six weeks extending back over the past two years. When questioned, Hershell, a popular member of the management team who had been with Midland for thirty-nine years, confessed that as payroll officer he had been drawing extra pay. He couldn't or wouldn't say what he had done with the money or even how much he had taken, and he couldn't return it. He had simply killed himself. Investigations had revealed Hershell had no assets.

For McMillan, this report had been the "straw that broke the camel's back." A

This case was prepared by Professor Kenneth J. Hatten and Research Assistant Mark T. Teagan as a basis for class discussion rather than to illustrate either effective or ineffective handling of an administrative situation.

strike at the company in 1974 had indicated that Midland was vulnerable. Now he wanted to replace Kincaid, or wait until the mess was cleaned up and sell the company.

Cushman, in contrast, was attached to Midland. It had been Great Lakes' second investment and it was the oldest investment in his SBIC's portfolio. When Great Lakes and Mid-Continent had bought Midland, they had hired Jeffrey Kincaid as President to replace the retiring owner. Sixteen years later, Kincaid was still Midland's President and had never suffered an unprofitable year. He had transformed the company from one with declining profits derived from precarious markets to one with steady profits from more stable markets. (See *Exhibit 1* for recent financial statements.) However, Cushman recalled that seventeen times he and McMillan had tried to convince Kincaid to acquire or merge with other companies to foster growth and increased profits. And seventeen times Kincaid had refused, claiming that the "marriage partners" were unsuitable. "If I'm going to merge with or acquire a company, I want any assumed product line to be in my backyard and not in something like hula hoops or pet rocks! Big isn't better—we're paying a bigger dividend than Penn Central or W.T. Grant!" he'd said the last time.

McMillan had made his money in textiles. In 1952, at the age of 46, he had invested $6,250 for a 5% share of an old textile company with sales of $12.5 million and a 5-year history of losses. As part of the deal he was elected President. By the time of his retirement in 1962 the company had made 27 acquisitions and had grown to sales of $424 million with earnings of $22 million. To top off his record, McMillan had made one investment of $62,450 in 1962 which, today, had a value of $206 million.

Cushman could understand McMillan's impatience with Kincaid and with Midland. Great Lakes was carrying its 25.5% equity interest on the books at $306,000 after 15 years—and McMillan was in the same boat.

McMillan felt that Kincaid could have fostered more growth than he had at Midland. Sales for 1975 were $3,148,578 compared to sales of about $2.1 million in 1960, the year prior to Kincaid's taking over. Although the investors had received a dividend each year since 1966, when Kincaid paid off the company's initial debt, Cushman wondered if his capital would produce greater returns and leverage elsewhere.

On the other hand, it was reassuring to have a stable company in his portfolio, and only recently Midland's reputation as a quality producer had enabled it to gain a major account with General Motors' AC spark plug division. The sales and profits derived from this account, and from others which had already flowed from it, could provide this renewed growth in sales and make Midland more profitable as well. In addition, Cushman recalled that, only a few months ago, Midland had received a Presidential "E" Award for its export performance in 1974 (the first received by any small company in Southern Michigan in the past 17 years). Cushman thought:

> Perhaps McMillan is right and we should seek higher returns either through Midland or through another investment. But, I'd sure feel foolish if I pulled out of a good company just before it got a lot better. My friends would give me a lot of grief if someone else took it public and got the P/E multiplier.

JEFFERY KINCAID

Impressed with Kincaid's background (*Exhibit 2*) and with his strong personal recommendation from one of the country's most famous management consultants, Cushman and

McMillan had hired Kincaid to take over Midland when the SBICs bought the company. At the time, sales and profits were declining (*Exhibit 3*). Cushman looked at the notes he had written while he and McMillan were contemplating hiring Kincaid:

> Some of the other investors think he may be young. They also worry about his background being primarily in sales. They think he should be more of an engineer. He looks good to me, though. Not all those successes at Giant Electric could have been due to luck.
>
> We thought we could attract him with a 2-year contract at $25,000 a year. He turned this down out of hand. He said 3 years was the absolute minimum time in which he could begin to turn the company around. I think he's right, too. If he can do it at all, results won't begin to show for some time.
>
> What bothers me about the company is its product line. The Big Three OEM (original equipment manufacturers) makers of spark plugs are tough competitors. And competition is cutthroat in contract precision machining and that's an even bigger part of Midland's business than spark plugs. If demand falls off you can't even look for much new business because it's hard to compete more than one or two hundred miles from home. And unless Midland can do something no one else can, margins are likely to be pretty slim.
>
> Any real future for Midland lies in developing new proprietary products which would capitalize on its skills. Its machines are modern and well maintained. What's more, it has some production and engineering people who seem pretty able. But, if it's to be turned around, I think someone from outside the company will have to come in and provide leadership.

Cushman said:

> We came back and offered him a 3-year contract at $22,500 a year. . . . He eventually accepted but only when we agreed to let him invest in the company. McMillan had been impressed by Kincaid's wanting to invest $10,000 for 10% of the company because he knew $10,000 was all Kincaid had and he felt it indicated Kincaid's faith in his ability to turn Midland around.

During his first few years with Midland, Kincaid spent much of his time on the road developing new customers as the basis for changing Midland's product mix. He succeeded in turning the company around, learned to love living in the rural Midland area and purchased a small house on the bank of nearby Lake Hobart. Kincaid liked running a small company:

> I came to Midland after working for Giant Electric for eight years. I had been on a fast track route at Giant Electric, holding eleven different jobs in the eight years and thus really learning the business. But I found that I didn't like the idea of getting everything approved through layers of authority, of writing reports back and forth, never knowing if and when anything would come of them. I didn't like the compartmentalization and the yes-men following close behind the big wheels. And by the time I was thirty-six, the time I came to Midland, I was in charge of a department employing men twenty years my senior. I could feel daggers pointed my way as I passed people in the hallway. You get to feel they'll be dancing at your funeral.

Although he had been President of Midland for sixteen years, Kincaid was one of its most junior personnel in terms of time with the company. Many of the workers and managers had been there for over thirty years. Only Kincaid had a college education. Kincaid liked to keep things simple and efficient; for example, he had no secretary and no air conditioning in his office. He personally answered many inquiries but had one of his clerical personnel sign routine letters with "J.P. Barnes, Vice-President, Marketing." Kincaid used this device so that potential customers would not think the company was so small that its president did everything. He himself signed letters of more importance, or those needing more bite.

Kincaid felt that the function of a small company was to do what large companies couldn't do or were unwilling to do. This philosophy lay behind his insistence on maintaining close customer contact and on working with customers to develop products. He also felt that the value of a small company lay not in its balance sheet but in its "state of mind"—that is, in its managers' and workers' attitudes and in the market position it took. Although Midland had a system which helped reduce inventory and production snarls, Kincaid felt an equally important part of cost control was a cost-conscious attitude, as manifested by such things as turning off lights.

THE COMPANY

Founded in 1910, Midland Spark Plug was one of the largest producers of specialty igniters used to trigger industrial oil and gas heaters, agricultural grain and cotton dryers, commercial jet engines, automobiles, lawn mowers and chain saws. The company also manufactured liquid-level control electrodes for use in the beverage, drug and chemical industries. Other products included electric feed-throughs and motor terminals used in heavy transformer and motor applications, and the observation ports used in steam boilers and gas generators. Approximately 10% of Midland's sales were exported.

A particularly large account with AC of General Motors for jet engine igniters was segregated for reporting purposes. Sales volume broke down as follows:

	% of Sales	
	1974	*1975*
Screw machine parts	15%	12%
Spark plugs	25	22
Engineered products	47	37
AC/GMC	13	29

Midland's plant and office was in an attractive red brick building located on seventeen acres of open land. Hanging over the front door was a red, wooden structure with tinted glass reputed to have once graced the entrance to the "House of the Rising Sun" in New Orleans. The factory was clean and orderly and had floors of old wooden "bricks." As Cushman had said on first seeing the plant, "The whole thing looks like it came from central casting."

Aside from attendance at occasional board meetings (to save time, most board business was done by phone), the SBIC managers had let Mr. Kincaid run the company his way. Kincaid held 29% of the outstanding stock and other senior employees held a total of 20%. The two SBICs each held 25.5%.

SCREW MACHINE PRODUCTS

The screw machine department produced metal casing for Midland's final products and other metal parts for outside, jobbed contracts. Parts produced for in-house use were priced at cost; those for external customers were priced at what negotiations determined the market could bear. Bill Reaske, the Executive Vice-President and a thirty-seven-year veteran of the company, oversaw the operation and estimated that, by value, 60% of the department's output was for in-house production and 40% for outside work. By machine time and materials used, the corresponding percentages were 75%, 25%.

Machinery consisted of twenty-two single-spindle National Acme screw machines and fourteen multiple-spindle Brown & Sharpe screw machines. The single-spindle machines, as the designation suggests, were able to process one bar of metal at a time; the multiple-spindles could process six bars. The machines could be set up to perform up to seventeen operations, such as drilling, grooving, threading and shaping the metal. The time required to complete operations varied but was much longer with the single-spindle machines, which had to perform operations in sequence. The multiple-spindle machines, in contrast, would normally require only the time needed for the longest of the set-up steps. Tooling costs for the multiple-spindle machines could be over twice those of the single-spindle machines, and set-up time could be four times as long. Having both types of machines lent Midland flexibility in scheduling long or short production runs and experimental design. In practice, the single-spindle machines were used primarily for outside jobs while the multiple-spindle ones were used primarily for making the casings used on Midland's own products.

The outside market in particular was cyclical because many of Midland's customers had in-house capability and subcontracted work to Midland when their own capacity was strained. When these same customers experienced business slowdowns, they naturally subcontracted fewer jobs.

Midland had found sales representatives unsatisfactory for gaining outside accounts because contracts had to be negotiated rather than bid. Sales reps were rarely familiar with Midland's capabilities and costs whereas Reaske had intimate knowledge of both and was able to modify his position on the spot without danger of entering a poor contract. Advertising was limited to a facilities brochure. The major outside customer was a firearms company which accounted for about 50% of outside billings. Other customers included shoe machinery and ignition manufacturers. Midland turned down short runs, except to service good customers for its other products.

There being many jobbers producing screw machine parts, Midland found it difficult to compete for business more than a few hundred miles from its Michigan location. Kincaid said most of the business was within half a day's drive from Midland—so a truck could deliver to a customer and return in a day. Freight costs could become quite high because of the weight of the metal products. For example, Midland had once done considerable business with a customer in Tennessee, but lost the account because Tennessee producers could offer a lower price after freight was included.

Technological innovation also constrained major sales expansion because, typically, mass production methods would be applied to a product as soon as demand justified it. For example, Midland had done quite well making pins for color television sets when they first hit the market. Midland had produced the pins on its screw machines for 2¢ apiece and sold them for 15¢. But, when color television sales took off, larger competitors created mass production processes which could produce the same pins for ½¢ a piece.

Despite these constraints, the screw machine department was almost fully scheduled; in fact, Mr. Reaske felt that the company might soon reach a point of conflict between internal and external needs. Midland occasionally bought screw machine products from other screw machine operations and Reaske felt it might be able to prevent scheduling problems if it did so more frequently. Increased subcontracting could also help Midland increase its sales, but Reaske felt that maintaining profit margins was more important.

Midland was rarely able to make more than 15% profit on its jobbed parts because its customers were usually familiar with the costs of production and could accept bids from competitors. Nevertheless, screw machine parts provided a good cash flow because orders usually called for the use of stock materials which Midland could draw out of its inventory. For those orders requiring non-stock materials, Midland purchased raw materials only after its receipt of a customer's order.

SPARK PLUGS

The spark plug department produced spark plugs for automobiles, power mowers, chain saws and snow-blowers. Automotive spark plugs were sold primarily through regional distributors. Customers were normally automotive service outlets which were unable to get credit with the Big Three spark plug manufacturers: AC of General Motors, Autolite of Bendix and Champion. Sales representatives had been unsuccessful because they had usually brought in more bad accounts than good ones. Final users were people who installed their own spark plugs and who believed that Midland plugs, especially those with three electrodes (*Exhibit 4*), would improve and extend the performance of their cars.

Power mower and other small engine plugs were sold through wagon jobbers,[1] repair shops, and catalog houses to hardware wholesale and large retail outlets. Kincaid estimated Midland had 10–15% of the market for power mower plugs with its sales of 1.2 million units a year. For small engine plugs, Midland used four sales representatives, three of whom sold on their own account as well as for commission. Midland's willingness to provide private-label imprinted boxing for small-engine plugs helped increase sales.

Both the OEM and replacement markets were dominated by the Big Three, who together produced up to 1 billion plugs a year compared to Midland's 2 million. Having to price competitively with the Big Three, but lacking their mass production facilities, Midland's plugs provided margins capable of absorbing burden, sometimes of breaking

[1]A wagon jobber is one who deals in several products and who makes a sale by delivering the purchased goods on the spot—i.e., ex wagon.

even, but never of making profits. However, staying in the spark plug business provided Midland with many advantages:

1 Midland could make full use of its screw machines and its skilled machinists.
2 The metal casings used on spark plugs were also used, with or without modification, on Midland's igniters. Without its own screw machines, obtaining casings could be more difficult and expensive.
3 Midland could gain more attention and lower prices when it ordered supplies (e.g., ceramic insulators) because it ordered more than it would if it did not make spark plugs.

Thus, though not directly profitable, spark plugs afforded Midland flexibility while absorbing overhead.

The production or assembly line consisted of special equipment arranged around a moving belt. Although not highly automated, the line was flexible. The foreman estimated that seven to nine changes per day could be made in the product mix with less than a 10% loss in production. Changeovers were made frequently to keep inventory low and delivery service rapid. One foreman commented:

> It's just as well we can. I get a schedule once a month, it's called the "hot list." Two or three days later, management wants something else. It's happened twice today. We get set up, then it's some emergency. . . .

Components were purchased from the screw machine shop at cost or from long-established vendors. The company's principal outside purchases were ceramic insulators and punch-press items such as bushings.

ENGINEERED PRODUCTS

Midland's line of engineered products included ignition assemblies[2] for industrial oil- and gas-fired burners, control electrodes for resistivity liquid-level control systems, electric feed-throughs for conducting current through a pressurized bulkhead for commercial and industrial applications, and observation ports for visual flame checks in commercial and industrial burner face-plates.

Sales had traditionally been to OEM accounts such as Westinghouse, GE, Carrier and Ideal. However, Midland's parts were being used in so many final applications that the replacement parts market was becoming a dominant factor. As Kincaid said:

> Recapturing the aftermarket is the name of the game. Replacement sales[3] to final users have passed OEM sales as a source of profits at Midland. We're constantly trying to develop the resale market by lining up distributors to reach minor users.

[2]Ignition assemblies were similar to spark plugs in their assembly, components and functions. They basically channelled electric current through an insulated device for the purpose of creating a spark. The spark might travel to an attached electrode as in the case of spark plugs, or to another, unattached electrical conductor.

[3]The replacement or aftermarket was created solely by the replacement of the same item previously sold to an OEM customer account. The product's ''life'' was primarily dependent on end-use application. However, following widespread trade practices, a product would normally be replaced under a service contract or maintenance schedule, whether needed or not (somewhat similar to automotive spark plugs being replaced, instead of cleaned and regapped, during an engine tune-up).

Typically, Midland's first new product sales to OEM accounts were made after its engineers had worked closely with engineers of the ''leader'' company to develop products which would have industry-wide use. Midland's entire observation-port line had been initiated in response to an igniter customer's informally telling Kincaid that a high-quality observation port would solve many of his igniter-related problems. Most of Midland's new products had evolved in this way—from solving an OEM customer's technological problems. The process was protracted, however, not only because of the need for testing the new product but also because often a new igniter necessitated the redesign and respecification of the OEM's product line. Although this process sometimes took up to five years, the product's use, once established, would normally extend over a long period. In addition, once Midland had sold a new product to a major account, minor accounts in the same field often followed quickly. For example, if Carrier made use of a new igniter unit in its air conditioners, other air conditioner manufacturers would quickly follow suit. Midland had also been successful in its efforts to constantly upgrade designs for existing OEM accounts. Kincaid estimated that over 80% of the engineered products' sales were dependent on the economic fortunes of six Midland customers.

The price/demand relationship for many of the company's engineered products was inelastic, especially since Midland was sole source for many of its products. Pricing changes to OEM accounts were always made with advance notice, usually on selected items. Kincaid's main objective had been not to overdo a good thing and risk the creation of another company.

Sales representatives had proven undesirable for this line as well as for Midland's other lines. Kincaid felt that reps were more concerned with volume sales than with landing profitable contracts. Midland's management felt confident that, in the U.S., almost every potential customer for its engineered products had heard of the company and came to it with any new needs.

Advertising and promotion were limited to coded classified advertising in Thomas' Register and to the company's irregular publication of new catalog editions. A new catalogue was printed whenever sufficient additional designs (in many cases those originally developed for a single customer at its request) warranted inclusion as possibilities for additional customer applications or for the aftermarket.

Midland became the largest North American producer of its kind of engineered products once AC had left the business by subcontracting it to Midland. The only companies making similar products were two small manufacturers which made igniters for residential burners. Kincaid felt that Midland could easily have entered this market because it was not capital-intensive. However, he felt that if Midland entered this market and gained a healthy margin, many ''garage operations'' would enter the market too and gnaw away at the margin. Instead, Midland had negotiated ''associated manufacturers'' distribution arrangements for the replacement aftermarket with the two producers now supplying the residential OEM market.

THE AC ACCOUNT

Although it was actually part of Engineered Products, the AC account was so large that Midland costed it separately. Midland had landed the account because AC's sales manager had been under pressure from GM headquarters to subcontract AC's jet engine igniters—the jet igniters did not fit in with AC's mass production methods. AC's sales manager contacted Midland primarily because Mr. King, Midland's plant manager, had worked at AC for twenty-one years before joining Midland in 1963[4] and had maintained contact with his former colleagues and kept them aware of Midland's capabilities.

Midland could produce the number of jet igniters needed more economically than AC because the design and number of units involved fitted in perfectly with Midland's assembly methods, while they were a nuisance at AC. The AC sales encompassed about thirty designs. Kincaid said:

> The price/demand relationship seems relatively inelastic, but I insisted that Midland put a lot of effort into developing a pricing strategy. I wanted to be sure we received adequate compensation for the difficulties inherent in forecasting AC's long-term demand. I expected that AC would be demanding in terms of quality and speed of delivery. Our price had to allow for the costs of quality control and I felt that Midland's in-process inventory would have to be increased to ensure that we could satisfy any short-notice orders from AC. In addition, I wanted to capture as much of any learning curve cost reduction as I could for Midland and I had to consider the need for depreciation on the specialized tooling we needed to service them.

AC had designed the igniters it needed, and depended on Midland to develop its own production processes. However, AC had provided much of the capital equipment like the lathes and arc welders at a token cost. For these reasons, Kincaid felt that, though the account was based on no patents or legal contracts, Midland would continue to be AC's sole source. The account had already led to $138,000 in additional sales for Engineered Products in 1975 as other companies followed AC's lead and placed orders with Midland.

SCHEDULING

Scheduling was done by Mr. King, the chief engineer, by forecasting sales by customer. These forecasts were based on recent monthly sales averages, on factors like the expected crop yields by region (which would affect igniter sales in grain dryer operators), and on industry trends. King prepared a six-month forecast every three months; the last three months of any forecast could be modified to reflect late changes. Forecast sales were then broken down to component items so that Mr. King could determine the number of common parts which would be needed. This step, in turn, enabled him to schedule long runs by component and sub-assembly rather than the shorter runs which would have been appropriate had he scheduled for end-product production. Stocking sub-assemblies lent Midland flexibility because many sub-assemblies were interchangeable in final products.

Mr. King used order points for standard components and raw materials. He took these into account while scheduling because many raw materials had to be ordered six to eight months in advance.

Even if a standard product was unlikely to be ordered for a few months, Mr. King would often schedule production of component sub-assemblies so that Midland would be

[4]King had left AC because, as one of 1,200 personnel in its engineering department, he had often found himself critiquing parts which he had never physically handled. He took the Midland job because he would be closer to the products on which he would be working and because he would have more varied responsibilities.

able to respond quickly when the demand for the end-product developed. For example, though lawnmower spark plugs were demanded infrequently between October and February, Mr. King built up stocks of the plugs and their sub-assemblies so that Midland could quickly fill orders when they did come in the late winter and early spring. This policy also enabled Midland to keep its machines and people working at a consistent pace, thereby minimizing layoffs and idle time. For these reasons, work-in-process inventory averaged about 80% of total inventory. During slack times, Midland also escalated its efforts in seeking external machining work.

Mr. King found scheduling assembly and handwork more difficult than scheduling the machines. Although Midland did not use time studies, Mr. King determined the output for assembly and handwork by working backward, i.e., looking at previous output per person per day. In 1976, Midland was still using a hand-entry cardex system for scheduling, pricing and inventory control, but King was looking forward to adapting a Hewlett-Packard mini-computer for these purposes.

PRICING

Mr. King was also in charge of pricing, for which Midland had a basic formula: Labor costs + component costs + 300% factory overhead + 50% SGA overhead + 10% profit + 5% sales commission + 1% discount = "cost."

Labor costs were based on Midland's analysis of employee output and the wages paid under the union contract; component costs had to be frequently adjusted to allow for inflation. The 300% factory overhead was based on labor hours and had been a standard figure for many years, as had been the 50% SGA overhead figure. The 5% sales commission was a remnant of times when sales agents and a salesforce had been used extensively; however, Midland felt the figure was still relevant insofar as it accounted for the time management spent on sales. The 10% profit figure was built in to assure that Midland would not inadvertently make unprofitable products. Once cost had been determined, management estimated what price the market could bear. In the case of spark plugs, competition kept prices below Midland's cost figures. In the case of other products, especially engineered products, the company was often able to price at a level considerably above cost.

Prices were reviewed annually and in 1976 Midland felt it would have to raise prices between 6 and 8%. The increases would not be uniform across the board but would vary, with increases of up to 20% for some products and no increase for others. Management sometimes found itself raising the prices of products on which it was making a profit even after three years of price stability just so its customers would not think Midland had been overpricing all along. A notification of price changes was sent to customers sixty days in advance. Midland had never experienced customer resistance after a pricing announcement.

PRODUCT DEVELOPMENT

The cornerstone of Midland's product development was satisfying customer needs rather than developing products and then marketing them. Most product development resulted from a customer's informing Midland of its new requirements, or through word-of-mouth referrals from its old customers to new customers. Most product developments were modifications of existing designs to meet evolving needs.

Product development was the full-time job of no one person, but several people were involved with it. Mr. Anderson, who had been with the company for five years, was the experimental engineer and spent approximately 80% of his time working on product development. Mr. Hardy, who had been with Midland for thirty-seven years, was the supervisor of the model shop which often made new product prototypes. And John Smiley, with Midland for thirty-six years, was a lab technician who spent much of his time tracking down customer problems. Although not involved with design, he supplied field-related input to the other two men. This group designed Midland's new products, built its prototypes, prepared the necessary tooling, and supervised production start-up.

In creating new products, Midland strived to keep as many common components as possible, in order to limit its inventory and to prevent frequently changing and short production runs.

SALES

Kincaid had always been the company's most active salesman. When he joined the company as President in 1961, he found that it was selling primarily cheap spark plugs to discounters, and was engaged in low-profit, cyclical government contracts. Feeling that the company's weak position stemmed in large part from its marketing and product mix, he decided that it should become a reputable manufacturer of spark plugs and a superior engineering house.

Changing its market for engineered products from government to industry took considerable effort and time. Kincaid said he spent three weeks to a month on the road during each of his first three years "smokestack calling" to develop accounts. Although his contacts at Giant Electric helped some, it was mostly a development-from-scratch process. "If I'd known what I was getting into, I never would have taken the job," said Kincaid in 1976, looking back on those tough years.

During that time, Kincaid had adopted the practice of leaving a lawnmower spark plug as his calling card; he felt that, as an inexpensive but usable item, it would leave a bigger and more durable impression than a business card which could easily be lost and casually discarded. He also developed the practice of writing customer profile sheets which he insisted be updated after each company visit. He felt the sheets helped Midland keep its customer contacts personal and lucrative. A sample customer profile sheet appears in *Exhibit 5*.

Kincaid remained Midland's most active salesman, especially for spark plugs, though he had tried to develop an attitude in the company that everyone was a salesman. Mr. Reaske handled the sales function for screw machine jobs by taking calls and helping the customers with their problems. Reaske felt there was no need to solicit business because Midland was using nearly all its capacity; established customers and word of mouth provided sufficient business.

Mr. King was the major salesman for engineered products. He felt that nearly all potential customers had heard of Midland and that potential new customers always made inquiries to the company, particularly since Midland was a sole source of many of its products. King could do his selling job on the phone or send Mr. Smiley to determine a customer's problems and requirements.

Management felt its sales work was primarily engineering sales: Midland had to sell customers' engineers on Midland's expertise in order to get them to adopt specifications which Midland's products could satisfy. Only after the customer's engineers were convinced did its purchasing agents order. Therefore, customer contact and trouble-shooting were major parts of the sales function. In fact, Midland sent a representative to the annual hardware trade show not to develop new customers so much as to talk with customers not often contacted during the year.

Reaske felt that the primary way in which Midland could increase sales would be through totally new products. He also felt if Midland subcontracted more of its business, the company could increase sales but would most likely suffer a decrease in its margins. King felt that the replacement market, if selectively and aggressively pursued, could yield increases in both sales and profits since prices to industrial users like utilities were much higher than the per-unit prices on multi-thousand unit orders for OEM markets. Midland was already enjoying increased sales to final users (*Exhibit 6*).

GROWTH POLICY

Kincaid pointed out that his policy had not been one of rapid growth but of evolving the product mix toward quality and high margins. Over 50% of Midland's products were new within the previous five years. He felt that if growth ever exceeded 20% a year, it would lead to a breakdown in quality and in organization control. Other constraints to growth were machine and electrical capacity, space, and access to skilled labor. Obtaining skilled labor was a major constraint because it took six months to train a foreman, and one year to train a screw machine set-up man. It was a continuous process to train an engineer. Kincaid also felt that many young people were unwilling to take manufacturing jobs because welfare benefits were so munificent.

In addition, he said, Midland had already penetrated its markets thoroughly; management was certain every potential customer had heard of the company and considered it when in need of new or modified products. Salesmen would most likely add less incremental profit than would be justified by their expense.

Kincaid knew that Midland was vulnerable because it served the same markets as the Big Three. For instance, Midland purchased its insulators from Bendix Autolite, which probably supplied its small competitor to avoid antitrust action. However, if Midland aggressively expanded its spark plug sales, Bendix, though it would most likely continue to supply Midland, could easily make things difficult—for example by delivering supplies late or by delivering the wrong supplies.

Though Midland could most likely expand its engineered product sales with little difficulty, Kincaid felt that it would be dangerous to increase the company's already healthy margins because higher profits might well provoke the establishment of competing companies. Kincaid said:

> Outsiders, including the owners, can easily recommend different courses of action, including rapid growth. But a detailed knowledge of the constraints should remind you that "your first bad decision in a small company is your last."

Kincaid believed that Midland's reputation as a good engineered-products house had led to its receiving the lucrative AC account. While tooling up and going through the learning period, Midland was having some capacity problems but Kincaid felt that once the AC operation was well-established, Midland would most likely receive more business from AC and from other companies which would follow AC's lead (as some had already done). Sales might well grow at 15–20% a year without a drop in margins or in quality as the learning curve took hold.

> Midland is a success. The owners could sell, and they have tax losses from fizzled deals to offset any capital gain, but autonomy is important to me and my senior managers. Job security isn't a problem for us, we all have had outstanding job offers from one of the Big Three. Another set of investors might be O.K., but operating ownership would make us think about other options.

Threat to leave.

LOUIS CUSHMAN

As Mr. Cushman reviewed his investment in Midland, he was torn between the possibility of getting a higher return by investing elsewhere and the stability Midland offered. Reviewing the SBICs' relationship with Midland, he noted that the SBICs had lent Midland $600,000 in convertible notes in 1961. They had been able to borrow the funds through the Small Business Administration at 3% while lending at 8%. After three years, Kincaid had paid off the debt by refinancing it through a machinery trust agreement. The SBICs had then each invested $30,000 for 30 shares of stock, which gave each 25.5% ownership of the company. Midland had paid no dividends until 1966. Since then it had steadily paid dividends totalling $225,000. *Exhibit 7* allows a comparison of Midland and representative companies in Mr. Cushman's Great Lakes portfolio.

Cushman had to consider whether Midland would continue to be stable. Engineered Products, the most profitable department, relied on one of its eleven customers for about one-half its OEM sales; on the other hand, it was the only operation of its kind in North America. The AC account, backed up by no contract, was assuming great importance for the company. If these major accounts pulled out, Midland's historic stability could be destroyed. Yet, the AC contract and the other business it was attracting could lead to Midland's returning more profits and dividends than it ever had before. If they waited a few more years maybe the company would be worth more.

In this light, another possibility was to replace Kincaid with a manager who would more aggressively pursue growth. On the other hand, perhaps Kincaid had pursued the only strategy available to a company in Midland's unique position. Other companies with more resources than Midland's had tried to take on the Big Three and had failed. The Supreme Court of the United States had acknowledged the difficulty of even a large company's succeeding in any confrontation with the Big Three (*Appendix 1*). And in products like igniters there were only so many final users; one of Cushman's assistants had estimated that the commercial airlines had a total fleet of around 3,000 planes and that there were about 15,000 private twin-engine jet planes in use in the U.S. But perhaps Midland could more aggressively pursue such markets as that for power mower spark plugs, or the larger engineered-products markets. Cushman thought:

I'm fond of this company and Kincaid, and I always enjoy our board meetings, but I should make this decision on a rational basis. It's a matter of whether Midland can be made a high growth company, with or without Kincaid, or whether it's just another attractive but unexciting small business.

EXHIBIT 1

MIDLAND SPARK PLUG CO., INC.
Balance Sheet
December 31, 1975 and 1974

Assets	*1975*	*1974*
Current Assets		
Cash	$ 47,353	$ 67,462
Accounts receivable—trade, less allowance for doubtful accounts, $3,500 each year	225,772	217,753
Inventories (Note 1)	967,081	978,907
Prepaid expenses	9,309	13,134
Total current assets	1,249,515	1,277,256
Cash surrender value—life insurance	78,717	74,340
Property, Plant, and Equipment, at cost (Note 1)		
Land and buildings	94,495	91,210
Machinery and equipment	413,334	416,950
Furniture and fixtures	15,465	12,618
Automobiles and trucks	1,825	1,825
	525,119	522,603
Less: Accumulated depreciation	382,436	368,554
Property, plant, and equipment—net	142,683	154,049
Other assets	425	425
	$1,471,340	$1,506,070

Liabilities and Stockholders' Equity		
Current Liabilities		
Notes payable:		
Stockholders		$ 80,000
Midland National Bank—Central		1,000
Accounts payable—trade	$ 59,040	128,025
Payroll taxes withheld and accrued	16,543	28,541
Federal and state income taxes	24,076	49,600
Accrued expenses	42,441	35,975
Total current liabilities	142,100	323,141
Stockholders' Equity		
Common stock—no par value; Authorized, 200 shares; Issued and outstanding, 116 shares	74,000	74,000
Paid-in capital	50,000	50 000
Retained earnings	1,205,240	1,058,929
Total stockholders' equity	1,329,240	1,182,929
	$1,471,340	$1,506,070

EXHIBIT 1 (Cont.)

MIDLAND SPARK PLUG CO., INC.
Statement of Income and Retained Earnings
Years Ended December 31, 1975 and 1974

	1975	*1974*
Gross sales	$3,148,578	$2,701,810
Less: Returns and allowances	93,280	13,870
Net Sales	3,055,298	2,687,940
Cost of goods sold	2,474,994	2,112,334
Gross profit	580,304	575,606
Selling and administrative expenses	274,125	248,371
Operating income	306,179	327,235
Other income		
Purchase discounts	4,314	5,200
Increase in life insurance cash value—net of premiums	1,521	2,466
Interest	19	1,126
Insurance premium refund and other	18,057	
Gain from sale of equipment	6,135	3,486
Total other income	30,046	12,278
	336,225	339,513
Other expenses		
Bad debts	704	1,288
Interest	1,607	874
Sales discounts	18,847	22,918
Total other expenses	21,158	25,080
NIBT Income before federal and state income taxes	315,067	314,433
Federal income taxes	118,614	127,260
Michigan State franchise tax	38,542	27,300
	157,156	154,560
Net income	157,911	159,873
Retained earnings—January 1	1,058,929	922,256
	1,216,840	1,082,129
Cash dividends per share, 1975—$100.00; 1974—$200.00	11,600	23,200
Retained earnings—December 31	$1,205,240	$1,058,929
Earnings per share	$ 1,361	$ 1,378

Note to Financial Statement

Note 1 Mr. Kincaid offered the following additional information in regard to liquidation values:

Date	*Inventory*	*Machinery*	*Auction Value of Fixed Assets*
9/30/61	$201,000	$102,000	$350,000*
12/31/75	960,000	120,000	500,000**

*Actual estimate by Botwinick of New Haven, a national auctioneer of general purpose machinery.
**Kincaid's own based on used equipment sales of certain hanger queens in 1974. This type of equipment on a used basis appreciates much more due to inflation than a straight line Schedule F depreciation reduction.

EXHIBIT 2 **(Oral) Resume of Jeffery Kincaid (May 1961)**

A *Present Situation*

1 Age: 36
2 Present position: Zone Manager, West Coast (responsible for eleven states), Air Conditioning Division, Giant Electric.
3 Present salary: $17,500 per year.
4 Net worth: $30,000 including equity in home.

B *Experience Before Joining Giant Electric*

1 1949.BS from Yale in engineering.
2 1950.MBA from Wharton in finance (completed MBA in 1½ years).
3 1950–1951. Salesman for Burroughs Corporation, Hartford, CT.
4 1951–1953. Served in the Air Force in Korea. Discharged as a Captain.

C *Record at Giant Electric*

1 1953–1954. Staff Assistant at headquarters Purchasing Department (studied reciprocity in purchasing at Giant Electric).
2 1954–1955. Buyer for the Transformer Division, Cleveland, Ohio.
3 1955. Assistant Purchasing Agent, Television & Radio Division, Erie, Pennsylvania.
4 1956–1957. OEM Sales Manager, Air Conditioning Division, Birmingham, Alabama.
5 1957–1958. Heat Pump Sales Manager, Air Conditioning Division (sent there to solve some problems with this new product; succeeded in doing so).
6 1958–1959. General Sales Manager, Packaged Products, Air Conditioning Division (packaged products amounted to about half of divisional sales).
7 1959–1961. Zone Manager, West Coast, Air Conditioning Division, Los Angeles (sent out to coordinate integration into Giant Electric of Frazer, Johnson Company, a new acquisition which had been causing problems for Giant Electric which Kincaid was able to solve).

EXHIBIT 3 **Midland Spark Plug Company Summary Income Data (1952–1960)**

Year	Gross Sales	Gross Profit		Selling and Administrative	Net Income After Other Income and Other Expenses (Before Federal Income Taxes)
		Amount	%		
1952	$2,044,475	$468,309	23.0	$297,257	$167,217
1953	2,305,214	506,999	22.0	316,946	181,217
1954	1,607,565	246,524	15.3	239,923	2,136
1955	1,650,585	246,529	14.1	236,356	1,980
1956	1,767,904	263,932	14.8	229,691	20,345
1957	1,749,954	295,233	16.9	259,652	23,175
1958	1,574,012	263,996	16.7	237,001	23,469
1959	1,801,963	342,658	19.0	265,001	75,308
1960*	1,197,153	309,763	26.9*	194,636	110,883

*Interim figures to 10/31/60 (ten months) subject to year-end audit.

EXHIBIT 4

WHY the new TORQUE-TIP® projected nose design is better for overhead valve engines

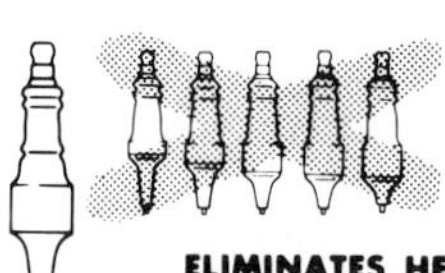

ELIMINATES HEAT RANGE PROBLEMS

The first spark plug suitable for both high speed and low speed operation, with top performance in either range. One plug takes the place of several standard nose type plugs.

RUNS HOTTER AT SLOW SPEEDS

Hot gas flow past projected nose heats plug up faster, prevents fouling by burning carbon and oil deposits away. You get: **• Smooth Idling • Reduced oil dilution • Flash starting • Faster pick-up • Better city gas mileage**

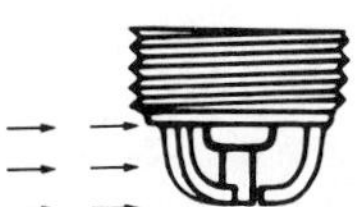

RUNS COOLER AT HIGH SPEEDS

The projected nose is fully exposed to the cooling action of air-fuel mixtures during open throttle driving. At high speeds this means: **• Pre-ignition is eliminated • No "high speed miss" • No overheating • Improved gas mileage**

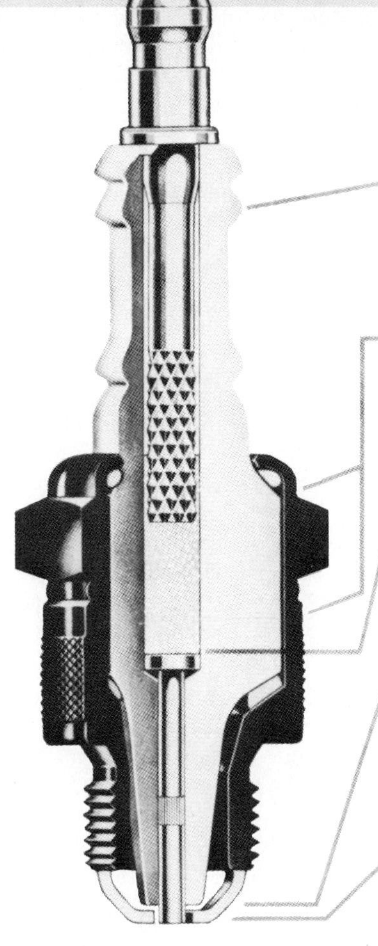

MULTI-RIB INSULATOR

Sure defense against flash-over.

HYDROLECTRIC HEAT-SEALED

This exclusive process gives positive assurance of a permanent gas-proof seal – not affected by heat or corrosion.

GLASS SEAL

Forms permanent lock against compression leakage.

NEW "ALLOY 524" ELECTRODE

An improved low sparking voltage nickel alloy. Resists burning away under any driving conditions. Maintains correct gap setting.

TRIPLE ELECTRODES

Three side electrodes (like an aircraft spark plug) instead of the usual one. More positive ignition for added power and gas mileage. Lengthens efficient spark plug life.

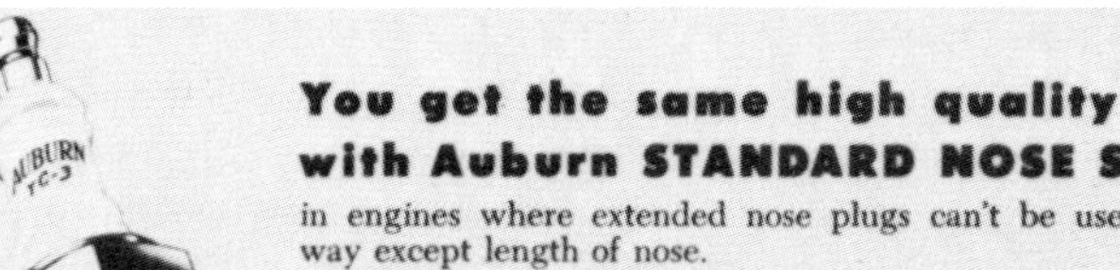

You get the same high quality construction with Auburn STANDARD NOSE SPARK PLUGS

in engines where extended nose plugs can't be used. Identical in every way except length of nose.

AUBURN TC-3
Triple Electrode

The ultimate in a high performance plug for toughest jobs and for long life without need for regapping.

SUPER AUBURN
Single Electrode

Finest spark plug made for regular duty in any vehicle or engine on or off the highway.

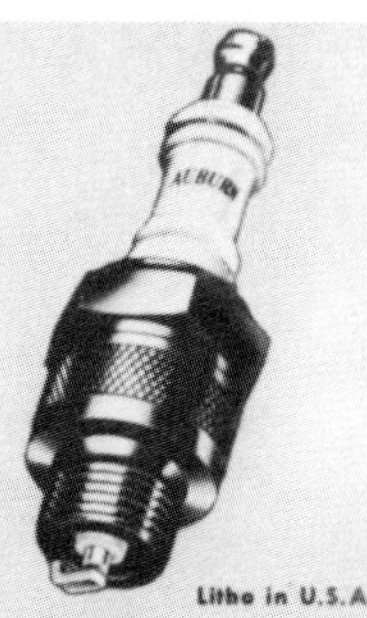

16

Litho in U.S.A.

EXHIBIT 5 Midland Spark Plug Company

Customer Profile Summary
(March 27, 1975)

Alladin Electric Company,
1203 Commercial Street,
Clinton, Pennsylvania,
Turbine Division.

- LOCATION—In Clinton, off Highway 203 (Exit 6) which connects to Commercial Street. A modest cab ride from Harrisburg Airport.
- ORGANIZATION—Constant turnover of non-supervisory personnel is the main difficulty in doing business on a consistent basis. Current contacts include:
  John (Jack) H. Deere (32?)—Purchasing (Buyer)
  —Single, conservative dresser, "very busy." New with Alladin and has only limited knowledge of product or application. Content to have correspondence directed to others with copy to him.
  —Supersedes Harold (Hal) Roberts, who in turn replaced Edward (Ed) Jones.
  James (Jim) Ellis (28?)—Engineering
  —Until six months ago was with turbine development at Boeing. Soft-spoken, flexible, authority unknown.
  Peter Marano (49?)—Service (Supervisor?)
  —Probably the most knowledgeable. Has the most experience—since 1959. Has most at stake since most of our sales are for resale to their aftermarket—he takes service function seriously. Has had problems with us and must be sold methodically and with hard data.
- METHOD OF DOING BUSINESS—Housed with two other divisions employing a total of about 3,000 people. Shielded igniters (with shielded harnesses) used for oil- and gas-fired small turbines which are built for stock with a price tag under $2 million each.
- PRODUCT HISTORY—Have been using the AEJ-39-22-3; have had few problems with them though they're getting tired of the ones they do have with their ground electrodes breaking and with poor service.

  As a result of this, Green and King derived three designs—the IT-35 (to combine with another customer's requirements), the IT-36 (directly interchangeable), and the IT-37 (to eliminate need for extension rods). Going back to initial visit in Clinton (5/30/71), and subsequently on numerous occasions, we have been on record as changing to a heavier-duty design.
  —In essence, this approach never seriously considered as interchangeability for field replacement was always the over-riding factor. The result was "giving the customer what we thought he wanted," carrying along all the old disadvantages with an escalating cost—a "flat" unit (AEJ-39-22-3) price of $1.30 to quantitative pricing on the IT-35 ($1.55 in lots of 1,000).
  —Total Annual purchases included:
  1972: $1,516 1973: $2,874 1974: $4,843
- PURCHASE POTENTIAL—While customer is willing to pay a higher OEM price, the real potential is in direct replacement sales to users. At present, the IT-37 has one of the highest user prices ($19.75) and profitability of any item we make.
- FUTURE COURSES OF ACTION
  Hopefully, the meeting of 3/18/75 (see Mr. King's trip report) accomplished objective of hastening Alladin's perceived need for the IT-35 series. It will perhaps give us time to come up with new design incorporating heavier electrodes and all-ceramic insulation on a non-crash basis and eliminate interim "band-aid" requests arising from field complaints.

EXHIBIT 6 Engineered Products (Aftermarket Sales Summary)

Year	*To Users*	*To Distributors*	*Combined Total*	*% Change*
1963	$ 7,465	$ 9,060	$ 16,525	
1964	8,074	13,119	21,193	(+28%)
1965	12,064	14,644	26,708	(+73%)
1966	16,512	10,842	27,354	(+ 6%)
1967	22,673	14,109	36,782	(+34%)
1968	23,403	16,191	39,594	(+ 8%)
1969	42,605	29,605	72,210	(+82%)
1970	55,132	38,165	93,297	(+29%)
1971	66,114	45,331	111,445	(+19%)
1972	83,833	49,668	133,501	(+20%)
1973	108,941	87,411	196,352	(+47%)
1974	122,573	92,113	214,686	(+ 9%)
1975	100,229	121,972	222,201	(+ 4%)
1976 (6 mos.)	60,798	72,711	135,509	

EXHIBIT 7
GREAT LAKES CAPITAL CORPORATION—MILWAUKEE
A Representative Sample of the Company's Investment Portfolio
March 31, 1975

		Dates of Investment		Notes Receivable at Cost	Stock			Total Investment at Cost	Fair Value[1]
		First	Last		Number of Stores	Great Lakes %	Cost		
Masonton Industries, Inc. Greenville, Ohio	Fire and security communications systems for commercial and residential buildings	9/61	12/73	$ 669,784	250	50.0%	$ 25,000	$ 694,784	$ 300,000
Midland Spark Plug, Co. Midland, Michigan	Proprietary electrical devices, spark plugs and screw machine products	9/61	—	—	30	25.5%	$ 30,000	$ 30,000	$ 306,000
Dennis Metals, Inc. Dexter, Oklahoma	Steel pressure tubing for heat exchanges used in refineries and power plants	9/73	12/74	$1,800,000	2,500	50.0%	$ 500,000	$2,300,000	$2,871,000
Kowan Pneumatics, Inc. Waco, Texas	Pumps and blowers	4/72	11/74	$1,092,023	806,783	39.1%	$1,022,489	$2,114,512	$2,114,512
Corba Electric Co. Fairport, Rhode Island	Electric components for diverse international markets	2/75	—	$1,941,707	—	—	—	$1,941,707	$1,941,707
Sand Springs Industries, Inc. Tucson, Arizona	Diversifed recreation company	2/62	—	—	48,000	31.8%	$ 141,702	$ 141,702	$ 963,500
Park Avenue Fashions, Inc. New York, New York	Ladies ready-to-wear clothing	9/61	11/73	$ 742,000	250	50.0%	$ 25,000	$ 767,000	$ 623,000
Concrete Systems, Inc. Hayward, Missouri	Concrete pipes for the construction industry	8/73	3/75	$ 600,000	45,975	48.1%	$ 150,000	$ 750,000	$ 150,000
Mobile Cola Bottling Co., Inc. Mobile, Alabama	Franchise to bottle soft drinks	7/69	4/73	—	31,592	100.0%	$3,078,250	$3,078,250	—

[1]All securities have been evaluated as of March 31, 1975 at their "fair values" as determined in good faith by the Board of Directors pursuant to the Investment Company Act of 1940. Such fair values do not reflect in some cases the amounts that could be realized upon an immediate sale nor the amounts that may ultimately be realized, which may be more or less. Nor do such fair values reflect taxes which might be incurred upon disposition. In establishing the fair value of portfolio securities, the Board of Directors has taken into consideration financial statements showing the financial condition and operating results of the portfolio companies, prices paid in private sales of such securities, market prices paid in public sales of unrestricted securities of the same class, the nature and duration of restrictions on disposition of the securities, the expenses and delays that would be involved in registration, the price and extent of public trading in similar securities of the portfolio company or comparable companies, the existence of merger proposals or tender offers affecting the securities, reports prepared by analysts and other pertinent information.

APPENDIX 1
FORD MOTOR COMPANY VS. UNITED STATES ET AL.

APPEAL FROM THE UNITED STATES DISTRICT COURT FOR THE EASTERN DISTRICT OF MICHIGAN
No. 70-113. Argued November 18, 1971—Decided March 29, 1972.

In 1961, Ford Motor Company acquired certain assets of Autolite in order to gain entry into the spark plug aftermarket. The government filed a complaint alleging a Clayton 7 violation.[1] The Michigan Eastern District Court found against Ford and ordered it to divest of its Autolite assets. On appeal to the U.S. Supreme Court, Ford again lost. Following are some excerpts from the Supreme Court decision which was delivered by Mr. Justice Douglas.

Describing the spark plug market, Mr. Justice Douglas said:

> The original equipment of new cars, insofar as spark plugs are concerned, is conveniently referred to as the OE tie. The independents, including Autolite, furnished the auto manufacturers with OE plugs at cost or less, about six cents a plug, and they continued to sell at that price even when their costs increased threefold. The independents sought to recover their losses on OE sales by profitable sales in the aftermarket where the requirement of each vehicle during its lifetime is about five replacement plug sets. By custom and practice among mechanics, the aftermarket plug is usually the same brand as the OE plug. . . . When Ford acquired Autolite, whose share of the domestic spark plug market was about 15%, only one major independent was left and that was Champion, whose share of the domestic market declined from just under 50% in 1960 to just under 40% in 1964 and to about 33% in 1966. At the time of the acquisition, General Motors' market share was about 30%. There were other small manufacturers of spark plugs but they had no important share of the market.[2]

Mr. Justice Douglas then quoted the District Court's judgment (the subject of the appeal):

> "Ford's acquisition of the Autolite assets, particularly when viewed in the context of the original equipment (OE) tie and of GM's ownership of AC, has the result of transmitting the rigidity of the oligopolistic structure of the automobile industry to the spark plug industry, thus reducing the chances of future deconcentration of the spark plug market by forces at work within that market. . . ."

[1]Section 7 provides in part: "No corporation engaged in commerce shall acquire, directly or indirectly, the whole or any part of the stock or other share capital and no corporation subject to the jurisdiction of the Federal Trade Commission shall acquire the whole or any part of the assets of another corporation engaged also in commerce, where in any line of commerce in any section of the country, the effect of such acquisition may be substantially to lessen competition or to tend to create a monopoly." 38 Stat. 731, as amended, 64 Stat. 1125, 15 U.S.C. 18.

[2]Autolite did not sell all of its assets to Ford and changed the name of the parts of its business that it retained to Eltra Corp. which in 1962 began manufacturing spark plugs in Decatur, Alabama, under the brand name Prestolite. But in 1964 it had only 1.6% of the domestic business. Others included Atlas, sponsored by Standard Oil of N.J., with 1.4% of that business, and Riverside, sponsored by Montgomery Ward, with 0.6%. As further stated by the District Court: "Most of the manufacturing for the private labels among these marketers is done by ELTRA and General Battery and Ceramic Corporation, the only producers of any stature at all after the Big Three." 286 F. Supp. 407, 435.

He continued:

It is obviously in the self-interest of OE plug manufacturers to discourage private-brand sales and to encourage the OE tie. There are findings that the private-brand sector of the spark plug market will grow substantially in the next decade because mass merchandisers are entering this market in force. They not only sell all brands over the counter but also have service bays where many carry only spark plugs of their own proprietary brand. It is anticipated that by 1980 the total private brand portion of the spark plug market may then represent 17% of the total aftermarket.

The District Court noted:

"To the extent that the spark [plug] manufacturers are not owned by the auto makers, it seems clear that they will be more favorably disposed toward private brand sales and will compete more vigorously for such sales. Also, the potential entrant continues to have the chance to sell not only the private brand customer but the auto maker as well." [315 F. Supp., at 378.]

Mr. Justice Stewart, concurring in the decision, said:

The habit among mechanics of installing replacement plugs carrying the same brand as the automobile's original plugs, reinforced by the unwillingness of service stations to stock more than two or three brands,[3] made possible the 'OE tie,' which rendered any large-scale entry into the aftermarket virtually impossible without first obtaining a large OE customer. Moreover, price competition was minimal, both in the OE market (where any reduction in the six-cent price would immediately be matched by rivals), and in the aftermarket (where spark plugs accounted for such a small percentage of the normal tuneup charge that price differentials did not have a significant impact upon consumer choice).

Mr. Chief Justice Burger, concurring in part and dissenting in part, in his remarks on the continued domination of the plug market by the Big Three, said:

Thus, it takes a position as supplier to a large auto maker to gain recognition in the spark plug replacement market. The Government conceded in the District Court, for instance, that American Motors, with 5% of the auto market, would not be able to create market acceptance for an independent brand of plug by installing it as original equipment in its cars.

The Chief Justice commented:

The strength of the OE tie is demonstrated by the inability of well-known auto supply manufacturers to gain a significant share of the spark plug market in the absence of an OE tie. As the District Court found, no company without the OE tie ". . . ever surpassed the 2% level. Several have come and gone. Firestone Tire and Rubber

[3]According to a 1966 survey, only 11% of all metropolitan area service stations stocked any brand of spark plug other than Champion, AC, or Autolite, and only 30% stocked all three of the leading brands.

> Company merchandised Firestone replacements for 35 years before it gave up in 1964. Although it owned some 800 accessory stores and successfully wholesaled other items to more than 50,000 shops and filling stations, it could not surmount the patent discrimination against brands not blessed with Detroit's approbation. Goodyear Tire and Rubber Company quit in only 3 years. Globe Union, a fabricator which had barely 1% of the nation's shipments, withdrew in 1960." [286 F. Supp. 407, 434–435.]
>
> Two small manufacturers survive, producing plugs for private-label brands. Thus 'Atlas' plugs, sponsored by the Standard Oil companies, has 1.4% of the replacement market; 'Prestolite' and Sears, Roebuck's 'Allstate' each have 1.2%; and Montgomery Ward's 'Riverside' Label has 0.6% of the replacement market. . . . With respect to Autolite itself, the District Court made several relevant findings. First, it found that Autolite is a fixed-production plant. In other words, it can be profitable only turning out approximately the number of plugs it now manufactures. It could not, for instance, reduce its production by half and sell that at a profit.

Then, commenting on the plug market and its distribution system, Mr. Chief Justice Burger continued:

> There is another set of relevant facts found by the District Court. The District Judge found that "there is a rising wind of new forces in the spark plug market which may profoundly change it." [315 F. Supp. 372, 377.] On the basis of the testimony of an executive of one of the producers of plugs for private labels, the court found that the private-brand sector would grow during the next ten years.
>
> This highly speculative observation of the District Court was based on a finding that the mass merchandisers are beginning to enter the plug marketing field in force. Not only do the mass merchandisers market private-brand plugs over the counter, but they are also building service bays. And in these bays many carry only their own proprietary brand of spark plugs. This witness predicted that the mass merchandisers would increase their share of the aftermarket from 4.4% to 10% by 1980. He further predicted that oil companies would enter the replacement market, resulting in a total of 17% of the replacement market being supplied by private-label plugs by 1980. The court concluded that these forces "may well lead to [the market's] eventual deconcentration by increasing the number of potential customers for a new entrant into the plug manufacturing business and reducing the need for original equipment identification." [315 F. Supp., at 378.]

However, in his final remarks, Mr. Burger said, "The District Court's suggestion that Autolite can find a niche supplying private-brand labels is unpersuasive. It cannot be predicted with any certainty that these sales outlets will grow to the extent predicted by one person in that line of the business. . . ."

N.V. PHILIPS' GLOEILAMPENFABRIEKEN (ABRIDGED)

In April, 1973, the three co-managers of the TV Article Group of Philips Electrical Limited—Mr. Ian Benton, Commercial Manager, Mr. George Franklin, Technical Manager, and Mr. Harold Crawford, Financial and Administrative Manager—were scheduled to meet with senior management of the Philips U.K. organization and with managers from other concerned operating units to decide how Philips should compete for the rapidly growing color television market in the United Kingdom. Mr. Benton described the problem they faced:

> Our problem is this. In our opinion, 1973 through 1975 are going to be cream years for color TV in the U.K. We are eager to exploit this demand and to regain some of our market share while the opportunity presents itself.
>
> Since we are now at capacity, it will be necessary for Philips to invest in additional manufacturing facilities and stocks to compete for this business. The volatility of the U.K. TV market in the past, however, has made senior management cautious with respect to it.
>
> We in the U.K. TV Article Group are close to this market and are convinced as to the soundness of our projections. The potential profits from this coming boom market more than offset the risks.

Mr. T. L. Koelman, Commercial Manager of the Video Main Industry Group (located in Eindhoven, Holland), was also scheduled to attend the meeting. He opposed the proposed expansion for the U.K. TV operation on the following grounds:

> Ian Benton is a very enthusiastic marketer who, by and large, is doing a good job for Philips in the U.K. In this instance, we believe that he and his Article Group colleagues have tended to overreact to the market when they boosted their forecasts of the market and Philips's share by some 15%. The U.K. has long been characterized by huge swings in demand and is a very difficult market to forecast.
>
> If we expand output and the market fails to materialize, Philips could lose money. The worst that would happen in holding at our present level is that the Group might have to sacrifice a little of its market share and to shave a bit off profits for 1973.
>
> The picture gets complicated when you put the U.K. into a broader perspective. Demand for color TV is going up in other countries as well, and it is part of my responsibility to see that the Philips concern allocates its resources in proper balance on a worldwide scale. While the U.K. is today the largest color TV market in Europe, Philips's long-term plans for TV rest heavily on other national markets as well.

This case was prepared by Professor Francis J. Aguilar as the basis for class discussion rather than to illustrate either effective or ineffective handling of an administrative situation. The names of all individuals have been disguised.

The contents of this case come from the following materials: Introductory Note to N.V. Philips' Gloeilampenfabrieken, 9-374-032; N.V. Philips' Gloeilampenfabrieken (B), 9-374-033; and N. V. Philips' Gloeilampenfabrieken (C), 9-374-034.

N.V. PHILIPS

N.V. Philips was founded in 1891 by Gerard Philips, a Dutch engineer who had developed an inexpensive process to manufacture incandescent lamps. The following account describes the firm's early successes:

> By 1914, Philips was Europe's largest producer of light bulbs. During the 1930s the company was the primary exporting member of the European light bulb cartel. In 1918, Philips entered the electronic tube business, and by the late 1930s it boasted 20% of the world's market for receivers.[1]

By 1972, N.V. Philips' Gloeilampenfabrieken had become the fourth-largest industrial company outside the United States and was reputedly the world's most widely known manufacturer of household appliances, television and radio sets, professional electronic equipment, lighting, and related products. *Exhibit 1* lists the company's major products and the sales volume for each product division.

The company had several hundred subsidiaries in 60 countries and operated plants in more than 40 countries (more than 200 plants in Europe) manufacturing thousands of different products. Of Philips's approximately 370,000 employees at the end of 1972, 45,000 worked in or near Eindhoven (site of the company's headquarters), another 52,000 in other locations in the Netherlands, 198,000 in other Western European countries, and 75,000 elsewhere. In 1972, 70% of corporate sales were made in Europe, 19% in other Western Hemisphere countries, and 11% throughout the rest of the world.

Although Philips's sales showed impressive growth between 1960 and 1972, profits were disappointing. The seriousness of the failure to increase earnings was reported as follows:

> Philips Lamps may not be the most puzzling enigma in world business, but it is certainly the biggest. Few companies, even in the United States, have devoted more effort to the scientific, productive and managerial technology of their businesses. Few, either by luck or design, have engaged in so attractive a range of fast-growing markets: color TV, data processing, audio equipment, communications—in such as these Philips has positions ranging from promising to dominant, founded, what is more, on the strongest geographic areas. Its product reputation is unsurpassed, and its brand-name (in stark contrast to a British group like GEC) runs worldwide. Yet the financial record of the past decade, the result by which management is supposed to be judged and to judge itself, is dismal. Between 1962 and 1971 sales all but trebled: yet 1971 profits were exactly the same as those of 1962 (if, that is, Philips is given the benefit of some helpful changes in applying its accounting principles in 1971).
>
> This fall from financial grace can't be blamed solely on the particularly miserable conditions of 1971 and 1970, when earnings fell by 34% and 16% respectively. Even in 1969, the former record year, sales were higher by two-and-one-half times compared to seven years before: but profits were only up by half.[2]

[1]*Business Week*, January 13, 1973, p. 66.
[2]*Management Today*, April 1973, p. 71.

The same article listed several reasons for the firm's poor profits: A sharp rise in costs led by a round of major wage increases for all its Dutch employees in 1970; a lag in demand because of economic recession in many countries; an increased interest burden for the company because of added debt to finance growth; and continuing company losses in its data processing business. On this last point, the article stated: "The big new data processing division was operating at a loss: its costs, about 1% of total turnover, are directly debited to the profit and loss account." Philips's cumulative bookkeeping loss on computers had exceeded $150 million through the end of 1971.

As can be seen in the financial review contained in *Exhibit 2,* Philips experienced a major improvement of earnings in 1972, moving the profit margin from 2.1% to 3.4%. (This compared to an estimated 6% or so for ITT-Europe, 5% for General Electric, and 3.8% for Westinghouse.) While pointing to a number of uncertainties for 1973—momentary unrest, inflation, and social tensions in important markets—the 1972 annual report predicted further improvement for the year to come.

THE PHILIPS ORGANIZATION IN THE U.K.

Philips Electronic and Associated Industries Limited (Philips Industries, Limited), one of the largest national organizations in N.V. Philips' Gloeilampenfabrieken, comprised several separate business units. Philips Electrical Limited, as one of these units, was responsible for the manufacture and sale of the company's line of consumer electrical products (articles) such as television, radio, phonographs, appliances, and lighting. The TV Article Group was responsible for the assembly and sales of both monochrome and color TV in the U.K. and accounted for a significant portion of Philips Electrical Limited's total sales in 1972. This dominant role of TV in the U.K. organization reflected the worldwide situation within the consumer companies for the total Philips concern.

The U.K. TV Article management team maintained close liaison with the Video Main Industry Group in Eindhoven, which was responsible for Philips's worldwide TV product policy. These managers also worked closely with Mullard Limited, since they relied on this sister company for most of the major components used to manufacture television sets—such as picture tubes, transformers, transistors and capacitors. (*Exhibit 3* shows the Philips organization as it related to the TV Article Group in the U.K.)

THE EARLY HISTORY OF MONOCHROME TELEVISION IN THE U.K.

The U.K. was one of the first countries in Europe to have TV on a major scale. This early popularity of TV in the U.K. was attributed primarily to the excellence of the British Broadcasting Corporation, a recognized pioneer in both transmission and programming. One Philips executive noted:

> The U.K. consumer came to see TV as a service. There was no snob appeal attached to TV in the U.K. as there was in other European countries. Once people got a set, they found it indispensable and were unhappy to be without a picture for even a single evening.

The high original cost of a television set, which was beyond the reach of most British families, was one of several reasons giving rise in the 1950s to a peculiarly British industry practice, television rentals. As one executive in the industry put it, "The average Englishman figured that he was buying nightly entertainment at ten bob a week. That was a price he could understand and a price he was willing to pay."

With rentals, the customer was also protected from repair costs. In this early period of television, the incidence of malfunction was relatively high and the quality of service generally available was spotty at best. Renting companies were obliged to provide rapid repair service if they were not to forfeit rentals.

It was generally agreed in the industry that renting did much to stimulate the growth of the U.K. television market. In addition to its impact on volume, the practice of renting sets also influenced greatly the nature of the television business in the U.K. The demands by renting companies for inexpensive, trouble-free television sets resulted in the design of less complicated circuitry and in the production of fewer chassis models and cabinet styles in comparison to the output on the European continent. Moreover, the sale of large volumes of TV sets to a relatively small number of firms and the widespread practice among renting companies to label TV sets with their own names in place of manufacturer brand names tended to alter the character of marketing activities in the U.K.

IMPACT OF GOVERNMENT REGULATION

While TV sales were sensitive to the general health of the British economy, they were extremely sensitive to governmental regulations of consumer credit directed at curbing sales of so-called luxury products. Mr. Robin Wright, head of commercial research for Philips Electrical Limited, described the impact of government regulations on the TV market:

> In planning for TV, once you have decided how many consumers may want to buy a product in a certain period, the most important step is to judge what the government will do, to what extent and exactly when—an extremely difficult task on which any two executives can disagree. It is also difficult because government's decisions are made on political as well as economic considerations.
>
> One of the basic weapons used in the last twenty-five years by the government to regulate the economy has been consumer credit. For example, in an effort to stimulate consumer demand in 1958, the government abolished all controls on the size of deposit and the period of repayment for hire-purchase of consumer durables and for TV rental contracts. The result was that the demand for monochrome TV shot up overnight. While the industry was expecting the government to take some such action, it did not anticipate it to be nearly so dramatic as it turned out to be. Philips, along with everyone else in the industry, lost sales as a result.
>
> Then in 1959, the entire industry expanded manufacturing capacity to serve what was to be a period of rapid growth during the first half of the 1960s. TV stocks had reached an all-time high when the government unexpectedly announced in April, 1960, the re-establishment of credit controls, with the result that demand dropped way off. The market was further perturbed in 1960 with the formation of the Pilkington Committee, which was to study technical standards for future television sets.

> The prospects of major technical changes helped to discourage sales even more. The entire TV industry in the U.K. was faced with a catastrophic situation with a 34% sales decrease within one year and a 45% sales decrease for the two-year period 1960 and 1961.
>
> By mid-1967 it was still the view of economists, government officials and businessmen that the U.K. economy would take a long time to recover, so the entire industry planned conservatively. Then, to everybody's surprise, the government eased up on its consumer credit controls in the autumn of 1967 and stimulated a substantial increase in television sales. However, within two months the government was forced to devalue the pound. Everybody anticipated that the government would tighten up consumer credit again in order to keep home consumption down and to stimulate exports. But the government made no such move for the best part of twelve months, and in the meantime television sales continued to rise. The company lost market share in 1968 because of our conservative stance and because of our inability to jack up production.

Exhibit 4 lists government regulation of consumer credit in the United Kingdom between 1955 and 1971.

COLOR TV PRODUCT DEVELOPMENT

N.V. Philips first undertook research in color television in 1951. Ten years later, the Video Main Industry Group began pre-development work on color television. Its objective was to develop a color TV chassis (the term used in the industry to refer to the internal configuration of the set) which could be sold in all European markets. This approach was based on the assumption that Europe would adopt a common system for broadcasting television. By 1966, however, it had become apparent that more than one color TV system would emerge within Europe and that each system would call for a particular circuitry in the receiving set. Ian Benton described the reactions of the U.K. TV Article Group to the emerging differences in color TV transmission:

> By 1966, it had become increasingly apparent to us that the work being done in Eindhoven on color TV would not really meet the needs of the U.K. market. There were certain unique problems that we had to face in the U.K. For example, the changeover from VHF to UHF transmission presented certain problems in product design. This changeover was not to be completed until 1971, and in the interim we had to produce a set which could handle both transmissions. For this reason alone we had to take the prototype chassis developed in Eindhoven and modify it for the U.K. market.
>
> As had happened with monochrome television, we found that we had to satisfy very different market conditions from those on the Continent. There, color TV sets were sold as prestige items and were consequently designed with all the extras. For example, as a piece of decorator furniture, it was considered important to make the TV set less boxy in appearance. Consequently, Eindhoven made a considerable effort to develop a 110° deflector picture tube in place of the standard 90° tube so that this component, which controlled the depth of a TV set, could be shortened. In the U.K., the depth of a TV set was unimportant.
>
> Other requirements in the U.K. also stood in marked contrast. For example, poor

> reception in certain localities on the Continent because of mountainous terrain and spotty transmission coverage called for a more sensitive tuning capability for the set than was required in the U.K., where excellent, strong signals were to be found. Moreover, our principal customers, the renting firms, were interested in only two things: low purchase price and dependable performance, which in turn meant low maintenance costs. We were told that the TV set would have to cost less than—let's say £100—and require no more than two service calls per year on the average.
>
> These requirements called for the simplest circuitry design possible. By 1968, we decided to proceed on our own to design an all-transistor color TV which would stress ease of manufacture, reliability of performance, and ease of service in the U.K. market. Admittedly, these sets manufactured in the U.K. can be used only in the U.K.

The U.K. TV Article Group employed about 300 design and production engineers.

COLOR TELEVISION IN THE U.K.

Color television was introduced into the U.K. in 1967. However, it failed to grow as rapidly as hoped for in the industry for several years. At the outset, only BBC 2 was authorized to transmit color programs. Since almost all of the popular programs were to be found in the BBC 1 and ITV channels, interest in changing from monochrome to color was effectively reduced. The government indicated that BBC 1 and ITV would be authorized to begin color transmission possibly by late 1969. Only in mid-1969 did the government finally confirm these plans, opening the way for a surge in demand for color television sets.

The renting companies were considered by the industry to have provided a major impetus for the rapid upturn in color TV sales in 1969. By not increasing the required down payment and simply raising the weekly rentals payment from 50p to 150p, these companies were able to trade up their customers from monochrome to color sets. Mr. Wright noted the effect of the rental practice on buying behavior and one implication for Philips:

> The fact that renting has dominated the U.K. TV market for so many years has led to a situation where there is now more distribution loyalty than brand loyalty on the part of the consumer. The consumer first asks himself or herself whether to rent or buy. The next question is, "What store?" The last question is, "What brand?" Consequently, we do little advertising for our product. For the past twelve years, specialist rental companies have been responsible for 75% to 80% of all TV product advertising expenditures in the press or on the air.

Government credit controls also played a key role in shaping the demand curve for color TV. In July 1971, the government once again abolished all controls on consumer credit. This unexpected decision caused an explosive growth in demand which the industry had not anticipated. The progress of color TV sales in the U.K. is shown in *Table 1*.

While Philips's sales of color TV in the U.K. had increased each year, its share of market began to slip in 1970 along with that of all British TV manufacturers. As with monochrome TV, this decline in market share was attributed in part to imports resulting

TABLE 1 Color TV Movements in the U.K. (thousands of units)

Year	Manufacturers' Sales	Consumer Offtake**
1967	30	20
1968	120	80
1969	155	170
1970	510	410
1971*	915	980
1972	1,780	1,680

*At mid-1971, the annual rates for sales and offtake were only 680 and 550, respectively.
**The television industry in the U.K. referred to consumer offtake as the volume of sets distributed to the final consumer either through purchase or on a rental basis.
Source: Company interview.

from the U.K. manufacturers' inability to satisfy demand. In 1972, Thorn held about one-third of the British color TV market. Philips, Pye, RBM, GEC, and the remaining British manufacturers as a group each held about 10% market share. Imports, which had increased dramatically from a negligible level in 1970, accounted for the remainder.

The nature of color TV imports into the U.K. was described in the following account of the industry:

> Imports in the last quarter of 1972 were around one-third of the market. They were concentrated in two areas, smaller sets being sold by the Japanese, Sony, Hitachi and National in particular, and the top of the market European brands, Grundig, Bang and Olufson, and Saba. However, there was a heavy proportion of mass market sets imported from a variety of sources in order to meet the U.K. production shortfall.[3]

As far as Philips was concerned, another factor contributing to its declining market share was the takeover of several independent distributors by other TV manufacturers. Thorn Electrical Industries had been particularly active in integrating forward into TV distribution and by the late 1960s had acquired four rental companies with about 1,000 specialty rental shops, as well as a 300-shop retail chain, in all accounting for about 19% of total U.K. monochrome sales and 24% of color.[4] Philips had a financial interest in two rental companies and a 600-store retail chain.

[3] *Financial Times*, July 12, 1973.

[4] Thorn Electrical Limited held a commanding lead in market share for both monochrome and color TV in the U.K. The year 1972 (ending March 31, 1973) was reported as its most successful, with profits before taxes of £70 million. *The Economist* tempered its report (July 21, 1973) of the company's positive performance and prospects with the following observation:

> The main reservations about Thorn are over what happens to the company after Sir Jules Thorn retires. He is 74. There is nobody on the board specifically from the rental side. And the 1972 accounts show that no employee outside the board earns over £10,000—not even among the top management of Radio Rentals and DER, the two largest television rental companies in the country. The Japanese threat is less important for Thorn than other manufacturers because of its vertical integration into rentals. The shares are a bargain, but is the future management?

THE 1973 COLOR TV OUTPUT TARGET

In December 1972, Benton, Franklin, Crawford and Wright met to discuss the TV Article Group's 1973 plans for color TV. Their recommendation to increase the production level about 15% per year had met resistance from other quarters in Philips. In recent weeks, even the 15% increase had begun to look inadequate for the demand these men anticipated for 1973. In view of this situation, they saw two alternatives before them: 1) to build a convincing case for the new sales forecast and hence for the expanded manufacturing capacity so that Philips could begin to increase its market share; or 2) to reassess pricing and TV set allocation policies in line with a likely shortage of color TV sets in 1973. They decided to press for expanded capacity so that Philips could compete aggressively for increased sales.

Discussions leading to a 1973 color TV output target had begun as early as April, 1972, when the Article management team had forecast its annual requirement for sets. Mounting sales during the summer and the expectation that the mid-1971 impetus to sales would carry over into 1972 and 1973 had led the TV Article Group to revise its market estimates upward.

During a September, 1972, meeting between Philips Electrical, Video Main Industry Group, Philips Industries, Mullard and Elcoma (see *Exhibit 3*), resistance mounted to expanding the Philips production output for 1973.

Ian Benton argued for still further expansion in 1973 on the following grounds:

> The U.K. is the largest and fastest-growing color TV market in Europe. This market is now developing faster than even the U.S. market did [see *Exhibit 5*].
>
> There are 18 million households in the U.K. By the end of 1972, 17% of these homes had a color set. With industry sales now reaching between 2 and 3 million sets per year, we will have several great years before saturation sets in. In view of our participation in rental and retail companies, it is not as if we do not have a good feel for market demand. We also have a few very large accounts, all of whom are willing to sign up for a considerably larger number of sets than we are now scheduled to sell.
>
> It is important to make these decisions early since it would take Mullard the greater part of a year to increase manufacturing capacity. We cannot expect Mullard to divert components to us that it had planned to supply other TV set manufacturers.

OTHER VIEWPOINTS

The U.K. TV expansion decision involved several other operating units in the Philips organization. As a consequence, these other units—Video Main Industry Group, Elcoma, and Mullard (see *Exhibit 3*)—were entitled to voice their positions concerning the decision. (*Appendix A* describes the N.V. Philips organization and its decision-making approach based on "coordination and consultation.") In general, these units opposed the proposed expansion—for various reasons.

The Video Main Industry Group View

In line with its worldwide profit responsibilities for television, the Video Main Industry Group management, located in Eindhoven, was active in planning production capacity for

TV throughout the Philips concern. For factories producing for local markets, the Video Group played an advisory role concerning investment proposals which went before the Central Capital Investment Committee in Eindhoven. Such capacity decisions were made in close conformity with those of Elcoma, which produced the picture tubes and most of the remaining components for television. Mr. T. L. Koelman, Commercial Manager of the Video Main Industry Group, noted:

> In allocating capital for new capacity, the Video Main Industry Group's major objective is to maximize the profits of the Philips concern as a whole and not necessarily the profits of any one national organization. Part of our analysis deals with optimizing the utilization of the plant capacity we already have. We are also constrained by Elcoma's investment decisions, since in time of rapid growth the availability of components often serves as a limiting factor. The situation in the U.K. for color television is a good case in point as to how these various elements influence our decisions concerning a major expansion of production capacity.

The Video Main Industry Group's decision to oppose an increase in the color television production capacity for the U.K. was based on several factors, some to do with the nature of the British television market and some with the Group's broad plans for Philips. Mr. T. L. Koelman commented on these reasons:

> We consider the U.K. television market particularly risky compared to other European countries for two principal reasons. The first of these stems from the dominant role played by the specialty rental companies in the U.K. For one thing, many of these rental companies are owned by manufacturing firms, thereby reducing the size of the market in which other companies can freely compete. For example, Thorn Electrical, which has almost 40% of the television market, controls about 40% of the captive rental outlets.
>
> Another disturbing aspect of the specialty rental companies is the ephemeral nature of their commitment to the manufacturer. In times of shortage, the rental companies will be most accommodating and accept most anything that is offered. At the first sign of a downturn, however, or in a period of oversupply, these companies can pressure a manufacturer with respect to price and to the terms of sale. After all, a rental company purchasing 120,000 sets from you in one year is under no commitment to buy 120,000 sets, or for that matter, any sets from you the following year. There are 6 to 8 rental companies controlling a major part of the non-captive market and 5 large manufacturers competing for their business. A TV manufacturer's share of market can fluctuate between 5% and 20% from one week to the next, depending on purchases from the rental companies.
>
> In contrast, a market share in Germany or elsewhere on the Continent is based on a consumer franchise. In these cases Philips can hold on to its market share from year to year. The consumer franchise in the U.K. is minimal, since most rental companies place their own brand name on the sets we supply them. In any event, brand name does not weigh heavily in the consumer purchase of a television in the U.K.
>
> Prices have not deteriorated too much in the U.K. so far, because of the short supply that has existed in recent years. Forecasts indicate, however, that the peak year for color television will be 1973 and that demand will begin to slow down in 1974. If past history is anything to go on, chances are excellent that prices will fall faster than demand in the U.K. From a Philips concern point of view, this makes other

European markets much more attractive. We believe that we can control prices on the Continent far better than in the U.K.

The second major problem with the U.K. market is the extreme difficulty associated with making accurate forecasts there. Since 1957, the U.K. market has been subject to violent swings in demand for consumer durables and TV in particular because of regulations by the British government controlling consumer credit. In 1961, we found ourselves with 150,000 monochrome sets in excess stock in the U.K. after the government had unexpectedly restricted consumer credit.

Since last June, Ian Benton has already revised his estimates of TV sales 3 times. Color TV sales for 1973 are now running at a level of 2.75 million sets for the year. Should the government decide that the economy is overheating and reinstitute consumer credit controls, the level of sales could easily drop by 1 million sets per year.

The efficient utilization of Philips's worldwide plant capacity was another reason why Video Main Industry Group management opposed the U.K. expansion. Mr. Koelman explained:

Our decision for the U.K. is also influenced by the current situation elsewhere in Philips and by our plans for the future. Specifically, we expect to have an excess capacity in one factory on the Continent in 1973, and it would be to Philips's overall benefit to utilize that capacity rather than to build new capacity in the U.K. Benton complains that the sets from this factory would be more expensive than those produced in the U.K. and that he would not be able to sell them at a satisfactory profit margin. Admittedly, these sets are overdesigned according to Benton's specifications and consequently more expensive. However, given the shortage of TVs in the U.K., I feel certain that he would have no difficulty in selling them at a profit.

Both Thorn Electrical and Sony have recently announced major capital expenditure programs for increasing capacity in the U.K. Unfortunately, it is very difficult to predict what effect these proposed expansions will have on Philips's market share in the U.K. If we underestimate the resulting impact, we could end up with a lot of costly inventory, since current U.K. sets are neither technically nor aesthetically suitable for export to the Continent. If we had a common European chassis, the risks would be considerably lessened insofar as the excess U.K. production could be channeled to other national markets.

Exhibit 6 shows color TV growth projections for the major European markets. *Exhibit 7* shows the European industry structure for television sets for 1970.

Elcoma

Elcoma was the Main Industry Group in Eindhoven with a world-wide responsibility for supplying electrical and electronic components to all the other Philips divisions as well as for sales to outside parties. Its five major customers within the Philips concern—Video, Audio, Computers, Telecommunications, and Professional Instruments—accounted for a significant part of its worldwide sales. As with the Video Main Industry Group, Elcoma had corresponding units within major national organizations which reported to those managements (e.g., Mullard in the U.K. reported to Philips Industries Ltd.).

Mr. H. de Vries, Commercial Planning Manager for Elcoma, described the problems it faced in trying to satisfy the component needs of both its internal and third-party customers:

> When Mr. Wim Hegener took over as Commercial Manager of Elcoma [Mr. Hegener had formerly been the Commercial Manager of the Video Main Industry Group], he was given profit responsibility for the Philips world-wide component business. Ever since, there has been a decided shift in emphasis from market share to profitability in making capacity decisions in this division.
>
> Our outside customers are an important influence on our investment decisions. They represent an important part of our business, and we must be prepared to serve them well. This is particularly true for a firm which depends almost wholly on us for all of its components. Since we supply our own divisions, we have to be particularly careful to demonstrate that we are not shortchanging our outside customers, or we can lose them very quickly. In the early 1960s, Mullard had a major setback when its largest customer, Thorn Electrical, decided to manufacture its own components. I do not mean to imply that we lost Thorn because of any inadequacies in the service we provided. Nonetheless, that event served as a strong reminder for us to be vigilant in satisfying our outside customers' needs with the same professional care with which we would serve our sister divisions.
>
> On occasion, the Product Divisions will take actions which cause us to change our plans substantially. For example, Video planned to concentrate much of its monochrome TV production in the Far East and advised us that it would have to go outside for components if we were unable to increase our capacity to serve them there. While our long-term plan had not called for an expansion in the Far East for several years, we accelerated these investments to accommodate the Video Group in this instance. In practice, there is a great deal of give and take as the various organizational units try to mesh their plans with each other. In contrast with the Far East decision, Video had to conform to our timetable in changing over from the 90° to the 110° color picture tube. It wanted to be the first one out with this new tube and the sooner the better. We decided not to move until we were convinced that the market justified the investments involved. Moreover, we did not intend to sell these tubes to Video alone, but to satisfy third-party customer demands as well right from the start.
>
> All our customers within Philips accuse Elcoma of being too conservative in its plans for expansion. This is true to some extent, but not without good reason. Elcoma is a capital-intensive operation. There is an old saying that capital investments for Elcoma are 2 zero's bigger than those for Video. Part of the reason for the larger investment is that Elcoma typically has to add 2 to 3 times the incremental volume required by in-house customers in order to meet its obligations to outside customers. For example, if Video requests an additional 100,000 picture tubes in the U.K. for 1973, we would probably have to increase volume by 300,000 tubes. If Philips Electrical is increasing its market estimate, our other U.K. customers are likely to be jacking up their forecasts and their demands on us as well. Moreover, the economic size of a picture tube plant has to be taken into account.

The interrelation of the various components and the degree of vertical integration of Elcoma's manufacturing facilities greatly complicated capacity expansion. For example, a demand for an increase in the number of color TV picture tubes would be accompanied by a similar demand for the other components to be used in the TV sets, such as capacitors, transistors, transformers, and the like. Moreover, some thirty-five items and chemicals went into making a color TV picture tube, and Elcoma manufactured thirty of them. These items were themselves often involved in one or more layers of manufacture and subassembly.

Mr. de Vries also described the process by which capacity decisions were usually arrived at in Philips:

In making our capacity decisions, we go through a series of negotiations with other Philips units. Prior to these discussions, we develop market forecasts for each of our customer's markets. This overview usually gives us a very good feeling for what is going to happen in each market, often better than any single manufacturer would have.

Now in the case of color picture tubes in the U.K., there are four other Philips units also making independent estimates of that market: the TV Article Group in Philips Electrical, Mullard, the Video Main Industry Group, and the Central Planning Department. Since these units, except Central Planning, have profit responsibility, each wants its own assessment of future market developments.

The next thing we do is sit down with each other and try to arrive at an agreed estimate of the market size and Philips's share of this market. This step is one of the more difficult and critical points in the planning process. Each of us has a different perspective of the situation, which tends to influence our judgments of the market. For example, under the present circumstances, where Ian Benton is trying to increase his output, we would fully expect that the TV Article Group would tend to estimate the total market on the high side, estimate its market share on the high side, and inflate its inventory requirements. Admittedly, we have our own biases.

The final forecasts are very important to us because we all base our production plans on them. Since each of the parties has its own goals, a bit of horse-trading goes on during these discussions, as you might expect.

Who sides with whom greatly influences the outcome of these negotiations. For example, if Mullard agrees with Philips Electrical concerning an increase in picture tube requirements, the chances are that Mr. F. Jonker [Managing Director of Philips Industries Ltd.] will be able to convince Mr. Koelman and Mr. Hegener that more capacity is needed in the U.K. If Sir Mark Baker [Managing Director and Commercial Manager of Philips Electrical] and Mr. Koelman agree but do not have the support of Mullard, it is not likely that Mr. Hegener will accommodate their requests so long as he agrees with Mullard. There is no set formula in this process, and the winds tend to blow differently each time.

Mr. Koelman described Video Main Industry Group's relationship with Elcoma as follows:

Vertical integration has both its advantages and disadvantages for us. In times of lower capacity, we find Elcoma most congenial. In times of shortage, we find that we are often the ones who have to tighten our belts, since Elcoma gives some preference to its third-party customers. In general, however, if Video Group can submit plans and programs with sufficient lead time for Elcoma to act, our needs are generally well served.

Mullard

Mullard Ltd., the Philips subsidiary producing electronic components and assemblies in the U.K., was the largest component supplier in the country, employing over 14,000 people and operating 7 factories. According to its Managing Director, Mr. Alan Johnson, Mullard served 3 primary customer groups: its U.K. sister companies (Philips Electrical and Pye of Cambridge); third-party customers including electronic equipment manufacturing companies, the U.K. government, and engineering concerns; and other Philips concerns outside the U.K. In 1972, roughly 20% of Mullard's annual turnover of £130 million went to U.K. sister companies,[5] 50% to third parties, and 30% to non-U.K. Philips units.

Production planning in Mullard was complicated by the wide range of products and large number of different customers served, both within Philips and without. Mullard was organized with five divisions: Consumer, Computer, Telecommunications, Instrument and Controls, and Government. As shown in *Figure 1,* there was a good deal of interchange among these divisions, the products of one division often finding appreciable sales to the customers of another. Changes in production capacity had to reflect these interdependencies.

Mr. Johnson commented on the nature of the relationships Mullard held with its sister divisions and its third-party customers:

> More than half of the manufacturing cost of a color set is its components. Our major customers buy most of their components from us. As you can see, Mullard can vitally affect the operations of these outside manufacturers. Thus, we have the responsibility to keep the set manufacturer in supply under these circumstances. For example, if we were to have a strike or for other reasons could not supply components from our facilities, we would feel compelled to obtain these supplies for the set makers in any way possible and would authorize our people to meet their obligations. In some ways product managers might be inclined to give more attention to third-party customers than to associated companies, but top management is careful to see that this does not happen and that all such customers as Philips Electrical, Pye, GEC and Bush are treated with the same consideration as each other.

Mullard was normally committed ahead for two four-monthly periods to its customers. Estimates of the total market and its production plans were based on what management expected the major manufacturers to do. In the case of color television, the staff built up its projections based on estimates for Thorn Electrical, for major third-party customers, for Philips Electrical and Pye, and for the remaining market. Finally, estimates of the requirements for Philips International and for customers abroad were added. Mr. Johnson noted:

> We must be very careful not to overestimate demand because of the size and nature of investments required in this business. For example, if we had to provide Philips

[5]Philips Electrical purchased components from Mullard on the basis of standard cost plus a 10% charge for interest and dividend payments. Standard cost included direct materials, direct labor, overhead, and allowances of up to 1% of total manufacturing costs each for research and for technological inefficiencies.

FIGURE 1 Examples of Product Exchanges Among Mullard Divisions

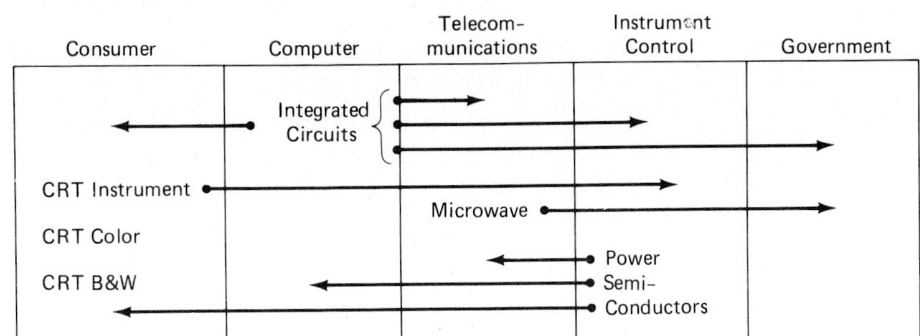

Electrical with an additional 50,000 color CRTs (television picture tubes), we would have to install a new glass tank, as our existing equipment is fully loaded. An economic glass tank takes months to build at a cost of over £2 million.[6] It can produce between 1.5 and 2 million face plates and cones per year and lasts about 4 years before requiring a major rebuild. Glass-making still contains an element of black magic, and so we can encounter other technical problems with a glass tank, especially during startup and during its later years. Clearly, we have to have a pretty good idea that the market demand for CRTs will remain high for some time before it would be appropriate for us to make this kind of investment.

With highly automated plants, we have little to fall back on to cut costs should the market drop. Accordingly, we try to maintain low inventory stocks and to monitor TV sales weekly. As a practical matter, we can live with a deficit production capacity of up to 7%. Within these bounds we can go to third parties for additional supplies, such as Plessey for coils and Siemens for transistors. Beyond that level we run into serious problems.[7]

Apart from the immediate economic considerations, the TV expansion proposal ran counter to one of Mr. Johnson's strategic aims. In 1972, about two-thirds of Mullard's sales went into consumer goods and one-third into professional equipment. Mr. Johnson wanted to reverse the existing proportions. He reasoned that the professional market was larger and less volatile in the long term than was the consumer market.

Maintaining a proper balance between long-term direction and short-term requirements called for Mr. Johnson's careful attention. He saw the U.K. management and Eindhoven as playing different roles in this balance:

The way we are organized, Mr. F. Jonker has the last say concerning our capacity. While Eindhoven can influence these decisions with respect to long-term considerations, it cannot really affect our short-term operations. For us, the customer is the ultimate criterion, and Eindhoven cannot possibly know fully what we have to do to satisfy our customers.

[6]The existing equipment could be overloaded for a short time to produce additional plates and cones to cover the construction period. This overload increased per unit costs somewhat and also increased the risk of equipment breakdown.

[7]This "7% reserve" represented an average figure. In April 1973, TV color picture tubes were in short supply world-wide.

U.K. Management

If operating units were unable to come to any agreement on an important decision, the matter would go before the main board of management at Eindhoven for final resolution (see *Appendix A*). As U.K. area managers, Sir Mark Baker and (especially) Mr. F. Jonker had considerable influence on the outcome. These men had an ultimate responsibility for the profitability of the U.K. operating companies.

Sir Mark Wilfred Baker, Managing Director and Commercial Director of Philips Electrical Limited, recognized a risk of overstocking inventories if the demand were suddenly to decrease:

> The U.K. television market has always been volatile and most difficult to forecast. Our best efforts in past years did not enable the company to avoid overstocking monochrome sets on at least two separate occasions. These errors with monochrome were costly. A similar mistake on color sets would cost us five to six times as much . . . and that would be unacceptable.
>
> If we are to decide upon higher production figures in order to increase our market share, we have to be alert to the risks involved. We must reduce these as far as possible by ensuring that our sales are estimated, forward-committed and monitored very carefully by individual outlets and that information is fed back rapidly to the factories in the event of a market downturn.

Exhibit 8 gives some indication of the forecasting experience in Philips with respect to color television sets. As can be seen, the volatile economic conditions, changing government legislation, and uncertainties in the rental market made color TV a particularly difficult market to forecast. Top management felt that the extent of vertical integration in the U.K. industry (links between manufacturers and distributors) caused problems in assessing both the total market and the firm's ability to change its market share. *Exhibit 9* contains two articles from *The Financial Times* describing the state of the color TV market as it was perceived around April, 1973.

Mr. F. Jonker, Managing and Commercial Director of Philips Industries Limited, was concerned with another problem. An expansion of capacity at Mullard involved a far greater investment than the corresponding investment to expand the assembly operations at Philips Electrical. A drop in the color TV market in 1975 or 1976 would jeopardize a profitable return on these investments. A sudden government regulation tightening credit—possibly prompted by the unsettled international monetary situation at the end of 1972—could cause such a downturn.

The TV Article team, while fully aware of these risks, felt confident that its analysis of the market, based on careful study and interviews, was sound and was anxious to proceed to build up market share.

EXHIBIT 1
N.V. PHILIPS' GLOEILAMPENFABRIEKEN
Product Divisions, Major Products and Sales, 1972

Name	*Major Products*	*Estimated 1972 Sales* (guilders million)*	*Percent of Total Group Sales %*
Lighting	Incandescent lights, fluorescents, lighting fixtures	2,300	11.5
Major Domestic Appliances Small Domestic Appliances	Washing machines, refrigerators, dryers, fans, heaters, shavers	1,600	8.0
Radio, Gramophone, and Television	Television sets, radios, and phonograph players	4,200	21.0
Elcoma	Electronic components, semiconductors, transistors	2,500	12.5
Electro-Acoustics (ELA)	Recording equipment, dictating machines, TV cameras	1,100	5.5
Telecommunications and Defense Systems	Dialing equipment, microwave units, radar	1,600	8.0
Polygram**	Records, music publishing and distribution	1,000	5.0
Data Systems	Computers	500	2.5
Industrial Equipment	Measuring, analyzing and monitoring devices		
Medical Systems	X-ray equipment, hospital monitoring systems		
Pharmaceutical and Chemical Products	Insecticides, animal vaccines, influenza vaccines and other human pharmaceuticals	5,200	26.0
Allied Industries	Cardboard, metals		
Glass	Glass		
	Totals	20,000	100

*These figures exclude intra-company sales which, for some divisions (notably Elcoma), add considerably to the level of operations.
**Polygram is a 50% joint venture with Siemens A.G.
Source: Various published articles.

EXHIBIT 2
GLOEILAMPENFABRIEKEN
Selected Items from Financial Statements, 1963–1972
(millions of guilders)

	1972	1971	1970	1969	1968	1967	1966	1965	1964	1963
Sales	19,924	18,120	15,070	13,023	9,721	8,695	8,069	7,545	7,002	6,224
Trading profit	1,975	1,315	1,280	1,354	1,121	901	862	908	935	826
As a percentage of sales	9.9	7.3	8.5	10.4	11.5	10.4	10.7	12.0	13.4	13.3
As a percentage of total capital employed	9.4	6.5	8.2	10.1	10.5	8.8	8.8	10.2	11.7	11.4
Net profit	717	343	435	518	439	355	347	399	405	366
As a percentage of net worth	10.1	5.3	7.3	9.7	8.8	7.5	7.5	9.2	10.1	9.8
Per ordinary share of f 10 (in guilders)	5.31	2.49	3.29	4.09	3.86	3.04	3.01	3.47	3.72	3.50
Dividend										
Per ordinary share of f 10 (in guilders)	1.80	1.60	1.70	1.90	1.80	1.80	1.60	1.80	1.60	1.60
Retained profit	447	110	193	255	210	126	125	170	206	175
As a percentage of net profit	62	32	44	49	48	36	36	43	51	48
Employees (in thousands) at end of year	371	367	359	339	265	241	244	252	252	234
Wages, salaries and social charges	7,433	7,046	5,890	4,913	3,621	3,234	3,076	2,833	2,509	2,146
Total fixed assets	8,788	8,608	7,921	5,976	5,378	4,736	4,345	3,861	3,448	2,943
Stocks	5,423	5,635	5,307	4,207	2,935	2,775	3,046	2,849	2,481	2,050
Debtors	6,106	5,800	5,117	4,264	3,286	2,836	2,648	2,383	2,147	1,989
Liquid assets	1,814	1,248	743	799	734	743	741	784	729	812
Total current assets	13,343	12,683	11,167	9,270	6,955	6,354	6,435	6,016	5,357	4,851
Total assets	22,131	21,291	19,088	15,246	12,333	11,090	10,780	9,877	8,805	7,794
Net worth	7,430	6,731	6,324	5,548	5,127	4,787	4,730	4,483	4,193	3,845
Minority shareholders' interests	907	840	748	681	237	171	166	151	145	124
Long-term liabilities and provisions	6,200	6,406	5,324	3,411	3,070	2,505	2,347	1,996	1,770	1,560
Short-term liabilities and provisions	7,594	7,314	6,692	5,606	3,899	3,627	3,537	3,247	2,697	2,265
Total liabilities	13,794	13,720	12,016	9,017	6,969	6,132	5,884	5,243	4,467	3,825
Total capital employed	22,131	21,291	19,088	15,246	12,333	11,090	10,780	9,877	8,805	7,794
Total liabilities as a percentage of total capital employed	62	64	63	59	57	55	55	53	51	49
Stocks as a percentage of sales	27	31	35	32	30	32	38	38	35	33
Trade debtors average credit term (in months)	2.6	2.8	2.8	2.7	2.7	2.7	2.8	2.6	2.6	2.6
Ratio of current assets to short-term liabilities and provisions	1.8	1.7	1.7	1.7	1.8	1.8	1.8	1.9	2.0	2.1

Source: N.V. Philips 1972 Annual Report.

EXHIBIT 3

N.V. PHILIPS' GLOEILAMPENFABRIEKEN

Partial Organization Chart, 1973

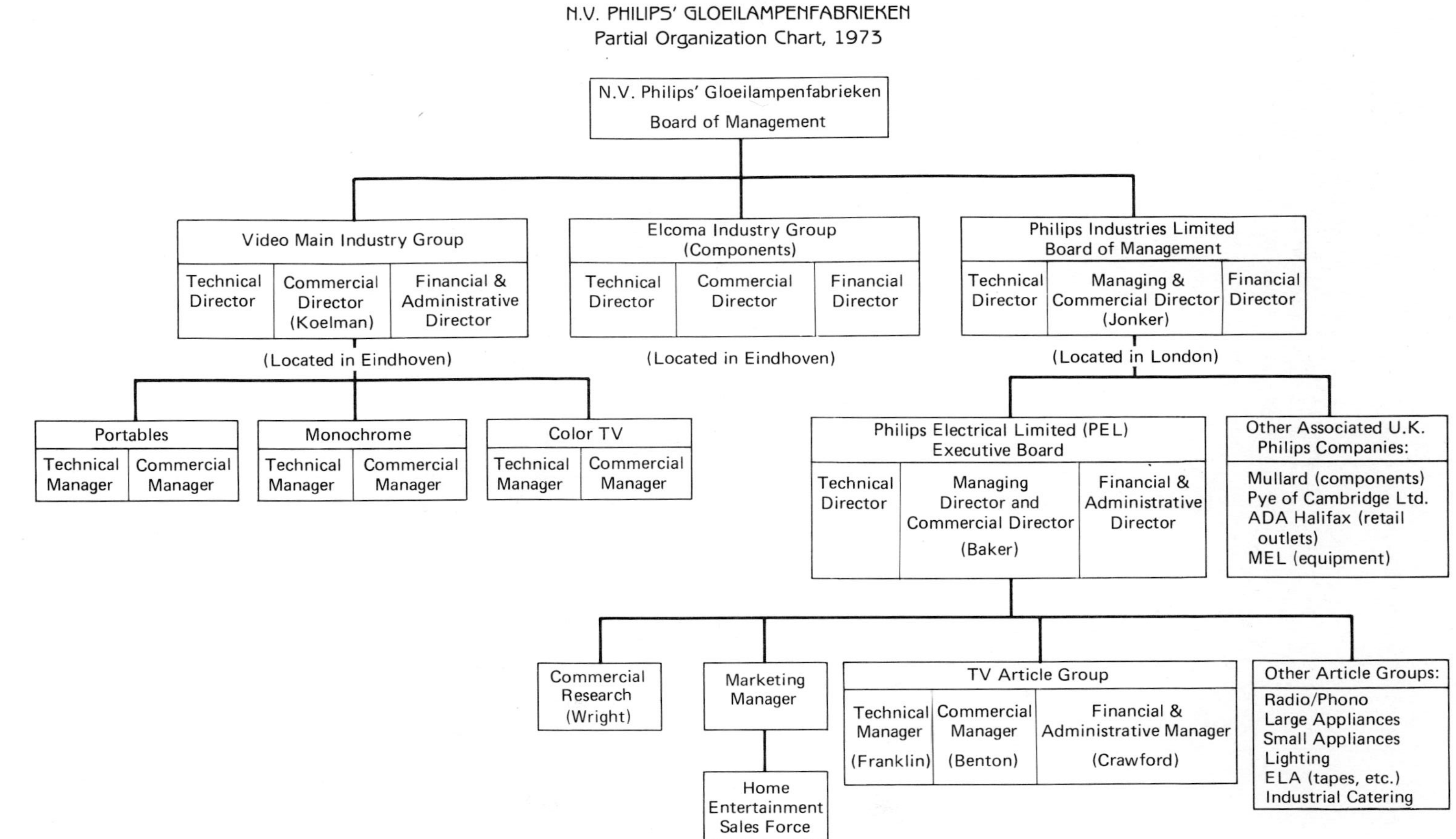

Source: Based on company documents.

EXHIBIT 4 British Government Regulation of Consumer Credit and TV Rental Contracts

	Purchase Tax	*Hire-Purchase*		*TV Rental Contracts*
Date of Change	*Effective Rate %*	*Required Deposit (%)*	*Payment Up To (months)*	*Rental Charge Required as Down Payment (weeks/months)*
October 1955	60			
February 1956		50	24[1]	9 months
September 1958		33	24[1]	First 4 months[2]
October 1958		Controls abolished		Controls abolished
April 1959	50			
April 1960		20	24[1]	First 3 months
January 1961		20	36[1]	
July 1961	55			
April 1962	45			
June 1962		10	36	
January 1963	25			
June 1965		15	36	First 20 weeks
July 1965		15	30	
February 1966		25	24	First 32 weeks
July 1966	27½+10% surcharge	33	24	First 42 weeks
April 1967	27½			
August 1967		25	30	First 30 weeks
March 1968	33			
November 1968	37	33	24	First 42 weeks
July 1971	30	Controls abolished		Controls abolished

[1]No deposit required if payment made in less than 9 months.
[2]No down payment required on any goods 3 or more years old.
Source: Based on company documents.

EXHIBIT 5 Growth of Ownership of Color TV in the U.K. and United States

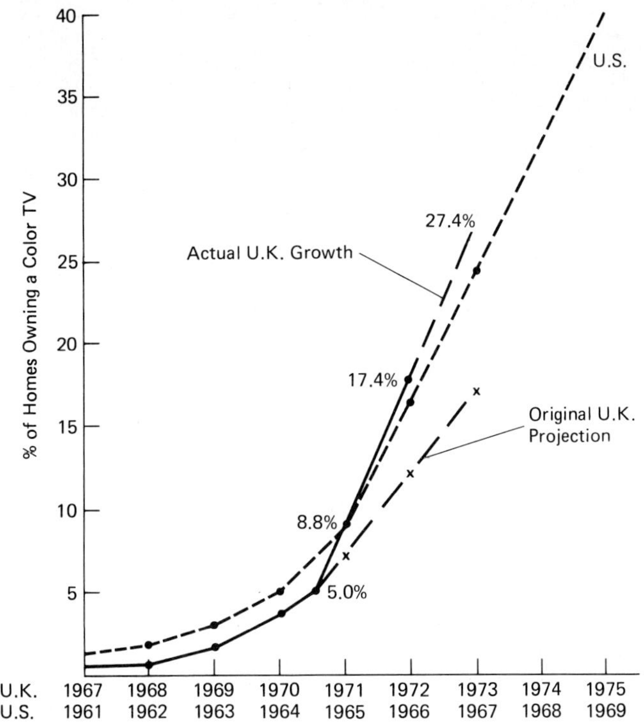

EXHIBIT 6 Color TV Market Penetration in Selected West European Countries

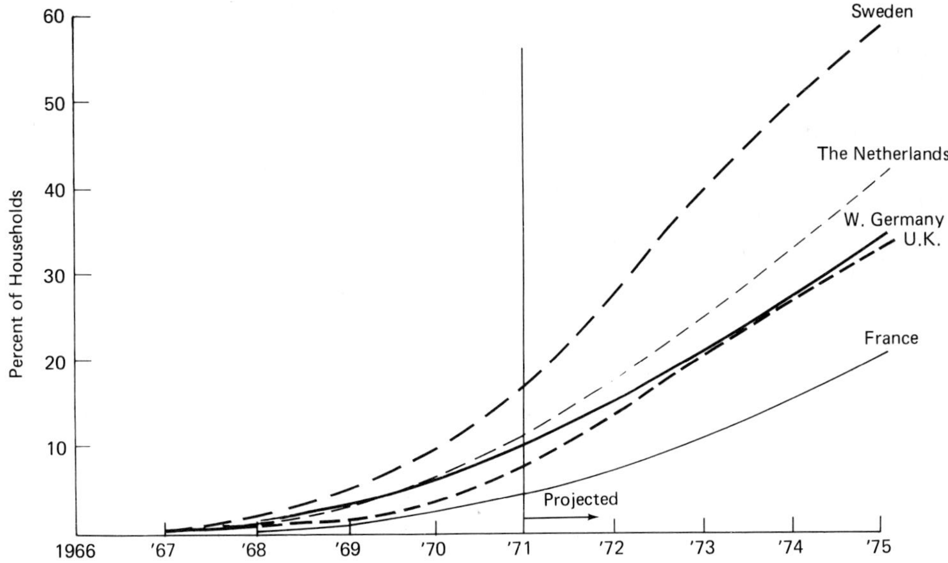

Source: Company planning document, 1971.

EXHIBIT 7
Important TV Manufacturers* in 1970 for Selected West European Countries

	France		*W. Germany*		*United Kingdom*		*Sweden*		*Italy*	*Spain*
	B/W	*Color*	*B/W*	*Color*	*B/W*	*Color*	*B/W*	*Color*	*B/W*	*B/W*
Philips Concern	X	X	X	X	X	X	X	X	X	X
Pye					X	X				
Schneider	X	X								
Grundig	X	X	X	X			X	X	X	
Loewe Opta			X	X						
Blaupunkt			X	X			X	X		
A.E.G./Telefunken			X	X			X	X	X	X
Nordmende			X	X						
Saba			X	X						
ITT	X	X	X	X	X	X				
Verzendhuizen			X	X						
Thomson Brandt	X	X								
Thorn					X	X				
Rank BM					X	X				
GEC					X	X				X
DECCA						X				
Vanguard										X
Inter										X
IBERTA										X
Philco-Ford									X	
Marelli									X	
Luxor/Skantic							X	X		
Luma							X	X		
Total Market Estimates (000 units)	1,330	203	2,125	615	1,815	505	210	130	1,450	570
Number of Major Suppliers**	4	3	4	4	4	5	3	3	3	2
Major Suppliers' Share of Market	72	82	44	52	71	85	59	63	29	23

*X's identify manufacturers with 3% or more market share. Foreign imports not included.
**Major suppliers are defined as holding 9% or more of the market.
Source: Company planning document, 1971.

EXHIBIT 8 **Estimates of Color TV Consumer Offtake,* 1964–1973 (thousands of units)**

Date of Estimate	*1969*	*1970*	*1971*	*1972*	*1973*	*1974*	*1975*	*1976*
September, 1964	75							
November, 1965	100	200						
March, 1966	150	250						
September, 1966	130	270	350					
May, 1967	180	290	450	550				
September, 1967	220	320	430					
October, 1967	260	375	440	540	630	730	830	
March, 1968	215	320	430					
October, 1968	190	300						
November, 1968	170	270	400	500				
September, 1969	110	220	350	480	620	800		
February, 1970		345	730	1000	1300	1450		
June, 1971			670	900	1050	1100	1150	
August, 1971			950	1300				
February, 1972 (U.S. Model)				1400	1580	1650	1700	
February, 1972 (U.K. Model)				1350	1400	1450	1500	
May, 1972				1600	1750	1900	1900	
December, 1972				1700	2100			
January, 1973					2310	2440	2400	2270
March, 1973					2600	2500	2300	
Actual	170	405	982	1681				

*The television industry in the U.K. referred to consumer offtake as the volume of TV sets distributed to the final consumer either through purchase or on a rental basis.
Source: Based on company documents.

EXHIBIT 9 **The British TV Market April/May 1973**

	*Color**	*Black and White*
January	198,000	151,000
February	197,000	131,000
March	233,000	115,000
Change Since First Quarter 1972	+75%	−17%

*At £250 per set this implies color sales of about £60 million per month, about half being rental.
Source: The Financial Times, April 19, 1973 and May 23, 1973.

APPENDIX A
N.V. PHILIPS ORGANIZATION AND DECISION MAKING

Over the years, N.V. Philips had developed what was fundamentally a three-tier management structure to relate its many products with its broad geographical interests.

A ten-man board of management was the top policy- and decision-making organ in the company. While the board members shared general management responsibility for the whole concern, each typically maintained special interest in one of the functional areas (e.g., R&D, sales, finance). Two board members worked with each product division.

Product policy throughout the world was the responsibility of fourteen product divisions. This responsibility was to be exercised in consultation with the general managements of the national organizations.

The general management boards of more than sixty national organizations were responsible for operations and overall Philips policies (in consultation with the product divisions) in each country. Most national organizations comprised a group of subsidiary companies ranging from pure marketing organizations to complete industrial enterprises.

The board of management, the product divisions, and the national organizations were supported by a number of staff departments and the research laboratories in Eindhoven and elsewhere. *Exhibit A* shows the broad structure of the N.V. Philips management organization.

DECISION MAKING

The management of N.V. Philips was based on coordination and consultation among these major units. The complicated relations were described in the following account:

> As Philips views its management process, Eindhoven's role is just to coordinate activities of the highly autonomous national organizations. Says one executive: "Coordination does not mean giving orders. It means negotiation."
>
> Much of the negotiating goes on between the product groups and the national companies, with the management board acting as referee and final arbiter. And even the management board operates by mutual agreement. The president has only co-responsibility with the other nine members.
>
> Even the simple matter of setting a sales target is negotiated, with the national company often setting a higher target than the product groups or central management is willing to support with advertising and sales promotion funds.[1]

Coordination was also the practice within organizational units in Philips, where typically a manager in charge of commercial affairs and a manager in charge of technical activities shared responsibility for general leadership of the unit. This diumvirate form of management, found at all levels in the Philips organization, had its origins when Anton Philips joined the firm as a salesman to complement his brother Gerard's talents as an engineer. Anton noted at a later date:

[1]*Business Week,* January 13, 1972, p. 67.

> From the moment I joined the company, the technical management and the sales management competed to out-perform each other. Production tried to produce so much that sales would not be able to get rid of it; sales tried to sell so much that the factory would not be able to keep up. And this competition has always continued; sometimes the one is ahead, sometimes the other seems to be winning.

In many national organizations, a third person—the financial manager who was responsible for accounting and cost-reporting activities—joined the commercial and technical managers to form a three-man Committee of Coordination and Direction.

The need to coordinate both within and among organizational units in making plans and deciding issues placed its own special demands on the Philips manager. As one executive surmised:

> There is always a lot of discussion and pressure from different directions working on the individual manager with respect to any major decision. I suppose one reason the system works is that when a man comes to work for Philips, more often than not, it is for life. I cannot think of an executive in our upper management levels who has not been with Philips since his twenties. During his time with the company he will occupy a number of different positions in different divisions (a Dutchman will normally undertake at least one extended tour of foreign duty). This experience tends to foster a set of informal relationships among managers throughout the organization and an intuitive understanding as to what can be done and what cannot be done. Another integrating device is the common working language. A man cannot reach a top position without being fluent in English, and all key documents are prepared in English. This practice permits an easier coordination and communication of ideas and problems between our national groups than is possible in many multinational companies.

In addition to these unifying practices, there were several headquarters staff departments responsible for coordination within the concern. These included Industrial Coordination, Technical Efficiency and Organization, Commercial Prognoses and Planning, Accounting, and Financial Affairs.

EXHIBIT A Company Organization Chart, 1972

BOARD OF MANAGEMENT

INTERNAL AUDIT

ORGANISATION

TECHNICAL SERVICES

- Industrial Coordination
- Technical Efficiency and Organisation
- Building Design and Plant Engineering
- Central Development Bureau

GENERAL SERVICES

- Financial Affairs
- Accounting
- Legal Affairs
- Fiscal Affairs
- Personnel Affairs
- Press Affairs
- Management Development

COMMERCIAL SERVICES

- Commercial Prognosis and Planning
- Concern Marketing Services
- Forwarding
- Advertising

RESEARCH LAB

PRODUCT DIVISIONS				
Lighting	Electronic Components and Materials (Elcoma)	Radio, Television and Record-Players* (RGT)	Major Domestic Appliances	Small Domestic Appliances
Telecommunications and Defense Systems	Medical Systems	Industrial Equipment	Electro-acoustics (ELA)	Data Systems
Allied Industries	Glass	Pharmaceutical Chemical Products		Music (Polygram)

REGIONAL BUREAUX

NATIONAL ORGANISATIONS		
Country A	Country B	Country C
Country D	– – –	– – –
– – –	– – –	– – –

DIRECT EXPORT

*In 1973, RGT was divided into two separate divisions: Audio Main Industry Group and Video Main Industry Group.

Source: Philips Charts and Tables, November 15, 1972.

ROBERTSON DISTRIBUTION SYSTEMS, INC.

Edward (Ted) Gaylord, the President of Robertson Distribution Systems, Inc., and son-in-law of its founder, L. M. Robertson, was looking forward to a clear, bright, early fall day as he rode the elevator to his eighteenth-floor Houston office on Monday, September 15, 1975. He walked through the foyer to his office, looked into the adjoining room and said, "Good morning. Has anything special come up?" His secretary said, "Not really, but Mr. R. asked if you'd call him back as soon as you could."

Ted thought to himself, "Well, there's nothing new about that." Sixteen months ago Ted had talked his father-in-law into stepping down from the board, but Mr. R., as he was affectionately known to many of the older employees, felt quite free to ask questions whenever they came to mind and he was never short of advice for his son-in-law—he was one of Robertson's larger shareholders. Ted dialed his father-in-law's home in Colorado Springs, Colorado, and was surprised to find the older man in good humor.

"I've got some good news for you, Ted," he said. "Louise's mother and I have informally agreed to sell the family's stock to Pakhoed for $22 a share. We know you and the rest of the family will follow our lead. I think it's a good price. They called me a week ago and asked me if I'd be prepared to sell. I said I would, and asked for $25. They rejected my offer, but I said, 'Alright, make it $22, and that's my last offer, take it or leave it,' and they accepted. You'd better let the board know today. Nothing official yet, Ted, because there are legal details and terms to hammer out, but . . ."

"Just a minute, Mr. R. Just whose shares are you agreeing to sell?"

"The family's, of course. Ours, yours, . . ."

"Well, hold on a minute, I'll decide for the Gaylord family."

His father-in-law coughed on the other end of the phone, and said, with a great deal of warmth, "Ted, now, we're all part of the one family. Louise's mother will be very upset if she thought you felt differently."

Ted managed to hang up before he or his father-in-law said anything either might later regret. He thought to himself, "That's the other side of 'relative ability.' " (He often told his friends that his business success was due to relative ability.) Looking out over the city, he barked an order to his secretary to get his assistant, Fred Sieber, then picked up the phone and dialed his friend, Charles Duncan, Chairman of Robertson Distribution Systems. "Charles," he said, "the old man has really done it. He's gonna sell this company right out from under me. Can we get the executive committee together tonight?"

Gaylord took out a notepad, signalled Fred Sieber to come in and sit down, and said, "Fred, work out what this company's really worth. Mr. R. is considering selling his stock and Louise's mother's to that Dutch company, for $22 a share. Louise's brothers will probably go along with him." As he spoke, he noted that it was less than twelve months since the younger of his two brothers-in-law, a former director and Vice-President, had left the firm. He remembered a close business associate's comment at the time,

This case was prepared by Assistant Professor Kenneth J. Hatten as a basis for class discussion rather than to illustrate either effective or ineffective handling of an administrative situation.

"Ted, you can't replace the founder and his son in three months and expect to keep control of the company." (Maybe he was right!) As Fred sat, waiting for more instructions, Gaylord said, "Fred, you might also look into the various ways in which we could fight a Dutch takeover attempt. They already have 5% of the company, and with the Robertson family stock they'd have near 40%. I expect they'd try to take control. See what you can work out, and get back to me at four o'clock; the executive committee will meet at five. And, Fred, give me whatever you come up with during the day. And, before I forget, see what our accountants have to say about the tax consequences of a takeover of the company, and make sure this press release gets out" (*Exhibit 1*).

THE COMPANY

Robertson Distribution Systems, Inc., was a Texas corporation, organized in 1946. Through its subsidiaries, it operated an integrated bulk distribution company serving major shippers of chemicals, petrochemicals, petroleum products, and construction materials in the Gulf Coast region of the United States. Robertson provided common and contract motor carriage, marine terminaling, bulk storage, and full-service truck leasing. Its financial statements for the years 1971 to 1975 are contained in *Exhibit 2* and amplified in *Appendices 1* and *2*.

Marine Terminaling

The company conducted its marine terminal operations through subsidiaries and in 1975 operated four terminals; two in the Houston, Texas, area and two in Tampa, Florida.

The Deer Park Marine Terminal, located on 102 acres owned by Robertson abutting the Houston Ship Channel, had 108 steel storage tanks, with capacities ranging from 1,000 barrels to 80,000 barrels, and with a total rated storage capacity of approximately 3.5 million barrels. The tanks were designed for the safe storage and handling of chemical, petrochemical, and petroleum products. The Deer Park facility included 4 docks. Pipelines within the terminal connected the storage tanks to the docks. Additional pipelines from the terminal provided direct connections for 2 major companies with whom Robertson had long-term contracts: Diamond Shamrock and Lubrizol. A railroad switch engine, 7,000 feet of track, and modern loading racks facilitated the handling of products to and from railcars and tank trucks.

The Galena Park Terminal, located on 37 acres owned by Robertson, was also on the Houston Ship Channel and had 77 storage tanks, ranking in size from 1,000 to 55,000 barrels with a total storage capacity of approximately 836,000 barrels. The facilities included a ship dock, a system of pipelines connecting the docks with tanks, modern railcar and tank truck loading racks, a 300-ton dry bulk storage facility, and warehouse space totaling 31,000 square feet. Robertson also operated two leased terminals in Florida which included tanks for liquid storage, grain silos, salt storage buildings, and other buildings for handling dry bulk products.

Motor Carrier Operations

Robertson conducted its interstate common carriage operations under operating authorities granted by the Interstate Commerce Commission (ICC) and also engaged in intrastate common and contract carriage in Texas and Louisiana under authorities granted by the Texas Railroad Commission and the Louisiana Public Service Commission. In addition to common and contract motor carrier service, Robertson provided full-service-maintenance leasing of trucks and tractor-trailers.

Robertson transported a wide variety of bulk products to most points in the continental United States, with a primary concentration in the South and Southwest. Bulk chemicals and petrochemicals such as acids, alcohols, caustic soda, resins, aromatics, paraffins, and chlorinated solvents were transported both intrastate and interstate, primarily from production sites in Texas and Louisiana. Petroleum products, such as heavy and light oils, liquified petroleum gas, gasoline and fuel oils, were transported primarily from refineries or bulk plants in Texas and Louisiana. Cement, asphalt, and other construction materials were delivered from point of manufacture in Texas to intermediate preparation points and to points of final use within Texas. Other products handled by Robertson on a regular basis included dry and liquid fertilizers, salt, syrups, sulphur, wood chips used in the production of paper, and several dry bulk products.

In Texas, Louisiana and Arkansas, Robertson owned, or leased, and operated fifteen truck terminal facilities which served as dispatching and en-route maintenance facilities for its motor carrier operations. In addition, a major maintenance facility for tractors and trailers was operational at Robertson's Deer Park truck terminal.

Robertson's motor carrier fleet in September, 1975, consisted of 510 tractors and 725 trailers. Of these, 65 tractors and 61 trailers were dedicated to the full-service leasing operations. As of September, 1975, approximately two-thirds of Robertson's tractors were less than five years old.

Customers

Robertson's principal customers were major oil companies, cement manufacturers, manufacturers and processors of chemicals, and wood pulp and paper companies. In 1975, Robertson's twenty largest customers accounted for approximately 52% of its consolidated revenues. No single customer accounted for more than 5.0% of its revenues during that period. Robertson's twenty largest customers in 1975, in alphabetical order, were:

- Air Products & Chemicals Company
- Centex Cement Corporation
- Diamond Shamrock Chemical Company
- Dow Chemical Company
- Eastex, Inc.
- Ethyl Corporation
- Exxon Chemical Company, U.S.A.
- Exxon Company U.S.A.
- General Portland Cement Company
- Gulf Oil Company—U.S.
- Ideal Cement Company
- Kaiser Cement & Gypsum Company
- Monsanto Company
- Olin Corporation
- PPG Industries, Inc.
- Procter & Gamble Co.
- San Antonio Portland Cement Co.
- Shell Chemical Company
- Shell Oil Company
- The Upjohn Company

Competition

The primary competitors for Robertson's marine terminal operations were the private marine terminal facilities owned and operated by oil refineries, chemical companies and other concerns. Robertson also competed with other marine terminal companies, which offered their services to the public (see *Exhibit 3*). One competing concern operated a nationwide network of terminals and, in the Houston, Texas, area, had terminaling facilities significantly larger than Robertson's.

Robertson's motor carrier operations competed with the private carriage of major shippers and with a number of specialized common carriers, several of which were larger than Robertson. The amount of direct competition to which Robertson was subject depended, among other things, upon the issuance of authorities by the various governmental agencies which regulated the common carriage business. The issuance of new certificates depended upon the hearing agency's determination of the adequacy of existing carrier service. To a lesser extent, Robertson's motor carrier operations were in competition with other modes of transportation, such as rail, barge and air transport. However, for the most part the services performed and rate structures were not homogeneous and, therefore, the level of such competition was not significant.

Regulation

Interstate carriers are regulated by the ICC and intrastate carriers are regulated by state regulatory agencies. The jurisdiction of the ICC, the United States Department of Transportation, and the various state agencies, is broad and covers practically every phase of a carrier's business. It includes the regulation of territories, rates, commodities shipped, equipment, safety of equipment and operations, work standards for drivers, accounting systems, certain financings, the issuance of securities, mergers, and acquisitions.

Robertson's carrier subsidiaries operated a call-and-demand service over irregular routes within the area of the authorities they held. They were permitted to operate over routes of their choosing within their authorized area, and were not required to use designated routes, as is the case with many carriers of general commodities.

The company's motor carrier subsidiaries were not permitted to pass increased costs through to their customers concurrently, but had to absorb these costs until rate increases were allowed by regulatory authorities. Applications for proposed rate increases are filed with the appropriate regulatory body. If shippers, the public or competing carriers object to the proposed rates, the agency may order hearings in which all protesting parties can be heard. During times of sharply rising costs, such as were experienced in 1973 and 1974, the company, and other motor carriers similarly situated, typically experienced a regulatory lag before higher costs could be recovered through rate increases. In September, 1975, the company's motor carrier subsidiaries were seeking rate increases covering a broad spectrum of products.

Lines of Business Comparison

Exhibit 4 is a schedule of the Company's revenues and earnings before income taxes and other items by lines of business for the four years ended December 31, 1974, and an estimate for 1975.

COMPANY HISTORY: FROM ENTREPRENEUR TO PROFESSIONAL

In 1942, L. M. Robertson was the owner-driver of a dump truck in Indiana. That year he moved to Houston and landed a job hauling petroleum and asphalt to air bases throughout Texas. The job lasted through the war years. In 1946 he incorporated his business and obtained a certificate from the Railways Commission to haul petroleum products intrastate.

Between 1946 and 1957, L. M. Robertson took the company from a one-man show to a corporation with an equity of $1 million (and no debt). Mr. Robertson's success was due to two things: his ability to extend the company's operating rights (from the ICC and state regulatory agencies) and his ability to satisfy his customers.

Ted Gaylord joined Robertson in 1957 and was made Executive Vice-President (Finance) in 1962. But it was not until 1967, when the health of the company's President failed, that Gaylord became President. This promotion heralded major changes in the company's development because Gaylord then had the opportunity to slowly introduce professional managers into what had been a substantially untrained but experienced group of old hands who had matured with the business.

The first two outsiders did not fare well at Robertson and quickly left, but Gaylord learned from the experience and took greater care with the third. Gaylord was part family and part hired manager and, because of this dual affiliation, could operate with either group within the company. When he hired Tom Clowe, the former general manager of a Dallas-based bulk hauling company which had a large share of the cement hauling business in Texas, Gaylord made him his assistant. This afforded Clowe the opportunity to establish himself within the company under Gaylord's mantle without direct operating responsibility. By 1968, when Clowe took over as V.P. Operations, he knew his way around Robertson and was able to function effectively within the firm.

Clowe recalled that the next major phase in Robertson's development began late in 1967, shortly after Gaylord's election as company President. Gaylord attended a YPO (Young Presidents Organization) meeting at the Harvard Business School where he heard an address by Professor Ted Levitt on the dangers of "Marketing Myopia." As a result of this address and subsequent discussions with fellow YPOers, Gaylord returned to Houston convinced that Robertson had to redefine its business and diversify.

DIVERSIFICATION

As many others have discovered, while diversification may be a useful grand strategy, it is not without its frustrations. Gaylord knew he wanted to diversify, but did not know how to do it. The unifying concept which slowly emerged was "distribution systems"—supporting other companies' distribution systems. The rationale was simple:

> Physical distribution is the third-largest cost of doing business (after manufacturing and marketing). Recognized experts acknowledge that it accounts for a full 20% of the cost of industrial goods. More people are engaged in handling and transporting raw commodities and packaged products throughout the United States than in any other basic job category.

> By balancing two or more elements of distribution (such as transportation modes, inventory control, investment in tank farms and warehousing, techniques of order processing), it is possible to reduce costs, improve service, or both. This concept of distribution—an equation with all parts subordinate to a clearly perceived whole—promises no less than a new path toward increased profits.

Unfortunately, the concept did not identify what should be done first. Then opportunity intervened.

Gene Johnson, Vice-President of Hess Terminals, a subsidiary of a major oil and gas producer, was introduced to Gaylord by a business acquaintance. Johnson was an entrepreneur, but undercapitalized. He had heard that Gaylord wanted to diversify and suggested the marine terminal business, pointing out that if a company could obtain control of storage facilities it would have the only uncommitted public storage in town. Johnson knew that the demand for storage was growing rapidly and that the only possible competitors did not have sufficient capacity to absorb it. Gaylord liked Johnson's idea and incorporated a subsidiary, with Johnson as President, to enter the marine terminal business.

They then discovered a virtually abandoned tank terminal on the Houston Ship Channel with a capacity of 240,000 barrels. Gulf Oil, which had owned the property since 1920, had been trying to sell it for almost 5 years.

Gaylord realized that Gulf would have to pay a substantial capital gains tax if it sold the property at 1970 prices. He wondered whether the asking price had been set high to allow for the tax on sale. He also wondered whether he might negotiate a more reasonable price if the capital gains tax could be deferred.[1]

Inquiries revealed that Gulf was in the market for property near the Loop freeways, about 6 miles from Houston's central business district. Gaylord and Johnson found a property which appeared to meet Gulf's requirements and, through Robertson Tank Lines, Inc., and with the aid of a mortgage from a Houston bank, acquired it as an investment at a total cost of $1,250,000.

Robertson then offered Gulf the Loop freeway site in exchange for the Ship Channel site. The offer was accepted and Robertson became a 60% owner of a tank storage terminal. Johnson held 40%. When Hess later closed some of its public storage capacity, Gaylord and Johnson were successful in attracting many of Hess's former customers. By late 1970, they were expanding their terminal's capacity to 600,000 barrels.

Growth and success brought problems, however. Robertson Tank Lines, Inc. and

[1]Tax deferred exchanges provide a means of disposing real estate assets and investing in new investment assets without paying capital gains taxes at the time of the disposition. This means of postponing the tax effect of a transaction is particularly important where there is a chance for a major appreciation in a particular property's values because of someone else's need for the property, possibly to change its use, and where the original owner still wants to be in the real estate business or wants another particular property.

To qualify for a full tax deferred exchange:

1 The property must be held for use in a trade or business, or as an investment. Property held for sale does not qualify.
2 There must be an exchange of property rather than a sale or reinvestment.
3 The property exchange must be of like kind.

If these conditions are met, the exchange provisions are mandatory. The provisions apply to both a gain and a loss so that if the conditions are met, a loss cannot be recognized, even if it is to the taxpayer's advantage.

particularly Johnson, who was an independent investor, were continuously stretched to raise the capital needed to expand the terminal. Then, in December, 1970, Johnson was killed in an auto accident. Robertson had prudently taken out an insurance policy on his life and so was able to survive the blow financially. But the company had lost a valuable man at a time when it was highly levered and sorely in need of new capital to expand the terminal side of the business.

Gaylord hired a new man to run the terminal company and came to the conclusion that Robertson's only way out of its financial bind was a public offering; but Robertson looked like just one more trucking company. Gaylord felt that a public offering would be expensive unless the company was made more marketable.

Once again, Gaylord knew what he wanted to do. The problem was how to do it. He wanted to expand the bulk storage terminal business as soon as possible. He would need about $5 million for the first stage of a project of the scale he felt was needed, and an additional $7–10 million to complete it. As he thought through Robertson's strengths and weaknesses, it was obvious to him that the terminal business and the trucking business were quite different but that there was a real opportunity to create synergy between them. *Exhibit 5* shows the major economic characteristics of Robertson's businesses.

Gaylord realized that the trucking business could be his source of funds. If he used his existing resources to expand the trucking business, he could kill two birds with one stone. He could accelerate the growth of the company—for example, by an acquisition—and use the growth to attract underwriter and market interest. And the expanded trucking operations could throw off cash which he could use in the terminal business.

His first move was to look around the trucking industry for an under-exploited opportunity. Tom Clowe's old company was in trouble. It was very thin on management and the cement companies which were its customers were complaining about the service they were getting. Some had even called Clowe asking for aid. Gaylord saw his chance and immediately acquired Materials Transportation Co., a small company with a certificate to haul cement intrastate. He added 100 trucks to its fleet of 30 and increased its sales from $600,000 to $2,500,000 in the first year.

GOING PUBLIC

In the interim, Gaylord had been preparing the Robertson family for public ownership. For many entrepreneurs, the idea of a public listing is appealing. It's nice to see your name in the *Wall Street Journal* every day. Fortunately, Mr. Robertson liked the idea. Although the name-change to Robertson Distribution Systems did not particularly appeal to him, he could understand the significance that a name had in the market. In 1972, when Robertson was preparing to go public, the P/E ratio for specialized trucking companies was 13.7; for distribution companies it was 19.4, a premium of over 40%. Gaylord's biggest headache was to get the Robertsons to realize the full implications of public ownership: it meant managing the company for all the shareholders, not just the family.

The major step Gaylord took to ensure that the family interests would not dominate those of all the shareholders was to add four outsiders, fellow YPOers, to his board. Thus he had four family members and four outsiders on the board, with himself positioned as the swing vote and representative of both camps.

At this time, Gaylord negotiated an option on a 110-acre site on the Houston Ship Channel, a few miles below the Galena terminal. A number of companies, Diamond Shamrock for example, already owned property in the area. Gaylord felt that if Robertson acquired the site he could take advantage of the general business activity in the area to boost revenues quickly. *Exhibit 6* shows the extent of industrial activity on the Houston Ship Channel in 1972 and the attractive locations of Robertson's new and proposed terminals.[2]

Control of a site was the final step in Gaylord's preparation for a public offering because it allowed him to set out how Robertson proposed to use the capital raised. The prospectus focused primarily on the track record of the company during his presidency and on the prospects of synergy between trucking and terminal operations in a distribution company.

With all the preparatory steps completed, Robertson went public on May 4, 1972, at a price of $20.50, a P/E of 14.5. Undoubtedly, Robertson was fortunate because it hit the market when the transportation index reached its peak. Between May, 1974, and September, 1975, Robertson's stock fell as low as $8.25, although it was hovering at about $10 when Mr. R. called Gaylord. As might be expected, very few of the initial investors were still shareholders. The publicly-held stock turned about once each year and most non-family owners had a tax basis of between $10 and $13 per share.

ROBERTSON, THE PUBLIC COMPANY

With the proceeds of the successful sale of 300,000 shares, about $5,564,000, Gaylord was able to increase Robertson's commitment to the terminal and bulk storage business, but not without risk. The company was relatively liquid, but when the ground was broken for the terminal project there was no major new business in sight. Then, as the project developed, Diamond Shamrock broke ground for a new plant adjacent to Robertson's terminal site.

Because it controlled the direct frontage on the Channel in front of Diamond Shamrock and because of its liquid position, Robertson was able to negotiate a deal attractive to both itself and Diamond. The companies signed a long-term contract under which Robertson supplied Diamond with storage and built a direct pipeline to connect Diamond's plant with the terminal and storage facilities. The contract freed capital for Diamond's production facilities; Robertson was able to use the Diamond contract as "security" for a loan to raise additional capital for new storage facilities for Diamond's use. Diamond's lease payments were fully tax deductible; Robertson got the tax credits and depreciation associated with ownership.

In 1973, with terminal construction consuming all available capital, the motor carrier division was suffering. To enable the company to compete effectively, Robertson broke with its traditions and hired 116 lease operators, owner-drivers, on a trip-by-trip

[2]When Robertson decided to go public in 1972 its plans were to build a new 3.2-million barrel terminal for an estimated $12.0 million to $15 million. By 1974, the company had spent $18.2 million and had 2.1 million barrels in service. At that time it expected to spend another $12.9 million to increase its Deer Park capacity to 3.5 million. In September, 1975, the final cost was expected to be $33 million.

basis. These independent operators worked under Robertson's aegis until the recession began to affect even Houston's and the Southwest's dynamic growth. Between mid-1974 and 1976 these independents were laid off. They had been paid a substantial premium above Robertson's employee drivers. (The latter were paid a base rate based on gross revenue earned and a bonus based on contribution to overhead and profit.) Most of the lease operators owned their tractors, subject to chattel mortgages, and many were forced to ''walk'' when the work ran out—they allowed the mortgagor to repossess their rigs to relieve themselves of their repayment obligations.

In 1974, when trucking was hit even harder by the recession and the decline in business activity associated with it, the demand for terminal storage increased; the variability of business conditions seemed to stimulate the need for storage. Simultaneously, Mr. Robertson was becoming more and more concerned by Gaylord's management of the trucking operations. The extent to which the trucking operations suffered during this period is reflected in the following set of figures.

Year	*% of Fleet Driven Less than 5 years*
1972	99%
1973	90%
1974	na
1975	67%

Matters came to a head in April, 1974. On the day before the annual meeting for fiscal 1973, Mr. Robertson, who was then Chairman, called one of the four outside directors and asked him to resign. The director naturally called Gaylord, wanting to know what was going on. Gaylord hit the roof, raised hell within the family and proclaimed that he wouldn't stand for it.

The outcome of this showdown was Mr. Robertson's agreement to step down from the board—when Gaylord came up with someone Mr. Robertson could respect and who would keep an eye on the company and its President. An uneasy truce reigned until May, 1974, when John Duncan, a Robertson board member and one of the founders of Gulf and Western, told Gaylord that his brother Charles, who had been President of Coca-Cola, had resigned and might consider the job. Even Mr. R. found it hard not to jump at this solution and, by October, Robertson had a new Chairman.

Three months after Mr. R. retired, Gaylord and the other managers of the firm were confronted with a serious problem. Gaylord's younger brother-in-law, who had a 6.5% ownership interest in the company and was a director and the Executive Vice-President of Robertson Tank Lines, was unhappy with Gaylord's policies. First Gaylord offered him alternative employment, but the offer was refused. Then Gaylord and his brother-in-law agreed to part company, although, to smooth the transition, Robertson signed a twelve-month consulting contract with him. Gaylord invited an outsider to take the vacant seat on the board.

In 1974, Robertson's stock hit its all-time low of \$8.50 and in the third quarter it had trouble holding even that price as it flickered between \$8.50 and \$9. Nonetheless, Gaylord persisted with his daily habit of reading the stock transfer notices. He did it out of curiosity, primarily to keep track of the confidence some of his personal acquaintances had in the business and in himself. One morning early in 1975, he realized that one account had been buying regularly. His interest piqued, he called the broker responsible for the purchases but received the expected "We can't reveal our client's name."

It was frustrating to watch the holding increase in size while being ignorant of the buyer's identity. As the holding approached 5%, the point at which the SEC must be notified of a buyer's interest, Gaylord briefly considered a treasury purchase to precipitate the revelation.

In May, 1975, Gaylord received a call from Pakhoed Holding, N.V., a company based in Rotterdam with subsidiaries in tank terminals, pipelines, transport and real estate. Gaylord was told that it was Pakhoed that had been buying, and that their motive was simply to invest in the low-priced stock of a good company. Although skeptical, Gaylord felt that with his and his wife's stock, and with either the Robertson family or the public proxy vote, he could maintain control if challenged.

Pakhoed had first taken an interest in Robertson in 1972. That October, Robertson's Vice-President for Terminal Operations had met with Pakhoed in Rotterdam to discuss possibilities for reciprocal business and joint ventures, but nothing had come of it. Then, in 1973, when Robertson's new terminal on the Houston Ship Channel began to take shape, Pakhoed had approached the company seeking a majority interest. Robertson had countered with an offer to sell 300,000 shares, a 30% share of the company, at $20 per share. Pakhoed responded with a request for warrants which would have allowed it to ultimately control Robertson. Mr. R. and Gaylord objected and the Dutch company had backed off.

1975

In 1975, Robertson had not had an opportunity to repeat the successful sorties into the fuel market which had contributed $650,000 to its earnings in 1973 and $330,000 in 1974. In addition, Robertson Tank Lines' revenues were running significantly lower than in 1974. Gaylord expected them to be probably 14% or 15% lower than in 1974 at the end of the fiscal year.

Already, however, the steps the trucking company was taking to improve its profitability were paying off. Robertson had sold 54 tractors and 144 trailers, about 14% of its fleet, freeing $1.1 million and realizing a gain of almost $300,000 on the sale. Tank Lines, under Tom Clowe's leadership, was consolidating its operations, eliminating unprofitable business where possible, and attempting to cut operating expenses.

Total shipments were down about 35% but the average trip distance was up 13% and revenue per mile was up 17% as of September. Clowe and Gaylord expected that these figures would hold until the year's end. Their biggest problem was a 1.4% increase in the motor carrier's operating ratio (the ratio of operating expenses, excluding interest, to operating revenue) to 97.3%.

Mr. R. was not on the board, but he felt free to tell Gaylord that he "didn't understand trucking." In addition, Mrs. Robertson, Ted's mother-in-law, who had refused to give up her seat on the board, leaned on her husband for advice. The Robertsons wanted Gaylord to increase the firm's investment in the trucking business which they felt offered good profit opportunities. They were not truly comfortable with the terminal operations which were beginning to dominate the company, perhaps because they had no experience in the marine storage business.

OWNERSHIP INTERESTS

When Ted Gaylord had been offered the job of President of what was then Robertson Tank Lines he accepted on the condition that he could acquire a substantial interest in the firm. Consequently, in 1968, when a buy-in contract was agreed to by Gaylord and his father-in-law, Mr. Robertson took the opportunity to arrange his estate. This decision led to part of the family's stock being owned by the Robertson children and grandchildren.

In 1972, when the company went public, the family's interest was substantially diluted both by the new shares sold and by the family's simultaneous sale of about 100,000 shares. It was diluted further when Charles Duncan joined the firm in 1974. He had been sold 20,000 shares at $10 a share (at a slight premium over the $8.75 bid—$9.25 market prevailing the day before the transaction) and various qualified and non-qualified options which entitled him to buy up to 100,000 shares at $10 per share.

In September, 1975, there were approximately 1,245,000 shares issued. The company's treasury held 81,000 and the rest were held or controlled as follows:

Mr. L. M. Robertson	98,000
Mrs. Elizabeth Robertson	119,000
Their two sons	125,000
Mr. Edward O. Gaylord and wife	125,000
Other directors and officers	118,000
Pakhoed Holding, N.V.	56,000
The public (about 800 holders of record)	522,000
	1,163,000
Treasury	82,000
Total issued	1,245,000

THE THREAT OF A TAKEOVER MAKES ONE THINK

Gaylord had many friends whom he knew were shareholders in Robertson, and the officers and outside directors of the Corporation held 118,000 shares plus 118,400 unexercised options to buy shares at an average price of $10.88. In addition, a few months ago, Gaylord had borrowed $450,000 from a Houston bank to increase his holdings in the firm. In fact, he had only until December, 1976, to acquire the shares his father-in-law had contracted to sell him back in 1966. This was a block of 50,000 shares at a price of $12.50. When he exercised this contract he would be $1,000,000 in debt.

The telephong rang, interrupting his thoughts. It was Charles Duncan. As they talked, it occurred to Gaylord that Pakhoed had not mentioned buying the whole company; they seemed to want only the Robertson family's stock. If the whole family sold, including the Gaylords, Pakhoed would have almost 50% ownership. If Gaylord held out he might block them. As a director, he couldn't see how he could sell. In 1973, Pakhoed had wanted control, but not the whole company; while it had well over 100 subsidiaries, its ownership, in the case of those outside the Netherlands, rarely exceeded 50%. For example, Pakhoed had set up two groups of wholly-owned subsidiaries to participate in two American joint ventures where its share of the operating businesses was exactly 50%.

"Charles," Gaylord said, "Mr. R. wanted me to go to Colorado Springs on the seventeenth to meet Pakhoed's representative, Arthur Penny. I've refused and pointed out to him that I can't sell my stock with his as things now stand and I've tried to explain that after seventeen years it wouldn't be fair for him to sell out and leave me locked in the company. I asked him to think of all his friends who own stock and I've told him that the deal should be all or nothing.

"Could you meet Penny in Denver and feel him out? You would represent all the shareholders. Let him know that I object to his offer, but be a little vague. Let's see how he reacts to a proposal of 100% or nothing. After reviewing their balance sheet, [*Exhibit* 7] my bet is that 100% will block him. With you doing that we should gain time and we might be able to frighten the Dutch off. Penny will be coming to Houston on the nineteenth to see me. By then Fred and I should have a full plan worked out to counter any moves Pakhoed makes."

He put down the phone. There was the family to consider. His wife's mother was in a tough spot; in addition to being a director of the company, she was caught between the Gaylords and her husband. He wondered what the personal costs of a fight with the Dutch company might be, and what the consequences would be if he refused to go along with the Robertsons, or if they refused to go along with him. He also wondered how the public shareholders would react to his decisions as a shareholder and director.

EXHIBIT 1 News Release

For Immediate Release

HOUSTON (September 15)—ROBERTSON DISTRIBUTION SYSTEMS, INC. (NASDAQ-RDIS)

Edward O. Gaylord, President of Robertson Distribution Systems, Inc., today announced that representatives of a substantial foreign corporation and the L. M. Robertson family have advised the company that negotiations are being conducted with members of the Robertson family for the acquisition of approximately one-third of the company's outstanding common stock. It is understood that the proposed purchase price is approximately $22 per share, payable in cash and notes to the family.

Gaylord stated that the Company has not been furnished sufficient detail concerning the proposal to determine what, if any, recommendations may be made to shareholders.

EXHIBIT 2

ROBERTSON DISTRIBUTION SYSTEMS, INC. AND SUBSIDIARIES
Consolidated Balance Sheet
Dec. 31, 1973 & 1974, & Projected for Dec. 31, 1975

Assets	*1975*	*1974*	*1973*
Current Assets			
Cash	$ 1,346,785	$ 2,630,939	$ 1,837,578
Receivables:			
Trade accounts	3,641,781	3,449,351	3,543,569
Estimated Federal income tax	—	—	138,541
Other	730,254	755,724	438,822
Inventories:			
Materials and supplies	785,253	793,147	672,539
Other	57,389	105,707	322,460
Deposits	151,444	448,732	262,320
Prepaid expenses	415,837	396,086	337,542
Total current assets	7,128,743	8,579,686	7,553,371
Property, Plant, and Equipment, at cost			
Revenue and service equipment	46,351,212	39,177,841	36,828,809
Plant and other equipment	12,455,943	9,781,808	8,593,147
Land	3,397,991	3,324,479	3,324,783
Construction in progress	3,174,370	5,265,290	680,073
	65,379,516	57,549,418	49,426,812
Less—Accumulated depreciation and amortization	18,414,557	15,649,340	13,119,940
	46,964,959	41,900,078	36,306,872
Other Assets			
Permits, at cost	448,257	443,781	437,449
Deferred charges and other	268,536	380,221	384,797
	716,793	824,002	822,246
	$54,810,495	$51,303,766	$44,682,489

Liabilities and Stockholders' Equity			
Current Liabilities			
Payables:			
Trade accounts	$ 1,872,036	$ 1,677,469	$ 1,584,345
New equipment purchases	—	43,786	320,308
Dividends	139,758	116,479	68,847
Accrued liabilities	2,006,705	2,010,656	1,479,307
Estimated Federal income tax	3,375	331,246	—
	4,021,874	4,179,636	3,452,807
Long-term debt due within 1 yr.	1,901,246	863,684	766,611
Total current liabilities	5,923,120	5,043,320	4,219,418
Long-Term Debt	25,849,484	25,370,731	22,344,129
Deferred Federal Taxes on Income	3,251,020	2,951,736	2,632,712
Other Liabilities	775,440	872,312	545,625
Stockholders' Equity:			
Common stock, no par; authorized 5,000,000, issued 1,245,426 shares	4,664,340	4,664,340	4,664,340
Additional paid-in capital	1,535,996	1,535,996	1,410,996
Retained earnings	13,851,029	11,890,302	10,121,768
	20,051,365	18,090,638	16,197,104
Less—Cost of 81,963; 80,790 and 98,435 shares in treasury (1975–73 respectively)	1,039,934	1,024,971	1,256,499
	19,011,431	17,065,667	14,940,605
	$54,810,495	$51,303,766	$44,682,489

EXHIBIT 2 (Cont.) Consolidated Statement of Earnings
For years ending Dec. 31, 1973 & 1974, & Projected for Dec. 31, 1975

	1975	*1974*	*1973*
Operating Revenues			
Transportation and thruput	$29,460,209	$33,684,456	$28,180,691
Rent and use charges	8,218,564	6,495,463	3,750,554
Other operating revenue	2,025,088	1,608,121	900,573
Fuel sales	—	743,626	1,341,900
Total operating revenues	39,703,861	42,531,666	34,173,718
Operating Expenses			
Salaries	3,539,092	3,253,458	2,787,439
Operating wages	10,659,647	11,849,122	8,775,049
Other compensation expense	2,113,992	1,800,085	1,356,410
Total	16,312,731	16,902,665	12,918,898
Operations and maintenance	5,540,981	5,641,812	5,193,400
Depreciation and amortization	4,669,463	4,541,553	3,974,591
Equipment rent	498,867	2,928,237	1,486,653
Selling and administrative	3,277,221	2,822,283	2,221,698
Taxes and licenses	2,200,685	2,406,093	2,054,488
Other operating expense	2,445,123	2,170,793	1,976,163
Cost of fuel sales	—	413,336	691,509
Total operating expenses	34,945,071	37,826,772	30,517,400
Earnings from operations	4,758,790	4,704,894	3,656,318
Other Expenses (Income), net			
Interest:			
Incurred	2,395,683	2,176,234	1,633,309
Income	(70,388)	—	—
Capitalized	(334,028)	192,590	290,500
Expensed	1,991,272	1,983,644	1,342,809
Gain on sale of equipment	(328,613)	(99,269)	(174,516)
Miscellaneous	(121,795)	(53,493)	143,426
Total other expenses, net	1,540,864	1,830,882	1,311,719
Earnings before taxes on income	3,217,926	2,874,012	2,344,599
Provision for Taxes on Income			
Current	483,375	457,794	136,406
Deferred	269,677	223,322	420,058
Total provision for taxes on income	753,052	681,116	556,464
Net Earnings	$ 2,464,874	$ 2,192,896	$ 1,788,135
Earnings per common share	$ 2.08	$ 1.91	$ 1.57

EXHIBIT 3

Public Storage Capacity
Houston Shipping Channel
1975

Company	*Capacity (barrels)**
GATX	9,770,000
Robertson Terminals, Inc.	4,500,000
International Terminal Company[1]	560,000
Anchor Tanklines, Inc.	500,000
Sea Coast Terminals	86,000
Hess Terminals[2]	6 to 7 million

[1]Controlled by Mitsui and expanding by about 1 million barrels
[2]Primarily trading on its own account and not normally in the public market; controlled by Hess Oil and Gas.
*1 barrel: 42 gallons

EXHIBIT 4

ROBERTSON DISTRIBUTION SYSTEMS, INC.
Revenue and Before-Tax Earnings

	Year Ended December 31 (000's Omitted)				
	1971	*1972*	*1973*	*1974*	*1975 Est.*
Revenues					
Marine Terminaling	$ 2,718	$ 2,913	$ 4,591	$ 7,578	$10,312
Motor Carrier	21,978	23,788	28,352	34,293	29,494
Fuel Sales	—	—	1,342	744	—
Corporate Items and Intercompany Eliminations	(147)	22	(111)	(83)	(102)
Consolidated Revenues	$24,549	$26,723	$34,174	$42,532	$39,704
Earnings					
Marine Terminaling	$ 385	$ 366	$ 407	$ 2,964	$ 3,685
Motor Carrier	1,640	1,400	1,588	1,445	1,220
Fuel Sales	—	—	650	330	—
Corporate Items and Intercompany Eliminations	—	603	(301)	(1,865)	(1,687)
Consolidated Earnings Before Income tax and Other Items	$ 2,025	$ 2,369	$ 2,344	$ 2,874	$ 3,218

EXHIBIT 5 Economic Characteristics of Robertson's Key Businesses

	Trucking	*Terminal*
Barriers to Entry	Low	High
Capital Intensity	Low	High
Labor Intensity	High	Low
Nature of Fixed Assets	Depreciating	Probably Appreciating
Cost Structure—% Fixed	50%	90%
Contribution Margin	5%–10% on Revenue	15%–40% on Revenue
Cash Payback Begins	Immediately	Not before 2 years
ROI	Low	High
Economic Life for Tax Purposes	6–8 years	20–30 years

EXHIBIT 6 Companies Active in Houston Ship Channel Area
Location of existing and proposed Robertson Distribution Systems, Inc. bulk storage and distribution terminals, and other existing Channel industries.

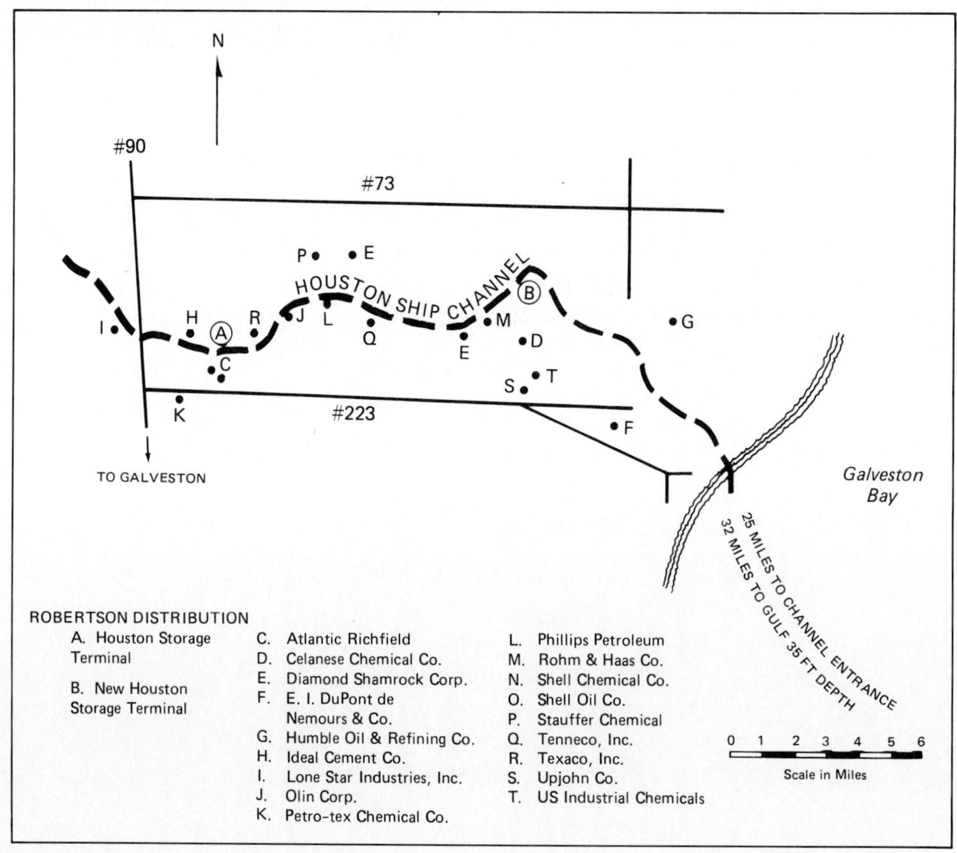

EXHIBIT 7

PAKHOED HOLDING, N.V.
Balance Sheets 1967 to 1975*
(in $; 000,000 omitted)

	1967	1968	1969	1970	1971	1972	1973	1974	1975
Land and buildings	36.3	40.9	42.9	47.1	46.5	47.4	56.2	58.3	88.1
Buildings under construction	4.9	5.2	2.4	5.3	6.6	9.7	7.8	9.4	10.4
Tank terminals and ancillary equipment	46.3	63.4	81.9	88.8	102.1	124.6	144.0	164.2	156.7
Machinery and equipment	8.1	9.1	10.3	7.7	7.0	7.8	9.8	11.3	16.4
Fixed assets	95.6	118.6	137.5	148.9	162.2	189.5	217.8	243.2	271.6
Intangible assets	—	—	—	—	—	—	—	—	4.1
Non-consolidated subsidiaries	11.1	18.8	24.2	25.1	27.9	30.9	29.7	52.7	88.5
	106.7	137.4	161.7	174.0	190.1	220.4	247.5	295.9	364.2
Current assets less current liabilities (working capital)	5.5	10.9	7.6	17.5	20.0	40.5	56.9	65.4	52.7
Total assets less current liabilities	112.2	148.3	169.3	191.5	210.1	260.9	304.4	361.3	416.9
Financed from:									
Shareholders' equity:									
Share capital at par value	14.1	16.7	17.8	18.6	19.3	22.0	22.9	27.2	28.3
Retained earnings plus contributed capital in excess of par value	27.2	36.5	40.0	42.8	46.4	56.5	61.7	84.6	92.4
Total shareholders' equity	41.3	53.2	57.8	61.4	65.7	78.5	84.6	111.8	120.7
Accumulated depreciation	32.1	37.8	42.7	48.8	53.7	60.3	67.7	76.0	70.0
Permanent capital	73.4	91.0	100.5	110.2	119.4	138.8	152.3	187.8	190.7
Deferred taxes and accrued liabilities	7.2	7.9	7.7	8.2	8.7	11.2	10.2	12.1	22.0
Long-term debts	31.6	49.4	61.1	73.1	82.0	110.9	141.9	161.4	204.2
Long-term liabilities	38.8	57.3	68.8	81.3	90.7	122.1	152.1	173.5	226.2
Total permanent capital and long-term liabilities	112.2	148.3	169.3	191.5	210.1	260.9	304.4	361.3	416.9

*Figures of 1967 to 1974 restated to permit comparison with 1975. (The original guilder amounts have been translated at the rate of US$ 1. — = Fl. 2.69)

(*continued*)

EXHIBIT 7 (Cont.)

Profit and Loss Accounts 1967 to 1974*
(in $; 000,000 omitted)

	1967	*1968*	*1969*	*1970*	*1971*	*1972*	*1973*	*1974*
Revenues	48.2	58.9	66.1	67.9	73.1	79.5	95.2	113.4
Expenses	−36.2	−44.0	−48.9	−46.1	−48.7	−53.5	−63.1	−76.5
Depreciation	− 4.8	− 6.2	− 6.3	− 7.1	− 7.7	− 7.8	− 8.9	−10.6
Operating results	7.2	8.7	10.9	14.7	16.7	18.2	23.2	26.3
Non-consolidated subsidiaries								
Income	1.5	1.7	1.7	1.4	2.9	3.6	2.5	3.4
Depreciation	− 0.3	− 0.4	− 0.7	− 1.0	− 1.0	− 0.9	− 0.9	− 0.9
Income after depreciation	1.2	1.3	1.0	0.4	1.9	2.7	1.6	2.5
Total	8.4	10.0	11.9	15.1	18.6	20.9	24.8	28.8
Net interest expense	− 1.6	− 2.7	− 3.6	− 5.0	− 5.3	− 5.3	− 7.0	− 6.9
Profit before taxation and extraordinary income and charges	6.8	7.3	8.3	10.1	13.3	15.6	17.8	21.9
Taxation	− 2.8	− 2.3	− 2.9	− 4.1	− 5.8	− 6.8	− 7.5	− 8.6
Profit before extraordinary income and charges	4.0	5.0	5.4	6.0	7.5	8.8	10.3	13.3
Extraordinary income and charges	− 0.2	− 0.3	0.1	0.1	− 0.3	− 0.3	− 0.6	− 0.3
Net profit	3.8	4.7	5.5	6.1	7.2	8.5	9.7	13.0

*Figures of 1967 to 1974 restated to permit comparison with 1975.

Figures per Fl. 20 share
(in $; adjusted for capital movements)

	1967	1968	1969	1970	1971	1972	1973	1974
Cash flow	3.22	3.74	3.84	4.38	4.89	5.04	5.70	6.42
Net profit	1.38	1.55	1.69	1.88	2.22	2.49	2.84	3.41
Cash dividend	0.61	0.63	0.71	0.80	0.89	1.03	1.07	1.32

(The original guilder amounts have been translated at the rate of US$ 1. = Fl. 2.69)

APPENDIX 1
ROBERTSON DISTRIBUTION SYSTEMS, INC.
Extracts from the Notes to Financial Statements

The accounting policies followed by Robertson Distribution Systems and all of its subsidiaries include the following:

The accompanying consolidated financial statements include the accounts of the company and all of its subsidiaries after elimination of all significant intercompany transactions.

Depreciation is calculated using the straight-line method over the estimated service lives of the respective assets.

Deferred income taxes are provided for timing differences between financial and tax reporting. Investment tax credits are recorded as a reduction of the provision for income taxes in the year in which the assets giving rise to credits are placed in service.

Interest is capitalized during the construction or development period for major projects, since interest constitutes an actual cost of the projects. Capitalized interest is computed monthly based on the average effective rate for all outstanding debt for the prior month. Net income was increased by $140,000 in 1974 and $249,000 in 1975 due to capitalizing interest.

Property, Plant, and Equipment

		Consolidated	
	Cost	*Depreciation*	*Net*
Revenue and Service Equipment			
Tractors, trailers and rail tank cars	$23,134,893	$12,049,896	$11,084,997
Tank storage systems	15,267,324	1,693,806	13,573,518
Docks and loading facilities	5,126,881	493,263	4,633,618
Service vehicles and equipment	2,822,114	1,178,727	1,643,387
Total revenue and service equipment	$46,351,212	$15,415,692	$30,935,520
Plant and Other Equipment			
Structures and surface improvements	$ 6,858,265	$ 1,146,825	$ 5,711,440
All other plant and equipment	5,597,678	1,852,040	3,745,638
Total plant and other equipment	$12,455,943	$ 2,998,865	$ 9,457,078

The estimated useful lives and salvage value percentages used in computing depreciation on various classes of property are as follows:

	Lives	*Salvage Percentages*
Revenue and Service Equipment		
Over-the-road tractors	6 Years	10%
Over-the-road trailers	8 Years	10
Terminal storage tanks	20–30 Years	10–15
Service equipment	4 Years	10–15
Liquid cargo docks	30 Years	15–33⅓

(continued)

	Lives	Salvage Percentages
Plant and Other Equipment		
Truck terminal buildings	20–25 Years	10%
Office and miscellaneous	Principally 3–10 Years	10
Leasehold improvements	Principally 5–30 Years	10–15
Other common facilities	15–30 Years	10–15

The excess of net book value of property, plant and equipment over tax basis was $8.93 million at December 31, 1974. By December 31, 1975, management estimated it would reach $9.5 million.

PROVISION FOR TAXES ON INCOME

A reconciliation of the current U.S. federal income tax rate of 48% to the effective tax rate in the consolidated statement of earnings for the year ended December 31, 1974, is presented in the following table:

	1974
Current U.S. federal income tax rate	48.0%
Increases (reductions) in tax rate resulting from:	
Investment tax credits utilized	(24.6)
Other, net	.3
Effective federal income tax rate	23.7%

The deferred income tax provisions of $223,000 for 1974 result from timing differences in the recognition of revenues and expenses for tax and financial reporting purposes. The tax effects of the timing differences in 1974 are detailed below:

(000s Omitted)	
	1974
Excess of tax depreciation over book depreciation	$645
Interest capitalized for book purposes, expensed for tax purposes	92
Difference in reserves not deductible until incurred	(124)
Difference in gains and losses recognized for book purposes from that recognized for tax purposes, net	(91)
Contract revenues deferred for book purposes but recognized for tax purposes	(97)
Other, net	21
	446
Less—investment tax credit utilized against deferred income tax provision	(223)
	$223

Total investment tax credits recorded as a reduction of the provision for federal income taxes amounted to approximately $706,000 for the year 1974.

In September, 1975, Robertson's management estimated that there would be a deferred tax provision of about $270,000 for 1975. It believed that the total investment tax credits to be recorded as a reduction of the provision for federal income taxes in 1975 would amount to about $778,000, leaving the company with an effective tax rate of about 23.4%.

Management expected that by December 31, 1975, the company would have $1,332,000 of investment tax credits available to reduce future tax payments. Most of these would expire between 1980 and 1982. Of such total credits by December, 1975, about $1,011,000 would have been applied as a reduction of deferred taxes.

APPENDIX 2
ROBERTSON DISTRIBUTION SYSTEMS, INC.
OPERATING SUMMARY (1971–1975)

The following table evidences in a statistical way the steady growth in the company's marine terminaling operations and the high degree of operating leverage which characterizes these operations.

	Year Ended December 31				
	1971	*1972*	*1973*	*1974*	*1975*
Barrels in Service (000's)	830	1,952	3,086	3,186	4,500
Operating revenues (000's)	$2,718	$2,913	$4,591	$7,578	$10,312
Operating expenses (000's)	$2,141	$2,342	$3,761	$4,644	$ 6,714
Operating earnings (000's)	$ 577	$ 571	$ 830	$2,934	$ 3,598
Contribution Margin	21.2%	19.6%	18.1%	38.7%	34.9%

Changes in common and contract motor carrier revenues (exclusive of leasing operations), expense, shipments, and miles operated are stated in the following schedule:

	Year Ended December 31				
	1971	*1972*	*1973*	*1974*	*1975*
Revenues (000's)	$ 20,234	$ 22,501	$ 26,578	$ 32,193	$ 27,624
Expenses (000's)	18,745	20,890	24,930	30,876	26,879
Shipments	200,347	223,082	224,788	228,875	149,319
Average round trip (miles)	178	168	197	203	229
Miles operated (000's)	35,669	37,680	44,476	46,598	34,199
Average revenue per mile	$ .567	$ .597	$ .598	$ .691	$ .808
Operating Ratio*	89.1%	89.6%	91.8%	95.9%	97.3%

*Ratio of operating expenses, excluding interest, to operating revenues.

PAKHOED HOLDING, N.V.

On September 17, 1975, Mr. Arthur Penny, acquisitions manager for the Dutch holding company, Pakhoed Holding, N.V., was at Kennedy Airport in New York waiting for his plane to make its long-delayed take-off for Denver, Colorado. Mr. Penny was on his way to Colorado Springs to meet Mr. L. M. Robertson, the founder of the Houston-based terminal and trucking company, Robertson Distribution Systems (RDS), at his summer home. The purpose of the trip was to wind up an informal agreement he had made with Mr. Robertson to acquire the Robertson family's stock at $22 a share.

Arthur Penny was anxious to get to Denver. He had received a phone call the day before from Charles Duncan, the Chairman of RDS. Duncan had suggested that they meet in Denver and discuss Pakhoed's offer to the Robertson family and the position of RDS's board.

Arthur's immediate problem, however, was rain. The weather in New York was awful; he hadn't seen so much rain since he left his native England. Planes were arriving and leaving hours behind schedule; Arthur's plane boarded for take-off an hour and a half late. "Not an auspicious start," he thought, wondering whether Mr. Duncan might become impatient. Arthur thought there was a good chance of it: Duncan, a former President of Coca Cola, was still a Coca Cola board member and was due at a Coca Cola board meeting later that afternoon.

While maneuvering his six-foot frame into his seat, Arthur noticed that the man on whose foot he was standing seemed to recognize him. Indeed, he himself knew the man; he was John W. Ingraham, Vice-President of First National City Bank, a member of RDS's board, and a close friend of its President, Ted Gaylord. "You Americans keep close tabs on a fellow," Arthur said.

Ingraham assured him that his presence was merely a coincidence and that he was on bank business. And, although both men were circumspect about their respective interests in RDS, Arthur was pleased that Ingraham would be with him on the flight and when he met Charles Duncan three and a half hours late. The flight captain had announced a revised arrival time as the plane waited for its clearance to take off. Storms were expected to slow the flight. The captain was right: the seat belt signs were on the entire time and visibility was comparatively good when one could see the wing lights.

As the plane struggled through the sky, Arthur reflected on the last few days. He had been with Pakhoed for a little over a year, having joined the company from the corporate planning and development group at British Petroleum. Now, as acquisitions

This case was prepared by Mark T. Teagan, Research Assistant, under the direction of Assistant Professor Kenneth J. Hatten and with the cooperation of Pakhoed's American manager, as a basis for class discussion. Some of the names and facts relating to the actual situation have been altered to facilitate such discussion. Some literary license has been taken with regard to direct quotations, personal reflections, and personal references. Also, certain descriptions of the negotiations involved have, for the sake of clarity and brevity, been condensed. Thus, the decision making process described here cannot be considered representative of that of Pakhoed Holding, N.V., or Robertson Distribution Systems, Inc. Similarly, the opinions expressed, whether overtly or implicitly, cannot be considered representative of those of the individuals involved.

manager, he was in charge of Pakhoed's American development program. Arthur felt that successful handling of Pakhoed's first U.S. acquisition and the company's largest acquisition to date would enhance his standing in his new company. He also felt that RDS was an excellent company, which would serve as a base for Pakhoed's further expansion of its terminal business into the U.S. and the Western Hemisphere. Though not knowing exactly to what extent RDS was facing an internal capital shortage, Arthur felt that Pakhoed's acquisition of the company was a now-or-never proposition. If the U.S. economy and the capital markets improved in late 1975 and early 1976, RDS might be able to obtain additional capital on its own. The market excitement generated by a major expansion would minimize the feasibility of any merger or acquisition by Pakhoed. If economic and capital market conditions didn't improve, both Pakhoed and RDS would have other problems.

Upon their arrival at Denver's airport, Ingraham and Penny walked quickly through the terminal to a limousine, which took them around the airport to Duncan's private jet. Penny wished he had taken the time to shave before the plane landed. Ingraham introduced the two men. Mr. Duncan was sympathetic when Penny apologized for being late, then immediately got to business. Duncan said that Pakhoed's offer would be acceptable to him, and most likely to the rest of the board, only if Pakhoed agreed to make the offer to all the shareholders and only if it was prepared to acquire 100% of the stock. Having previously determined just what he could and could not accept, Arthur was ready with a quick answer: "That's fine with us." "Then there should be few problems," replied Duncan. "Except that Ted has some reservations and may be hard to swing around."

Insofar as Ted Gaylord was RDS's President and CEO, a board member, the son-in-law of the founder, and one of the company's largest shareholders, Arthur Penny felt any reservations Ted might have could easily amount to at least a few problems. But he felt pleased with himself; his quick and assured response to Duncan's statement seemed to have surprised Duncan and Ingraham. In only a few minutes Duncan stood up, shook hands, and said he had to leave, offering Penny the use of his plane for the trip to Colorado Springs.

PAKHOED HOLDING, N.V.

Pakhoed Holding was a Netherlands-based international holding company. The parent company was responsible for planning, financing and employee policy; its three divisions—Paktank, Paktrans, and Blauwhoed—enjoyed a large measure of operating independence.

The Paktank division leased tank terminals and pipelines to the petroleum and chemical industries and rendered other logistical services. It had been in the terminal business since the 1800s and had built Europe's first tank terminal. With nearly nine million cubic meters of tank storage capacity, Paktank was the largest independent tankage company in the world. Facilities were located in Western Europe (primarily Rotterdam), in North America, and in the Caribbean.

With energy conservation continuing in Europe, and with a shift from oil consumption to other forms of energy, Paktank expected an average growth rate of only 4% per annum for oil storage over the next few years. As a result, Paktank expected to achieve a more moderate expansion in Europe than it had in the past. Emphasis in Europe would be placed on broadening the range of services offered.

Looking toward the United States, Paktank saw completely different opportunities from those available in Western Europe. Paktank believed that the increasing and continuing need for oil imports would call for changes in the American distribution system—in particular, a greater reliance on independent oil storage facilities. With these opportunities in mind, Paktank had already entered joint ventures in Philadelphia and in Los Angeles. In addition, the first crude oil was about to be discharged into the transhipment tanks of the Bonaire Petroleum Corporation in the Netherland Antilles, a joint venture of Paktank and Northville Industries Corporation of Long Island. Paktank planned to spend approximately $40 million to complete the Bonaire project. Although Bonaire was in the Caribbean, the terminal was intended for supplying oil to the U.S. The crude oil came from Africa and the Middle East in supertankers and at Bonaire was transferred to smaller tankers which could dock in U.S. harbors. By utilizing supertankers for the long voyage, and then switching the oil to smaller vessels, considerable savings on the total transport cost of oil could be effected.

The Paktrans division consisted of 20 operating companies active in various modes of distribution. Unlike the Paktank division, it had not expanded beyond Western Europe. Activities included specialized road and air transport, servicing the offshore oil industries, stevedoring, transhipment, forwarding, warehousing, and refrigerated storage. In 1975, Paktrans had suffered operating losses. The division had acquired the remaining 50% interest in the French road transport company ONATRA, a move which put Paktrans's earnings into the red. Paktrans had already cut ONATRA's fleet of vehicles, tightened its organization and reduced its total work force (by more than 200) to 800. These measures had improved operating results. Paktrans was looking forward to further improvement because of the chemical industry's recovery, which was of great importance to ONATRA. Improved sales in 1976 would have a strong effect on the results of the now substantially leaner company.

Pakhoed's other division, the Blauwhoed division, managed development and investment real estate in Europe and the United States. Its income had more than doubled in 1975 over 1974. Profits on real estate sales, rentals, and managed real estate funds all increased, as did the capital invested in the division. Management expected a similar pattern in coming years. See *Exhibits 1* and *2* for Pakhoed's income statements and balance sheets for 1974 and 1975.

ROBERTSON DISTRIBUTION SYSTEMS, INC.*

Robertson Distribution Systems, Inc., was a Texas corporation, organized in 1946. Through its subsidiaries, it operated an integrated bulk distribution company serving major shippers of chemicals, petrochemicals, petroleum products and construction materials in the Gulf Coast region of the United States. Robertson provided common and contract motor carriage, marine terminaling, bulk storage and full-service truck leasing.

Marine Terminaling

The company conducted its marine terminal operations through subsidiaries and in 1975 operated four terminals: two in the Houston, Texas, area and two in Tampa, Florida.

*See Robertson Distribution Systems case, p. 911, for more detail.

The Deer Park Marine Terminal, located on 102 acres owned by Robertson abutting the Houston Ship Channel, had 108 steel storage tanks with total rated storage capacity of approximately 3.5 million barrels. The tanks were designed for the safe storage and handling of chemical, petrochemical and petroleum products. The Deer Park facility included 4 docks with berths for 8 barges, and 2 ship docks situated on a turning basin. Pipelines within the terminal connected the storage tanks to the docks. A railroad switch engine, 7,000 feet of track, and modern loading racks facilitated the handling of products to and from railcars and tank trucks.

The Galena Park Terminal, located on 37 acres owned by Robertson, was also on the Houston Ship Channel and had 77 storage tanks with a total storage capacity of approximately 836,000 barrels. The facilities included a ship dock, a system of pipelines connecting the docks with tanks, modern railcar and tank truck loading racks, a 300-ton dry bulk storage facility and warehouse space totaling 31,000 square feet. Robertson also operated 2 leased terminals in Florida which included tanks for liquid storage, grain silos, salt storage buildings and other buildings for handling dry bulk products.

Motor Carrier Operations

Robertson conducted its interstate common carriage operations under operating authorities granted by the Interstate Commerce Commission (ICC). It also engaged in intrastate common and contract carriage in Texas and Louisiana under authorities granted by the Texas Railroad Commission and the Louisiana Public Service Commission. In addition to common and contract motor carrier service, Robertson provided full-service-maintenance leasing of trucks and tractor-trailers.

Robertson transported a wide variety of bulk products to most points in the continental United States, with primary concentration in the South and Southwest. Products shipped included bulk chemicals and petrochemicals, petroleum products, construction products such as cement and asphalt, dry and liquid fertilizers, salt, syrups, sulphur, wood chips used in the production of paper, and several dry bulk products.

Robertson owned, or leased, and operated fifteen truck terminal facilities in Texas, Louisiana and Arkansas, which served as dispatching and en-route maintenance facilities for its motor carrier operations.

In September 1975, Robertson's motor carrier fleet consisted of 510 tractors and 725 trailers. Of these, 65 tractors and 61 trailers were dedicated to the full-service leasing operations. Approximately two-thirds of Robertson's tractors were less than 5 years old.

Customers

Robertson's principal customers were major oil companies, cement manufacturers, manufacturers and processors of chemicals, and wood pulp and paper companies. In 1975, Robertson's twenty largest customers accounted for approximately 52% of its consolidated revenues. No single customer accounted for more than 5% of its revenues during that period. Robertson's twenty largest customers in 1975, in alphabetical order, were:

Air Products & Chemicals Company	Dow Chemical Company
Centex Cement Corporation	Eastex, Inc.
Diamond Shamrock Chemical Company	Ethyl Corporation

Exxon Chemical Company, U.S.A.	Olin Corporation
Exxon Company U.S.A.	PPG Industries, Inc.
General Portland Cement Company	Procter & Gamble Co.
Gulf Oil Company—U.S.	San Antonio Portland Cement Company
Ideal Cement Company	Shell Chemical Company
Kaiser Cement & Gypsum Company	Shell Oil Company
Monsanto Company	The Upjohn Company

Competition

The primary competitors for Robertson's marine terminal operations were the private marine terminal facilities owned and operated by oil refineries, chemical companies and other concerns. Robertson also competed with other marine terminal companies which offered their services to the public. One competing concern operated a nationwide network of terminals and, in the Houston, Texas, area, operated terminaling facilities significantly larger than Robertson's (*Exhibit 3*).

Robertson's motor carrier operations competed with the private carriage of major shippers and with a number of specialized common carriers, several of which were larger than Robertson. The amount of direct competition to which Robertson was subject depended, among other things, upon the issuance of authorities by the various governmental agencies which regulated the common carriage business. The issuance of new certificates depended upon the hearing agency's determination of the adequacy of existing carrier service.

Regulation

Interstate carriers are regulated by the ICC and intrastate carriers are regulated by state regulatory agencies. The jurisdiction of the ICC, the United States Department of Transportation, and the various state agencies, is broad and covers practically every phase of a carrier's business. It includes the regulation of territories, rates, commodities shipped, equipment, safety of equipment and operations, work standards for drivers, accounting systems, certain financings, the issuance of securities, mergers, and acquisitions.

The company's motor carrier subsidiaries were not permitted to pass increased costs through to their customers concurrently, but had to absorb these costs until rate increases were allowed by the regulatory authorities. Applications for proposed rate increases are filed with the appropriate regulatory body. If shippers, the public or competing carriers object to the proposed rates, the agency may order hearings in which all protesting parties can be heard. During times of sharply rising costs, motor carrier companies typically experience a regulatory lag before higher costs can be recovered through rate increases.

Lines of Business Comparison

Exhibit 4 is a schedule of the company's revenues and earnings before income taxes, and other items by lines of business, for the four years ended December 31, 1974, and an estimate for 1975. *Exhibit 5* contains a more extensive financial statement by RDS.

Edward O. Gaylord

Ted Gaylord joined Robertson in 1957 when the company had equity of $1 million and no debt. He was made Executive Vice-President (Finance) in 1962, but it was not until 1967, when the health of the company's President failed, that Gaylord became President. This promotion heralded major changes in the company's development: Gaylord slowly introduced professional managers into what had been a substantially untrained but experienced group of old hands who had matured with the business.

After the establishment of a professional management team, the next major phase in Robertson's development was diversification. Having decided that, as a trucking operation, Robertson was in the distribution business, Gaylord viewed marine terminaling as a logical and profitable extension of current operations. By 1972, Gaylord had been able to get Robertson started in marine terminaling at its Galena Park Terminal on the Houston Ship Channel and was planning a major new terminal at Deer Park. To raise the capital needed for this expansion, he first increased the scope of the trucking operation, thereby providing cash for the capital-intensive marine terminals and a steady and growing earnings stream. This would make Robertson attractive for public issue.

Robertson went public on May 4, 1972, at a price of $20.50, a P/E of 14½. In some ways, the timing was fortunate because Robertson hit the market when the transportation index peaked. Between May, 1974, and September, 1975, Robertson's stock fell as low as $8.25; it was hovering around $10 when Arthur Penny was attempting to effect Pakhoed's acquisition of the Robertson family's stock. Very few of the initial public investors were still shareholders; the publicly-held stock turned about once each year and inquiries had revealed that most non-family owners had a tax basis of between $10 and $13 per share.

RDS AND PAKHOED

In 1972, the Vice-President of Robertson's terminal operations, who was reputed to have an excellent eye for potential deals, was on a business trip in Europe. Having heard of Pakhoed, he thought there might be some interesting and synergystic possibilities in combining Robertson's American and Pakhoed's European operations in a joint venture. The contact was informal and produced nothing beyond increased mutual awareness.

In 1973, when Robertson's new terminal on the Houston Ship Channel was beginning to take shape, Pakhoed approached RDS seeking a majority interest. Robertson countered with an offer to sell 300,000 shares, a 30% interest. Pakhoed responded with a request for warrants, which would ultimately have allowed it to control Robertson. Though negotiations got to the stage at which both parties thought a press release was necessary to protect themselves and to comply with SEC regulations, objections by Mr. L. M. Robertson and Ted Gaylord led to Pakhoed's backing off.

PAKHOED IN THE U.S.

When Arthur Penny joined Pakhoed in January, 1974, he was assigned the task of creating and coordinating an American development program for Pakhoed. Arthur and his project team recommended that Pakhoed become a major presence in marine terminaling on the American East and West Coasts and at a major Gulf port. Pakhoed's management accepted the recommendations and was determined to implement them.

On the East Coast, Pakhoed entered into a joint venture with Philadelphia-based Thoroughfare Petroleum, Inc. in March 1974. The venture developed well and, by late 1975, Pakhoed planned to broaden its scope.

On the West Coast, Pakhoed entered into a joint venture in Los Angeles with Pacific Lighting, in June 1975. Compliance with environmental restrictions had posed problems, primarily a greater than anticipated capital investment and a later than anticipated commencement of earnings.

Only the Gulf Coast remained without a Pakhoed presence. Pakhoed prepared market studies of Houston, New Orleans, Lake Charles and two other major Gulf Coast locations before finally selecting Houston as the number-one target—primarily because of its dynamic growth and its proximity to major oil and chemical activity.

In Houston, Pakhoed was interested in a controlling interest in an existing company for two major reasons. First, its management wanted to maintain a steady 12% growth in EPS as reported in its public statements, especially since a large share of its ownership lay with institutional investors. Second, Pakhoed had to maintain stability in its balance sheet.[1]

Penny's acquisition team had determined that a ''grass-roots operation,'' building terminal facilities from scratch, would take approximately three years to become operational and another year to become profitable. During this period, the value of fixed assets would lag behind the value of the long-term loans needed to create them, and there would be no earnings. On the other hand, buying outright would produce immediate earnings. In addition, Pakhoed had structured the necessary cash into its balance sheet a year in advance by allocating part of its increase in debt and equity to working capital.[2] Management believed that the cash was available and that an acquisition would not change Pakhoed's debt/equity ratio. Of course, taking construction loans for a new terminal would directly increase the company's debt.

By May 1975, Pakhoed had acquired 4.7–4.8% of Robertson stock—an amount

[1]When accounting for those subsidiaries in which Pakhoed had ownership of 50% or less, a category which included its American joint ventures, only the net results of the participations were included in Pakhoed's financial statements—that is, only Pakhoed's share of the income or loss was reported; its share of assets and debt was not. This was done for two reasons: first, it had been done for many years and Pakhoed wished to maintain accounting consistency; and second, it enabled Pakhoed to leverage up joint ventures without affecting its own balance sheet. If Pakhoed's interest exceeded 50%, assets and debt were also consolidated on its financial statements.

[2]Pakhoed was confronted with a unique problem in gathering the cash with which to buy RDS. In the Netherlands, the amount of equity a domestic corporation can export is limited to the increase in equity created during the previous year. Any investment in foreign subsidiaries beyond that amount is considered a loan, which is assessed an interest rate. The interest is not deductible for tax purposes and so is shown as earnings.

In the United States, the IRS has thin capitalization guidelines. If the IRS deems a corporation to have too little equity, a portion of the debt will be deemed to be equity and the interest to be non-deductible. Pakhoed thus had to inject enough equity to avoid thin capitalization rulings but could not export so much equity from the Netherlands as to come under that country's equity export limitations.

Pakhoed would want to keep RDS's and its own debt/equity ratios near their present 60/40. Therefore 40% of the $26 million would have to come from equity sources inside and outside the Netherlands, keeping in mind the above restrictions. Pakhoed had confronted this problem in its previous American dealings and knew it was approaching a thin capitalization problem in the United States. If the RDS deal were to go through, Pakhoed hoped to restructure its entire U.S. capitalization.

just short of the 5% ownership which requires disclosure of such ownership to the SEC and the company. At this point, Pakhoed decided to make an all-out effort to acquire a controlling interest in Robertson.

A member of his staff had provided Arthur with a general description of the advantages and disadvantages of different methods of acquisition (*Appendix 1*). In Rotterdam, Arthur's team had studied Robertson and calculated its value from many points of view. Pakhoed emphasized earnings streams in its valuations—both those earnings reasonably to be expected under current management[3] and those which might occur with Pakhoed's expanding operations. In neither case did Pakhoed assume it could improve the efficiency of the company because Pakhoed had great respect for RDS's management. A present value of future earnings model (net of taxes, interest and investment tax credits) yielded the following values for RDS stock:

1972	1973	1974	1975	1976	1977	1978	1979
$13	$12.90	$14.80	$15	$18.50	$21	$24	$27

In its valuation, Pakhoed had to rely solely on its own experience and RDS's published information. However, Penny had commissioned Morgan Guaranty and a private consultant to conduct studies of the trucking and marine terminal markets. The trucking study helped convince Pakhoed's board of directors that the American trucking industry was not in as bad straits as Paktrans's experience in Europe might have suggested. The marine terminal study stated that there was a strong and growing U.S. market. In addition to analyzing basic trends in marine terminaling, the study included an analysis of many marine terminal operations based on interviews with their customers. Pakhoed was pleased that the study was highly complimentary to Robertson and that it contained no surprises.

Although Pakhoed took these market studies into consideration, as well as replacement values and the market value of operating permits, it insisted that the price paid for the company had to be justified by an earnings analysis. The replacement value of Robertson's marine terminals in particular could well be greater than book value. Although marine terminals were depreciated over twenty years for book purposes, Pakhoed knew from experience that a well-managed marine terminal could have had a useful life of approximately fifty years. In addition, inflation, particularly in the construction industry, would make it more expensive to duplicate Robertson's facilities than to buy the company. One expert estimated that a new storage facility like RDS's would have an all-inclusive cost of about $12 per barrel. And, although environmental conditions seemed more favorable in the Houston area, Pakhoed had learned in its California joint venture how expensive a delay in obtaining permits could be. Such factors influenced Pakhoed,

[3]The basic difference between Pakhoed's evaluation model and a simple value based on RDS's current operating results was Pakhoed's treatment of the investment tax credit (ITC). Having spent over $30 million on new marine terminal facilities, RDS has available sufficient ITCs to reduce the effective federal tax rate from 48% to 23.7% in 1974 and to 23.4% in 1975. Pakhoed, in valuing Robertson, assumed that the ITCs would eventually expire (although it wasn't certain when) and used the 48% tax rate in its valuations.

In this respect Pakhoed did the same thing the stock market seemed to be doing. RDS's P/E was always below that of the market unless one subtracted the ITCs from reported earnings, in which case RDS's modified earnings led to a P/E roughly in line with the market average.

but normally they did not affect the company's decision to proceed with an acquisition unless some factor was so out of line (negatively) as to demand an effective veto of the deal.

When he presented his proposals to Pakhoed's board, Arthur learned that Pakhoed would go along with the acquisition only if Robertson's management stayed on. Although Arthur was told to aim for a price of $21 a share, it was indicated that $24 or $25 could be acceptable, barring any substantial new information which would have a negative impact on Robertson's value.

Having evaluated Robertson and received his board's approval, Arthur now had to plan how to approach the company. In early September, 1975, he decided to call L. M. Robertson, founder, retired Chairman of the board, and the largest shareholder of Robertson. Arthur told him that Pakhoed would be interested in acquiring the Robertson family's stock, which then amounted to approximately 35% of the stock outstanding. Mr. Robertson said he would be interested at $25 a share. Arthur felt he would have to get Pakhoed's board's approval to meet this figure, and, besides, it was a first offer. So he rejected it, saying that $25 was really much too high. To Arthur's surprise, Mr. Robertson replied, "Alright, Mr. Penny, make it $22 and that's my last offer, take it or leave it!"

Arthur believed that he was serious. Mr. Robertson was a former truck driver and had begun his business career with only an eighth-grade education; but he had founded and developed a $40 million corporation. Arthur felt that this sort of man wasn't kidding when he said "take it or leave it." So, given that the $22 price was reasonable and would be approved with little effort, he accepted informally. Arthur made plans to meet with Mr. Robertson; if everything went off all right, he would then meet with the Chairman of the board and with Robertson's President and CEO.

FOLLOW-UP: TED GAYLORD

After his meeting with Charles Duncan, Arthur felt the major likely stumbling block to the merger would be Ted Gaylord: Arthur's flight to Mr. Robertson's home on Duncan's private jet and his short stay in Colorado Springs were both pleasant, especially when contrasted to the flight from New York. Mr. Robertson and his wife (who sat on the RDS board) merely stated the same two conditions Duncan had. Arthur concluded that the family was not only very willing to sell but that they had had it in mind for some time. Arthur also sensed that there may have been some disagreements between Mr. Robertson and his son-in-law, whom he knew owned 10.7% of Robertson's stock. When asked, Mr. Robertson had said, ". . . sure, Ted will go along." But Arthur wondered why Mr. Robertson had retired as Chairman of the board. He also remembered noticing that Mr. Robertson's younger son, who had been an officer and a director, was no longer listed in either capacity in the annual report. And the hesitancy with which Mr. Robertson had said that Ted would go along hardly inspired certitude about it.

After Duncan's statement that Ted would have reservations and Mr. Robertson's hesitancy, Arthur was more concerned about the upcoming meeting with Gaylord than he had been about the others. As he flew to Houston to meet Gaylord, he thought about Gaylord's position and likely concerns.

Arthur understood why Gaylord might be reluctant to let go of a company he had worked so hard to build. Yet Arthur knew that if Gaylord threatened to walk out,

Pakhoed's board might well not go through with the deal. Arthur sensed that Robertson's board and Gaylord shared a mutual respect. Although Gaylord ran the company, he would give serious consideration to the board's advice—which, in this case, seemed to be in Arthur's favor. In addition, Gaylord might feel, as Pakhoed's board did, that it would do great damage to Robertson if he left precipitately. His self-image and his pride in the company could well dictate against his allowing that to happen. Of course, Gaylord could use the threat of walking out as a negotiating point.

Gaylord could also decide to recommend that the shareholders hold out for a better price. If he demanded an extra $1 per share, Pakhoed would most likely pay it without resorting to a tender offer. If Gaylord asked for more than that, Pakhoed could withdraw or go through with the tender offer, which Arthur had prepared in case of such a contingency. The tender offer could be registered and ready to go within a few days.

In backing up his demand for a higher price, Gaylord could value the stock on replacement value. Arthur knew that a liberal replacement value estimate would place the price per share above $22.

For Gaylord, another possible tactic would be recommending to the board and to the shareholders not to approve the merger at all. He could claim that the stock was worth more, or perhaps even come up with another buyer—perhaps a minority investor—who would leave him in charge.

Finally, Gaylord might try to prevent the merger, or even a tender offer, through the U.S. court system. The courts had often been used to create delay and expense for an acquiring corporation in the hope that it might back off.

On the other hand, Arthur realized that there were several factors which would help prevent Gaylord's taking any action unfavorable to Pakhoed. Though he wasn't certain, Arthur felt that RDS might be facing a cash shortage due to its recent extensive capital expansion in marine terminals. With the poor capital markets of 1975, Gaylord could most likely obtain new funds only from board members. Although many of them were wealthy, with the Robertson family wanting to sell and apparently in some conflict with Gaylord, such a step might prove difficult.

Another factor Arthur knew Gaylord had to be considering was his and Robertson's other directors' liability if they were to recommend against the merger or in favor of holding out for a higher price. Whether or not the Robertson family sold, if RDS's stock price then fell back to, say, $12, or went even lower, there would most likely be shareholder suits accusing the present board of negligence, or inside dealing, or both. And, in late 1975, experts were almost evenly split about the future direction of the economy—a condition which made the market flighty, unstable and litigious.

Arthur rode the elevator up to the eighteenth floor, where he got out and entered the Robertson offices. A few people were waiting in the sitting area for appointments with various executives. The receptionist took Arthur's name. He and his team had prepared an extensive list of the questions, and reservations that Gaylord and other Robertson officers might have, and had formulated Pakhoed's responses. Arthur knew he would have to be in command of all that information (as well as the relevant financial analyses) to be prepared for any possible tactical or strategic move Robertson might make to counter Pakhoed's plans. There was a short wait until Mr. Gaylord, tanned and smiling, appeared. Gaylord was courteous and easy-going, in a "down home" sort of way. Arthur remembered that one of his bosses at British Petroleum had said long ago: "When a Texan starts coming on as though he's just a little ol' country boy—that's time to watch out!"

EXHIBIT 1
PAKHOED HOLDING, N.V.
Balance Sheets 1967 to 1975[1]
(in $; 000,000 omitted)

	1967	1968	1969	1970	1971	1972	1973	1974	1975
Land and buildings	36.3	40.9	42.9	47.1	46.5	47.4	56.2	58.3	88.1
Buildings under construction	4.9	5.2	2.4	5.3	6.6	9.7	7.8	9.4	10.4
Tank terminals and ancillary equipment	46.3	63.4	81.9	88.8	102.1	124.6	144.0	164.2	156.7
Machinery and equipment	8.1	9.1	10.3	7.7	7.0	7.8	9.8	11.3	16.4
Fixed assets	95.6	118.6	137.5	148.9	162.2	189.5	217.8	243.2	271.6
Intangible assets	—	—	—	—	—	—	—	—	4.1
Non-consolidated subsidiaries	11.1	18.8	24.2	25.1	27.9	30.9	29.7	52.7	88.5
	106.7	137.4	161.7	174.0	190.1	220.4	247.5	295.9	364.2
Current assets less current liabilities (working capital)	5.5	10.9	7.6	17.5	20.0	40.5	56.9	65.4	52.7
Total assets less current liabilities	112.2	148.3	169.3	191.5	210.1	260.9	304.4	361.3	416.9
Financed from:									
Shareholders' Equity									
Share capital at par value	14.1	16.7	17.8	18.6	19.3	22.0	22.9	27.2	28.3
Retained earnings plus contributed capital in excess of par value	27.2	36.5	40.0	42.8	46.4	56.5	61.7	84.6	92.4
Total shareholders' equity	41.3	53.2	57.8	61.4	65.7	78.5	84.6	111.8	120.7
Accumulated depreciation	32.1	37.8	42.7	48.8	53.7	60.3	67.7	76.0	70.0
Permanent capital	73.4	91.0	100.5	110.2	119.4	138.8	152.3	187.8	190.7
Deferred taxes and accrued liabilities	7.2	7.9	7.7	8.2	8.7	11.2	10.2	12.1	22.0
Long-term debts	31.6	49.4	61.1	73.1	82.0	110.9	141.9	161.4	204.2
Long-term liabilities	38.8	57.3	68.8	81.3	90.7	122.1	152.1	173.5	226.2
Total permanent capital and long-term liabilities	112.2	148.3	169.3	191.5	210.1	260.9	304.4	361.3	416.9

[1]Figures of 1967 to 1974 restated to permit comparison with 1975. (The original guilder amounts have been translated at the rate of US $1.00 = Fl. 2.69)

EXHIBIT 2
PAKHOED HOLDING, N.V.
Profit & Loss Accounts 1967 to 1975[1]
(in $; 000,000 omitted)

	1967	1968	1969	1970	1971	1972	1973	1974	1975
Revenues	48.2	58.9	66.1	67.9	73.1	79.5	95.2	113.4	150.7
Expenses	−36.2	−44.0	−48.9	−46.1	−48.7	−53.5	−63.1	−76.5	−110.9
Depreciation	− 4.8	− 6.2	− 6.3	− 7.1	− 7.7	− 7.8	− 8.9	−10.6	−13.0
Operating results	7.2	8.7	10.9	14.7	16.7	18.2	23.2	26.3	26.8
Non-consolidated subsidiaries									
Income	1.5	1.7	1.7	1.4	2.9	3.6	2.5	3.4	5.1
Depreciation	− 0.3	− 0.4	− 0.7	− 1.0	− 1.0	− 0.9	− 0.9	− 0.9	− 1.0
Income after depreciation	1.2	1.3	1.0	0.4	1.9	2.7	1.6	2.5	4.1
Total	8.4	10.0	11.9	15.1	18.6	20.9	24.8	28.8	30.9
Net interest expense	− 1.6	− 2.7	− 3.6	− 5.0	− 5.3	− 5.3	− 7.0	− 6.9	−11.0
Profit before taxation and extraordinary income and charges	6.8	7.3	8.3	10.1	13.3	15.6	17.8	21.9	19.9
Taxation	− 2.8	− 2.3	− 2.9	− 4.1	− 5.8	− 6.8	− 7.5	− 8.6	− 5.1
Profit before extraordinary income and charges	4.0	5.0	5.4	6.0	7.5	8.8	10.3	13.3	14.8
Extraordinary income and charges	− 0.2	− 0.3	0.1	0.1	− 0.3	− 0.3	− 0.6	− 0.3	− 0.2
Net profit	3.8	4.7	5.5	6.1	7.2	8.5	9.7	13.0	14.6

[1]Figures of 1967 to 1974 restated to permit comparison with 1975.

Figures per Fl. 20 share
(in $; adjusted for capital movements)

	1967	1968	1969	1970	1971	1972	1973	1974	1975
Cash flow	3.22	3.74	3.84	4.38	4.89	5.04	5.70	6.42	7.50
Net profit	1.38	1.55	1.69	1.88	2.22	2.49	2.84	3.41	3.82
Cash dividend	0.61	0.63	0.71	0.80	0.89	1.03	1.07	1.32	1.49

(The original guilder amounts have been translated at the rate of US $1.00 = Fl. 2.69)

EXHIBIT 3 Public Storage Capacity, Houston Shipping Channel, 1975

Company	Capacity (barrels)*
GATX	9,770,000
Robertson Terminals, Inc.	4,500,000
International Terminal Company[1]	560,000
Anchor Tanklines, Inc.	500,000
Sea Coast Terminals	86,000
Hess Terminals[2]	6 to 7 million

[1]Controlled by Mitsui and expanding by about 1 million barrels.
[2]Primarily trading on its own account and not normally in the public market controlled by Hess Oil and Gas.
*1 barrel: 42 gallons.

EXHIBIT 4 **Revenues and Earnings by Line of Business, Robertson Distribution Systems, Inc. and Subsidiaries**

The following table evidences in a statistical way the steady growth in the company's marine terminaling operations and the high degree of operating leverage which characterizes these operations.

	Year Ended December 31				
	1971	1972	1973	1974	1975
Barrels in Service (000's)	830	1,952	3,086	3,186	4,500
Operating revenues (000's)	$2,718	$2,913	$4,591	$7,578	$10,312
Operating expenses (000's)	$2,141	$2,342	$3,761	$4,644	$ 6,714
Operating earnings (000's)	$ 577	$ 571	$ 830	$2,934	$ 3,598
Contribution Margin	21.2%	19.6%	18.1%	38.7%	34.9%

Changes in common and contract motor carrier revenues (exclusive of leasing operations), expenses, shipments, and miles operated are stated in the following schedule:

	Year Ended December 31				
	1971	1972	1973	1974	1975
Revenues (000's)	$ 20,234	$ 22,501	$ 26,578	$ 32,193	$ 27,624
Expenses (000's)	18,745	20,890	24,930	30,876	26,879
Shipments	200,347	223,082	224,788	228,875	149,319
Average round trip (miles)	178	168	197	203	229
Miles operated (000's)	35,669	37,680	44,476	46,598	34,199
Average revenue per mile	$ .567	$ .597	$ .598	$ .691	$ .808
Operating Ratio*	89.1%	89.6%	91.8%	95.9%	97.3%

*Ratio of operating expenses, excluding interest, to operating revenues.

EXHIBIT 5
ROBERTSON DISTRIBUTION SYSTEMS, INC. AND SUBSIDIARIES
Consolidated Balance Sheet
December 31, 1973–1975

Assets	1975	1974	1973
Current Assets			
Cash	$ 1,346,785	$ 2,630,939	$ 1,837,578
Receivables:			
Trade accounts	3,641,781	3,449,351	3,543,569
Estimated Federal income tax	—	—	138,541
Other	730,254	755,724	438,822
Inventories:			
Materials and supplies	785,253	793,147	672,539
Other	57,389	105,707	322,460
Deposits	151,444	448,732	262,320
Prepaid expenses	415,837	396,086	337,542
Total current assets	7,128,743	8,579,686	7,553,371

(*continued*)

EXHIBIT 5 (Cont.)

Assets	*1975*	*1974*	*1973*
Property, Plant, and Equipment, at Cost			
Revenue and service equipment	46,351,212	39,177,841	36,828,809
Plant and other equipment	12,455,943	9,781,808	8,593,147
Land	3,397,991	3,324,479	3,324,783
Construction in progress	3,174,370	5,265,290	680,073
	65,379,516	57,549,418	49,426,812
Less—Accumulated depreciation and amortization	18,414,557	15,649,340	13,119,940
	46,964,959	41,900,078	36,306,872
Other Assets			
Permits, at cost	448,257	443,781	437,449
Deferred charges and other	268,536	380,221	384,797
	716,793	824,002	822,246
	$54,810,495	$51,303,766	$44,682,489
Liabilities and Stockholders' Equity			
Current Liabilities			
Payables:			
Trade accounts	$ 1,872,036	$ 1,677,469	$ 1,584,345
New equipment purchases	—	43,786	320,308
Dividends	139,758	116,479	68,847
Accrued liabilities	2,006,705	2,010,656	1,479,307
Estimated Federal income tax	3,375	331,246	—
	4,021,874	4,179,636	3,452,807
Long-term debt due within 1 yr.	1,901,246	863,684	766,611
Total current liabilities	5,923,120	5,043,320	4,219,418
Long-Term Debt	25,849,484	25,370,731	22,344,129
Deferred Federal Taxes on Income	3,251,020	2,951,736	2,632,712
Other Liabilities	775,440	872,312	545,625
Stockholders' Equity			
Common stock, no par; authorized 5,000,000, issued 1,245,426 shares	4,664,340	4,664,340	4,664,340
Additional paid-in capital	1,535,996	1,535,996	1,410,996
Retained earnings	13,851,029	11,890,302	10,121,768
	20,051,365	18,090,638	16,197,104
Less—Cost of 81,963; 80,790 and 98,435 shares in treasury (1975–73 respectively)	1,039,934	1,024,971	1,256,499
	19,011,431	17,065,667	14,940,605
	$54,810,495	$51,303,766	$44,682,489

(continued)

EXHIBIT 5 (Cont.)

Consolidated Statement of Earnings
December 31, 1973–1975

	1975	1974	1973
Operating Revenues			
Transportation and thruput	$29,460,209	$33,684,456	$28,180,691
Rent and use charges	8,218,564	6,495,463	3,750,554
Other operating revenue	2,025,088	1,608,121	900,573
Fuel sales	—	743,626	1,341,900
Total operating revenues	39,703,861	42,531,666	34,173,718
Operating Expenses			
Salaries	3,539,092	3,253,458	2,787,439
Operating wages	10,659,647	11,849,122	8,775,049
Other compensation expense	2,113,992	1,800,085	1,356,410
Total	16,312,731	16,902,665	12,918,898
Operations and maintenance	5,540,981	5,641,812	5,193,400
Depreciation and amortization	4,669,463	4,541,553	3,974,591
Equipment rent	498,867	2,928,237	1,486,653
Selling and administrative	3,277,221	2,822,283	2,221,698
Taxes and licenses	2,200,685	2,406,093	2,054,488
Other operating expense	2,445,123	2,170,793	1,976,163
Cost of fuel sales	—	413,336	691,509
Total operating expenses	34,945,071	37,826,772	30,517,400
Earnings from operations	4,758,790	4,704,894	3,656,318
Other Expenses (Income), net			
Interest:			
Incurred	2,395,683	2,176,234	1,633,309
Income	(70,388)	—	—
Capitalized	(334,028)	192,590	290,500
Expensed	1,991,272	1,983,644	1,342,809
Gain on sale of equipment	(328,613)	(99,269)	(174,516)
Miscellaneous	(121,795)	(53,493)	143,426
Total other expenses, net	1,540,864	1,830,882	1,311,719
Earnings before taxes on income	3,217,926	2,874,012	2,344,599
Provision for Taxes on Income			
Current	483,375	457,794	136,406
Deferred	269,677	223,322	420,058
Total provision for taxes on income	753,052	681,116	556,464
Net Earnings	$ 2,464,874	$ 2,192,896	$ 1,788,135
Earnings per common share	$ 2.08	$ 1.91	$ 1.57

APPENDIX 1
A GENERAL DESCRIPTION OF THE ADVANTAGES AND DISADVANTAGES OF DIFFERENT METHODS OF ACQUISITION

PURCHASE OF ASSETS

Our legal department would prefer a straight purchase of assets arrangement because it will enable us to buy the assets without assuming any liabilities or warranties. Any hidden liabilities and legal problems would be left with Robertson. Such deals consist merely of the purchaser buying the seller's assets with cash, and the seller paying off its shareholders. The purchaser obviously prefers to assume no liabilities; the seller obviously would prefer to be free of them.

Insofar as trucking and terminaling are both highly litigious businesses, Robertson would most likely not accept such an arrangement or would do so only for a hefty premium.

Robertson would probably demand a high price under a purchase of assets arrangement, because it would have to pay a recapture tax on accelerated depreciation and on tax credits taken on recently-acquired depreciable equipment (whether new or used) not yet used for the time specified under American tax law. Another problem is that Pakhoed may have difficulty retaining the present management team. Since the board prefers that we send as few managers as possible to new acquisitions, this would be a major drawback.

You should note that to be tax-free under American law, a purchase of assets must normally be done only with the buyer's voting stock. We would have to register our stock with the SEC; such registrations are expensive and time-consuming.

TENDER OFFER

The biggest drawback posed by a tender offer is the necessity of registering such offerings with the SEC. Since Robertson is closely held, a tender offer is most likely unnecessary. (It would perhaps be the most feasible method if Robertson's stock were more widely distributed.)

We in the legal department aren't wild about tender offers anyway. As the buyer, Pakhoed would receive no representations or warranties from Robertson, thus leaving us unprotected and subject to unwelcome surprises.

A tender offer is often unwelcome to the potential seller's management since the buyer essentially bypasses them and goes directly to the stockholders. However, sometimes, particularly when management owns a fair amount of stock, management may attempt to force a tender offer in order to delay the acquisition or to negotiate the price upward.

STATUTORY MERGER

In America, a statutory merger automatically results by operation of law if the parties comply with the requirements dictated by the home states of the involved corporations. A merger results in one of the joining corporations surviving as a legal entity. (In a consolidation, none of the joining corporations continue to exist, and a new corporation is created.)

We would most likely want to structure the deal so that Robertson remains a legal entity. Almost any form of acquisition in which Robertson is not the surviving taxable legal entity will cause depreciation to be recaptured on operating assets. In addition, investment tax credits (ITCs) which have been taken on these properties may be subject to recapture at the time of sale. Without financial statements more detailed than annual reports, it is difficult to calculate how much accelerated depreciation and ITC recapture would amount to. We would have to estimate by how much net book value of property, plant and equipment exceeds their tax basis. This figure would have to be added to deferred federal income taxes and the current flow-through of the ITC. The total would be taxable at ordinary income rates.

IMPLEMENTATION

We should avoid any deal which would entail stock or notes, in order to avoid registering with the SEC. Most likely, Robertson shareholders would not want to receive stock traded only on foreign exchanges.

An installment sale arrangement may possibly benefit the Robertson family from a tax viewpoint. However, their tax situation is peculiar to them. An installment sale would require the issuance and therefore the registration.

If we can get the Robertson family to go along with our offer, we can most likely avoid the necessity of a tender offer; $21 a share, a 64% premium (over current market prices), should make most shareholders amenable to a statutory merger.

Thus, to avoid SEC registration we should offer cash for shares; to avoid tax recapture, we should use the statutory merger form with Robertson as the surviving legal entity. Robertson's directors would have to approve the merger, as (under Texas law) would two-thirds of the shareholders.

BIG D DRUG, INC.

Big D Drug, Inc. and its underwriter, Phillips and Company, successfully completed an SEC Regulation A offering of $500,000 in September, 1973. On September 6, 1974, Big D's chairman and president, Louis Gentry, addressed his company's first annual meeting at the Hotel Buena Vista in downtown Heaton, West Aloe, and announced:

> At the end of our first fiscal year, June 30, 1974, we had chalked up sales of $1,106,509 and a net income after tax of $3,063. . . . I am pleased that we have completed our first fiscal year of operations in the black.

Now, on May 14, 1975, Gentry was reading a letter which his attorney had sent him by special delivery.

LAW OFFICES OF
BURGETT E. JASON
HEATON, WEST ALOE

PERSONAL AND
CONFIDENTIAL

May 13, 1975

Mr. Louis Gentry
Big D Drug, Inc.
710 Mapleton Drive
Heaton, West Aloe

Dear Louis:

As I have communicated with you in the past, I am getting more and more distressed concerning the obvious deteriorating financial condition of Big D Drug, Inc. and its cash flow problems.

As you know, we have been barraged by a series of lawsuits from trade creditors indicating that the company is unable to pay bills as they reasonably mature. While we can fend off creditors in litigation for some time (by reason of the normal court trial delay schedules), ultimately a decision must be reached concerning the viability of the company as a going concern.

You have indicated to me that you are in the process of disposing of certain stores and certain merchandise, but nonetheless, the cash flow crunch continues. *Further, I have an indication that, to fund your business, you might be utilizing money-order trust funds which results in constant delay in payment of money orders to the*

This case was prepared by Assistant Professor Kenneth J. Hatten as a basis for class discussion rather than to illustrate either effective or ineffective handling of an administrative situation.

bank handling same. This, of course, violates the banking laws of the state of West Aloe with respect to trust funds. It may have deeper implications than just an inability to pay trade creditors as debts mature.

I spoke to you briefly about the availability of Chapter XI of the Bankruptcy Laws of the United States. This statute provides general relief to a debtor while permitting it to remain in business in order to develop a Plan of Arrangement to compromise its unsecured creditors. The Plan of Arrangement may be to delay creditors and to cause a 100% pay-out, but in an extended period of time. It also has the effect of staying all litigation to permit the Plan to go forward.

I recognize your aversion to proceedings of this type. However, if Big D Drug, Inc. is to remain a viable organization, it needs an injection of capital immediately, in the form of either equity or debt capital. If this is unachievable, you may wish to consider the availability of the aforesaid Chapter XI proceedings.

Please do not think that I am questioning your judgment. However, as president of a public company, you must do everything possible to continue the viability of that company without the continued legal harassments that you are presently experiencing because of your inability to pay bills as they reasonably mature. Chapter XI was written for companies like yours, and many have taken advantage of this procedure.

I do not mean further to suggest that the above is a panacea for all problems, but it certainly has given companies an opportunity to regroup, make some definite plans, and proceed with their business affairs.

Your immediate attention to this is requested, and I would be more than happy to sit down with you and explain further the legal ramifications of this procedure. If you do not avail yourself of this or a substantial recapitalization of the company, I fear that you will simply go deeper and deeper and ultimately be required to answer to the Securities and Exchange Commission and your shareholders for a business failure, and for your unwillingness to take certain definitive steps to keep the company a going concern.

I consider this matter of urgent import and your attention is requested. We stand ready and able to assist you in all phases of this matter.

Very truly yours,

Burgett E. Jason

Burgett E. Jason
BEJ:mjb

Gentry had called Jason and Big D's accountants a few days earlier, seeking advice. He felt he could save his company and wanted to hear their ideas on measures to get things back on a sound basis. He was surprised and worried by Jason's suggestion to take the public company into a Chapter 11 bankruptcy. He wondered if such a drastic step was necessary. Furthermore, if that step were taken, could the company ever be rebuilt, especially if the Chapter 11 resulted in serious loss to general creditors? The economy was beginning to show signs of recovery and, although the Big D stores had sales on average of 15–20 percent below last year's, Gentry believed that, if credit could be re-established, the promotional merchandise necessary to rebuild sales could be obtained.

Gentry wondered whether to take Jason's advice and go into Chapter 11. He realized that if he rejected Jason's counsel he would quickly have to come up with a plan to work Big D out of the mounting crisis which threatened to engulf it. Big D's financial statements are set out in *Exhibit 1*.

THE COMPANY AND ITS AFFILIATES

Big D Drug, Inc. was a wholesaler to a loose-knit confederation of drug stores which traded under the Big D banner. The retail stores were owned by Louis Gentry, by members of Gentry's family, by some close friends, by a number of independent pharmacists and store-keepers, and one by the publicly-held company, Big D Drug, Inc. The following extracts from the company's August 10, 1973, prospectus describes Big D and Louis Gentry's relationship with it:

The Company

Big D Drug, Inc. was organized under the laws of the state of West Aloe on February 22, 1973. Big D was organized to engage in the business of selling wholesale and retail drug and sundry items and, specifically, to open or purchase five to seven (depending upon location) retail drug stores in various locations throughout metropolitan Heaton, an isolated city of about one million persons in West Aloe in the growing Southwest sector of the U.S.

It proposed that the various retail drug stores be located in neighborhood and community shopping centers and not in downtown Heaton. Stores have a prescription drug department and carry a broad selection of both traditional drug-store merchandise and other merchandise not normally found in neighborhood drug stores. In addition, one of the stores includes a retail package liquor outlet. (Local regulations are restrictive, one license for each owner.) A substantial amount of the company's merchandise will be priced at a discount, competitive with prices of other retailers selling comparable merchandise. Approximately $35,000 to $50,000-worth of furniture, fixtures and equipment are needed for each store. It is anticipated that some of these items will be leased or financed directly with the manufacturer or independent sources.

Big D also proposes to sell wholesale to approximately ten existing Big D drug stores located throughout the Heaton metropolitan area. While some of these drug stores are presently owned and controlled by executives of the company, the company will have no interest therein other than as a wholesale distributor.

Big D does not propose to engage in any other aspect of the drug or retail business, and will not be engaged in the manufacture of drugs of any other items. . . .

Affiliates

Big D, through common ownership of Louis Gentry, has various affiliates, some of whom own and operate various Big D drug stores throughout metropolitan Heaton. These affiliates are in competition with Big D with respect to the ownership and operation of retail drug stores in the metropolitan area. Big D has no equity interest in these various drug stores.

In addition, Promotions Unlimited, Inc., a West Aloe corporation wholly owned by Louis Gentry, has entered into a contract with Big D to provide various central advertising and promotional functions for the company and its proposed drug stores. Big D will pay to Promotions Unlimited, Inc. 2.5% of gross retail sales (excluding sales of any products covered by a liquor license), which monies will be utilized for advertising and promotion in connection with Big D's proposed business. In connection with sales made under a liquor license, the company will pay Promotions Unlimited, Inc. 0.5 of 1% of gross sales plus $50 per month. All advertising allowances which may be allowed by suppliers will be retained by Promotions Unlimited, Inc., and will be additional compensation to the affiliate.

It is anticipated that the existing Big D drug stores, some of which are owned and controlled by Louis Gentry and affiliate corporations, will also join in this advertising program and pay their proportionate fees (based on gross retail sales).

In addition, Promotions Unlimited, Inc.,[1] which previously sold wholesale to the various Big D drug stores, has agreed to refrain from any wholesale sales. Big D proposes to engage in this phase of business. . . .

Mr. Gentry is also a majority shareholder (90%) in Capital D, Inc., a West Aloe corporation which owns or controls four operating Big D drug stores in the Heaton area. He has no financial or other interest in other Big D stores. Other than in the ordinary course of business, there will be no business relationship between the company and this affiliate. However, Capital D, Inc., through the ownership and operation of the various existing Big D drug stores, will be a competitor of Big D and its proposed retail drug units.

Certain members of Mr. Gentry's immediate family and some of his close associates have interests in or control four other operating corporations whose business is to operate four Big D drug stores in the Heaton area. These also will be competitive with Big D units.

Big D has no interest in, nor will it acquire any interest in, any of these operating drug stores or affiliate corporations, nor will it have any business relationships therewith, other than in the normal course of business. Mr. Gentry, through his position as an executive officer and substantial shareholder of the company, and through his ownership and position in the various operating Big D drug stores, and in Promotions Unlimited, Inc., may profit directly and indirectly through the operations of the company and existing Big D drug stores.

In addition, it is proposed that Big D will perform certain accounting, bookkeeping, and billing functions not only for its own stores, but also for some of the ten existing Big D drug stores. The company will be paid $300 per month per store for such services. Naturally, there is no obligation on the part of any of the existing Big D drug stores to utilize this service.

Mr. Gentry will continue to own and operate through Capital D, Inc. his interests in various existing Big D drug stores located in the state of West Aloe. As well, he will own an interest in the company, Big D Drug, Inc., and act as its chief executive officer.

[1]Mr. Gentry had once indicated that Promotions Unlimited operated on the Peter and Paul principle: "You buy from Peter and then you buy from Paul. You sell Peter's goods and then you sell Paul's goods, using the money generated to pay Peter. Then you buy from Peter, using the money generated from selling the second batch of Peter's goods to pay Paul. By being one step behind, you can use your suppliers' money (goods in this case) to finance not only your inventory, but your receivables as well." In 1973, Promotions Unlimited, Inc. reported sales of $1,234,583 and a gross profit of $275,972. After operating expenses its net profit before tax was $67,014. In 1970, 1971 and 1972 its net profit before tax was ($554), $1638, and $2865. At the end of the 1973 fiscal year the company had working capital totalling $59,206 and stockholders' equity of $80,963.

Exhibit 2 illustrates the interrelationships between the various business entities and Mr. Gentry.

LOUIS GENTRY

After earning his MBA (with high distinction) in 1962, Louis Gentry worked in various management capacities with a number of retail drug companies before joining the Republic Drug Company of Heaton in 1966. By 1968 he was made executive vice-president of the company, which owned drug stores in suburban Heaton and acted as a supplier on an agency basis for a number of independent stores. These paid 3% of total sales to belong to the group. The benefits included a competitive advertising program and the privilege of buying from the warehouse at prices better than normal wholesale. Republic was the professional advisor to client stores and acted as a central buying agency for them. This arrangement gave the stores some of the benefits of economies of scale in buying merchandise, contracting for advertising, and general management services enjoyed by national and regional drug store chains such as CVS and Walgreens.

In early 1969, after a policy disagreement with the president of Republic over the future direction of the company, Louis Gentry resigned. After a few weeks in the limbo of the unemployed, during which he worked on a plan to start his own drug store chain, Gentry received a call from Giles August, the owner of one of Republic's independent drug stores. At Republic's policy meetings, August had always impressed Gentry as being intelligent and shrewd.

August asked Gentry if he would be interested in starting a "new Republic" to service five independent drug stores. August said he was representing the owners of these stores, who were unsatisfied with the way Republic was being managed. They felt that they were being given little say in the important management decisions that affected their businesses. They were prepared to leave Republic when their annual contracts were up for renewal.

A NEW REPUBLIC: PROMOTIONS UNLIMITED, INC.

Meeting with August and the other store owners, Gentry was impressed with their commitment to support a new organization. He agreed to set up a Republic-like business on the condition that he would have sole ownership rights. The store owners agreed, subject to the board being made up of representatives of each participating store, with decisions made on the basis of one vote for each store and one for Gentry. Gentry accepted this condition realizing that the five independent stores and the newly formed company, Promotions Unlimited, Inc., would provide a protective umbrella under which he could develop his own chain of stores.

Promotions Unlimited, Inc. acted as the advertising and buying agent for the de facto chain on a fee basis. PUI also coordinated store promotions, warehoused promotional goods, and provided accounting services for those stores which needed them. In the first two years of operations, PUI was a harmonious and cooperative venture. The democratic decision process which had been built into the company's structure appealed to the store owners, who invariably adopted Gentry's recommendations. Word of mouth and the obvious success of the stores attracted others, including additional former Republic stores.

When some stores left Republic, that company went into receivership. Gentry picked up the pieces. He had little trouble convincing his board that Republic's plight was a boon for PUI. After some negotiation, Gentry paid $180,000 for Republic's inventory, which he believed had a market value of $500,000 if properly merchandised.

With a steady set of ten to twelve independent stores under its wing, and the Republic windfall gain, PUI was profitable. By early 1970, Louis Gentry had accumulated the capital needed to begin his own drug store chain. In March, 1970, Gentry acquired his first privately-owned store and in September, he bought his second. Because West Aloe allows one individual or entity to hold only one liquor license and because drug stores in West Aloe traditionally sell liquor, Gentry bought the stores through partnerships with close and trusted friends, using members of his family as the nominal controlling owners. He kept the stores outside PUI's corporate form, but contracted with PUI for its various services. In early 1971, Gentry acquired his third store and gave PUI its fifteenth affiliate.

At this point, the owners of member stores wanted their own warehouse so that PUI could supply them with even greater cost effectiveness by buying in larger lots from major suppliers. Already PUI was distributing merchandise worth $1 million annually from the basement of one of Louis Gentry's stores.

Gentry realized that PUI would need additional capital if it was to expand further. It would need a larger capital base to finance the purchases of merchandise. Moreover, a larger capital base would enhance the company's credit worthiness and so allow the company to more readily lease suitable properties on favorable terms. Consequently, Gentry was pleased when the president of Powerhouse Drug, Inc., a national drug chain with $150 million in sales, called to see if he was interested in selling PUI and its associated stores by merging them all into a larger chain.

Although Gentry liked running his own show, he recognized the need for capital to sustain the growth rate already achieved by the organization. Therefore, he negotiated a complete sell-out deal to Powerhouse Drug in which he would become the divisional manager in the Heaton region and many of his agents would become store managers for Powerhouse Drug. However, this deal required the assignment, on reasonable terms, of all outstanding store leases. A few of the landlords involved became greedy and refused to assign their leases unless hold-up terms were met by Powerhouse Drug. Tired of waiting for clear title, Powerhouse regretfully withdrew its offer.

Gentry looked around him and decided that PUI would have to go it alone. Over the next year he acquired five additional stores, pyramiding them on top of the three he already owned. The total number of the stores in the larger organization remained constant, however. Some conflicts developed among the agents, causing a few of them to withdraw from the program.

THE REPUBLIC BECOMES A MONARCHY

The start of 1973 found Gentry acquiring control over a ninth unit, a store which previously had been owned by an independent agent. For the first time, the remaining eight independent agency stores constituted a minority in the Big D program. Agency meetings became abrasive as the independents grew restless and began to dispute Gentry's business judgment. It appeared that they resented the greater success which some of Gentry's own units seemed to enjoy when compared with their own results. One independent told Gentry he was building the success of his own stores by exploiting the independents in the group. On the other hand, Gentry felt that, in his own units, he could carry out the Big D promotional program as it should be done. He believed that the lesser success enjoyed by most of the independent agency units was due to their half-hearted commitment to Big D's promotional efforts.

EXPANDING THE EMPIRE: CAPITAL

At this point, Gentry was introduced by a mutual friend to Peter Phillips, head of Phillips and Company. Phillips suggested that his company could underwrite a public offering that would bring Gentry the capital he needed to continue development of the Big D drug chain.

Phillips had founded Phillips and Company, a small, local stock brokerage house, two years earlier. At first he specialized in supplying information and brokerage services concerning the sale of over-the-counter stocks of local businesses. In the previous year, 1972, he had successfully carried out approximately a dozen equity underwritings for local companies, varying from $200,000 to $500,000. Phillips's account executives had developed a large number of local accounts, professionals and business people, who looked to them for advice on investing in local Heaton businesses.

Phillips told Gentry that the SEC allowed two types of offering: a Reg A offering permitting him to raise up to $500,000 and involving legal fees of approximately $20,000, and an S-1 offering for any amount over $500,000, which would involve legal fees of a minimum of $100,000. While Gentry felt he had a need for more than $500,000 of new capital, Phillips argued that a good first step would be a Reg A offering of $500,000 on a "best efforts only" basis. In view of the heavy expenses associated with an S-1 offering and the questionable ability of a firm the size of Phillips and Company to market a $1 million or better offering, Gentry decided to go with the $500,000 Reg A offering.

Much to the surprise of both Phillips and Gentry, the 500,000 share issue ($1 per share) was oversubscribed by $400,000 on its first day. Apparently, the growth of Big D and its advertising in the Heaton market had been noticed by many people. In retrospect, it was apparent that a $1 million or better offering could have been accomplished had the effort been made. Big D's net proceeds from the offering, after all expenses and underwriting commissions, were $412,500.

EMIGRES

At this point, Big D Drug, Inc. was ready to set up a full-scale warehouse operation and provide virtually all of the services that the independents had requested. However, seven of the eight independent agency units now decided to pull out of Big D and set up a "third Republic," taking Gentry's vice-president of operations from PUI as their leader.

Much later, reflecting on the independents' actions, Gentry said:

> It seemed to me that the independents were like passengers entering a railway station at the end of the line. They find a train sitting in the station, waiting to begin its journey. They jump on and wait for the train to get going. After a long wait, they lose patience, get off, and step out of the train onto the platform. At that very moment, the doors slam shut and the train takes off without them.

In effect, the independents had asked for full-scale warehouse operations and other supportive functions that could not be provided without more capital. Now that the capital for the warehouse had been obtained, seven of the eight franchisees left before they could begin to enjoy the advantages it promised.

The seven independents of the "third Republic" met with little success. Giles August and Gentry's vice-president of operations ran some ads at first, but after a few months they stopped. One of their best stores was sold and the new owner rejoined Big D. In the next year, two more stores were sold to independents who remained totally independent. The remaining four stores continued under the "third Republic" name but did no mutual promotion or buying.

Although Big D regained one of the seven stores, the lost fees and buying volume created a major problem for Gentry. To maintain the level of promotion and buying that the company had developed, Gentry would have to obtain more independent agency stores or acquire more units. Ironically, now that he had the 20,000-square-foot warehouse so badly needed in the past, he had lost much of the volume required to make the warehouse operation profitable. Gentry maintained the high level of advertising Big D had established and attempted to recruit more independent stores. However, he discovered that the independents preferred their independence to the high profit and volume that membership of the Big D chain could bring. Apparently, if the lost volume was to be regained, Gentry would have to attempt some other type of expansion.

MR. PHILLIPS CALLS

On July 13, 1974, Gentry received a telephone call from Peter Phillips. Phillips, who had heard that Big D might break even in its first year, suggested that Gentry should get his company into the retail business before his first annual report was sent to his shareholders. Phillips told Gentry that if he wanted to maintain Big D's stock price, he had better have something exciting to report to the shareholders.

Phillips and Company, through its clients, controlled 70% of Big D's stock and held, in fact, 56% of the stock in its trading account. During the negotiations prior to the stock offering, Gentry had told Phillips that the high-margin sector of the drug business was retailing and that Big D Drug, Inc. would enter it as soon as possible. Consequently, he felt that Phillips's impatience was understandable. For almost a year Gentry had searched for a good retail unit so that Big D's first entry into the retail drug market would be a success. There was always a risk in starting a new store; such ventures were rarely profitable from day one.

THE O'CONNELL DRUG STORE

Now, fortunately, the O'Connell Drug Store unit, in which Gentry had been interested for several years, had become available. The store was located in Bakerville, twenty miles outside of Heaton and farther from the city center than any of his other stores. The area was not yet fully developed but was growing rapidly.

The owner, Jack O'Connell, had died and his widow, unable to run the store profitably, was under pressure to sell. In view of the store's problems, Gentry had second thoughts about its potential, but even though the widow and her teenage son were "rank amateurs in the drug business and doing few things right," the store appeared to be generating sales of over \$50,000 per month. And he knew that the store, being in a prime location, would not remain available for long.

Louis Gentry met with his operations vice-president and his treasurer and controller to discuss the O'Connell store. The figures supplied by Mrs. O'Connell's accountant and the operating results of a typical Big D store are shown in *Exhibit 3*.

Concerning finance, the treasurer and the controller stated that right now Big D did not have the money to consummate the deal comfortably and run the store through the Christmas period. On the other hand, Gentry had been promised a loan of \$250,000 by a local bank at the end of the year. This would supply adequate funds to relieve any pressure that developed. Furthermore, profits would be forthcoming from Christmas sales at the end of the year. As far as Gentry was concerned, the major points against buying appeared to be the need to turn around a losing situation, the need to learn about the high-priced camera department and adapt it to something Big D could successfully work with, and the need to seek and secure good local management.

On the positive side, the store was doing \$600,000 annually in sales under the poorest possible management; sales might well increase to over \$1 million annually under the impact of Big D promotion and advertising. Gentry's first store had gone from \$250,000/year to \$500,000/year in one year under his management. Gentry also suspected that someone had been stealing Mrs. O'Connell blind. If this could be curbed, large increases in profit might result. The need certainly existed for Big D to show prosperity and growth to suppliers and the independents (who had seen seven stores leave the group), and the chain needed the "shot in the arm" which a \$1 million store could provide. Another advantage was the low price: payment of net worth plus \$25,000 for good will.

In spite of references to the recession by various staff members, Gentry was optimistic about the economic climate. He had found, in the past, that Heaton's growth rate had more than counteracted several national recessions.

ANOTHER TALK WITH PHILLIPS

Gentry was mulling over these arguments when he was interrupted by a telephone call from Phillips. Phillips told him in no uncertain terms that the stock price was under considerable pressure. It had dropped from 87 cents to 62 cents in the past 7 days. Phillips admitted that the entire market was dropping but he felt that some good news for investors—for example, the purchase of a store—would encourage them and allow the price of Big D stock to rise again. Phillips emphasized the fact that his company had put a lot of money into stabilizing the price of Big D's stock: it now held 57,000 shares for its own account. In addition, the company was holding over 300,000 shares for its clients. A major piece of good news was essential.

As the staff left the room for lunch, Gentry remarked, "If we don't give Phillips the news he wants, it will be tough to face him at the stockholders' meeting. If we're going to stay in this business we'll need him on our side. Let's go ahead with it. We've turned worse situations around."

A NEW PROBLEM

The problem now facing Gentry was Big D Drug's cash flow. However, he had the bank loan and Christmas sales to fall back on. Gentry felt he could outlast the tight cash situation until Christmas, due to the firm's ability to buy Christmas merchandise on long-term dating.[2] Furthermore, only a small payment was due Mrs. O'Connell. The bulk of the money Gentry would have to find was owed to Mrs. O'Connell's creditors and he felt confident that he could negotiate with these people for extended dating since many of them were the same people with whom he worked every day.

THE ANNUAL MEETING

On September 6, at the first annual meeting of Big D Drug, Inc., Gentry was happy to make the announcement of the purchase of Big D's first retail unit. Much to his surprise, only one of the more than 400 stockholders came to the meeting and that man owned only 100 shares. Due to pressing business matters, Peter Phillips did not attend, but his stand-in, the sales manager of Phillips and Company, was present. He was obviously pleased with the announcement but appeared subdued and depressed, unlike his normal, optimistic self.

PHILLIPS IN THE NEWS

Two weeks later, the announcement of the demise of Phillips and Company hit the front page of the business sections of Heaton's two newspapers. Phillips and Company had apparently tried to support the prices of many of the small issues which it had underwritten. The decline of prices in the stock market was particularly severe in small, local issues. Evidently, Phillips and Company was caught holding far too many shares of the issues it had placed on the market. As a result of its demise, the stock it held for its

[2]The largest portion of Christmas merchandise (toys, appliances, cosmetics, and seasonal goods) was sold on seasonal dating. The terms of this dating were normally 2% 10, net 30 as of January 1. Frequently, goods would be delivered as early as July or August. In the case of a chain such as Big D, this might mean delivery to the company of $350,000 worth of goods in July and August, much of which could be sold before October, although none would have to be paid for until January 10.

customers in its trading account was distributed to these customers and the SEC halted trading in all of the stocks Phillips had underwritten in the previous two years.

There appeared to be no company prepared or able to immediately "make" a market in these stocks. Before trading ceased, the price of Big D common hit an all-time low of 25¢ per share. Several weeks later, Gentry was informed that among the assets of Phillips and Company were over 50,000 shares of Big D stock which would have to be disposed of before any stock trading company would consider trying to make a market for Big D's stock. Much to Gentry's surprise, not one stockholder called his office or contacted him. When Phillips and Company had been in business, it seemed they were calling continuously for news for their "interested" stockholders.

At this point business looked good to Gentry and he believed his timing in buying the O'Connell Drug store was right. He could use the Peter and Paul principle to get by yet another tight financial situation.

THE ENVIRONMENT

The Heaton business community, like that of many major cities in the Southwest, had been little affected by the 1973 or 1974 business recessions which had been felt severely in other areas of the United States. For example, unemployment in West Aloe was only 4% while in New England it had climbed to over 12%. This had also been true for several minor recessions in the late 1960s and early 1970s.

However, in November of 1974, West Aloe elected a liberal governor on an anti-development and anti-business platform. Anti-expansion environmental people, policies and programs dominated the news. Business leaders, and even ordinary citizens, became cautious. The effects of this caution were felt first in the West Aloe real estate and construction industry and then in the economy of West Aloe as a whole. For the first time in modern history, real estate prices in West Aloe fell and overall unemployment rose significantly while business activity in general declined. Although there appeared to be no real justification for it, the community seemed to be talking itself into a recession.

PLANNING FOR CHRISTMAS

Louis Gentry planned to follow his traditional business strategy of heavy promotion of department-store-type merchandise at discount-store prices through December 17 or 18. Then, as usual, he planned to cut prices during the final week of pre-Christmas sales to an even lower level to ensure clearing his inventory. During the two weeks following Thanksgiving, sales were slightly below plan but this did not seem serious. Gentry felt his slightly lower than normal sales were the usual moderate reflection of the national recession in West Aloe. He had heard rumors, however, through salesmen that the department stores were having disastrous post-Thanksgiving sales.

. . . A Little Bit Late

On the second Sunday of December, Gentry was disturbed to see that local newspapers were full of huge advertisements by Heaton's major department stores announcing ridiculously deep price-cutting on merchandise that these stores had never before reduced until after Christmas. Apparently, the rumors had been true. Now the department stores began to unload their merchandise, almost in a panic.

Due to the lead time needed to set advertisements, Gentry could not begin his own close-out rock-bottom pricing program until the final week before Christmas. In the meantime, department store prices considerably undercut Big D prices on most name-brand goods. Furthermore, in the week before Christmas many department stores went to below-cost pricing. As a result, Big D's prices through the final two key weeks of the Christmas selling season were, for the first time in six years, considerably higher than the department stores'.

AFTER CHRISTMAS, 1974

When the dust settled, Gentry found that his overall Christmas sales had fallen 15% below his target figures. Sales of Christmas goods were almost 40% below the target and he still had significant inventories of all types of Christmas merchandise. The effect of the recession on sales in the market as a whole had been relatively mild (a 5% overall decline as opposed to the normal 10% annual increase) but the panicky price-cutting by the major department stores in Heaton had worked to accentuate the effect of the recession on Big D. The large Christmas volume and cash flow he had expected had not materialized.

In thc three weeks following Christmas, Gentry tried to move the left-over Christmas inventory by heavy promotions at virtually cost prices. However, the traditionally bargain-happy shoppers of Heaton seemed to be buying only what they needed and, then, only after prices were cut spectacularly low. Many of them, too, had stocked up on the unusual pre-Christmas sales. It was apparent that the recession had changed their buying habits. Big D's advertisements did not generate their normal high sales volume. Instead, the cost of these ads merely cut profits further and used up cash.

The December 31, 1975, financial statements (*Exhibit 1*) revealed that Big D Drug had been marginally profitable in the Christmas quarter but there was still the Christmas inventory to move and the dated "trade" payables to deal with. Gentry felt that the situation represented a serious business problem because his suppliers would not date their deliveries unless their accounts were paid off. But, given time, Gentry was sure the problem could be overcome. In any case, he had his friendly Heaton banker to fall back on.

DISAPPOINTMENT

The recession intervened again. Daylin, a $650 million retail drug store chain astounded the industry by going "belly-up." Unfortunately for Big D, the announcement of Daylin's Chapter 11 filing had an immediate and direct effect on the Heaton bank with which Gentry dealt. It was a correspondent of the major Los Angeles bank which had backed Daylin. After putting off Gentry for several weeks, the bank's president agreed to meet with him. Following polite preliminaries, Gentry was told that the bank was worried about the retail drug business and that, in fact, it had taken a small loss on a correspondent loan to Daylin. The president said the bank would prefer to wait until Big D's June 30, 1975, year-end results were in, showing that the company was in a sound position, before going ahead with the promised loan. The president of the bank said he "hoped this delay would not be inconvenient."

After his initial dismay and disappointment abated, Gentry became angry. Hadn't the bank assured him of a $250,000 loan back in August? Gentry decided to visit other banks in the Heaton area to seek their assistance. Three weeks passed in futile discussions with local bankers who seemed uninterested in talking to Big D, much less in lending it money. West Aloe was posting new highs in unemployment and several mid-sized local companies announced bankruptcy. This time a recession was hitting the state for real. Furthermore, instead of announcing major programs to help stimulate business, the environmentalist, conservation-minded state government heralded the economic recession as being good for West Aloe because it would slow or stop the rapid and persistent growth that had become the state's trademark.

THE O'CONNELL STORE

The results at the O'Connell store were most disappointing. The first six months of operation saw three store managers follow each other out the door. It seemed to be very difficult to hire good management personnel in Bakerville. Furthermore, it became painfully obvious that local advertising was absolutely essential to Big D's operations. Big D's Heaton ads did not generate sales at Bakerville, even though the Heaton papers had excellent circulation there. Apparently, Bakerville's shoppers had been conditioned to look to their local papers for news of local sales. The cost of local advertising was completely out of line with the volume of a single store.

The store experienced a sales loss due to competitors' discount pricing and a drop in sales of specialty camera equipment, as well as the loss of sales generated from personal connections of the O'Connell family in Bakerville. These losses were only barely overcome by the increases generated by an active advertising program combined with an effective discount price structure.

DESPERATION

Gentry felt desperate. What was he going to do? Less than half the "dated" merchandise had been paid for, few accounts had been paid in full, and it was the beginning of March. His creditors were beginning to harass him and his staff, wanting to know when they would be paid. Normal sales in the stores were down for the first time in six years. Since he had not fully paid either Peter or Paul, his sources of new merchandise to promote and sell were drying up. Big D was losing its ability to buy. Gentry was running out of fast moving goods. Worse, the *Heaton Valley Voice* had put Big D on a double COD policy and was demanding full cash payments for any new advertisements and a reduction of Big D's outstanding accounts in advance of any promotional effort. This move forced Gentry to cut Big D's promotional activity which, in turn, cut sales further.

RELIEF?

March 9 brought a surprise. McGregor Cavandish, president of Nucleonic Drug, Inc., a fast-growing, integrated drug company, left a message for Gentry to call him as soon as possible. Gentry returned the call and was amazed and then relieved to be asked if he was interested in selling out. Remembering his grandfather's advice at a cattle sale in 1946—"Don't let them know what you're thinking"—Gentry played it cool but agreed to fly to Houston on March 16. Unfortunately, it quickly became obvious to Gentry that Nucleonic was a scavenger. It wanted to pick Big D's bones but there would be no value left for the company's shareholders or for Gentry. Gentry broke off the discussions and returned to Heaton.

ONE MORE TRY

Upon his return to Heaton, Gentry called Powerhouse Drug and attempted to develop a deal with them. Powerhouse showed some interest and this time the landlords were in a cooperative state of mind—even those who had been so stubborn the year before. However, Powerhouse was feeling the effects of the recession, and after several weeks of consideration, decided against making a deal.

BACK IN THE STORE

Gentry had imposed stringent measures in early January with the goal of reducing the inventory of each store by $20,000 (15%). He hoped to use this freed working capital to pay off some of his most vociferous and persistent trade creditors. But the inventory had become hard to move. Gentry knew that Big D needed new merchandise if it was to generate a healthy cash flow. As he walked through the warehouse he realized just how slowly his total inventory had been turning. A large portion was Christmas goods. These could probably be sold for 90 cents on the dollar in December but, thinking back to Republic's fate, Gentry felt that if Big D shut its doors, he would be lucky to get 30 cents on the dollar for its inventory.

To make things worse, he now discovered that the news of Big D's troubles was spreading. Many accounts which had allowed sixty to ninety days to pay in the past were now demanding payment in thirty days and, as each day passed, more were asking for cash on delivery. The cash generated by inventory reduction was needed to maintain stocks of essential merchandise in the stores, merchandise which could no longer be purchased on credit terms. Even firms which had allowed dating and had always been patient were now demanding their money on delivery. Apparently the recession, which had hit the retailers first, was now moving back through the distribution channels, putting pressure on wholesalers and jobbers whose accounts-payable financing had helped Gentry's chain grow. Their increasing reluctance to extend credit cut Gentry's working capital even further. Occasional bankruptcies by small independents began to panic even the major wholesalers in Heaton. The old Peter and Paul principle was no longer valid.

In mid-April, Gentry decided to close the three lowest-volume stores he controlled personally, in order to free additional working capital. These stores held over $400,000 worth of goods, and if they could be liquidated effectively by late May, the capital freed would enable Big D to survive. Gentry recognized that such action would undoubtedly affect the overall profitability of each link in the Big D chain of stores and probably result in the first "red ink" for the chain as a whole. However, drastic steps were necessary in order to salvage the remainder of the chain.

DISMAY, A SURPRISE, AND ANOTHER DECISION TO MAKE

Much to Gentry's dismay and consternation, most of the money generated by the closing of the three stores was absorbed by Big D's suppliers, who all switched the chain to a COD basis. This dried up even more of his working capital. (With the smaller number of stores and his normal credit terms, Gentry felt he could easily have made payments to suppliers.) As a result, mid-May found Gentry with a slowing inventory and still facing a host of old bills on the books, some dating back to the previous June. In addition, some creditors had instituted lawsuits. Gentry was pleasantly surprised to discover that these lawsuits could be postponed for six months to a year with no problem, but he realized that there would be judgments against Big D at that time unless he had paid the bills.

Big D's end-of-March figures became available to Gentry in mid-April (*Exhibit 1*). By May, when he called his lawyer, Gentry was thinking in terms of selling his interest in two or three more stores in order to obtain more working capital. A few of Gentry's associates in the ownership of some of the company-associated Big D stores had expressed concern that "their" stores might be sucked into the whirlpool that was Big D Drug, Inc.; Gentry thought he might be able to raise some money by selling them "his" part of the store for cash. While ultimately this move could mean the loss to the chain of several more stores, he felt that that was unlikely; it might bring in enough capital necessary to re-establish Big D's credit. Besides, now he had Jason's letter to consider.

EXHIBIT I
BIG D DRUG, INC.
Balance Sheet

Assets	*June 30, 1973*	*June 30, 1974*	*September 30, 1974*	*December 31, 1974*	*March 31, 1975*
Current Assets					
Cash	$27,709	$ 16,109	$ 7,713.58	$ 6,002.25	$ 7,093.15
Accounts Receivable, Trade, (less allowances for doubtful accounts of $0, $4,200, $6,260, $6,200, $6,360)	—	517,022	412,341.18	448,720.32	314,434.87
Accounts Receivable, Money orders (Big D Stores)	—	215,390	323,248.50	503,469.12	465,318.65
Accounts Receivable—Other	—	1,289	3,365.07	7,421.88	6,448.47
Merchandise Inventory	—	160,101	415,520.05	429,256.21	383,822.68
Prepaid Expenses	10,450	2,325	1,435.86	2,978.55	8,242.80
Total Current Assets	$38,159	$912,236	$1,163,624.24	$1,397,848.33	$1,185,350.62
Property and Equipment					
Motor Vehicles	—	22,978	22,978.42	22,978.42	22,978.42
Warehouse Equipment	—	700	699.95	699.95	699.95
Furniture and Fixtures	—	10,508	19,219.33	19,210.33	22,719.33
		34,186	42,897.70	42,897.70	46,397.70
Less Accumulated Depreciation		4,552	7,658.74	10,021.05	12,471.18
Total Property & Equipment	—	29,634	35,238.96	32,876.65	33,926.52
Other Assets					
Deposits	—	6,781	11,710.00	11,335.00	10,000.00
Unamortized Organization Costs	541	460	433.20	406.13	379.06
Investments	—	—	29,126.79	29,176.79	29,126.79
Total Other Assets	541	7,241	41,269.99	40,867.92	39,505.85
Total Assets	$38,700	$949,111	$1,240,133.19	$1,471,592.90	$1,258,782.99
Liabilities and Stockholders' Equity					
Current Liabilities					
Accounts Payable—Trade	$ —	$380,778	$ 621,081.53	$ 846,551.62	$ 619,582.47
Accounts Payable—Money Orders (Bank)	—	102,289	135,460.34	113,652.82	117,789.95
Accounts Payable—Other	—	9,988	—	22,022.52	26,608.35
Accounts Payable—Investment	—	—	4,361.15	4,361.15	4,361.15
Notes Payable (Current Portion)	—	—	8,500.00	—	13,268.80
Accrued Payroll	—	645	6,681.80	1,758.90	6,460.84
Payroll Withholding and Accrued Payroll Taxes	—	2,344	7,125.31	4,091.73	7,826.95
Accrued Liabilities	1,450	3,150	30,534.54	25,857.33	29,571.74
State Income Tax	—	224	224.18	—	—
Total Current Liabilities	1,450	499,418	$ 813,968.85	$1,018,296.07	$ 825,470.25

Long-Term Liabilities					
Notes Payable	—	—	—	—	7,234.70
Stockholders' Equity					
Common Stock	37,250	446,580	446,580.03	446,580.03	446,580.03
Paid in Capital	—	50	50.00	50.00	50.00
Retailed Earnings	—	3,063	(20,465.69)	6,666.80	(20,551.99)
Total Stockholders' Equity	$37,250	$449,693	$ 426,164.34	$ 453,296.83	$ 426,078.04
Total Liabilities and Stockholders' Equity	$38,700	$949,111	$1,240,133.19	$1,471,592.90	$1,258,782.99

Statement of Income and Retained Earnings

	The Year Ended June 30, 1974	Year to Date September 30, 1974	Year to Date December 31, 1974	Year to Date March 31, 1975
Net sales	$1,106,509	$281,267.42	$965,708.97	$1,160,993.43
Cost of sales	992,234	235,922.97	813,512.18	957,074.86
Gross Profit	$ 114,275	$ 45,344.45	$152,196.79	$ 203,918.57
Other Income				
Accounting Fee Income	21,675	7,650.00	15,600.00	25,050.00
Finance Charges	46,386	18,724.23	33,699.27	50,107.08
Money Order Income	—	—	4,955.02	3,059.24
Miscellaneous Income	—	—	3,382.05	8,270.93
Total Profit	$ 182,336	$ 71,718.68	$209,833.13	$ 290,405.82
Costs and Expenses				
Salaries and Wages	89,414	41,036.10	92,782.03	143,924.78
Payroll Taxes	6,542	2,420.95	6,045.67	9,303.33
Professional Fees	31,610	19,867.10	33,445.30	48,641.30
Rent	15,126	11,168.04	24,014.56	38,671.33
Utilities	6,239	2,577.93	4,928.41	10,039.94
Depreciation	4,891	3,106.84	6,631.64	7,919.28
Other	25,227	15,070.82	38,382.13	55,521.26
Total Expenses	$ 179,049	$ 95,247.78	$206,229.74	$ 314,021.22
Net Income (Loss) From Operations	3,287	$ (23,529.10)	$ 3,603.39	$ (23,615.40)
Less Tax	224	—	—	—
Retained Earnings at June 30, 1974	$ 3,063	3,063.41	3,063.41	3,063.41
Retained Earnings at Date	$ 3,063	$ (20,465.69)	$ 6,666.80	$ (20,551.99)

(continued)

SELECTED NOTES TO FINANCIAL STATEMENTS

Credit Terms

Customer receivables are due and payable twenty days after the billing is made. Thereafter, the company charges interest at the rate of 1.5% per month on the then outstanding account balance arising from the sale of merchandise.

Money Order Receivables and Payables

As a sales promotion device, the affiliated retail stores sell money orders to their customers. Money order proceeds received by the company from the retail stores are forwarded to the commercial bank on which the money orders were drawn. "Accounts Receivable—Money Orders" represents money order receipts yet to be collected by the company; "Accounts Payable—Money Orders" represents the amount of money orders written which the company has not forwarded to the commercial bank. Income and costs relating to this service are not significant in amount.

Interest Expense

Interest expense arose as the result of a $250,000 line of credit which Big D Drug, Inc. obtained during the 1974 fiscal year at 11.5%. Amounts outstanding fluctuated during the year, reaching a maximum of $250,000. All amounts borrowed have been repaid and the line of credit has been discontinued.

Rental Commitments

The minimum rental commitments under non-cancelable leases (not reduced by sublease rentals) for the next 5 years averages $36,241 per annum.

EXHIBIT 2 Gentry's Interests in Big D Drug, Inc. and Affiliates

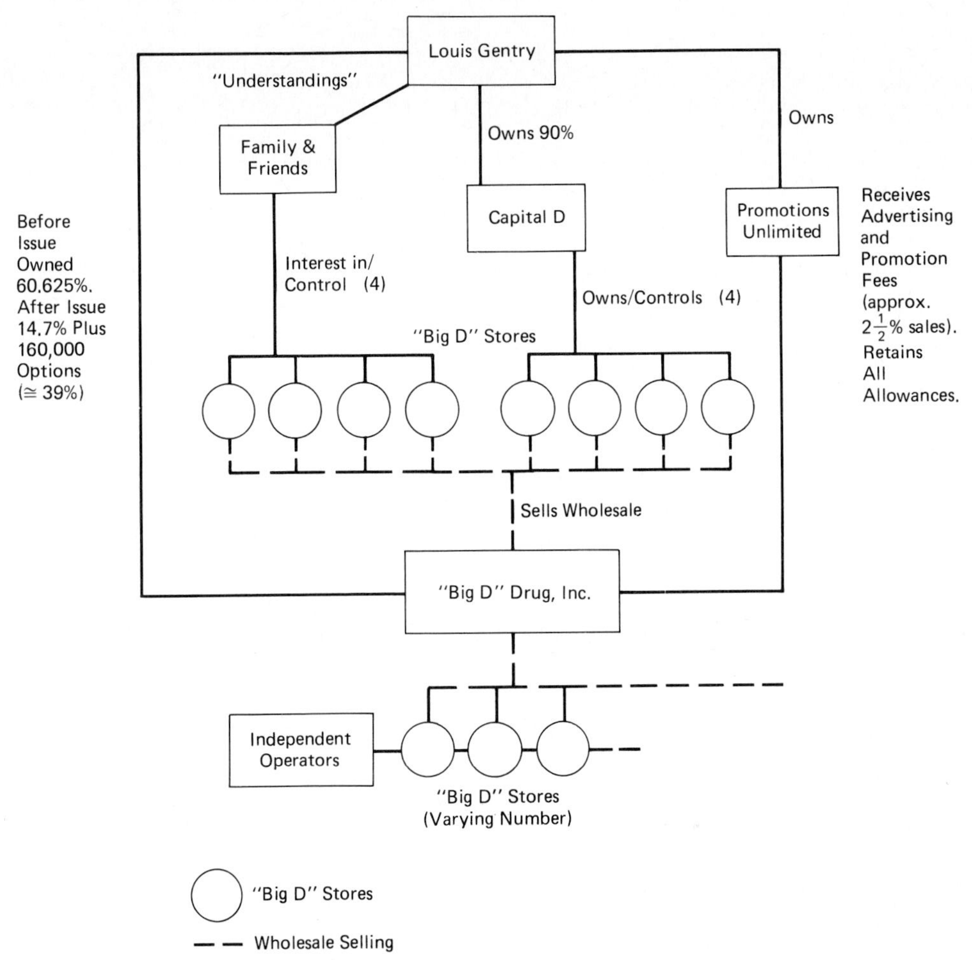

EXHIBIT 3 Comparative Statements; A Typical "Big D" Store and the O'Connell Drug Store

Balance Sheet

	Feb, 28, '74 Big D Store #3	Aug. 23, '74 O'Connell Store
Assets		
Current Assets		
Cash	$ 693	$ 4,786
Accounts Receivable	26,959	14,552
Loans Receivable	29,500	—
Inventory	149,449	149,142[1]
Total Current Assets	206,601	168,480
Fixed Assets		
Store Fixtures	6,335	57,987
Furniture & Fixtures	15,403	8,406
Vehicles	5,834	1,311
Leasehold Impr.	13,261	21,204
Less Accum. Depreciation	(19,567)	(80,196)
Total Fixed Assets	21,266	8,712
Investments	1,272	—
Other Assets	5,300	598
Total	$234,439	$177,790
Liabilities & Stockholders' Equity		
Current Liabilities		
Notes Payable—Officer	$ —	$ 8,500
Accounts Payable	107,169	160,235
Accrued Payroll	373	5,826
Payroll & Sales Taxes Payable	3,034	7,171
Accrued Liabilities	18,740	10,385
Total Current Liabilities	129,316	192,117
Other Liabilities	2,384	—
Stockholders' Equity		
Capital Account	39,385	15,500
Retained Earnings	63,354	(29,827)
Total Stockholders' Equity	$102,739	$(14,327)
Total	$234,439	$177,790

Income Statement

	Year Ending	
	Feb, 28, '74 Big D Store #3	Aug. 23, '74 O'Connell Store
Sales	$505,633	$597,324[2]
Cost of Goods Sold		
Beginning Inventory	152,613	193,480
Purchases	350,780	410,838
	503,393	604,318
Less: Ending Inventory	149,449	149,142
Cost of Goods Sold	353,944	455,176
Gross Profit	151,689	142,148[3]

(continued)

EXHIBIT 3 (Cont.)

	Feb, 28, '74 Big D Store #3	Aug. 23, '74 O'Connell Store
Operating Expenses		
Advertising	263	3,586
Auto Expense	669	758
Bad Checks and Debts	469	1,159
Cash Short	668	854
Common Maintenance	1,000	—
Depreciation Expense	2,896	2,463
Dues & Subscriptions	250	208
Agency & Management Fees	13,339	—
Group Insurance	584	2,719
Insurance—Other	1,866	3,560
Miscellaneous Expense	804	2,731
Office Expense & Supplies	336	—
Rent	19,587	24,421
Accounting & Legal	—	5,422
Repair & Maintenance	416	1,634
Salaries—Officers	9,015	26,076
Salaries—Other	38,296	95,135
Service Charge—Credit Cards	1,189	4,503
Store Expense & Supplies	4,144	3,254
Taxes & Licenses	2,593	1,570
Taxes—Payroll	2,065	7,486
Telephone	866	1,399
Utilities	3,401	3,270
Total Expenses	104,716	192,208
Net Profit from Operations	46,973	(50,080)
Other Income		
Cash Discount	2,100	5,848
Fee Income (Money Orders)	340	—
Miscellaneous Income	1,602	4,860
	4,042	10,708
Other Expense		
Interest	132	1,237
Net Profit 7/1/71 to 2/28/72	$ 50,883	$ (40,589)

[1]The O'Connell store's ending inventory by department was as follows: drug, $69,932; magazines, $1,697; tobacco, $1,131; photo, $69,531; liquor, $6,851.
[2,3]The source of the O'Connell store's sales and gross profit by department were:

	Sales % Whole	*Gross Profit as % Sales*
Drug	43.3%	28.8%
Magazine	3.3	.4
Tobacco	3.3	(3.0)
Photo	34.4	25.2
Liquor	15.7	17.7
	100.0%	23.8%

BIG D DRUG, INC.: DENOUEMENT

Rather than accept Burgett Jason's suggestion regarding Chapter 11, Louis Gentry pushed on in an effort to save the combined companies. The group survived May through the addition of $15,000 of outside capital raised from Gentry's close friends and relatives. In June, the sale of a partially-owned store to Gentry's partners raised $30,000. Gentry expected to get by July with tax refunds expected that month. However, on July 23, his 49% partners in the largest, most profitable store used their control of the board of directors to seize majority control of the company by voting themselves the right to buy additional stock while not giving Gentry an equivalent right.

In an associated, and equally unexpected, move, his erstwhile partners stopped normal payments on their accounts with Big D Drug, Inc., thereby cutting Big D's cash flow by almost $35,000 in the first week after the takeover.

Gentry's lawyers informed him that the only legal remedies would merely tie up the assets and assure failure for everyone. They pointed out that it would be impossible to obtain a firm, final, legal decision in less than three years. He realized that a legal attack on his partners would not help Big D Drug, Inc. It would only create problems for his partners and destroy the value of the residual and minority ownership he had in the store. Lacking the planned-upon cash flow from this unit, Gentry had no way to pay off and thereby turn Big D's money order payables with the bank.[1] He had no alternative but to take Chapter 11 and so file for bankruptcy. He announced this to the shareholders in a letter of July 25, 1975 (*Exhibit 1*).

The attempt at rehabilitation under the protection of Chapter 11, lasted for over six months but, in the end, a majority of the unsecured creditors voted against the plan of arrangement. It was questionable whether the resources remained to carry out the plan even if the unsecured creditors had supported it. The firm was then liquidated. All secured creditors received full payment and unsecured creditors received approximately 25¢ on the dollar. Gentry felt this result was primarily due to the fact that the Chapter 11 plan did not have the flexibility within it to allow for advertising and promotional buying for the stores.

RETROSPECTIVE ASSESSMENT

Gentry commented: "A crucial turning point was the departure of the independents. Some method should have been found to maintain their voice in the decisions of the organization so they could continue with Big D. The departure of the independents meant insufficient

[1]Big D Drug, Inc. sold money orders through its agency stores. There was normally a three-week lag between the sale of a money order and its presentation to the bank on which it was drawn. The money order payables were turned on a weekly basis. Once Big D failed to pay the bank, money order sales had to cease.

This case was prepared by Assistant Professor Kenneth J. Hatten as a basis for class discussion rather than to illustrate either effective or ineffective handling of an administrative situation.

volume for the profitable operation of the new warehouse facility, and insufficient advertising fees to support the growing promotional efforts.

''Basic planning for Big D was really planning for success and did not consider the possibility of failure due to environmental conditions. This attitude worked so long as the economy was favorable. However, maintaining this posture indefinitely invited eventual failure. The purchase of O'Connell Drug really was the beginning of the end. Careful analysis would have pointed up the danger and also have indicated a real lack of ability on the part of Phillips and Company to force the deal. Who else could they get to manage the company? On the other hand, similar gambles had been taken for six years and in every case they had worked out. This alone can cause one to assume that he could safely make 'one more trip to the well.'

''The earlier one takes Chapter 11, the more likely one is to survive. Once it was clear that the company would not make it, the attempt to continue to pay down the accounts payable was a debilitating step that reduced the resources available for rehabilitation under the protection of Chapter 11. But, would survival have been possible if a few of my partners had not revolted?

''Finally, one must bear in mind the advantages and disadvantages of a complex organizational structure not only under conditions of success, but also under conditions of stress.''

EXHIBIT 1

July 25, 1975

Dear Shareholder:

Since my last letter to you, our cash flow problem has deteriorated until it has now become extremely critical. Although the company believes it has assets in excess of liabilities, it is unable to pay its debts because of the lack of sufficient cash flow. Most of the funds received are now being used to pay for resupply of inventory and we are on a COD basis.

The board of directors has recognized that the company is experiencing substantial inability to pay its obligations as required and is aware of various lawsuits which have been instituted by suppliers and vendors. In addition, the company has been selling money orders under the name of "Guardian." Due to a shortage of funds, many of these money orders are being returned by the depository bank and the company is unable to honor these as presented.

Consequently, a petition under Chapter 11 of the bankruptcy laws of the United States will shortly be filed with the United States District Court. The ability of the company to file an acceptable plan of arrangement is subject to many factors which are unpredictable at this time. The plan of arrangement is subject to approval from both the creditors and the Court. This approval cannot be assured. It is hoped that, within the confines of the Chapter 11, all obligations can be taken care of and the company can rehabilitate itself and pay its creditors. This, of course, is unknown at this time.

Your management will strive to overcome these financial problems and we will keep you advised.

Sincerely,
Big D Drug, Inc.

Louis Gentry

Louis Gentry
President

LG:df

CHRYSLER IN THE U.S. AUTO INDUSTRY: 1921–1980

EARLY CHRYSLER HISTORY

Chrysler Corporation began as a turnaround operation in 1921 when Walter P. Chrysler purchased the ailing Maxwell Motor Company. The first Chrysler car was designed in 1924 around Walter Chrysler's new high compression engine, and the firm's objective was "offering the majority of American motorists a passenger car with beauty, acceleration, performance and quality previously available only in more expensive models."

Indeed, by 1946 Chrysler had a 25.7 percent market share, second only to General Motors, and had achieved a reputation for sound engineering. However, in 1950, Ford sold more cars than Chrysler, and Chrysler slid to third place in the Big Three. It began to add debt to cushion it from the cyclical swings in demand and, to maintain its attractiveness to investors, pursued a GM-type dividend payout policy.

Henry Ford's idea, an inexpensive car for the masses, still dominates Ford Motor Company. GM's concept, developed by Alfred P. Sloan, Jr., in the early 1920s, of "a car for every purse and purpose" is still the company's strategy. AMC exploits its heritage from the Nash—innovative, well-styled small cars. And Chrysler saw itself as dominated by its engineering department. Chrysler broke the boundaries of "the river of thought" in automotive engineering; an example of Chrysler's innovative engineering was a push-button transmission on its 1959 models.

Lynn Townsend, a former Touche, Ross accountant who was Chrysler's CEO during the 1960s, expanded Chrysler into worldwide production by building plants in Europe, South America, South Africa, and Australia. And he attempted to match every Ford and GM product line with a Chrysler offering, while neglecting to modernize his core facilities. One consulting report at the time noted Chrysler had direct manufacturing costs per vehicle that were 10 percent higher than those of Ford. *Fortune* in 1978 described Townsend:

> Lynn Townsend seemed more like an old-style Hollywood film czar than a midwestern auto company chief. He was a handsome and dictatorial leader who enjoyed a high reputation as a numbers man, but he never seemed to understand the fundamental business of his company. . . . At one point the company was running marginal or losing operations on every continent except Antarctica.

Indeed, Townsend's foreign ventures represented major drains on Chrysler's cash. For example, his European acquisitions, Simca in France and Rootes Motors Ltd. in Britain, were failing companies when acquired. They siphoned off funds just when the company should have been massing its resources in the U.S. to meet growing fuel-economy, emission, and safety pressures.

In the 1960s, Chrysler suffered from a severe image problem, since the public perceived Chrysler as years behind the other auto companies in styling and even in engineering. *Fortune* described its muddled image:

> Any schoolboy knows that a Pontiac is "better" (i.e., higher in price and prestige) than a Chevrolet. But not all schoolboys know that a Dodge is supposed to outrank a Plymouth.

About 70 percent of new-car buyers decided to purchase the same make of car again in the 1960s. But Eugene Cafiero, Chrysler executive, noted that, compared with Ford and GM, "our buyers are a little older. Their incomes are a little lower in almost every category of car. In the lower end of the market, they are blue-collar workers." As such, Chrysler buyers purchased fewer options, retained their cars longer, and so were potential customers less frequently. An executive at another auto company was more blunt as he remarked that a lot of Chrysler buyers "are losers. These are people who didn't make it someplace."

Under Townsend, Chrysler had unsuccessfully tried to appeal to a younger buyer and may have alienated its own customers. In the early 1960s, most of Chrysler's intermediate-sized cars offered a hot-rod image to compete with Pontiac and Ford's "muscle" cars, GTOs and Mustangs. The Dodge Charger and Coronet and Plymouth Road Runner and Satellite grabbed 19–22 percent of the intermediate market. Similarly, the "Dodge Rebellion" campaign of the 1960s featuring cowgirls and hoopla left the bulk of non-rebellious Dodge owners confused and resentful of Chrysler's threat to their image. Later, when environmental issues surfaced, Chrysler found that its older and more conservative buyers abandoned it; its younger buyers found Chrysler had no appealing cars when they wanted to trade their Chargers and Road Runners.

THE SEVENTIES AT CHRYSLER

In Chrysler's US product line, Townsend chose to redesign Chrysler's big cars in the early 1970s rather than develop smaller cars for the market. He gambled that small cars were just a passing fancy (see *Exhibit 1*) and spent $450 million restyling his full-size line. Indeed, Townsend recalled that "we struggled here in the late 50s to do a rear-engined car (to compete with GM's Corvair) and we couldn't. Our engineers were not willing to go with the weight distribution that it would entail. There was no way this management could have even ordered that engineering department to do a rear-engined car." And so, early in the 1970s, Chrysler had no subcompact. By contrast, GM introduced the subcompact Vega in 1971, Ford brought out the Pinto, and AMC began selling the Gremlin in the same year. Chrysler's new big cars entered the market in the fall of 1973, just months before the Arab oil embargo destroyed the traditional luxury car market in the United States. The same year, GM introduced the Chevette, the first successful U.S. minicar.

In the fall of 1974, when the auto market had nearly disappeared to a 7.4 million-unit level, Townsend came up with a plan to lower the company's breakeven point so Chrysler would be profitable even if the U.S. car market fell to 6 million units from its normal 10 million. At Chrysler, thousands of designers and engineers were either laid off or fired; the engineering staff was cut by 80 percent. At some Chrysler plants in 1975, only people hired before 1965 still had jobs. *Fortune* described the plan from a 1978 vantage point by noting:

> The cost cutting required . . . was awesome; the effect on future car development at Chrysler nearly fatal. . . . Product programs were so seriously delayed that every model the company has introduced since then has been from four to eight months late.

In 1975, Townsend retired at midyear, a $260 million loss for Chrysler, and John Riccardo became Chrysler's CEO. Formerly a Touche, Ross accountant like Townsend, Riccardo had been President during Chrysler's 1969 and 1970 retrenchment and had earned the nickname of "Flamethrower" for his tough management style.

Yet, as Riccardo took over, Chrysler had an unexpected strength. In the midst of its muddled image and preoccupation with big cars and racy intermediates, it continued to build its compact Dodge Darts and Plymouth Valiants to keep its dealers happy. These cars, not subject to much annual tampering as Chrysler concentrated on larger cars, won an image for quality and reliability, just the characteristics the usual Chrysler buyers wanted. The company's mild attempts to liven them up did not work as planned; the Dart Swinger was bought mostly by people over 45. And amazingly, these compacts held 40 percent of the small-car market in 1974, even though Chrysler's all-around market share was only 12.4 percent in that year. Even with no subcompacts, Chrysler had a reputation as a quality US small-car manufacturer in spite of itself.

Riccardo's tasks for turnaround in the mid-1970s ranged from organizational problems—for example, product plans had always been on one calendar, profit plans on another—to reading the minds of federal regulators of fuel-economy, safety, and emissions standards. Riccardo was to supervise the "downsizing" of Chrysler as it sold smaller, lighter cars both to compete with Ford and GM and to meet regulatory standards. The change required heavy advance planning in an industry where new model development took five years and new engine development seven.

The task proved arduous from the beginning. The Plymouth Volare and Dodge Aspen compact models, planned under Townsend and introduced in 1976, were plagued by delays and launch and quality problems. They went through eight recalls, prompting many loyal Chrysler customers to vow, "Never again!" David Healy, an analyst at Drexel Burnham Lambert, wrote:

> The company has been known in recent years for neither its prestige nor the advanced styling of its cars—it must sell its "me too" line at attractive prices in order to retain customers.

Riccardo's rescue plan was designed to move Chrysler along with the market to smaller cars. The plan called for Chrysler to bring out all new models each year for four years, starting with its 1979 model cars. First the standards, then the intermediates, then compacts, and finally trucks and vans would be brought to the market, each new line coming from a plant that would be gutted and refitted to produce it.

But Chrysler's launch in fall 1978 of its standard-sized St. Regis in a market unreceptive to large cars was a disaster. Chrysler couldn't get models to dealers in time to coincide with its heavy promotional program. By February, the company had a 381-day supply of St. Regises, with only 307 days remaining in the sales year.

Riccardo's full implementation of his plan was delayed as Chrysler waited for the government to finalize its regulations. By late 1977, when the regulations were set, the price tag for the program, which was earlier estimated to cost $5.5 billion, was $7.5 billion, and there was evidence that Chrysler could no longer hope to finance it internally.

GOVERNMENT REGULATION HITS THE AUTO INDUSTRY

The impact of the energy crisis and growing environment and safety consciousness on the auto industry in the 1970s was severe, and the combined effects of these factors were not always those expected by industry analysts. Government attempts to blunt rising gasoline prices, reduce U.S. dependence on foreign oil, control pollution, and increase product safety resulted in a regulatory patchwork that proved hard to predict and required expensive measures for compliance by the automakers.

A trend to smaller cars for the United States existed as early as 1959, as the smaller imports held 10.7 percent of the market. But although small-car sales grew immediately in response to the Arab oil embargo in 1973 and the Iranian oil crisis in 1979, the fluctuations in the import market share were large enough (see *Exhibit 1*) that automakers were reluctant to switch quickly away from their profitable large cars. In his book *On a Clear Day You Can See General Motors,* John Z. DeLorean, a former GM vice-president, noted that it was possible to build a Cadillac for $300 more than a Chevrolet and then sell it for $3,000–$10,000 more. And Henry Ford II summed up the industry's feeling that "mini cars mean mini profits," since small cars carry nearly the same costs but consumers are much more price-sensitive toward them.

Federal energy policy contributed to the confusion the automakers felt over consumers' size preference. OPEC raised prices in 1973 and 1974 by over 500 percent, but gasoline was the only commodity on which Nixon's wage-price controls were maintained in force. Although OPEC was selling oil for $12/barrel, Congress controlled U.S. oil prices to $8.65/barrel from new wells and $5.25 from established wells. And to cushion the impact on the consumer still further, Congress rolled back the oil price $1/barrel in 1976, managing both to reduce the U.S. auto buyers' incentive for conservation and to increase U.S. reliance on OPEC oil.

In longer-term policies, however, corporate average fuel-economy (CAFE) standards year by year required auto manufacturers to be responsible for conservation, and required them to build a certain percentage of fuel-efficient vehicles in order to attain fleet CAFE standards, whether the market existed or not. *Exhibit 2* shows projected CAFE standards for 1976 to 1985.

Environmental restrictions on building oil refineries virtually stopped. At the same time, however, emission standards required development of expensive technology for compliance—as well as unleaded gas, which used more petroleum to produce. And energy-efficient diesel engines were permitted high emission and particulate levels. *Exhibit 2* shows Federal and California emission standards for 1976–1985.

Safety regulations required both more new technology and heavier cars carrying airbags and rollbars; small cars were portrayed as death-traps. Indeed, New York Chevy dealers sponsored a 1980 ad campaign, embarassing to the industry, which showed mangled imported subcompacts in graphic accident scenes with the headline, "But it got 43 miles per gallon" above copy reading, "In What Are Your Children Driving Tonight?"

Complex regulations required the companies to incur steep development, tooling, materials, and production costs for compliance. For example, cheap steel was being replaced with more expensive (either in terms of tooling or the material itself) aluminum, high-strength low-alloy steel, graphite fibers or molded plastics. Estimates of regulation-related costs ranged from $450 to $675 per vehicle. More fully integrated manufacturers like GM had an advantage over Chrysler, which bought most of its components outside. GM could institute internal cost cutting measures to improve margins; Chrysler had to pay whatever its suppliers charged.

The industry criticized the regulations as not in the public interest. Airbags, effective only in frontal collisions at speeds faster than 25 miles per hour, cost $600 new and nearly double that for replacement; a seatbelt shoulder harness cost $75 and provided better protection in more situations. Ford noted that the three-way catalyst to reduce three pollutants to 5 percent of their uncontrolled levels cost $59 million per percentage point of reduced pollution. By contrast, Ford spent $7.7 million per point pollution reduction from 1968–1977 when pollutants were reduced by more than 80 percent.

IMPLEMENTATION OF RICCARDO'S TURNAROUND

As Chrysler's market share and financial resources continued to dwindle in the 1970s, Riccardo began to finance his $7.5 billion capital spending program to move Chrysler into the emerging 1980s markets and regulation requirements by issuing a block of preferred stock. Despite a speculative rating by Moody's and Standard and Poor, and no institutional interest, Merrill Lynch successfully promoted the offering in the summer of 1978 to retail customers with an 11 percent dividend yield, and Chrysler increased the issue from $150 million to $250 million. In addition, Chrysler borrowed heavily from banks and insurance companies; Manufacturers Hanover is Chrysler's lead bank.

As part of his systematic turnaround scheme (which included the unsuccessful 1979 standard-sized St. Regis), Riccardo recognized Chrysler's lack of a subcompact. In January, 1978, he introduced the Dodge Omni and Plymouth Horizon, cars with sideways-mounted engines and front-wheel drive. Two years ahead of GM's front-wheel-drive X-Car compacts, *Motor Trend* magazine named them 1978 Car of the Year.

But in July, 1978, *Consumer Reports* featured the Omni and Horizon cover photo that *Motor Trend* had used, with the words "Not Acceptable" stamped across the cover. *Consumer Reports* tests, although later criticized by experts in the industry as made under highly unusual circumstances, indicated that the car had a dangerous directional instability, a tendency to sway from side to side when, at 50 miles an hour, "we twitch the steering wheel smartly and then let go with both hands. . . ." For the first time in ten years, a U.S.-made car had been branded "not acceptable."

The impact on the Omni/Horizon was catastrophic, and Chrysler's reputation and sales were weakened in its other lines as well. Riccardo's conversion expenses and the Omni/Horizon introduction added to Chrysler's financial woes, resulting in a $204.6 million loss for 1978.

LEE IACOCCA HEADS FOR CHRYSLER

Lee A. Iacocca, former president of Ford, was named Chrysler's president in December 1978 by John Riccardo, who announced plans to retain Chrysler's chairmanship but turn over the duties of CEO to Iacocca within a year.

Industry observers were enthusiastic about the change in leadership. Iacocca was a graduate engineer and marketing whiz fired the year before by Henry Ford II over a disagreement on the timing of smaller, more fuel-efficient models for Ford's line. Iacocca recalled the offers that followed his July, 1978, firing:

> I wanted to stay in the business that I'd spent my whole life in, that I was as good or better at than anyone else. When someone suggested I take over an aircraft manufacturer, for example, I said, "You want me as a professional manager, but how many years will it take before I know what the hell is going on in that business?" So I decided I wanted to stay in autos. I got some foreign offers, but I didn't want to move. Chrysler was the only game in town.

Iacocca and product planner and designer Harold Sperlich, hired by Riccardo two years earlier after a similar disagreement with Henry Ford II, had been responsible in the mid-1960s for the very successful Mustang that updated Ford's stodgy image and introduced a new class of small, personal cars.

With yet another turnaround ahead at Chrysler, Iacocca's success required both remedial work on Chrysler's image and obvious operating improvements. Maintaining Chrysler's position as a full-line manufacturer, he hired Kenyon and Eckhardt to build the Dodge image as sporty and fun-to-drive, and to stress Plymouth's reputation for stability and good handling. He added dealer incentives and five-year, 50,000-mile warranties on some slow-moving models to boost sales.

Exhibit 3 shows Chrysler's financial standing in the U.S. auto industry. *Exhibit 4* gives Chrysler's ten year financial statistics through 1978. *Exhibit 5* and *6* detail market share and dealer position.

Chrysler had never built solely to dealer order as was the practice at Ford and GM. Instead, Chrysler produced half its cars to dealer order and half for its own inventory or "sales bank" and then sold to dealers from inventory, a practice termed "forcing the market." Iacocca commented to *Automotive Industries* in July 1979:

> There's only one thing wrong with that. You miss the market, usually because you don't know what the hell to put in the bank. Also, you carry hundreds of millions of dollars in carrying costs. The cars are in there thirty, sixty, or maybe ninety days. When you add all the concomitant damage that goes with it—it's not the way to do business.

So, moving to the Ford and GM norm, Iacocca told *The Wall Street Journal* in a September 10, 1979, interview, "I'll be damned if I'm going to build one car without a dealer order." Retraining of sales reps and dealers required six months before Iacocca's system was fully operational, and dealers were signing orders one and two months in advance.

Although Townsend had said his proudest achievement as Chrysler president was gaining one-third of Chrysler's sales overseas, Iacocca continued the international retrenchment begun by Riccardo. Riccardo had worked out a deal with the British government to help bail out Chrysler-UK long enough to sell it and all other Chrysler European manufacturing and finance companies to Peugeot-Citroen in 1978, gaining $300 million in cash and 25 percent equity in the French company, and wiping off almost $400 million in debt from his balance sheet.

Iacocca continued the "fold or fix" strategy by:

1 A deal with VW to triple the capitalization of Chrysler do Brazil, with VW acquiring two-thirds equity in exchange for providing the additional funds.
2 Sale to GM of its car and truck assembly facilities in Venezuela and its equity in a Colombian assembly operation.
3 A deal with Mitsubishi under which Chrysler and Mitsubishi would put $30.2 million into Chrysler-Australia in exchange for a combined one-third equity in the company.
4 Sale of its Turkish plants and 75 percent of its South African company.

Automotive market movements did not make Iacocca's turnaround task easier. The political crisis in Iran resulted in a gasoline shortage, and consumers moved en masse to the 30 mpg. minicars. Sales of Chrysler big cars, pickup trucks, and vans "dropped like a rock," and the company reported first quarter losses of $53.8 million.

Even the soaring demand for Omni/Horizons couldn't stem the tide; there was a worldwide shortage of the four-cylinder engines that went into them. Volkswagen, Chrysler's original supplier of 300,000 four-cylinder engines for the Omni, as well as Mitsubishi of Japan, which supplied engines for Chrysler's Colt and Sopporo models, would not have additional four-cylinder engine capacity before August, 1980. Chrysler's own Trenton, Michigan, plant was being retooled to produce four-cylinder engines beginning in the spring of 1980. By 1980 Chrysler would have capacity to provide its own four-cylinder engines.

Iacocca was betting that the introduction of the fuel-efficient front-wheel-drive K-Cars with the model year would win consumer support and profits for Chrysler. The K-Cars were to replace the ill-fated Aspen/Volare models and compete with General Motors' fuel-efficient, front-wheel-drive X-Cars. As well, Iacocca had scheduled slightly larger front-wheel-drive cars to be introduced in 1984 and 1985.

But introductions of the all-new models required for Chrysler's recovery demanded resources, and Chrysler's first quarter 1979 loss made it apparent to Iacocca and Riccardo that Chrysler could not make it to the 1981 model without assistance.

EFFORTS FOR ASSISTANCE BEGIN

Early in June 1979, Riccardo began lobbying Washington to emphasize Chrysler's financial plight. He organized a lobby of dealers, suppliers, UAW union representatives, and most of the Michigan congressional delegation to demonstrate that a Chrysler collapse would start a tidal wave through the U.S. economy. Riccardo's own position was that the 1979 sales slump was unexpected and, coupled with the spending required to comply with federal regulations, made profitability of Chrysler temporarily impossible. Riccardo offered a program of special tax credits to cover part of the expenditures necessary to meet regulations; Chrysler in the long run could then meet its full tax obligation with higher than normal tax payments on future earnings. As well, Riccardo suggested a two-year postponement in complying with federal emission standards, which he said would save Chrysler $600 million.

In July 1979, Chrysler reported a second quarter loss of $207 million. At this time, Chrysler Financial had $1.3 billion worth of commercial paper outstanding and had been downgraded by the investment services. Corporations that usually sold paper feared the collapse of the market and began to activate bank credit lines instead.

Chrysler was blocked from obtaining funds on the short-term market and so it, too, was forced to activate backup lines of credit at about 300 banks. Led by Manufacturers Hanover, Chrysler also negotiated a $400 million credit line in Japan, $70 million in Canada, and $94 million from Prudential Insurance Company and Aetna Life Insurance Co., Chrysler's two largest long-term lenders.

In August 1979, Chrysler Financial sold its retail receivables (car loans to retail customers) to Household Finance Corporation for $500 million and wholesale receivables to General Motors Acceptance Corporation for $230 million. Chrysler Financial then converted its backup credit line to revolving credit. Revolving credit is available to a borrower as soon as a loan is paid off, in contrast to backup credit lines, which can be activated only under certain financial or operating conditions as stipulated by contract.

During the first week of August, 1979, John Riccardo called a press conference, where he announced that Chrysler was asking the U.S. government for a $1 billion cash advance against future income. He said,

> We have taken all the prudent steps that could be taken to make our way. . . . We are not talking about bailout, we are not talking about handout, we are not talking welfare. We are talking equity. We are talking about money we intend to repay.

Two weeks before the press conference, Michigan's two senators had personally taken the word to President Carter. Three days after Chrysler "surprised the world," UAW President Douglas A. Fraser rejected Iacocca's request that Chrysler be exempted from August contract negotiations between the UAW and the U.S. automakers and that wages and benefits be frozen for two years. But he said, "They've hollered wolf so many times, I'm concerned about people taking them seriously. I think they *must* be taken seriously."

Early Response

Rejecting Chrysler's plea for $1 billion cash, the administration requested that a detailed Chrysler survival plan be sent to the Treasury.

With Riccardo having been hospitalized in May for cardiac insufficiency and now spending four to five days a week in Washington gaining support for Chrysler from legislators and officials, Iacocca's tasks lay in Detroit, where he tried to gain more control over Chrysler's dwindling resources with:

1 Suspension of common stock dividends.

2 Suspension of an employee "thrift stock" plan under which the company matched half the funds invested by salaried employees in Chrysler stock. Chrysler had contributed $15.8 million to the plan in 1978; the plan was scheduled to resume when Chrysler became profitable, it was hoped in 1981.

3 Rejection of all price increases from suppliers and requests to suppliers for extended payment terms. Although most suppliers agreed, many immediately purchased insurance to cover their accounts receivable.

4 Meetings with the UAW to try to gain concessions from the union.

5 Public relations and ad programs in 50 major newspapers and magazines, outlining the predicament under the headline, "Would America Be Better Off without Chrysler?" and declaring, "We're going to get well . . . because it will be good for the automotive business and for America."

6 Sale of Chrysler Realty Corporation to Abko Realty, Inc., a privately-held Wichita, Kansas, investment company formed especially to purchase it. Under a new name, it continued to lease its 780 dealership facilities to Chrysler dealers. The sale netted $200 million in cash and reduced debt by $70 million. Chrysler was looking for buyers for Chrysler Marine to net about $20 million. Chrysler Financial was profitable, and Chrysler was the thirteenth-largest defense contractor in the United States with $742.5 in military business.

7 A $400 rebate offer direct from factory to customers on all Chrysler light trucks, vans, and cars except Omni/Horizon subcompacts. The rebate was popular with Chrysler dealers, who held more than 350,000 vehicles on August 1, 1979. Iacocca himelf appeared on Chrysler's TV ads before the rebates, saying, "I'm not asking anyone to buy a car on faith. I'm asking you to compare." A month later, Iacocca commented that the rebate had generated enough interest that Chrysler's sales bank, its 80,000 car inventory, had been trimmed by 53,000 cars.

8 Layoffs of workers. With the elimination of the sales bank policy, which maintained production despite lack of dealer orders, Chrysler had laid off 25,800 from a total of 100,000 hourly workers by August, 1979. Following Riccardo's request for federal aid, 1,800 hourly workers were indefinitely laid off at plants that manufactured Chrysler's slowest-selling large cars, Dodge St. Regis and Chrysler New Yorker and Newport models. In addition, more than 2,500 employees of Chrysler in Canada, and all nonessential white collar employees, were laid off. Offices had rows of empty desks.

9 Executive salary cuts. Riccardo's and Iacocca's $360,000 base salaries had drawn public criticism, so in late August they announced they were giving up all but $1 per year until the company was again profitable. Also, 17,000 other top executives took salary cuts, averaging 10 percent for the vice-presidents and 2–5 percent for those with lower base salaries. The salary reduction plan allowed the executives to gain their deferred salaries if Chrysler became profitable on schedule in 1981, and represented a savings of less than $3 million.

10 Strategic marketing changes. Chrysler lowered prices on the Aspen and Volare below 1979 prices for cuts of more than $100, several hundred dollars below the popular Omnis and Horizons. It also announced new three-year, unlimited mileage, corrosion warranties on all its cars and trucks, similar to warranties in the rest of the industry in 1979.

Despite its efforts, Chrysler anticipated the loss of at least 200 of its dealers by 1980. Iacocca noted the irony of Chrysler's plans to have fuel-efficient cars available in 1981 as he quipped that the ousting of the Shah of Iran in 1979 came just two years too soon. Government forecasts predicted the price of gasoline would rise to 76.6 cents per gallon in 1981 and $1.38 by 1990.

VIEW FROM THE CARTER ADMINISTRATION

The Administration did not buy Chrysler's plan for a $1 billion cash advance, but instead preferred to approach the problem through loan guarantees, in the same way as it had averted the economic ripple effects in the Lockheed and New York City emergencies. It had earned $31 million in fees for guaranteeing up to $250 million in loans.

President Carter said at a town meeting in Burlington, Iowa, that there should be shared responsibility between Chrysler employees and officials, with the private sector most responsible for assisting Chrysler, minimum federal involvement, and maximum security for any government guaranteed loan. It "would be a good investment, I believe, if we do it that way, keep Chrysler operating, aid auto industry competition, hold prices down, and keep several hundred thousand Chrysler employees working," Carter said.

On September 8, 1979, after a meeting with Riccardo and Iacocca, the Treasury stated it would not accept a plan giving the company tax credits "or the equivalent of the government's taking an equity interest in Chrysler." Treasury Secretary G. William Miller objected to a tax credit plan as interest-free to Chrysler. He also said $750 million was the outside range of federal help for Chrysler.

Sen. William Proxmire (D. Wisc.), chairman of the Senate Banking Committee, viewed Lockheed as a "terrible precedent" and loan guarantees as "a gross interference with the private sector."

Rep. Henry Reuss (D. Wisc.), chairman of the House Banking Committee, was similarly unenthusiastic about federal loan guarantees to "a company that is about to expire because it has insisted on making gas guzzlers."

THE PLAN

On September 15, 1979, Chrysler formally presented its recovery plan to the Treasury, requesting $1.2 billion in federal loan guarantees, which, along with $900 million it would raise from the sale of unspecified assets and "other actions," would give it the $2.1 billion it needed by 1982 to implement its product plans.

The recovery plan included Chrysler's projection that by 1982 it would realize $593 more per car than in 1979. The $593 included:

- $25 gained because its products would be more competitive, sell better, and use design techniques incorporating cheaper materials and manufacturing techniques.
- $89 per unit from more optional equipment.
- The rest in variable profit margins from production efficiencies, less costly parts, and reduced warranty expenses from design and manufacturing improvements.

The plan included forecast of an anticipated loss of $1.07 billion for 1979 and, even with federal help, a $482 million loss for 1980. Chrysler also announced that it was negotiating with VW for sale of its Argentina business and with Mitsubishi about another part of its interest in Chrysler Australia.

Chrysler also released results of studies done by the Department of Transportation and Data Resources, Inc., showing the effect of a Chrysler bankruptcy on Detroit and the

U.S. economy. According to DRI, national unemployment would grow by .5 percent and Detroit unemployment could reach 16 percent, with heavy impact on blacks and other minorities—approximately 38,000 unemployed minority workers—since Chrysler's plants were primarily located in older, inner-city areas. DRI also estimated the net impact of lost tax revenue and needed extra social spending on federal, state, and local governments at $16.5 billion, with a loss in GNP of over $30 billion. As well, the DOT study forecast a $7.2 billion unfavorable effect on the U.S. balance of payments for 1979–1981, since imports were likely to gain 40 percent of Chrysler's market share. DOT also estimated that for every Chrysler production worker laid off, two people employed by Chrysler's suppliers and related businesses would also be laid off. In 1978, Chrysler had employed 131,758 employees, paying total wages and salaries of $2.9 billion.

Another problem was Chrysler's pension plan, with an unfunded pension liability of $1.1 billion in 1979, $250 million of which was uninsured. The balance was insured by the Pension Benefit Guaranty Corporation, an agency of the federal government. PBGC had accumulated a net deficiency of $130 million in 1979 from the termination of 664 plans that had lacked enough assets to cover their pension liabilities, and was not prepared to confront a major corporate liquidation. Henry Rose, general counsel to the PBGC, said in *Fortune:*

> If Chrysler did terminate its pension plan, the funded portion of the total liability ($1.4 billion) would be sufficient to meet the needs of the beneficiaries for the next seven years.

In the meantime, the agency could raise revenues by increasing premiums on other corporate plans, if Chrysler should go bankrupt.

CHRYSLER'S MANAGEMENT CHANGES

Citing his strenuous efforts in Washington, which had aggravated a heart condition discovered earlier in the year, John Riccardo announced his resignation as chairman and chief executive officer on September 17, 1979. He stated:

> In the minds of many, I am closely associated with the past management of a troubled company. It would be most unfair to the new management . . . if my continued presence as Chairman should in any way hinder the final passage of our request.

Industry observers were surprised by his move, and Chrysler officials stated that the decision was Riccardo's own, with no pressure from Chrysler's directors, bankers, or the government.

On September 20, 1979, Lee A. Iacocca was elected chairman and chief executive officer by Chrysler's board. Two of his long-term associates at Ford, Paul Bergmoser and Gerald Greenwald, joined him at Chrysler as president and executive vice-president, finance. Bergmoser had been a former Ford Motor purchasing vice-president who, at 63, had come out of retirement earlier in 1979 to join Iacocca. Greenwald had been the president of Ford's Venezuelan subsidiary and joined Iacocca in May at Chrysler.

In an interview following his appointment, Iacocca said he would spend ''at least half'' his time running the company and the rest negotiating with federal officials. ''I came to run an auto show. I don't want to do it in Washington. I'd rather do it in Detroit,'' he said.

Iacocca was not pleased to turn to the government for help; he had said in Detroit a week before Chrysler's proposal that going to the government for money ''gets you in a bureaucratic and political tangle, and I don't like it. That should be stronger—I detest it.'' Nevertheless, Chrysler's financial crisis was ''more than we're able to bear,'' he said. ''Hell, I don't care what form [the aid] takes now. I'm very innovative.''

REACTION TO CHRYSLER'S SITUATION

In July 1979, the rumor of a Chrysler-VW merger swept Wall Street and was vehemently denied by both Chrysler and Volkswagen. A Paine Webber Mitchell Hutchings analysis declared:

> . . . We regard it as wishful thinking to expect a white knight to appear out of Europe, or elsewhere, to buy the company in its entirety. Realistically, foreign car companies will wait for the "garage sale" which would accompany financial reorganization.

Others suggested that a Chapter XI bankruptcy might be Chrysler's wisest move, since under the recently revised federal bankruptcy code, the court could retain the present management rather than automatically appointing a trustee. *Newsweek* wrote:

> [Chrysler] would be protected against its creditors and temporarily relieved of its burden of debt. The Company could fire unproductive managers, shed its unprofitable lines, continue to make cars and provide employment, and with any luck emerge a few years later a leaner, healthier company. "Chrysler will still be in business if it doesn't get any government help—just a smaller company than it is today," one analyst argued.

One New York banker observed, ''A reorganization could bring 70 to 80 cents on the dollar. With the government in, we don't know what our chances of recovery would be.''

Leaders of the UAW and Senate members, including Senate Majority Leader Robert C. Byrd (D. W. Va.) and Senate Finance Committee Chairman Russell Long (D. La.), had suggested that government aid ought to be contingent on Chrysler workers being able to own a piece of the corporation, or at least influence decision making ''at all levels of the corporation,'' as the UAW said. Employee Stock Ownership Plans (ESOPs) were discussed whereby Chrysler would have to set up an ESOP and give it 10–20 percent of company equity in new stock in return for federal loan guarantees. It was estimated that $1 billion in equity would give the trust about a one-third interest in the corporation.

Economist Robert Lekachman endorsed government acquisition of an equity interest in Chrysler, saying:

> This is probably the most promising avenue of gradual socialization of the American economy. In the grim economic environment of the next decade, Chrysler will be only

the first of numerous chances for government to become an active partner of corporate enterprise.

Business worried about Chrysler's rescue as setting up a dangerous precedent of federal help for failing private companies, and some thought that federal loans would only forestall the inevitable, since Chrysler might be beyond repair. Phil R. North, president of Tandy Corporation, said:

> The government should be trying to . . . help its winners instead of . . . help the losers. If government would pay as much attention to helping GM compete worldwide as they do to help Chrysler, which is only the victim of mismanagement, then GM might be selling a lot more cars abroad.

Consumer advocate Ralph Nader found himself agreeing with conservative economist Milton Friedman that Chrysler should go it alone. When General Motors chairman Thomas A. Murphy agreed, United Auto Workers President Douglas A. Fraser snapped, "Murphy is a horse's ass. He hasn't got any goddam business injecting himself into this!"

Howard S. Clark, a member of the executive committee of American Express and a former Chrysler director, changed his mind from his early opposition to Chrysler aid:

> Government has become involved in lots of ways in business. Government spends as much as $15,000 per person training people for jobs, and here it has a chance by guaranteeing loans for Chrysler to save 400,000 jobs. That's a pretty efficient way to go about maintaining employment levels.

Dave Stockman, Republican congressman from Michigan, however, took issue with the projections of unemployment from a Chrysler failure:

> The longer term prospects for Chrysler's 120,000 direct employees are not entirely bleak. Nearly two fifths are white-collar, supervisory, or skilled production workers with strong prospects for reemployment. Another 22,000 are employed at modern efficient plants . . . with good prospects for a new owner.

Freda Ackerman, director of Moody's municipal bond department and an authority on local government finances, had a high opinion of the managerial astuteness of Coleman Young, mayor of Detroit, and his ability to guide Detroit through a Chrysler reorganization. She said, "Everybody thought that Seattle would never survive the Boeing contraction and that Youngstown could never sustain its loss, but both of them did."

GM chairman Thomas A. Murphy said GM was not "opposed to federal government assistance . . . so long as the aid is in the form of relief from the excess burden of regulation and is applicable to all automotive companies." Ford executive vice-president William O. Bourke commented that "the thought of my company's taxes being used as an incentive to sell against me doesn't give me a warm and comfortable feeling."

The "orphan car syndrome" afflicted many potential Chrysler customers, discouraged about Chrysler's possible bankruptcy and its effect on warranties and dealer service. Warranties would be simply another creditor claim, dealers to process recalls might be nonexistent, resale value of the cars would decline, and parts—although likely to be still available, since the parts supply business is profitable—might be harder to find as time went by.

Maryann Keller, an auto analyst at Paine Webber, commented:

> You can be philosophically in favor of bailing out Chrysler, but when it comes to spending your own money, it is a different matter. Chrysler could sell cars only if they were cheaper or substantially better than the competition. This is a consumer product, after all. How would it change your life if Chrysler were not there?

OCTOBER 1979

Hearings began before the Senate Banking Committee on the Chrysler situation on October 11, 1979. Officials of the Federal Trade Commission and the Department of Transportation indicated that they were unconvinced of Chrysler's long-term ability to continue to compete as a full-line auto maker and were skeptical of Chrysler's plans to increase its market share.

On October 15, Chrysler's Lee Iacocca personally appeared before the UAW's rank and file bargaining committee to bring them up to date on the company's efforts for government aid. Contract negotiations with the UAW were resumed; they had been suspended since August 3 pending UAW contract settlements with GM and Ford.

Seven Japanese commercial banks announced that they had stopped underwriting Chrysler's imports of Mitsubishi cars and trucks on October 17, because Chrysler's financial position dropped below the level specified in loan agreements between Chrysler and the Japanese banks. Key U.S. bankers continued to stand firm in their existing credit agreement, after hasty afternoon meetings called by Chrysler.

On October 18, Iacocca submitted to the Treasury a request for federal aid that complied with the $750 million level specified by the administration. The company said it was willing to consider disposing of its Canadian and profitable Mexican operations (Chrysler was Mexican profit and volume leader), its defense division (Chrysler was the thirteenth-largest U.S. defense contractor), and possibly some of its Peugeot stock (Chrysler owned 15 percent of both Peugeot and Mitsubishi) to secure loan guarantees.

Simultaneously, the UAW announced it had agreed to permit Chrysler to defer $200 million in pension fund payments for one year. Such deferrals were allowed under federal pension law and did not jeopardize future benefit payments.

That afternoon, Iacocca appeared before the House Banking Subcommittee. He said that all the groups from whom the company was seeking help were waiting for a firm commitment of federal aid before agreeing to aid in the overall recovery plan. He noted that the money provided by possible federal loan guarantees was "almost overshadowed by the importance of the government's vote of confidence needed to keep our present creditors in line." Under questioning, he admitted that if the economic climate did not improve by the latter part of 1980, "the cash flow projections and other parts of the survival plan could turn out to be overly optimistic." He conceded that he "would feel more comfortable with" the $1.2 billion Chrysler had earlier requested.

On October 22, a Booz Allen and Hamilton study, requested and paid for by Chrysler, was released. It noted that Chrysler might need government help to raise $1.5

billion from outside sources by 1982, although the October 18 plan had Chrysler estimating its cash needs at about $2.1 billion during the intervening years. The report included an assessment of the effect of rising interest rates and possible further slowdowns in the economy as a result of the Federal Reserve Board's credit-tightening moves taken in early fall 1979.

On October 25, Chrysler and the UAW reached agreement on a three-year national labor contract that was expected to save Chrysler $203 million in labor costs over two years compared to what its costs would have been if it had reached terms similar to those of GM and Ford. UAW president Douglas A. Fraser was nominated for election to the Chrysler board of directors at the company's annual meeting in May 1980. Stockholder approval would make the UAW the first major U.S. industrial union to obtain a seat on the board of such a large company. Chrysler shied away from making the move seem precedent-setting, saying, "Mr. Fraser was nominated as a man of outstanding ability, not as a representative of labor." Fraser, however, said, "I'm going to represent the United Auto Workers on the board and speak out on their behalf," and denied that his presence on the board would create a conflict of interest.

On October 31, Iacocca issued a shareholders' letter announcing a $460.6 million loss in the third quarter 1979, second only to the record Bethlehem Steel quarterly loss of $477 million in the third quarter 1977. GM and Ford also had third quarter losses, although their tax credits put them in the black overall; GM's first loss in 9 years resulted in a sharp reduction of its year end dividend.

Chrysler also disclosed that its short-term debt outstanding at the end of the third quarter had more than doubled, to $586.4 million from $217 million at the end of the second quarter; short-term debt was $143.8 million a year earlier. Chrysler also told its shareholders that its working capital had dropped to $356 million at the end of September from $800 million at the end of the second quarter and $959 million at the end of the third quarter 1978.

NOVEMBER 1979

On November 1, Treasury Secretary G. William Miller announced a Carter administration proposal of a $1.5 billion federal loan guarantee program for Chrysler. In order to qualify, the company would be required to raise an equal amount of new capital that would *not* be protected by government guarantees, through additional borrowing, the sale of assets, and concessions from those with an economic stake in the company; anything raised after October 18 would qualify. "The impact of developments in the auto industry forced the change," said Miller.

Chrysler's board showed its good faith by suspending the quarterly dividend on 10 million shares of the company's preferred stock, saving Chrysler $27.5 million annually. It was in serious negotiations with the seven states where it had major operations. The state of Michigan was planning to mortgage Chrysler's Highland Park headquarters for $150 million.

Within the industry, the pace of new car sales, including imports, plunged 17 percent during October, 1979 (although sales of imports during October accounted for just over 19 percent) from sales in October, 1978. On November 5, 1979, Chrysler announced a new series of cash rebates, offering $300 payments for the purchase of a new 1979 or 1980 model car or truck; rebates were not offered on the Omni-Horizon or the Japanese imports that Chrysler sold.

Also in November, Miller said he would not disapprove of Russell Long's amendment to the administration proposal requiring Chrysler to establish an ESOP for its employees, but disagreed with Chairman Henry Reuss (D. Wisc.) of the House Banking Committee, who proposed an amendment requiring the company to produce vehicles for mass transit. Miller said, "We have to get [Chrysler] healing before we put them into another area." Miller released Treasury estimates that a Chrysler failure in 1979 would cost the government $2.75 billion in 1980–81 lost revenue and payments for unemployment and other forms of compensation. It would also add $1 billion yearly to the U.S. trade gap.

Douglas Fraser, UAW president, said "We're going to lobby like hell" to push the loan guarantees program for Chrysler through Congress.

By mid-November, all three automakers had begun rebate programs to help the deteriorating car sales in the country and to unload remaining 1979 models. General Motors gave $100–$400 incentives to its dealers; Ford offered its dealers $200–$500 on its eight-cylinder sporty cars, full-sized and luxury models, and most vans and light trucks. Chrysler's program, by comparison, was a $300 per car direct cash rebate program to all customers on all vehicles except its compacts. With declining sales, all three manufacturers continued to initiate temporary plant closings and production cutbacks. By late 1979, there were 100,750 auto workers indefinitely laid off in the United States.

On November 21, 1979, the Defense Department authorized the army to obligate an additional $189.7 million to Chrysler for work on the M1 tank, with plans to spend a total of $711.3 million in the year before September 30, 1980, compared to $463.7 million the preceding year. Chrysler was also awarded a $6.8 million army contract for spare parts for the tank. Chrysler had begun building the first 110 production models of the tank in the earlier fiscal year. The army wanted to order an additional 352 tanks in the 1979–1980 fiscal year and hoped that it could convince the Defense Department that the army could move ahead of schedule with the proposed 7,000 tank program.

Also in November, Walter Wriston, chairman of Citicorp, and John McGillicuddy, chairman and president of Manufacturers Hanover Trust, Chrysler's chief bank, appeared before the Senate Banking Committee and agreed that financial markets could survive a Chrysler bankruptcy. McGillicuddy reiterated that his bank would not commit itself to lending more to Chrysler, saying, "We don't lend money in circumstances in which we don't expect to be repaid, and that's where Chrysler Corporation is." Wriston called the federal aid attempt a "distortion . . . a movement of economic resources to places where they wouldn't otherwise go."

And on November 20, Chrysler announced plans to offer $250 million of new preferred stock to parties having a particular interest in the company, such as its suppliers and dealers.

DECEMBER 1979

On December 5, 1979, Chrysler presented a plan to the Canadian government to invest $1.2 billion in Canadian auto production facilities over the next five to ten years if Ottawa provided loan guarantees or other assistance. While Canadian officials expressed interest, they said they would make no commitments until action was taken by the U.S. government.

Chrysler also announced plans on December 9, 1979, to close the aged Hamtramck, Michigan, assembly plant six months ahead of schedule, on January 4, 1980; this was the "Dodge Main" plant that had operated for 70 years and was the largest automobile plant in the world. In January 1979, more than 5,000 workers has been employed at this plant, and its closing resulted in the loss of nearly 3,000 jobs. Also on December 9, Chrysler disclosed an agreement to sell its unprofitable Chrysler Boat Corporation unit to a group of the unit's executives and reported that it was continuing to seek a buyer for its unprofitable marine engine division.

Also in December, the company's Chrysler Financial Corporation unit announced the negotiation of the sale of a 75 percent interest in its Chrysler Credit Australia Ltd. unit to an Australian affiliate of the Barclays Group for about $10 million.

On December 19, *The Wall Street Journal* wrote:

> Chrysler is in far worse shape than anyone expected. Its loss this year will exceed its official $1 billion estimate and its cash is bleeding away at the alarming rate of $6 million to $8 million a day.

On December 19, the House approved a $3.43 billion package of aid, which included $1.5 billion in federal loan guarantees. Under the terms of the bill, Chrysler's unionized workers had to contribute $400 million; non-union employees were to contribute $100 million. Domestic bankers were required to provide up to $500 million, foreign banks $150 million, state and local governments $250 million, suppliers and dealers $180 million. Chrysler had to raise $300 million more through the sale of assets and an additional $50 million through the sale of stock, and issue $100 million worth of stock to its workers. Speaker Thomas O'Neill concluded his remarks in support of the legislation with a warning of a huge increase in unemployment if Chrysler failed. He said, "That's how recessions start. That's how depressions begin."

On December 20, the Senate approved a bill that differed slightly from the House version, requiring a $525 million contribution from union workers and $125 million from Chrysler's non-union employees.

Late on December 20, before congressional adjournment on December 21, 1979, House and Senate conferees agreed on a compromise package calling for a $462.5 million contribution from Chrysler's union workers and a $125 million contribution from non-union employees, as well as Chrysler's issuance of $162.5 million in stock to its workers. They agreed that the federal government would waive its status as senior creditor on $400 million of new bank lending, on lending from state and local governments, and on loans of $100,000 or less from small suppliers. The bill also established a five-member government board to monitor the rescue package and set a fee of .5–1.0 percent to be paid to the federal government for its loan guarantees.

The $3.5 billion aid bill, including $1.5 billion in federal loan guarantees, was passed on December 21, 1979. Iacocca was exhausted but elated, and he gave an upbeat view of his turnaround strategy while emphasizing that many of the biggest risks facing Chrysler "are beyond the company's control because we're playing in such a volatile market."

Iacocca went on to note that for January (1980) alone, Chrysler would need between $100 million and $200 million of interim financing to help pay its bills and meet its payrolls. ''We'll be looking to the banks for some help,'' Iacocca said. ''Nobody wants to be the first in line, but some of the banks are saying they want to be last'' to make firm commitments of help. (*Exhibit 7* details Chrysler's financial standing and results for 1978 and 1979.) The interim funds were needed through the end of March 1980, because it was expected to take at least that long to assemble the complete financing package spelled out in the law. Until the package was assembled, the company could not begin using the federally backed loans.

CHRYSLER IN 1980

While assembling its stakeholders to put together the package that would qualify it for $1.5 billion in federal aid, beginning with $800 million and standby for $700 million, Chrysler continued to try to sell its 1980 model cars. Its Omni/Horizon minicars continued to lead the way, but Chrysler felt that its full-line strategy, although costing $13.6 billion through 1985, would cushion a drop in any one segment and give dealers greater variety. In the West and Southwest, some Dodge dealers were earning more than half their profits from sales of Dodge trucks.

Iacocca predicted a $1.3 billion operating profit in 1985. Meanwhile, Chrysler expected to lose $1 billion in 1979 and $500 million in 1980, although its fourth quarter 1980 would be profitable by ''either $1 or up to $250 million,'' according to Iacocca, with a $400 million profit in 1981.

Chrysler introduced a thirty-day money back guarantee on its cars, with only .5 percent of its cars being returned and most of those traded in for larger models, as buyers complained that the cars they had originally bought were too small. Chrysler also conducted discussions with Household Finance on buying a piece of Chrysler Financial in 1980.

In April 1980, Federal Reserve efforts to curb inflation raised interest rates to unheard-of levels, with the Federal Funds rate going as high as 26 percent and the prime rate hovering in the high teens. The effect on the automobile industry was devastating. In May, adjusted annual sales for domestic manufacturers were 5.3 million, versus 9.7 million in the 1973 record year. And the refusal rate on auto loans rose from its usual 10–15 percent level to as high as 50 percent as interest rates raised payments for the few consumers who still tried to buy cars. In 1979, the average age of all cars in the United States had risen to 6.3 years from its level of 5.5 years in 1974, and the industry worried that consumers would be forced by such Federal Reserve actions to extend the life of their cars still further. (The average age of automobiles had increased to 8–9 years during World War II while the automakers were doing defense work.)

Chrysler's hopes for 1980 hinged on its 1981 models. Chrysler's 1981 fleet received higher mileage ratings from the EPA than did GM and Ford. But both before and after a $9 million Chrysler ad campaign in the summer of 1980, 75 percent of consumers still thought Chrysler built gas guzzlers.

The front-wheel-drive K-Car introduced in September 1980 received the heaviest promotion in Chrysler's 1981 lineup, and its pricing policy required sensitivity. Henry H. Pyle, vice-president of Chrysler's U.S. automotive sales, said: ''When the Omni was hot, we had trouble moving people up to a larger car because the size gap was so big. That won't be a problem with the [mid-priced] K-Car.'' But Chrysler's director of advertising and merchandising described Chrysler's newest problem:

> We call it our beauty-and-beast syndrome. We can't afford to get so caught up in selling those beautiful K-Cars (500,000 capacity) that we forget about the other models we have to sell (700,000 for breakeven in 1981).

With its growing four-cylinder engine capacity, Chrysler hoped to sell 1 million front-wheel-drive Omni/Horizons and K-Cars in 1981. The city of Detroit had given it a major tax break on its front-wheel car assembly plant.

Chrysler also continued preliminary discussions with foreign companies interested in acquiring it. Indeed, the real rationale behind the board's action may have been best publicly expressed by the former chairman of the guarantee board, former Treasury Secretary G. William Miller. He hoped the reduction in Chrysler's debts would make it a more attractive merger partner to someone interested in Chrysler's $1.7 billion losses as a tax shield for its profits. Lee Iacocca told a press conference that Chrysler's lightened debt load ''makes you a more attractive partner to dance with.''

EXHIBIT 1 **U.S. Franchised Dealer; New, Used, and Imported Vehicle Sales 1955–1978**

Year	*New Cars*	*New Trucks*	*Used Cars*	*Import New Car*	*Import Market Share*
1955	7,408,000	957,000	10,139,000	58,500	.8%
1956	5,844,000	927,000	8,902,000	98,200	1.7%
1957	5,826,000	879,000	8,770,000	206,800	3.5%
1958	4,289,000	731,000	7,805,000	378,500	8.8%
1959	5,486,000	928,000	8,728,000	614,100	11.2%
1960	6,142,000	925,000	8,808,000	498,800	8.1%
1961	5,556,000	908,000	8,221,000	378,600	6.8%
1962	6,753,000	1,068,000	8,863,000	339,200	5.0%
1963	7,334,000	1,230,000	9,285,000	385,600	5.3%
1964	7,617,000	1,352,000	9,393,000	484,100	6.3%
1965	8,763,200	1,533,000	9,784,200	559,400	6.4%
1966	8,377,400	1,613,600	9,294,800	658,100	7.9%
1967	7,567,900	1,519,200	8,854,400	779,200	9.7%
1968	8,624,800	1,805,400	9,040,100	985,800	11.4%
1969	8,464,000	1,929,000	8,945,800	1,061,600	12.5%
1970	7,115,500	1,746,100	8,296,300	1,231,000	17.3%
1971	8,676,300	2,009,000	9,005,000	1,487,600	17.1%
1972	9,321,500	2,530,600	9,384,000	1,529,400	16.4%
1973	9,669,700	3,008,200	8,987,900	1,719,900	17.8%
1974	7,448,900	3,586,600	7,666,100	1,369,100	18.4%
1975	7,050,100	2,351,000	7,943,100	1,501,000	21.3%
1976	8,606,600	3,043,900	9,056,900	1,446,600	16.8%
1977	9,104,400	3,485,500	8,878,900	1,973,075	21.7%
1978	9,308,000	3,913,900	8,766,900	1,950,393	21.0%

Source: Compiled by Robert Bosch Corp., *Ward's Automotive Yearbook*.

EXHIBIT 2 Emission and Fuel Economy Standards 1976–1985

Model Year	Emission Standards: Federal HC GM/MI	Federal CO GM/MI	Federal NO_x GM/MI	California (a) HC GM/MI	California CO GM/MI	California NO_x GM/MI	Fuel Economy Standards USA MPG	Fuel Economy Standards USA L/100 KM
1976	1.5	15.0	3.1	0.9	9.0	2.0	—	—
1977	1.5	15.0	2.0	0.41	9.0	1.5	18.0	13.1
1978	1.5	15.0	2.0	0.41	9.0	1.5	18.0	12.4
1979	1.5	15.0	2.0	0.41	9.0	1.5	19.0	13.1
1980	0.41	7.0	2.0	0.41	7.0	1.0(d)	20.0	11.8
1981	0.41	3.4(b)	1.0(c)	0.41	3.4	1.0(d)	22.0	10.7
1982	0.41	3.4(b)	1.0(c)	0.41	3.4	0.4(e)	24.0	9.8
1983	0.41	3.4	1.0(c)	0.41	3.4	0.4(e)	26.0	9.0
1984	0.41	3.4	1.0(c)	0.41	3.4	0.4(e)	27.0	8.7
1985	0.41	3.4	1.0	0.41	3.4	0.4(e)	27.5	8.6

(a)Federal Standards Applicable to Diesel Engines
(b)Waiver for Up to 7 GM/MI Possible
(c)Waiver for Up to 1.5 GM/MI Possible (Diesel or Innovative Technology)
(d)1.5 GM/MI Alternatively at 100.000 MI instead of 50,000 MI
(e)1.0 GM/MI Alternatively at 100,000 MI instead of 50,000 MI
Source: Compiled by Robert Bosch Corp., *Ward's Automotive Yearbook.*

EXHIBIT 3
Five-Year Average Ranking of Auto Firms Among 1,000 Largest Firms, 1972–1977

	General Motors		Ford		Chrysler		American Motors	
	5-Year Average	Ranking	5-Year Average	Ranking	5-Year Average	Ranking	5-Year Average	Ranking
Profitability								
Return on equity	16.9%	274	12.2%	597	4.2%	929	1.1%	954
Return on capital	15.4	133	10.2	447	4.0	925	2.2	958
Growth								
Earnings per share	5.6	675	6.4	643	−8.1	898	N.A.	N.A.
Sales	10.3	718	10.8	684	11.1	655	15.1	370
Stock market performance								
5-year price change	−18.6	583	−30.3	688	−66.5	946	−18.5	848

Source: Forbes, January 9, 1978, 30th Annual Report on American Industry.

EXHIBIT 4
THE CHRYSLER CORPORATION
Ten-Year Financial Statistics

Operating Data	*1978*	*1977*	*1976*	*1975*	*1974*	*1973*	*1972*	*1971*	*1970*	*1969*
Motor vehicles sold (in thousands of units)	2,212	2,328	2,371	1,773	2,015	2,423	2,192	1,898	1,794	1,851
Net sales	$13,618	13,059	12,240	8,572	8,389	8,983	7,749	6,431	5,606	5,793
Interest expense	$ 166	106	101	121	101	72	63	66	74	45
Maintenance and repairs	$ 426	439	351	230	277	328	251	204	175	220
Taxes other than on income	$ 308	278	249	190	187	189	156	423	362	433
Research and development	$ 344	286	237	161	202	211	161	123	113	140
Depreciation	$ 154	130	108	93	131	123	129	133	136	158
Amortization of special tools	$ 198	190	229	149	124	168	173	165	161	164
Taxes on income (credit)	$ (81)	72	152	(9)	(61)	163	167	47	(20)	87
Earnings (loss) from continuing operations	$ (205)	125	328	(207)	(41)	266	226	92	—	107
A common share (in dollars)	$ (3.54)	2.07	5.45	(3.46)	(0.73)	4.99	4.38	1.82	—	2.26
Net earnings (loss)	$ (205)	163	423	(260)	(52)	255	220	84	(8)	99
A common share (in dollars)	$ (3.54)	2.71	7.02	(4.33)	(0.92)	4.80	4.27	1.67	(0.16)	2.09
Average shares outstanding (in thousands)	61,679	60,278	60,205	59,942	56,421	53,182	51,643	50,214	48,693	47,391
Common stock dividends paid	$ 52	54	18	—	79	69	47	30	29	95
A share (in dollars)	0.85	0.90	0.30	—	1.40	1.30	0.90	0.60	0.60	2.00
Net earnings as a percent of sales	$ (1.5%)	1.2%	3.5%	(3.0%)	(0.6%)	2.8%	2.8%	1.3%	1.3%	1.7%
Expenditures for facilities other than special tools	$ 338	386	227	164	226	331	169	114	174	375
Expenditures for special tools	$ 333	337	197	220	242	298	166	136	242	272

Source: Company annual report 1978.

EXHIBIT 5 Estimated Manufacturers' Share of the Domestic Automobile Market (Model Years)

	1972	*1973*	*1974*	*1975*	*1976*	*1977*	*1978*
GM	44.6	44.3	42.4	42.6	46.7	46.6	46.9
Ford	24.4	23.4	24.6	22.8	23.4	22.0	23.3
Chrysler	13.9	13.6	13.6	11.7	12.8	11.3	10.3
AMC	2.8	3.2	4.1	3.6	2.7	1.9	1.6
Foreign	14.3	15.5	15.3	19.3	14.4	18.2	17.9
	100.0	100.0	100.0	100.0	100.0	100.0	100.0

EXHIBIT 6 Number of Domestic Dealers

	1976	*1977*	*1978*
GM	11670	11610	11565
Ford	6712	6722	6723
Chrysler	4811	4822	4786
AMC	1690	1612	1661

Source: Company statistics

EXHIBIT 7

CHRYSLER CORPORATION AND CONSOLIDATED SUBSIDIARIES
Consolidated Balance Sheet

	December 31	
	1979	1978
	(in millions of dollars)	
Assets		
Current Assets		
Cash	$ 188.2	$ 123.2
Time deposits (1979 includes $68.2 million restricted)	120.8	248.8
Marketable securities	165.3	150.8
Accounts receivable (less allowance for doubtful accounts: 1979, $34.9 million; 1978, $16.7 million)	610.3	848.0
Inventories—at the lower of cost (substantially first-in, first-out) or market	1,873.8	1,980.8
Prepaid insurance, taxes and other expenses	102.3	109.7
Income taxes allocable to the following year	60.0	60.5
Refundable taxes on income	—	40.0
Total Current Assets	3,120.7	3,561.8
Investments and Other Assets:		
Investments in and advances to associated companies outside the United States	411.4	449.1
Investments in and advances to unconsolidated subsidiaries	702.9	896.9
Other noncurrent assets	69.2	50.5
Total Investments and Other Assets	1,183.5	1,396.5
Property, Plant, and Equipment:		
Land, buildings, machinery and equipment	3,733.1	3,391.3
Less accumulated depreciation	2,097.1	1,963.9
	1,636.0	1,427.4
Unamortized special tools	712.9	595.5
Net Property, Plant and Equipment	2,348.9	2,022.9
Total Assets	$ 6,653.1	$ 6,981.2
Liabilities and Shareholders' Investment		
Current Liabilities		
Accounts payable	$ 1,530.4	$ 1,725.0
Accrued expenses	807.9	698.0
Short term debt	600.9	49.2
Payments due within one year on long term debt	275.6	12.4
Taxes on income	16.8	1.2
Total Current Liabilities	3,231.6	2,485.8
Other Liabilities and Deferred Credits		
Deferred employee benefit plan accruals	301.4	91.0
Deferred taxes on income	83.0	107.1
Unrealized profits on sales to unconsolidated subsidiaries	47.7	66.4
Other noncurrent liabilities	134.9	96.1
Total Other Liabilities and Deferred Credits	567.0	360.6
Long Term Debt		
Notes and debentures payable	880.7	1,082.6
Convertible sinking fund debentures	96.0	105.9
Total Long Term Debt	976.7	1,188.5
Obligations Under Capital Leases	15.4	15.0
Minority Interest in Net Assets of Consolidated Subsidiaries	38.3	4.8
Preferred Stock—no par value	218.7	217.0
Common Stock—par value $6.25 a share	416.9	397.7
Additional Paid-in Capital	692.2	683.1
Net Earnings Retained	496.3	1,628.7
Total Liabilities and Shareholders' Investment	$ 6,653.1	$ 6,981.2

(continued)

EXHIBIT 7 (Cont.)

	December 31	
	1979	*1978*
	(in millions of dollars)	
Consolidated Statement of Operations		
Net sales	$12,001.9	$13.618.3
Equity in net earnings of unconsolidated subsidiaries	2.4	22.1
Net earnings from European and certain South American operations	—	29.4
	12,004.3	13,669.8
Costs, other than items below	11,631.5	12,640.1
Depreciation of plant and equipment	180.6	154.0
Amortization of special tools	220.0	198.2
Selling and administrative expenses	598.5	572.1
Pension plans	260.6	262.3
Interest expense-net	215.4	128.9
	13,106.6	13,955.6
Loss Before Taxes on Income	(1,102.3)	(285.8)
Taxes on income (credit)	(5.0)	(81.2)
Net Loss	(1,097.3)	(204.6)
Dividend requirement on preferred shares	29.1	13.6
Net Loss Attributable to Common Stock	$ (1,126.4)	$ (218.2)
Loss per share of Common Stock	$ (17.18)	$ (3.54)
Average number of shares of Common Stock outstanding during the year (in thousands)	65,552	61,679

Source: Chrysler Corporation Annual Report, 1979.

CHRYSLER IN CRISIS

THE TURNAROUND

"Chrysler Corporation is now on the leading edge of a dramatic recovery. . . . We are on our way back. We are a fighting company that is leading the industry out of its worst depression in fifty years," said Lee A. Iacocca, chairman of Chrysler Corp., at a Washington press conference on September 23, 1980.

Lee Iacocca's pronouncement was part of his effort to effect a turnaround of the third-largest U.S. automaker, after it had won $1.5 billion in loan guarantees from the federal government on December 21, 1979, to aid its bailout following losses in 1978 ($205 million) and 1979 ($1.1 billion). Its loss for the first three quarters of 1980 was $1.5 billion.

His company's 1981 model line was introduced in September, 1980. Iacocca told a press conference that Chrysler's product was "great," giving Chrysler "fuel economy leadership" and "leadership in front-wheel drive"; the cars came from "six of the most modern plants in the world."

Iacocca went on to forecast that Chrysler would have a 35 percent increase in unit auto sales in 1981, gaining 12 percent of the ten-million unit U.S. car market, a substantial rise from its market share during 1980 of 8.5 percent, which would give it a $9.23 billion reserve. The fourth quarter of 1980, Iacocca continued, would be profitable "by either a dollar or up to $250 million," giving Chrysler "a historic turnaround."

Iacocca's plan rode on the success of the 1981 K-Car. The stylish front-wheel-drive cars, the Dodge Aries and Plymouth Reliant, were competitive with General Motors' X-Cars, introduced 18 months earlier (the Chevrolet Citation, Buick Skylark, Oldsmobile Omega, and Pontiac Phoenix), and the K-Cars were slightly better than the X-Cars in both fuel-efficiency and interior space. The K-Car was priced close to the X-Car at its base price of $6,700. With options, the average price to the customer was nearly $8,000.

Iacocca termed the K-Cars "probably the center of the market for the next decade." The government's loan guarantee board noted in April 1980 that "the company's viability in the coming year depends on its success in building and selling the K-Car at a profit."

DISAPPOINTMENT

The fourth quarter 1980 saw Chrysler posting a $235 million loss, and its annual results showed a $1.7 billion deficit, far below Iacocca's projected results. Indeed, when questioned by *The Wall Street Journal* in September, 1980, about Chrysler's earlier optimistic profit projections, which were presented to the government as the basis for the loan guarantees to finance the turnaround, Chrysler executive vice-president Gerald Greenwald exclaimed, "You didn't really take that stuff seriously?" Chrysler's operating loss for the fourth quarter was $157 million, and the company took an annual charge of $78 million for its Dodge main plant, which it shut.

The K-Car's performance by early 1981 had been far less than expected. Iacocca blamed high interest rates for the model's sales problems, saying, "This latest crippling action by the Fed will have its desired effect on Chrysler's financial results" as the interest rates began rising on November 6.

Against forecasts of 70,000 K-Cars to be sold in October and November 1980, and 492,000 volume for 1981 (41,000 cars per month and 85 percent of capacity), its first two months' sales totaled only 34,273 units. By contrast, Ford's new subcompacts, the Lynx and the Escort, had achieved over 45,000 volume in the same two months, and GM's X-Cars, practically unchanged from the 1980 models, sold three times the volume of the K-Car. Compared to GM dealers, who were holding a 54-day supply of X-Cars in late November, 1980, Chrysler dealers held a 98-day supply. Auto industry experts generally agree that manufacturers consider about a 60-day inventory as the most desirable.

Chrysler's Omnis and Horizons, which had been early entrants in the U.S. market of fuel-efficient subcompacts at their introduction for the 1979 model year, also were hard hit in 1980. By late November, only 222,814 units had been sold of a year's forecast volume of 394,000, since Ford and GM by 1980 had both introduced competing models. Chrysler dealers in late November held a 134-day supply of the subcompacts.

Also lower than projected were sales of Chrysler's Imperial, added to the model line in 1981 for the first time since 1976. The 1981 Imperial was a luxury model necessary to Iacocca's bid to have Chrysler remain a full-line auto manufacturer. Heralded with massive print and TV ads, including dialogues between Iacocca and Frank Sinatra praising the car, it sported the latest in digital control technology, plush carpeting as standard equipment, and a Cartier crystal hood ornament. But sales of 1,885 units in October and November were less than half the forecasts.

REACTION

Iacocca responded to the poor showing of his 1981 models with rebates, linked to the prime interest rate, that amounted to $380 to $1,200 a car. Chrysler's market share rose to 10.7 percent for December 1980 and January 1981.

Iacocca returned to the loan guarantee board for another $400 million infusion. (Of the $1.5 billion authorized by Congress in late 1979, Chrysler had already drawn down $800 million.) And since the law governing the loan guarantee required that Chrysler match every withdrawal of loan guarantees with an equivalent sum from other sources, such as cost reductions or asset sales, Iacocca also unveiled, on December 17, 1980, a 1981 cost-cutting program to save over $1 billion.

Chrysler's cost cutting program included:

- A wage freeze for Chrysler's blue-collar labor force, whose earnings currently averaged $21 per hour, saving $250 million in 1981.
- A 5% reduction in prices charged by suppliers for 90 days, and a freeze for the rest of 1981.
- A $755 million cut in investment in new plant capacity and new product development.
- A request to its lenders to convert $572 million in debt to preferred stock, thereby reducing its interest payments by $100 million a year.

The loan guarantee board, however, termed Chrysler's plan inadequate and required further concessions. In negotiations, Chrysler got a bit less than it asked from labor and suppliers, and so it was forced to press its lenders harder. The banks and insurance companies agreed to the gradual elimination of all debt held by them, almost $1.2 billion (the rest of Chrysler's debt was primarily notes and debentures), converting about half the loans to preferred shares and allowing Chrysler to pay off the rest of its bank debt in 1981 for 30 cents on the dollar. The lenders apparently preferred "a little cash in hand and a gamble on Chrysler's long-term survival to standing in line in bankruptcy court," according to *Fortune* (February 2, 1981).

The loan guarantees were tentatively approved by the board, which apparently believed that the cost-cutting measures were practical. The board also, as the law required, determined that under the new plans Chrysler would be a "going concern" in the automobile business after December 31, 1983, with no further need for federal help. Chrysler's latest forecasts showed that its losses would be cut to $224 million in 1981, and that it would turn a $349 million profit in 1982 and $1.1 billion in 1984. This forecast was based on a 9.1 percent share of a 9.6 million-unit U.S. car market in 1981; observers felt that the US market estimate was reasonable. And after the current restructuring, Chrysler would be carrying $2.4 billion in debt: $1.2 billion in guaranteed loans and $1.2 billion in unfunded pension liabilities. While it had 141,000 employees in August, 1979, Chrysler employed 79,000 in December, 1980, with more reductions to come (see *Exhibit 1*).

Tentative board approval of the latest Chrysler plan, however, did not assure success. Fifteen days had to elapse in mid-February before the guarantees could actually be granted, during which time the unions had to ratify the pact and all 125 lenders had to agree. The deal would collapse if any refused.

Exhibit 2 details Chrysler's financial results in 1980 as well as its 1978 and 1979 performance.

EXHIBIT 1 Where the Jobs Are: Chrysler Employment, 1981

Michigan	42,500 employees
Indiana	8,200
Delaware	5,900
Ohio	5,000
Illinois	4,700
New York	2,700
Missouri	2,500
Alabama	1,600

Source: Chrysler 10K Report.

EXHIBIT 2

CHRYSLER CORPORATION AND CONSOLIDATED SUBSIDIARIES
Consolidated Statement of Operations

	Year Ended December 31	
	1980	1979
	(In millions of dollars)	
Net sales	$ 9,225.3	$12,001.9
Equity in net earnings (loss) of unconsolidated subsidiaries	(56.5)	2.4
Net earnings from European and certain South American operations	—	—
	9,168.8	12,004.3
Costs, other than items below	9,132.5	11,631.5
Depreciation of plant and equipment	261.5	180.6
Amortization of special tools	305.8	220.0
Selling and administrative expenses	561.3	598.5
Pension plans	302.4	260.6
Interest expense—net	275.5	215.4
	10,839.0	13,106.6
Loss before Taxes on Income	(1,670.2)	(1,102.3)
Taxes on income (credit)	39.5	(5.0)
Net Loss	$ (1,709.7)	$ (1,097.3)
Loss per share of Common Stock	$(26.00)	$(17.18)
Average number of shares of Common Stock outstanding during the year (in thousands)	66,871	65,552

Consolidated Balance Sheet

	December 31	
	1980	1979
Assets	(In millions of dollars)	
Current Assets		
Cash	$ 101.1	$ 188.2
Time deposits	2.6	120.8
Marketable securities—at lower of cost or market	193.6	165.3
Accounts receivable (less allowance for doubtful accounts: 1980, $40.3 million: 1979, $34.9 million)	476.2	610.3
Inventories	1,916.0	1,873.8
Prepaid insurance, taxes and other expenses	101.6	102.3
Income taxes allocable to the following year	70.1	60.0
Total Current Assets	2,861.2	3,120.7
Investments and Other Assets		
Investments in associated companies outside the United States	353.3	353.3
Investments in and advances to 20% to 50% owned companies	30.5	58.1
Investments in and advances to unconsolidated subsidiaries	702.3	702.9
Other noncurrent assets	150.5	69.2
Total Investments and Other Assets	1,236.6	1,183.5

(continued)

EXHIBIT 2 (Cont.)

	December 31	
	1980	1979
Property, Plant, and Equipment		
Land, buildings, machinery, and equipment	3,877.9	3,733.1
Less accumulated depreciation	2,158.7	2,097.7
	1,719.2	1,636.0
Unamortized special tools	800.8	712.9
Net Property, Plant, and Equipment	2,520.0	2,348.9
Total Assets	$ 6,617.8	$ 6,653.1
Liabilities and Shareholders' Investment		
Current Liabilities	(In millions of dollars)	
Accounts payable	$ 1,179.6	$ 1,079.8
Short-term debt	150.5	600.9
Payments due within one year on long-term debt	166.2	275.6
Employee compensation and benefits	616.6	349.8
Taxes on income	12.3	16.8
Other taxes	113.3	100.8
Interest payable	44.6	40.6
Accrued expenses	746.2	767.3
Total Current Liabilities	3,029.3	3,231.6
Other Liabilities and Deferred Credits		
Deferred employee benefit plan accruals	353.0	301.4
Deferred taxes on income	71.6	83.0
Unrealized profits on sales to unconsolidated subsidiaries	31.0	47.7
Other noncurrent liabilities	190.4	188.6
Total Other Liabilities and Deferred Credits	646.0	620.7
Long-Term Debt		
Notes and debentures payable	2,321.4	880.7
Convertible sinking fund debentures	83.9	96.0
12% Subordinated debentures ($32.1 million issued, $45.9 million subscribed but not issued)	78.0	—
Total Long-Term Debt	2,483.3	976.7

(continued)

EXHIBIT 2 (Cont.)

CHRYSLER CORPORATION AND CONSOLIDATED SUBSIDIARIES
Consolidated Statement of Changes in Financial Position

	Year Ended December 31	
	1980	1979
Additions to (Uses of) Working Capital	(In millions of dollars)	
From operations:		
Net loss	$ (1,709.7)	$ (1,097.3)
Depreciation and amortization	567.3	400.6
Depreciation and amortization—European and South American operations	—	—
Changes in deferred income taxes—noncurrent	(11.4)	(24.1)
Equity in net (earnings) loss of unconsolidated subsidiaries	56.5	(2.4)
(Gain) loss on translation of long-term debt	(5.4)	2.6
Funds provided by (used in) operations	(1,102.7)	(720.6)
Effect of June 24, 1980 debt restructuring	910.4	—
Proceeds from long-term borrowing	1,145.1	123.7
Proceeds from sale of common stock	1.9	28.3
Proceeds from sale of $2.75 preferred stock and warrants	—	—
Conversion of debt to 1981 preferred stock	342.9	—
Proceeds from sale of European operations	—	—
Retirement of property, plant and equipment	89.8	17.3
Increase (decrease) in other liabilities	36.7	264.4
Other	6.4	4.7
Total Additions (Uses)	1,430.5	(282.2)
Dispositions of Working Capital		
Cash dividends paid	—	33.5
Increase (decrease) in investments and advances	28.3	(234.1)
Increase (decrease) in other noncurrent assets	81.3	18.7
Expenditures for property, plant and equipment	439.9	406.6
Expenditures for special tools	394.7	341.9
Reduction in long-term borrowing	543.5	338.1
Deconsolidation of European and South American operations	—	—
Total Dispositions	1,487.7	904.7
Increase (decrease) in working capital during the year	$ (57.2)	$ (1,186.9)

	Increase (Decrease) in Working Capital	
	1980	1979
Changes in Components of Working Capital		
Cash and marketable securities	$ (177.0)	$ (48.5)
Accounts and notes receivable	(134.1)	(277.7)
Current and deferred taxes on income	14.6	(16.1)
Inventories	42.2	(107.0)
Accounts payable and accrued expenses	(362.0)	84.7
Short-term debt	450.4	(551.7)
Payments due within one year on long-term debt	109.4	(263.2)
Other	(.7)	(7.4)
	$ (57.2)	$ (1,186.9)

THE DORAL CORPORATION

In 1978, The Doral Corporation was one of the largest manufacturers and retailers of men's quality footwear in the United States and a major producer of adult work and outdoor recreational shoes and boots. The company had been founded in St. Louis in 1889 as the Bush Shoe Manufacturing Company. Its name was changed to Doral in 1966.

Doral's men's footwear was sold through 127 company-owned Doral stores, 25 leased departments in leading department stores, and 2100 other retail outlets across the country. These outlets were operated by approximately 1600 independent dealers.

Adult work and outdoor recreational shoes and boots were manufactured by Ross Shoe, which produced the leading high-quality brand in the northern United States, and Boone Shoe, which marketed boots primarily in the Southwest. These products were sold through an estimated 3200 independent retail outlets, including shoe stores, sporting goods shops and clothing stores, and 10 franchised stores known as Boone's Frontier Stores.

In the Company's 1977 annual report, Doral's Chairman and CEO, Mr. Paul Serry, reported that the company's sales in 1977 were $89 million. He made the following statement to shareholders, which describes the company's then-current position and gives some insight into its strategy:

> The Doral Corporation has just completed a five-year period of growth in both sales and earnings. This performance has been achieved during a time of adverse conditions in the economy and the industry.
>
> Although the company maintained its trend of higher sales in 1977, there was only a modest increase in earnings from the record level of 1976. Net income in the past year was $5,184,000, up from $5,017,000 in 1976. Earnings per share, based on a somewhat higher number of shares outstanding in 1977, were $2.13, compared to $2.09 a year ago.
>
> There were three principal reasons for this slower earnings growth in 1977.
>
> Demand for men's footwear declined at the beginning of the year. With inventories at the retail level high, and consumer spending down, production levels were lowered substantially. With fewer units to absorb fixed costs, profit levels were lower than expected. At mid-year, conditions within the footwear market began to improve. Retailers had brought their inventories into line, and fall buying—after a somewhat later-than-normal beginning—strengthened. This trend gathered momentum in the fourth quarter and appears to be continuing into 1978. We have been increasing production, which is bringing unit costs back into line.
>
> A second factor affecting 1977 earnings was a significantly higher interest expense during the year. Average borrowings in 1977 were $13,608,000, up substantially from $7,452,000 in 1976. These additional borrowings were used primarily for the purchase of Boone. Interest expense totalled $1,020,000 in 1977, nearly double the $545,000 in interest paid in 1976.
>
> Finally, although Boone added sales volume in 1977, it detracted from earnings. At the time of purchase, we recognized the need to improve the management and the quality of its product line. A great deal of corporate time, energy and expense has been directed to Boone during the past year and much has been accomplished. This

investment is now showing some return and Boone should add to corporate earnings in 1978. With its strong market position in the Southwest, this company is a natural addition to our involvement in adult work and recreational footwear.

The company's ability to respond to adverse conditions in men's footwear over the past several years attests to the strong market position of the Doral name among quality-conscious American men. By maintaining high quality standards, and by stressing customer service with retailers, we are confident that Doral will continue to prosper in this marketplace.

Our Retail Division ended fiscal 1977 with 152 outlets, up from 134 a year earlier. This Division continues to assume a more important role both in the distribution of the company's footwear products and in its contribution to company earnings.

Five years ago, all of Doral's sales were of men's dress footwear. Today, this market accounts for 70% of sales, with the remaining 30% coming from adult work and recreational footwear. The acquisition of the Ross Shoe Company in December, 1973, established the company's position in the adult work and recreational footwear market. Ross manufactures a high-quality line of work shoes and recreational boots and has a major market share in the northern United States. Since its acquisition, Ross's profits have increased steadily, and 1977 was its best year ever.

During the past year, Doral successfully negotiated a $12.5 million long-term financing agreement. These funds were used to retire a term loan, to finance the Boone acquisition, and to provide additional working capital. Our financial resources are adequate to support continued expansion within our existing businesses and also permit us to explore new opportunities.

On January 16, 1978, the Board of Directors voted to raise the quarterly dividend payment to $.25 per share, or an annualized rate of $1.00. This is an 8.7% increase from the 1977 dividend rate and will be the fourth consecutive year of higher dividend payments to shareholders.

We enter the new year with a positive assessment of both near-term and long-term prospects for the Doral Corporation and look forward to reporting additional progress to you.

Paul Serry
Chairman & Chief Executive Officer
January 16, 1978

Mr. Serry's statement emphasized recent changes in the company's product/market and financial strategies. It illustrated the company's willingness to change with the times—and adaptiveness seemed to have been one of the major features in Doral's success. The extent of this success can be gauged from the company's sales and income growth during its life as a public company from 1965 to 1977. Sales grew from $27,633,000 to $89,000,000 and income from $2,030,000 to $5,184,000. Moreover, this growth occurred as the U.S. shoe manufacturing industry itself suffered a major decline.

THE U.S. SHOE INDUSTRY

The United States shoe manufacturing industry developed from a "cottage" scale to become one of the country's earliest industrial exporters. At first, it was concentrated in the New England states, which supplied significant numbers of boots for overseas military operations in both World Wars. In 1964, Massachusetts, Maine and New Hampshire together accounted for 30% of the total U.S. shoe production, but by 1973 they produced only 22% of total U.S. shoe output.

Shoes have historically been made in small towns, and the trend continues today, with 74% of shoe manufacturing towns having populations less than 20,000. Indeed, some shoe manufacturing operations are major (and often critical) sources of employment in these small towns, and companies are often induced to begin or continue operations under favorable tax and rental agreements.

The government classifies footwear as either rubber or non-rubber. Generally, non-molded, non-rubber shoes require more, and more complicated, operations for a closed ladies' shoe; a men's dress shoe might require 150 operations. Although most operations are performed by machines, shoe manufacturing is labor-intensive. This is because the machine operations are manually directed and require high levels of dexterity and hand and eye co-ordination. Machines need to be reset to produce shoes of varying size and width, and human control is required because of the variability in the quality of shoe materials, particularly leather. It is not surprising, then, that productivity in the industry remains near the 1919 level.

Doral's 1969 annual report throws some light on the matter:

> Back in 1919, the company had fewer than 100 employees producing some 800–1000 pairs of men's shoes per day. Currently Doral has 2000 employees turning out 5 million pairs of shoes annually—an average of 20,000 pairs per day.

However, while reported productivity figures show that rates of around 1.52 pairs per man hour have prevailed nationally for some decades (*Exhibit 1*), industry representatives point out that the situation is more complex. Although refined work methods, new materials and new production technology have increased productivity, this increase has been offset by the shorter production runs imposed on manufacturers by the complexity of the product. Consumers demand different sizes, widths, styles and materials, making it virtually impossible to fully automate shoe production.

While reported productivity has remained relatively stable, so too has the U.S. consumption of non-rubber shoes—ranging from 3.3 to 4.1 pairs per capita per year (*Exhibits 2* and *3*). Footwear has consistently accounted for 1.1–1.4% of disposable personal income. The major recent change in the shoe market has been an increased emphasis on fashion in every segment of the market, bringing with it inventory headaches and shorter production runs. Furthermore, because many customers perceive imports as trend-setters, fashion-consciousness has helped imported shoes gain market share in the U.S. (*Exhibit 3*).

The industry, however, attributes the real success of imported shoes in the U.S. market to their price competitiveness, the result of lower labor costs. Direct labor averages 30% of shoe manufacturing cost and, although U.S. shoe workers are generally paid on a piece-work basis, they averaged $3.82 per hour in 1975 compared with as little as $0.20 per hour in some exporting nations.

Because US per capita consumption of non-rubber shoes has been steady and because US consumers have spent a stable percentage of their disposable income on shoes over recent years, it seems reasonable to see imports as a major problem for U.S. shoe manufacturers. Indeed, since 1960, imported shoes have taken an increasingly large share of the U.S. market. For example, imports held 20% of the U.S. market in 1968; by 1977 their market share (in units) had increased to 49.3%. And while the median profit margin in the shoe manufacturing industry in 1964 was 2.0% of sales, by 1974 it had fallen to 1.55%. *Exhibits 4* and *5* give additional detail on profit performance in the non-rubber shoe manufacturing industry.

Employment in the industry dropped from 242,000 in 1960 to 164,000 in 1977, partly because of this loss of market. The number of pairs of non-rubber shoes produced annually in the U.S. fell from an average of 608.5 million in 1960–1964, to 384 million in 1977. The impact of this reduction in U.S. production is also reflected in the 299 plant closings reported between 1963 and August, 1976.

In the men's market (*Exhibits 6* and *7*), imports held 17.1% in 1968. This figure expanded to 32.2% by 1975 and to 38.2% in 1976. As the following table shows, many companies fell by the wayside:

Number of U.S. Companies Producing Men's Shoes

	1967	*1969*	*1974*
Athletic	91	81	67
Men's work	94	79	54
Men's (other than work)	135	122	119
Youths' and boys'	101	80	63

Generally speaking, as imports have gained strength in the U.S. market, the more successful U.S. manufacturers have either diversified out of the shoe business or integrated forward into retail operations, often franchising their operations. With this latter strategy they are able to sell imported footwear in their retail outlets and thus share the profits earned by imported shoes.

Imports, coupled with stable U.S. demand, have also put pressure on the U.S. non-rubber shoe companies to keep their factories fully utilized and thereby spread their fixed costs. As *Exhibit 8* shows, they have found the going rough.

Yet many U.S. companies are consistently profitable. *Exhibit 9* shows general industry-wide data for 1975. *Exhibit 10* shows the ROE for a number of large shoe manufacturers from 1971 to 1976. Market concentration is little changed except at the top end, as *Exhibit 11* suggests.

Unions have supported U.S. shoe manufacturers in lobbying against imports, and industry leaders state that union activity is not a hindrance to productivity in the industry today. Generally, they say, there is little difference in operating costs between union and non-union factories.

U.S. management has other worries, in addition to imports. Worker turnover in the shoe industry is high. Some operations, which are generally considered efficient, have annual turnover rates as high as 100%. This turnover usually occurs in the least desirable 10% of the jobs in any one plant, which may turn over as many as ten times per year.

Although the shoe industry is labor-intensive, technology for the industry is developed by a relatively small number of specialist companies. United Shoe Machine, International Shoe Machine, and Compo Industries supply most of the machines used in shoe manufacturing. Until the United Shoe Machine antitrust case in 1964, most manufacturing companies leased their production machinery. At that point, the owners of many companies bought the equipment their companies were using at prices near its depreciated value and leased it back to their own businesses at the former rates. More recently, shoe manufacturers have been leasing equipment from the machinery manufacturers themselves.

DORAL: EARLY HISTORY

Founded in 1889 in St. Louis, the Bush Shoe Manufacturing Company gradually became well known for its high-priced, high-quality men's footwear, sold under the Doral brand. Peter and Philip Bush, the sons of the founder, managed the company through most of the twentieth century. Peter was the company's marketer; Philip was in charge of production. The company has been described as generally well run.

As a marketer, Peter was understandably pleased with his company's leadership in the high-quality segment of the men's shoe industry and with its exclusive dealer network. In the early 1960s, however, the Bush Shoe Manufacturing Company sought to protect and strengthen its position in what it believed would be a growing men's market.

Outside directors on Bush Shoe's board urged management to acquire complementary men's footwear lines. Townsend, a manufacturer of high-fashion men's shoes, headquartered in Davis, Missouri, was acquired in 1963. Style was gaining importance as a factor in men's dress footwear and management believed that Townsend would augment the offerings of the Doral line at the top end of the price range. Townsend produced only to order and so had no inventories to assure availability to dealers.

In April, 1964, Bush Shoe acquired Mohawk, a manufacturer of high-quality moccasin-type casuals produced under a patented construction system. To extend its product line even further, Doral also introduced a sneaker line in 1964. Men could wear Doral shoes year-round, allowing the company to maintain year-round customer loyalty. This prevented competitors from gaining a foothold in the market in the summer, with the prospect of carrying that success over into the fall.

In late 1964, the management team was slightly shuffled when Philip Bush retired. Winthrop McDonald became President, Peter Bush moved to Chairman of the board, and David Bush became Executive Vice-President.

The family's pride in Doral's quality and value and its experience in the industry remained an important factor in the maintenance of Doral's commanding position in men's footwear through the 1960s. Summarizing the company's position in 1964, Peter Bush reported that quality, value, and fashion as well as unmatched dealer service gave it a competitive edge in men's footwear.

Peter Bush maintained the company's former policies. Doral shoes were produced in only one factory, which Philip had seen as the limit of his supervisory capacity. Of Doral's manufacturing equipment, 95% was owned rather than leased, since the company believed ownership was cost-effective. The 100% in-stock inventory policy was maintained and was a source of pride in Doral's dealings with retailers.

In 1965, the company went public and changed its name to the Doral Corporation.

1965 sales revenues were reported at $27,633,000, up 135% over 1959, with net earnings of $2,030,000. That year, the 100% in-stock policy meant carrying an inventory of between 290,000 and 480,000 pairs to respond to customer orders within 24 hours of receipt. Bush's inventory policies and its merchandising arrangement with its dealers show how important dealer relations were to the company. Bush's dealers handled the Doral men's line exclusively. In return, Bush dealt with only one retailer in any sales territory. In New York City, for example, this meant that only one department store—Macy's—carried Doral.

Expansion continued, through acquisitions and internally. In 1965, Mohawk closed its original Massachusetts plant, moved to Maine, and introduced a new line of casual shoes for big boys and youths. Townsend leased a second factory in Missouri and Doral itself began operating in an expansion to its plant and warehouse in St. Louis.

Doral introduced a new line of warm weather casuals in 1966, seeking to increase the fashionableness of its offerings as well as its summer market position. In management's eyes, fashion was becoming increasingly important in the market, particularly in the effort to capture the affections of the younger male. The company noted in 1966's annual report, "These original Doral designs have been created to satisfy the ever-growing demand of both young and more mature men for a fashionable product."

Through this period of growth, Doral's management insisted on maintaining the company's dealer selection procedures, exclusivity, and 100% in-stock inventory policy—even though the high fashion component of its line had expanded and the policy necessitated large markdowns as fashions changed. The balance between traditional quality and changing tastes was delicate, but Doral felt it had to respond to "the public's insistence upon, and its ability to pay for, nothing short of the best." The price of Doral shoes was commensurate with their high quality but many men were apparently unwilling to entrust their feet to anything less.

Then, late in 1966, Doral chose to depart from its traditional role as manufacturer and became a retailer to boot, with the acquisition of the Loebe Shoe Co. With this addition, Doral obtained sixty-seven leased department and retail store shoe outlets for men's, women's, and children's shoes in the East and Midwest. Thoughts turned to the need for divisional sales managers and more salesmen as Doral's distribution system grew. Volume production was also required.

Bush's managers discussed this pressure for growth in their 1966 annual report, stating that they were fulfilling a two-fold responsibility:

> . . . to secure a consistent quality product and to secure a consistent profitable business position in a world of rapid change. To achieve both, we must maintain a delicate balance between individual craftsmanship and mass production mechanisms. We believe neither can, or should, replace the other. But each can increase the other's potential, as our newly expanded faciliites demonstrate.

Thus, accompanying Doral's foray into retailing was a stated goal of adopting the most modern production techniques. Doral occasionally tested new equipment for United Shoe Machine (USM), International Shoe Machine (ISM) and Compo Industries, Inc., and so was generally immediately aware of production innovations. Increased efficiency was necessary to secure the consistently profitable business position it sought.

In spite of its apparently well-laid plans, however, 1967 was a year of poor financial performance for Doral. With diversification into retailing and broadening of the markets, earnings declined. A strike hit the company in January, and the settlement resulted in rising labor costs. A cold winter and early Easter necessitated large inventory write-downs. The problem management faced was to cut costs while maintaining quality.

At this time, Doral was the acknowledged leader in high-priced, high-quality, high-fashion men's shoes. Its fashion image was further buttressed in 1968 by Townsend's new line of casual shoes, the products of additions Townsend had made to its creative design staff. By 1968, Mohawk had doubled its dollar volume from 1963 levels, with a broader product line and the new outlets its association with Doral had opened to it. Formerly, Mohawk had been precluded from many outlets by Doral's exclusive distribution agreements with its dealers. Doral also added a high-priced, high-quality line of dress shoes for big boys and youths in 1968, adding further variety to the company's offerings.

In another market expansion move in March, 1968, Doral acquired Jarrah Shoes and thereby entered the men's mid-priced market. This acquisition added Jarrah's Ziptonville, Arkansas, plant to the company's manufacturing facilities. Significantly, it also opened the door of a new type of retail distribution to the company through Jarrah's private branding arrangements with a number of major national retail and discount chains. The acquisition of Jarrah put Paul Serry, Jarrah's founder, on the board of Doral and on its management team as Vice-President. Serry maintained his status as head of Jarrah but, with a substantial stock holding in Doral, his interest in the company's continued financial success was high. He was particularly welcomed by the Bush family when he successfully terminated Doral's negotiations with a conglomerate which wanted to add Doral to its holdings and then sell out to Penn Central.

A NEW CEO

Serry's knowledge of the retail shoe business had given him familiarity with Doral and its products before the acquisition. But, shortly after the companies merged, members of Jarrah's salesforce told him that retailers were complaining that they were noticing a slow decline in Doral's traditionally high product quality.

On another front, Serry himself noted that the Townsend and Mohawk plants were very high-cost producers, primarily because their capacity was being underutilized. When these concerns were raised at a board meeting, and he suggested that Doral shoes could be made at the subsidiaries' plants, he was advised that Doral shoes could be made only at Doral plants and that the quality complaints were unfounded.

Some weeks later, Paul Serry stood in his Boston office next to two racks of men's dress shoes. "Can you identify the Dorals? I made the others in my factory." Without hesitation, the Doral foreman chose the shoes on the left, saying confidently, "That's easy—your stitching's not straight; the soles aren't properly attached." The shoes he chose were produced in Serry's Ziptonville plant. While some of Doral's managers made the same error, with equal confidence, one man, Mace Hass, impressed Serry by identifying the Doral's correctly and asking Serry how he had made them.

His demonstration of declining Doral quality was important to Serry since it raised the possibility of manufacturing Doral shoes at the acquired subsidiary plants outside St. Louis. However, this was not to happen until some months had passed.

Mr. Serry became Chairman and CEO of the Doral Corporation later in 1969 in the wake of Winthrop McDonald's resignation and Peter Bush's death. His 1969 message to shareholders referred to "our new, young management team"—fifteen out of seventeen of the company's senior executives were replaced in his first year, due to resignations, retirements, and forced separations. Mace Hass became President and Chief Operating Officer. David Bush held his position as Executive Vice-President.

So began the updating of Doral. The family company was pushed hard by the non-family managers. Net sales rose from $41,018,000 in 1967 to $77,341,000 in 1976. Simultaneously, net earnings rose from $1,946,000 in 1967 to $5,017,000 in 1976. In 1976, the company's margin was 6.5% of sales, up from 4.7% in 1967.

The changes that led to these results began with Serry's two-rack demonstration of Doral's decreasing quality. The fact that Doral's quality could be equalled by another company's factory vividly pointed up the need for changes in production practices.

Employing a "why not" philosophy upon taking over Doral, Serry's marketing changes emphasized both product quality and dealer service. On the efficiency side, he employed new production techniques for Doral and focused the production of different shoes in separate facilities. For the first time Doral shoes were produced outside Doral's St. Louis plants: at Mohawk in Maine, Townsend in Missouri, and Jarrah in Arkansas. Such focused factories (focused first by process and then by product) improved productivity levels. Indeed, such focusing proved successful with Mohawk as well as with Townsend's operations in boys' casual shoes.

Serry explained the change in the company's 1969 report:

> *Realignment of Production.* In the past, each of our plants had been devoted to the production of a specific brand regardless of production techniques involved. During 1969 steps were taken to make each individual plant responsible for a specific manufacturing process. These changes should reduce costs, smooth out peaks and valleys in production and enable us to make more efficient use of the manufacturing skills we have developed in each plant.

Serry believed that, although up-to-date manufacturing technology had not been critical to Doral's survival, technological changes had contributed to the maintenance of the company's profit margin. Focusing further helped the company respond to the market with a consistently high-quality product. Doral was a company which selectively took advantage of available shoe manufacturing technology and, although a larger percentage of its production equipment was leased after Serry assumed control, the company continued its traditional policy of owning much of its own equipment. Serry characterized the most important new technologies being adopted by Doral as:

1 An in-house ability to produce unit soles via injection molding; and
2 Computer stitching, used for both decoration and construction.

He noted that "nothing we could have done (with other new technology) would have made any real difference to us."

On another technological front was Doral's use of the computer as a management tool. Doral began using the latest information-processing technology when it installed a new EDP system in 1969. At the time, the company's hope was that the computer would be a useful tool in all phases of the company's operations as the following additional extract from the 1969 annual report suggests:

> *Data Processing.* Shoe merchandising in the fashion market requires timely and accurate information flow between manufacturer and retailer. Doral has always recognized the value of electronic data processing. Effective use of EDP equipment should materially strengthen production and warehousing techniques while adding to the effectiveness of the company's merchandising program and retailer service.
>
> During the year, newer and more sophisticated equipment was installed in our large data processing center. Conversion to the new system presented many problems, including high initial costs. However, improved inventory control enable us to sense style changes and to project sales trends much faster than previously.
>
> We are now looking forward to building a totally integrated management information system involving all phases of our business.

Integrating the computer into the management system appeared to be particularly attractive in an industry where fashion was continuing to gain importance and mistakes in planning were becoming increasingly costly. However, it proved difficult and costly, as *Barron's* reported in a June 1970 article on Doral:

> Last year, however, difficulties with a computer, which caused widespread shipment delays, and the late introduction of a new high-fashion Doral line resulted in a sharp profits drop. . . .

As he had focused his factories, Serry also focused his firm's product market strategy and was in large part responsible for the sale of the sixty-seven Loebe stores. In Serry's view, the fact that only 10% of Loebe's sales were in men's footwear meant that Loebe did not provide a good fit with Doral's desired market and unnecessarily diluted Doral's strengths and expertise in marketing men's shoes. The company's 1970 report, distributed shortly before Serry became President, stated "Because of the company's decision to concentrate on the manufacture and sale of men's quality footwear, it has been orally agreed in principle to sell these retail operations." Thus Doral retreated to its former role as a men's quality footwear manufacturer.

Doral increased its dealer support in many ways. TV advertising was used successfully, as well as a harder sell in print. Quality was stressed in ads which proclaimed, "Shoes that do as much for your peace of mind as they do for your foot."

With a new senior management team in place, Serry reorganized the Doral Corporation on a functional basis, discarding its former divisional structure. He replaced the outsiders on the company's board with members of his own choosing. He alleviated the seasonal nature of high-fashion shoe production and sales with the introduction of a Townsend dual purpose sport/dress shoe for the adult male and further expanded the Doral line to serve the needs of the big boys' and teenage markets. Thus Doral's dealers had both a broader and better quality line, and a higher level of service from the more efficiently managed Doral Corporation.

High inventory levels (96% in-stock) were maintained to ensure response to dealer requests for shoes: all orders were filled within 24 hours of their receipt. While expensive, this was somewhat cheaper and more realistic than the previous policy of 100% availability with "no limit" on order size. Serry's slightly lower inventory levels only negligibly affected dealers' perception of the service they obtained from Doral. Indeed, in 1970, 97.5% of dealer orders were immediately available, and finished goods inventory levels were maintained at 1.3 to 1.7 million pairs. Some move to lower in-stock order-filling capabilities was essential due to the high costs of such a policy in the fashion goods market, where up to 50% of the line changed every six months and large markdowns were required to move obsolete goods.

Service within the community was also important to Serry. Doral's location in the depressed Carthage area of St. Louis provided substantial employment in a region of severe economic hardship. In addition, Doral was one of the first companies in the U.S. to provide in-house day care for children of its employees and the community as well.

When he took over, Serry made haste to remedy Doral's absence from the highly successful shopping-center market, seeing it as a gap in the company's distribution system. Generally, Doral's lines were represented, if at all, only by the anchor stores in the centers. At rents of $14 per square foot rather than the $3 they were used to paying, many old Doral dealers would not enter the centers independently. And Doral's exclusive distribution practice (only one dealer in a retail market) precluded their entry as a men's shoe store in the malls where Doral was already represented by the anchor.

Serry, however, thought that the practice of exclusivity unnecessarily constrained sales, so he tested the effect of a second dealer on the company's existing business in Jarrah's home town in the Arkansas market. Despite the initial protests of the original Doral retailer, Doral found that their dealer's sales were unaffected. Indeed, the market expanded for the two dealers, since the single retailer had apparently been unable to tap the full potential of the market.

In 1970's annual report, Serry announced a set of changes which flowed from his experiment:

> We engaged a marketing consulting firm to do a four-month study of the U.S. men's footwear market by metropolitan areas. Analyzing our brand penetration of each market against its determined potential gave us a sound basis for realignment of territories and upward revision of sales quotas for '71, '72, and '73.
>
> The study also led to re-evaluation of the nature of our coverage. To maintain our influence and increase our rate of growth, our field men were given larger responsibilities with incentives to match. With intensive and ongoing training, they will act as business advisors to their accounts, transcending the traditionally limited salesman's role. They will be supervised closely by three new regional sales managers who will assist in liaison with top management in each area.
>
> Expanded distribution plans required an expanded staff to locate desirable store sites throughout the country and negotiate leases as needed. The objective is to insure prime locations, particularly in shopping centers, for existing and prospective customers.

One business publication, in an article titled "Doral's Fight for Higher Profits" wrote:

> Doral has changed its traditional policy of limited dealerships. Under the old system, a dealer was given virtually exclusive domain in a territory, whether that would be a shopping center or other busy locale. However, Doral now has modified this concept. Other retailers are being recruited on a more intensive basis. However, they have to agree to handle only the Doral line, plus possibly other company brands, for the men's trade. The strategy reflects the fact that though the basic demographic factors favor expansion of Doral's market, the company fundamentally is seeking to snare a bigger share of the business.
>
> Moreover, production and distribution have been streamlined. Especially noteworthy is that Doral has improved warehouse operations so that the progress of receiving, packing and shipping shoes has been speeded up to 42 pairs per man hour, from 33; the ultimate goal is set at 50. A Townsend facility in Davis, Missouri, has been switched to turning out big boys' footwear, where production is reasonably constant the year round. In addition, an unprofitable Massachusetts unit recently has been sold, roughly at a price to offset Doral's investment in it.
>
> Doral's shoes are in the upper end of the men's footwear market, priced at $18 to $20. Prices were increased last year, but not this year. Jarrah shoes, marketed on a private-label basis to such chains as Penney and Sears, and also under Doral's own labels, are priced at $12–$20.

Doral opened its first company-owned stores in 1971, maintaining its long-standing relationship with its dealers by giving them a right of first refusal on the new outlets and an offer of financial assistance should they want to participate in the new venture. Doral's management believed that the personal motivation of their independent dealers played an important part in the company's success and they wished to encourage it.

Doral's commitment to retailing ultimately had two effects on dealer relations. First, as the company dealt with retail problems first-hand, it gained a healthy respect for its dealers and a new sensitivity for their problems. Second, Doral dealers seemed to take more notice of the company, apparently feeling that Doral understood their concerns and had experience to back its advice. This had been one of the hopes of the ill-fated Loebe acquisition in 1967.

Over time, Doral came to prefer to aid an aspiring dealer financially, rather than to own stores itself. The company believed that the presence of an enthusiastic independent dealer could substantially improve store performance over that of a company-owned and managed store; a personal interest in customers was clearly important under Doral's customer service concept. The independent dealer put up about $20,000 as equity and Doral—as a 'AAA' company, more attractive to center developers than a small independent shoe store—negotiated a ten-year lease. This, the independent sublet for three years, subject to Doral's renewal. By the end of 1977, Doral owned and operated 127 stores. This, however, was a small number compared with the company's approximately 2100 independent outlets.

As noted earlier, expansion into retailing was a strategy followed by many successful shoe manufacturers during the 1960s and 1970s since it allowed them to take share in the profits derived from the sales growth of imported footwear, and reduced their dependence on dwindling manufacturing profits. For Doral, however, the expansion into retailing required patience and hard work and, initially, did little to improve its financial performance.

Mr. Serry was quoted in *Barron's* (January, 1972) as follows:

> We're netting 8% on our wholesale business and hopeful of netting 5% on retail stores. Retail margins won't be the same but the business will have a good impact on overall sales and earnings.

However, the business press reported that Doral's retail stores "operated at a loss since inception and just turned into the black in fiscal '75 (*under a new management team*)."

In 1972, recognizing that Doral was the dominant brand in the company's product line, the decision was made to drop the other brands and focus all promotional efforts on Doral. Even its shoes for the 15–20-year-old market carried the Doral name, reflecting the company's efforts to create allegiance to the Doral brand.

While Doral was adapting its market strategy—its product line and its distribution system—to the realities of a shifting marketplace, it was matching its manufacturing strategy with that market strategy so that marketing and manufacturing could work together harmoniously. However, while these changes were being made, imports were changing the U.S. shoe industry.

DORAL AND IMPORTS

In its 1976 annual report, Doral's management explained the company's success in the face of imports:

> Within the U.S. footwear industry, there are a number of different market-segments. For Doral, the most important is the high-quality men's footwear market, which accounted for more than 80% of the company's shipments in 1976. This portion of the market has definite characteristics which differentiate it and its competitive climate from the broader footwear industry.
>
> For example, imports have steadily increased their penetration of the domestic footwear market in the past decade, but their impact on Doral's primary market, high-quality leather footwear, has not been significant. . . . By 1976, the penetration of imports had increased to almost 40%. In high-quality men's leather footwear, however, imports only accounted for about 20% of the U.S. market.
>
> Foreign manufacturers have concentrated on the less expensive and lower-quality segments of the domestic market. Imports tend to be available in one width only, which is insufficient for the fit-conscious American consumer of high-quality footwear.

DIVERSIFICATION

Despite the success of Doral's men's dress shoe business, and the growing earnings reported in the early 1970s under his leadership, Serry was concerned about the impact of imports and inflation on the company. He realized that even superb performance in a contracting market could not ensure the long-term viability of the company. Since Doral held all its assets in one potentially threatened market segment, diversification was needed. Serry searched for the best direction to take.

A movement away from men's dress shoes was essential. In Serry's view, shoe manufacturing and marketing were Doral's areas of greatest competence. Forward integration, via Doral's retail outlets, was meeting with success, but still tied the company to the men's dress shoe market. Backward integration was not attractive for a number of reasons, including the dominance of USM and the lower ROI of suppliers to the shoe industry. Women's shoes were risky because of their high fashion component and the import threat; they therefore seemed an unattractive diversification opportunity. The children's high-priced shoe market was dominated by Stride Rite and seemed unappealing for a newcomer.

Realizing its niche in men's shoes had protected it from imports and the fate of much of the U.S. shoe industry, Serry searched for another protected masculine area. Ultimately, Doral purchased Ross Shoes, a Heaton, PA, manufacturer of workshoes. With a high-quality product and high brand name recognition, Serry saw Ross as a stable but underexploited company which had no interlocking distribution system to give it the synergy in the marketplace which Doral enjoyed. And since Ross's weaknesses were exactly the strengths which Serry saw in Doral, he believed Ross would be a profitable acquisition which would give Doral improved long-term growth prospects in a distinct market.

Serry was correct. Ross had reported sales of $10.5 million and after-tax earnings of $130,000 the year before the acquisition. By the end of the third year after its acquisition by Doral, its sales had increased to $17.8 million with before-tax earnings of $2 million—after Doral's corporate and capital charges.

After the initial successes in the adult workshoe market, Doral's management decided to expand the company's commitment to this profitable market segment (see *Exhibit 12*). So, in 1977, after the board had approved the company's taking $12.5 million in long term debt at 8.45%, Doral acquired Boone Shoes, a San Antonio, Texas, workshoe manufacturer. Serry believed that, with Boone, Doral could replicate Ross's northern success in the South. Serry characterized Boone's quality as initially inferior to Ross's but he believed it would be improved with Doral's experienced management.

However, although Serry had not expected the company to be profitable until some time after the purchase, Boone's troubles proved to be more severe than he had anticipated. The worst of its problems was high personnel turnover—100% every quarter. For example, the senior cutter, a man holding one of the most skilled craft positions in the operation, had only eight months seniority.

Serry's response was to transfer experienced Doral executives from St. Louis to San Antonio. One of their first projects was to take a close look at Boone's personnel practices. As a result, new hires showed greater stability than Boone's former workers. The high and very costly turnover and the attendant quality problems seemed to be under control.

It is interesting to note that Doral's strategy in the work, service, and sports boot market appeared to be a replication of its strategy in the men's dress shoe market. Doral sought a niche which was at least partly sheltered from import intrusion. Then it tried to protect it by growing.

One key element in the company's efforts to protect its business was its product quality. Another was its dealer relations, characterized by a highly responsive service policy anchored by the large in-stock inventory. The company expanded its market by widening its product line by acquisition and took an active role in developing new retail outlets for its product—in both the dress shoe and the work boot markets. Moreover, it learned from its experiences. For example, the new Doral Stores and the Boone Frontier Stores were franchised, not owned.

In part, the company's success was due to its willingness to change management whenever there was either a serious difference in philosophy or demonstrably unsatisfactory performance. The company adopted new technology and new production practices selectively and carefully, often after a partial experiment.

In fact, the essence of Doral's success seemed to be conservative risk management and the considered adaptation of the company to the realities of the market. The essence of this adaptation was a focusing of management effort in the market and in the factory.

The later growth of the company was a diversification away from its traditional market, but the company's *modus operandi* seemed substantially unchanged. The Doral strategy based on focused factories and a segmented market place was simply shifted to a new territory. Once again, the company was growing through acquisition and business development. *Exhibit 13* summarizes Doral's acquisition history. *Exhibit 14* provides an unadjusted record of the company's financial performance. *Exhibit 15* shows some relevant operating data.

THE FUTURE

Paul Serry believed that inflation was a great threat to the continued progress of the U.S. economy, pointing out that movement of the Wholesale Price Index for shoes showed how severely the shoe industry had been affected (*Exhibit 16*). Serry noted that the margin between Doral shoes and lower-priced men's shoes increased from a $7 premium when he took over in 1968 to a $15 premium a decade later, due to inflation. "Every time we raise prices," he said, "we just pray that the margin won't be too great for consumers to maintain their loyalty to us."

As an indication of the company's adaptability Mr. Serry pointed in 1978 to Doral's success in the "action shoe" market:

> The fastest-growing segment of the shoe market is action shoes, which have evolved from traditional sneakers into a whole line of fashionable footwear.
>
> Historically, Doral had a relatively small share of the men's sneaker market. The market was not large, exhibited little real growth, and was price-sensitive. Approximately three years ago, however, new trends began to evolve. Athletic footwear was developing a stronger appeal among consumers for all-purpose wear, and the footwear itself was taking on a fashion ingredient.
>
> In 1976, Doral made a major commitment to expand in this market segment and introduced a line of athletic footwear—"Harts." Consumer reaction was immediately positive, and sales have grown significantly each year. In 1977, Harts sales were 147% higher than the previous year, and accounted for 13.5% of Doral's non-work boot sales. Today, Doral is a significant factor in the action shoe market.

The company introduced its Harts line using US manufacturers which sold a competitive branded product. However, these companies never quite met Doral's needs for quality and delivery. Subsequently, the company switched to a large importer, whose performance was also unsatisfactory. The company then decided to deal directly with an independent foreign manufacturer. Harts came to exhibit the same quality and workmanship as Doral's leather footwear.

Doral was also well positioned in the warm-weather casual shoe market. It introduced its summer line using another U.S. manufacturer. However, once the success of the line was proven, Doral switched to in-house production to better match demand and production capacity. Annual sales of these summer shoes increased to almost 800,000 pairs in the 1972–1977 period.

In spite of these successes, Serry saw the effect of imports on the dress shoe market as worrisome since Doral still made 70% of its sales in that market. ''Our goal is a 50-50 distribution, between dress shoe and work boot sales,'' he said. Thus, Doral saw the expansion of Ross and Boone in the work shoe and sports boot markets as important to the achievement of that goal. The company continued to be open to other acquisitions.

EXHIBIT 1 Non-Rubber Footwear: Output per Production Worker and per Man-Hour

	Output per Production Worker		Output per Man-Hour	
	Quantity	*Index (1967 = 100)*	*Quantity*	*Index (1967 = 100)*
Year	*Pairs*		*Pairs*	
1965	2,996.2	101.4	1.52	101.3
1966	2,998.6	101.5	1.50	100.0
1967	2,955.7	100.0	1.50	100.0
1968	3,103.4	105.0	1.56	104.0
1969	2,914.1	98.5	1.52	101.3
1970	3,031.3	102.6	1.57	104.7
1971	3,086.4	104.4	1.58	105.3
1972	3,058.7	103.5	1.54	102.7
1973	2,982.3	100.9	1.51	100.7
1974	2,936.5	99.3	1.53	102.0
1975	2,929.6	99.1	1.53	102.0
Jan.–Aug.				
1975	1,894.4	[1]	1.47	98.0
1976	2,044.5	[2]	1.54	102.7

[1] Index is 64.1. Adjusting this value to make it comparable to the year value gives 96.2.
[2] Index is 69.2. Adjusting this value to make it comparable to the year value gives 103.8.
Source: U.S. Department of Commerce, Bureau of the Census, *Current Industrial Reports, Shoes and Slippers, by Type of Construction and Price Line, 1975*, September 1976.

EXHIBIT 2
U.S. Footwear Consumption
('000 pair)

	Domestic		Imports		U.S.	Per Capita Consumption, Pairs		Spending on Footwear
	Non-rubber	*Canvas/Rubber*	*Non-rubber*	*Canvas/Rubber*	*Consumption*	*Non-rubber*	*Rubber*	*as % of Personal Consumption Expenditure*
1960	600,000	110,440	26,639	30,435	767,514	3.46		
1964	630,062	167,728	75,352	29,063	902,225			
1965	650,157	188,138	87,632	33,363	959,290	3.68	1.03	1.23
1968	659,031	194,495	175,292	49,200	1,075,123	4.09	1.02	1.29
1970	576,879	152,187	241,560	49,726	1,020,352	3.93	0.92	1.23
1972	556,738	163,700	296,665	53,020	1,075,123	3.94	1.02	1.21
1974	483,221	150,571	294,457	67,922	996,171	3.40	1.01	1.21
1975	423,763	124,901	319,411	73,080	941,158	3.30	0.97	1.21
1976	445,243	124,173	369,815*	115,355	1,054,586*	3.70	1.07	1.18

*1976 Figure adjusted to exclude disposable footwear

Source: AFIA Record Footwear Manual, 1976, Table 23; 1977, Table 21 (American Footwear Industries Association records).

EXHIBIT 3
Non-Rubber Footwear[1]

Period	U.S. Production (million pairs)	Imports[2] (million pairs)	Exports (million pairs)	Apparent Consumption (million pairs)	Ratio of Imports to Consumption (percent)	Ratio of Imports to Production (percent)	Per Capita Consumption (number of pairs)
3-year average:							
1954–56	569.2	10.0	4.6	574.6	2	2	3.46
1957–59	607.4	27.0	4.0	630.4	4	4	3.60
1960–62	608.7	57.0	3.0	662.7	9	9	3.61
Annual:							
1963	604.3	67.0	2.8	668.5	10	11	3.53
1964	612.8	80.7	2.8	690.7	12	13	3.60
1965	626.2	96.0	2.5	719.7	13	15	3.70
1966	641.7	101.7	2.7	740.7	14	16	3.77
1967	600.0	133.3	2.2	731.1	18	22	3.68
1968	642.4	181.5	2.4	821.5	22	28	4.09
1969	577.0	202.2	2.3	776.9	26	35	3.83
1970	562.3	241.7	2.2	801.8	30	43	3.91
1971	535.8	268.6	2.1	802.3	33	50	3.88
1972	526.7	296.7	2.3	821.1	36	56	3.93
1973	490.0	307.5	3.6	793.9	39	63	3.77
1974	453.0	266.4	4.0	715.4	37	59	3.38
1975	413.1	287.7	4.6	696.2	41	70	3.26
Jan.–Sept.							
1975	301.0	213.8	3.5[3]	511.3	42	71	2.40
1976	347.8	289.8	4.6[3]	633.0	46	83	2.95

[1]Data on imports of so-called disposable paper slippers from Mexico, which were entered in substantial quantities beginning in 1973, have been excluded from this table. Such imports amounted to an estimated 32 million pairs in 1975. Data on zoris have also been excluded from this table; such imports amounted to 20 million pairs in 1975.
[2]Data for 1954–63 partly estimated.
[3]Estimated.
Source: Compiled from official statistics of the U.S. Department of Commerce, except as noted (AFIA).

EXHIBIT 4

Profit-and Loss Experience of Producers of Footwear, Except Protective-Type and Canvas, on Total Establishment Operations in Which Such Footwear was Produced, 1970–74

Size-of-Output Group and Year	*Net Sales (1,000 dollars)*	*Cost of Sales (1,000 dollars)*	*Gross Profit (1,000 dollars)*	*Selling, Administrative, and General Expenses (1,000 dollars)*	*Net Operating Profits (1,000 dollars)*	*Other (expense), Net (1,000 dollars)*	*Net Profit or (loss) before Taxes (1,000 dollars)*	*Ratio of Net Operating Profit in Net Sales (Percent)*
Less than 200,000 pairs								
1970	63,744	44,517	19,227	15,714	3,513	(585)	2,928	5.5
1971	73,268	49,205	24,063	18,975	5,088	(525)	4,563	6.9
1972	81,916	55,055	26,861	20,761	6,100	(239)	5,861	7.5
1973	98,280	64,945	33,335	24,968	8,367	(211)	8,156	8.5
1974	115,191	77,922	37,271	30,659	6,612	(489)	6,123	5.7
1975	109,844	69,857	39,987	30,103	9,884			9.0
200,000 to 499,999 pairs								
1970	207,371	169,400	37,971	33,862	4,109	(2,904)	1,205	2.0
1971	201,216	158,272	42,944	34,460	8,484	(1,646)	6,838	4.2
1972	223,254	177,166	46,088	38,130	7,958	(1,253)	6,705	3.6
1973	238,194	195,762	42,432	40,157	2,275	(2,327)	(52)	1.0
1974	274,828	218,483	56,345	44,197	12,148	(2,413)	9,735	4.4
1975	204,170	165,100	39,070	31,483	7,587			3.7
500,000 to 999,999 pairs								
1970	210,488	166,322	44,166	35,347	8,819	(1,968)	6,851	4.2
1971	250,343	199,188	51,155	37,970	13,185	(1,212)	11,978	5.3
1972	285,781	227,976	51,805	43,526	14,279	(1,289)	12,990	5.0
1973	312,723	246,425	66,298	59,835	15,463	(1,531)	13,932	4.9
1974	353,998	275,587	78,411	58,081	20,330	(4,875)	15,455	5.7
1975	514,035							

1,000,000 to 1,999,999 pairs								
1970	429,079	341,497	87,582	60,027	27,555	(4,100)	23,455	6.4
1971	471,877	370,747	101,110	75,003	26,127	(4,927)	21,200	5.5
1972	483,734	395,517	88,217	78,167	10,050	(3,461)	6,589	2.1
1973	545,998	451,917	94,081	83,000	11,081	(6,604)	4,477	2.0
1974	545,588	449,925	95,658	85,916	9,472	(9,379)	363	1.8
2,000,000 to 3,999,999 pairs								
1970	471,060	351,459	119,601	86,813	32,788	(8,880)	23,908	7.0
1971	479,963	358,130	121,833	91,504	30,329	(5,920)	24,409	6.3
1972	547,914	412,605	135,309	99,003	36,306	(6,144)	30,162	6.6
1973	599,035	455,373	143,662	113,230	30,432	(7,534)	22,898	5.1
1974	616,855	463,085	153,770	123,779	29,991	(13,792)	16,199	4.9
More than 4,000,000 pairs								
1970	1,558,037	1,156,238	401,799	282,899	118,900	(7,884)	111,016	7.6
1971	1,651,428	1,224,827	426,601	302,504	124,097	(4,853)	119,244	7.5
1972	1,847,418	1,395,535	451,883	326,973	124,910	(4,570)	120,340	6.8
1973	1,910,333	1,433,057	477,276	350,732	126,544	(6,453)	120,091	6.6
1974	1,951,981	1,450,424	501,557	375,534	126,023	(13,060)	112,963	6.5

Source: U.S. International Trade Commission.

EXHIBIT 5
Profit-and-Loss Experience of Producers of Footwear, Except Protective-Type and Canvas, on Footwear Operations Only, 1970–74

Size-of-Output Group and Year	Net Sales (1,000 dollars)	Cost of Sales (1,000 dollars)	Gross Profit (1,000 dollars)	Selling, Administrative, and General Expenses (1,000 dollars)	Net Operating Profit (1,000 dollars)	Other (Expense), Net (1,000 dollars)	Net Profit or (Loss) before Taxes (1,000 dollars)	Ratio of Net Operating Profit in Net Sales (Percent)
Less than 200,000 pairs								
1970	38,652	29,796	8,856	7,862	994	(653)	341	2.6
1971	41,223	31,086	10,137	9,227	910	(707)	203	2.2
1972	43,020	32,594	10,426	8,978	1,448	(481)	967	3.4
1973	47,143	35,357	11,786	10,288	1,498	(413)	1,085	3.2
1974	54,608	41,683	12,925	12,098	827	(645)	182	1.5
200,000 to 499,999 pairs								
1970	200,504	164,531	35,973	32,443	3,530	(2,920)	610	1.8
1971	193,947	153,033	40,914	33,072	7,842	(1,654)	6,188	4.0
1972	213,195	169,502	43,693	35,932	7,761	(1,284)	6,477	3.6
1973	229,104	187,161	41,943	37,833	4,110	(2,340)	1,770	1.8
1974	268,780	213,904	54,876	43,111	11,765	(2,051)	9,714	4.4
500,000 to 999,999 pairs								
1970	207,397	164,086	43,311	34,817	8,494	(1,635)	6,859	4.1
1971	246,404	196,323	50,081	37,320	12,761	(824)	11,937	5.2
1972	280,717	224,323	56,394	42,695	13,699	(876)	12,823	4.9
1973	305,986	241,618	64,368	49,759	14,609	(1,079)	13,530	4.8
1974	335,876	264,404	71,472	56,633	14,839	(555)	14,284	4.4

1,000,000 to 1,999,999 pairs								
1970	413,977	329,167	81,810	57,578	27,232	(3,759)	23,473	6.6
1971	448,455	351,130	97,325	72,813	24,512	(4,580)	19,932	5.5
1972	455,661	372,122	83,539	75,362	8,177	(3,189)	4,988	1.8
1973	509,311	421,136	88,175	79,830	8,345	(6,010)	2,335	1.6
1974	510,987	420,878	90,109	82,983	7,126	(7,892)	(766)	1.4
2,000,000 to 3,999,999 pairs								
1970	471,060	351,459	119,601	86,813	32,788	(8,880)	23,908	7.0
1971	479,963	358,130	121,833	91,504	30,329	(5,920)	24,409	6.3
1972	539,248	406,062	133,186	97,802	35,384	(5,743)	29,641	6.6
1973	598,026	454,851	143,175	112,561	30,614	(7,767)	22,847	5.1
1974	616,855	463,085	153,770	123,779	29,991	(13,792)	16,199	4.9
More than 4,000,000 pairs								
1970	1,474,660	1,106,889	367,771	251,635	116,136	(7,911)	108,225	7.9
1971	1,568,850	1,175,923	392,927	272,004	120,923	(4,628)	116,295	7.7
1972	1,755,280	1,342,372	412,908	292,919	119,989	(4,727)	115,262	6.8
1973	1,818,462	1,380,415	438,047	314,329	123,718	(6,798)	116,920	6.8
1974	1,854,918	1,396,619	458,299	336,639	121,660	(13,209)	108,451	6.6

Source: U.S. International Trade Commission.

EXHIBIT 6
Per Capita Consumption of Shoes (Except Slippers & Athletic) 1964, 1967–1976

	Men's (10 & Over)			*Women's (10 & Over)*			*Juvenile (Under 10)*		
Year	*Market (million pairs)*	*Population[1] (million)*	*Per* Capita	*Market (million pairs)*	*Population[1] (million)*	*Per* Capita	*Market (million pairs)*	*Population[1] (million)*	*Per* Capita
1964	133.4	73.2	1.82	320.7	77.5	4.14	133.8	40.4	3.31
1967	143.3	76.4	1.88	348.5	82.0	4.25	127.3	39.0	3.26
1968	152.4	77.6	1.96	408.6	83.5	4.89	135.1	38.3	3.53
1969	153.7	78.9	1.95	373.3	85.0	4.39	132.9	37.5	3.54
1970	164.7	80.3	2.05	390.2	86.4	4.52	130.9	37.1	3.53
1971	171.2	81.8	2.09	382.1	87.8	4.35	133.1	36.6	3.64
1972	185.6	83.4	2.23	381.7	89.2	4.28	138.3	35.9	3.85
1973	178.1[2]	84.9	2.10	381.2[2]	90.5	4.21	126.1	35.0	3.60
1974	158.3[2]	86.2	1.84	340.5[2]	91.9	3.71	112.4	33.8	3.33
1975	155.9[2]	87.2	1.79	335.8[2]	93.0	3.61	107.9	33.3	3.24
1976	177.1[2]	88.1	2.01	361.1[2]	94.1	3.84	140.8	32.9	4.28

[1]Population is the total resident population as on July 1.
[2]Excluding disposable footwear for one-time use.
Source: Prepared by AFIA based on data from U.S. Department of Commerce.

EXHIBIT 7 Percentage Distribution of Domestic and Imported Non-Rubber Footwear, by Types and by Price Ranges

Type and Price Range	1976				1974			
	Percent of Domestic Production		Percent of Imports		Percent of Domestic Production		Percent of Imports	
Men's dress and casual shoes	15		11		16		12	
Less than $6.00		13		26		9		26
$6.01–$10.00		40		25		38		12
$10.01–$14.00		28		20		30		23
$14.01–$18.00		8		13		8		17
Greater than $18.00		13		16		14		22
Total		100		100		100		100
Men's boots and dress and casual shoes (except work), ankle-height or higher	3		1		4		2	
Less than $6.00		3		6		1		17
$6.01–$10.00		6		36		17		18
$10.00–$14.00		32		11		21		12
$14.01–$18.00		28		20		33		26
Greater than $18.00		30		28		32		28
Total		100		100		100		100
Men's work shoes, ankle height or higher (including steel-toe)	6		2		6		1	
Less than $6.00		5		67		2		18
$6.01–$9.00		16		29		8		49
$9.01–$12.00		35		4		22		11
$12.01–$15.00		21		0.3		40		13
Greater than $15.00		23		0.1		27		9
Total		100		100		100		100
Youths' and boys' shoes	4		2		4		2	
Less than $4.00		23		76		13		48
$4.01–$6.00		40		9		26		34
$6.01–$8.00		22		6		36		7
$8.01–$10.00		12		5		20		4
Greater than $10.00		3		3		5		7
Total		100		100		100		100

(continued)

EXHIBIT 7 (Cont.)
Imports as a Percentage of Market Supply by Types 1966–1977

Year	Men's	Youths' & Boys'	Women's	Misses'	Children's	Infants' & Babies'	Athletic	Slippers	Other	Total
1966	11.1	8.2	18.3	6.3	8.7	8.6	14.1	3.7	25.6	13.0
1967	13.7	10.6	25.9	10.4	13.3	8.5	16.9	3.1	31.0	17.7
1968	17.1	13.3	30.5	13.8	18.2	8.3	17.0	2.7	50.0	21.4
1969	23.8	16.3	36.2	17.1	27.1	12.7	21.7	2.0	20.0	25.9
1970	27.3	17.4	41.0	23.2	31.7	14.7	31.8	1.9	20.6	30.0
1971	31.3	19.9	45.8	24.0	33.0	17.5	39.6	1.7	21.4	33.4
1972	31.8	20.5	49.4	25.2	42.5	25.5	41.6	1.7	27.6	36.0
1973	33.3	22.7	53.0	35.3	37.0	23.2	39.0	1.6	26.5	38.6
1974	30.5	28.0	51.0	34.2	37.2	22.2	45.6	1.6	21.1	37.0
1975	32.2	41.5	54.1	36.4	37.4	22.2	68.0	0.8	15.0	40.9
1976	38.2	52.4	56.8	46.8	42.9	30.1	77.5	0.9	32.3	46.7

Source: U.S. Department of Commerce and AFIA.

EXHIBIT 8 **Utilization of Plant Capacity in Non-Rubber Footwear Industry 1968–1975**

	1968	1969	1970	1971	1972	1973	1974	1975	1976
Plant Capacity (million pairs)	776.4	741.9	738.6	695.8	673.0	653.4	619.4	598.2	568.4
Actual Production (million pairs)	642.4	577.0	562.3	535.8	526.7	488.3	453.0	413.1	444.1
Percent Utilization of capacity (%)	82.7	77.8	76.1	77.0	78.2	74.7	73.1	69.1	78.1

Source: American Footwear Industries Association data.

EXHIBIT 9 **Footwear: Ratio of Net Operating Profit (Loss) to Sales, Accounting Year 1975**

		U.S. Producers with 75% or More of Production Consisting of:	
Size-of-Output Group	All U.S. Producers	Women's and Misses'	Men's, Youths', and Boys'
Less than 200,000	2.2	5.9	2.3
200,000 to 499,999	3.4	1.1	6.2
500,000 to 999,999	2.8	(2.6)	5.6
1,000,000 to 1,999,999	5.5	(1.6)	10.8
2,000,000 to 3,999,999	7.5	8.9	7.8
Over 4,000,000	5.7	1.0	

Source: Compiled from data submitted in response to questionnaire of the U.S. International Trade Commission by producers of non-rubber footwear.

EXHIBIT 10
Performance of Some of the Largest U.S. Shoe Companies, 1976

Company	Sales $ Million	% Sales Shoes	% of Shoes Sold Retail in Company Stores	Net Income $ Million	Assets $ Million	Equity $ Million	Return on Equity—%					
							71	72	73	74	75	76
Brown Group, Inc.	845.3	67%	50%	21.0	383.2	207.5	12.3	12.4	13.1	9.2	7.3	12.2
McDonough	284.5	63%	56%	16.5	155.5	99.8	14.8	14.1	15.1	14.1	14.1	15.6
Hanover Shoe, Inc.	60.2	100%		3.1	38.0	28.4	9.0			9.2	11.5	10.9
Melville Shoe Corp.	1228.2	59.6%	98%	61.0	472.3	250.4	22.7	23.0	21.5	15.5	21.5	24.4
Stride Rite Corp.	95.5	100%	20%	6.2	54.7	36.5	16.0	16.2	11.8	14.0	15.5	17.0
United States Shoe Corp.	552.6	71%	31%	25.7	277.0	139.1	17.0	16.9	12.0	11.3	10.5	18.4
Weyenberg Shoe Mfg. Co.	78.9			36.8	3.2	24.3	14.1	13.8	13.1	9.2	10.1	13.2

EXHIBIT 11 **Non-Rubber Footwear: Number of U.S. Producing Companies, by Size of Output**

	Number of Companies				Percent of Total Output			
Size-of-Output Group	*1967*	*1969*	*1974*	*1975*	*1967*	*1969*	*1974*	*1975*
Less than 200,000 pairs	226	192	139	129	2	2	2	2
200,000 to 499,999 pairs	170	146	105	92	10	8	8	7
500,000 to 999,999 pairs	121	113	65	71	14	14	10	12
1,000,000 to 1,999,999 pairs	100	93	57	42	24	24	17	14
2,000,000 to 3,999,999 pairs	42	32	22	23	19	15	13	15
4,000,000 pairs or more	16	21	21	21	31	37	50	50
Total	675	597	409	376	100	100	100	100

Source: Compiled by U.S. International Trade Commission from data supplied by the U.S. Bureau of Census.

EXHIBIT 12 **Work Footwear**

Period	*Production*[1] *(million pairs)*	*Imports (million pairs)*	*Apparent Consumption*[2] *(million pairs)*	*Ratio of Imports to Consumption (percent)*	*Ratio of Imports to Production (percent)*
1968	36	2	38	5	6
1969	35	2	37	5	6
1970	38	2	40	5	5
1971	38	2	40	5	5
1972	35	2	37	5	6
1973	29	3	32	9	10
1974	27	3	30	10	11
1975	25	2	27	7	8
Jan.-Sept.					
1975	18	2	20	10	11
1976	19	4	23	17	21

[1]The data reported for years prior to 1973 include all work shoes regardless of ankle height; those for 1973 and subsequent years include only such shoes of ankle height or higher. (In 1972, production of work shoes less than 6 inches high amounted to 8 million pairs.)

[2]Production plus imports without an allowance for exports, which are believed to be negligible.

Source: Compiled from official statistics of the U.S. Department of Commerce by United States International Trade Commission in Report to President on Investigation No. TA-201-18 under Section 201 of the Trade Act of 1974. USITC Publication 799, Washington, D.C., February 1977.

EXHIBIT 13
THE DORAL CORPORATION
Major Acquisitions

Date	Company	Terms	Prior Track Record: Year	Prior Track Record: Sales $(000's)	Prior Track Record: Net Income $(000's)	Subsequent Record: Year	Subsequent Record: Sales $(000's)	Subsequent Record: Net income $(000's)
1962	Townsend Shoe Co., Inc., Davis, MO	Exchange for 46,000 shares of Common	'58	1693	50	'68	$2737	
			'59	1750	50	'70	2708	
			'60	1974	53	'71	1920	
			'61	2230	81			
April, 1964	Mohawk Shoe Co., Lawrence, MA	Exchange for 80,400 shares of Common	'60	910	27	'68	$3164	
			'61	1050	33	'70	2321	
			'62	1287	34	'71	1880	
			'63	1406	55			
August, 1966	The Loebe Shoe Company	Exchange for 120,000 Common; divested for cash equal to book value	'62	8300	98	'66	$8361	
			'63	6312	115	'67	8238	
			'64	7686	210	Divested		
			'65	8058	236			
March, 1968	Jarrah Shoe Company, Ziptonville, AK	40,000 shares of convertible preferred, plus $500,000 cash	'63	3737	116	'68	$3516	
			'64	3389	161	'70	5030	
			'65	3423	160	'71	5490	
			'66	4056	254			
December, 1973	Ross Shoe Co., Heaton, PA	$1,640,000 cash, plus assumption of liabilities	'73	10854	136	'74	$11832	284
						'75	13623	
						'76	15508	
						'77	17804	2050
January, 1977	Boone Shoes, Inc., San Antonio, TX	$4,000,000 cash, plus assumption of liabilities	'77	Ten-month sales $8,300				

EXHIBIT 14
THE DORAL CORPORATION
Consolidated Balance Sheets as Reported at Date and Unadjusted

	November/December									
	1968	*1969*	*1970*	*1971*	*1972*	*1973*	*1974*	*1975*	*1976*	*1977*
Current Assets										
Cash	847	323	681	1,312	1,033	1,190	1,349	1,742	1,499	2,594
Marketable Securities	1,632	83	407	2,043						3,240
Accounts Receivable	3,823	4,705	4,580	4,292	4,841	4,821	7,586	8,527	8,575	11,600
Inventories										
Finished Goods	4,979	5,570	6,994	6,743	10,092	9,052	12,777	13,188	16,873	16,586
Work in Progress	986	1,400	1,110	1,191	1,315	1,313	1,364	1,630	1,582	2,292
Raw Materials & Supplies	1,342	1,680	1,645	2,006	2,445	2,385	2,809	3,128	3,557	4,730
Total	7,307	8,650	9,749	9,940	13,852	12,749	16,950	17,946	22,012	23,608
Other Current Assets	237	453	584	612	709	493	635	657	654	850
Current Assets	13,846	14,214	16,001	18,199	20,435	19,254	26,520	28,872	32,740	41,893
Property Plant, & Equipment										
Land	595	624	626	586	620	620	645	667	710	832
Buildings	4,840	5,150	5,857	5,642	5,655	6,020	6,808	7,255	7,356	8,232
Machinery & Equipment	2,795	3,080	3,003	2,791	3,218	3,526	4,308	4,586	5,510	6,894
Leasehold Improvements	117			251	1,324	2,010	2,651	2,667	3,015	3,148
	8,347	8,854	9,486	9,270	10,817	12,177	14,412	15,175	16,591	19,106
Less Accumulated Depreciation	3,105	3,319	3,568	3,418	3,590	3,762	4,312	5,062	5,779	6,675
	5,243	5,536	5,918	5,852	7,227	8,415	10,100	10,113	10,812	12,431
Other Assets	867	964	738	736	669	600	486	635	790	1,152
Total Assets	19,955	20,713	22,657	24,787	28,331	28,270	37,106	39,620	44,432	55,476

Liabilities & Stockholders' Equity										
Current Liabilities										
Short Term Debt					2,268	1,215	1,458	810	2,430	
Accounts Payable	1,067	1,352	1,361	1,582	1,776	2,198	2,679	3,485	3,195	3,942
Federal Income Taxes	1,654	855	1,245	1,133	624	38	1,207	1,277	815	878
Accrued Expenses	723	1,168	1,159	1,327	1,484	1,541	2,822	2,752	2,976	3,457
Dividend Payable	335	367	367	369	377	392	392	421	478	562
Current Liabilities	3,779	3,742	4,132	4,411	6,529	5,384	8,558	8,745	9,894	8,839
Deferred Taxes	90	96	128	163	275	288	394	480	605	703
Provisions under Employment Contract	223	166	170							
Long Term Debt							3,749	3,719	4,246	12,795
Stockholders' Equity										
Preferred at Par	32	32	32	19						
Common at Par	3,519	1,173	1,173	1,235	2,638	2,638	2,638	2,638	2,638	2,638
Capital Surplus	572	2,948	2,948	2,913	1,552	1,550	1,550	1,384	1,415	1,332
Earned Surplus	14,017	14,801	16,310	18,119	20,114	21,187	22,994	25,431	28,535	31,487
Total	18,140	18,954	20,463	22,286	24,304	25,375	27,182	29,453	32,588	35,458
Less Treasury Stock	2,277	2,243	2,236	2,073	2,777	2,777	2,777	2,777	2,991	2,320
Stockholders' Equity	15,863	16,711	18,227	20,213	21,527	22,598	24,405	26,676	29,597	33,138
	19,955	20,713	22,657	24,787	28,331	28,270	37,106	39,620	44,342	55,476

EXHIBIT 14 (Cont.)
THE DORAL CORPORATION
Consolidated Income Sheets as Reported at Date and Unadjusted

	1968	*1969*	*1970*	*1971*	*1972*	*1973*	*1974*	*1975*	*1976*	*1977*
Net Sales	35,253	35,165	38,693	39,218	42,740	46,364	61,559	67,997	77,341	88,999
Operating Expenses								43,729	48,402	56,377
Cost of Sales	23,290	23,880	25,883	26,148	28,218	31,091	40,125	15,828	18,830	21,929
Selling & Administrative	5,842	5,893	6,516	6,477	7,906	9,995	14,147		67,232	78,306
Depreciation	376	389	418	427						
Income from Operations	5,745	4,640	5,875	6,167	6,616	5,277	7,287	8,439	10,109	10,693
Other Income (expense)	78	80		83	36	28	6		28	87
Interest Expense (other charges)	47		(86)	29	53	277	833	(524)	(545)	(1,020)
Income Before Federal Taxes		4,720	5,790	6,250	6,652	5,028	6,459	7,911	9,536	9,761
Provision for Federal Taxes Loss on Discontinued Operations	2,922	2,470	2,812	2,971	3,131	2,389	3,083	3,767	4,519	4,577
Net Income	2,824	2,251	2,978	3,279	3,521	2,639	3,376	4,144	5,017	5,184
Net Income per Share	2.44	1.93	2.60	2.83	1.47*	1.09	1.39	1.70	2.09	2.13
(fully diluted)	2.27	1.84	2.44	2.68	1.43	1.09	1.39			
Depreciation	376	389	418	427	752	929	1,049	1,222	1,375	1,633

*100% Stock Split, 1972.

EXHIBIT 15
DORAL CORPORATION
Operating Statistics

Year	Number of Pairs Shipped: Men's & Youths' (millions)	Number of Pairs Shipped: Men's Workboots (000's)	Number of Outlets	Number of Company-owned Stores	Advertising $ (000's)	Number of Pairs in Inventory (millions)	Percent of Line Covered	Percent Men's not Subject to Fashion Changes
1969	5.17							
1970								
1971	5.7		1700			1.3–1.8	93%	70%
1972	6.1		1700			1.5–1.9	94%	55%
1973	5.7	650	1850	78		1.3–1.9	93%	50%
1974	5.8	730	2650	103	$960	1.6–1.8	90%	50%
1975	6.1	770	2700	100	1070	1.7–2.0	90%	50%
1976	6.1	790	2700	108	1570	1.6–2.2	90%	45%
1977	5.9	1220	3200	127	2110	1.9–2.4	90%	45%

EXHIBIT 16
Indexes of U.S. Wholesale Prices for Footwear and Other Selected Commodities (1967 = 100)

Period	Footwear (BLS Code 043): Total	Footwear: Women's and Misses'	Footwear: Men's and Boys'	Footwear: Children's and Infants'	All Commodities	Nondurable Manufactured Goods	Wearing Apparel	Leather
1960	87.6	89.7	84.8	86.5	95.9	92.6	94.5	94.1
1961	88.0	90.2	84.8	86.8	95.5	92.4	94.5	95.9
1962	88.9	90.8	86.5	87.5	94.8	95.1	95.4	97.7
1963	88.7	90.8	86.5	87.5	94.5	94.8	95.4	92.3
1964	88.9	90.3	86.8	87.8	94.7	94.7	96.4	93.2
1965	90.7	91.6	89.4	90.1	96.6	96.8	97.3	97.7
1966	96.8	96.8	97.0	96.6	99.8	100.0	98.2	109.6
1967	100.0	100.0	100.0	100.0	100.0	100.0	100.0	100.0
1968	104.8	109.3	103.6	107.4	102.5	101.5	103.2	101.9
1969	109.5	110.1	108.1	112.9	106.5	104.6	107.1	108.5
1970	113.3	114.1	111.7	117.0	110.4	108.2	111.0	107.7
1971	116.8	117.1	115.7	119.8	113.9	110.5	112.9	112.5
1972	124.5	123.3	125.9	126.1	119.1	114.7	114.8	140.3
1973	130.5	125.4	137.9	130.2	134.7	131.0	119.0	160.1
1974	140.0	132.8	140.0	138.5	160.1	159.5	129.5	154.3
1975	147.8	140.2	159.3	143.7	174.9	176.6	133.4	151.5
1976 (Jan.–Aug.)	156.0	145.5	172.0	148.9	181.5	181.2	138.6	185.7

Source: Compiled from official statistics of the U.S. Bureau of Labor Statistics (AFIA).

Index

D

E

F

M

N

O

P